THE WORLD'S RELIGIONS

The World's Religions

EDITED BY

Stewart Sutherland
Leslie Houlden
Peter Clarke
and
Friedhelm Hardy

ROUTLEDGE

First published in 1988 by
Routledge
11 New Fetter Lane, London EC4P 4EE

Printed in Great Britain

British Library Cataloguing in Publication Data

The World's religions.
1. Religion — History
I. Sutherland, Stewart R.
291'.09 BL80.2

ISBN 0-415-00324-5

Contents

General Introduction

Stewart Sutherland

This book is offered as an aid to the disinterested study of religion. It is offered, that is to say, to those who are certainly interested in religion and religions, but whose first aim is to seek knowledge and understanding. Of course, it may well be that the reader's ultimate aim is to discover or formulate beliefs—to come to a view of what it is that one does believe or what one might believe. However, the assumption of the editors is that understanding is not a barrier to belief: indeed, sometimes it is quite the reverse. It may pose problems for certain specific beliefs, just as an understanding of fairly elementary principles of the working of the Solar System will prove to be an obstacle to the belief that the earth is flat, or acquaintance with foreigners may change one's belief that all strangers are to be feared. But in each case the knowledge or understanding does not simply negate beliefs, it gives rise to new beliefs—that the earth is round, or that at least some strangers are to be welcomed.

Inevitably a single-volume work cannot be completely comprehensive in its range of topics and there has been selectivity based on general as well as specific principles. The general divisions are indicated in the contents list. The more specific principles operating are of three types.

The first is to indicate the range and variety of religions, religious beliefs and religious forms of life that are found in the world today. Thus in addition to devoting whole divisions of the volume to the Judeo-Christian tradition, to Islam and to the complex of religious beliefs and practices in South and East Asia, we have provided accounts of the indigenous religions of the Americas, of Africa, of Australia and Melanesia. In these latter cases we have been selective and this is true also of the contents of the last division of the volume, devoted to New Religious Movements.

This leads naturally to our second principle, which is to be selective in a way that illustrates the relative weight, size and significance of the various groups under the five general headings. However, not *every* Christian or Buddhist group can be discussed or even mentioned, but those that are discussed exemplify the basic patterns of belief within that system. Thus although mention is made of Sri Lanka we have not devoted a separate chapter to the form of Buddhism which has flourished there, on the grounds that, for our purposes, it does not illustrate points that are not covered elsewhere in the book. Equally, traditional religions have existed in all periods of human history and are found in every continent today. In this work there is necessarily here also a selection of examples, rather than an over-reaching attempt to be completely comprehensive. The examples are chosen to bring into dialogue the nature of the subject matter with the type and range of interests which a reader may have.

The third principle is to produce a book which is a series of interlinked essays, each of which has its own discrete coherence, as well as its place within a wider and more complex tapestry.

Thus for the many reasons examined in the essays of the opening section, there has been no attempt to impose a single over-arching structure, based on a single comprehensive method. The assumption of the editors is that no such method would be sufficient in itself to explore the rich conceptual geography of the idea of religion and religions. Equally no single 'theory' or definition of religion will be offered, and again the reasons for this are explored in the opening essays.

However, although the book is planned as a single volume it is written to be read also by those who prefer to sample essays according to the particular issues or questions which are of moment or interest to them.

The Richness of the Tapestry

What are we to make of the variety and richness which is displayed in the pages that follow?

As with any worthwhile study or series of studies the ultimate intention must be that the reader should see beyond and indeed come to ignore the writers. This applies in the case of the general as well as the specific and it is the universal character of religion to which this book as a whole must finally point. Above all a study of the world's religions by its breadth and plan and (albeit selective) study of detail must remind us of the universality of the phenomena of belief, experience and practice which we call 'religion'. We are reminded further that what for want of a more economic phrase I shall call 'the religious impulse' is deeply embedded both in the individual human soul and in human society.

The very phrase '*the* religious impulse' can, however, mislead the unwary into assuming a monotony of similar manifestations in diverse times and places which require no separate attentiveness from those who wish to learn. It would be a similar folly to be misled by talk of 'the artistic impulse', into assuming that studying the arts of India would add nothing to a moderate acquaintance with the Dutch Masters, or even that those who know well the paintings of Turner will find little additionally to appreciate in the sculpture of Henry Moore. Indeed the broader one's perspective and sympathies the less the danger of trying to 'sum up' *the* artistic, or *the* religious impulse.

Nonetheless, we do use the terms 'religion' or 'art' to encompass what is diverse in detail and emphasis within one focus of attention, and this volume offers an overview of what (again sometimes by selective example) should fall under the heading of 'the world's religions'. The question of drawing even notional boundary lines is less simple than might appear at first glance, and in addition to chapters dealing with some of the philosophical issues which arise, there are separate essays devoted to the near neighbours of religion—ideology, agnosticism and atheism.

One common thread in the tapestry is that religious beliefs and practices are not best seen as 'additions' to the already full and well-organised lives, or as minor modifications to social structures which can be easily detached from them. Whether for the individual or for society, religious belief and practice is a means of structuring or focusing, not something that comes after the establishment of perspective and pattern. This is not to say that there are not secular alternatives to religion. The crucial point is that religious belief and practice do not belong to the fringes of either social or individual lives. Their abandonment or their adoption implies radical change even if as a matter of fact such change comes about gradually. To reject or adopt 'religion' is not like taking up or laying aside a hobby or a club membership. If it seems like that, then there is misperception somewhere. This is perhaps why David Hume wrote, 'Whereas mistakes in philosophy are merely ridiculous, those in religion are dangerous.' This raises the difficult question of what constitutes 'a mistake' in religion and who, if anyone, is in a position to determine whether or not a mistake has been made.

At one level this book will certainly help here, for *within* all of the various traditions discussed there are clear indications of what, within *that* belief system, counts as error and falsehood. The major problems arise when the focus takes in beliefs and practices belonging to more than one religion, and I shall refer to this further in due course. By way of preparation, however, I wish to make two further points.

One of the emphases which is found in religious belief and practice is that far from simply being an adjunct to other areas of life it provides a point of perspective in terms of which to evaluate and organise them. The view provided thus differs from one religious tradition to another, but what they do offer is the possibility that human life is not simply a chronicle of things and events which ultimately are as self-contained as they are random. Within the beliefs or the organising symbols of the ritual is implied a refusal to accept that human life is or need to be an uncoordinated procession of sights, sounds, places and people. It is a refusal to accept as a final statement on human life the picture, in the words of a once popular song, of life as 'one damn thing after another'.

A differing but not incompatible emphasis is the importance attached to seeing not only what is true about this world, but the possibility of relating to what lies beyond it. There is clearly much diversity here, for some religions focus very centrally upon 'escape' from this world and seek to discern in the world the points, structures or moments of transparency which are the keys to 'right living' and, depending upon emphasis, 'right believing'.

To summarise briefly, I am suggesting that in the variety, diversity and richness of the tapestry there is no single framework or grid within which a neat taxonomy of religions may be produced. The evidence for this is reiterated in detail in the book which follows. Nonetheless, there is in that mosaic of beliefs and practices which we unhesitatingly include under the general heading of 'religion', and even in some which are at best distant relatives, a series of points of interest of a very general nature. The first is the universality of these phenomena. This is not to say that every human being is a religious devotee, or that every society is affected in equal manner, but undoubtedly the elasticity of the term 'religion' and the variety of forms of religion throughout history raise conceptual as well as empirical problems about the identification of a society wholly devoid of all traces of religious beliefs, practice and attitude.

The second point follows from this and reminds us of the dangers of regarding such an observation as a licence to pronounce in general terms about religion without an awareness of the diversity which this book takes as its *raison d'être*. What is apparent however is that religious belief and practice are not in essence coincidental or peripheral, though they may become so, and thus gradually decay. Religion which is peripheral to the life of believer or community is in decline. Thus religious belief and practice is the particular rather than the general, to be found on a line of tension between two different but not necessarily incompatible emphases. On the one hand they provide a home, or at least a bivouac, in the buzzing, blooming confusion of this world, and on the other a means of seeing through and beyond the immediacy of what surrounds us.

Comparing and Contrasting

For some to gaze in wonder, perhaps awe, and occasionally distaste may be sufficient. For others however the question of where if anywhere in this variety truth lies will be the central issue. Certainly for believers, as distinct from observers, the question must arise. Even for those who are not believers the question prompted by Hume's remarks about the danger of mistakes in religion is a real one. There are deep and important questions here which have provoked an extensive literature. To tackle them adequately would be to depart from the main aim of this volume and would require at least another volume on the philosophy of religion. However, there are points which would arise in such a study which are treated in the first section of this volume and the brief comments now offered may be initially pursued by considering the issues presented there.

There is inevitably a temptation in our competitive and judgemental world to begin with points of comparison and to end up with a 'league-table' of religions. Theology has sometimes followed certain patterns of belief by emphasising this. There are two general comments which I offer on such a tendency.

The first is that the most important single factor in determining religious allegiance or affiliation is place of birth. I hazard the guess that there are few devotees of the Eskimo female deity Sedna in Chelsea, London, or living by the banks of the Ganges. This must be the fundamental starting-point of any discussion of truth and error in religion.

The second general comment is that, notwithstanding the relativity of all of our respective starting-points, it is undoubtedly the case that many religions are so structured that the commitment demanded from believers is of a *non-relative* kind. Those who were born in Chelsea and who are Christians do not preface the affirmation of the Creed with, 'Most probably because I was born in Britain rather than northern Greenland, I believe in . . .'

The resolution of the tensions implicit in these two comments is not easy and cannot be achieved in the brief compass of a few remarks here. However, there is a distinction which it is important to draw and which will point us in a more helpful direction. We must contrast the complex affirmation and recognition of the existential 'I believe . . .' of the credo of the believer with something which is rather different, but with which it has often been confused. This is the standpoint of the Ideal Observer or of the Ultimately Wise Man who affirms, 'All things considered the X religion is nearest to the Truth.' There is no human being who is in the position of the Ideal Observer, and indeed it is arguable whether the position of total detachment implicit in such a conception is itself intelligible. On the other hand the supposed Ultimately Wise Man who is in the position to say truthfully '*All* things considered' can be none other than an omniscient God.

One central danger of which Hume was too well aware is the equation of the existential 'I believe', with 'God says'. This is not to underestimate the importance of an affirmation sincerely made that 'I believe that God says x or y [or *mutatis mutandis*, the comparable affirmation where it exists in other religions].' Rather it highlights what such a confession is—an act of human piety.

What the study of religions and indeed of *The World's Religions* does do, however, is to alter the believers' perception of what they are doing. It does not rule out (nor for that matter compel) belief, but it emphasises the fact that belief is in the first instance contextual. One's beliefs are held, sometimes explicitly, sometimes implicitly, but always in a context which is demarcated by the social, intellectual and experiential options open to one. As that context changes one's beliefs may, indeed probably will, alter, sometimes fundamentally but most often in limited fashion. However, the fact that beliefs are in principle revisable in the light of growth should not be confused with the paralysing claim that belief must therefore always be tentative and decisions postponed. That we *might* be wrong should not in itself be a veto on acting appropriately on the beliefs which we have, though it ought to provoke more reflection in many believers than it does.

The general point is this. Growth in awareness of other cultures and other religious beliefs and practices is bound to bring reflection upon any religious commitments which we have. As such it can be disturbing, but need not be negatively disruptive. In any case these issues arise not only in inter-religious contexts, for all of the major world religions and many other of the world's religions also have diversity and change *within* them. Indeed their strength is in part located in their capacity to respond to as well as to initiate change. A believer must in the nature of his or her commitment recognise that fact.

The study of *The World's Religions* is intended in part to aid the enquirer—whether or not they have particular or firm religious commitments—to engage in and perhaps to contribute to reflection upon these issues. Equally, however, this book is an invitation to increase both our understanding of and our wonder at the rich if incomplete and ever-changing tapestry which is signalled in its title.

Part 1 *Religion and the Study of Religions*

Editor:
Stewart Sutherland

1 Religion and the Religions

Peter Byrne

Introduction

The aim of this book is to offer a survey of the world's religions. We must ask ourselves at the outset what is the general character of the thing the more specialised chapters describe. There are three important questions which must be considered prior to any detailed description of the religious life of mankind in history: What is religion? What kind of unity does it possess? How far is it available for disinterested study? Each of the questions will be considered in separate subsections below.

Before they are tackled it is worth while to note some important features of the context in which they are considered—features which also help to reveal some of the assumptions underlying the approach behind this entire work. So it is vital to understand that what is offered in these pages is a work in the study of religions and not in theology. Theology is an attempt to express or articulate a given religious faith (see Smart, 1973: 6). Theology thus begins, and is shaped by, the fundamental beliefs of, say, Christianity. The theologian in his development of these beliefs may offer historical accounts of the scriptures or church of his religion, but such accounts will be part of an attempt to state and defend the fundamentals of his faith for his fellow believers and the age in which they live. The student of religion attempts to offer a reflective account of the various facets of one religion or of many. He aims at detachment and disinterestedness in observation so far as these are possible. In describing the beliefs, practices and institutions of a particular religion he seeks neither to defend nor attack them, but only to understand. So it should be possible to offer a study of religion (or of religions) without committing oneself or one's reader to the truth or falsity of that religion (or religions). Whereas to present a theology is to claim endorsement of some religious beliefs. It is in the spirit of detachment and disinterestedness that the present volume is offered.

The degree to which a detached study of religions can be successful in reaching a full understanding of religious traditions will be discussed when our third question about the general character of religion is considered below ('How far is religion available for disinterested study?'). We may note now how the aims behind the study of religions, as opposed to theology, give a distinctive sense to these questions about the general character of religion. For the student of religion and the theologian will be inclined, because of their divergent interests, to give quite different answers to the question 'What is religion?'. A typical theological account of the nature of religion is to be found in the writings of the great systematiser of medieval Catholic thought, St Thomas Aquinas (?1225–73). 'Religion' here figures as the name of a moral virtue, the virtue of offering due worship and service to God (see Aquinas, 1974: 2a2aeQ81). It is opposed to the vices of idolatry and superstition (see Aquinas: 2a2aeQ92 and 94). Thus one cannot recognise the presence of religion in someone's life without judging the truth and adequacy of his beliefs about God and the theological appropriateness of the forms of worship he engages in. But the student of religion tries to use the concept of religion as a neutral, descriptive category. He neither desires nor needs to judge of the truth of someone's beliefs in deciding that person is engaged in religion. Concerned to give an impartial treatment of religions as important historical and social phenomena, he does not contrast religion with idolatry or superstition, but with those other aspects of individual and social life, e.g. politics, art, science and economics, which are worthy of separate treatment from the student of human nature.

The use of 'religion' to signify a descriptive category is relatively new in European thought, as is the concern for an impartial historical and sociological survey of religions. Three important movements of thought seem to be essential to this use of 'religion' and the study that underlies it. First there is the detachment already remarked upon, which involves a readiness to stand back from the religious traditions of one's own culture. This leads to the second thing: comparison. In standing back from the faith of one's own people, one will be ready to look at the faiths of other cultures and to see one's own as but one instance of a general phenomenon to be found throughout culture. The third underpinning of this approach is an historical perspective upon religion. Detachment and comparison will inevitably bring with it a readiness to see the ways one's own and other nations' religions have changed in the course of time and have been enmeshed in the general progress and decay of human societies.

We are now able to turn to our first question about the general character of religion: 'What is religion?'. We must consider whether the detachment, comparison and historical reflection behind the study of religions presupposes or leads to some definition of religion that will fix its essential nature, or sum up in a sentence or two what we are looking to study in various societies or epochs.

What is Religion?

At first glance it seems as if a clear definition of 'religion' is both desirable and necessary for the study of religion. A clear understanding of what religion is is needed if, in advance of historical and sociological enquiry, one is to know what is to be rightly included within the scope of study. Only with the kind of understanding a definition of 'religion' (and hence of 'a religion') provides will one know what is to count as a religion for the purposes of study. And after a survey of world's religions has been completed it would seem desirable to sum up the general conclusions reached about the nature of religion in the course of the survey by improving, filling out and making more precise the original 'operational definition' on the basis of which enquiry was launched (for this argument see Wiebe, 1981: 11–13). The way in which an operational definition of religion might be constructed appears straightforward. One would examine the definition of 'religion' implicit in ordinary usage, adapting it and making it more precise in the light of the scholarly purpose one has in using the word (in this case picking out in a neutral fashion a particular historical and social reality in human life).

The search for definition is common enough in branches of the human sciences, but it faces enormous difficulties in the case of 'religion'. For the rest of this subsection we shall treat of the problems that arise in giving an initial, operational definition of 'religion'. These difficulties begin with disputes arising from the ordinary usage of 'religion' and from the conflicting purposes scholars may bring to the business of defining and studying religion.

The clues to defining 'religion' that come from the ordinary use of the word are best considered by separating the denotation and connotation of 'religion'. The denotation of 'religion' is given by listing all those systems of belief, or whatever, we would normally agree on calling religions or examples of religion. Its connotation includes the properties or features of these systems we take to be constitutive of their being religions. The problem with ordinary usage as a guide to an operational definition of 'religion' is that the denotation and connotation of 'religion' are both confused and contradictory therein (see Ferre, 1967: 31–4). There is no question that we could *begin* to set out the denotation of 'religion'. We would start our list of religions with: Christianity, Judaism, Islam, Hinduism, Buddhism. But we would get no clear guidance from ordinary usage as to whether Confucianism was to be included here or under the denotation or 'ethical systems', or as to whether Voodoo was a religion or a mere system of magic. Further we might, without solecism in either case, say that Maoism in the 1960s and 1970s was the new religion of China *and* that China then had no religion because its dominant ideology was so fiercely atheistical. Reflection upon the connotation of 'religion' will produce similar results. Thinking of items on our list of religions like Christianity, Judaism and Islam we might conclude that the chief feature that made something a religion was the presence of a given doctrine: belief in God. Reminding ourselves now of obvious instances of polytheistic religions (e.g. Homeric religion) we may broaden the connotation to 'belief in gods or spiritual beings'. But so seemingly obvious a definition will run into trouble very quickly. It will rule out from the denotation of 'religion' things ordinary usage would at the very least have us pause over (i.e. forms of Buddhism which are apparently atheistic, Jainism, Confucianism and Taoism) and definitely include things like magical practices usage would bid us be hesitant about. If we modify the statement of the belief said to be crucial in making something a religion so that it refers now to something broader (say, 'belief in sacred things or things of ultimate value') we will still be in difficulty. For ordinary usage will be happy to list in the denotation of 'religion' tribal or folk-religions ('the religion of the Eskimos', 'the religion of the Nuer' etc.) in which the element of doctrine/belief may be undeveloped and unimportant. The nineteenth-century anthropologist William Robertson Smith argued that the ancient, tribal religions of mankind were largely systems of rites. They were 'series of acts and observances' in which doctrine and myth were secondary (W.R. Smith, 1927: 20–1). And if this is even half true, to define 'religion' simply in terms of a kind of belief may be quite misleading.

Ordinary usage not being clear about the denotation of religion, and giving no sure guide even to the genus into which 'religion' fits, there is plenty of scope for scholars with different interests in the study of religions to resort to different operational definitions. The possibility of bringing different purposes to the definition of 'religion' reflects the fact of their being different kinds of reflection upon religion and different aims and purposes behind these modes of reflection. Thus a definition of 'religion' may be influenced by avowedly theological purposes even though it wishes to treat 'religion' as a descriptive category. When Max Mueller defines religion as 'A disposition which enables man to apprehend the Infinite under different names and varying guises' (Mueller, 1893: 13) he is modifying an element present in the ordinary connotation of 'religion' (i.e. 'religion is belief in God') to suit a theological purpose behind his study, a purpose which becomes evident when he concludes that all religions place the human soul in the presence of God, despite their surface differences (see Mueller, 1893: 192). Equally a definition could be advanced by a sociological theorist of religion to suit the purpose of showing that religion was a wholly social and human construct, as the following definition appears to do:

> a religion is (1) a system of symbols which acts to (2) establish powerful, pervasive and long-lasting moods and motivations in men by (3) formulating concepts of a general order of existence (4) and clothing these conceptions with such an aura of factuality that (5) the moods and motivations seem uniquely realistic. (Geertz, 1966: 4)

Given that different scholarly interests provide divergent ways of resolving the vagaries of ordinary usage, we must be clear as to the purpose of the study now in hand. Since this purpose is to provide a neutral survey of the broad sweep of mankind's religious life, it seems to call for a definition of 'religion' which does not immediately imply any controversial claims about religion's truth or origin and which preserves as broad a denotation for 'religion' as possible. The definition should allow us to make the necessary discrimination between the religious aspect of human life in history and, say, its economic or political aspects, whilst begging as few questions as possible over which particular forms of belief and practice illustrate this aspect. Boundary questions, such as those concerning the relation between religion and magic, can thus be commented on in the course of surveying tribal religions, rather than being settled arbitrarily in advance.

In producing a definition to meet the above purpose, the first requirement is to establish as broad a genus for 'religion' as possible. So we shall define 'religion' as a type of human institution. It is a complex to be found in human history having the following four important dimensions: the theoretical (e.g. beliefs, myths and doctrines), the practical (e.g. rites, prayers and moral codes), the sociological (e.g. churches, leaders and functionaries) and the experiential (e.g. emotions, visions and sentiments of all kinds). A religion is an institution in human life showing a significant mixture of this complex of theoretical, practical, sociological and experiential dimensions (see Wach's definition in Kitagama, 1967: 41 and Smart, 1971: 15ff.). It is an institution which may be further distinguished by three types of differentiae which qualify the dimensions making up its genus. These may be specified as the *object* of this complex, its *goal* and its *function*. The object of the complex of dimensions that make up the institution that is religion is given in describing the content of its theoretical dimension and the focus of its practical and experiential ones. Its beliefs will concern God, or the gods or more generally sacred things. Its practices and characteristic experiences will be devoted to and focus on supernatural beings or sacred aspects of reality. The goal of this complex will be shown in its practical and sociological dimensions (and in part defined by its theoretical). This goal will be salvation or the achievement of some ultimate good or well-being. The function of the entire system of dimensions will typically be to provide an overall meaning to an individual's life, or in the case of the religion of a group, to integrate and unify the society which they form. To sum up: a religion is an institution with a complex of theoretical, practical, sociological and experiential dimensions, which is distinguished by characteristic objects (gods or sacred things), goals (salvation or ultimate good) and functions (giving an overall meaning to life or providing the identity or cohesion of a social group).

A number of points now need to be made about this definition. We may see first that its very broadness provides a way of understanding the great variety of more specific definitions which have competed with one another in scholarly literature upon religion. For each of these rivals will usually be found to select only some of the dimensions of religion to provide its genus and to fasten upon some limited differentiae to fix the species to which religion belongs. Thus E.B. Tylor's famous definition of 'religion' as 'belief in spiritual beings' (Tylor, 1903: 424) selects the theoretical element as the most important aspect of religion's genus and differentiates it by a particular kind of belief. Religion becomes a kind of philosophy, which Tylor distinguishes from other types by the label 'Animism' (a general view that the world is moved and controlled by superhuman and spiritual beings) and its other dimensions are then but secondary. By contrast the following definition from a recent author initially selects two of our dimensions to provide the genus and picks out the particular function of these dimensions to fix the species:

> Religion, then, can be defined as a system of beliefs and practices by means of which a group of people struggles with these ultimate problems of human life. It expresses their refusal to capitulate to death, to give up in the face of frustration, to allow hostility to tear apart their human aspirations. (Yinger, 1970: 7)

Such a difference in selection by Tylor and Yinger leads to a difference in fixing religion's denotation: Tylor's definition will make us hesitate about including the 'atheistic' religions in the denotation, whilst Yinger's will see the downgrading of belief in personal gods as unimportant in the light of the common function the beliefs and practices of theistic and atheistic religions share. These different definitions with their attendant consequences can now be seen to be selections from the dimensions which give religion its genus and from the various differentiae of these dimensions. Such selection can be motivated by a variety of reasons: the impressiveness of a certain aspect of the ordinary use of religion (or of a chosen example of religion) or the bringing of a specific purpose to the business of definition. No such reasons lie behind our definition so it eschews such selection and remains as inclusive as possible.

The inclusiveness of our definition shows that it is in good measure vague. We allow in the first instance that a religion need not clearly show all four dimensions in developed form. We can thus accept that at the penumbra of religion there may be primitive, ancient religions which, as Robertson Smith suggested, display the theoretical dimension in but a weak fashion. We can equally accept the Society of Friends as practising a religion in which the sociological dimension has atrophied to a large extent and in which the ritual aspects of the practical dimension have all but disappeared. We look only for a 'significant mix' of these four dimensions. We have also allowed for a number of diverse differentiae so that we produce yet further species of our genus. Moreover many of these differentiae are themselves vague. Thus one of the most important differentia of religion relates to its object and is given by the great French sociologist Durkheim thus: 'A religion is a unified system of beliefs and practices relative to sacred things ...' (Durkheim, 1976: 47). The advantage of this way of fixing the object of religion is that the object becomes broad enough to include religious realities (such as nirvana) which are none the less not divine. But how is the sacred to be defined itself? We may contrast sacred objects and realities with profane on the grounds the former are thought of as transcendent, extraordinary and beyond anything in normal experience, but a full understanding of the nature and range of the sacred can only come with an actual study of the complexity of beliefs about the sacred that can be found in religious history. It is impossible to give an adequate idea of this complexity in some simple formula (cf. Eliade, 1958: xii).

Vague though our definition is, it will still serve to pick out the religious aspect of human life in history from other aspects of that life. It is useful, for example, to be able to distinguish religions in history from systems of belief we say are 'merely philosophies' even though they may have an object, goal and at least personal function which parallel those of religion proper. The demand that the theoretical dimension to religion be significantly linked with at least some of the other three enables us to do this. We might, on the other hand, come across institutions in human life which display the four dimensions of theoretical, practical, sociological and experiential but from which are absent any of the differentiae which mark out religion in the genus. In such institutions there would be no concern with the divine or the sacred, no attempt to rise beyond utilitarian goals and aims and no desire to function as the ultimate source of meaning or identity in life. Political institutions may thus show the dimensions of religion but lack any significant combination of the differentiae of central examples of religion. Some indeed regard the combination of science and technology in the modern world as a significant instance of the displacement of religion by something parallel but different to it. But though our definition has some obvious discriminating power, it will not, because it is vague, sort out the nicer boundary disputes which occur, say, in distinguishing religion from magic. For in some magical systems we may have elements of the four dimensions and at least one of the important differentiae of religion in the presence of belief in spiritual, superhuman beings. Yet other differentiae will be lacking. The goal and function of a system of magic may be entirely mundane and utilitarian, being concerned solely with the attainment of worldly and limited ends. Whether such a system is likened in the end to a crude kind of religion or a crude kind of science/technology (as Sir James Frazer famously does in the opening and closing chapters of *The Golden Bough*) will be left to a detailed study of its relation to central examples of religion.

We may summarise the above points by saying that our definition of religion serves to pick out religion as a recognisable aspect of human life in history but does so in an open-ended way. It serves the purposes of a broad enquiry into religion by giving it a general direction whilst not settling in advance important questions which can only be properly decided upon after detailed study has finished. This kind of operational definition of 'religion' works by listing the more important features which contribute to something's being an instance of religion, but refuses to say exactly what combination of such features is essential for something's being a religion and refuses to define in advance what each feature precisely means (cf. Alston, 1967: 142–3). To some this will seem like the abdication of the attempt to define 'religion' at all, since the operational definition given does not state in unambiguous terms the necessary and sufficient conditions for something's being a religion. A statement of religion's necessary and sufficient conditions would be a list of precise features such that, if an institution lacked them, it could not be classed as a religion, and if it did possess them, it could not fail to be a religion. All that our list of dimensions and differentiae of religion does is allow a number of different statements of sufficient conditions for something's being a religion to be produced, since we know that the possession of a significant number of these features in varying combinations will be enough to enable something to be a religion. But we neither close the list of possible combinations of religion-making features, nor do we attempt to define each feature precisely. But how may we suppose that 'religion' has a meaning we can understand, if we cannot thus state necessary and sufficient conditions for the use of the term?

One answer to the above question would be this: 'religion' is a family-resemblance term and religions form a family. Ludwig Wittgenstein explained the family-resemblance idea of meaning in the following way (he is discussing the words 'language' and 'game'):

> Instead of producing something common to all that we call language, I am saying that these phenomena have no one thing in common which makes us use the same word for all—but that they are all *related* to one another in many different ways. And it is because of this relationship, or these relationships, that we call them all 'language'... Consider for example the proceedings that we call 'games'... What is common to them all?—Don't say 'There *must* be something common, or they would not be called 'games' '—but *look and see* whether there is anything common to them all.—For if you look at them you will not see something that is common to *all*, but similarities, relationships, and a whole series of them at that ... we see a complicated network of similarities overlapping and criss-crossing: sometimes overall similarities, sometimes similarities of detail. I can think of no better expression to characterise these similarities than 'family resemblances'; for the various resemblances between members of a family: build, features, colour of eyes, gait, temperament, etc. etc. overlap and criss-cross in the same way.—And I shall say: 'games' form a family. (Wittgenstein, 1958: 31–2)

If the family-resemblance idea of meaning applies to 'religion' then we should expect to find the following facts in our understanding of the word. 1. There will be a characteristic set of features found in examples of religion (such as those described above). 2. There will be no single set of such features to be found in each and every example of religion. 3. There will be no limits to set in advance to the kind of combinations of the characteristic features newly discovered or developing religions could be found to exemplify, nor will there be absolute limits to the additional features such new examples could add to the set. 4. The various examples of religion will be related to one another not therefore by them all sharing a single set of features but through a series of significant overlaps in the features they possess; there will be a network of relationships but no one set of things they all share. 5. The meaning of the word 'religion' will none the less be projectible, that is, having rehearsed the characteristic features of religion in an inclusive definition like that given above or having gained a knowledge of some central examples one will be able to say of newly-found examples whether they are religions or not.

The merit of accepting, at least initially, a family-resemblance meaning for 'religion' is that it agrees with our intuition that religion is an open-ended and ever-developing aspect of life. To think there social existence to be drawn in advance is to falsify our perception that religion will enmesh and intermingle with what surrounds it. Since, too, religion is part of human history it will be ever-changing and therefore it would be wrong not to be open to the possibility that new forms of religion await to be discovered, forms which indeed could extend our apprehension of what religion can be and amount to. The analogy with a family, an ever-developing unity of diverse yet organically-related elements, is more than apt to bring out these facts about religion. We should also be ready to extend the family-resemblance model to the prior picture we have of the particular religions.

This last point is worth stressing. Many believe that to be able to identify different religions and baptise them with names such as 'Hinduism' and 'Christianity' presupposes that there is some easily definable common element that distinguishes them from one another. But if we can legitimately distinguish a host of Indian forms of belief and worship by the term 'Hinduism', this is not because there is some essential unity among them that can be seen on the surface. We have, in fact, coined an umbrella term which refers to a mass of phenomena which does not aspire to be a unity and which is not united by any single item of belief, mode of worship etc. (see Smith, 1978: 65–6). The use of the single term to cover all these phenomena rests only on there being a significant family likeness between them of the sort Wittgenstein has described for us. Nor is this lack of unity simply a feature of the religious traditions of India. In Christianity there is evidently a greater desire to present the religion as a unity and its various sects will accordingly tend to present themselves as representatives of '*the* Church of Christ'. But even in this instance, the actual forms of religion to which we give the label 'Christianity' have shown, and continue to show, the most astonishing variety. Consider in this light the difference between the Christian Unitarianism to be found in parts of Victorian England and the Catholic

Christianity of the peoples of Latin America. Even an alleged common feature in all, such as 'the preaching of Christ' (or '. . . the Gospel' or '. . . the New Testament') will be found to take different shapes in different examples of the religion and to bring with it no essential likeness. Again we will have to fall back upon a family-resemblance picture.

The reason for the variability within specific religions is the same as that for the variability of the general phenomenon, 'religion'. To speak of 'Hinduism' or 'Christianity' is to refer to aspects of the belief, practice, organisation and experience of human beings. These aspects of human life show the variability that human beings show. We might wish as students of human life that human beings believed and behaved more uniformly but they do not. There is limitless scope for novelty and for receptivity to the differing influences of time and place amongst human beings. It is the humanity of religion and the religions which commands that we begin our study with an open-ended definition of 'religion'.

What Kind of Unity does Religion Possess?

The difficulties in giving a clear operational definition for 'religion' do not reflect an inability to pick out the general area of human life that the study of religion is concerned with. The problems surround the precise description of its distinguishing features and the search for uniformity in those features. We have in this latter source of difficulty a reflection of a general problem in all attempts to classify phenomena, for all classification is an attempt to seek unity in diversity. Many students of religion have thought that the attempt to seek unity in the diversity of religious phenomena cannot stop merely with the acknowledgement of the problems confronted in giving a precise operational definition. These problems, they will argue, show only the great divergence in the outward characteristics of the various things we call 'religions'. Further study will reveal an inner unity amongst them, an identity, or sharing, of fundamental characteristics that only comes to light once one has penetrated the varying outer forms of religion. All religions, they argue, share an inner core of some sort, which underlies their outward characteristics.

The relation between the alleged common core to religions and their outward characteristics can be understood on the model of 'essence and manifestation'. The common core to all religions is then said to be the essence of religion. There are different religions because this essence is manifested in different historical and cultural contexts. The unique features of a particular religion can be explained by showing how the core features of religion would produce the outward characteristics of the religion in question, given the particular setting that this religion is placed in. The core features of religion are thus believed to be its true essence in that they are the unvarying, underlying features fundamental in explaining all else.

Such a definition of 'religion' that arose from a search for religion's inner essence or core would have two distinct advantages over an operational definition. It could, in the first place, be said to be a true account of the nature of religion. An operational definition on the other hand would at best be a true summary of ordinary usage, but its adequacy would largely be a matter of its suitability to the purposes behind it. But if we discovered an inward core to religion we would be able to describe the true source of religion's unity and the true explanation of its manifold characteristics. Such a definition would produce a second valuable consequence in so far as it would be the means of settling the boundary disputes over the demarcation of religion in a sure and non-arbitrary fashion. The religions shown to possess the core would have been linked together in fundamental respects. Those things our operational definition had previously allowed to be marginal examples of religious phenomena but which did not possess the core of religion would have been shown to be essentially unlike the central cases.

The power of an account of religion's essence to produce a strong, clear demarcation of religion points to the way one could test any such account. If the account excludes from the denotation of 'religion' central examples of religious phenomena according to a reasonable operational definition, then it is false and inadequate. If we cannot come up with any precise specification of a common core to all religions which does not exclude some such examples, then all religions do not have a common core and religion does not have an essence.

There seem to be two main sources of the belief in an essence to religion, in the belief that all religions share a common core. One we may call 'theological', the other 'scientific'.

The theological source of the belief arises from a concern with the truth of religion. Those who wish to contend that religion in general is correct in its claim that there is a sacred realm beyond the profane or that there is a God will naturally be embarrassed by the apparent diversity and conflict amongst the contrasting beliefs of the world's religions. Divergence and disagreement will also cast a similar shadow over the belief that there is in human religion a valid concern with a transcendent goal or meaning to life. One way of avoiding the worst consequences of these conflicts is to claim that the differences conceal an underlying unity. In essence, by reference to some inner core of belief, experience or ethic, the major religions at least will be found to be in harmony. Underneath their outward differences they offer the same truth and way. This concern with religious truth and an inner core to religion is frequently felt by those who wish to construct a theology of world religions as part of articulating and expressing their own faith. The problem posed by many parts of the human race following religions different from one's own is overcome if a harmony at the level of inner essence is discovered. Many Christian theologies of world religions proceed along these lines and the apologetic value of postulating this deeper harmony is increased if the inner core is shown to commit other faiths to the perceptions of the Christian religion. Furthermore, a theory of religion's inner core may be of apologetic value if it could be shown that, by reference to the core, one's own religion is the highest, most fully developed example of religion: the specific form of faith in which religion's inner essence is given fullest, most perfect expression. Many Christian accounts of 'other religions' have been inspired by just such theological aims (cf. Smart, 1973: 60–1).

Given the terms of this study, we cannot endorse so evidently theological a motive in searching for religion's essence. But we can take cognisance of another source of the search. One might well believe that a truly scientific treatment of religion must be committed to the belief in a common core to all religions, for only if this belief is true will the world's religions be explicable in a truly scientific way. The student of religion will be able to see his investigation into religion by analogy with the way a scientist investigates the nature and properties of a natural substance. If a chemist is investigating the properties of, say, water or gold he knows that, since he is dealing with a natural substance, it is no mere matter of linguistic custom that things are or are not examples of water or gold. We may feel inclined to call substances which look and behave like water and gold by these terms, but it is a question of *truth* whether they are properly so called, for all true examples of these substances will share the common essences of them. A sample of liquid, a piece of metal will either have the molecular structure of these substances or it will not. It is by this criterion that we say no matter how much 'fool's gold' looks and feels like gold it is not as a matter of truth and fact real gold. The real, as opposed to merely conventional, unity of the objects he investigates enables the scientist to delimit the scope of his enquiries in a precise way and to seek genuinely true laws to explain how that which he investigates behaves. There are laws descriptive of the behaviour and properties of water, because all examples of the substance share a common inward constitution which determines their behaviour and properties in a strict fashion. To sum up: we can have a true science of natural substances only because they have common essences as well as common outward properties, for this in turn means that we can classify them in a precise and non-arbitrary manner and explain their myriad properties and reactions in terms of genuine laws.

The attractiveness of the belief in an essence to all religions to those who wish the study of religions to be a true science lies in the thought that a precise delimiting of the object of study and the true laws to explain its characteristics are thereby possible. With a common core there is a real non-conventional and non-arbitrary way of picking out 'true' examples of religion and there is hope of being able to explain the many facets of religion by generalisations from its essence. In considering examples of suggested cores for religion we thus need to bear two questions in mind. We must ask whether any suggested essence really does show a real, inner unity in the central examples of religion. If no account of the core does this, but all force us to dismiss from the category of religion some central cases (on our preliminary classification) then the scientific analogy behind the belief in religion's essence is weak. We must further ask if the suggested accounts of religion's essence really seem to explain the many characteristics of the various central examples of religion our operational definition of 'religion' gives us. If no account of an essence to religion seems to have this explanatory power then, again, the scientific analogy is weak.

The entire question of whether a true science of religion is possible is an important one and we shall touch upon it later in considering how far a disinterested study of religion is possible. In now turning to sample accounts of religion's essence or common core, we shall discuss examples of theories which locate the essence/core in religion's beliefs, in its origins and in its experiences.

An early example of an attempt by a Western scholar to find an essence to all religion comes from the work of the seventeenth-century humanist Edward Herbert. Exhibiting very clearly the theological motives that can lie behind the search for a common core to all religions, Herbert argues that, if God exercises a universal providence over the whole of mankind, we should expect to find in all religions a reliable account of how God is to be served. There must therefore be some 'common notions' in religion or 'catholic articles' which all true religions agree in. Herbert thinks he has found these common notions in the following five simple beliefs: 1. 'That there is one supreme God'; 2. 'That he ought to be worshipped'; 3. 'That virtue and piety are the chief parts of divine worship'; 4. 'That we ought to be sorry for our sins and repent of them'; 5. 'That divine goodness doth dispense rewards and punishments both in this life and after it' (Herbert, 1705: 3–4). The brevity of the list of common notions in religion, and the generality of individual items in it, points to one of the major problems in attempting to unite all religions around a set of common beliefs. (It is a problem which carries over into other attempts to seek a common core as well.) The set of beliefs has to be both vague enough to stand a chance of being seen to be behind the theologies of many outwardly different religions and yet it must be precise enough to point to a factor which really unites those many different religions. What Herbert has done is to locate this vague but genuinely unifying factor in monotheism and an awareness of right and wrong. To this day this has remained a popular way of seeking a unity in the world religions.

The problem that we have pointed to facing Herbert's attempt at unity shows initially in how he links both Christianity and Classical paganism together by reference to his common notions in religion. The Classical world apparently believed in many gods who were often regarded as being identical with parts of the natural world (e.g. sun, heavens, moon) rather than as supreme and transcendent. Ancient heathenism and

Christianity are still linked, however, for, according to Herbert, the heathens' worship of the sun etc. 'was symbolical' (Herbert, 1705: 31). Thus he is forced to seek a 'true', 'inner' meaning behind the outward form of pagan beliefs. Such an inner meaning *ought* to be there if his belief about God's presence in all religions is correct, but can we follow him in this 'symbolical' interpretation of Classical polytheism if we do not accept his theological starting-point? The question here raised about the attempt to see a common theology in all faiths gains force upon noting that Herbert acknowledges *popular* polytheism could not be interpreted symbolically. Polytheistic and pagan beliefs were taken seriously by many with the result that in place of religion, defined by the common notions, we had superstition and idolatry (see Herbert, 1705: 381–2). But now all religion is being unified by Herbert's common core of belief only at the cost of setting aside many forms of theology and worship as superstitious and idolatrous. We have: not an attempt to seek a common core to all religions, but a theological judgement that all correct, worthwhile religions will share certain beliefs. Herbert's theology is more unifying than some, because it is less specific, but he is none the less trying to establish what is correct in religion rather than what is essential to all its manifestations.

When we reflect, as Herbert could not, on the greater variety of doctrine and myth apparent with the recognition of non-theistic religions, the normative, theological character of attempts to see a single set of beliefs as unifying all religions is even more evident. Only if we are prepared to wield the distinction between 'true' and 'false' religion with vigour can we hope to unite all religions around a common set of beliefs. But that this is so, shows in turn that this form of the search for a common core to religion has no place in a disinterested, neutral survey of mankind's religious life throughout the world and its history.

The second form of the belief in an essence to all religions we wish to consider focuses upon the idea that all religions are identical in origin. There is a common essence to all religions because they all spring from the same original root (see Alston, 1967: 141). This approach to the search for religion's essence is popular wherever a strongly evolutionary perspective upon human life is influential. For if one thinks that human life and culture is the product of an evolutionary process, one may be led to conclude that the key to understanding it will lie in its origins. Since it is reasonable to suppose that human culture had similar origins in different parts of the world, one can assume a uniform starting-point for mankind's religions. Accepting the crucial role of origins in an evolutionary account of any aspect of cultural life, one will conclude there is common essence (i.e. explanatory key) to all religions.

There are numerous examples of this version of the essence theory, for it was particularly in vogue amongst late nineteenth-century scholars in Europe impressed by the success of evolutionism in biology and other fields. Thus E.B. Tylor argues in his famous work *Primitive Culture* that all religions share in a common root, which is also their essence, through 'animism'. Animism is the first philosophy of life and nature primitive man can be supposed to have thought out. It shaped the first human societies, the first religions from which all the rest flowed and is still at the heart of the religious faiths found today. It consists of the simple belief in souls (i.e. spiritual, non-material personalities) which animate man and his environment and control nature. Because of the centrality of the evolutionary origins of religion, animism in Tylor's account is the key to understanding the manifold beliefs and practices now extant and is the hidden unity beneath that manifold. Despite the popularity of searching for the essence of religions through origins, there are a number of grave difficulties in this approach. They can be instructively set out by reference to Tylor's theory. How, we may first ask, could we know that animism was or was not the first philosophy of life and nature from which all religions sprung? We have no direct access to the period of human history when culture and religion first arose, for by definition it occurred long before written records were possible. We can investigate the archaeology of the first human communities, but the traces they have left behind are meagre, rarely found and leave only the slimmest basis for inference as to the shape of the earliest human religions. Tylor overcomes this problem by largely basing his account upon the evidence of the beliefs of contemporary primitive peoples. These are tribal peoples who employ a low standard of technology and food production by European standards and can thus be taken to be living examples of the very first human communities. Leaving aside the much debated point of whether their religious life is really united by the philosophy of animism, it may be doubted whether they truly fill the evidential gap that threatens the anthropologist's speculations about the origins of all religions. For how do we know that their material culture has not developed slower than their spiritual? How do we know that either one or both are not degenerations from a state more sophisticated than that enjoyed at present? Even if their religious life were uniform, no sure clue is provided to the earliest origins of all religious life.

In fact the search for origins can be seen as a misleading detour in the search for religion's essence. For granted that all religions originate from, say, the same philosophy of nature, this will not unite them now unless they are all still true to that origin. It is an obvious fallacy (the 'genetic fallacy') to assume that because something originated in X it must still be essentially X and no more. Thus Tylor still has to show that all religions are *still* united in essence by the animistic philosophy (a point recognised in Chapter 11 of *Primitive Culture*). But then the origins theory of religion's essence collapses into one of the other types of theory. In Tylor's case it becomes another version of the view that all religions are united around a common belief or beliefs, but in his case a vague philosophy of nature has replaced the minimal theology Herbert lays down.

There is good reason to doubt whether any single philosophy of nature is or has been shared by all the central examples of religion. Animism, as defined by Tylor, will not do. For we read that in early Buddhism (to take but one example), though a variety of beings, including *devas* (gods), populate the universe, they occupy a secondary place, being impermanent and subject to a higher, impersonal cosmic law (see von Glasenapp, 1970: 30). The 'gods', therefore, did not occupy a fundamental role in the theoretical, practical, sociological or experiential dimensions of this central example of a religion.

The two sample accounts of religion's essence so far considered flounder upon the doctrinal and theological complexities exhibited by the world's religions. Given these complexities it is hard to find a common set of beliefs shared by all, or a common philosophical outlook in which they all agree. One way of continuing the search for religion's essence which bypasses the doctrinal and philosophical differences among religions is provided by the notion that we must look for the shared possession of a certain type of experience. A shared mode of experience underlying doctrinal differences is the common core to all religions and the essence of religion, the key to understanding its other dimensions.

Numerous writers have prosecuted the search for religion's essence in this fashion. One of the most famous is Rudolf Otto, who in his influential work *The Idea of the Holy* describes the numinous experience and of it concludes 'There is no religion in which it does not live as the real innermost core, and without it no religion would be worthy of the name' (Otto, 1950: 6). This experiential essence to religion is described by Otto as having three essential features: mystery, power and love. The religious experience is firstly an experience of something 'wholly other', that is, of something felt to be totally different from mundane objects of awareness. It is of something alien, foreign and transcendent. It does in addition strike those who have it with a sense of immense power. Before it awe, dread and fear are appropriate. The human subject of the experience feels himself and the objects around him as nothing in comparison with what is revealed in the numinous experience. The third important feature of the experience is shown in the way that, despite the mystery and power given in it, it draws and fascinates those who have it. They are not repelled, but rather their interest and concern is demanded by what is shown to them in the experience.

There are reasons for believing that something like Otto's numinous experience is present in many religions otherwise different in points of doctrine or explicit philosophical outlook (why this is so will become apparent below). Despite this there are a number of grounds for doubting whether we have stumbled upon the essence or common core to all religions. Some of these grounds relate to the specifics of Otto's account, others apply generally to accounts placing religion's essence in experience.

A specific point of criticism comes from the difficulty of seeing that Otto's analysis fits the character of many types of mystical experience. In mysticism the object of religion is sought through contemplation and inner quest. The characteristic result is a unitive experience in which the object is not felt as 'wholly other' but as identical with, or somehow within, the self. A concentration upon numinous experiences has been held to come from over-attention to the strand of worship in the religions, worship being a religious attitude or discipline which encourages the idea of a gulf between the believer and the object of his devotions (see Smart, 1964: 129–31).

A further question mark over the status of the numinous as the essence to all religion casts doubts about the validity of any search for religion's unifying essence in a mode of experience. The reason why the numinous experience looks like an important unifying feature, binding together at least all those religions in which worship is an important strand, is because its description captures many of the general features of man's experience of the sacred. But 'the sacred' is not the name of a *specific* object common to all religions; no more is it the name of a *specific* experience. Otto's description is unifying because it picks out some of the *generic* features (transcendence, power and attraction) that specific experiences of the sacred exemplify. We must be clear, however, that specific experiences of the sacred exemplify these generic features in different ways. This is not an accident. It arises through the mutual interaction of experience and doctrine in the religions. Those religions which all may be said to have as their generic object 'the sacred' differ enormously in the beliefs they hold about what specifically for them is sacred, and these idiosyncratic beliefs naturally colour in part how the sacred is experienced in religion. Otto's appearance in *The Idea of the Holy* of presenting a precise, specific, non-generic experience is created by the concentration upon Jewish and Christian sample experiences used to illustrate the numinous, for here we have experiences coloured and shaped by similar and overlapping beliefs about the object of experience. Otto himself affirms that the true essence of religion is not the numinous in isolation but the category of 'the Holy' (see Chapters 14 and 17 of *The Idea of the Holy*), this being the numinous experience mediated, interpreted by some definite conceptions and beliefs. They turn out to be elements of conception and belief associated with the concept of God as we find it in the philosophical theology of the Christian tradition. No wonder then that, if organisation around the category of the Holy is the mark of the full development of something as an example of religion, 'we find that Christianity . . . in this as in other respects, stands out in complete superiority over all its sister religions' (Otto, 1950: 142). Here, then, we have a general point of principle against any attempt to seek a specific religious experience that will unite all religions despite their doctrinal and philosophical differences. There is no such specific experience because doctrines shape experiences, so the specifics of doctrine will affect the specifics of experience. Only if experience and doctrine in religion were sharply separable (with perhaps differing doctrinal structures floating free above a unifying, specific experience to be found in all religions) could this be otherwise.

There are other ways of seeking an essence to religion than by the three modes we have illustrated (belief, origin and experience). Another important approach, for example, undertakes to discover a common, unifying feature in the function religion might have in personal and social life (see, e.g. Durkheim, 1936). In the course of discussing our examples of the quest for religion's essence we have noted one crucial problem that faces all such attempts. They have to locate religion's essence in something sufficiently precise enough to have a real unifying and explanatory force, but sufficiently general not to be tied to the specifics of some central examples of religion rather than others. Our discussion also throws up another general difficulty for all forms of the quest. We see that it is hard to find a core with the right combination of precision and generality in any of the beliefs of the religions or in anything that is fundamentally affected by their differing beliefs (such as their different philosophical outlooks or modes of experience). The measure of the difficulty in finding a core to religion which bypasses doctrine and belief may now be shown. For we can hope to find a common essence to religion only if we can hope to demonstrate that the theoretical dimension to religion is strictly secondary in making institutions examples of religion and in explaining their fundamental characteristics.

One may feel that this goal of relegating to the secondary and consequential the theoretical dimension in religion is too far-fetched to make the task of seeking an essence and common core to all religions seem at all attractive. Abandoning the task, one may still hope that the study of religions will produce interesting facts from one religion which illuminate our general conception of religion, and through that, other religions as well. One will have given up, however, any attempt to discover an absolute, definitive unity amongst religions or to explain the characteristics of religion by universal laws modelled on those in science.

Is Religion Available for Disinterested Study?

If our brief discussion of the search for religion's essence raises a question mark over a fully scientific explanation of religion, it remains to be considered how far a more modest scientific approach to religion is possible. In offering this volume as a work of detached, disinterested scholarship we have in fact been claiming that an acceptably modest scientific description of religion in history is possible. This is a description free of doctrinal commitment and bias, based upon objective, scholarly research. Such an approach, being distinct from that of theology, presupposes that one may seek to understand the world's religions without being a committed participant in them. It assumes, in short, that understanding a religion is possible without believing it.

Whether belief and understanding can thus be separated is something we must now pursue, as well as the related issue of how the historian's or sociologist's description of a religion is related to the beliefs of those who actually practise it. Many have thought that a neutral understanding of religion is impossible in some degree or other. This may reflect either a worry about a neutral approach to any human institution or doubts arising from the specific institution religion is. To tackle these doubts we must remind ourselves that we have defined 'religion' in terms of genus and differentiae. Its genus is a human institution—a complex of theoretical, practical, sociological and experiential dimensions. Its differentiae are provided by the characteristic object, goal and function of this complex. Our question about whether it is possible to have a neutral, outsider's understanding of religion now divides into two: Is it possible to have a neutral understanding of *any* complex of human belief, behaviour etc.? Can we have such an understanding for the *specific* types of belief, behaviour etc. that we find in religion?

The general question about the relation between understanding and belief raised here is important because of the common recognition that human behaviour has an 'inside' as well as an 'outside'. This distinction is evident if we reflect on the difference between the behaviour of an inanimate object and even a moderately complex piece of human behaviour, such as a gesture of greeting. The difference between say, describing a kettle boiling and describing something like the latter is shown in the way an account in terms of mere externals will do in the first case but not in the second. A kettle's boiling is a sequence of physical changes and to describe it is to do no more than plot these changes. But a description of the externally observable events that constitute one person's act of greeting to another would leave out some vital features of the act altogether. It would ignore those features which gave it its meaning as this act rather than another. It is an act of greeting because it has a certain kind of point. Its having this point is a matter of its being informed by beliefs and desires of a given kind and of it conforming to accepted conventions and rules for giving expression to those beliefs and desires. Unlike a sequence of mere physical changes, we may say that a piece of human behaviour has an 'inside' as well as an 'outside'. It is informed by beliefs and desires, and is related to conventions and rules of a human community. This 'inside' to human behaviour is even more apparent if we consider the experience and feelings that accompany behaviour and which also inform and shape it. Attention to both the externals and the inside of human behaviour is necessary if its meaning is to be discovered and hence if it is to be understood.

We might seem able to conclude quickly that an understanding of any human institution cannot be separated from the beliefs of those who participate in it. For any such institution will have an inside as well as an outside. Discovery of its inside will be necessary to determine the meaning of its component parts but will include precisely the beliefs of its participants. The beliefs of the participants will shape the meaning of the institution. But we must note the very limited nature of this conclusion. If to uncover the meaning of a human institution is in part to uncover the beliefs of those who participate in it, this is not to say that we must *share* those beliefs. It is only to say that we must describe them in describing the 'inward' side to the institution on pain of missing its meaning. As non-participating observers we should look to the beliefs and conventions present in the institution in helping us complete our description of it. We need sympathy, imagination and insight to uncover these beliefs, but this does not entail that we share them. We need to describe the beliefs of the participants to describe the institution in its fullness, but we do not need in addition to hold them.

If we equate a scientific approach to the description of religion with one that is neutral, scholarly and disinterested, we have not ruled it out in noting the importance of the 'inside' to any human institution. A scientific approach would only have been defeated if we assumed that neutrality, scholarship and disinterest meant being confined to the externals of an institution only. But there is no reason to suppose that the elements of objective study exclude the sympathetic and imaginative insight needed to penetrate beyond the externals of an institution. In the case of human belief and behaviour sympathy and imagination turn out to be the preconditions for the discovery of the whole range of data needed by objective scholarship.

This conclusion about the relation between belief and understanding drawn from the general character of a human institution can be applied to the specific case of a religion in the following way. Consider a scholar describing the meaning of the ritual of the Eucharist in a particular Christian denomination. No adequate description of this rite could confine itself to the externals of what goes on. It would have to mention and delineate its point—let it be an act of remembrance of the Saviour. In characterising the point of the rite many beliefs about the object of Christianity (i.e. God-in-Christ) would have to be mentioned and explained. The worshippers' beliefs about the object of their religion would thus need to be called upon to make up the description of the rite. But this does not entail that the scholar himself shares these beliefs, only that he be ready to uncover and use them in his account. All the beliefs about Christ and the Eucharist mentioned in his account would be in reported speech, and thus neither endorsed nor denied. Though the object of the religion would figure very considerably in the observer's account, it would, to use the technical expression, be 'bracketed' (see Smart, 1973: 57). All the statements about God and Christ in the description of the Eucharist would, on this score, be preceded by an explicit or implicit 'The participants believe that . . .' The nature of the object of religion would figure in the description only in and through the participants' beliefs about that object. So the 'inside' of the ritual could be grasped in the scholarly account without committing either the scholar or his readers to the actual existence of a religious object having that nature.

Our brief discussion of the general difficulties in describing human institutions has revealed a complexity in the relationship between an outsider's understanding of them and a participant's beliefs and experiences. The latter are crucial in yielding an understanding of the institution but not because endorsing them is a precondition of understanding them. Rather, uncovering and describing them will reveal to the outsider the full meaning of what goes on in the institution. The object of the outsider's reflection and, he hopes, understanding is in large measure the participant's beliefs. If we wish to restrict the possibility of an objective, neutral study of religion we must seek something more specific in religion to block this kind of approach to it.

One common way of arguing from the specifics of religion to the impossibility of a neutral understanding of it has been found in its experiential dimension. Thus it has been argued that religion's essence lies in its experiential dimension and that in the case of religion the experiential dimension is beyond definition or description (see Wiebe, 1981: 9–10). If this were the case, the only means of understanding the 'inside' to the institution is actually to have the experiences which determine it. Since they are beyond description nothing believers say or write can help the non-participant understand religion. Only by becoming a participant can one understand the unique, inexpressible experience that lies at the heart of religion. This line of thought is suggested by Otto's comments on the numinous experience:

> This mental state is perfectly *sui generis* and irreducible to any other, and therefore, like every absolutely primary and elementary datum, while it admits of being discussed, it cannot be strictly defined. There is only one way to help another to an understanding of it. He must be guided and led on by consideration and discussion of the matter through the ways of his own mind, until he reaches the point at which 'the numinous' in him perforce begins to stir, to start into life and into consciousness. (Otto, 1950: 7)

No doubt part of the reasoning behind Otto's conclusion that we can understand religious experience, and thus the core of religion, only if it is awakened in us lies in his stress upon it as the experience of something 'wholly other'. The observer of religion doesn't merely confront beliefs about and experiences of objects he happens not to have met himself, but could still understand. For he cannot be apprised of the character of these alleged objects by the use of general categories of which he has had experience in other cases. The objects of religious belief and experience, being transcendent, are not well described by general categories of description into which objects of common acquaintance also fit. Thus the believer himself feels the presence of a gap between the descriptions he offers and the object of his religion, just because those descriptions are drawn from ordinary things. Here we have a point which reflects the general character of the sacred as a class of objects of belief, ritual and experience. The sacred is other than the ordinary, the mundane, and thus not easily defined by ordinary descriptions and classifications.

There can be no question that the content of religious beliefs and experiences is out of the ordinary in a quite special sense and that this creates peculiar difficulties in understanding. The resources of imagination, sympathy and insight that the neutral scholar must employ will have to be greater than in the description of many other aspects of human life. Further reflection, however, will show that he is not without important aids in understanding even the content of beliefs and experiences focusing on the sacred.

One source of interpretation comes from the fact that beliefs and experiences concerning the sacred do not exist in isolation. It is, for example, clear from Otto's discussion of the numinous experience that it is in concrete cases always found connected with a web of notions and doctrines in particular religions. It is shaped by these connections and in turn contributes to the concepts and beliefs that surround it. In its developed forms it is not a bare experience but an encounter with the object of a specific religion. Thus its character can in part be ascertained by noting the connections established between it and other things in the various dimensions of a religion. The fact that particular beliefs and experiences concerning the sacred are connected with other beliefs and experiences, and with practices and sociological structures, brings with it a further source of understanding for the non-participant. These connections entail that such beliefs and experiences are parts of a publicly shareable and shared human institution. Experiences of the sacred may in a manner be private and unique but they are bound up with dimensions of belief, behaviour, experience and social organisation that define a human, cultural phenomenon (see Wiebe, 1981: 9–10). Being a cultural phenomenon religion exists as a public entity. The experiential dimension to religion does not militate against this fact. For what makes an individual's experiences of the sacred *religiously* significant (as opposed to being merely private experiences of one knows not what) is that they do connect with and contribute to the public phenomenon that is a religion. To be counted as experiences of the sacred they must be characterised as experiences of something, where the relevant concept used to delineate the object is recognisably drawn from some system of religious thought or other, even if it is a system initiated by the experience itself. This entails that all experiences of the sacred have the public connections described if they are to be counted as experiences of the sacred. If someone had an experience that was literally indescribable or literally of nothing, there would be no more reason to classify it as a religious experience than there would to classify it as belonging to some totally different area of life.

One cannot deny that there are esoteric experiences in the religions. There are experiences (sometimes associated with forms of mysticism) described as being of the Ineffable or of Nothingness. Such experiences do of course create a problem for the interpreter. But it should be noted that words like 'Ineffable' and 'Nothingness' do function here as descriptions: they are means of positively characterising the experiences in question, which in turn connect the experiences with doctrines, rituals etc. in comprehensible ways. Thus 'Ineffable' gets its force from associations with doctrines to the effect that the sacred object surpasses and is distinct from all mundane things. 'Nothingness' as a characterisation may be connected with doctrines and practices associated with the religious importance of the extinction of the self or of the emptying of mind of all discrete, finite objects of consciousness. Such characterisations do not, then, blunt the force of what has been urged concerning the publicity and connectedness of individual religious experiences and beliefs. In the last analysis the force of these characterisations is derived from what comes before and what comes after them in the life of religion.

A further source of help to the observer trying to understand the character of beliefs and experiences comes from the undoubted fact that the sacred connects with the mundane in countless ways. Thus, to cite Otto's particular account of the sacred again, it is evident that both the numinous experience itself and the concepts used to rationalise it are connected with experiences and descriptions of the ordinary and everyday. Otto notes how the numinous experience has 'numerous analogies' with other experiences, despite being qualitatively *sui generis* in some sense. He mentions the experience of the sublime in nature as a closely analogous feeling (Otto, 1950: 44). If the experience is rationalised in the manner of Christian theology (in terms of an all-powerful, all-good creator God), then it is being shaped by concepts derived from public conceptions of mundane things (power, goodness, making). For all the unique and 'wholly other' character of the numinous, one who has not had experience of it is not without bearings in understanding it. A general truth about the character of the sacred here emerges. The characteristic objects of religion may be regarded as distinct from ordinary, mundane things in various and varying respects. But they are all regarded as connected with and related to ordinary things in important ways.

There are two strong reasons from within the dynamics of religion why the sacred should thus be connected with the ordinary. In the first case: if it were not it would be of no interest and importance. Religion does not merely focus on realities felt to be extraordinary but on ones which are vital to human life. They must be realities which suggest a goal for human striving, the following of which will have an important role in human individual or social life. They must therefore be thought of as interacting in important ways with ordinary life and its concerns. In addition, if the sacred were not related to ordinary things and realities there would be no route into religion for even those who aspire to be participants. Religion would be a completely closed book quite incapable of being comprehended by anyone. Nothing else in human culture would provide a means for being able to understand or participate in it. Not only the phenomenon of conversion, but also the obvious interpenetration of religion and the other aspects of human culture shows the connectedness of religious belief and experience with other things. If religion were completely esoteric, it would be of no interest to anyone; and it would not exist. We do not, again, deny that religion may speak of the 'ineffable' or the 'utterly mysterious'. One way of relating a felt reality to ordinary things may be the way of differencing and distinguishing it from them. The importance for us of the religious object might lie in its unlikeness to anything ordinary. We can describe and relate one thing to another by stressing unlikeness and difference.

If we consider the differentiae of religion as a human institution, we must conclude that it has many aspects which will stretch the sympathetic and imaginative resources of the neutral scholar to the uttermost. We have not, however, found anything to suggest that, unlike other phenomena in human culture, it is not available for disinterested study. 'Disinterest' and 'neutrality' are not labels for 'lack of sympathy' or 'external observation'. The scholar must get to grips with the living 'inside' of religion, but he need not share the beliefs, experiences etc. which make up that 'inside'. Nor need he govern his research and observation by the desire to make them prove preconceived theological commitments.

Conclusion

Much has been said in the last section of the difference between a theological approach to religion and an approach of disinterested scholarship. The point of view of the believer has likewise been distinguished from that of the non-participating observer of religion. It would be wrong to leave the impression that such distinctions were hard and fast.

It may, for example, be very important for one who is a committed participant in a particular religion to adopt on occasion the stance of a disinterested observer of the religious scene. The fruits of others' neutral scholarship may equally be of great importance to the participant. No one is any the better for being ignorant of the actual historical or sociological details of his own religion. To stand back from one's own faith, to examine it and other faiths with disinterested scrutiny, may be of great importance in fully understanding what one believes and why one believes it. Scholarly enquiry into one's own faith may be the means of uncovering beliefs and assumptions about one's religion that are best dismissed as prejudiced and harmful. Looking at the faiths of others may give one a new insight into one's own, in revealing how people of different cultures have coped with common problems, such as suffering and death. It may be a powerful check to the parochialism which assumes that one's own culture represents the experience of humanity as a whole.

For the kind of reason mentioned above much theology has in fact been engaged in scholarly historical and critical research. Much of the pioneering work in the West in the global study of religions was undertaken by theologians interested in discovering the facts of the relationship between Christianity and the larger religious life of mankind. The best theologians have understood that one cannot articulate one's faith without understanding it. Acts of disinterested reflection which take in what others have thought and believed may be an aid to such understanding. An understanding of one's own religion, and of religion in general, is not given just in being a participant in it.

As we reflect upon religion in the contemporary world it is with a heightened sense of the facts of the historical antiquity, and geographical variety and extent of human culture. More and more we will come to realise accordingly the truth of Max Mueller's dictum of 100 years ago: he who knows one religion, knows none (Mueller, 1893: 13).

Bibliography

Alston, W. P. 'Religion', in P. Edwards (ed.), *The Encyclopedia of Philosophy* (Macmillan, New York, 1967), pp. 140–5.

Aquinas, Thomas *Summa Theologiae*, tr. Dominican Fathers (Eyre & Spottiswoode, London, 1974)

Durkheim, E. *The Elementary Forms of the Religious Life* (Allen & Unwin, London, 1976)

Eliade, M. *Patterns in Comparative Religion* (Sheed and Ward, London, 1958)

Ferre, F. *Basic Modern Philosophy of Religion* (Scribners, New York, 1967)

Frazer, J. *The Golden Bough*, abridged edn (Macmillan, London, 1922)

Geertz, C. 'Religion as a Cultural System' in M. Banton (ed.), *Anthropological Approaches to the Study of Religion* (Tavistock, London, 1966), pp. 1–46

Glasenapp, H. von *Buddhism—a Non-Theistic Religion*, tr. Irmgard Schlögel (Allen and Unwin, London, 1970)

Herbert, Edward *De Religione Gentilium*, tr. as *The Antient Religion of the Gentiles* by William Lewis (London, 1705)

Kitagawa, J. 'Primitive, Classical and Modern Religions' in Kitagawa (ed.), *The History of Religions* (University of Chicago Press, Chicago, 1967), pp. 39–65

Mueller, F.M. *An Introduction to the Science of Religion* (Longman, London, 1893)

Otto, R. *The Idea of the Holy*, tr. J. Harvey (Oxford University Press, Oxford, 1950)

Smart, R.N. *Philosophers and Religious Truth* (SCM, London, 1964)

—— *The Religious Experience of Mankind* (Collins, Glasgow, 1971)

—— *The Science of Religion and the Sociology of Knowledge* (Princeton University Press, Princeton, 1973)

Smith, W.C. *The Meaning and End of Religion* (SPCK, London, 1978)

Smith, W.R. *Lectures on the Religion of the Semites*, 3rd edn (Black, London, 1927)

Tylor, E.B. *Primitive Culture*, vol. 1, 4th edn (Murray, London, 1903)

Wiebe, D. *Religion and Truth* (Mouton, The Hague, 1981)
Wittgenstein, L. *Philosophical Investigations* (Blackwell, Oxford, 1958)
Yinger, J. M. *The Scientific Study of Religion* (Macmillan, New York, 1970)

Some of the material for this chapter is taken from an article by the author in *The Scottish Journal of Religious Studies*, Vol. 1, No. 1 (1980), and is reproduced by kind permission of the editor.

2 *The Study of Religion and Religions*

Stewart Sutherland

There are many reasons or motives which may lead someone to study religion or particular religions. One may simply be *interested* in the subject, or in some aspect of it. Alternatively one may be engaged 'existentially' with some of the questions to which religion and religions offer answers: that is to say one may be looking for a belief or set of beliefs. More mundanely one may be sitting examinations which will test one's knowledge of these matters.

To focus upon the reasons or motives however is at this stage not very helpful. What is more important is to try to grasp what the successful outcome of the study of religion or religions should be. In one sense this is a straightforward matter, for the successful outcome of anything worth studying ought to be an extension of knowledge and understanding. This obvious answer, however, raises as many questions as it settles. There are three main types of question which arise, and they are all central to the nature and rationale of this book:

1. What will one know if one knows more about religion(s) and what is it that one will understand if one has a greater understanding of religion(s)?
2. If one seeks such knowledge or understanding where should one focus one's attention?
3. What methods should one use to increase knowledge or understanding?

Let us answer these questions in turn, recognising at the outset what will become even more apparent as we proceed: the answer to any one of these questions is ultimately dependent upon the answers given to the other two.

Knowledge and Understanding

What will one know, if one knows more about religion(s) and what is it that one will understand if one has a greater understanding of religion(s)?

In his discussion of the idea that all religions may have a common core (see pp. 3–28), Peter Byrne considers the comparison some had drawn between looking for knowledge or understanding of religion, and looking for knowledge or understanding of a substance in the natural world. This someone who 'knows' what gold is, knows how to distinguish it from what looks like it, 'fool's gold', and ultimately such knowledge is based upon knowledge of the properties which the substance gold has. Now it would be very nice if knowing about religion or religions could be characterised in an equivalently straightforward way. However, for all the reasons spelt out in Peter Byrne's chapter, such a comparison is too simple and simplified.

A fundamental difficulty in such a comparison is that gold is gold, with its various physical properties whatever human beings may believe about it, or whatever value they attach to it. It is part of the natural world which is there and is what is, without reference to what we may or may not think of it. Religion, however, is not part of the natural world in that way, for if there were no human beings there would be no religion: whereas there was gold before there were any human beings, and there may well still be gold after the human race is extinct. This is an element of what we mean when we say that religion is in part at least a social phenomenon. It has to do with what human beings do and think and say. Thus in studying religion(s) one is studying, amongst other things, human beings and human societies. To grasp this is to have avoided many of the pitfalls of the study of religion. It is also, as we shall see, to have given ourselves some hints about where we must focus our attention, and also of the methods which we must use.

It will be useful to pause briefly to underline this point. Some regard the study of religion(s) as at best distracting, and at worst impossible. They do this because they believe that the study of religion(s) is and can only be the study of 'God' or of what is 'transcendent'. They then recall or point out that if God is God, or if we do really mean 'what transcends human thought', then study in any acceptable sense will be impossible, for God is above all knowing and beyond all of our limited conceptions and is not a suitable candidate for study: for worship, or love, or even hatred, yes, but not for the cool reflective gaze of the student. Now there are many questions which could be raised here, which are not the concern of this book, but which are properly the focus of theological enquiry (for example St Thomas Aquinas's *Summa Theologiae*, or Karl Barth's *Church Dogmatics*, both of which consider with great subtlety the question of the knowledge which we may have of God). These questions are not our concern because the study of religion(s) is not, for example, the study of what God is, but is the study of what men and women *believe* or *say* that God is. Equally the study of religion(s) is not the study of what we must do to have eternal life, but is the study of what human beings *do* in pursuit of eternal life, and of what they *say* we must do to find it. Thus the study of religion(s) must at least begin with the study of human beings and their doings and sayings.

Of course for many it will go well beyond this. On the one hand there are those who would also press the question of whether what such human beings say and believe is true, and on the other, there are those who might, in assuming that it is not true, look for an explanation of why human societies should, without exception, include people who do engage in religious practices and/or hold religious beliefs.

If it is clear that the study of religion(s) is founded in the study of human beings and human society, are we any nearer answering our first question of what it is that we hope to know or understand through the study of religion(s)? We are a little nearer, but we still have some considerable way to go. For some the idea of study is the amassing of facts or information so that they may achieve a reputation for erudition, whether in playing *Trivial Pursuit* with their relatives, or entering television quiz-games, or with more *gravitas*, in the arena of scholarship.

Thus they might be seeking, in magpie fashion, knowledge of a number of facts about religion, e.g. that in Brazil the number of Protestants in 1890 was 143,743, in 1940 was 1,074,857 and in 1961 was 4,071,643, or that an Islamic writer named al-Ghazali wrote a book called *The Incoherence of Philosophers* in which he attacked the growing influence of philosophy on Islamic theology. Or we may be interested in such facts as that in 1976 211 of the 236 adults resident in Hardenburgh, New York State, became ministers of the Universal Life Church. (The explanation of this apparently massive response to a veritable trumpet-blast of religious vocation is that evidently, in the USA, citizens who are ministers or clergy may be exempt from some taxes. An enterprising though almost illiterate former hobo called Kirby J. Hensley founded the Universal Life Church to provide a mail-order ordination service, thus allowing the recipients of his airmail dog-collars to reclassify their homes as churches and thereby to save on taxes payable!)

Now knowledge of such facts which are in each case, in some sense, knowledge of facts about or of religion, may well be important in non-trivial ways and in some cases essential for further study or deeper understanding. Indeed of such facts there is virtually no end and drawing upon and analysing them is a precondition of the discussions of all the contributions to this book. In putting the point in that way I am implying that the search for knowledge and understanding may rest upon, but it must go far beyond, the acquisition of such snippets of information.

This suggests a second answer to our question of what sort of knowledge or understanding we hope to attain. On this view we may be seeking knowledge in the sense of the specific sort of understanding which an expertise or particular discipline can give us. Thus, for example, an historian can tell us much about the historical fortunes of a particular religious tradition, or a sociologist can inform us about the statistical correlations between particular social groupings and classes on the one hand, and membership of particular religious groups or branches of the Christian Church on the other. Or an expertise in ancient Greek and Hebrew can contribute an understanding of the Scriptures of the Christian religion which is not possible for those who study these Scriptures only in translation. These are all examples of the application of a skill or a discipline to the analysis of facts, and the extension of the understanding of religion(s).

What each example makes plain is that understanding or knowledge may take many forms and draw upon many disciplines, and the consequent fragmentation of knowledge and understanding is a fundamental feature of the world in which we live, whether we think of understanding religion(s) or understanding agriculture. To that extent it is a feature also of this book, for the multi-faceted nature of religion(s) requires a variety of skills and techniques in its analysis. Equally the interests of any particular reader may best be served through the use of one particular discipline rather than another (see below).

What is true, however, is that it is unlikely that any *one* discipline will provide a universal key to unlock all the secrets of religion(s) to those in search of understanding and knowledge. In addition to the answers to specific questions (e.g. Is there a correlation between industrialisation and the decline of religion?, or, Is Islamic Fundamentalism best understood as a political movement?, or, Do any of the Gospels present an accurate picture of the historical Jesus?) there are questions of a much wider nature, where it is not clear that an historian *qua* historian or a sociologist *qua* sociologist can provide adequate answers.

This shows itself in two ways. In the first instance there are many questions about religion(s) which require the skills of more than one discipline to answer them. Thus for example even within the limited range of the exegesis of religious texts practitioners will use historical, linguistic, textual, and increasingly also, anthropological and sociological skills. In the second place we do seem to return to the further group of questions of a much wider nature already mentioned which are perhaps more easily formulated than answered.

These questions are for many the driving force behind the study of religion(s) and are questions which signal the desire for a third and much less easily definable knowledge or understanding. We might for example be puzzled about what religion is, or about how to understand a particular religious practice. Someone who is not a Muslim might be puzzled about why some of his colleagues or neighbours kneel and bow low five times each day, facing always in the same direction. He may begin to understand if he is told that they are praying, but his puzzlement may go deeper than that. It may show itself in the further question of '*Why* do they pray five times daily in that way?', but it may in fact be a question about what prayer is.

One answer to the question, 'Why do they pray five times daily?' may be found in the teachings of the Qur'an and in the traditions of Islam and an answer which spells out the details here will be an increase in knowledge and understanding. What it will not do, however, is give the sort of understanding which the questioner seeks. The puzzlement may be about what prayer is, or about why men and women should pray at all. Two centuries ago the philosopher Kant wrote of Christian prayer that a man might be embarrassed to be found alone in a room on his knees. Now Kant knew perfectly well what the practices and conventions of Christianity are regarding prayer, and someone who wanted to contest his view, or to imply that he did not 'really' understand what prayer is, would have to do rather more than reiterate biblical injunctions about the manner of and the importance of prayer. He would have to give Kant an account of the nature of prayer which justifies other descriptions than 'a man alone in a room on his knees'. On the one hand he would have to persuade Kant that the practice of prayer has a point or meaning which Kant has missed, and on the other, in the course of that, he would have to give content and meaning to expressions such as 'watch and pray that ye may not enter into temptation', or 'worship the Lord in the beauty of holiness'. Whether a practitioner or believer can help in providing such an understanding of this practice for a non-believer is of course one of the major questions of the study of religion(s), and preparing to answer it requires reflection, study and great care.

It is often helpful to look for comparisons and contrasts in such a situation, and there are forms of puzzlement from other areas of life which have, at least, common roots in the human condition, which as we have already seen is the starting-point for the study of religion(s). We may be a little puzzled if in some tropical swampland we came across someone wearing only a pair of shorts standing quite still by the edge of a pool of water. We may be even more puzzled when we see that he is apparently using his body as live bait for mosquitoes. Now if we ask him why he is standing there, the reply that this is a good place for being bitten by mosquitoes will not remove the question marks which we have set against his behaviour. Indeed it might increase the significance which we attach to them! There are further unanswered questions, which we may have difficulty in formulating clearly, but which are a clear indication of our problem in trying to understand what this man is doing (cf. Kant's problem about a man alone in a room on his knees).

Rather different examples are the difficulties which an American may have in helping an Englishman understand what is going on in a game of American Football, or the parallel but reverse difficulty of explaining what is going on in a game of cricket. If a non-initiate asks a cricket fan, 'Why is the captain asking those fielders to move?', there may be an elaborate but clear answer in terms of strategy. If, however, that was the first of a series of questions which ends up with 'And why should grown men want to spend five days doing that, here, now?', then there surely is a problem which *may* be one of understanding, but may on the other hand be one of taste.

If we compare these two examples with the religious example, a number of points emerge, which might help us appreciate the complexities involved in some of the very general questions which arise about understanding religion. If, in the case of the human mosquito bait, we learn that this man is one member of a research team working on the control of mosquitoes in an area where malaria is a serious problem, and if we learn further that it is necessary to catch and breed from live mosquitoes and that this is the most efficient way of catching them, our puzzlement goes. We no longer doubt the man's sanity and we understand what he is doing. We cease to ask questions about it. It is not perhaps that we understand the fine and important detail of the design of the research, nor of the complex microbiology underlying it. There is, however, a degree of satisfaction and we can 'place' the activity in a larger context. Now many questions about religion(s) are of this sort and answering them requires a broadening of the context and of our knowledge of the context. Careful study of this book will answer, or at least significantly help in answering, such questions. This is one of the central reasons for the variety and range of the book.

There is, however, another feature of the example which is important. We accept as satisfactory a limited answer because we can place the activity, 'standing alone by the edge of the pool wearing only shorts', not only as part of its immediate context, 'facilitating a piece of research', but also as part of a much wider context, namely the diminution of illness and suffering, which we accept as important.

In the case of the cricket match, however, 'standing alone in the outfield clad in white' may well be something which the questioner can see in a wider context, and to that extent 'understand', but may well still leave a sense of dissatisfaction. Thus there may be an appreciation that the tactics of the game, the fact that there is a leg-break specialist bowling from this end, make prudent the presence of Willoughby minor on the boundary, but still no equivalent satisfaction to that marked by the response, 'Ah, I see, you are trying to eliminate malaria from this region'.

Not only is it agreed that there is an ultimate point to standing alone by the edge of the pool wearing only shorts, but there is an understanding of what the point of this is, and also, in this case, that the point is important. In the cricket example, however, one might see that standing alone on the boundary clad in white makes it more likely that the batsman will be caught out, but still not be satisfied that 'there is a point to all this', or that if there is that it has any importance.

In the religious case some of the questions which we ask, and some of the knowledge or understanding which we may seek, is of this wider sort. One may be wanting to know what the point of all this is; 'Very well,' we may say, 'I see that they are praying to Allah, or that he is praying to God, but I am not convinced that this is important, or perhaps even that it ultimately has a point.'

A further variation on the mosquitoes example might help here. Suppose instead of a swampy tropical region we were in a rather cool temperate region by a fast-flowing, rather chilly looking, river. Suppose further we saw not a near-naked mosquito-catcher, but a well-wrapped Englishman wearing thigh-length rubber boots and carrying a fishing-rod. We might well grasp that he is hoping to catch fish rather than mosquitoes and to that extent 'understand' what he is doing. But we might well also shake our heads and say, 'If he wants trout for supper it would be cheaper and much less uncomfortable to buy it from the fish farm down the road.' That is to say, whatever the million or so fishermen in Britain 'see' in this pastime, we do not. Or is it the case that if necessary we might be persuaded to act as mosquito-bait because we see the importance of this, whereas we are not convinced of the importance of acting as assistant to our friend who is quite sane apart from his desire to stand up to his thighs in cold water from time to time? In the one case we might overcome our lack of taste for the activity, whereas in the other we shall not.

This comparison does help highlight some of the features of the religious example of prayer. Now it may be that some disagreements over religion(s) are matters of taste—'you prefer candles and incense, I prefer sermons and metrical psalms'. But in that case there is no disagreement about importance, or possibly about understanding. If, however, the disagreement is of the pattern—'You prefer candles and incense, I prefer going to the theatre, or playing golf'—then not only is there a disagreement about taste, there is also a disagreement about importance, for believers are not inclined to accept that anything is even of equal importance to the practice of religion. Our question must be whether this is properly described as a difference in understanding, and if so whether the study of religion(s) can play any part in removing such a possible lack of understanding. This is an area through which we must tread with great care for it contains many intellectual land-mines.

There are two main ways in which these very general questions about the ultimate importance or 'point' of religion(s) are tackled. Some, including particularly those who belong to the great monotheistic religions, would want to say that the importance of religion derives from the *truth* of the central beliefs involved. If it is not true that we are creatures in a world created by a just and loving God then prayer has neither importance nor 'point'. Others would claim that the argument is not quite so straightforward. Persuading someone to say, 'Our Father, which art in Heaven', as a believer says it, is first and foremost persuading him that the words have a meaning by showing him what the meaning is.

To appreciate this point is to appreciate that we have moved from the realm of the study of religion(s) as it is variously practised in this book, to the philosophical discussion of the implications of questions raised in and through the study of religion(s). I shall return to these matters briefly in due course.

In brief summary, however, we have seen how the search for knowledge and understanding in the study of religion(s) can take a variety of forms, as can the types of knowledge and understanding to be found in such study. This is the reason for the range of approaches and methods followed in this book. The approach or the method used in any particular section or page will depend upon the particular issue being discussed. Before elaborating on this, however, it would be useful to raise a rather different question.

The Focus of Attention

One of the reassuring things about study rather than speculation or free association is that study is always study *of* something. Study has an object upon which we focus our attention and which helps define the nature of the study. Hence it is reasonable to ask, 'If one seeks knowledge and understanding through study where should one focus one's attention?'

We have already spent some time analysing the variety of really rather different possibilities which are included under the general heading of 'Knowledge and Understanding', and there is no need to retrace our steps in detail. Rather we should be applying what we have already learned.

We have also noticed the importance of drawing a distinction between the study of religion (singular) and the study of religions (plural). This will be the starting-point for our short excursion into identifying the focuses of attention in our study. Again, of course, the variety which we find will depend upon the variety of types of knowledge or understanding which we seek. There are three different types of focuses of attention.

In the first place in setting out to study religion(s) we may be interested in some specific aspect of religion or religions. Two different examples of such study can give some indication of the range of possibilities and the implications of this range.

In a classic work first published at the beginning of the century, *The Protestant Ethic and the Spirit of Capitalism*, Max Weber examined the question of the relation between the development of capitalist civilisation and the type of ethical outlook and practice which he believed lay at the heart of Protestant and in particular Calvinistic religion. This is to focus one's study upon a very specific aspect of one particular religion. It also illustrates the intimate connection between the specific nature of the focus of attention, the type of method used, and determining both of these, the question set about the psychological conditions which made possible the development of capitalist society. Much of what counts as the study of religion(s) will be of this form and since the possible questions are without limit so in one volume, while accepting the constraints of finitude, we must attempt to give some sense of the range of possible specific focuses of attention which are required by the search for answers to specific questions.

The temptation to oversimplify is ever present and, in his foreword to the English translation, R.H. Tawney expresses it well:

> It is the temptation of one who expounds a new and fruitful idea to use it as a key to unlock all doors, and to explain by reference to a single principle phenomena which are in reality the result of several converging causes. (p. 7)

Weber is less guilty of this than most, but the danger is inevitably there.

A rather different example of focusing on one aspect of religion is to be found in another classic of the same decade, William James's *The Varieties of Religious Experience*. James's book, subtitled *A Study in Human Nature*, is clearly centred upon close observation of and classification of the variety within one aspect of religion—religious experience. But there is not, as in Weber's case, the organising pressure of a single question. The study is classificatory and extends as widely as this aspect of religion and human nature require. Equally there is not the constraint of a single method brought to bear on a recalcitrant subject matter, and as a study in 'religion' so evidence is produced as it is considered relevant from a variety of 'religions'.

These two examples show how the type of question asked—the sort of knowledge or understanding sought—require a focus upon some aspect of religion which may belong to only one religion, or which may span several religions. The method or methods to be used will vary according to the question asked.

A second general type of focus of attention is not some aspect of religion, but is a particular religion or religious tradition. Here one might be studying—seeking knowledge or understanding of—the religion in question *as a religion*, not for example as a social or anthropological phenomenon. This clearly differs from Weber's interest which is in an aspect of a religious tradition as an explanation of particular social changes. The appropriate form of study here is usually called the History of Religions and is to be distinguished from Comparative Religion which is the comparative study of more than one religion or religious tradition.

It may be that in defining this focus of attention we are on much clearer and firmer ground, but we do run into some of the problems already uncovered in Peter Byrne's essay on 'Religion and Religions'. How do we define what counts as a religion? It is consonant with his arguments there and with the general approach of this volume that there will be borderline cases, and some of the general issues arising out of this are discussed in Anders Jeffner's essays on 'Religion and Ideology' and 'Atheism and Agnosticism'.

The uncertainties there are as nothing, however, when compared with the problems of the third most general focus of attention. What if, as is a fairly widespread desire on the part of many students of religion, one wishes to focus not upon particular traditions, nor particular aspects of religion, but upon religion as such. By now we ought to realise that there is an element of intellectual hubris in such a hope, but perhaps of such things are real scholars made. If our aim is to understand religion, then we ought to aim to do so with the widest possible focus of attention which we can achieve.

The unclarities and uncertainties of such an aim, however, have been documented at some length and I shall not repeat them again. One point of summary and recapitulation will suffice. Attempting to focus one's attention upon 'religion in itself' or 'religion in general' is to focus upon what is diffuse and infinitely varied and it is to do so with a variety of methods which are subject only to the nature and scope of the question being asked.

Methods

The ground which we must briefly cover under this heading has already been well tilled. To the question, 'What methods should one use to increase knowledge or understanding?' the answer must be, 'It depends upon the question being asked.' Some questions, such as those of Weber, required the methods of historical and social analysis. Other questions may require linguistic and archaeological as well as historical skills. It would be impossible to study the forms which religion takes in some cultures without invoking the methods of social anthropology.

In rather different contexts, if for example claims about the Turin Shroud were to be regarded as religious claims, the techniques of chemical analysis would be a precondition of answering some questions. The psychology of religion as a branch of psychology has its own contribution to make, but again always depending upon specific questions being asked. However, there are some general points about method as such which can be illustrated by a brief discussion of one of the most stimulating contributions to the psychology of religion which has been published this century. I refer to Freud's *The Future of an Illusion*.

Freud's writings in this and other essays illustrate well both the strengths and the potential pitfalls of developing and using a specific method and applying it to the study of religion. Freud was clearly intrigued by religious belief and practice and in a number of works including *The Future of an Illusion* set down his reflections on the matter. By that time (1927) he had fully developed his psychoanalytic method of treating illness, and with it a fairly elaborate theory of human nature. His puzzlement about religion was based on his observations of what people do and say. His resolution of that puzzlement was to apply a theory developed in the context of the study and treatment of mental illness to this area of human experience also. Indeed all the indications are that Freud believed his theories to have general application to all areas of human life and his followers have certainly taken this view.

Effectively he regarded religious behaviour as analogous to neurotic behaviour. His characterisation of religion as 'an illusion' is not, he insists, its classification as 'error' (although the onus is firmly on the believer to show that it is not), but it is to claim that religion is based on wish-fulfilment—on what we *want* to be true. Now there is much of interest in such a claim and undoubtedly human beings are prone to believe what, in some sense, they want to believe. The particular twist in Freud's account is that we are not in this case aware of these deep-seated, unconscious, wishes. This is an interesting and important view about which much might be written, but our present task is to focus upon some general features of the application of this method to the study of religious belief and practice.

There is no doubt that there are those whose religious belief and practice are based upon what they want to believe rather than what they have other reason to believe. As such, Freud's observation is clear and accurate. However, what is also true is that Freud may face the same danger as that which Tawney signalled in Weber's case (see p. 36 above)—he seems to want to apply a single method of enquiry and explanation which may well have great significance in one context, as if it were 'a key to unlock all doors'. That is to say, it may well be correct to infer that Mr Enderby's religious belief and Miss Crimpel's religious devotions are, in Freud's sense, 'illusions', without wishing to imply that this is the appropriate account to give of the belief of Thomas Aquinas, or of Franz Jaggerstäter (see *Zahn*) or Billy Graham and so on. Now in each of these cases if there is a clear 'explanation' to be given the explanations will be severally different, but that is just the point. The difficulty and indeed implausibility of Freud's view is that in the end there is only one explanation and that is the same explanation for everyone. This is the greatest single potential pitfall facing the application of specific methods or disciplines to the study of religion(s)—a forced uniformity arising from an illusory universality. Hence the need in this volume to use as many methods as are necessary to answer the variety of questions which arise in the study of religion(s).

The other major point which is illustrated by the example taken from Freud could equally well apply to all such general theories of religion which are derived from the application of a single method of enquiry. In each case, whether we think of Freud, or Marx, or Durkheim, or whomsoever, the method either boasts or conceals a particular theory of human nature. The first and most obvious point is that if we accept Freud's or Marx's respective definitions of religion (and we cannot consistently accept both!) then we are *ipso facto* accepting the correlated theory of human nature which underpins that definition. We should certainly ask for considerable evidence and argument before taking on board such a major intellectual structure. The second point of course is that very often what is offered by religious belief is a theory of human nature which is quite clearly seen as an *alternative* to the non-religious diagnoses of the human condition. We must not allow the adoption of a method in any way to mask or hide that deep point of difference.

Summary and Interim Conclusions

We have surveyed briefly in this essay three interrelated topics, all of which have a central bearing upon the study of religion and religions. The question of the type of knowledge or understanding which we seek in such study clearly has a number of answers, of which we selected three main types. The focus of our attention, and the method of enquiry which we should follow, have equally in each case a number of possible answers. The outcome is a grid of considerable detailed complexity if we were to fill in all possible variables, and which would require at least three dimensions to represent. The point here is not to distract the reader into trying to visualise such a grid, but rather to indicate the reasons for the degree of variety and flexibility of approach which will be necessary in a single volume devoted to the study of *The World's Religions*.

Bibliography

Aquinas, Thomas *Summa Theologiae*, Latin text and English translation in 60 volumes (Eyre & Spottiswoode, London, and McGraw-Hill, New York, 1964ff.)
Barth, Karl *Church Dogmatics*, English translation (T. & T. Clark, Edinburgh, 1936ff.)
Freud, S. *The Future of an Illusion* (Hogarth Press, London, 1928)
James, W. *The Varieties of Religious Experience* (Collins Fontana, London, 1960)
Weber, M. *The Protestant Ethic and The Spirit of Capitalism* (Unwin, London, 1930)
Zahn, G. *In Solitary Witness* (Chapman, London, 1964)

3 Religion and Ideology

Anders Jeffner

Bertrand Russell, in his *History of Western Philosophy*, claimed that there are many structural similarities between Christianity and Marxism.[1] If we call Marxism a political ideology, this indicates an interesting relationship between a religion and an ideology. If, on the other hand, we accept the Marxist concept of ideology—which is to say false consciousness—then a given religion can be labelled an ideology in contradistinction to Marxism.[2] These examples will perhaps serve to demonstrate that the terms 'religion' and 'ideology' point in different ways to a field in the world of human ideas and reactions that deserves closer examination. It is also obvious, however, that anyone wishing to study the relationship between religion and ideology risks getting stuck in a conceptual bog. The term 'ideology' has acquired a bewildering number of different meanings, while the problems involved in defining the concept of religion are well known. In the following, we will first select and define a useful concept of ideology, and make some remarks on the concept of religion. It will then be possible to point to some relationships between religion and one of its neighbours.

The term 'ideology' is sometimes used in a very wide sense. But since we are interested in a restricted field of human reactions, one in which we can compare such entities as conservatism and Judaism, it will be more useful for our purposes to adopt a more narrow concept. If we go back to Karl Mannheim's distinction between 'total' and 'partial' ideology—as most writers on ideology do—it is clear that the more interesting concept in our context is that of partial ideology. To define a partial ideology, we must first decide how to single out an ideology from other products of human endeavour.

There seems to be a considerable agreement among writers on ideology that ideologies consist of certain interrelated theoretical convictions, evaluations and norms. Various scholars have then tried in different ways to delimit precisely the class of such phenomena that should be labelled 'ideology'. Let us consider, in order, various delimitations relating to truth—value, adherents, function and content.[3]

As I have already mentioned, one influential Marxist concept of ideology restricts the theoretical aspects of ideologies to false convictions. A similar way of thinking is reflected in a modern dictionary in which ideologies are presented as 'selected or distorted ideas about a social system or a class of systems'.[4] Most convictions which we label as ideological may indeed be false, but it is hardly reasonable in our context to include statements as to truth or falsity in the actual definition of an ideology. We have at least to leave the door open for the possibility of true ideological ideas. Can we talk about an ideology embraced by only a single person? This would seem to conflict with all common usages of the term. If we are to call a set of ideas an ideology, they must be held in common by a group of people. This we will therefore accept as one defining characteristic of an ideology.

Ideologies are said to have many important functions for the group of people among whom they prevail. One such function pointed out in the classical literature (Marx and Pareto) is that of justification.[5] Ideologies justify actions and attitudes. They reinforce social rules, and defend a social order that promotes the interests of the group or class. Even certain cognitive structures can be justified by an ideology. Related to the function of justification is the integrating function that has been pointed to by many Marxists. The ideology can be the factor that actually creates the group, as, according to Marx, does the class-consciousness of the proletariat.[6] Many specifically political functions are in fact ascribed to ideologies, such as securing the existence of a political organisation, or a legitimate political authority or leadership. It might well result in all too narrow a concept of ideology were we to select any of these specific functions as defining characteristics: it seems reasonable, however, to stipulate that a set of ideas must have some social and/or political function if it is to be termed an ideology. Let us say that a system of ideas has a socio-political function when it fulfils certain vital needs of a group, and is used in situations that occur with some frequency. A socio-political function is thus a defining characteristic of an ideology, in our sense of the term.

Is it meaningful to point to any given common content of ideologies? E. Schill speaks of ideologies as 'comprehensive patterns of cognitive and moral beliefs about *man*, *society* and the *universe in relation to man and society*'.[7] This gives us a wide concept of ideology. A more narrow one will be obtained if we see the content of ideologies in C.J. Friedrich's terms, as 'reasonably coherent bodies of ideas concerning practical means of how to change, reform or maintain a political order'.[8] I think the wider concept is to be preferred here, since it allows us to see such interesting ideas as Marx's concept of man, or the various powerful Utopias, as parts of an ideology.

In our discussion, we have come across such terms as 'coherent', 'interrelated', and 'system' applied to ideology. This points to an important feature of such systems as Marxism, liberalism and humanism. The theoretical aspects of the system sustain or back the evaluations and norms it contains. Marxist ethics acquires its force from theoretical ideas about nature and society; and what could any liberal political or moral ideal amount to without the theory of the freedom of decision? The relationship can also work in the other direction. Some powerful practical norm or strong evaluative pattern in a society can help to keep alive a given theory. When speaking of the 'interrelatedness' of parts of an ideology, we shall be referring to a relationship between its theoretical and evaluative or normative parts which can be vaguely described as supportive. It seems necessary to include something about interrelatedness in our definition of ideology, in order not to make every theory part of an ideology.

Let us now sum up the discussion, and stipulate a definition of an ideology: an ideology consists of interrelated theories, evaluations and norms about man, society and the universe in relation to man and society, which are held in common by a group and have a socio-political function.

This concept of ideology is vague. To avoid this, a very long discussion resulting in numerous precise concepts would have been necessary, and such an enterprise would not have been worth the effort for our present purposes. The criteria guiding our definition have been usefulness, and the actual usage of the term. Marxism, in our terminology, is an ideology as are conservatism, liberalism and humanism. Existentialism is a borderline case because of its individualistic character, but it often has sufficient of a group function to count as an ideology. In Western societies there exist widespread ideologies, influential among ordinary people, which have no recognised label. One interesting study of such ideologies is to be found in Robert E. Lane's well-known work, *Political Ideology* (1962). The ways of life studied by Charles Morris are also aspects of general, usually unnamed ideologies.[9]

The attentive reader will perhaps already have noticed an apparent problem in our definition. We have selected it to enable us to study the relationship between religion and one of its neighbours, but according to it many religions must count as ideologies. This is a quite deliberate complication, and, as will soon become clear, it has certain advantages.

It is necessary at this point to devote a few words to the concept of religion. We will not, however, enter the great debate about the definition of religion. What we shall point to is a core activity in all religions, namely relating in prayer or meditation to the ultimate power that governs the universe. Every religion, consequently, must contain a theory about the ultimate power, a theory of transcendence. The devotional attitude and practice, and the theories corresponding to it, will here be termed the devotional–transcendent element in religion. Nothing lacking this element will here be regarded as a religion.

We are now in a position to draw up a map that may facilitate our orientation in the common terrain of religion and ideology. This we will do in the form of a cross-table, containing six cells.

The element of an ideology which we have called its socio-political function can be seen as a variable assuming three values, which we will call 'strong', 'weak' and 'lacking'. In the same way, we can think of the devotional–transcendent element as also varying from strong to lacking. The appearance of the table will then be as in Table 3.1.

Table 3.1: Religion and Ideology

The socio-political function of a system of thought	The devotional–transcendent element in a world-view		
	A strong	B weak	C lacking
1. strong			
2. weak			
3. lacking			

When different existing ideologies and religions are placed in this matrix, some interesting relationships become apparent. All the cells will be of interest except C3: an intellectual entity that lacks both a socio-political function and a devotional–transcendent element is by our definitions neither an ideology nor a religion.

Let us start with A1. Many ideologies have both a strong socio-political function and a strong devotional–transcendent element. The most obvious example is perhaps Islam in Iran. Medieval Christianity is another clear example, as are certain forms of present-day Zionism. Christianity can still belong to this cell, as is probably the case among certain South American groups with a liberation theology, or, in another form, in Poland. Ideologies belonging to this group are of equal interest from the political and religious points of view. They are both religions and ideologies, and it can be convenient to label them 'religious ideologies' or 'ideological religions'. It would be a misleading description of an important realm of intellectual reality to isolate doctrines about God, religious practices etc. and call these aspects a religion and the social and political ideas and rules an ideology.

Moving on to B1, we again come across some important ideologies. Take, for example, conservatism. Its theoretical aspects include religious ideas, and religious practices are also considered important even if they do not play a foreground role. The same is true of classical liberalism, and I do not think it unfair to refer to this group the ideology of most parties in present-day Western democracies that call themselves Christian.[10]

The socio-political function of, for example, a conservative ideology is of course a strong one, but we notice an important difference as compared with the A1 systems. In an ideology like political Islam or Zionism, the theoretical aspects of the ideology—theories about the revealed transcendent reality—lend very strong support to the various moral and political rules and practices. In fulfilling a given social practice you are acting as the servant of God, and doing his will. In an ideology like conservatism, the situation is different. Theories relating to the growth of a society, for example, are of importance in the shaping of practical social and political rules. We have here the back-up constituents of an ideology. But the backing they provide does not, for better or worse, lend them the same psychological force. Neither ideological martyrs nor political fanatics are common among the adherents of B1 ideologies. This is an internal difference between the two types of ideology, and it does not mean that B1 ideologies do not have a strong socio-political function. The personalised difference between the two types of ideology is roughly that between Joan of Arc and Margaret Thatcher, or between Ayatollah Khomeini and Ronald Reagan. We will return to this difference when considering type C1.

C1 ideologies are entirely lacking in the devotional–transcendent element. A clear example is Marxism, in its Leninistic form. However, many modern secularised, democratic political ideologies can belong to this group, including liberalism and the social democratic ideologies. Religious elements often play no role whatsoever for the function of these ideologies, and the socio-political function is pronounced. This, however, is not always the case, as has been observed by Bell and in the debate on the 'death of ideologies'.[11] Consequently, modern democratic ideologies with no religious elements are sometimes better classified under B2.

To refer now to the issue of force, we can easily see that there is a difference between the various ideologies belonging to this group. Marxism, in its different forms, possesses a remarkable force of the same type as do the religious ideologies. This is perhaps what people mean when they say that Marxism functions as a religion. But let us try to go a step further, and ask what constitutes this similarity. As we have already said, the transcendent–devotional element of an ideology can back the rules of that ideology by giving them the status of the will of God. But another element can also lend force to a religious ideology. As a rule, a religious ideology offers an integrated, holistic view of the universe. Man acting in society is part of a vast system, and his work is integrated in a meaningful development. To act according to the ideology is to act according to the internal rules of the universe. It is quite possible also for a non-theistic system of religious metaphysics, such as Buddhism, to constitute an element in a forceful ideology. In fact, political Buddhism is gaining in importance on the ideological scene. To return to Marxism, it is obvious that as clearly as it denies the first trait of religious ideologies—theories of a God—it shares the second—an integrated, overall view of the universe. It is a plausible hypothesis that the likeness in force can be explained by this common trait. It also explains structural similarities. Both ideologies contain metaphysical theories of the same general type. The Marxist theory of a socialist society can be compared to Christian eschatology etc. It was similarities of this kind that Bertrand Russell was observing in the passage referred to above. It is perhaps worth making one further observation concerning force. The elements of an ideology that lend force to some of its rules seem to some extent to be independent of the content of those rules. In South Africa, Christian ideas of God seem to be able to strengthen both the apartheid laws, and the struggle against these.

Let us now go on to column A2, and ask whether any ideologies in the defined sense could be characterised in this way. It looks as if the Christian religion in many Western societies is precisely an ideology of this kind. The devotional–transcendent element is strong. It has a socio-political function, and to some extent colours social life. This function, however, is weak and cannot be compared in any way with the political function of the Catholic Church in Poland, or the role of Islam in Arab societies. From the standpoint of the non-religious Western ideologies, religion in its A2 form can be tolerated, actually regarded as positive. The force of religious convictions can even be used to strengthen parts of the non-religious ideology. The secularisation of Western societies seems now partly to involve a movement of Christianity from A2 to B2. The question of whether Christianity in a given society is an ideology of type A2 or B2 is one to be decided by sociological research. Such an enterprise would presuppose operational definitions of 'strong' and 'weak'—a problem we cannot deal with here, but which it is perfectly possible to solve. Secularisation in the direction A2 to B2 is a different process from the movement from A1 to A2, which can also be called secularisation. We can notice, finally, that even if the socio-political function of Christianity as a whole is often weak, the mechanism of force is still at work and can become apparent in certain issues, for example the problem of abortion.

In cell C2 we encounter non-religious political ideologies which function largely as decorative elements in pragmatic political movements. In the history of religions we sometimes speak of a *deus otiosus*. In the same way we could speak about dormant ideologies. When it comes, however, to the empirical question of how far the ideologies in prevailing Western societies have acquired this character, it is wise to be careful. The empirical grounds for generalisation and prognosis are weak.

Moving now to C, we are leaving the realm of ideologies. Nothing, in our definition, can be an ideology without at least some socio-political function. But we are not leaving religion. Some people, indeed, would say that we have now come to the core of it. In C1 we find the 'inner religion', and certain forms of mysticism. The devotional–transcendental element is strong, but the relationship between the religious man and his God does not greatly affect his life in society and has nothing to do with his political convictions, if any. The function of the religious group is devotional, and nothing else. Christianity may perhaps be like this, but hardly a religion such as Islam. The political and social aspects of the Islamic ideology are too firmly tied up with its theology. I have said that Christianity can perhaps exist without a socio-political function. There is reason to emphasise the word 'perhaps'. In most cases a devotional practice seems to have social and political consequences, which takes us back to A2. Let us consider an introvert form of Christianity, like that of the Quakers. It functions, surely, as a forceful political ideology, and not only in questions of war and peace. From the standpoints, however, of the non-religious political ideologies belonging to C1, it sometimes seems as if A3 is regarded as the ideal form of religion. This is the form of religion that can be tolerated in most Marxist societies; and, according to non-religious liberal ideologies, a private religion of this kind can be seen either as a positive source of satisfaction for the individual, or as a form of superstition which must be given the freedom to exist. As we have said above, liberal and, say, social democratic ideologies are of course also open to religions tending towards cell 2, in so far as they have a socio-political function of a non-dominant kind. But when religions are ideologies of the A1 type, embracing in their concept for example civil law, as in the case of Islam, the concept of freedom of religion becomes problematical. In Communist societies like Russia, the Church has officially accepted a role that accords with A3 but in practice seems to function more like A2.

Are there any religions to be referred to B3? This is a question that cannot be answered without a closer discussion of the definition of religion. It is certain, however, that the conventional, disengaged adherence to a traditional church in many Western countries is a mental activity belonging to this type. The devotional–transcendent element is weak. God probably does not exist. There is no harm in sometimes saying a prayer, but it is surely of very little importance. In daily life and in politics, religion plays no role whatsoever. How far this kind of thinking characterises ordinary people in a secularised Christian society is a question that remains to be investigated.

What I hope has become clear from this survey is that the field common to religion and ideology is not easily described. There are no clearly defined entities to be characterised and compared. A religion such as Christianity assumes many different shapes and functions when seen in the context of the political ideologies, and a complex network of similarities and dissimilarities is evident between the doctrines and functions of religions and ideologies. We find patterns of ideas, rules and attitudes that display similarities and dissimilarities in their content and function, and we can describe certain aspects of this intellectual reality by using such concepts as religion and ideology, and by using more specific labels such as humanism and conservatism. Clear comparisons between the content of different ideologies, philosophies, theologies etc. can only be made if we restrict ourselves to specific authors, or to certain normative textbooks. And even such sources require careful analysis. It is not, for example, certain that similar theories in different ideologies and religions are supposed to answer the same questions, or play the same role in the totality of the view. Against this background, I have no desire to offer the usual brief summaries of the more common ideologies and philosophies. In order, however, not entirely to neglect a presentation of the content of different modern views, I will outline some characteristic ideas from ideologies that are sometimes seen as alternatives to religion, and discuss their relation to different religions.

The first of these ideas is taken from existentialism, and it says that an objective, impersonal attitude never gives us any true knowledge regarding the situation of man. We have to be personally concerned, make an unguarded choice, and live ourselves into the reality of human existence. True knowledge is knowledge from the inside. Kierkegaard says

> For an objective reflection the truth becomes an object, something objective, and thought must be pointed away from the subject. For a subjective reflection the truth becomes a matter of appropriation, of inwardness, of subjectivity, and thought must probe more and more deeply into the subject and his subjectivity.[12]

This idea provides to a large extent the basis for subsequent existentialist authors. Kierkegaard was a Christian theologian, and he surely saw it as a Christian idea. It has been greatly used in later Christian theology, but it is also central to such atheist authors as Sartre. To compare existentialism and Christianity is a complicated task. Existentialist ideas like this can in fact be incorporated in the theology of various religions.

Then we have an important ideological standpoint clearly opposed to that just described. According to this view, the only factual basis of private and social actions must be the results of strictly objective empirical science. We are now on the ground of behaviourism, turned into an ideology. Skinner is here the standard example, especially in his programmatic book, *Beyond Freedom and Dignity* (1972). This idea, the implications of which cannot be discussed in this context, is incompatible not only with existentialism but also with most religious standpoints. It can, however, be rendered more precise in such a way as to become compatible with Marxism, even if Skinner would have denied this.

One fundamental Marxist idea which plays a prominent role in many modern discussions is that the socio-economical circumstances of a society are causally primary to its intellectual, cultural and political development. Modified forms of this idea can be combined with religion—both Christianity and Islam—as has also been done both in practical and theoretical terms.[13] In a weak form, involving little more than the assignment of great importance to socio-economical factors in history, it has become commonplace.

The ideologies that we call materialistic have in common the idea that some form of matter is primary, ontologically and causally, in the universe. If something other than matter exists, then it can be causally explained from matter and the laws governing matter. This ideological element has been alive since antiquity, and acquired a powerful form through Marx. It is still a clearly anti-religious element in our culture, but it can be incorporated in various secular ideologies, for instance secular liberalism.[14]

A powerful idea of quite another kind which has been incorporated in modern ideologies, both secular and religious, stems from psychoanalysis. This is that every human being has a powerful unconscious, which to a large extent governs his actions and thoughts.

I think it will now suffice to take one more example, and one from the evaluative field. Let us take the idea that most men live in a corrupted state. This can be found in Marxism, and the reason given for the corruption is the predominance of the class structure of human societies. The actual idea of such corruption, however, is easily recognisable also in different forms in the Christian theology. A clear difference is also evident in this respect between Christian and Muslim anthropology.

This list of isolated ideas in no way negates the possibility of comparing and choosing between overall systems. It is intended simply as a warning against excessively general comparisons, and a reminder of the floating limits of religions and ideologies. This last thesis will be illustrated once again in the next section, when we move on to make some preliminary remarks on the problem of making a reasonable choice between different religions and ideologies. The main aim of this section is not to solve the general problem of such a decision but simply to point out some further traits that can characterise both religion and ideology.

To a certain extent, we grow up into a religion or ideology. Or at least we unconsciously acquire, through our social environment, a certain way of thinking and reacting. This, however, does not contradict the fact that we are able as grown-up, rational human beings to choose between different standpoints in the field of religion and ideology. The problem at this point is that some ideologies and religions affect even the rational standards for such a choice. The rationality is defined by the ideology. This is the case in the moral field, when the good is defined as what is in accordance with the will of God, and his will is regarded as being known only within a given religion. The same situation exists regarding a decision as to the theoretical aspects, if the ability to arrive at the truth is restricted to a given class, or to those in receipt of special gifts from the Holy Spirit. The mere statement that a rational choice is possible—in principle for all men—in the field of religion and ideology seems to involve the repudiation of certain ideologies and religions.[15] For my own part, I regard such a repudiation as reasonable. A rational choice will then involve four steps. The first is to compare the content of the evaluative parts of the ideologies concerned with our own moral convictions and experiences. We may perhaps find that a democratic ideology is to be preferred to a totalitarian one, or that a pessimistic view of man's moral powers is more realistic than an optimistic one. The next step is to look at those theoretical parts of the ideology or religion which can be tested by scientific methods within the disciplines of social, economic or natural science, and historical research. An ideology or religion which is open to scientific research, and does not contradict obvious scientific results, is then to be preferred to one which does. The third step is the most difficult. This is to test the metaphysical aspects of the views entailed—such as theories about transcendental realities, or the ultimate source of order in nature and society. There is no agreement among philosophers whatsoever as to the possibility of a rational metaphysics, or about the rational standards of any possible metaphysics. I cannot deal, here, with this philosophical question. My conviction, however, is that a rational metaphysics exists, but that some basic choices in metaphysics are of a more personal nature than can be contained within scientific reasoning. The final step in the procedure is to study the internal relationships between different parts of the religion or ideology. Do they mutually support each other, or are there tensions—or even contradictions—within the system? Obviously, a choice of the kind now hinted at deserves ideologies and religions that are clearly formulated and explicit. In spite of its obvious dangers, the intellectual comparison we mentioned above therefore has some value.

These brief remarks point to a similar decision-making procedure for religions and ideologies, a fact that again underlines their close relationship. Perhaps, indeed, it is inadequate to call them neighbours. 'Members of the same family' would be more adequate.

Notes

1. Bertrand Russell, *History of Western Philosophy* (New York, 1945), Ch. IV.
2. See for example J. Plamenatz, *Ideology* (London, 1970), pp. 23ff.
3. My way of delimiting the concept ideology here is influenced by discussions

with Professor Robert Heeger of Utrecht. See for example R. Heeger, 'Vad är en ideologi?', *Statsvetenskaplig Tidskrift*, 1972, pp. 307–25.

4. H.M. Johnson in *International Encyclopaedia of the Social Sciences* 7, 1968, p. 77.

5. K. Marx, F. Engels, *Werke XIX*, p. 190 (Berlin, 1969). V. Pareto, *Oeuvres Complètes* (Geneva and Paris, 1956), III § 1043, IV § 2173 and § 2440.

6. See K. Marx, F. Engels, *Werke III* (Geneva and Paris, 1958), p. 70.

7. *International Encyclopaedia of the Social Sciences* 7, 1968, p. 66.

8. C.J. Friedrich, *Man and his Government, an Empirical Theory of Politics* (New York, 1963), p. 90.

9. Charles Morris, *Varieties of Human Value* (Chicago, 1956).

10. Conservatism here means the stream of ideas going back to Edmund Burke (1729–97). Classical liberalism is the political ideology of for instance J. Locke (1632–1704) and J.S. Mill (1806–73).

11. See Daniel Bell, *The End of Ideology* (New York, 1960).

12. S. Kierkegaard, *Samlade Værker*, utg af A.B. Drachmann, J.L. Heidberg og H.O. Lauge, VII:159f. (Copenhagen, 1901–6).

13. The dialogue between Marxists and Christians has resulted in a great number of books and articles which cannot by listed here. See further J. van der Beat, *The Christian–Marxist Dialogue. An annotated bibliography 1959–69*. WCC 1969 and for an analysis Peter Hebblethwaite, *The Christian–Marxist Dialogue and Beyond* (New York, 1977).

14. Different types of materialism will be discussed in the paragraph on atheism below.

15. See my article 'Några problem vid livsåskådningsanalys', *Svensk Teologisk Kvartalskrift*, 46 (1970).

4 Atheism and Agnosticism

Anders Jeffner

The great Icelandic writer of sagas Snorri Sturluson relates an interesting episode about the Norwegian king, St Olaf. While assembling his army to proceed to Trondheim, he was approached by two brothers from the wilds, Gaukapórir and Afrafasti. They were bigger, stronger and braver than all other warriors. 'Are you Christians?' the king asked. Gaukapórir answered:

> We are neither Christian nor pagan. We and our brothers have no faith, other than in our own strength and skill, and our own fortune in war. This has so far sufficed. Or is there, king, in your army any Christian man who has performed in a day greater deeds than we?[1]

Are we encountering here an articulate atheist, in this obscure time of great religious change in the wilds of northern Europe? In a way, I think it is reasonable to say yes. This is a clear example of a reaction to religion which it makes sense to call atheism. Atheism will then mean a deliberate rejection of all the religious alternatives available at the time. We will take this as the first sense of the term 'atheism' to be considered. As we shall see later on, 'atheism' like so many other terms in the field of religion is used in many different senses.

Atheism in our first sense seems to be an eternal companion to religion. We know that some kind of religion exists in every culture; what is not so frequently observed is that one can also find traces of religious denial and disbelief in practically every religious milieu.[2] The examples from Greece are fairly well known; they can be studied in the numerous legal proceedings against people accused of denying the gods, especially in the fourth century BCE. In early Greek culture we find complaints about *asebeía*, which means a lack of respect for the rules based on belief in the gods; it also, however, involves a clear theoretical disbelief in all gods. This is atheism in our first sense. In his dialogue *The Laws* (884–90),

Plato prescribes severe punishment for those who do not respect religion, arguing that a theoretical denial of basic theological assertions is the root of anti-religious behaviour. People who reject religion are also mentioned in texts from ancient Israel and India. Among peoples and tribes without a written language, we find examples of unbelief in the many narratives about men who disregard the gods, and are later struck down by their wrath. It is not my intention here to list such examples of the refutation of religion in different cultures, and I will simply refer the interested reader to the books mentioned in notes 1 and 2.

I hope it has become apparent from what we have already said that it is simply not true that there was a time when all men were religious. The assumption of a religious point of view always seems to involve a personal element which renders it neither intellectually nor socially irresistible. There is always an opening towards atheism in our first sense.

It should be observed that anyone in a Buddhist society who rejects Buddhism as well as other religions is an atheist in our first sense, despite the fact that the Buddhist doctrine itself can be termed atheistic. This last example affords us another meaning of atheism, to which we will now address ourselves.

The term 'atheism' is often used to refer to an argumentative denial of a more specific core-element of religion—the belief in personal gods, or in a personal God. The epithet 'personal' means that the god in question is believed to bear a likeness at least to such human abilities as thinking, willing and communicating. The term 'argumentative' in the definition implies that this view is a theoretical standpoint, adopted on the basis of some kind of reasoning. Atheism in this sense is something more than a dislike of religion, or a neglect of religious practices. A man can, of course, be an atheist in both our first and second senses, as indeed was the Norwegian soldier in our example. He denied a personal God, and he presented a kind of argument. But it is possible to be an atheist in the first sense and not in the second, or in the second and not in the first. An example of the latter is provided by a modern author such as Julian Huxley in his book *Religion Without Revelation* (1957). He offers reasons for not believing in a personal God, while none the less adhering to religious practices and rules. As mentioned above, a Buddhist can belong to this category.

We will discuss here two types of atheism in the sense of an argumentative denial of personal gods or a personal God. The difference between these two forms lies in the argumentative approach. The ground for a repudiation of theism can be a philosophical critique of the doctrine of a personal God in all its forms, as in the philosophy of logical positivism. This is the first type. But atheism can also be based on a positive alternative system of metaphysics, which may be of a religious character (as in the case of Buddhism) or totally non-religious (as in the case of Marxism).

It is naturally impossible in our present context to offer any survey of the philosophical arguments for and against the existence of a God. Such surveys can be found in most textbooks on the philosophy of religion.[3] They are often instructive, but a word of warning may well be in place. Short summaries of philosophical arguments can be very misleading without being totally wrong, and all these summaries of 'The five ways of Aquinas' along with the critiques of Kant and Hume seem to me excessively boring. My advice to a reader interested in the critical side of these matters is to study Hume's *Dialogues Concerning Natural Religion* in the original, and without abbreviation. I agree with Hume himself: 'nothing can be . . . more artfully written'.[4] The general warning I have now given can also be applied to the following short summary of the one argument that seems to me to constitute the strongest case against theism. It is inspired by the philosophical tradition known as empiricism, which dates back to Greek philosophy. It flourished in the eighteenth century, and one of its champions was Hume. In our own century it has taken the form of logical empiricism, associated with names like Schlick, Carnap and Russell. The enigmatic Ludwig Wittgenstein also belongs to this tradition.

The argument starts from a very simple principle, which has been called the principle of intellectual morality.[5] It says: 'Do not believe in anything for which you cannot give good reasons.' At first sight, few people would reject this rule. It appears to be the basis of a rational life, and a starting-point for all kinds of scientific and scholarly activity.

The second step in the argument is to try to establish what kinds of reason we can give for the existence of anything whatsoever. In daily life we refer in questions of existence to our common-sense experience. If we together see or hear something, then it must in some way exist in the real world; and if it is possible to experience it, then it is possible that it exists. Many things, however, cannot be familiar to us in this direct way, for example the particles of which physicists speak or various remote astronomical objects. But if the assumption of the existence of an entity is necessary in order to explain what we become acquainted with through our senses, then we have good reasons to believe in it. It is not necessary of course that the 'we' in these sentences should include every human being. One of the basic conditions of human knowledge is that we have to rely on the testimony of others. One single, unprejudiced person can suffice, provided that his judgement is open to control by others. The reasons I have just described can be called empirical reasons. They undoubtedly govern our ordinary lives, and scientific theories as to factual conditions in the real world are based on such reasons. It can now be claimed that there are no other good reasons for the existence of anything, except reasons based on some possible sense-experience. We have to use other tools in exploring reality, such as logic and mathematics, but these tools cannot without any reference to the senses afford us any knowledge about what exists, and what does not exist. We are referred exclusively to our senses. This standpoint is the second premiss of the argument.

The third premiss, of course, is the claim that we cannot offer any empirical reasons for the existence of God. No reliable person has seen or heard a God in a way which is open to control. There was a time when the God-hypothesis seemed necessary in order to explain certain phenomena or regularities in the experiential world, but scientific development has made the God-hypothesis entirely superfluous. The supposition of a personal God has no anchorage in our experience.

From the second and third steps in this argument, the conclusion follows that there are no good reasons for believing in any personal God. Then, according to the maxim contained in the first premiss, we should not believe in a personal God.

This is an example of philosophical atheism. It is a weak form of atheism, since the argument does not claim actually to disprove the existence of a personal God. It seems correct, none the less, to call it atheism. It is a refutation of the belief in God. If the form of atheism is weak, the actual argument, on the other hand, is strong. It does not involve any complex philosophical theories. It is based on common sense and science, without being tied to any given, current scientific theories. As a whole, it reflects an undogmatical attitude. The theist, of course, can deny all the premisses. He can refuse to accept the rule of intellectual morality, but this involves being an irrationalist—which is a difficult and uncomfortable position. It is also possible to try to present empirical reasons for the existence of God, and thus refute the third premiss. I do not, however, know of anyone who has completely succeeded in this. The best approach for the theist, in my view, is to question the second premiss. He can argue that there are more good reasons for existence-claims than references to the senses. It can be claimed, for instance, that religious experiences, or our conscience-reactions, or our I–Thou relations, give us access to reality. Arguments for the existence of a personal God could perhaps be built up on such a ground. It is not my intention to discuss these possibilities further, but I do feel that there is an interesting field here for argumentation between theists and atheists.

Let us now turn to the second type of argumentative denial of a personal God. This is the form of atheism which offers an elaborated metaphysical alternative to theism. The classical example, which is still important, is materialism. Materialism in its various forms is a strong and powerful stream of Western philosophical thought. (One well-known German history of Western materialism covers 1,099 pages.[6])

The most important of the Greek materialists is Democritus, and we can take his theories as a standard example of strict classical materialism. In his philosophy, only matter is existent or real. Even mental states consist of a kind of matter. Democritus introduced the term 'atom' for the smallest constituent of matter. Democritus' ontological materialism was developed in an interesting way by the Roman Epicurean philosopher Lucretius, in his great poem *De Rerum Natura*. It seems evident there that strict materialism is incompatible with belief in a personal God. But this is only true if we also accept the premiss that God is not material. Most materialists have indeed done this, but not all of them. Epicurus, for instance, who based his metaphysics on Democritus, reckoned with the actual existence of gods, even if he thought that we need not bother about them, just as they do not care about us.

If Democritus affords a typical example of classical materialism, the hero of modern materialism is Marx. Some modern materialists, as we shall see later on, would deny this, but he undoubtedly has the greatest influence. Marxist atheism is the strongest atheistic movement of our time.

There are two basic differences in principle between strict, classical materialism and that of Marx, quite apart from the fact that they have emerged against quite disparate cultural and scientific backgrounds. The first is that Marx reckons with the existence of something other than material entities. Mental states are seen as real, although dependent on a material basis which is causally primary. This doctrine is generally called 'epiphenomenalism'. According to the Marxists themselves, the most important difference between Marxist and other forms of materialism is that Marxist materialism is 'dialectical'. According to Marx and Lenin, there exist in the material world certain fundamental dual opposites, which meet and produce a development towards a synthesis of opposing forces. According to Marx, the basic laws governing the development of matter can be clearly formulated and they are termed 'dialectical laws'. One of these, formulated by Engels, is called 'the law of the transformation of quantity into quality and vice versa'. By the help of such laws, Marxist materialism can be applied to social development. It can be explained, for example, in materialist terms how a gradual change in the material basis of a society suddenly gives rise to a qualitatively new kind of society. The application of basic dialectical materialism to human conditions and human societies is called in Marxist philosophical terms 'historical materialism'. Historical materialist theories also explain, according to the Marxists, why and how the false belief in a personal God will disappear in the future. In Leningrad, a former church has been made into a museum for the history of religion and atheism. Those interested in the application of historical materialism to religion will find there many very skilful illustrations.

Apart from strict, classical materialism and Marxist materialism, it may be sufficient to consider one further form, which we can refer to as explanative materialism. Its basic idea is that everything can be explained in terms of matter, or of matter and energy. Many of the results achieved in modern science point in this direction. It is also supposed that matter is always causally primary in relation to everything else. These ideas are compatible with the existence of mind, and epiphenomenalism seems to be a generally accepted theory in most forms of modern materialism. Even if explanative materialism can be included in Marxist materialism, it is a much more modest standpoint. An explanative materialist need not accept the dialectical laws, or the theory of historical materialism *in toto*. A clear example of this form of materialism, in which the atheistic consequences are drawn, is provided by Ernest Nagel, who calls his view 'naturalism'.[7]

Before leaving the subject of materialism, we should underline the fact that we have dealt here only with the theoretical type of materialism. 'Materialism' can also refer to the normative view that owning material things, or possessing economic wealth, is the highest goal of human life. The two forms of materialism need not be combined in any way. On the contrary, theoretical materialists have often been and are idealists in the sense of striving at higher spiritual or moral goals, or sacrificing their own welfare for the benefit of their fellow men.

From materialism, we will now take a step to what may appear to be its absolute opposite—mysticism. As we shall see, however, the great mystical traditions include patterns of thought which allow no room for a personal God. They tend towards atheism in our second sense—an argumentative denial of a personal God. Two traits common to many mystical traditions are of importance here.[8] In the mystical experience, the mystic claims to be in contact with the deepest level of reality. Now for many mystics, both in the Christian and other traditions, experience of this reality means an annihilation of their own personality. 'The visionary is himself One', says Plotinus. This is *Unio Mystica*. St Teresa of Avila, one of the great Christian mystics, wrote 'It is plain enough what unity is—two distinct things becoming one.' This transcendence of the personal 'I', and total unity with something else, is quite a different experience from meeting a person. If such mystics meet God, it is not a personal God. Mystics of this kind have consequently been regarded with great suspicion by the representatives of such religions as Christianity and Islam even to the point of persecution. The condemnation of the great medieval mystic Meister Eckhart ('The knower and the known are one') can serve as an example from Christian history, and from the Muslim world we can mention the mystic Mansur al-Hallaj, who was killed in 922 for his claim of identity with the divine. It must be observed, however, that not all mystical experiences are of this non-personal kind. Nathan Söderblom speaks of a kind of mysticism which he calls 'personal mysticism'.[9] And then we have the great Jewish religious figure Martin Buber: his type of religious experience bears a similarity to mystical experience, but its very kernel is an 'I–Thou' relationship. The mystical tradition seems to move between two poles, from the deep personal encounter to a unity beyond all personal categories.

One further trait in the mystical tradition should be mentioned. What is felt in the mystical experience is impossible to describe, lies outside the reach of human language; it is ineffable. Nearly all mystics are in agreement about this. If, however, the ultimate reality is impossible to describe, then it must be wrong to talk about this reality as a personal God. But it is also a fact that many mystics, despite the doctrine of ineffability, try to say something about their experience with the help of symbols and metaphors. Mystics often balance on the edge of the ineffable, without being totally silent.

Among the many meanings of atheism a third and powerful one may be observed. This involves denial of the existence of a personal God with certain specific attributes: if a personal God is to have such-and-such characteristics, he does not exist. In many religious traditions, including the Jewish and the Christian, God is said to be Almighty and Good. Very early on in our intellectual tradition, people found it difficult to combine this belief with the experience of the factual evils of the world. This gave rise to the so-called problem of theodicy, and if it insoluble it is easy to make it into a proof of the non-existence of a Good and Almighty God. This is a powerful line of thought in both the ancient and modern history of atheism. A pioneer in this field is the Greek philosopher Sextus Empiricus.

We can now conclude this passage on atheism with an interesting observation. For each form of atheism, there are kinds of theism which correspond and come very close to the atheistic position. This I say not in order to blur the demarcation line between the different ideologies, but to point to the possibility that an interesting position may be found at some of the points at which theism and atheism touch each other.

Our first kind of atheism involved the rejection of all currently available religious alternatives. This, however, is also the position of a deeply religious theist like Dietrich Bonhoeffer. He was seeking a God behind the religions, striving towards a non-religious Christianity. We can simply note this for the present, without further discussion. The type of atheism which we defined as the argumentative rejection of a personal God took many different forms. The most interesting relation to theism is to be found in the last of these, namely mystical atheism. But let us first note that the intellectual basis of those theists who wish to fight superstition is the principle of intellectual morality, and interestingly enough this also opens one of the best ways for the theist to combat atheistic metaphysics, such as materialism. It may be possible for the theist and the atheist to travel a long way together when it comes to the question of rational reasons, but at some point they must separate, and the theist has to accept religious experience, for instance, as part of the ground for an existence-claim. The materialist type of atheism lies a long way from theism on the theoretical side but, when in practice, the extent of the views they hold in common can be remarkable, as evident in the dialogue between Marxists, Christians and Muslims. Let us now proceed to mysticism. The reflected forms of belief in a personal God always seem to contain an awareness of the absolute unintelligibility of God. God is seen as transcending all our concepts. Even concepts of a person are used in another sense when applied to God. In the skilfully elaborated doctrine of analogy, St Thomas Aquinas tries to safeguard the otherness of God, without rendering the description of him as a person entirely meaningless. When we come to a modern Christian theologian such as Paul Tillich, one may doubt whether anything whatsoever of the personal character of the Christian God has been preserved. The point, however, is that a deep form of personal theism comes very close to non-personal mysticism. Finally, a word about those who deny the existence of a Good and Almighty God. This denial is part of the constant struggle among Christian and Jewish theists, and its model is the biblical person of Job.

Apart from different forms of theism and atheism, there is also a third position, namely agnosticism. Let us quote directly a famous agnostic, the Greek philosopher Protagoras: 'About the gods I do not know if they exist or do not exist. There are many circumstances which prevent one from knowing that: the obscurity of the matter and the shortness of human life.' Agnosticism can be defined as suspending one's judgement on the question of the existence of God. Let us compare this position with the forms of atheism which we have dealt with. The first form of atheism was a rejection of all available religious alternatives. An agnostic would not reject religion but he would refuse to say yes or no to it. It must then be observed that an agnostic of this kind will often be seen in the same way as an atheist from the religious point of view, following the principle that 'he who is not with me is against me'. The argumentative rejection of belief in a personal God cannot be accepted by an agnostic, although he can come very close to the argument based on the principle of intellectual morality. Some, perhaps, would call this form of atheism a kind of agnosticism. I think, however, that it is better terminology to speak of agnosticism only if the second and third premisses are modified. An agnostic would say that there exist *at present* no rational reasons for believing in God. This, perhaps, is the best example of an agnostic position. An agnostic corresponding to our third kind of atheism has to leave open the possibility of a solution of the theodicy problem, even if he cannot see one.

An interesting agnostic position is what perhaps can be called 'methodological agnosticism'. This involves not adopting any definite standpoint as to the existence or non-existence of a divine reality, when dealing with a scientific or scholarly problem. In this sense, a high proportion of modern religious studies are agnostic—including the present chapter.

Notes

1. This passage from Snorri Sturluson's life of St Olaf in the *Heimskringla* is here translated from a quotation in Tor Andrae, *Die Frage der Religiösen Anlage* (Uppsala Universitets Årsskrift, 1932), p. 32.

2. The article 'Atheism' in the classical *Encyclopaedia of Religion and Ethics* ed. by J. Hastings from 1909 is still a useful introduction to atheism in different cultures.

3. See for instance John Hick, *Philosophy of Religion* (Englewood Cliffs, N.J., 1963). A historical survey of Western atheism is given in Fritz Mauthner, *Der Atheismus und seine Geschichte im Abenland*, 1–4 (1922–4). This work embraces over 2000 pages.

4. *The Letters of David Hume*. Ed. by J.Y.T. Greig, 1932 II, p. 334.

5. My way of formulating the argument is influenced by the Swedish philosopher Ingmar Hedenius.

6. Friedrich Lange, *Geschichte des Materialismus* 9th edn (Leipzig, 1914–15).

7. See for instance his contribution in *Proceedings and Addresses of The Am Philosophical Association* XXVII.

8. For common traits in mystical experiences see for instance W.T. Stace, *Mysticism and Philosophy* (London, 1961).

9. Nathan Söderblom, *Uppenbarelsereligion* (Uppsala, 1903). See also his *The Living God* (London, 1933).

Part 2 Judaism and Christianity

Editor:
Leslie Houlden

5 Introduction

Leslie Houlden

The approach to the religions of the world used in this book is phenomenological; that is, it sees them as instances of 'what is', in past and present, as expressions of the human attempt to relate to God or the transcendent. Such an approach is so broad that there is room for a number of variants on the general theme. Anyone interested in questions of method will observe them, and will note how various parts of the subject might have been dealt with in other ways. From that point of view, there is undoubtedly an arbitrary element in the arrangement of the topics.

For example, it is not self-evident that Christianity and Judaism should be joined together to form one major part of the book. They could have been handled in some other way—geographically, for instance, with the material dispersed in a treatment of religion country by country. Or Islam could have been brought in alongside them, as springing historically from the same biblical roots and sharing monotheistic faith. In any case, Christianity and Judaism, and movements related to them either closely or tenuously, figure inevitably in other parts of the book. For many centuries, and all the more so now, religions do not live in sealed compartments.

All the same, there are excellent reasons for associating these two religions in a work of this kind. Some belong to history, some to the present day. In terms of its origins, Christianity was an offspring of Judaism, and Jesus was a Jew. To say that is, however, not to say all, either about those origins or about subsequent developments. To take first the crucial situation at the start of our era. The Judaism from which Christianity took its beginning was that of first-century Palestine, within the Roman Empire and exposed, often happily, to Greek culture. Within a very short time, the new movement began to incorporate non-Jews on a footing of equality, to extend the expression of its beliefs in Greek intellectual terms, and to focus its devotion concentratedly on Jesus in a way that set it at odds with its Jewish context and began to raise the question of its separate identity. Already in those early decades, almost every possible view of the relation between the two emerged. Christianity fulfilled Judaism; or else it superseded it; or it was built upon it; or it was the true Judaism; or it was a complete novelty. And from a more detached standpoint, it is still difficult to say when the two faiths should be thought of as distinct. Even as institutions, the separation probably proceeded piecemeal and slowly over the first hundred years and more of the Church's existence. The relation between the two had to be defined not just in social and organisational but also in theological terms. From a Jewish point of view, Christians came to be seen as having abandoned the Law and given honours to Jesus which belonged to God alone. Christians speedily identified 'the Jews' as responsible for the execution of Jesus which had been perpetrated by Pontius Pilate in collusion with the Temple authorities in Jerusalem. All the same, there is much to be said for the view that, despite their crucially distinct beliefs, the more mainstream Christians were precisely those who stuck closest to their Jewish roots, above all in the retention, albeit reinterpreted, of the Scriptures they came to call the Old Testament.

Such were the beginnings of the relationship between Judaism and Christianity. Their diversity and complexity is worth pondering, if only to put a brake on over-simplified views of their relationship, whether then or now. The growth of those seeds has taken endlessly different forms, but, for good or ill, and often with much distortion and anachronism, the mark of those early stages has remained upon them. The continued Christian use of the Scriptures of Judaism is its most obvious and problematic outward sign. The relations between the two are still often discussed in first-century terms, as if the two religions had not developed with infinite richness and subtlety in the period between then and now. The truth is that, whatever the stereotypes, the relationship has taken many forms, chiefly in the setting of European society, where they have lived together through the entire period. Each has gone its own way, Christianity becoming the religion of the vast majority, backed by and backing political power in many different ways since the fourth century, and itself subject to division and diversity of expression; and Judaism living usually precariously as the small minority of strangers, now tolerated for their economic usefulness, now savagely persecuted, now flowering amazingly. Yet persistently, Christians held over Judaism the charge of deicide, and Jews saw Christians as blasphemous apostates, each side bearing for ever in the eyes of the other the stigma of those first years—as if in essence nothing could ever change.

There is irony in the fact that it has taken the intellectual developments of the modern secularised Western world to break the mould. They alone have made possible a historical and phenomenological perspective such as that adopted here. On the scholarly side, one result has been a growing consensus between Jewish and Christian writers on biblical and historical matters, including those relating to Christians origins. Its effects have been felt in the religious sphere itself, as the major Christian churches have abandoned old anti-Jewish formulas, seeking reconciliation, friendship and dialogue. Despite even recent setbacks like the Papacy's alleged failure to do enough to oppose Nazi persecution of Jews, we have seen Vatican II erasing talk of deicide and a Pope preaching in the Rome synagogue. If the softness of liberal Europe may be blamed for not nullifying the outrageous climax of the anti-Semitic tradition in the holocaust of the Nazi period, its instinct for justice and objectivity can be credited with the emergence of a more detached, historically sensitive and charitable spirit in the relations of the two traditions. Such detachment, overcoming both anachronism and old hostility, is now to be found widely spread among firm adherents of both Christian and Jewish faiths, and it makes its mark not only academically but also in the kind of official pronouncements where change can often be least expected.

Their common exposure to these intellectual developments provides another reason for associating Christianity and Judaism in a survey of the world's religions. Not only have they lived side by side for so many centuries, especially in Europe, but they are the only two of the great religions of the world to have opened their doors, in varying degrees and modes, to scientific investigation of many kinds. Despite powerful forces to the contrary, some crude, some sophisticated, both have found their Scriptures subjected to minute historical and literary scrutiny and their beliefs given over to philosophical enquiry—all this largely by scholars among their own members. In both Europe and North America, the tension brought about by such enquiry, conducted in the secularised atmosphere of the modern university, is perhaps the most important single item on the agenda concerning the future viability of both religions. Will they be able to respond to the questions raised by intellectual analysis in such a way as to maintain a hold on educated Western opinion, or will they lose more and more of that traditional market? Will they become (or continue to become) ghetto movements, strange phenomena, outlandish in the setting of Western culture as a whole? Will such a future even be a source of a kind of strength, perhaps a condition of survival? Judaism is well accustomed to such a position; for Christianity, it is in many ways a novelty, contemplated only with difficulty, except where the French Revolution gave an early opportunity to become used to some of its aspects.

Those elements in both religions which resist a future in a cultural ghetto do it sometimes for the deepest religious reasons: a refusal to lose hold on God-given truth, from whatever quarter it derives. They take many forms: the liberal Jewish movements in North America, bringing historical perspective to bear on the Torah, whose tensions with traditional Hasidic Judaism are so vividly depicted in the novels of Chaim Potok; liberation theologians and basic church communities in South and Central America, seeing their Catholicism as the response of the gospel to the injustices of the local political setting; liberal forces in North American Protestantism resisting the resurgence of biblical fundamentalism and the intolerance of 'the moral majority'; American Orthodox Christians beginning to question the tenacious conservatism of Orthodox Christianity on matters such as biblical criticism and the role of women in the Church; and liberal theologians and churchmen in Europe criticising the antiquated authoritarianism of the Papacy or the traditionalism of those who oppose changes like the ordination of women.

Some of these tensions direct attention to yet another feature shared by Judaism and Christianity in the modern world. It is the combination of universality and parochialism which has come to characterise both, each in its own way, and more problematically in the case of Christianity. To Judaism indeed, such a combination has long been second nature. From before the beginning of the common era, Judaism held together a sense of single identity and wide cultural diversity, relating to the different cultural settings in which Jews had come to live. That capacity has not diminished in recent times. In the present century, it has received a new impetus and visible focus in the creation of the State of Israel.

In the case of Christianity, the combination has taken new and paradoxical forms. In Catholicism, there has never been a time when the universality of the Church has been more obvious, available to every television viewer, in the pastoral visits to every corner of the globe by Pope John Paul II, as it was indeed in his election to office, a Slav breaking a centuries-long Italian monopoly. Yet there is a constant pressure, symbolised above all in the use of the vernacular instead of Latin in the liturgy, towards more and more diversification in the light of local needs: may clerical marriage be permitted here, or wider birth control there? May there be alliance with guerrilla movements in this setting, or with feminist protest in that? Similarly, all the major churches have developed in recent decades organisational structures on the international scene. The ecumenical World Council of Churches has come to be paralleled by world denominationalism—universal organs of Lutheranism, Anglicanism, Presbyterianism and Methodism. Anglicanism indeed, stimulated by the growth of the British Empire and with its episcopal structure, began to possess such an expression of itself a hundred and twenty years ago. At the same time, as such centralised organs have grown in formality, on an issue like the ordination of women, some Anglican provinces have felt free to proceed without seeking universal agreement. The Orthodox churches, now planted in societies, such as the USA and Australia, far removed from their traditional homes, share the same tendency towards the creation of universal instruments but are equally affected by local variations of ethos and circumstance.

The approach taken in this part of *The World's Religions* is in many ways straightforward and traditional. While being phenomenological, in the sense of treating of Christianity and Judaism as parts of 'what is', it is for the most part simply historical in arrangement. In successive essays, the reader is presented with an account of the development of ancient Israel and Christian beginnings, and then of the Church through Eastern and Western Europe, together with an account of Judaism's life in its midst. From the sixteenth century, with the gradual spread of Christianity to India, South and North America, Africa and elsewhere, the approach becomes more regional as well as historical. A final essay, contemplating a vast and varied scene, highlights certain tendencies in the present situation of Christianity, which may (or may not) turn out to be points of creativity and change. Others have been indicated in the course of this introduction, relating them also to Judaism. The future of both religions is of course unpredictable. For Judaism, no doubt the biggest single tangible factor is the State of Israel, itself poised between religious and secularised Judaism and related precariously to both its Islamic Arab neighbours and Western (above all American) post-Christian society, from which so much of its culture and so many of its citizens derived. For Christianity, the relatively long-standing ecumenical movement still has life within it and unity negotiations between the major churches proceed relentlessly but with few notable results, treading a well-known circuit of ideas and largely unremarked by most Christians. It is accompanied by constant small acts of initiative, responding to local needs and circumstances. These are, as we have seen, sometimes liable to be at variance with the centralised organs of the churches. In all these ways, Catholicism, mainstream Protestantism and Orthodoxy have much in common. In the meantime, the centre of gravity of Christianity, in terms of numbers and vitality if not of the official structures, has undoubtedly moved to Africa and South America, with considerable anarchy, and with unforeseeable consequences for both Christianity itself and for the other religions alongside which it lives and worships.

6 *Israel Before Christianity*

R.J. Coggins

Christian Old Testament and Hebrew Bible

The body of writings most commonly known as the Old Testament is perhaps unique in that it is revered as Scripture by two of the world's great religions: Judaism and Christianity. (It is also of vital importance for Islam, whose own sacred writings incorporate many Old Testament traditions, but that is beyond our immediate concern.) It is necessary to realise at the very outset that the term 'Old Testament' is in a sense a polemical one, part of the long-standing hostility between Christianity and Judaism, since it implies a sequel, which for the Christian Church is, of course, to be found in the New Testament. We shall use the term 'Old Testament' here, because it has come into general use, sometimes even among Jews themselves, but it is important to remember that it is a Christian title. For the Jew the same writings may be called Tenak (a made-up word which incorporates the initial letters of Torah, Nevi'im and Ketubim, Law, Prophets and Writings, the three component parts of the Old Testament), or Miqra, meaning that which is read (in the solemn assembly of the synagogue).

There is another important element in the anti-Jewish polemic which is implicit in the term 'Old Testament'. The claim is often made that the Old Testament writings point beyond themselves in some way to a more complete fulfilment in the future, and that here Christians have the advantage over Jews. For them, the fulfilment has been realised: the life, death and resurrection of Jesus are held to be the fulfilment of all that the Old Testament had been looking forward to. This would imply that Judaism is simply the religion of the Old Testament. Such an approach ignores the fact that for Judaism, as for Christianity, the promises of the Old Testament are in large measure seen as having been fulfilled. The voluminous collection of later writings which makes up the Mishnah and the Talmud provides the structure of Jewish religious observance, just as the New Testament provides the structure of Christian belief.

One could indeed go further. It would be possible, and in many ways legitimate, for Jews to claim that they have remained loyal worshippers of the God who has revealed himself in the Old Testament, whereas Christians have in practice largely replaced devotion to God by devotion to Jesus Christ. Sometimes he is regarded simply as God; often it is stressed that there is no access to God save through Jesus. Assertions of this kind are deeply offensive to Judaism, which sees such devotion as replacing true commitment to God, the father and saviour of his people.

It is right to mention differences of this kind right at the outset, for the Old Testament writings are both the common heritage of Jews and Christians and a cause of their deepest misunderstandings. What is more, there can be no denying that Christians have been the worse offenders, not only in the appalling history of anti-Semitism, but also in their failure to take Jewish religious claims with due seriousness. However that may be, the fact remains that the writings of the Old Testament are regarded as holy both in Judaism and in Christianity. This fact remains true even though there are certain differences in detail both about the content of the material and in its arrangement.

For Jews, as already noted, the term Tenak denotes a threefold division: Law, Prophets and Writings. These three collections are best envisaged as three concentric circles. The innermost circle, the most holy part, is the Torah or Pentateuch: Genesis, Exodus, Leviticus, Numbers and Deuteronomy. Here, in books traditionally ascribed to Moses, is set down the guidance God has given to his people. Indeed, part of the meaning of Torah is 'Guidance': simply to render it 'Law' can convey a negative impression, such as is found in the Christian polemic which has contrasted the freedom of the Gospel with the negative demands of the Law. Even where it has the character of law, it has been turned in many cases into prayer, as for example in the *Shema* ('Hear, O Israel') (Deut. 6:4), one of the prayers used daily by observant Jews.

The second circle consists of the Prophets. This material is not confined to the books of the prophets in the sense understood by Christians. Rather, it consists of two sections, the Former Prophets (Joshua, Judges, Samuel, Kings) and the Latter Prophets (Isaiah, Jeremiah, Ezekiel and the Twelve Minor Prophets, Hosea–Malachi). In traditional Judaism these books are understood as commentary upon the Torah, and there are religious groups related to Judaism which have limited their Scripture to the Torah; the Prophets, though revered, are only commentary. The Samaritans, who still survive as a small community in Palestine, are a case in point; for them the Torah alone is Scripture.

Finally, there is the third and most heterogeneous collection, simply called the Writings: Psalms, Proverbs, Job, the five

Megilloth or Festal Scrolls (Song of Songs, Ruth, Lamentations, Ecclesiastes and Esther), Daniel, Ezra–Nehemiah and Chronicles. These are writings of much more varied origins, and though the Psalms in particular have played an important part in Judaism in general and in its worship in particular, they are on the whole of less significance for our understanding of Judaism.

The books listed in the preceding paragraphs are also those regarded by Protestant Christians as the Old Testament, though as we shall see in a moment there are differences of order which may be significant. All of these books were written, wholly or in part, in Hebrew. (Those parts not in Hebrew had as their original language Aramaic, a language closely akin to Hebrew, in which parts of Daniel and Ezra and a single verse in Jeremiah were written.) But Catholic Christians include in their Old Testament a number of other writings which were originally written in Greek or have survived in that language even if there was once a Hebrew original. The book called Ecclesiasticus, for example, was composed in Hebrew, but for a long period only survived in Greek and Latin translations; a Hebrew form of the greater part of this book has been discovered as a result of archaeological work within the last century.

For the most part the early Christian Church was a Greek-speaking body, and so its Bible was a collection of writings in Greek, and for a long time it seems as if no sharp differentiation was made between books originally written in Hebrew and those which had been composed in Greek. Eventually, however, there was dispute among the Church fathers of the fourth and fifth centuries whether the Church's Old Testament should be limited to that which survived in Hebrew, or whether the larger Greek collection should be accepted. The latter view, upheld by the influential figure of St Augustine, prevailed.

Only at the Reformation in the sixteenth century did the dispute arise again in acute form, and from that time the Protestant usage has been to limit its Old Testament to the Hebrew canon, while the Catholic Church has accepted also those books which are commonly called the Apocrypha. The ambivalent status of these books has been recognised even in Catholic circles by the custom of referring to them as 'Deutero-canonical'.

As a postscript to the above discussion it may be noted that in recent years, though no church has changed its official teaching, unofficial attitudes have changed. Many Protestant bodies now recognise the value of the Apocryphal books for study, even if not for formal doctrinal purposes, and so the use of such translations as the RSV Common Bible, the Jerusalem Bible and the NEB has meant the availability of these texts, though to speak of familiarity would certainly be an exaggeration.

But is not only with regard to the actual number of books that some Christian usage differs from that of Judaism; their order is also significant. Whereas in

Judaism the appropriate model is, as we have seen, a series of concentric circles, the Christian Old Testament can more appropriately be pictured as a series of points on an extended line. That line runs from past to future. The first part of the Christian Old Testament has traditionally been understood as historical in character, beginning at the every beginning, with the account of Creation in Genesis 1, and then describing God's dealings with his people in a succession of historical books down to Esther. There follows a series of books dealing with life in the present: Job and the problem of human existence; Psalms as the hymns of the religious community; Proverbs as a series of maxims for the right ordering of life; Ecclesiastes and the Song of Songs as reflection by the greatest of wise men, Solomon, on the ambiguities of life and the pleasures of sexual union. The remainder of the Christian Old Testament consists of the prophetic books, including Daniel, not part of the Prophets in the Jewish canon, but understood as such in the Christian Church as early as New Testament times (Matt. 24:15). And in the Christian tradition, the role of the prophets has essentially been understood as foretelling the future.

Such an outline may help to explain how the Old Testament came to reach its present shape. It will at once be obvious that much in our modern experience renders it no longer applicable. The advance of the physical and life sciences means that it is no longer possible, save by very special pleading, to accept Genesis 1 as an accurate account of the creation of the world; an increased historical awareness warns us against accepting at its face value much that is found in the remaining 'history-like' sections. Different, but just as serious, difficulties arise in taking the prophetic parts of the Old Testament as having a future reference. It is clear, therefore, that the lasting value of the Old Testament, whether in a Jewish or a Christian context, will to a large extent be dependent upon the contents of the books rather than upon any external principle of order which they may exhibit. Put another way, this means that any authority which may be granted to the Old Testament will now be based upon what it says rather than on any preconceived idea of divine inspiration. It is to the contents of the Old Testament that we must now turn.

Old Testament or History of Israel?

The latest part of the Old Testament (perhaps the Book of Daniel, which probably reached its final form *c.* 165 BCE) is well over 2,000 years old. For the earliest parts (possibly the Song of Deborah, Judges 5, which some scholars would date before 1000 BCE) we may need to go back nearly another 1,000 years. It is obvious that no writing of such antiquity can speak to us direct; we live in what is, in many respects, a different world of thought.

At the most basic level the texts will need to be translated, for few will be able to handle them with confidence in their original language. To an overwhelming extent, however, the mechanics of translation rest upon an agreed consensus. Of course there are individual words and phrases which pose problems. Thus, if one were to compare different translations of the Book of Job, very different renderings of the poetic sections could soon be found. But even here there is no dispute about the essential shape of the story, and in most parts of the Old Testament the difficulties are far fewer. Indeed, when there has been discussion concerning the translation of the Old Testament into English, it has focused much more on the appropriate English style to be adopted rather than on the difficulty of rendering the Hebrew. It is therefore very unlikely that this consensus will be shaken in its broad outlines by any fresh discoveries of ancient texts. (The theories put forward from time to time that the Old Testament's origin is quite different from that normally supposed, to take a recent example that it originates not from Palestine but from Arabia, normally die with their propounder and rarely get beyond the crankish.)

We may therefore reasonably be confident that we can make sense of the actual words, but how are they to be interpreted? Here we are confronted with a much more basic issue of principle.

Until the Renaissance in the fifteenth and sixteenth centuries CE, the Bible was mainly taken as a body of texts which could be used to prove the truth of Jewish or Christian beliefs. From that period on, however, a dominantly historical method of approach has gradually prevailed. It could be said to be laid down by the very first words of Genesis, 'In the beginning'. (This translation of what is actually the first word in the Hebrew Bible, *b^e^reshith*, appears to be common to all the main modern versions.) From the very outset, that is to say, it appears as if we have to do with a story of humanity's past, a story which begins with the creation of the world itself and then of human beings, and then concentrates its attention upon a particular people through their various adventures.

We have just seen that the beginning of Genesis seems to invite a historical approach; in fact, of course, for at least a century the early chapters of Genesis have proved to present the main difficulty for such a historical approach. The creation of the world in six days; a paradise garden; a talking snake; the possibility of all humankind being descended from one primeval pair; a universal flood—these and other difficulties have meant that for most people Genesis 1–11 cannot be taken seriously as history but must be understood as stories setting out one understanding of human origins. We shall return later to consider what significance can legitimately be attributed to this material if it is not history.

From Genesis 12 onwards, however, it is remarkable that for a very long time serious and reputable scholars (including those who were not themselves believers) felt able to affirm the basic historicity of the biblical material. Details have, of course, been questioned, such as the great age to which the figures in the remote past are said to have lived, but these have been regarded as peripheral to the main thrust of the story. The idea of semi-nomads from the East entering Palestine, as is told of Abraham and his clan (Gen. 12); the movements within the land of patriarchal figures such as Abraham and Jacob (Gen. 12–35); links with Egypt in times of famine (Gen. 37–50); the oppression and expulsion by the Egyptians of unwanted intruders from the desert fringes (Exod. 1–15); wilderness groups eventually seeking possession of a fertile land (Exod. 16–Joshua)—all of these themes have been widely accepted as supplying the basis for a story which can by and large be regarded as historical.

From that point onwards in the biblical text historical uncertainties become steadily fewer. In Judges we read of an experiment in a form of government which failed to respond to the realities of external pressure, and so the usual form of government for states in the ancient world—kingship—was resorted to, though not without misgivings (1 and 2 Samuel). From then on the little states of Judah and Israel existed in a world where the great powers posed an increasing threat to their independence, and both eventually succumbed, Israel to Assyrian and Judah to Babylonian invasion (1 and 2 Kings). There followed the experience of exile; and again an apparently agreed historical consensus has been achieved. For the northern kingdom, Israel, the exile to Assyria appears as the end of the story; these were the 'ten lost tribes' of later legend. By contrast, those from the southern kingdom, Judah, who were exiled to Babylon, retained their identity, and were able to take advantage of the greater tolerance of the Persians, who succeeded the Babylonians in power. In due course the exiles returned to Jerusalem, rebuilt the Temple, and established themselves anew in the service of their God (Ezra). From that time on historical records are much scantier, and it is not until the time of the Maccabee uprising against Syrian domination in the 160s BCE that we are able once again to reconstruct a more detailed picture of Jewish life and religious practice. But that is virtually the end of the historical period of the Old Testament; the most detailed account comes in the Book of 1 Maccabees, which is in the Apocrypha and not part of the Hebrew Bible.

Some such account as this would be recognised by many as a rough outline of the Old Testament seen as a historical record of the community's experience, with particular emphasis on the way in which it perceived God's dealings with it. It can be reinforced by placing within the appropriate historical contexts the life and teaching of the various prophets whose message is so distinctive a part of the Old Testament. Some of these (Samuel, Elijah, Elisha) are the subject of stories in the Books of Samuel and Kings; others have books named after them, recording the words with which they condemned the people either in the time of Assyria's rise to power in the eighth century (Amos, Hosea, Isaiah, Micah), or at the time of the Babylonian threat in the sixth century (Jeremiah, Ezekiel), or when Persian rule allowed the re-establishment of the Jerusalem community later in the same

Table 6.1: Chronological Table

As is indicated in the text, there are many uncertainties concerning the history of Israel and its forebears, particularly with regard to the pre-monarchical period. The table below is therefore no more than a rough guide: the *italic* entries for the earlier period are no more than approximations. For the later period, greater precision (to within a decade) is usually attainable, and where there is corroborating evidence from other sources (e.g. the Babylonian Chronicle referring to the last years of the kingdom of Judah), a high degree of chronological accuracy can be achieved.

c. 1900–1500 BCE	*The Patriarchs (Abraham, Isaac, Jacob).*
15th or 13th cent.	*The Exodus.*
1250–1200	*Settlement in Canaan.*
1200–1000	*The 'Judges' Period.*
1000–920	Saul. David. Solomon, The Division of the Kingdom.
850	First Assyrian Invasion (not mentioned in OT). Ahab.
750–720	Eighth-Century Prophets active (Amos, Hosea, Isaiah, Micah).*
722	Fall of Northern Kingdom to Assyria. Southern Kingdom reduced to vassal status.
630–600	Decline of Assyria, rise of Babylon. Josiah of Judah bids for independence but is killed.
597	Capture of Jerusalem by Babylonians (Nebuchadnezzar). King Jehoiachin and leading citizens exiled.
587/6	Rebellion against Babylon leads to destruction of Jerusalem and its Temple.
539	Persians (Cyrus) capture Babylon; reconstruction of Jerusalem Temple permitted.
515	Second Temple completed.
458 (or 398)	Mission of Ezra.
333	Conquest of Palestine by Alexander the Great (not mentioned in OT).

The last events referred to in the Old Testament are almost certainly those of the period of rebellion against Hellenistic rule (the successors of Alexander), *c.* 165; the Book of Daniel in its completed form almost certainly dates from this period. The so-called 'intertestamental period' is usually regarded as beginning at approximately that time; see the chapter in this volume on 'The First-Century Crisis' (pp. 91–110).

* These dates refer to the lifetime of the prophets whose words have been gathered in books; the books themselves, all of which contain substantial later additions, cannot be precisely dated.

century (Haggai, Zechariah). Within such an outline by far the greater part of the Old Testament is successfully accommodated; only the Psalms and, in particular, the wisdom books (Proverbs, Job, Ecclesiastes), which by their very nature are timeless and resist a historical approach, have to be treated in a different manner.

The broad outline sketch which has just been set out will for many people provide the kind of framework upon which their knowledge of the Old Testament is based. Certainly many of the most widely used and influential introductory books about the subject follow such an outline. Yet in recent years its appropriateness has increasingly come to be questioned. This questioning has arisen in three distinct, but interrelated, areas. First, there are doubts as to the historical reliability of such an outline: is the consensus which has been built up in fact a securely based one? Secondly, there are difficulties concerning the relation between a historical approach of this kind and the religious conviction of the community which the Old Testament enshrines. To take an obvious example: if the Exodus from Egypt could be established as in some sense 'historical fact', how would that fact relate to the people's continuing belief in God, one of whose mighty deeds had been the deliverance from Egypt of their forefathers? Thirdly, questions are raised as to the propriety of understanding the Old Testament in so exclusively historical a manner. Whatever else they may be, the books of the Old Testament are literature; would it not therefore be appropriate that they should in the first instance be treated as literature rather than being assessed as witnesses to a historical development? These questions will perhaps give sufficient indication that Old Testament studies are currently in ferment, and that the agreement on basic issues which appeared to be within the grasp of an earlier generation now seems to be very remote.

Historical Difficulties

First of all, then, we must consider the kind of historical difficulties which would now be widely felt to be passed over much too lightly in the outline given above. There it was implied that something like a reliable historical outline could be begun with the arrival of the patriarchs in Palestine, perhaps in the nineteenth to eighteenth centuries BCE, the period referred to by archaeologists as the Middle Bronze Age. By contrast, recent studies both of the material in Genesis and of the history of the Bronze Age, in so far as it can be reconstructed by archaeological and other means, have radically questioned this assumption. Many scholars would doubt whether we have any grounds for speaking of historical figures called Abraham or Jacob; others would accept the likelihood of their existence, but would feel it to be quite impossible to disentangle any reliable evidence relating to their life or historical context from the religious significance which has been given by a later age to the stories which it told about them.

The problems relating to Moses and the story of the Exodus are slightly different. Here a useful starting-point is provided by the fact that Moses is an Egyptian-type name; it is in fact precisely comparable with that of the Egyptian Pharaoh Ra-meses, without the prefix of an Egyptian god's name. It is indeed likely that a band of slaves did at some point escape from Egyptian domination, but this is a far cry from the story in the Book of Exodus, Chapters 7–15, in which a series of devastating plagues reaches a climax with the death of all Egypt's first-born and the destruction of its army. Such events would have had shattering and long-lasting effects on the history of any society, yet the well-documented history of ancient Egypt offers no hint of any such crises. Here as elsewhere the folk-memories of particular groups of people, shaped by their expression in the worship of their God ('I am the LORD your God who brought you out of the land of Egypt', Exod. 20:1) have misleadingly come to be regarded as if they are the very stuff of history.

Historical elaboration of a rather different kind has been at work in the Books of Joshua and Judges. In Joshua, the story of Israel's establishment in the 'promised land', Canaan, has been set out in the form of a series of glorious conquests. Unfortunately the two chief stories, describing the destruction of Jericho and Ai (Josh. 2–8), are very far from being supported by the evidence from archaeological excavation, which suggests that neither of these cities was the site of significant habitation at any possible time of Israelite invasion. In Judges, the impression is given of a deliberate experiment, under divine command, with a form of government which would differentiate Israel from all her neighbours. Others had kings, whereas Israel was to be ruled by 'judges', raised up for them by God. In fact it seems much more likely that this represents not so much a historical account as the religious reflection of a later period. Israel, like other nations of that time, came to kingship as the only conceivable form of government when it had developed sufficiently to take on the characteristics of a nation-state.

Recent scholarly discussion has raised another issue which in many ways would put the historicity of the earlier biblical books even more into question. The biblical tradition appears to state beyond the possibility of dispute that the ancestors of Israel had come into Canaan from the wilderness, after a long period when they had led a nomadic or semi-nomadic existence. This tradition has recently been challenged, and it is now maintained that Israel's establishment in Canaan was a matter of a rising of an oppressed lower class rather than of immigration from elsewhere. It is almost certainly true that the very sharp contrast between Israelite and Canaanite set out in, for example, the Book of Deuteronomy is much exaggerated. Whether the more drastic suggestion, that Israel never experienced that way of life conventionally pictured as the forty years in the wilderness before entering the land flowing with milk and honey, will win general favour is as yet uncertain.

Whether or not the particular hypothesis just discussed is accepted, the point is now very widely recognised that the apparently historical picture of the people's development set out in the books from Genesis to Judges cannot be taken at face value as a historical record. Rather, in its final form it represents the religious viewpoint of a much later age. This is not to deny that ancient traditions are embedded in these books; that is a matter for the detailed discussion of particular episodes. It is rather that the overall presentation offers a continuous story of a group developing from a family into a nation, a story which is simply not borne out by detailed historical or archaeological research.

Uncertainty as to historical reliability remains even into the time of the monarchy. It is noteworthy that both David and Solomon are credited with the round figure of forty years as the length of their reign, which suggests that exact information is not available. It is also striking that the accounts of their lives contain much of a legendary character: David and Goliath; Solomon and the two mothers with one child. Clearly, though, the historical basis is by this time becoming more secure. We have detailed lists of court officials from the reign of David, which suggests that a formal basis of court annals was emerging; and this increasing precision of historical detail is characteristic of the period of the divided kingdoms, from the death of Solomon down to the fall of Jerusalem to the Babylonians (*c.* 920–597 BCE).

The last century and a half of this period has also had a great deal of light shed upon it by the fact that the royal annals of the Assyrian and Babylonian kings have become available as a result of excavations in modern Iraq, the Tigris–Euphrates basin. By and large this material can be correlated in a good deal of detail with the biblical record of the period in 2 Kings, and it is very clear that by this period we are on firm historical ground, whatever may be said of the historicity of the earlier Old Testament stories.

Even so, however, difficulties in the way of reconstructing a clear historical outline remain. Two major problems in particular may be noted. The first of these concerns the understanding of the period from the Exile onwards. In the biblical account a sharp distinction is made between the fate of the exiles from the two kingdoms. Those from the northern kingdom, Israel, who were sent into exile by the Assyrians in the eighth century, simply disappear from view; their exile is described in 2 Kings 17, and then no more is said. From this silence has arisen the legend of the 'ten lost tribes', though that is not itself biblical. By contrast, great stress is laid on the idea of the exile of the Jerusalem community as being an event of strictly limited duration, which came to a datable end (Ezra 1–2).

This sharply contrasted presentation almost certainly owes more to religious polemic than to historical accuracy. There never were ten 'lost' tribes; the Assyrians themselves (not given to modesty in their claims) refer to the deportation of some 27,000 people, a tiny proportion of the population of northern Israel. In other words, life in the former northern kingdom will have continued under Assyrian rule, no doubt with additional hardship, but without the dramatic changes implied by 2 Kings 17.

Again, the exile of the Jerusalem community is presented in some of the texts in theological rather than historical terms. It became an article of faith, for example in the Book of Ezra, that the true community consisted of those who had been through the purging experience of exile in Babylon. But once again history and theology point in different directions. The historical record is likely to be close to that in Jeremiah 52, which speaks of 4,600 exiles, rather than the total depopulation implied in the Books of Chronicles and in Ezra, looking back from a later standpoint. In 2 Chronicles 36, we have a picture of the land as completely deserted during the exile; Ezra 1–2 picture a mass return of exiles from Babylon. Such a picture is very unlikely historically; the Persian rulers allowed a greater diversity of local cults, so that permission to rebuild the ruined Jerusalem Temple may plausibly be seen as part of their policy. But mass migrations of former subject peoples is much less probable, and it is very unlikely that there was a large-scale return of exiles in the later part of the sixth century. Instead, we should envisage from that time on a continuing Jewish community in Babylon.

In some respects, the lack of knowledge of the development of the Jerusalem community during the Second Temple period, that is, from 515 BCE until 70 CE, has had still more serious effects on modern understanding. Too often Jesus and his earliest followers have been pictured, not as the products of the Judaism of their own day, but as rebels against it, whose Old Testament links were exclusively with the earlier period, and with the prophets in particular. In fact, there is little evidence to support such a view; rather, for a proper understanding of the 'Jesus-movement' it is essential to see him against the background of contemporary Judaism, about whose religious beliefs and practices our knowledge has greatly increased through such discoveries as the Dead Sea Scrolls. In this wider context, it soon becomes apparent that the followers of Jesus had much in common with other groups in Judaism whose prime concern was a total commitment to God's service. So, for example, despite the bitter opposition to the Pharisees characteristic of some parts of the New Testament (e.g. Matt. 23), we can now see that there was a great deal in common in belief and practice between the Pharisees and the earliest followers of Jesus.

The other weakness in the type of historical sketch offered at the outset of this section relates to its handling of the work of the prophets. What is commonly called the historical–critical method lays down certain preconditions for the right understanding of the prophetic books. If they are to be seen in their true historical contexts, then it is essential that it should first of all be established which parts really do come from the supposed historical period. So a great deal of scholarly attention has been devoted to the analysis of the present form of the books, with the declared intention of stripping away those parts held to be 'secondary'. And the word 'secondary' has come to mean not only 'of later origin' but also 'of lesser importance'. There has, of course, been one great exception to this general rule. In the case of the book of Isaiah it has been agreed on all hands that Chapters 40–66 are from a historical setting later than that of Isaiah himself, and for Chapters 40–55 in particular it has been argued that another setting—Babylon in the 540s—can confidently be postulated. And so we have a modern scholarly creation: an anonymous (and quite possibly imaginary) figure, the prophet known as Second or Deutero-Isaiah. Thus a wealth of well-loved and profound material is saved from the charge of being 'secondary'.

Such an approach to the prophets can be questioned in various ways. Two particular difficulties can be mentioned here. First, concentration on the parts of the material judged to be original has meant an excessive concern with particular sections dotted through the final form of the existing books; and the existing form of the prophetic books has either been ignored or regarded as purely fortuitous. This seems to be a very curious approach to any piece of literature. Secondly, a dangerous process of circular argument is often involved. The state of Israelite society in the eighth century, for example, is often asserted to have reached a particularly decadent condition; and the ground for such an assertion is the preaching of the prophets like Amos. But the claim is also made that God raised up Amos and the other prophets because of the peculiar decadence of the society of his day. Apart from the logical fallacy involved, this takes no account of the possibility that polemic may have been a part of the preacher's art, and accepts at face value charges which are at least as likely to involve some measure of poetic exaggeration. After all, what preacher worth listening to would ever say that his congregation were not so wicked after all?

One final comment must be made relating to the mainly historical type of approach to the Old Testament, since it affects a particular way of understanding the Old and the New Testaments together which has been much in vogue among some scholars. It involves the form of argument that there was a radical difference of understanding of the historical process in ancient Israel by comparison with other ancient peoples. For Israel, it is alleged, history was linear, purposive, an unfolding of the purpose of God. Other peoples, by contrast, held it to be cyclic, a constant return to the point of departure, a conception based on a religious understanding rooted in the fertility of nature as experienced in the recurring seasons of the year.

In fact there is little evidence which would support the claim to so drastically different an understanding. Certainly Israel did see in the unfolding of events the hand of its God at work: the books from Joshua to 2 Kings, often called the 'Deuteronomistic History', provide a clear illustration of this. But other nations in the same way saw the hand of their gods guiding their own history. Thus, the 'Moabite Stone', discovered in the nineteenth century, shows how the successes and failures of Moab, a people bordering on Israel, were believed to correspond to favour and punishment bestowed by Chemosh, the god of Moab. The extent of the Old Testament means that it can supply us with more elaborate examples of this principle of divine responsibility, but the principle itself could certainly be applied to the history of other nations.

It should also be remembered that there was much in Israel to show the importance of the seasonal round of fertility in its religious observance. The festal calendar, as set out several times in Exodus–Deuteronomy with minor variations, is based on three festivals at fixed times of the year, whose observance was intimately bound up with the need for continuing fertility in the land. (It is important for readers in northern climes to remember that in Palestine the time of new birth is not the spring, after winter bleakness, but the autumn, after the parching heat of summer has dried up the land; the first rains of autumn, the 'former rains', are the signs of new life, when the land can once again be worked.)

The implications of this résumé of some of the problems posed when we attempt to take the Old Testament material as straightforward historical record may seem overwhelmingly negative; but this would be a false impression. For those who brought the Old Testament to its final form a primary means of understanding God's dealings with his people was to set them out in history-like terms, as an extended story. To achieve that purpose many ancient traditions were used which can throw much light on the history of the ancient Near East. But the purpose itself was inspired by religious aims, rather than by any motivation which we should describe as historical. In other words, we must not suppose that the history of ancient Israel is itself the key to unlock the door of true understanding of the Old Testament. Taken simply as a history book, the Old Testament would be seriously defective; and to attempt to understand it in those terms would be equally unsatisfactory. For an understanding both of ancient Israel and of the Old Testament religious motives have to be taken into account.

The Religion of Ancient Israel

Modern service books in Judaism and Christianity commonly contain both the actual words to be used in the service, and instructions to the participants as to how the service is to be carried out, with instructions as to how the role of each is to be fulfilled. A basic problem in any attempt to understand the religion of ancient Israel consists in the fact that the instructions how worship is to be ordered appear in one part of the Old Testament, the main surviving worship texts in another. The Book of Leviticus especially offers detailed and precise instructions concerning the carrying-out of sacrificial worship in particular; whereas it is to the Psalms that we must turn if we are to learn more of the 'innerness' of worship, from the viewpoint of the participant. In the Psalms what is implicit in many other parts of the material becomes quite explicit: the Old Testament is a religious collection, bearing witness to the religious aspirations of the community which brought it together. And those aspirations are expressed more directly, and often in more memorable language, in the Psalms than anywhere else.

One meaning of the word 'psalm' is: one of the 150 such pieces that make up the Book of Psalms. But a wider meaning would be: a hymn of praise addressed to God. If we take that wider meaning we shall see that 'psalms' are not confined to the Book of Psalms. Other parts of the Old Testament also reflect this felt need for the expression of praise to God. So at times the flow of a narrative is 'interrupted' (as we should feel it to be) by a 'psalm': such is the thanksgiving for the deliverance of the Exodus (Exod. 15), or the song of Hannah at the birth of the child Samuel (1 Sam. 2), or the hymn uttered by Jonah in the belly of the fish (Jonah 2). At other times the collection of prophetic words, normally directed toward the people in the fashion of a preacher or messenger, includes praise directed to God. We find such passages in Amos, normally the most severe in his condemnations of the people (Amos 4:13); or in the hymn in Isaiah 9:2–7 familiar to many from its use in Handel's *Messiah*. Psalms, whether in the Book of Psalms or elsewhere, remind us that the Israel which gathered its traditions together did so as a worshipping community.

Praise and prayer addressed to God are characteristic responses of a religious group, and go beyond any specific time and place; and so it is not surprising that many Psalms, or phrases from them, retain their impact even when most of the rest of the Old Testament is completely unknown. 'The LORD is my shepherd', 'The heavens declare the glory of God', 'By the waters of Babylon'—these opening words of Psalms 23, 19 and 137 are among many which can still resonate even beyond a formal religious setting. But the Psalms were surely not free lyric compositions; they did emerge from a particular context of worship, and much scholarly effort has been devoted to attempts to reconstruct the detailed form of that worship.

Such an attempt is much more difficult than might at first be supposed. It is probable that many of the Psalms originated in the time when Judah was a nation-state, with its own king ruling in Jerusalem, where the Temple was a national cult centre. (The Psalms are often referred to as 'Psalms of David', and though this need not imply that he was the author of any that have come down to us, it does remind us that the king, a religious figure, was at the centre of the nation's cultic life.) But if most of the Psalms originated in the time before the Exile, in the form in which they have come down to us they represent a collection gathered for the worship of a later period, the time of the 'Second Temple', which lasted from *c.* 515 BCE until its destruction by the Romans in 70 CE. In other words, like many of the hymns in a modern hymn-book, psalms that originally had been composed for one situation came to be used in quite a different context, and the details of the earlier situation are now lost to us, perhaps beyond recall.

There is one important consequence of this for our understanding. In so far as we *can* reconstruct the character of the worship in the earlier age, it appears to have had a natural joyous character, expressing itself with dance and music, and perhaps with sexual rites, which became quite unacceptable from the viewpoint of a later period. At that time what we might regard as a more 'puritan' ethos had emerged. The community had come through the harrowing experience of exile; God had shown his displeasure with the people once, and might do so again. So the texts relating to worship, in the form in which they have come down to us, are dominated by an awareness of sin, and an anxiety that everything possible might be done to remove the taint caused by sin.

This emphasis is very clearly marked in the Psalms, where nearly half of the 150 individual pieces are of the form known as 'laments', where the community or an individual (perhaps speaking as representative of the community) express awareness of sin and plead to God for forgiveness. It is even more characteristic of Leviticus, where, as we have seen, detailed instructions are provided for the carrying-out of a variety of rituals in the proper manner. Overwhelmingly the emphasis is on the maintenance of the proper standing of the community before God by a series of rites, of burnt offering and the like, all concerned with the need for the proper expiation of sin. In many ways the climax of the Book of Leviticus is provided by the strange rite described in Chapter 16, to be performed on what came to be known as the Day of Atonement (Yom Kippur), a day which continues to be central to the observances of modern Judaism.

Such a change of emphasis meant that many Psalms, which had no doubt originally been used in the performance of joyous rites of thanksgiving to God, came to be interpreted as referring to the future, to a time when the people could once more be assured of the divine favour. For the present the community could no longer assume that its relation with God was basically secure; always the appropriate rituals had to be carried out to ensure that it might be so. The consequences of this concern for human sinfulness were to be very deep-rooted in both Judaism and Christianity.

It is from such a standpoint as this that we can achieve an important insight into the role of the prophets. Neither the traditional Jewish approach to the prophets, as interpreters of the Torah, the Law of Moses, nor the traditional Christian understanding of them as foretellers of the future, is wholly satisfactory. The prophets were clearly men who were addressing what they believed to be messages from God to their own contemporaries; to that extent the description of the prophets as 'forthtellers, not foretellers' is reasonable enough. But too often the prophets have been regarded as set over against the religious establishment, free preachers opposed to the cultic orthodoxy of their day. So the denunciations of sacrificial worship found in all the main prophetic collections—Amos and Hosea, Micah and Isaiah from the eighth century, Jeremiah and Ezekiel from the sixth—have been understood as calls for a religion free of the trammels of cultic detail. Thus when Hosea, in perhaps the best-known of these passages, proclaims in God's name

I desire steadfast love, and not sacrifice,
  the knowledge of God, rather than burnt offerings

(Hos. 6:6)

this has often been taken as an outright rejection of all forms of sacrificial offering.

Such an understanding is almost certainly misleading. It would, for a start, be completely anachronistic to suppose that free individual religion without involvement in the cultic practice of the community would have been a possible option in the eighth century BCE; that is a concept much more characteristic of the Liberal Protestantism of the last century or so. But even in Old Testament terms to picture the prophets as opposed to cultic practices is misleading. Rather, it was precisely because of its importance that any corruption in the people's worship was to be condemned severely. Other parts of the Old Testament, for example the Books of Exodus, Leviticus and Numbers, spell out in great detail the importance of sacrificial worship; the prophets are not to be seen in opposition to such practice, but as messengers bringing warnings. And one of those warnings most frequently expressed was concerned with the dangers of corruption in worship.

The possible causes and nature of such corruption might, of course, differ according to circumstances. In Hosea it seems as if he was combating the supposition that sacrifice and burnt offering could make the community acceptable to God regardless of its failure to observe God's will in the rest of its life. In Amos, a southerner preaching in the north, we find sweeping denunciations of social ills, but also the underlying assumption that the very existence of particular northern sanctuaries was a matter for condemnation. The irony of

Come to Bethel, and transgress,
  to Gilgal, and multiply transgression

(Amos 4:4)

seems to make it clear that the very act of joining in worship at those sanctuaries was wrong; only at Jerusalem could the Lord's voice truly be heard. And so it would be possible with the other prophets to pick out particular emphases in their denunciation. But all would be motivated by the same basic conviction that Israel's worship must reflect its unique position as a nation specially chosen by God.

The prophets were, that is to say, part of the religious and political establishment of their day, but they were also prepared to rebel against the viewpont of that establishment if it appeared to them to be right to do so; and herein lies one of the lasting values of the Old Testament. There are scattered pieces of evidence that elsewhere in the ancient Near East religious functionaries were prepared to reject the official line, to act under the conviction that they had received a direct command from God, but nowhere is that independence carried as far as among the Israelite prophets. It may well have been due to the great prophets that the conviction arose that Yahweh, the God of Israel, alone could properly be worshipped, that no other god was acceptable; it was certainly part of their message that his worship demanded worthy forms of behaviour which must pervade all aspects of human life.

Some of these prophetic concerns are carried still further in the Book of Deuteronomy, though the language employed there is for the most part less stirring. Deuteronomy is often regarded as a kind of repository of much of prophetic preaching. Though ostensibly a series of sermons from the mouth of Moses given before the people had ever entered the Promised Land, it is in fact almost certainly a product of the period leading up to the Exile, when Israel's existence in Canaan was once more in jeopardy. Here are set out some of the convictions that have shaped the expression of Judaism ever since, notably the *Shema*: 'Hear, O Israel: the Lord our God, the Lord is one; and you shall love the Lord your God with all your heart, and with all your soul, and with all your might' (Deut. 6:4). Here is expressed the belief that Israel's relation with its God was a wholly unique one, quite unlike that of other surrounding peoples. This is clearly a religious judgement rather than a historical one. Israel is not to be regarded simply as a state among states; it is essentially a religious community, set apart from all other peoples.

The particular way of expressing this belief in Deuteronomy was by use of the word 'covenant', a concept which has been of immense significance in Judaism and Christianity ever since. (What we habitually speak of as the Old and New 'Testaments' would more accurately be called 'Covenants'.) The two great prophets roughly contemporary with Deuteronomy, Jeremiah and Ezekiel, both make frequent use of this way of describing the people's past history, which they saw as largely a story of religious infidelity, and of its hopes for the future based on a 'new covenant' (Jer. 31:31–34, a passage much used in the New Testament and applied to the work of Jesus; Ezek. 34:25–31, another passage of importance for the New Testament because of its use of the theme of the 'good shepherd').

The idea of covenant was no doubt not a wholly new one at the time of Deuteronomy and the sixth-century prophets, but it does seem as if that was the period at which the word was employed most creatively and extensively. Characteristically it was projected back to the very beginnings of human experience, so that the deliverance of Noah from the great flood was pictured in terms of an everlasting covenant (Gen. 9:8–17). Similarly, the act of the giving of the Law on Mount Sinai, the conventional mode of describing the guiding principles by which the community's life was to be determined, was expressed in terms of a covenant (Exod. 24:3–8). By such means was the community enabled to come to terms with the greatly changed situation which its overthrow as a nation-state imposed upon it; in future, its relation to its God would increasingly be that of a religious community rather than that of a nation-state. The whole notion of a 'covenant people' is one which is much more appropriate to the religious group than to the secular state.

Deuteronomy is in many ways the book which best conveys to the modern reader the central concerns of the Old Testament, and there is much else in its contents which could legitimately be discussed here: for example, the particular emphasis on the *one* community worshipping the *one* God at the *one* holy place. But there is one particular emphasis in Deuteronomy and the literature associated with it (e.g. the Deuteronomistic History, Joshua–Judges–Samuel–Kings) which must be considered, for it has provided one of the strengths and one of the problems of theistic belief ever since.

One of the central concerns of Deuteronomy is to show that the community is rewarded or punished in accordance with its behaviour. The climax of the speech or sermon put into the mouth of Moses emphasises the two ways which are open to the people, and the inevitable consequences of each course of behaviour (Deut. 30). A large part of the Deuteronomistic History is devoted to showing how the people's behaviour had in fact been a choice of the wrong way, falling away from the worship of the one God, and that this had been the real cause of the disasters that had befallen them. The defeats that had been inflicted by their enemies, the Philistines, the Assyrians, the Babylonians, had all been the result of God's own action in punishing his faithless people.

Some kind of theology of history along these lines is essential for the maintenance of belief in a God whose demands are in any way to be predictable, and it is a type of theology which has played a major part in the Judeo-Christian tradition ever since: what happens in history is held to be in accordance with the divine will and purpose. But whatever may be said of this view with regard to the history of whole communities, it poses acute problems if the attempt is made to apply it to individuals, as if their success or misfortune could also be directly correlated with good or bad behaviour. Certain parts of the Book of Proverbs seem to inculcate this belief (e.g. Prov. 10:3), and it is also found in some Psalms. The Book of Psalms contains individual psalms of a type very different from those which we considered as witnessing to Israel's worship; such is Ps. 37:25:

> I have been young, and now am old;
> yet I have not seen the righteous forsaken
> or his children begging bread.

Perhaps the most thoroughgoing exposition of this view, that one can assess another's virtue by his prosperity or its absence, is put into the mouth of the friends of Job. But when we come to consider the Book of Job, we have left all strictly historical considerations far behind; the Book of Job is in a real sense timeless, and it is now appropriate to consider the third of our questions (p. 75 above): is there not a case for approaching the Old Testament as literature, without particular regard for historical questions? Though attempts have been made to discover a historical context for the Book of Job, the interest and passion that it has aroused have overwhelmingly been caused by the fact that it is perceived as great literature.

The Literary Study of the Bible

The study of the Bible has for the most part been undertaken by those who have had some active link with the believing community, Jewish and Christian. For a variety of reasons, that has led to the strongly historical concern which we have already noted. It may well be that one reason for the decline of a purely historical concern is the fact that there has been an increased interest in the Bible (and the Old Testament in particular) as a literary phenomenon; and this interest has been by no means confined to those who are themselves religious believers.

Before considering this point more generally, however, we may return briefly to the Book of Job, which of all Old Testament books has exercised great fascination for literary figures from the widest possible background. William Blake, Thomas Carlyle, H.G. Wells, C.G. Jung are figures that come to mind, and in an often quoted judgement Job has been compared with Dante's *Divine Comedy* and Goethe's *Faust* as part of the great literature of the world. Yet it is also religious literature, and poses in the most acute form imaginable (for the context of the poem is a bet laid in heaven, of which human beings can know nothing) the problem of the inexplicability of human affairs. The supposition of Job's friends, arguing along the lines set out for the community in Deuteronomy, that human prosperity reflects acceptability with God and ill fortune implies wrong behaviour, is rejected. In the end Job is vindicated and his fortunes are restored; and arguments still rage whether this is a satisfactory ending to the Book. Clearly, in life good behaviour is not always rewarded: should the Book of Job have reflected that ambiguity? It is striking that the Old Testament also contains another treatment of this theme, in the book Ecclesiastes, which is in many ways even more questioning of the accepted religious solution that good behaviour always receives its due reward.

Job and Ecclesiastes offer us two timely reminders. First, neither of them can be placed in any historical context; the ascription of Ecclesiastes to Solomon is universally agreed to be simply a literary device. Secondly, they demonstrate in a remarkable way the ability of the particular religious system which brought the Old Testament into its final shape to include within its canon of sacred writings at least two which raised basic doubts concerning the divine–human relation which was at the very heart of that system. Whatever else they are, Job and Ecclesiastes are works that challenge received beliefs.

One of the most striking features of the approach to the Bible in the first instance as a piece of literature is this capacity for raising disturbing questions. Some of the stories that have had the deepest effect on our culture come into this category. A prime example would be the command to Abraham to sacrifice his only son Isaac, told in Genesis 22. It will always be a profoundly disturbing account; yet if historical questions are to the fore, then it becomes possible to envisage it as illustrating changing social and religious conditions, the abandonment of an earlier custom of human sacrifice, and the like. Explanations of this kind, it is now widely agreed, are wide of the mark; and if we read Genesis 22 as a story, then it is no longer possible to avoid the issues it raises as to the kind of God who could be pictured as making such commands, the nature of Abraham's response, and so on.

Similar points can be made about the stories in the opening chapters of the Old Testament, concerning Creation and the universal Flood. As historical record these stories are clearly unacceptable. By using such labels as 'myth', we may get some insight into the processes which underlie the telling of such stories. In Genesis 2 and 3, for example, it is easy to see how the story sets out to explain aspects of human existence which may be puzzling or even terrifying: the ambivalence of relations between the sexes, the fascination/repulsion of snakes, the pain experienced by women in childbirth, the need for and the unproductive nature of manual labour. All these questions are set within a context of divine creative activity. But underlying all these detailed points is the power of the story in itself. This is not simply a didactic message given story form to make it more acceptable; the story has its own compelling force. As with the parables of Jesus, we are first gripped by the story itself; only subsequently do we reflect upon its implications for our leading of our lives and understanding of them.

Not surprisingly, therefore, this literary approach has spawned a whole new area of biblical study, and the disputes which have often reached bitter proportions in other literary studies, concerning structuralism, semiotics and the like, have not left biblical scholars unscathed. (Indeed, the expression 'literary criticism', when applied to the Bible, is now very ambiguous: sometimes it means the type of historical and source criticism referred to earlier in this article, sometimes it is concerned with the type of literary study here being discussed. *Caveat lector!*)

Of more immediate relevance is the relation of this type of study to the authority of the Bible within a religious community. Perhaps not many would now wish to maintain the historical inerrancy of the Bible in the sense that the accuracy of every statement in it is an essential prerequisite if the Bible is to retain any authority. But there are very many who would feel, in more general terms, that the historical approach outlined earlier did provide the possibility of objective criteria which are no longer available if the Bible is to be approached primarily as literature, which seems a much more subjective matter. (Whether that last point is indeed true is an issue that is much discussed, but can hardly be raised here.) In fact the objective/subjective tension corresponds closely to another division which is widely experienced among religious believers. There are those who regard their faith as a series of propositions, which must be substantially true if the faith itself is to be maintained; this approach corresponds closely to the desire to have a series of verifiable historical claims. There are others who would express their conviction rather in terms of accepting the Jewish or the Christian story as that which makes best sense of the world in which they live and reflects most closely their own deepest feelings; for them a more subjective approach will not be a weakness.

There is one other aspect of the literary approach to the Old Testament which even the briefest survey must note. As we have seen, traditional study of the prophets by historical–critical methods has been much concerned to establish what was original to the prophet in question, with what was secondary being in effect discarded. Thus with Amos, for example, critical scholars have been almost unanimous in regarding the last few verses of the book (9:11–15) as a later addition, a kind of 'happy ending' which had no place in the preaching of Amos himself. Here, as will be seen, is a tension which can never be entirely resolved. If our main concern is with the individual figure of the prophet Amos, preaching a devastating message of doom to his contemporaries in the eighth century BCE, then we shall regard all the probably later additions as detracting from the 'real' message. If, on the other hand, our first concern is with the Book of Amos, part of the sacred tradition of the Jewish (and later Christian) community as it has been handed down through the centuries, then the message will be a different one: a conviction that beyond imminent and very real disaster a happy outcome could nevertheless be awaited. According to whether we seek the history and religion of ancient Israel, or the sacred writings handed down, we receive a different message. Neither is 'right' at the expense of the other; their difference should still be recognised.

Conclusion

The material which we call the Old Testament is commonly found as a single book, either by itself or with the Christian writings called the New Testament. Yet we also speak of 'the Book of Genesis', 'the Book of Exodus' and so on. There are insights to be gained from each approach: the Old Testament is both a single book and a collection of separate books.

The Old Testament (and here we are thinking of the Hebrew Bible, as described in the first section of this article) is the gathering together of the sacred traditions of the Jerusalem community of the Second Temple period. Though very diverse in origin, as to both time and place, they have been given a unity by the nature of the editorial process. For the most part these traditions were shaped in the form of history, particular events in the community's experience in which God's decisive action was discerned, with the Exodus from Egypt, the settlement in the promised land, and the establishment of David as king the three especially prominent themes. We have already seen that there is great difficulty in treating many of these traditions as historical in the modern sense of the term; and another problem arises from the fact that all subsequent events tended to be seen in terms of these decisive events in the past. The people were once again in exile from the promised land, and so were to look forward once again to a new exodus-deliverance and a new settlement in the promised land (Isa. 40–55 develops these themes with great poetic power); equally they might hope for a new David to arise to restore past glories to the people. Even the least 'historical' or narrative parts of the material, books such as Proverbs, share these underlying assumptions. They are not simply foreign wisdom literature translated into Hebrew. The Old Testament is one book; and as such it has played a vital role in shaping the religious and cultural perceptions of the Judeo-Christian tradition.

But the Old Testament is also a collection of diverse books, and those who have studied this collection down the ages have been confronted with the fact that basic religious matters are treated very differently in different books. Human kingship is a divine gift in the Psalms, but a usurpation of divine power in 1 Samuel 8. Cultic worship is the life-blood of the community in Leviticus, but a cause of cynical manipulation in Amos and Hosea. Prosperity is a mark of divine favour in Deuteronomy, and ill fortune a clear sign of wickedness; the Book of Job says that such matters may depend upon a wager in heaven between God and his entourage. And so one could go on. Though the Old Testament is a unity, that does not imply that all except an officially approved view has been edited out. Its diversity remains to warn us against seeking easy and tidy answers to many of our most basic questions.

Bibliography

The first three books listed are useful introductions to Old Testament study; the remainder provide further material on the points raised in the text of this article, as briefly indicated in the comments after each.

Charpentier, E. *How to Read the Old Testament* (SCM Press, London, 1982)
Rogerson, J. (ed.) *Beginning Old Testament Study* (SPCK, London, 1983)
Sawyer, J.F.A. *From Moses to Patmos* (SPCK, London, 1977)

Anderson, B.W. *The Living World of the Old Testament*, 3rd edn (Longman, London, 1978) (an introduction to the material arranged around a historical outline)

Barr, J. *Old and New in Interpretation* (SCM Press, London, 1966) (on the relation between Old and New Testaments)
Barton, J. *Oracles of God* (Darton, Longman & Todd, London, 1986) (on the interpretation of Scripture)
Barton, J. *Reading the Old Testament: Method in Biblical Study* (Darton, Longman & Todd, London, 1984) (on literary and other approaches to the Old Testament)
Blenkinsopp, J. *A History of Prophecy in Israel* (SPCK, London, 1984) (on the role of Israel's prophets)
Bruce, F.F. *History of the Bible in English from the Earliest Versions*, 3rd edn (Lutterworth Press, Guildford, 1979) (on the characteristics of different translations)
Caird, G.B. *The Language and Imagery of the Bible* (Duckworth, London, 1980) (on the literary heritage of the Bible)
Ramsey, G.W. *The Quest for the Historical Israel* (SCM Press, London, 1981) (non-technical introduction to the difficulties of historical reconstruction)
Schmidt, W.H. *The Faith of the Old Testament* (Blackwell, Oxford, 1983) (introduction to the significance of Israelite religious practice)

7 *The First-Century Crisis: Christian Origins*

John Muddiman

The period covered in this chapter, from the death of Herod the Great, King of the Jews, in 4 BCE to the end of the second Jewish war with Rome in 135 CE, is a period of lingering and terminal crisis in the history of Israel. Within it and from it arose two of the world's religions, Christianity and Rabbinic Judaism. Both had, in a sense, foreseen what was to come; and both responded in different ways to the same basic problem, of how a people who believed themselves to be specially chosen by God could live with a past but with no earthly future.

A few days before his death, Herod altered his will. He nominated Archelaus to the throne, the son most like his father in brutality, but ensured that even in the grave he would not be outshone by making provision for other possible claimants, his sons Herod Antipas and Philip. Amid threatened rebellion in Palestine, the Roman Emperor on appeal partitioned the kingdom between them. The northern territories were secure, but in Judea, Archelaus lasted only ten years. At the request of the Jews themselves, Rome deposed him and annexed his territory to the Empire as a third-rate and underfunded province.

The tax census which followed sparked off a new movement of uncompromising opposition. The rebellion of Judas in 6 CE, though unsuccessful, was to inspire a succession of Zealot uprisings. From a Roman perspective, the Judean problem at first appeared settled. 'Under Tiberius, all was quiet' commented one historian. But the local perception was rather different. Pontius Pilate, the fifth and one of the longer serving prefects in charge of the province, deliberately offended Jewish scruples by a series of provocative acts. Later in 40 CE the ill-fated Emperor Caligula himself threatened to desecrate the Temple. The plan was foiled by his assassination, but it painfully reawakened old memories from the Maccabean period, 'the abomination of desolation standing where it ought not'. After a brief, vain attempt at restoration of a Jewish monarchy, soon it was back to business as usual, a quick succession of Roman governors, quisling hierarchs and opportunist revolutionaries. Provoked by an exceptionally corrupt prefect, and with the Empire weakened at the centre under Nero, the forces of opposition were galvanised into a united front. This Zealot war ended with a siege of Jerusalem, the firing of the Temple and the massacre of its inhabitants (66–70 CE). Rebel bases in the countryside were gradually eliminated; the last, heroic stand at Masada and the group suicide of its defenders symbolised the national despair. With the disappearance of the Temple cult as the focus of Israel's identity, resistance in Palestine waned for a time, but when the Emperor Hadrian commanded a pagan shrine to be built on the sacred site and forbade the practice of circumcision, the Jews revolted again under Simon called Bar Kochba (the 'Son of the Star' of David). His defeat made Jerusalem a forbidden city to Jews. The divine promises of land and peace in which to worship their God appeared irreparably broken.

Within this political crisis, other disintegrating factors were at work. The period was marked by extensive inroads of Greek culture into Palestine. New cities modelled on Greek lines with theatres and gymnasia, mixed races and mores, were established. The very precincts of the Temple reflected the vogue in Hellenistic architecture. The rural poor became cultural aliens in their own country. Confiscations of property and the creation of large estates owned by absentee landlords drove the surplus population to emigration, vagrancy or brigandage. The economic problems were compounded by the increasing burden of taxation and periodic natural disasters like famine and epidemic.

Not even Israel's religious institutions could supply the element of cohesion needed in this situation, for they too were the object of controversy and division. The Jerusalem Temple was run as a profitable business for the benefit of a small group of families and their clients. Its corruption was such that some Jews on conscientious grounds abandoned the practices of pilgrimage and sacrifice, while others, both in Palestine and in the Diaspora, did so for simple economic reasons. The priestly aristocracy was pragmatic in politics and conservative in religion. In alliance with the landed gentry, the elders, they formed the Sadducean party, which accepted only the letter of the written Law and rejected all innovation, including belief in life after death. This life alone had to be made as comfortable as possible.

The scribes, the intelligentsia who constituted the other half of the Jewish Senate, attempted to apply the Law to changing circumstances. For this they appealed to authoritative oral tradition, traced back to Moses himself and expounded in the Jerusalem legal academies by different teachers who often disagreed sharply among themselves. Many scribes were attracted into the party of the Pharisees, a strict, separatist movement concerned with such matters as purity, tithing and Sabbath obedience. Once more active politically, they had retreated into quietism and the abandonment to divine providence. For them the focus of religion was not so much the Temple as the local synagogues. But the moralistic rigour of their teaching drove a wedge between the pious and ordinary folk.

In addition to Sadducees and Pharisees, there were other distinguishable sects in first-century Palestine. The Qumran settlement and its library known as the Dead Sea Scrolls probably belonged to a more widespread Essene movement, practising celibacy and ritual washing. Its ideology was to return to the wilderness to recapture the purity of Israel's faith. They were more prophetic and mystical in temperament than the Pharisees, producing new sacred literature of their own as well as commenting on the Scriptures. Alongside monastic communities like Qumran, there may have been individual hermits and prophets who followed the Essene way, among them perhaps John the Baptist. Their stance on the political question was ambiguous and could easily be construed as incitement to rebellion and active involvement. As the prospect of all-out war loomed in the sixties, the Zealots emerged as a further distinct party, dedicated to repossession of the land.

Thus, Jewish religious institutions, the Temple and the priesthood, the scribes, the law and the synagogue, the reawakening of prophecy, and the ideology of wilderness and land, were disparate factors emphasised differently by competing sects, Sadducees, Pharisees, Essenes and Zealots, as the Jewish historian Josephus analyses them. They lacked a coherent synthesis and were unable to provide the religious unity needed to combat the crisis of political, cultural and social disintegration. This is the matrix in which Christianity and Rabbinic Judaism were born.

Jesus of Nazareth and the Early Church

Roman and Jewish historians writing at the end of the first century independently attest the existence of Jesus and derive the Christian movement from him, but their meagre notices contribute no information not already available from Christian documents. These are our only substantial sources and therein lies the basic problem for the modern historian.

Our oldest material is the genuine letters of Paul, written in the fifties, twenty or so years after the crucifixion of Jesus. Much can be gleaned from them concerning the structure and internal conflicts of Gentile Christian congregations established by then in the main urban centres of the eastern Mediterranean and in Rome. But as letters, they often deal with local, ephemeral issues, and so tell us very little about the origins of the movement as such. And composed by a Greek-speaking convert from

Judaism, who had not known Jesus personally and whose relations with those who had were not always harmonious, they distort our perception of the nature of Christianity if read in isolation.

The New Testament Gospels appear to give detailed, connected biographies of Jesus' public career and fate, and in one case, Luke's, the account continues into a second volume tracing the earliest missionary expansion of the Church. However, the Gospels and Acts are documents of religious propaganda. Their general aim is to inspire and confirm the faith, and they blur the sequence of events with frequent anachronisms, reading later beliefs, especially about the person of Jesus, back into the narrative. This is particularly the case with the Gospel of John. A further complication arises from the fact that the other three Gospels, the Synoptics, are in some way interrelated as texts, Mark's usually being considered the oldest. And comparisons between them reveal extensive editorial alterations of detail and emphasis. Despite traditional attributions to well-known figures of the first generation, the documents are anonymous works dating from 65 to 100 CE and preserving the corporate memory of various Greek-speaking Christian communities. It is likely that, before they were written down, these traditions were handed on orally, through a process of transmission in which they would have been separated from their original contexts, smoothed down, translated and adapted to contemporary congregational needs. The Gospels and Acts, therefore, can be used as sources for the origins of Christianity only with extreme caution.

The general picture of Jesus which emerges from a critical reading of the Gospels is, however, reasonably consistent and historically credible. He was an Aramaic-speaking Galilean, of rural rather than urbanised Hellenistic culture, an amateur teacher not a professional scribe. Despite similarities between facets of his teaching and that of Pharisaic and Essene sectarianism, he seems to have aligned himself with the common people, with the 'poor' and 'sinners', rather than the pious. He was renowned as a healer and exorcist, like others we know of from the period, such as Rabbi Haninah ben Dosa. After a short period of prominence in Galilee and later in Judea, he was accused and executed by the Roman method of crucifixion as a pretender to messianic kingship.

Other more detailed facts about his life and thought can be deduced with some degree of probability. He was associated with the figure of John the Baptist, a latter-day prophet of doom, who summoned the nation to signify its corporate penitence in a ceremony of ritual washing—later to be adopted by the Church as a Christian sacrament. Jesus responded to this summons himself, though he did not preach baptism as part of his own programme. The lifestyles of the two were markedly different (Matt. 11:18f), but they were categorised together, at least by Herod Antipas (Mark 6:14) who discerned perhaps in Jesus' rejection of divorce (I Cor. 7:10; cf. Mark 10:11f) the same implied criticism of himself, which the Baptist had made to his cost (Mark 6:18 and 28). John may also have denounced Temple corruption since, after the disturbance in the Court of the Gentiles, when Jesus overturned the tables of the money-changers, he appealed to John's authority for the action (Mark 11:29f). It is sometimes claimed that Jesus was originally a disciple of John and took over from him the main tenets of his prophetic teaching. On this view, the Christian tradition largely redrew its picture of John to disguise its embarrassment, representing him as a conscious forerunner and witness to Jesus (Mark 1:7f). Historically, John may have been more agnostic about Jesus (Matt. 11:3). But taking into account the striking differences between them, it is safer to argue that they were partly parallel figures with complementary missions.

The movement initiated by Jesus was located not in the desert retreats favoured by John, but in small towns and villages. He attracted to himself a circle of followers. Remarkably for a religious teacher of the time, it included a number of women (Luke 8:2f). The group, like the Pharisees, seems to have been held together by its common meals and table-fellowship, but unlike them it was characterised by its openness to all, not by exclusivist scrupulosity in the observance of food laws. The disciples lacked any constitutional structure, special training in exegesis of Scripture, distinctive rites or forms of prayer (cf. Luke 11:1ff, where the Lord's Prayer follows a standard synagogue pattern). They were not a definable sect. An inner group, the 'twelve' were itinerant like their leader, and shared in his activities of preaching and healing. Although the tradition is somewhat hazy about the exact list of their names, the admission that one of them, Judas Iskariot, later betrayed him, authenticates the historicity of the 'twelve'. The number is probably symbolic, recalling the patriarchs or perhaps the twelve elders who assisted Moses, but their appointment had to do not with present function but with a future role (Matt. 19:28; cf. 16:16–18 where a special role is promised to Simon Peter in particular).

The miracle stories, which occupy the largest portion of the Gospel accounts, were once neglected by scholarship in its search for the Jesus of history; they were treated as late legendary accretions, conforming him to the type of a Hellenistic wonder worker. More recently, however, they have been given closer attention, as similarities with other Palestinian charismatic healers have been pointed out. The high incidence among them of exorcisms is noteworthy, and is consistent with the widespread popular interest in demonology during the period. While the Evangelists draw theological conclusions from the miracles, regarding the final inbreaking of God's reign or the status of Jesus, it is unclear whether he did so himself. He did not regard his own activity in this field as unique (cf. Mark 9:38f and Matt. 12:27). They were apparently not a point of issue at his trial, although a much later Jewish tradition claims that he was condemned as a sorcerer. Paul could write as though miracles formed no part of the gospel of Jesus (1 Cor. 1:22).

The original forms of Jesus' teaching and its distinctive content have been the subject of continuous debate among scholars for over a century, and little can be asserted with any certainty. He committed nothing to writing. His methods of teaching were informal, brief wisdom or prophetic sayings and vivid analogies and example stories (the parables). These would not have been as accurately memorised by his followers as the legal judgements of the scribes were. The practice of the later Church of expounding them in the context of preaching—a practice which underlies the more connected form of Jesus' discourses in the Gospel of John—raises the question of how far the thinking of early Christian communities has suppressed, modified or added to the thought of Jesus himself. Nevertheless, certain emphases recur with sufficient frequency in different settings, and are expressed so strikingly that they ought probably to be considered authentic.

Jesus proclaimed the imminent coming of a new age, when God's sovereign rule would again be powerfully established (Mark 9:1). By repentance and faith, the Kingdom could already be entered and celebrated in advance. Condemnation at the coming judgement could be avoided by decisive action in the present (Matt. 11:20–4). This future hope is often described in language derived from the tradition of Jewish apocalyptic, but whether its reference was to the literal end of the world within one generation, or to an earthly restoration of Israelite theocracy, or to a spiritual order of reality, or by turns to all three, is hotly disputed by modern scholars. Even when full allowance has been made for changes of perspective introduced by the Church later, none of these referents can be altogether excluded. For the Kingdom is never defined in the teaching of Jesus; it is evoked parabolically in a variety of verbally inconsistent images: its coming is both with signs (Mark 13:7) and without signs (Luke 17:20), its suddenness can be pictured negatively as a thief (Matt. 24:43) and positively as a bridegroom (Matt. 25:6). The Kingdom image conveys the idea of both corporate solidarity and personal allegiance. It is national but not xenophobic, universal without being merely inward and spiritual.

The nearness of the Kingdom corresponds to the emphasis in Jesus' teaching on the nearness of God, and the immediacy of knowledge of his will. Torah, the Law of God, is to be received not through scholarly study but by intuitive grasp of its essence (Matt. 7:12). Later rivalry and mutual suspicion between the Church and the Synagogue is clearly reflected in the Gospels, especially Matthew's, where the scribes and Pharisees are placed under blanket condemnation as evasive and hypocritical casuists (Matt. 23). In many respects, however, Jesus was very close to the scribes in their understanding of Torah (Mark 12:34). He remained within the accepted bounds of Torah-obedience. The accusations that he committed or abetted infringements of Sabbath law were without substance. The Hellenistic Christians, who preserved the traditions of controversies over the Law and were themselves opposed to those commandments pertaining to special

Jewish identity like the Sabbath, would have every reason to mention serious breaches of the Law on Jesus' part, had any occurred. Probably what brought him into conflict with the scribes was not liberal principles of interpretation, but paradoxically, the rigorist implications of certain parts of his preaching, his denunciations of anger, lust, dishonesty and vindictiveness (Matt. 5:21ff). Such exaggerated language threatened the place of Torah in Judaism not by failing to meet its requirements in practice, but by overshooting its standards in theory and thus endangering the whole system by a humanly impractical idealism.

Did a particular view of his own status form part of Jesus' message? Certainly the person of Christ was the central motif of early Christian preaching, and the confessional titles, Son of God and Lord, may well have been read back into the tradition at certain points. But whereas teaching on Jesus' person is explicit in the Gospel of John, in the other Gospels it is often more a matter of implication. Thus our question needs to be phrased in a more general way: how did Jesus conceive of his relation to the coming of God's Kingdom? Obviously the answer we give will depend on what the latter is taken to mean. Starting from the three main possibilities noted above, we could say that Jesus saw himself as a herald, preparing for the End of history, and determining in advance the outcome of future judgement through the responses people made to his preaching; or that he saw himself as Messiah-designate, destined by faithful endurance of suffering to reign with his followers in a restored Israel on earth; or again that he saw himself as the bringer of God's Kingdom, and its embodiment in the present. Or indeed elements of all three self-understandings may be authentic.

The implications of Jesus' attitude to the Law should also be noted. For he delivered his message on his own authority, and expressed it in a highly personal way in poetic stories and sayings. He did not base his appeal on the generally accepted source of authoritative knowledge, the Scriptures. Some scholars have detected in the irregular Aramaic construction 'Amen I say to you...' evidence for a peculiar assumption of authority on Jesus' part.

It has also been argued that Jesus' frequent references to the fatherhood of God, and his use of the Aramaic word Abba in addressing him, imply a specially intimate sense of filial consciousness. But examples of a similarly homely piety can be adduced from certain contemporary spiritual masters, and the actual evidence for Abba is not extensive (Mark 14:36). Nevertheless, father–child imagery is firmly rooted in the tradition (e.g. Matt. 11:25–7), and although Jesus probably did not intend it to be applied exclusively to his own relation to God, it prepared the ground for post-Easter developments.

The self-designation which occurs most frequently in the Gospels, and has a strong claim to be treated as historical, absent as it is from the doctrinal vocabulary of the later Church, is the Son of Man. The phrase is awkward in Greek, and must represent a Semitic original. Depending on what background for it is presupposed, many different interpretations are offered. It could reflect the standard Hebrew poetic expression for Man (cf. Ps. 8:4), or echo God's address to a prophet like Ezekiel, or be a visionary, symbolic representation of the redeemed community, the saints of Daniel 7:13ff. (This passage of Daniel was later interpreted in Judaism to refer to an individual heavenly figure, God's viceregent in the age to come, but the date of this development cannot be ascertained with certainty.) Recently, a more popular idiomatic background for 'son of man' has been proposed. In Aramaic, a speaker might refer to himself in this oblique, generalising way in certain contexts, out of modesty, hesitation or gentle self-mockery. Unless whole categories of the Son of Man sayings in the Gospels are to be rejected, it is necessary to allow for more than one sense in the expression on the lips of Jesus. But if so, the juxtaposition of its different nuances, solidarity with humankind, destiny to prophetic suffering and hope for the vindication of Israel and God's visitation in judgement and grace, is highly evocative, and it was but a short step for the gospel tradition to run these together into a unified concept. However, it should be emphasised that this was a Christian innovation; 'the Son of Man' was not a messianic title in pre-Christian Judaism and was not an explicit claim to particular status on Jesus' part.

The account given so far of the mission of Jesus makes its connection to the circumstances and manner of his death very problematic. Why should such a person have been thought worthy of such a punishment? While each of the Gospels tells roughly the same story of the Passion, they differ on many of the vital historical details: the extent of Jewish involvement, the attitude of the Roman prefect, the wording of the charges, the relevance and temporal relation to his arrest of incidents like the cleansing of the Temple. With these and many other points in doubt, it is not surprising that some very radical reconstructions of the history have been offered, most persistently that which presents Jesus as a violent revolutionary, justly condemned by the Romans to crucifixion, and the Gospels, therefore, as elaborate fictions to cover the truth.

In dealing with a complex historical problem such as the reasons for Jesus' death, it may be false to assume that all parties to the affair must have acted rationally and in full cognisance of all the relevant facts, so that their motives are open to scientific analysis. The modern historian is predisposed to finding momentous issues at stake here. To have to admit that the death of Jesus was a minor miscarriage of justice and in a sense a chapter of accidents is aesthetically unsatisfying, but may be truer to the facts and, incidentally, to one of the ways Christians have traditionally understood the Cross as scandalous in its very particularity. Nevertheless, the Jewish and Roman trials, as recorded in the Gospels, are not implausible in broad outline as they stand. The High Priest and his circle examined Jesus on his attitude to the Temple, and they may have been willing to entertain false accusations concerning his violent prophecies against it. They would also have wanted to learn more of Jesus' attitude towards Messiahship, for if he were reluctant to disclaim the title, they could safely transfer the case to Pilate, confident that he would be convicted for sedition and given a deterrent sentence. Since the early Church was to find little use for the title 'Christ' (Greek *christos*, equivalent of Messiah) and quickly reduced it to an alternative proper name for Jesus, its origin must be traced back to what was said of Jesus by some in his lifetime, which he was unable or unwilling to refute at the end.

Jesus' mission was a response to the first-century crisis. He managed to integrate fragmented elements of Israel's life and faith, not in a theological system, but in a practical synthesis, which lasted—in its original form—only as long as he was present himself to embody it. The event which transformed Jesus' response into an organised movement and eventually into a religion distinct from Judaism was the proclamation of his resurrection from the dead. The proclamation may itself be called an *event*, for it occurred suddenly and decisively. It did not result from a gradual process of theological reflection on the completed life of Jesus; nor did it resolve the enigma of a crucified Messiah. It was rather the starting point for a completely new way of understanding him. Historical criticism is unable to determine any other sense in which the resurrection of Jesus might be called an event. The objectivity of reported visions of the risen Christ, or the veracity and significance of the empty tomb, remain problematic.

The framework in which the message of the resurrection was interpreted was that of Jewish apocalyptic. His followers believed that Jesus had been raised not to continued earthly existence, but to the life of the age to come. In the light of this conviction, the apocalyptic dimension of Jesus' own preaching was given special emphasis, almost at first to the point of eclipsing its other aspects. In particular, the expectation that God was about to intervene for judgement and salvation became concentrated on the hope for the imminent return of Jesus himself 'on the clouds' at his Parousia (Greek equivalent of coming, presence). But at the same time, the resurrection message had the effect of partially realising eschatological expectations. The End-time conditions (as already envisaged in Judaism)—the conquest of sin and death, the demonstration of God's righteousness, the conversion of the Gentiles, the gift of the Spirit and sonship—must already be available through him to others. Those who were thus incorporated into Jesus became a new, eschatological Israel, for which the apocalyptic term was 'the saints'. Earliest Christianity apparently drew no sharp distinction between the risen Christ and the community. Similarly, it did not distinguish between the risen one and the Spirit of God which he bestowed. Thus, its new understanding of Jesus based on his resurrection involved from the first an exalted view of the nature both of the Church and of the person of Christ. And it is these ideas which were rapidly and explicitly worked out in the writings of early Christianity and which were the chief causes of its divergence from Jewish tradition.

The Earliest Christian Churches

We cannot tell precisely how or when the Christian movement spread outside Palestine and began preaching to Gentiles. One possibility is that it gained a hearing among members of the Greek-speaking ('Hellenist') synagogue in Jerusalem (Acts 6:5) and through them converted pilgrims at major Jewish feasts (Acts 2:5). Within a very short period, there were adherents of the 'sect of the Nazarenes', as it was called (Acts 24:5), in the chief cities of Syria, such as Antioch. This is clear from the fact that the Church began almost immediately to attract persecution from Diaspora Pharisaism represented by Paul of Tarsus.

We first encounter Paul about 35 CE at Damascus in Syria, attempting to use the disciplinary procedures of the synagogue to dissuade Christian Jews from consorting with Gentiles (Gal. 1:13). His objections to the new movement were probably of a practical rather than doctrinal kind. It was guilty of unfair competition with his own sect. For it offered to the Gentiles, as a privilege of the End-time, full membership in the community through water-baptism without the accompanying rite of circumcision, and thus undermined the basis of the Pharisaic, proselytising mission. Paul's visionary experience of the crucified and glorified Messiah of Christian preaching vindicated the claims of those he was persecuting, and the movement suddenly acquired in him a brilliant and energetic apologist, the extent of whose work and influence soon outstripped that of its original leadership.

What do we know about Paul? If we possessed only the Acts of the Apostles, we should have almost as much difficulty in answering this question of Paul as we do of Jesus. Fortunately, in this case primary evidence is available in Paul's genuine letters. Acts, for example, presents him to us as both a Roman citizen and a graduate of Gamaliel's school in Jerusalem, equally at home in the Greco-Roman and Jewish worlds. But there is nothing in Paul to corroborate either claim. He appears rather to have been a marginal figure, culturally speaking. He was unmarried, of artisan background, whose education was limited to the resources of the Diaspora synagogue, the Greek Old Testament and the dialogue between Judaism and popular pagan philosophy. In his writings he uses the stock images of Greek city life, but he shows little real appreciation for the higher achievements of Hellenism. He was brought up a strict adherent of the Law (Gal. 1:14)—the only safeguard against the threat posed in his environment to the Jewish identity he cherished.

His career as a Christian missionary spanned the first three decades of church history. At first he stayed within his own native region of Cilicia and Syria (Gal. 1:21). But after a meeting with Peter, John and James the Lord's brother at Jerusalem in 49 CE he branched out further afield. They approved his vocation to preach the gospel to the Gentiles in the cities around the Aegean, with the proviso that he should organise a financial collection in support of the poor and persecuted churches in Judea—the Christian equivalent, as it were, of the Temple Tax (Gal. 2:1–10; for a rather different version of events see Acts 15:1–29). For the following ten years, he and his associates built up congregations in Macedonia, Achaea, on the coast of Asia Minor and inland. In order to keep control of such a wide area, he resorted to writing pastoral letters to his communities advising them on the problems they faced; for instance, the different conclusions being drawn from belief in the nearness of Christ's return (1 Thess. 4:13; 1 Cor. 15:12), the contrasts in social status (1 Cor. 11:18f) or religious background (1 Cor. 10:32) of different groups in the same congregation, excessive enthusiasm or asceticism (1 Cor. 12:1; Col. 2:23), competition from rival Christian missionaries (2 Cor. 11:4f; Phil. 1:15), and above all, the resurgence of Pharisaic persecution, imitating the tactics Paul himself had used in Syria, and attempting to sabotage the success of the Gentile mission (Gal. 3:1; Rom. 3:8; Phil. 3:2).

While concrete issues like these predominate in his letters, Paul continually reverts to the essential gospel that the End-time has begun with Jesus' resurrection. The Church, therefore, cannot be just another sect or philosophy, for it is already in its corporate and sacramental life an anticipation of the age to come; it is destined soon to embrace all Israel and the fullness of the Gentiles (Rom. 11:25f) in one humanity redeemed in Christ (Gal. 3:28). For Paul, Jesus' resurrection replaces the Jewish Law as the final revelation of God's righteousness; and characteristics formerly attributed to the Law are transferred instead to the person of Christ. He is pre-existent, active in creation, the history of salvation and ultimate redemption, the bringer of freedom, life and light (cf. 2 Cor. 4:4–6; Phil. 2:6–11). Paul's contribution to the development of Christian thought rests chiefly in his concepts of the Church as the Body of Christ, and of Christ as the Last Adam and Wisdom of God.

As he feared (Rom. 15:31), Paul was denounced by unbelieving Jews, as he tried to deliver the collection in Jerusalem, was arrested, and after a lengthy imprisonment in Caesarea was shipped to Rome. Whether he was ever brought to trial there, or was caught up in the Neronian purge, or was released to continue his mission, or died undramatically in prison of illness and old age, we do not know.

Paul's career is simply the best documented segment of a much wider expansion of Christianity in the first generation. Congregations were being established at the same time in Rome, Alexandria and in the oriental Jewish Dispersion. Within Paul's own sphere of influence, parallel missions were operating, like those of Peter and of the group which eventually produced the Johannine literature. By the end of the first generation, therefore, the movement had penetrated into the chief provinces of the Empire, and into many levels of society. It had no central organisation, but was a loose federation of local congregations and independent missions, held together by a common eschatological faith.

For all its Jewish roots, Christianity was a highly attractive religious option for non-Jews, dissatisfied with the sterility and political cynicism of state religion and excluded from the sectional and elitist constituencies of the philosophical sects and mystery cults. For them, Christianity offered a non-violent but revolutionary message, which corresponded well to the instability of the times and the helplessness felt by ordinary people. It built upon the appeal of Israel's ethical monotheism, but replaced the cultural drawbacks like circumcision, dietary regulations and animal sacrifice, with intense devotion to the person of the risen Saviour. It transformed a potentially damaging point, the execution of Jesus on a Roman cross, into a major asset, by making it the prime example of the mystery of God's compassion. It offered to those who, for whatever reason, saw themselves as socially disadvantaged, the security and identity of fellowship and the faith that they belonged in the centre of the divine purpose for the world.

The outline we have just given of the early development of Christianity has been rejected by several scholars in the modern period, and it is appropriate here to add a note of caution. Reacting against the over-idealised picture of Church harmony in the Acts of the Apostles, they have gone to the opposite extreme, and posited deep divisions in the movement from the very beginning. Alongside the form which Christian faith took in the case of Paul, two other distinct types have been detected, Jewish Christianity and Gnosticism. Second-century catholic orthodoxy, then, is seen as a fusion of certain elements of all three, while the main tendencies continued directly into various 'heresies'. This radical hypothesis, however, depends so heavily on reading what it presupposes behind and between the lines of the surviving New Testament literature, and on tracing back later developments necessarily into the earlier period, that it can never be substantiated. If 'Jewish Christianity' is defined in the narrow sense which involves strict adherence to the whole Law and the rejection of developed Christology, there is no evidence for it in the early period. Similarly there is no first-century evidence for 'Gnosticism', if by that we mean the myth of a divine redeemer disguised in human form, and not just intellectualised ideas of salvation.

The more plausible, alternative view followed here is that early Christianity, for all its local variations in language, culture and organisation, retained an essential unity around its eschatological gospel; and that it only began to separate into distinct forms as it entered its second generation and awoke to the realisation that the End was to be delayed. The attempts to cope with the consequences of this unexpected survival into the 'post-apostolic' era covered a wide spectrum. For various reasons, not all of them purely doctrinal, some of these developed into the 'heresies' of the second and later centuries; the rest achieved a degree of recognition, signalled by their ultimate inclusion in the New Testament canon, and marked the boundaries of legitimate diversity within catholic orthodoxy.

Although its long-term effects for the structure of Christian doctrine were considerable, the delay of the Parousia did not, it must be emphasised, cause an immediate crisis of confidence. The certainty that the last days had begun with the resurrection of Jesus was not shaken by his failure to return within the lifetime of the Apostles. For one thing, the motif of unaccountable delay in God's intervention was a regular feature in the story of Israel. Furthermore, Jesus' own teaching was equivocal on this very point; and Paul had long since counselled the over-excited to adopt a reverent agnosticism. The fall of the Temple in 70 CE in the first instance reinforced the belief that at last the End was near. It was some time before it became necessary to revise the programme in this regard (Luke 21:21–4). But even before that, an alternative interpretation of the event was suggested, namely that the Jews were thereby receiving their just reward for the rejection of the Messiah and of the Christian gospel (Matt. 22:7). Later writers are diplomatic about the precise timing of the End (John 21:22f), even when they strongly resist the temptation to abandon belief in it (2 Pet. 3:8–10). Under the threat of Roman persecution, the apocalyptic genre might be dusted off, and redeployed, as in the Book of Revelation, but the future, visionary element in that work is more strictly controlled by exegetical and theological tradition than is often recognised.

Eschatology, in the post-apostolic period, becomes less a means of interpreting the course of history, and more the ground and sanction for ethical exhortation. The prospect of ultimate judgement was morally if not temporally certain. Matthew allegorises several of the parables along these lines (see 13:24–30), and Luke inserts example stories in which the imminent death of an individual substitutes for public End-expectation (see 12:16–20). While eschatology was retained as the indispensable framework of Christian ethics, it was no longer able alone to determine its content. Marriage (Eph. 5:21ff) and civic duty (1 Pet. 2:13ff) had to be rehabilitated alongside the ideals of celibacy and martyrdom. It would be mistaken to interpret these changes simply as a decline from radicalism into social conformity, for imminent eschatology could induce passivity, as in the case of attitudes to slavery, where a more down-to-earth approach could lead to actual changes in the social structure, at least within the confines of the Christian community.

The earliest Church had rejected Israel's Law as the chief focus of its spirituality, but, in spite of some strong rhetoric from Paul, had allowed its influence tacitly to continue as an ethical code, through pressure from Christian Jews in the community. However, with the failure of the mission to the Jews in the post-apostolic period, the composition of the Church became increasingly Gentile, and Christian moral standards required explicit restatement. At the same time, the hostility between post-70 Judaism and Christianity meant that no open concessions to the Jewish tradition could be made. So Matthew's Gospel, for example, has to walk a tightrope between moral exhortation and anti-Pharisaic polemic. And those who refused, on the authority of Paul, to adjust to the new situation and relearn the language of obedience to commandments, had to be silenced in his own name (2 Tim. 2:14–19) or one of comparable weight (Jas 2:18f). The same phenomenon, of simultaneous Judaisation and anti-Judaism, is apparent elsewhere. In this period we witness the beginning of a long development in Christianity of standard orders of ministry, the structures of church government and discipline, set forms of liturgy and prayer, an ecclesiastical calendar, places of worship and pilgrimage, a Christian canon of Old Testament Scripture and methods for interpreting it, and a parallel New Testament canon. Thus, in competition with Rabbinic Judaism, Christianity reinvented equivalents for the religious institutions of Israel which had disappeared in the first-century crisis.

As we have seen, the delay of the Parousia gradually forced the Church to come to terms with the problems of ethics and its institutional life. Not surprisingly, when its own internal unity was threatened, chiefly by extremist solutions to the problems it was facing, it was tempted to meet the challenge out of these resources. Loyalty to the hierarchy and the test of practical morality often substitute for theological argument with dissidents (see Titus 1:8–16; 2 John 6; 3 John 9). But at a higher level, criteria for legitimate development do emerge from the later controversies with Jewish opponents and Christian heretics—the historical criteria of apostolic tradition and the finality of Christ. The two volumes of Luke-Acts are the clearest instance of this twofold appeal.

Apostolic tradition is not to be thought of as an authoritative body of doctrine. Paul's letters, for example, yield no such thing. When the attempt was made, in the middle of the second century by Marcion, to reduce them to a theologically coherent system, the result was rejected as heresy. Tradition consisted rather of a willingness to identify with the Church's own historical past, at the same time as trusting to the Spirit to guide it into the future. The fashion for writing pseudonymous letters, Ephesians, the Pastorals, 1 Peter, James, 2 Peter and Jude, is a graphic expression of this appeal in practice. Whatever needed to be said to preserve the health and unity of the contemporary Church was placed under the aegis of its founding fathers. The function of this criterion was to be a safeguard against discontinuity and radical innovation, and a brake on the free exercise of charismatic authority. It was rather a blunt instrument in its original form, which demanded and received considerable refinement as the Christian centuries proceeded.

The finality of Christ was already for Paul the one test of genuine apostolate (1 Cor. 3:11). In the later period it became, more than it was for him, a historical criterion. This is perhaps the main difference between the apostolic and the post-apostolic age, that while the one looked forward, to future verification of its claims about Jesus, the other turned back to history to justify those claims. The Synoptic Evangelists may well have been motivated principally by their own contemporary concerns, but the medium in which they chose to express them was that of historical narrative. The identity between the earthly Jesus and the transcendent glory of the risen Christ was to be maintained, however difficult the conjunction of humanity and divinity might be to understand. When, as in the case of the Fourth Gospel, post-Easter preaching and apologetic largely replace the tradition of Jesus' own words, the historical realism of the Passion and the theological assertion that the word became flesh (1:14) provide the counterbalance. In the other great work of creative doctrine from the post-apostolic age, the Epistle to the Hebrews, a conscious attempt is made to lay equal stress on the historical and eternal, the human and divine aspects of the person of Christ (1:1–3; 2:14–18). The Christological criterion was not as precise as it had to become later. It left many questions still open for discussion, like how exactly the oneness with God of the risen Christ could be reconciled with monotheism, or the oneness with man of the earthly Jesus reconciled with his sinlessness. But the degree of clarity that was achieved in this period removed any further threat to the structure of Christian faith from continued disappointment of Parousia hope. The revelation of God in Christ was already complete; his future coming would only confirm, it would not change or add to it. Christology also provided the answer to the question of the relations between the Church and reconstituted Rabbinic Judaism; a decisive break had occurred, for all their similarities, between Christ-centred and Law-centred forms of Israel's religion.

Rabbinic Judaism

The origins of Judaism may be located as far back as the Exile or as far forward as the writing down of the Mishnah (*c.* 200 CE) but its essential character as a world religion was forged, like that of Christianity, in the crisis of the first century. The religious, cultural and political disintegration described at the beginning of this chapter makes it impossible to speak of Judaism as a unified entity before the Jewish War of 66–70 CE. But with the disappearance of the last visible expressions of Israel's nationhood, the Temple and the Sanhedrin, all serious rivals to the triumph of Pharisaism were removed, and that tradition emerged as the sole source of continuity and reconstruction.

Enquiry into this crucial period of Judaism is hampered by similar problems in the extent and nature of the surviving historical evidence as those affecting research into Christian origins. The works of Josephus, *The Jewish War* (published *c.* 77 CE) and the *Antiquities* (*c.* 94 CE), give a full account of the period 66–70 and its background in earlier Jewish history and culture, but they do not cover the post-war period, and are biased towards Rome. Interest in the continuing history of Israel survived only in marginal, apocalyptic works such as 2 Esdras and the Apocalypse of Baruch which were later repudiated and are extant only in translation. The evidence for Rabbinic Judaism reaches us through much later sources which lack a chronological framework. They are of two kinds: oral law (*halachah*) codified in the Mishnah and expanded with commentary later into the two versions of the Talmud; and scriptural exegesis (*haggadah*) contained in a series of expositions of the Hebrew Bible known as Midrashim. The dangers of anachronism and idealisation are thus very great; critical research can provide only a tentative outline of the historical and theological development of Rabbinic Judaism.

It may be helpful to focus attention on one particular figure, who was in several respects Judaism's equivalent of Paul, namely Rabbi Jochanan ben Zakkai. Born at roughly the same time, he was the youngest and most promising of the pupils of Hillel. He inherited from his teacher a lasting aversion to violence as the solution to Israel's plight. Between 20 and 40 CE, he lived in semi-retirement in Galilee, supporting his wife and child, rarely consulted on legal matters and with only one recorded pupil, the healer and sage Haninah ben Dosa. He claimed, as he left, that 'Galilee hated Torah'; its religion was too enthusiastic and unscholarly for his taste. He returned to Jerusalem to become the leading spokesman of Pharisaism against the corruption of the Temple establishment, which he, like Jesus of Nazareth, saw as a threat to its very survival. In this more successful period of his career, he attracted many ordinary priests into the Pharisaic movement, which was to prove an important factor in broadening its base of support later. Eventually, he succeeded Gamaliel I, as joint leader with the latter's son of the Hillelite school, and he numbered among his disciples five of the most influential teachers of the next generation. He abandoned Jerusalem before the fall of the Temple, and took refuge in the town of Jamnia (Yavneh) on the coastal plain to the west of the city, and with the permission of Vespasian set up a new school which quickly became the centre of restoration. After a brief but formative period of leadership, he stepped down in favour of the more forceful personality of Gamaliel II, and ended his long life in a small Judean village, revered by many as the one light in the choas and madness of Zealotism, as a forceful opponent, a 'mighty hammer', against the Sadducees, and as the pillar of Judaism renewed in its obedience to Torah.

As Pharisaism at Jamnia assumed responsibility for Israel as a whole, it had first to put its own house in order. Disagreements between the schools of Hillel and Shammai had from the early decades of the century weakened the movement; these were now reconciled or resolved, with the less stringent and nationalist opinions of the former often prevailing. The earliest attempts were made to bring order into the varied judgements of legal experts by arranging them into standard thematic groups. The authority of oral law was put beyond question by tracing it back through Ezra and the Prophets to Moses himself. The Pharisaic movement, which had earlier been characterised by prominent lay participation, became 'clericalised' in a manner comparable to that in contemporary Christianity. The courtesy title 'rabbi' was granted as an official designation to all qualified legal scholars; they were appointed to their office by a rite of ordination, the laying on of hands. The successors of Jochanan even assumed the title *Nasi* (patriarch or president).

From Jamnia, the jurisdiction of the rabbis was extended to cover all Jews, wherever they lived. Since the destruction of the Temple, Palestine was itself becoming part of the Diaspora. There was no longer any logical ground for making the distinction. All Israel now lived in exile. This gradually had the effect of reintegrating the Hellenistic and Palestinian forms of Jewish thought. Less emphasis began to be placed on the themes of election and covenant, and more on those of creation and universal moral obligation. But, at the same time, other trends in Hellenistic Judaism, the philosophical syncretism and allegorism of Philo for example, were firmly rejected, and his works survive only because Christians took an interest in them. The Septuagint translation into Greek of the Hebrew Scriptures, used by Philo and taken over by the Church, was eclipsed by a more literal Greek translation better fitted to the precise rules of textual interpretation which were being developed. The boundaries around the threefold Jewish canon, the Law, the Prophets and the Writings, were marked out more clearly over against opposing Sadducean and Hellenistic (chiefly Christian) views.

In some respects, then, Rabbinic Judaism was inclusive and comprehensive. It synthesised scribal teaching into a common stream of tradition, and bridged the gap between Palestine and the Diaspora. But it also consolidated its position by reducing the variety of permitted views and by excluding deviations from them. In particular, it defined itself in conscious opposition to Christianity, just as the Church did in relation to the Synagogue. At Jamnia, a curse against Nazarenes and heretics was inserted into the liturgy, so that any remaining Jewish Christians in the Synagogue could be rooted out. Whatever else one might be inclined to believe about Israel's hoped-for Messiah, the opinion that he had already arrived with the coming of Jesus was no longer to be tolerated. At a later period, during the religious persecutions under Trajan, some eminent rabbis were censured and banned merely for showing sympathy for suffering Christians. An anti-Christian motive may also lie behind the change of emphasis in Jewish spirituality from the Decalogue, appealed to frequently by the Church against the elaborations of oral law, to the *Shema* with its vigorous insistence on monotheism.

The rabbis at Jamnia were faced with an even more important task than the integration of their own tradition and its differentiation from Christianity; they had to show that the Torah alone was sufficient to preserve the faith of Israel without the support of Temple worship and without even the pretence of political independence. Jochanan ben Zakkai had foreseen the destruction of the Temple, but when vindicated, he could not simply applaud its passing as the judgement of God upon Israel's disobedience to Torah. That would have been to invite unfavourable comparison with the patriotism of those who had given their lives in its defence. Moreover, the Temple occupied too central a place in the Torah for it to be simply dispensed with. Confronted with this dilemma, Rabbinic Judaism adopted a paradoxical stance. It proceeded on the one hand to elaborate in great detail the rules for the conduct of Temple worship, and on the other hand to propose practical alternatives to their implementation. The strange obsession with cultic rules has often been interpreted as a great act of faith in the future, implying that one day the Temple will be rebuilt. But it could equally be seen as a retreat from hard reality into the abstract beauty of a legal system developed for its own sake. Rabbinic judgements even on non-cultic matters were often delivered 'in remembrance of the Temple'; the motive of piety towards the past was at least as important as that of hope towards the future.

Many Jews reacted to the loss of the Temple with penitence and fasting. So much so that the rabbis began to counsel moderation in the use of ascetic practices. Excessive sorrow would only exaggerate the importance of what had been lost and make it appear irreplaceable. They preferred to promote the pious duties of the Synagogue, prayer, fasting and especially almsgiving, as a socially and religiously more positive replacement for the discontinued offerings in the Temple. 'I desire mercy not sacrifice' (Hos. 6:6) was a favourite text for the rabbis, as it was for post-apostolic Christianity (Matt. 9:13). Israel had been along this path before. In the Babylonian Exile it had to cope with the same problem. The difference in the Rabbinic response to the destruction of the Second Temple was that it established permanent practical substitutes for the Temple cult in the worship of the Synagogue, and particularly in the study of Torah and in the deeds of mercy.

The attitude of Rabbinic Judaism towards the political vacuum created by the defeat of 70 CE was as ambivalent as its attitude to the Temple. The Jamnia Academy reserved to itself full liturgical authority, for example in relation to the calendar, and its composition of 72 scholars consciously reflected that of the old Jerusalem Sanhedrin, but it did not attempt to exercise the political powers of that body or to have the High Priesthood restored. The possibility was at first left open that by patience and co-operation with Rome, Israel might at some future date recover the freedom it had lost. Consistently, Jochanan warned against messianic speculation and enthusiasm: 'If you have a sapling in your hand,' he is reported to have said, 'when they tell you the Messiah has come, plant it first and (when it has grown into a tree) only then go out to meet him.' But it took more than this to dislodge eschatological expectation from its place in first-century Jewish thought. The apocalypses of Ezra and Baruch mentioned above are evidence for its persistent hold on the imagination, despite the object lesson in its impracticality so recently given. In 115–17 CE, a widespread revolt broke out among Diaspora Jews, in support of a messianic pretender from Cyrene, but it did not touch Palestine. However, when enough time had elapsed for the trees to grow again, messianic activism flourished briefly, before it was finally eradicated in Bar Kochba's rebellion of 132–5 CE. Rabbinism, in the person of Akiva, endorsed his claim to Messiahship and suffered the consequences, when that humble scholar and exegete was martyred with the words of the *Shema* on his dying lips. In the heroism of that act, Rabbinic Judaism expunged any taint of cowardice attaching to the generation of Jamnia; but equally, in its patent futility, it abandoned all earthly means to secure the advent of the promised Messiah. Eschatology was subordinated to Law in Judaism, just as it was subordinated to Christology in post-apostolic Christianity. Only if Israel repented and obeyed Torah perfectly, would Messiah come. That possibility was in principle always near; one or two sabbaths properly observed would suffice to bring it about. But in practice it was always far off and receding. The Scriptures contained no revelation about the course of future history for Israel; God had revised the programme and all previous dates for the End had expired. The matter now rested solely on obedience to the scriptural summons to repentance and good works. As Jochanan ben Zakkai said: 'Happy are you, O Israel! When you obey the will of God, then no nation or race can rule over you!' In Torah there was both an explanation of why the End was delayed, and also the possibility of a partial realisation of the freedom it promised.

The response of Rabbinic Judaism to the crisis of the first century was to mobilise the resources of the Synagogue and Pharisaic tradition to fill the gaps left by the destruction of Jerusalem and Israel's life as a nation. The past could not of course be forgotten. Idealised blueprints of Temple and Sanhedrin were reverently preserved. The glories of Israel's history were permanently fixed in a closed canon of scripture. But the way forward into the future was determined by the practical ordering of one's domestic concerns in accordance with Torah. Through legal and spiritual exegesis of Scripture, clear answers could be given to all questions of immediate relevance. The dubious speculations of philosophy, mysticism or apocalyptic were idle, if not positively dangerous, and were suppressed. True religion had to do with the study of Torah, the development of moral character and with the values of family life. Within its forced limitations,

Rabbinic Judaism followed that definition of the whole duty of man provided by the prophet Micah (6:8): 'What does the Lord require of you, but to do justice and to love mercy and to walk humbly with your God?'

Further Reading

Bornkamm, G. *Paul* (Hodder & Stoughton, London, 1971)
Dunn, J.D.G. *Unity and Diversity in the New Testament* (SCM Press, London, 1977)
Kee, H.C. *The Origins of Christianity* (SPCK, London, 1980)
Kümmel, W.G. *Introduction to the New Testament* (SCM Press, London, 1975)
Meeks, W.A. *The First Urban Christians* (University Press, Yale, 1983)
Rivkin, E. *What Crucified Jesus?* (SCM Press, London, 1986)
Rowland, C. *Christian Origins* (SPCK, London, 1985)
Sanders, E.P. *Paul and Palestinian Judaism* (SCM Press, London, 1977)
——*Jesus and Judaism* (SCM Press, London, 1985)
Theissen, G. *The First Followers of Jesus* (SCM Press, London, 1978)
—— *The Shadow of the Galilean* (SCM Press, London, 1987)
Vermes, G. *Jesus and the World of Judaism* (SCM Press, London, 1983)

8 Judaism

Albert H. Friedlander

Rabbinic Judaism

The history of Judaism cannot appropriately be divided into periods. Rabbi Leo Baeck, one of the great teachers and leaders of the Jewish community of our time, saw Judaism as a perennial revolution, constantly renewing itself, a 'history of rebirth from epoch to epoch, of rebirth which created epochs—epochs which gave the old ideas new expression; this was the gift of prophetism to Judaism'.[1] Yet these epochs do not conform to the rigid patterns of most historical systems. The renewal of Judaism, its constant return to its biblical roots, can be a withdrawal from the world of the Renaissance or an affirmation of the golden age of Islam; it can and does combine the teachings of the rabbis from the time of the destruction of the Temple (70 CE) with the interpretations of a French rabbi a thousand years later. It stands, as it were, outside history, in its own continuum, and still responds to every aspect of the society in which it finds itself at any moment of time. Examining Jewish life and teachings from the time of the Mishnah to the present, we cannot ignore any of these dimensions of Judaism.

The two centuries before the destruction of Jerusalem by the Romans had seen a turbulent Jewish life in Palestine. Forces of religious syncretism and sectarianism battled with one another and created the sectarian movements of Pharisees, Sadducees, Essenes, New Covenanters and other sects. Messianic speculations, Hellenistic teachings, and older traditions created patterns and systems of thought which were only partially shattered by the tragedy of the Fall of Jerusalem. Jerusalem had fallen before: older teachings of consolation and of hope for rebirth came from the Babylonian experience. But this destruction was different. They were still in the land, and the land was not theirs. The Temple had fallen; and this spelled the end for the Sadducees. Pharisaism took over, and the other groupings disappeared. The new period brought about new leadership: the rabbinate emerged. Here was a blend of scholar, judge and religious leader whose authority was derived from a new literature which the rabbinate itself created. As Nicholas de Lange notes, the origins of the rabbinate are obscure: its roots are diverse and include priestly, scribal and pietistic elements. After 70 CE, it achieved extraordinary powers through its acquisition of political privileges and the wooing of support from the scattered Jewish communities who earnestly desired a central authority. The Pharisaic approach—and serious scholars are now agreed that this was an authentic, concerned application of Jewish law to the needs of the common people—and the spiritual authority of its rabbinic leaders established rabbinism as the enduring core of Jewish life.

Under the leadership of Rabbi Jochanan ben Zakkai and his successors, Pharisaic Judaism reformulated the whole system of Jewish beliefs and practices. Ben Zakkai had fled Jerusalem and established a Jewish academy in Yavneh (Jamnia) which gave a new focus to a scattered people. The Jews could not disappear among the nations. The Roman world stressed ethnic classifications, and Jewish life itself contained a deep desire for identity and cultural autonomy. Roman tolerance left room in its Empire for Jewish religious communal life, and for its schools. And these schools became the Jewish internal government. The successors of ben Zakkai (R. Gamaliel and other descendants of the Davidic house of Hillel: another basis of leadership for the rabbis linked to the royal line) were granted the authority of the patriarchate by Rome (from 85 to 425 CE). They emended the liturgy, so that the Temple rite became part of synagogue worship. They gave a response to the calamity: personal piety, observance of ritual, life within the synagogue which had replaced the Temple. And Palestine was to remain central to the Diaspora: its rabbis determined the calendar for all Jewish communities, established the rule and made its rabbis the final authority.

Behind the rabbis stood the written Law: the Torah. All laws emanated from it, with the rabbis as its interpreters. The rabbis were not charismatic figures (there were exceptions), but teachers and lawyers who established the normative rules and guided community observances. Variations were possible; the rabbis recognised minority opinions, and could not deny the brilliant Hellenistic culture of Alexandrian Jewry. There, one could not know whether 'Philo wrote like Plato, or Plato wrote like Philo'. Many followed Philo (d. *c.* 50 CE) into a world where symbols became abstractions, crystallising monotheistic thought within philosophy: the God of Abraham was seen as the transcendent First Cause. But Palestinian Jewry could not rejoice in the outer world; its suffering had turned it inward. God was thought of in utterly human terms: he wept with his children—the Shekinah (God as 'dwelling' with his own) went into exile with them. Nevertheless, the rich symbolism and imaginative interpretations of the Hellenistic world entered the teaching of the rabbis as homiletic interpretations, as the poetry of *midrash*. *Midrash* was the creative imagination of the rabbis, applied to the biblical texts. There was *Halachic* (legal) *Midrash*, an exegesis applied to the problems of daily conduct. A collection of texts (the *Mechilta* on Exodus; *Sifra* on Leviticus; and *Sifre* on Numbers and Deuteronomy) became the *Halachic Midrash* offering hermeneutical conclusions moving from biblical texts to daily events. There was the *Tosephta* and the *Baraitot*, texts running parallel to the great collection Rabbi Judah the Prince brought together shortly before 200 CE as the *Mishnah* (see below). And there was the *Haggadah* of *Midrash*: the delightful dreams, stories, poetry and sermons which linked the people to the old texts with a new love.

The text of the Torah, the Written Law, was sacred. Nothing was to stand alongside it. Nevertheless, over the centuries, new interpretations had kept it relevant to life, and various hermeneutic rules had preserved the flexibility of the law. The rabbis believed that these interpretations should not be written down: oral law, and oral transmission, came to be established. It was claimed that Moses had received the Oral Law at Sinai as well: all that the rabbis did was to rediscover that aspect of revelation. Yet the Oral Law kept growing and was more difficult to memorise. The rabbis surrendered to the needs of the present, and prepared their own written summaries. Throughout the second century, starting with Rabbi Akiva, continuing with Rabbi Meir and concluding with Rabbi Judah the Prince, these were collated and became the *Mishnah*, a systematic code divided into six sections and sixty tractates. The rabbis quoted in this body of law, this super-commentary upon the Torah, were called the *Tannaim*, and their authority endured through the centuries. The *Mishnah* ensured the homogeneity of Jewish usage and Jewish community organisations for the Jews of Syria and Rome, of Persia and Egypt.

The process of the Oral Law continued. The next sages, called the *Amoraim*, made their commentaries and explanations upon the Mishnah. Using all of the material from the earlier period—*midrash*, *halachah*, *haggadah*, texts not included in the *Mishnah*, and their own knowledge and training in logic, they created their own body of law, emanating from the great Jewish academies of learning which developed in Babylonia as the academies in Palestine declined. The Palestinian rabbis also continued their work; but the growing anarchy after Constantine meant that their *Gemara* (Completion) was never finished. It was Babylonia, with great academies in Sura, Pumpeditha, Nehardea, Mehoza and Nersh, active from 200 CE until the Arab conquest (*c.* 640 CE), which fashioned that marvellous structure of Jewish law called the Talmud.

There is a Babylonian Talmud and a Palestinian Talmud. Both may be viewed as records of discussions held in the rabbinic academies (it would be a mistake to think of the Talmud as 'a book'). They resemble Hansard or the Congressional Record: complete accounts of the discussions within a legislative assembly, including asides, poetry, stories, anecdotes, minority opinions and the final decisions on legal points. There are academic notes, cases cited; exegesis deriving laws from Torah texts; biographical notes on the great rabbis and their clashes with one another; astronomy, folklore and anything which could arise within a group which combined the functions of legislation, study, enforcement, creation of liturgies and living within a host culture. One of the first great *Amoraim*, Sh'muel (a friend of the Sassanid ruler Shapur I) had enunciated the principle of *dina d'malchuta dina*—the law of the land is binding and in some cases superior to Jewish law. The Jews of Babylonia created patterns of conforming to the surrounding culture. This is also reflected in the Talmud; and the Babylonian Talmud came to be the authority for Jewish life in all lands up to the present time. The process of Oral Law continued: commentary followed upon commentary, and a rabbinic court today will still view itself as rediscovering the revealed Law of Sinai; but it is generally guided by the thoughts and precepts of the Talmud. The *Talmud Bavli* (Babylonian) is the heart of *Halachah*, of normative Jewish law through the centuries. The *Talmud Yerushalmi* (Palestinian) does have its legal sections, primarily dealing with the first three tractates of the *Mishnah* on Damages, and a compendium of commentaries on other sections, probably edited in Tiberias before 400 CE. Theodosius II abolished the patriarchate a few years later; and the texts we have give fascinating insights into a vanished Jewish life but cannot compete with the Babylonian Talmud as the centre of Jewish life and law.

Babylonia replaced Palestine. The thousand years after the fall of the Temple mark a development and inner growth within Judaism which was fashioned in Babylonia. The head of the community was the *Resh Galuta*, the Exilarch, recognised by all Jewish communities once the Palestinian Patriarchate had been abolished. The Exilarch was a prince, deemed a descendant of David, third in rank at the Babylonian court. He appointed the judges and was the civil ruler of Jewry, with a splendid court of his own. Yet the polarities of Jewish life set another force alongside him: the heads of the great Jewish academies. The Gaon (Excellency) of Sura and of Pumpeditha ruled Jewish religious life by reason of scholarship, and the period from 600 CE to 1000 CE often came to be called the Geonic Period by Jewish historians. The gains of the Talmudic Period were consolidated, with the knowledge that the law, the *Halachah*, kept growing, and that answers to legal questions, 'Responsa', had to continue as a link between the academies and Jewish life throughout the Mediterranean areas.

Other texts developed throughout that period, within the Talmud and alongside it. In the ninth century, Rav Amram Gaon compiled the first complete prayer book in response to the needs of Spanish communities. One cannot ignore the *Siddur* (Prayer Book) as an abiding expression of Jewish faith which grew and developed through the ages. Here, the rabbis expressed their theology of the near and far God ('Our Father, our King'), and affirmed the complementary divine attributes of *rachamim* (loving-kindness) and of *din* (justice). In good times and bad, the Jews turned to the *Siddur* to affirm the moral order which filled the universe. All aspects of Jewish life—suffering and martyrdom, teaching about the one God who requires moral actions from his worshippers, remembrance of the dead and the assuming of responsibility for the living and their needs—all entered the Prayer Book. At various times, various languages were used: the vernacular was always considered proper within worship—had not a translator stood alongside Ezra when he read the Law? But the Hebrew and Aramaic tongues linked Jewry together throughout the Diaspora. The *Targumim* (translations) of the late Talmudic time give insights into the process of acculturation; but the knowledge of the original texts within a profoundly literate Jewry stands behind all translations.

There have always been challenges to rabbinic Judaism and to the Oral Law. In late Geonic times, when Saadya Gaon was the intellectual leader of Jewry, he had to oppose the Karaite sect. Karaites only recognised the Written Law, the Torah interpreted most literally. Karaism rejected the customs and ceremonies developed in Palestine and Babylonia, the minutiae of Talmudic law. The founder, Anan ben David, failed in his attempt to become Exilarch, and broke away to found a sect which was joined by many Jews in search of simplicity and antagonistic to rabbinic authority. Saadya (892–942 CE) was the greatest Jewish mind of his time, a philosopher and leader who re-established Babylonian authority over the reviving claims of Palestine, and who was able to give rational, clear answers to the Karaites which contained them as a sect at a time when they were growing in authority. Saadya's Arabic translation of the Bible is still in use. He was a pioneer of Jewish grammar, a liturgist of note, scholar of mystic texts and a great legal authority. His central philosophic text, *Beliefs and Opinions*, was written in Arabic, since Arabic philosophy had influenced it. It is a text of extreme rationalism: Judaism is completely in line with reason, with revelation there to advance our knowledge but not to deny the dictates of reason. Saadya proves God's existence through rational proofs, and dismisses the anthropomorphic language of the Bible: whatever contradicts reason must be seen as allegory.

In his texts, and in the writings of the other Geonim, Babylonia reached out to instruct the communities now developing under Islam. There was a creative encounter between religions which developed here, but the centre of Jewish life slowly began to shift away from Babylonia. The Spanish Jewries were beginning to set up their own academies, to turn to their own scholars. Jews under Islam, Jewish communities within a Europe of the Middle Ages, came to create new patterns. Sephardi and Ashkenasi Jewish life began to form different patterns. Yet all this built upon the rabbinic Judaism established during the thousand years after the destruction of the Temple. The Talmud would receive different commentaries—French rabbis as well as Spanish sages—and would realise itself within varying communal organisations; but it remained the centre of the Jewish world. The

Oral Law led to medieval codes, but also to teachings of universalism, to the vision of humanity engaged in the quest for a better world in partnership with God. It was a most necessary vision for the centuries ahead of a Jewish community entering a period of much darkness and some light.

The Middle Ages: An Introduction

Wherever Jews lived in the Middle Ages, they felt themselves first and foremost as the people of Israel who had crossed the Red Sea and had stood at Sinai, who had seen Jerusalem burned by the Babylonians and by the Romans, who had studied in the Babylonian academies of Sura and Pumpeditha and in the successor schools of Muslim Spain. Their link to that past was not historiography, although *Yosippon* (a history attributed to Josephus but actually written in Italy in the tenth century) was a popular text used to explain the present through the ancient past. Familiar archetypes of suffering were reassuring, particularly when they could be linked to messianic hopes. The 'wars of Gog and Magog' could be applied to any period as the necessary upheaval of society heralding the coming messianic age. The *Akedah* (the 'Binding of Isaac', told in Genesis 22) could be applied to the Jewish children slaughtered by the Crusaders just as our age linked it to the concentration camps. Not the specific events of history, but the ongoing pattern of persecution had to be fitted into a divine plan. Striving to understand Jewish historical thinking in the Middle Ages, Professor Gerson Cohen writes, 'Schematology always betrays a very superficial interest in the events themselves, but a deep desire to unravel their meaning and their place in the plan of history as a whole.'[2] But meaning and purpose, within the continuum of medieval Judaism, were found in the examination of Jewish law beginning at Sinai and moving into the rabbinic decisions of one's own time—the *shalshelet ha-kabbalah* (chain of tradition). The medieval Jew lived within that law and experienced all of past history within his own life. In Yosef Yerushalmi's words: 'In the Middle Ages, as before, Jewish memory had other channels—largely ritual and liturgical—through which to flow, and only that which was transfigured ritually and liturgically was endowed with a real chance for survival and permanence.'[3] The medieval experience entered Judaism in that fashion, albeit incompletely: penitential prayers, fast days and certain rituals recorded those events alongside the communal records, but only as one aspect of a Jewish faith which remembers the paradigmatic and non-historical events of the Book of Esther with far greater clarity than the massacre of Mainz.

The medieval period had to encompass within itself that flow of Jewish history which had moved from biblical times through the Hellenistic period and the Talmudic age into the world of Islam where rabbinic Judaism flourished. Often assigned to Central Europe, the Judaism of that time cannot be understood unless one sees the commingling of

'Ashkenasi' (Germany and Central Europe) and 'Sephardi' (Spanish and Mediterranean territories) Jewry. The standard text of Jewish life, Joseph Caro's *Shulchan Aruch* (first printed in 1567), describes the Sephardic experience; its commentary stresses the Ashkenasi variants. The legal codes of medieval Jewry rise out of the Babylonian Talmud; but that text is seen and mediated by the great Sephardic interpreters, notably Maimonides. The Fourth Lateran Council of 1215 had tried to isolate the Jews from the outside world: Jews and Christians were not to dwell together, trade together, work together. Medicine, handicrafts, almost anything except pawnbroking and the old-clothes trade was closed to them. They were driven from the rural areas, and confined to what became ghettos in the city. Isolated, persecuted (expelled from England in 1290, from France in 1306 and 1394, from Spain in 1492, from Portugal in 1497, from most German cities during the Black Death in 1348–9), they yet achieved their particular identity as Jews and as a people at that time—it may well have been their chief contribution to the medieval world.[4] An indomitable optimism and assertion of this world as against the world-to-come, a nonconformity in terms of the outside structures of thought and a total programme of continuous education had fashioned a Judaism which permitted the existence of the most isolated, smallest Jewish communities. The synagogue was the expression of their corporate identity; and from the rabbis and their meetings there issued *takkanot*—social legislation which dealt with civil and religious matters under a system of self-government which yet kept in touch with the world outside. It was not a perfect system: the rich and the scholars were slow to share their privileges; but Judaism stressed the prophetic vision of social justice, and education was far broader than that of the neighbours. Underneath rabbinic formalism there was always the quest for universal meaning, for a shared life of Jewish testimony to the world. The *Siddur*, the Jewish prayer book, expressed the rabbinic theology of the near and far God. The Crusades and pogroms brought knowledge of the far God; but the experience of martyrdom by Israel, God's 'suffering servant', reached towards an awareness of the near God which was taught by mystics but lived by the common people.

The Golden Age of Sephardic Jewry

Much had come together within medieval Judaism. Islam and Arabic had changed the practices and teachings of Babylonia. By replacing Aramaic, a new world of thought was opened up within a benign environment. The Christian Goths in Spain had oppressed the Jews, but the Arab conquest gave the Jews entrance into commerce, the professions, literature, science and philosophy. Islam and Judaism met, and there was much to share, including the Greek philosophers who had been preserved in Arabic texts. Together, they built the Alhambra and a better society. Samuel Ha-Nagid (993–1055) was the Vizier of Granada, its general, statesman, and a grammarian and poet. A golden age of Jewish life developed in Spain. Jewish philosophy and theology utilised the rational teachings of Muslim *Kalam*; but Bachya ibn Pakuda's *Chovot Ha-Levavot* (Duties of the Heart), published in Saragossa in 1040, drew upon Neoplatonism and ascetic Sufi mysticism. This text was a model of personal piety and ethics, set within a Jewish tradition which kept the individual firmly within the community and prevented a full flight into mysticism.

Poets could be philosophers in this world. Solomon ibn Gabirol (1021–69) celebrated his vision of God as the metaphysical absolute, united with the world by his divine will, in poetry still recited in the synagogue. His *Keter Malchut* (Royal Crown) remains a poetic adornment to the liturgy, while his great philosophic work *Fountain of Life* strayed into Christian theology as the *Fons Vitae*, assumed to be the teaching of a Christian scholar Avicebron—a mistake not corrected until the nineteenth century. Moses ibn Ezra (1080–1139) was a poet and religious thinker of delicate sadness, overshadowed by his great contemporary Judah Halevi (1086–1143). Halevi reassured Israel of its special role in God's plan, as a people endowed with the gift of prophecy, with the ability to hear God. His poems sing of Israel's love for God and for Zion. His philosophic dialogue *Kuzari* is a brilliant religious polemic, telling the story of the Black Sea kingdom of the Khazars who chose Judaism over Islam and Christianity. Against their opponents, Judaism could claim the direct revelation given on Mount Sinai, witnessed by the multitudes and preserved by the people through the millennia. Faith, not reason, was the way to God; yet reason had its role, subordinated to the experience and faith of the Jewish people who had known God and his miracles through the ages. This emphasis on religious experience (partially influenced by the Muslim al-Ghazali) and upon Jewish life again stressed the special nature of Israel as 'the heart of the nations' with its suffering as the badge of its election.

The greatest teacher of this Jewish world was Moses Maimonides (1135–1204), who was born in Cordoba, taken to Morocco by his father, and finally settled in Egypt, where he was the first physician of his day at the court of Saladin. His medical treatises still command respect; but it is through his life as the Jewish leader of his time, as *the* philosopher and theologian within all of Jewish history, that he personifies the greatness of Sephardic Jewry. His *Mishne Torah* (Repetition of the Torah) is a compendium of rabbinic law up to his time, together with a statement of Jewish beliefs, ethical attitudes and ideals of Jewish practice. It contains a statement of thirteen principles of faith which later entered the liturgy (although no Jewish community has ever agreed upon the authority of a firm set of dogmas or a 'catechism'):

Maimonides taught that every Jew should accept

1. That God exists.

2. That He is One in a unique and perfect sense.
3. That He is immaterial, and not be compared to anything else.
4. That He is eternal.
5. That prayer must be addressed to Him alone.
6. That God revealed Himself to the prophets.
7. That the prophecy of Moses is unique and superior to all other revelations.
8. That through Moses God gave us the Torah.
9. That God will never change or revoke the Torah.
10. That God's providence observes our actions and our inner motives.
11. That man is rewarded or punished according to his deserts.
12. The coming of the Messiah.
13. The resurrection of the dead.[5]

Many Jewish scholars, then and now, argue that one must view the entire Torah as fundamental and not elevate some teachings above the rest. Others disagreed upon the teachings (Joseph Albo, in the fifteenth century, stressed three fundamental beliefs: God, revelation and retribution). But Maimonides' statement, now the *Yigdal* of the daily service, is still sung in the synagogues.

Maimonides' philosophy developed the Jewish dialogue with Aristotelianism. In his main work, the *More Nevuchim* (Guide for the Perplexed), he tried to show that faith is not opposed to reason; the chief doctrines of Judaism can be demonstrated in a rational manner, in harmony with philosophy. Beyond that, they offer insights which reason alone cannot obtain. In a later, less generous age, within a Jewish community under attack, this book was denounced to the Christian authorities (in Provence) as heretical, and was consigned to the flames. Even in his time, Maimonides evoked great hostility—the philosopher was distrusted because he was so great an authority upon the Talmud. Unsophisticated worshippers wanted to use anthropomorphic terms, denied to them by his teaching that no attributes can be ascribed to God except as a denial of imperfection. One may only say that 'God is not weak, not ignorant'. The *via negativa* was difficult to walk. Maimonides' world was an Aristotelian system of concentric spheres ending in the tenth sphere with the *sechel ha-poel*, the creative instinct which imposes form on life and also gives humans the faculty of prophecy. But all can develop their rational faculty through the discipline of Torah. It fosters soundness of mind and body with all its laws, helping man achieve the greatest good: the contemplation of God, given to all in the time of the Messiah. Intoxicated with the intellectual love of God, reason here built firmly upon faith. Halevi, by contrast, had reared his edifice of faith with the tools of reason. Here, too, one must bring in the next generation of great Jewish teachers who disagreed with Maimonides, particularly Nachmanides (Moses ben Nachman of Gerona, 1194–1270) who denounced those who deny the existence of realities unperceived by the senses and who suppose that what their little minds cannot grasp must be untrue. Nachmanides was also a profound Talmudist, and a pioneer of *Kabbalah*, of Jewish mysticism. God-given laws need no reason. The Babylonian scholar Rab had taught that the precepts were given for no other purpose than to refine people. Nachmanides used this to show that worship of God and obedience to the Torah have the effect of inculcating virtue and good character, making humans more God-like. It is the aim of the precepts 'to eradicate every evil belief from our hearts, to make the truth known to us and to remind us of it at all times'.[6] The creative interplay of faith and reason is evident in all these teachers, and the differing emphases engaged one another in a creative conflict within an open society. All too soon, that society changed.

Sephardim and Ashkenasim

The Diaspora had become divided into two areas: the Sephardim of the Mediterranean world and Spain confronted the Ashkenasim of Germany and Central Europe where the Church ruled. They differed greatly. Leo Baeck defined the Sephardim as 'the piety of culture' and the Ashkenasim as 'the culture of piety'.[7] Sephardic scholars wrote in Arabic and affirmed the outer culture. Ashkenasim wrote in Hebrew and lived within the culture of the Torah. The Sephardim became systematisers; the Ashkenasim, commentators. The giant of them all, Rashi of Troyes (1040–1105), introduced French words into his commentaries. Yet he is only understood within an Ashkenasi community which could only find culture, education and intellectual dialogue in what was their own and in their tradition: only where there was Torah could there be *chochmah* (wisdom); piety engendered culture for them. And, to establish their identity, they had to start with the simple meaning of their basic texts, the *peshat*, as expounded by Rashi and his school of Tosaphists. The most tangled legal arguments of the Torah and Talmud were reduced to their basic meaning in Rashi's commentaries. Where the Sephardim struggled with the outside culture, Rashi refined and sharpened the understanding of the ancient teachers. A simple unquestioning faith in the rabbinic tradition remained isolated from the turmoil and doubts of the outer world of science and philosophy. The anguish of the Crusades commencing in 1096 tore at their bodies, decimated their communities, made martyrdom a daily reality—and reaffirmed their links with the ancient texts, restored to them by the crystal-clear commentaries of Rashi and his successors. Christianity was instructed by Rashi as much as by Maimonides. In the Middle Ages, much of ancient and contemporary Judaism was admired and respected—while the Jewish people themselves were hated and persecuted. The Crusaders gained practice at killing Jews as they marched through France and Germany; by the time they captured Jerusalem, they were trained enough to herd the Jews there into a synagogue and to burn it and them.

In Europe, the feudal system had removed the Jews from the soil, and the guilds kept them out of crafts. They were assigned the role of money-lenders, with most of the profit going to the crown, until the Church realised that it could charge interest by not calling it interest! Then, Jewish life became truly marginal, and the Ashkenasi Jew could only assert his individuality through the daily customs, ceremonies and observances which somehow assured him that even in his lowly estate he continued to be God's witness in the world.

Mysticism developed. Alongside the *musar*, the simple ethical instructions for the righteous life, there had to be an escape into a world the persecutors could not enter. The *hasside ashkenas* (pious Jews of Germany) stood alongside the great Talmudic scholars, giving an inner glow to the lives of the lowly, in apposition to the *chochmah* of mysticism which developed in the Sephardic lands. Against the brilliant systems and speculations of the profound Sephardic vision, theirs was a quiet, daily experience as seen in the *Sefer Hasidim* (Book of the Pious Ones), described by Baeck as 'as much a book of ethics as of mysticism. Life cannot be experienced without morality. The heart begins to open itself and to speak . . . to the questions of human needs.'[8]

The ritual and communal Jewish life became their profession of faith, organised into structures of law by the rabbis. German rabbis often left for other lands where life was more secure, although their greatest teacher, Meir of Rothenburg, was imprisoned and held for ransom in 1286 when he tried to leave for Palestine. In order not to set a precedent, he refused to be ransomed and died in prison. But Asher ben Yechiel (1256–1328) found a haven in Toledo, and the Sephardim welcomed a man of Talmudic learning even if it was closed to the outside culture. His son, Jacob ben Asher, presented Jewish life with an important code, *Arbaah Turim* (Four Rows), which was a summary of Jewish law in its most recent developments. Joseph Caro, writing in Safed, built upon this edifice; his *Shulchan Aruch* became the definitive code for the centuries which followed. Caro was part of the mystic circle around Isaac Luria of Safed, and felt the presence of a spiritual mentor in all of his life. The legal structure of the Ashkenasim here began to shimmer with the glow of Sephardi mysticism.

The Kabbalah

Kabbalah (Tradition) refers to the transmission of mystic truths from ancient times to the present. The Spanish teachers of the eleventh century (Azriel ben Solomon in Gerona and others) spoke of secret doctrines for the elite which in time became teachings of comfort to the many. Jewish mysticism was a search for harmony which would unite the upper and lower worlds and would eliminate the evil in the world. The heart of the system was the prophetic teaching, and it turned to Ezekiel's chariot and the story of creation. The first mystic text, the *Sefer Yetzirah* (Book of Creation), utilised Neoplatonic ideas and a philosophic approach which could challenge radical evil. A path led upwards from that lowly sphere to ever higher forces blessing the world; and those benign forces also streamed downward, through the spheres, offering hope and salvation. In contrast to outside forms of mysticism seeking total union with God, Judaism strove more towards communion—*d'vekut* (cleaving unto God), which implied no loss of identity.[9] God was the *En Sof*, infinitely distant, the *deus absconditus* of their Christian neighbours. But in the *Zohar*, the basic text of Jewish mysticism which received its final form in the thirteenth century, the near God is always encountered. The Ashkenasi Jew had invested the small actions of daily life with a mystic glow; the Sephardi thinker hurled his mind through the universe. They were one in striving to redeem the world. Their mysticism broke into two aspects: the speculative type, which studied the nature of the spiritual world as related to the world below and to the place of humanity within that structure; and the practical type, which attempted, through powerful rituals, wonders and actions, to change the world and make it a better place.

The practical *Kabbalah* of the German school was ecstatic, centring primarily on prayer, inner meditation and contemplation. The alphabet and numerology of the *Sefer Yetzirah* found its fullest expression here, together with theurgical actions which provided escape from the lowly and persecuted position Jews occupied in Germany during the twelfth and thirteenth centuries. Judah the Chasid (d. 1217) and his disciple Eleazar of Worms (d. 1238) combined ethics and piety with the mystic vision of the Divine Glory which the simple *Hasidim* (pious ones) could achieve through humble, dedicated and ethical lives, in which they could come to love fellow human beings as they came to love God.

Meanwhile, the happier Jewish life in Provence and Spain fashioned the 'speculative' type of mysticism. Philosophic thought was subjugated to faith and used to search out the truths of each word of sacred text. It had to establish the world as within the *En Sof* (the Endless), but, since the world is imperfect, the *Sefirot* (the spheres) were interposed as the medium through which God irradiates the elements of the universe without diminishing his power. Nachmanides taught that the Torah was made up of divine names, with each letter containing powers waiting to be released. Then came the *Zohar* (Book of Splendour) probably compiled by Moses de Leon of Granada (d. 1305), which unites all the themes of Jewish mysticism, particularly the teachings on good and evil, human nature, the Messiah and redemption. As a different type of Torah commentary, it searched for the hidden meanings of the text. It was *midrash*—homiletic interpretation of the Torah, the Song of Songs and Ruth; and it was genius. It saw the spheres as a Jacob's Ladder, with divine light moving down to man, and human aspiration reaching upward and creating angels of its own. Striving to understand evil and suffering, it drew the form of *Adam Kadmon* (Primordial Man) with

God's justice and punishment moving through the left side of the cosmic body and bringing human suffering. Evil is in the shells, the husks surrounding the sparks of light. The task of redemption is the stripping off of these husks, letting the light shine forth. And one must still wait for the Messiah. Meanwhile, Israel's special task is to achieve that great unity (*Yichud*) in which the Indwelling Presence of God (*Shekinah*), attached firmly to Israel in a covenant relationship, is reunited with God in the time of the Messiah. The Torah, seen through the *Zohar*, is the tool for that task in which the ethical and mystical aspects of Judaism are firmly joined together. Study, devout prayer (*Kavanah*) and love lead every soul back to the source from which it emanated. With these teachings, the *Zohar* moved out to all the areas of Jewish wanderings where its light and hope illumined the dark world.

Kabbalah reached its finest development in Safed in Palestine. The speculative school was represented there by Moses Cordovero (1522–76) whose *Pardes* (Orchard) was a poem of reason and of mystical thought. He saw the *Sefirot* as *Kelim* (Vessels) containing the unchanging light of the *En Sof* which is reflected in various ways due to the differing qualities of the *Kelim*. But it was his compatriot Isaac Luria (1514–72) who developed this thought to its conclusion. The great central figure of Jewish mysticism, combining speculative and practical motifs of mysticism, Luria developed the theory of the *shevirat ha-kelim* (the breaking of the vessels), as the imperfect containers could not contain the rush of light entering them. The light became sparks, illuminating parts of the world, with evil residing in the dark areas. Yet light and darkness became so intermingled within the universe that all evil contains some good, all good contains some evil. Central to the Lurianic system was the concept of *zimzum* (contraction) where the *En Sof*, the Infinite, contracts in order to make room for the finite. The intermingling of good and bad, of the souls created at the time of Adam and flawed by his sin, creates a world in which evil flourishes; but harmony will be restored with the coming of the Messiah. Meanwhile, Jewish wanderings through the world serve the task of *tikkun* (restoring the harmony of the world). These teachings, and the customs of *Safed*—joyous celebrations, all night studies, special fasts and observances—all left their mark upon the generations which followed. And it moved from there to most other countries, particularly to Poland. There, Isaiah Horowitz (1570–1630) brought the teachings of *Safed* to a great centre of Jewish life which made his text of ethics and mystical lore *Sh'ne Luchot Ha-Brit* (Two Tablets of the Covenant) a cherished part of life for the learned and for some laymen. Yet it was not until much later that the rise of Eastern Hasidism brought the mystical teachings of joy and inner devotion into the life of the masses.[10]

Messianic Stirrings

If Talmudic learning and mystical speculations linked Jews in the many lands of their dispersion, it must also be noted that their most shared thought was the hope for redemption, for the coming of the Messiah. This hope could live in dark or bright areas where they resided. After the Inquisition and the expulsion from Spain (1492) many of them had moved into Italy. The great Don Isaac Abravanel, the last of the great Jewish statesmen of Spain, turned from the world around him to the world of the Bible; but his son Judah (Leone Ebreo 1465–1535) wrote the famous *Dialoghi di Amore*, affirming the Renaissance culture surrounding him. Popes Leo X and Clement VII, in the first part of the sixteenth century, welcomed the Jews and even expressed interest in a strange messianic figure who arrived in Rome in 1524. David Reubeni claimed to be the brother of a king of a far-away Jewish kingdom and was accepted joyfully by Jews and Christians. One of the *Conversos* (Jews whose families had been forced to convert to Christianity), called Diogo Pires, joined Reubeni when he came to Portugal with letters of introduction from Pope Clement. Diogo changed his name to Shlomo Molcho, and began to think of himself as the Messiah. He was killed as a heretic in Mantua in 1532; and Reubeni later perished in an *auto-da-fé* in Portugal. Yet they were early representatives of a yearning which brought about a tragic episode in Jewish life and thought: Sabbatai Zvi, born in Smyrna in 1626.

The complex history of his life unites all trends within the *Kabbalah* in a figure of flesh and blood. He lived out the legends and the prophecies, much of this managed by Nathan of Gaza, a brilliant pseudo-Messiah figure happy to assume the lesser role of Elijah and able to fashion a religion around the charismatic, mysterious Sabbatai Zvi. Nathan was more like St Paul, busy in organising letters which covered all of Europe with the good tidings that the Messiah had come. In most synagogues, prayers were offered on behalf of 'Our Lord, King and Master, the holy and righteous Sabbatai Zvi, Anointed of the God of Israel'. A vast literature of prayers, poems and exhortations drew the Jewish community together in a mass hysteria in the course of which children were married so that the remaining souls might enter bodies to hasten the coming redemption. Sober business people sold their possessions, and the Amsterdam stock-market crashed once 1666 was announced as the time of redemption. Spinoza saw no rational reason why Sabbatai Zvi's claims might not come to pass; and Pepys informs us that Jews were offering odds of 10 to 1 in favour of the man from Smyrna being the King of the World. The end of the strange fantasy was arrest and imprisonment in Turkey, where the Sultan gave Sabbatai the choice between death or Islam. Sabbatai became a Muslim. Yet this was not the end. 'He is testing us', said the disciples. And many turned to Luria's teaching on the light that had to be taken out of the husks. Sabbatai Zvi, they argued, had let the final degradation come upon him to suffer for the sake of the world and to liberate the sparks of divinity held captive in the shells of Islam. There are still believers of Sabbatai Zvi today, although the sect of the Donmeh in Turkey has all but disappeared.

The Sabbatian heresy divided the Jewish community in the centuries which followed. Some of its followers questioned the oneness of God, believed in a return which would lead to the abrogation of the Torah, and even embraced acts of licentiousness and challenged the moral authority of the rabbis. There were corresponding excesses on the other side: saintly teachers like Moses Luzzatto were forced out of their communities, the most brilliant rabbis engaged in bitter fights (the Emden vs. Eybeschuetz controversy in Hamburg), and there were Sabbatian 'cells' in many communities challenging established authorities.

The Eastern Jewish community opened itself to this mysticism, just as it had become a stronghold of Talmudic learning. A Podolian adventurer, Jacob Frank (actually Jacob Leibovitz), returned from Turkey as a messianic figure demanding and receiving royal honours from his people. He claimed to be the reincarnation of Sabbatai Zvi, and taught a cult of ending evil by entering upon acts of licence and thus fighting evil from within. Immorality became a religious commandment. Excommunicated by the Jews, Frank and his followers joined the Church, having maligned the Jewish community with the Blood Libel and causing the Talmud to be burned after disputations in Lemberg in 1757 and 1759. Frank was imprisoned for many years; but he and the Frankists continued to flourish. He died in 1791, in Offenbach, Germany, holding court as a self-styled baron, and his daughter Eve continued as the 'Holy Mistress' of the sect, surrounded by admirers. These and other excesses weakened the fire of messianic hopes, and Jews began to look elsewhere for salvation.

Light and Darkness in Eastern Europe

Judaism has always been an amalgam of contrasting experiences in many lands and the transmission of ancient teachings containing within themselves the power of renewal and development. Ashkenasi and Sephardi Judaism give one example of the polarities which shape Jewish faith, just as the struggle between rationalism and mysticism must be seen as a creative dynamism always present in Jewish thought. The countries which opened themselves to the Jews play their part in this development. After the expulsion from Spain (1492) Poland had become a place of refuge. Where Central Europe became a place of persecution, Poland and Eastern Europe offered new hope and opportunity. Great Jewish centres developed, and the Council of the Four Lands, a natural development once King Sigismund Augustus had granted the Jews self-government in 1551, legislated for a community grown rich not only in material but also spiritual possessions. Great scholars arose, academies were established and the time of Babylonia seemed about to re-emerge. But appearances were deceptive. Economic circumstances changed, and the Jews became the outsiders, used as scapegoats which the nobility interposed between themselves and the peasants. For example, church keys would be held by Jews, so that a poor couple could not enter the church to have their child baptised until the fee was paid. Jews were used to collect taxes. It was not only the church teaching of deicide, but also such tactics as these which created a virulent and enduring anti-Semitism in Poland and Russia.

Anti-Semitism had taken on a most particular shape in the Middle Ages. Xenophobia here mingled with the hatred of an exposed community who were used both as scapegoats and as outlets for rebellion against Judaism's ancient teachings. Yet it was the Christian insistence upon the Jews as Christ-killers and 'defilers of the Host' (both accusations were used to shore up loyalty to church doctrine) which proved most destructive. Martin Luther is often cited here, with his pamphlet, *Concerning the Jews and their Lies*. Here is an almost complete outline of the Nazi tactics: 'destroy and burn their books, their synagogues, their homes, enslave them, imprison them'. But these were the teachings of a man grown old, sick and afraid; the young Luther had written a book acclaimed by many Jews, *That Jesus Christ was a born Jew*, in which he spoke in favour of that persecuted people. The Jews welcomed him, and even changed Kabbalistic prophecies to apply to him (in 1524, Rabbi Abraham took a messianic prophecy and wrote, 'We first thought that the man prophesied by the stars would be the messiah, the son of Joseph; now it is proven that he (Luther) is the man about whom all speak, who is noble in all his actions. . .').[11] Yet at the centre of Luther's teaching was the awareness that the Old Testament which he loved had to be taken away from the Jews; and that the Christians, not the Jews, were the chosen people. Christians defined themselves in terms of the Jews; and Jews had to assert their identity against Christianity, in Eastern as in Western Europe.

Enormous pressure had descended upon the Jews of Eastern Europe. Their life had been narrowed, compressed, intensified in the cauldron of suffering. In the process, they achieved an adamantine identity, with the rough surface concealing the deep brilliance of the precious centre. The persecutions damaged the social structure: an alliance of the few wealthy and powerful with the rabbinic scholars made life even more difficult for the Jewish masses. But the deep learning and great academies, the encouragement given to education, and the knowledge of both Talmudic and mystical sources, created a storehouse of religious treasure here which feeds Jewry even today. The few remnants left after the Holocaust show how much greatness rested beneath that grim exterior of Jewish life in the East. Even if much of that learning seemed wasted by the *pilpul* interpretation of Talmudic texts (mental gymnastics, more concerned with showing brilliance than meaning, taught first by Rabbi Jacob Pollak (d. 1541)) and was not applicable to daily life, it gave an intellectual excitement and a standard of excellence to that rabbinic learning which has not been surpassed.

Hasidism

The impoverished peasants who had little time for study suffered under this dictatorship of the intellect which did not consider the unlearned Jew to be an equal partner in acts of worship or in the life of the community. They could not read the Talmud; they could not read the *Zohar.* They even had trouble with the *Siddur* (the Prayer Book); yet they needed the warmth and hope of Judaism more than any of the others. And so a teacher came, a simple man from Podolia, Israel ben Eliezer (1700–60). The stream of piety and hope, of laughter and visions for the future, emerged from underground and encouraged a great new movement: Hasidism. Its leader became known as the *Baal Shem Tov* (the good 'Master of the Name'—a term applied to wonder workers who used the name of God). Many became disciples of this gentle yet charismatic teacher who stressed piety over scholarship. All could approach God on their own terms, through song and dance and joy far more than through mortification of the flesh. True, there were *Zaddikim* (Righteous Ones), who were close to God and whose intercessions helped; but teachers needed disciples. And the *Baal Shem Tov*, in his wanderings and his story-telling, sowed the seeds for Hasidic communities formed around the students and disciples who became the heart of a large movement.

Set against the gloomy asceticism of Lurianic *Kabbalah* and against the excesses of Sabbataism, the new pietism also challenged the rigorous intellectualism of *pilpul* Talmudism which responded by persecuting the *Hasidim.* The *Mitnagdim* (Opponents) became the party of traditionalism, led by the great Elijah ben Solomon, the Vilna Gaon (1720–97). They tried to excommunicate the new movement and much internal conflict ensued, which changed both groups. The Hasidic doctrines of humility, and *hitlahavut* (enthusiasm), of the *Zaddik* who becomes a channel of divine communication and the reliable spiritual guide to his flock, whose simplest action—tying his shoelaces, for example—becomes a word of Torah, the pattern of song, dance and celebration as worship: these were anathema to the religious scholars of the *Mitnagdim* party. The Vilna Gaon would not talk to Rabbi Schneur Zalman, head of the Lithuanian *Hasidim*, and the *Hasid* wound up in a St Petersburg jail, denounced by the *Mitnagdim.* Yet in Russia, the Hasidic movement came to include scholarship, particularly under the leadership of Dov Baer of Mezerich (1710–72). The simpler Polish Hasidism (which spread into Hungary and Rumania) responded more to the marvellous tales and charismatic leadership of men like Levi Yitzchak of Berdichev, whose songs and prayers could even challenge God on behalf of the oppressed Jews.

Sadly, the early enthusiasm and joy of simple pietism came to deteriorate as it developed into a formal movement. The *Zaddikim* became hereditary rulers over their flock, and held court for their simple followers. The joyous sabbath meals became magical sacraments, with disciples scrambling for the bits of food (*Sh'rayim*) left on the *rebbe*'s plate. They demanded amulets and expected miracles. Competing sects developed, followers of rival dynasties: Lubavitch, Satmar, Bobover and *Hasidim* had little use for one another. And yet the mystic vision endured, sometimes in strange ways. The 'Dead *Hasidim*' of Bratzlav kept an empty chair at their table for their great teacher Rabbi Nachman, whose parables and teachings reached out to an ever-growing public after his death. And Hasidism, once viewed as the great enemy of traditionalism, is now the bulwark of Orthodoxy, of traditional observances. Its teachings and insights are at the centre of modern Jewish thought, mainly through its reinterpretation and popularisation by Martin Buber. Outer pressures often determine the inner forms.

The medieval period, despite its persecution of the Jews, was a long era of law and order of a corporate society in which the Jews found themselves a separate corporate body with a clearly defined identity. In the home, it was centred upon family life, values and tradition. In the synagogue, rabbinism had created a leadership where the central figure was a scholar, a judge, a preserver of the Talmud and its commentaries. As the Jews began to move into a new structure of uncertain identities, of former corporate groups striving to find new patterns, the Hasidic *rebbe*, a mystic, charismatic figure, replaced the scholar—only to become a scholar himself in due course, with Hasidic commentaries now written for the old texts. But this was only one solution of many developments as the Jews entered the modern age. Traditionalism also surged forward. And Progressive Judaism, previously a component part of a stable, isolated Jewish life, came to express itself in new institutions and formulations of Judaism which responded to the new environment. All of Jewish life and thought continued to build upon the Bible and the traditions established through the centuries: the family, the synagogue and the knowledge of the Jews' special fate links all the ages and periods of Jewish life and thought into the continuous 'chain of tradition' which is the heart of Judaism.

The New Period: An Introduction

There was no magic moment in which the world changed for the Jews. Sephardi Jewry, particularly in Arab lands, had achieved an equilibrium enabling the Jew to survive within an almost closed system, although Italian and French developments gave warning of changes to come. In Eastern Europe, medievalism was slow to crack; Jews moving from Eastern to Western Europe literally jumped across the centuries. The Enlightenment, emanating from the Netherlands and Germany, found its full political expression in France, where it culminated in the Revolution and in the Declaration of the Rights of Man, changing Jewish status. Its effect on the mind, with its doctrine of the autonomy of reason challenging all dogma, authority and tradition, first evidenced itself in Germany. Suddenly, Jews found themselves viewed as individual human beings. The medieval religious prejudices were challenged by the new system of economics which could see Jews as part of the gross national product—a human resource to be developed rather than destroyed or isolated for religious reasons. As the Age of Reason came into its own, the commercial middle class gained power and confidence, and there was a lowering of religious and class barriers. A sane and ethical deism, not tied to institutions, heralded a new world. C.W. von Dohm (1751–1820) wrote his *Concerning the Civil Amelioration of the Jews* in which he argued that improvement in Jewish status would result in improving the Jews whose 'flaws' were simply injuries inflicted upon them by persecution. Frederick II of Prussia could understand this; he could still hate Jews, but would give special status to those Jews who would improve the economy of Prussia. And then there was Moses Mendelssohn.

Moses Mendelssohn (1729–1786)

Mendelssohn came out of the Eastern environment, trained in the tradition of Talmud and observance, but yearning for the new bright world of the Enlightenment. Behind Lessing's celebrated picture of him in *Nathan the Wise*, there stands the frail figure of a little hunchbacked Jew, who came to Berlin as a poor student and who became the new Socrates of the Western world. He became a philosopher whose essays were placed alongside those of Kant, a classical scholar and outstanding stylist surrounded by an admiring Christian world; and he remained a traditional Jew, following the precepts and observances of Eastern European Jewry. How could he reconcile the two worlds? The answer he gave, which reconciled reason with faith, made him the father figure of modern traditionalism—and of modern Reform Jewish life. 'I recognize no eternal truths except those which cannot only be conceived but also be established and verified by human reason,' he declared in his *Jerusalem*.[12] Filled with admiration for the Enlightenment and its teachings, he saw his surroundings as a world which had, through God-given reason, achieved knowledge of the truth which Jews had been granted long ago, in the Bible. The truths of the Bible were accessible to the universal human mind. Yet there was also revelation: the special instructions given to the Jews in the Bible, the customs, ceremonies and observances were a particular revelation to the Jews as a priest-people, to be kept by them in obedience to God's will. Jews could thus partake of the modern world of rationalism, and still remain true to their heritage.

Yet how could the Jews, still half in the ghetto, enter this modern world? They did not understand the language, and non-Jewish texts were not permitted by the rabbis. Mendelssohn's answer was to translate the Pentateuch into German, written in Hebrew letters—a 'Rosetta

Stone' enabling the Jews to enter the new culture through its language. He and his disciples established free schools for the next generation, and fought for political rights for his generation. His *Jerusalem* argued for freedom of thought, and insisted that the individual and not the state must decide what to believe (since Judaism was revealed practice, not dogma). Jews could thus be rational, traditionally observant *and* cultured Europeans. For a moment, in a rational, tolerant world, this was an approach which could work for at least some individuals. But the world changed, and so did the Jew.

Not every Jew yearned for emancipation. Some would have remained in their secure enclave; but Napoleon and other factors in European history swept away those enclaves, and attacked medieval religious institutions—the Church and the Synagogue. The ghetto walls were destroyed, to be replaced soon enough by invisible walls. European Jews had various options now. They could re-establish the old traditionalism, particularly in Eastern Europe, where great Jewish scholars rebuilt the walls of *Halachah* as a bulwark against modernism. They could try to be traditional *and* modern. 'Be a Jew in your home and a *mensch* (a cultured human being) in the street' was taught in the East and West. A new term emerged—'neo-Orthodoxy'—describing an enlightened traditionalism as taught by Samson Raphael Hirsch. But that, too, was assimilation. The Revolutionary Assembly in Paris had listened to the statement: 'To the Jew as a human being, everything; to the Jew as a Jew, nothing!' And it did not occur to many Jews and Christians that one could really be a Jew in the street, or that an abstract definition of humanity might give way to the reality of a living Jewish people who had emerged out of their seclusion. Mendelssohn achieved this; but he was the exception to the rule.

The Science of Judaism

Other options were chosen. Mendelssohn's children and grandchildren saw their Judaism as a barrier to the new culture; and they became Christians. Felix Mendelssohn-Bartholdy entered the world of music. Other grandchildren, the Veit brothers, became devout Christian painters. In the world of the Christian Prussian state it was a prerequisite for government service, university teaching and other professions that one should be a Christian. Many Jews entered that Christian world and were absorbed by it. But there were special islands of self-expression. The ladies of the salons (e.g. Henrietta Herz, Rahel (Levin) Varnhagen, Dorothea Mendelssohn, Fanny Arnstein) created areas of contact between artists, writers and politicians and a world of high Jewish intellect which gave more than it received and began to set a pattern for a secular Jewish survival.

There were brilliant Jewish scholars and writers who did not want to cease being Jews but who yearned for the top of the pyramid: a university lecturership. But how could a Jew teach 'Christian' history, theology or philosophy? Hoping that a more liberal administration would permit Jews to teach, they decided that not only Jews but Judaism should enter the new world. Judaism itself should be taught at the university—and who was better equipped to teach this than a Jew? A group of young scholars, Eduard Gans, Leopold Zunz, Immanuel Wolf (joined by Heinrich Heine, one of the greatest of German writers) came together in a *Verein fuer Kultur und Wissenschaft der Juden* (Association for the Culture and Scholarly Study of the Jews). An important new concept emerged here: modern science and scholarship could be applied to the history, philosophy and basic texts of Judaism. Philology and archaeology would examine aspects of Jewish life hitherto held sacrosanct. Traditional thinkers were appalled: science had to remain subservient to religion. The Association only existed for a few years (1819–23) and many of its members converted as their passport to careers in a Christian world. Yet some (notably Zunz and Jost) persisted. Almost singlehandedly, Leopold Zunz (1794–1886) created a Science of Judaism which became a towering bastion of Jewish scholarship upon which the whole of modern Jewish thought has founded its new learning. This learning has remained opposed to much of traditional Judaism; yet it made possible a new approach to Judaism emerging at that time: Progressive Judaism.

Progressive Judaism: the First Phase

In the ghetto, the closed Jewish community contained conservative and progressive thought, with much leeway given to the free-thinker and sceptic (even Spinoza was offered a generous living if he would only refrain from publishing). But once dogma, customs and ceremonies seemed the only way to remain Jewish, progressive thought was challenged. However, traditionalism was no longer enforced by civil law, although the Christian authorities often listened to the plea of the new traditionalist 'Orthodox' party to curb innovations within the Jewish community. Central to the new 'Reform' party was the leadership of the laity. They wanted a service resembling the pattern they saw in church: choirs, mixed seating in family pews, organ music, confirmation and the use of the vernacular tongue. In achieving this, partly through the work of Israel Jacobson (1768–1828), a lay leader of ability and wealth, they still remained Jews. Zunz proved that the sermon had traditionally been preached in the vernacular. The option for anyone leaving Judaism was conversion or rejection of any religion, so that Reform proved to be a viable alternative to total assimilation. Rabbis came forward bringing old proofs for new practices, notably Abraham Geiger (1810–74). Their teachings spoke the language of their time: rational, liberal, rejecting the old dream of national life to be reborn in Palestine by affirming that perfection could be found where they lived (which also meant an attack upon the messianism and mysticism then flourishing in Eastern Europe). Often, the rabbinic writings built upon Kant and Hegel rather than Maimonides or Judah Halevi.

Neglecting the links to Jewish nationhood which were to re-emerge later in the century, Western Judaism faced the danger of becoming more of a sect and less of a living faith. In France, Napoleon had convened a 'Sanhedrin' of Jewish notables programmed to give conformist answers, in accordance with the pattern of state-dominated Consistories into which he pressed both Church and Synagogue (1806). But alternative patterns also developed. Almost from the beginning, Orthodoxy found its spokesmen in great scholars like Moses Sofer of Pressburg (1763–1839). Against the rejection of the Oral Law, which now viewed the Talmud and the later Responsa historically rather than theologically, traditionalism found ways of preserving the 'chain of tradition' connecting modern Jewry with the exponents of the Torah through the centuries. And there was also a median way, espoused by Zarachiah Frankel (1801–75), called 'Historical Judaism', which accepted the need for change and the principle of Progressive Revelation but strove for a minimum of new additions and a maximum of links with the historic Jewish community and its teachings. Freedom of inquiry was granted, but the collective experience and observances of the Jewish people were not to be rejected.

Germany was the place for radical Reform, born out of political circumstances as much as out of the presence of a group of scholarly and progressive rabbis ready to storm the heavens. England, by contrast, moved slowly and cautiously. The beginning of its Reform movement was more a rebellion against an old autocracy than a radical shift in theology. However, by the middle of the nineteenth century, the West London Synagogue became a centre for a Reform movement which established its ideology along with its changes in ritual. And, with the turn of the century, the more radical Liberal movement, still building upon a radical, rational and optimistic pattern already crumbling in Europe, brought to the fore a group of new teachers such as Lily Montagu, Israel Mattuck and C.G. Montefiore. Traditional Judaism, centred upon the Chief Rabbinate and its Seminary (Jews' College, founded 1855), maintained its leadership then as now. Yet the 'progressive' community became a dynamic and growing element in Anglo-Jewish life; and Liberal and Reform eventually joined in establishing the Leo Baeck College in 1956 (see below). The full development of Progressive Judaism can only be seen by examining the growth of American Jewry, where all aspects of Jewish life have discovered new life for themselves over the past 150 years.

Jewish Life in the United States

The beginnings of Jewish life and thought in the USA take us back to the colonial period and to the seeds planted at that time by the Sephardi Jews who played a small but significant role in the founding of the new republic. Their very presence assured Judaism of free development under a system which separated Church and State. A quiet traditionalism maintained the customs and traditions of home and synagogue, but outwardly adjusted to the new world. Great changes came after 1848, when the failure of revolutionary uprisings in Germany and elsewhere in Europe sent a new wave of Germans—and German Jews—to an expanding United States.

In the Old World, Jews desirous of change confronted patterns of observance and belief that had changed little over the centuries. In the New World, in an atmosphere of change, the Jews moved to the south-west, mid-west and California. The small communities often had no kosher butchers or ritual baths. They had few scholars; and they fervently affirmed the values of a new land which had welcomed them into a freedom they had seldom known. The outward religious pattern was congregationalist and made for independent communities. This became part of American Jewish life, where no Chief Rabbinate ever developed. The rabbis who gave ideology and substance to this new development were the German Reform rabbis who arrived after 1848. Isaac M. Wise (1819–1900) had radical vision but a moderate temper. His great achievement was in the field of organisation. He established the Hebrew Union College (1875), now the oldest and most influential Jewish seminary in the world; the Union of American Hebrew Congregations (1873), which united American Jewry for the first time; a Jewish newspaper, a prayer book (*Minhag America*—expressing the hope that there would be one united American Jewish community); and the first rabbinical Conference (1889). However, his willingness to go along with traditional thought (i.e. to give lip-service to the Oral Law) was negated by the fiery teacher of radical Reform, David Einhorn (1809–79), who transferred the most radical aspects of German Reform—anti-nationalism, rationalism, rejection of most rituals—to the American scene and filled Wise's institution with an uncompromising Reform which led to a split within American Jewry. Other German thinkers (Samuel Hirsch, Samuel Adler, David Lilienthal) strengthened and developed American Reform as the leading expression of America's Jewry. And then, the world changed again.

In the 1880s, pogroms swept the Eastern Jewish world; and a great wave of Jewish immigrants came to the United States. Previously, Jews had arrived as individuals, had been caught up in the movements of a developing America ('Go West, young man'), and had been absorbed within the American scene. The new group arrived as *landsmannschaften*—unified groups from individual communities who were transplanted as they had been before the move: even the synagogues, brick by brick, accompanied them. At the same time, the changing economic scene meant that the flow across the continent was stopped. The small factories of the eastern seaboard wanted and needed them. Often, they kept their own language: aspects of Europe were rebuilt in New York and Boston. The Jews they met were strange to them. Sephardi traditionalism had remained a small aristocratic enclave. The German Jews had created an accommodating pattern of Jewish life in America which combined pragmatism, independence and strong nationalism within an American Judaism which viewed the older European customs with mixed emotions. Zionism seemed a threat to the established community: 'America is our Palestine, Washington our Jerusalem', they proclaimed: the new arrivals must be 'Americanised'.

Conservatism and Orthodox Judaism in America after 1900

The Reform community, in its 1885 Pittsburgh Platform,[13] had embodied a statement of radical progressive Jewish thought which had rejected the Oral Law, ritual, the centrality of Hebrew and Zionism together with nationhood. It had added a strong emphasis on social justice and on the Jewish mission to bring about the messianic age, while rejecting the person of the Messiah. Fifty years later, in its Columbus Platform, it came back to ritual, Zionism, more tradition and an affirmation of Jewish nationhood. But alongside it there had emerged a strong central position of Conservative Judaism, building upon the teachings of Zechariah Frankel's Historical Judaism. The Jewish Theological Seminary in New York (founded 1886) gave the scholarly Solomon Schechter (1848–1915) an instrument for creating a strong Conservative community with ever-growing traditional practices, even though much of its thinking was progressive and refused to submit itself to the discipline and interpretations of the Orthodox rabbinate.

No central Orthodox authority could establish itself in the United States. The congregationalist pattern was too strong, and Europe was too far away. There had been great traditional thinkers (Isaac Leeser, Benjamin Szold and the many rabbis who came with their own communities including, later on, the heads of Hasidic dynasties). They were able to supervise traditional observances, and maintained contact with the great Halachic authorities of Eastern Europe. In time, major *yeshivot* (seminaries) were established in the Midwest and the East, and New York's Yeshiva University is a tower of traditional strength today. A vibrant and strong traditionalism maintained itself in the Jewish East End of New York and in the major cities, and much of the European way of life and thought continues to exist in the United States. But Orthodoxy could not become the normative way of expression for American Jewry. Throughout the twentieth century, it has stood alongside Conservative and Reform Judaism—sometimes as an unwilling partner, but also as an influence for greater observance and traditional rituals among the rest of America's Jews.

Out of Conservative Judaism there also arose a small splinter movement, Reconstructionism. Its founder, Mordecai Kaplan (1881–1983), viewed Judaism as a religious civilisation (Durkheim's influence), God as a process and the State of Israel as basic to Jewish life. His rejection of supernaturalism evoked a response among pragmatic Jews adjusted to the American scene and more aware of Jewish identity outside a pattern of belief. The group has remained small but is not without influence. In the period between the two World Wars, American Jewry developed along predictable lines. The Holocaust and the establishment of the State of Israel caused a radical change within American Jewish thought. Since that community leads world Jewry (Conservative, Reform and Orthodox American Jewry number well over a million in each section, with perhaps two million Jews unaffiliated), its dynamic tension with Israeli Jewish life and thought (over two million Jews) is part of any definition of contemporary Judaism.

Foundations for Contemporary Jewish Thought

Communal institutions and shared observances, a sense of identity and family feeling, kept Western Jewry from being absorbed by an outside world, where, all too soon, rejection of the Jew soon reasserted itself after the Enlightenment period. Its seminaries—Berlin had added Hildesheimer's Orthodox Seminary alongside Geiger's Hochschule—formulated the Reform and Traditional theology. Yet much of Western Jewish belief was sustained and vitalised through the influx of Eastern Jewry and its teachers who moved out of a persecuting society into the happier atmosphere of the West. Disciples went out from the great *yeshivot* of Voloshin in Lithuania (founded 1802), Moses Sofer's Pressburg *yeshiva*, the later *Slabodka Yeshiva* of Kovno (founded 1882), and other places of deep Talmudic learning and piety, many of them influenced by the *Musar* (ethical pietism) taught by the great Israel Salanter in Vilna after 1842. The *Musar* movement strove for morality through education, to be achieved through the subjugation of evil by discipline of will; the admitting of personal flaws through honest self-analysis; and conscious effort to improve oneself. Just as the *Mitnagdim* and Hasidim had confronted each other within Eastern Jewry, so this pietism set itself against the Eastern development of European Enlightenment, the *Haskalah*, which had developed in Russia and Poland as a revival of Hebrew, secular philosophy, poetry and non-traditional Jewish scholarship. Eastern Europe presented the choice between traditional observance and belief and secular citizenship or else assertion of Jewish peoplehood; there was no place for a strong Reform movement. Transplanted to the West, it gave additional strength to the new traditionalism of the Frankfurt school which had followed S.R. Hirsch. And the secular Eastern thinking became part of the new Zionism enunciated by Moses Hess' *Rome and Jerusalem* (1862). Zionism became a fully developed political movement with the emergence of Theodor Herzl at the end of the century. Jewish literature was shaped by I.B. Levensohn (1788–1860), Abraham Mapu (1806–67) and J.L. Gordon (1831–92), a great poet representative of many, who shaped European

Judaism into a national culture with its religious and secular aspects. Once Herzl's *Judenstaat* (*Jewish State*, 1895) had established a programme for a national Jewish home in Palestine, the secular messianism of the Zionists (and Jewish socialism share the same character) was soon joined by religious teachers who brought the return to Zion into Orthodox and Reform theology. The cultural Zionism of Ahad Ha-Am (1886–1927) had dissociated the ethical ideas of Judaism from its theology, making ethics an innate, unconscious force within the Jew while still clinging to the messianic notion of the return to the land as a precondition for the messianic time. The mystics also rediscovered the land of Israel. The bulk of Western European Jewry only found it through the rise of anti-Semitism, from the Dreyfus trial (1849) to the coming of the Nazis. Today, neither the Jews nor Judaism are comprehensible except in relation to the events establishing the State of Israel and the tragedy of the Holocaust.

The optimism and rational approaches of the nineteenth century entered the twentieth century alongside mystic, romantic and secular trends. Much of modern Jewish thought to this day cannot be understood without Immanuel Kant. The first great teacher of twentieth-century Jews was Hermann Cohen (1842–1918), who tried to save the great visions of a happier age by teaching Judaism as a religion of duty, derived from the sources of reason. This great neo-Kantian philosopher, founder of the Marburg School and critical idealism, saw a symbiosis between 'Germanism' and Judaism which denied Zionism. The Jews were a people, with a mission to teach righteousness, partners to states which housed them for this God-given task. With Talmudic learning, Cohen defended his people against the old-new charges made by scholarly anti-Semites. And he joined the best of modern philosophy with his religious insights. In Baeck's words, 'He received the dynamism of philosophy in the stronger dynamism of his religion, and it became his final harvest.'[14]

Cohen had three disciples: Martin Buber, Franz Rosenzweig and Leo Baeck. In what might have become a golden age of European Jewry in Germany, these men shaped modern Judaism. Much of what they created survives; more died in the Holocaust.

Martin Buber (1878–1965) was a genius towering above the experts in many fields. He was perhaps the greatest modern Jewish educator. He became an expert in Hasidism rescuing the stories of the Hasidic masters even when he added his transforming poetic touches. He was a Zionist, an ideologist of cultural Zionism who stressed the humanistic task of a nation restoring the land by acts of compassion and brotherhood, desiring a bi-cultural state for Arab and Jew. He was a great Bible scholar, a theologian and philosopher. Perhaps his most lasting contribution to Jewish thought is the epistemological breakthrough of his 'I–Thou' concept in philosophy, the awareness that knowledge rises out of relationships which move from the impersonal 'I–It' encounter of reality to the dialogue of response as central to the 'I–Thou' encounter between humans (who fall back into the 'I–it' relation) and God, the eternal Thou. His language became central to much of modern thought and faith—his impact upon Christianity was perhaps greater than upon the Jewish community, which viewed his non-affiliation with its religious institutions with some suspicion.

Buber's monumental Bible translation was done in partnership with Franz Rosenzweig (1886–1929), who has been canonised by contemporary Jewry for his life of suffering and his teachings (hermetic, existential), which are still in search of students. His great text, *The Star of Redemption*, was composed on daily postcards sent to his mother from the (German) trenches. It was a work which challenged the comfortable bourgeois Judaism of his time, drawing upon the insights of Hegel and Schelling, but ultimately rejecting philosophic wisdom for the existential encounter of divine revelation. Rosenzweig shaped an often bitter dialogue between Judaism and Christianity. It was creative: his vision of a Double Covenant saw both faiths as authentic. The Jew was a meta-historical figure, already with the Father, confirming the role of the Christian moving through history to bring the world to God. It explored the limits of language-philosophy; and Buber and Rosenzweig tried to translate the Bible as a text to be spoken aloud, a revelation always addressing the reader. Franz Rosenzweig became ill early in life with a progressive paralysis which rendered him mute and immobile. His wife Edith became a courageous interpreter, and one is stunned to realise that his poetic texts were ultimately conveyed by the flicker of an eye to recited letters of the alphabet: words from a 'mattress grave'. Rosenzweig affirmed the traditional way of life, but not by accepting outside authority of rabbinate or community. There had to be the inner response: 'law' had to become 'commandment' (Buber) as a free decision. It was the way for the contemporary intellectual into the authentic tradition; and it was a middle way which shaped modern Orthodoxy and modern Progressive Judaism.

In many ways, the mantle of Hermann Cohen fell upon Leo Baeck (1873–1956), who came to be the leader of German Jewry during the darkness of the Nazi epoch. Rosenzweig had been part of communal Jewish life: his Frankfurt *Lehrhaus* has been a breakthrough in adult education which had placed his hopes with the people more than with the scholars. Buber also taught there, but his main work was with the scholars. Baeck stood between the two. He was a rabbi in the fullest sense of that term. A servant of the community as well as its leader, he occupied a great variety of roles which included chaplain on the Eastern and Western Fronts during the First World War (but later a leading pacifist); head of German Jewry's *B'nai Brith* fraternal order; head of the *Keren Ha-Yesod* which purchased land in Palestine (but also a leading figure in non-Zionist circles); a communal rabbi and lecturer at the Berlin Hochschule (the progressive seminary). In 1905, responding to Harnack's *The Essence of Christianity*, he had published *The*

Essence of Judaism, still a classic text, defending Hermann Cohen's vision of the religion of duty, of rational faith, of the response to the 'Ought', the categorical imperatives of the moral law. Yet, in its 1922 revision, the 'religion of polarity', the recognition of the 'Mystery' alongside the 'Commandment', began to emerge: the ethical act leads to the encounter with God, the encounter with God leads to the ethical act.

Baeck was also a New Testament scholar, with an incisive challenge against 'romantic Christianity' set next to 'classic Judaism'. And he was an explorer of Jewish mystic texts who pointed the way to a new understanding of that world. However, in 1933, the dreams, visions, institutions and all foundations of German Jewish life crashed. Overnight, the Jews of Germany became an imprisoned minority, and had to elect a leader to deal with their captors. Baeck was elected the head of the representative Council. All funds were cut off, and contacts with the outside world were limited. A new educational structure was established, all communal responsibilities to the poor, the orphans, the sick and those who still needed education and vision had to be assumed. It could be said that Judaism grew stronger at that time—but the Jews who could not escape the trap died. The thousand-year-old history of the Jews in Germany had come to an end.

Holocaust and the State of Israel

The historical structure of that time is complex, outside the scope of this essay. The Holocaust transformed the whole of Jewish life: its destruction of Sephardi Jewry is often ignored, partly because the enormity of the destruction of Eastern European Jewry overshadows everything else. So much learning, so many teachers and students died with the destruction of the *yeshivot* in that part of the world. Jews have never been ignorant of the millions who died alongside the six million Jews who perished; yet their role of remembrancers, of lighting candles for their own families, could not be set aside. To understand contemporary Judaism, one must begin with the knowledge that the task of mourning and remembering cannot be terminated by a fortieth or fiftieth anniversary of the end of a period. Jews have never been more aware of their role as witnesses for God and against evil than at this time.

Leo Baeck had refused to leave his community for the many offers which had come to him. As shepherd, he remained with them, and entered a concentration camp (Terezin). It was one of the 'better' camps—almost 20,000 of the 170,000 sent there survived! Baeck continued to be a teacher, and wrote a book on scraps of paper (*This People Israel: The Meaning of Jewish Existence*), a clear movement from 'essence' to 'existence'. In it, he affirmed the 'people Israel' as a divine revelation, and discovered the dimensions of their faith through their life, as he had earlier seen the teachings defining the Jews. It was a steadfast faith. Baeck continued to teach, to guide, to be a 'beacon of light'—as others saw him in that darkness. And he survived to continue his instruction to the next generation. The Leo Baeck College in London is a monument to his work.

The survivors and the next generation often challenged the traditional faith at this point. For the Orthodox, the Holocaust was often the 'third *Churban*' (time of destruction), following upon the two destructions of the Temple in 586 BCE and in 70 CE. There was the old teaching of *mipne chatta-eynu* (for our sins), viewing Jewish suffering as a punishment for sins committed (many of the old traditionalists saw the accommodation of Jews to Western culture as the sin concerned). There were those who spoke of *chevle ha-moshiach*—the 'messianic pains' ushering in the final stage of world history. Most rabbis turned to the Book of Job: can human beings ever understand the divine plan? Martin Buber and others spoke of God 'turning his face from the world for a moment'. And, where the rabbis said that they could not understand, they tried to heal: the Book of Ezekiel, a post-*Churban* text, also tries to revive a shattered faith and people, and it looks toward the land of Israel.

We cannot ignore those who refused such teaching. Often, both the poets and writers who died and those who emerged from the camps left their teaching which has entered Jewish life and thought. Paul Celan's *Death Fugue* and his *Psalm addressed to 'No-One'* are a challenge into the void which yet waits for an answer. Elie Wiesel's body of work is a profound spiritual testimony and a continuing search for a God who will yet be found. Images from his texts (*Night* tells of the child hung between two adults and has become central to Christian Holocaust theology: where is God? There, hanging upon the gallows) can lead to misinterpretation: the basic teaching is that God is with the sufferers and not the oppressors. And the child is not a symbol—it lived and died. Auschwitz and Calvary cannot be seen together: one means death, the other meant life.

Rabbis also struggled with the concept of a God who permits such evil. Richard Rubinstein is the first and clearest challenge; but he moved from a 'God is dead' theology to the mystic's search for the *En Sof*, the Ultimate Nothingness which still gives unlimited frontiers to the seeker. *After Auschwitz*, his first book, changed Jewish theological inquiry; his later texts on the technology of death informed contemporary historiography. The best known response came from Rabbi Emil Fackenheim, who combined profound philosophical knowledge with an affirmation of faith. He heard 'God's commanding voice' from Auschwitz as an imperative to Jews that they *must* survive (the '614th commandment'), and later built his love and faith in the future of the State of Israel into that teaching. Against this, it is important to note the modern traditionalism as expressed by Eliser Berbovits in his *Faith after the Holocaust* (1973).

The State of Israel, by its very existence, constitutes one answer to the anguish of the Holocaust. At times, the answer must be questioned, as in the frequent assertion of *shlillat ha-galut* (negating Diaspora life) which sees Israel as the one viable option of Jewish life. Yet its remarkable achievements in all areas of Jewish life: scholarship, literature, Hebrew reborn as a living language, the saving of the remnant, the haven for Sephardi life threatened in Arab countries (which forced as great an exodus from their lands as the Palestinian Exodus from Israel with its tragic consequences)—all these make us see the centrality of Israel to contemporary Jewish life and thought.

Israel has seen a rebirth of traditional Jewish learning, with the seeds of Eastern European *yeshivot* producing new harvests. Its presence has been a foundation for the self-assertion of the secular Jew who at times makes Zionism his religious faith. It is the centre of a new Hebrew culture, and unites Jews from all over the world who find at least part of their identity in its presence and in its future. As such, it cannot be ignored in any contemporary definition of Judaism—even its challenges bring new vigour to all aspects of Jewish theological discourse.

A Closing Word

Contemporary Judaism expresses all of the past and present we have examined within the existence of the Jew as he is encountered in the world. There is an overarching pattern of religious observances (S.R. Hirsch once stated that 'the Jewish calendar is the Jew's catechism'). All the festivals express religious teachings within historical events. *Rosh Hashana* (the New Year) is the continuing moment of Creation; *Yom Kippur* (the Day of Atonement) is repentance and return within all of life; *Sukkot* (Tabernacles) is the harvest celebration acknowledging human dependence upon nature, but adds ethical values to pagan knowledge of the world; *Chanukah* (the dedication Feast of Lights) changes midwinter solstice observances into the vision of religion as light and life; *Purim* (the Feast of Lots) looks at past and future anti-Semitism; *Pesach* (Passover) sees the home table as altar and rediscovers the Covenant and the Exodus from slavery to freedom in all times; and *Shavuot* (Weeks) is the Pentecost celebration of the giving of the Law at Sinai which unites all Jews.

Customs and observances, in all their different interpretations, still unite the Jewish community. Dietary laws and the Sabbath can vary as religious statements, but always affirm tradition. In the end, they are a fence for one Judaism, moving from biblical to rabbinic and medieval formulations, possessing a many-faceted present, but it is still a proclamation of ethical monotheism where the One God is affirmed by righteous actions which will ultimately establish God's kingdom in the world.

Notes

1. Leo Baeck, *Epochen der juedischen Geschichte* (ed. Hans Bach) (Kohlhammer Verlag, Mainz, 1947), p. 127.
2. Gerson Cohen, quoted in Yosef Hayim Yerushalmi, *Zakhor: Jewish History and Jewish Memory* (Jewish Publication Society of America, Philadelphia, 1982), p. 39.
3. Yerushalmi, *Zakhor*, p. 40.
4. Cf. Cecil Roth, 'The European Age' in Leo W. Schwarz (ed.), *Great Ages and Ideas of the Jewish People* (Random House, New York, 1956), pp. 272ff.
5. Moses Maimonides, 'Commentary on the Mishna' quoted in Bernard Bamberger, *The Story of Judaism* (Union of American Hebrew Congregations, New York, 1957), p. 177.
6. Moses Nachmanides, 'Commentary on the Pentateuch' (on Deut. 22:6), quoted by Louis Jacobs, *A Jewish Theology* (Darton, Longman & Todd, London, 1973), p. 183.
7. Leo Baeck, *This People Israel* (transl. A.H. Friedlander) (W.H. Allen, London, 1965), pp. 266ff.
8. Ibid., p. 271.
9. Cf. Gershom Scholem, particularly his *Major Trends in Jewish Mysticism*, 3rd edn (Thames & Hudson, London, 1955).
10. Cf. Bamberger, *The Story of Judaism*, pp. 243ff.
11. Abraham Farrisol quoted in H. Kremer (ed.) *Die Juden und Martin Luther* (Neukirchen, 1985), p. 175. See also A.H. Friedlander, 'Martin Luther und wir Juden' in Kremer, *Die Juden und Martin Luther*, pp. 288ff.
12. Moses Mendelssohn, *Jerusalem* (English translation by H. Samuels) (London, 1838), II, p. 98, cited by I. Epstein, *Judaism* (Penguin Books, Harmondsworth, 1959), p. 287.
13. A.H. Friedlander, *The Pittsburgh Platform* (Union of American Hebrew Congregations, New York, 1956), pp. 2ff.
14. Baeck, *This People Israel*, p. 376.

Further Reading

Bamberger, B. *The Story of Judaism* (Union of American Hebrew Congregations, New York, 1957), pp. 451–3
Epstein, I. *Judaism* (Penguin Books, Harmondsworth, 1959), pp. 325–32
Jacobs, L. *A Jewish Theology* (Darton, Longman & Todd, London, 1973), pp. 323–31

In the area of Holocaust literature and theology, an overview can be found in
Friedlander, A.H. (ed.) *Out of the Whirlwind: The Literature of the Holocaust* (Schocken Books, New York, 1976)

Two new one-volume histories of Judaism are highly recommended:
Johnson, Paul *A History of the Jews* (Weidenfeld & Nicolson, London, 1987)
Goldberg, David and John Rayner *The Jewish People: Its History and Religion* (Penguin and Viking Press, London and New York, 1987)

9 Christianity in the First Five Centuries

William Frend

Conflicts with Authorities, to 135 CE

In John Muddiman's chapter (pp. 91–110), the origins of the Christian movement were set in the Judaism of the period. It showed how Jesus and his first followers should be viewed chiefly within that context. It showed also how the Church began to expand to move outwards from its centre in Jerusalem, above all under the impulse of Paul. His mission succeeded in establishing congregations of Jewish and Gentile Christians in many urban centres in Asia Minor and Greece, and others too founded churches in Rome itself and elsewhere. In that early period, the dynamic impulse to spread the gospel, derived from the death and resurrection of Jesus, dominated the scene, despite certain tensions among those engaged in the work. However, within thirty years or so, serious difficulties and conflicts arose, presenting Christianity with its first major trials.

The equilibrium between Paul and the more conservative Jewish leadership in Jerusalem was ended by a series of events between 62 and 70 CE. First came the judicial murder of James by the combination of high-priestly rancour and the violence of the fickle Jerusalem mob, that had proved fatal to his brother thirty years before. Secondly, Christians in Rome came into violent conflict with the imperial authorities, and thirdly, the repercussions of the fall of Jerusalem to Titus in 70 CE had a profound influence on the future of the faith.

Up to the point where Acts breaks off its account of Paul, relations between the Roman authorities and the Christians had called for little comment. Luke, in his treatment of Sergius Paullus (Acts 13:7–12) and Gallio (Acts 18:12–18), attempts to show that senior Roman officials were friendly to Paul and his companions and were prepared even to protect them against the assaults of the Jews. In 64 CE all this changed. On 19 July of that year, a conflagration swept through Rome and destroyed two entire quarters of the city. Suspicion fell on the Emperor Nero (54–68 CE), known for his grandiose schemes of town-planning, for which a fire in the old quarters of the city would have been a help. The emperor had to find a scapegoat and whether or not he was put up to the idea by Jews and their sympathisers at court, such as the Empress Poppaea, he handed the blame on to the Christians. As the historian Tacitus wrote fifty years later, 'Nero fastened the guilt and inflicted the most exquisite tortures on a class of men, hated for their abominations, called Christians by the populace' (*Annales*, xv:44). Many were done to death in the Circus of Gaius and Nero. Though this persecution was an isolated event, it was remembered, and it put the Christians on the wrong side of legal precedent.

Equally fateful were events in Jerusalem. James had no capable successor. In 66 CE the Jews rose against Roman rule. However one may interpret the evidence, the Christians appear to have stood aside in the struggle. They survived, but had no share in the triumphs and disasters of the war that imprinted the names of Jerusalem and Masada for ever on Jewish history. With the reorganisation of Judaism and its revival as a religious (but not political) force by the Pharisees, the Christian position in Palestine became intolerable. Something of the hostility between Jews and Christians between 70 and 90 CE can be gleaned from the Gospels of Matthew and John, which were written at this time. With the exception of slow progress north-eastward into the Aramaic-speaking areas of Syria, and the still independent kingdom of Osrhoene, Christianity became a 'Western' religion with western Asia Minor as its centre and Greek as its language. The Pauline mission formed the basis for future Christian expansion.

The later books of the New Testament, written between 70 and 100 CE, and works by writers immediately after this period, show that the Church was still linked culturally to the synagogue. Its members accepted the Jewish Scriptures, eschatology, messianism, and the ethics of Judaism. They claimed to be 'saints' (i.e. set apart), just as did the Jews themselves (Jude 3, Heb. 6:10), their leaders continued to wear distinctive Jewish insignia of office (such as the *petalon* or gold band on the forehead), and their inspired writings were directed to the 'twelve tribes which are in the Dispersion' (Jas. 1:1). Only for them, the messianic prophecies in Scripture had been fulfilled by Jesus, and by Jesus alone. Otherwise, as the writer of the best-known Christian book of this period, the First Letter of Clement, indicates, the New Israel was the true successor of the Old.

For the Roman authorities, however, it had become clear that Christians and Jews were separate entities. In the 90s the Jews finally won their battle with the Christians for the right to be called 'Israel'. In a rough and ready style, the Roman authorities regarded those who kept the Law of Moses (i.e. were circumcised) as Jews, and those who did not could not claim the privileges of Jews. If they refused to worship the Roman gods they could be adjudged atheists and punished. In 112 CE Pliny, who had been sent by the Emperor Trajan (98–117) to stamp out maladministration in the Black Sea province of Pontus–Bithynia, had to deal with groups of individuals who had been denounced to him as Christians. He knew Christianity was an offence and the first batch of those brought before him was hauled off to execution. When some Christians recanted or claimed that they had ceased to be Christians, Pliny was in difficulties and wrote to the emperor requesting his advice. Trajan affirmed the illegality of the new religion, but conceded that they should not be sought out, and if they recanted they were to be pardoned (Pliny, *Letters*, x. 96 and 97). In *c.* 124, his successor, Hadrian (117–38), enlarged the scope of these concessions by obliging an accuser to prove that his intended victim had offended against the laws. If he failed to do so, the charge would rebound on him. Few, only determined adversaries of Christians would care to take that risk, and so long as the Church remained an insignificant Judaistic sect, its members were relatively free from molestation.

Opponents and Advocates of Orthodoxy

By about 130 CE the character of the Church was changing. Its mission had taken it far beyond the areas visited by Paul. It was beginning to attract pagans such as Justin Martyr (*c.* 100–65) who had no experience of the synagogue, and some of its intellectual leaders were attempting to find common ground between the Christian message and contemporary Greek philosophy. Prominent among these last were the Alexandrian Gnostics.

Since 1945 a great deal has come to light concerning the Gnostic movement, following the discovery of fifty-two Gnostic texts in a Christian cemetery at Nag Hammadi, near Luxor in the middle Nile valley. *Gnosis*, or knowledge, was already beginning to be claimed as the way of salvation alongside or even in preference to baptism in the period immediately after the Pauline mission (1 Tim. 6:20). The Gnostics were, as their name implies, individuals who took the gospel precept 'Seek and ye shall find' (Matt. 7:7) literally. Their quest for truth, if based on Jewish and Christian literature and ideas, sought to integrate every form of religious experience, derived from all sources, into their faith. They were prepared to loose Christianity from its historic links with Jewish prophecies relating to the Messiah and replace these with current Platonic and Stoic teaching through which the Scriptures would be interpreted. The incipient Christian hierarchy of bishops, priests and deacons, was replaced by the Gnostic teacher and his disciples. The salvation of the immortal soul replaced the concept of the resurrection of the body.

Yet for all their strange teaching, the Gnostic leaders, Basilides, Valentinus and Heracleon, dominated Christianity between 130 and 180; and Alexandria, where they were active, was the centre of the Church's intellectual life. It was, however, realised at the time that even if Christianity could no longer ignore philosophy, so radical a break from the Jewish Scriptures did not represent the tradition of the Gospels, even as interpreted by Paul.

Outstanding both as a leader and disciple of Paul was Marcion (*c.* 85–*c.* 160), son of the Christian 'bishop' of Sinope on the Black Sea. Marcion accepted the Old Testament as the history of the Jews, but this had nothing to do with Christianity. Christ 'had made all things new' and the contradictions between the teaching of the Old and New Testaments argued against Jaweh being his father and the Old Testament being the word of God. The story of man's redemption was contained in Luke's Gospel, Christ 'suddenly appearing' in the fifteenth year of Tiberius Caesar. Only Paul understood properly this message of redemption, and his letters together with Luke's Gospel made up the Christian canon of Scripture. Marcion's was a bold attempt to free Christianity from Judaism but like that of the Gnostics, it was too radical for acceptance at this time.

During the second century the 'Great Church', as it was often called (after the Great Congregation of Old Israel referred to in Neh. 5:8 and Ps. 22:25), had to concentrate on two main problems. First, there was the need to defend itself against its growing number of adversaries, Gnostics, Jews and the increasingly hostile pagan majority. Secondly, it had to establish its own identity as a third (religious) race, independent of Judaism and paganism, by systematising its beliefs, organisation and liturgy.

By 150, Christianity had become an identifiable cult organised on an urban basis under a bishop with a staff of clergy dependent on him. It was strongest in the towns of western Asia Minor, but like the Jewish Dispersion before it, had spread among other Greek-speaking communities, including the lower and immigrant classes in Rome. Its members, however, were not popular. Refusing to worship the gods, they were regarded as 'atheists' and darker rumours circulated about happenings during the celebration of their cult. The second half of the century witnessed sporadic but savage persecutions fuelled by popular suspicions and anger. One such outbreak at Smyrna in *c.* 165 cost Bishop Polycarp his life. In 177, forty-eight Christians were done to death in the amphitheatre at Lyons. Increase in numbers began to attract the hostility of educated provincials. One such, Celsus, a Platonist, probably from Syria, wrote *The True Doctrine*, branding the Christians as an illegal association that merited punishment (Origen, *Contra Celsum*, i:1), and warning his fellow provincials that even though they might be simply rebels from Judaism with characteristic Jewish beliefs (Origen, *Contra Celsum*, ii:2 and 4), they could no longer be ignored. Christians, however, were ready to take up the challenge. Between 140 and 190, educated members of the community wrote a series of tracts (Apologies) refuting pagan charges and setting out what Christians believed. These

Apologists, most notable of whom are Justin Martyr, Melito of Sardis, Athenagoras and the first Latin Christian writer, Tertullian, poured scorn on pagan beliefs and accusations against Christianity. Instead, they asserted that the Christians worshipped one God through Jesus Christ, who had fulfilled the prophecies relating to the Messiah in Scripture, and they claimed a moral superiority over paganism and Gnostic heresy alike.

This movement culminated in the teaching of Irenaeus (*c.* 140–*c.* 197), an immigrant to Gaul from Asia Minor, who became bishop in Lyons after surviving the massacre there. His five books *Against the Heresies* (*c.* 185) were directed mainly against the Gnostics, and followers of Marcion (*c.* 85–160). In the course of his argument, he set out a Rule of Faith based on the confession of Trinitarian orthodoxy, the birth, ministry, death and bodily resurrection of Jesus Christ, the work of the Spirit, the coming Judgement, and the universality of this message. He asserted the validity of both Testaments to demonstrate (against the followers of Marcion) that the same God who created the world was the Father of Jesus Christ, and finally, church government must be in the hands of presbyters who stood in the succession of the Apostles and on whom the charisma of the Spirit had fallen. Though he left a loophole for the Spirit imparting itself to others, not least Christian prophets, Irenaeus, through his teaching on doctrine and organisation and his stress on order and orthodoxy, deserves his title as the 'first Catholic theologian'. By the end of the century, with its Rule of Faith respected in all major episcopal sees, the selection of the canon of New Testament Scripture almost completed, and a set pattern of eucharistic service, based on the biblical account of the Last Supper which stressed the memorial aspect of the Lord's command and forgiveness of sins, the Christian Church was probably the strongest single religious force in the Greco-Roman world, except for the religion of the immortal gods of Rome.

A Century of Advance, 200–303 CE

The third century witnessed another transformation in the development of the Church. Up to this time, except for the Aramaic-speaking Christians in eastern Syria and beyond the Roman frontier towards Parthia, the language of the Church had been Greek. This had been an important factor strengthening the Church's organisation, liturgy and propaganda in the previous half-century. By 180, however, Christianity had taken root in Carthage and a Latin-speaking Church came into being, strengthened when in *c.* 230 Latin became the language of the Church in Rome. By 200 the historian becomes aware of the emergence of four or five main centres of Christianity, each with an independent interpretation of the faith. Rome, Alexandria, Antioch, Carthage and sometimes Ephesus were destined to dominate the history of the Church through the next two centuries. Their bishops would wield authority over wide areas surrounding their episcopal cities. These formed the basis of the patriarchates that came into being in the fifth century.

The third century was a period of continuous advance. The Church recovered its missionary sense that had been lacking largely since the time of Paul. By the 230s, the Church historian, Eusebius of Caesarea (*c.* 269–339) declared, 'Then, as was fitting, the faith was increasing and our doctrine was proclaimed boldly in the ears of all' (*Eccles. Hist.*, vi:36). Those who heard it included increasing numbers of the upper, literate classes in the eastern provinces of the Empire. The Church, too, was beginning to hold property, the first catacomb, that of Pope Callistus (San Callisto) dating from *c.* 200, and the number increased steadily as the century wore on. The art of the catacombs, realist, serene but powerful, drawing at this stage largely from the Old Testament and the baptismal and eucharistic liturgy, was another sign of self-confidence. A third was the construction of the first churches such as that at Dura Europos on the Euphrates frontier *c.* 232, with its paintings and frescos rivalling those of the Roman catacombs. With these developments went a strengthening of the administration through the emergence of the diaconate as the Church's administrators, while Rules of Faith developed into creeds that could be used as tests of orthodoxy.

Throughout the century the Church became stronger, wealthier and increasingly a challenge to the religion of the Empire. Not surprisingly, popular hostility to the Christians continued. During the reign of Septimius Severus (193–211), there were vicious outbreaks against the Christians in half a dozen cities of the Empire, including Rome, Carthage and Alexandria. For the government, Christianity had become a major internal issue. First, the Emperor Maximin Thrax (235–8) attempted to strike at the leadership, and then fourteen years later, Decius launched the first official persecution of the Church, in order to force its members to join Empire-wide sacrifices for the welfare of the state (250). Commissions were set up in every large centre, and all were called upon to sacrifice to the Roman gods. Each who had done so received a certificate (*libellus*) testifying to the fact. Some forty-three of these certificates have been found in Egypt. Though few were martyred, the blow to the Church's organisation and self-confidence was great, as when confronted with the choice of showing loyalty to the Empire or the Church, most Christians did their duty by the former. Nine years later, the Emperor Valerian (253–60) again unleashed a persecution, this time aimed at Christian leaders and property. His victims included Pope Xystus II and his deacon Laurence (August 258) and Cyprian, Bishop of Carthage (14 September 258). The measure was carried out energetically by the provincial governors. Bishop Frumentius of Tarragona had the following brief discussion with the provincial governor.

Governor Are you the bishop?
Frumentius I am.
Governor You were.

And Frumentius was hurried off to execution.

Even so, these massive storms were weathered and, when in *c.* 260 the Emperor Gallienus restored to the Church its property and acquiesced in its *de facto* existence, its survival was assured.

Expansion, however, brought its own problems. By 200, hopes of an immediate Second Coming of Christ had faded, except among some groups of Christians mainly in Phrygia (in Asia Minor) and North Africa. But, if Christ would not be returning, how was he to be worshipped as a God? Between 190 and 230, Rome became the centre of obstinate controversies, involving different schools of thought on this question. As a preliminary, a dispute over the dating of Easter enabled the Church to move away from dependence on the Jews' dating of the Passover (14 Nisan) for the Christian celebration of Easter, and incidentally brought the Papacy's claims to direct the churches' affairs from Gaul to Osrhoene into public debate for the first time. Then, opposite opinions were canvassed concerning the relations of the Persons of the Trinity. One group (known as Modalists) argued that the Son was simply an aspect (or 'mode') of the Father, who therefore himself participated in the suffering on the Cross. Another took the contrary view, that the Son was a human being who had been sanctified at baptism and 'adopted' into the Godhead on account of his pre-eminent virtues (Adoptionists). Though both ideas were deemed unorthodox, much was to be heard of them in the Trinitarian and Christological controversies of the next two centuries.

The major division of Christendom, however, resulted from the emergence of a Latin Church in North Africa centred on Carthage (in modern Tunisia). Throughout its history, which lasted until *c.* 700, the North African Church was to be a church of the martyrs, boasting saints such as Perpetua and Felicitas (executed in Carthage in March 203) and Bishop Cyprian (on 14 September 258), as well as fervent Apologists such as Tertullian. The North Africans regarded holiness, both collective and personal, as the key to salvation. The Church was a body of the elect, 'a society with a common religious feeling, a unity of discipline and a common bond of hope', wrote Tertullian in *c.* 197 (*Apology*, 39:1). It was also a society fed on the books of God, with a profound belief in the necessity of the presence of the Holy Spirit in all its members and in its rites, especially baptism. Its members accepted the reality of God's approaching judgement and hence the need of complete separation from pagan society, and indeed the state itself.

In the Greek-speaking East, on the other hand, Christianity was seen in spiritual and philosophical terms. The Christian moved towards God step by step and in a way which allowed pagan philosophy a positive role in that progress. Scripture was interpreted allegorically and not literally as in the West, and judgement was deemed to be remedial rather than punitive. Ultimately, the harmony of God and his creation lost at the Fall would be restored, and all would achieve salvation.

The differing tendencies of Eastern and Western Christian thought can be illustrated from the careers of two leaders, almost contemporaries, both of whom share the credit of contributing to ultimate Christian victory: Origen (185–254) of Alexandria and Cyprian, Bishop of Carthage from 248 to 258.

Origen was born probably of mixed Alexandrian Greek and Egyptian Jewish parentage, and his father, Leonides, became a Christian. As the historian Eusebius of Caesarea claims, 'he was noteworthy from the cradle' (*Eccles. Hist.*, vi.2:2). From the outset, he had an enormous interest in reading both secular literature and the Bible. In 202–3 his father was martyred during the persecution that struck Alexandria that year, and Origen's first thought was to join him, a venture in which he was frustrated as his mother hid his clothes! At the age of eighteen, he was appointed head of a school for instructing enquirers into Christianity that had been established in Alexandria. There was, however, a streak of fanaticism in his character, for not only would he have nothing to do with any heretic, but he took Matthew 19:12 literally and became a eunuch. This was to be a great disadvantage to him in his dealings with clerical superiors throughout his life.

At this stage, *c.* 210, however, he took a further and quite different step that was to influence his ideas profoundly. He attended lectures on philosophy under the Neoplatonist scholar, Ammonius Saccas. Whatever heritage of classical learning derived from his father was now awoken in him, and henceforth he would interpret the Christian Scriptures and message in terms of Neoplatonic philosophy. Thereby he would set the course for the great tradition of Byzantine and Orthodox theology.

Origen, however, remained a controversialist. His early works, down to 230, were directed mainly against the Gnostics and Jews. In a major work, *Peri Archōn* (On First Principles), begun *c.* 225, he sought to demonstrate, within the framework of the Alexandrian Rule of Faith, that existence began with God, but that God could never be without the active quality of love, which was transmitted continuously by his Son, or Word and Wisdom. The Holy Spirit was the highest of the angels created by God. Evil, like death itself, was not a positive force as the Gnostics claimed, but a negative element in creation that would gradually be eliminated as mankind achieved progressively greater harmony with God. Evil deeds would be punished but the aim of punishment was always remedial. Finally, God and creation would once more be in complete harmony. It was an optimistic creed, with the weaknesses that it depended too little on a literal understanding of Scripture and that the prospect of universal salvation included Satan himself—which ordinary Christians could not take.

Scripture, even though interpreted allegorically, as a philosopher was wont to interpret Homer or the legends of the Olympian gods, remained Origen's foremost interest. Before he died, he had written commentaries on practically every book in the Bible. That on John's Gospel, started *c.* 227, was a vast work in some thirty-two books and was directed against the commentary of the Gnostic teacher Heracleon written some fifty years before. There were elements of continuity between the two Alexandrian theologies.

Scripture still meant primarily the Old Testament, and many Christians resented that the copies they had to use had been compiled by Jews, whom they suspected of falsifying certain key texts. As early as *c.* 212, Origen, having gained a working knowledge of Hebrew, set to work to establish as near as possible a true text. The *Hexapla*, so called because the text was written in six columns, enabled readers to compare the Hebrew text of the Old Testament with the Septuagint and other texts in circulation. Demonstrating his inquiring mind, Origen added an additional text of the Psalms which he claimed to have found in a pot near Jericho. This vast work took nearly forty years to complete but proved that the Church possessed scholars and biblical critics of a high order.

Origen's career at Alexandria was interrupted in 231 by a long-standing quarrel with Demetrius, the Bishop of Alexandria. He was forced into exile and the last twenty-two years of his life were spent at Caesarea, the capital of Roman Palestine. Here, paganism (he wrote *Against Celsus* in *c.* 248), Monarchianism (to Origen, an over-simplified concept of the oneness of God), and the ever-present commentaries occupied his life, but he also left his mark as a teacher. We have a letter of thanks from one of his distinguished pupils, Gregory the Wonderworker, setting out in detail Origen's method of instruction. Origen believed that nearly all existing systems of philosophy were useful; but that Christianity alone could answer the problems that philosophers posed, and provide a truly rational understanding of the universe.

Origen was arrested and imprisoned during the Decian persecution, and died in 254. Before that, he had been consulted by the governor of the province of Arabia, and by the wisest of those emperors (Alexander Severus and Philip the Arabian) who had some sympathy with Christianity. His theology was never to be far from the minds of the contendents in the doctrinal disputes of the next century, but his true legacy was that he put reason into the forefront of the values for a Christian.

Cyprian was an entirely different person. If he was drawn from a rather higher class of society than Origen, his view of Christianity was almost diametrically opposed to his. If Origen was concerned with the nature of the Trinity and man's salvation through a right understanding of orthodox doctrine, Cyprian was concerned with the nature of the Church, and how salvation was to be achieved through it. For him the issue was who belonged or did not belong to the Church. Origen believed in the ultimate harmony of interest between Church and Empire, Cyprian did not. Paganism, whether cult or society or philosophy, was the work of the Devil and to be renounced and repudiated. In no way did the learning of this world assist the Christian on his way to salvation. Cyprian saw the Church as a united, hierarchically governed body, each community being under a bishop whose authority was as plain as was his responsibility for his flock on the Day of Judgement. There was no salvation outside the Church governed by Cyprian and his fellow bishops.

His legacy of fifteen treatises and eighty-two letters deals almost exclusively with the period of the Decian persecution (249–50) and its long aftermath. With the onset of the persecution, Cyprian had left Carthage. Control in a confused situation had fallen to the confessors (i.e. those who affirmed or 'confessed' their faith when challenged), mostly laymen, and these claimed the right of forgiving those who had lapsed. With no little skill Cyprian wrested control over the reintegration of the lapsed, and consequently the right to forgive sins, from Spirit-inspired laity to councils led by bishops. The council which he assembled after Easter 251 proved to be a major step in asserting the authority of the clergy over penances in the Western Church.

Cyprian's correspondence shows that the affairs of Carthage and Rome were closely interrelated. While Cyprian conceded to the Bishop of Rome a senior status, and regarded the see of Peter as providing the origins of episcopacy, he was not prepared to accept jurisdictional authority from Rome. In two disputes with Pope Stephen (254–7), Cyprian established principles which were to be lasting importance in Western Christendom.

First, in the autumn of 254, two Spanish congregations appealed to Cyprian over the head of Pope Stephen to prevent the latter restoring to office their bishops who had lapsed during the Decian persecution. Cyprian's council decided that no cleric who had committed a deadly sin, such as apostasy, and who no longer possessed the Holy Spirit, could remain in office and administer the sacraments. Congregations were in duty bound to separate themselves from such a minister. In September 256, in a dispute over the validity of baptism dispensed by Novatianist schismatics, another Carthaginian council attended by eighty-seven bishops decided, against Stephen, that no sacrament given by a minister not in communion with the Church was valid. Cyprian's martyrdom on 14 September 258 set a seal of sanctity on these decisions, though they prepared for the schism which was to rend the Church in North Africa through the whole of the next century.

During the last forty years of the third century, the Church attained the *de facto* status of an autonomous group within the Empire, under its own law and organisation. Its influence now began to extend to the countryside, the most obvious sign being the emergence of the monastic movement among the native Egyptians of the Nile valley, symbolised by the decision of Antony (250–356) to retire to the desert to practise the ascetic life in *c.* 270. By the end of the century the Church's power, especially in the eastern provinces of the Empire and in North Africa, would be proof against all efforts by the imperial authorities to reduce it to submission to the pagan state.

Diocletian and Constantine

The final test of strength came in 303 when Diocletian (284–305) had been emperor for nineteen years. Why this otherwise dour, canny ruler sought conclusions with the Christians is obscure, but the most likely reason is that he came to see the Christian Church as the single great independent organisation in an Empire which he and his colleagues were administering increasingly on unitary lines. It was a dangerous rival to the state that must be made harmless.

The persecution that began on 23 February 303 lasted for nine years. It started with administrative measures aimed at destroying the Church's organisation and literature. Churches were destroyed, Scriptures had to be handed over to be burnt, and clergy were forced to sacrifice to the gods. In addition, the lives of ordinary Christians were made burdensome by withdrawing any privileged status from upper-class (*honorati*) Christians and denying them the right to plead at law. There was, however, to be no bloodshed, and this in general was observed. After Diocletian's incapacity through illness (early 304) and abdication (1 May 305), however, power fell to his more anti-Christian successors, in particular Galerius (Caesar 292, Augustus 305–11) and his deputy (Caesar) Maximin (d. 313). A series of edicts extended the persecution to the laity and made death the penalty for refusal to sacrifice. Repression was especially severe in North Africa during 304 and in Egypt from 308 to 311. There, hundreds died in savage acts by the authorities. To this day the Coptic era counts from the accession of Diocletian. In retrospect, his reign marked the Church's baptism of blood.

In the spring of 311, however, Galerius fell ill. In desperation he sought the help of the Christian God. On 30 April 311, six days before he died, he signed an edict that effectively ended the persecution. In this edict he accepted that the displeasure of the Christian God could not be provoked without danger, but the immortal gods of Rome were still the guardians of the state. Christians might exist again, so long as they behaved themselves ('did nothing contrary to good order').

In the West, however, the persecution had ended in 305. Galerius' colleague, Constantius, had not reopened it. When he died at York on 25 July 306, his son Constantine was immediately proclaimed emperor by his father's troops. A period of confusion ensued, but by the spring of 312 Constantine was effectively Emperor of the western Roman provinces and only Maxentius, son of Diocletian's western colleague, Maximian, stood in his way to Rome and sole power. The decisive battle at the Milvian Bridge some five miles north of Rome on 28 October 312 was won by Constantine and he entered the city in triumph.

In 310 Constantine had had a vision of Apollo, promising him a victorious reign of thirty years, and so far that promise had been kept. On the eve of the decisive battle with Maxentius, however, he had had a second vision, this time susceptible of a Christian interpretation. 'Constantine', says a contemporary Christian author, Lactantius, 'was directed in a dream to mark the heavenly sign of God on the shields of his soldiers and thus join battle. He did as he was ordered and with a cross-shaped letter X with the top bent over, he marked Christ on the shields' (*On the deaths of the Persecutors*, Ch. 44).

Contemporaries believed that Constantine had benefited by some form of divine aid, and there can be little doubt that from that moment on he moved towards acceptance of the Christian faith. For some years however, his personal inclination towards Christianity was balanced by his regard for the Sun God whose companionship he continued to claim on his bronze coinage (i.e. that with Empire-wide use by ordinary people) until *c.* 325. His actions, however, foreshadowed future developments; from the moment of his victory over Maxentius he was determined that the last embers of the persecution against the Christians should be extinguished. In February 313 he met his colleague Licinius, who was emperor in the Balkan provinces of the Empire, and there at Milan drew up the famous Edict which marked the official end of the Great Persecution. In contrast, however, to that of Galerius nearly two years before, Constantine and Licinius, while proclaiming religious freedom throughout the Empire, gave no place to the immortal gods, but on the other hand, the Christians were mentioned by name. Pagans were referred to as all others. Within a dozen years, when Constantine convoked the Council of Nicea in May 325, the immortal gods, who had sustained the Roman Republic and Empire for more than a thousand years, had been replaced by the God of the Christians. Few revolutions in the religions of mankind have been so swift and decisive.

Before that moment was reached, Constantine found himself obliged to deal with two serious disputes in the West and East respectively, which in their turn foreshadowed the future development of Western and Eastern Christendom. The Donatist movement arose from the situation in North Africa after the Great Persecution. The Church there was rent between those who were prepared to accept back Christians, including clergy, who had lapsed, on relatively easy terms, and those who regarded anyone who had sacrificed or handed over the Scriptures to the authorities as 'Betrayers' (*Traditores*). Following the decisions of Cyprian's councils, they regarded sacraments dispensed by these clergy as invalid and separation from them by their congregations as justified. In 311, however, an election to the vacant see of Carthage saw the consecration of a moderate, the archdeacon Caecilian, to this position of authority. He was challenged immediately by a coalition of interests, the most powerful of which was the Numidian Church. Constantine, however, angry that there could be divisions among the Christian ministry, backed Caecilian from the start, ordering his officials in North Africa to provide him with a considerable sum of money (winter 312/13). The opposition appealed to the emperor with a request for impartial episcopal judges (from Gaul) to adjudicate between them and Caecilian. For three years there was incessant legal activity between the opposing factions. Constantine first delegated the case to the Bishop of Rome, Miltiades (311–14), himself a North African; then, on his judgement being rejected by the opposition, summoned a council of bishops at Arles in August 314, the first episcopal council for the whole of the West, which included three bishops from Britain. Finally judging the case himself and finding Caecilian innocent (November 316), he declared him to be true Bishop of Carthage. His opponent, Donatus, by origin a Numidian, was condemned. In vain, the majority of North Africans supported Donatus. The remainder of Christendom stuck to Caecilian and this in the end assured his 'Catholic' supporters the upper hand in a schism which was to last as long as Christianity in North Africa.

In the East also, dispute arose out of events in the Great Persecution; but whereas in North Africa the issue was ecclesiastical and disciplinary, in the East it affected fundamentals of doctrine and belief. If the origins of the Donatist controversy extended back to Cyprian and the puritanical tradition represented by Tertullian and the martyrs, the Arian controversy had its roots in the tensions within Alexandrian theology represented by Origen and his opponents.

The issue appeared to come into the open suddenly, in *c.* 318, with a theological disagreement between Bishop Alexander of Alexandria and Arius, one of his senior presbyters. To quote the words of a fifth-century historian, 'Alexander attempted one day, in the presence of presbyters and the rest of his clergy, too ambitious a discourse about the Holy Trinity, the subject being "Unity in Trinity".' Arius, one of the presbyters under his jurisdiction, a man possessed of no little logical acumen, thinking that the bishop was introducing the doctrine of Sabellius the Libyan (i.e. the Modalist concept of the relationship between God and Christ), from love of controversy advanced another view diametrically opposed to the opinion of the Libyan, 'and agreed that if God begat the Son, there must have been when he was not, and in addition, as part of the order created by God, he must have possessed free will and was capable of vice as well as virtue' (Socrates, *Eccl. Hist.*, 1:8).

These ideas were repudiated by Alexander and his colleagues, but however absurdly Arius may have pressed them, they were a corollary of Origen's teaching seventy years before on the relations of God, Jesus and creation. Moreover, Arius had offended a powerful group of puritan-minded clergy (the Meletians) who had wanted sterner treatment of those who had lapsed in the Great Persecution than adjudged by Alexander. Arius had once agreed with them, but had changed sides. The Meletians were glad of the chance of embroiling him in a charge of heresy. Egypt and soon the whole of Eastern Christendom were split by the controversy, when in 321 Licinius, now emperor in the whole of the East, revived measures of harassment against the Christians. For him the 'Supreme God' was always Jupiter, while for Constantine he had become identified with the Christian God. The issue could not be avoided. Constantine attacked Licinius and defeated him at Chrysopolis on the Bosphorus on 18 September 324. Shortly afterwards, in a manifesto addressed to his newly acquired provinces, he proclaimed his faith in Christianity, offering only a scornful toleration to his pagan subjects. He now turned to the division within Eastern Christianity itself.

Constantine first tried to shame Arius and his opponents into agreement. This failed, and in the spring of 325 he ordered bishops from all over the Empire to meet at Nicea in western Asia Minor. The dispute raised by Arius and a variety of other controversies, such as the continuing problem of the date of Easter, were to be solved, and peace was to be established throughout the Church.

While this aim was not achieved, the Council of Nicea (20 May–July 325) was extraordinarily important. The summons by the emperor (as well as his active participation in its proceedings) showed the way to lay participation, if not control, in the affairs of the Church from that time onwards. Arianism was condemned, and the Creed of Nicea recognised Christ as active in the process of creating, and not as belonging to the created universe. The credal definition 'God from God, Light from Light, True God from True God, begotten not made, consubstantial with the Father', has survived with slight modifications to our own day. Nicea throughout the patristic period was the touchstone of orthodoxy with which in the fifth century even papal decisions must accord. It marked finally the Church's triumph over paganism. Henceforth, Christianity was to be the predominant religion of the Greco-Roman world.

The seal was set on this process by Constantine's dedication, on 11 May 330, of Constantinople as a Christian city that was to be his capital henceforth. His baptism at Easter 337, five weeks before his death, completed a religious progress that began with distaste for Diocletian's religious policy and some admiration for the Christians, and led to his being the architect of a religious revolution that was to change the course of the history of a large portion of mankind.

The Triumph of Christianity, 330–400 CE

The century and a quarter that separate the Councils of Nicea and Chalcedon (October–November 451) is the classic Age of the Fathers. It is the period that saw the definition of Trinitarian and Christological doctrine in the form that has survived to our own time. In the West, the Papacy emerged as the authoritative centre for ecclesiastical discipline and order, and relations with the Empire were delimited through the statecraft of Ambrose of Milan. Western theology found its great exponent in Augustine of Hippo whose ideas concerning the nature of the Church, of Grace and Free Will were to influence European theology across the divides of Reformation and Counter-Reformation. In the East, on the other hand, the conversion of Constantine led to the opposite process of integration of Church and State and the distinctive Byzantine polity that lasted until the fall of Constantinople in 1453, and, through the Tsars, in Russia until the revolution of 1917. These movements of thought produced leaders of equal calibre, in the East, the Cappadocian Fathers, Cyril of Alexandria and John Chrysostom, in the West, Augustine, Ambrose, Jerome and Pope Leo. The fourth century was an age of great changes in the intellectual and economic life of the Mediterranean and the Western European peoples. It was not a period of decline and decay.

Under Constantine's three sons (Constantine II, Constantius II and Constans) who succeeded him, much of this was already taking place. The advance of Christianity in the period down to the death of Constantius II in 361 demonstrated that the faith was not to be merely a state religion. The numbers of bishoprics multiplied; extensive Christian quarters, such as at Salona on the Dalmatian coast, and Hippo and Djemila (Cuicul) in North Africa, grew up either outside or within the boundaries of the cities; bishops became advisers to the emperor and prominent at all levels of civic and political life. The names of no less than 1,100 clergy, from pope to humble presbyters and deacons, have survived in contemporary records of the age.

In much of the Empire, some of the earlier Christian militancy had modified. North Africa was indeed torn by the Donatist schism, and the Donatists reflected the intransigencies of an earlier age. Elsewhere, however, Christianity was tending to absorb and convert traditional pagan values, and provide a climate in which a Christianised, but still recognisably Classical education flourished, extending, it is to be noted, to women. For the first and last time until the Renaissance and Reformation, laymen and women contributed significantly to the formation of Christian doctrine.

In its triumph, however, the Church was not to be united. Apart from fundamental differences of outlook between East and West, in the East itself the Creed of Nicea had opened up serious rifts. To the misgivings of a majority of Eastern bishops over the formula 'of one substance with the Father' as applied to Christ, was added the personality of Athanasius who had succeeded Alexander as Bishop of Alexandria in June 328. His long episcopate of forty-five years in all (328–73) was punctuated by five periods of exile which testified to his turbulent spirit as well as his uncompromising defence of the Creed of Nicea. Though Arius was not restored as a presbyter of Alexandria, Athanasius was condemned for unruly behaviour by a council held at Tyre in 335 and exiled to Trier by Constantine himself (November 335). While the Eastern bishops considered that the Creed of Nicea failed to distinguish adequately between Father and Son, the West accepted the Creed. In 340 Pope Julius (337–52) wrote to the Eastern bishops requiring them to justify their sentence against Athanasius or restore him forthwith. Not surprisingly the Easterners refused, and at a council held at Serdica (Sofia) in 342/3 bishops from the two halves of the Empire failed to agree, parting not even on speaking terms. The seeds of permanent schism between East and West had been sown.

Athanasius returned in triumph to Alexandria in October 346, but another thirty-five years were to elapse before the Second Ecumenical Council held at Constantinople in 381 finally accepted the Nicene formula with changes acceptable to the Eastern episcopate, thus formally ending the Arian controversy.

In the 350s East and West clashed again, this time over the emperor's authority in the Church. The Emperor Constantius had tried to impose on the Western bishops a formula of belief regarding the Son that replaced 'of the same substance' (*homóousios*) as the Father, by 'of like substance' (*homoíousios*). The aged Hosius, Bishop of Cordoba, who had accompanied Constantine to his victory over Maxentius in 312, spoke for the Western bishops, drawing on the analogy of the two swords (taken from Luke 22:38) to point to the distinction between imperial and ecclesiastical rule, with the implication that the latter was more authoritative. The emperor had no right to impose changes on beliefs affirmed by bishops in council. He must desist from harassing Athanasius. Constantius failed to get his way. In the West, an important precedent against imperial control of the Church had been established.

The pagan reaction under the Emperor Julian (the Apostate, 361–3) did not halt the progress of the Church, except perhaps in Britain. It did, however, destroy some of its self-confidence, and in North Africa, the restoration of the Donatist bishops who had been exiled by the Emperor Constans gave their church another thirty years of superiority over their Catholic rivals. In the East, however, Julian's reign incidentally contributed towards driving the factions within the Church to accept a uniform statement of belief based on the Creed of Nicea. It was the Cappadocian Fathers' (Basil of Caesarea, his brother Gregory of Nyssa and his friend Gregory Nazianzen) lasting claim to renown that the stark wording of that Creed was modified to include a definition of the work of the Spirit and interpreted to accord with the Platonic insights shared by most of the Eastern episcopate. When in 380 the Emperor Theodosius I (379–95) decreed that Catholic Christianity should be the sole religion of the Empire, East and West would agree on the definitions of the relations of the Persons of the Trinity as expressed at the Council of Constantinople in 381.

One further movement accompanied the triumph of Christianity, namely asceticism. What Antony had started in Upper Egypt in the reign of Diocletian took on. Alongside the individual call to the desert, there was growing up the view that ascetics could fulfil their vocation even better by living in communities. In Egypt, Pachomius, an ex-soldier (*c.* 290–346), decided to establish monasteries on communal lines, organised as self-sufficient villages. The idea became popular. At the end of the century, Jerome described how 'brethren of the same trades were lodged together in one house under its own superior. Manual work was encouraged. Excesses were discouraged.' Yet excesses, competitions even in fasting and abstinence, did take place, and in Syria, where monasticism seems to have developed independently, extreme rigours of individual ascetic achievement were the rule. In the next century, the pillar saints, such as Simeon (d. 459) or Daniel Stylites (d. *c.* 480) combined ascetic life on the lofty eminence of the capital of a column with a social purpose. They became tribunes of the people, settling disputes, forwarding petitions to the authorities, even the emperor, and denouncing evil-doers, as well as converting crowds of heathens who came to listen to their preaching. In Asia Minor, however, another aspect of the work of the Cappadocian Fathers was to bring monasticism there under the control of the episcopate and direct its energies towards social welfare in town and countryside alike. Hospitals, orphanages and schools began to flourish under their guidance. The monastic Rules drawn up by Basil of Caesarea have remained valid in Orthodox Christianity to our day.

In the West, on the other hand, asceticism evolved in contrary directions. In North Africa, the Donatist rejection of the idea of a Christian Empire and insistence on the irreconcilable distinction between Church and Empire produced a strange popular movement among the peasants on the High Plains of Numidia, part religious and part social-revolutionary, which drew its teaching from a literal understanding of the Gospels and the Book of Revelation. These Circumcellions, as they were known, saw the Devil at work in inequalities of wealth and in the existence of slavery. They ambushed wealthy landowners and forced them to change places with their slaves, running behind their own carriages. They prevented creditors from collecting debts and they freed slaves. The intensity and violence of their convictions was demonstrated by their ultimate aim of gaining the martyr's crown, even by leaping over precipices.

At the other end of the social scale, Christians including some of great wealth were interpreting a life dedicated to Christ as one requiring complete renunciation and estrangement from the world (*alienatio*). Men and women such as Martin of Tours, Jerome, Paulinus of Nola, Honoratus of Lérins and Melania the Elder and Younger, set examples of self-abnegation, and founded the first religious communities in the West. At the same time, their refusal to undertake public office and wholesale unloading of vast properties on to the market contributed to the weakness of the Empire when confronted by massive barbarian inroads in the first decade of the fifth century.

By this time, the Greco-Roman world was overwhelmingly Christian. One of the last bastions of the old religion was the senatorial aristocracy of Rome, but even this had succumbed by the end of the century. With a sure sense of self-preservation, its members became within a generation or so the most ardent supporters of the Papacy. All over the Mediterranean world, the period 380–410 witnessed the final phase of religious transformation, shown by the building of churches, the creation of parishes and the establishment of a religious life that had a considerable place for relics, martyrs' shrines and pilgrimages. Medieval Christianity had come into being.

The West: Ambrose and Augustine

Two men were responsible for major changes of direction in the Church of their day which affected Western Christianity for centuries to come.

Ambrose was born in 339, the son of Aurelius Ambrosius, the head of one of the few major Christian families in Rome, who had risen to be praetorian prefect of the Gauls (Britain, Gaul, the German provinces, Spain and a small area round Tangier). His father's comparatively early death, *c.* 340, left Ambrose in the care of the women members of the household and ensured him a pious Christian if also a good Classical education, which included what was becoming rarer in Rome, a sound knowledge of Greek. Ambrose followed his father into the administrative service. By 373 he was governor of the important north Italian province of Aemilia Liguria in which stood Milan, one of the imperial headquarters. In December 373 unexpected events resulted in his choice as Bishop of Milan by popular acclamation.

Ambrose contributed to the recognition of the ascetic way of life as the highest service to Christ but placed it firmly under episcopal control. He destroyed the remnants of Arianism in the West, and in 382–4 warded off the last great effort by the then pagan majority in the Roman Senate to safeguard the outward symbols of the pagan past in the Senate-house at Rome. His most lasting contribution to Western Christianity, however, concerned his dealings with the successive emperors, Valentinian II (375–92) and his mother Justina, and Theodosius (379–95).

Valentinian's court at Milan, though Christian, was not Catholic-orthodox. The young emperor was under the influence of his mother, a liberal-minded Sicilian named Justina, and considered the Creed of Ariminum of 359, that defined the Son as 'like the Father', as a reasonable statement of orthodoxy. To Ambrose, however, it was Arianism, and when early in 385 Justina requested a church outside the walls of Milan for the use of those who accepted Ariminum rather than Nicea, Ambrose refused. On 9 April, a memorable interview took place between the bishop and high officials of the court. The latter declared that the emperor was within his rights in asking for the church, 'as he has supreme power over all things'. To this Ambrose replied that 'if he required what is my own, my estate, my money and the like, I would not refuse it, although all my property belongs in reality to the poor, but sacred things do not belong to the Emperor'. Valentinian was told that if he wished to maintain his authority he should submit himself to God. The court gave way, as it did again next year in a similar situation. The superiority of the Church to the State in ecclesiastical affairs had been conceded.

The decisive moment came in 390. Now the emperor was Theodosius I. He had moved into Italy in 388 to defeat the usurper Magnus Maximus, whose army from Hadrian's Wall had made a bid for power in the West. Magnus Maximus was defeated and Valentinian sent to Trier to rule the Gallic provinces. Theodosius chose Milan as his headquarters. He was an able but headstrong ruler, and when a riot broke out in Thessalonica resulting in the death of one of his senior officers, he prepared a drastic punishment for the townsfolk. They were lured into the amphitheatre on the promise of a spectacular show, and when they were there, soldiers massacred 7,000 of them.

By any standards this was a terrible deed, made worse by Theodosius having indicated to Ambrose that less serious penalties would be imposed. Ambrose reacted calmly. In mid-September 390, he wrote to Theodosius. He praised his eminent qualities of statesmanship and zeal for the true faith, but his temper had got the better of him. He must be excommunicated. 'I dare not offer the Sacrifice. That which may not be done when the blood of one innocent person has been shed, may it be done where many have been slain? I believe not.' The effect has been lasting. Ambrose had asserted successfully the superiority of moral law over all expediency of state. The dead of Thessalonica could not be revived, but the Church in the West had shown that its voice could be heard. Emperors would experience the same treatment from popes in the Middle Ages.

Augustine's contribution to Western theology and ethics was different but just as lasting. He was a North African, being born at Thagaste (Souk Aharas) in Numidia (eastern Algeria) on 13 November 354. For once the date is important because it falls in the period of Catholic ascendancy in North Africa which lasted from 347 until 361. Thagaste had been a Donatist town before this, but switched allegiances and did not return to Donatism after the Emperor Julian had given complete toleration to all the Christian churches (in the hope that they would tear each other to pieces). Though some of Augustine's relations were Donatists, his experience was wholly within the Catholic Church in North Africa. The *Confessions*, which he wrote in 397, provide an outline of his early life and some insights (but by no means a complete picture) into his outlook. He was promising but not brilliant at school. Though never inclined to revert to his father's pagan religion, he had little sympathy with the religion of his mother Monica, for its moralism and literal acceptance of Scripture, particularly the Old Testament. When he went to the University of Carthage in 372, his mind was opened by the works of Cicero and his religious sense satisfied by the questioning, rationalist, yet wholly dualist interpretation of Christianity put forward by the Manichees. These were disciples of the Persian religious reformer, Mani (216–77), who preached a universal faith based on Gnostic dualism with the addition of Buddhist and Zoroastrian elements. In North Africa, the Manichees formed cells, often within the Catholic Church, among the literate members of the community. They rejected the Old Testament, emphasising instead the dualistic passages in the Pauline Epistles, and venerated Mani as 'the apostle of Jesus Christ'. It was to this sect that Augustine belonged for nine impressionable years (373–82).

Augustine's ambitions were towards a career in public service. His ability as a speaker gained him the position of Professor of Rhetoric and official spokesman at the court of Justina and Valentinian II at Milan in 384. There, the pressures were on him to revert at least nominally to orthodox Christianity and to marry a suitable heiress. His faithful mistress was returned to North Africa. He heard in the sermons of Ambrose a more acceptable, allegorical interpretation of the Scriptures. His own reading of Neoplatonist works freed him finally from the dualism of the Manichees. His mother's arrival in Milan and his own inability to reconcile himself to a two-year wait for his prospective wife strengthened the ascetic ideal in his conscience. He was ready to listen to stories of the conversion of Neoplatonists (such as Marius Victorinus in Rome) and brilliant young civil servants (like himself) to ascetic orthodox faith. His conversion came in August 386 and he was baptised in Milan Cathedral at Easter 387.

Augustine did not have the chance to escape from the world, as Paulinus of Nola had done. His mother died at Ostia in October 387. Augustine returned to Africa. At first he established a monastery at Thagaste, but in 391 (while on business for his monastery) he found himself ordained priest at Hippo on the coast of Numidia. Four years later he was bishop.

The ideas for which Augustine is famous grew directly out of the two great controversies in which he was engaged throughout the rest of his life, first with the Donatists, from 399 to 412, and secondly with Pelagius and his followers, from 413 to 430. Against the Donatists, Augustine was able gradually to marshal imperial and official aid and finally have them proscribed after a three-day conference at Carthage in June 411. The issues had been the nature of the Church and the relation of Church and State. Against the Donatist claim that integrity was the hallmark of a true church, Augustine stressed the universality of the Church, recalling God's promises to Abraham, to make him father of many nations (see Gen. 17:5), and the fact that the rest of the world had kept communion with Caecilian. He won his case, but in having the Donatists banned by law he opened a new chapter in the history of the Church's relations with the State. The emperor, he argued, had the duty of suppressing schism and heresy, and indeed of putting pressure on heretics to oblige them to convert. 'Compel them to come in' (Luke 14:23) was given a new and unsuspected meaning. Augustine had become the father of the Inquisition.

If freedom inevitably meant freedom to err, Augustine was unlikely to have much sympathy for those who like Pelagius believed in the inborn ability of man to live by God's commands: 'Be ye perfect, as your Father in heaven is perfect' (Matt. 5:48) would not have been ordered if it was impossible. For Augustine, however, the fall of Adam had bequeathed to all his successors a legacy of sin, from which only God's grace, given to a pre-ordained few, would rescue the sinner. Again, backed by the superb organisation of the North African Church he prevailed, this time over the south Italian episcopate and the instincts of the Papacy itself. The Pelagians were condemned in 418, though the issues of Free Will and Grace continued to be argued down to Augustine's death in August 430, and beyond. On the very eve of the barbarian invasions, Western Europe was bequeathed the legacy of the Augustinian teaching on Predestination and Grace.

What Think Ye of Christ?

The answer given to this question by Eastern Christendom in the fifth century was very different from that found in the New Testament. The Easterners had not been convinced that Pelagianism was a heresy, and letters of Augustine (newly found by Professor Johannes Divjak) show him using all his powers to persuade the Bishops of Alexandria and Constantinople that these views did indeed merit condemnation.

The East was concerned with metaphysical problems of salvation and redemption through Christ as God. But how? The Creed of Nicea had defined Christ as 'of the same substance as the Father'. What then was his relation to man? The Arians had claimed that the divine Word had occupied the same place in Christ as the human mind does in an individual, only that it was 'created' and was subject to human weakness as well as being exalted in its glory. These views were condemned, but the problem of the nature of Christ remained.

In the 370s one of the most active anti-Arians, Apollinaris, Bishop of Laodicea in Syria, wrote a series of tracts setting out in trenchant terms his belief that 'there is but one incarnate nature of God the Word, to be worshipped in the flesh with one worship'. This one nature (Monophysite) Christology was criticised by the Cappadocian Fathers as distancing Christ too far from humanity ('What he did not assume he could not redeem'), and it was condemned at the Second Ecumenical Council at Constantinople in 381. It corresponded, however, to what many people in the East, especially in Alexandria, believed. The Alexandrians were further angered by the decision of the council that Constantinople as New Rome should have precedence over the other sees in the East, yielding honorary precedence only to Old Rome.

Between 381 and 451 issues of precedence were inextricably confused with disputes over doctrine. Down to 449, Alexandria and Rome worked together in opposition generally to Constantinople and Antioch, though the emperors never lost control of the situation. Thus in 403, when Theophilus of Alexandria attempted to have John Chrysostom of Constantinople (398–404) removed from office on disciplinary grounds, the imperial court intervened to prevent this, only to order John into exile the next year on its own account.

By this time a new development was taking place which ensured that the Christological issue would not be allowed to die. After nearly three-quarters of a century, a school of theological beliefs was emerging in Antioch and its surrounding bishoprics that contrasted in almost every way with that of Alexandria. For the Alexandrians represented by Cyril who became bishop in 412, the key passage in the New Testament that described Christ's personality was John 1:14, 'the Word was made flesh and dwelt among us', i.e. the divine nature assumed humanity at the Incarnation, without being changed in any way. Jesus therefore was God in every sense. Against this Word-flesh Christology, the Antiochenes believed that Jesus possessed a fully human personality as revealed in the New Testament, but that God dwelt in him to a unique degree, the divine nature being joined to the human, enabling him to offer a perfect pattern of virtue for the redemption of humanity.

In 428, the Emperor Theodosius II (408–50) appointed an Antiochene presbyter named Nestorius as Bishop of Constantinople. Within two years his theology and that of Cyril had come into serious conflict. In particular, Nestorius was not prepared to accept that the Virgin Mary was *Theotokos* (Bearer of God), arguing that she was mother only of the man, Jesus. The Third Ecumenical Council, assembled on the orders of the Emperor Theodosius at Ephesus in June 431, favoured Cyril. His doctrine was held to accord more closely with the Creed of Nicea than that of Nestorius, and the latter was deposed. Alexandria emerged as the most powerful see in the East, and had the support of the Papacy.

A peace was patched up between Cyril and John of Antioch (428–41), and in this Formula of Reunion, agreed in April 433, Cyril was willing to accept that Christ should be confessed 'in two natures' (i.e. divine and human). The Antiochenes for their part were willing to agree the orthodoxy of the term *Theotokos* as applied to the Virgin.

The uneasy truce lasted until Cyril's death in 444. His successor, Dioscorus (444–51), was more intransigent than Cyril had been, and in a few years set about eradicating what he conceived as the remains of Nestorianism. This time he found an ally in Constantinople, in the Archimandrite Eutyches. The latter, having been condemned by his bishop, Flavian (446–9), for holding Monophysite opinions concerning the nature of Christ, appealed to the other major sees of Christendom, but in particular to Rome and Alexandria. Supported by the emperor, Dioscorus presided at a second council at Ephesus in August 449, and was able to pronounce sentence of deposition on Flavian and also on Domnus, Bishop of Antioch. Papal legates who had attended were insulted. The letter which they brought with them from Pope Leo known as the 'Tome of Leo', arguing the two nature Christology and requiring adherence to it, was refused a reading.

Two years later, the wheel turned full circle. Theodosius died suddenly (28 July 450). His successor Marcian (450–7) preferred communion between Old and New Rome to the supremacy of Alexandria. In the autumn of 451 a council of no less than 520 bishops assembled at Chalcedon on the east side of the Bosphorus. Dioscorus was deposed for indiscipline (not for heresy), and the Christological belief of Christendom was defined in balanced phrases providing a compromise between Alexandria and Antioch and accepting also the orthodoxy of the Tome of Leo.

The crucial passage, which remains the faith of Christendom, runs as follows:

> Following then the Holy Fathers, we all unanimously teach that our Lord Jesus Christ is to us one and the same Son, the self-same perfect in Godhead; the self-same perfect in Manhood; truly God and truly Man; the self-same of a rational soul and body; consubstantial with the Father according to the Godhead; the self-same consubstantial with us according to the Manhood; like us in all things, sin apart; before all the ages begotten of the Father as to the Godhead, but in the last days, the self-same, for us and for our salvation (born) of Mary the Virgin Theotokos as to the Manhood; one and the same Christ, Son, Lord, only-begotten; made known to us in two Natures, unconfusedly, unchangeably, indivisibly, inseparably; the difference of the Natures being in no way removed because of the Union, but rather the properties of each Nature being preserved and concurring into one Prosopon and one Hypostasis; not as though he were parted or divided into two Prosopa, but one and the self-same Son and only-begotten God, Word, Lord Jesus Christ; even as from the beginning the prophets have taught concerning him, and as the Lord Jesus Christ Himself hath taught us, and as the symbol of the Fathers hath handed down to us.

The council also confirmed Constantinople's position as senior bishopric, barring only Old Rome's primacy of honour (Canon 28).

Chalcedon was a triumph for the Emperor Marcian, who with his lay advisers oversaw the proceedings of the council and, practically speaking, piloted the Definition through the acrimonious debates of the bishops. It was a triumph, too, for Cyril's theology, as modified by the terms of the Formula of Reunion. It was also an historic effort at compromise involving Alexandria, Antioch and Rome, and a supreme attempt to find a common interpretation of the faith acceptable to both Greek and Latin Christianity. Chalcedon remains one of the landmarks in the history of the Church.

The sequel, however, showed how brittle even the most finely constructed compromises can be. Rome never accepted Constantinople's standing. Apostolic foundation, its Popes argued, could not be compared with any civil status, such as was now Constantinople's as the Empire's capital. In addition, the majority opinion in the East outside Constantinople remained wedded to a Monophysite definition of Christ's person, and disliked Chalcedon. In 482 the Emperor Zeno (474–91) attempted to appease this opinion by publishing the *Henotikon* or Letter of Unity addressed to the Church of Alexandria, which acknowledged that Christ was 'One and not two', but did not repudiate Chalcedon. This and other similar efforts by his successors could not avert the gradual break-up of the religious unity of Christendom, until by the end of the sixth century, the great divisions of Latin, Orthodox, Nestorian and Monophysite had come into being and were destined to remain for centuries to come.

In five centuries the Church had moved from the position of reforming sect within Judaism to that of a world religion. To account for this, there was the contribution of the Jewish Dispersion which provided the Church with communities throughout the Mediterranean lands in which to work and the basis of an organisation and liturgy. But there was also intense conviction in the truth and relevance of the message itself and a willingness to die for it. Christian apologies were not always convincing; miracles were usually no more than what was expected of a religious movement; but to proclaim that death was liberation was a new phenomenon among the provincials of the Greco-Roman world. This, combined with worldwide organisation ensured that Christianity would survive pressures against it and prevail.

Further Reading

Baynes, N.H. *Constantine the Great and the Christian Church*, 2nd edn (Oxford University Press, Oxford, 1972)

Brown, P.R.L. *Augustine of Hippo* (Faber & Faber, London, 1967)

—— *Religion and Society in the Age of Saint Augustine* (Faber & Faber, London, 1972)

Chadwick, H. *Early Christian Thought and the Classical Tradition* (Oxford University Press, Oxford, 1966)

Fox, R. Lane *Pagans and Christians* (Viking, Harmondsworth, 1986)

Frend, W.H.C. *Martyrdom and Persecution in the Early Church* (Blackwell, Oxford, 1965)

—— *The Rise of the Monophysite Movement*, 2nd edn (Cambridge University Press, Cambridge, 1979)

Grant, R.M. *Early Christianity and Society* (Harper & Row, New York, 1977)

Greenslade, S.L. *Church and State from Constantine to Theodosius* (SCM Press, London, 1954)
Kelly, J.N.D. *Early Christian Doctrines*, 5th edn (A. & C. Black, London, 1978)
Robinson, J.M. *The Nag Hammadi Library* (Harper & Row, New York, 1978)
Stevenson, J. *A New Eusebius* (SPCK, London, 1957)
Young, F.M. *From Nicaea to Chalcedon* (SCM Press, London, 1983)

10 *Eastern Christianity since 451*

Hugh Wybrew

Chalcedonians and Non-Chalcedonians

The Council of Chalcedon (cf. p. 164) in 451 was a turning-point in the development of Christianity. For those who would come to be known as Orthodox it provided the basic dogma of the nature of Jesus Christ as both God and Man, united 'unconfusedly, unchangeably, indivisibly, inseparably'. It also marked the decisive victory of the imperial capital Constantinople in its struggle for supremacy in church affairs over its chief rival in the East, Alexandria. Constantinople was to be henceforth the centre of both Church and Empire, the symbol of their unity and the focus of the Christian universe.

But it was also the cause of the first major and lasting schism in the Church. For those who were to be termed by their opponents Monophysite, the dogmatic definition of 451 was unacceptable both as doctrine and as symbolic of the predominance of Greek culture over the other cultural traditions included within the Roman Empire. The Christians of Egypt, and in particular the numerous monks, saw the council as a betrayal of the teaching of Cyril of Alexandria. Christians in Syria detected in it signs of Nestorius' doctrine (p. 163). In both countries the monks were the spearhead of the defence of the local theological tradition against the domination of Hellenistic culture. The result was a powerful separatist movement inspired by both religious conviction and national sentiment which the Empire was unable either to contain or to suppress.

For two hundred years the struggle between Chalcedonians and non-Chalcedonians dominated imperial politics and church life. The Emperor Marcian tried to impose the Chalcedonian dogma on the Empire by force. After his death in 457 attempts were made to reach a compromise with the Monophysites. In 482 the Emperor Zeno promulgated the *Henoticon*, or Act of Union, devised by Acacius of Constantinople and Peter Mongus, Patriarch of Alexandria. It condemned Nestorius and Eutyches, affirmed the Creed of Nicea-Constantinople and the teaching of Cyril of Alexandria. It avoided any reference to the crucial question as to whether there were two natures or one in the Incarnate Christ. Rejected by Rome, it failed ultimately to satisfy either Chalcedonians or Monophysites, and caused a schism between Rome and Constantinople which lasted until 519. The churches in Egypt and Syria chose Monophysites as Patriarchs of Alexandria and Antioch. Constantinople often appointed Chalcedonian patriarchs, who were not accepted by the vast majority in those churches. The few who adhered to them were called Melkites—emperor's men—by the rest. State persecution only reinforced anti-imperial sentiment in Egypt and Syria. The last attempt to impose Chalcedonian bishops there was made by the Emperor Justinian (527–65), whose overriding ambition was to restore the unity of the universal Roman Empire. Its failure was followed by the development of an independent Monophysite episcopate alongside the imperial Orthodox episcopate. The schism between the Jacobite (Syria) and Coptic (Egypt) churches, and the Church of the Empire, became final. Such was the religious and political hostility of these churches towards the Empire that when the armies of Muhammad overran Syria and Egypt in the seventh century they were welcomed almost as liberators.

The Development of Byzantine Christianity

The Council of Chalcedon did not put an end to theological controversy even within the Byzantine Church. The influence of the third-century Alexandrian theologian Origen was still strong, particularly in monastic circles in Palestine. Some aspects of his teaching were condemned by Justinian in 543 in a letter to Mennas, Patriarch of Constantinople, and later that year at a council in Constantinople. Not long after, the Emperor also condemned some aspects of the teaching of Theodore of Mopsuestia, Theodoret of Cyrrhus and Ibas of Edessa, noted teachers of the Antiochene school closely linked with Nestorius. To resolve the continuing doctrinal disputes Justinian called the Council of Constantinople, the Fifth Ecumenical Council, in 553, which, under Monophysite pressure, condemned these so-called 'Three Chapters'. Rome, in the person of Pope Vigilius, was unhappy about the condemnation, but finally accepted the council's decision.

Controversy over Christological doctrine continued in the seventh century. The Empire had not abandoned all hope of reconciling the Monophysites, and renewed its efforts for union in the face of Persian invasion. After discussions with Monophysite leaders, the Emperor Heraclius (610–41) proposed making Chalcedon more acceptable to them by explaining that although there were two natures in Christ there was only one energy, or will. On the basis of this monothelite ('one will') doctrine, approved by Patriarch Sergius of Constantinople and Pope Honorius of Rome, a union between Orthodox and Monophysites was agreed in 632. It was opposed by Sophronius of Jerusalem. Heraclius tried to impose the new doctrine on the Church by his *Ekthesis* of 638, which forbade discussion as to whether there were one or two energies in Christ, and insisted there was only one will. It was accepted by two councils in Constantinople in 638 and 639, but Rome, under Pope Martin, opposed the new policy, which was resisted strongly within the Empire by Maximus the Confessor. Constans II withdrew the *Ekthesis* in 648, and issued a new edict, the *Typos*, forbidding the assertion of either one or two wills in Christ, and limiting teaching on the nature of Christ to what the first five Ecumenical Councils had defined. The Council of Constantinople of 680–1, the Sixth Ecumenical, reaffirmed the doctrine of Chalcedon, and insisted that two wills and two energies, human and divine, in Jesus Christ were a necessary consequence of Chalcedon. Attempts to heal the Monophysite schism by doctrinal compromise finally came to an end.

If the Church in the Empire was becoming firmly Chalcedonian, it was also becoming strongly imperial. Justinian saw himself as the Christian Emperor ruling the Christian Empire, which was the instrument on earth of God's purposes. That instrument, in the belief of the New Testament and the early Church, was the Church itself. But since Constantine's acceptance of Christianity, Church and Empire had come to be more and more coterminous. In Justinian's view, there was no place for a Church whose identity differed from that of the Empire. It came to be a commonplace in Byzantine thought that Church and Empire were related as body and soul. The earlier problem of relations between Church and State was replaced by that of relations between Patriarch and Emperor, the twin pillars upholding Byzantine society. It was a view deriving more from the pagan vision of the theocratic state than from Christian sources, and one which saw religion as a function of the State. The Church, and even monasticism, existed, according to this view, for the benefit of the Empire. Although this view was incompatible with the Church's own self-understanding, the Church in the Byzantine Empire was often too ready to accept the State's evaluation of its role in Byzantine society.

The centuries between the Council of Chalcedon and the outbreak of the iconoclastic controversy in the eighth century were formative for the Orthodox tradition. The Fifth Ecumenical Council of 553 approved a list of earlier Christian writers whose authority was undisputed. On the basis of their teaching Orthodox theology was consolidated. The doctrines of the Incarnation and the Trinity received their final form. The life of the Church was regulated by the canons issued by the council 'in Trullo' of 692, sometimes called the Quinisext, since its canons supplemented the doctrinal decisions of the Fifth and Sixth Councils, which did not concern themselves with disciplinary matters. Its forms of worship, deriving immediately from the tradition of Antioch, but influenced by the traditions of Jerusalem and other neighbouring churches, developed under the dominant influence of Justinian's Great Church of the Holy Wisdom in Constantinople. The growing cult of the Virgin Mary, Mother of God, and the saints, and the ascetic tradition within the Church, made their contribution to the services of the Byzantine Church and its calendar. Their main lines were laid down in this period, and were determinative of subsequent Orthodox worship.

The Byzantine Empire provided the historical and cultural setting in which the Orthodox tradition took shape, and which moulded it in all its aspects, doctrinal, liturgical, canonical, iconographic and devotional. But the Empire was constantly shrinking. Muhammad conquered Mecca in 630. By the time of his death in 632 he had united the Arab tribes on the basis of a new religious faith, which inspired their military expansion throughout the Middle East. By 642 the forces of Islam had overrun Persia, Syria, Palestine and Egypt. The barbarian invasions had already detached the West from the Roman/Byzantine Empire. Now the Empire finally lost the non-Greek part of the East. Byzantium became a Greek state rather than an international empire. The horizons of the Byzantine Church correspondingly narrowed. Constantinople was the only patriarchal see left within the Empire, and its position was as a consequence enhanced.

The Iconoclastic Controversy

Against this background the Church was torn, in the eighth century, by the bitter controversy over the use of icons. Representations of Christ, his Mother and the saints had been widely used in the Eastern Church for several centuries. Painted on board or made of mosaic, portable or attached to churches and other buildings, icons had come to play an important part in popular piety. Superstition often attached to their veneration, and the danger of idolatry was never far away. A powerful movement against the use of icons developed in the first half of the eighth century, and was supported by the Emperor Leo (717–41), who in 730 deposed Patriarch Germanus I and replaced him by the iconoclast Anastasius. Under his son Constantine those who venerated icons—iconodules—were openly persecuted. A council called by the Emperor in 754 in Constantinople condemned both the veneration and the making of images. Fierce persecution of the iconodules, chief among whom were the monks, followed. It came to an end under Leo IV, on whose death in 780 his widow the Empress Irene prepared the way for the restoration of icons. In 787 a council, the Seventh Ecumenical, met in Nicea, and proclaimed the Orthodox teaching on icons and their veneration, which had been formulated in the earlier part of the century by John of Damascus. The council endorsed his view that the legitimacy of icons derived from the

Incarnation itself, by which the invisible God became visible in Jesus Christ, and by his Incarnation sanctified the material creation. Icons were to be made and placed, together with the image of the cross, in churches and houses, inside and outside, and were to be venerated with the worship of reverence, clearly distinct from that of adoration, reserved for God alone.

Persecution of iconodules was renewed after Irene's death in 802, and continued until 842, under Leo V, Michael II and Theophilus. On the first Sunday of Lent 843, under Theophilus' widow Empress Theodora, icons and their veneration were finally restored. So integral to Orthodox faith and worship had icons become that the 'Triumph of Orthodoxy' has been commemorated annually ever since on the first Sunday in Lent. The council of 787 was the last of the Ecumenical Councils which defined Orthodox dogma, and the Orthodox Church came to think of itself as the Church of the Seven Ecumenical Councils.

Church and State after Iconoclasm

Iconoclasm, though originating within the Church, had ended as a policy which the Empire attempted to force on the Church. The flaw in the 'symphony' of Church and State of which Justinian had been the architect became apparent. The eighth-century emperors, fighting to defend and preserve the Empire, sought to subordinate the Church to the State, seeing themselves as responsible to God for both aspects of Byzantine life. In persecuting the monks, the chief defenders of icons, the iconoclastic emperors were also engaged in conflict with that element in the life of the Church which was most conscious of the distinctive vocation of the Church to be in the world but not of it, and so to distance itself from the State. The revival of monasticism in the early ninth century under the inspiration of St Theodore of Studios (759–826) contributed to a reappraisal of Church–State relations within the Church, from which there emerged the late-Byzantine pattern of the theocratic state. This pattern was embodied in the introduction to Basil I's law code issued towards the end of the ninth century. Known as the *Epanagōgē*, it set out the respective functions within the Christian Empire of emperor and patriarch. Each had his God-given task to perform, and neither was subordinate to the other. The image of the pious emperor kneeling before Christ became a frequent one in the centuries after the defeat of iconoclasm, and reflected a different understanding of the emperor's position from that held by Constantine, Justinian and the iconoclastic emperors. In practice the balance in the relationship between emperor and patriarch often failed to correspond to the theory, and with the gradual weakening of the Church, and the increasing pressure exerted by the emperors, the position of the patriarch became more and more subordinate to that of the emperor. The Church became thoroughly Byzantine, losing any awareness of itself as called to any kind of prophetic role within the Empire.

The Fixing of the Orthodox Tradition

The iconoclastic controversy was the last major doctrinal dispute within the Byzantine Church. Once it was settled, the Church entered a period of doctrinal stability. Any who might have disturbed the consensus which had been reached were now outside the bounds of the Empire, and therefore also of the Church. Imperial policy, recognising the harmful effect doctrinal controversy had on the State as well as on the Church, encouraged conservatism rather than creative thinking in the Church. The *De Fide Orthodoxa* of St John of Damascus (*c.* 675–*c.* 749) referred constantly to what previous theologians had said, and from then on the tradition was faithfully handed on as a fully developed whole. The worship of the Church, too, became fixed. A period of creative writing in the eighth and ninth centuries, which produced liturgical texts of great beauty and spiritual depth, was followed by the standardisation and fixation of liturgical texts and rules, so that little development took place after the tenth and eleventh centuries.

Only one further doctrinal controversy of any significance occurred. Mount Athos, in northern Greece, became from the tenth century the centre of Byzantine monasticism, and it was the one remaining home of speculative theological thinking. In the fourteenth century the hesychastic movement in monastic spirituality gave rise to a dispute as to the exact nature of the light which shone forth from Christ at the Transfiguration, and which some of the monks claimed to be able to see in prayer. Gregory Palamas (*c.* 1296–1359) defended the monks' teaching against the attacks of the monk Barlaam, a Greek from Calabria who had come under the influence of Western nominalism and taught the complete unknowability of God. Gregory defended the method of prayer practised by the hesychasts, and affirmed the possibility of a real union with God through his deifying grace. He distinguished between the essence of God, which is unknowable, and his energies, consubstantial with his essence, through which he communicates himself to the world. At a council in Constantinople in 1341 Palamas' views were upheld, and Barlaam condemned. His teaching was accepted by two more councils at Constantinople in 1347 and 1351, and became an integral part of Orthodox doctrine.

Relations with the West

The Council of Chalcedon was accepted equally by Old Rome and New Rome. But relations between the western and eastern parts of the Church gradually became more and more strained. The East, while usually tacitly accepting papal claims from Leo the Great (440–61) onwards, increasingly resented them. The insertion of the *Filioque* (the Spirit proceeds from the Father *and the Son*) in the Creed of Nicea–Constantinople in the West, though resisted in Rome itself until the early eleventh century, provided potential material for dogmatic conflict. The collapse of the Western Empire under barbarian attack in 476 and the consequent political separation of West and East contributed to the further alienation of the two parts of the Church, which the growing preoccupation of the Empire with the East after Justinian only intensified. Developing in very different political and cultural circumstances, East and West gradually ceased to communicate much with each other. The establishment of the Carolingian Empire with the support of Rome in 800 increased the political rivalry between the two different worlds, which were becoming self-contained and self-sufficient. A major conflict broke out between them in the ninth century, when in the course of the so-called Photian Schism Photius, Patriarch of Constantinople, wrote in 867 a letter setting out Eastern objections to the *Filioque* and pointing to the divisive nature of the papal claims. Later contacts between East and West were the result, from the eleventh century, of the Byzantine Empire's need for Western help in resisting the Turks, and the Papacy's need for Eastern help in dealing with the Normans. Negotiations for union, focused on the Council of Lyons in 1274 and the Council of Florence in 1438–9, continued until the fall of Constantinople in 1453. The formal schism of 1054, when the Roman legate Cardinal Humbert excommunicated Patriarch Michael Cerularius, who in turn anathematised Humbert, took place against the background of negotiations for mutual political assistance. The arguments revolved around ritual rather than doctrinal divergences. The schism was neither complete nor final. Complete separation and irreconcilable hostility came about only as a consequence of the Crusades, and the capture and sack of Constantinople by the Fourth Crusade in 1204. From then on, whatever agreements between East and West were reached by church leaders under the pressure of political necessity were rejected by the instinctive hostility and mistrust of the mass of the Orthodox people towards Rome. Orthodoxy became finally Eastern, and turned its back on the West.

The Conversion of the Slavs

While the Empire was contracting, and the Byzantine Church becoming more conservative, a remarkable expansion of Orthodox Christianity was beginning. Slav tribes had moved into the Balkans from the sixth century. From the seventh century they were gradually converted to Christianity in those areas where they had settled. The great apostles of the Slavs were two brothers, Greeks of Thessaloniki, Constantine and Methodius, who learnt the local Slav dialect. In 862 the Emperor Michael III sent them to Moravia, where they carried out extensive missionary work with the approval of both Constantinople and Rome. Constantine, by now the monk Cyril, died in Rome in 869. When Methodius died in 885 the Moravian mission collapsed. But the two brothers had laid the foundation of Slav Christianity by devising the Glagolitic alphabet for the Slav language, and translating the Bible and essential theological and liturgical texts into the Slav language.

The Bulgarian Empire was the first Slav state to adopt Christianity as its official religion. From the eighth century the pagan Bulgar Khans were consolidating their rule over Slavic tribes which had settled within the Empire. By 852 when the Khan Boris began his reign an independent Bulgar state had emerged out of prolonged wars with the Empire. Byzantine culture exercised a powerful attraction on the Slavic peoples, even while they sought to conquer the Empire for themselves. Since Byzantine culture and Christianity were inseparable, they wished to be baptised. At the same time they had no intention of surrendering their national independence. Boris, baptised in 869 after a defeat inflicted on the Bulgars by the Empire, became a devout Christian who ended his life as a monk.

The Byzantine Empire saw the baptism of Boris as a means of keeping the Bulgar state within the Empire. Boris saw it rather as the first step towards an independent empire for himself and his people. Another was the establishment of an independent church. After fruitless negotiations with both Rome and Constantinople for an independent archbishopric, he finally persuaded the latter to let him have a semi-autonomous archbishop. In the course of the next hundred years the work of Cyril and Methodius bore abundant fruit in the Bulgarian Empire. Under Tsar Simeon (892–927), who received the title of Emperor from Rome and whose archbishop became Patriarch of an autocephalous church, with his see first at Preslav and then at Ohrid, the Bulgarian Church took up and developed their work. The Glagolitic alphabet was replaced by the Cyrillic, closer to Greek, and many Christian writings were translated into Slavonic. Bulgarian Christianity was in fact Byzantine Christianity translated into Slavonic, and it was the source from which subsequent Slav Christianity derived.

The first Bulgarian Empire came to an end in 972, defeated by the Byzantine Emperor Basil II 'the Bulgar-Slayer', and with it came to an end the effective independence of the Bulgarian Church. The empire revived towards the end of the twelfth century, and the patriarchate, suppressed by the Byzantines in 1018, was re-established at Trnovo in 1235. Under Simeon the Bulgarians had made their own the theocratic vision of Byzantium: Empire and Church, Emperor and Patriarch, went hand in hand. Orthodoxy and nationhood were inextricably linked. The quest for national independence led to war against Byzantium, and the Christianisation of the Slavs led paradoxically to the first civil war in the Orthodox world.

The characteristics of Bulgarian Orthodoxy were also those of the Serbian Church. In the ninth century Christianity in its Byzantine form took firm root among the Serbs. While Byzantium and Bulgaria fought, the Serbs, influenced now by the one, now by the other, grew into national self-consciousness. When Prince Mutimir (860–91) was baptised, Christianity was made the national religion. Like the Bulgarians, the Serbs maintained relations with both Rome and Constantinople, before finally adhering to the latter. Under the Grand Zupan Nemanya at the end of the eleventh century, the Serbs were united in independence of Byzantium. In the reign of his son Stephen the First-Crowned, the Serbian Church gained recognition of its autonomy from the Byzantine emperor in Nicea. Stephen's younger brother Rastko had become a monk with the name of Sava on Mount Athos in 1191. When his father Stephen Nemanya retired there in 1196, they founded the Serbian monastery of Hilandari, which became the centre of Serbian religious life and culture. Sava returned to Serbia to be abbot of Studenica, and in 1219 was consecrated by the Greek Patriarch in Nicea as the first archbishop of the Serbian Orthodox Church. From his seat at the monastery of Zica he established a complete church organisation in Serbia, and effected a thorough renewal of the nation's religious life. In 1233 he retired from office. Since his death he has been venerated as the true founder of both Serbian Church and Serbian State.

Under Stephen Dushan (1331–55) Serbia reached a peak of achievement. In 1346 Dushan was crowned as Emperor of the Serbs and the Greeks, and in the same year gave the archbishop the title of patriarch, with his seat at Pec. His aim was to unite Byzantines, Bulgarians and Serbs in a single empire, but he died in 1355 on the eve of a campaign against Constantinople. The Byzantines recognised the Patriarchate of Pec in 1375.

While the Bulgarians and the Serbs gained their ecclesiastical independence of Constantinople, the Church in the two Romanian principalities of Wallachia and Moldavia, and the Romanian Orthodox in Transylvania, remained under Constantinople. Christianity had been brought to the Roman province of Dacia at least by the fourth century, and a Latin-speaking Church grew up among the Romanised Dacians. Little is known of its history in the Middle Ages, but by the fourteenth century it was firmly within the sphere of influence of Constantinople. Although the language of the people was derived from Latin, Slav influence had made Slavonic the language of worship. The Orthodox Church was the one organisation which united the Romanian people, politically divided, and as in Bulgaria and Serbia it became inseparable from the Romanian sense of nationhood.

Orthodoxy under Turkish Rule

In 1453 Constantinople fell to the army of the Turkish Sultan Muhammad II. By 1460 Bulgaria, Serbia and Greece were parts of the Ottoman Empire, and the Romanian provinces soon came under Turkish suzerainty, although they were never incorporated into the Empire. With the exception of Russia, the whole of the Orthodox world was to remain under the Muslim Turkish yoke until the nineteenth century.

The Turks in theory allowed the Church considerable freedom. In practice the Sultan possessed absolute power, and Christians were often treated as cattle. As the Turkish Empire grew weaker and more corrupt, so the treatment of Christians grew worse. The seventeenth and eighteenth centuries were particularly difficult times for the Orthodox in the Empire. Financial oppression, persecution and frequent killings reduced the Christian population to misery, and not a few Christians apostatised and became Muslims.

The Turks regarded Christianity as the religion of the Greeks, and the Patriarch of Constantinople as the head of the Greek *milet*, or nation, as well as their spiritual leader, and so as responsible for their civil administration. Completely dependent on the sultans, patriarchs were frequently deposed and replaced by the civil power. In 1821 Gregory V was hanged at the gate of the Patriarchate in Istanbul on Easter Day for his support of the Greek revolt against Turkish rule. The position of Christians actually grew worse when in 1856 they were given equal rights with Muslims within the Empire, which deprived them of the possibility of outside protection.

During the Turkish period education, both general and theological, declined. From the sixteenth century Western influences, both Catholic and Protestant, made serious inroads into the Orthodox tradition. The Confession of Cyril Lukaris, Patriarch of Constantinople, published in 1629, had a decidedly Protestant character. Persistent efforts were made by Rome to persuade the Orthodox to recognise the Papacy, and through their provision of schools Catholic missionaries exercised considerable influence on the Greeks. But in spite of the political and economic oppression to which the Orthodox were subjected, in spite of the decay of education and the pressure exerted by Western Churches, and in spite of the narrowing effects of nationalism within the Church, the inner life of Orthodoxy was not quite extinguished. The publication in 1782 in Venice of the *Philocalia* is evidence of the continuing vitality of the Orthodox spiritual tradition. A collection of ascetical and mystical writings from the fourth century to the fifteenth, made by St Macarius and St Nicodemus of the Holy Mountain (as Mount Athos was called), it was translated from Greek into Slavonic in 1793 by Paissy Velichkovsky, a monk of Russian origin living at the monastery of Neamt in Moldavia, and has become one of the most valued books in modern Orthodoxy and in other churches.

The Turkish period saw the final stage in the process by which Orthodoxy became, in the Greek mind, inextricably linked with Hellenism. After the Crusades Orthodoxy became Eastern and Greek, in opposition to the Latin West. Increasingly Hellenism, which for the early Church Fathers meant paganism, came to be regarded as the source of the Greek national tradition. The fall of the Byzantine Empire only served to reinforce the significance of Hellenism, whose symbolic embodiment became the Ecumenical Patriarch. The Patriarch inherited, in part, the role of the Emperor, and used, as all Orthodox bishops came to do, some of the imperial insignia: the *sakkos* (the emperor's formal robe), the mitre, and the double-headed eagle. Increasingly, under Turkish rule, the Patriarchate of Constantinople tried to impose Greek culture on the Slav and Romanian Churches. From 1397 Greek clergy were sent to Bulgaria. The last trace of Serbian ecclesiastical independence vanished in 1775 with the suppression of the Patriarchate of Pec. The Arabic-speaking Orthodox churches in the Middle East came under the authority of Constantinople, which appointed Greek patriarchs to Alexandria, Antioch and Jerusalem. Orthodoxy, having first become Eastern, under the Turks also became national. The non-Greek Orthodox were forced into an anti-Greek attitude in order to preserve their own national traditions. When the Turkish Empire began to decay finally in the nineteenth century, national liberation movements led to the establishment of independent Greek, Bulgarian, Serbian and Romanian states, each with its own national Orthodox Church aspiring to complete independence from Constantinople. In 1833 the Church of Greece became self-governing under its Holy Synod, presided over by the Archbishop of Athens. The Orthodox Church in Romania claimed independence in 1859, and it was granted in 1885. In 1879 the Serbian Church became autocephalous (i.e. independent within the Orthodox fold), with the approval of Constantinople, and in 1920 the Patriarchate was restored in Belgrade. The Bulgarian Church claimed autocephaly under an Exarch in 1870, and was excommunicated by Constantinople for the heresy of philetism, or nationalism. Only in 1945 was the breach healed. The Metropolitan of Sofia took the title of patriarch in 1953, receiving recognition by Constantinople in 1961. In Romania the Holy Synod was replaced as supreme church authority by a patriarch in 1923.

Christianity in Russia

From Byzantium Christianity in its Orthodox form spread to Russia at least from the ninth century. The baptism of Vladimir, Prince of Kiev, in 988 made Christianity the religion of the Kievan state. Imposed in its Slavic Byzantine form on the people by the state, Orthodoxy quickly struck deep roots, and developed its own Russian qualities. It was nourished by the Slavonic literature stemming from the work of St Cyril and St Methodius, and soon by native writing. The spiritual centre of the Kievan Church was the Monastery of the Caves in Kiev, founded by St Anthony in 1051 and organised by St Theodosius, the father of monasticism in Russia. Church and state worked together in Kievan Russia to create a society inspired by Christian ideals. But paganism remained strongly entrenched among the ordinary people; and the fact that Russia had inherited an Orthodoxy already fully developed and to a large extent fixed meant that Russian Orthodoxy was marked from the beginning by intense conservatism.

The Kievan state was destroyed by the Tartar invasions of 1237–40. Under Tartar domination the centre of state power in Russia moved north, first to Suzdal and then to Moscow. The Metropolitan of Kiev also moved north, settling in the early fourteenth century in Moscow. The Church gave its full support to the princes of Moscow in their policy of uniting under their own rule all the Russian lands, in order to drive out the Tartars, but in doing so came increasingly under the domination of the state. Church as well as state underwent spiritual and moral decline as a result of the Tartar yoke.

Meanwhile Russian monasticism, nourished by the hesychastic revival on Mount Athos in the fourteenth century, flourished under the guidance of St Sergius of Radonezh (1320–92) and his disciples. The monastery of the Holy Trinity at what is now Zagorsk became a national religious centre, and the many monasteries in the north of Russia founded by St Sergius and his followers were centres both of missionary activity and spiritual culture, sources of light in a society often brutal and corrupt.

The union with Rome signed by the Greeks at Florence in 1439 deeply shocked the Russians, and encouraged them to declare their ecclesiastical independence of Constantinople in 1448, when Metropolitan Jonah was elected by a Russian council of bishops. The fall of Constantinople in 1453 seemed just punishment for the betrayal of Orthodoxy by the Greeks. The marriage of Ivan III of Moscow in 1472 to the niece of the last Byzantine emperor, and the final liberation of Russia from the Tartars in 1480, encouraged the Muscovite Church to take up the view, first formulated by the monk Philotheus, that the Christian Empire, having passed from Old Rome to New, had now passed from New Rome to Moscow, the third Rome, whose emperor was now responsible for the future of Orthodoxy. The adoption of the Byzantine concept of the theocratic state served to reinforce the autocratic character of the Muscovite princes, and to complete the process of subordinating Church to State.

In 1503 a dispute broke out between two groups of monks over the question of property. The so-called 'possessors' led by Joseph of Volokolamsk held that the monasteries needed to have wealth in order to fulfil their social responsibilities. The 'non-possessors' led by St Nil of Sorsk held to the original concept of monastic poverty. Their suppression by the Tsar, and the victory of the Josephites, further weakened the spiritual freedom of the Church and contributed to its growing subservience to the State.

Under Ivan IV the Terrible this process reached its climax. Although the Council of the Hundred Chapters in 1551 marked the full achievement of Russian Orthodox self-consciousness, the murder by the anointed Tsar of Metropolitan Philip of Moscow in 1569 finally extinguished the Church's ability or willingness to protest against the abuse of power by the State. When in 1589 Metropolitan Job was made Patriarch of Moscow and All Russia by Constantinople, the Church finally identified with the State.

Spiritual freedom continued to find a home in the remote north of the country, but the tradition of spirituality became increasingly detached from the life of the Russian state, and even from that of the institutional church. The Muscovite Church's intense conservatism caused it to withdraw into its own fixed tradition, reacting against any outside influence, not least from Greek Orthodoxy.

Meanwhile Russian Orthodoxy in the Kievan metropolitanate was being forced into contact with Western thought. Politically within the Lithuanian, and later the Polish, states, Orthodoxy came under strong pressure from Roman Catholicism. By the Union of Brest–Litovsk in 1596 many Orthodox recognised the Papacy. The Orthodox metropolitans of Kiev continued to defend Orthodoxy, but in doing so increasingly came to use the categories of Western theological thought. Peter Mogila, Metropolitan of Kiev (1633–47), was an enthusiastic Westerniser, and introduced Latin thought as well as the Latin language into the teaching of Orthodox theology, which became progressively more Westernised.

Suspicion of the West, and of everything non-Russian, lay in part behind the schism of the Old Believers from the official Russian Church. The immediate cause of the split was the correction of the Slavonic liturgical books used by the Russian Church on the basis of existing Greek texts. Patriarch Nikon (1652–8) forced the reform through with the backing of the Tsar in the face of fierce opposition from conservatives, led by the Archpriest Avvakum. He saw reliance on Greek books printed in Catholic Venice as undermining the validity of the native Russian Orthodox tradition. Excommunicated in 1667, those who refused to accept the reform became known as Old Believers, or Old Ritualists. Often fiercely persecuted by the Empire whose authority over the Church they rejected, their numbers increased under Peter I when many opponents of his policy of Europeanisation joined the Old Believers. Deprived of bishops, they were split into two groups, those with priests and those without. In 1846 a deposed Bosnian bishop, Ambrose, provided the former with an episcopate. The priestless Old Believers were still further divided. The Church of the Old Believers continues to exist in the Soviet Union.

Under Peter the Great (1676–1725) the Patriarchate was abolished in 1721, and replaced by a governing Holy Synod. The Synod was a government department, presided over by a lay Chief Procurator. The change was part of Peter's policy of transforming Russia into an absolutist monarch on the Western pattern, and was the culmination of a long process by which the Church in Russia, inheriting the ambiguous relationship of Church to State in the Byzantine world, became finally subordinate to the State, which treated it like any other government department, whose decisions were taken only by permission of the Emperor. The Church continued to think of its relationship with the State in terms of Byzantine theocracy, viewing the anointed Tsar as the image of the Christian Empire. The synodal period in the life of the Russian Orthodox Church, which lasted until 1917, saw extensive westernisation in Russian theological thinking and education. But theological learning remained alive, and the monastic tradition produced remarkable spiritual leaders and centres. By the beginning of the twentieth century a renewal of Orthodoxy was beginning to become apparent, to be cut short tragically by the Bolshevik seizure of power in 1917.

The Council of the Russian Church, which had begun its work just before the Revolution, re-established the Patriarchate, and elected Metropolitan Tikhon of Moscow as Patriarch. The Bolshevik government disestablished the Orthodox Church, and secularised all education. Church activity was effectively confined to church buildings. Persecution soon broke out, and many church leaders were killed or imprisoned. In 1923 Tikhon declared his loyalty to the Soviet State, but when he died in 1925 it proved impossible to elect a successor, and Metropolitan Sergius of Moscow became Patriarchal *Locum Tenens.* Sergius aligned the Church with the Soviet State, but his loyalty did not prevent the devastation of the Church by fierce persecution. By 1939 the Church as an organised body had virtually ceased to exist. In 1943 Stalin, in order to rally behind the government all sections of Russian society in the defence of the Fatherland against Nazi Germany, allowed the Church to come into the open and reorganise itself. Sergius was elected Patriarch, and many churches were opened for worship. Eight theological seminaries and two academies were allowed to function to train new clergy. In 1945 Metropolitan Alexis of Leningrad was elected to succeed Patriarch Sergius. After the war the Church enjoyed some freedom to worship, and its external structure was built up. Renewed pressure was applied by the State after the death of Stalin, and in the early 1960s roughly half the working churches were closed, together with five of the eight seminaries. Under Alexis' successor, Patriarch Pimen, the church leadership has continued to co-operate with the State, not least in matters of foreign policy. Recently it has beome prominent in the 'peace movement'. Perhaps because of the difficulties experienced by Christian believers in keeping alive their faith in a state whose official philosophy is hostile to religion, Russian Orthodox Christians, like other Christians in the Soviet Union, often display great fervour in the practice of their religion.

The Orthodox Churches Today

Since the end of the Second World War all the Orthodox Churches of Eastern Europe have found themselves under Marxist governments: the Churches of Bulgaria, Serbia and Romania, and the smaller Churches in Estonia, Latvia and Lithuania, and in Poland, Czechoslovakia and Hungary. Their constitutional position is usually closely similar to that of the Russian Orthodox Church. Freedom of worship is guaranteed, though not freedom of propaganda. Educational activities are restricted to the training of future clergy, and the publication of theological works and other religious literature is tightly controlled. Relations with the State are conducted through a government department for religious affairs, with which the church leadership has close contact. The Byzantine tradition of co-operation between Church and State, and the close link which Turkish rule forged between Church and Nation, have perhaps made it easier for the Orthodox Churches than for some others to live within the limits imposed by governments in whose philosophy there is no permanent place for the Christian or any other religion. Soon after the end of the Second World War the Uniate Churches (Eastern in liturgy but giving allegiance to Rome) in the Ukraine and in Transylvania were reunited, under pressure, with the Russian and Romanian Orthodox Churches respectively. The Church of Greece is the only major autocephalous Orthodox Church which still enjoys the position of a recognised national Church. A similar position is held by the Church of Cyprus, autocephalous since the Third Ecumenical Council of 431.

The ancient Patriarchates of Alexandria, Jerusalem and Antioch survive as much diminished communities, representing the Churches which once formed the heartlands of Christianity. The Patriarchate of Alexandria, whose head has the title of Pope and Patriarch of Alexandria and All Africa, has in recent years established new congregations in Central and East Africa, where numbers of local Africans have joined the Orthodox Church. The Patriarchate of Jerusalem, which is largely Arabic although its hierarchy is Greek, has control of the Holy Places, chief among them the Church of the Holy Sepulchre in Jerusalem, access to which is guaranteed to all the major Christian churches for services. The Patriarchate of Antioch and All the East, with its seat in Damascus, has congregations in the Middle East, South India and South America. Included with these autocephalous churches, living in countries for long Arab and Muslim (the Patriarchate of Jerusalem is now in the State of Israel), is the Church of Sinai. The abbot of the Monastery of St Catherine on Mount Sinai, founded by Justinian in the sixth century, is archbishop of the smallest of the self-governing Orthodox churches, which has been independent since 1575. Its archbishop is consecrated by the Patriarch of Jerusalem.

Meanwhile, Orthodox Christianity has been spreading outside traditionally Orthodox countries. The Russian Orthodox Church carried out extensive missionary activity in the territories absorbed into the Russian Empire in the eighteenth and nineteenth centuries. At the very end of the eighteenth century, Russian missionaries began to work in Alaska and soon laid the foundations of an Orthodox Church in North America. A Russian diocese was set up in 1840. Immigration from Greece and other Orthodox countries in Europe led to the establishment of Greek, Bulgarian, Serbian and Romanian parishes, which were at first under the jurisdiction of the one Russian diocese. But in the early twentieth century separate ethnic jurisdictions were set up, fragmenting the original unity of

Orthodoxy in America. Political conditions in Europe in the twentieth century have still further increased the numbers of immigrants from Orthodox countries. Those in diaspora from countries under Marxist rule have tended to split along political lines. Some recognise the authority of the patriarchates in the mother country. Others refuse to do so, doubtful of their spiritual independence from the government. Largest among the jurisdictions which are independent for political reasons is the Russian Orthodox Church Abroad, or in Exile. Its existence derives from the Synod of Russian bishops which soon after the Russian Revolution gathered at Karlovci in Yugoslavia. Since the 1950s it has had its centre in the USA. On the other hand, in 1970 the Patriarchate of Moscow granted autocephaly to the Russian Metropolia in America, which, as the Orthodox Church in America, became the fifteenth local autocephalous Orthodox Church. Its existence as such has not been recognised by the older patriarchates, and it has yet to be seen whether or not the hope that it might become the basis of a truly American Orthodox Church will be realised. Through Russian Orthodox missionary work, too, Orthodox churches, not big enough to be fully self-governing, have been founded in Japan, China and Korea. Following Orthodox custom they use the vernacular in worship. Orthodoxy has the same pluriform character in countries of Western Europe.

The existence of parallel, national, episcopates is a denial of the Orthodox understanding of the Church, which affirms the principle that there can be only one bishop in any one place, as the focus of the unity of all local Christians. But the strength of the national traditions within Orthodoxy has so far proved greater than that of strict Orthodox theology, and *émigrés* from Orthodox countries often regard their church as their one remaining link with their native land and culture. Nevertheless the spread of Orthodoxy to most parts of the world by emigration has meant that Orthodoxy has ceased to be exclusively Eastern. In most places where they have settled, Orthodox Christians have attracted converts from among the local population, and the vernacular has increasingly come to be used in worship. In Western Europe, North America, Australia and elsewhere Orthodoxy now lives side by side with other Christian traditions, and is in contact with them locally, as well as through its now strong involvement in the international ecumenical movement.

All the Orthodox churches are united by a common faith and by common forms of worship. They recognise a primacy of honour in the Ecumenical Patriarchate of Constantinople. The immediate jurisdiction of the Ecumenical Patriarch has suffered severe losses since the end of the First World War, when conflict between Greeks and Turks led to the emigration to Greece and elsewhere of the majority of the Greeks in Turkey. But his jurisdiction extends to all Greek Orthodox living outside Greece and Cyprus.

It includes, too, Mount Athos, which forms a self-governing monastic community within the Republic of Greece. In recent years the Holy Mountain has experienced a renewal of monastic life, with significant numbers of young and often well-educated men joining the monasteries. Monastic life remains important throughout the Orthodox Church, and it is from the monks that bishops are always chosen.

The Non-Chalcedonian Churches

The Chalcedonian definition of the Orthodox faith in Jesus Christ as both God and Man was intended to exclude the views attributed to Nestorius on the one hand and Eutyches on the other. It was unacceptable to followers of the former, as well as to those who favoured Cyril of Alexandria's doctrine, although for quite different reasons. Two distinct groups of non-Chalcedonian Christians emerged, known as Nestorian and Monophysite.

The Nestorian Church

The followers of Nestorius had already refused to accept the decisions of the Third Ecumenical Council of Ephesus in 431, giving to Mary the title 'Theotokos' (Mother of God). They predominated among the East Syrians, who, existing largely in the Persian Empire, had been ecclesiastically independent of Antioch since the Synod of Markabba in 424. After 431 they gradually formed themselves into a Nestorian, Diophysite (i.e. stressing Christ's human as well as divine nature) Church, which was Syriac-speaking. Within the Empire the theological school at Edessa became, under Bishop Ibas (435–57), the centre of Nestorian teaching. Ibas' successor Nonnus was a Monophysite, and Monophysite pressure on the followers of Nestorius caused many of them to leave the Empire and settle in Persia. The Emperor Zeno (474–91) finally expelled the Nestorians from Edessa and from the Empire, and Nisibis became the theological centre of Nestorianism. Ibas' pupil Barsumas, Bishop of Nisibis from 457, founded an important school there. The Fifth Ecumenical Council of Constantinople in 553 condemned Theodore of Mopsuestia and other representatives of the school of Antioch, and outlawed Nestorianism in the Empire.

The ecclesiastical centre of the East Syrian Nestorian Church was Seleucia-Ctesiphon on the River Tigris in Mesopotamia, and its head was known from 498 as Patriarch of the East. *The Book of Union* by Mar Babai the Great, composed at the end of the sixth century, expressed definitive Nestorian teaching on the person of Christ. For several centuries the Nestorian Church flourished, with a strong monastic life, and engaged in extensive missionary activity in Arabia, Central Asia, India and China, making it the most widely spread of all the churches. The Sigan-Fu Stone, found in north-west China in 1625, testifies to the introduction and spread of Christianity in that region in the seventh and eighth centuries. It began to decline in the ninth century, to be extinguished by Timur Lane at the end of the fourteenth.

By 651 Persia had fallen completely under Arab rule. The Muslim caliphs were on the whole tolerant towards the Church, and Christians often played an important part in the political and cultural life of the country. There were occasional outbreaks of persecution, under Caliphs Omar II (717–20) and Mutawakkil (847–61). In 775 the seat of the Patriarchate was transferred to Baghdad, where the Patriarchs retained a position of relative political significance as heads of the Nestorian community even after Mongul rule replaced the Arab Caliphate in 1258.

After the Mongol rulers accepted Islam in 1295, the Church became subjected to intense persecution and declined rapidly. Under Timur Lane (1396–1405) the Nestorian churches in Asia and China were wiped out, and Nestorians soon disappeared from Persia and Mesopotamia. They survived chiefly in the region of the Hakkiari Mountain in Kurdistan, in great poverty and ignorance, almost unknown to the rest of the world until the nineteenth century. The Patriarchate, and subsequently the episcopate, became hereditary, descending from uncle to nephew.

Known as Assyrians, because of their legendary descent from the Assyrians of Old Testament times, they have survived as a community until the present day. Depleted by Kurdish massacre in the nineteenth century, many left their homeland during the First World War and fought with the Allies against the Turks. Stranded in Iraq after the war, many were massacred in 1933. The Patriarch went to live in Chicago, and the remnant of the Assyrians now live in exile in Syria, Iraq, Lebanon and the USA.

Though venerating Nestorius the Assyrians claim not to be Nestorians in the heretical sense. In their eucharistic worship they use three eucharistic prayers, or *anaphoras*, ascribed to Theodore of Mopsuestia, Nestorius, and Addai and Mari, the last of which reflects a very early tradition. Among their literature is *The Bazaar of Heracleides*, written by Nestorius in exile towards the end of his life and the only major work of his to have survived. It was discovered by Western scholars at the end of the nineteenth century and published in 1910. The Archbishop of Canterbury's Mission to the Assyrians, begun in 1885 but building on earlier contacts, gave valuable assistance to the Assyrian Church in printing liturgical and other books and established friendly relations between Nestorians and Anglicans. The Nestorian Church in Turkey and Persia was brought into contact with the Roman Catholic Church by missionaries in the thirteenth century. Negotiations for union were begun, which in 1830 resulted in the formation of a uniate church (owing allegiance to Rome), known as the Chaldean Church.

The Monophysite Churches

The Monophysites, after their final break with the Empire and with Orthodoxy, formed three independent Churches: the Coptic and Abyssinian, the Syrian Jacobite and the Armenian.

The Church in Egypt and Ethiopia. The Coptic (i.e. Egyptian) Church was the most determined in its rejection of Chalcedon. When the Chalcedonian Proterius was appointed Patriarch of Alexandria (452–7), a rival Monophysite Timothy was elected by the Copts. From then on rival patriarchs confronted each other for most of the time, the Monophysites enjoying popular, and especially monastic, support, the Melkites relying on that of the imperial forces. The last Patriarch under the Empire, Cyrus, appointed in 631, led a fierce persecution of the Monophysites, which set the seal on Coptic hatred of the Empire and all things Byzantine. But in 641 Cyrus surrendered Babylon to the victorious Arabs, and with the fall of Alexandria in 642 Egypt was finally lost to the Empire.

The Arabs treated Melkites and Monophysites alike. This meant a considerable improvement in the situation of the Copts, who were able to take over many church buildings and other property abandoned by the Greeks. Copts occupied many administrative, financial and legal offices in the government of the country. Financial oppression led to occasional uprisings and caused many Copts to embrace Islam in order to avoid taxation. In 705 Arabic was made the official language, and Coptic gradually declined as a spoken language, surviving as such until the late Middle Ages and as the liturgical language of the Copts until the present day. Under the Fatimid caliphs (969–1171) the Copts enjoyed their most prosperous period under Arab rule. Influential in the State, they enjoyed considerable religious freedom, and Coptic arts and craftsmanship flourished. Caliph al-Hakim (996–1021) unleashed a violent persecution of the Copts, destroying some 3,000 churches, and causing many to become Muslims. His successors re-established religious liberty. In the eleventh century under Christodoulos (1046–77) the Patriarchate was moved from Alexandria, first to Damru, in the Delta, then finally to Cairo. Good relations were established with the churches in Nubia and Abyssinia.

The Crusades were disastrous for the Copts. They provoked Muslim hostility towards all Christians and led to harsher conditions for the Copts. In addition, the Latin rulers of the Holy Land were hostile to the Monophysites, and prohibited Coptic pilgrimages to the Holy Places. The accession to power, first as Vizier then as Caliph, of Saladin inaugurated the Ayyubid Sultanate (1169–1250), which witnessed the beginning of the decline of the Coptic people. Under the Mamluk dynasty, which took power in 1250, the Copts were subjected to repeated popular Muslim harassment. Churches and monasteries were destroyed, and the economic position of the Copts declined. At the Council of Florence (1438–9) the Copts were involved in negotiations for union with Rome, but the act of union was never put into effect.

The Turkish conquest of Egypt in 1517 by Selim I marked the beginning of a long period of economic and cultural decline for the whole country, from which the Coptic community inevitably suffered. Copts continued to hold high office in the government. Ibrahim Gauheri, towards the end of the eighteenth century, used his wealth to benefit the Church, and was responsible for the building of St Mark's Cathedral at Ezbekieh, the seat of the Patriarchate.

From 1798 to 1801 the French under Napoleon ruled Egypt, and made use of the Copts in their administration. The Coptic Church was relieved of oppression, and the seed of Egyptian nationalism sown. A little later, good relations existed between the Viceroy of Egypt, Mohammed Ali, and Patriarch Peter VII (1809–52). Peter's successor, Cyril IV (1854–61), initiated a programme of reform in the Church which laid the foundation for the modern revival of Coptic Christianity. He was particularly concerned to promote education and encouraged the growth of an educated laity. A theological school was set up in Cairo in 1875. Under the conservative Cyril V (1875–1927) the reform movement was taken up by lay leaders. During the patriarchates of Cyril VI (1956–71) and Shenouda III (1971–) the numbers of educated clergy and monks have increased, giving the Coptic Church and people leadership of a high quality. Lay participation in the life of the Church is widespread, and many benevolent societies have been set up to provide for the spiritual, educational and social needs of the people. Appreciation of the value of the Coptic religious and cultural tradition has motivated widespread renewal in the life of the Church, which has founded an Institute of Coptic Studies in Cairo, and has begun to extend its mission to other parts of Africa. The Coptic Church is by far the largest of the non-Chalcedonian Churches and has a numerous diaspora in different parts of the world.

The beginnings of Christianity in Ethiopia, or Abyssinia, in the fourth century were closely connected with Egypt. Frumentius, one of the first missionaries, was consecrated by Athanasius of Alexandria. The Church was reinforced at the end of the fifth century by the Mission of the Nine Saints. They encouraged the translation of religious literature into Ge'ez, which has remained the liturgical language of the Church. For a while Christianity flourished in close contact with the Monophysite Copts, and Axum became the religious as well as the political centre of the country. The spread of Islam in Africa caused Christianity to decline in Ethiopia. From *c.* 650 to 1268 the Ethiopian Church lived in almost complete isolation, save for the consecration of its metropolitan by the Coptic patriarch. The chief religious monuments of this period are the rock churches of King Lalibela (1181–1221). The influence of both paganism and Judaism was strong, and a number of church practices of Jewish origin have remained. The struggle between Christianity and expanding Islam continued.

In 1268 the old Ethiopian dynasty, claiming descent

from Solomon and the Queen of Sheba, was restored. Under the Abuna Takla Haymanot the Church regained considerable vitality. From the thirteenth century attempts were made to reconcile the Ethiopians with Rome. A representative of the Church took part in the Council of Florence (1438–9). Ethiopia's need for Western help against Islam in the late fifteenth and sixteenth centuries enabled the Portuguese to introduce Roman Catholic missionaries, who remained after the final defeat of Islamic forces in 1578. A Latin patriarch and two bishops were consecrated by the Pope at the request of Ignatius Loyola. Although the Jesuit mission failed, Roman attempts to convert the Ethiopians persisted, and Alphonso Mendez, consecrated Patriarch by Rome in 1624, was recognised by the King. In 1626 Catholicism was made the official religion of Ethiopia, and Mendez tried to impose it by force. Popular opposition and the accession of Fasildas in 1632 brought this attempt to an end. Continuing activity, especially in the nineteenth and twentieth centuries, led to the creation of a small uniate Church, largely in Eritrea. A titular Bishop of Suzusa was consecrated in 1950.

Since 1959 the Ethiopian Church has been independent of the Coptic Church, while retaining close links with it. Always intimately linked with the State, its situation was changed dramatically when the Emperor Haile Selassie was overthrown and a Marxist government took power. Deprived of its vast wealth, the Church has suffered considerably, and is faced with the need to make painful readjustments to a new political situation as well as to the contemporary world.

The Syrian Jacobite Church. Antioch had been the home of the school of theology from which Nestorius ultimately emerged. After 451 its church leaders at first supported Chalcedon. But Monophysite tendencies grew more influential. Peter the Fuller, who became Patriarch in 465, was deposed for his Monophysite views, but accepted the *Henoticon* of Zeno in 482 and was restored to office. The most distinguished Monophysite in Antioch was Severus, Patriarch from 512 to 518. Deposed by Justin I, he took refuge in Alexandria, and died in 538. He was one of the greatest of the moderate Monophysite theologians. He was succeeded by rival patriarchs, one Chalcedonian and Melkite, the other Monophysite. The Monophysites, persecuted by Justinian, were rallied and finally organised as a separate church by Jacob Baradaeus, after whom they have been known as Jacobites.

In 542, with the assistance of the Empress Theodora, Jacob was consecrated as Metropolitan of Edessa by Theodosius of Alexandria, in prison for his Monophysite faith near Constantinople. Travelling widely all over the East, he ordained bishops and priests for the persecuted Monophysite communities, and consecrated Sergius, Severus' successor as Patriarch of Antioch. By the time of his death in 578 he had firmly established the Monophysite Church in west Syria, and also in Persia, where it coexisted with the Nestorian Church. It possessed a strong monastic life, which produced a remarkable series of so-called stylite saints, who following the example of St Symeon Stylites (389–459) spent years on the top of pillars. The monasteries were centres of Syrian culture and education as well as of the Syrian spiritual tradition.

The Syrian Jacobites, like the Nestorians, were outlawed by the Empire, but unlike the Nestorians remained within it. The Arab conquest gave them relief from imperial persecution and the possibility of missionary expansion within the territories under Arab rule. They produced a number of distinguished church leaders and writers, such as Jacob of Edessa (633–708), George, Bishop of the Arabs (686–724), and Moses bar Kepha (d. 903), and played a significant part in the political, commercial and cultural life of the Arab empire.

But from the ninth century growing Turkish influence contributed to a less tolerant policy towards Christians. From the tenth century the Jacobite Church began to decline. A temporary revival of theological culture took place in the twelfth and thirteenth centuries, associated with Dionysius Bar Salibi, Michael the Syrian and Gregory Bar Hebraeus. By this time Arabic was becoming the normal literary language, and after the thirteenth century Syriac was used only in liturgical worship. Like the Nestorians, the Syrian Jacobites suffered much from Mongol attacks and depredations. Many churches and monasteries were destroyed by Timur Lane, and further destruction was inflicted by the Ottoman Turks. The Syrian community dwindled rapidly in numbers and morale. In the seventeenth century a Uniate patriarchate was set up, whose seat was transferred to Beirut under the distinguished Syriac scholar Patriarch Ignatius Ephrem Rahmani (1898–1929). In the nineteenth century Protestant missions encroached further on the small Syrian Church. The majority of present-day Syrian Jacobites are in India.

The Armenian Church. The Armenians, who became independent of Caesarea, their mother church, in 374, and in the first part of the fifth century adopted Armenian as their liturgical language in place of Syriac, were not drawn into the doctrinal disputes leading up to Chalcedon, being since 430 under Persian rule. They took little part in the council itself, which in 506 at the Synod of Dwin they rejected as not in accord with the teaching of the school of Alexandria, which the Council of Ephesus of 449 had endorsed. Political as well as theological reasons lay behind this rejection. In 651 the Synod of Manzikert rejected the union with the Greeks concluded in 629 by the Catholicos (i.e. chief bishop) Ezra, and again condemned Chalcedon.

Political subjection, first to the Byzantine and Persian Empires, then to successive Arab, Mongol, Egyptian and Turkish conquerors, only reinforced the national character of the Armenian Church. In 856 a new Armenian dynasty, the Bagratids, established itself and maintained a virtual independence under Arab suzerainty until 1071, when the Seljuk Turks defeated the Byzantine Emperor Romanus Diogenes and overran Armenia. Many Armenians then left their homeland in Greater Armenia, and settled in Cilicia, founding in 1080 a new kingdom of Lesser Armenia, with its capital at Sis, which preserved its independence from the end of the eleventh century until the Egyptian Mamluk conquest in 1375. Political necessity forced the Cilician Armenians into contact with Rome and the West. Under the Catholicos Constantine I (1221–67) a union with Rome was proclaimed and maintained at Sis until 1441. But a Monophysite catholicosate continued on the island of Aghthamar in Lake Van. In 1441 the Catholicosate of Etchmiadzin was restored, that at Sis remaining as the second main centre of the Armenian Church. Two more patriarchates were subsequently founded: in Constantinople in 1461, and in Jerusalem in the early eighteenth century. In modern times Aghthamar has ceased to be a patriarchate, and the patriarchate of Sis, most of whose people were exiled during the First World War, has been transferred to Antelias in Lebanon.

The Armenians in Turkey suffered severe losses as a result of Turkish massacres at the end of the nineteenth century and the beginning of the twentieth. Since the Russian Revolution of 1917 the Catholicosate of Etchmiadzin has lived under Marxist rule. Its patriarch is recognised as the Catholicos of All Armenians. The Catholicosate of Sis has jurisdiction over Armenians in diaspora. Although scattered widely throughout the world, Armenians have retained a strong sense of national identity, closely bound up with the Armenian Church.

In 1740 a Catholic Armenian patriarchate was founded in Lebanon, building on the links which Cilician Armenians in Syria and Turkey had kept with Rome since the Crusades. The union of all Armenians with Rome which was proclaimed at the Council of Florence was never translated into reality.

The Armenian liturgical tradition derived from that of Caesarea in Cappadocia and Antioch, and so is closely related to that of the Byzantine Orthodox Church. Latin influence at the time of the Crusades was responsible for its assimilating a number of Western characteristics. Armenian dogma is defined by the teaching of the first three Ecumenical Councils only (i.e. excluding Chalcedon).

The St Thomas Christians of India. Claiming to have been founded by the Apostle Thomas, the Christian community in Kerala in South India was certainly in existence by 550, and probably owed its foundation to contacts with east Syria. For centuries it received its bishops from the Nestorian Patriarchate in Seleucia–Ctesiphon, and later Baghdad. Its liturgical language was Syriac. In the course of the later Middle Ages links were formed with the Syrian Jacobites.

The advent of the Portuguese in 1498 brought with it Roman Catholic influence. At the Synod of Diamper in 1599 the bishops, mostly appointed because they were favourable to Rome, condemned Nestorian teaching and recognised the supremacy of the Pope. All books suspected of heresy were destroyed, making modern study of early Indian Christianity impossible. But despite Roman vigilance contacts were kept with the Coptic, Jacobite and Nestorian Churches. When a Syrian Jacobite bishop arrived in 1652, he was arrested, and in 1654 burnt by the Inquisition. Widespread hostility to Rome led to secession from papal authority, but a Carmelite mission in 1657 succeeded in persuading some two-thirds of the Indian Christians to return to the Roman obedience. Before the Jesuit bishop Joseph was expelled by the Dutch in 1663, he had consecrated the first native bishop, Chandy Kattanar, as Bishop of Megara.

The anti-Roman Christians meanwhile elected their own bishop, Mar Thoma I, irregularly consecrated by twelve priests. A Syrian Jacobite bishop was sent to Malabar in 1665. Further divisions among the Indian Christians followed. A Nestorian bishop, Mar Gabriel, arrived in 1708, and won over some of the Roman parishes. A Nestorian community has survived in Trichur to the present day. Towards the end of the eighteenth century, the British replaced the Dutch as rulers in south India, and with them, in 1816, came Anglican missionaries, who were allowed to preach in Jacobite churches. Although the Anglicans did not intend to proselytise, a group of Syrians was influenced by Protestant ideas. Led by Abraham Malpan, they were at the origin of a reformed Syrian Church, known as the Mar Thoma Church, which is in communion with the Anglican Church.

The Indians in communion with the Syrian Jacobite Church suffered a further split, when in 1909 the Syrian Patriarch visited India and excommunicated Metropolitan Dionysius VI. Some followed the patriarch, and have remained in communion with Antioch. Others formed an autonomous church, of which Mar Ivanios eventually became Catholicos. In 1930 Mar Ivanios recognised the authority of Rome and led part of his church into a union, forming the Malankarese Church. The autonomous Syrian Jacobite Church has retained its Catholicos, while recognising the ultimate authority of the Patriarch of Antioch.

The Maronite Church. From the fourth century the Monastery of St Maro on the Orontes was the centre of Christianity and of Christian missionary work in Lebanon. It was founded by the disciples of St Maro (350–433). In 628 Heraclius visited the monastery and persuaded the monks to accept monothelitism, the doctrine that there is only one will in Jesus Christ. Although, as we saw, this attempt to reconcile Chalcedonians and Monophysites failed, the Maronites became firmly monothelite and were excommunicated by the Council of Constantinople of 680. In 685 they elected St John Maron as their own Patriarch, with the title of Antioch and the East.

The Monastery of St Maro was devastated by the Byzantines in 694, and finally destroyed by the Arabs, during the wars in which both were engaged in Lebanon. The Maronites removed to the mountains. It was at this time that the name Maronite came to be used to denote both Church and people.

During the Crusades the Maronites came under Western and Roman influence. They welcomed the Crusaders as allies in the struggle with Islam. In 1182 they renounced monothelitism and recognised papal supremacy. Contact with Rome was sporadic after the Muslim reconquest of the Holy Land, completed in 1291 with the capture of Acre. Close relations date only from the sixteenth century. The Maronite College in Rome was founded in 1584. The Maronites retained their Eastern customs and their Syriac liturgy. A synod held in 1736 reinforced the union with Rome, and extended Latin influence in the Church's life and practice. Romanisation was carried further during the Patriarchate of Paul Mubarak (1854–90).

In the second half of the nineteenth century relations between the Maronites and the Muslim Druzes in Lebanon deteriorated. Encouraged by the Turks, Druzes clashed with Christians, and in the 1860s many Maronites were massacred, and churches and monasteries were destroyed with villages. In 1861 Lebanon became an autonomous province under the sultan, with a Christian governor. Still worse massacres were perpetrated under the Turks during the First World War. In 1926 Lebanon became a republic whose constitution provided for a Maronite President, a Sunni Muslim Prime Minister, a Shi'ite Muslim Chairman of the Chamber of Deputies and a Druze Minister of Defence. The Patriarch and church leadership became highly influential in the political life of the country.

Towards the Healing of Schism

With the development of the ecumenical movement, representatives of the Chalcedonian Orthodox and the non-Chalcedonian Eastern Churches have met each other, and have come to realise the need to overcome the divisions which go back to the fifth century. A series of theological consultations between theologians of both families of churches was held from 1964 to 1971. The conclusion was reached that both traditions could agree on the essentials of Christological doctrine, and that the way was open for a formal theological dialogue. Preparations for such a dialogue were put in hand in 1973.

Further Reading

On the non-Chalcedonian Churches:
Atiya, Aziz S. *A History of Eastern Christianity* (Methuen, London, 1968)

On the Orthodox Churches:
Hussey, J. *The Orthodox Church in the Byzantine Empire* (Oxford University Press, Oxford, 1986)
Meyendorff, J. *The Byzantine Legacy in the Orthodox Church* (St Vladimir's Seminary Press, 1982)
Runciman, S. *The Great Church in Captivity* (Cambridge University Press, Cambridge, 1968)
Schmemann, A. *The Historical Road of Eastern Orthodoxy* (Harvill, London, 1963)
Vlasto, A.P. *The Entry of the Slavs into Christendom* (Cambridge University Press, Cambridge, 1970)

On the Orthodox (and other) Churches in Eastern Europe today:
Beeson, T. *Discretion and Valour*, rev. edn (Collins, London, 1982)

11 Christianity in the West to the Reformation

Christopher Harper-Bill

Popes and Emperors

Throughout the Middle Ages the Papacy occupied a central position in the life of the Western Church. The supremacy of the Bishop of Rome might be challenged at various times by secular rulers jealous of his authority within their kingdoms, by bishops who resented papal interference within their dioceses, or by dissident heretical groups who questioned the fundamental premisses on which papal claims were based; yet from the period of the conversion to Latin Christianity of the various Germanic tribes until the Reformation, no area of Western Europe was immune from the doctrinal and jurisdictional authority of Rome, and the history of the Papacy provides a common thread running through a long period of dogmatic and ecclesiological development.

When Leo I ascended the papal throne in 440 CE, imperial authority in Western Europe was already in decline. The emperor, in his new capital at Constantinople, increasingly neglected the backward and unproductive western provinces and concentrated the defence of the Empire in the East. Leo and his successors did not eagerly emancipate themselves from imperial tyranny; rather they were compelled to fill the vacuum left by the inertia and incapacity of emperors who nevertheless desired to preserve in full their theoretical authority in the abandoned Western provinces.

The Council of Chalcedon in 451 CE, at imperial instigation, declared the parallel jurisdiction of the Patriarch of Constantinople, an equality which was anathema to Rome. Yet the imperial government was still glad of any agency which might hold together the Western provinces. The decree of the Emperor Valentinian III in 455, supporting the Bishop of Rome against an assertion of independence by the churches of Gaul, is traditionally taken as marking the establishment of the unchallenged supremacy of the Pope as Patriarch of the West. During the previous century successive popes had formulated a sophisticated theory of church government. In 381 Pope Damasus I had countered the claims of the Council of Constantinople by stating that the authority of Rome was derived from no synodal decision, but from Christ's commission to St Peter (Matt. 16:18–19). Jerome's translation of the Bible into Latin (the Vulgate, commissioned by the same pope, not only rendered the sacred texts accessible to a far larger audience in the West, but also couched the Word of God in Roman jurisdictional terms. The power to bind and loose granted to Peter was now a statement of legal competence; Christ had not only established Christian society, but had instituted a form of government appropriate for that community. While every apostle had received sacramental powers, transmitted to all the bishops of the Church, only Peter had been entrusted with governmental authority, which he had bequeathed to his successors as Bishop of Rome. Pope Leo I evolved the concept of the Pope as the 'unworthy heir of St Peter'—by Roman law the heir assumed the legal status of the deceased, and the unworthiness of any particular pope did not affect this, for power resided in the office, not in the individual. Moreover, Leo declared that whereas each Bishop of Rome succeeded his predecessor sacramentally as bishop, governmentally as pope he succeeded St Peter directly, and therefore was not bound by the decisions of his predecessors. Because of the authority passed from Christ to Peter to Pope, the Pope became like Christ an estate set above the Church, which was committed to his charge and had no independent powers of its own. Therefore the Church had no means of depriving the Pope of his position. The Pope exercised a totality of power—*plenitudo potestatis*—and the jurisdictional authority of the episcopate was delegated to its members by the Pope. A papal ruling was the actualisation on earth of the Word of God.

This elaborate theory was not devised to free the Papacy from imperial domination. For three centuries successive popes continued to look to the emperor for leadership, support and protection. Rather, it was intended to consolidate and magnify the position of the Papacy within the Church. In the fifth century Vandal domination of the Mediterranean isolated the Western Church from its Eastern counterpart, and from the great religious and intellectual centres of Jerusalem, Antioch and Alexandria, and the influence of Rome inevitably increased in the Western provinces, which were gradually transformed into the new Germanic kingdoms. The gulf between East and West was subsequently widened, and rendered permanent, by the Islamic conquests of the seventh century. In the meantime the prestige of the Papacy had been increased by Leo I's negotiations with Attila the Hun in 452, and subsequently by Gregory I's independent dealings designed to avert the threat from the Lombards in the late sixth century.

The Germanic tribes who settled in the West had a great admiration for the traditions of Rome, and as the institutions of imperial government gradually crumbled in the fifth and sixth centuries, they came to regard the Latin Church, and especially the Papacy, as the sole effective expression of the Roman spirit. A papal missionary strategy, culminating in Gregory I's dispatch of the English mission in 596, gradually restored the lost provinces to Catholic Christianity. As conversion proceeded, the popes added to the prestige which they enjoyed as governors of the imperial city and heirs of the Caesars that reverence which was accorded by peoples whose new religion was more fetishistic than rational to the guardians of the relics of SS Peter and Paul and of so many other martyrs buried in the catacombs.

The initial efforts of the missionaries were directed towards the barbarian war-lords. Their conversion was often ascribed to divine intervention, as when Clovis, during his progress from tribal leadership to the kingship of the whole Frankish folk, on the eve of battle (*c.* 503 CE) saw a cross in the sky, and was converted. The parallel to Constantine was obvious to contemporaries. Yet in reality, shrewd calculation cannot have been absent from the minds of both Germanic chieftains and Catholic bishops. The invaders were attempting to establish their control over a sub-Roman population by whom they were heavily outnumbered. In the early days of settlement the exclusiveness of the closed senatorial aristocracy had prevented that integration into the Roman world which the newcomers so desperately desired. In provinces whose invaders had been converted to Arian rather than Catholic Christianity, religious differences made peaceful coexistence, and hence profitable exploitation of the land, even more unlikely. The heretical beliefs of the new rulers, and tales of persecution, gave justification to the Emperor Justinian's reconquest and brief occupation of the Mediterranean provinces (536–65). The reception of the Catholic faith was the passport to acceptance in a world still dominated by the ethos of Rome, and conversion to orthodoxy was as crucial as military capacity in ensuring Clovis' success in the conquest of almost the whole of Gaul, from which the heretical Visigoths were expelled.

The Catholic bishops realised that a royal conversion would provide the opportunity for evangelisation among a receptive people. Strong government was an essential prerequisite for effective missionary work, and the episcopate placed at the disposal of successful tribal leaders the ideology which would transform them from barbarian war-lords into Christian kings. A catena of biblical texts was forged to emphasise that subjection to a lawfully constituted prince was ordained by God. The ultimate sign of divine approval was, according to Frankish tradition, bestowed upon Clovis. At his coronation the oil for his unction descended from heaven on the back of a dove. This legend of the *Sainte Ampoule* was an important element in the political theology of the French monarchy far beyond the Middle Ages.

On Christmas Day 800 Charlemagne, King of the Franks, whose territory he had greatly extended, was crowned by the Pope as Emperor of the Romans. In the face of the violent indignation of the imperial authorities in Constantinople, he subsequently denied that he had ever sought this honour, yet his elevation was a recognition of political realities. Charlemagne, conscious imitator of both King David and of the Emperor Augustus, was regarded by the intellectuals at his court as the new Melchizedek, both priest and king. His rule was theocratic; he stood as the representative and the mirror image of God on earth. He was the channel by which the Divine Law was transformed into a code of legislation designed to establish a state of peace in which his subjects might pursue their quest for salvation.

The unity imposed by Charlemagne was ephemeral, and disintegrated under the pressure of pagan attack from all sides. In the short term the status of the Pope, liberated from imperial control, was enhanced, as he arbitrated between the claims of Charlemagne's grandsons to the imperial title. Ultimately, however, the Papacy suffered from the breakdown of public order and the fragmentation of authority which characterised the first 'feudal' age of Western European history, from the mid-ninth to the mid-eleventh century. The Papacy, like almost every bishopric in the West, became secularised, the prize for competing local families who appreciated the value to their own kin group of the annexation of spiritual authority. In the tenth century the Papacy sank to its nadir, and became the plaything of central Italian factions. The alternative, in the brief intervals of the restoration of imperial power, as under the three Ottonian kings of Germany (962–1002), was that the Bishop of Rome should become merely the senior domestic chaplain of a northern ruler.

The first attempts to reform the clerical order and to free the Church from the unscrupulous exploitation of lay lords were made north of the Alps in the tenth century by a group of monastic houses, of which the most prominent was Cluny, in Burgundy. The ideology of purification was implanted at Rome when in 1046 Henry III, King of the Germans and Western emperor, an ardent reformer himself, deposed three rival claimants to the papal throne and installed his own candidate. After two short pontificates, he appointed his own cousin. Pope Leo IX (1048–54) was determined, with imperial co-operation, both to extricate the bishopric of Rome from the mire of central Italian politics and to inaugurate a programme of moral reform within the Western Church.

The twin evils which were attacked by Leo and his enthusiastic advisers were simony and clerical concubinage. The former signified the buying and selling of ecclesiastical office, which was no less than trafficking in the grace of the Holy Spirit, and was condemned as heretical. Clerical marriage had been commonplace in Western Europe for centuries, but the reformers regarded any relationship, however stable, between a priest and a woman, as immoral. It was intolerable that the minister who officiated at the miracle of the Mass should be tainted by what was seen as sexual squalour, while the begetting of sons by priests created the danger of an hereditary priestly caste, passing on churches from generation to generation irrespective of the individual's suitability for the cure of souls. Leo implemented his reforms by taking the papal court on tour, convening a series of councils throughout Germany and France during which he expounded his radical legislation and deposed erring prelates. The impact of Pope Leo's travels was extraordinary. He had announced firmly that the Bishop of Rome would no longer stagnate in his see, a mere custodian of relics, but intended rather to provide leadership for Western Christendom and to enforce reforms which would inevitably offend powerful vested interests. His idealism, however, attracted the support of many secular rulers, masters of the Church within their own dominions, such as Duke William of Normandy, and it is remarkable how quickly Leo's premisses, upheld by his successors, were accepted throughout Western Europe. Abuses did not cease overnight, but within half a century it was generally agreed that simony and the keeping of women by priests were aberrations to be carefully concealed, rather than the norm of clerical life.

The Papacy was deprived of its greatest ally by the death in 1056 of the Emperor Henry III; the ensuing royal minority, accompanied by factional strife, left it unprotected. It was self-defence which led Pope Nicholas II in 1059 to promulgate a decree which attempted to circumvent the Roman aristocracy by entrusting the election of the Pope to the cardinals. Only later would this legislation be used to exclude also the emperor. In the same year, realising that the power vacuum in Germany and northern Italy left the Papacy vulnerable, Nicholas formed an alliance with the newly established Norman principalities of southern Italy, who would fulfil the vital role of protector of the Church of Rome. Practical necessity had loosened the ties between pope and Western emperor. At the same time, a group of theologians at the papal court arrived painfully at the conclusion that the greatest evil within the Church was not simony or immorality; these were merely symptoms of the degradation caused by lay domination of the Church at every level, from the local lord who appointed his kinsmen to a church on his estate to the emperor and kings who, sacrilegiously regarding themselves as the ministers of God within their domains, installed bishops and abbots according to their will and utilised the Church as an instrument of government.

The practical consequences of this view were seen in the pontificate of Gregory VII (1073–85), who thought of himself as a conservative, attempting to recreate the purity of the apostolic age and to revive the supreme authority which he believed, sincerely but misguidedly, to have been exercised by the Bishop of Rome in the years following the conversion of the first Christian Caesar. He utilised the Donation of Constantine, an eighth-century forgery only detected as such in the fifteenth century, which described how the emperor had ceded to the Pope not only spiritual authority over all churches, but also supreme temporal power in the West. It was soon realised, however, that the Donation was susceptible of an imperialist interpretation, for what the emperor had given his successor might take away. Increasingly the Pope and his publicists emphasised the direct delegation of dominion to the Papacy by Christ himself. Gregory VII's successors, indeed, adopted the title of Vicar of Christ, rather than Vicar of St Peter. The powers claimed by Gregory as a consequence of the divine commission were all-embracing. Not only should he exercise unrestricted authority within the clerical order, with complete discretion to determine matters of faith and Christian ethics, he also claimed the right to arbitrate in all matters in any way pertaining to the Christian commonwealth, which transcended all national and feudal frontiers. The feet of the Pope were to be kissed by all princes, he might depose emperors, he might absolve the subjects of unjust rulers from their oath of fealty. This was a doctrine of revolution. For seven hundred years the Church had provided Roman emperors and Germanic kings with an armoury of theological justifications for their paramount position within Christian society. Now the Bible, seen by all as a textbook from which could be abstracted God's plan for the governance of the world, was reinterpreted in order to locate all directive authority within the priestly hierarchy, culminating in the Pope, and to reduce the lay ruler to the role of an executive officer, existing merely to fulfil, under the direction of the priesthood, the functions of law enforcement and punishment, necessary only because of the fallen state of man. Theocratic kingship was interred, and the ground-plan for papal monarchy was delineated.

Secular rulers did not, of course, acquiesce passively in this attack on their status, and because of the long-standing and intimate relationship between pope and emperor, the inevitable conflict broke first and most violently, once Henry IV attained his majority, in Germany and northern Italy. A dispute in 1075 over appointment to the important archbishopric of Milan rapidly escalated into a bitter confrontation over matters of fundamental ideological significance. The ensuing struggle is known as the Investiture Contest, since the question of whether a new bishop or abbot should be invested with ring and staff by the king or by his ecclesiastical superior became a convenient symbolic issue on which to focus the wider questions of control over the selection of the higher clergy and the rightful distribution of authority within the Church. This was a clash between two rival theories of world government, for both of which was claimed divine institution, the one sanctioned by long usage, the other revolutionary but allegedly a reconstitution of the pristine purity of a primitive golden age. The result was half a century of physical and intellectual violence, and the first great propaganda war in modern European history. Gregory excommunicated Henry and declared him deposed. The king ultimately appointed his own rival pope, whom in 1084, after a prolonged siege, he enthroned at Rome—there were to be eleven imperial anti-popes in the next hundred years. Gregory had by now been deserted by many of his own cardinals, who had come to believe that his policies of confrontation retarded rather than advanced reform within the Church at large, and the Pope died in exile in southern Italy in 1085, after the Holy City had been sacked by his own Norman allies. The conflict was not immediately resolved, but Gregory's successors, if less charismatic figures, had a greater appreciation of the realities of power, while the kings of western Europe came to terms with the loss of their sacral status, for which they compensated by the institution of bureaucratic forms of government designed to maximise the exploitation of their secular resources. In 1122 the Investiture Contest in the Empire was ended by the Concordat of Worms, based on an earlier agreement in the Anglo-Norman realm. The king abandoned investiture, but retained the right to take, or to refuse, from newly elected prelates homage for the lands of their church, which gave him an effective power of veto. Elections, moreover, were to be held in the king's presence, and in practice monarchs throughout the Middle Ages retained considerable control over the appointment of the higher clergy, on whom they relied so heavily for the efficient conduct of government.

The compromise of 1122 was hardly in accord with the principles enunciated by Pope Gregory VII, and it is extremely doubtful if he, or his twelfth-century imitator Thomas Becket, Archbishop of Canterbury (1162–70), could have achieved the full implementation of their idealistic programme. The Church could neither isolate itself from the world, nor could it succeed in dominating entrenched secular institutions. It is arguable that more effective measures of reform were implemented by popes and prelates who sought accommodation with the lay power, enlisting the support of pious rulers and utilising the machinery of the State to facilitate the Church's great mission of the salvation of souls, than by those who invited confrontation by insisting on the inviolable privileges of the clerical order. Yet Gregory VII, if he died in exile with his work apparently in ruins, exercised a profound and lasting effect on Western ecclesiology and political thought. He established the principle that there are criteria, divorced from *raison d'état*, by which the actions of the secular ruler must be judged. While papal authority was almost universally accepted, this standard was provided by the Divine Law, revealed to and interpreted by the pontiff. Thereafter, with the breakdown of unity and even the decline of religious belief, the measure came to be provided by the conscience of the individual. The Western tradition, forged by the eleventh-century Pope, is very different from that of the medieval Byzantine Empire and its modern successor states, where religion (and subsequently ideology) has been expected, in the tradition of imperial Rome, to provide justification for the policies of the state.

The Concordat of Worms did not end hostility between the Papacy and the Empire. In the late twelfth and thirteenth centuries there remained ideological differences between the two authorities, aggravated by the attempts of the Hohenstaufen emperors to resurrect the ancient prerogatives of the Caesars and to provide the German Empire with a tradition older than Christianity itself. The main issue, however, was territorial. The emperors sought, for political and fiscal reasons, to render more effective their dominion over northern Italy and to extend their authority southwards to Rome. The situation for the Papacy worsened considerably when Frederick II of Hohenstaufen, regarded as a dangerous free-thinker and seen by some as Antichrist, in the early thirteenth century united the Empire with the kingdom of Sicily, inherited from his mother, thus encircling papal territory in central Italy. If the Papacy was to remain an independent institution, and the corner-stone of the unity of the Church in the West, it was essential that it should remain free of imperial domination, and to achieve this freedom it was necessary to maintain around Rome a cordon sanitaire of territory under its own control. Pope Alexander III (1159–81) was successful in orchestrating the resistance of the quasi-independent northern Italian cities against the Emperor Frederick I, but the Peace of Venice of 1177, which provided temporary respite, solved none of the fundamental problems. Between 1227 and 1250 the Papacy fiercely resisted the efforts of Frederick II to unite all Italy under his rule. Holy war was preached against the Emperor, civil strife was fomented in Germany by papal legates, and the clergy of western Europe were heavily taxed in order to finance papal campaigns. Ultimately, but only after Frederick's death, the Papacy was successful in breaking the Hohenstaufen dynasty, but the means to which it resorted were regarded by many as a perversion of the powers committed to the Vicar of Christ. The victory, moreover, was achieved only by inviting Charles of Anjou, younger brother of the French king, to invade the kingdom of Sicily, and once established he was as eager as his German predecessors to control the apostolic see. Once more a constant factor in papal history was emphasised: the popes desperately needed the support of a strong secular ally to guarantee their independence, but any ruler strong enough to give effective protection would himself seek domination.

In the interval between two periods of imperial aggression, however, the medieval Papacy had apparently achieved the summit of its authority during the pontificate of Innocent III (1198–1216). He was elected at the extraordinarily early age of thirty-seven, and capitalised extremely ably on propitious political circumstances. He utilised the internal conflicts in Germany to secure, albeit with great difficulty, the elevation of his own candidates for the imperial title. He exploited King John's difficulties in order to reduce England to the status of a papal fief. A lawyer by training, as were all but one of his predecessors and successors between 1159 and 1303, he formulated with logical clarity the fully evolved theory of the papal monarchy based on the vicariate of Christ, and he strove manfully to reform the government of the Papal States and the machinery of curial bureaucracy. He was also a religious leader of great vision. In the face of strong episcopal resistance, he supported the radical and inspirational interpretation of the Christian ideal propounded by Francis of Assisi, and presiding over the

Fourth Lateran Council (1215), he co-ordinated a programme of general ecclesiastical reform designed to purge the Church of the laxity and opulence which had recently attracted so much criticism. Yet even so able a pontiff was frequently at the mercy of external forces. The reunion of the Greek and Latin Churches under the Bishop of Rome, so ardently desired by the papal court since the breach had gradually widened into schism in the late eleventh and early twelfth centuries, was achieved only at the expense of the scandalous sack of Constantinople by Western armies in 1204, which the Pope had never desired but was forced to condone. The extirpation of the Cathar heresy, which in northern Italy was peacefully eradicated by Franciscan preaching, in southern France was achieved only by a bloody crusade, initiated by the Pope but ruthlessly exploited by the acquisitive aristocracy of the north. Even Innocent's imperial policy, apparently successful during his lifetime, bequeathed to his successors the bitter legacy of Frederick II's ambition. If in 1215 it appeared that the Bishop of Rome was the arbiter of the affairs of Europe, and that Gregory VII's ambitions had been fulfilled, it was because an extremely able Pope had strained the resources of the apostolic see to the limits in order to exploit a situation of temporary advantage.

There is a clear contrast between the apparently successful pontificate of Innocent III and the ultimate degrading failure of Boniface VIII (1294–1303), yet the two popes pursued identical policies, to which they were bound by tradition, and which may be summarised as the determined assertion, by legal and ideological means, of the papal plenitude of power in every matter connected, however remotely, with the spiritual welfare of mankind. In a society still regarded by papal publicists as a unitary Christian commonwealth, matters in which the Pope could and indeed was bound to intervene were almost limitless. When Boniface VIII stated that it was absolutely necessary for salvation for every creature to be utterly subject to the apostolic see, he was proposing no radical new thesis. The thirteenth century, however, had witnessed a radical shift in the European balance of power. The French monarchy had risen from insignificance to a position of dominance in the West, and a French cadet house ruled southern Italy. The effective power of the Empire, with its unrealistic universalist pretensions, had been broken by the Papacy, but in the process the concept of universalism had been shattered. In the late thirteenth century, for the first time in over two centuries, the ideological basis of papal authority was effectively challenged. The reception, through contact with Islam, of the political thought of Aristotle had led to the questioning of the dictum that the secular state had been established merely as a remedy for sin, necessary because of mankind's flawed nature and therefore tolerated by God as a regrettable evil. An alternative view was now proposed that the state was the outcome of man's natural tendency towards association, which was positively approved by God. The king was rehabilitated. No longer was power mediated to him through the Pope; rather it was granted to him by the voice of the people, which was equated with the voice of God. When Boniface VIII clashed with King Philip IV of France over the royal right to tax and exercise jurisdiction over the clergy of his realm, the Pope was confronted not only by superior physical force, but by an independently based ideology of the state which owed nothing to papal interpretation of the Bible. Undermined within the Papal States by a rival clan, the kindred of former popes who resented his monopolising of office within his own family, Boniface was extremely vulnerable. His seizure by French agents at Anagni in 1303 and his almost immediate death were symbolic. The power of the Papacy was not broken, but henceforth it would increasingly be forced to accommodate the aspirations of secular rulers and to compromise with their determination to control the Church within their kingdoms.

The nationalistic tendencies within the late medieval Church were emphasised and aggravated by the papal residence at Avignon from 1305 to 1378. The popes were driven to this city not so much by French royal pressure—Avignon was in fact an independent papal enclave—as by the anarchic condition of central Italy, which for seventy years they attempted to reduce to order from their stronghold north of the Alps. They were fiercely criticised, however, not only by Roman businessmen crippled by the absence of a great household noted for its conspicuous expenditure and by Italian humanists mortified by the decline in status of the imperial city, but by the nationals of all those countries diplomatically aligned against France. The situation was greatly worsened by the outbreak in 1337 of the Hundred Years' War between France and England, and the consequent division of western Europe into two armed camps. Successive popes attempted to act as honest brokers in this conflict, but while they thereby failed to satisfy the French king, they were nevertheless castigated by France's enemies as tools of the Valois monarchy who had abnegated their universal responsibilities. An English tag had it that 'as the Pope has become French, so has Jesus become English'.

The tensions within western Europe were reflected within the College of Cardinals, no longer as in the eleventh century the intimate assistants of the Pope, but representatives of national and sectional interests. The return of the Papacy to Rome in 1378 was shortly followed by schism, when the French cardinals set up at Avignon a rival Pope against Urban VI. The 'Great Schism', which lasted until 1415, shocked contemporaries and provided much ammunition for heretical critics of the Church, but whatever solutions were put forward by theologians, the political conflicts within western Europe perpetuated the division. Every ally of France repudiated the Roman line of popes, while no friend of England would recognise the claimant at Avignon. The belated attempt of the cardinals of both obediences to assert their collegial independence by summoning a general council of the Church at Pisa in 1409 resulted not in the healing of the rift, since both Popes refused to accept their deposition, but in a third competing pontiff. The failure of the cardinals led to an increase in episcopal demands for a wider collegiality in the Church—an aspiration with deep roots, which had been rigorously repressed by the Papacy since the Gregorian reform. The kings of Europe, however, were content with a divided Papacy, from which they could the more easily wring concessions, and it was only the initiative of Sigismund, elected Holy Roman Emperor in 1411, whose hereditary power base was Bohemia, home of the Hussite heresy which fed on the divisions within the Church and which was thought to threaten secular as much as ecclesiastical authority, which secured the convening of the Council of Constance in 1415. The Council triumphantly asserted its orthodoxy by burning John Hus, the Bohemian heresiarch, and proceeded to heal the schism by electing Martin V as undisputed Pope. With the support of the other European rulers, however, it ignored the Emperor's pleas to reform the Church at large, and the papal *Curia* in particular, before the election, and the new Pope and his successors, supremely conscious of their legacy, devoted the greater part of their energies to the undermining of plans agreed at Constance for regular and effective councils of the Church.

The Church in France had during the schism assumed an independent existence, looking increasingly to the king for the leadership hitherto expected from Rome. Martin V and his successors, desperate for support, negotiated concordats with other European rulers recognising their *de facto* authority within the national churches. Reformist elements within the Church continued to debate at the Council of Basle (1431–49) even after the papal dissolution of the council, but its success in negotiating with the Bohemian heretics was countered by the papal *rapprochement* with the Byzantine Church, so long in schism; and its efforts towards reform were vitiated by the fear of secular rulers, eagerly fomented by the Papacy, that a demand for wider consultation within the Church signified an attack upon the developing trend towards autocracy within the state. Finally, appeal to a general council was declared to be heretical and treasonable. The Papacy, in order to defeat the conciliar movement, had sacrificed much of its authority to the national monarchies, and become increasingly preoccupied with its own political concerns in central Italy. The popes of the late fifteenth and early sixteenth centuries were of necessity territorial princes. Their ability to influence the spiritual life and ecclesiastical politics of western Europe had been eroded by the concessions made by their predecessors in order to ward off the threat of conciliarism.

Monks and Friars

The Papacy was responsible for the souls of all Christians, but throughout the Middle Ages it showed special solicitude for the welfare of the religious, those men and women who devoted themselves to the communal, celibate and impoverished quest for the grace of God. The foundation charter of Western monasticism is the Rule of St Benedict, written in the middle of the sixth century. The document is not unique, for many monastic leaders composed such rules, and the community at Monte Cassino for which Benedict wrote probably did not survive the sack of their house in 581. Yet because of its inherent excellence, the admiration expressed for the abbot by Pope Gregory I and the desire of Charlemagne for religious uniformity, Benedict's Rule had by the ninth century become the blueprint for monastic life throughout western Europe. The author called his work 'a little rule for beginners'. It was intended not for spiritual athletes, who could scale the heights of asceticism as hermits, but for those who sought a school of religious observance under the direction of an autocratic abbot, elected for life, advised but not governed by the counsel of his monks. The liturgy was set firmly at the centre of communal life, but the monk's day was to be divided between prayer, study and manual work.

The Rule of St Benedict was in some ways a reaction against the monasticism of Syria and Egypt, which had expanded so rapidly because many fervent believers, conscious after 312 CE that the purity of Christian observance had been diluted by compromise with the secular power, sought individual salvation through a life of austere isolation, or forming into groups, waged from their desert retreats a violent campaign against paganism and the classical tradition. Benedict and his Western contemporaries, living in the shadow of the distintegration of the Roman Empire in an era of violent uncertainty, existed in a state of siege. Within their communities they struggled to create a refuge wherein Roman social ideals and classical culture were preserved. Unlike the holy men of the East, they were not wild radicals, but conservatives. They imagined that their new barbarian rulers were both irreligious and philistine. Yet once the initial stage of evangelisation, the conversion of the Germanic war-lords, had been completed, the monasteries came to be highly valued as the only surviving repositories of that *Romanitas* so ardently admired by the new rulers of western Europe.

Because of their monopoly of education in the early Middle Ages, rulers looked to monasteries to provide training for those clerks essential for the servicing of their rudimentary bureaucracies, for written government distinguished a Christian king from a barbarian chieftain. As successful tribal kingdoms extended their frontiers, Christianisation and colonisation went hand in hand, and the monks were in the vanguard, establishing outposts of evangelisation and royal influence in newly conquered territories. Election of an abbot by his monks was soon replaced by royal appointment, and as the monasteries accumulated vast estates, from which the king expected military service as from any others, the religious superiors provided a counterweight to the secular aristocracy, whose interests often conflicted with those of the crown. In countless ways the monastic order buttressed royal authority, and lesser lords obtained as many benefits from their own religious foundations.

The primary motivation for the establishment of monasteries was, however, surely religious. Early medieval theology was dominated by the Old Testament. The vengeful God of Israel was ideally suited to the tribal society of the barbarian kings, and there was little emphasis upon the love of Jesus. Men lived in perpetual fear of the Last Judgement and the pains of Hell, vividly portrayed sculpturally and in wall-paintings. Preachers constantly emphasised that the aristocratic and military classes, who in this harsh competitive world had to fight to survive, were in the greatest danger of damnation. The penance imposed by the priest on earth, however, and the debt due to God after death, might in this world, where little store was set by individualism, be discharged by others. The prayers and religious exercises of the monks might be credited to their founders and benefactors. By founding a monastery, great men created for themselves a mausoleum, to be staffed for all time by a community whose *raison d'être* was intercessory prayer. Lesser benefactors stipulated that, in return for their gifts, they should on their death-beds be clothed as monks, and treated as such at the divine tribunal. The monks, knights of Christ, were engaged in a constant battle against the forces of darkness for the souls of mankind, and especially of those who had made a spiritual investment in their community. They took upon their shoulders the sins of the world.

In the late eleventh century there was a sudden but widespread reaction against the integration of monasticism with the world. This was intimately connected with that intellectual movement known as the 'twelfth-century Renaissance', which was characterised by pronounced concern for the individual and by an attempt to return to primitive ideals. This rejection of past monastic glories was led by young monks, influenced by the new theology which emphasised the love of the human Jesus, sent to be a companion and exemplar, and seeking to establish a personal relationship with him through meditation conducted in an environment divorced from feudal politics and the manorial economy, which was to be a conscious recreation of the life of the apostolic community at Jerusalem or the Desert Fathers of the fourth century.

In the twelfth century, the monolithic structure of Benedictine monasticism was shattered, and many versions of the 'apostolic and evangelical life' were offered to those in search of perfection. The Carthusians, most austere of the new orders, combined the solitude of the desert with the discipline of a conventual structure. The Augustinian canons, whose modest establishments attracted the patronage of the lesser gentry and prosperous merchants, undertook pastoral work and administered hospitals. The military orders, both in the Holy Land and in Spain, combined the monastic vocation with the chivalric ethos, and constituted the most efficient fighting machine of the age.

The most successful and influential of the new orders, however, was that of Cîteaux. The Cistercian interpretation of the Rule of St Benedict, which was to be followed to the letter, their determination to found communities in places far removed from the conversation of men, their rejection of involvement in the complexities of feudal government and their avoidance of superfluous elaboration in architecture and liturgy convinced many people across western Europe and the Christian Levant that the life of the White Monks provided 'the surest road to heaven'. The path to salvation was opened not only to the knightly class, from which the choir monks were still exclusively recruited, but to many thousands of illiterate members of the lower ranks of society admitted as lay brethren, who in earning their salvation provided a highly efficient work-force. In an attempt to preserve the pristine purity of the founding fathers in an order which had by 1152 expanded to 328 abbeys, the Cistercians evolved a constitution based on a yearly meeting of all abbots and the annual visitation of all monasteries. This model was later applied by the Papacy to all religious orders, in an attempt to override the traditional autonomy of the ancient Benedictine houses. Cistercian influence on the ecclesiastical politics of twelfth-century Europe was increased immeasurably by the career and writings of Bernard of Clairvaux, a spiritual and theological genius who ardently, if sometimes stridently, combated sin and sloth wherever they were perceived. No king, bishop or scholar was exempt from his criticism, which was directed most fiercely against the alleged laxity of traditional Benedictinism. It is sad, although perhaps not surprising, that the primitive zeal of the early Cistercians could not be sustained in perpetuity. By the end of the twelfth century social critics found it hard to distinguish them from the Benedictines, except perhaps that their avarice was greater.

The function of radical reform within the thirteenth-century Church was fulfilled not by monks, but by a new form of religious institution, the mendicant orders of friars. The institutions of the Church had in the late twelfth century come under attack from various groups of fundamentalist critics, regarded by the hierarchy as heretics. A challenge to Rome was mounted by the very existence of the Cathar faith, firmly entrenched in southern France and with a strong presence in northern Italy. This was a religion closely akin to Christianity rather than a Christian heresy, whose adherents believed in the coexistence of good and evil gods, whose eternal strife was represented by incessant conflict between spirit and matter; this was an unacceptable accentuation of tendencies in Christian, and especially monastic, theology. The presence of dissident groups within the Christian community, such as the Waldensians, was probably the long-term result of Pope Gregory VII's incitement of pious laymen to open criticism of unworthy priests as part of his programme to purify the Church. Many felt themselves betrayed by the more cautiously bureaucratic popes of the twelfth century and became increasingly alienated from the structure and practice of contemporary sacerdotal religion, until their strictures became so abrasive that they were excluded from the Church.

The challenge of the heretics was met by Dominic's organisation of the Order of Preachers, a disciplined body of skilled theologians trained to excel in popular preaching, and by the spontaneous joy in God's creation expressed by Francis and his followers, whose enthusiastic imitation of the poverty of Christ evoked such a response in northern Italy that the pessimistic Cathar heresy simply withered away. Dominic deliberately set out to create a highly motivated elite corps; Francis, whose interpretation of the Gospel message was closely akin to that of many heretical leaders, but who unlike them was unwavering in his loyalty to the Papacy, reluctantly accepted an organisational structure for his followers when it became obvious that the alternative was spiritual anarchy. The poverty of the order—as opposed to the monastic vow of individual poverty, often fulfilled within a rich corporation—was an ideal for Francis, whereas for Dominic it was a means towards the end of counteracting heretical criticism of the Church. The Dominican and Franciscan Orders borrowed heavily from each other, and with their international organisations they became the front-line troops of the Papacy in the battle against heterodoxy and religious dissent. It is symptomatic, however, of their very different origins that the Dominicans, as well as achieving much that would be considered laudable by any Christian, provided the staff of the Holy Inquisition, while the Franciscans were themselves racked by schism when a vociferous minority of the brethren reacted strongly against the alleged corruption of the primitive ideals of the founder by his successors as Minister General, and were themselves condemned as heretical.

The resolution of the friars to live by begging forced them into the towns to survive, and in consequence they fulfilled one of the greatest needs of the medieval Church, which since the decline of the Roman Empire had been orientated towards agrarian society. By their charismatic preaching the friars often succeeded in harnessing the potentially anarchic religious enthusiasm of the urban masses to aims approved by the Church. They provided for the poor, in return for the smallest contribution, the services of intercession which their social superiors expected from the monks, and during outbreaks of plague they acquired an enviable reputation for the care of the sick and dying. This evangelical and social work was combined with a formidable record of academic attainment. Within a few years of the foundation of the orders, university teachers of the highest reputation were recruited to their ranks, and the majority of outstanding theologians of the later Middle Ages were members of the mendicant orders, who also established networks of lowers schools across Europe, and led the way in the study of languages and the natural sciences. The friars, however, attracted much hostility from bishops jealous of their exemption from episcopal control, parish clergy fearful for their offerings and academics whose reputations and fees were jeopardised. The price paid by the Papacy for the establishment of this international militia was the concession that no new rule of religious life should be sanctioned in the future. When by the early fourteenth century the friars had lost their initial radical impulse, there was an embargo on the establishment of any innovative and reforming body within the Church. This surely accounts for the proliferation of heretical groups in the later Middle Ages and the inflexibility of the Church in the face of any criticism.

Christian Belief and Thought

The transformation of Western theology, and the development of a distinctively medieval interpretation, coincides with the rise in the early twelfth century of the cathedral schools, from which the new universities were to grow. Early medieval theology, which had been dominated by the monastic ethos, had been derivative and highly conservative. The great need had been to consolidate. Thinking men were convinced that all the great questions surrounding the Christian religion had been answered by the Fathers of the Church, and it was only the inadequate powers of contemporary scholars which retarded comprehension. There was a total reliance on authority, and a great mistrust of the exercise of reason.

Then, in the late eleventh century, six hundred years after the magisterial contribution of Augustine, men began with remarkable suddenness to ask fundamental questions about the faith: why should men believe in God? How could God be One and yet threefold? Why was God made man? This outbreak of theological speculation is one of the main strands of the intellectual and artistic Renaissance of the twelfth century, and resulted from the vastly increased confidence of a society newly freed from external pressure and enjoying an economic miracle, whose basic principles were nevertheless questioned by Jews within and by Muslims beyond its frontiers. It was a sign of security and of maturity that Christian thinkers were now eager to meet the challenge of other faiths not merely by the recitation of biblical and patristic texts, but by rational argument. Anselm, considered today by many to be the medieval theologian most relevant to the modern world, offered rational proof, without recourse to any authority, of the existence of God and the necessity for God's incarnation. Faith provided him with the insights which allowed him to construct this proof, yet he believed that it could not be controverted intellectually by those who lacked faith.

Revealed truth, indeed, dictated certain parameters within which logical discussion must be conducted, and to traverse these boundaries invited condemnation by the common consensus of Latin Christian thinkers, which was visited on Peter Abelard in his lifetime. Abelard's influence, however, was profound. He emphasised the role of the human

Jesus, sent to be an exemplar and friend to mankind, thus humanising the image of Christ in majesty, the dreadful Judge of the Last Day, which dominated early medieval theology. He stressed the relationship of the individual with his creator, which should be based on love tinged with awe, rather than on terror of a vengeful God. Individual intention for him was all important, for it was on this, rather than on the consequences of any act, that judgement was passed by a God far more percipient than the tribal deity of the early Middle Ages intent only on receiving his judicial due. Above all, in his relationship with Héloïse and more especially in the correspondence resulting from their separation, Abelard rejected the monastic theology of the past and asserted that salvation was not restricted to the celibate inmates of the cloister, but was open to men and women in a wide variety of Christian vocations which were consonant with the will of God.

Early medieval thinkers had accepted that the Bible presented to mankind the divine plan for the organisation of society, and that it was the inadequacy of fallen man that prevented its realisation. Such was the self-confidence of the theologians of the twelfth and thirteenth centuries that they believed that the power of reason, with which man alone in creation was endowed, could compensate for the ravages of sin. The experience of their own age, which was confirmed by the observations of human society contained in those works of the ancient Greek philosopher Aristotle newly rediscovered in the West through contact with Islam, indicated that the idealised lifestyle of the earliest Christian community was unattainable by the generality of mankind. Rather than simply accept the shortcomings of contemporary Christians, the new generation of rational theologians, whose endeavours culminated in the magisterial synthesis of Thomas Aquinas (d. 1274), embarked upon a detailed analysis of the Divine Law and presented a series of subtle distinctions. Private property, profit and the waging of war, all condemned by the Bible, were discovered to be justified in certain circumstances, which corresponded closely to the current practice of western Europe. The biblical account of the apostolic community was now seen as an historical description of the Church at an early stage of its development, rather than as the divinely ordained exemplar of Christian life for all time. A dramatic official endorsement of this view came when in 1323 Pope John XXII, in the face of radical Franciscan criticism of ecclesiastical wealth, condemned as heretical belief in the absolute poverty of Christ and the apostles. Aquinas and his contemporaries expressed a sublime certainty in the worth of western society, in which natural man, in accordance with God's grace and by his own endeavours, was fulfilling the divine plan for the world.

Earlier theologians, following Augustine, had differentiated sharply between grace and nature. For Aquinas grace perfected nature. The natural condition of man was not one of degradation resulting from his fall. God did not merely tolerate human society as a consequence of sin, but willed that man should develop according to his natural inclinations, which God had instituted. Aquinas saw the main characteristic of God as intelligence and reason. Man, created in the image of God, was endowed with reason, clouded but not obliterated by the fall, and was therefore capable of comprehending, albeit imperfectly, objective and eternal truths. Intellect rather than will provided the pathway towards the ultimate contemplation of God, whose existence could be demonstrated not merely by direct revelation, but by human reason. The existence of God was certainly not contrary to human reason; rather it was the only explanation available to human reason for existence itself.

This theological certainty and self-confidence in the destiny of mankind was rapidly eroded in the fourteenth century. Western Europe lost its sense of direction as economic conditions worsened, plague became endemic, expansion ground to a halt and the twin universal authorities of Empire and Papacy were successively humbled. The optimism of Aquinas now seemed misplaced, and Thomism, although it was resurrected in the sixteenth century as the intellectual orthodoxy of the Roman Catholic Church, found few enthusiastic followers in the later Middle Ages, whose theology was fideistic rather than rational. William of Ockham (d. 1349), despite excommunication for his antipapal political writings in support of the Emperor Lewis of Bavaria, was the most influential theologian of this period, for his nominalism reflected the uncertainty of the age. He denied the capacity of man's mind to comprehend concepts beyond the experience of the senses. God could not be reduced to a glorified likeness of human rationality. In contemporary Europe it appeared obvious that the world was subject to evil and that man was limited. God by definition was infinitely powerful, and the only explanation of current events was that God was subject to no laws and acted merely at his pleasure. Things which men generally agreed were just could be unjust if God so willed it. God could not be approached by reason, and conformity with the Divine Law became an exercise in uncomprehending obedience. There was a return to the dread of a terrifying and arbitrary deity which had been felt in the earlier Middle Ages, and a wedge was once more driven between theology and philosophy, which in the days of optimism had apparently been reconciled.

Closely allied with theological enquiry was the vital task of translating the Divine Law revealed by God in the Bible into a code of legislation by which Christian society might be governed. The corpus of canon law of the Western Church represented a monumental jurisdictional achievement. In the twelfth century the divergent penitential codes of Christianised tribal societies and the contradictory rulings of church councils and bishops were first tentatively reconciled, in a private compilation by the Bolognese monk Gratian, the *Concordance of Discordant Canons* (1140), into a universal system based on the authority of Rome. Subsequent popes, by their rulings on individual cases submitted to them, created a comprehensive body of international law, codified in the *Corpus Iuris Canonici* of 1234 and continually analysed in the voluminous writings of learned commentators. Canon law has often been regarded as the primary instrument of the extension of papal 'political' power, but the relationship between Church and State was far from being the sole concern of the canonists. Papal decisions of the late twelfth century, for example, humanised the Christian law of marriage and created a code for the implementation of poor relief. The papal court, moreover, never intervened directly in any case; it acted only upon appeal, made either in order to obtain clarification of a difficult legal point, or against the ruling of an inferior court. The influence of the Papacy throughout western Europe was greatly increased by the activities of the various central courts at Rome and of judges-delegate in the provinces, but papal justice became firmly entrenched because the popes offered a superior legal product, for which numerous clerks and laymen were willing to travel and to pay.

Practical and Popular Religion

The speculative thought of the universities and the subtle distinctions of the lawyers had little direct effect upon the religious beliefs of the generality of the population of western Europe, although in the thirteenth century a great effort was made to disseminate at parochial level the essential elements of the new pastoral theology through the publication of manuals for confessors and parish priests. Medieval Western Christianity was a sacerdotal religion, and the exclusive status of the priestly caste had been emphasised by the Gregorian reformers. Theory did not, however, correspond to reality. There was a great divide between those 'sublime and literate persons' from whom were recruited bishops and the higher clergy, and the vast majority of village priests whose economic condition was little better than that of their parishioners, and whose learning was often enough limited to the mere recitation of the offices of the Church. The laity were bound to support their local minister by the payment of tithe and various obligatory offerings, which was enforced by law, and this naturally led to grumbling and tension. That allegedly rampant late medieval anti-clericalism, however, which is so often cited as a cause of the success of the Reformation, was not directed at the priesthood as a whole, or its function within Christian society. Vociferous complaints were directed at isolated instances of flagrant immorality or neglect by parish priests, but general resentment was reserved for exploitative ecclesiastical landlords and for the agents of the ecclesiastical courts, whose jurisdiction touched so many aspects of life.

For the vast majority of western European Christians, the church of their village or market town was the focus not only of their spiritual but of their social life. The Mass was the channel of mediation between God and man, but it was also an assertion of corporate identity during which blessing was invoked upon the extended brotherhood, living and dead, and enemies of the group were anathematised. The festivals of the

Church clearly delineated the divisions of the agricultural year, and the course of human life was marked by baptism, marriage, the purification of women after childbirth and the requiem. In the church or churchyard the penitent would discharge his debt of guilt to God and to his local community. The priest, on the instructions of king or archbishop, transmitted to his flock news of momentous events and arranged processions to pray for the success of royal armies, for deliverance from plague or for clement weather. In every parish church lights were maintained in honour of various saints, and most especially in honour of the Blessed Virgin Mary whose cult, as the supreme mediatrix, attained tremendous popularity in the twelfth century. In larger churches a chantry chapel might be established by the lordly patron or by a rich merchant, dedicated to his patron saint, wherein prayers for the soul of the founder and his kin would be offered for all time. There might also be a guild or confraternity, an association established for pious, charitable and social purposes, whose members would organise the maintenance of the poor and the commemoration of deceased brethren, and in towns would produce cycles of mystery plays which provided both entertainment and instruction. The church building itself was a teaching medium of vital importance. The rood, set on a screen separating the congregation from the mystery of the altar, displayed Christ's sacrifice for mankind. Above the door was often depicted the Last Judgement, a stern warning of the consequences of unrepented sin. The walls were covered with colourful representations of the Bible story and the lives of saints. The central position of the parish church in the corporate and religious life of medieval communities is clearly demonstrated by the vast resources invested in frequent rebuilding. In England, for example, the sumptuous wool churches of the Cotswolds and East Anglia are an expression of ostentatious wealth, but also of a determination to rebuild on a grand scale to the greater glory of God.

Beyond the confines of their own parish, Christians might make gifts or death-bed bequests to the religious orders, and increasingly in the later Middle Ages to the four orders of friars or to one of the increasing number of hospitals for lepers, the insane or the aged. They were encouraged to acts of piety and charity by the issue of indulgences, that is the promise of remission of a specified number of days or years of those penalties due for sin which in the later twelfth century were embraced within the concept of Purgatory. Such remission could be granted by the Church because of the existence of the Treasury of Merits, an inexhaustible store accumulated mainly by Christ, but supplemented by the saints, who had far more than were needed for their own salvation. The bishops' power of remission was restricted to forty days, but the Pope, because of his plenitude of power, might grant whatever pardon he wished. The plenary indulgence, granting complete immunity for all sins committed before it was acquired to those contrite, confessed and of good intent, was originally offered to crusaders, but it was gradually extended to contributors to the holy war and other papally approved causes. In 1300 Boniface VIII offered a plenary indulgence to all visitors to Rome in that year and in subsequent Jubilee years, and the interval between Jubilees was gradually reduced from a hundred to twenty-five years. In the later Middle Ages full remission of sins was granted to visitors to various holy places at specified times. This explains the extraordinary popularity of pilgrimages, usually to churches which were the repositories of outstanding relics. No doubt many pilgrims were motivated by a desire to see the world, and proceeded in the holiday mood described in Chaucer's *Canterbury Tales*, but behind this jovial sociability lay the utterly serious purpose of the search for salvation, achieved through the veneration of the tomb of Thomas Becket at Canterbury, the Holy Blood of Hailes or the Holy Rood of Bromholm. Every region had its quota of such shrines, and the adventurous from all over the continent would journey to sites of international repute such as the sanctuary of Santiago de Compostella. From the mid-fourteenth century, however, the Papacy increasingly granted indulgences which allowed the recipient to obtain from his chosen confessor at the moment of death full remission of all his sins. The charge for this wonderful benefit was remarkably small, and it is hardly surprising that subsequent Roman Jubilees never attracted the huge concourse of pilgrims which descended on the Holy City in 1300.

The crusade indulgence was one of the main inducements for men to embark on those armed pilgrimages which expanded the frontiers of Western Christendom in the twelfth and thirteenth centuries. The desire for salvation and for worldly gain was nicely balanced in the minds of participants in expeditions to the Holy Land, the *Reconquista* by which Spain was recovered from Islam, and the *Drang nach Osten*, wherein German eastward expansion was fused with the Christianisation of the northern Slavs. Endemic warfare against Islam had far-reaching consequences for the West, and was one of the formative factors in the development of Western European civilisation, although in the Muslim world the Crusades were seen as no more than minor frontier conflicts. The Papacy gained great prestige from the launching of the First Crusade in 1095 and its supervisory role in subsequent expeditions, and the holy wars may be seen as the logical culmination of the peace movement preached in the eleventh century by the French bishops, an attempt to redirect the bellicose energies of the feudal aristocracy away from internecine strife into a common effort against the enemies of the faith. In the wake of the First Crusade knighthood became a Christian vocation, by the conscientious practice of which salvation might be achieved outside the monastic cloister. Through the Crusades the Christian Church, in its origins pacifist, became reconciled to the regrettable necessity for armed action, and Latin theologians and canon lawyers evolved a theory of the just war which has been echoed down to the present day.

Contact with the superior civilisation of Islam in the Near East, and more especially in Spain and in Sicily, conquered from the

Muslims by Norman princes who in the twelfth century encouraged the development of a remarkably tolerant and cosmopolitan society, led to great advances in the West in philosophy and all branches of the sciences. There were, however, less happy consequences. Norman participation in the Crusades increased hostility between those fierce but pious adherents of muscular Latin Christianity and the Byzantines, whom they had recently ejected from southern Italy, and Norman pressure on the Papacy caused the rift between Latin and Greek Churches to develop into schism, finally rendered permanent by the Western sack of Constantinople in 1204. Moreover, the new sentimental regard for the holy places associated with the life and sufferings of Christ led on the eve of the First Crusade to violent recrimination by popular preachers against the Jews and to widespread massacres, shamefully repeated thereafter at regular intervals.

There was no element in the life of the Western Church in the period from 1100 to 1500 which did not attract vociferous criticism from groups who were convinced that Latin Christianity had strayed far from the pathway of perfection described in the New Testament. The hostility of the hierarchy to their sincere, if sometimes naïve, strictures was paralleled by the paranoiac conviction of secular rulers that any challenge to ecclesiastical authority would lead to the undermining of the established structure of society. Christian fundamentalists—the Waldensians and the English Lollards—were persecuted as vigorously as members of the lunatic fringe, such as the adherents of the Free Spirit, who believed that their special relationship with God freed them from all moral restrictions. The final collapse of the medieval religious system was not, however, brought about by the attacks of any heretical group, but by the growing conviction among increasingly well-educated and completely orthodox men and women, such as the Brethren of the Common Life, that the organisational framework of the Catholic Church was of little relevance to their search for salvation, which might best be achieved not through unquestioning obedience to the Papacy, donations to the religious orders or participation in holy war, but by a sincere attempt to follow the precepts of the most popular of later medieval religious treatises, Thomas à Kempis's *Imitation of Christ*.

Further Reading

Barraclough, G. *The Medieval Papacy* (Thames & Hudson, London, 1968)
Brooke, C.N.L. *The Monastic World* (Paul Elek, London, 1974)
Brooke, C. and R. *Popular Religion in the Middle Ages* (Thames & Hudson, London, 1984)
Moore, R.I. *The Origins of European Dissent* (Allen Lane, London, 1977)
Morris, C. *The Discovery of the Individual 1050–1200* (SPCK, London, 1972)
Oakley, F. *The Western Church in the Later Middle Ages* (Cornell University Press, Ithaca, 1979)
Riley Smith, J. *What were the Crusades?* (Macmillan, London, 1977)

Southern, R.W. *Western Society and the Church in the Middle Ages* (Penguin, Harmondsworth, 1970)
Sumption, J. *Pilgrimage—an Image of Medieval Religion* (Faber & Faber, London, 1977)
Tierney, B. *The Crisis of Church and State 1050–1300* (Prentice-Hall Inc., Englewood Cliffs, 1964)

12 *Christianity in Europe: Reformation to Today*

Sheridan Gilley

Reform and Counter-Reform

The sixteenth century was notable for two great changes which have shaped the subsequent history of the Christian West. First, Spain and Portugal acquired vast new empires in the Americas and the Far East which made Christianity a global religion. A king of Spain gave his name to what still remains the only Christian country in Asia, the Philippines, while a Roman Catholic population was formed in Latin America which is now the largest in the world. Second, Protestantism ended forever the religious unity of western Christendom under the Pope, as in the years after Luther's revolt in 1517 most of northern Europe declared its independence of Rome and has preserved it to the present day. Yet that Protestant rejection of the Papacy provoked a massive Catholic reaction, the Counter-Reformation, which left Europe more religious in 1600 than it had been in 1500, as two in some ways rather similar movements of spiritual renewal strove for mastery, in more than a hundred years of religious war.

The origins of the Catholic revival predated the Reformation, and lay in the new strength achieved by Iberian Catholicism from the union of the Spanish kingdom under Ferdinand V the Catholic (1452–1516) and his wife Isabella (1451–1504). These 'Catholic Sovereigns' patronised the church-reforming programme of the Queen's Observant Franciscan confessor, Cardinal Francisco Ximénez de Cisneros (1436–1517), the scourge of unreformed conventualism, founder of the humanist University of Alcalá, and patron of its most famous production, the Complutensian Polyglot Bible, with its parallel texts in Hebrew, Latin and Greek. Ferdinand and Isabella also favoured the Spanish Inquisition established in 1479, which, under its most famous Grand Inquisitor, Tomás de Torquemada (1420–98), reinforced national as well as religious unity against former Jews and Moors deemed as 'Marranos' and 'Moriscos' to have been inadequately converted to Christianity. The royal expulsion of the remaining Spanish Jews in 1492 moved the heartland of Jewish culture to the Low Countries and central and eastern Europe, though in Catholic states they were increasingly confined to 'ghettos'. The Spanish conquest of Granada in 1492 also removed the last Muslim state from western European soil, and led to the forcible conversion or expulsion of the Moors. Many devout and eminent Spanish Christians had non-Christian forbears, but an 'Old Christian' ideology, founded on pride in 'purity of blood' and directed against 'New Christians' suspected of lingering Jewish or Moorish sympathies, reinforced an orthodoxy also impregnated with the chivalric crusading idealism which was given brutal expression in Central and South America in the 1520s and 1530s, in the conquests of the Aztecs and Incas.

A militant and military Spanish Catholicism was to have an equal influence on the wider European stage: the disputed Aragonese overlordship of southern Italy led to two centuries of Spanish domination of the Italian peninsula, while Ferdinand the Catholic's grandson Charles V (1500–58), also grandson of the Habsburg Holy Roman Emperor Maximilian I (1459–1519), inherited both the Spanish Empire and the Habsburg dominions in Austria, Germany and the old Burgundian Netherlands. Charles was elected emperor in 1519, and his efforts to contain the Protestant challenge within his ramshackle Holy Roman Empire was to be sustained by Spanish soldiers and silver as well as by Spanish sanctity. Charles's Spanish empire in the Old and New Worlds was inherited by his son Philip II (1527–98), whose armies championed the Catholic cause not only in his own possessions in Italy and Flanders, but in France and Germany, and against England, indeed wherever the Catholic Church had need of new crusaders.

Spanish sanctity also produced the principal spiritual defender of the Roman Catholic Church in the ex-soldier Ignatius Loyola (1491–1556), who after periods of mystical ascetism and some belated university study, laid the foundations in Paris in 1534 of the Society of Jesus, approved by the Papacy in 1540 and destined soon to become, under its 'General', the 'Black Pope', the most impressive, powerful and hated of the propagandist orders of a new Catholicism. Loyola's original inspiration was the old medieval one of pilgrimage to Jerusalem, and his first thought for his Order was the conversion of the heathen, a vision realised by the most famous of his early companions, Francis Xavier (1506–52), in spectacular missionary journeys to India and Japan. Loyola's own religious teaching, embodied in his *Spiritual Exercises*, harnessed medieval techniques of meditation involving the training of the senses, the imagination, the reason and the will, to an activist ideal of sanctity, which was to be pursued not by withdrawal to the cloister but by working in the world. The Inquisition suspected

Ignatius and dealt harshly with the illuminist mystics known as the *Alumbrados*, as with the humanist religious circle of Juan de Valdés (*c*. 1500–41); yet it did not prevent the considerable theological activity of divines like the Dominicans Dominic Soto (1494–1560) and Melchior Cano (1509–60), or the spiritual writings of the Carmelite reformer and visionary Teresa of Ávila (1515–82), who set forth the profoundest of analyses of the whole range of mystical experience from discursive meditation to the highest states of union with God. Teresa's circle included Peter of Alcántara (1499–1562), founder of the Spanish Discalced Franciscans, the great preacher John of Ávila (1500–69), the 'Apostle of Andalusia', and the Carmelite poet John of the Cross (1542–91), who, with the Dominican Luis of Granada (1505–88) made the second half of the sixteenth century the golden age of Spanish mystical religion. The Orders also furnished a host of heroic evangelists, to redeem the barbarities of white colonists by evangelising the peoples of the New World. The intensity of Hispanic Christianity was captured by its favourite painter, Domenico Theotocopuli, known as El Greco (1541–1614), whose strangely elongated, surrealist, neo-Byzantine saints and martyrs still communicate the Spanish longing for the eternal.

Yet Spanish Catholicism also exalted the royal authority dominant in the Church. There was a similar tendency to national religious independence both in France, where it was embodied in the Pragmatic Sanction of Bourges (1438) and the Concordat of Bologna (1516), and in England, where it was symbolised by the wealth and power of a great royal protégé and statesman, Cardinal Thomas Wolsey (*c*. 1474–1530). Indeed, outside Spain, secular authority contributed to the disorganisation of Catholicism by permitting monarchies and aristocracies to exploit her; and while the aspiration to reform the Church was universal, the chief institutional effort to realise it, the 'conciliar movement' to renew Christendom by universal general councils like those of Constance (1414–18) and Basle (1431–49), was defeated by the Papacy after 1450 as a rival to its own ecclesiastical power.

The Papacy was a large part of the Church's problem. From the mid-fifteenth century, a sequence of able, unscrupulous and increasingly secular-minded popes became entirely absorbed in the sordid and murderous intricacies of Italian politics and the enrichment of their own families. The Papacy reached its moral nadir with the pontificate of Rodrigo Borgia, Alexander VI (1431–1503), though a still greater notoriety for political ruthlessness was won by his soldier–son Cesare Borgia (1475–1507). Their work for the consolidation of the central Italian States of the Church was continued by the warlike Julius II (1443–1513), but the greatest achievement of the Renaissance Papacy lay in its patronage of the visual arts, which were overwhelmingly religious in content, and Julius II was especially notable for his employment of Donato Bramante (1444–1514), Raphael (Raffaele) Sanzio (1483–1520) and Michelangelo Buonarroti (1475–1564), who gave Christianity some of its most enduring images, the new St Peter's, the

Sistine Madonna, the Pietà and Sistine Chapel frescos. Julius also convened the Fifth Lateran Council (1512–17), but while it defended papal authority against conciliar theory, it made no major reforms, and left the Roman Church under the pleasure-loving Giovanni de' Medici, Pope Leo X (1475–1521), wholly unprepared for the religious storms whipped up by new religious values and ideals.

The causes of the Reformation are only partly to be found in the pastoral and moral failures of late medieval Catholicism, as orthodox Catholics had deplored as much as heretics the concubinage, pluralism, neglect of religious duty and venality of many of the clergy. Much of rural Europe was poorly served by uneducated or absentee priests, but though the religiosity of the Middle Ages has been much overrated, the growth of guilds and chantries attested to the vigorous spiritual life of the towns. Medieval religion was a house with many mansions, with room for considerable philosophical disagreement, as between 'realists' and 'nominalists', and for both the individualistic mysticism of such masters of the spiritual life as the English Richard Rolle (*c*. 1300–49) and the German Johann Tauler (*c*. 1300–61), and the *devotio moderna* of the Brethren of the Common Life, a Dutch and German religious movement given its most diffused expression in the *Imitation of Christ* of Thomas à Kempis (*c*. 1380–1471). The spiritual seriousness of the Brethren influenced the tone and preoccupations of Renaissance humanism in northern Europe, and of their most celebrated pupil Desiderius Erasmus (*c*. 1466–1536), a Dutch-born but internationally-minded and free-ranging intellectual indifferent or hostile to local and ecclesiastical tradition and custom, and given to brilliantly witty satire of the Papacy, his own monasticism and of popular religion. This he regarded with a true intellectual's disdain as contaminated with monkish superstition. From the mid-fifteenth century, the invention of printing by Johann Gutenberg (*c*. 1396–1468) multiplied Bibles and Testaments in northern Europe, and Erasmus' edition and translation of the Greek New Testament represented a scholarly recall to the sources of Christianity, to recover its simplicity, purity and power.

The Erasmian reforming programme, learned but rather untheological, at first captured the educated religious mind of Europe. In Germany, this 'New Learning' was the subject of attacks on the Hebrew scholar Johannes Reuchlin (1455–1522), but it flourished in England in the early humanist ideals of St Thomas More (1478–1535) and John Colet (1466–1519) and in France in the circle of Jacques Lefèvre d'Étaples (1455–1536). The future lay, however, with the German Augustinian friar and biblical professor of Wittenberg, Martin Luther (1483–1546). Luther was both a much more human and a more violent man than Erasmus, an emotionally and intellectually complex character influenced by theological nominalism and Tauler's mysticism. He was converted to monasticism by a vow made to St Anne during a thunderstorm, and thereafter was a prey to terrible internal suffering over his conviction of his own sinfulness. He resolved his inner crisis by finding the central message of the Scriptures not, like Erasmus, in the Gospels, but in the Epistles, and especially in the Pauline conviction that the divine gift of faith, in 'justification', converted God's justice from an instrument of condemnation of sin to one of pardon: thus the man of faith is forgiven his sins, not in any degree by virtue of his own works and merits but by his faith alone in the merits of Christ. Luther's original objection to Rome in his '95 theses' of 1517 was a moderate one, centred on the scandalous methods of selling the papal indulgences which applied the 'treasury of merit' earned by Christ and the saints to relieve the 'temporal punishment' due to sin, especially the penal sufferings of the dead in Purgatory; the money raised by the sale was for the Renaissance rebuilding of St Peter's, though some of it was creamed off by German bishops and bankers. By 1521, when Luther was excommunicated by Leo X, his theology had advanced to the doctrine of the 'priesthood of all believers', which overturned the authority of a separate ministerial order of mass-saying priestly intermediaries between man and God, and which defined the Pope as Antichrist. Luther also distanced himself from the older Catholic humanists, and denied the freedom of the human will in 1525 in controversy with Erasmus. The German reformer defended the principles of *sola Scriptura* (against tradition), *sola gratia* (against the idea of human merit) and *sola fide* (against salvation by good works). In marrying a nun, he specifically repudiated monasticism and asceticism as forms of salvation by works, and through the 1520s he enriched his own new church order with its greatest spiritual treasures, new vernacular catechisms, Scriptures, commentaries, liturgy, hymnody and scatological polemics, landmarks in the history of the German language and literature as well as of German religion.

Luther owed his appeal in part to patriotic German resentment of Roman taxation and abuse of power, and to the lack of an effective central imperial authority to restrain the princes, cities, knights and peasants who rallied to support him. He repudiated the violence of the Peasants' Revolt of 1525 and its Anabaptist leader Thomas Müntzer (*c.* 1490–1525), and it was the princes who proved to be his most important allies in the creation of a new Lutheran church order, even if they were also moved by greed for church property. The Grand Master of the Teutonic Knights became in 1525 the first Hohenzollern Duke of Prussia, and the very word 'Protestant' itself arose from the protest of the Lutheran princes at the Diet of Speyer in 1529. In 1530, Luther's most attractive and eirenic younger disciple, the humanist Philipp Melanchthon (1497–1560), was chiefly responsible for framing the first of the great Protestant confessions of faith, that of Augsburg. In 1526, the Ottoman Turks overran most of Hungary, and Charles V, too occupied with these and other threats to his vast dominions, did not break up the Schmalkaldic League of Protestant princes until 1547. He failed in the attempt to impose a religious settlement on the Empire in the

Interim of Augsburg of 1548, and the Peace of Augsburg of 1555 acknowledged the existence of Lutheranism as well as Catholicism, on the principle of confessional absolutism, *cujus regio ejus religio*, that the religion of the ruler should decide the religion of his people.

The Lutheran reform was also officially victorious by 1540 in Denmark and newly independent Sweden, where it greatly strengthened royal authority over the nobility as well as the Church, and whence it was spread by force and royal command as well as by evangelism to the dependent regions of Norway, Iceland and Finland. Later Roman missions left undisturbed this nearly total Lutheran monopoly of Scandinavian Christianity. In 1528, a Lutheran martyr, Patrick Hamilton, was burnt at the stake in Scotland. In England a Lutheran circle formed around Thomas Cranmer (1489–1556), who was secretly married to the niece of the German reformer Andreas Osiander (1498–1552). As Archbishop of Canterbury from 1532, Cranmer provided Henry VIII (1491–1547) with the theological justification to break the Church in England's ties with Rome in 1534. A more radical reform was reserved to the brief reign of Edward VI (1537–53). Again by 1560, Lutheran ideas in Austria and southern Germany were attracting a majority of the population. By that date, however, outside Scandinavia and northern and central Germany, where there was a steady consolidation of the Lutheran pastoral ministry, the Protestant advance took place on more radical lines than Luther's, as the Reformed tradition disputed with Lutheranism the division of the Protestant world.

Luther's liturgical instincts were conservative, and he quickly repudiated the lawless iconoclasm and violence of his disciple Andreas Carlstadt (*c*. 1480–1541) and of the spirit-filled 'Zwickau prophets'. The first architect of Reformed Protestantism was the Zurich pastor Ulrich Zwingli (1484–1531), a former chaplain to Swiss papal mercenaries, who converted the Mass into a simple vernacular memorial communion service, and banished all images, statues, vestments, organs and ritual from the churches in an effort to confine Christianity to the explicit teaching of the gospel. Zwingli lacked Luther's earthy peasant realism, the German's instinctive feeling for the concrete and the material, and in 1529, at the Colloquy of Marburg, Zwingli denied Luther's doctrine that the Body and Blood of Christ coexist in the Eucharist with the bread and wine. Though Zwingli fell in battle with the Swiss Catholic cantons in 1531, his Swiss type of reformed Protestantism was given an international influence through the reformation of the French-born John Calvin (1509–64).

Calvin was an organiser of genius who in a long ministry at Geneva (1536–8; 1541–64), refined the ecclesiological experiments of his predecessors like Martin Bucer (1491–1551) in Strasbourg into a new church order for Protestantism, a fourfold ministry of presbyters, elders, teachers and deacons, with authority over the religious, moral, educational and charitable life of the Church, its courts of discipline and congregations. Calvin was also a theologian of genius, a master of French and Latin prose, who gave Protestantism a systematic theology based on a crystalline conception of God's providence for all his creatures, containing an infinitely consoling assurance to the elect that he had chosen and predestined them to salvation from all eternity.

The doctrine of predestination was not new; it was rooted in Scripture, it was taught by Augustine and Aquinas, and there was much in the logic of Reformed ideas to thrust it to the foreground, as in harmony with the Augustinian emphases on the sovereignty of grace, the power of original sin and the unfreedom of the human will. But St Ignatius Loyola urged that predestination was no part of ordinary Christian teaching and preaching, and it was Calvin who transformed it, albeit without some of the refinements of his successors, from a theological conundrum into a central strand of popular religion. By 1620, the negative aspect of Calvinism was producing a revolt against it in the very churches it had helped to form. But at first its power was wholly positive, and this power was apparent even before Calvin's death, in the rise of the 'Huguenot' Church in France, with two thousand congregations in 1560; in the triumph of the Reformation, in Scotland in 1560, under Calvin's disciple John Knox (*c*. 1513–72); and in the return of Protestantism to power in England on the accession of Elizabeth I (1533–1603) in 1558, after the brief Catholic reaction under Mary Tudor (1516–58), though here the Elizabethan church settlement combined a Calvinist theology with a liturgy respectful of tradition, and with the traditional episcopal church order. Calvinism also spread under noble patronage into Hungary and Poland, and Calvinists made a contribution wholly disproportionate to their numbers to the Dutch revolt against Spanish rule from 1566, which led in 1579 to the division of the Catholic south from the increasingly Calvinist north, the origin of modern Belgium and Holland.

The most important of the territories disputed between Catholicism and Calvinism was France, where more than thirty years of civil war (1562–94) were ended by the conversion to Catholicism of the Protestant King Henry IV (1553–1610), and by the Edict of Nantes of 1598, granting a measure of political autonomy and of freedom of worship to the Protestant minority. The Huguenots lost their political privileges in 1629 at the hands of the French statesman Cardinal A.J. du Plessis Richelieu (1585–1642), who saw them as an obstacle to French national unity, and the last vestiges of religious toleration were destroyed by the revocation of the Edict of Nantes by Louis XIV (1638–1715) in 1685. Most Protestants conformed to Catholicism or fled into exile, and despite desperate Calvinist 'Camisard' risings in the Cévennes in 1702 and 1709, Protestantism remained proscribed until 1787, so that Calvin hardly survived as a prophet in his own country.

Not that Calvin favoured religious toleration any more than Catholicism. One interconfessional form of persecution, the late medieval European witch craze, lasted in Protestant countries as well as in Catholic middle Europe until the later seventeenth century. Catholics and Protestants also united against the 'Radical Reformation'. Just as Zwingli in the 1520s drowned Anabaptists, so Calvin, acting on information from Catholics, was responsible for the burning at the stake of the Antitrinitarian Spaniard Michael Servetus (1511–53). Hostility to orthodoxy, Catholic or Protestant, seems to have been the special characteristic of the small number of Spanish or Italian Protestants: Socinianism, the denial of the full divinity of Christ, owes its name to Fausto Sozzini (1539–1604), who carried his teaching to Transylvania and Poland where he founded Unitarian churches; and Poland was also the scene of mission of the Protestant former Capuchin Bernadino Ochino (1487–1564), who repudiated both Calvinism and the Trinity. Protestants were historically correct in rejecting the radical spiritualist teachings of the Anabaptist leaders of the 1520s, Thomas Müntzer, Balthasar Hübmaier (1485–1528) and John Denck (1495–1527), for Anabaptism, especially in its apocalyptic element, owed less to the Reformation than to the late medieval heresies, and by denying infant baptism, albeit with some good Protestant arguments, the Anabaptists repudiated the principle of a Church conterminous with the whole community. The Protestant Landgrave of Hesse joined with the Catholic Bishop of Münster to rescue that prelate's cathedral city from the rule of an Anabaptist madman, Jan of Leyden (executed in 1535), but more pacific Anabaptist communities of Mennonites and Hutterites developed in Holland and Moravia, and after enduring many persecutions established still surviving co-operative colonies in the New World. The pre-Reformation Bohemian (later Moravian) Brethren also survived, by adopting a Lutheran confession.

If the Protestant fringe might seem to discredit the Protestant appeal from the Church to the Bible, the Protestant failure to present a united front to Rome, and the jealousies between Lutheranism and Calvinism especially, in part explains the Protestant inability to acquire any significant new territory from Catholicism after 1570. Lutheranism was itself divided by controversy between the compromising Philippists who followed Melanchthon and the Gnesiolutherans under Matthias Flacius Illyricus (1520–75), who developed Lutheranism into a stern unbending orthodoxy without the spirit which in Luther gave it life. Calvinism also hardened into the rigid systems of Theodore Beza (1519–1605), Calvin's successor at Geneva, and of Francis Gomar (1563–1641) of Leyden, whose controversy with Jacobus Arminius (1560–1609) led in 1610 to the 'Remonstrance', a statement of the Dutch 'Arminian' position that Christ died for all and not only the elect, and that divine sovereignty was compatible with human freedom. The Remonstrants were condemned by the Synod of Dort (1618–19), but the influx of Arminian opinion into the Church of England in the 1620s led to the consolidation of a more distinctively 'Anglican' theological school, stemming from the writings of Richard Hooker (*c*. 1554–1600), with a more definite theological defence of episcopal order and formal liturgical worship. The movement received the patronage of King Charles I (1600–49) and William Laud (1573–1645), Archbishop of Canterbury, and precipitated both a Calvinist rebellion in Scotland in 1637, which restored Presbyterian church order, and from 1641, a civil war in England, in the course of which the king and archbishop were executed and a Puritan republican Commonwealth was established under the protectorship of Oliver Cromwell (1599–1658). The Westminster Assembly of 1643 drew up the Calvinist Westminster Confession, but Presbyterianism did not everywhere prevail, and though episcopacy and Catholicism were proscribed, the extraordinary efflorescence of Protestant free thought produced many Independent and Baptist congregations, and the pacifist Society of Friends established by the Quaker mystic George Fox (1624–91). The experiment ended with the permanent restoration of the monarchy and the Church of England in 1660, though Scottish episcopacy, which was also then restored, faced great opposition and was replaced by Presbyterianism in 1690.

England was by far the largest and most important of the conquests of the Reformation, and after 1600 the emergence of her first American colonies, with those of the vast new trading empire of Holland, gave Protestantism its most important modern role, in the rise of a great Protestant state in the New World. But while Catholicism in England survived as a genuine native growth, it was restricted to an aristocratic and gentry-dominated minority, especially in remote parts of Lancashire and elsewhere in northern England. There was, however, no adequate Protestant effort to evangelise the Irish, who remained obdurately Catholic through four centuries of rule by English heretics, though after 1600 a Protestant minority was introduced by dispossession of the Catholic landlord class, and Protestant immigrants, mostly Presbyterians from Scotland, became a majority in one province, Ulster.

In Europe, Protestantism was in retreat after 1590, having made all its conquests over the medieval Catholicism still unreformed by the Council of Trent (1545–63). The council was a predominantly Italian and Papacy-controlled affair, which with theological subtlety and clarity reaffirmed and redefined the doctrinal and devotional content of Roman Catholicism. The origins of this Italian Catholic reform lay in the Oratory of Divine Love established in Rome around 1517 by Pietro Caraffa, later Pope Paul IV (1476–1559), the founder, in 1524, with the gentle Cajetan (1480–1547), of the Theatines, the first of the new evangelist and activist orders of priest 'Clerks Regular'. These orders were supplemented by the most numerous and popular of all the Counter-Reformation religious institutes, the Franciscan Capuchins, established in 1529 by Matteo di Bassi (d. 1552). No reform, however, was achieved in the short pontificate of the well-meaning Dutchman, Hadrian VI (1459–1523). The brutal sack of Rome by imperial troops in 1527 rang the knell of the secular Roman Renaissance, and sent Gian Matteo Giberti (1495–1543) back to his diocese of Verona to set a new pastoral standard for the episcopate; but it was only in 1537 that the Farnese Pope Paul III (1468–1549) began effective reforming measures with the radical recommendations of the *Consilium de emendanda ecclesia*. A last attempt was made by Cardinal Gasparo Contarini (1483–1542) and the moderate reform-minded *spirituali* to find ground for a reconciliation with the Protestants at Ratisbon in 1541, but after its failure, the conservative *zelanti*, led by Caraffa, prevailed in Rome, and a new Roman Inquisition began the repression of Italian heresy in 1542. The spiritual regeneration of Rome itself was the work of the most delightful of Counter-Reformation saints, Philip Neri (1515–95), the 'Apostle of Rome', whose congregation of priests, the Oratory, gave its name to the *oratorio* deriving from the spiritual songs composed for Oratorian devotional use, some of them by Neri's penitent Giovanni Palestrina (*c*. 1525–94), the modern founder-patron of Catholic church music.

After the savagely puritan pontificate of Paul IV, who banished the Roman prostitutes and published the first *Index of Prohibited Books*, a succession of dedicated if ruthless pontiffs restored the religious prestige of the Papacy. Pius IV (1499–1565) confirmed the decrees of Trent and published the summary *Profession of Tridentine Faith* known as the 'Creed of Pius IV'. Pius V (1504–72) reformed the Roman Missal, Breviary and Catechism, Gregory XIII (1502–85) reformed the Calendar and Sixtus V (1521–90) revolutionised Roman town planning, rid the Papal States of bandits and reorganised the government of the Church under fifteen congregations of cardinals. Outside Rome, much reform rested on individual or local initiative, as in the great archdiocese of Milan, in which the Archbishop, Charles Borromeo (1538–84), Pius IV's nephew, made the Tridentine decrees effective through a unique personal combination of pastoral efficiency, compassion and charismatic sanctity.

Outside Italy, however, acceptance of the council depended on secular authority, and in southern Germany and Austria the most efficient instrument of the Catholic revival was the Jesuit Order, under the propagandist direction of Peter Canisius (1521–97), as its scores of new schools and universities founded after 1556 reconciled the educated laity to the Roman Catholic Church. Their most willing pupil was the Archduke Ferdinand (1578–1637), who eliminated Protestantism from his domains in Inner Austria after 1595 and carried his crusade into the Thirty Years' War (1618–48) after becoming emperor in 1619. In the 1620s, Bohemia was recovered from Calvinist rule and forcibly re-Catholicised, and the Edict of Restitution in 1629 demanded the return of all territories in the Empire Protestantised since 1552. The Protestant cause in Germany was saved from disaster in the 1630s by the armies of Gustavus II Adolphus (1594–1632), King of Sweden, and by his Catholic ally, France, which feared too powerful an empire. The Peace of Westphalia in 1648 signalled the end of a century of religious war, the failure of the Catholic *reconquista* and the legal existence in the Empire of Calvinism, which also survived in Turkish Hungary under Ottoman protection. All ecclesiastical power was now the weaker for the rise of the nation-state, a fact of which the Papacy was only too aware. Yet the Protestant share of Europe had fallen to a fifth by 1650, as Catholicism kept what it had reconquered. One signal success of wholesale re-Catholicisation was in Poland-Lithuania, where religious toleration of Protestants declined during the long reign of Sigismund III (1566–1632). After 1650, the final touches to St Peter's by the supreme architect and sculptor of the age, Gian Lorenzo Bernini (1598–1680)—the colonnades to the Piazza and the huge bronze reliquary for St Peter's Chair—marked the triumphant resurgence of Roman Catholicism.

Spirituality and Reason

The seventeenth-century Counter-Reformation achieved its most significant victory in absolutist France. Its first notable spiritual figure was Francis of Sales (1567–1622), Bishop of Geneva, who with Jane Frances de Chantal (1572–1641) founded the Visitation Order for teaching girls, and who infused lay piety with a new sweetness of spirit in his *Introduction to the Devout Life*. The later international cultus of the Sacred Heart arose from the revelations of the Visitandine nun Margaret Mary Alacoque (1647–90). The Spanish Carmelite tradition was fed into the aristocratic mystical revival pioneered by the founder of the French Oratory, Cardinal Pierre de Bérulle (1575–1629), while the Oratorians and Jesuits created French secondary education. The quality of the French parochial clergy was gradually transformed by the extension of seminary training by John Eudes (1601–80) and Jean-Jacques Olier (1608–57) of Saint-Sulpice. French missionaries carried the gospel to Canada and Vietnam, and the care and evangelisation of the poor and of prisoners and galley slaves were undertaken by Vincent de Paul (1580–1660), with the assistance of his 'Lazarist' missionary order of priests and of St Louise de Marillac (1591–1660), with whom he founded the Ladies and Daughters of Charity. Just as notable was the revival of Catholic intellectual life. The reformed Maurist Benedictines revolutionised the critical study of church history, in a work comparable to the contemporary achievement of the Jesuit Flemish Bollandists in transforming the scientific study of hagiography; while French Catholic scholars of international reputation included the Jesuit Dionysius Petavius (1583–1652), the biblical scholar Richard Simon (1638–1712), and the acutest of polemicists and greatest of French orators, Jacques Bénigne Bossuet (1627–1704), Bishop of Meaux.

Yet like Protestantism, Roman Catholicism suffered a fundamental theological division over the roles to be assigned to divine grace and human freedom. Two famous Spanish Jesuit theologians, Luis de Molina (1535–1600) and Francisco de Suarez (1548–1617), the most influential modern reinterpreter of the scholasticism of Aquinas, tried to safeguard the realm of human freedom by making the gift of grace dependent on God's foreknowledge of the needs of the recipient, a position opposed by the Dominican Domingo Báñez (1528–1604), and defended by the Jesuit Leonhard Lessius (1554–1623) against another Louvain theologian, the Dominican Michel Baius (1513–89). The matter was not decided by the Papacy, but the stricter Augustinian position, designed to protect the gratuity of grace, was enunciated by a posthumously published work, the *Augustinus* of Cornelius Jansen (1585–1638), Bishop of Ypres. The Abbé de Saint-Cyran (1581–1643) introduced Jansen's Augustinian teaching to the Benedictine convent of Port-Royal near Paris, under its reforming Abbesses, Mère Angélique Arnauld (1591–1661) and her sister Agnès (1593–1671); and their brother 'le grand' Antoine Arnauld (1612–94) became the acknowledged leader of the devout Jansenist aristocrats of the capital, through his attack in 1643 on what he claimed to be Jesuit exhortations to the unworthy reception of frequent communion. When in 1653, Pope Innocent X (1574–1655) condemned five Jansenist propositions allegedly from the *Augustinus*, many of the Jansenists as good Catholics accepted the *droit* of the condemnation, but denied the *fait* that the propositions were Jansen's. The movement received its most illustrious adherent through the 'definitive conversion' of the scientist Blaise Pascal (1623–62), one of the most gifted of all Christian apologists, who from a 'rigorist' viewpoint attacked the 'laxist' moral casuistry of the French Jesuits in the brilliant *Lettres provinciales* (1656–7). Jansenism attracted many bishops and secular clergy jealous of Jesuit influence, and raised the difficult issue of papal authority in France. Many Frenchmen rallied to the defence of the 'Gallican liberties', defined by the Church with royal approval in 1682 to deny papal infallibility and to restrict active papal interference in France, at a time when Pope Innocent XI (1611–89) was in dispute with Louis XIV about the royal right of *régale* over the Church. Jansenism complicated this warfare of competing jurisdictions at the heart of Counter-Reformation Catholicism; the Jansenist controversy became as much about authority as about grace, and it received a new formulation from the *Réflexions morales* on the French New Testament by the Oratorian Pasquier Quesnel (1634–1719). The Jansenists aroused the special enmity of Louis XIV, who regarded them as a persistent irritant to his own absolutism, and in 1710 he ordered Port-Royal to be destroyed. In 1713, he secured the bull *Unigenitus* from Clement XI (1649–1721), condemning 101 propositions from the *Réflexions morales*. In Holland a small Jansenist Catholic minority in 1723 seceded from Rome to form a church centred on Utrecht, and the French Jansenists, as 'Appellants', appealed against Rome to a future General Council. The conflict took a sensational turn when Jansenist 'Convulsionaries' worked miracles in 1731 at the tomb of a Jansenist deacon in the Parisian cemetery of Saint-Médard, and it continued to involve and to discredit the Papacy, the Crown, the bishops and the *Parlements*, passing through an especially virulent phase in the 1750s, and dividing the French Church as it faced the onset of the most anti-Christian phase of the European Enlightenment.

Catholicism was also weakened by the discrediting of its own mystical tradition, through the fall into disgrace of Miguel de Molinos (*c*. 1640–97), a Spaniard who achieved a large spiritual following in Rome itself, and whose 'Quietist' teaching on the highest passive states of prayer appears to have dispensed with the need for conventional moral effort as well as conventional devotion. A similar dispute in France over the value of mystical religion between Bossuet and François Fénelon (1651–1715), Archbishop of Cambrai, marked the end of the golden age of French piety, at the very time that, on the Protestant side, a more affective pietism in the hands of the pastor Philipp Jakob Spener (1635–1705) was challenging a dry and lifeless High Lutheran orthodoxy with a new lay movement of 'heart' religion. The pietists were patronised by the rising power of Protestant Prussia, which supported the University and philanthropic institutions of Halle established in the 1690s by Spener and August Hermann Francke (1663–1727); and their simplified Protestantism, largely devoid of learned theology, harmonised with the revivalist religion of Protestants still persecuted in the German and Habsburg Catholic lands.

One body of Bohemian refugees from Catholic rule was transformed into a new international missionary movement by their Moravian bishop, the visionary enthusiast Count Nikolaus von Zinzendorf (1700–60). His Moravians stressed the need for a heartfelt conversion to faith in Christ in the emotional assurance that he had died to redeem the sinner from his sin. Zinzendorf saw the Moravians, as they spread to all the Protestant-ruled states of the Old and New Worlds, as a light to enlighten the churches on the true inner meaning of the gospel. The Moravians' most illustrious convert was a Church of England clergyman, John Wesley (1703–91), who with his hymn-writer brother Charles (1707–88) combined revivalist preaching with the organisation of converts into disciplined 'Methodist' societies. At his death they had more than a hundred thousand members.

Wesley's work was the never finished one of Christianising Europe: its revivalist parallel in the Catholic countries was the equally emotive evangelism of the Passionist order, established in 1725 by Paul of the Cross (1694–1775), and of the Redemptorist order, founded in 1732 by the most influential of the Roman Church's modern moral theologians, Alphonsus Liguori (1696–1787). In central Europe, the century from 1650 was also one of Christian reconstruction.

Austrian Catholicism entered on its most triumphant phase as the borders of Christendom moved east and south out of Hungary in the wake of the retreating Turk, whose defeat was celebrated in the architectural glories of a century of building new pilgrimage and abbey churches. Christendom also expanded through the recovery of Orthodox Russia, an independent patriarchate from 1589, which survived the Old Believer schism provoked by the liturgical reforms of the Patriarch Nikon (1605–81), to become, without a patriarch, an instrument of the autocratic Caesaropapalist Russian state in the hands of the ruthless and brutal moderniser Peter the Great (1672–1725). The religious genius of 'Holy Russia' lay less in the official theology of divines like the Metropolitan Philaret Drozdov (1782–1867), than in the fervour of the peasant masses, which was distilled into the holiness teaching of the *staretz* or spiritual counsellor, men such as the thaumaturge-ascetic St Seraphim of Sarov (1759–1833). Russia steadily expanded west, east and south through the eighteenth and nineteenth centuries, and posed as patron to the Orthodox Christians under Ottoman rule in the Near East, the Slav Balkans and Greece. This Orthodoxy resisted both Roman and Protestant blandishments from the seventeenth century. Dositheus (1641–1707), Patriarch of Jerusalem, was the chief influence on the definition of Orthodox doctrine against the Calvinist ideas of Cyril Lucar (1572–1638) at the Synod of Jerusalem in 1672, and equally attacked the Polish-Ruthenian Uniat churches with eastern liturgies and married priesthoods in communion with Rome, under the Union of Brest-Litovsk of 1596.

Protestant creativity achieved its loftiest cultural expressions in the Christocentric art of the Dutch Rembrandt van Rijn (1606–69), and the religious music of J.S. Bach (1685–1750) and G.F. Handel (1685–1759), whose Lutheran masses and English oratorios are as untroubled as the south German baroque by the new political and intellectual challenges to Christianity from within.

These arose from those Christians who after 1600 tried to define a common Christianity above the warfare of the churches, like the Dutch jurist and theologian Hugo Grotius (1583–1645). Holland was largely free of religious persecution, and gave a refuge to the Bohemian bishop and Utopian educationist J.A. Comenius (1592–1670); to the Jewish pantheist Baruch Spinoza (1632–77); and to the sceptical Huguenot refugee Pierre Bayle (1647–1706), whose *Historical and Critical Dictionary* (1695–7) drove a wedge between religion and reason, and between religion and morality. It was also in Holland that the English philosopher John Locke (1632–1704) developed the arguments for the religious toleration of all Protestant Trinitarians actually achieved in England in 1689. Locke expounded a reasonable 'Latitudinarian' Christianity reduced to faith in God and Christ's Messiahship and the fulfilment of the moral law. Some of Locke's disciples, like the Deists John Toland (1670–1722), Anthony Collins (1676–1729) and Matthew Tindal (1655–1733), denied that Christian revelation properly understood was more than a republication of the universal truths of a natural and rational religion, and ridiculed the scriptural arguments for Christianity from Christ's performance of miracles and the fulfilment of prophecy. Yet the appeal to enlightened reason in religion in England was generally along the more orthodox lines suggested by Locke, and took place primarily within the churches; philosopher-theologians like Joseph Butler (1692–1752) and George Berkeley (1685–1753) were more than a match for any of their non-Christian opponents except the Scottish sceptic David Hume (1711–76).

The rationalist systems of G.W. Leibniz (1646–1716) and Christian Wolff (1679–1754) constituted the equally orthodox first phase of the Protestant *Aufklärung* (Enlightenment) in Germany. The 'reform Catholicism' of Ludovico Muratori (1672–1750) was protected by the learned Pope Benedict XIV (1675–1758) in Italy; while in France, the self-confident rationalism of the Catholic René Descartes (1596–1650) was put to good philosophical use by both Catholics and Protestants, like the Oratorian Nicolas Malebranche (1638–1715).

But in France, there was also an undercurrent of scepticism and materialism deriving partly from classical philosophy and partly from the Catholic essayist Michel de Montaigne (1533–92); and, despite state censorship, Locke's philosophy and English Deism combined with the anti-clerical and free-thinking libertine element in the native Gallic tradition to turn the playwright and novelist François-Marie Arouet, under his literary pseudonym Voltaire (1694–1778), into one of the wittiest and most devastating opponents of Christianity. Voltaire's crusade to 'crush the infamy' of religious intolerance and superstition had its most celebrated victory in his vindication of the name of Jean Calas, a Protestant falsely tortured and executed in 1762 for killing his son. Voltaire claimed to be a theist. A less cerebral, more devout and sentimental Deism was propounded by the proto-romantic Jean-Jacques Rousseau (1712–78), who was to influence the romantic Catholicism of writers like the Vicomte F.R. de Chateaubriand (1768–1848). But a yet more radical literary circle of materialists and atheists formed in Paris after 1750 around the brilliant and industrious novelist, Denis Diderot (1713–84), whose editing of the multi-volume *Encyclopédie* deployed a vast new body of knowledge, some of it technical and scientific, against all religion in general and Catholicism in particular.

Voltaire and Diderot exerted an enormous influence on the court circles dominated by French culture, as in the Prussia of Frederick the Great (1712–86) and the Russia of Catherine the Great (1729–96). There was also a more radical German critique of Christianity after 1750 in the writings of G.E. Lessing (1729–81), who edited the *Wolfenbüttel Fragments* of H.S. Reimarus (1694–1768), who with greater learning than his English Deist predecessors opened up the modern era of destructive Biblical Criticism. Still more fundamental was the attack on traditional metaphysics by the philosopher Immanuel Kant (1724–1804), who answered Hume's scepticism by deriving religious knowledge not from rational cognition but from the moral imperatives of conscience. Kant was an influence on the ethical and idealist pantheist systems of J.G. Fichte (1762–1814) and F.W.J. von Schelling (1775–1854). Another response to scepticism was developed by Friedrich

Schleiermacher (1768–1834), who defended religion as a subjective sense of dependence on God, in an emotive and affective conception of Christianity drawing on German pietism and romanticism.

There were, therefore, two different legacies from the Enlightenment: a movement of ideas opposed to Christianity, and the hope of renewing the tradition with the aid of modern science and criticism. The anti-Christian Enlightenment was only dominant in France: elsewhere in both Protestant and Catholic states, it is easier to discern a current of eighteenth-century educated opinion towards a simplified, less dogmatic and more tolerant Christianity, appealing to a practical and prudential moralism and shading into Freemasonic Deism or illuminism. There were, however, signs that the centre would not hold, and that reason was parting company from imagination, and head from heart, as the extra-ecclesiastical religious fringes tended to Socinian rationalism or irrationalist pietism. The later anti-rationalist mysticism of the Nonjuring divine William Law (1686–1761), who had influenced John Wesley, was inspired by the spiritualist teaching of the German Lutheran cobbler Jakob Boehme (1575–1624). Still stranger were the angelogical revelations and speculations of the scientist visionary Emanuel Swedenborg (1688–1772), a Swedish bishop's son with an international discipleship crystallised into the New Jerusalem Church by his Methodist followers in 1787. The anti-rationalist extreme was touched by the English poet-painter William Blake (1757–1827), whose private antinomian mythology made the most powerful if inverted use of Christian symbols and ideas. The other, rationalist extreme was represented by the gifted Socinian metaphysician divine Samuel Clarke (1675–1729), the most important early English influence on Rousseau. A new Socinian 'Unitarian' Church arose after 1770 from the ministries of Theophilus Lindsey (1723–1808) and the scientist Joseph Priestley (1733–1804).

Such 'enlightened religion' posed the modern Christian dilemma, whether to modify traditional belief in the light of new attitudes and knowledge, and so risk the sacrifice of the essentials of the faith; or whether to reject any such accommodation and so risk identification with intellectual and sometimes political conservatism. As yet, however, this was a choice for the few, and it is difficult to relate elitist or minority movements of ideas to popular irreligion or active de-Christianisation. It has been argued that the failure of the English state to enforce churchgoing after 1690 led to a decline in ordinary religious practice, and it was the Church of England after 1750 which first failed utterly in its pastoral duty to the new urban proletariat created by the Industrial Revolution. Yet in France, there was also a decline in moral and religious discipline in some eighteenth-century cities; and in areas of rural de-Christianisation, especially in central and southern France, the tavern or Sunday labour exercised a greater attraction than the parish church. Yet the evangelistic activities of Louis Grignion de Montfort (1673–1716) in the Vendée, and the wandering career of the pilgrim-beggar Benedict

Joseph Labre (1748–83), point to the vitality of the movement of Christianisation; and it is in France that a modern set of sociological methods has penetrated furthest below the imposing façades of semi-uniform religious practice under the *ancien régime*, to distinguish the regions of lukewarm piety from those marked by a sometimes novel fervour, in patterns which became more pronounced when the State ceased to enforce church attendance after 1790.

There was also an increase before 1790 in aristocratic domination of the French and English churches, which contained the danger of discrediting religion by over-identifying it with a privileged social order. In Protestant Prussia, England and Scandinavia, the clergy were by 1750 primarily servants of the State, and in the second half of the eighteenth century, absolutist Catholic reforming administrations also asserted their authority over the Church to restrict the power of Rome and of Rome's special servant, the Society of Jesus. The Jesuits were expelled from Portugal in 1759, from France in 1764 and from Spain in 1767. Though they were protected by Pope Clement XIII (1693–1769), his successor Clement XIV (1705–74) gave way to the demands of the Catholic powers by suppressing the Society in 1773. It owed its survival primarily to the non-Catholic protection of Frederick in Prussia and Catherine in Russia, and was not restored by Rome until 1814. The popes were also buffeted by attacks from the great German Archbishop-Electors, and of their priest pamphleteer Johann von Hontheim (1701–90), who wrote under the pseudonym 'Febronius'. The Febronian demand for a greater local Catholic autonomy was given practical expression by the Emperor Joseph II (1741–90), who expropriated monastic property in order to finance new parishes and bishoprics and so extend and improve the pastoral ministrations of the secular clergy. This Catholic reforming preference of the active to the contemplative life recurred in the amalgam of Jansenist, Josephist and Gallican proposals adopted by the Synod of Pistoia in 1786 under the aegis of Scipione de' Ricci (1741–1810), Bishop of Pistoia-Prato, and his patron Joseph II's brother Leopold, Grand Duke of Tuscany (1747–92).

Revolution and Revival

The climax of state power came in the French Revolution, which seized the vast possessions of the Church, dissolved all religious orders, reordered diocesan boundaries to coincide with civil departments and turned the clergy into a semi-egalitarian bureaucracy of state employees. This 'Civil Constitution' was imposed in 1790 and denounced by Rome in 1791. It caused a schism between the French 'Constitutional Church' recognised by the state and a 'refractory' Church underground or in exile. Thirty thousand priests became *émigrés* abroad, and in 1792 the Catholic Vendée rose in rebellion against the revolutionary regime, which in 1793 declared a terror on its enemies, and tried to secularise French culture by persecuting even the Constitutional Church and by imposing patriotic Deist or atheist ritual substitutes for Christianity. Though persecution lightened after 1795, the French occupation of Rome made Pope Pius VI (1717–99) a prisoner of France. As First Consul of the Republic, Napoleon (1769–1821) restored Catholicism in 1801 by a Concordat with Pope Pius VII (1740–1823) and even compelled the pontiff to assist at his coronation as Emperor in Notre Dame in 1804; but the unprecedented if only temporary revolutionary rejection of Christianity by a European Christian nation had created both a new cultus of martyrdom and a counter-revolutionary mentality in much of French Catholicism, which explains both the strength and limitations of its nineteenth-century revival.

That revival was given its pro-papal 'neo-Ultramontane' character by the French Revolution's abolition of the countervailing powers to the Papacy in the Roman Catholic Church. Napoleon secularised the German ecclesiastical electorates and prince-bishoprics, the Holy Roman Emperor became Emperor of Austria, and even the humbled French Gallican Church was restored by agreement with Rome, though the Pope's authority in France remained restricted by the Organic Articles of 1802. But the Church's 'Gallican liberties' now looked like the liberties which the State could take with her, and Gallicanism was equally attacked by the arch-conservative polemicist Count Joseph de Maistre (1753–1821), who saw in the Papacy the ultimate guarantor of social and political order, and Félicité de Lamennais (1782–1854), who wanted the Pope to give an infallible sanction to the liberties of Catholic peoples. Indeed by 1830, Catholicism had forged its still enduring links with radical nationalism, in Ireland, then governed by English heretics, and Poland, partitioned in 1772, 1792 and 1795 among Austria, Russia and Prussia, and only briefly restored by Napoleon. Orthodox Greece achieved its independence from the Ottoman Empire in a religious and national rising which began in 1821, and modern Belgium owes its creation to the union of Catholics and Liberals in 1830 to overthrow the rule of Protestant Holland. There were to be similar religious contributions to the modern definition of national and regional identities from the Basque country to the Balkans, in which a number of Orthodox states arose from the ruins of the Ottoman Empire, Serbia, Rumania and Bulgaria; though the Holy Alliance of Austria, Russia and Prussia formed in 1815, equally invoked the sanction of Christianity for traditional constituted authority, as did the restored Bourbon monarchies of France, Spain and Naples.

In this division between peoples and princes, the Papacy backed the princes. The States of the Church were restored in 1815, but were increasingly threatened by lay secret societies of Italian revolutionary nationalists who rose in rebellion in 1831 and 1848. The Roman revolution of 1848 transformed the saintly Pius IX (1792–1878), the longest ruling Pope since Peter, from a moderate liberal into the most stubborn and intransigent opponent of the pretensions of the nineteenth-century liberal mind. The anti-clerical challenge to the authority of the Church over education and morals, and to the survival of the religious orders, in Spain and Latin America, also contributed to papal conservatism, as did the expropriation of church property by the government of Piedmont-Savoy from 1848 as it adopted the cause of Italian unity. By 1860, most of Italy was united in a new secular nation-state, which seized its capital, Rome, from the Pope's rule in 1870.

Pius' hostility to the liberal idea of 'a free church in a free state' lost him the support of some of the pioneers of the Liberal Catholic revival in France like the Count Charles de Montalembert (1810–70), but it was in France especially that the Pope won a vast popular following, among the readers of the newspaper *L'Univers*, marshalled by its peasant-born editor, Louis Veuillot (1813–83). The rising tide of French 'neo-Ultramontane' devotion to the Pope accompanied the revival of the modern cultus of the Virgin Mary, encouraged by Pius in his definition of the doctrine of her Immaculate Conception in 1854, and by the Marian apparition to a peasant girl, Bernadette Soubirous (1844–79) at Lourdes in 1858. The French Catholic revival was sustained by an unprecedented growth in charitable and educational orders of religious women, by the sanctity of the Curé d'Ars, Jean-Baptiste Vianney (1786–1859), patron of parish priests, and the Carmelite contemplative Thérèse of Lisieux (1873–97), the much-loved 'Little Flower', and by the recovery of the French missionary spirit, which was given a new international outreach after 1850 in the creation of new Catholic churches in Asia and the Pacific, and in the French Empire in Africa.

The outcome of the Catholic revival was the victory of a militant and monolithic Catholicism, which received its twin cap-stones in the papal condemnation of 'progress, liberalism, and modern civilization' in the Syllabus of Errors of 1864, and in the definition, agreed by the First Vatican Council of 1869–70, of the Pope's infallibility in faith and morals as a doctrine binding on Roman Catholics. There was opposition to defining the doctrine at the council, which was well informed of the historical objections argued by the German church historian Ignaz von Döllinger (1799–1890) and his English Liberal Catholic disciple John Acton (1834–1902). The Vatican decrees were also rejected after 1870 by small middle-class 'Old Catholic' churches formed in Germany and Switzerland, by the 'Los von Rom' movement in Austria after 1897, by the Marian 'Mariavites' in Poland, and in 1920 by the Czechoslovak national Church. These movements were insignificant, however, beside the chorus of Liberal and Protestant protest, which produced the Prussian government's anti-Catholic *Kulturkampf*, enshrined in the May Laws in the 1870s, and a new bout of anti-clerical persecution in France in the 1880s, culminating in 1905 in the abrogation of the Concordat under the Law of Separation. Such external pressures, however, stimulated the rise in the 1880s of a new political Catholicism, most notably the Catholic Centre Party founded by Ludwig Windthorst (1812–91) in Germany, which began to threaten the dominance of liberal elites in the new parliamentary democracies. A social Catholicism, alive to the grievances of the industrial working class, also opposed the rising power of anti-religious and anti-clerical Socialism, and an anti-Socialist reforming programme received the blessing of Pope Leo XIII (1810–1903) in the Encyclical *Rerum Novarum* of 1891.

Leo gave official patronage to a scholastic revival based on the works of Aquinas, but the attempt to defend Catholicism on a more radical intellectual basis by the French biblical critic Alfred Loisy (1857–1940), the Anglo-Irish theologian George Tyrrell (1861–1909) and the German-Scots metaphysician Friedrich von Hügel (1852–1925) was condemned as the 'Modernist heresy' by Pope St Pius X (1835–1914) in 1907.

The power of the Papacy was also enhanced by the rise of missionary Catholic churches, like those of England, Scotland, the United States and Australasia, largely built up by emigrants from Ireland. These churches were not subject to State interference: so that it was through the realisation of the liberal principle of 'a free Church in a free State' that the Papacy in 1900 enjoyed a more untrammelled jurisdiction over the whole Catholic world.

Protestantism like Catholicism benefited from the conservative reaction to the French Revolution, to enjoy a massive nineteenth-century revival. In England, the former radical Unitarian S.T. Coleridge (1772–1834) defended the union of Church and State on the basis of a Neoplatonic and neo-Germanic idealist philosophy, while the Church of England Evangelicals of the 'Clapham Sect', under the lay leadership of William Wilberforce (1759–1833), the arch-opponent of the slave trade, offered a philanthropic if conservative alternative to violent revolution. A similar social-reforming Evangelicalism was given practical expression in the crusades of the seventh Earl of Shaftesbury (1801–85) against the exploitation of child and female labour. The Evangelicals also produced the first great Protestant missions to the heathen overseas, while under Evangelical influence the English Nonconformist Churches grew between 1790 and 1850 to a near parity in numbers with the Church of England. The Nonconformist and radical subversion of the Anglican confessional state, aided and abetted by Irish and English Catholics, produced from 1833 a conservative High Church reaction in defence of the Church of England led by Edward Bouverie Pusey (1800–82) and John Henry Newman (1801–90), who after his submission to Rome in 1845, became one of the most original of modern Roman Catholic theologians. This ecclesiastical hostility to a more liberal reforming State also occurred in the new Calvinist secession churches of Holland, Switzerland and Scotland, where a Free Kirk, formed under the leadership of Thomas Chalmers (1780–1847) in 1843 by the disruption of the official Church of Scotland, professed to act in defence of the 'Crown Rights of the Redeemer' against secular tyranny. There were Evangelicals still more other-worldly: the Scots Edward Irving (1792–1834), inspirer of the Catholic Apostolic Church, and the Irish J.N. Darby (1800–82), founder of the Plymouth Brethren, denounced the existing churches as apostate, and looked for deliverance to the Second Coming to usher in the Millennium. Their literalist understanding of Scripture is the foundation of modern fundamentalism. Other churches, like the Methodists, also divided. Yet underlying the warfare of the mainstream rival denominations were shared tendencies towards the revival of higher doctrines of Church, ministry and sacrament, the formation of a more professional clergy, and the adoption of a more formal liturgy and Gothic architecture and symbolism, and even of a more distinctive clerical dress.

This wholesale renewal of the institutional fabric of the Protestant Churches was, however, largely middle class in character, and repelled a large majority of the urban poor in the new industrial towns. One of the few successful proletarian Christian movements was the Salvation Army, founded by William Booth (1829–1912), with both evangelistic and philanthropic aims. The social and educational achievements of the Protestant Churches were generally impressive, if inadequate to the sheer magnitude of their task, and the Christian Socialism of well-meaning clergymen like F.D. Maurice (1805–72) was better at interesting Christians in Socialism than in converting Socialists to Christianity. The growth of the British Empire, however, enlarged the field of action of Protestant Christianity, while the advent of Protestant Prussia as the principal industrial and military power on the continent was confirmed by the proclamation of a new German Empire in 1871. The learned Protestant apologists for Prussia included the philosopher G.W.F. Hegel (1770–1831), who, though his system was near to pantheism, exercised an enormous influence in his defence of Christianity as the Absolute Religion, corresponding in imaginative terms to the highest scientific realisation of Absolute Idealism, as defined in his own romantic philosophy.

Challenge and Decline

German thought was also a dissolvent of orthodoxy. Hegel's system could be recast in atheist form, as by Ludwig Feuerbach (1804–72), while the biblical critic David Strauss (1808–74) applied an extraordinary erudition to demonstrate that the New Testament was a work of historical mythology. Strauss's methods were refined by the Tübingen School of F.C. Baur (1792–1860), who understood the formation of the New Testament and of the Catholic Church as the second-century resolution of a conflict between Jewish and Gentile Christianity. Though Baur was refuted in England by J.B. Lightfoot (1828–89), a radical attitude to the New Testament underlay both the transcendental apocalyptic Christianity of scholars like Johannes Weiss

(1863–1914) and the medical missionary Albert Schweitzer (1875–1965), and the rival Liberal Protestant syntheses of Albrecht Ritschl (1822–89) and Adolf von Harnack (1851–1930), who expounded a modern ethical and spiritual religion to the more doubting and progressive sections of the German Christian middle class. The chief recent theological fruit of this radical Biblicism has been the demythologised Christianity of Rudolf Bultmann (1884–1976).

Another cause of doubt about the biblical world-view was suggested by geologists and biologists like Charles Darwin (1809–82), whose evolutionary theory was charged with contradicting Genesis and denying the special spiritual status of man as a distinct divine creation. A number of Christian theologians gave evolutionary theory an orthodox interpretation as in the English Liberal Catholicism of Charles Gore (1853–1932), and, more recently, in the optimistic cosmology of the Jesuit Pierre Teilhard de Chardin (1881–1955), but its anti-religious implications were stressed in England by the agnostic T.H. Huxley (1825–95) and Herbert Spencer (1820–1903), and in Germany by the materialist Ernst Haeckel (1834–1919). In France, Auguste Comte (1798–1857) set out a scientific 'Positivism' as a sanction for an atheist 'Religion of Humanity', while in Germany, the philosopher Friedrich Nietzsche (1844–1900) denounced the Christian values of meekness and endurance of suffering as the slave morality of the herd, and urged their replacement by the aristocratic and military ethic of the future Superman's will to power. Such sophisticated philosophies touched only a middle-class intellectual minority. More significant for the future was the Communist materialism of the Jewish-born Karl Marx (1818–83), based on an atheistic application of Hegelian dialectic to economic relationships, which inspired much of the secularist Socialism of France and Germany after 1860, and which became a world-transforming force as the secular religion imposed by the Bolshevik revolution on Russia after 1917.

Though tainted by association with the Tsars, the Orthodox Church in Russia retained its sense of identity with the nation, a role acknowledged in the Second World War, and despite recurring persecution, it survived among the peasantry who formed the bulk of the population. But the advent of the world's first enduring atheist state, territorially the largest in the world, meant the exclusion of Christians from public life, the prohibition of Christian education and evangelisation, the closure of churches at official whim, and the confinement of religious activity to the performance of a liturgy remarkable for its transcendent and other-worldly mystery and power.

The First World War saw the breakup of two other Christian empires, the German and Austrian, but it also led to the resurrection of Poland, whose self-understanding as the 'Christ of the nations' infused Christianity with messianic nationalism. At the other geographical extreme, the Easter Rising in Ireland against British rule in 1916 produced in 1922 the most devoutly Christian nation in western Europe. The re-

Catholicisation of Ireland by the Ultramontane movement as part of the modernisation of a demoralised society was one of the most signal triumphs of nineteenth-century Christianisation. It widened the gulf, however, between the Catholic mass of the population and two minorities, the English-descended landowners in the Protestant Church of Ireland, disestablished in 1869, and the Scots-descended Presbyterians, the largest religious body in the six counties of Ulster which remained outside the new Ireland. The Irish Catholic refusal to accept this partition and the equal Protestant determination to preserve it is inextricably a part of the most violent and intractable religious dispute in the British Isles, perhaps the most intractable in Europe.

The First World War also marked the beginning of the end of European hegemony with the rise of the United States as a great world power. The resulting loss of self-confidence accompanied the eclipse of the more sanguine religious liberalism of the nineteenth century, and gave a new prominence to the hitherto neglected existentialist theology of the Danish Søren Kierkegaard (1813–55), who influenced the neo-Orthodoxy of Karl Barth (1886–1968), the most considerable of modern Protestant theologians. The intellectual vitality of Catholicism was represented by such lay theologians as the Augustinian voluntarist Maurice Blondel (1861–1949) and the neo-Thomists Jacques Maritain (1882–1973) and Étienne Gilson (1884–1978), as of Eastern Orthodoxy by the Russian Vladimir Lossky (1903–58). Churchgoing fell between the wars where it was already weak, as the Church surrendered many of its voluntary activities in education and charity to the State, but Christianity also flourished as an adjunct to official civic religion and political conservatism, which strengthened religious practice in the peasantry and middle classes and further decreased it in the urban proletariat. The Virgin's appearance at Fatima in 1917 not only reinforced Portuguese popular religion, but gave a supernatural sanction to Catholic hostility to Communism, while a classic confrontation was the polarisation of Austrian politics in the 1920s and 1930s between a clerical government supported by a largely believing countryside and an anti-clerical Socialist administration in Vienna. Benito Mussolini (1883–1945) made peace between Italy and the Papacy with the Lateran Treaty of 1929 establishing an independent Vatican State; while, though the republican Basque country is one of the most Catholic regions of Spain, the victory of the Nationalist Francisco Franco (1892–1975) over the anti-clerical Spanish Republic was regarded by most Catholics as a Christian triumph. Despite the overt atheism of Nazism, only a small minority of Protestants and Catholics opposed the rise of Adolf Hitler (1889–1945) to power in Germany, and though a Protestant minority led by Martin Niemöller (1892–1984) and Dietrich Bonhoeffer (1906–45) gave an impressive witness in the 'Confessing Church', the Nazi 'German Christians' achieved a greater influence over German religious life. Peasant clerical nationalism actually united with Fascism to produce German puppet regimes in Vichy France, Croatia and Slovakia, while the failure of

Pope Pius XII (1876–1958) to condemn the Nazi extermination of six million European Jews became a matter of lively post-war controversy. Against this must be set the Church's local efforts to save European Jewry, as in Rome itself, whose Chief Rabbi subsequently became a Catholic, taking the Pope's Christian name, Eugenio.

After the defeat of Germany, eastern Europe passed under Russian Communist rule, and despite rigorous persecution, at its worst in Albania where religion is officially proscribed, Christianity has shown an impressive resilience as a spiritual refuge from secular totalitarian state power, and is at its most impressive in Catholic Poland, in which the Solidarity movement is largely Catholic in inspiration, and has drawn much of its strength from the patronage of the present Polish Pope, John Paul II (b. 1920). Elsewhere, Christian experience of Communism has varied from the continuous harassment practised in Czechoslovakia to the *modus vivendi* achieved after great suffering in Hungary. The Catholic Uniat Churches of Russia and Rumania were forced by the Communist authorities in 1946 and 1948 to renounce the authority of Rome. The Eastern Orthodox experience of Communism has ranged from the Russian-style repression of Bulgaria to the degree of encouragement and support which Rumania extends to the Church as a pillar of the nation. The most courageous Protestant witness under Communism has been that of the Baptist Churches created by nineteenth-century missions, especially in the Soviet Union, in which outlawed Baptist bodies exist as well as the congregations officially tolerated by the State. The often tragic and heterodox, and highly emotional, Russian Christian literary tradition associated with the novelists F.M. Dostoievsky (1821–81) and Leo Tolstoy (1828–1910), has been worthily continued by Alexander Solzhenitsyn (b. 1918), and Christianity retains a curious position in Russia as the only intellectual rival to a Marxism which otherwise tolerates no influence but its own.

In western Europe, the Christian contribution to post-war reconstruction came primarily through the Christian Democratic parties, which combined a modernising and moderately reforming influence with a commitment to religious tradition. Their following was concentrated in classes and regions of persisting Christian strength: strong in Brittany, Flemish Belgium and the Rhineland, weak in such heartlands of nineteenth-century anti-clericalism as Belgian Wallonia and the Italian Red Romagna. There was, however, a lightening of such anti-clerical hostility in France and Austria, as Catholicism became less wholly identified with the political Right. There was also a marked eclipse of the four-hundred-year-old antagonism between Protestants and Catholics, and of that spirit of denominational rivalry which had so sustained the church revivals of the nineteenth century. A new ecumenical spirit among Protestants deriving from the Edinburgh World Missionary Conference in 1910 bore fruit in the formation of the World Council of Churches in Amsterdam in 1948, while the decline of old sectarianisms encouraged church reunions like the amalgamation of the sundered branches of Scots Presbyterianism in 1929 and of English Methodism in 1932. The ecumenical outreach of Roman Catholicism was pioneered by Father Paul Couturier (1881–1953) and the gifted theologian Yves Congar (b. 1904); and at the Second Vatican Council (1962–5) called by the enormously popular Pope John XXIII (1881–1963), the Roman Catholic Church set out to modernise the presentation of its teaching. The outcome was the translation of the Latin Mass into the vernacular languages, a new openness to Christians of other traditions, and the controversial renewal of Catholic theology associated with the post-Kantian experientialism of Karl Rahner (1904–84) and the Protestant-influenced radicalism of Hans Küng (b. 1928).

These changes coincided, however, in the 1960s with the subversion of traditional religious values by a newly affluent neo-pagan mass culture, hedonist, consumerist and materialist, leading to the individualisation and disintegration of the loyalties of Christian as well as Socialist blocs of collective practice and opinion, and to the widespread adoption of permissive moral norms and a much sharper decline in church-going. This revolution was given a kind of sanction by the vulgarisation of the psychoanalytic theory of the Jewish-born Sigmund Freud (1856–1939), who dismissed religion as an illusion connected with personality disorder and sexual repression, though a more favourable view, of the imaginative power of primordial religious archetypes, informed the writings of Carl Jung (1875–1961). The impact of secularisation has, however, been very uneven, and has been influenced by every local circumstance of religious and political tradition. De-Christianisation has been most marked in those parts of Europe in which the Church was already weak: thus the largely Communist, under-churched former latifundia of southern Portugal remain much less religious than the small peasant proprietors of the north, while at the other extreme of Europe, western Norway preserves a pietist tradition against secularist Oslo. Sweden offers the contrast of a Church establishment embracing almost the whole population with one of the lowest percentages of churchgoers in Europe, while in England, in which the largest single body of regular worshippers is now a Roman Catholic one of largely Irish descent, a Church of England establishment survives, to give a general sanction to civic and folk religion and to act as an institutional framework for warring church parties, Protestant and Anglo-Catholic, conservative and liberal. There are constitutional Christian monarchies in the Low Countries, Spain and Scandinavia, and religious behaviour remains a significant feature of the lives of some of the wealthiest and best-educated sections of European society, as well as of some of the poorest and least literate.

In other ways, the picture is a very mixed one. Traditional Christian attitudes continue to influence human relations at every level, but in the specific matter of regulating sexual mores by Christian laws, most of Europe has ceased to be Christian. Science and medicine may have diminished the importance of certain traditional consolations of religion, and, less rationally, shaken belief in the possibility of miracles; but scientists and doctors are not noticeably less believing than the professional classes from which they come. If heavily urbanised populations are cut off from the Christianised calendar of the agricultural year, the widely varying levels of religiosity from city to city are less a consequence of a uniform experience of urbanisation than of the equally varying degrees of religious practice in their respective surrounding countrysides.

For all the complexities of these new developments, however, there has been a perceptible weakening of Christian institutions, a displacement of religious commitment from public allegiance to private conviction, and a softening of the terrors of a properly Christian belief in sin, Satan, hell and judgement. Not that European man is more 'rational' than his forebears, but his favourite superstitions seem remoter from Christianity. Even such bastions of the faith as Ireland have seen an erosion of belief and practice, especially among the young, and most of the statistical indexes, which speak of an ageing religious population, indicate a still further future decline. The Church's response has not been encouraging. The recent experiments, both Protestant and Catholic, with radical theologies and liturgies, have attracted Christian minorities, but they often appear to amount to an internal desacralisation of religion, which has disoriented and disheartened traditional worshippers and made no significant conversions from among the ranks of unbelief. The only major expanding forms of Western European religious life in the age of ecumenism have been upon the fringes, among the ecstatic Pentecostal or conservative revivalist and 'fundamentalist' Protestant sects, especially those with a strong apocalyptic message; various imported, often adapted or syncretic, oriental religions; and the Muslim faith professed by Pakistani, Algerian and Turkish immigrants into Britain, France and Germany.

Against so pessimistic a conclusion it might be said that the roots of European Christianity lie deep, and it has been possible here to give only the most fleeting glimpse of the splendours and miseries of the Christian legacy: enshrined in the lives and works of princes and peasants, doctors and confessors, saints and scholars, warriors and persecutors, liberators and blood-stained villains and martyr-heroes; the innumerable company of all blessed and faithful people, and a good many less faithful; men and women of every sort and condition, a goodly portion of that multitude which no man can number who have bowed the knee at the name of Jesus. In the present ahistorical climate, their witness, in all its variety, is discounted, and so is the religion which, for good and ill, has been at the heart of European history. But it is now no longer clear that it will remain so. Having been during most of its two-thousand-year history predominantly the religion of Europe, Christianity is now showing a much greater vitality in former mission fields in the Third World, and it now seems more likely to survive in

Europe under Communism than in the increasingly sceptical, pluralist and secular societies west of the Iron Curtain. There, perhaps, like its Founder, it may have to die before its rise again.

Further Reading

For an efficient survey of the literature, see Owen Chadwick, *The History of the Church: A Select Bibliography*, 3rd rev. edn (Historical Association, London, 1973). There are short surveys, again with bibliographies, in *The Pelican History of the Church*, vols. 3, 4 and 5, by Owen Chadwick, G.R. Cragg and Alec R. Vidler, and in *A Short History of the Catholic Church* (London, 1984), by J. Derek Holmes and Bernard W. Bickers. Of the projected definitive volumes in the *Oxford History of the Christian Church*, only one, *The Popes and European Revolution* (Oxford, 1981), by Owen Chadwick, essentially on the eighteenth-century Catholic Church outside France, has so far appeared. Volumes 3 and 4 in K.S. Latourette, *A History of the Expansion of Christianity*, new edn, 7 vols. (London, 1971), and the modern volumes of A. Fliche and V. Martin (eds.), *Histoire de l'Église* (Paris, 1934–) from a Protestant and Roman Catholic viewpoint respectively, provide more detailed and conventional surveys of the subject, while a more sociological approach is to be found in two magnificent survey volumes by Jean Delumeau, *Naissance et affirmation de la Réforme* (Paris, 1968), and *Le Catholicisme entre Luther et Voltaire* (Paris, 1971); in John Bossy, *Christianity in the West, 1400–1700* (Oxford, 1985); and in Hugh McLeod, *Religion and the People of Western Europe, 1789–1970* (Oxford, 1981).

On the history of thought, see H. Cunliffe-Jones, *Christian Theology since 1600* (London, 1970), and J.C. Livingstone, *Modern Christian Thought: From the Enlightenment to Vatican II* (New York, 1971), and, more heroically, C. Andresen (ed.), *Handbuch der Dogmen-und Theologiegeschichte* (Göttingen, 1980–4): though after 1600, the history of ideas tends to be treated out of context with a wider religious, political and social history. For individuals and movements, see F.L. Cross and E.A. Livingstone (eds.), *The Oxford Dictionary of the Christian Church*, 2nd edn (London, 1974), and J.D. Douglas (ed.), *The New International Dictionary of the Christian Church* (Exeter, 1974), the former with excellent bibliographies. Cross and Livingstone take a more 'Catholic' perspective, Douglas a more 'Protestant'. Also indispensable are the larger religious encyclopedias, *Die Religion in Geschichte und Gegenwart* (1957–65); *Dictionnaire de Théologie Catholique* (1903–); *The New Schaff-Herzog Encyclopedia of Religious Knowledge* (1951–4); and the *New Catholic Encyclopedia* (1967–), all of which contain a wealth of specialist information. Much about the history of the Church can also be gleaned at a general level, from the new *Fontana History of Europe*, and at a specialist level, from *The New Cambridge Modern History*.

13 *Christianity in Africa from 1450 to Today*

Peter Clarke

Introduction

There have been broadly four phases in the development of Christianity in Africa. The first of these, which is not part of our main concern here, relates to North Africa where by the middle years of the second century a strong Christian community had emerged, centred on both Carthage and Alexandria. It was presided over in turn by such influential theologians as Clement of Alexandria (*c.* 150–215 CE), his pupil Origen (*c.* 185–254); 'the brilliant, exasperating, sarcastic, and intolerant yet intensely vigorous and incisive in argument' Tertullian (160–220), who determined the terminology of Latin theology for the future and was to join the ecstatic religious sect, the Montanists; Cyprian, Bishop of Carthage, who was martyred in 258; Athanasius, the long-serving Bishop of Alexandria (*c.* 296–373); and Augustine, Bishop of Hippo (354–430), most influential of all (see Chapter 9).

Schism, persecution, failure to sink its roots among the ordinary people, and in the seventh century the advance of Islam, severely curtailed the expansion of the North African Christian Church. With the exception of Egypt and Ethiopia, where the Coptic Church with its strong monastic strain is still even today relatively large, Christianity in North Africa was reduced to a number of very small and scattered communities which, although they were allowed to practise their faith, were forbidden to evangelise.

Moreover the Sahara Desert made missionary work among the peoples of sub-Saharan Africa a virtual impossibility. The Christian evangelisation of this region of Africa was in fact only to begin in the wake of Portugal's seaborne expansion which got under way in the middle years of the fifteenth century. This marks the second phase in the development of Christianity in Africa which was to cover the period *c.* 1450–*c.* 1800. The modern missionary movement followed and lasted until the era of independence, which began for many African states in the late 1950s and early 1960s. The fourth phase covers the period from independence to the present. The rest of this article is concerned with the second, third and fourth phases of the history of Christianity in Africa.

Sub-Saharan Africa, *c*. 1450–*c*. 1800

Prince Henry the Navigator (d. 1460) was the architect of Portugal's geographical and navigational explorations which occasioned the involvement of Christian missionaries in sub-Saharan Africa during the second half of the fifteenth century. He not only mapped out the plans but also launched the expeditions for the charting of the African coastline, and was given authorisation in a papal Bull in 1455 to go forth and conquer far-off lands and take possession of their wealth. The explorations that followed had a strong religious as well as economic, scientific and political purpose, though in practice it was not always possible to distinguish the religious from these other interests. The Portuguese were not only anxious to establish Christian kingdoms in Africa with a view to spreading Catholicism but also saw these kingdoms as potential trading partners, African gold and slaves being two of the commodities that were of increasing interest to them at the time, and as allies in their struggle against Islam.

The year 1482 saw the arrival of a Portuguese ship at La Mina (Elmina) in present-day Ghana (formerly the Gold Coast) and the beginnings of Catholicism on the West African mainland. Mass, according to tradition, was celebrated under a tree and prayers said for the 'conversion of the natives from idolatry and the perpetual prosperity of the Church'. But it was further south in Benin, in modern-day mid-western Nigeria, that the first serious attempts were made in 1485 to establish those Christian kingdoms envisaged by the Portuguese. Little was accomplished either here or in the nearby kingdom of Warri over the following three hundred years. Some of the more important reasons for this were the shortage of missionary personnel, the deep involvement of some of them in trade, including the slave trade, rather than evangelisation, the dislocation and insecurity caused by the traffic in slaves, the economic and political rivalry between the European powers with interests in the region, the failure to train an indigenous clergy and the reluctance of many African rulers to convert to Christianity and thereby undermine the authority and support they derived from their position as both priest and king in the traditional African politico-religious system.

Somewhat greater success was achieved in the kingdom of the Kongo in present-day Angola, where by the 1550s the ruler and some five hundred of his subjects had converted to Christianity. This success, however, was relatively short-lived for by the opening of the nineteenth century there was little trace of a Christian presence in the region. The early history of Christianity in East and South Africa followed a similar pattern to that in West and Central Africa. Although Bartholomew Dias had rounded the Cape of Good Hope in 1488, followed by Vasco da Gama who arrived at Mombasa in present-day Kenya in 1498, Christian missionary work did not get under way in East Africa until the 1590s with the building of a church at Fort Jesus at the entrance to the mouth of the Mombasa harbour. During the next half century several hundred people in the immediate vicinity and in nearby Malindi and Zanzibar (now part of Tanzania) were converted to Christianity. But soon after, the struggle between the Portuguese and the Arabs for hegemony in the region began, and most of the Christians died in the ensuing conflicts. These ended with the Portuguese leaving the area in the middle of the eighteenth century.

Missionary activity in the hinterland was spearheaded by the Jesuits who reached Sofala (to the south of Mombasa in present-day Mozambique) in 1560. From there they advanced further inland to the Monopatapa (Mutapa) kingdom, in Zimbabwe, where they succeeded in converting the ruler in 1652, the same year that the Dutch entered the Cape and laid the foundations of what was to become the foremost Christian Church in South Africa, the Dutch Reformed Church (Nederduitse Gereformeerde Kerk, NGK).

At the outset the Dutch, more widely known today as the Boers, did nothing to convert the indigenous population, concentrating instead on obtaining clergy to minister in their own churches. Missionary work in the Cape only began after the British had taken it over from the Dutch in 1795. While the Anglican and Roman Catholic Churches were at the outset to adopt much the same attitude towards the indigenous people of the Cape as the Dutch, other missionary societies, among them the London Missionary Society (LMS), the Methodists and the Rhenish Mission, became the leading pioneers of missionary endeavour here and elsewhere in Southern Africa. As for the Dutch, they began their historic trek northwards from the Cape which between 1835 and 1848 took them to the Orange Free State, Natal and the Transvaal.

The vast majority of the missionaries during this second phase were Roman Catholics, and with a few exceptions it was not until the last quarter of the eighteenth century that the Protestant churches directed their attention to the African continent. By that time the Christian Church in Africa had almost nothing to show for its efforts during the previous three hundred years. Some of the reasons for this have already been mentioned. To these we can add other serious drawbacks, such as the missionaries' dependence on the secular arm for financial support, transport to and from Africa, and even for permission to carry out their duties outside certain specified areas. During the third phase, this dependence on the state lessened somewhat as missionary societies became more self-supporting and more international in character. The growing opposition to and the eventual abolition of the transatlantic slave trade also facilitated missionary activity in this third period.

Sub-Saharan Africa, *c.* 1800–*c.* 1960

The Nineteenth Century

The origins of this third phase of the Christian missionary movement in Africa owe much to the concern to remedy the evil effects of the slave trade and to replace it by what were termed 'legitimate' trade and commerce and by agricultural development, all of which was to be inspired by Christian virtues and values, an approach to evangelisation usually referred to as that of the Bible and the Plough.

In West Africa the modern missionary movement began with the establishment of Christian colonies in Sierra Leone in the late eighteenth and early nineteenth centuries. The so-called problem of the 'black poor' in Britain, exacerbated by the ruling of Lord Chief Justice Mansfield in 1772 that the holding of slaves was illegal and by the arrival of black soldiers who had fought on the British side during the American War of Independence (1776–83), preoccupied humanitarians and abolitionists such as Thomas Clarkson, Granville Sharp, Samuel Hoare, Henry Thornton and Zachary Macaulay, all members of or associated with the Evangelical wing of the Church of England known as the Clapham Sect. Some were also connected with the Sierra Leone Company. The solution devised to deal with the problem of the 'black poor', which at the same time would enable the evangelisation of Africa to begin, consisted in settling these black people in Sierra Leone, an ideal entry point to the hinterland, it was believed. It was also a place where the settlers would have little difficulty in finding land and, through 'legitimate' enterprise grounded in Christian values, acquire wealth. In this way a prosperous and virtuous African middle class would in time emerge and lead their fellow Africans along the twin paths of Christianity and 'civilisation' and away from 'darkness' and 'idolatry'. Europe would also benefit from having helped to raise up a new African business and trading elite, with whom it could enter into 'legitimate' commerce and thereby offset any economic disadvantage that might ensue from the abolition of the slave trade.

The first of these settlements, notably Granville Town, named after Sharp (also euphemistically known as the 'Province of Freedom'), were largely unsuccessful, as also were later attempts. Similar ventures in Liberia by the American Colonization Society in the first quarter of the nineteenth century also started inauspiciously. In fact, by the end of the nineteenth century, while there were several thousand Christians in

Freetown and Monrovia, capitals of Sierra Leone and Liberia respectively, Christianity had made almost no impact at all on the peoples of the hinterland in either country.

The aim of most Protestant missionary societies in the nineteenth century was the establishment of self-supporting, self-governing African churches, a policy pursued with conviction and determination by Henry Venn, secretary of the Church Missionary Society (CMS) from 1841 to 1875. To this end Venn emphasised the absolute necessity of engaging Africans as equal partners with European missionaries in the work of Christian evangelisation and of establishing a practical, relevant Christianity, which would contribute not only to the spiritual development of the people but also to an improvement in their quality of life. As a result, an industrial school was opened by the CMS in the 1840s at Abeokuta in western Nigeria, and agricultural and other relevant schemes were introduced. Moreover, many of these societies appointed Africans to posts of responsibility. For example, the CMS in the 1850s placed the Nigerian Samuel Ajayi Crowther in charge of the Niger Delta Pastorate, which covered what is today a large part of Nigeria. In 1864 Crowther was consecrated a bishop at Canterbury. However, some European missionaries were not prepared to accept the authority of Africans and even questioned their competence to manage the affairs of the churches in their charge. This kind of opposition not only forced Crowther to resign his post in 1890 (in reality he was displaced) but also contributed, as we shall see, to the rise of what are known as the African independent churches.

There were, of course, other missionaries like Christina and François Coillard of the Paris-based Protestant Evangelical Missionary Society (SME) who worked both for and with the local people. The Coillards, for example, found themselves working with Mohesh and his people as they struggled to save their kingdom in the Drakensberg mountains from English and Boer domination. There were many others who followed a similar path, among them David Livingstone, Johannes Vanderkemp, Robert Moffat and John Philip of the London Missionary Society (LMS), who sought to co-operate with rather than rule over Africans. Livingstone pioneered the beginnings of Christianity and 'legitimate' commerce between 1842 and 1874 in parts of what are today Zambia, Malawi, Mozambique and Tanzania, while other Scottish missionaries of the LMS were to consolidate his work and that of others in these areas. Yet others were to make a notable contribution to the development of Christianity in both East and South Africa. By the middle of the nineteenth century not only the LMS but many missionary societies were expanding their activities in South Africa, among them the Wesleyan Methodists, the Moravians, the Lutherans and several Presbyterian societies. From the last emerged the entirely black Bantu Presbyterian Church and the mainly white Presbyterian Church of Southern Africa. In 1836 the Dutch Reformed Church began its first mission to blacks, a move that contributed much to one of several schisms within this church during the nineteenth century.

Despite the impression conveyed so far, the nineteenth-century missionary movement was not an exclusively Protestant affair. In fact Roman Catholic missionary societies had been engaged in the task of evangelisation from the first quarter of the nineteenth century when the French order of nuns, the Sisters of St Joseph of Cluny, undertook hospital and teaching work in Senegal and the Gambia. Catholic priests had returned to South Africa in 1805. Later in the century other Catholic missionary orders, among them the Society of African Missions (SMA), the Holy Ghost Fathers and the White Fathers, all three French foundations, established themselves in North, West, East, Central and South Africa, and competed fiercely with their Protestant counterparts for influence and converts. Intra- and inter-denominational rivalry—and rivalry with Islam—characterised much of Christian missionary endeavour in this period.

There were numerous instances of this Catholic–Protestant and Christian–Muslim rivalry, late nineteenth-century Uganda providing one of the best known examples of both. It was there in 1892 that Catholics from the mission-stations of the White Fathers and Protestants from the CMS engaged each other in open combat for power and influence among the Buganda. This followed on the Christian–Muslim war of 1889, which had not only brought the Christian leaders into political power but had also established the principle of *cujus regio ejus religio*.

During the nineteenth century the Catholic Church was to make most headway in what became during the last quarter of that century and the first decade of the twentieth century French, Belgian and Portuguese colonial territories, for example in the former French and Belgian Congo (Congo Brazzaville and Kinshasa respectively), the Ivory Coast, Senegal, Guinea (Conakry), the People's Republic of Benin, Togo, Cameroon, Gabon, Angola, Rwanda-Burundi and Mozambique. The Cape Verde Islands and São Tomé and Príncipe were a virtual Roman Catholic monopoly from the fifteenth century, the presence of Protestant missionaries only being tolerated in recent times.

Although the first Roman Catholic church was built in South Africa at Mossel Bay, Natal, in 1501, and Jesuits had visited the Cape in 1685, followed, as we have seen, by other priests in 1805, Catholics only began regular missionary work in earnest in that country in 1820. Even then progress was slow, one of the reasons being that they were not officially granted freedom of worship until 1870.

By the end of the nineteenth century, Christian missionary societies were involved in the work of Christianising and 'civilising' Africa, from virtually every country in Europe and from North America, from those already mentioned to the Finnish Lutherans active among the Ovambo in Namibia and their Swedish colleagues in the Congo and

Ethiopia. While, as we have seen, this renewal of missionary involvement in Africa was triggered in large measure by the anti-slavery campaign, it was also a response to the Evangelical Revival which swept through parts of Europe and North America in the eighteenth century and to the gradual opening up and greater knowledge of the continent made possible by explorers, settlers and traders. As others had become in the second half of the eighteenth century the pathfinders of the missionary in Africa, the missionary himself had, in the opinion of some scholars, become one hundred years later the 'flag-bearer of colonialism' on that continent.

This, however, would seem to be something of an over-simplification; for while there were cases where missionaries encouraged and even appealed to governments to intervene and establish a presence in Africa (the British bombardment and annexation of Lagos, Nigeria, in 1851 and the French conquest of the western Sudan (Mali) in the late 1880s being cases in point) missionaries tended on the whole to be somewhat sceptical of the benefits to be derived from large-scale, direct Western political and economic involvement in Africa. As it turned out, the first stages of formal colonialism from the mid-1880s to the outbreak of the First World War were, in Uganda and elsewhere, remarkably favourable in somewhat different ways not only to Christianity but also to Islam.

Finally, while during the nineteenth century much more had been achieved by European and North American missionaries, both black and white, in terms of the number of those converted to Christianity, the building of churches, schools and hospitals and the introduction of 'legitimate' commerce in among other places the Zambesi valley where the slave trade had once flourished, than during the whole of the period from *c.* 1450 to 1800, it was bands of neophytes, organised by lay Africans, sometimes not yet baptised, who were the most effective vehicles for the spread of Christianity. The Christian churches, however, with one or two notable exceptions, such as the Basle and Bremen missions in West Africa and for a time the Niger mission of the CMS under the leadership of the Nigerian bishop Samuel Ajayi Crowther until 1890, had made little headway in establishing self-supporting, self-governing churches in Africa, nor were they to accomplish very much more before the end of the colonial period.

The Twentieth Century

During the colonial era, which in the case of most African states had come to an end, at least in a formal sense, by the mid-1960s, Christianity made rapid progress in the so-called 'pagan' areas, that is in those areas which had not been heavily influenced by Islam. Where Islam had taken root, for example in northern Nigeria, the northern Sudan and in large areas of former French West Africa, it made virtually no headway, despite its earlier optimism that African Muslims would flock to the Christian churches immediately on seeing what were regarded as the obvious benefits to be derived from membership when compared with allegiance to Islam, Western education and medicine in particular. However, apart from the fact that Christian missionary activity was prohibited or severely restricted by colonial governments in certain Muslim areas, such as northern Nigeria, African Muslims generally turned out to be more secure in and committed to their religion than was expected, and Islam sometimes exercised greater appeal than Christianity, even in the designated 'pagan' areas such as the Ivory Coast.

It was nevertheless the case that Christianity, wherever it opened schools and even more wherever it made full use of the catechist or lay African evangelist, made considerable gains in influence and in numbers of converts. The upheaval and dislocation resulting from the colonial takeover of the region facilitated change, eastern Nigeria being one striking example of the phenomenal growth of mission Christianity in this period. It was a growth that had much to do with the school approach to evangelisation adopted by both Catholics and Protestants. Senegal is a striking case of the expansion achieved as a direct result of the greater use made of catechists in the teaching and preaching of the Christian faith. Moreover, during the First World War, in parts of both East and West Africa where German and French missionaries had to withdraw for chaplaincy service and other reasons, their mission-stations and churches advanced and prospered under African leadership. After the war when the rail and road networks were appreciably extended to reach far into the interior, and with the introduction of the motor-bicycle and the motor-car, the scope and pace of missionary work widened and quickened, producing dramatic results as far as the numerical growth of Christianity was concerned. Furthermore, an increasing number of educated Christians began to enter the professions and the modern sector of the economy, achieving thereby more status and influence in society. While this was largely unintentional on the part of the mission churches, this educated, relatively prosperous elite which they were helping to create became the leaders of the independence movements that began to take shape in the 1930s and 1940s.

Other important developments in this period include the slow but steady increase in the numbers of indigenous clergy, two of the best examples being in eastern Nigeria and Cameroon, and the change in attitude to both Islam and African 'traditional' religion. The former came to be regarded less and less by the Christian missionary as an inferior religion, a post-Christian heresy founded by a corrupt, immoral and psychologically disturbed, self-proclaimed prophet, and more as a genuine religion, and although fundamentally in error, one that should be treated with greater tolerance, sympathy and understanding rather than with the scorn and ridicule which had been until then characteristic of the Christian approach to Islam.

As for African 'traditional' religion, this had been widely attacked as little more than a bundle of primitive superstitions. Some missionaries in the very early years of this century, like the Catholic bishop Shanahan, in eastern Nigeria, had taken a more positive approach, recognising that Africans did have a concept of and faith in a Supreme Being, and that this could provide a useful vehicle for introducing them to the Christian idea of God. But on the whole, as far as written sources are concerned, missionary interpretations of and approach to African 'traditional' religion were almost entirely negative; it was in fact an evil and harmful influence from which African converts were to be protected and shielded. This explains much about the location of the Christian churches which were sited away from the ordinary, everyday world of the African. The writings and research of missionaries like Father Schmidt, who in the 1930s argued that African religions were in 'origin' at least monotheistic, and of Father Tempels who in his *Bantu Philosophy* used the Bergsonian notion of 'vital force' to interpret the unifying idea underlying all Bantu cosmology, ethics and ritual, thereby attempting a dialogue between African religious thought and Western philosophical categories, did much to change the climate of opinion and approach to 'traditional' religion.

However negative and hostile its view of and approach to African 'traditional' religion, Christianity in Africa was never able to escape from its influence and today seeks positively to integrate into its own liturgy and teaching elements of African ritual, beliefs and practices. Many of the traditional life cycle rituals in the religious and cultural life of African Christians such as birth, marriage and funeral rites, and practices such as the veneration of ancestors, once frowned upon by mission Christianity and which consequently were simply allowed to run parallel to (where they were not deemed actually to collide with) the so-called orthodox version of the faith, have now been incorporated in one form or another into the Church's liturgy. It is not an exaggeration to say that in certain respects the Christianity introduced by the mission churches, for the most part very Western in organisation, content, character and style, has undergone considerable transformation as a result of its encounter with the 'traditional' religious culture of Africa.

Nevertheless, as independence drew near it was still very much a mission Church and one that in several respects had not prepared itself for this new age in African history. Certainly a glance around Africa as it was in the 1950s will show that much had been achieved. There were by then some twenty-five million Christians in Africa from the Sahara to the Cape, and in the former Belgian Congo (Zaire) alone there was an estimated Catholic population of over three and a half million, while the Protestant churches, somewhat surprisingly in this 'Catholic' colony, had over one and a half million members. They had around three million in the Union of South Africa, the Methodist Church being the largest of the Protestant mission churches there. The Anglican Church was present wherever Britain was the colonial power, a presence that was considerable in Nigeria and Uganda in particular. Of course its character varied from 'evangelical' in these and other countries, where it had been introduced by the CMS, to Anglo-Catholic in Zanzibar, Malawi, Zimbabwe and South Africa, where either the Universities Mission to Central Africa (UMCA) or the Society for the Propagation of the Gospel (SPG) was its chief support or standard-bearer. In addition to their remarkable growth, the mission churches also enjoyed a virtual monopoly of primary and secondary education, which in parts of Nigeria and elsewhere was to be lost shortly before or soon after independence.

But these churches were not as strong as they looked. They had become too dependent on the school approach to evangelisation and on outside financial support and expatriate leadership. With no more than a handful of African bishops and a comparatively small number of African clergy, many of them at independence still bore the appearance of colonial churches. There were other churches, generally referred to as independent churches, that were much more African in character. To a brief consideration of these we now turn.

Independency

African independent or, as they are sometimes called, separatist churches can be counted in their thousands, the largest number being in South Africa, which perhaps has the greatest proliferation of such churches of any country in the world. Founded by African Christians, these churches first began to appear in the closing decades of the nineteenth century and today are an established and familiar part of the religious and cultural life of many African countries, and especially in those areas where Protestant Christianity prevailed.

The early independence churches that emerged in South Africa and Nigeria in the late nineteenth and early twentieth centuries were an appeal to mission churches to adapt to the local conditions and, even more, a protest against European domination of these churches. As we saw in the case of Nigeria, Africans were being demoted rather than promoted to positions of leadership in the churches in this period, the case of Samuel Ajayi Crowther being one of the best-known instances. However, the issue of white leadership was to come to a head in Nigeria in the Baptist Church in Lagos in 1888, when most of its members joined the dissident African-led African Baptist Church founded by the Nigerian Mojola Agbebi. This was followed in 1891 by a schism within the CMS in Lagos which saw the establishment of the United Native African Church, dedicated to the evangelisation of Africa by indigenous agents and to the replacement of alien rituals and ceremonies by African ones.

While they placed considerable emphasis on African leadership and independence from the mission churches and are therefore sometimes referred to as 'Ethiopian' (Ethiopia being both long Christian and uncolonised, and therefore symbolic of African independence) some of these churches modelled themselves where liturgy, organisation and doctrine were concerned on the mission churches from which they had seceded.

Somewhat different were the separatist churches that began to emerge not long before, during and just after the First World War. These are known by different names, such as 'zionist' in South Africa (in no way connected with Jewish Zionism), *aladura* (prayer) in Nigeria and 'prophetic' and 'spirit' churches elsewhere. It was not deliberate policy on the part of these churches to break away from the mission churches. Their principal preoccupation was with healing through prayer, and they strongly opposed the use of all forms of medicine, traditional or Western. Led by charismatic, prophetic figures they attracted both Christians and non-Christians alike and in due course became churches in their own right.

The Harrist Church in the Ivory Coast, inspired by the teaching and preaching of the Liberian 'prophet' William Wade Harris, is a case in point. Harris's preaching tour of the southern region of the Ivory Coast and south-west Ghana in 1913–14 was perhaps the most remarkable conversion campaign ever undertaken in Africa, leading to the baptism of an estimated one hundred thousand people. It was not undertaken in opposition to the mission churches or with a view to founding a separatist church, which only came much later. In fact Harris advised his followers at this time to join the mission churches, either Catholic or Protestant; while later, in the 1920s, it appears that he issued instructions that they were to seek membership of the Protestant churches only. In Nigeria, it was Moses Orimolade who in the 1920s inspired the praying bands that had developed into the popular and now widespread Cherubim and Seraphim societies and churches, one of them being the Church of the Lord (*Aladura*), founded by the former Anglican Josiah Oshitelu. In South Africa the best known of the quasi-messianic, prophetic leaders of the zionist churches of roughly the same period was the soft-spoken, reserved, former Baptist, Zulu healer and hymn-writer of genius, Isaiah Shembe, who founded the Church of the Ama Nazaretha. Today in South Africa some 20 per cent of the African population belong to one or other of the country's many independent churches, while the *aladura* churches have millions of followers in Nigeria and have spread to other West African states and even to Europe and North America.

Although they did not unite in pursuit of political independence, these churches did contribute to that cause in its wider sense and in particular to the religious and cultural independence of Africa, preserving, albeit on a selective basis, African rituals, hymns, prayers, names and beliefs, and providing through their organisations and schools a means for Africans to acquire experience in running their own affairs.

On occasion, colonial governments and mission churches reacted (and not always without some justification) as if these churches were, or were likely to become, simply 'fronts' for political movements. The prophet Harris, mentioned above, was expelled from the Ivory Coast by the French colonial administration for fear that he might incite the people to rebellion. John Chilembwe, founder of the Providence Industrial Mission in Nyasaland (Malawi), a mission with over nine hundred students in seven schools in 1912, did in fact organise and lead an uprising which resulted in the death of several European settlers in 1915. This brought about the immediate closure of his mission and schools and caused all independent churches to appear suspect to the colonial authorities and the missions. Some leaders of independent churches, although they did not necessarily regard themselves as such, were seen by sections of their followers more as nationalists and revolutionaries than as Christian prophets. Simon Kimbangu, in whose name was founded in the 1920s, in the Belgian Congo (now Zaire), the Church of Jesus Christ on Earth Through the Prophet Simon Kimbangu, is one well-known example. Although this former catechist with the Baptist Missionary Society presented himself as a messenger or prophet of God and healed in the name of Jesus, he opposed separation from the mission churches, condemned the spirit cult associated with charms called *menkisi* and advised the people, unlike some of the Nigerian prophets of the same period, to pay their taxes to the government. Nevertheless, he was eventually arrested and sentenced to death. The sentence was commuted by the King of the Belgians and he died in solitary confinement in 1951. Kimbangu's preaching with its strong millenarian strain—a new God was to come more powerful than the state—and his large following made him a threat to the authorities, as did what was said and done by groups of his followers in his name if not necessarily with his approval (such as the non-payment of taxes).

On the other hand, certain movements that started off as political became over time religious. For an example of this we turn this time to the former French Congo and to Simon Matswa, who founded the Amicale in Paris in 1926. This was a secular protest movement at the outset and brought the Lari people into confrontation with the French colonial administration, while Matswa himself died in a colonial prison in 1942. At this point the movement turned away from direct political action to a passive millenarianism as followers awaited deliverance through the second coming of 'our sovereign Father Matswa', as they now called him. Like the mission or historic churches as they are sometimes known, the independence churches grew at a rapid pace between 1945 and 1960, by which time many of them had become increasingly respectable and would soon receive state recognition.

Christianity in Africa since Independence

Great change amid continuity has characterised the very recent history of Christianity in post-independence Africa. The hierarchy is for the most part

African and many of the Protestant mission churches are self-governing. There has also been a vast increase in the number of indigenous clergy, though in many countries expatriate missionaries are still in the majority, especially in Catholic areas. The catechists, however, remain the principal agents of evangelisation and the fact that Christianity in Africa today, with its estimated one hundred million adherents can no longer be regarded as merely an exotic appendage of so-called mainstream Christianity, owes much to their unstinting work in the villages across the length and breadth of the continent.

Since independence there has been greater co-operation and tolerance both between the older Christian churches, and between these churches and the independence churches, some of which have come to resemble increasingly those older, more established churches themselves. Moreover attitudes towards and relations with Islam have improved considerably, and much greater esteem and respect are now shown to 'traditional' religion. Some of the branches of the Dutch Reformed Church in South Africa are an exception to all or most of this and the NGK has continued to defend the historic role of the Afrikaner to protect Christian civilisation from anti-Christian forces and as recently as October 1986 ceased to justify apartheid on theological grounds, but still supports segregated schools and housing. By way of contrast, 'black theology', a development of the late 1960s and early 1970s, has attempted to address itself, by 'black' self-awareness, to this and other issues and experiences that have shaped much of the history of Africa and its peoples during the five hundred years of Christianity sketchily outlined here: the slave trade, colonisation, urbanisation, individual freedom and human rights, industrialisation, religious pluralism, and nation-building within the context of massive poverty and inequality, the political solutions for which have often been one-party states and military rule.

Further Reading

Ajayi, J.F.A. *Christian Missions in Nigeria 1841–1891. The Making of a New Elite* (Longman, London, 1965)

Barrett, David B. *Schism and Renewal in Africa: an Analysis of Six Thousand Contemporary Religious Movements* (Oxford University Press, Nairobi and London, 1968)

Clarke, P.B. *West Africa and Christianity. A Study of Religious Development from the 15th to the 20th Century* (Edward Arnold, London, 1986)

Fasholé-Luke, E., Gray, R., Hastings, A. and Tasie, G. (eds.) *Christianity in Independent Africa* (Rex Collings, London, 1978)

Groves, C.P. *The Planting of Christianity in Africa*, 4 vols. (Lutterworth Press, London, 1948–58)

Hastings, A. *A History of African Christianity 1950–1975* (Cambridge University Press, Cambridge, 1979)

Kendall, E. *The End of an Era. Africa and the Missionary* (SPCK, London, 1978)

Oliver, R.O. *The Missionary Factor in East Africa* (Longman, London, 1965)

Peel, J.D.Y. *Aladura: a Religious Movement among the Yoruba* (Oxford University Press, London, 1968)
Ranger, T.O. and Weller, J. (eds.) *Themes in the Christian History of Central Africa* (Heinemann, London, 1975)
Sanneh, L. *West African Christianity. The Religious Impact* (C. Hurst & Co., London, 1983)
Shorter, A. and Kataza, E. (eds.) *Missionaries to Yourselves. African Catechists Today* (G. Chapman, London, 1972)
Sundkler, B.G.M. *Bantu Prophets in South Africa*, 2nd edn (Oxford University Press for the International African Institute, London, 1961)
Turner, H.W. *African Independent Church*, vol. 1: *History of an African Independent Church: the Church of the Lord (Aladura)*; vol. 2: *African Independent Church: the Life and Faith of the Church of the Lord (Aladura)* (Clarendon Press, Oxford, 1967)

14 *Christianity in North America from the Sixteenth Century*

Richard Carwardine

In 1650, when the first permanent settlements within the boundaries of what was to become the United States and Canada were still less than a century old, a perspicacious traveller to the New World would already have been able to discern in their infancy many of the later distinctive features of Christianity in North America. By that date five European nations had established colonies there and had carried their national churches with them. To the south, Spanish efforts to secure a base in Florida had established a settlement at St Augustine in 1565 from which other Spanish colonies and Catholic missions to the Indians spread over the next century along the southern and south-western edge of the later United States. To the north, the early seventeenth century saw the beginnings of settlement in New France: the founding of the trading station of Quebec in 1608 encouraged a vision of a vast French Catholic empire that would, through mass conversion of the Huron Indians, extend far beyond the Great Lakes. Between the two Catholic powers, along the eastern seaboard stood the colonies of the Protestant English, principally those of Virginia (1607) and the New England settlements of Plymouth (1620), Massachusetts Bay, Connecticut and New Haven, in all of which at the outset the non-Separatist Puritan element of the Church of England held sway. Each of the small and relatively short-lived colonies of New Netherland (centred on Manhattan Island) and New Sweden (Delaware) saw the transplanting of the established religion of the mother country, Reformed and Lutheran respectively.

In the very diversity of these official establishments our traveller might have foreseen the future heterogeneity of North American religious life. Moreover, America's particular form of religious pluralism, in which denominations would compete freely one with another, neither aided nor hindered by formal state support, was foreshadowed in the presence of dissenting groups within each colony—Huguenots in New France, Separatists in New England, German Lutherans in New Netherland—and in the existence of colonies without any establishment at all, as in Rhode Island, established by Roger Williams as a haven for Separatist, Baptist refugees from Massachusetts Bay, and in Lord Baltimore's shelter for Roman Catholics in the proprietary colony of Maryland. Given that the English colonies were growing much faster than the others he might have guessed that Protestantism rather than Catholicism would provide the principal key to America's religious development, while the relative strength of Puritanism within those colonies hinted that in America would develop the most Protestant of all Protestant societies, biblicist, evangelical and salvation-focused. Already by 1650 the interrelationship of religious attachment and loyalty to ethnic and national grouping, evident throughout North American history, was well established. So too was a prevalent and enduring sense of America's special mission in the fulfilment of God's plan and of her duty to stand as an example to other nations. Governor John Winthrop told the settlers of Massachusetts Bay that 'the eyes of all people are upon us'; their Bible Commonwealth was to be 'as a city upon a hill'.

The diversity of colonial Christianity continued to increase with the march of time and population. In New England the Congregational Calvinist establishments unsuccessfully threatened fines, disenfranchisement, imprisonment and even execution to keep intrusive Baptists and Quakers at bay. Anglican worship was introduced into Massachusetts in the 1680s. The ending of a religious test for exercising the suffrage in the same colony, and the Salem witchcraft tragedy further weakened the Puritan system. In Rhode Island and in the middle colonies various churches took advantage of conditions that favoured religious liberty. Large numbers of Quakers, following George Fox's visit to the colonies in 1672–3 and encouraged by William Penn, arrived to settle in Pennsylvania, as did Anabaptists from Germany, Scots-Irish Presbyterians, and General and Particular Baptists from Britain. Even in the southern colonies, where the Anglican establishment extended beyond Virginia to take root in Maryland and the Carolinas, there was a growing religious heterogeneity as Presbyterian, Baptists and Quakers, disproportionately the churches of the less well-to-do, won rights for themselves. During the eighteenth century the founding of Protestant churches began in earnest in Canada, but it was not until the great Loyalist migrations during and after the American Revolution that a truly influential Protestant community emerged.

Despite the multiplication of churches—or perhaps because their growth threatened the concept of a cohesive Christian commonwealth—by the second and third decades of the eighteenth century there was a widespread sense of *malaise* in many colonial churches. In their jeremiads preachers criticised the growing materialist spirit and worried about the lowering of standards associated with the 'Half-Way Covenant', the arrangement by which children of non-professors could be baptised; orthodoxy seemed in danger of melting under the early rationalist rays of the Enlightenment; the majority of the population were unchurched. A series of dramatic revivals, collectively known as the Great Awakening, drawing tens of thousands of converts into the churches, represented the reaction of orthodox evangelicalism to this decline, a movement paralleling the eighteenth-century Evangelical Revival in Britain and the flowering of Pietism in continental Europe, but one with its own indigenous sources and characteristics. The Awakening is commonly seen as originating in the middle colonies in the 1730s. Preaching a forceful evangelical Calvinism, the Dutch Reformed pastor Theodorus Frelinghuysen, the Presbyterian Tennent family and the English itinerant George Whitefield set an example to hungry revivalist elements and brought the movement to a climax in the early 1740s. A 'surprising work of God' in Northampton, western Massachusetts, under the ministry of the formidable Jonathan Edwards was the forerunner of a parallel awakening in New England that by the mid-1740s had reached most churches and all ranks of society. Nothing so intense or concentrated affected southern churches, but at different times between the 1740s and the 1770s the Presbyterians, the Separate and Regular Baptists and finally the fledgling Methodists profited from this pietistic movement. The Canadian Maritime Provinces of Nova Scotia and New Brunswick saw similar results in their evangelical Protestant churches, particularly through the work of Henry Alline and William Black.

The Awakening had profound consequences. In the short term it divided many churches into Old Lights, fearful of its disruptive 'enthusiasm', and separatist New Lights. It gave a new vigour to evangelical Protestantism, establishing new colleges and hundreds of new churches. It saw the clear emergence of a permanent tension between rationalist, Enlightenment emphases in American religious thinking and the pietistic, revivalist thrust of 'heart' religion. It ensured that the revivalist strain would be the dominant one in American religious life: those churches, especially the Anglican, which opposed the movement were destined to a minority status. It reinforced anti-Catholicism. The egalitarian, democratic and individualist aspects of its theology and practice, its millennialism, its apparent confirmation of America's special mission and its fostering of an intercolonial sense of nationhood were to have profound political effects during the Revolutionary era.

One by-product of the struggle for independence—which was strongly supported by most American churches—was the dismantling of all but three of the colonial religious establishments and the commitment of the emergent federal government to religious freedom: under the Constitution of 1787 there was to be no religious test for office nor might Congress set up any national church. The experience of an increasing religious toleration through the colonial period, the proportionate increase in the strength and diversity of dissenting churches consequent upon the Great Awakening, and the formidable coalition of Enlightenment rationalists and pietists behind a movement for the separation of Church and State created an irresistible momentum for change. Once Massachusetts had dismantled her establishment in 1833 all churches were voluntary institutions that depended for survival and growth only upon their own persuasive powers. The pluralist, competitive, revivalist, denominational pattern of American religious life was now firmly settled. It would make American Protestantism uniquely diverse and fissiparous.

The diversionary effect of the Revolution on spiritual life, the threat posed to revealed religion by Deism and other forms of 'infidelity' (particularly diabolical in its French Revolutionary guise), the shift in the demographic centre of gravity as millions crossed the Appalachian range, the emergence of a national market economy, and the growing democratisation of American politics and society in the late eighteenth and early nineteenth centuries: all demanded an evangelical response. The Second Great Awakening (*c*. 1795–*c*. 1840) originated in the orderly revivals of predominantly Calvinist New England and in the tumultuous, emotional revivalism of the frontier regions. In Kentucky and Tennessee conversions multiplied under revivalists whose preaching at vast, noisy outdoor gatherings, as at Cane Ridge in 1801, produced 'physical exercises' in their hearers. The frontier revivals split Presbyterian churches worried about good order, but the democratic theology and flexible, itinerant-based organisation of Arminian Methodism and the social and theological accessibility of Baptist preachers won huge numbers of converts to both those denominations. In the extraordinary work of the celebrated Charles G. Finney in the north-east, the middle Atlantic states and the old north-west, the emotional, cruder revivalism of the frontier and the more orderly traditional approach coalesced into a self-conscious, high-pressure revivalism based on an activist, Arminianised Calvinism. This 'new measures' revivalism became the orthodoxy in American Protestantism by the mid-nineteenth century.

Revivals encouraged a millennialist optimism in the perfectibility of American society through Christian activity. Partly a product of a dream of evangelical Protestant unity, led by men but disproportionately dependent on women, such interdenominational agencies as the American Bible Society, American Education Society, American Home Missionary Society and American Temperance Society formed a 'benevolent empire' committed to changing the world from within. (In contrast, a small minority of revival-inspired evangelicals withdrew into separatist communities, of which the Shaker colonies and the Oneida community of John Humphrey Noyes are the best remembered.) More problematic for Protestant evangelicals was their proper response to slavery. Finneyite revivalism drove many northern evangelicals to demand an immediate end to slavery, but the majority remained hostile to abolitionism. In the south the Awakening prompted missions to the slaves, and fashioned a Christian defence of slavery. Schisms in the Methodist Episcopal Church (1844) and in the Baptist missionary bodies (1845) over the proper Christian response to slaveholding undoubtedly impeded evangelical advance, as had the division in 1838 of the Presbyterian Church into New and Old Schools, and the disillusionment that followed the failure of the pre-millennialist prophecies of the Baptist William Miller in 1844. None the less, on the eve of the Civil War evangelical Protestantism was clearly the most influential subculture in American society.

At the same time, other forms of Christianity were influential in the United States. Some Protestants resisted new measures revivalism. Liberal, Arminian, rationalist and anti-Trinitarian critics of orthodox New England Calvinism drew towards Unitarianism, centred on a Boston elite, and Universalism, more demotic and rural-based. High-churchmen in the Episcopal Church stressed the importance of liturgy and 'catholic' traditions; a parallel movement in the German Reformed Church benefited from the writings of the Mercersburg theologians, as did conservative Lutherans of the Missouri Synod, whose presence was dramatically increased by mid-nineteenth-century immigration. The greatest beneficiary of this immigration was the Roman Catholic Church, growing from fifty thousand members in 1800 to over four million by 1860; some of this growth, however, which made the Church the largest denomination in the United States, followed the incorporation of an indigenous Catholic population as the United States successively acquired Louisiana territory, Florida, and Mexican lands that included California. The Church was reorganised to meet this challenge but was not wholly successful in dealing with internal conflicts over the power of lay trustees and over the place of poorer Irish and German immigrants in an institution historically dominated by American, English and French. Additionally, it faced a fierce anti-Catholicism, ever present in this culturally Protestant society, but now exacerbated by the Church's moving from the margins to the mainstream of American life. Worried by the poverty and political illiteracy of the immigrants, frightened by the Church's 'superstition' and despotic structure, and dismayed by its challenge to public school education, anti-Catholic nativists responded with threats, violence and attempted political proscription. The American commitment to religious toleration was stretched to its limits.

Similar questions—of the relationship between Protestant and Catholic, and between Church and State in a rapidly growing society—affected the Christian community in British North America in the years before Confederation in 1867. However, Canadian Catholics were able to protect themselves more easily than their co-religionists in the United

States: they were historically and socially entrenched and not even the eighteenth-century defeat of the Catholic French by the Protestant British had left them wholly without some privileges of establishment in Quebec (Lower Canada). In Upper Canada to the west and the Maritime Provinces and Newfoundland to the east the privileged and protected Anglican Church faced the increasing muscle of Methodists, Presbyterians, Baptists and other dissenting groups. One controversial issue was that of state help for denominational education; even more intense and bitter was the conflict over the disposition of the Clergy Reserves, millions of acres of land set aside for the endowment of the Protestant clergy and virtually monopolised by the Church of England. The outcome was the overturning of the establishment and the acceptance of a voluntary system, although the separation of Church and State was never to be as strict as in the United States.

During the later nineteenth and early twentieth centuries Christian churches in both societies had to face a variety of social and intellectual challenges emanating from immigration, urbanisation, industrialisation, war and Darwinian thought. Immigration drew into the United States many non-Christians, particularly Jews, swelled the Lutheran family of churches into the third largest Protestant grouping in the country, established a significant Eastern Orthodox presence and trebled the size of the Catholic Church between 1880 and 1920. The arrival of many southern and eastern Europeans intensified ethnic conflict within Catholicism, polarising around the 'Americanists', who stressed the compatibility of Catholicism and American traditions of democracy and religious pluralism, and the conservatives, opposed to Anglo-Saxon culture and arguing for separate dioceses for each nationality ('Cahenslyism'). Pope Leo XIII's settling of the issues in the 1890s ensured that American Catholics would follow a conservative route until the mid-twentieth century. In Canada, Catholics were likewise divided, between natives and newcomers, and between an 'ultramontane' party and liberals in Quebec.

Evangelical Protestants in the United States sought to preserve their predominance in the face of pluralist, secularising forces by expanding their home missionary work and devising new forms of urban evangelism, most notably through the work of Dwight L. Moody. The clearest symptom of evangelical success was in the extraordinary growth of black churches, particularly Baptist and Methodist. Black religion, so important before emancipation in combating the dehumanising tendencies of slavery, continued to offer blacks a social and spiritual focus in their marginal existence. Revivalistic, emotional and theologically uncomplicated, it suffered few of the crises that attended the Darwinian challenge to biblical literalism within white evangelicalism. Many northern liberals, Congregationalist and Methodist in particular, sought successfully to unite an historical approach to the Bible with a Christ-centred profession of faith. Conservatives, strong in the south but by no means confined there, centred intellectually on Princeton, and reinforced by the millenarian 'dispensationalism' of John N. Darby, fought back strongly in defence of 'the fundamentals' of faith provided by an inerrant Bible. Conservative biblicism and revivalism were the hallmarks of the new, schismatic holiness movements of the late nineteenth century, notably the Nazarenes, and of the Pentecostalist movement, which reached the poor in particular through a blend of glossolalia, faith-healing, physical emotionalism and millennialism. Conflict between conservative and liberal was further aggravated as Washington Gladden and Walter Rauschenbusch, representing Protestants for whom *laissez-faire* individualism was a bankrupt social philosophy, fashioned a new 'Social Gospel' out of socialist and progressive ideas. Conservatives continued to stress the need for individual, not social, regeneration. In Canada, even though many churches employed Moody-style revivalism, Christocentric liberalism and the social gospel made faster headway and was more widely accepted. A smaller number of major Protestant denominations dominated religious life in that country especially after the drawing together of Congregationalists, Methodists and most Presbyterians to become the United Church of Canada in 1925, and their adherence to social Christianity helped preclude the traumatic quarrels between liberals and fundamentalists that marked church life in the United States.

Growing secularisation has marked North American life through the twentieth century, but the weakening of Christianity's hold has not been uninterrupted (nor, in the light of recent developments, would all consider it irreversible). The 1920s and 1930s saw a general loss of Protestant morale: missions and church attendance declined, the social gospel lost its vigour, the anti-evolutionists' hollow victory at the Scopes trial in 1925 and the growth in black, holiness and pentecostal churches could not hide a general spiritual decline. But a clear revival of religion developed after the Second World War, originating in the neo-orthodox theology of the brothers Reinhold and H. Richard Niebuhr. Church membership and attendance figures increased in both newer and older denominations. Conservative evangelical Protestantism in particular enjoyed a resurgence, aided by the efforts of the mass evangelist Billy Graham, whose preaching combined patriotism, anti-Communism and old-fashioned Southern Baptist theology. Roman Catholic status and numbers also grew and some slackening of the historical tension between Catholic and Protestant was evident, symbolised by John F. Kennedy's election to the presidency in 1960 and further encouraged by the pontificate of John XXIII. The period saw a number of ecumenical and co-operative movements both within and between denominational families, including the Canadian Council of Churches (1944), the National Council of the Churches of Christ (1950) and the United Church of Christ (1957–61). The social traumas of the 1960s, generated by racial and ethnic conflict and foreign war, threw up radical new theologies and religious movements but also brought the earlier revival to an end. Yet the return of a more conservative political mood in the 1970s and 1980s was accompanied by a resurgence of the conservative evangelicalism of the 1950s and by a growth in pentecostal and charismatic movements. A majority of North Americans in the 1980s continued to attend a Christian church, many of them as convinced as had been the continent's first white settlers of their unique role in the unfolding of God's plan.

North America's contribution to the history of Christianity has been distinctive and profound. The circumstances of its settlement and its ethnic heterogeneity have generated denominational pluralism, theological diversity and religious freedom. The churches' dependence on voluntary efforts has resulted in much experimentation, particularly in the United States. Revivalism, in conjunction with the democratic, egalitarian emphases in American culture, has encouraged lay power and the emergence of a female ministry. It has also thrown up hundreds of new sects and denominations, some of them theologically orthodox offspring of traditional churches, others (such as the Seventh-day Adventists, Jehovah's Witnesses, Christian Scientists and Mormons) offering variants of conventional Christianity, many of them ephemeral, but all of them adding to a religious life in North America that has been as rich and heterogeneous as the wider culture.

Further Reading

Ahlstrom, Sydney E. *A Religious History of the American People* (Yale University Press, New Haven, 1972)

Gaustad, Edwin S. *Historical Atlas of Religion in America*, rev. edn (Harper & Row, New York, 1976)

Handy, Robert T. *History of the Churches in the United States and Canada* (Oxford University Press, Oxford, 1977)

Herberg, Will *Protestant, Catholic, Jew: An Essay in American Religious Sociology* (Doubleday and Co., Garden City, New York, 1955)

McLoughlin Jr, William G. *Modern Revivalism: Charles Grandison Finney to Billy Graham* (Ronald Press Co., New York, 1959)

Smith, James Ward and Jameson, A. Leland *Religion in American Life*, 4 vols. (Princeton University Press, New Jersey, 1961)

15 *Christianity in Latin America from the Sixteenth Century*

D.A. Brading

I

In 1524 a band of twelve barefooted Franciscan friars walked from Veracruz to Mexico City, there to be welcomed by the Conqueror, Hernán Cortés, kneeling in the dust before the assembled nobility, both Spanish and Indian. The mendicants summoned the children of the native elite to their priories for instruction both in Spanish and in the Christian faith, thereafter employing these boys as their interpreters and chief lieutenants in their campaign to extirpate idolatry and preach the gospel. All pagan images were destroyed, temples razed to the ground, and any obdurate native priest or chief who resisted the imposition of the new religion was whipped, imprisoned or, on occasion, even executed. Within a generation, the Indian population, by then suffering grievously from the onslaught of epidemic diseases introduced from Europe, was resettled in new villages, all laid out on a grid system, invariably dominated by a handsome parish church. Evangelisation was thus accompanied by acculturation, with the native elite serving as both collaborators and intermediaries. If the mendicants acted as the instruments of Spanish dominion, with the conquest justified by its harvest of souls won for the Church, nevertheless they also dedicated their lives to the service of their flock with remarkable austerity and devotion. In particular, Bartolomé de las Casas, a Dominican, denounced the cruelties and oppression of the conquerors and settlers and obtained from the Spanish Crown some measure of redress. The spiritual foundation of the Catholic Church in Spanish America rested on the apostolic zeal of the Franciscans and the prophetic thirst for justice of Las Casas. The Papacy had entrusted the governance of the New World to the Kings of Spain and Portugal on condition that they ensured the conversion of its inhabitants to the Christian faith, a task which they in turn entrusted to the mendicant orders. Throughout the three centuries of colonial rule, the Crown maintained the right to appoint to all ecclesiastical benefices, so that the Church, then supported by its own taxes and courts, constituted a parallel arm of government. Indeed, only the common practice of Catholic liturgy united the diverse races and classes that inhabited Latin America, otherwise separated by language and culture.

By the start of the seventeenth century the leading cities and provincial capitals of the New World were blessed with a plethora of ecclesiastical institutions, all created primarily to serve the needs of the European settler community, with wealthy merchants, landowners and officials vying to endow convents and colleges. The Creole children of the first settlers poured into the ranks of the priesthood or entered nunneries. By 1614 Lima, the capital of the viceroyalty of Peru, housed 1,194 priests, both religious and secular, and 1,245 nuns, which together accounted for nearly a tenth of the city's population of 25,400. The cathedral, the university, the Jesuit colleges, the mendicant priories and the convents all supported veritable battalions of often contentious clerics, their physical fabric and churches dominating entire blocks of the city. Moreover, as architecture entered a cycle that moved swiftly from the classical simplicity of the Renaissance to the extravagant splendours of the Baroque and Churrigueresque, so churches in Mexico, Peru and Brazil became filled with elaborately carved altars that soared to the vaults, their walls covered with paintings and sculpture, and their liturgy celebrated with the maximum of pomp.

From the outset, therefore, the Catholic Church in America was both a European transplant and a missionary enterprise, catering for the needs of Spanish and Portuguese settlers, and seeking to convert Indian peasants and African slaves. At both levels, in the cities and in the countryside, among the elite and the masses, the clergy taught much the same kind of religion, introducing the cult and ethos of late medieval Catholicism as practised in the Iberian Peninsula. Moreover, as the process of miscegenation between Europeans, Africans and Indians gathered momentum, yielding a numerous population of mestizos and mulattos, the simple antithesis of Hispanic elite and native masses made way for a variegated society characterised by regional diversity and ethnic complexity. At all levels, however, religious devotion and its public practice occupied a central place in men's lives. African slaves and free blacks in Brazil organised brotherhoods in direct imitation of their Portuguese masters, building chapels, parading through the streets, each inspired by devotion to their particular image or patron saint. So too, Indian religion came to centre on the veneration of images and the celebration of the liturgy, with feast days distinguished by processions and banquets. In both cases, social identity and local hierarchy within each community found expression in institutions such as confraternities and *mayordomias*, whose principal purpose was the celebration of religious cult. What requires emphasis here, against the views of sceptical anthropologists, is that the Christian faith sank deep roots within the fertile ground of popular religion in Latin America. The appearance of millennial movements both in Mexico and Brazil attests to the strength of that influence. At the same time, the failure of the mendicants to educate or ordain a native priesthood provoked enduring resentment. In southern Mexico both in 1712 and in 1846 Indian rebellions were led by native prophets who assumed the rank and office of the Catholic priesthood. Nevertheless, the Creole clergy sought to advance local saints and devotions. In Lima, the black Dominican lay brother, Martín de Porras, became the object of popular veneration and was later canonised. In Mexico, the devotion of Our Lady of Guadalupe became the vehicle of sentiment that was as much patriotic as religious, in which both Creoles and Indians joined to venerate an image where the Virgin Mary was depicted as an Indian or mestiza, miraculously imprinted, so it was affirmed, on the cape of a poor Indian, Juan Diego, to whom the Mother of God had appeared, promising protection for the people of Mexico. The popularity of this cult at all levels of society illustrates the degree to which Tridentine Catholicism succeeded in uniting elite and masses, clergy and people in common devotion.

By the middle years of the eighteenth century the chief ministers of Portugal and Spain had become disenchanted with the preponderant weight of clerical institutions in the sphere of education and culture. In particular, the Jesuit order attracted their hostility. For since their arrival in 1570 the Jesuits had grown steadily in numbers, wealth and influence, opening colleges for the education of the Creole elite in all leading cities, ministering to the urban poor, especially to black slaves and free men, and maintaining an extensive circuit of mission-stations on the frontiers of empire, their multiple operations supported by an evermore prosperous chain of great estates. In both Amazonia and in Paraguay the Jesuits effectively governed thousands of Indian neophytes, with settlers excluded from their domains. Whereas the mendicant orders had fallen into disorder and decay, the Jesuits had preserved their discipline, rigorously expelling all backsliders from their society. Although many cultivated the Creole elite, others still followed the apostolate of St Peter Claver, who had devoted his life to serving slaves at Cartagena brought in from Africa. But Jesuit achievements bred pride, yielded great wealth and influence, and in turn provoked the inordinate jealousy of religious, bishops, royal governors and colonial landlords. At the same time, there occurred within the Catholic world a shift in sentiment, in part attributable to Jansenism, in which the Tridentine emphasis on liturgy and religious life was replaced by a preference for education, good works and simple piety. So too, baroque extravagance was condemned and a frigid neo-classicism introduced by royal fiat. Portugal, under the influence of the Marquis of Pombal, took the lead in expelling the Jesuits, an example followed in 1767 by Charles III of Spain. Enlightened despotism would brook no rivals to its power. At the same time, the parishes still administered by the mendicants were handed over to the secular clergy. There followed an entire campaign directed against the Church, inspired by an attempt to nullify ecclesiastical jurisdiction, expropriate, where possible, church wealth and curtail the public manifestation of popular religion. By the close of the eighteenth century, as the Enlightenment entered the Hispanic world, anti-clericalism offered a cloak for outright religious scepticism among the educated classes. The very clergy were affected, with hundreds of religious seeking release from their vows. This crisis of belief and devotion obviously centred among the elite: the masses remained loyal to traditional faith, more offended than attracted by the Crown offensive against often cherished practices and cults. Moreover, a gulf had opened between the outlook of the clerical elite and popular religion.

The achievement of independence for the countries of the region in the early nineteenth century plunged the Church in Latin America still further into crisis, since in most countries it suffered a profound loss in authority, wealth and numbers of clergy. In Brazil Emperor Pedro II, a typical liberal of that epoch, continued to assert state control over all clerical appointments, leaving the Church to wither through shortage of funds and curtailment of activity. By 1860 a population of fourteen million people was served by little more than 700 priests. With the advent of the Old Republic in 1889 Church and State were separated and the religious orders temporarily expelled. So too, in Mexico the clergy who had led out the masses in insurgency against the Crown in 1810, their followers marching under the banner of Our Lady of Guadalupe, were subsequently the object of Liberal attack, a campaign which culminated in the 1850s with the separation of Church and State, the expropriation of all Church property and the expulsion of the religious orders. Elsewhere, the religious orders were affected by the loss of their Spanish members and the continuing decline in vocations. In the Andean countries, particularly in Peru and Bolivia, the absence of a numerous middle class led to a severe decline in the number of clergy, both secular and religious, so that the Church retained but a shadow of its past predominance. By the middle years of the nineteenth century the educated elite who directed public affairs in Latin America viewed Catholicism as a remnant of the past, still dangerous, however, by reason of its influence among the masses. Education was secularised and was soon dominated by the doctrines of Positivism, with science accepted as the gospel of progress. The State thus became actively hostile to the pretensions of the Church to act or to pronounce on matters of public or social concern; its only tolerable sphere of action was private devotion and corporate worship.

Despite, or possibly because of, this Liberal assault, the Church in Latin America experienced a marked revival in the late nineteenth and early twentieth centuries. By this period, however, national characteristics had become pronounced, so that the process of revival exhibited a different momentum and scope from country to country. Throughout the New World, however, the Papacy now intervened to secure control over all clerical appointments, thus acquiring a power it had never exercised during the colonial period. An epoch of Romanisation now ensued. The Holy See established a college in Rome for the education of the clerical elite of Latin America, thereafter frequently promoting these favoured priests to dominant positions in the national hierarchies. The Papacy also acted to create new dioceses, urging bishops to open seminaries and to divide existing parishes into smaller units. In Brazil the number of dioceses thus increased from a mere twelve in 1889 to no less than fifty-eight in 1920. At the same time, the Papacy mobilised the religious orders, so that over the years several thousand missionaries arrived in Latin America, training the local clergy in seminaries, opening colleges and schools, and entering the parochial ministry. This reliance on European clergy, when combined with the new-found authority of Rome, aroused Liberal charges that the Church in Latin America was no longer a national body, but rather an instrument of papal intervention. However, it must be remembered that in the same period Latin America received millions of immigrants from Europe, so that much of the efforts of the imported clergy went to serve the needs of this new population. This was especially the case in Argentina, Uruguay and southern Brazil. Moreover, in countries such as Peru and Mexico, which did not receive a mass immigration, the urban middle class was reinforced by European merchants and artisans, who often strengthened the constituency of the Church. Romanisation thus should be viewed within the context of the reincorporation of Latin America in the North Atlantic economy, a process characterised by massive transference of population, capital and trade goods.

Emphasis on external influences should not lead us to neglect the internal forces which also assisted in the revival of the Church. In several countries, notably in Mexico, Columbia and north-eastern Brazil, the Liberal assault and erosion of elite adherence drove the Church back into the countryside and into provincial towns where the priesthood, now often recruited from the sons of prosperous farmers and shopkeepers, still wielded influence as leaders of their communities. At times, new bishoprics were established in such towns and their seminaries became the centre of local cultural life. In Brazil a series of messianic movements erupted, culminating in the 1890s in the rebellion at Canudos led by Antonio the Counsellor, a wandering mystagogue, who defied the might of the new republic in the name of traditional beliefs. In Mexico during the 1920s the western peasantry rose in rebellion against the anti-clerical measures of the revolutionary regime of President Calles, assuming the name of Cristeros. In both countries the enduring influence of popular Catholicism drove the rural masses to challenge the Liberal ideology of the urban political elite.

By the 1930s the intellectual climate of Latin America had changed sufficiently to prompt a revival in the cultural appeal of Catholicism, a shift in part attributable to the influence of German idealism on the modernist movement at the turn of the century. In Brazil Jackson de Figueiredo and in Mexico José Vasconcelos exemplified the new-found attraction of the Church for intellectuals. Moreover, the colleges and universities established by the Jesuits and other orders now began to bear fruit in the emergence of a class of educated laity and clergy anxious to controvert the dominance of Liberalism. It has to be confessed that many Catholics of this period flirted with Fascism, participating in the Integralist movement in Brazil and in the movement of the Sinarquistas in Mexico. With the defeat of the Axis, however, political action entered a democratic phase, and the 1940s witnessed the emergence of Christian Democratic parties in Chile and Venezuela, both of which succeeded in winning elections and forming governments. But the mounting problems caused by economic modernisation in Latin America, a process of rapid growth accompanied by mass migration to the cities and by rapid population increase, ushered in a phase of revolutionary idealism and savage military reprisals that offered a stark challenge to the Christian conscience of all socially concerned Catholics. The seizure of power by Fidel Castro in Cuba strengthened yet further the attraction of Marxism as the one ideology that united a critical analysis of capitalism to an advocacy of revolutionary action. If young militants from the universities were prepared to lay down their lives in this cause, what role did the Catholic clergy and committed laymen have to play in such an agitated continent? In Nicaragua priests joined the Sandinista rebellion against the Somoza dictatorship and thereafter participated in the revolutionary government, defining the achievement of social justice as an essentially Christian goal. By contrast, the growing number of evangelical Protestant communities, essentially the creation of fundamentalist missionaries sent in from the United States, tended to embrace right-wing doctrines of a free enterprise variety. Their appeal derived from their emphasis on lay action and self-help as against the clerical dominance of the traditional Church.

The Church in contemporary Latin America offers a bewilderingly complex picture to any observer, with different strata of its history still present in many countries. The folk Catholicism of Indian communities still survives in the Andean highlands or in Mesoamerica virtually untouched since the colonial period, with veneration of images still generating customary consolation. At the same time, the reliance on foreign missionaries, now as much North American as European, continues, with no less than 60 per cent of priests in Peru recruited from overseas. Throughout Latin America, however, the Church is confronted with the challenge of rapid, mass urbanisation, a process which threatens to bring to a summary end its influence among the masses. In reaction the clergy have organised the laity into 'base communities', groups of devout Catholics engaged in mutual help and social welfare, recruited from the poorer strata of the urban populace. Whether these groups will become a permanent vehicle of social organisation only time will tell. Whatever the result, the Church, both at the level of its national hierarchies and on the part of individual priests, has increasingly expressed a public voice and concern on matters of social justice. The theology of liberation has adopted a prophetic voice, placing the issue of social justice at the very centre of the Christian message. The poor are defined as Christ's own flock, blessed in their deprivation. Proponents of these doctrines differ as to the morality of armed insurrection against tyranny, with most theologians advocates of peaceful solutions. At the same time, the hierarchy in countries such as Brazil and Chile, subject to military rule, have emerged as spokesmen of human rights and political liberty. Once more, it is the pressure of circumstances that has driven the Church into intervention in political affairs. By contrast, in Mexico the hierarchy preserves a discreet silence, seeking to maintain its institutional life without challenge to the authority of the State. In sum, with Latin America caught in the maelstrom of massive, all-pervasive economic and social change, the Catholic Church seeks desperately to preserve its hard-won position, adapting the message of the gospel to modern conditions. As it began, so it now continues, characterised (at its best) by a Franciscan zeal for the popular apostolate and a prophetic plea for social justice reminiscent of Las Casas.

Further Reading

Bruneau, Thomas C. *The Church in Brazil* (Texas University Press, Austin, 1982)
Cara, Ralph de la *Miracle at Joaseiro* (Columbia University Press, New York, 1970)
Dussel, Enrique D. *A History of the Church in Latin America* (Eerdmans, Grand Rapids, Michigan, 1981)
Fawiss, N.M. *Crown and Clergy in Colonial Mexico* (Athlone Press, London, 1968)
Levine, Daniel H. *Religion and Politics in Latin America* (Princeton University Press, New Jersey, 1981)
Meyer, Jean *The Cristero Rebellion* (Cambridge University Press, Cambridge, 1976)
Ricard, Robert *The Spiritual Conquest of Mexico* (University of California Press, Berkeley, 1966)

16 Christianity in India from the Sixteenth Century

Ian Clark

When the Portuguese explorer Vasco da Gama reached the Indian coast in 1498 he came as the representative of a European Latin Catholicism which was soon to face the challenge of the Protestant Reformation and the rise of non-Catholic nations which would compete with Portugal for commercial control of Asia. The Indian sub-continent, too, was about to undergo major upheaval. In the ensuing five hundred years Christianity took root in India in a variety of forms and underwent a process of transformation as Christians sought to express their faith within patterns of Indian thought, symbol and rite. At the same time, the presence of Christianity as a small but not negligible minority has itself contributed to the changes which have revolutionised at least some aspects of Indian life since the sixteenth century.

By 1500 the great formative period of Hindu religious development was over and other faiths were already established. A divergent group, the Jains, had long been accepted as having a separate identity, and now Guru Nanak (d. 1539) was laying the foundations of the 'reformed' version of Hinduism which was to coalesce as the Sikh community. Buddhism had been rejected by the northern areas in which it originated; but Islam, an 'alien' religion, had struck deep roots since the eighth century. Kabir (d. 1518) sought to combine elements of Hinduism and Islam, and this openness was encouraged by the Muslim dynasty, the Moguls, who were to rule much of India for three hundred years. Christianity, which had allegedly been introduced by the apostle Thomas in the first century, was flourishing in the south-west where there is clear evidence of a Christian presence from at least the sixth century. This community was in touch with churches in the Middle East, and had been strengthened by the arrival (between 1490 and 1503) of five bishops sent by the Nestorian Patriarch of Babylon. The 'St

Thomas Christians' were proud of their ancient customs and liturgy, stemming from Syrian rather than Greek or Latin origins, and had become a respected community under their Hindu rulers.

The Portuguese base at Goa, with its baroque churches and monasteries, embodied a more aggressive 'Western' Christianity which appeared strange to Indians. Goa was, nevertheless, a centre for vigorous missionary activity led by Franciscan and Dominican friars and, from 1542 onwards, the new Jesuit Order. It was one of the latter, Francis Xavier, who reaped the first 'mass movement' in India among the despised and illiterate Parava fishermen on the Coromandel coast. His methods were rough and ready, including much learning by rote; but the area has remained staunchly Catholic to this day. Very different was the approach of another Jesuit, Robert Nobili (d. 1656) who spent fifty years at Madurai, a centre of Hindu Tamil culture dominated by its enormous temple. Nobili set himself to win the upper castes, living as a Brahmin himself and adopting their customs in dress, diet and even worship. Despite opposition from fellow Christians and trepidation in Rome, where Counter-Reformation piety boggled at his experiments with indigenisation, Nobili poured out a stream of writings in Tamil and raised questions about dialogue and cultural penetration which are still being worked out today. Meanwhile, with a sure instinct for the seat of political power, other Jesuits from Goa responded eagerly to an invitation from the Mogul Emperor Akbar to send a mission to his court in the north. He was gratifyingly pleased to see them, and much inconclusive discussion took place. A precedent was set for a Christian presence near to government. In post-Independence India, Christians have been found in the corridors of power out of all proportion to their actual numbers, and have often held politically sensitive posts.

In theory the Archbishop of Goa had jurisdiction over all Christians within the Portuguese possessions in India and was answerable through the King of Portugal to the Pope. For the ancient St Thomas community this had serious implications. Their historical connection had always been with the various patriarchs of western Asia, some of whom were on at least nodding terms with Rome, but suspicious of interference. At first a certain amount of timely reform was accepted by the Christians of Malabar from the Portuguese, though not always with a good grace. They resented being referred to as 'pestilential Nestorian heretics', and Portuguese clerics could be tactless. In 1599 the autocratic young Archbishop Menezes began a Visitation of Malabar, ordaining new *cattanars* (priests) to replace the old, and extracting from them an oath of obedience to the Pope and repudiation of the Patriarch of Babylon. At the Synod of Diamper that year the St Thomas Christians were placed under the jurisdiction of Menezes, and relations went from bad to worse as Roman customs were imposed on the unwilling community. In 1653 resistance came to a head with the dramatic episode of the Koonen Cross Oath by which they re-established their old independence. This in fact reflected the decline of Portuguese power in India. A decade later Protestant sailors from Holland appeared on the Malabar coast and a new era of encounter began.

The subsequent history of the Orthodox communities in India is tangled but colourful. In 1665 a bishop was sent to India by the Patriarch of Diabekir. He belonged to a line which had never recognised the Council of Chalcedon (451) and was technically at the opposite end of the ecclesiastical spectrum to the Nestorian Church which had supplied bishops to India in the past. The Nestorian Catholicos today presides over a community of several thousand at Trichur. The Syrian Christians number millions, and are divided between those who look to the Patriarch of Antioch, and those who acknowledge a Catholicos in Kerala as their leader. In the nineteenth century, under the influence of Protestant missionaries, a portion of the Syrian community broke away to form the Mar Thoma Church which is Reformed in doctrine but uses a modified version of the old Orthodox liturgy. Others in Kerala today adhere to the Roman Catholic Church but use Orthodox forms of worship. All are conscious of representing an age-old Christian presence in India, and can be understandably resentful of condescension from 'younger' Christians in the West.

When we turn to the impact of Protestantism the picture becomes very confusing. While it is not entirely true to say that the missionaries followed the merchants and the merchants followed the flag, it is certainly the case that patterns of Christian distribution in India today were to some extent determined by the accidents of military, commercial and colonial activity by European nations in the past. A short voyage up the River Hooghly, for example, will take the traveller from the neo-Gothic spires of eighteenth- and nineteenth-century Calcutta (which also contains an ancient Armenian, and later Greek Orthodox church, and a Scots kirk, amongst many other sacred edifices) to Serampore, a former Danish possession which sports a Lutheran church dedicated to St Olaf and the great college founded in 1818 by the English Baptist shoemaker, William Carey, outside the East India Company's territory, where for some thirty years he and his companions translated the Bible into twenty-four Indian languages. Further upstream the former French settlement at Chandernagore is dominated by its Roman Catholic church and *hôtel de ville*. Further still lies the old Portuguese enclave of Bandel with a small whitewashed pilgrimage church and devout population. On his way the traveller might have speculated about the enormous cathedral-like structure at Belur, which is in fact the temple of the Ramakrishna community whose founder was not uninfluenced by Christianity in the nineteenth century.

The two and a half centuries which separate the arrival of the first Protestant missionaries, the Germans Ziegenbalg and Plütschau in Tranquebar in 1706, from Independence and the beginnings of restriction on missionary activity from outside India in 1947, are best seen as a period of encounter between the very diverse peoples of India and the equally variegated forms in which Christianity was presented, usually by 'professional' missionaries seeking 'conversion'. Alongside this primary goal most missionary activity acknowledged a need to break down social attitudes (such as caste) which oppressed individuals and communities, to stimulate education, to introduce higher standards of health-care and to foster new agricultural and industrial methods. It was not always easy to distinguish between the aspirations of the missionaries and the aims of the British rulers who increasingly controlled the sub-continent. Originally it had been the policy of the East India Company to exclude missionary enterprise among Indians, but successive revisions of the Charter between 1793 and 1833 coincided with the Evangelical Awakening in Europe, and by the middle of the century there were Anglican diocesan bishops, a network of chaplains and mission-stations, and a field wide open to missionaries from all churches and many lands (including, increasingly, North America).

Priorities and emphases varied, and many mistakes were no doubt made. Educated urban Indians looked out upon a sort of vast ecclesiastical cafeteria in which everything was on offer. The millions in the rural areas and tribal regions were usually only aware of the brand available locally, be it American Methodist, Welsh Baptist or Tractarian Anglican, to name but a few. The nature of the response varied enormously, from enquiring Brahmin (Nehemiah Goreh, d. 1895) or Muslim (Imad-ud-din, d. 1900), nationalist and poet (Narayan Vaman Tilak, d. 1919), evangelist (Solomon, d. 1909, apostle of the Nicobar Islands), Bengali intellectual (K.C. Banerji, who called himself a Hindu Christian) or wandering sadhu (Sundar Singh, who vanished into the Himalayan snows in 1929). For many millions the way into the Christian community lay through one of the rural mass movements whose precise mechanisms are still obscure. In other areas it was tribal peoples who opted for a Christianity which replaced their animism but bypassed the Hinduism which they associated with their overlords.

The missionary era, with its hospitals, schools and colleges and the variety of Christian communities which it evoked, and the permeation of social and political attitudes which it sometimes achieved, cannot be assessed in merely numerical terms. Historians calculate that in the nineteenth century Protestants made the greatest percentage advance, but in 1914 Roman Catholics still outnumbered them. In some tribal areas today Christians form a majority of the population and have long since replaced foreigners as agents of evangelism. The figure of 2.6 per cent which is usually given for the whole Christian community represents an actual Christian presence of some sixteen million. Much less quantifiable are such factors as the influence of Christian ideas on Gandhi, architect of Independence, through his English friend C.F. Andrews; or the changed perceptions of social justice through the writings of the Mar Thoma theologian M.M. Thomas; or the activity of an Anglican priest, the late Subir Biswas, in the *bustees* of Calcutta—less well known but no less charismatic than the Albanian-born Mother Teresa.

Long before the end of the missionary era it was apparent that out of the variety of responses to Christianity, the lineaments of an authentically Indian Church were beginning to emerge. At times it has been hindered by insensitive interference by foreign churches and their reluctance to let go. Equally, it has been inhibited by a sense of insecurity as a minority in a surrounding sea of other faiths. Insecurity has sometimes bred extreme conservatism, a litigious preoccupation with property, and a complacent dependence on overseas funding. These factors are outweighed, however, by the gradual articulation of a Christianity which is rooted in the soil of India. Sometimes this has been the conscious programme of a great Christian leader (e.g. Bishop Azariah of Dornakal, first Indian Anglican bishop in 1912). Often it has been a quiet process of spiritual insight at humble village level.

Dialogue with other faiths, pursued in the stillness of 'the cave of the heart' by men such as Swami Abhishiktananda and others in ashrams and pilgrimage centres from Cape Cormorin to the Himalayas, is perhaps a precondition for this rooting process. At a less rarefied level most of the mainstream communities have moved towards an explicit Indianisation not only of the externals of worship, but of the inner structures of theology. Catholics and Protestants alike have increasingly brought traditional symbols into their worship: the oil-lamp and the offering of flowers, the use of *agabatti* (incense-sticks), Christianised forms of ancient invocatory chant, and the gestures, posture and architectural setting which come naturally to Indian worshippers. The rich regional musical tradition has been absorbed into a new Christian *bhakti*, bringing with it deeply rooted Indian thought-patterns which are used both to articulate the gospel and communicate it. Artists have focused the classical tradition of painting on the themes of the Incarnation and transposed symbols which go back deep into the Indian consciousness. The interior of the aggressively 'foreign' St Paul's Cathedral in Calcutta came alive for many in the 1960s during the Bangladesh freedom-struggle and against the sombre background of the ongoing battle for dignity for the poor of the city, as the young Sudhir Bairagi gradually filled it with images of a Bengali Christ in a Calcutta Gethsemane, or standing triumphantly risen beside a fetid slum tank where, surprisingly, lotus and water-hyacinth blossom. Jyoti Sahi's work in the chapel of Vidyajyoti College in Delhi carries the same vision of a Christ who fulfils the integral Indian experience, 'secular' as well as 'religious'.

What some have attempted in music and colour, others have seen as a programme for theology. Brahmabandhab Upadhyay (d. 1907), uneasy Roman Catholic convert, wrestled to formulate the Christian concept of the Trinity within the framework of *advaita* (non-dualist) Vedanta drawn from the philosopher Shankara. In a different tradition which comes from Ramanuja, the Protestant theologians Vengal Chakkarai and A.J. Appasamy explored the Hindu concept of *avatāra* as a vehicle for understanding the Incarnation, fully conscious of the danger of a simplistic search for equivalences. The lay theologian and judge, Pandippedi Chenchiah (d. 1959), called for a rethinking of all inherited Western doctrine, in order that India might achieve *pratyaksa* (direct encounter) with what he called 'the raw fact' of Christ. The paradox with which Indian theologians have had to grapple is perhaps best summed up in the titles of two formative books. In 1964 Raymundo Panikkar wrote in *The Unknown Christ of Hinduism* of the task of unveiling the Christ who has been present all along in the Hindu experience, as he was within the Jewish and Hellenistic context of the Early Church: a truly 'Indian' contribution to the Christ of universal Christian faith. In *The Acknowledged Christ of the Indian Renaissance* (1968) by contrast, M.M. Thomas pointed to the great array of social reformers (such as Rāmmohan Roy, d. 1833) in the nineteenth century who responded eagerly and with devotional reverence to the Christ whom they encountered from the West, but who found the Church singularly unattractive.

The discovery of an Indian identity by Christians is reflected also in the part they played in the nationalist movement which culminated in Independence in 1947. From its foundation in 1885, Christians took a prominent part in the National Congress, as they had done in the intellectual preparation for it earlier in the century. During the first all-India General Elections in 1952 Dr V.E. Devadutt pointed out that the secular democracy to which India had committed herself stood much closer to Christian ideals of human value and social responsibility than did the classical Hindu tradition. Chandran Devanesan, S.K. Chatterji and many others have sought to bring a prophetic critique to bear upon defining goals of social change, freedom for victims of inherited social structures and the building of a more just society. M.M. Thomas, whose *Christian Response to the Asian Revolution* (1966) was itself rather revolutionary, and the publications of the Christian Institute for the Study of Religion and Society, have helped to wean Christians away from unthinking adherence to the Congress Party, and to explore the implications of other cross-currents in the process of nation-building.

Finally, the self-identity which the Indian churches have gained in these various areas has undoubtedly acted as a catalyst in the achievement of ecclesiastical unity. The realisation that Western denominational differences hampered mission and made little sense on Indian soil anyway slowly dawned on Indians and expatriates alike in the nineteenth century. A series of decennial Conferences, with increasing Indian participation, culminated in the Edinburgh World Missionary gathering in 1910 and the establishment of the principle of comity to obviate overlapping of work and local 'poaching'. Joint institutions (e.g. Madras Christian College, and the foundation of a number of united theological colleges) fostered the desire for closer organic unity between churches, and after long negotiation the Church of South India brought together Anglicans, Methodists, Presbyterians and Congregationalists (the two latter already united since 1908) in the first successful union of episcopal and non-episcopal traditions. Although the procedure for union, which involved the mutual recognition of existing ministries, led to thirty years of estrangement from the Anglican Communion, the CSI's ability to grow together, evolve a remarkable consensus of liturgical practice and establish an identity which impressed itself on the government and people of India, spurred Christians in the north to follow suit. The Church of North India, inaugurated in 1970, was formed on a Plan which provided for the sharing of ministries through a mutual laying on of hands which allayed Anglican scruples. A much greater hurdle, the question of infant and adult baptism, was successfully surmounted and it has been possible for many former Baptist congregations to join the CNI. In 1978 the CSI, CNI and Mar Thoma Church formed a Joint Council and are pledged to seek deeper federal union.

As long ago as 1923 the newly-formed National Christian Council looked forward to the day when the Indian Church would be united, self-sufficient in resources and personnel, truly national in ethos and theology, and self-propagating. There is nothing in the record of Indian Christianity to suggest that, despite set-backs, that goal will not eventually be attained.

Further Reading

Boyd, R.H.S. *An Introduction to Indian Christian Theology* (Christian Literature Society, Madras, 1969)

Brown, L. *The Indian Christians of St Thomas*, rev. edn (Cambridge University Press, Cambridge, 1982)

Matthew, C.P. and Thomas, M.M. *The Indian Christians of St Thomas* (ISPCK, Delhi, 1967)

Neill, S.C. *The Story of the Christian Church in India and Pakistan* (Eerdmans, Grand Rapids, Michigan, 1970)

—— *A History of Christianity in India: The Beginnings to AD 1707* (Cambridge University Press, Cambridge, 1984)

Pickett, J.W. *Christian Mass Movements in India* (Abingdon Press, New York, 1933)

Sundkler, B.G.M. *The Church of South India: the Movement Towards Union, 1900–1947* (Lutterworth Press, London, 1954)

17 Christianity in China from the Sixteenth Century

Robert Whyte

The Secular Context

The establishment of the People's Republic of China in 1949 marked the end of an era that began with the first Opium War in 1840 when China was compelled to open her doors to the outside world. The weak and hidebound Qing dynasty gave way in 1911 in face of a revolution inspired by a social-democratic nationalism borrowed from Europe and led by Dr Sun Yat-sen, a Christian overseas Chinese. 1911–49 was a period of intellectual and political ferment. The May 4th Movement in 1919 represented the first modern opposition to the West in reaction to the First World War and China's intellectuals became increasingly committed to the pursuit of 'modernisation' through revolution. The Kuomintang (Nationalist) Party now led by Chiang Kai-shek, through its corruption and failure to resist the Japanese invaders, lost support as people turned to the Communist Party. The Communist revolution was also a nationalist revolution and when in 1949 Mao Zedong declared, 'The Chinese people have stood up', he voiced the feelings of a nation.

The Place of Christianity

The association of the churches from 1840 with foreign imperialism helped to ensure that Chinese nationalism would take a secular form and that the Church would sooner or later be confronted with this negative aspect of its history. Modern Chinese history is often interpreted according to a 'revolutionary' paradigm and the history of Christianity in the years immediately after the revolution is best understood from this point of view. However, an exclusive reliance on this model distorts our understanding of the overall process. An alternative, or rather complementary, model concentrates on China's search for modernisation. The former approach serves to highlight the link between Christianity and imperialism but the latter is able to present a more subtle account of the place of Christianity in China's modern history.

The Churches Face the Revolution: 1949–66

The nationalist critique of Christianity was, after 1949, inevitably joined to a Marxist–Leninist critique of religion in general. Chinese Christians were thrown on the defensive and most were ill-prepared to deal with the crisis. Few understood the process of the Chinese revolution and in past years had remained either politically uncommitted or had supported Chiang Kai-shek. Nevertheless, many were patriotic and some had become convinced of the need for radical social change—notably those involved in the YMCA and YWCA. Since the 1920s there had been attempts to break free of foreign controls expressed in the goals of self-support, self-administration and self-propagation (the 'Three Selfs'). After 1949, the state asked for Christians to demonstrate their loyalty to the new system by breaking overseas connections and, while Christians may have disliked the political pressure, many welcomed the chance to implement the 'Three Selfs'. In 1951 the Three Self Patriotic Movement was launched amongst non-Catholics, to be followed after a long gap by the establishment, in 1957, of the Catholic Patriotic Association.

The religious policy of the Communist Party in the early part of this period seems to have aimed at limited toleration but with political control by the state. Like all previous Chinese governments it did not like religion to interfere in public life. Christians could only choose between acceptance or resistance. The majority chose to co-operate but there was fierce opposition in certain areas from Catholics, notably in Shanghai led by Bishop Gong Pinmei, and from some Protestants such as the independent evangelist Wang Mingdao and the leader of the Little Flock, Watchman Nee. Chinese political life swung to the left in 1957 and these three men were sentenced to long prison terms.

There was also a decline in the morale of the Church, which can only in part be accounted for by political pressure. Professor Zhao Fusan, a well-known Christian scholar, articulated this in an essay published in 1958 in *Essays in Anglican Self-Criticism*:[1]

> We did not weep with them that wept in old China, neither do we rejoice with them that rejoice in the new. We seem to have become pitiful strangers in our own country and among our own people.

The leftist policies after 1957 led finally into the Cultural Revolution of 1966 when all public religious activity was stopped. By the early 1970s most observers were inclined to accept the official Chinese view that Christianity was a spent force.

Christianity and Chinese Culture

The Limits of the Revolutionary Model. The crisis of the post-revolution Church in China can thus be understood as in part the result of the 'foreign' associations of Christianity. However, the overall question of Christianity's relationship to China is best approached from a wider framework which looks at the impact of Christianity on Chinese culture and values. There are deep continuities between Chinese tradition and official and unofficial attitudes today. While cultural values undergo constant modification this is a slow and complex process in which alien value systems such as Marxism and Christianity are themselves modified. What impact then did Christianity have on Chinese culture and its values? The revolutionary model is of little help here—a fact that is now coming to be recognised even in China.

The Jesuit Mission. Chinese culture, of all the major cultural traditions, has been the most confined to one region of the world. Before the sixteenth century Christian culture had barely touched East Asia. The brief Persian 'Nestorian' mission of the seventh century made no long-term impact on things Chinese, even if its use of Chinese Buddhist and Taoist categories is of some interest. The Franciscan mission to the Mongol court in the twelfth century was even more peripheral. It is the Jesuit mission begun by Fr Matteo Ricci in 1582 that represents the first major encounter between the two cultural traditions—perhaps the only serious Christian approach to Chinese culture. Ricci and his distinguished successors were theologically conservative but they were also open to Chinese culture and tradition—unlike their Catholic and Protestant counterparts in the nineteenth century. Although the mission was part of the Age of Expansion, 'imperial' attitudes towards other cultures had not really developed. Nor did the Jesuits go to China under the protection of their governments. The relationship of equality finds expression in the words of Valignano, Visitor to the Far Eastern Jesuit missions: 'A confrontation with the intellectual aristocracy on its own level of language, social customs and superior talent.' Their learning, adoption of the dress of the scholar-officials and their willingness to conform to Chinese customs earned them the (sometimes grudging) respect of the official class. The Jesuits acknowledged a degree of truth in Confucian doctrine and accorded respect to Chinese tradition so that 'conversion' did not imply alienation from Chinese culture. They were prepared to accept ancestor rites within the Church, an attitude inexplicable to Rome, whose rejection of the Jesuit position led to the 1724 ban on Christianity by the Yongzheng Emperor.

The Missionaries Return. Robert Morrison was the first Protestant to establish a foothold on the Chinese mainland, in 1807.

There were few results until, to the consternation of the missionaries, their preaching inspired Hong Xiuquan, the leader of the Taiping uprising which devastated central China between 1850 and 1864. After the Opium Wars both Catholic and Protestant missionaries were able gradually to extend their work throughout China. But by 1900 Protestants, small in numbers, had had little success in recommending their faith to the Chinese, although this failure was masked by the extent of their medical and educational work. Catholics, building on the foundation that had survived from the eighteenth century and working amongst the poor, could at least boast ten to twenty times the number of Protestant converts.

Cultural Confrontation. A pietistic theology, that in its preoccupation with the need for individual conversion never questioned the cultural values of its own society, informed both Catholic and Protestant missions in the nineteenth century. Religious fervour went alongside cultural narrowness. To Dr William Milne, a colleague of Morrison, China was 'a land full of idols; a land of darkness and spiritual death'. Hudson Taylor, founder of the China Inland Mission, although advocating the adoption of Chinese dress and lifestyle, based his appeal for support on the assertion of 'four hundred millions of souls, having no hope and without God in the world'. The Jesuit acceptance of the partial validity of Chinese tradition had been replaced by a theological dichotomy between revelation and culture of doubtful orthodoxy. As time went on some missionaries became convinced of the need for social reform in China and, while retaining a pietist theology, they sought to introduce Western notions of education and economic improvement. Foremost amongst such people was the British Baptist, Timothy Richard. In the twentieth century the Protestant Church in China of new 'returned renouncer' movements, from that of Rāmmohan Roy (founder of the early nineteenth-century *Brāhmo Samāj*) to Swami Vivekānanda, with his Ramakrishna Mission, and other founders of religious Movement.

The return of the missionaries coincided with the decline of the Qing dynasty and the decadence of official culture. It hardly seemed worth taking seriously and the 'modernising' values taught by the missionaries speeded the dissolution of the bonds that held the imperial system together. Chinese intellectuals began to adopt the modernising ideas but showed scant regard for the faith of the teachers. They became aware of the 'scientific' attack on religion in Europe and saw the First World War as demonstrating the bankruptcy of Christian culture. So they turned to Marxism and found an alternative faith that in the Red Bases after 1927 also offered a new form of society that appeared to work. The churches' attempts at social reform seemed irrelevant.

The 'revolutionary' model points to Christianity's links with imperialism. Looking from the alternative perspective of 'modernisation' it appears to have performed the role of a midwife, assisting at the birth of Chinese Communism. Both nineteenth-century pietism and twentieth-century liberalism appear to have failed to establish the Christian faith as a living reality within the Chinese world. In 1949 it remained an alien presence. It was the trauma of the subsequent years that was to lead to a new dawn for the Church.

The Growth of the Church

The Spiritual Dynamic. Our account so far has largely ignored the internal dynamic of the Church itself. Missionary attitudes towards Chinese culture could never be fully shared even by the most Westernised Chinese. Thus unselfconsciously in the lives of individual Christians faith was in encounter with Chinese tradition. To date there have been few attempts to elaborate a Chinese theology out of the Chinese experience but the profound spiritual experience is not to be denied and will one day bear theological fruit. Bishop K.H. Ting, President of the China Christian Council, speaks of the 'thing that has become the most real and most precious to us . . . after these last thirty years. It is the faith in the Risen Christ.' He continues:

> How strongly many Chinese Christians feared at the time of the liberation in 1949 that we were losing so many things dear to us, only to find later they were mostly just excess baggage. But it was during the Cultural Revolution . . . that the Chinese people suffered so much and we Christians suffered so much with them. We felt the gospel to be something precious, but the Red Guards and the so-called rebels thought of it as nothing but poisonous weed. We had no means of communicating it or of answering the attacks in the big-character posters. Not a single church remained open. There was no government organ to protect us from lawlessness. We had no rebel group of our own to support us, nor any bandwagon to ride on. It would be fortunate if we could just worship in a small group in a home. We were very weak indeed, a little flock. By all human reckoning Christianity, perhaps for the fourth time in Chinese history, was again breathing its last breath.[2]

The Rebirth of the Church. Three years after the formal end of the Cultural Revolution in 1976, a public meeting in Shanghai announced the restoration of 'normal' religious activities and the rehabilitation of religious leaders. Revolutionary values took second place to the needs of 'modernisation' and there was a re-emphasis on the 'united front' policies of the early 1950s, but this time in a very different international climate. Christianity seemed no longer to be regarded as a foreign religion. The state remained concerned to limit the social impact of religion but appeared willing to allow a much greater degree of freedom than before.

It was in this context that the two patriotic Christian organisations were restored at the respective national conferences in 1980. At the same time new organs were established to deal with internal church affairs—an interesting and significant indication of more freedom. Catholics established a Bishops' College and National Administrative Commission and Protestants set up the China Christian Council. The state oversees the general religious situation through its national and local Religious Affairs Bureaux. Christian leaders have to operate within a complex and shifting political reality. On the one hand they are expected to inculcate values acceptable to the State and on the other hand their Christian constituency relies on them for defending the position of the Church in society. The Religious policy of the State retains certain ambiguities and many local officials are still influenced by the 'leftist' values of the past, as indeed are some church officials.

The development of church life between 1979 and 1987 has been quite remarkable. Almost 4,000 Protestant churches have been reopened and around 1,000 Catholic. Both groups have a national seminary and six or more regional colleges. The China Christian Council organises lay training in many localities and a monthly syllabus is sent out to about 40,000 lay leaders in rural churches. The Council claims that ten thousand home meeting-points are in touch with them and estimates the number of Protestants as around three to four million, a fourfold increase over 1949. This is generally considered to be a conservative estimate but it is likely to be closer to the actual number than the figure of twenty-five or even fifty million sometimes quoted in non-Chinese Christian publications. The number of Catholics is officially stated as three million, the same as in 1949—again probably a cautious estimate.

The China Christian Council has published the Bible in Chinese, Korean, Miao and Lisu. A Catechism produced in 1983 forms some sort of common theological basis for the diversity of traditions that coexist under the Council's auspices.

Ecumenical Contacts. The China Christian Council is considered to represent an intermediate stage on the road to a united non-Catholic Church. In the meantime Christians from different backgrounds are learning to co-operate together in local churches. However, while a variety of liturgical and other practices can be accommodated and even a considerable agreement over doctrine discovered it has not so far proved possible to reach consensus over the most appropriate form of church government. It is hoped that the unity being developed locally will lead in the end to a solution of the national problem.

Ecumenism in China does not extend to seeking closer links between Catholics and Protestants. In the nineteenth century there was overt hostility, and Protestants developed their own Chinese theological vocabulary even to the extent of rejecting the Catholic term for 'God'. To this day most Chinese regard the two branches of Christianity as different religions—not surprisingly in view of the fact that the Chinese for

'Protestant' means 'Christian' (*Jidujiao*), while Catholics are termed followers of the 'religion of the Lord of Heaven' (*Tianzhujiao*). Today the hostility has gone but the differences remain profound.

Chinese Catholics and Rome. The political atmosphere in the 1950s made continued links with the Vatican problematical—yet for Catholics the Pope is the living visible expression of the catholicity of the Church. Events in this period were therefore particularly traumatic for Catholics torn between two loyalties. The first national Catholic conference in 1957 declared its loyalty to the Pope in spiritual matters but asserted its right to deal with matters relating to Chinese church affairs. Crisis came over the nomination of new bishops, and when no agreement with Rome was forthcoming the consecrations went ahead, leading before long to a break with Rome. The problem remains unresolved and has deeply wounded the Church. Yet it appears unlikely that this issue is in the forefront of the minds of the laity who seem willing to accept the services of priests working under the autonomous structures. The future is uncertain: a reconciliation is probably desired by all but a small minority of Catholic leaders, but on terms acceptable to China. A long-term failure to resolve the problem could lead to an irrevocable break, and reference is made to the precedent of the English Reformation.

Some Protestant Issues. Protestant problems stem from isolation. At its simplest this means nothing more than geographical isolation, a problem shared with the Catholics. But there is also the isolation stemming from sectarian origins or in some cases resulting from the influence of modern sects such as the 'Shouters'—a group who infiltrated Chinese Christian communities after 1978 and caused much trouble. Problems of isolation relate to the controversial question of the role of the home meetings in China. There appear to be three sorts of home meetings: those linked to the official church structures, those which are not directly linked but have occasional contact and groups who have no contact. Some of these last refuse contact on theological grounds which also relate to the issue of co-operation with the State. Disagreement amongst observers concerns the number of these last groups. The limited evidence that is available suggests that they constitute only a small proportion. The majority of Christians are gradually being drawn into the networks being established by the China Christian Council.

Conclusion

In this survey of the relationship between Christianity and Chinese culture and tradition, we have attempted to show how the Christian presence in China has been related to political and social developments and how the fate of Christianity after the Communist revolution was closely related to the long-term failure to come to terms with Chinese culture. However, we then had to offer a corrective to this analysis by discussing the internal spiritual dynamic of Chinese Christianity—a dynamic that has surpassed the failures in theological understanding in the past and today presents the Christian world with a renewed Chinese Church firmly rooted in Chinese culture.

Notes

1. David M. Paton (ed.) *Essays in Anglican Self-Criticism* (SCM Press, London, 1958).
2. Bishop K.H. Ting: Address in Lambeth Palace Chapel (1 October 1982).

Further Reading

Bush Jun., Richard C. *Religion in Communist China* (Abingdon Press, New York, 1970)

Cary-Elwes, Columba *China and the Cross: Studies in Missionary History* (Longman, London, 1957)

Fung, Raymond *Households of God on China's Soil* (World Council of Churches, 1982)

Hanson, Eric O. *Catholic Politics in China and Korea* (Orbis, Maryknoll, New York, 1980)

Latourette, Kenneth Scott *A History of Christian Mission in China* (SPCK, London, 1929)

Paton, David M. *Christian Mission and the Judgment of God* (SCM Press, London, 1953)

Treadgold, Donald W. *The West in Russia and China*, vol. 2, *China 1582–1949* (Cambridge University Press, Cambridge, 1973)

18 Christianity Today

Simon Barrington-Ward

A Crucial Divide

Critical views of Christianity and the part it plays in our present world are not hard to come by. It is worth trying to listen carefully to what they are saying. A Kenyan writer, Ngugi Wa Thiongo, gives a harsh caricature of the Church in his own country in his novel, *Petals of Blood* (London, 1977). He seems to assign to the Church the role accorded to it by Marx, depicting it as a means of making people content with the status quo.

The novel focuses on some poor villagers coming out of the belt of arid scrubland which flanks the fertile highlands around Nairobi. They set out on a pilgrimage to the heart of the capital city, seeking to attract financial and political aid to their own area. There is a poignant encounter when they come to the large house and grounds of a well-known leader of one of the 'main-line' churches in the country. He is preoccupied, entertaining some fellow members of the elite, of the same ethnic group as himself. He dismisses the shabby little group at his door with a blessing and a swift farewell.

Here we have the 'establishment' on the one hand, and on the other an 'alternative' church, a white-robed, singing, dancing, healing 'prophet-movement'. In this body the poor seem to be at home, and are ministered to as individuals. But in fact they are shown to be manipulated by the same kind of political forces as those which are already sustained by the 'established' church structure.

Of course one's first temptation on reading this is to react against such a manifest distortion and over-simplification. Both images, that of the larger denominational Catholic and Protestant institutional churches, and that of the indigenous African Christian movements, are evidently unjust. There are in Kenya effective 'main-line' church leaders living and caring simply and fruitfully for the poorer people in their areas.

There are indigenous churches which have long offered a genuinely independent alternative community life and worship, and which are strengthening their programmes of training and of social responsibility.

Yet there is also something that rings true about Ngugi's critique. He has put his finger on, or at least near, something that is true of Christianity not only in Kenya, but, as we shall see, in other parts of Africa and all over the world. There is a crucial divide here between two types of Christian life and expression. The first is connected with the rational, businesslike forms of secular, Westernised society. The second is rooted in a romantic, mystically minded, pietistic or pentecostal 'counter-culture'.

In many societies there has been a divergence between what could be called the official, central cults of the ruling group (usually male) and the more free-ranging, innovative spirituality of nonconformist underlings (often female). Robin Horton drew attention to this kind of interplay long ago in his studies of the Kalabari of the Niger Delta (e.g. 'Types of Spirit Possession in Kalabari Religion' in Beattie and Middleton (eds.), *Spirit Mediumship and Society in Africa* (London, 1969)). Ioan Lewis built up a whole theory of 'ecstatic religion' on a similar basis (I.M. Lewis, *Ecstatic Religion* (London, 1971)). But the controlling framework in these traditional world pictures was never in doubt. There was an underlying unity within which prophetic or mystical movements could arise, become absorbed into the centre and 'established', or just fade away.

What is different about the disintegrated religion depicted by Ngugi is that a radically new type of society, dominated by Westernised economic and political forces, has broken in. It is served by the new educational system required by a new technology. And it brings with it a divided spirit and a divided culture. Here people are swaying between privately held traditional interpretations of life and traditional values, such as prevail in the 'prophet' movement, and the publicly accepted, modern, secular atmosphere of a commercial city. There is a secularisation of the centre of the society and a spiritualisation at the periphery.

Modern Christianity has been shaped by this conflict, a religion seemingly divided within itself. The tension between head and heart, between the secular style implicit in modern technology and the fragmented habits of thought and practice of a more sacred order inherited from the past, sets in motion an inner strife. It goes back to the first missionaries' appearance. During the period of the expansion of Europe from the seventeenth to the twentieth century this conflict has deeply and irreversibly penetrated all faiths and cultures. Indeed, it accounts for the disintegration and the relative numerical decline encountered by every world religion. European Christendom was the first religious world to experience this disintegration. Arguably, it was latent in its whole development.

Yet it could be true that out of world-wide Christianity today there may be emerging the first hint of a reintegration, a healing of the division. Some Christians would claim that this healing has also been latent from the beginning in the heart of their faith. They would see as their calling and opportunity the bringing of a fresh coherence into the broken worlds of all faiths. This coherence would be very different from the spiritual uniformity of the past.

The Expansion and Contraction of Christianity

The world-wide spread of Christianity over the last two centuries cannot be attributed to the effects of European political or economic dominance alone. It is rather that European technology, and the form of rationality that accompanied it, created a social and spiritual ferment within which the Christian message and the Church offered a means of interpreting and grappling with new experience.

The growth of Christianity has been a striking phenomenon. David Barrett's *World Christian Encyclopaedia* estimates that Christians of all kinds at the beginning of the 1980s numbered 32.8 per cent of the world's population. The percentage had increased rapidly during the nineteenth century, at the rate of 1.2 per cent each decade. In the twentieth century, the rate of increase slowed down, especially after 1914, and in Europe gradually turned into an ever-growing rate of decrease. However, in the Third World Christianity grew from 83 millions in 1900 to 643 millions by 1980. In Africa alone, the growth was from 9.9 millions in 1900 to 203 millions in 1980, with a present net increase of six millions per year. 'During the twentieth century Christianity has become the world's most extensive and universal religion. There are today Christians and organised Christian churches of some kind in every inhabited country on earth. The Church is therefore now, for the first time in history, *ecumenical* in the literal meaning of the word; its boundaries are coextensive with the *oikoumene*, the whole inhabited world.' (Barrett, p. 3)

However, in spite of the great numerical increases of almost all kinds of Christians, there has been a gradual numerical decline when these figures are looked at as percentages of the world's total population. This is a characteristic of all religions in the second half of the twentieth century. Apparent increases are offset by overall decline. While there is a persistent survival of localised religions that were once thought likely to vanish, there is also evidence of the rise in apparently secularised areas of new religions, cults and sects.

Meanwhile, the growth of Christianity in Latin America, Africa and South and East Asia is amply documented. This new vitality shows signs of effecting a substantial shift in the patterns of Christian life and sensibility which developed during the long period of its exclusive involvement with the culture of Europe.

Over the past few centuries, that culture has become

more and more disintegrated—in several different ways. Not only have there been the divisions along national and church lines, but, especially since the eighteenth century, human self-awareness has fragmented. Head and heart, thought and feeling, group loyalty and individual assertion have become more and more in tension. Christianity could scarcely avoid becoming a victim, as the demands of objectivity in the quest for scientific and historical truth seemed at variance with the claims of faith and human integration.

In Western society the process which is called 'secularisation' had meant not so much a total loss of religious awareness as a split consciousness. The so-called 'spiritual' dimension can become increasingly confined to the inward, the subjective, the private aspects of life.

In North America the culture as a whole may still be imbued with a faint trace of the old New England spirit, reinforced by the revivals of the early nineteenth century and overlaid by the rich variety of religious contributions from a whole collage of fragments of cultures, black or Spanish, Italian, Jewish or East European. But there is a sense even here of jostling competition and variety, in the midst of which any church, even the great traditional churches that in Europe or the East were once the framework of society, becomes one more optional club.

In Britain and Europe, secularisation has eaten its way even further into life. The sense that churches are part of the whole established order of things is increasingly attenuated. Not only is there a dramatic decline in their membership but that membership itself has long been confined, in the urban and industrial north of Europe (apart from Ireland) at least, to the middle class, and is strongest in some parts of the countryside and in the suburbs. Paradoxically it is where such a church is attempting most consciously to renew itself, to strengthen its corporate sense and to modernise its liturgy a little or intensify its worship, that it is most in danger of becoming even more of a withdrawn sect, a club for the converted.

Yet the whole culture is still, in all its aspects, in its arts and science and technology, in its politics, in its sense of history and its self-understanding, in its moral confusion, in its very self-questioning, deeply derived from Christian roots.

A general religious consciousness survives in amazingly persistent varieties of folk religion. There is a fascination in the media with sensational new heresies or religious controversies between conservative and radical, such as the conflict over the ordination of women. Secularisation itself is supremely a particularly post-Christian phenomenon.

The central areas of political and economic debate and struggle, of art and the performing arts, may seem to be almost defiantly stripped of all spiritual reference, even though Christian intellectuals, artists or scientists may seek to make their own contribution.

But where the Church has genuinely and deeply involved itself in the quest for a new shape to society, where, learning from the poor and disadvantaged, it has succeeded in generally embodying its own distinctive feeling for wholeness, there it is surely pressing its costly way back into the mainstream in a new humbler guise, gently repenetrating the very consciousness it once helped to shape. In this task the Church of the North needs help from the Third World.

Some of the new springs of Christian life, in areas or sectors of society (e.g. the poor of Latin America) less deeply affected by the force of this European heritage, show signs of transcending these divisions and producing new patterns of Christian perception and sensibility.

By contrast, none of the old, Europe-centred churches has been immune from these tensions, which have been exported and have thus had a deeply felt effect also among the Christian intelligentsia of Latin America, Africa and Asia. This heritage finds its expression in the gatherings of the World Council of Churches, while the more spiritualising side of the division finds expression through the activities of the Lausanne Committee for World Evangelization.

The Roman Catholic Church has also, in its own circumstances, become divided along comparable lines. Under Popes John XXIII and Paul VI, and the impulse of the Second Vatican Council of 1962–5, many, especially laity and members of religious orders in North America and northern Europe, were deeply affected by the ideas and practices of renewal and *aggiornamento*. But more recently, under Pope John Paul II and his advisers, there has been a pressing back into older patterns. The Rome Synod of 1985 offered a fascinating picture of the success of 'centrists' in mediating between implacable traditionalism and dangerous radicalism. Meanwhile, Western Christianity, save for the Roman Catholic Church in Ireland and southern Europe, has become less and less of a folk religion and more and more of the private, 'leisure' pursuit of those attracted to it.

The Impact in Africa

The enormous growth of the Christian Church in Africa south of the Sahara in the last decades, seemingly outpacing the growth of Islam and still expanding even within what are primarily Islamic areas, has tended to obscure the real nature of the movement. Essentially, the rise of Christianity in Africa is one aspect of the response of peoples shaped by small-scale localised cultures to the intrusion of Western power. At the centre of the religious systems of such cultures was a common kind of pattern. The whole social and natural order was seen as the product of a remote, abstract High God, within whose overall control lay a wide range of spirit powers underpinning the community and its segments. There were the central spirits and founders, of a particular ethnic group, then the 'clan' spirits and founders, and then the 'living dead' or spirit forebears of families. But over against these there was a peripheral, shifting fringe of more free-ranging and dynamic spirits, often using for their mediums women or younger people, who were able to contain and interpret the unexpected or the innovative energies in the society.

Western commerce and government shook these smaller-scale cultures. The more fixed parts of the pattern were weakened. In the new towns and centres of power a more secularised, Westernised mood prevailed, publicly at least. Western-style education and administration became dominant. Christianity itself became a central religion of the establishment, expressed in Westernised Catholic or Protestant forms.

Meanwhile, for those on the fringes of the new centre, the free-ranging spirit movements mediated by women and younger men took on a variety of creative forms, as new cults, 'churches', prayer movements, or religious societies like the Jehovah's Witnesses or the Rosicrucians came on the scene. From time to time some of these have sought to move into the relative spiritual vacuum at the centre, claiming to recreate community and, in an apocalyptic spirit, to shape 'a new heaven and a new earth'. Sometimes they have taken on violent forms and been repressed by governments. Usually they withdraw to the sidelines to offer, in innumerable 'clinics', Bethels, chapels, societies and churches, fragments of an alternative modernity, a spiritual technology for obtaining prosperity and well-being. Hence, a bewildering diversity of movements, symbolic systems and experiments exists within a more or less Christian or sometimes Islamic framework. There is a divide between the institutional, more rationalised centres of power and control in the churches, Catholic and Protestant, which are in the hands of a prestigious clerical and lay hierarchy, and a seething, ever-growing mass of small, local congregations in both rural and high-density urban areas less and less amenable to control from government or ecclesiastical superstructure.

If the whole concept of the divine has been modified, so also has the concept of evil and of evil powers. The causes of sickness and misfortune have come to be diagnosed less as an offence against social rules and relationships and more as a generalised tension and disruption, matching the intuitive sense of a breakdown of the social and political order. Evil becomes attributable to the activity not only of a variety of newly perceived demonic forces, but also of a more generalised power of witchcraft, pervading society, symbolising new forms of ambiguity and mistrust in the society. All these require some kind of exorcising and cleansing away by the new religious movements, with their 'witchcraft-eradicating' potential, as they present the possibility of new forms of community and of wholeness. Christianity provides a new mine of symbolic resources for this constant quest for power that can mediate between modernity and the fragments of tradition, between individual or group and the new social order, between centre and periphery. And there is in fact a wide spectrum of experiment, innovation and acceptance or rejection of various aspects of Christianity in various African settings.

In the dreams, visions, messages and liturgical forms of the churches of a Simon Kimbangu in Zaire or an Isaiah Shembe in South Africa there are to be found new perceptions of Christ and of the Christian message, often relating to the ills of society. 'Black theology' in South Africa has sought to make the identification of God with struggling and suffering Africans both explicit and socially and politically effective. But in doing so it has only drawn out the unconscious implications of many inchoate spirit movements, striving to offer an alternative social and spiritual form that could move in and possess the Westernised centre.

For the most part there remains a gulf between the more Westernised, institutionalised centres of power and the local and popular struggle to find wholeness and new community. This struggle has been expressed in Christian forms newly emergent among the last Africans to face modernity, the nomadic cattle peoples, the Fulani and Maasai, in a conscious attempt to re-express and universalise their traditional values 'in Christ'.

The attempts to recreate community and spirituality are numberless. They range from cults in which Christ figures as the wounded healer, the divine Nganga standing between his people and the evils oppressing them, to one of the most substantial and longest lasting of all such efforts at restoration, the East African Revival, which has spanned several countries for over half a century. This movement for rediscovering mutual trust and cleansing through placing secret evil thoughts and past wrongs 'under the blood' of Christ has always tended to fall short of becoming a public, open reality, dropping rather into a private world of inner, individualised piety. But at its most full and vital it has been able to generate the integrity, courage and moral power which characterised some of the finest leaders of the Church anywhere in Africa, men like the martyr Archbishop Jnani Luwum in Uganda. At the moment of his confrontation with President Amin, the gap between centre and periphery, public and private, inner and outer worlds was bridged and an authentic African wholeness and holiness emerged.

The Impact in the Islamic World

In Islamic, as in African, religion and society there was always an inherent divide between the ordered hierarchy centring on the Caliphate and sustained by the institutions and legal traditions of Sunni Islam at their greatest, a framework for a widely spread, rich and intricate culture, and the more apocalyptic, romantic impulses of Shi'a Islam, with its eschatological yearning for a once and future Imam, and Sufist mysticism in all its varied forms.

With the coming of Western modernity, as the centres of government have become more secularised and liberalised, the traditional spiritual leaders have often tended to be pushed into the wings, in effect into the urban slums and the rural fringes. Christians have always stood to benefit from the more liberal, secularised mood at the centre. Ancient churches, whether Chalcedonian like the Orthodox, Nestorian like the Assyrians, or Monophysite like the Copts, Syrians and Armenians, gradually began to emerge from their second-class citizenship in the old Ottoman Empire into a new era wherein Western influences gave hope for a new deal. Aspiring modern Christians, often educated by Western missions, have always sought to participate in movements for greater openness, tolerance and modernisation. Many of them have been the pioneers of an Arab literary renaissance in the nineteenth and early twentieth centuries. While many of them have indeed been attracted by the West, their ideal has had to be the mutual tolerance sought by a leader like Charles Malik in Lebanon, who wanted to see his country not a confessional state but rather a 'pilot country' (*pays pilote*) for the development of a new kind of society. Something of the same vision was shared by members of an earlier generation of Jews in Palestine, such as Martin Buber.

The building of the modern state of Israel, and the interventions and pressures of the great powers, have served to intensify a developing radical, popular revivalism in Islam. This has created a new, narrowly puritanical, scripturalist mood, attractive to the poorer dispossessed, feared by many moderates and liberal Muslims, as also by their Christian counterparts. No room is left within such reconstructions of an idealised Islam for any such being as an Arab Christian. When, in Iran, Lebanon or Egypt, the disenchantment of the poor with those Westernised and secularised regimes which have not yielded enough fruit has led to eruptions of frenzy, the hopes of Christian or Muslim compromisers have been shaken. A fanatical egalitarian, Utopian energy has driven its proponents to clamber out of the abyss of what they have felt to be the humiliation of Islam under Westernised hands to attempt to seize control of the faltering liberal centre. Some Christians have been tempted to withdraw into militarism, and the aggressive exclusiveness of some of the Phalangists in Lebanon springs from such a source.

Where Christian energies flow into reconstruction, reconciliation and patient witness, as amongst some of those working with the Middle East Council of Churches in Beirut, the tradition of the ancient churches, in a witness of worship and service, offers the seeds of a new Christian movement within the Islamic world, penitent for the arrogance of the West. This movement can be strengthened by a sensitive Western Christian presence.

The Impact in the East

Within the religious worlds of the East as much as in the West, in Africa, or Islam, there has always been the same potential dualism. The social order and indeed the whole universe are seen as sustained by the great unfolding of a spirit that seeks only to return ultimately to itself. All steadily moves, in the great cosmic dance, in 'the commonwealth of transmigration' (reincarnation), through innumerable phases of existence towards the final purification and reunion. The social order, the pantheons of gods, the castes of humans, gradually process through degrees of impurity to the ultimate purity. Kings and rulers are charged with maintaining the temporal order while it lasts to enable all to attain to the eternal.

But there have always been spiritual alternatives, which broke out of the normative pattern to offer a more immediate access to the divine, the so-called 'renouncer movements'. The renouncers quitted worldly society, left their place at the hearth to reach beyond all the gods and, like Kipling's Purun Bhagat, to seek final liberation. In Hinduism they were the founders of sects, in Buddhism the most dedicated monks. The convention was that the 'renouncer' would not return. Even the Bodhisattva, the Buddhist who *does* postpone his enlightenment painfully to stay and help others, is still essentially orientated towards final liberation from this world.

The arrival of Western commerce, culture and political rule posed a new threat to the pattern. Their powerful stress on this world and its material transformation, together with new resources, skills and knowledge, has shifted the Eastern emphasis. It could be argued that Christian missionaries and teachers, with their hospitals, schools and good works, have emphasised *karma*, the way of selfless service propounded in the *Bhagavadgita*, to a point where it has presented a new mode of spiritual response, in order to deal with the new stress on this world. This mode is that of the renouncer who does return. Churches, missions and the person and story of Christ have thus provided a more secularised, reformist style of religious action. Christian influence has helped to generate a vast succession of new 'returned renouncer' movements, from that of Rāmmohan Roy (founder of the early nineteenth-century *Brāhmo Samāj*) to Swami Vivekānanda, with his Ramakrishna Mission, and other founders of religious societies, churches, *samājs* and ashrams. The whole so-called Hindu renaissance, with its peak figures such as Rādhakrishnan, a distinguished President of India, or Gandhi himself, as well as its populous foothills of Sai Babas, Rajneeshes, Maharishis and the like, has its Christian connections. While the old centres of Hindu orthodoxy, such as the schools of the pundits in Varanasi, have been relatively neglected, the Westernised movements have laid a new emphasis on fragments of the tradition, on mere extracts from the *Upanishads*, and supremely on the *Bhagavadgita* itself, peripheral to the main literature of the past, as a kind of 'New Testament' in its own right. The story and person of Christ have widespread appeal and influence in such circles.

The Church itself, on the other hand, with its Westernised forms and its seemingly exclusive emphasis on baptism, has won far less ground. It has been more a part of modern secularised society than of the traditional scene, and more attractive to the harijan outcastes, with their mass movement into Christianity, than to the higher castes. Indeed it could be shown that even in the Church, which has sought to oppose the caste system, as have other sectarian movements before it and the neo-Buddhist movement since, there has in fact been a subtly pervasive influence of caste. The churches in the north of India, the area where traditionally new religions have to win their way if they are to have any widespread success, are still fragmentary and scattered, a kind of remnant of the raj, with a heritage of large British-style buildings. Although there are movements to unity among Protestants in the Church of North India, and in the far stronger Church of South India, in the area where ancient Indian Christianity began, Protestants are still divided by lawsuits and other forms of conflict. In spite of their impressive contribution to society through their hospitals, rural community developments and social action, in spite too of Mother Teresa and the work of the old Oxford Mission to Calcutta, their churches remain largely extraneous, seemingly Westernised institutions. The exceptions are the many Christian ashrams, exploring Hindu–Christian dialogue along the lines made famous by Abishiktanda and Bede Griffiths, both indigenised Westerners. But even here, and in the communities of the ancient Syrian Orthodox Church and its more modernised offshoot the Mar Thoma Church, there is no real mediation, which could be its gift, between the two halves of Indian consciousness, the modern, urban, materialistic, pragmatic aspect once personified by Nehru and the vast inchoate tradition.

Even in East Asia there is the sense of an unfulfilled potential confronting Christian churches in the face of social and material change. In the modern commercial and capitalist centres such as Hong Kong, Singapore, South Korea, or indeed Japan, traditional religions have tended to fade and disintegrate at the centre. New religions and new religious movements have once again offered a haven for some, a way of dealing with modernity in an enclosed community. The Christian churches have provided impressive institutions—colleges, schools, hospitals, church buildings. In Hong Kong the Church still has overtones of power and patronage from the past. It is an effective organisation. There are also dynamic evangelistic groups at work. But the Church often wears the appearance of an efficient business. It could, with advantage, release a more profound yet socially and materially effective spiritual dynamic. In modernised Japan with its polarisation of intimate, private spiritual remnants on the one side and a streamlined, neutral public machine on the other, the Church remains a largely Westernised fragment with a 'high threshold'. New Catholic monastic and Anglican charismatic movements offer a hint of change. In Singapore, South Korea, Java and parts of Indonesia the churches are thriving and growing. In these areas of more recent expansion, a genuine spiritual and communal dynamic is apparent. Real needs are being dramatically met and lives touched and changed. But even here the realisation of a corporate gospel is tantalisingly incomplete. The movement has not yet provided an integrated approach to the whole society and the issues confronting it. Those Christians who are concerned for a political and social witness seem sometimes, as in the West, to be isolated and to lose touch with their spiritual roots. Those in the wider movement of renewal and evangelism remain content to provide what is still often a private, inward leisure activity, not greatly affecting the social context. There are outstanding exceptions, for example Tom Takami's Asian Rural Institute in Japan, High Rise House Churches in Singapore, Batak Christian communities in Indonesia and Catholic community witness in the Philippines. Yet that integration and mediation, the 'marriage of East and West', have still to be attained in both.

Prospects of World-wide Christianity Today

Christianity, emanating from the West, has today become part of the problem with which all faiths are grappling. The divide between spiritual and material confronts all cultures now. It originated in the eighteenth-century Enlightenment era in western Europe, as the product of a Christendom which had already lost sight of the potential integration of human society latent in its own faith. It was, arguably, the distinctive relationship between heaven and earth, divine and human, implicit in the message of the Incarnation, which gave Western culture its particular grasp on reality. It may be claimed that while this led to its capacity to develop natural science and technology, new forms of commerce and democracy, Western society's original realisation of its own faith proved in this context to be both socially and conceptually inadequate. Christianity expanded beyond its European confines at precisely the period when its own inner spiritual, intellectual and social resources were proving inadequate to the multiple challenge posed within the European setting itself.

The relative decline of all faiths in this era of global crisis, in which religious revivals often appear as symptom rather than cure, can be clearly charted. All cultures and societies are fundamentally disintegrating. They desperately require a new mediation between a sceptical, urbanised materialism, individualist or collectivist, and a romantic nostalgia or Utopian yearning; between public institutions, centres of economic or political power, and private quests for both personal fulfilment and true community; between a just social order and universal liberty; between public control and personal freedom; between the rational and the intuitive. The expansion of Christianity has been one crucial aspect of this universal breakdown. In its fragmented Westernised form it has appeared in many cultural settings to be more part of the problem than of the solution, especially in its complacent and aggressive forms. However, the possibility is emerging that there could yet be within Christianity the means of a fresh realisation of its meaning and potential. There is the hint of a kind of Church transcending west and east, north and south, coming into being across the globe. Where this happens, there is a sense in which the Christian way discloses once again the seed of a healing, a bridging of the great divide.

Pilgrims

Some of those who have discerned this possibility most clearly are people on the fringes of Christian faith. They may even be living across the frontiers between faiths. But so many of those in the West who cross over into Islam, into the circle surrounding some newly fashionable guru or yogi, into a Buddhist monastery, into a new religion or a new version of an old, seem to have fallen away into an alternative half-world under the pressures of contemporary secular experience. They do not represent an attempt to break new ground in enabling Christianity to find fresh expression within a world-wide context.

To cite a specific example: one striking 'Pilgrim of the Absolute' who lives on the edge of an Asian city has suggested that the only expression of the Christian mystery that is anywhere near faithful to its original integration of earth and heaven is to be found in Russian Christianity. He did not want to study Western theology for fear of its anaemic abstraction. Asian thought had not yet truly come to terms with the 'demythologised humanism' of the West. So it was Dostoevsky who spoke to him more effectively than any other of Christ in modern dress. It would be those capable of living between two worlds who would find an authentic form for the Christian message, itself a marriage of East and West, in our time. This insistence recalls the way in which Khomiakov, a contemporary of Dostoevsky's, visiting the West, found its churches, Catholic and Protestant alike, cold, grey, individualised and suffering from a profound inner dichotomy. For this Asian pilgrim, Father Zossima in *The Brothers Karamazov* spoke most truly of the indissoluble marriage of earth and heaven in Christ.

The Persecuted

Russian Christianity also afford striking examples of a second aspect of vitality and creativity in Christian life today. Persecution has come to be part of its existence. The usefulness of the Church to Stalin during the Second World War saved it from the near extinction it had reached in two decades after the Revolution, but Khrushchev resumed harsh persecution and restriction. The situation has since eased a little but the limited freedom of the Church is always precarious. On the one hand, church leaders like the Patriarch Nikodim and his successor Pimen remained cautiously conforming in relation to the system, in order to enable the liturgy to be maintained and the Church to survive. On the other hand, famous dissidents like Father Glev Yakunin, Lev Regelson or Father Dimitri Dudko have been arrested, brain-washed and crushed. The Baptists have grown significantly and have attracted the young. Solzhenitsyn's Baptist in *One Day in the Life of Ivan Denisovich* is a representative figure in our time. In the life and testimony of such Russian Christians there is the integrity and vitality which Solzhenitsyn describes as the 'radiant ethical atmosphere in which our morals have been grounded'. It contrasts with the stale, spiritually bankrupt atmosphere of much of Soviet Communist society, and indeed of much of the capitalist world of the West.

Among other Eastern European Christians, a similar rediscovery of the true integrity of the Christian gospel is being made. Here, too, significant examples of creativity are to be found, striking notes that are in one sense traditional but in another sense novel, so that they are 'pointers' within present-day Christianity, viewed as a world religion, transcending their local context.

The faith of the Polish Church, still inspired and epitomised by the experience of the priest Maximilian Kolbe in the concentration camp of Auschwitz, who offered himself up to death in place of another prisoner, is going beyond its roots in popular religion. The Church may indeed be the guardian of the nation's language, history and culture, but in its alliance with the Solidarity political reform movement, its Masses in shipyards and factories, its martyr priest Jerzy Popieluszko, it has identified itself with the suffering and survival of the people. That is where the real integration lies.

Other parts of Eastern Europe afford comparable examples, where new Christian ground is being broken. These are the Christian heirs of Dubček in Czechoslovakia, members of the Protestant Church of the Czech Brethren or the Catholic 'Oasis' movement in Slovakia, living in faithfulness to the vision of a 'socialism with a human face', all persisting despite pressure from the regime. There are the two to four thousand 'basic Christian communities' in Hungary where Church and State are coming to terms with each other, the struggling martyrs of Albania where the Church has been systematically crushed, the continuing witness against atheism of the steadily surviving Church in Bulgaria, with its brutally assaulted Pentecostals, and the strong and flourishing Church and monastic life of Rumania. In East Germany, as in Yugoslavia, a Western type of secularism and materialism is a more serious cause of decline now than political pressure. There has of late been a degree of relaxation by the government and some acknowledgement of the place and role of the Church. In all these countries a profound witness is being worked out which Western Christians need to understand more deeply, and in which the social and political failures of the Church of the past can often be faced and acknowledged. In such settings, the Church begins to discover a new identity, a new sense of belonging to the people, a way which goes far beyond its previous associations with the powerful and the oppressive.

Perhaps nowhere have persecuted Christians so much atoned for and lived down this distorted past as in China. There, where Christian missionaries were once linked in the popular mind with the shameful ravages of Western intruders with Opium Wars and gunboats, and with China's era of frustration and division, they had indeed much to live down. The 'Three Self' Christian movement originally arose in a reaction against this embarrassment. It was a controversial effort by some liberal Chinese Christians for self-government, self-support and self-propagation—old ideals, enforced by the Communists through a semi-official body in the 1950s. It could not save Christianity in the traumatic era of the Cultural Revolution of the 1960s. Then, Evangelical indigenous churches, like the Little Flock or the Jesus Family, and institutional mission-led churches, Catholic and Protestant, reactionary and modernist, all went under together. It seemed the end of *Yang Jiao*, a foreign teaching, 'a religion of love spread by force', as one Chinese Christian critic called it. In the 'dark night' of the Chinese Church, the period of stripping of the altars, when buildings were lost, Bibles trampled upon and leaders led away in shame, often to die in prison and disgrace, there was some kind of real purgation of its alienness.

Two years ago, on the steps of Lambeth Palace in London, Bishop Ting, the leader of the revived 'Church of China', the Three Self movement reconstituted, declared, 'We have been through a death and a resurrection.' There had emerged across the country a widely scattered series of Christian communities with an integrity, an attractive power and a moral force proved in persecution which were infectious. Now the renewed churches are far more numerous than before and the buildings which are being returned to their aged leaders cannot house them all. Seminaries are coming into being. The main Christian bodies include a 'post-denomination' Protestant Church and a divided Catholic Church, part linked to Rome, part separated. Meanwhile, more and more descriptions of how little Christian groups came into being, grew secretly and spread rapidly are emerging. Some could only pray together 'in the parks ... with our eyes open and mouths smiling, as if we were talking and sharing a joke'.

In the moral and spiritual vacuum of post-Maoist China, where a whole generation 'lost out', the disillusioned young are searching for more meaningful patterns of life, and the Church can have a special attraction. In the setting of Chinese society it is distinctive, offering different features from the revivals of Taoism and Islam which China is also seeing. For the Church appeals as something modern, something which has embraced and contained technological, scientific and social change, something open to today's more pluralist, relativist world.

The Poor

Throughout the world, those who are embracing a revitalised Christian vision most effectively of all are those for whom the original gospel of Christ crucified and risen always was supremely good news: the poor. And a movement has begun in the area where the Church has had its crudest identification with power and oppression, where Christianity has often been seen not as crucified but crucifying—Latin America. The movement is that of the 'basic Christian communities'.

After the failure of the great struggle of Friar Bartolomé de Las Casas (1474–1566) and the Jesuit missions to defend the Indians from the tyranny of their conquerors, the Church in both Portuguese and Spanish America became identified with the wealthy and the powerful. As the Peruvian song has it:

> They say God cares for the poor
> Well, this may be true or not,
> But it's the mine-owner he dines with.

The Church, the rich and the army formed a mutually supportive triumvirate. Individuals will, of course, here and there have played a more compassionate role. But the bishops and the whole organisation of the Church were part and parcel of an extremely unequal and unjust society. It is all the more remarkable therefore that over the whole of Latin America, and especially in Mexico and Brazil, a movement of 'grass-roots' Christian communities has spread through the Catholic Church. They may be in little units of seven to twelve, like the house groups popular in the West, and they may often also be linked into larger combinations of several such groups. They meet for prayer and Bible study, for mutual support and exchange of experience, and to encourage each other to social and political action. This they see as the outworking of Christian love. The famous, or notorious, 'liberation theology' has developed out of reflection on the experience of such 'base communities', and at the same time given them an articulation and a rationale.

At first sight the movement may appear to be once again a romantic or Utopian alternative to the necessary structures of Church and society. Sometimes the language of its apologetics strays into a Marxist jargon with an unreal ring of propaganda about it. And it is true to say that some of the organisers and so-called 'conscientisers', in attempting to make poor people aware of the 'social' cause of their plight, have become increasingly politically ideological; and their disciples have learnt to echo them.

But there is far too much vigour and independence of spirit in the members of the base communities themselves for them to fall for such a typically Western style. Although in the days of its origins liberation theology had overtones of a Marxist dogmatism, a fanatical optimism and a naïve belief in the inevitable processes of history (the imminent emergence of the 'New Man' and the like), this was soon modified by sometimes bitter experience.

In 1968 the famous Second Assembly of the Latin American Episcopate of the Catholic Church took place at Medellin, Colombia. In the Statement resulting from the Assembly the bishops drew on personal experience and on the experience of hundreds of priests and lay members of base communities from all over the region. There was a firm realism about the personal as well as the social nature of sin, and about its cosmic and demonic character. There was thus a recognition of the need for grace, faith, the Bible, prayer and the sacraments in the struggle for the transformation of people and society. The Church, while not expecting instant change, nor indeed identifying the will of God with any one political party or philosophy, must seek to be made into a sign of self-giving, materially worked-out love to the whole of humanity.

The biblical accounts of the liberating Exodus of the Israelites from Egypt and their subsequent long Captivity in Babylon both came to assume for these Latin American Christians a profound significance. To endure patiently a long political struggle, they began to feel the need for all the resources of the Spirit. They were to build up a new middle way between institution and community, the spiritual and the material. They were to fuse worship and prayer with practical action. The meditations of Archbishop Helder Camara, the story and witness of Archbishop Romero or the American missionary sisters murdered soon after him in San Salvador, reveal a fresh integration of faith and love. The mood is epitomised in the book of the Peruvian theologian, Gustavo Gutierrez, priest-adviser to groups of students and workers, *We Drink from our own Wells* (London, 1983). Moving beyond his earlier 'Theology of Liberation', he has come to stress the distinctively Christian and spiritual dimension, the dimension of grace. For him, theology arises from the experience of prayer, worship, Bible study and the active struggle for justice, described as 'praxis'. Theology should be written and taught out of action, prayer and then reflection. Similarly, for Mortimer Arias, a Uruguayan Methodist bishop, writing after a time in prison, 'Jesus Christ came in the Spirit, and he came to liberate, so here together you have the charismatic and liberating dimension of the Gospel. In Jesus Christ, it is one, but we have put asunder what God has joined together. We have a polarisation of the two. But I believe we have to open both windows' (D. Winter, *Hope in Captivity* (London, 1977), p. 48).

This is very much the quality of the Asian theology of liberation of a remarkable mystic and radical, the Jesuit Aloysius Pieris in Sri Lanka, who has been critical of the earlier Latin American liberation theology as being too materialistic and obsessed with 'freedom from poverty', the goal of Western technocracy. Pieris wants less of a Marxist, more of a monastic flavour. He wants not just the 'praxis' of Marxism and Latin

American liberation theology but a '*theo*praxis', God-centred not man-centred, involving an *askesis*, a spiritual discipline, and a *darsana*, a vision. The 'Minjung' folk-theologians of Korea and the writing and witness of the Christian Korean poet, Kim Chi Ha, stress a Christian and spiritual third way, an alternative to Western socialism and capitalism, rooted in a costly discipleship and a contemplative struggle for justice. A similar spirit has infused 'base communities' in the Philippines and the whole mood underlying what was so largely a Christian uprising there during the Marcos–Aquino struggle of 1985–6. The quality of a number of Christian communities in Tondo, the slums of Manila, and other parts of the country, with their radical faith, prayer and courageous obedience, has been a major source of the humane character of the Filipino revolution.

It remains to be seen whether Christianity can exercise a similar role in other parts of the world where issues concerning the transfer of power remain to be decided. Foremost among them is South Africa. Within the black townships as much as in the white suburbs of Johannesburg or Cape Town, there is everywhere a Christian leadership that is committed to justice. It is brave, patient and far-sighted. The black Christian leaders have so far been able to carry with them their more violent young followers, and to reach out to include the more repentant and sympathetic whites. Whether the Church can retain its spiritual lead much longer without Western intervention (as happened in the Philippines) is doubtful.

In all these manifestations, the stress is on the value of the person, the quality of relationships, the role of women as well as men, and the importance of the poorest, the least confident and the uneducated. The group is usually actively involved in social and political concerns but not essentially politicised. Rather, it has its own identity and approach, inspired by faith, worship, word and sacrament. It has about it something of the joy and freshness of the gospel message. 'This joy', says Clodovis Boff of Brazil, 'differentiates members of a basic community from the political militants of the left and from bourgeois Christians. The deepest and most intimate core of the Gospel is felt in basic communities.'

This is the quality of many groups springing up all over the world. Within such an ambience there is often a great openness to other faiths and an intermingling with adherents of those faiths, a respect for them, a readiness for mutual exchange. The secret of this openness is that there is a conviction shared by Christian pilgrims, persecuted and poor, as they explore new expressions and forms of their faith and transcend old barriers, that they are caught up in a movement of the Spirit, spanning the globe. The old religious systems and institutions are seen to be shifting and disintegrating. A new common humanity is emerging from the divided worlds of earlier days. We are entering a spiritual and cultural melting-pot. And yet in the midst of this confusion there is a healing, and what is believed to be the integrating disclosure of God alongside us, in the form of Christ, broken, stripped and excluded from an outworn system, who offers the possibility of holiness. Here there can be seen the hope of a humane faith, a life transfigured by the Spirit and available to all, that will be true to the heart of all Christianity's inherited fragments of faith, true to Semitic, Hellenistic and localised folk cultures, true also to East and West. Perhaps that is why a Muslim Sufist, Hassan Askari, has written, 'The Cross is a sign of the relationship between God and man for people of all faiths.' This can be the only real meaning of Christianity today, as it was at the time of its beginning.

Further Reading

Barrett, D. *World Christian Encyclopaedia* (Oxford, 1982)

Bourdeaux, Michael *Rhythm Indeed* (Darton, Longman & Todd, London, 1983)

Donovan, Vincent *Christianity Rediscovered: Epistle from the Maasai* (SCM, London, 1982)

Gutierrez, G. *We Drink from our own Wells* (SCM, London, 1983)

Hastings, Adrian *History of African Christianity 1950–75* (Cambridge, 1981)

Hebblethwaite, Peter *Synod Extraordinary* (Darton, Longman & Todd, London, 1986)

Sobrino, J. *The True Church and the Poor* (SCM, London, 1985)

Part 3 Islam

Editor:
Peter Clarke

19 Introduction

Peter Clarke

Since its introduction in the Arabian peninsula in the early years of the seventh century CE Islam has come to embrace over one-sixth of the world's population and stretches almost continuously over wide and diverse areas from, for example, Mauretania in the west to China in the east. This makes it easier to point to those parts of the world, such as Australia and South America, where to date Islam has had little or virtually no impact, than to enumerate the numerous regions where it is the religion of a majority or a substantial minority of the population or those, such as the Iberian peninsula, where it once had a strong presence and has left a very distinctive mark on the culture and history.

One of the most striking aspects of this religion as it has travelled and developed beyond its original homeland is, to use the biological concept of homogenesis, the likeness of the offspring to the parent body, and this sameness is in the words of one scholar 'all the more puzzling in the theoretical absence of a Church, and hence of a Central authority on Faith and Morals', for 'There is no obvious agency which could have enforced this homogeneity.'[1] While this is so, the fact that Islam is a religion of a book, the Qur'an, dictated to the Prophet Muhammad by the Angel Gabriel and which is for Muslims in a most literal sense the word of God, and that it has in Mecca a focal point to which believers throughout the Muslim community are linked by prayer and the hadj or pilgrimage, make for a considerable degree of unity and cohesion.

However, while the idealist portrait of this faith is inclined to leave things there, stating that Islam is one and the same thing wherever it is found, it is also clear, as contributions to this section of the volume show, that the reality is somewhat different. Islam is not some kind of seamless, monochromatic garment-like entity without either variation or division, nor did the Prophet Muhammad ever imagine it would be so.

Although Muslim communities in Africa are very often recognisably believing in and practising what is essentially the same faith as those in Central Asia or China or Europe, there exist, all the same, certain differences of emphases, style, practice, content and intensity of commitment. Moreover, even within the same community there are more often than not at least two sides to Islam, one 'official' and grounded in a scrupulous concern for right belief and even more for orthopraxy, and the other 'popular' and sometimes shaped and moulded as much by the local culture as it is by so-called 'pure' Islam.

Although the coverage provided here is by no means comprehensive, several of the case studies enable the reader to glimpse something of the variety and difference as well as the homogeneity in Islam as found in, among other places, North Africa, Iran, the Indian sub-continent, Turkey, China, Indonesia, the Middle East, sub-Saharan Africa, western and eastern Europe, and the United States. Adaptation or assimilation, however, has often given rise to dispute between the *ulema*, religious experts who may be regarded as the custodians of Muslim values, and those who have 'mixed' Islamic practice with local custom, although not all local belief and practice is considered as false and therefore to be rejected. However, very often in the history of Islam what some authors refer to as the *smaller jihad* or *jihad of the sword*, as distinct from *greater jihad* which denotes a more spiritual activity like fighting one's evil inclinations or even studying the *fiqh*, Islamic jurisprudence, has been waged in response to such syncretism, the stated purpose being to purify Islam.

The idea of 'pure' Islam from a Muslim perspective consists essentially in submission in faith to God's will revealed to his prophets and finalised in the series of revelations in Mecca and Medina to the last of the prophets, the Prophet Muhammad (*c.* 570–632 CE). These revelations were collected together soon after Muhammad's death to form the holy book or scripture of Islam, the Qur'an. This book lays stress time and again on the Oneness of God, and the Muslim confession of faith or *Shahada* reads: 'There is no god but God and Muhammad is his Apostle.' God is totally other and must never be likened to or associated with anything finite and to do so is to commit the most grievous of offences, *shirk* or association, and especially the association of a companion with God in the sense of polytheism or the worshipping of another besides God. On the other hand, God is 'closer to man than his own jugular vein' (Qur'an 2, 182), one of the qur'anic statements which the Sufis or mystics of Islam refer to in justification of their practices.

While from very early times *Sufism* has been part of the Islamic tradition, its position within that tradition has not always been secure. The way in which the quest for a mystical experience of oneness with God has been pursued, and the technical terms such as *fana* or annihilation which are used to interpret that experience, often wrongly compared to the Buddhist notion of Nirvāṇa, has led on occasion to bitterness and conflict between mystic and scholar, the latter concerned to preserve the doctrine of *Tawhid*, or the oneness of God, the basis as we have just seen of all the articles of belief of Islam. It was for this reason that al-Husein ibn Mansur al-Hallaj, the Iranian mystic, was executed in 922 CE. There was also, and to an extent still is, the fear amongst the *ulema* that inherent in Sufism was the tendency to emphasise the importance of the interior or inward path of faith in and submission to God at the expense of outward observance of the Shari'a or sacred law of Islam discussed below.

Of course, not all Sufis have been given to making extravagant claims or equivocal pronouncements, and through the teaching, writing and influence of the Iranian mystic al-Ghazzali (1058–1111 CE) Sufism and 'orthodoxy' were in theory reconciled. This great and highly controversial thinker, who became an absolute sceptic to the possibility of any certain knowledge, religious or otherwise, and who eventually appears to have turned whole-heartedly to Sufism, was to argue that it was only through *marifa* or personal experience that the truth of prophetic revelation could be established and that while their doctrines were correct the systems of the speculative theologians possessed no intellectual certainty. However, he also insisted that while Sufism provided the gateway to the true knowledge of God the mystic would not achieve this end without the guidance of a sound orthodox education in Islamic faith and practice. And for the 'simple' believer, he maintained, the safer path was through observance of the law. Throughout the Muslim world there have emerged numerous Sufi orders or brotherhoods, *turuq*, which have played a vital role in the development and spread of Islam.

In addition to the confession of faith already mentioned, there are four other obligations which make what are known as 'the Pillars of the Faith'. There is the performance, with sincere and right intention, *niya*, of *salat* or the five daily prayers, the payment of *zakat*, a percentage of annual revenue handed over to the local authorities for the relief of the poor and needy and similar works of charity, *sawm* or fasting during the month of Ramadan, and the *hadj* or pilgrimage, providing one has the finances and the health, to the holy mosque and shrine in Mecca during the month of pilgrimage, *Dhul-Hijja*. There is also the wider question, of which these obligations form part, of the observance of Shari'a or sacred law which is regarded as mandatory, immutable and universal and, therefore, binding not only on Muslims but on all mankind. The Shari'a has been described as 'the constitution of the Muslim community, the pattern of its communal order' and is, Muslims believe, contained in substance in the Qur'an.[2] It, therefore, requires no supplementing but only clarification and the elaboration of its texts where method, application and interpretation are concerned, and for this resort is made to authentic Tradition, *hadith*, handed down from the 'Companions of the Prophet', otherwise first-generation Muslims, and the *Sunna*, practice, of the Prophet which supersede any other practice or any form of speculation. There are, however, differences between Sunni Muslims, followers of the practice of the Community or *umma* at large, and the Shi'a Muslims, followers of Ali, son-in-law and cousin of the Prophet Muhammad, regarding the conditions required for authenticity of Tradition. The former, who hold to the doctrine of *ijma*, consensus of the Community, recognise all rulings of the four main schools, *madhahib*, of Islamic law, concerning what constitutes valid Tradition, while the latter reject ijma on the grounds that only the imams, leaders, from the House of Ali, can interpret the law. This in turn sheds light on the different constitutional arrangements found in Sunni and Shi'a Islam, the former being more democratic and the latter more monarchical. In the light of what has been said here about the Qur'an and the Shari'a, it is no surprise to find among Muslims an intense preoccupation with the past, with the first Muslim community, a preoccupation which is often today labelled misleadingly 'fundamentalism' as if it were simply confined to a minority of narrow-minded fanatics opposed to all that they regard as unIslamic. It can in fact be just as much an inspiration for change and adaptation in the modern world as for regression, for seen and understood in its 'purity', as many Muslims point out, Islam not only accepts as authentic the Judeo-Christian prophetic tradition but positively pursues 'knowledge' wherever it is to be found. Moreover, as some scholars have shown, far from being incompatible with 'modernity' it can be a progressive faith and a force for modernisation, as those familiar with its impact on the development of the natural sciences, medicine and architecture, among other things, are aware.[3]

In its 'pure' form then, Islam is, in the words of Gellner, 'the blueprint of a social order. It holds that a set of rules exists, eternal, divinely ordained, and independent of the will of men, which defines the proper ordering of society . . . and thus there is in principle no call or justification for an internal separation of society into two parts, of which one would be closer to the deity than the other.'[4] There is in theory no clergy, no church structure and no religious virtuosi and for this reason no orthodoxy in the Christian sense, the nearest equivalent being the *Sunna*, the way of life and practice of the Prophet Muhammad, his companions and immediate successors known as the four rightly guided caliphs. Therefore, commitment to Islam is first and foremost expressed in the acceptance and practice of Islamic norms and way of life, obedience to the caliph or head of state and loyalty to the community. Deviation in these respects and rejection of the belief contained in the confession of faith cited above constitute the closest thing to heresy as understood in the Christian tradition. This is but one of the ways in which Islam differs from Christianity, another being the absence in the former of that division which is found in the latter between the spiritual and temporal spheres. An even more fundamental difference exists over the question of Jesus, who is regarded and respected by Muslims as a prophet, but is not believed by them to be the Son of God. Muslims, further, do not accept the Christian idea of God as Father, or the interpretation and authenticity of Christian gospel as presented by the Christian Church. To find out the truth about Jesus one has to turn to the Qur'an.

It can be noted here with reference to the establishment of what is authentic and what is not in matters relating to belief and practice, that there is not to be found among Muslim scholars the same 'critical' approach to Muslim scripture and early Muslim history as exists among theologians and historians of the Old and New Testaments and early Christianity. Moreover, there is comparatively little in the way of documents for the first five hundred years and more of the history of Islam, although inscriptions and coins to some extent fill this gap. Meanwhile, some Western students of Islam have applied the approach and methods used in examining any historical document or oral tradition to the Qur'an and early biographies of the Prophet Muhammad. As to the Qur'an, attempts have been made to elucidate further, among other things, its structure, on the grounds that the traditional revision into Meccan and Medinan *suras*, chapters, can no longer be accepted on historical grounds. Moreover, it has been pointed out that the Qur'an contains material about trade, for example, that is taken to be historical fact but which is not easily supported by external evidence.

However, with regard to Muhammad there is no doubt about his existence; both internal and external sources confirm that he was a historical figure, but the latter, *if they are right*, suggest that Muslim tradition is not entirely accurate on a number of important aspects of his career. These and related matters are taken up in this section; but it is worth pointing out here that the student of Islamic history enters a field where a great deal of basic research still has to be done and that some of those who take this more 'critical' approach to Muslim sources are as persuaded as the more conservative historians of the great innovations and achievements of Muhammad, perhaps the most notable being his revival 'of the radically monotheistic polity enshrined in the story of Moses'.[5]

While Muhammad accomplished this in Arabia, he is recognised today as the last of the prophets in a great many different cultural settings. The contributions to this section, written from a variety of perspectives including that of the historian, political scientist, sociologist and linguist, show how the message he proclaimed has been widely accepted in its fundamentals, and in other respects developed, extended and if not changed then greatly modified by peoples and generations living at times and in societies and cultures very far distant from his own.

Notes

1. E. Gellner, *Muslim Society* (Cambridge University Press, Cambridge, 1983), p. 99.
2. H.A.R. Gibb, 'Islam' in R.C. Zaehner (ed.), *The Concise Encyclopaedia of Living Faiths* (Hutchinson, London, 1977), p. 171.

3. See for example O. Wright, 'Science' in J. Schacht and C.E. Bosworth (eds.), *The Legacy of Islam*, 2nd edn (The Clarendon Press, Oxford, 1974), pp. 425–89.
4. Gellner, *Muslim Society*, p. 1.
5. M. Cook, *Muhammad* (Oxford University Press, Oxford, 1983), p. 86.

20 Early Islam

Julian Baldick

The subject of early Islam is both extremely important and extremely fascinating. It is important because hundreds of millions of Muslims believe, or are supposed to believe, that every detail of their lives should be determined in accordance with what was allegedly said or done in Arabia in the seventh century CE. It is fascinating because at the moment a profound change is taking place in the study of the evidence, as what was previously repeated without question is now being challenged or discarded.

Let us look, first of all, at the background to the rise of Islam, at the Near and Middle East in the 620s and 630s, when the activities of a preacher, called Muhammad, and his Arab followers first enter history. The world, as it concerns us here, was divided between two superpowers: in the West, the later Roman (or early Byzantine) Empire, and in the East the Persian (or Iranian) Empire.

The Roman Empire had for long possessed Egypt, Syria, Palestine and what is now Turkey. Its main religion was Christianity. In the previous hundred years it had been badly weakened: by over-expansion in the western Mediterranean, by overtaxation in the eastern Mediterranean, by plague, by war, by autocracy, by internal struggle and, most significantly, by religious persecution. This last had been aimed at the vigorous and independent Christian traditions of Egypt and Syria, often branded as 'heretical', as well as at the Jewish and Samaritan minorities in Palestine. The Roman Empire's rich eastern provinces were ripe for revolt from within or easy conquest from without, ripe for a new solution of sectarian differences and quarrels between religious communities.

The Persian Empire had for long consisted mainly of Iran and Iraq. Its main religion was Mazdaism ('Zoroastrianism'), a faith weakened by the persecuting, archaic, inward-looking and class-bound character which it had assumed by that time. The Persian Empire itself had been weakened, in the previous century, by war and by the bloody repression of a communistic revolt, as well as by its inability to come to terms with a variety of religious movements and creeds. In Iraq the Jewish and Christian components of the population offered radically different and challenging alternatives.

In the first three decades of the seventh century dramatic events took place on a large scale, as the forces of the Persian Empire swept into the eastern provinces of its Roman adversary, only to suffer defeat and invasion in their own turn. As the holy places of the Near East changed hands literature was composed which spoke of messianic hopes and even more cataclysmic occurrences.

In sum, then, we can say that conditions had never been so propitious for the advent of a new religion, or at least a religion that has been seen as new, and never so propitious for a military explosion and expansion often viewed as little short of miraculous. The impetus was to come from another quarter: the Arabian peninsula.

Very little is known of the Arabs before Islam. The literary materials are late and open to the charge that they represent Islamic preoccupations, attempts, for doctrinal purposes, to create a certain image of the society in which Islam appeared. The northern Arabs, the 'Saracens', were wanderers of the desert, 'Bedouin', often used by the superpowers for military purposes. In the south lay the ancient sedentary civilisation of the 'happy' Arabs, conquered for Iran in the sixth century CE. In Arabia there were some Christians and Jews, some partly Christianised and Judaicised Arabs, and, for the most part, worshippers of many indigenous Arabian gods.

An older generation of Western scholars still continues to concentrate on the specifically Arabian evidence as important for the study of the origins of Islam. They stress the value of examining present-day Arabian tribes, and the archaeological materials, notably in southern Arabia. Against this, younger Western scholars have emphasised that just as Islam has projected its teachings backwards into the life of Muhammad, so too it has projected its beginnings back into the Arabian peninsula, thereby disguising its indebtedness to the civilised territories, from Egypt to Iran, which the Arabs were to conquer.

It is with this in mind that we must now consider the traditional version, given by the Muslims themselves, of the rise of Islam. Of this historical tradition it must be said from the outset that it is found in late works, not considered reliable by some contemporary Islamicists. For example, the earliest and most-used biography of Muhammad dates from the mid-eighth century, and is preserved in a recension of the early ninth.

According to this traditional account Muhammad would have been born around 570 in the city of Mecca, in central western Arabia. An orphan, he would have engaged in trade, received revelations, acquired followers, been persecuted, fled to Medina, some two hundred miles to the north, formed an alliance of Arabs and Jews there, engaged in local warfare, conquered Mecca and died in 632 in Medina. In the meantime, in addition to the revelations received, and quickly collected as the Qur'an (Recitation), he uttered an enormous number of important sayings, and gave an enormous number of examples of conduct, while approving others by his silence. These sayings and examples were remembered by his Companions and transmitted by them in oral form to succeeding generations (as 'Traditions'). Taken together with the Qur'an, they formed the basis of Islam: a complete guide to all human activity. In sum, the Prophet Muhammad would, with the help of divine intervention, have instituted a religion in a remarkably short period of time.

After this, the Islamic historical tradition continues to relate, the Muslim community was ruled by a 'caliph' (deputy), called Abu Bakr, from 632 to 634. It would have been his successor, Umar (634–44), who began the conquest of Palestine, which was quickly accompanied by that of Syria, Egypt, Iraq and Iran. The murder of his successor, Uthman (644–56), started the First Civil War, between Ali, both cousin and son-in-law to Muhammad, reigning from 656 to 661, and a family known as the Umayyads. The latter, who ruled over the Muslim community from Syria until 750, are considered to have been bad and unIslamic, unlike their successors from 750 onwards, the Abbasid dynasty, which ruled from Iraq.

At this point we might remark, first of all, that since the history books were written under the Abbasid dynasty it is not surprising that their predecessors should receive a rather hostile treatment. Then we have to consider the whole nature of the Islamic historical tradition in the same way. It is late, biased and, in its portrayal of early religious developments, difficult to accept for anyone experienced in the comparison of historical and literary materials. That it should have been largely accepted for so long by orientialists is an extreme example of the results of over-specialisation in universities after the First World War.

The standard Muslim biography of Muhammad, composed well over a hundred years after his death, and edited in the ninth century, is the earliest extended narrative that we possess. Today no serious student of early Christianity would imagine that its beginnings could be reconstructed, or the life of Jesus convincingly retold, if so lengthy an interval existed between our sources and the period to which they refer. Although lives of other alleged founders of religions, such as the Buddha and Zarathushtra, still continue to appear, based on tardy and legendary materials of the same kind, the historian can only smile. As for 'modern' portraits of Muhammad, in which Marxist sociological surveys rest on the flimsiest tatters of historical 'fact', and Freudian psychoanalysis is brought to bear on a personality who remains a shadow, the less said the better. Ironically, such productions tend to come not from those who speak at the greatest length of 'methodology'. To admit, as many do, that the sources are entirely unreliable, and then to construct a narrative based upon them, is indefensible in logic.

Thus the *Sira*, or standard biography of Muhammad, composed by one Ibn Ishaq in the middle of the eighth century, produces, as one might imagine, a justification of the new, Abbasid dynasty and a reflection of Jewish and Christian traditional lore about what a prophet should be like. It represents the results of long processes of sectarian and regional rivalries. Not only does it project back into the life of Muhammad developments that must have taken much longer than a single life-span; it also projects back into Arabia a vast array of elements that belong to Palestine, Syria and Iraq.

It is at this point that we must consider sources outside the Islamic historical tradition. Not much can be gleaned from the surviving inscriptions, papyri, coins and archaeological evidence relating to early Islam. That leaves us with Christian and Jewish sources, in practice almost entirely the former. These sources are often much earlier than the Islamic ones, and, when they are not so old, can be seen as preserving very old traditions, owing to the fossilising character of the Christian minorities of the Near and Middle East. Now these materials have recently been used, with very great talent, to offer a speculative reconstruction of the course taken by Muhammad and the Arabs after him. Here it must be said that such attempts are in themselves admirable and very long overdue. For them to be conducted more successfully, however, it is necessary first of all to examine the Christian writings more closely, in order to determine as accurately as possible not only when they were written, but from what sectarian positions in relation to others, and in order to judge how the various statements, made from differing perspectives, stand with reference to one another.

Another view would be that these Christian sources for the life of Muhammad and the activities of his successors are, like the Muslim ones, so fragmentary, biased and ill-informed that no reconstruction of the events is possible, and we should confine ourselves to purely literary analyses of both these and the Islamic materials: we should study only the games which authors play, and texts play unbeknownst to them, in the pursuit of attacks upon religious adversaries. Such a view can, while opposing the attempted reconstruction of 'what really happened', indirectly assist it, by improving historians' appreciation of what they read.

In the perspectives of the Christian sources the origins of Islam appear in a very different light. They seem to be situated on a Palestine–north Arabia axis, instead of a Mecca–Medina one in central west Arabia. Here corroboration is afforded by the geographical indications of the Qur'an itself and the orientation of the earliest mosques. As for the alliance with the Jews, it seems to have lasted for some time after Muhammad's death, and not to have been dissolved in his lifetime, as the Islamic tradition claims. The orientation of worship towards Mecca, ascribed by the Muslim sources to the Prophet himself, would appear to be much later. As for the death of Muhammad, placed by Islamic historians in 632 in Medina, there is much evidence to suggest that he was alive and leading the conquest of Palestine in 634.

In a way, there is a common thread to the standard Muslim version of Muhammad's life on the one hand and what has been reconstructed of the rise of Islam on the basis of the Christian sources on the other. In both, there is an initial preaching on Muhammad's part; then there is an alliance with the Jews; then there is a break with the Jews, followed by an orientation of worship towards Mecca. We can suspect what anyone might naturally have suspected: a compression of events into one man's career as they are projected backwards into the past. From this we can now proceed to a consideration of the Qur'an.

Islamic tradition gives different and contradictory accounts about how the Qur'an was put together. They unite in agreeing that this was done very early on, at the latest within a quarter-century of Muhammad's death. This the modern specialist may doubt. The external indications, as we have seen, point to a prolonged period of development for the germination of the new creed. The internal evidence of the Qur'an is one of the most marked confusion. Widely disparate teachings, at considerable variance with one another, again point to a long period of development. As for the chronology furnished by Muslim tradition, it seems largely to answer the demands of moral edification and the lawyers' doctrine that some verses were 'abrogated' by others. It goes along with the biography discussed above. As for the practice of assigning some parts of the Qur'an to a Meccan period, and others to a Medinan one, often on the basis that poetic, 'inspired' passages must be early and Meccan, and that prosaic legal ones must be late and Medinan, it must be said that some contemporary scholars would find this procedure somewhat arbitrary.

The field of Qur'anic studies, until recently virtually untouched by the methods applied by modern biblical criticism, is now a very open one, in which the most widely divergent interpretations can easily be offered. In form the Qur'an is extremely disjointed. It switches rapidly from one subject to another. It is repetitive, often telling the same story in variant versions and in content markedly multivoiced. Dominated by the praise of God, it gives biblical stories, attacks on opponents, references to contemporary events and legal prescriptions, all very much mixed together. It does not tell us much about Muhammad, unless one combines it with the traditional biography and chronology already discussed.

The Qur'an is immensely important for Muslims, but primarily as what it is held to be, namely the speech of God, rather than for what it says and in its immediate presence to the believer, memorised in his heart. But its actual words do not appear, in themselves, to have had a great influence on the early growth of Islamic beliefs and institutions. Muslim theologians, like Jewish and Christian ones, seem to have constructed their doctrines largely independently of scripture, doing so often in response to Christian theology, as both adversary and model. Some Muslim lawyers have bypassed the Qur'an in the founding of Islamic jurisprudence, which rests mainly on Jewish elements in the form of 'Traditions'. Muslim mystics have preserved Eastern Christian spirituality without overt assistance from the Qur'an, which on the surface at least gave them little encouragement. All these classes of thinkers refer constantly to the Qur'an: none of them owe much of their historical genesis to it. Indeed, recent research indicates that in the eighth century CE the Qur'an and the Traditions were considered to be on the same level, equal in authority. In some of these Traditions God speaks in the first person: divine speech is not restricted to the Qur'an alone.

Proceeding now to what has been attributed to Muhammad's successors, we find that here again the sources are determined by literary and doctrinal considerations. As for the First Civil War of 656–61, the sectarian interpretations and accounts of the ensuing period preclude any confident reconstruction. It was desperately important for later Muslims to decide which side one should have supported, that of Ali on the one hand or that of the Umayyads on the other, or what further alternative or compromise would have been correct. The various sects of Islam largely defined themselves by their retrospective positions in this complicated tale of internecine disarray, as they applauded the noble stands attributed to their predecessors. Our present hopes of disentangling the consequent reworking of 'history' are slim.

It is only later in the seventh century CE that the proto-Muslims seem to begin to produce the actual framework of an independent Islam. Muslim coinage, Muslim inscriptions and Muslim architecture, along with the reconstruction of the beginnings of Islamic theology and Tradition-collecting, all point to the 690s and 700s as the period in which the emergent faith finally blossomed. It is at this time too that real historical events come into focus. But it is not until late Umayyad times that detailed reconstruction of the religious developments becomes at all possible (and some would doubt that) and even after the Abbasid take-over in 750 the sources continue to blind the observer with mirror-like reduplications of earlier narratives.

At this point we must turn our attention to the rise of the Muslim Traditions and the closely allied field of Islamic law. The word *hadith*, usually rendered in English as 'Tradition', means a report of something said, done or tacitly accepted by a leading figure of early Islam. Eventually it was to mean, for most Muslims, a report about Muhammad, or, for the minority Shi'ite sect characterised by its extreme devotion to his family, a report about one of the early 'leaders' (imams) therein. Now main-line Islam accepts the authenticity of a large number of canonically established Traditions about Muhammad. Upon these Islamic law, doctrine and practice are largely based. Western scholars, however, have challenged the authenticity of these Traditions. They have argued that the content reflects the social, economic, political and doctrinal history of the first three centuries of Islam. They have also argued that originally Traditions were reports about persons other than Muhammad, and that these reports were then transformed into ones about the Prophet himself. They have attacked the 'pedigrees' which precede the Traditions as guarantees of authenticity. In these A says that he has heard from B, who heard from C, and so on, that Muhammad said or did this or that.

Now it is obviously easy to forge a pedigree, just as it is easy to forge a Tradition. It is also easy to extend a pedigree backwards a bit to reach Muhammad. The Muslim exponents of the discipline in which the Traditions are studied concentrate on the pedigrees. They try to determine whether B and C could have met, and whether they were reliable transmitters. These Muslim scholars have accepted that forgery, backward extension and other 'improvements' of pedigrees were practised on a large scale. None the less, they have maintained that, especially given the apparent confirmation of authenticity by multiple pedigrees for some Traditions, a reasonably extensive bed-rock of sound materials remains.

Recent study in the West has pointed to the beginning of the eighth century CE as the period in which the majority of the most ancient Traditions originated, and to Iraq as the region of their first major expansion. Thus it was in Iraq that the greatest effort was made in developing Islam in the eighth century, and it seems reasonable to connect this, as far as law is concerned, with the important Jewish minority there, which showed considerable vigour (unlike the Jews of Palestine, who were largely cowed by persecution). From this comes the Jewish character of many of the Muslim Traditions which relate to jurisprudence. Traditions of a mystical character, on the other hand, seem to reflect the work of the Christians of Iraq, and notably the Nestorians, who were close to and on good terms with the Muslims, and the authors of a rich literature of spirituality. As for the men mentioned in the pedigrees, the large number of people alleged to have had the same unusual name, coupled with the same father's name, and studying with the same master is such as to raise considerable doubt. As for what was eventually to become main-line Muslim dogma, namely, that all of the Prophet's Companions were truthful in transmitting Traditions, this is not directly contradicted by recent Western research, in which it does not appear that they were transmitting at all. Here again, one must regret the naïve and literalistic acceptance of materials by previous Western writers, who failed to recognise the complicated interplay of the factors involved.

When we turn to the rise of Islamic law, we may first of all remark that this has usually been considered an extremely tedious subject. It is indeed true that the books about this field are distinctly dry. But

Muslim jurisprudence could be studied in a lively manner, and deserves to be, since it includes not just what is usually understood as 'law', but also politics and ethics. The Iranian Revolution of 1978–9, dominated by the figure of a jurist, the Ayatollah Khomeini, amply demonstrates Islamic law's importance. Law has always been the main discipline within Islam, however much it has been despised by those who saw themselves as the mystical elite.

As regards the early history of Islamic law, we are largely dependent upon the reconstruction put forward by the late Joseph Schacht, whose work is also fundamental to the study of the Traditions. According to him law would appear to have been based originally upon local, provincial custom, and upon a judge's appeal to his own common sense. Later on it is principally in Iraq that the development of jurisprudence, in a specifically Islamic way, takes place, in the course of the eighth century CE. In this development the Traditions are brought in, and eventually it is decided that only Traditions going back to Muhammad himself have authority, along with the Qur'an. By the middle of the ninth century the ancient provincial 'schools of law' had been transformed into new, Islamic schools of law, consisting of the followers of individual masters, not regions. In the ninth century the old theory of 'consensus', according to which the local, regional agreement of legal experts was considered binding in a given question, was renewed in the same way, as the consensus of each new school of law. These schools were to differ in their theories of how 'personal discretion' was to be used alongside the Qur'an, the Traditions and consensus: whether one should use 'analogy', 'personal preference', or 'having regard for the public interest', or avoid using one's own discretion at all. Eventually, as some schools of law died out, only four remained among the great majority of main-line (Sunni) Muslims, each recognising the perfect respectability of the others.

Now the localisation of early Islamic jurisprudence in Iraq, and the similarity of Islamic law to Jewish law, in their common universality, in their recognition of individual scholars as having authority and in a vast number of individual details, undoubtedly point to the Babylonian Jewish community of Iraq, with its rich independent culture, as the source. Indeed, it is a noteworthy example of self-criticism in Islam that Muslim lawyers are considered to have erred by being too like the Jews, while Muslim mystics are considered to have erred by being too like the Christians.

By the end of the ninth century CE it was felt that the main problems of Islamic jurisprudence had been answered. From now on, in mainstream (Sunni) Islam, it was considered that independent, personal discretion should be abandoned in favour of the decisions of the old masters. An unthinking and pedantic attitude prevailed, doubtless increased by the circumstance that Islamic law, in criminal matters at any rate, was usually found too liberal to be applied in practice. In the minority Sh'ite sect, however, characterised by its extreme devotion to the family of Muhammad, the freedom to interpret and decide anew remained. The actual details of Shi'ite law, none the less, are extremely similar to those of the Sunni majority, in spite of the differences in theory. The important distinguishing factor in Sh'ite jurisprudence is not so much its emphasis on Muhammad's family, constituting the source of law, as the independence in political action which it bestows upon the qualified jurist. Here the contemporary significance emerges when one considers the Iranian Revolution of 1978–9 and the ensuing exercise of power by prominent legal experts.

We must now turn to the rise of Muslim theology, and the early divisions into sects. Here too our sources are extremely obscure. The student must be warned that some of the Arabic materials on which European studies are based have been attacked as forgeries, and that the difficulties of authentication and chronology are enormous. In general it would seem that Islamic theology grew up largely in imitation of, and in hostile response to, Christian theology. The central debates, as to whether God determined human actions, whether God's speech was created and whether God's attributes were identical with his essence, had their roots in Christianity and followed Christian patterns. But theology was never to have in Islam the pre-eminence that it assumed in Christianity. The lawyers and the mystics, not the theologians, were to dominate the Muslim community.

As for the various sects or sub-sects presented by our sources, many of them are doubtless fictitious, invented in a sustained effort of personal literary creation. This is often the case with the multiple varieties attributed to Islam's principal minority, the Shi'a, literally the 'Party' of Muhammad's family. Now this Party is not only distinguished by its veneration for, and loyalty to, Fatima, the Prophet's daughter, and Ali, seen as her husband, along with their descendants; it is also noted for its belief in the infallibility of Ali and other 'leaders' (imams), who, the Shi'ites consider, should be the rulers both spiritual and temporal of Islam.

Thus the Shi'a, the Party, bears a resemblance to the Roman Catholic Church, with its belief in papal infallibility. It is a sect of mediations, unlike the Sunni majority, which resembles Protestantism, placing the individual believer alone and immediately before his Maker. The Shi'a also is characterised by, among other things, its sophisticated development of theory and its political aspects, notably its messianic appeal to an ideal of justice, and its hostility to the established authorities.

The Shi'a's two most significant sub-sects are the 'Twelvers' and the Ismailis. The Twelvers are so called because they recognise twelve 'leaders' in succession to Muhammad. Of these the last is thought to have disappeared and to be waiting for the right moment to come back as an ideal ruler, the Mahdi or 'divinely guided one'. The concept of such an ideal ruler exists in mainstream Islam as well, but in Twelver Shi'ism he assumes an overriding contemporary psychological, political and cosmic importance, present in the hearts of the faithful, guiding the political decisions of the leading jurists and holding the life of the universe together. The Twelvers are also largely concerned with the subject of martyrdom, and notably the killing of Ali's son Husein. This event is commemorated in annual festivals, in which popular emotion is mobilised against the unjust temporal powers of this world.

As for the Ismailis, they are much less numerous, and indeed by their very nature constitute a severely restricted elite. Named after a figure in an early dynastic split, which cuts them off from the Twelvers, they recognise a continuing line of 'leaders' up to the present day, the best-known claimant being the Aga Khan. They were celebrated in early Islam for their clandestine propaganda and jealously guarded esoteric lore, both preserved in a tightly knit hierarchical organisation. Their dramatic view of history as a series of cycles, their emphasis on the value of different civilisations and their boldness in political adventures made them an exciting and serious challenge to mainstream Islam.

Similarly adventurous, but outside Shi'ism and in contrast to it, were the Kharijites, literally the 'Goers-out', who would 'go out' of the Muslim community and start armed rebellions. The sources present them as extremely democratic, notably in their elections of leaders, who could be deposed for the most trivial of sins, owing to the sect's marked puritanism. Not surprisingly, they ended up as a marginal force in outlying areas. Their discussions of who is and who is not a Muslim remain of prime importance, as this issue is debated today with burning vigour.

More prudent were the Murjiites, the 'Suspensionists', who cautiously suspended judgement on difficult theological and political questions, leaving them to the ultimate decision of the Deity. This lack of confidence in human reason may represent a continuation of the Sceptical/Empirical tradition of philosophy in the ancient Greco-Roman world. Little is known of this sect, and its apparent ineffectiveness was soon followed by its disappearance.

Equally doomed were the Qadarites, called after the term *Qadar*, which denotes the 'decree' of God. They, however, held that man could decree and decide his own acts, a position which seems to come from Christianity, and was rejected by mainstream Islam. Also maintaining the doctrine of man's free will, but more important, were the Mutazilites, the 'Withdrawers', who did indeed cut themselves off from the rest of the Muslim community in their arrogant intellectual conceit. They borrowed the arguments and methods of Greek philosophy to attack main-line views which they saw as vulgar, such as the belief that the faithful will actually see God in the next world, and the opinion that the Qur'an, as God's speech, is eternal and uncreated. Some European writers have seen them as 'liberal', enlightened rationalists. In reality they were bigoted persecutors who used the apparatus of the State to torture their opponents into recantation. They were to give way to a new school of theology, which brought about a compromise between them and their opponents.

This school was that of the Asharites, named after their founder, al-Ashari (d. 935). It adopted a series of half-way positions, in which God creates men's actions but men acquire responsibility for them, the Qur'an is uncreated speech in one aspect but created in another, and so on. The believer has to accept these combinations 'without asking how'. The Asharite school thus acquired a reputation of safe if not profound respectability. It must be borne in mind, however, that many Muslims were against the use of theology completely, and Muslim mystics were to hold it in low esteem.

It is indeed time for us to consider the principal movement of Islamic mysticism, Sufism. Recent research has emphasised the existence of mystical currents outside Sufism, notably in Sh'ism and Islamic philosophy, but old-fashioned writers continue to speak of the main movement as the sole manifestation of Muslim spirituality.

The Arabic word *Sufi*, meaning an adherent of the movement, is derived from the Arabic for wool, *suf*. This is because the early members wore wool, in the manner of Christian ascetics. Here we have the first of many indications that Sufism is mainly a continuation of Eastern Christian elements. Other explanations of the word can be rejected as philologically unsound.

It was in Syrian Christianity that the mortification of the flesh was carried to its greatest extremes—carrying heavy weights, living off roots and so on, without the intellectual and academic superiority of Iraq. Thus in Syrian Islam the beginnings of the spiritual life are naturally represented in our sources as marked by asceticism: voluntary poverty, 'weeping', vigils and fasting.

This world-denying tendency, accompanied by the fear of God, is indeed shown by the sources as dominating the beginnings of Sufism everywhere. But we must be aware of the legendary and fragmentary character of the materials, and the constructions erected upon them by early Western orientalists. The latter have, for example, tended to dismiss the Traditions most used by Sufis as ninth-century creations, and Sufism itself as coming into Islam after the latter had already been established as a severe religion without the prospect of love and intimate communion between God and man. Indeed, recent research has shown that there are no good grounds for believing that the Traditions used by the Sufis in the ninth century are any later in origin than the rest. But the student need not take as historical the claims that Muhammad himself started the movement, secretly initiating founders who then began 'pedigrees' of successors. These pedigrees are not to be taken as genuine for the earliest period. Nor need the student accept the view, often repeated, that Sufism grew up naturally out of a Qur'anic revelation to Muhammad and his own teachings.

It is rather in Iraq, under the shadow of the Nestorian Christian Church, and doubtless in the minds of converts to Islam who preserved their original culture, that we are to find the continuation of ideas. In Iraq, in the ninth century, we find historical Sufi individuals with texts to their credit, exposing the themes of repentance, poverty and the love of God. A rich anecdotal literature attests to early Sufi interest in Christian practices and institutions, and Sufi contacts with and conversions from Christianity.

It is against this background that we must consider also the possibility of Indian influences. Over the centuries there was undoubtedly considerable borrowing in the form of meditational techniques, but at the level of doctrine there does not appear to have been any significant effect. An exception is the case of the Iranian Abu Yazid (d. *c.* 874), whose unmistakably Indian utterances, such as 'Glory be to me!', and 'I sloughed off my self as a snake sloughs off its skin: then I looked into my self and lo! I was He', along with the rejection of this world, seen in the form of a tree, as a deceitful illusion, undoubtedly point to the teaching of an Indian master. This has been powerfully demonstrated by the late R.C. Zaehner. It is beyond the bounds of possibility that such an accumulation of Indian expressions could have occurred without a direct historical influence.

Zaehner errs, however, in imagining that Abu Yazid completely changed the course of development of Islamic mysticism, and brought it from being theistic, oriented towards God, into monism, the doctrine that there is only one Being in all existence. If one examines the works of the sophisticated Sufi leaders in Baghdad, it is clear that they were certainly interested in this somewhat eccentric provincial, but did not want what he had to offer. They continued on their own path, aiming at the restoration of a primordial union of the mystic with God, expressed in a pre-eternal covenant between God and man. Thus the Sufi's aim was to become once more an idea in the mind of God, as one was before one's temporal creation. This is achieved by 'annihilation', in which the mystic experiences the passing-away of his separate, earthly existence.

The dangers inherent in Islam's uneasy blend of Christian spirituality and Judaic legalism were strikingly demonstrated in the execution of Sufism's most famous martyr, Hallaj (d. 922). His name has always been associated with the unwise popular divulging of secret Sufi doctrine, and in particular a supposed claim of being identical with God, although Sufism in fact denies that it has any such teaching. Whatever really happened in his colourful career, and whatever his ideas may actually have been, the Muslims certainly believed that in his case there had been an alarming lurch towards alien belief, one that could not be allowed to happen again, since it threatened the delicate balance achieved in Islam through careful compromise.

Equally dangerous in the eyes of the Muslims was the menace posed by Greek philosophy. We must now consider the beginnings of the Islamic philosophical tradition in its Hellenised background. For this tradition is really the continuation of a number of sciences, ranging from astronomy to logic, from ethics to medicine, from music to alchemy, inherited from the world of late antiquity.

Now it has been fashionable in the past, and it is still common among some writers, to view Islamic philosophy as a brief episode of transition, from ancient Greek philosophy on the one hand to medieval European thought on the other. This narrow perspective has naturally led to dull and uninspiring studies, in which the rich flowering of later Muslim thinking has been ignored. But in the present survey we are limited to the consideration of early Islam, and are therefore prevented from analysing the manifold achievement and profusion of Islamic thought.

The process of translating Greek philosophical literature out of Syriac, the language of Christians under Muslim rule, into Arabic was naturally dominated by the Christians themselves, who were also the masters of philosophical teaching in the first centuries of Islam, and notably in the first half of the ninth century, when the Abbasid caliphs patronised a wide range of inter-cultural activities. Not surprisingly, philosophy was seen as alien to and hostile to Islam. This was not without good cause. A variety of thinkers with bizarre, impious or sceptical ideas came into view, but one line dominated, that of Neoplatonism, defined in Islamic terms in the tenth century, and constituting the basis of most subsequent Islamic philosophy. In this God's creation of the world was denied: the universe was rather deemed to 'emanate' from him in a process of overflowing. God's intimate knowledge of particular things was also denied: he was said to know things only in a 'universal' way. His future bodily resurrection of the dead, also a cornerstone of mainstream Muslim belief, was furthermore denied by the philosophers of the Islamic world.

Thus the philosophers would be denounced as non-Muslims, as unbelievers, by the theologians and jurists, who were supported by the violence of the populace. As they were to turn for protection to the rulers of the day they were naturally to be identified with tyranny. But their ideas continued to be taken over, adapted and used by their enemies, notably the Sufis. A tiny and marginal minority, the philosophers none the less exerted enormous influence.

Our consideration of the patronage given to philosophers brings us briefly to review the progress of the Abbasid line of caliphs, who reigned from 750 onwards, making Baghdad their capital. After their grand period of splendour in the first half of the ninth century, in which they favoured both the translation of philosophical works and the Mutazilite school of theology, they declined as local, provincial rulers came to the fore, and also as the slave soldiers on whom they came to depend turned into their masters. From the tenth century, as Shi'ite dynasties temporarily took over in much of the Muslim world, the Abbasid caliphs continued as religious, rather than as temporal leaders.

With this short historical sketch behind us we can now examine the main lines of Muslim belief and practice, as they emerge from the early development, in the majority grouping, the Sunnis, so called because they concentrate on what they see as the 'established custom' (*sunna*) of Muhammad. We shall use the traditional headings of the 'five pillars' of Islam, although they do not really reflect the variety of Muslim doctrines and institutions.

First, there is the attestation of belief, that there is no god except God and Muhammad is his Messenger. In fact the Muslim has to believe much more, notably that there is no Trinity and that God has no Son; that Muhammad is the last of a line of prophets, which includes Jesus, accepted as the Christ but not as divine, and that there will be a bodily resurrection, heaven and hell.

Secondly, there is the ritual worship, five times a day, performed either where one happens to be or in a place set aside for worship, a mosque. The worship consists of a series of bodily movements, along with the recitation of given formulas. It gave the Muslims a discipline of the body that European Christians, outside the monastic orders, were not to find until modern times. It does not exhaust the category of 'prayer', or indeed of religious exercises in general, which were much developed by the Sufis.

Thirdly, there is the alms-tax, the *zakat*. Recently Michael Cook has done well to point out the decisively overwhelming evidence for the Judaic character of this term, in which the acquiring of merit for oneself is indissoluble from the act of giving away a proportion of one's wealth for the poor.

Fourthly, there is the fasting during daylight in the month of Ramadan. This has been noted as in fact much more important than the ritual worship, since in traditional Muslim societies in which the latter has been largely neglected the fast, at least in public, has been observed by all.

Fifthly and finally, there is the pilgrimage to Mecca. This is rather less important for the ordinary Muslim, since only a small minority of Muslims have in practice been able to perform it. Thus, although it demands the suppression of social differences and class distinctions during its actual performance, it serves to reinforce such barriers through the added prestige which it confers on those wealthy enough to afford its accomplishment.

Sometimes added to these five is the duty of holy war, a perpetual obligation incumbent on the Muslim community as a whole. However, it is important to avoid the popular myth that conversion to Islam was universally imposed and achieved at the point of the sword. In practice it appears to have been brought about largely through taxation, which discriminated in favour of the Muslims. It grew doubtless also through dissatisfaction with existing creeds.

Such, then, are some of the main aspects, divisions and movements of Islam as it emerged up to the mid-tenth century. This early period is usually called the 'formative' one, wrongly, since an early period of germination is by no means necessarily more 'formative' than a later one of structuring, systematisation and definitive codification. Thus it is only later that we encounter in Islam the important institution of the college, the *madrasah*, which was everywhere to dominate legal life. It is only later that we find the appearance of organised brotherhoods in Sufism, operating as political forces, and above all the extreme veneration accorded to leading Sufis, alive or dead. It is this last feature which casts its shadow over the succeeding centuries, and which, from the thirteenth century onwards, constitutes a kind of 'Counter-Reformation' in Islam. For the veneration of these figures to some extent resembles that of the saints in Catholicism.

This leads us to consider the parallel often drawn between the Protestant Reformation and the rise of Islam. To be sure, the Sunni majority has much in common with Protestantism. Islam does not actually present itself as a new religion, but as the restoration of an old one, freed from the corruptions brought in by Jews and Christians. So it sees itself as the restored religion of Jesus, accepted as the Christ.

But along with the comparison with the Reformation we can make another one, which at first sight may seem surprising: with the European Enlightenment of the eighteenth century. For Islam has no Church and no clergy (although Western writers often, and wrongly, so designate the Muslim jurists). It has no Trinity, no Incarnation, no Redemption, no Original Sin. Thus it avoids certain main features of Christianity which the deists of the eighteenth century ridiculed. Perhaps we can see in early Islam the same attempt as that made in the Enlightenment, to produce a simple, lowest-common-denominator religion. Just as the commercial interests of Europe were to demand a simplification of religious belief, so that sectarian squabbles over non-essentials would not impede the progress of trade, so too we may perhaps discern, in the activities of the proto-Muslims and their successors, a similar accommodation to mercantile imperatives. Early Christian and Muslim sources agree that Muhammad himself was a trader; the early Muslim literature is full of the vocabulary and preoccupations of merchants. But here the field is full of traps and technical terms that defy comprehension: the analysis cannot, for the moment, be taken further.

Early Islam, then, is a complex mixture of varied elements, brought together over a long period of time. The mere cataloguing of these elements, however, and the identification of their provenance, indispensable though that is, cannot provide either an 'explanation' or an understanding of a religion. Nor, for that matter, can the delineation of a 'structure'. What one must do is try to appreciate the nature and functioning of the various articulations by which contrary elements in Islam work together: the Jewish and the Christian, the legal and the mystical, the monarchical and the tribal, the urban and the nomadic. Therein lie the mysteries of Islam. The word *Islam* itself, alongside the usual translation of 'submission', has been seen as having different original meanings, such as 'entering into a state of peace'. It is doubtless in the ambiguous and ambivalent character of Islam, both as religion and as society and civilisation, that its capacity for radically new initiatives resides.

Further Reading

Arberry, Arthur John (tr.) *The Koran Interpreted* (Oxford University Press, Oxford, 1983)

Cook, Michael *Muhammad* (Oxford University Press, Oxford, 1985)

Coulson, Noel J. *A History of Islamic Law* (Edinburgh University Press, Edinburgh, 1978)

Smith, Margaret *Studies in Early Mysticism in the Near and Middle East* (London, 1930), reprinted as *The Way of the Mystics* (Sheldon Press, London, 1976)

Sourdel, Dominique *Medieval Islam* (Routledge & Kegan Paul, London, 1983)

Watt, William Montgomery *Islamic Philosophy and Theology* (Edinburgh University Press, Edinburgh, 1979)

Zaehner, Robert Charles *Hindu and Muslim Mysticism* (Shocken, New York, 1970)

21 Islam in North Africa

M. Brett

North Africa is formed by the bloc of the Atlas mountains between the Sahara and the Mediterranean. The ranges, 4,000, 8,000 and 12,000 feet high, run parallel to the desert and the sea, enclosing a great upland stretching from Morocco across Algeria to Tunisia. In the west they open on to lowlands that spread down to the Atlantic coast to Morocco, and in the east on to the plains and coastal districts of Tunisia. Along the length of the coast runs a belt of Mediterranean climate that gives way to steppe and then to desert inland. The pattern is repeated in Libya, where the hills are lower and the Sahara closer to the sea. Corresponding to this diversity of landscape and climate, an equal diversity of ways of life—urban and rural, agricultural and pastoral, settled and nomadic—is still recognisable despite the pressures of modernisation. Different forms of the one religion go with this variety, modified but not yet abolished by the secularism of the twentieth century, and by the standardisation of the faith that has accompanied the formation of national societies. These forms and their various combinations over the centuries represent North African Islam.

At its introduction into North Africa in the seventh and eighth centuries, Islam was the faith of foreign conquerors, the Arabs. These conquerors found a region which was politically divided between the Byzantine Empire in the east and native peoples in the west. The Byzantine province of Africa, comprising Tunisia, Tripolitania and eastern Algeria, was ruled from Carthage near Tunis. In the towns and the more settled regions on the coast and inland, the population spoke Latin, and was Christian. In the mountains and deserts, on the other hand, the population was Berber, that is, speaking the indigenous language of North Africa called after the Latin *barbarus*, barbarian. Although this population might be controlled from Carthage, it was not for the most part under direct rule. It was tribal, by which I mean 'stateless' or 'acephalous' in the anthropological sense of peoples who basically governed themselves according to custom enforced either by the feud or by some collective sanction. These peoples had names of vague and shifting application, such as Lawata, Hawwara, Zanata and Sanhaja; they had their elders and their war-chiefs and sometimes their princes, allies or enemies of the imperial government in a tradition stretching back to the kings of Numidia and Mauretania at the time of the Punic Wars. Berbers like these delayed the Arab conquest of Byzantine Africa until *c.* 700 CE, but once the province had been annexed to the Arab empire centred on Damascus in Syria, the invaders moved rapidly westwards through wholly Berber territory to Tangier, then on into Spain, which they had conquered from the Visigoths by 715.

The Arabs were an army of the faithful, *muminun*, men who had put their faith, *iman*, in God, his Prophet, and his Prophet's successors as Commanders of the Faithful, or caliphs. This faith, in the old English sense of a promise to be kept by both parties to an agreement, separated them from the rest of humanity, whom it was their mission to subjugate. As a militant community of the faithful, they were physically set apart in the *misr* (pl. *amsar*), the garrison city set up by the Arabs as a base camp at each stage of their advance, which then developed into the capital of each region. Beginning with Fustat in Egypt, on the site of Cairo, these garrison cities were first Barqa (Barce) in Cyrenaica, then Tripoli, Qayrawan (Kairouan) in Tunisia, Tlemcen, Tangier and finally Cordoba in Spain. Those whom they conquered became tax-paying subjects. In Egypt this was simple. As Christians the inhabitants were declared to be 'People of the Book', believers in God under the *dhimma* or protection of the faithful who believed in his final message: in return for this protection they paid a special poll-tax in addition to their other dues. In Byzantine Africa, now Ifriqiya, the same regime could be imposed on the Latin Christians. Rightly or wrongly, however, the tribal Berbers were not counted as Christian, and when conquered were therefore obliged to make their submission to the Arabs and to God. This submission was called *islam*, and those who made it, *muslimun*. These Berber *muslimun* or submitters were in an ambiguous position. On the one hand they were conquered people and subjects required to pay tribute; this tribute was typically a tribute of slaves, male and female. On the other hand, they were affiliated by their *islam* to the Arab community of the faithful. Some chosen Berbers, most of whom were probably first enslaved, were therefore taken into the army of the faithful as *mawali* (sing. *mawla*), 'clients' of the Arabs. Others, still tribesmen, joined the army's campaigns. Thus after the Berber resistance in Byzantine Africa had been overcome, a large force was assembled for the rapid march on Tangier and Spain.

The problem arose after the conquest of Spain, when the horizon of the conquest was far away on the Pyrenees, and the Umayyad caliphs at Damascus endeavoured to bring North Africa under regular administration by insisting on the tribute due from conquered Berber peoples who had identified themselves with the conquerors. The rebellion which broke out at Tangier in 739 was intended as a revolution to replace the caliph of the Umayyad dynasty at Damascus with a new Commander of the Faithful. Its leaders were Kharijites, from *kharaja*, to go out, who believed that the bad ruler was a sinner who had 'gone out' of the community, and should be replaced by the best believer, not necessarily an Arab. But the Kharijites in North Africa were divided between the Sufrites (Yellows), at Tangier and Tlemcen, and the Ibadites (Whites), at Tripoli and Qayrawan, and the revolution they planned was accomplished instead by a different movement based on a different principle, the exclusive right of members of the Prophet's family to succeed to the Caliphate. This was the Abbasid movement, based in north-eastern Iran, which took power in 750. Nevertheless the original unity of the empire and the community was broken. Andalus, that is Spain, became independent. In North Africa, the Ibadites established a capital at Tahart (Tiaret) in western Algeria under their own imam or leader of their community; his followers extended through the Djerid in southern Tunisia and the Jabal Nafusa in Tripolitania to the Fezzan in the central Sahara. Sufrites ruled at Tlemcen, while towards the end of the century the alternative principle of government by a member of the Prophet's family produced the Idrisid dynasty at Fès in northern Morocco in opposition to the Abbasids. Partly as a result of this Idrisid challenge, in 800 the Caliph Harun al-Rashid permitted the governor of Qayrawan to become the hereditary emir or ruler of Ifriqiya in exchange for recognition of the caliph's suzerainty. Under the Aghlabid dynasty which the new emir founded, this erstwhile province became independent in its turn.

The burning question of the right to lead the community of the faithful and to rule its empire, which resulted in the breaking-up of both in North Africa, was symptomatic of the rapid growth of the community and the development of its ideas. By the eighth century, the community of the faithful was ceasing to be identical either with the Arabs or even with the army. Continuous recruitment from outside and natural growth from within was turning it into a cross-section of the population in all the lands it had conquered. One result was that the distinction between *muminun* and *muslimun*, Arabs and clients, lost its force; *islam* (submission), became Islam, the proper name of the true religion, and Muslims that of the true believers. A second result was that the army became professional, and sometimes not even Muslim; it was segregated along with the ruler, his household and his ministers in great fortified palaces built outside or apart from the original garrison cities. These palaces, or royal towns, were modelled on the new Abbasid capital Baghdad; in North Africa they first appeared around 800 at Fès, newly founded by the Idrisids, and outside Qayrawan, the garrison city which was the capital of Ifriqiya and centre of the Aghlabid dominions. Thereafter it was normal for each new dynasty to build itself a residence of this kind.

With the government of the community thus physically removed from the old garrison cities, these became populated by civilian subjects whose life revolved around the Great Mosque in the middle. This served all the purposes of the Roman forum as a place of meeting, assembly, administration, justice, marketing and even defence, as well as worship, with this difference, that by the ninth century the seat of government had been moved away; the market area was in the surrounding streets; and the central enclosure had been built and rebuilt as a single edifice whose prime function was communal worship. The Great Mosque of Qayrawan, the greatest of its kind in North Africa, was finally completed in 864; it consisted of a vast prayer-hall, a huge court surrounded by colonnades, and a fortified tower. In and around this building, Islam developed in important ways.

Collective worship, resembling a military drill, had always been central to the life of the militant community, whose zeal had been further stimulated by preachers whose sermons, based on parables, had conveyed the exciting message of the holy war. The growth of the community turned the prayer at midday on Friday into a more stately occasion, when prayer was offered in the name of the reigning monarch. Meanwhile the simple preacher was displaced as the keeper of the community's conscience by the jurist or *faqih* (pl. *fuqaha*). The *faqih* was the scholar of the Holy Law, a concept fully formulated by the middle of the ninth century on the basis of scripture. This scripture was not only the Qur'an, the Book of God, but the record of the Sunna, the divinely-inspired practice of the Prophet and his four immediate successors, provided by traditions of their words and deeds which had been progressively reduced to writing. Upon this scripture was based a description of the Shari'a, the Law of God, a heavenly code covering every aspect of human behaviour. Its description by human beings could never be perfect, and differed somewhat from school to school, but was broadly agreed by 850. In the various doctrines of the schools, the Muslim community had a standard of reference authenticated and preserved by the scholarly jurists who handed it on by their teaching from generation to generation. In the jurists, comprehensively called the *ulema* (sing. *alim*), the wise, the community had a body of guardians of the divine science who alone could give an authoritative opinion as to what the Law might be in any particular case. At Qayrawan, they came to belong to the Malikite school, thanks to the work of the greatest among them, Sahnun (d. 854), who produced the *Mudawwana*, a definitive version of Malikite teaching upon which all subsequent elaboration was based. Jurists like these were indisputably supreme in matters of faith.

Their supremacy affected the government of the community by the *sultan* or man of power, such as the Aghlabid emir in his palace city. As leader of the community, the sultan was required to uphold the Law which he could neither make (since that was for God), nor define (since that was for the *alim*, the man of wisdom), but only enforce. In fulfilment of his narrow duty, therefore, he appointed to each main city a *qadi* or judge from among the ranks of the jurists to decide in accordance with the Law. In fulfilment of his wider duty to govern, however, he heard complaints and gave judgement himself. Moreover, he reserved the right to police and tax his subjects as he thought fit, thus restricting the jurisdiction of the qadi to public morality and personal or 'civil' matters such as contracts, marriage, inheritance and so forth. The qadi stood in an equally odd relationship to his fellow jurists, who in principle shunned his job as one entailing mortal sin: error was inevitable when a human being made binding judgements on behalf of God. Both he and they endeavoured to mitigate the offence by consultation: they gave him their opinion as to what the Law should be in any particular case, and he acted upon it in good faith. On the other hand he was a person of immense prestige, representing the justice of God on earth; without such an authority to lay down the Law and see that it was obeyed, the community itself would perish. Through him, the Great Mosque with which he was especially associated became not only a centre of scholarship, where the jurists studied and taught. It continued to play a major role in government.

Militancy and zeal were not dead, but became associated with a different building, the *ribat*. This was originally a frontier fortress garrisoned against the infidel—in Ifriqiya, a castle on the coast for defence against Byzantine Christian raids from Sicily. But in the ninth century Sicily was conquered by the Aghlabids in a fresh holy war, and the *ribats* of Ifriqiya became the home of ascetics shut off from the world. The term *murabit*, man of the *ribat*, the acquired two meanings, on the one hand the dedicated holy warrior, on the other the hermit. At the same time it began to acquire a third, that of the man of God who called the people to the holy war. Such a person carried on the tradition of the popular preacher of the original armies of the original community. His target was the same—enmity to God and his Prophet. Enmity was above all the condition of unbelievers who had not yet submitted to the rule of the faithful, so that the message in its simplest form was an exhortation to continue the fight against the infidel beyond the pale of Islam. But enmity was also present in sin, and then the message was turned in upon the community of believers. In fulfilment of his pious duty to 'command the right and forbid the wrong', the zealous *murabit* became a prophet who denounced iniquity and summoned the people to hear and obey the orders of God. Such a call was revolutionary, and politically threatening. Where the more sophisticated jurists regretfully accepted the fact that the emir or sultan ruled with wide discretion, and often tyrannously, the *murabit* was ready to condemn and oppose the monarch. People were only too liable to listen.

By the end of the ninth century, this was the situation in Ifriqiya, at the capital Qayrawan and in the surrounding region of

Tunisia which was the heart of the Aghlabid dominion. There, the native Christian population was probably already in a minority, doomed to disappear entirely within the next two hundred years as the Muslim community grew demographically as well as by conversion. Outside this very limited area, Islam was evolving in the same way, but in the different context of a largely tribal society. The Ibadites, for example, had shared in the original rising of believers against a sinful ruler in the middle of the eighth century. Defeated and expelled from Qayrawan, they developed their own doctrine of the Law, separate from but comparable to those of the Malikites and other Sunnite schools. As this doctrine failed to win acceptance from the majority of the *ulema* as an orthodox variant of the Shari'a, so the Ibadites became a sect apart from the rest of the community. Nevertheless in their new capital city of Tahart in western Algeria they produced a dynasty of rulers, a body of scholarly jurists and a class of dissenters who objected to the monarchy. Tahart, however, was no more than a city-state, and the bulk of the Ibadites who recognised its authority were not under its jurisdiction but as far away as the Fezzan. They were tribal Berbers among whom the jurists of the sect had only a moral authority which they used sometimes to judge in accordance with the holy Law, but more often to arbitrate in disputes in accordance with tribal custom.

Custom implies a stability which did not exist. Not only was tribal custom founded in violence, upon the need to repay killing with killing, in the first or the last resort. The peoples themselves were under pressure. In the desert, trans-Saharan trade affected their society and economy. In the mountains and oases surrounding Qayrawan and its territory, they were repressed by the military expeditions of the Aghlabids and their governors to collect taxes and ensure safe travel. At the same time they were required to be Muslim, at the very least to profess the faith as a sign of obedience to the dominant order. They were thus peculiarly susceptible to the appeal of the Muslim zealot preaching both for and against that order—for the right which it represented and against the wrong which it did. Such preachers might be Sunnite or Ibadite; but the critical prophecy when it came was that of Abu Abd Allah, a missionary from the Middle East who preached the coming of the Mahdi, the Muslim Messiah. He belonged to the Ismaili sect of the Shi'ite branch of Islam, hitherto (and subsequently) unrepresented in North Africa; his success came in the first place, however, from the universal attraction of that kind of message to peoples under the long-standing influence of the biblical tradition of Judaism, Christianity and Islam. It lent urgency to the demand to root out iniquity and gave it point—the overthrow of the Aghlabids in readiness for the Lord. Accordingly, the Kutama peoples of the mountains of the Petite Kabylie in eastern Algeria responded to the preacher's summons to make a new *islam* for a new community of the faithful under his command. Paradoxically, then, they were transformed, from a stateless society without rulers into an embryonic state under the absolute dictation of a single man. In that state, they were primarily soldiers, providing an army which drove out the Aghlabids in 909, and installed the Mahdi whom Abu Abd Allah introduced as the new ruler of Ifriqiya, the first of the Fatimid dynasty.

The Fatimids came, and in 972 went, moving to Egypt in pursuit of their claim (never realised) to rule the entire Muslim world. Their importance for North African Islam lay partly in their failure. They changed neither the nature of the state, nor the nature of the Law, nor the nature of tribal society. The Malikite school of Qayrawan was strengthened by its opposition to their doctrines; the Kutama reverted to their old ways. But they had popularised the notion of the Mahdi as a saviour in times of distress. More importantly, their prophet Abu Abd Allah had set an example of revolution which was swiftly followed, with or without the justification of Mahdism. The Fatimids themselves were almost overthrown in the 940s by Abu Yazid, an Ibadite leader who imitated their movement among the tribes of the Aures mountains. Morocco proved still more susceptible.

Central government had disappeared from North Africa to the west of Ifriqiya with the break-up of the Arab empire in the Maghrib in the eighth century. Small cities served as the capitals of petty dynasties in western Algeria and northern Morocco, and as markets for local tribes. In central and southern Morocco, a chain of ports and caravan cities ran down the Atlantic coast and to the south and east of the High Atlas, forming a pattern of Muslim settlement and trade in a huge region which had escaped the Arab conquest almost as much as the Roman. Here, Muslims in their townships and along their caravan trails confronted more or less pagan Berbers in the plains, mountains and deserts. These Berbers were nevertheless influenced by the Muslim presence and by the idea of Islam; in the ninth century an imitation Prophet with an imitation Qur'an, in Berber, created an imitation Muslim community called the Barghawata on the Atlantic plains, which lived by holy war upon its neighbours. Again we see the force of prophetic appeal to tribesmen on the margins of civilised Islam, and also its result: in the absence of a Muslim state to overthrow, the Barghawata created a state of their own. Thereby they anticipated the still more striking achievement of Ibn Yasin and his mission to the Berber tribes of the western Sahara.

Ibn Yasin was the *murabit par excellence*, a prophet of sternly orthodox conviction inspired by the Malikite opposition to the Fatimids, who set out to compel the tribesmen to obey the Law, and in so doing formed them like the Kutama and the Barghawata into an army and a state. His followers were called al-Murabitun, *the* Murabits or Almoravids, because they had joined together to live by the Law and to fight for it. A formidable army, between 1050 and 1100 they conquered the whole of Morocco, western Algeria and Muslim Spain, ruling an empire with its capital at Marrakesh. Fifty years later the Almoravids were themselves overthrown by the movement of yet another prophet, Ibn Tumart, who preached to the tribes of the High Atlas. Ibn Tumart claimed to be the Mahdi, come to insist on the unity of God; therefore his followers were called al-Muwahhidun, the Unitarians or Almohads. Once again they formed an army under a statesmanlike commander, which not only took over the Almoravid empire, but added Ifriqiya as well. Thus the whole of North Africa was politically united by the energies of peoples naturally without rulers, but transformed by the preaching of Islam.

As with the Fatimids, it is important to realise what the Almoravids and Almohads did not do. The empire they created was cumbersome, and in the thirteenth century broke up into four dynastic states in Ifriqiya, western Algeria, Morocco and Granada in southern Spain. Like the Kutama in Ifriqiya, the tribes which composed the two movements first became closed military aristocracies, and then reverted to their tribal ways of life. Despite the Mahdism of the Almohads, the Malikite orthodoxy upheld by the Almoravids became still more firmly established. Nevertheless, for the first time in history, they incorporated the whole of Morocco into a state. That state survived the break-up of the empire, to become an essential part of the Muslim state system which then covered the entire region. That system in turn provided a framework for the uneasy relationship between royal government, city and tribe which now became typical of the whole of the Maghrib. The principle of the system was the need for a *sultan* to uphold the Law without which the community would perish in sin. In practice the framework was sufficiently flexible to avoid further overthrow by the revolutionary preacher and prophet. That was partly because it allowed for the development of new forms of religion.

Behind any new forms lay the development of Islam as a way of life. In the cities, the accent fell on respectability and decency, privacy at home and seemliness abroad. For those who practised it, such a lifestyle was the proof of their Islam. It was structured by religion in all kinds of ways—by the Islamic observances of prayers, fasting and feasts; by Islamic rules of marriage and inheritance which governed the patriarchal family; and by the Islamic character of the administration. This was the responsibility of the three officers required by Law: the *wali* or governor on behalf of the sultan; the qadi or judge; and the *muhtasib* or market inspector on behalf of the qadi. Their duties were minimal rather than maximal: to keep the peace and collect taxes; to give judgement in court; and to ensure fair trading. The onus of the Law was upon the individual to behave properly, not upon the city to tell him what to do. The individual in question was pre-eminently the sane adult Muslim male, who had the greatest legal capacity, over and above women, children, slaves and of course non-Muslims like Jews. He was nevertheless under heavy social constraint, in which Islam came once again into play, not as a form of legislation, but as an element in the social order. The city was ruled by its governor, a military man as a rule appointed by the monarch; but its society was dominated by its bourgeoisie, whose wealth came from trade and property, and its prestige from religious learning. Typically, the chief families would provide the principal merchants, the principal landlords, and the principal *ulema*, including the qadi. Divided by faction, allied or opposed to the *wali*, the members of this class formed an influential elite respected for its tradition of Islamic scholarship and largely hereditary monopoly of office as imams or prayer-leaders, *khatibs* or preachers, judges and notaries (*udul*, sing. *adl*), and *muftis* or jurists.

The equivalent of this scholarly, sociable Islam in the tribal countryside was provided by the shaykhs of the Ibadites in the oases and villages of the Sahara and its Ifriqiyan borders. But from the tenth century the Ibadites dwindled into a minority even in their own region, and orthodox Islam had no ready substitute. The sense of mission to the tribes which provoked the great revolutions more often led to ignorant practitioners, with little knowledge of the Law, who relied more upon the mystique of Islam to find their niche in tribal society. Affected by the animism underlying the beliefs of the people, who saw the supernatural in trees, stones, springs and so forth, they were likely to resort to what the more educated called conjuring tricks and witchcraft to satisfy their clients. Nevertheless, in the course of time, such figures were drawn into a reputable tradition.

The origins of that tradition lay in *zuhd*, asceticism. In the ninth century asceticism had produced a person in strong contrast to the scholarly jurist who set out to direct the community, or the ardent preacher who set out to inflame it. This was the hermit or recluse who took the name of *murabit* from the *ribats* in which he took refuge after they had been abandoned as fortresses in the holy war. This was a form of the religious life which the jurists in principle condemned as antisocial, against the proper life of the community according to the Law. Certainly it led to extremes of austerity and emaciation among individuals apparently obsessed with mortification. On the other hand, asceticism retained its appeal and its justification as a form of godliness, and continued to be practised in varying degrees by educated and uneducated alike. The pious ascetic, sometimes a man of great learning, became a familiar figure, typically occupying a small abandoned mosque or shrine, a *ribat* or other building, inside or outside the city. Such a person had a reputation for saintliness, evidenced by the gift of second sight and other miraculous powers. Thus blessed by God, his *baraka* or power of blessing benefited those who came into contact with him before and after his death, when his residence became his tomb and a place of sanctity for those who lived nearby or came as visitors. Thereby his contemplative style of holiness took on considerable social significance. Meanwhile the term '*murabit*', while keeping its association with the holy war and militant righteousness, extended its meaning of hermit to a rather broader type of holy man.

Against this background, then, we see by the Almohad period in the twelfth century the beginning of two important and interconnected tendencies—the acquisition of disciples by some at least of these *murabitic* holy men, and the introduction of Sufism. The one gave asceticism its own tradition in the Islamic manner of passing on wisdom from master to pupil, the other reinforced that tradition with new beliefs and new insistence upon a communal mode of living. *Tasawwuf*, the profession of wool or Sufism, from the woollen robe of the ascetic, came from the Mashriq, the Muslim East, where it had already developed into mysticism associated with brotherhood and devotion. For the greatest adepts, the mysticism was of a high intellectual order; taken up in the twelfth century by students of philosophy as well as theology in Muslim Spain, it gave rise to one of the great mystics of all time, Ibn al-Arabi. But Ibn al-Arabi left Spain for the Mashriq at the beginning of the thirteenth century, and North Africa owed much more to his fellow-countryman Abu Madyan, who lived at Fès and Bejaia (Bougie), and died at Tlemcen in 1198. As a pupil of Moroccan holy men (one apparently unlettered) he stood at the beginning of the tradition of instruction. As a teacher himself, he added to the piety of his masters a measure of formal learning in theology and meditation. His teaching was followed by his disciples, notably Ibn Mashish in Morocco and al-Dahmani in Ifriqiya, so that it became the intellectual foundation of the ascetic, Sufi tradition in the Maghrib. In the course of the thirteenth century this tradition developed rapidly, producing another of the great figures of Sufism, the Moroccan al-Shadhili. Although Al-Shadhili and many of his fellows removed themselves like Ibn al-Arabi to the Mashriq, by the end of the century the tradition was not only well established in North Africa. Despite the hostility of the purists among the Malikite *ulema*, it was winning acceptance as a supplementary rather than an alternative form of Islam, to be followed alongside, in addition, to the orthodox tradition of the Shari'a.

Ideally, the holy man lived on charity, giving nothing but his blessing in return. But, again during the thirteenth century, he began to make his mark as a colonist, cultivating land which he had reclaimed from the waste, or which had been given to him. He might live there alone, or at the head of a colony of disciples. Equally, he became associated with travel and trade. His residence then was the *zawiya*, literally 'niche' or 'corner', but meaning when it was first introduced into North Africa a hostel giving food and shelter to poor travellers. As the residence of a holy man, the *zawiya* was naturally a sanctuary protecting its visitors from brigands and marauding nomads; its protection followed them on their way, giving them safe conduct across the surrounding territory. It might easily attract a market where trade could be carried on in peace maintained by the sanctity of the holy man who lived there. For the *zawiya* to operate in this way, its saintly occupant clearly required not only the respect of the local population, but a measure of obedience. Certainly in Ifriqiya, this was obtained in a time of troubles begun by war and continued by the presence of warlike Arab nomads, when people looked to the *baraka* of the man of God to establish some kind of order. In the course of the fourteenth century, both as a colonist of the land and as a colonist of the caravan trails, the holy man who had originated as an ascetic recluse became a familiar figure in a very different capacity, more or less actively engaged in the regulation of rural, largely tribal, society. This murabit, as he was generally known, differed not only from the hermit of the same name, but also from the militant prophet personified by Ibn Yasin. Whereas that murabit had set out drastically to change the way of life of his audience, the purpose of this one, as perceived by his parishioners, was to moderate and sanctify an existing, customary manner of living which may or may not have been strictly in accordance with the Law. For this reason it is useful to distinguish him by a different name, not murabit, the classical Arabic term applied to him in the literature, but the colloquial version with which Europeans eventually became familiar, and rendered into French as *marabout*.

The marabout effectively put an end to the great days of the prophet, to whose disturbing message he offered a more reassuring alternative. Militancy and zeal were by no means dead, but expressed within a new framework. That framework was the rural equivalent of Islam in the social order of the city, where a scholarly class set the tone of society, and that tone was the faith. Maraboutism in the countryside gathered up all previous beliefs and practices into a form of religion increasingly identical to the social structure of the countryside and its traditional outlook. Within the long-standing animist tradition, for example, the marabout became a legendary figure associated with the supernatural quality of nature located in places and things. Likewise he became a miracle worker, with second sight, the ability to be in two places at once, to alter the reality of the material world, and to command the jinn or spirits who, for good or evil, inhabited the earth. Upon his reputation as a virtuous master of the occult depended much of his authority in practical matters, the righting of wrongs and the arbitration of disputes, in which his word might well be law. For such services to the community, essential to the peace of a largely self-governing society, he would receive gifts. He himself might decline them, to the benefit of his reputation, but take the wealth nevertheless for redistribution to those who sought his charity and protection. As a patron, then, he became a centre of attraction in another way, drawing a following which formed part of his wider clientele. Over time, his central position in the neighbourhood would be confirmed by heredity. His holiness would remain in the place where he was buried, which would become a shrine and a place of pilgrimage, while it reappeared in his offspring, who would form a holy lineage. More than that, he might well become the ancestor of an entire tribe of people who claimed descent from him as his disciples or his protégés. Over the centuries, whole populations were restructured in this way, regrouped as nomads or cultivators around some maraboutic settlement, and reassorted into kindreds which were largely fictitious, but served the important purpose of identifying each group and its rights in relation to its neighbours. Such maraboutic tribes were often in contrast to more warlike peoples who lived by the sword and claimed a more heroic ancestry; but these too had their patron saints, and came within the scope of the holy men and their operations. In all this, there may have been little of formal Islam, but Islam it essentially was for the peoples concerned.

Formality itself, however, was not lacking. While many marabouts were doubtless ignorant, and undoubtedly rustic, as a class they were increasingly informed by the growing tradition of education in the concepts and practices of Sufism. That in turn involved a certain education in the basic sciences of the Law. The marabout was first a pupil who learned his texts, and at the same time acquired the techniques of abstinence, worship, prayer and meditation which might one day qualify him as a saint. Texts varied, and so did the techniques, but typically consisted in the endless repetition of prayers to induce a state of trance, or in pondering on the allegorical meaning of the Qur'an and the writings of the great masters. The pupil himself was likely to be a wanderer from place to place and teacher to teacher, as far away as Mecca and Medina; he might establish himself in the end very far from his birthplace. When at last he did so, however, he too was likely to be a teacher, passing on what he had learned and what he himself had come to think and do. This might be highly intellectual and deeply spiritual; the new master might be a scholar to rank with any *alim* as well as a mystic of great subtlety and difficulty. Even those of less exalted attainments were often distinguishable from the *ulema* of the cities only in their choice of the maraboutic profession. For by the fifteenth century it had become normal for anyone who aspired to education to train himself as a Sufi as well as an exponent of the Law, and at the higher levels of scholarship and saintliness the learned elite was becoming one and the same.

This was most evident in the development of the *zawiya* from a wayside hostel to an institution which met the spiritual needs of the marabout as well as the requirements of his social role. At its most elaborate, it contained within itself every kind of building associated with the practice of Islam, from the mosque downwards. It was a complex at whose heart was the tomb of the founder, which hallowed the place, and brought the visitor as nearly as possible into the presence of the other world. With the tomb, typically enclosed by a railing in the centre of a domed chamber, went a mosque with its prayer-hall, and with the mosque a *madrasah* or school with its reading-room. The hospice remained, offering food and lodging, perhaps with special accommodation for the sick. In and around was the housing for the permanent residents—the holy man and his family; his students; his staff; and his servants. Somewhere there was a library; a reception room where the master would give audience; and a refectory. This last was central to the whole. Materially and spiritually the master or shaykh 'spread a table': his earthly hospitality expressed his heavenly welcome: the flock was fed. Nourishment depended upon the head of the house. But for the disciple it was likely to be arduous—long hours of readings, recitations and prayers which either began, completed or carried on his education in Sufism. For him, the *zawiya* was an institution to match and complement the great mosque of the city, traditionally associated with the sciences of religion, above all with jurisprudence. For others, the *zawiya* met other needs, economic, social and political, according to circumstance, but all within the general meaning of Islam for those concerned.

The *zawiya* naturally varied in size and importance, and by no means all were so complete and self-contained. But by the fifteenth or sixteenth century, earlier in Ifriqiya, later in Morocco, the full-blown *zawiya* in town as well as countryside represented the climax of a cumulative process which had brought the *murabit*, the holy man, in from the margin to the midst of North African society. As the marabout, he spanned the gulf between the literate scholar of the city and the rustic saint. Moreover, as he closed with his *baraka* the wide gap between the Law of God and the custom of the people, so too he stretched across the deep divide between the state and its subjects. That divide was a major feature of the society. The Muslim state in the Maghrib was an historic achievement, the product of the Arab conquest and the three great prophetic revolutions which had brought the whole of North Africa within the one system. Despite the determination of an Ibn Yasin to 'command the right and forbid the wrong', however, the mechanism of government not only remained far from the religious ideal of conformity to the Law, but also limited in scope. On the one hand the sultan, the man of power or ruler, was the shepherd of his sheep, his *raiya* or flock, as his subjects were known. On the other, his majesty as defender of the faith and pillar of justice was upheld in the post-Almohad era by the Marinids of Fès, the Ziyanids of Tlemcen and the Hafsids of Tunis through the collection of taxes and tributes to support a royal household and army. This kind of government is defined by the name which it eventually acquired in Morocco, that is *makhzan* or treasury. It lived largely for itself, taking its dues and exacting obedience while leaving the various communities of its subjects, even in the cities, as far as possible to govern themselves. The marabout in consequence was called upon to play a vital political and administrative role.

When the state was strong, as in Ifriqiya under the Hafsids in the fifteenth century, the marabout kept the peace on behalf of the sultan by his authority in local disputes. At the same time he protected the local population from the excesses of the tax-collector and the army. Receiving pious gifts from the men of power, he was able to distribute that much more to his own people, and so increase his standing even further. With his fellow heads of *zawiyas* and the *ulema* who were his cousins in the same milieu of piety and learning, he was a member of a class of religious notables highly influential in the counsels of the monarch. When the state was weak, on the other hand, as it was throughout the Maghrib in the first half of the sixteenth century, the marabout might join the struggle for power, on behalf of some claimant to the throne or in his own right. The Saadian dynasty came to power in Morocco in the sixteenth century with the help of the marabouts and the tribesmen they controlled. At the same time in western Algeria, another such holy man acquired the aura of the expected Mahdi, come to restore the reign of justice and righteousness. His cause came to nothing, but in what is now Tunisia, a marabout with a tribal following founded at Qayrawan (Kairouan) a short-lived dynasty, the Shabbiya. Much more spectacular, although equally short-lived, were the maraboutic principalities which ruled Morocco in the middle of the seventeenth century, most notably that of the *zawiya* of Dila in the Middle Atlas, which at its height covered two-thirds of the country and was on the point of establishing a permanent monarchy. These great adventures show the extent to which the marabout had taken over from the *murabit* as holy warrior and as statesman. Unlike the prophet who came from outside, he was already integrated into tribal society on the strength of his *baraka*, his all-purpose holiness. From that *baraka*, rather than any prophetic mission, came the ability to turn on occasion from an authority in tribal affairs into a ruler equipped with the state's apparatus of coercion, tax-gathering and repression. Nevertheless, by comparison with the achievements of the prophets of the three great revolutions of the Fatimids, the Almoravids and the Almohads, the marabouts of the sixteenth and seventeenth centuries failed to make good their power. New dynasties of warriors forced them back into their customary role.

Politically, the eighteenth century saw the modern states of North Africa take shape within their present boundaries. In Morocco, the Alawite dynasty which overthrew the *zawiya* of Dila in the 1660s established itself as the ruling house to which the present king belongs. Like the Saadians before them in the sixteenth century, the Alawites claimed the throne as *sharifs* (Arabic pl. *shurafa*) or descendants of the Prophet. Sharifianism in the Maghrib dated from at least the fourteenth century, but only became widespread when it became royal. Sharifian lineages then proliferated, creating an elite of no particular profession but high esteem, which overlapped the *ulema* and marabouts who formed the religious aristocracy. Still greater emphasis was thus placed upon hereditary holiness, upon the notion of families in whose blood ran a godliness which showed itself from generation to generation in gifted individuals. But although the holy men aspired to royalty as the royal family became holy, the division between the two remained hard and fast. The traditional relationship between the sultan and the *alim*, the man of power and the man of wisdom, was not destroyed.

To the east of Morocco, political and religious change was of a different kind. Provinces of the Ottoman Empire since the sixteenth century, Algeria, Tunisia and Libya became independent in all but name by the eighteenth century, but still under the government of Turks or rulers of Turkish descent. These formed in each country a small but powerful ruling class, distinguished from their North African subjects by, among other things, their Islam. The Turks belonged to the Hanafite rather than the Malikite school of the Law, equally orthodox, but characterised by its own mosques and its own *ulema*. These came in the main from learned families of Turkish origin, who because of their association with the state exercised a disproportionate influence. More important was the principle which they represented, of political and administrative distinctions on the grounds of religion. This dated from the Arab conquests, which had divided the faithful from their non-Muslim subjects, but had almost vanished in practice from North Africa, whose native Christian population had disappeared, leaving only the Jews. Nor had there been much need to distinguish, as in the Middle East, between different kinds of Muslims with their own doctrines and religious leaders. Malikism had eliminated all formal differences between Muslims in the Maghrib except for the Ibadites, whose communities were now small and scattered, and as far as the state was concerned, on the same footing as tribes. But the introduction of the Hanafite school by the Turks was a reminder of how important a difference of religion could still be to the Muslim community and its government.

Formal differences had nevertheless entered into North African Islam, although because they did not affect the Law they did not fall into the same category as the Malikite-Hanafite divide. These differences turned on points of Sufi teaching rather than legal doctrine, on the so-called *tariqas* (Ar. pl. *turuq*) or spiritual 'ways' of the Sufi masters which their disciples followed. Those who followed a particular *tariqa* were likely to form a particular group or brotherhood. The older the *tariqa*, the larger and more diffuse the brotherhood was likely to be, stretching across the Muslim world with no particular organisation. But within such *tariqas* new masters could arise, and other masters could break away to establish their own. The newer the *tariqa* thus revived or created, the more likely it was to generate a closer and more active community, very often centred upon some parent *zawiya*. That was especially so in the Maghrib, where the notions of *tariqa* and brotherhood readily coincided with and reinforced the relationship between a marabout and his clients in tribal society. From the fifteenth century onwards, therefore, and certainly by the eighteenth, we find a proliferation of names of brotherhoods covering the whole range of maraboutism, and to some extent scholarship as well. Some of these names went back for centuries, notably Qadiriyya to the Iraqi Abd al-Qadir al-Jilani in the twelfth century, and Shadhiliyya to the Moroccan al-Shadhili in the thirteenth. Others were more recent, and their brotherhoods much more closely associated with their founders. Some were distinctly local, reflecting the position of the founder and his successors in the locality. Others had a more general appeal.

Sometimes this was a matter of lifestyle. The Isawiyya (Aïssaoua) were exhibitionists, eating fire and cutting themselves in ecstasy, the most extravagant of those who lived in holy beggary on the fringe of society, the successors of the murabit in his extreme repudiation of the world. Much more respectable, the Qadiriyya traded on the immense reputation of its eponymous founder, one of the great saints of Islam. In between, however, was the holy man who attracted not only disciples, and not merely the allegiance of peoples in the vicinity, but a wide and popular following which cut across community and class. The first conspicuous example of such a person was al-Jazuli in Morocco in the fifteenth century, who ranged the country at the head of an itinerant horde drawn by his promise of immediate entry into his 'way' and subsequent salvation. After his death and burial in the western High Atlas, his Jazuliyya order settled into a normal maraboutic practice in the region. But there were others, and at the end of the eighteenth century appeared a whole set of shaykhs whose *tariqas* and confraternities were as much revivalist movements as the routine operation of Sufism within the maraboutic system. In eastern Algeria and southern Tunisia sprang up the Rahmaniyya in the belief that reverence for the founder, his tomb and his *tariqa* was security against damnation. In western Algeria the Qadiriyya was reintroduced by a sharif with a commission from the order in Baghdad and Cairo; his *zawiya* near Mascara rapidly became a focus for the whole Turkish province of Oran. From western Algeria also came al-Tijani, who considered himself directly inspired by the Prophet to establish the one true brotherhood which everyone should join, but join to the exclusion of all others. His centre was in Morocco, where his puritanical message, which disapproved of the more extravagant forms of piety, contrasted with the *tariqa* of al-Darqawi, which emphasised holy poverty and ecstasy. The Tijaniyya was for a while in favour at court, while the more popular Darqawiyya became associated with rebellion. In Algeria likewise the new orders were of political importance in the last days of Turkish rule. In both countries they were associated with conflicts of ideas and discontents with established order which threatened a century of revolution.

In the event, the revolution of the nineteenth century in North Africa was brought about by European intervention. The French conquest of Algeria from 1830 onwards was contested by the brotherhoods down to the Margueritte affair in 1903. In Abdelkader (Abd al-Qadir) the Qadiriyya produced Algeria's national hero, who between 1832 and 1847 briefly created his own state to replace that of the Turks and defy the French. For this he drew upon the influence of his marabout father over the tribes to make himself emir, on the one hand a ruler, on the other a leader of the holy way against the infidel. He was doomed: he needed to fight the French to keep the loyalty of his followers, but peace with them to organise his power. In the end he lost both. Subsequently it was the turn of the Rahmaniyya in eastern Algeria, then of the maraboutic families and tribes of the Awlad Sidi

Shaykh in the south and south-west. When all else failed, prophets and mahdis made their appearance to call for a general rising—Bu Maza, Man with a Goat; Bu Baghla, Man with a Mule; Bu Amama, Man with a Turban; and others. Later still, in the twentieth century, the Fadiliyya under the great marabout Ma al-Aynayn and his sons resisted the French and the Spanish in the Moroccan Sahara down to 1934. In Libya from 1911, the Italians encountered the Sanusiyya, a brotherhood which survived the destruction of its *zawiyas* to organise a guerrilla war and finally to provide the newly independent state of Libya with its first head, King Idris.

The Sanusiyya was unique in its ability to transform itself from a traditional religious into a modern political movement, and to found a modern state instead of a traditional sultanate. It did so in unique circumstances, largely because of British support. All other orders which opposed the European conquest succumbed to military defeat before either their appeal or their leadership, wide as these might be, could develop into nationalism and national government. Some, like the Tijaniyya in Algeria, collaborated from the first. Once subdued, the brotherhoods were first patronised by the European administration as traditional agents for the control of traditional society, then attacked by Muslim reformers for their backwardness and compliance. French ethnography, which was employed as a tool by French government to create a detailed picture of North African society for the purpose of surveillance, gave substance to a pejorative image of maraboutism as a highly unorthodox form of Islam, riddled with superstition and verging on paganism, which on the one hand justified a managerial approach to a primitive culture, and on the other, sharp criticism of the degradation encouraged by colonial rule. Both positions were theoretical. North African society was changing rapidly, causing the marabouts and their brotherhoods to lose many of their old functions as tribal life lost much of its independence or simply ceased to exist. The corresponding growth of a population either dislocated or restructured by the colonial economy created a new constituency, but one in which maraboutism began to contrast and conflict with the Islam of the Law.

Both the Law and its guardians, the *ulema*, were fundamentally affected by the French conquest and annexation of Algeria from 1830, the establishment of the French Protectorates of Tunisia in 1881 and Morocco in 1912, and the Italian conquest and annexation of Libya between 1911 and 1940. In each case, a powerful European type of state, based on legislation, working through bureaucracy and regulating sphere after sphere of activity, took the place of the previous *makhzan* type of government based on tax-collection and the army. In each, the maintenance of the Islamic Law became only one among other purposes of government; the Law itself depended on legislation rather than divinity to have any legal force; its administration was incorporated into the bureaucracy; and its application was much more strictly limited, for the most part to family matters. Thus reduced as far as possible to what the French in Algeria called a *statut personnel* or personal statute, the Law nevertheless served an important administrative purpose as the definition of a Muslim as distinct from a Frenchman or an Italian. This use of Islam, which recalls the traditional use of religion in a Muslim state to separate Muslims from non-Muslims, and to some extent Muslims from Muslims, excluded the bulk of the Muslim population of Algeria from French citizenship, and everywhere meant the application of different laws of other kinds to the native as opposed to the immigrant European population.

The *ulema* who administered the Law in the courts, who taught it especially in the university mosques of the Zaytuna (Zitouna) at Tunis and the Qarawiyyin (Karaouiyine) at Fès, and who staffed the mosques with prayer-leaders and preachers, reluctantly accepted the need to serve under the new regimes. Willingly or unwillingly they then co-operated with the European authorities, either because it was profitable to do so, or because of an even stronger dislike for the new generation of Westernised North Africans whose secular attitudes seemed to threaten their traditional values. To such as these they preferred colonial governments which for their own good reasons gave their approval to traditional Islam as a defence against modern twentieth century agitation for national independence. In this position the *ulema* came to resemble the marabouts as clients of the colonial state which provided them with a niche of their own. A vocal minority nevertheless continued to protest at such an unnatural state of affairs, in which Islam was not free and not supreme. From 1900 onwards these belonged broadly to the Salafiyya, the movement for Islamic reform associated with the name of the Egyptian *alim* (scholar), Muhammed Abduh (d. 1905). The Salafiyya called for the *aggiornamento* or updating of Islam to meet the exigencies of the modern world, by a return to the religion of the *salaf*, the ancestors, to the original principles of the faith. Once the accumulation of traditional interpretations had been removed, Islam could once again become the principle of human progress. In the pre-colonial period, those who thought in this way had looked to Muslim rulers to introduce the necessary reforms, but in the colonial period the task fell to the people. How it was to be accomplished was a problem. Some thought that Islam should be simply a personal faith and a moral standard, others that immediate political independence was required to reintroduce Islam into the structure of government and society. The main line from Muhammad Abduh held that the faith should be inculcated and the Law reinterpreted before the community was ready for independence and the final triumph of religion.

Despite opposition from the conservative *ulema*, who feared that the Salafiyya was blasphemous in the revisions of the faith which it contemplated, the demand for independence was pressed in Tunisia by the Cheikh Taalbi (Shaykh al-Thaalibi) and in Morocco by Allal el-Fassi, both men of religious training and conviction who became leaders of nationalist parties. In Algeria, where the demand for independence was tantamount to treason in a country which was officially part of France, the Cheikh (Shaykh) Ben Badis formed an association of reforming *ulema* to campaign for equal rights for Muslims with Europeans, and in particular for the right to be educated in classical Arabic and the sciences of Islam. His campaign was combined with a strong attack upon maraboutism and its Sufi practices as representative of the very worst in traditional Islam, keeping the people in ignorance and subjection. In this way he sought to raise the level of Muslim consciousness to a new standard of literacy and faith.

As a result of the preaching, teaching and campaigning of these leaders and their associates, their ideas were doubly effective. On the one hand they helped to identify the old concept of the Muslim community with the new principle of the nation, and to assign a role to Islam in national culture. On the other, they served to discredit the more conservative *ulema*, but most especially the marabouts and their confraternities, as poor Muslims and bad patriots. This was a considerable achievement on the part of a movement which depended very much upon individual effort to accomplish the dual task of presenting an Islamic alternative to Western secularism, and at the same time bringing Islam up to date in the modern world. It was not, however, enough to form an effective nationalist movement for political independence, or to provide North African states which had just achieved independence with a comprehensive programme of government. This was because the means which religious leaders had traditionally employed to organise a wider following—tribe, *zawiya*, brotherhood and mosque—had lost their old political efficacy; and religion was not the only criterion for the modern alternative, the political party. Still less were the reformers in a position to capture the bureaucracy that was the modern alternative to the *makhzan*; the hope of Muhammad Abduh that a new doctrine of the Law could be devised to replace the old was far from realisation.

In Tunisia the Cheikh Taalbi was the most popular leader of the Old Destour, the first nationalist party, founded in 1920, which stood for constitutional rights including the rights of Islam as the national religion. But from 1934 the Old Destour was eclipsed by the Neo-Destour of Bourguiba, a Westernised leader who relied on the appeal of Islam but opposed its representatives. In Morocco Allal el-Fassi remained at the head of the Istiqlal, easily the largest nationalist party, which he founded in 1944. But in his case, the cause of the party was subordinated to the cause of the Sultan, who became the focus of religious sentiment for political purposes. In Algeria the successors of Ben Badis turned away from self-government as an immediate objective, with the result that they played a very limited part in the Algerian revolution. Their choice is nicely illustrated by the publication in 1954 of Malek Bennabi's *La vocation de l'Islam*, a book which argued that Muslims must purify their inner faith before taking political action, in the year when the Algerian war was begun by militants who would wait no longer. In terms of Islam, the war was ambiguous. The newspaper of the FLN (*Front de Libération National*) was called *El Moudjahid* (Al-Mujahid), the fighter in the holy war; guerrillas were called *fidain*, self-sacrificers, and *musabbilin*, the dedicated, both terms with religious connotations; the observance of Islamic prohibitions upon drinking and smoking was brutally enforced to solidarise the Muslim population. On the other hand, the war was never declared to be a jihad, a holy war upon the infidel; down to the end in 1962, Algerian citizenship was to be irrespective of religion; and many Muslims fought for the French.

This ambiguity survived the independence of Tunisia and Morocco in 1956, and of Algeria in 1962. It led in 1965 to an article by the American scholar Leon Carl Brown which is almost an historical document of the 1960s, recording the impression created in the period immediately after the end of French rule. Brown observed a sharp contrast between a Muslim past and a largely non-Muslim present. The pervasive maraboutism of the old Maghrib had, he said, been supplanted by the radicalism of Islamic reform, which had inspired the struggle for independence; but with independence, it seemed that Islam had been put aside, having served its historical purpose. He noted the non-Islamic forms of government inherited from the French, and the secular objectives of the new regimes, which in the case of Bourguiba's Tunisia were positively anti-Islamic; a Westernised lifestyle was in demand. At the same time, anti-Islamism had its limits. Islam was in all cases the state religion; there was no anti-clericalism directed at the *ulema*; and while the mosques were emptying, Bourguiba had been obliged to abandon his attempt to abolish the fast of Ramadan. Although the future seemed to lie with secularism, its triumph was not quite certain.

The history of the twenty years since Brown wrote has seen the situation develop while the question remains. In 1965 the populist president of Algeria, Ben Bella, was overthrown by the puritanical commander of the army, Boumedienne; a radical modernist who seemed to flout Islam in the name of Marxism was replaced by a leader of good Muslim education and profound conviction who had named himself after the great saint Abu Madyan. In the novel circumstances of the twentieth century, Boumedienne was almost a *murabit*, a man with a self-appointed mission to establish an Islamic government. But as in the empire of the Almoravids, this commitment did not radically alter the character of the state, which followed the standard practice of the twentieth century as a bureaucratic insitution in pursuit of its citizens' welfare, in this case by state socialism. Public observance of Ramadan, for example, was compulsory, as befitted one of the most important duties imposed upon the community by the Law; it constituted a form of national discipline. In most respects, however, the state religion was confined to the sphere of cult and culture under a minister appointed for the purpose. Islam, in other words, achieved the position sought for it in the

French state by Ben Badis, along with classical Arabic, which became the language of education. But there was little or no attempt to rethink the structure of government and administration, or its legislative foundation, and thus to achieve the ultimate aim of the Salafiyya.

Much the same could be said of Tunisia and Morocco. Islam has been a principle of legitimacy in whose name governments have felt justified in keeping power and ruling in the national interest. All three regimes have accordingly attracted opposition from Muslims who have felt that the anti-colonial revolution has been betrayed to the advantage of privileged classes and to the detriment of Islamic justice. This opposition has found expression in Islamic fundamentalism, the call for a return to the elementary letter of the Law as stated above all in the Qur'an, disregarding both traditional legal doctrine and the arguments of the Salafiyya for reform and reinterpretation. Such fundamentalism has been linked with the name of the Muslim Brethren, the Islamic radicals and revolutionaries of Egypt, and seemed especially alarming after the overthrow of the Shah in Iran, when crowds in Tunisia listened to popular preachers, and mosques in Algeria filled with stern young men. But any threat has so far been stifled by governments which continue to enjoy large measures of support and goodwill, and extensive powers of repression. Westernisation has maintained its force, even if religion may have inhibited overt secularism.

From the point of view of Islam, however, the most dramatic political event in the Maghrib since Brown wrote in the mid-1960s was the revolution in Libya in 1969 which substituted Colonel Gadaffi (Qadhdhafi) for King Idris, a radical anti-Western regime for one denounced as a pro-Western clique. The revolution itself, in a country made unexpectedly rich by oil, was more political than religious, despite the religious origins of the monarchy. Nevertheless Gadaffi has been truly radical in religion as well as politics. Opposed to government by elected representatives of the people and by man-made laws, he has introduced a scheme of government by popular committees. These, composed of the people themselves, will take decisions in accordance with 'the law of society', which for Muslims is the Law of God. This should mean that they will be the interpreters of the Law in accordance with the old legal maxim: 'my people (i.e. God's) will never agree upon an error'. Thus the Law is not only to be taken out of the hands of the *ulema*, but introducted at every point into government, in place of bureaucracy and its norms. The theory is sketched in Gadaffi's tract *The Green Book*, but in practice it has taken years to organise the committees, and meanwhile Gadaffi has remained a dictator. In that capacity it is he, rather than the people in committee, who has become the national authority for the Law, declaring that the Qur'an alone, rather than the whole corpus of scripture and commentary upon which Sunnite jurisprudence rests, is its source. Not only, then, does he provide a second example of an individual inspired to lead a modern community in the path of righteousness, but the sole example in North Africa of a fundamentalist in power. While Gadaffi's policies may have been inconsistent and changeable, they have in consequence been vigorous, and often violent. From the Qur'an he has taken the moral authority for a continuous revolution which is only Islamic by his definition, but socialist in its redistribution of wealth and more dubiously in its committee system. Meanwhile his definition of Islam makes an important addition to the scope of religion in North Africa today.

Where, then, does Brown's case for secularisation now stand? Reports are conflicting. From Tunisia we hear that traditional Islamic attitudes gained strength at a time (1967–73), when the regime had ceased to be so openly secularist, and from Morocco that secularism has flourished under a government which has been notably tolerant in religious matters. Morocco will probably strike the visitor as more, Tunisia as less, traditionally Islamic. In Algeria, the country which may seem most like Europe, the *zawiyas* denounced by Ben Badis have been criticised for their continued hold upon the upper as well as lower levels of society. Religious observances like prayer of course continue, and religious institutions like mosques naturally remain. The pilgrimage to Mecca, which the French once sought to prevent, is still popular and respectable. Mosques are places for men to meet or pass the time as well as pray—though prayer is a ritual which must be learnt by imitation, by praying 'behind' one who knows; and not all Muslims have done so. The countryside is covered with the domed tombs of holy men which are themselves called marabouts, some ruined, some well maintained, visited mainly by women. The *zawiyas* are still centres of brotherhoods frequented by their *khouan* (*ikhwan*, brothers); the tombs of their founders are equally sought by supplicants, both men and women. The wilder, more ecstatic orders survive, though do not noticeably prosper. Festivals are celebrated, either nationally, like the canonical feasts of sacrifice and breaking the fast at the end of Ramadan, or locally, like the *moussems* (*mawsims*, seasons, sc. monsoon), annual gatherings at a shrine. The Mawlid or Prophet's birthday is a popular occasion. The ban on pork is almost universally observed, the fast of Ramadan fairly generally; but alcohol is drunk, and smoking common.

Change, on the whole, is in the direction favoured by the state. With the spread of education, the movement of people into and out of the countryside, and the development of mass communications, the tendency is towards a standard of religion set by reformers, basic learning in place of popular belief. Approximation to this standard goes with the development of the national community, just as conformity to it is an element in national consciousness. Conformity may often be conventional, with little conviction; but it may equally be intensified by nationalism. From this point of view the national society is taking over from the traditional, and Islam is acquiring a new social and political function in place of all those it has lost to the state. To a greater extent than Brown anticipated, therefore, modern Islam has counterbalanced the continuing growth of secular attitudes to match the growth of secular society and institutions. From another point of view, however, this is misleading; the problem itself is different, and must be rephrased—not secularism versus Islam, but modernity, religious or otherwise, versus tradition which is still far from done.

This, the original problem of the Salafiyya, has remained despite the achievement of independence, which for others beside Brown should have completed the transformation of traditional values in the course of the battle for freedom. Another American scholar, David C. Gordon, writing at the same time as Brown, saw tradition rather as a lingering obstacle to be overcome only by a long struggle in which the state would play a crucial role. Tradition in this sense clearly does not mean the way of life of pre-colonial North Africa, but those elements which have endured, either because they are associated with poverty and backwardness, or because they have in fact proved useful in the competition to survive, or because they are so basic that they have remained when so much else has gone. In all three categories we find the Muslim family.

Islamic Law does not recognise the family, only the rights and duties of its members, giving more to adult males and fewer to women and children. These rights and duties, however, govern the traditional Muslim family, which is recognised by custom as part of the Muslim way of life. Custom has varied from country to city, where the Law is most in evidence, and where women have been most secluded. In general, however, it has confirmed the father as the head of the household and the elder brother as the head of the line. Women have belonged in principle inside the house, with a separate sphere of activity from the men; this separation extends to religion, where women worship at the shrines of saints while men worship in the mosques, and where they have a reputation for magic, white and black. Modern city life has reduced the barriers, and for many women has brought extensive Westernisation; but the tradition remains extremely strong. Independence brought no sudden change, as Frantz Fanon, the writer of the Algerian revolution, predicted; the veil is still much in evidence, and the sexes widely segregated.

The problem about the position of women is one of attitudes to the subject as much as facts. In the colonial period, Europeans were accustomed to consider Muslim women as degraded, and their degradation as the result of Islam. Even the sympathetic Budgett Meakin in Morocco about 1900 quoted the North African adage, 'a donkey by day and a darling by night', to epitomise their servitude. Since then, the association of inferiority and oppression with Islam has produced a corresponding identification of emancipation with Westernisation. As a result, an argument about modernisation has been confused with the argument over secularisation. The Salafiyya has concerned itself with women's rights, but its most celebrated attack on tradition in this matter, that by Tahar Haddad in Tunisia in the

1930s, led to his disqualification as a teacher. Approaching the question from a different angle, Germaine Tillion has tried to take the subject out of religion by demonstrating that the position of Muslim women in North Africa is only a variation of that of women in Mediterranean Europe as well as the Middle East. But the most celebrated piece of legislation in favour of women, the prohibition of polygamy in Tunisia, was enacted by Bourguiba in his most defiantly secularist vein. Polygamy in fact is not a great problem, since few can afford it, or wish to do so; and the slave concubine disappeared with slavery itself, prohibited and abolished from the mid-nineteenth century onwards. Traditional views are nevertheless firmly held not only in the population at large, but by many who feel that the Muslim family is of the essence of the nation. Non-Muslims, on the other hand, are generally critical. The argument is not very well informed, and only recently have good descriptions begun to appear to clarify the issues. Eventually it may be possible to distinguish between what women have, what they want and what they are entitled to. Meanwhile an emotive subject continues to involve Islam in principle and in practice in the battle for the future.

Further Reading

Berque, J. *French North Africa. The Maghrib between two World Wars* (London, 1967)

Brett, M. and Forman, W. *The Moors. Islam in the West* (Orbis, London, 1980)

—— 'Islam in the Maghreb', *The Maghreb Review*, II, 3 (1977), pp. 18–22; II, 4 (1977), pp. 14–18; III, 5–6 (1978), pp. 6–9

—— 'Mufti, Murabit, Marabout and Mahdi: four types in the Islamic history of North Africa', *Revue de l'Occident Musulman et de la Méditerranée*, XXXI (1980), pp. 5–15

Brown, K.L. *People of Salé. Tradition and change in a Moroccan city, 1830–1930* (Manchester Univesity Press, Manchester, 1976)

Cambridge History of Africa, 8 vols. (Cambridge University Press, Cambridge, 1975–86)

Encyclopaedia of Islam, 1st edn (Leiden and London, 1913–38); 2nd edn (Leiden and London, 1954, in progress); *Shorter Encyclopaedia* (Leiden and London, 1961)

Evans-Pritchard, E.E. *The Sanusi of Cyrenaica* (Oxford, 1949)

Geertz, C. *Islam Observed. Religious Development in Morocco and Indonesia* (New Haven, 1968; University of Chicago Press, Chicago and London, 1971)

Gellner, E. *Saints of the Atlas* (Weidenfeld & Nicolson, London, 1969)

Jenkins, R.G. 'The Evolution of Religious Brotherhoods in North and Northwest Africa, 1523–1900', in J.R. Willis (ed.), *Studies in West African Islamic History*, I, *The Cultivators of Islam* (Cassell & Co., London, 1979), pp. 40–77

Julien, Ch.-A. *History of North Africa: from the Arab conquest to 1830* (Routledge & Kegan Paul, London, 1970)

Keddie, N.R. (ed.) *Scholars, Saints and Sufis. Muslim religious institutions in the Middle East since 1500* (University of California Press, Berkeley, Los Angeles and London, 1972)

Le Tourneau, R. *Fez in the Age of the Marinids* (Norman, Oklahoma, 1961)

Martin, B.G. *Muslim Brotherhoods in Nineteenth-Century Africa* (Cambridge University Press, Cambridge, 1976)

Mernissi, F. *Beyond the Veil. Male-female dynamics in a modern Muslim society* (Halsted Press, New York, 1975)
Stewart, C.C. with Stewart, E.K. *Islam and Social Order in Mauritania. A case study from the nineteenth century* (Oxford University Press, Oxford, 1973)
Trimingham, J.S. *The Sufi Orders in Islam* (Oxford University Press, Oxford, 1971)
Westermarck, E.A. *Ritual and Belief in Morocco*, 2 vols. (London, 1926; reprint New York, 1968)

22 *Islam in Iran*

Julian Baldick

Islam in Iran, although it is now a subject that attracts attention by virtue of the revolution of 1978–9 and its reverberating aftermath, needs to be viewed in the perspective of a long historical process. Indeed, no other subject could provide a more powerful justification for the discipline of history: the present resurgence of traditional elements is incomprehensible without an examination of the distant past. Moreover, the varying interpretations of that past form a major and integral part of contemporary political activity.

A massive problem confronts us. To what extent is it right to speak of an 'Iranian Islam'? How much of the pre-Islamic heritage that was specifically Iranian went into Islam as practised and conceived in Iran? Here one essential fact dominates consideration of the question. Since the sixteenth century Iran alone has had as its official faith Twelver Shi'ism, which represents the principal minority sect in Islam, and is characterised by its extreme devotion to Muhammad's family, notably to twelve 'leaders' therein. But how Iranian is this development? How far is it prefigured in Iran's earlier religious history?

The field is overshadowed by the studies of one man, the late Henry Corbin, whose extremely personal approach and difficult style have given rise to much misunderstanding. He argued that the structures of Mazdaism ('Zoroastrianism', Iran's principal and official pre-Islamic faith, distinguished by its preoccupation with an epic struggle between the forces of Good and Evil) were to reappear in Iran under the guise of Islamic mysticism. Now this argument has been misinterpreted, by over-zealous partisans and opponents alike, as implying actual continuity of Iranian doctrines, handed down from Mazdean to Muslim, from teacher to disciple, across the Islamisation of Iran from the seventh century CE onwards.

This misinterpretation has led Iranian nationalists and some academics, heavily subsidised by the late Shah, to engage in a predictable and massive exaggeration of the indebtedness of Islam to Mazdaism, in line with the Shah's glorification of Iranian culture as a continuous and pure self-expression of the Aryan race. On the other hand, in an extreme reaction, some specialists have tried to deny the existence of mystical elements in the thought of leading Iranian Muslim philosophers, claiming that they were entirely rational; similarly, the attempt has been made to deny the existence of Shi'ite elements, or elements conducive to the acceptance of Shi'ism, in the thought of leading Iranian mystics before the Shi'ite take-over in the sixteenth century.

Recent research points to a different solution: it is not the main-line Iranian faith, Mazdaism, or the pre-Islamic monarchical tradition of Iran, or, in general, specifically Iranian elements that were to have a real continuity and be preserved in Islam. Rather, it was the mystical and insurrectionary traditions opposed to Mazdaism and the old Iranian state that were to go on in Muslim form. These traditions would appear not to be specifically Iranian, though they had flourished in Iran, but to come, like most things in Islam, from Iraq, with ideas previously expressed in Greek. Indeed, it must be stressed that before the Islamic period Iran and Iraq constituted a cultural and political unity, and in the Islamic period must always be viewed together. If Shi'ism belongs in its historical origin to any country, it is to Iraq. In a wider perspective one could see its central ceremonies which evoke, with a heavy emphasis on the supply of water, the martyrdom of the Shi'ites' third 'leader', Husein, as a prolongation of the fertility cults of dying semi-divine figures (Adonis, Attis, Jesus) in the ancient Near East.

Let us begin with the various religious movements in Iran after the Arab conquest in the seventh century CE. Here it must be said that our sources are very late and unreliable, and represent main-line or respectably moderate positions in their vilification of people portrayed as wicked extremists and 'heretics'.

Central to these movements is a type of Shi'ism usually seen as constituting a sub-sect: Zaydism, so called after an unsuccessful rebel from Muhammad's family. This tendency is defined by its insistence on armed insurrection with a view to installing a proclaimed leader in power. It was to find a strong foothold among the warlike mountain tribesmen of northern Iran.

Alongside this we may see attempts by other insurgents to combine Islam with older religious practices against the official Mazdean clergy. In such a context the appearance of new and short-lived prophets, uniting Muslim and Iranian elements, can be seen as a continuation of the tradition of the prophet Mani (d. *c.* 274 CE), the founder of a new religion called after him Manichaeism, and one's interpretation would vary according to how one saw that faith: either as syncretism, the deliberate mingling together of different creeds, or as the adaptation of a secret, mystical religion to local beliefs. In either interpretation the tradition is one coming from Iraq.

This is certainly the case with the continuation in Muslim dress of Mazdakism (with a 'k', not to be confused with the mainline Mazdaism). This pre-Islamic religion, called after its leader at the end of the fifth century CE, Mazdak, who is held responsible for its famous socialistic character, did indeed grow out of Manichaeism (and thus owed its original inspiration to Gnosticism, a movement which, in its emphasis on a hidden knowledge reserved for an elite, was independent of any regional colouring). It was to live on in Islam, its rebellious adherents being known as the *Khurramiyya*, 'people of joy'. According to one firsthand Muslim source some of them considered sexual promiscuity, and in general any harmless pleasures, to be lawful. But one need not take seriously the usual Muslim accusation that they advocated or practised the communal possession of women (a charge often made, without evidence, against nineteenth-century European socialists and communists). On the other hand, both their Islamic messianism and their Manichaean belief in Light, partially sullied by darkness, as the source of this world's existence, are well attested.

It is against this background of Zaydi and Mazdakite insurrectionism that one must see the secret propaganda of the small Ismaili sect of Shi'ism, which recognises a continuing line of 'leaders' up to the present day. Apparently the Ismailis and Mazdakites were not really connected; but the latter indirectly assisted the former's missionary activity, which found fertile soil from north-western to north-eastern Iran. The result, as we shall note, will be Ismailism at its most extreme, both in its recourse to assassination and its messianic rejection of Islamic law.

We must now consider the extent to which the Abbasid dynasty of caliphs, reigning from 750 onwards, and installing its capital in Baghdad as opposed to Damascus, might be seen as representing an Iranisation of Islam. The shifting of the capital, the fact that the revolution which brought them to power was effected by forces coming from north-eastern Iran, and their re-creation of the court ceremonial of the Persian Empire, all used to be taken to indicate a fully-fledged Iranian revival. But in recent years, after this nineteenth-century view was discarded, as it was observed that the Abbasid revolution was really the work of the Arabs themselves, leading specialists have pointed to the course of the Abbasid caliphate as following an internal logic of its own. To be sure, at the new court conventional Mazdean ethical formulas would be transposed literally into Arabic, and Indian animal fables would be translated from Middle Persian, but the real ferment of ideas would be Christian, Jewish, Greek, Manichaean and Gnostic.

We may note, under the Abbasids, the movement of the *Shuubiyya*, the party of the peoples, against the ruling Arabs. But it is important to remember that this is really a literary phenomenon, representing a type of writer. To be sure, this provided a cover for the disgruntled non-Arab bureaucrats, whose ancestors had had to become inferior 'associate members' of Arab tribes to qualify for Muslim status. Arabs were called 'lizard-eaters' and the past glories of Iran were extolled. But one must be extremely doubtful about modern specialists' use of literary anecdotes, with their romantic localisations of isolated poetical fragments, to show an alleged 'strength of Persian national sentiment' in the population as a whole, or its use for political purposes.

With these considerations in mind, we may now examine the political decline of the Abbasids in the ninth century and their fall in the tenth, along with the rise of regional dynasties in the Iranian world. In the past this process was also seen as a specifically Iranian phenomenon: one of Aryans casting off the Semitic yoke. Nowadays it would be attributed to the inner contradictions of the Abbasids, who claimed the right to rule as kiṇsmen but not as actual descendants of Muhammad, and to their use of slave soldiers, who were to become their masters. The rise of regional dynasties is not peculiar to Iran: it happens, noteworthily with Shi'ite rulers, in Egypt and North Africa and in Syria in the tenth century.

Moreover, the new dynasties in Iran were not always markedly Iranian. They varied from local governors whose position became hereditary to anti-sectarian vigilantes who got out of control. As for the Samanids, who ruled in north-eastern Iran and Central Asia from about 875 to 999, we may note with interest the observation made about their achievements by R.N. Frye, that whereas in Iran itself the rigid caste system of Mazdaism prevented the absorption of indigenous elements into the new religion, the relative absence of such class distinctions in Central Asia enabled Iranian culture to be preserved. When, however, he claims that the Samanids 'liberated Islam from its narrow Arab bedouin background and mores and made of it an international culture and society', we must agree with A.K.S. Lambton in dismissing this as 'arrant nonsense'. To give such a view of early Islam, which entirely abolishes the role of Abbasid Iraq, is as if one were to pretend that seventeenth-century France brought Europe out of the Middle Ages, and thereby exclude the intervention of the Italian Renaissance.

This brings us to the Shi'ite dynasty of the Buyids, who descended from their north Iranian homeland to take over Iraq and western Iran in the first half of the tenth century, capturing Baghdad in 945 and thereby severely reducing the position of the Abbasid caliphs. We encounter here a problem which is to recur, notably today: what are Shi'ites to do when they have succeeded in seizing power? The Buyid solution seems markedly cynical and opportunist, but also tolerant and pacific in its chosen compromise. The Shi'ite, Buyid military rulers were to coexist with the Sunni, Abbasid caliphs, who continued to command the loyalty of most Muslims. Each side would recognise the other and give it legitimacy. Thus the Buyids adopted and largely gave shape to the main, 'Twelver' subdivision of Shi'ism, in which the twelfth 'leader' is held to have disappeared. Meanwhile the Buyids tried, without success, to revive the old Iranian monarchy, resurrecting the ancient title *Shahanshah*, King of Kings, and reproducing an old coronation rite. We may see here, as in other periods of Iranian history, a striking illustration of what has been put forward as a general rule: the State is always an attempt to restore and imitate a lost oriental original, with all its pomp and autocracy, an attempt that is bound to fail, since the pristine tradition has been forgotten, and only the outward trappings can be recalled. In any case, the new sharing of authority can be seen as the fulfilment of an old Abbasid dream of collaboration with the Shi'ite sect, brought into effect by the influence of rich Shi'ites in Iraq, rather than as the result of an authentically Iranian interference. As for the outcome, the Buyids were inevitably unsuccessful, falling as they did between the two stools of Sunnism and Shi'ism, unable to find the support of the former and unwilling to try to impose the latter.

We may here consider the most famous of Islamic philosophers, Ibn Sina (Avicenna, d. 1037), who was intimately connected with the Samanid and Buyid princes as physician and political adviser. Here again Islam and Iran illustrate most emphatically a general tendency, that of philosophers and monarchs to engage in mutual support. Much controversy has surrounded Ibn Sina's avowed attempt to produce a mystical, 'Oriental' thought, superior to the conventional Greco-Islamic philosophy which he inherited. He does not seem to have succeeded in making a real break with the latter, but on the other hand one specialist's denial that he was a mystic on the grounds that Catholic theology 'reserves the word for one whose whole life is a great love of God' is hardly a serious contribution to the history of religions. In Ibn Sina's literary production, as in that of other Muslim thinkers, we find both straightforward clarification of the work of predecessors on the one hand, and on the other short stories in which personal and spiritual self-realisation is expressed in symbolic form.

The dynasties just mentioned were to give way to new rulers, Turks coming from their original homeland in Central Asia. These rulers were main-line, Sunni Muslims, and they were to bring about a restoration of Sunnism and the collapse of Shi'ism's political domination in the eastern Islamic world. The Sunni caliph in Baghdad, much against his will, it would seem, was 'rescued' from his comfortable arrangement with the Shi'ite dynasty of the Buyids in 1055. One family, that of the Seljuks, was now to hold sway over most Muslims in the East. They and their Iranian collaborators were to exploit all the resources of their strong and powerful state, and the institutions thereof, in order to impose upon the population a strict and respectable form of Islam. Thus a relatively new institution, the college (*madrasah*) was used to fight minority views condemned as 'heretical'. Well-subsidised students were trained in these colleges to be the official judges and jurists of the future. At the same time the lodge (*khanaqah*) of the Sufis would be used, with suitable endowments, to prevent excessive divagations and indulgence in libertinism on the part of the mystics. Political theorists were found to justify the conditions that had been imposed by force upon the caliphate, and in which the new sovereigns had effective power.

But alongside these tendencies of a restrictive character we can see others, in the opposite direction, connected with the influx of nomadic Turks from the north-east. The wilder practices of the Sufis, and of the more extended and popular class of world-renouncers called 'dervishes', of which the Sufis are a part, received a powerful stimulus from Central Asia. The discipline of 'gazing at beardless boys' in order to perceive the Divine Beauty manifested therein, and the accompanying use of song, music and dance, with the deliberate provoking of 'blame' from respectable society, were all strengthened by the Turks' original religion of shamanism, distinguished by the cultivation of ecstasy, magic and the initiate's experience of 'flying'. To be sure, these practices can be seen as originating elsewhere, among the Greeks, the Christians and the Cynics of late antiquity, and some are found everywhere; but the massive immigration of Turks was to reinforce these elements as characteristic of their tribal, nomadic society, not as 'influences' casually crossing frontiers. These themes were to overshadow, in content and background, the Persian poetry of Sufism, seen by the peoples of the eastern Islamic world as constituting their very highest cultural achievement.

Alongside these developments of an institutional and ecstatic character we may observe the extremist activities of an Ismaili sub-sect, which, from 1090 to 1256, maintained a small state of its own, based in an isolated mountain castle in northern Iran, and recognising a separate line of 'leaders'. Its notorious 'Assassins' would strike fear into the hearts of political opponents, while its secret propaganda constituted the perennial bogy of main-line Islam. At one point its chief actually proclaimed that the Last Day, the Resurrection (understood symbolically) had come and Islamic law was nullified.

As Seljuk rule declined in the second half of the twelfth century there appeared a figure central to the concept of 'Iranian Islam', the philosopher Suhrawardi, put to death, for reasons which must remain obscure, in 1192. He divided his time between Turkey and Syria, but we cannot ignore him here. The founder of the school of 'Oriental Illumination' (*ishraq*), he claimed to revive an ancient wisdom common to Greece and Iran, and dominated by the theme of Light as the all-pervading reality. But here there is no continuity of Iranian ideas from teacher to disciple. Suhrawardi himself said (as Corbin has stressed) that he had no predecessor in this enterprise, and it appears that he found no suitable pupil. His first successor in the school, Shahrazuri (*fl.* 1281), was not, as has been imagined, in contact with any of Suhrawardi's students. To be sure, Suhrawardi uses the names of Iranian angels (accompanied by royalist sentiments), but it would be wrong to see here any continuation of Mazdaism on the level of the structures themselves, which remain essentially Greek. Any similarities, for example that between a spiritual geography in Mazdean Middle Persian literature and Suhrawardi's vision of a mysterious 'No-where-place', are to be explained in terms of Greek influences in later Mazdean thought, corresponding to Platonic elements in Suhrawardi's system. As for the similarities between Plato and the oldest Iranian doctrines, with the Greek triad of reason, anger and lust corresponding to the proto-Mazdean triad of religion, war and fertility, they are explicable in terms of an original ideology of the Indo-Europeans, the linguistic ancestors of the Iranians and the Greeks.

In the same way, it is a Greek, not an Iranian structure that dominates the Sufi didactic poetry produced by Iranians in this period. Thus the poet Attar (d. 1221) presents the Spirit as having six sons, in three pairs: the experiencing of God's unity, and poverty; reason and knowledge; the lower or carnal soul and the Devil. These three pairs correspond to Neoplatonism's triad of the One, Reason and the Soul. The resemblances with Mazdaism's six Archangels and its original triad of religion, war and fertility are only partial and again understandable as due to a common Indo-European heritage.

In the thirteenth century Iran, like many other countries, was subject to invasions, enormous massacres and conquest at the hands of the Mongols. Islamic apologists often attribute the apparent decline of their religion and civilisation to this momentous intervention. Against this it has been said that the seeds of decline were visible before the Mongols' advent, and came to fruition in countries not overrun by them. At any rate, as far as Islam is concerned, it can be said that the Mongol conquest acted as a catalyst in a transformation that was to some extent prefigured and need not necessarily be viewed as a 'decline'.

Two elements dominated in this transformation, in the course of the thirteenth century. One was that of the Sufi organisations. Arising shortly before the Mongol conquest, and emphasising the important role of the Sufi master, they had to respond to the devastation that now ensued and provide leadership for Muslim society beneath non-Muslim rule. The result was inevitably a higher degree of collaboration with temporal authority, enrichment and political involvement on the one hand, and the even greater glorification of the individual Sufi teacher on the other, as the caliphate of Baghdad was overthrown.

The second dominant element was the introduction of the mystical doctrine of the Andalusian Ibn Arabi (d. 1240), Sufism's main systematiser. This was to overshadow all subsequent Muslim thinking, and effectively take over Sufi theory in the eastern Islamic world, notably in Iran, where it found a particularly fertile soil. Ibn Arabi's system is called that of 'the unity of existence' and comes dangerously close to monism, the belief that there is only one Being in all existence. It also emphasises the cosmic role of the mystic as a 'Perfect Man', an interface between God and this world of appearances.

Thus whereas in the pre-Mongol period main-line, Sunni Muslims stood before God without an intermediary, and Sufis, as Sunnis, were seen as natural enemies by the Shi'ites, intent on the mediation of their 'leaders', by the fourteenth century much had changed. The Sufi master, alive or dead, was accorded an all-important veneration. Sufism and Shi'ism now both represented a 'catholic' spirituality. An Iranian Sufi Shi'ite could write with justification that 'he who Shi'ises Sufises and he who Sufises Shi'ises'. In the fourteenth and fifteenth centuries Shi'ism and Ibn Arabi are the principal influences in Persian Sufi literature. To be sure, the writers usually cited as evidence for the advance of Shi'ism were often Sunnis, who made violent attacks upon the Shi'a as a sect. But their veneration for the family of Muhammad, akin to that of an Anglo-Catholic for Mary, was expressed more and more strongly. The boundary between Sunni and Shi'ite was not so clear as it was later to become.

The Mongol Empire was to split up into regional commands, and the rulers in Iran were to be converted to Islam before losing their power in the chaos and confusion of the fourteenth century. Then various attempts were made by the indigenous population to govern themselves. Rebels arose, notably in a Shi'ite district in north-eastern Iran, where an extensive 'republic' was set up, constituting a remarkable exception to the usual run of dynasties. But this state was weakened by a fight between a faction of Shi'ite dervishes and a conservative oligarchy, and the latter submitted to a new Central Asian conqueror, Timur (d. 1405).

In the fifteenth century yet more disorder and agitation ensued. Of particular interest is the synthesis made by Ibn Abi Jumhur (*fl.* 1474–99) of Shi'ite theology, philosophy, especially that of 'Oriental Illumination', and Sufism, thereby prefiguring a later mixture that was to be popular in Iran, and, in its originality, affording a refreshing contrast to the more academic, backward-looking character of Sunnism at this time. It was in this period that what had been a quietly respectable Sunni organisation of Sufis, presided over by a family known as the Safavids, turned to Shi'ism and political and military activities, with all-important results for Islam in Iran.

At the end of the fifteenth century and the beginning of the sixteenth a revolution was begun and successfully carried out by a son of this family, at the time a mere boy, who, as Shah Ismail (1501–24), founded the Safavid dynasty of kings and brutally imposed Twelver Shi'ism as the official religion of Iran. This was done thanks to his nomadic followers, Turks, who invaded Iran from the West. Today no serious student would repeat the nineteenth-century view that the Safavid revolution was an expression of Iranian nationalism. On the contrary, as Jean Aubin has done well to emphasise, it was fully impregnated by the old Central Asian tribal traditions of Ismail's Turkish supporters, which were now manifested in cannibalism and using the skull of the enemy as a cup. Ismail's massacres and use of torture were horrific even by the standards of the day. However, one must be sceptical about the interpretation by some specialists of his verses to mean that he claimed to be God 'incarnate'. The idea of incarnation is expressly rejected by the Sufi poetical tradition in which these verses must be seen. That said, his followers certainly gave him immense veneration, which, added to their messianism, posed a considerable problem for the new state. Again there arose the question of how a successful revolution could be continued. Shi'ite Sufis have tended to see, or be accused of seeing, the present heads of their organisations as in some way identical with the twelfth 'leader' of the Twelver Shi'ites, considered to have disappeared and to be awaiting the right moment to return and fill the world with justice. But there was to be no fulfilment of messianic hopes, and thus the Safavid state was fatally flawed from the outset.

Accordingly, when Shah Tahmasp (1524–76) was proclaimed as the Mahdi, the divinely guided ruler whose advent was expected, by some Sufi supporters in 1554–5, he felt obliged to execute their chiefs. He preferred the more cautious policy of diplomatic marriages between his family and the religious classes. Shah Abbas (1588–1629) was able to restrain the tribal and dervish elements to which the dynasty owed its initial success. He tried to present himself as the Sufi master whose disciples would be the population as a whole. With him the family achieved its greatest power and splendour.

But the rise of the Shi'ite jurists, consequent upon the imposition of their creed, was to weaken the dynasty that had enforced its acceptance. Thus later in the seventeenth century discussion centred on a question of great contemporary interest: should society be controlled by an outstanding jurist, in the absence of the 'twelfth leader', or should it be ruled by descendants of one of the 'leaders', as the Safavids claimed to be? The Shahs did their best to check the jurists, by bureaucratic control and keeping legal proceedings out of their grasp. But as the state grew more feeble and less religious the jurists became increasingly an opposition to it.

We must now consider a phenomenon of the very greatest importance, sadly neglected by many previous writers: the brilliant revival of philosophy in Safavid Iran. Why did this take place, when in the rest of the Muslim world philosophy, and indeed theology, had effectively been suppressed? One particular reason is that a thirteenth-century collaborator of the Mongol conquerors had diverted religious trusts in order to subsidise the philosophical sciences in Iran, and consequently they continued to be studied there. A more general explanation is to be found in the theological positions of Shi'ism, taken over from the Mutazilite sect, which had borrowed its methods from Greek philosophy. Yet another is to be seen in the pro-philosophical leanings of strong monarchies, such as the Safavid Empire at its height of glory.

The philosophical revival is dominated by the figure of one man, Mulla Sadra (d. 1640), who brought about a great revolution in his discipline, and founded a kind of 'existentialism'. For he insisted that existence itself is original and prior to the essences of things, and he developed a system on this basis for the first time. Being, in its acts of existing, produces essences, which, since they are not original, are not unchangeable, as is usually the case in Islamic thought, but go through infinite degrees of alteration in a process of movement which actually operates within substances themselves. Thus Sadra was able to go much further than his predecessors in Iran in liberating philosophy from its conventional self-restrictions, while incorporating Ibn Arabi's Sufi doctrine of the 'unity of existence' and applying the whole to the Shi'ite canon of 'Traditions'. The result was to inspire an impressive progression of philosophical thinking up to the present day.

Complementing Sadra's work in philosophy is that done in law by Majlisi (d. 1699). In him Shi'ite learning finds its definitive and most comprehensive expression and codification, notably in the field of the 'Traditions' attributed to the 'leaders' in Muhammad's family, and constituting the main source of jurisprudence. Thus he and his colleagues, in contrast to Sadra and his school, represented a greater concern with externals, and manifested a considerable hostility, which was to be continued to the present day, towards Sufism, as improperly transferring veneration to the heads of the organised 'brotherhoods'. Unfortunately, Majlisi also had considerable hostility for Sunnis, and it was largely thanks to him that they were persecuted, so that Sunnis from Afghanistan duly revolted and overthrew the Safavid Empire in 1722.

There now followed a peculiar episode. A new monarch, Nadir Shah (1736–47), tried to find a diplomatic solution to heal the rift between Shi'ite Iran and the Sunni exterior. For the existence of the Shi'ite, Safavid Empire between two Sunni empires, the Turkish, Ottoman Empire on the one hand and the Indian, Mogul Empire on the other, had hardened the divisions between the two main sects of Islam. Nadir thought that by depriving Shi'ism of its most offensive aspects, the rejection and the public vilification of Muhammad's first successors as usurpers, and by restyling it as a 'Jafarite' school of law, so named after the sixth 'leader' of the Shi'ites, he could get it accepted as a fifth respectable school of law alongside the four established among the Sunnis. As it happened, the Ottoman Empire and its jurists refused to agree to this, and in any case Nadir's extreme cruelty led to his murder. One must severely doubt the viability of his enterprise. After him the most powerful ruler in Iran, Karim Khan Zand (*c.* 1751–79), was a loyal and tolerant servant of both Shi'ism and the continuing shadow of Safavid legitimacy, which retained popular support despite the actual fall of the dynasty, owing to its claim to descent from Muhammad's family.

During the violent chaos of the eighteenth century many Iranian religious scholars took refuge in the Shi'ite centres of Iraq, and there something happened which was to have immense reverberations in our own time. For a long time, Shi'ite lawyers had been divided between two factions, the Akhbaris or 'Traditionites', who insisted that one should simply conform to the canonical 'Traditions', and the Usulis or 'Principlites' who held that the qualified jurist could use his own judgement. Now whereas in the early eighteenth century the 'Traditionites' carried all before them, by the end of the century they were effectively beaten for ever. The attraction of the opposite position doubtless lay in the massive political power which it conferred on the jurists, whom the ordinary believer was required to obey.

It would be wrong, however, to imagine that the 'Traditionites' were mere dusty pedants. On the contrary, they gave rise to a number of original thinkers in the field of mystical philosophy, and notably the Shaykhi school, so called after its founder, Shaykh Ahmad Ahsai (d. 1826). This movement, though small in itself, continuing up to our own time in one family in an out-of-the-way provincial city, has none the less given birth to a large and world-wide development in the history of religions. For this school's spiritual emphasis on a secret *Bab* or gate, that is an unknown person acting as intermediary between the hidden twelfth 'leader' and his followers, was to lead to the appearance in the nineteenth century of someone publicly claiming to be the *Bab*, and the consequent founding of a new sect, Babism, and a new religion, Bahaism.

Also in the late eighteenth century, and on the mystical side, we must observe the revival of Sufism, and the return of Sufi masters after a long period of exile in India. The Safavid state and its jurists had persecuted these dervishes in the past: now, when the Sufis came back after the fall of the empire, the lawyers were to hound several of them to their deaths.

We now come to the history of the Qajar dynasty (1785–1924). The religious aspects of this period have been admirably presented by Hamid Algar, in a study that shows us many elements which have resurfaced violently in recent years. This dynasty did not have the aura of legitimacy conferred on the Safavids by their claim to descent from Muhammad's family. Real power lay in the hands of the Shi'ite jurists: but, unlike their contemporary counterparts, they chose to exercise it without taking over the apparatus of the State, for which they evinced an undisguised distaste. Here they found a natural ally in the merchant class, which was also independent of the government and hostile to such un-Islamic innovations as customs duties and foreign loans. Opposition to the monarchy found expression in the public recitation of verses evoking the martyrdom of Husein, the third 'leader' of the Shi'ites, and in the association of the reigning house with the rulers responsible for his killing. As in recent years, opposition to the

Shah from a jurist brought the latter increased popular respect, while one who collaborated with the dynasty found himself unable to exercise the ultimate authority of the expert considered to have the greatest knowledge.

Of particular interest is the massacre of the Russian Legation in Tehran in 1829. Here the religious scholars showed their ability to mobilise rioters in defence of Islam: it was alleged that the Russians were detaining Muslim women. The Shah had to threaten a counter-massacre, that of the populace, in order to ensure the departure of the religious leader who had been most prominent in the agitation.

In the reign of Muhammad Shah (1834–48), the government was in the hands of his Sufi teacher. Resistance was led by a jurist who was not only the spiritual, but also the temporal master of a former capital, Isfahan, and ruled as an extremely rich man, revered by the population, with a mysterious organisation of brigands to help him. The reign of Nasir al-Din Shah (1848–96) was marked by tyranny and yet more resistance from the Muslim leadership. Violence surrounded Europeanisation, special concessions given to foreigners, the rise of the new sect of Babism, and the right of sanctuary, which was exercised not only in shrines but also in mosques and the houses of the scholar-jurists.

Antagonism reached its height in the tobacco crisis of 1891–2. The monarchy had given a monopoly of all commercial activities involving tobacco to a British company. The religious leaders and merchants united to force the government to cancel this. Their success demonstrated the Shi'ite loyalty of the population, who boycotted the use of tobacco when copies of a legal opinion were circulated, declaring smoking to be equivalent to war against the twelfth 'leader' of Muhammad's family. One should notice in this affair, the classic use, still practised nowadays, of the jurist's highly effective threat to go away and deprive his supporters of his spiritual guidance, and also the practice by demonstrators of dressing themselves in their shrouds in preparation for martyrdom.

In 1905 a beating inflicted upon some merchants for opposing the government provoked the scholar-jurists into actually leaving the capital. In 1906, as the agitation continued, they did so again and forced the monarchy to agree to the grant of a constitution. The constitution gave the religious leaders a right of veto over legislation, but in practice this clause remained a dead letter. Britain and Russia cynically intervened to divide the country between themselves. The resulting disorder gave rise to a new dynasty, that of the Pahlavis, founded by Rida (Reza) Shah (1925–41).

This potentate had secured his power by having Chopin's Funeral March played during the main Shi'ite period of mourning, thus falsely convincing the scholar–jurists that he was on their side. He now embarked upon a series of measures designed to Europeanise Iran and deprive the country of its Islamic character. He tried to ban the veil and believed that progress could be achieved by making men wear a Western style of hat.

Although his own limited literacy occasioned many a jest, his regime tried to impose examinations upon students of the religious sciences, who had managed perfectly well without them for centuries. Not surprisingly, positive achievements were few. The Shah's open pro-Nazi sympathies were to provide a pretext for another British and Russian intervention in the Second World War, and he left his relieved subjects for South Africa.

His son and successor, Muhammad Rida Shah (1941–79), was also to hold views characteristic of the losing side of the Second World War. He had to be restored to power by American intelligence officers in 1953, and later concentrated upon the fulfilment of increasingly grander visions, which he identified with 'civilisation'. Money from oil revenues was lavished upon Western academics, whose obliging panegyrics replaced the court poetry of yore, and who discovered an enlightened tolerance in pre-Islamic Iranian kings. Torture was carried out on an unparalleled scale, presumably illustrating the continuity of ancient 'national' traditions, now elevated above the Semitic intrusion of Islam.

In 1963 the regime gunned down a large number of the religious leaders' supporters, in an action which was later saluted by the British Ambassador of that time as the very highest masterpiece of statesmanship. The population was to take a different view. One leading scholar–jurist, the Ayatollah Khomeini, had distinguished himself by his outspoken stance, and was thus able, in long years of exile, to command the allegiance of his fellow-countrymen. In the later 1970s the Shah's self-identification with Iran's pre-Islamic past became increasingly divorced from practicability, as the regime tried to replace the Islamic calendar with an 'Imperial' one, and had Khomeini denounced as a British agent. By now the religious leadership and the population in general had had enough, and after further attempts to intimidate his subjects by mass shootings had failed the Shah left, for Khomeini to return in 1979.

The continuation of the Revolution, with the establishing of an Islamic Republic, has followed a pattern normal in revolutions, with inevitable disappointments, excesses and abuses. Added to this, an attack from a Sunni regime in Iraq, ruling a very large Shi'ite population, and the ensuing long war, with huge loss of life, provided a tragically significant underlining of the two countries' interdependence in religious history. In general, with regard to recent developments, it must be said that the more privileged classes of Iranian society (along with American and British meddlers) should bear a heavy burden of blame for their irresponsible conduct under the Shah. Their absurd efforts to ape the manners of the West, while losing touch with the lower classes and the latter's traditional, Islamic culture, along with the Shah's failure to develop genuinely representative institutions, were bound to result in chaos. Not surprisingly, they now complain that they do not receive more money, food and influence than their social inferiors.

Recent political activity, then, points to a real continuity in the insurrectionary traditions of Islam in Iran, as opposed to the discontinuity of the monarchical failures to revive a forgotten past. It seems better to speak of 'Islam in Iran' rather than 'Iranian Islam': it was Muslims who changed the country, rather than Iranians who changed the religion. The strange form of Islam in Iran, a poignant cult of martyrdoms, is dominated by paradoxical features that owe their origin to the early development of the religion itself: Twelver Shi'ism has become a Catholicism without the phenomenon of a Church, and involves a messianism whose infallible Messiah can apparently never come, since the elite who would confirm his legitimacy seem to view his interior presence as excluding his physical advent. The result is a Papacy without a Pope, while on the other hand the rich tradition of Persian Sufi poetry, with its glorification of ecstasy against conventional worship, vigorously expresses the sentiments of anticlericalism without a clergy as such to attack. But such paradoxes are inherent in the nature of both mysticism and religion, and it is difficult to see how any viable solution to Iran's present problems could be expressed in terms other than Islamic.

Further Reading

One may wish to read Chapters 20 and 34, 'Early Islam' and 'Mazdaism' in conjunction with this chapter.

Algar, Hamid *Religion and State in Iran 1785–1906* (University of California Press, Berkeley, 1969)

Bakhash, Shaul *The Reign of the Ayatollahs* (Tauris, London, 1985)

Corbin, Henry *Spiritual Body and Celestial Earth* (Princeton University Press, New Jersey, 1977)

—— *The Man of Light in Iranian Sufism* (Shambhala Publications, 1981)

The Cambridge History of Iran, vols. 4–5 (Cambridge University Press, Cambridge, 1968–75)

23 Islam in the Indian Sub-Continent

F.A. Nizami

Introduction

In sheer numerical terms, the Islamic presence in the Indian sub-continent is far more significant than is generally appreciated. Put together, the Muslim population of Bangladesh, India and Pakistan is greater than that of the Middle East. Intellectually, this region has made one of the biggest contributions to the corpus of Islamic literature. Socially, it has given rise to powerful movements of cultural syncretism or religious revitalisation, some of which continue to be important today. In the realms of culture, art and architecture, the sub-continent boasts a rich heritage. A short chapter cannot bring out the various dimensions and complexities of this story. Here only a synoptic overview of some of the major trends in what are now Bangladesh, India and Pakistan has been attempted. Generalisations and lacunae are inevitable in such a treatment but it is hoped that this account will provide a broad understanding of the subject.

An obvious indicator of the Islamic presence in any region is the existence of Muslim political institutions at any given time. This is no doubt true of the sub-continent as well, but historically, in this region, Islam and Muslim political authority have not necessarily been conterminous: the grand edifices of the medieval empires drew their inspiration and often indeed their legitimation from Iranian notions of kingship rather than the Shari'a (religious law) and in that sense they were not Islamic, although they are ascribed that meaning in a symbolic, political sense; and in independent India, alongside a predominant Hindu majority, exists a substantial Muslim minority larger in size than the entire population of Pakistan.

Islam reached the sub-continent before the Muslim armies. The earliest contact between India and the Islamic world was essentially commercial and cultural. Over time this had resulted, prior to the actual conquest, in the growth of Muslim settlements on the coastal regions and the northern boundaries of the country. By the twelfth to thirteenth centuries small indigenous Muslim communities, often centred round immigrant teachers and saints, had cropped up in the interior of the country such as at Nagaur, Ajmer, Badaon and Qannauj.

Merchants and navigators were the nexus between Islamic Arabia and pre-Muslim India. Trade documents, known as Geniza records, have revealed the existence of brisk commercial activity between the two regions and also the existence of corporate institutions, such as *Karim*, to oversee international trade. On the western coast of India, small Arab settlements had grown up, along with a new ethnic element, *Baysar*, the offspring of Indian mothers and Arab fathers. Arab settlers enjoyed freedom to practise their own juridical system and indeed introduced many Islamic practices albeit on a rather restricted scale. There are references to the appointment of Muslim judges by Hindu rajas which again points to the existence of pockets of Muslim population in different parts of the country. A corollary to Arab settlements in India was the existence of small Indian communities near Arab seaports which came to be known as *Arz al-Hind* (Land of India).

Commercial contact inevitably promoted cultural interaction and indeed exchange of knowledge. As early as the time of the Prophet, Indian pickles were available in Arabia. In later years, an Indian physician was summoned for the treatment of the Prophet's wife, Ayesha. Languages borrowed words from each other: Arab navigational terms became prevalent in India; names of Indian commodities found their way into Arab vocabulary. With linguistic interaction, intellectual exchange was inevitable.

The different social roles performed by enterprising Arab traders, Muslim learned and holy men, and indeed adventurous military commanders and soldiers, created the channels through which Islam reached the sub-continent. Equally important in the processes of Islam's development were the impact of Islamic egalitarian and monotheistic ideas on the Indian social structure; the increase in the Muslim population by large-scale migrations from Islamic lands; and the strength that indigenous Muslim communities derived from the growth of an Indo-Islamic social and cultural order as reflected in lifestyles, language and literature, towns and urban institutions, and above all, dispensation of justice.

When the Umayyads (661–750 CE) embarked on an era of imperial expansion, their forces, led by Muhammad bin Qasim, son-in-law of Hajjaj, captured Sind in 711 CE. *Chachnamah*, the earliest history of Sind, records this encounter and also quotes the Brahmanabad Declaration which Muhammad bin Qasim issued after his victory. Complete religious and economic freedom was assured to the Indians. They were retained in all government positions and even the status of *Ahl al Kitab* (people with a Revealed Book with whom a covenant is permitted) was accorded to them. The generous treatment meted out to the vanquished created the right climate for the consolidation and extension of Muslim power in Sind. The lure of complete equality with the rulers was later held out to those who embraced Islam and consequently some tribes became Muslim. However, the Islamisation of Sind as a consequence of this first encounter was short lived. With Muhammad bin Qasim's recall to Syria, his bust also joined the earlier pantheon of idols and Sind lapsed into its pre-Islamic beliefs.

Under the Abbasids (750–1258 CE), particularly the Barmakids, a phase of closer cultural contact between India and Baghdad ensued. A large number of Indian scholars—especially physicians and mathematicians—were invited to the Abbasid court. At Baghdad a bureau was entrusted with the task of translating Indian works into Arabic and a hospital was established which specialised in Indian medicine. Inevitably this led to the growth of a class of bilingual scholars who became the transmitters of ideas between the Islamic world and the sub-continent.

With the rise of the post-Abbasid dynasties of Afghanistan a new phase started which was marked by the effective establishment of Muslim political authority in north India. The Ghaznavids under Sultan Mahmud (998–1030) consolidated and expanded their territories. During the early decades of the eleventh century, Sultan Mahmud led seventeen military campaigns into India but did not annex any territory until 1026–7 when Multan and Lahore were incorporated into the Ghaznavid sultnate. These invasions to a certain extent introduced the elements of power and force into the relationship between the sub-continent and the Islamic world and thereby altered the nature of cultural interaction that had taken place since the time of the Abbasids. Often Mahmud's expeditions have been looked upon as holy wars but the desire for plunder and booty seem predominant. Non-Muslim generals assisted Mahmud, and his devastation of some famous temples was less a manifestation of pious iconoclasm than an attempt to gain the centuries-old hoarded wealth of India. Alberuni, a great philosopher and scientist, who visited India during that period, observed in a perspicacious remark that Indians developed a hostility and aversion towards Islam because of the wanton destruction wrought by Ghaznavid armies. During the next hundred and fifty years, while the penetration of Turkish military power into northern India was stoutly resisted by the Rajputs, Muslim learned and holy men settled in different Indian towns and became the focuses for the growth of small Muslim colonies.

Mahmud's motives may not have been religious but he and large numbers of his soldiers were Muslim. They carried with themselves Islam into the heartland of north India and when they withdrew left behind the occasional convert such as Rai Hardat, ruler of Baran; or the fallen soldier, whose tomb, as in Bahraich, became a shrine; or indeed the itinerant scholar-saint who devoted himself to explaining the faith to the common man both by precept and practice. When, in the twelfth century, Ghurids replaced the Ghaznavids in Afghanistan, parts of north India were incorporated not only into a Muslim political system but increasingly within the ambit of Islamic cultural and ideological influences radiating from Central Asia. Towards the close of the twelfth century, the ruler of Ghur (a small principality in Afghanistan), Shihabuddin Muhammad, started attacking India and gradually the region from Multan to Delhi was occupied. In 1206, Qutbuddin Aibek, a slave general of Shihabuddin Muhammad, broke away from Ghur and laid the foundations of an independent sultanate with its capital at Delhi.

The Delhi Sultanate, the Mogul Empire and the Modern States

Within the general rubric of the Delhi Sultanate are included five dynasties that ruled north India from Qutbuddin Aibek onwards: Mamluks (1210–90); Khaljis (1290–1320); Tughluqs (1320–1413); Saiyyids (1414–51); and Lodis (1451–1526). They all had Turko-Afghan origins and in terms of the nature of state organisation they represent certain elements of continuity. The Delhi sultans attempted to control the centrifugal forces prevalent in Rajput India: they tried to liquidate feudal fiefs and established a centralised monarchy with a system of appointment, promotion and transfer of officers. The Mamluk state was basically racist: power rested with the Turks alone and slaves occupied an important position in the governing class. Sultan Iltutmish (1210–36) was the first to seek an Islamic legitimation for his authority when, in 1229, he sought and obtained an investiture from the Caliph of Baghdad. Iltutmish conquered Bihar, Rajputana and Multan. The Khaljis incorporated various sections of Indian society within the power structure and in that sense transformed the state into an Indo-Muslim state. Alauddin (1296–1316), the most famous Khalji sultan, introduced significant changes in the collection of land revenue, attempted to control prices of essential commodities, embarked on an era of expansion of the empire and was the first ruler to try and enforce prohibition—a measure not born out of religious zeal but the need to control the nobility. Alauddin established diplomatic relations with the Il-Khanids and their famous historian, Rashiduddin Fazlullah, visited his court as an emissary. Muhammad bin Tughluq (1324–51) marked the next stage in the evolution of the Indo-Muslim state when he admitted non-Muslims to military and government offices and ensured complete religious freedom to all. He conquered parts of the Deccan and even tried to build an outpost of Indo-Islamic culture in the south by attempting to create a second capital at Daulatabad. He established diplomatic relations with the Asiatic powers, strengthened the political and administrative unity of the country, introduced token currency and welcomed scholars from various parts of the Islamic world. The two centuries following Muhammad bin Tughluq witnessed the invasion of Timur (1398), the rise of Saiyyids (1414–51) and Lodis (1451–1526) as well as of small, independent regional principalities. In the growth of Islamic culture and society in the sub-continent, the provincial dynasties of the Deccan, Gujarat, Malwa, Bengal and Jaunpur have performed a significant function. At the time of decadence of the sultanate, they kept the vitality of Muslim political authority intact on the peripheries of the empire. To varying degrees they articulated and Islamised local sentiments, traditions and art forms. Under their patronage, regional languages developed, creating new vehicles for the transmission of ideas. Regional dynasts patronised saints, made huge endowments, and generally facilitated the flowering of an urban aristocratic Indo-Islamic culture. Some of the noteworthy provincial dynasties were the Bahmanis (1347–1686) in Bijapur; the Qutb Shahis (1491–1688) in Golconda; and the Husain Shahis (1494–1538) in Bengal.

The last of the five dynasties of the Delhi Sultanate, the Lodi, was swept aside in 1526 by the successful forces of Babar who laid the foundation of the Mogul empire. Except for a brief interregnum when Babar's son Humayun was displaced by the Afghan ruler Sher Shah, the Moguls ruled the sub-continent in their full glory until the death of Aurangzeb in 1707. For a century thereafter the dynasty survived with fluctuating fortunes in the face of strident and assertive regional forces. In 1803, the Mogul emperor virtually became a puppet in the hands of the English East India Company but he tottered on until finally the British Crown took over in 1857.

The Moguls ensured religious freedom to all people. Akbar (1556–1605) entered into matrimonial alliances with the Hindus, patronised temples and received Jesuit missionaries. Aurangzeb (d. 1707), the last of the Great Moguls, reimposed *jiziya* (poll-tax) on the non-Muslims but freedom of opportunity continued. The Moguls dismantled the racist governing class of the sultans, in some ways bureaucratised the nobility, embarked on a large-scale expansion of the empire and greatly patronised arts and architecture. Mogul culture was truly cosmopolitan: Turkish, Iranian and Indian elements were equally present in it. The imperial court set the cultural pattern for the urban elite but there were also other institutions, such as the *diwan khanas*, which articulated it. With the decline of centralised Mogul authority, regional princely states such as Hyderabad and Awadh assumed virtual independence, though for a long time they continued to pay token allegiance to Delhi. The British entered into alliances with these states and incorporated them into a network of collaboration. For quite some time, after the decline of Mogul authority, these princely states provided alternative patronage to Indo-Islamic culture and stood out as the symbols of Muslim political and cultural dominance in the sub-continent.

In 1857, Indian soldiers serving in the army of the English East India Company joined hands with large sections of the population in a big uprising against foreign domination. This has been described by British historians as a mutiny, and by the nationalist historians as a war of independence. The uprising was mainly centred in north India and was successfully suppressed by the British forces. Muslims, who had played a prominent part in it, bore the brunt of the repressions that followed: thousands were hanged and shot; many had their lands confiscated; and the community generally came under suspicion. The Mogul emperor who was considered to be the rallying point for opposition to foreign rule was deposed and sent to Burma. In the post-1857 period, Muslim leaders like Sir Syed Ahmad Khan tried to ameliorate the position of their community by exhorting Muslims to take to modern education, to improve their social and economic position, and above all to adopt a loyalist attitude towards the British.

When, in December 1885, the Indian National Congress was formed as a channel for the peaceful and constitutional expression of the discontent felt by educated Indians, some Muslims like Badruddin Tyabji participated in it. The Congress soon became the vehicle for the presentation of nationalist aspirations, but in certain quarters it came to be regarded as a predominantly Hindu organisation. In 1906 some Muslims formed a separate body called the All Indian Muslim League as the organ for articulating the political aspirations of Muslims in the sub-continent. It is noteworthy that even after the formation of the League, many Muslims continued to play an important part in the Congress. The Muslim League demanded and secured separate electorates for Muslims. In 1916, it entered into a pact with the Congress to wage a joint struggle for India's freedom. However, the meeting of ways between the Congress and the Muslim League was short lived. After the First World War, Muslims, supported by other Indians, launched a mass struggle known as the Khilafat movement, in support of the restoration of the Caliphate in Turkey. Maulana Muhammad Ali was the outstanding leader of this movement.

Under the leadership of Muhammad Ali Jinnah, the Muslim League argued that in an independent India with universal adult franchise, Muslims would be swamped by the Hindus and would have no effective say even in their own affairs. Hence, various safeguards were demanded. Politics, personal ambitions, mutual fears and suspicions on either side combined to thwart any agreement. The Muslim League called for a separate homeland for Muslims. This view was not shared by the whole community. Political leaders, like Maulana Abul Kalam Azad, and religious scholars, mainly from Deoband, such as Maulana Husain Ahmad Madani, remained opposed to it. However this demand gained strong support in certain areas and, when the British finally left, the sub-continent was partitioned into two independent countries, India and Pakistan. The latter consisted of West Punjab, Sind, North-West Frontier, Baluchistan and East Bengal. The eastern and western wings of Pakistan were separated by a distance of nearly a thousand miles. Demands for greater provincial autonomy, better distribution of resources and discontent at the unequal economic development of the country at the expense of the eastern wing led, in 1971, to a civil war in Pakistan which finally resulted in a conflict with India. It culminated in the splitting up of Pakistan and the declaration of independence by the eastern wing as the independent state of Bangladesh. Both Bangladesh and Pakistan have a predominantly Muslim population while in India Muslims constitute the single largest minority.

Indo-Muslim Society

With the expansion of Muslim political power, the sub-continent experienced the inevitable growth of religious, educational and cultural institutions innate to Islamic lifestyles. Mosques for congregational prayers, *madrasahs* for religious instructions, and Sufi hospices—*khanqahs*—for spiritual culture sprang up either as direct or indirect consequence of political expansion. These institutions, manned by individuals who in a sense were the exemplars—the 'ideal types'—of an Islamic personality, often aloof and detached from the lust and greed of power, became far more potent vehicles for transmitting the faith than all the fear or temptation that successful military commanders could generate.

In pre-Muslim India, religion, custom and tradition all advocated a strict division of society on caste lines. Alberuni informs us that non-caste people were not even permitted to live within the city walls. With the establishment of the Delhi Sultanate fundamental changes took place in the organisation of cities: from being caste cities, they became cosmopolitan in character. The political support for the notion of hereditary caste disappeared; the economic, social and cultural demands of Muslim towns created opportunities for people from all strata of society; and, at least at the theoretical level, the notion of Islamic egalitarianism challenged the ideological underpinning of the caste system. Considerations of family status in matters of matrimony which have been prevalent amongst Muslims, or the racism of the early sultans, could never have the same social implications as the hereditary nature of the Indian caste system. Islamic egalitarianism, as epitomised by an ordinary Muslim itinerant, scholar, trader or teacher, attracted many non-caste Hindus. A large number of conversions to Islam took place among lower castes and professional groups. This process was facilitated by the message of love and kindness which the Sufis (mystics) propagated. They approached the oppressed masses not with the fiery zeal of a proselytiser but with the understanding and sympathy of a fellow human being. Chishti saints like Shaykh Muinuddin at Ajmer and Shaykh Fariduddin (d. 1265) at Pakpattan attracted hundreds of Hindus to their hospices. Recent researches have shown that Sufis played a major role in the conversion of non-Muslims to Islam. Increase in the Muslim population on the sub-continent was also caused by a continuing influx of refugees into India in the wake of Ghuzz and Mongol invasions of Islamic lands. Then there were those scholars, artisans and soldiers from Central Asia, Iraq and Persia who came looking for the medieval Indian El Dorado. This population influx into the sub-continent performed a twin function: on the one hand, it reinforced the Muslim presence in numerical terms which inevitably extended and intensified the process of Islamisation; and, on the other, this fresh inflow of population from regions where Islam was firmly entrenched as a religious and cultural system assisted the development of a high Islamic tradition and provided a check against uncontrolled assimilation and syncretism in the Indian environment.

With the reorganisation of administration in conquered lands, new opportunities were created for people well-versed in Islamic law and Persian language. Initially immigrants filled these positions but gradually educational institutions (*madrasahs*) which provided such instruction grew in number. Intellectual contact between Islam and the sub-continent might have been independent of the political encounter but the latter certainly enhanced it. The efflorescence of an urban aristocratic culture also owed much to official patronage.

Sufis charted out the sub-continent into spiritual dominions (*wilayat*) and the areas where they settled became centres of religious learning and spiritual devotion. They facilitated the transmission of Islam to those parts of the sub-continent where political power had not reached or where the officers of the state had no reason to be present. The main Sufi orders were the Chishtiya, the Suhrawardiya, the Firdausiya, the Shattariya, the Qadiriya and the Naqshbandiya. The Chishti order spread out all over India; the activities of the Suhrawardis were mainly confined to the Punjab and Sind, and the Firdausis concentrated on Bihar. The important hospices of the Shattaris were located in Gujarat and Bengal while those of the Qadiris were in the Punjab. The Naqshbandi order reached India during the sixteenth century and soon established centres all over the sub-continent. Ideologically the Chishtis and the Shattaris were closer: they believed in the unity of Being (*wahdat al-wujud*). The Naqshbandis and, to a certain extent, the Suhrawardis represented, in varying degrees, a second approach characterised by opposition to pantheistic ideas and emphasis on adherence to the religious law. The Firdausis, in some ways, attempted to adopt a middle course by reconciling *wujudi* (unity of Being) and *shuhudi* (unity of Vision) ideas.

The Chishtis and Shattaris worked with great success among the non-Muslims and the Suhrawardis among the Muslims. The energies of the Naqshbandis were also directed mainly towards their co-religionists; they tried to imbue them with a spirit of revitalisation of the faith and to attract them to the path of the Shari'a (religious law) and *Sunna* (path of the Prophet Muhammad).

The Sufi attitude towards preaching is well summed up in this remark of the famous Chishti saint, Shaykh Nizamuddin Auliya (d. 1325): 'Example is better than precept.' The Sufis tried to draw people towards Islam by setting a personal example and by bringing solace to the hearts of those who came to their hospices. They emphasised cultivation of human emotions as a means of attaining direct communion with the Ultimate Reality. Often they identified themselves with local practices and customs. Sufis were not opposed to the Shari'a (religious law) but emphasised that the spirit underlying it was equally important. However, in certain areas and groups many practices were adopted which came to be strongly criticised for being un-Islamic.

The *ulema* (religious scholars) generally performed the role of guardians and upholders of Islamic law and in that sense protected the social and cultural identity of the Muslim community. Some of them latched on to state power and often compromised their position. Others remained unaffected or aloof from it and ensured that neither the political expediencies of the rulers nor the liberalism and accommodation of the Sufis compromised the essence of Islamic belief and lifestyle. They accepted offices and performed various administrative functions in the judicial and revenue departments. Very often they came into conflict with the Sufis over some of the practices adopted by the latter and strongly criticised all accretions and innovations. Sufis criticised them for taking a rigid legalistic approach towards religion and missing out its spirit. By the eighteenth to nineteenth centuries there was a drawing together of some strands within these two traditions and often an individual combined in himself the roles of a Sufi (mystic) and an *alim* (scholar).

Islamic Religious Thought

India inherited the conceptual framework and the ideological parameters prevalent amongst the scholars in the Islamic world during the eleventh and twelfth centuries. This was the period when in the wake of the Mongol cataclysm, a fresh interpretation of religion had given way to the desire to preserve and protect existing beliefs. In the sub-continent, during the course of succeeding decades, faint rumblings of the Asharite and Mutazilite debate continued to be heard but, on the whole, the emphasis remained on preservation rather than creativity. Commentaries on the Qur'an and the Traditions of the Prophet and a few treatises on mysticism and jurisprudence defined the broad boundaries of enquiry. Raziuddin Hasan Saghani's *Mashariq al-Anwar*, a selection of Traditions from the collections of Bukhari and Muslim, remained the main text of *hadith* (sacred tradition of the Prophet Muhammad) in India until the sixteenth to seventeenth centuries when Shaykh Abdul Haq Muhaddith introduced other collections.

The ideas of Mansur al-Hallaj reached India through Aush, Farghana, from whence came the famous Chishti saint, Shaykh Qutbuddin Bakhtiyar Kaki (d. 1235/6). Fakhruddin Iraqi, a famous mystic poet, brought Ibn al-Arabi's *Fusus al-Hikam* and *Futuhat al-Makkiya* to Multan. These works gradually spread all over the sub-continent. They found a particularly ripe climate for dissemination partly because the idea of unity of Being (*wahdat al-wujud*) could in some respects be identified with that of pantheism in Hinduism. The concept of unity of Being provided an ideological meeting-ground for Islam and certain strands of Hinduism but when translated by Sufis as a working principle in social life it upheld egalitarianism and undermined the caste system. In their lives and writings saints and scholars, like Saiyyid Muhammad Ghauth of Gwalior, Abdur Rahman Chishti and Dara Shukoh, represent the tradition of bringing Sufism and the thought of the Upanishads closer to each other. Sufis utilised the vehicle of Persian poetry, especially Rumi's *Mathnavi*, for the dissemination of *wujudi* ideas (principally the idea of unity of Being). In the fourteenth and fifteenth centuries distinguished scholars wrote commentaries on the works of Ibn al-Arabi in different parts of the country, such as Saiyyid Ali Hamdani (d. 1384) in Kashmir, Sharafuddin (1392) in Delhi and Shaykh Ali (d. 1431) in Mahaim. The last even attempted a commentary on the Qur'an, inspired by Ibn al-Arabi's thought. Firuz Shah (1351–88), the Tughluq ruler, tried very hard to suppress the expression of pantheistic ideas and in his autobiography mentions the various punishments he inflicted on those who advocated Hallaji views, but paradoxically enough, at the Madrasah Firuzi such ideas continued to be studied. During Firuz's reign, Masud Bak and Amir Mah propagated the ideas of Ibn al-Arabi in verse and prose but their most outstanding exponent was Shaykh Muhibullah Allahabadi, a contemporary of the Mogul Emperor Shah Jahan. Muhibullah Allahabadi believed that the concept of unity of Being should guide social relationships and wrote to Dara Shukoh, the Mogul prince, that the state should not distinguish between Hindus and Muslims just as God did not discriminate between his creations and sent the Prophet as a 'blessing for all the worlds'.

In the aftermath of Mongol devastations, two main trends had crystallised in Muslim lands. One was represented by the mystics who charted out the Islamic world into spiritual dominions (*wilayat*), turned their backs on state and politics and concentrated on the reform of morals as a panacea for all the ills of society. The second approach propounded by Ibn Taimiyya emphasised that state and religion were twins and that any attempt at regeneration should cover all facets of life. Abdul Aziz Ardbili who came to the court of Muhammad bin Tughluq (1324–51) greatly influenced the Sultan with the ideas of Ibn Taimiyya. Muhammad bin Tughluq dealt firmly with the mystic orders and forced them to take up government service, but his successors did not continue this policy. Ibn Taimiyya's ideas did not have a major impact until the eighteenth and nineteenth centuries when the reformist and revivalist movements, such as that of the *mujahidin*, took them up.

The ideas of Ibn al-Arabi were challenged mainly because of the pantheistic tendencies they unleashed amongst certain mystics. The *ulema* (scholars) produced a whole corpus of religious literature during the fourteenth century emphasising the strict Islamic position on monotheism. The famous Chishti saint Shaykh Nasiruddin Chiragh (d. 1356) attempted to bridge the gulf between the *ulama* and the Sufis by advocating close adherence to the Shari'a (religious law) and giving up certain Sufi practices. His disciple in the Deccan, Saiyyid Muhammad Gisu Daraz, continued to be extremely critical of the ideas of Ibn al-Arabi. Increasingly, however, the philosophy of *wahdat al-wujud* reasserted itself. In the context of its ideological parallels with the ideas of the Upanishads, this process attained a unique ambivalence: whereas on the one hand it facilitated the presentation of Islamic religious thought to a Hindu populace, on the other, to the horror of the *ulema*, it aided in the encroachments made by Indian traditions and beliefs into standard Islamic precepts and practices. The drawing together of Islamic and Indian ideas had far-reaching social implications. During the fifteenth and sixteenth centuries, the Bhakti and Raushaniya movements and various Sufi orders such as the Shattariya, attempted to emphasise the spirit of the faith at the expense of its form and structure. The Bhakti movement was an upshot of Islamic influences on Hindu society. It was a protest against the caste system and drew its leadership from the lower strata of society—weavers, cobblers and so on. Bhakti saints such as Kabir, Nanak, Chaitaniya, Dadu, Pipa and Sena advocated direct relationship between God and man and challenged the position of priests and mediators.

Ideological interaction obviously worked both ways. Hindu mystical ideas and practices were borrowed by the Sufis: Shaykh Muhammad Ghauth introduced Hindu yogic beliefs and practices into Sufi circles through his Persian translation of the *Amrit Kund*. The religious experiments of the Mogul Emperor Akbar, who attempted to draw elements from different faiths into a new amalgam—the Din-i-Ilahi—further intensified this trend but in doing so it also triggered off that process of going back to the Qur'an and *hadith* that one so often finds in Muslim societies.

Shaykh Abdul Haq Muhaddith (d. 1642) initiated a powerful movement of the study of the Traditions of the Prophet, which inevitably led to greater Islamisation. The most direct attack on *wahdat al-wujud* and the religious and socio-cultural implications of that ideology, however, came from the Naqshbandi saint, Shaykh Ahmad Sirhindi (1564–1624) who is often referred to as the 'Renewer of the Second Millennium'. He openly criticised the religious experiments of Akbar, rejected the views of Ibn al-Arabi and argued that the Creator and creation are distinct (*wahdat al-shuhud*, unity of vision). He preached adherence to the Shari'a and the Traditions of the Prophet, rejected mystic music and preferred sobriety to ecstasy. His influence percolated down into the Mogul nobility: Jahangir did not pursue Akbar's religious ideas and his two successors—Shah Jahan and Aurangzeb—came under the influence of Shaykh Ahmad's disciples. However, the debate between the *wujudis* and *shuhudis* was never fully resolved. Dara Shukoh, Shah Sarmad and Muhibullah Allahabadi continued to espouse the *wujudi* position. When Bernier visited India during the eighteenth century even he noticed that the debate between the two schools was raging all around him.

Within two centuries of Shaykh Ahmad's condemnation of Ibn al-Arabi's ideas, a couple of his outstanding Naqshbandi successors, Mirza Mazhar (d. 1780) and Shah Waliullah (d. 1762), were attempting a reconciliation between these different positions. Shah Waliullah argued that the difference between the ideas of Ibn al-Arabi and Shaykh Ahmad Sirhindi was one of style and metaphor, not of essence or substance. He emphasised recourse to *ijtihad* (reinterpretation of Islamic law), adjustment of law to space-time requirements, and attached equal importance to both the structural and spiritual elements of Islam. He believed in recourse to all the four Sunni schools of law instead of blind adherence to any one of them. He characterised the Mogul state as exploitative but was upset when it was shaken by Maratha and Jat invasions and wrote to the neighbouring Muslim rulers asking them to restore Islamic political authority. He translated the Qur'an into Persian (1736) and laid great emphasis on following the *hadith* (sacred tradition). He advocated balance and adaptability, tried to bring different Sufi and juristic schools closer, but remained critical of the Shias. Shah Waliullah's mission was carried forward by his sons, Shah Abdul Aziz, Shah Abdul Qadir and Shah Rafiuddin. The last two translated the Qur'an into Urdu.

Shah Waliullah's thought inspired three main trends: first, a renewed emphasis on the study of the Qur'an and the *hadith*; second, a struggle for the creation of an Islamic state; and third, reform of the beliefs, morals and customs of Muslim society. The first was epitomised in the Madrasah-i-Rahimiya over which Shah Waliullah presided and where he was succeeded by his elder son Shah Abdul Aziz. To this educational institution are connected the major figures of eighteenth- to nineteenth-century Islam in India. The reformist trend inspired by Shah Waliullah had striking resemblance to the Wahhabis of Nejd. Its leading light was Saiyyid Ahmad Brelvi (d. 1831) who was severely critical of the accretions to the faith, excessive devotion to shrines and saints, and the populist dimensions of Sufism. The most prolific writer of this school was Shah Muhammad Ismail (d. 1831). Saiyyid Ahmad's (d. 1831) *mujahidin* movement was intended as a holy war against the sikhs and the British with the aim of establishing an Islamic state.

When in the nineteenth century Muslim society in the sub-continent found itself threatened by Western imperialism with its concomitant social, cultural and economic implications, initially the *ulema* and Sufis tried to strengthen the defensive mechanism of the community by an insistence on the letter of the law. Shah Abdul Aziz (d. 1824) declared British India *dar al-harb* (Land of the Enemy) but with great foresight permitted the acquisition of Western learning as long as it did not contradict one's religious beliefs. The religious elite combated Christian missionary activity, intensified preaching and religious education, utilised the lithographic press and even adapted Western institutional models (e.g. at Deoband) for the purpose of imparting religious education. Sir Syed Ahmad Khan established a modern educational institution on the pattern of Oxbridge at Aligarh to ensure that Muslims, while being steadfast in their faith, did not lose out in the race for this world. *Ulema*, such as Rahmatullah Kairanvi and Wazir Khan, engaged in debates with Christian missionaries, and using the critical writings of German scholars tried to prove the point of corruption and interpolation in the text of the Bible.

Towards the end of the nineteenth century, various ideological strands had crystallised into different movements: the *ahl al-Qur'an* regarded the Qur'an as sufficient for the formulation of legal principles and the *hadith* as unnecessary for that purpose; the *ahl al-hadith* laid emphasis on both the Qur'an and the *hadith* as sources of law but did not accept the finality of the four schools of jurisprudence. To these controversies, centred around the sources of law, was added another major one, emanating from different attitudes towards Sufi practices, the position of the spiritual mentor, and the style of showing reverence to the Prophet. Soon these differences manifested themselves in two different schools: the Barelvis under Maulana Ahmad Raza Khan (1856–1921), who upheld traditional Sufi beliefs and practices, and the Deobandis under Maulana Muhammad Qasim Nanautavi (d. 1880) and Maulana Rashid Gangohi (d. 1905), who criticised devotion at shrines, ceremonies associated with the birth and death of saints and so on. These differences still persist.

Sir Syed Ahmad Khan (d. 1878) attempted to instil a rationalist attitude in matters pertaining to religion and denounced blind adherence to tradition. He emphasised reinterpretation of Islamic law and even attempted to study Islam and Christianity on a comparative basis. Sir Syed inspired a new generation of modernist Muslims, outstanding amongst whom were Chiragh Ali (d. 1875) and Saiyyid Amir Ali, who was amongst the first Muslims in the sub-continent to write on Islamic history in the English language.

Other important personalities of eighteenth- and nineteenth-century Islam in the sub-continent were Shah Ghulam Ali (d. 1824), a Naqshbandi saint of Delhi, and Shah Muhammad Suleiman (d. 1850), a Chishti saint of Taunsa. Shah Ghulam Ali's influence reached Turkey, Syria and Iraq through his disciple Khalid Kurdi. Shah Suleiman concentrated on spreading religious knowledge in the rural and tribal areas of the Punjab and established a large number of *madrasahs*. Haji Imdadullah (d.

1899), a scholar and saint of the Chishti-Sabiri order, greatly influenced his contemporaries in many ways. The founding of the schools of Deoband and Nadwa owed much to his guidance and inspiration.

Dr Muhammad Iqbal (1876–1938) and Abul Kalam Azad (1888–1958) continued the process of reorientation of Muslim religious thought. Iqbal brought to bear his knowledge of Western philosophy and history on an understanding and reformulation of Muslim religious ideas. He emphasised the dynamism of the Islamic message and denounced traditionalism and inertia. He exhorted man to struggle in order to attain his destiny, criticised Western notions of nationalism, advocated pan-Islamism and left a deep impact on contemporaries and posterity. Paradoxically, despite his opposition to nationalism, he became the poet-philosopher of the demand for Pakistan. Abul Kalam Azad (d. 1958), imbued with the ideas of Jamaluddin Afghani and Rashid Rida, articulated a modern and dynamic approach towards religion. He dismissed attempts to reconcile religion and science as futile and instead attempted a direct and simple commentary on the Qur'an which reflects the influence of Western utilitarian and humanistic movements. He presented religion as a message of love and service to mankind.

Islamic Movements and Organisations

Since the advent of Islam on the sub-continent various movements and organisations have emerged. Professor K.A. Nizami has pointed out that they represent four broad tendencies: movements starting from the twelfth to the sixteenth century aimed at the 'expansion' of Islam and Muslim society in India; during the seventeenth century the emphasis shifted to 'reform' of beliefs and society; during the eighteenth century the concern was 'regeneration'; and finally in the nineteench century attempts were made at 'reorientation' either in the light of classical Islamic viewpoints or Western influences.

The main Sufi orders which contributed towards the spread of Islam were, as we have seen, the Chistiya, the Qadiriya, the Suhrawardiya, the Firdausiya, and the Shattariya. Although these orders differed amongst themselves *vis-à-vis* their attitudes towards the state, sobriety or ecstasy, emphasis on Shari'a and so on, yet they were united in the view that service of mankind was possible only by translating Islamic ideals into practice. Sufi orders adopted many Hindu and Buddhist practices usually in so far as they did not compromise essential Islamic precepts. This syncretism was not always the reassertion of popular religion but very often the Islamisation of local religious forms.

The reformist tendency was epitomised in the Naqshbandi order which was introduced in India by Khwaja Baqi Billah (1563–1603) and reached its zenith under Shaykh Ahmad Sirhindi, whose influence on posterity has already been discussed. At a time of political decline during the eighteenth century not only did Shah Waliullah make his seminary, Madrasah-i Rahimiya, the centre for a movement of regeneration but even Sufis such as the Chishti saint, Shah Kalimullah (d. 1729) attempted to revitalise that order, extend its influence in north India and rid it of its non-Islamic accretions.

From the eighteenth to nineteenth centuries onwards, Mujahidin and Faraidi movements attempted to restore political power to the Muslims by trying to reform society according to Islamic principles. The Deoband seminary (1867) was established with the aim of promoting religious learning. The MAO (Mohammedan Anglo-Oriental) College at Aligarh (1875) was the outcome of an attempt to adapt Western education to the requirements of Muslim society and initiated a process of reorientation in social, religious and educational ideals. The establishment of Nadwat-ul-ulama (1891) at Lucknow marked a synthesis between the rejection of the West as represented at Deoband and its assimilation as symbolised by Aligarh. These institutions have contributed tremendously to the development and growth of Muslim society in India.

The writings of Maulana Ashraf Ali Thanvi (d. 1943) encouraged the remodelling of lifestyles according to Islamic principles and created a scripturalist attitude towards Islam. But perhaps the most significant and far-reaching movement to emerge in modern times is that of *Tabligh*, started by Maulana Muhammad Ilyas (d. 1944), which aims at propagating the message of Islam through bands of volunteers. This movement has now turned international. The *Jamaat-i Islami*, founded by Abul Ala Mawdudi (d. 1979) in 1941, has inspired a large number of modern educated youth and has advocated the Islamisation of politics and society. It emphasises the indivisibility of religion and politics.

The Shi'ites

Among the non-Sunni religious groups the Shi'ites constitute a major sect with certain distinct beliefs and practices. They do not recognise the legitimacy of the succession of Abu Bakr, Umar and Uthman to the caliphate. Instead they claim that Ali directly succeeded the Prophet.

The Shi'a sect split into two groups on the question of the number of imams. The *Ithna-i Ashariya* believed in twelve imams and the Ismailis recognised only seven. The majority of Shi'as belong to the *Ithna-i Ashariya*. In India it was the Ismaili sect which entered first and established its power in Multan. Sultan Mahmud of Ghazna (d. 1030) overthrew the Multan dynasty and adopted stern measures against them and the Carmathians. Shihabuddin Muhammad of Ghur (d. 1206) continued Mahmud's policy of stern action against Ismaili strongholds and as a consequence Ismailis became fiercely opposed to Sunni governments. They were suspected of being involved in the assassination of Shihabuddin and even planned the overthrow of two Delhi Sultans, Iltutmish and Raziya. The

Sultans of Delhi, particularly Alauddin Khalji and Firuz Shah Tughluq, adopted rigorous measures against all forms of Ismailism.

The *Ithna-i Ashariya* came into prominence with the establishment of the Shi'a states in the Deccan. The Adil Shahi rulers of Bijapur (1489–1686), the Nizam Shahis of Ahmadnagar (1490–1633), and the Qutb Shahis of Golconda (1512–1687) adopted Shi'ism as state religion and actively propagated Shi'a doctrines. In northern India Shi'a influence increased during the sixteenth century after the return of the Mogul Emperor Humayun from Persia. The Safavid ruler, Tahmasp, who was a devout Shi'a, supported Humayun in regaining the throne of Delhi from the Afghans. Tahmasp even prevailed upon Humayun to adopt certain Shi'a practices. Large numbers of Shi'a poets and scholars came to India during the reign of Akbar and their numbers in the Mogul nobility also increased. The entry of Nur Jahan into the harem of Jahangir (d. 1627) further consolidated the Shi'a position. The most important Shi'a scholar of the Mogul period was Qazi Nurullah Shustari. From the time of Jahangir, polemics between the Sunnis and Shi'as started and during the succeeding centuries books were written by scholars on both sides to show why the other was wrong.

The Shi'as have developed certain practices and institutions of their own. They have separate buildings, called *imambaras*, where they perform their religious ceremonies and offer prayers. During the month of Muharram (the month in which Imam Husein was martyred), they take out skeleton-effigies (known as *tazias*) representing the tombs of the martyred imams and bury them in graveyards. Elegies (*marsiyas*) are recited during the first ten days of Muharram. Muhammad Quli of the Qutb Shahi dynasty of Golconda was one of the first reciters of elegies in Urdu.

Among the Ismaili Shi'as, the Khojas and the Bohras are the best organised communities, and are mainly engaged in business. The Khojas are Nizari Ismailis and are the followers of the Agha Khan. Initially the Nizaris in India acknowledged the imams in Iran but subsequently when Agha Khan I moved to Bombay in 1845 the Immamat was transferred to India. The Bohras developed the concept of *dai-i mutlaq* when their imam, Mustali, disappeared in 1133. Originally established in Yemen, they later moved to India.

Education and Learning

Along with the establishment of Muslim political and administrative control over the sub-continent, educational institutions developed at all levels—*maktabs* for primary education and *madrasahs* for higher learning. Some of these institutions were established by rulers or nobles while others were run by public charity. The Muizzi, the Nasiri and the Firuzi *madrasahs* were founded by the Delhi Sultans and were considered the highest seats of learning in the country. The Firuzi *madrasah* provided board and lodging to both the teachers and the taught. During the time of Muhammad bin Tughluq (1324–51) there were one thousand colleges in Delhi alone. In the early nineteenth century every small locality in Delhi had dozens of *madrasahs*. Though female education was confined to certain elite sections of society and was arranged inside the houses, there are some references to institutions for women in the Deccan.

Indian educational institutions maintained close contact with the intellectual centres of Islamic lands. The works of Ibn al-Arabi, Rumi and other important thinkers became known to Indian scholars almost during the lifetime of these scholar-saints. Alam bin Ala had access to almost every important work on jurisprudence written by his contemporaries, while preparing his *Fatawa-i-Tatar Khaniyah*. From the Deccan Mahmud Gawan corresponded with Jami; the rulers of Bengal extended invitations to Hafiz. By the time of Akbar the desire to know about developments in the West also increased. Danishmand Khan, a Mogul noble of the seventeenth century, engaged Bernier, a French traveller, to explain to him theories about the circulation of blood.

The syllabus in the *madrasahs* was broadly categorised into *ma'qulat* (rational subjects) and *manqulat* (traditional subjects). The rational subjects included mathematics, philosophy, logic, medicine, and so on; the traditional subjects included Qur'an, *hadith*, *fiqh* (jurisprudence), *tasawwuf* (mysticism) and *ilm-i-kalam* (scholasticism). In the beginning there was greater emphasis on traditional subjects but by the close of the fifteenth century Maulana Abdullah of Tulanba and his brother increased the content of rational subjects in the syllabus. Although the influence of Mir Fathullah Shirazi (d. 1588) and Akbar worked in favour of rational subjects, the main thrust of education remained towards religious and traditional disciplines. In the eighteenth century Mulla Nizamuddin of Sihali (d. 1748) introduced some changes in the syllabus at Firangi Mahal, an outstanding seminary at Lucknow. The curriculum that he prescribed came to be known as the *Dars-i Nizami* (the syllabus of Nizami) and for more than a century and a half it remained the basis of instruction imparted in most *madrasahs* on the sub-continent.

Literature

Indo-Muslim scholarship made significant contributions to both religious and secular literature. The religious literature is broadly divided into Qur'anic (pertaining to the Qur'an, exegesis, syntax and so on), *hadith* (collections of the sayings of the Prophet and principles of their critique), *fiqh* (jurisprudence), *tasawwuf* (mysticism) and *ilm-i Kalam* (scholasticism). Shah Waliullah's (d. 1762) translation of the Qur'an into Persian made it intellectually accessible to a large number of people. Qazi Thanaullah Panipati's (d. 1810) *Tafsir i Mazhari* runs into several large volumes and is perhaps one of the most comprehensive works on exegesis produced in the sub-continent. In the light of the exigencies of the time, scholars adopted different approaches in their study of the Qur'an. Sir Syed (d. 1898), in his commentary, attempted to resolve the conflict between religion and science; Abul Kalam Azad's (d. 1958) *Tarjuman al-Qur'an* is characterised by the subtle influence of humanistic and utilitarian trends in Western thought; and Abul Ala Mawdudi's (d. 1979) *Tafhim al-Qur'an* endeavours to emphasise the indivisibility of religion and politics and in some ways attempts to meet the challenge of Marxist ideas.

Shaykh Abdul Haq Muhaddith (d. 1642) and Shah Waliullah (d. 1762) made significant contributions to the study of *hadith* by incorporating various collections of Traditions of the Prophet in the syllabus of the time. Shaykh Abdul Haq concentrated mainly on the *Mishkat* and wrote commentaries on it in Arabic and Persian. Shah Waliullah selected *Muwatta* and also wrote commentaries on it in both the languages. During the last hundred years large numbers of works on the study of *hadith* have been produced in Urdu.

The two most productive periods for juristic literature in India were the fourteenth and seventeenth centuries. Firuz Shah Tughluq (1351–88) and Aurangzeb (d. 1707) were keenly interested in Islamic jurisprudence and as a result many scholars turned their attention to *fiqh*. During the time of Firuz Shah, the *Fatawa-i Tatar Khaniyah* was compiled; Aurangzeb himself supervised the compilation of *Fatawa-i-Alamgiri*. Both these works received recognition outside the sub-continent. It is surprising that in the juristic literature produced in the sub-continent there is almost total absence of any discussion of the position of the Hindus. The books take the non-Indian milieu into consideration but completely ignore the Indian situation.

The sub-continent's contribution in the sphere of mystic literature is next only to that of Iran. The art of compiling day-to-day conversations of mystic teachers was introduced in India during the time of Shaykh Nizamuddin Auliya (d. 1325) whose conversations, compiled under the rubric *Fawaid al-Fuad*, laid the foundation of *malfuz* literature in the sub-continent. In the centuries that followed, enormous *malfuz* literature was produced by the Chishti, Suhrawardi, Firdausi, Shattari, Qadiri and Naqshbandi saints. This literature gives us a glimpse into the problems of the common man. Under Maulana Ashraf Ali Thanvi (d. 1943) *malfuz* writing became an essential part of the *khanqah* routine. The earliest Persian work on mystic ideas and ideals was produced in India during the eleventh century by Shaykh Ali Hajweri at Lahore. It is known as *Kashf al-mahjub* (Light for the eyes of the blind) and Shaykh Nizamuddin Auliya regarded it as the best guide for one who was without a teacher. The letters of Shaykh Ahmad Sirhindi (d. 1624), known as *Maktubat-i Imam Rabbani*, are a major contribution to the evolution of Islamic religious thought in India. These letters contain criticism of Ibn al-Arabi's pantheistic philosophy and have been translated into Arabic and Turkish.

The *Hujjatullah al Baligha* of Shah Waliullah ranks pre-eminent in the scholastic literature produced in the sub-continent. It deals with the basic principles of faith and the fundamental laws of Shari'a in the light of the spiritual, moral, biological and psychological needs of society and does not even ignore the economic background of human institutions. The secular or non-religious literature produced by the Muslims in India covers poetry, history, epistolatory collections, stories, philosophical treatises, books on mathematics, medicine and the art of government. The earliest work on the art of warfare—*Adab al harb wa shujaat*—was written by Fakhr-i Mudabbir in Persian during the thirteenth century.

Among the Persian poets who flourished in India and gained recognition outside the sub-continent as well were Amir Khusrau (d. 1325), Faizi (d. 1595), Urfi (d. 1590) and Bedil (d. 1720). Khusrau wrote a rejoinder to the famous Persian poet Nizami; Faizi's *qasidahs* (panegyrics) raised him to a pre-eminent position; Urfi spoke about the dignity of man and his egocentric approach gave a new turn to panegyric writing in Mogul India. Abdul Qadir Bedil's verses with their philosophic content and deep pathos became famous in the Persian-speaking lands. Asadullah Ghalib (1797–1869) gained a formidable reputation for his Persian and Urdu poetry and continues to be popular today.

The Indo-Muslim period was characterised by the production of an enormous historical literature. Ziyauddin Barani's *Tarikh-i Firuz Shahi*, which contains an account of the Delhi Sultans from Balban to Firuz Shah Tughluq, is one of the most fascinating historical accounts of medieval society and culture. Abul Fazl (d. 1602) has supplied in his *Akbar Namah* and *Ain-i Akbari* interesting historical details and statistical data about the administrative measures of Akbar and the life of the court and the common man.

Anecdotal literature of the period is also varied and interesting. The *Tuti namah* and the *Gulriz* of Ziyauddin Nakhshabi are valuable. In the *Tuti namah* birds have been used as a medium for communicating ethical and didactic lessons.

As a result of interaction between the local population and Muslims, a new language, Urdu, grew up. Grammatically based on north Indian dialect, its vocabulary and metaphors are drawn from Persian. Muslim religious and literary activity found expression in the Urdu language. Urdu poetry—particularly *ghazal*—became a powerful vehicle for the expression of romantic ideas.

Indo-Muslim culture developed in harmony with local cultures and brought about a synthesis between Islamic and Indian traditions. The growth of regional languages in Bengal, Gujarat and the Deccan was helped by the efforts of the Muslim elite and mystics. Important

Arabic and Persian classics were rendered into regional languages, especially in Bengal and the Deccan.

Art and Architecture

Art and architecture were particularly patronised by the Muslim rulers and the elite. The sub-continent is studded with monuments of all types—mosques, minarets, *khanqahs*, forts, bridges, water-reservoirs, gardens and mausolea. A recent study by a Japanese team has brought to light a variety of waterworks that operated in Delhi alone during the Sultanate period. The Muslim rulers of India displayed keen interest in the founding of new cities such as Firuzabad, Jaunpur, Farrukhabad, Fatehpur Sikri, Hyderabad, Shah-jahanabad, Moradabad, Daulatabad and so on. This urbanisation facilitated the proliferation of the Indo-Islamic culture. The grandeur, beauty and humming trade activity of Fatehpur Sikri, the city founded by Akbar, has been described by European travellers. Cities were generally beautified by the construction of mosques, minarets and gates. In Delhi, Iltutmish built the Qutb Minar which resembles a minaret recently discovered at Jam in Afghanistan. The Buland Darwaza constructed by Akbar at Fatehpur Sikri is one of the loftiest gates. The Attala Mosque at Jaunpur, the Fatehpur Sikri Mosque and the Jama Masjid of Delhi are noteworthy for their architectural beauty. Akbar's palace of Fatehpur Sikri has survived intact. Akbar's style of architecture represents a blending of Indian and Islamic traditions: arches and domes go hand in hand with flat stone beams and ornate decoration. In fact the tradition of combining Indian and Muslim motifs had become very prominent from the Tughluq period onwards when Hindu *chatri* or kiosks, heavy stone and balustrades were borrowed. The Mogul Emperor Shah Jahan (1592–1666) was a great builder. He built a new city, Shahjahanabad (Old Delhi). Its Great Mosque, the Red Fort and big bazaar—Chandni Chawk—shaded by trees and cooled by a stream, rivalled the Chahar Bagh of Isfahan. The tomb that he built for his wife Mumtaz Mahal is known as the Taj Mahal and is the finest Mogul monument, unique in symmetry, delicacy and grandeur.

The Moguls were fond of laying out gardens. The Shalimar gardens in Kashmir and Lahore bear testimony to their interest in gardening. Large numbers of flowers, fruits and trees were brought from Central Asia and Iran and planted there. Their tombs are surrounded by beautiful gardens.

Barring one or two hazy specimens, no paintings of the Sultanate period have survived but there are references to mural paintings during the early medieval period. Under the Moguls, particularly Akbar and Jahangir, painting made great progress in India. Akbar's studio had more than one hundred painters drawn from different parts. Nearly 24,000 manu-scripts were illustrated for his library. These manuscripts comprised not only

Persian works but also Indian classics. This provided an opportunity for the intermingling of Indian and Iranian traditions of painting. An illustrated manuscript of the *Akbar namah* in the Chester Beaty Collection gives a good idea of the standard achieved in the painting of landscapes, selection of colours, depiction of figures and communication of immutable feelings and emotions. Mansur was one of the most outstanding painters of the Mogul period. His paintings of the natural world, birds and flowers are superb. Jahangir, who was a leading connoisseur of art, greatly encouraged painting. During his reign some Western influences also became visible in Indian paintings.

Music was developed as an art in the courts and in the hospices of saints. Both male and female musicians performed at the courts of Kaiqubad and Jalaluddin Khalji. Amir Khusrau was an expert in music and invented certain melodies which combined the Indian and Iranian forms. Tan Sen, a famous Hindu musician, joined the circle of Saiyyid Muhammad Ghauth Gwaliyari's disciples and attempted to unite Indian and Sufi melodies. Two classical works on music—*Ghunyat al munyah*, by an anonymous writer during the reign of Firuz Shah Tughluq, and Faqirullah's *Rag Darpan*, compiled in 1666—give a good idea of the traditions of Indian music and the way Iranian influences moulded them into a new form.

Calligraphy was developed as an art during the Sultanate and Mogul periods. Babur invented a new style of calligraphy and had his memoirs written in it. Akbar was so fascinated by calligraphy that he did not approve of the printing-press. Calligraphy flourished unchallenged till the early nineteenth century when the printing-press increasingly started to replace it.

Further Reading

Ahmad, Aziz *Studies in Islamic Culture in the Indian Environment* (Clarendon Press, Oxford, 1964)

—— *Islamic Modernism in India and Pakistan 1857–1964* (Oxford University Press, London, 1967)

—— *An Intellectual History of Islam in India* (Edinburgh University Press, Edinburgh, 1969)

Ashraf, K.M. *The Life and Conditions of the People of Hindustan 1200–1556*, 2nd edn (New Delhi, 1970)

Brown, Percy *Indian Painting under the Mughals* AD *1550 to* AD *1750* (Clarendon Press, Oxford, 1924)

—— *Indian Architecture*, 2nd edn (D.B. Taraporevala Sons & Co. Ltd, Bombay, 1942)

Cantwell-Smith, Wilfred *Modern Islam in India* (Victor Gollancz Ltd, London, 1946)

Chand, Tara *History of the Freedom Movement in India*, 4 vols. (Publications Division, Ministry of Information and Broadcasting, Government of India, Delhi, 1961–72)

Encyclopaedia of Islam, new edn (Leiden and London, 1960–78)

Habib, M. and Nizami, K.A. *The Delhi Sultanat*, vol. 5 (People's Publishing House, Delhi, 1970)

Islam in the Indian Sub-Continent

Habibullah *The Foundation of Muslim Rule in India*, 2nd edn (Central Book Depot, Allahabad, 1961)
Hardy, Peter *The Muslims of British India* (Cambridge University Press, Cambridge, 1972)
Jafar, S.M. *Education in Muslim India* (Idarah-i Adabiyat-i, Delhi, 1973)
Metcalf, Barbara D. *Islamic Revival in British India: Deoband 1860–1900* (Princeton University Press, Princeton, New Jersey, 1982)
Mujeeb, M. *The Indian Muslims* (George Allen and Unwin Ltd, London, 1967)
Nizami, K.A. *Some Aspects of Religion and Politics in India during the 13th Century*, 2nd edn (Idarah-i Adabiyat-i, Delhi, 1978)
Qureshi, I.H. *The Muslim Community of the Indo-Pakistan Sub-Continent (610–1942)* (published for Near and Middle Eastern Studies, Columbia University, by Mouton & Co., The Hague, 1962)
Sadiq, Muhammad *A History of Urdu Literature*, 2nd edn (Oxford University Press, Delhi, 1984)
Schimmel, Annemarie *Islam in the Indian Sub-Continent*, (E.J. Brill, Leiden and Cologne, 1980)
Spear, T.G.P. *A History of India*, vol. 2 (Pelican, Harmondsworth, 1981)
—— *The Twilight of the Mughals* (Cambridge University Press, Cambridge, 1951)

24 The Turks and Islam

J.D. Norton

Introduction

The Turkish involvement with Islam provides vivid examples of how a religion affects a people and how a people affect a religion. This article traces the story of that involvement from the adoption of various forms of Islam by the Turks, through their rise to become the strongest champions of the faith, their subsequent decline, loss of empire, proclamation of secularism in the Republic and on to the present where the struggle over the place of Islam in the state is still being fought.

Turks came to Islam in different ways. In their original Central Asian homelands they had followed shamanistic practices and in the course of time had come into contact with Buddhism, Manichaeism and Nestorian Christianity. But when they started moving westwards and encountered Arabs carrying their new faith into and beyond Iran it was Islam that made the greatest impact upon them and thereby changed the course of history.

Among the various categories of convert were: the warrior taken into the service of Muslim armies; the tribe or community following its leader's example; and the convinced individual. In the first category come the Turks like those that the Abbasid Caliph Mutasim (833–42 CE) recruited for his bodyguard. Their martial prowess brought them swift advancement until soon they themselves were in control and had reduced the caliphs to powerless figureheads. An example of the second type of conversion is provided by the Seljuks who became Muslims at the behest of their leader, Seljuk, after whom the tribe was named. By becoming Sunnis they strengthened this orthodox branch of Islam when it had appeared to be in decline. Some other tribes came under the influence of various Sufi orders, both Sunni and Shi'a. As for the individual converts, they include many Turks who were attracted to the faith by Muslims with whom they came in contact; some became strictly orthodox, whilst others joined the dervish orders.

These dervish, or Sufi, orders—known in Turkish as *tarikats*—were to play an important part in Turkish history. Some of them were Sunni orders and others Shi'a. Many orthodox Sunnis maintained that several of these tarikats were heretical, whereas other orthodox believers themselves joined Sunni tarikats. One feature common to all the tarikats was the total allegiance owed by devotees to their leaders (who often bore the title *seyh*). This gave the heads of the main tarikats political as well as spiritual power.

Conversion meant different things to different people. To many the adoption of Islam lent religious encouragement for what they would probably have done anyway, namely take possession of land in Anatolia. To some it meant the abandonment of old ways and the substitution of a new lifestyle that required among other things the performance of ritual prayers five times a day. To yet others it meant simply putting an Islamic gloss upon old beliefs and customs. This was particularly true in the case of many of the nomadic and semi-nomadic Turkoman tribes that would have found the formal demands of orthodox worship inconvenient. Among them in particular the tarikats with strong heterodox elements and distinct traces of shamanism found favour. The roots of religious schism among Turkish Muslims go back to these days. But although the interpretations of Islam to which Turks subscribed varied widely, the common acknowledgement of the one God did provide a focus for unity among the Turkish tribes.

Moreover, all these Turkish Muslims eagerly accepted the demand of their faith that they should extend its territorial bounds. (This was in contrast to the pacific attitudes fostered by some other creeds that had been held to blame for the weakness of some Turkish tribes in pre-Islamic times.) It was natural therefore that they should seek to wrest Anatolia from the enfeebled grasp of the Byzantine Empire. Turkish raiders had penetrated to Konya in central Anatolia as early as the middle of the tenth century but had not then attempted settlement.

The Seljuks

After the Seljuks under Alparslan inflicted a crushing defeat on the Byzantines in 1071 at the Battle of Manzikert near Lake Van in eastern Anatolia, the land lay open for their occupation, and wave after wave of Turkish immigrants moved in. The Seljuks established a capital at Nicea (modern Iznik) in 1078, but after the armies of the First Crusade had forced them back to the centre and east of Anatolia they set up a new capital in Konya.

Seljuk dominance in Anatolia lasted for two centuries, a period that witnessed religious developments whose consequences were felt throughout subsequent Turkish history and still have an influence upon events today. The Seljuk rulers' control was by no means uniformly effective throughout the whole of the areas newly occupied by Turks. Sectarian divisions tended to accentuate economic, social and political differences. Then, as always in Turkish history, the Islam of the rulers was very different from the Islam of many of their subjects. The Seljuk elite acquired land, privileges and a preference for city life. They attracted scholars and established theological colleges to train the *ulema*, the body of learned men in the Islamic establishment with the dual role of interpreting and implementing the Shari'a (the sacred law of Islam). They lent authority to the sultan's claim to rule but they circumscribed that power by making sure he did not deviate from the *şeriat (*=Shari'a). Sufis of the more refined variety also came to the cities. The most notable example is Celaleddin Rumi who was to become the patron saint of the Mevlevi or Whirling Dervishes, a Sunni tarikat in close touch with the established political rulers. A very different type of dervish was to be found in the rural areas. The tarikat practices there often owed rather more to other religions and ceremonies than they did to Islam. Influences of customs the Turks had followed in Central Asia and those they had found in Anatolia as well as Shi'a teachings and esoteric interpretations of the Qur'an were all to be found in some of the dervish groups that held sway outside the towns. Numerous communities and tarikats preferred the Shi'a to the Sunni expression of Islam. In Turkey these have commonly gone under a variety of names such as *Alevi* and *Kızılbaş*, which are often used inconsistently and imprecisely. Most of these groups were characterised by strong community loyalty, endogamy and secrecy. They customarily rejected four of the five 'pillars' of Islam, almsgiving being the only exception. Common to many of them was the belief that a Mahdi or divine deliverer would come to end oppression and impose a reign of justice.

Rebellions occurred periodically throughout Turkish history when particularly adverse economic conditions and oppressive rule combined to make rural communities receptive to reports that the eagerly awaited Mahdi had appeared. One of the first such uprisings, the Babai Rebellion in 1240, nearly overthrew the Seljuks. It happened in response to the misrule of Giyasuddin Keyhusrev II who seized the sultanate in 1237. At a time when the Turkoman tribesmen were already suffering from land shortage caused by the flood of new immigrants pouring into Anatolia to escape the Mongol hordes, the sultan's demands for higher land-taxes brought resentment to the boil. A dervish leader, Baba Ilyas, then declared himself to be a prophet and the rightful ruler, and his follower, Baba Ishak, called upon the Turkoman tribes to rebel. Followers flocked to his banner in characteristically unswerving obedience to their tarikat leaders, and encouraged by the Baba's promise that all would receive equal shares of the spoils of victory. In a series of major confrontations they inflicted heavy losses on the Seljuk armies sent to crush them but were eventually beaten in a critical pitched battle in Central Anatolia when Christian mercenaries played a crucial part in the Seljuk success. Although the Seljuks won the day, the rebellion had revealed their weakness and three years later the Mongols came and temporarily made the Turks of Anatolia tributaries of the Ilhan dynasty. The rural Turkoman tradition of opposition to the central authority persisted and flared up periodically throughout Turkish history, receiving support from tarikats such as the Bektashis that inherited the mantle of these first rebellious babas.

The Ottomans

Of the rival emirates that emerged after the Seljuk defeat, the Ottomans were destined to achieve dominance and establish an empire that lasted for six centuries. Having been granted lands at Söğüt in Western Anatolia bordering on Byzantine territory, the Ottomans attracted to their ranks large numbers of *gazis* (warriors eager to expand the frontiers of Islam) since this region offered the best prospects of success against the Christians. Most of the *gazis* were fierce Turkoman tribesmen who were devotees of the rural tarikats. The early Ottoman rulers, starting with Osman I, showed considerable skill in maintaining the loyalty both of these warriors and of the Sunni townsmen and settled agriculturalists and directing the energies of all of them not against one another but against the neighbouring Christian territories whose capture was lauded by all branches of Islam.

It would be wrong, however, to conclude that unrelenting enmity towards Christians was a constant feature of the Turkish expansion into Anatolia. We have already seen how Christian mercenaries helped the Seljuks crush an uprising of disaffected heterodox Muslims. More than once Turkish troops, with the approval of their rulers, fought for Byzantines who sought their aid against other Christians. Many Turks, even at the highest level, married daughters of Christian families. In areas that were overrun by the Turks, Christians, as 'People of the Book', received the privileged treatment afforded them by Islamic law. Thus, provided they were not captured fighting against Islam, they were guaranteed life, liberty and sometimes property too. If they did not convert to Islam they had to pay a poll-tax and contribute financially to Muslim armies and accept a number of other discriminatory measures but they were free to practise their religion and were exempt from military service. Many Christian families of Anatolia found that these conditions compared so favourably with those they endured under the Byzantine yoke that they actually welcomed the Turks. Some converted to Islam, many of them finding the sort of Islam practised by the rural dervish orders particularly easy to accept. At the same time, sizeable territories in Cilicia and around Trebizond had been left in the hands of Christian rulers, and the degree of fraternisation between Seljuk and Byzantine rulers sometimes drew stern rebukes from zealous Muslims.

Since our primary concern here is with religion in Turkey we shall not dwell upon the conquests, marriage settlements and other means by which Ottoman boundaries were expanded to cover a vast empire with its capital in Istanbul but we shall instead examine the place of Islam in the organisation of the Ottoman state.

When working at its best the unique Ottoman system of government made a considerable contribution to the effectiveness of control over a vast empire and won the admiration of such astute analysts as Machiavelli. Many historians have portrayed this system as comprising two rival institutions keeping one another in check: the 'Muslim Institution', consisting of the *ulema* who ensured that the *şeriat* was observed, and the 'Ruling Institution' containing the personnel who formulated and implemented government policies, waged war and maintained security. This traditional analysis tends to obscure certain important realities such as the constant struggle for power waged between rural and urban interests and the often parallel struggle by certain tarikats and other unorthodox Muslims against the Sunni establishment. To understand these realities it is necessary to look more closely at some of the important power groups within the empire, noting the effect religion had upon each of them.

At the top was the Sultan, the 'Shadow of God upon earth' and, after the assumption of the caliphate, the 'Representative of the Prophet' too. With this important religious role to perform it might be supposed that the ruler could behave as an unfettered autocrat. But the need to maintain the support of the various power groups placed considerable restraints upon every sultan's freedom of action.

The group most obviously concerned with ensuring that the sultan kept strictly to the path of Islam was the *ulema*. They based their claim to exercise authority upon their expert knowledge of the Qur'an and *şeriat* which they gained by study under a *müderris* (teacher) at a *medrese* (an institute of higher theological education, normally autonomous and situated within a mosque complex in a city). Most *medreses* were funded by a *vakif*, an Islamic charitable foundation, so tuition, accommodation and food were provided free, thus giving the chance of advancement to intelligent and pious sons of Muslim families. Islam dominated the curriculum; students were taught—mostly by rote learning—Qur'anic studies, Islamic law and jurisprudence, Arabic and calligraphy and a few other subjects. Upon graduation a student received from his *müderris* an *icazet*—a certificate of competence—and he was then eligible to follow a career as a member of the *ulema* in law, teaching or administration. In all three of these branches knowledge of the *şeriat* was of the greatest importance.

A *medrese* graduate who chose a career in law could expect to be sent first to some small town or district as *kadı*, a post whose duties included not only those of judge and public prosecutor but also involvement in food distribution, road maintenance and the conscription system, ensuring that the orders of central government were implemented, and keeping a watch on other state officials and reporting irregularities. In addition to his daily wage, which was based on his grade, the *kadı* received a fixed sum from the parties involved in the cases he tried. The promotion path took a successful *kadı* to increasingly prestigious places. To progress beyond certain levels he had first to go back to a *medrese* and spend time teaching at an advanced level. He could then become a *kadı* of a whole province and go on to hold the post of *kadı* in one of the eight most important cities: Mecca, Medina, Edirne, Bursa, Cairo, Damascus, Aleppo and Jerusalem. The only rungs then left on the promotion ladder were *kadı* of the capital, Istanbul, *Kadıasker* of Anatolia, *Kadıasker* of Rumelia, and at the very top *Şeyhülislam* (Shaykh of Islam). Members of the *ulema* who had achieved certain levels of promotion were eligible for appointment to the sultan's staff. The *şeyhülislam* and both *kadıaskers* were members of the *divan*, the imperial council. The oath of allegiance of the twelve senior *kadıs* to a new sultan signified religious approval of his rule, and it was the same twelve officials who could authorise his deposition. A sultan required the approval of his *şeyhülislam* for important decisions such as the declaration of war. This limitation on his power was the price the sultan had to pay to retain the support of his Sunni orthodox subjects, as they accepted the authority of the *ulema*.

It may be remarked here that another of the *şeyhülislam*'s tasks was to issue *fetvas*—formal opinions on questions put to him. Throughout the empire *müftis* at lower levels issued *fetvas* in their own areas. As the Ottomans upheld the Hanafi legal school and appointed only hanafi judges, only *fetvas* issued by Hanafi *müftis* were admissible in Ottoman courts. The work of interpreting the *şeriat* fell to the *müftis*, while the *kadıs* had to see it made effective. The *müftis* did not go so far as to claim the right to new interpretation since, unlike the religious authorities in Iran, they accepted that there was no longer any room for innovation in establishing religious precedent. (In the words of the traditional saying, 'the door of *ictihad*—religious innovation—was closed'.) This left scope for the sultan to introduce legislation (*kanun*) based on accepted custom and the requirements of the state to deal with matters on which the *şeriat* was not explicit. He could not issue laws contrary to the *şeriat* and the *ulema* were ever watchful to prevent him strengthening his own position at their expense. Since in Islamic theory the goal of Muslim society and individual alike was perfection achieved through observance of the *şeriat*, the position of the *ulema* as interpreters and implementers of the *şeriat* was extremely powerful in the lives of all who accepted their authority. Although in theory Islam has no place for intermediaries between the believer and Allah, in practice the *ulema* as trained and professional experts in the *şeriat* achieved a position of authority over orthodox Sunni Muslims and were extremely influential in the Ottoman Empire.

A major rival to the *ulema* in the struggle for power within the empire was what many historians have dubbed the 'Ruling Institution'. Its ranks were filled mostly by men who were technically slaves owing complete allegiance to the sultan. The reason for this odd arrangement lay in the severe limits the *şeriat* imposed on the rights a ruler could exercise over free-born Muslims. To get round this problem 'slaves' were appointed to serve the sultan in the standing army, the bureaucracy and the palace. Over this category of person the sultan had the power of life or death. The source of these slaves was originally the sultan's share (one fifth) of prisoners captured in war. But in time a levy system known as *devşirme* provided most of the new male recruits for the ruling institution by taking a proportion of the boys from Christian families, mostly in the Balkans, and sending them to Turkey to be trained for the sultan's service. The most promising were sent to palace schools to be groomed for high government office. After intensive training there followed by a period of personal service to the sultan in the palace, they were sent at about the age of twenty-five to gain experience in battle or in administrative posts in the provinces. Progress thereafter took the most successful through the various ranks of officialdom right up to that of Grand Vizir, second only to the sultan himself and with precedence over the *şeyhül-islam*. The boys not selected for the palace school were sent off to Anatolia to learn the Turkish language, Turkish customs and the new faith into which they had been inducted upon arrival in Istanbul by making the declaration: 'There is no god but God, and Muhammad is the Prophet of God', and undergoing circumcision. For a few years they developed their physical strength and stamina before they were enrolled into the Janissaries, the elite foot-soldiers of the sultan's standing army that in their heyday constituted the world's finest fighting force. Because they had not been born Muslims these members of the ruling institution remained technically slaves and as such, although they could acquire great wealth, prestige and power, their fortunes were dependent upon the sultan's pleasure and even a grand vizer could be executed at the sultan's whim. This threat was by no means remote; so dangerous was the post in the reign of Selim I (1512–20) that the words, 'May you become Selim's vizier!' became a familiar curse.

The system of filling vacancies in the ruling institution with the children of subject peoples of a different religion was designed to ensure their dependence upon and loyalty to the sultan and prevent the rise of powerful families within the palace establishment. But as well as maintaining the allegiance of those engaged in ruling the empire the sultan also had to beware of alienating the people who were ruled, the important subject class. These produced the revenue needed to keep the empire going: tradesmen, merchants, craftsmen, peasants, shepherds and so on. They themselves had organisations that were forces to be reckoned with. For example, among Turkish craftsmen and small traders the trade guild called *ahilik* (brotherhood) was a particularly influential body of which sultans had to take note. It not only set standards of workmanship and strict ethical conduct based upon Muslim principles for its members at recognised grades from apprentice to master craftsman, it also played a conspicuous part in maintaining order in the community, particularly in areas where the central government's control was weak. Early Ottoman sultans accepted formal positions in this brotherhood.

Many members of the subject class belonged to tarikats. The tarikats continued to reflect the Sunni–Shi'a schism and often the urban–rural divide too. Some attracted royal favours and even royal members. Others became associated with rebellious elements, taking part in the disturbances that broke out periodically in echoes of the Babai uprising of Seljuk times. Shi'a tarikats were the most disaffected, as the Shi'a detested the Sunni rule of the Ottomans, and in the early sixteenth century many Shi'a tribesmen and peasants threw in their lot with the Safavid Shah Ismail of neighbouring Iran. Acting decisively against this internal and external threat to Ottoman supremacy, Selim I moved first against the Shi'a of Anatolia, putting 40,000 of them to the sword, then routed Shah Ismail at the Battle of Chaldiran in 1514. Although he went on to enhance his prestige as the most powerful Muslim ruler of his day by establishing Turkish rule over Syria, Egypt and the Hejaz—thus assuming guardianship of the holy cities of Mecca, Medina and Jerusalem—Selim is still execrated by Shi'a Turks for his ruthlessness towards them. His victory over the Shi'a was also a victory for the *şeyhülislam* and the *ulema* in their bitter struggle against the Shi'a tarikats.

Within the subject class non-Muslim communities were granted considerable autonomy under what was known as the *millet* system. In effect the sultan authorised the religious leaders of the different communities to run their affairs—not only spiritual but also judicial and educational—and accept responsibility for their conduct. From the fifteenth century there were separate *millets* for Orthodox Christians, Armenian Gregorians and Jews. More *millets* were recognised in the nineteenth century. Ottoman tolerance towards non-Muslims attracted 100,000 Jews to major Turkish cities in 1492 when they fled from persecution in Spain and Portugal.

While the Ottomans recognised religious differences, they did not distinguish between members of any religion on racial grounds. So, Turks, Arabs and Kurds were all treated as members of the Islamic community. Muslims actually constituted under half the total population of the Ottoman Empire at its height, and they did not form a separate *millet* but were subject to direct rule. Unlike non-Muslim subjects they were liable for military service (members of *millets* paid a poll-tax instead), so in this respect could be considered less privileged than members of *millets*, though non-Muslims were deemed inferior and suffered other disadvantages.

Nationality was, however, important when certain Western European powers gained special privileges for their citizens who were living in the Ottoman Empire conducting business. Under the *capitula-*

tions system, these people became subject to the jurisdiction of their own consular courts and were exempt from local taxes. Naturally this arrangement gave these foreigners considerable advantages. In time the capitulations system became the subject of scandalous abuse and had an increasingly harmful effect upon the Turkish economy.

The Golden Age of Ottoman Rule

Between 1451 and 1566 the Ottoman Empire achieved its greatest glories under three successive sultans: Mehmet II, Selim I and Süleyman I (known in the West as Süleyman the Magnificent). Its territories eventually stretched from Algiers to Aden, from Buda to Basra and from the borders of Poland to those of Sudan. The Ottomans naturally regarded this success as a divine reward for their services to Islam. Manifestations of their Muslim faith were evident in all aspects of their lives: they had adopted the Arabic script; the language used by the Ottoman elite contained so much Arabic and Persian (both words and grammatical structures) that it was largely incomprehensible to the mass of Turkish subjects (and further widened the gap between rulers and ruled); the education system was dominated by Islamic teaching; magnificent mosques were the greatest glories of Ottoman architecture; Turkish artists, barred from the sort of painting familiar in the West because of Muslim objections to the representation of living beings, excelled in calligraphy, and Turkish craftsmen demonstrated their devotion as well as their skill by producing masterpieces to the glory of God in wood, metal and textiles; many of the most splendid Turkish carpets were prayer-rugs.

Decline

But it needed more than faith alone to maintain the empire. Only leaders of exceptional vision, ability and integrity could defend such vast territories against threats from within and without. After the glorious reign of Süleyman the Magnificent (1520–66), a succession of incompetent sultans could no longer sustain Turkish supremacy in the face of a resurgent Europe benefiting from the discovery of the New World, new trade routes and trade patterns, and the development of new industrial and agricultural techniques. By the beginning of the eighteenth century it was clear that the West had outpaced the Turks. In fact, most of the Ottoman religious establishment had for a long time fiercely resisted 'infidel learning', as they termed scientific and technical discoveries made in Europe. As early as 1580 the Janissaries, incited by the *ulema*, had destroyed the observatory in the capital. And because of pressure from religious reactionaries no printing-press was allowed to produce works in Turkish until 1727—nearly three centuries after Gutenberg had invented movable type! The hostility of the *ulema* towards the rational sciences in the sixteenth and seventeenth centuries led to a concentration on law studies which stunted intellectual development and caused a stagnation in Ottoman learning whose woeful consequences are well illustrated in the report by Captain Beaufort, the English hydrographer who conducted a survey in Turkish waters in 1811–12:

> There is no subject on which the Turks are in general more ignorant than geography. The Mediterranean bounds their ideas of the ocean; and a Pasha of high rank maintained to me with earnestness, that England was an island in the Black Sea, with which there was another channel of communication besides the Dardanelles. They have indeed copies of English and French charts, printed at Constantinople, with the names in Turkish; but their naval officers disdain to understand them, and confide entirely in their Greek pilots.

A sad decline indeed from the days of Piri Reis (1465–1554), the distinguished Turkish admiral and cartographer whose world map included America!

Short-comings in learning were paralleled by weaknesses in the administration. When the *devşirme* system of recruitment fell into disuse and sons of officials and Janissaries were admitted to government service, nepotism as well as corruption seriously blemished Ottoman rule. The previously peerless Janissaries deteriorated into a rebellious rabble more dangerous to the state than to its external enemies. Moreover, the Turkish armed forces generally became increasingly outclassed.

Degeneration went beyond the official institutions; it affected the tarikats too. At some earlier stages of Turkish history these Sufi orders had played a major part in converting inhabitants of occupied territories to Islam. Offering enthusiastic Muslims a popular and colourful alternative to the teaching and example of the *ulema* and sometimes contributing to the education of the common people, they also played a significant social role by providing opportunities for people of different classes and backgrounds to come together in the *tekkes* where tarikat meetings were held. But the *ulema* usually resented these rivals for the allegiance of the Muslim community and frequently intrigued against them, thus adding to the instability of the state. In the mid-seventeenth century the Grand Vizier temporarily suppressed several tarikats by force. In 1826 Sultan Mahmud II tried to wipe out the Bektashis when he annihilated the Janissaries with whom they had a centuries-long close association. At various times standards in many of the tarikats deteriorated markedly as their leaders began shamefully to exploit the blind obedience of their devotees.

But moral decay was not confined to Muslims in the empire; the Christian *millets* too became a reproach to religion, riddled with corruption and intrigue. Even after Mahmud II hanged the Greek Orthodox Patriarch Gregorius in 1821, the Christian minorities continued to mix religion with politics, and foreign powers used them as an excuse to interfere in Ottoman internal affairs and to encourage separatist demands. The Jewish *millet*, however, was less involved in politics, its members preferring to concern themselves with occupations for which few Muslims showed much inclination such as trade and interpreting.

The Beginning of Secularisation

Although the Turks chose to turn a blind eye to much of the growing evidence of deterioration of their empire, the one aspect they could not ignore was the weakness of their armed forces. To remedy this they had no alternative but to look to the West. But it was not possible to retrain and re-equip the armed forces in isolation. The new army and navy needed personnel with qualifications the traditional schools and *medreses* could not provide. Inevitably contacts with the West, particularly with the French, increased. Equally inevitably, French ideas on political philosophy and the place of religion in the state began to penetrate Turkey. These ideas and growing European interference in Ottoman affairs sparked off a soul-searching debate among Turkish intellectuals on what should be the Ottoman response to the challenge of the West.

Different possibilities were examined. In 1822 Akif Efendi said Muslims would have to choose between vigorously defending the whole of their territory, withdrawing to Anatolia, or being reduced to slavery. He urged the first choice, and it is significant that his words were addressed to *Muslims* not to *Turks*; the concept of Turkish nationality had not by then arisen. Soon after this many Muslim subjects felt their privileges were being eroded by the nineteenth-century *Tanzimat* reforms that introduced some limited secularisation. Moreover, through their French contacts some Turkish intellectuals became familiar with the idea that religion could be regarded as a matter for the private belief of the individual. Since this concept was totally at variance with the traditional teaching that Islam should govern every aspect of life and form the foundation of the state and society, it met fierce resistance. Once Turks had also grasped the concept of nationalism, three rival remedies were offered for the empire's ills, each offering a different basis on which unity might be achieved. In 1904 these were listed as: Ottomanism—a common citizenship and loyalty of all subjects of the empire without regard to religion or race; Islamism (or pan-Islamism)—the union of all Muslim peoples; and Turkism (or pan-Turkism)—the unity of peoples speaking Turkic languages. The Young Turks who came to power after the 1908 Revolution wrestled with these concepts, but in the event neither Ottomanism nor Islamism could prevail against the rising tide of nationalism even amongst the Muslim subjects.

The Young Turks introduced limited secularising measures that offended the religious conservatives. The power of secular courts was increased at the expense of the religious courts, *kadıs* and religious employees came under closer state control, a Family Code and new educational and work opportunities brought changes to the position of women. In response to such developments members of the Nakşibendi tarikat led three uprisings in 1919–20 in Anatolia aimed at enforcing the reimplementation of the *şeriat*. The place of the *şeriat* in Turkish life was actually to remain the subject of fierce controversy in Atatürk's day and even now the argument rumbles on.

Atatürk and the Creation of a Secular State

Defeat in the First World War left Turkey without an empire, and religious issues were of great importance in the subsequent Turkish War of Independence (1919–22) during which Mustafa Kemal (1881–1938)—later to receive the name Atatürk—organised resistance to Turkey's occupation by the victors of the World War. The Sultan and his government in Istanbul were subservient to Allied demands and regarded opposition as hopeless. The Sultan ordered wide distribution to be given to a *fetva* issued by his *şeyhülislam* calling upon the faithful to kill Mustafa Kemal and his 'rebels'. Mustafa Kemal countered a month later, on 5 May 1920, by getting the *müfti* of Ankara to issue a *fetva*, endorsed by 152 other *müftis* in Anatolia, declaring the *şeyhülislam*'s *fetva* invalid because it had been issued under foreign duress, and calling upon Muslims to 'liberate their Caliph from captivity'. But this was not enough to prevent serious attacks upon Kemal's Nationalists by men who unquestioningly accepted as always the authority of the Sultan, his Grand Vizier and his *Şeyhülislam*. Mustafa Kemal needed to retain the support of all who were prepared to give it; he could not afford to alienate anyone by disregarding their religious susceptibilities. His effective campaign against the Greek invaders eventually swung many Muslims to his side: the Christian Greeks could be seen as enemies of Islam as well as of Turkey.

Mustafa Kemal used the prestige and power gained from his victory in the War of Independence to bring about a most remarkable and thoroughgoing transformation of his people. He combined within his person the qualities of bold visionary and clear-sighted practical politician. He therefore kept his ultimate goals to himself, never losing sight of his objective but never making a move towards it until he calculated he could muster enough support to cajole his Grand National Assembly into approving the next step along the way. By this means he effected the dismantling of the long-established religious apparatus and turned the erstwhile theocracy into a secular state.

He started at the top with the Sultan–Caliph. With difficulty he managed to persuade the Turkish Grand National Assembly that the sultanate and the caliphate should be separated and the former office abolished. On 1 November 1922 the last sultan–caliph was therefore dismissed, and on 18 November his cousin, Abdülmecid, was appointed caliph. It had required all Mustafa Kemal's formidable powers of persuasion to achieve that much; it would not have been possible to abolish the caliphate at the same time because that office was still held in such high esteem by multitudes of the faithful. In fact, as far back as the sixteenth century Ottoman sultans had used the title caliph, but it was not until the nineteenth century that they laid much stress upon this role. Abdülhamid (1876–1909) used it in a calculated bid to maintain the support of his Arab Muslim subjects, and at the outbreak of the First World War Sultan Mehmed V used the title caliph in an unsuccessful bid to turn Muslim subjects of the British and French Empires against their rulers. But within Turkey itself a considerable number of devout Muslims accepted the early Sunni tradition that the caliph must receive unhesitating obedience and to rebel against him was to rebel against God. Nevertheless, Mustafa Kemal saw the caliphate as an obstacle to progress and he was determined to remove it. In 1924 he seized an opportunity to persuade Parliament to abolish the office on the grounds that foreign intriguers were trying to use it to interfere in Turkey's affairs. He took the same opportunity to deliver further heavy blows at the religious establishment: the abolition of the post of *şeyhülislam* and the Ministry of Şeriat and Evkaf and the transference of all religious schools and *medreses* to the Ministry of Education. These drastic measures caused deep unrest, and in February 1925 the Nakşibendi Şey Said of Palu led a serious rebellion of Kurds in the south-east of Anatolia aimed at ending the republic and restoring the caliphate and the *şeriat*. This uprising was crushed and its forty-seven leaders were executed at the end of June 1925.

The revolt had shown that the tarikats remained a powerful force in Turkey, and Kemal determined to destroy them. He considered their arcane mysteries had no place in the modern world he wanted Turkey to join, and he knew that throughout history various tarikats had sheltered dissident elements and engaged in subversive activities—indeed some of them had lent him vital support during the War of Independence and in his struggle against the sultan. He grasped the nettle in November 1925 and banned all tarikats and their activities and closed their meeting-places. He declared that Turkey no longer had need of them. In their place he offered his vision of an enlightened society based on scientific learning. 'The straightest and truest tarikat is the tarikat of civilisation', he declared.

Kemal was determined that Turkey should achieve the level of civilisation enjoyed by advanced nations in the West. He therefore set about bringing his country into line with Western Europe. This process affected almost every aspect of his people's lives. He banned the wearing of the fez and discouraged the veil, he adopted the Western calendar and the international 24-hour clock (instead of the Muslim system based on the time of sunrise), and made Sunday the weekly day of rest. He ousted the Arab-based script and introduced a Latin-based alphabet. He made surnames compulsory, taking for himself the name 'Atatürk' (Father of the Turks). He encouraged sculptors and artists to produce works in the Western style, so statues and paintings of living things at last became familiar to Turks.

He strove to exclude the influences of Islam from national life. In a move of fundamental importance he introduced new laws based on European models to replace what was left of the *şeriat*. He gave women the vote and encouraged them to stand for election. He banned religious education in schools and closed the Faculty of Theology. He set up a new Department of Religious Affairs under direct contol of the prime minister. Its task was, in effect, to ensure that religion was used in the service of the state—a complete reversal of the old Ottoman concept that the purpose of government was to implement the will of Allah. The nation itself was now to become the focus of devotion. Nationalist fervour was instilled into the people almost as a substitute for religion, although all citizens remained free to practise their faith in their private lives. In keeping with the emphasis on Turkishness, the Arabic call to prayer was banned and a Turkish formula substituted. In 1937 the constitution was amended to define Turkey as a *secular* state.

Developments since Atatürk

All these reforms were imposed by Atatürk and a band of enthusiastic supporters in what they believed to be the best interests of the people. But many devout Muslims deeply resented these measures, although they rarely dared to express their opinions openly. After the Second World War, however, with the introduction of multi-party politics they had at last an opportunity to make their views felt. In 1950 they voted out of office the Republican People's Party, the champions of Kemalist reforms, and elected the Democratic Party, which they believed would be responsive to the public will. The Republican People's Party had itself come to realise the unpopularity of some of the anti-religious legislation and in 1949 it had allowed religious education again in primary schools and had set up a Theology Faculty in Ankara University.

During their decade of power the Democratic Party repealed the ban on the Arabic call to prayer and showed themselves to be generally sympathetic to Muslim sentiments. The proliferation of Qur'an courses for children and of schools to train preachers and other Muslim functionaries bore witness to this party's greater tolerance towards religion.

But, to the disappointment of certain fervent groups, the Democrats did not dare to revoke the more fundamental Kemalist reforms. These fervent groups included members of the Ticani tarikat, who achieved notoriety by smashing statues of Atatürk, and movements such as Nurculuk and Süleymancılık that called for the restoration of Islam as the foundation of the state. Said Nursi (1873–1960), the founder of the Nurcu movement, claimed to be the *mücedded* (divinely appointed reformer of Islam) for the twentieth century, and the fact that he had been one of Atatürk's boldest critics and frequently in trouble with the authorities enhanced his prestige and increased his following among those Muslims who yearned for a return to what they regarded as the glorious era of Islamic rule. The Süleymancıs—a secretive group founded by Süleyman Hilmi Tunahan, who died in 1959, and now led by Kemal Kaçar—also made vigorous attempts to win new members. Like the Nurcus, they have set up student hostels in university towns to aid their recruitment drive.

On 27 May 1960 the armed forces, in their role as 'guardians of Kemalism', ousted the Democratic Party, which had developed dictatorial tendencies. The struggle to determine the place of Islam in the state has continued and proved to be long, bitter and occasionally bloody. The forces engaged represent the full spectrum of political opinion and a wide range of Muslim views. The extreme right-wing Nationalist Action Party sought to mobilise ultra-nationalists and keen Sunnis in a campaign against the Left. Another party, the National Salvation Party, founded in October 1972, defied the constitutional ban on exploiting religion for political purposes and expressed a desire for an Islamic state based on the principles of the *şeriat.* Some of its instant success was attributed to links with the Nakşibendi order, one of the many tarikats that had cautiously started to re-emerge decades after Atatürk's 1925 suppression of all such movements. Some of the tarikats now studiously avoided political involvement; after all, they were still prohibited by law. Others became associated with the political struggle. The Left, seeing that the Right was making an open bid for Sunni support, sought to enlist the Shi'a to its ranks. Clashes, mainly of a political nature but often with religious ingredients, proliferated. One attack, in December 1978, upon the population of the largely Alevi town of Kahramanmaraş in south-east Anatolia left 117 dead and over 1,000 wounded. The combination of the Left and the Shi'a clearly saw themselves as maintaining the long tradition, going right back to the Babai rebellion of 1240, of championing the victims of Sunni oppression.

Right-wingers in Turkey had for many years labelled their opponents as Communists, a smear intended to imply treacherous allegiance to the godless regime of the traditional enemy, Russia. While this epithet deterred some conservative Muslim voters from drifting leftwards, it was so overused that almost any proposal for social reform became branded as Communist with the result that many people began to think that 'Communism'—whatever that might be—was perhaps their only way to a better life. This all contributed to the increasingly bitter division of Turkish society in the 1970s.

Most Turks welcomed the military coup on 12 September 1980, convinced that it was the only alternative to a full-scale civil war enflamed by both political and religious passions. The new rulers reaffirmed Kemalist principles, enshrined them in the constitution and tried to make them the basis for national unity. The preamble to the 1982 Constitution states: 'as required by the principle of secularism, there shall be no interference whatsoever of sacred religious feelings in state affairs and politics'. Article 24 grants freedom of religion and conscience, and Article 136 says the Department of Religious Affairs is to exercise its duties 'in accordance with the principles of secularism, removed from all political views and ideas, and aiming at national solidarity and integrity'. Thus the authorities still considered religion should serve the interests of the state rather than the other way round.

This view is exemplified in the religious instruction made compulsory again by Article 24 of the same constitution. The official textbooks, emphasising the virtue of national unity, give Sunni teaching without any reference to Shi'a views and are at pains to reconcile the Kemalist interpretation of secularism with the teachings of Islam. The lessons are intended to instil a sense of patriotism and civic responsibility as well as basic religious knowledge. But just as religion is called in aid of the Kemalist state, so too are selected sayings of Atatürk quoted to claim his seal of approval for belief in Islam and to predispose pupils accordingly.

By no means all Turkish Muslims support the stance of the Religious Affairs Department. The Department gives no aid or encouragement to the Shi'a, to tarikats or to any of the new Sunni movements that have appeared in recent years. Many of these people deprecate the Department's activities, particularly its promulgation of state secularism. As we have noted, some of these groups, such as the Nurcus and the Süleymancıs, want a return to a state governed according to the *şeriat*. But, as a state organisation, the Department has to do as it is told by its government masters, though by the mid-1980s its officials were generally content with the government's attitude.

The shortage of religious leaders with a respectable level of learning has posed acute problems. In 1961, for example, of over 60,000 religious leaders in the country only 5,191 had completed even elementary education. The Religious Affairs Department has taken this matter seriously and as well as offering more education in Turkey is sending the best students abroad to acquire advanced qualifications. The fact that money for their training comes from a Religious Affairs charitable foundation to which Turkish Muslims at home and also those working abroad have donated generously that it has become an immensely wealthy institution indicates the solid support for Islam that still persists among very many Turks. Similar deeply-held convictions are evident among the thousands who still flock to the tombs of saints and celebrate festivals peculiar to their own religious group.

At the international level, Turks have endeavoured to capitalise on the fact that some 98 per cent of their population is Muslim. In an attempt to obtain economic aid and political support from the Muslim world Turkey joined the Islamic Conference—a move which some Turks condemned as being at odds with Turkey's secular status, in disregard of

Atatürk's principles, and harmful to Turkey's chances of gaining admission to the European Economic Community. In trade, the fact that Turks are Muslims gives them some advantages in Arab markets, for example as suppliers of halal meat. It has also made it easier for their numerous contract workers to adapt to conditions in the Arab world, but by the same token it makes it more difficult for the far greater number of Turks in Europe to adjust.

Conclusion: an Islamic Revival?

In the mid-1980s there was renewed speculation about the possibility of a radical Islamic revival in Turkey. It was claimed that reactionaries, with foreign backing, were in the ascendant. The boom in religious publications, a more widespread observance of the Muslim month of fasting, new restrictions some councils placed on the sale of alcohol, an increase to some 30,000 a year in the number of Turkish pilgrims to Mecca, the re-emergence of tarikats, and the building of an average of 500 new mosques each year were cited as evidence of such a revival. In early 1987 many secularists were alarmed by open fundamentalist clamour for Turkey to implement the *şeriat*. They condemned Iranian provocation and deplored Saudi financial support for fundamentalist groups in Turkey.

Prominent among those clamouring for an Islamic state was Cemalettin Kaplan, a former *Müfti* of Adana living in voluntary exile in Germany. He branded Kemalism as 'rebellion against Allah', and video cassettes of his fundamentalist sermons circulated in Turkey in their thousands. The situation became sufficiently serious for the President of the Republic to condemn Kaplan in particular and Islamic reactionaries in general, stating that they represented as great a danger as Communism.

Private religious observance by individuals, however, is not discouraged and it is natural that some Turks turn increasingly to Islam for solace amid the hardships they have to suffer in an economically struggling nation that is seeking to modernise and industrialise in order to support its rapidly growing population. But certain open manifestations of faith may provoke major confrontations such as the fierce controversy, renewed in 1987, over whether female students should be allowed to wear Islamic-style headscarves at university. On such matters Prime Minister Turgut Özal, no doubt anxious to avoid alienating religious voters, took a markedly softer line against the fundamentalists than did President Evren, who was not eligible for re-election.

Secularists' fears were heightened by reports that Nurcus had infiltrated military schools and fundamentalists were plotting to win over the armed forces. Everyone regarded the armed forces as the ultimate bastions of Kemalism; no fundamentalist design could succeed in the face of their determined opposition. As Atatürk had decreed that Islam should not determine the policies or conduct of the state, and as Turkish military leaders have been taught since their schooldays to cherish Atatürk's reforms, the armed forces are unlikely to remain passive if faced with a serious risk that Turkey might be turned into a religious state. So the actual extent of any Islamic revival in Turkey is likely to remain limited.

The example of Iran is not one that many Turks feel inclined to follow. Even when in 1987 secularists were surprised and alarmed to rediscover the intensity of Islamic fundamentalist attachment manifest in Turkey, opinion polls indicated that at least 80 per cent of the population had no desire to see the *şeriat* implemented. And that is a measure of the change Atatürk brought about.

Further Reading

Berkes, Niyazi *The Development of Secularism in Turkey* (McGill University Press, Montreal, 1964)

Birge, John K. *The Bektashi Order of Dervishes* (Luzac, London, 1965)

Chambers, Richard L. 'The Ottoman Ulema and the Tanzimat' in Nikki R. Keddie (ed.) *Scholars, Saints, and Sufis* (University of California Press, London, 1972), pp. 33–46

Friedlander, Ira *The Whirling Dervishes* (Wildwood House, London, 1975)

Inalcik, Halil *The Ottoman Empire: The Classical Age 1300–1600* (Weidenfeld and Nicolson, London, 1973)

Holt, P.M., Lambton, Ann K.S. and Lewis, Bernard (eds.) *The Cambridge History of Islam*, vol. I: *The Central Islamic Lands* (Cambridge University Press, Cambridge, 1970)

Lewis, Bernard *The Emergence of Modern Turkey*, 2nd edn (Oxford University Press, London, 1966)

Lewis, Geoffrey *Modern Turkey*, 4th edn (Ernest Benn, London, 1974)

Mardin, Şerif 'Religion in Modern Turkey', *International Social Science Journal*, XXIX, no. 2 (1977), pp. 279–97

Martin, B.G. 'A Short History of the Khalwati Order of Dervishes' in Nikki R. Keddie (ed.) *Scholars, Saints, and Sufis* (University of California Press, London, 1972) pp. 275–306

Norton, J.D. 'Bektashis in Turkey' in Denis MacEoin and Ahmed Al-Shahi (eds.) *Islam in the Modern World* (Croom Helm, London, 1983), pp. 73–87

Repp, Richard 'Some Observations on the Development of the Ottoman Learned Hierarchy' in Nikki R. Keddie (ed.) *Scholars, Saints, and Sufis* (University of California Press, London, 1972), pp. 17–32

Schimmel, Annemarie 'Islam in Turkey' in A.J. Arberry (ed.) *Religion in the Middle East: Three Religions in Concord and Conflict*, II (Cambridge University Press, Cambridge, 1969), pp. 68–96

Shaw, Stanford *History of the Ottoman Empire and Modern Turkey*, 2 vols. (Cambridge University Press, London, 1976 and 1977)

Trimingham, J. S. *The Sufi Orders in Islam* (Oxford University Press, London, 1971)

25 China's Muslims

R. Israeli

In view of the basic demand of Islam that Muslims should live, to the greatest possible extent, under Islamic rulers, there are many problems surrounding the survival of Muslim minorities under non-Islamic rule. We are not only talking about majority–minority and host culture–guest culture relationships, but also about some basic requirements, short of which a Muslim minority is bound to rebel against the ruling government and even to try to secede from the state institutions. This issue, which has repeatedly recurred in the history of many Muslim minorities throughout the world, is perhaps more acute in China these days due to the extraordinary convergence of several major factors:

1. Chinese society and culture, which has a long tradition of assimilating foreign cultures, had to contend in this case with a self-confident guest culture which does not lend itself to acculturation;
2. Chinese Communism, which has been until recently unitarian and strictly anti-religious, has been opening up of late, thus possibly creating a more accommodating environment for the reassertion of Islamic norms;
3. The current revival of Islam throughout the world, coupled with the growing interest of the Islamic core in the minorities of the periphery, have raised the probability of Islamic renewal in these remote fringes of the Islamic world.

It is therefore timely and important to examine Islamic China not merely as a historical exoticism but mainly as a prototype of a vital Muslim minority that may be undergoing significant developments in response to the winds of change that have been sweeping through the vast Islamic world which now encompasses some forty-odd countries and more than eight hundred million believers.

Historical Background

Islam came to China as early as the T'ang period (seventh to ninth centuries), probably during the eighth century. The first Muslim settlers in China were Arab and Persian merchants who travelled via the sea routes around India and soon found the Chinese trade remunerative enough to justify their permanent presence in Chinese coastal cities. In those days, the Muslims dwelled apart in separate quarters and actually maintained the Muslim mode of life which they had imported with them, and this seclusion was facilitated by the almost extraterritorial rights they enjoyed. They preserved their Arabic names, their original dress, their Persian and Arabic tongues, and conducted their religious and social life independently of the Chinese. Moreover, many of them married Chinese women or bought Chinese children in times of famine, thus not only consciously contributing to the numerical growth of the Muslim community, but also unwittingly injecting into the midst the first germ of their ultimate ethnic assimilation.

The Yuan (1279–1368) rule in China considerably boosted Muslim existence in the Middle Kingdom inasmuch as the Muslims, together with other non-Chinese groups (ssu-mu) were superimposed by the Mongol conqueror upon the Chinese. The Muslims, both those who had settled in China in previous centuries and the newly arrived allies of the Mongols from the Muslim sultanates of Central Asia, indeed wielded a great deal of power, the most prominent example being Seyyid Edjell who conquered Yunnan for the Yuan and was nominated by the Khan as the first governor of the province. The borders of Central Asia were wide open for trade and ideas during the Mongol rule and considerable numbers of Muslims moved to settle in the north-western and south-western provinces of China; strong ties were established and cultivated between the Muslims of China and the lands of Islam.

The retrenchment of the Ming (1368–1644), and the self-isolation that came as a reaction to the rule of the Mongol barbarians over China, constituted a major watershed in the fortunes of Chinese Muslims. From then on, one could indeed speak of 'Chinese Muslims' and no longer about 'Muslims in China'. The Muslims adopted Chinese names, became fluent in the Chinese speech and in most cases, at least as far as China proper was concerned, they became outwardly indistinguishable from the Chinese. This same trend continued throughout the 'High Ch'ing', that is until the end of the Ch'ien-lung reign (1796).

The decline of the Manchu Dynasty, which was accompanied by the symptomatic plights of demographic explosion, scarcity of resources, devolution of power and the rise of anti-establishment groups such as secret societies, was, in this instance, also coupled with a startling Muslim revivalist movement in China. This movement, which gathered momentum during the nineteenth century, was contemporaneous with a similar outburst of Muslim fundamentalism in India, known as the Wahhabiyya, and was generated by the spread of the Naqshbandi Sufi order from Central Asia into China. The most dramatic development resulting from this movement was the avant-garde role that the 'New Sect' of Chinese Islam played in Muslim rebellions during the final years of the Ch'ing. Indeed, the Muslim revolts of the mid-nineteenth century, which threw most of China's north-west and south-west into chaos, were apparently connected with the 'New Sectarians'.

The Muslim revolts were mainly initiated in provinces where the Muslims constituted a large portion of the population. In Kansu, the rebellion was led by the messianic figure of Ma Hua-lung, who attempted to establish a Muslim state during the 1850s and 1860s, but it ended in failure. In Yunnan, Tu Wen-hsiu proclaimed himself 'Sultan Suleiman' and governed a secessionist Muslim state for about sixteen years (1856–72) before he succumbed to the imperial forces. The same fate awaited the Sinkiang revolt of the Uighur Muslims (in the 1870s). But although these rebellions were quelled, amidst a terrifying bloodshed, the Muslims never gave up either their separate identity as Muslims or their messianic craving for a schism from the Chinese polity. Indeed, some outbursts of Muslim secessionism were recorded at the turn of the century, and again during the Communist rule when the Hundred Flowers campaign of the mid-1950s was proclaimed.

Chinese versus Muslims

Intellectually as well as practically, the Chinese of the Confucian tradition could hardly tolerate a guest culture such as the Muslims in their midst. This is all the more so under the Communist regime of contemporary China, the best evidence for that being the generally harsh policy of the Peking regime towards the minorities in general and the Muslims in particular.

In traditional China the reasons for this uneasy coexistence could be identified mainly in the wide intellectual hiatus that separated the two communities. In fact, the Muslims differed from all other minority groups in that, although they were concentrated mainly in marginal areas of the empire, they were present in virtually every province and every sizeable urban agglomeration throughout the country, and their presence was not merely statistical. They had large communities in the capitals (Nanking and Peking), they handled some trade in many places and left their impact (though more as individuals than as a collective) all over the country. This may explain the ubiquitous nature of the hatred, jealousy and contempt in which they were held by the Chinese at large. Conversely, from the authorities' point of view, no crash programme in a certain territory could force all the Hui to acculturate, since there was no such single territory. For this reason, while the other major minorities were handled under the Ch'ing by the Li Fan Yuan, which controlled them by controlling their territory, the Hui were free from such control.

Secondly, since the Muslims could not accept the principle of filial piety or participate in the ceremonies of the Ancestral Shrines in the Court, through which the Chinese attempted to 'civilise' non-Chinese barbarians, they chose to remain outside the pale of the sought-for 'refinement and virtue'. Neither was the stratagem that the Ch'ing used with un-Chinese aborigines workable with the Muslims. The Hui had their own sense of superiority, their own festivals and religious symbolism, their own learning and culture, and needed no 'uplifting' to the heights of Chinese civilisation. In short, they did not yield to the *mission civilisatrice* of their Chinese hosts.

From a Chinese intellectual's point of view, then, if Confucius means nothing to the Muslims, this signifies that they are outside the pale of civilisation. More specifically, if they lack adherence to the Confucian principle of filial piety, as exemplified in their ignorance of ancestor worship, then all the socio-political and religio-ethical tenets that bind the Chinese together do not apply to Muslims. That is to say:

1. If Muslims are outside the framework of the father–son relationship, then they are bound to be unruly *vis-à-vis* their family hierarchy, the local authority and even the emperor. As such, they are detrimental, at least potentially, to the social order in particular and to the Chinese polity in general.
2. If Muslims do not respect the rituals due to ancestors and other spirits, they are exposed to the malicious needs of those spirits, and thus one had better keep away from them.
3. If the blessings of Heaven are transmitted to earth through the Son of Heaven, the Muslims, by being unfilial to the emperor, cannot rejoice in those blessings and thus cannot partake of Chinese civilisation.
4. Since the emperor, though claiming no superiority over Heaven, is the ruler of both temporal and celestial orders, the Muslims, claiming that celestial powers are beyond the emperor's authority, are likely to fall short of respecting the Chinese monarch and what he represents. How, then, can they be expected to be his loyal subjects?
5. In general, ancestor worship and filial piety imply the acceptance of the ways of the Ancients. If the Muslims have their own calendar, celebrate their own festivals, have no attachment to their locale or domicile, and pay no attention to the Chinese way, how can they be considered Chinese?

Indeed, in the eyes of the Chinese literati, who would formulate their objections to Muslims in intellectual and rational terms, the gap between the two communities might have looked so hopelessly unbridgeable that they could easily come under the sway of popular stereotypes, which tended to make the gap look even wider.

Religion in China was closely intertwined with intellectual life and with the political and social institutions of the nation. Confucianism was identified with scholarship and was deeply entrenched in the habits of thought, affections and loyalties of the educated people. The state was committed to the existing faiths, especially Confucianism. Confucian classics were the basis for education and the examination system. Ceremonies were associated with Confucianism and maintained at public expense. Officials, including the emperor, performed many of the duties usually assigned to a priesthood in other cultures. The very political theory on which the state rested derived its authority from Confucian teachings.

Religion also formed part of the village life. Temples were maintained by villages, festivals and ceremonies took place through general contribution. Guilds had patron gods and other religious features. Above all, the family, the strongest social unit, had as an integral part of its structure, the honouring of ancestors by rites that were religious in origin and retained a religious significance.

Muslims were out of place in this setting, since their social and religious norms were so different and could not displace the already well entrenched Chinese philosophies and traditions. They went their own ways in prayers and ceremonies, in their calendar and festivals, in their weddings and burial of the dead, in their socialising and eating habits, in their travelling and dwelling. So, no matter how much the Muslims wished to put on an appearance of being Chinese they were and remained Hui people, that is non-Chinese in the eyes of the Chinese.

Chinese Muslims, for their part, felt they were alien people, more akin to other members of the world Muslim community—the *umma*—than to their Chinese neighbours. Their main concern was their religion and their identity focused on the universal umma, and thus the deeply ingrained Chinese tradition of identification with the locus of domicile did not pertain to them. The specific congregation to which a Muslim belonged had for him a functional and temporary quality, not the intrinsic and immutable value that the Chinese felt for his village, county and province.

The Muslim community consistently underwent indoctrination on various levels. First, the Muslims kept from becoming Chinese; they reinforced their sense of superiority and distinctiveness, and encouraged the Muslim to remain socially and economically as independent of the Chinese as possible. Second, the Muslims became better members of their community through strong communal organisation, inculcation of Islamic values, communal worship and activities, a total and unqualified identification with their fellow Muslims in the congregation and moral submission to the authority of the imam. Third, the Chinese Muslim was made a conscious member of the world Muslim community. This was achieved by cultivating in the Muslim the centrality of Arabia, Islam, the Islamic Empire and Islamic traditions and values. But this was not all.

The daily prayers in the mosque were not only a communal worship, but also a way of identifying with all Muslims who faced the same *qibla* (direction of prayer)—Holy Mecca, the place of inception of Islam and conception of the Prophet. Some Chinese Muslims who could afford it went on the hadj (pilgrimage), and participated with the Muslim multitudes in common rituals that must have generated a feeling of religious exaltation. On the way to and from Mecca some Chinese Muslim notables visited Islamic centres such as Cairo and Constantinople, and on their return home they told their fellow Muslims of the marvels of the Islamic world and of their brethren there.

Muslims from Persia, India and Turkey seem to have paid sporadic visits to Muslim communities in China. Some of them, especially scholars, stayed for long periods of time and presumably shared their knowledge with their co-religionists. Chinese Muslims also met other Muslims in Asia on their way to the hadj. They received hospitality in mosques in Colombo, in Singapore and Hanoi. From Yunnan, Chinese Muslims maintained a permanent correspondence with Muslim scholars in Arabia and South-east Asia whence they sought advice when they faced problems of interpretation of the Shari'a.

The Muslims Resist the Assimilatory Pressures

The Muslim-Chinese literature of the Ch'ing period made valiant efforts to convince the general public that the Hui people were not so different from their Chinese hosts. The manifestations of the Muslims' smoothing over the built-in incongruencies between their faith and Confucianism do not necessarily have to be conceived as a conscious diversionary tactic on the part of the Muslims, but rather as a defence mechanism which sought to soften the intensity of hostility emanating from the Chinese dominant culture. True, the Muslim attitude as manifested in some of their writings can also be construed as an erosion of the sense of Muslim uniqueness and identity. But, judging from the Muslim revivalism of the eighteenth and nineteenth centuries, this erosion affected only the margins and surface of Chinese Islam, while its core retained a dormant vigour that became evident when the extreme anti-Muslim oppression under the Ch'ing Dynasty necessitated a vigorous Muslim reaction.

One of the main factors which enabled the Muslims in China to withstand these tensions and to continue to prosper as a community was their numerical strength. It is very difficult to ascertain how many Muslims were in China at any particular time, or even now. No reliable census has ever been taken, and evaluations, some of which were made through conscientious field work, still vary greatly, from 10 to 80 million, depending on the religious denomination or the political commitment of the author, and on the definition of who is a Chinese Muslim. The typical figure given by Muslims—Arabs and Chinese—is around 50 million. Muhammad Tawadu, for example, wrote back in the 1940s:

> The total population of China amounts to 473,237,335 people, and the Muslims constitute no small part of it. Their number is around fifty million, according to the most reliable views. Some researchers have exaggerated the figure and put it to eighty million, while others have reduced it to a mere thirty million.

This is not the proper place to go any deeper into this question, which will have to remain unanswered for the time being. Suffice it to say that the figure of 50 million is greatly inflated. Its recurrence in Arab and Chinese Muslim writings reflects, however, a state of mind that defies facts and reality as long as the Muslim ego can be boosted. (China's population today, however, is over 1 billion, which means that Tawadu's figure of 50 million Muslims should at least be doubled.)

One thing is certain—all of these estimates include the Muslims of Sinkiang, a Turkic ethno-linguistic group completely separate from the Hui, who have actually become Chinese in race and language. At any rate it is evident that the Hui community in China by Ming times had a membership of many millions and constituted the majority group or a very sizeable minority in many places throughout the country, especially in the north-west and the south-west, as well as a strong presence in virtually all the major cities of China. The Ming period was the crucial watershed because, as a result of the intensified Sinicisation under that dynasty, only minorities which had been numerous enough to form their own moulds of life previously could survive the assimilatory process thereafter.

During the Ming, many mosques were built in the pagoda shape of Chinese temples, eliminating the minarets which are typical of Muslim houses of prayer elsewhere, making them indistinguishable from Chinese temples. With the obliteration of the minaret, the muezzin could no longer call the believers to prayer in the traditional way. But the muezzin stood indoors, behind the entrance to the mosque, and urged Muslims to join in the prayer. When one entered the mosque, one was struck by the traditional Muslim flavour: cleanliness and austerity. Except for the Emperor's Tablets that were mandatory in any house of prayer, there was no sign of Chinese characters or Chinese characteristics. On the walls there were Arabic inscriptions of verses from the Qur'an, and the west end of the mosque (the *qibla*) was adorned with arabesques. Once the believers were inside the mosque, they put on white caps, shoes were taken off, elaborate ablutions were ritually performed, and the prayers began in Arabic, with hearts and minds centred on Mecca. When prostrating themselves before the Emperor's

Tablets, as required, the Muslims would avoid bringing their heads into contact with the floor (which they do when they worship Allah). Thus, Muslims could satisfy their conscience since they avoided the true significance of the rite, and the prohibited worship of the Tablets became invalid because it was imperfectly performed.

Muslims used their Chinese names and spoke Chinese in public, but with other Muslims they would use their Arabic names and speak a Chinese mixed with many Arabic and Persian words. They greeted each other in Arabic '*al-salam alaykum*' and got the reply in Arabic '*alaykum al-salam*'. This situation persists in both Chinas to this day.

In their domestic life Muslims also adopted a double standard of behaviour. Outside their homes, they pasted up red Chinese strips, like all other Chinese, but inside usually no Chinese paintings were in sight. The scrolls that adorned the walls bore Arabic script rather than Chinese characters, specifically verses from the Qur'an or from Islamic traditions. One of them, for example, mentions the caliph and the vizier, not the emperor or the mandarin. The same applies to Muslim *objets d'art*, dating from the Ming period and still treasured by Muslims in China. Their style and design are typically Chinese, but the ornaments and inscriptions are unmistakably Islamic.

In the art of calligraphy, also, a combination of Chinese and Arabic was worked out. Muslim artists first formed the outlines of a Chinese character and then filled it with Muslim proverbs or poems in Arabic. So, in a large Chinese *hu* (tiger) or *shou* (long life), Arabic phrases could be detected on closer examination. Another form of calligraphy was the writing of Arabic words in Chinese transliteration.

Islamisation and Sinicisation are obviously a contradiction in terms, because these processes entail a clash between two very powerful and self-confident cultures. The proposition that Muslims in China have simply become Chinese Muslims is thus, and indeed turns out in historical perspective to be, a superficial observation at worst and a reckless generalisation at best. Chinese Islam, though it underwent a long process of coexistence with Confucianism during which it had to bend before the prevailing Chinese winds, preserved a surprising vitality that never allowed it to break. The vital power of Islam was manifested in the sweeping revival of eighteenth- and nineteenth-century Chinese Islam, which gathered momentum concurrently with the mounting oppression of Islam in China, and erupted in a series of violent rebellions which held the Muslim community in China in a deep messianic spell, and threw the whole country into chaos for a quarter of a century.

It is clear that the widespread appeal that the Muslim rebels had in nineteenth-century China stemmed from the social, economic and political difficulties which plagued China as a whole. But what made the Muslim rebellions crystallise around the novel ideology of the New Sect, despite its seemingly deviationist religious idiosyncracies, were, basically, the concepts that are likely to stir any Muslim's emotions—the Mahdi and the jihad. Since these two concepts are common to both Sunni and sectarian Islam, though with different emphases and interpretations, an outlet presented itself into which all Muslims could channel their frustrations. Hence, although the New Sect took the lead in the uprising, 'rebel' was not necessarily identical with 'New Sectarian'. Perhaps members of the New Sect were more liable than others to participate in the rebellions, but not all rebels were part of the New Sect. Many non-sectarian Muslims who did not rebel probably sympathised with the rebels, but they waited to see the trend of success before taking sides.

The capacity of the New Sect to produce an over-arching organisational umbrella which would tie together the scattered and decentralised Muslim community or parts thereof, and the unmistakable political ambitions of this militant movement, i.e. the establishment of a separate Muslim state in China, were no doubt the traits that appealed to the anxieties and passions of the Muslim populace and to its belief in the imminent coming of a rightful leader who could end misery and evil, and thus inaugurate a new age of plenty and justice. These traits formed an ideology which, according to Geertz's definition, 'bridges the emotional gap between things as they are and as one would have them be, thus realizing the performance of roles that might otherwise be abandoned in despair and apathy'.

From the Chinese viewpoint, it was these very same traits which made Muslim sectarianism dangerous and therefore liable to persecution. Not only did the movement have a 'heterodox' ideology from the Chinese view, but it had forged the organisational tool to carry it out as an extra-imperial, and therefore anti-imperial, corporate activity. Ideology and organisation, efficiently combined, looked so alarming to Chinese authorities that they could not help likening the New Sect to the Chinese White Lotus. Thus, by both Chinese and Muslim standards, the militant movement of the New Sect, headed by Ma Hua-lung, was the thing to watch, although each side saw it its own way. Where the former saw danger, the latter saw hope. What was eminently destructive for one, was imminently promising to the other.

The interesting thing about the New Sect is that, although it raised the banner of Muslim rebellion and made no secret of its Muslim essence and Islamic ideals, it still needed Chinese symbols in order to make itself relevant in the Chinese environment. So, the Muslim leaders of the rebellion used Chinese as well as Arabic, and Ma Hua-lung, the head of the rebelling New Sectarians, resorted to Chinese heterodox symbols in order to make sense in the Chinese as well as the Muslim context. Paradoxically, only if he resembled one of the Chinese sectarian lords (such as the master of a secret society) could he be trusted by his Chinese Muslim followers as their Mahdi (similar to the Maytreya Buddha of the White

Lotus). Only if the symbol was a Chinese one as well as a Muslim one was it likely to be a living symbol, through which Chinese Muslims would share the experience of the Chinese sectarian movements at large.

Muslim disaffection in nineteenth-century China was universal and generated millenarian cravings in all parts of Chinese Islam; but it was in areas where Muslims constituted a major portion of the population that the Chinese-Muslim confrontation was the most acute. Thus, invariably, major Muslim rebellions in China took place in the north-west and the south-west where the sizeable Muslim population was both something of a threat to the Chinese host culture, and numerically strong enough to initiate a rebellion and maintain a revolutionary (if we can use a non-millenarian term) *élan*. It was no coincidence that Lanchou, the 'Mecca of Chinese Islam', which was largely populated by Muslims and situated in a heavily Muslim area, was also the scene of the inception and growth of the New Sect. It was also no coincidence that some of the great luminaries among Chinese Muslims, including Ma Te-hsin, who played a prominent part in the revivalist movement of nineteenth-century Chinese Islam, were from the densely Muslim populated province of Yunnan.

The rebellious wave of Chinese Muslims can be conceived as an impulse to revive Islamisation by a Muslim minority which lived under the stress of forced Sinicisation under the Manchu rule. The north-west in 1764 and 1781, and again in 1862–76, Yunnan in 1820–8, 1846, and again in 1855–73, were the staging areas of the momentous Muslim uprisings which cost millions of lives, and at times seemed on the verge of sweeping much of the Chinese Empire under the sway of Islam.

The rebellious wave, which was promoted in Central Asia in about 1760 by Muslim Khojas who raised the banner of *jihad* against the Chinese, was transmitted through the medium of the New Sect to north-west China and thence to the south-west. It took half a century of New Sectarian ferment in Central Asia and the north-west before the rebellious impulse reached Yunnan. This may be explained in terms of the proximity of the north-west to Central Asia, where rebellion was rife. By contrast, adjacent to the south-west was India, where the revivalist movement of Shah Waliullah was contemporary with the Chinese Muslim revivalist movement in general, which took a less militant stance at the outset and stressed ritual purity and the restoration of old Islamic values.

By the middle of the nineteenth century, when persecution of the Muslims by both the Manchus and the Chinese reached its peak, the junction was made between Chinese Islam in the north-west and the south-west, and the uprising, under the unifying symbols of the Mahdi and jihad, finally took the shape of a full-blown Chinese versus Muslim struggle. Thenceforth, it was no longer a question of merely defending Islam and preserving it, or an internal strife between the new and the old sects, but a definite trend of Muslim separatism, imbued with the militant ideas that had seeped through Kansu to Yunnan. The whole Muslim East was in turmoil (Central Asia, India and China), and the contagious sense of unfolding fateful events must have swept the Muslim community from the Indus to the Yellow River.

It was an age of unique opportunity for Chinese Islam to rise and take its fate into its own hands when the feasibility of secession from Chinese domination looked favourable, due to the breakdown of the Chinese bureaucratic system and the impotence of the imperial Chinese troops. It was an era of widespread rebellion in China, of mushrooming secret society activities, of socio-political fragmentation and power devolution which demanded that particularistic new forces under charismatic leadership should fill the vacuum. So, Chinese Muslim separatism, while it was generated and nurtured by its particularistic inner dynamics, was certainly not incongruent with the outer Chinese context in general.

The swing between Islamisation and Sinicisation was due to the fact that although Chinese and Muslims could be classified into two different networks, they could not help interacting between themselves. After all, there was an interdependence between the two, the Muslims depending on the Chinese market for certain basic commodities, and the Chinese depending upon Muslim traders and artisans for others. But the interaction was structured by a categorical dichotomisation in the minds of both groups, of people who are like oneself and with whom one could have relations in all spheres of activity, and people different from oneself, with whom one could only interact in a limited scope of capacities. This situation is somewhat analogous to the relationship and communication between two different register-groups belonging to the same culture; they speak the same language but they can communicate only on a very limited level (e.g. an intellectual and an artisan, a taxi driver and a professional, etc.).

This peculiar relationship was the sum total and the outcome of the contradictory pressures to which Chinese Muslims were subjected. On the one hand, they were not pariah groups whose boundaries are usually strongly maintained by the excluding host majority—if anything, the Chinese majority would have welcomed them on an individual basis into Chinese culture, and it did co-opt those who wanted to join. On the other hand, under the disability of a stigmatised identity, Muslims sought to qualify themselves as Chinese, thus developing techniques to avoid sanctions from the Chinese majority: apologetic writings for the learned Chinese and material acculturation for the illiterate populace; thus, they were making efforts to show all Chinese their 'Chineseness', at least in time of peace and coexistence. Like the Lapp people of Norway, however, their guest relationships, language behaviour, dilemmas of identity, *esprit de corps*, orientations and social aspirations, all smacked of the cultural specific.

Chinese Muslims learned to differentiate between the general public sphere and their closed Muslim space and to behave self-effacingly outside, albeit determined about their goals inside. It was the Muslims' desire to be nothing but themselves which also occasioned their uprising against the authority when they sensed they were pressured to forgo their identity. Their only recourse, then, would be separation from the state in order to find their own selves again.

Were Muslims who lived in China Muslims in China or Chinese Muslims? They certainly were both, at one time or another, and they have even attempted to go out of China while remaining there, by seceding from the empire. So, it appears that as no large-scale process of Islamisation of Confucianism has been possible in China, so no intensive and far-reaching Sinicisation of Islam has been feasible. The confrontation has been between two very self-confident cultures, both having a long history of swallowing others rather than being swallowed up. Their mutual inability to overwhelm each other, which was underlined by occasional outbursts of confrontation between them, persisted even when they encountered each other on a majority–minority basis. This is due, of course, to the potent sense of belonging to the universal umma, whose basis of power and centre of creativity, being outside China, kept feeding the inner strength of the Muslim Chinese community and its sense of self-confidence.

Paradoxically, only as long as Sinicisation was not pressed by the Chinese rulers, would this process go on unhindered, and more and more Muslims on the margins would fall off to Confucianism. But when Sinicisation was forced or Islam oppressed, the main body of Muslims would rise up, shrug off the outer signs of material acculturation, forget the amenities of good neighbourhood with the Chinese, and raise the banner of a separate identity. This seems to have been the case not only in imperial China, but under the Communist realm as well.

Muslims in Contemporary China

In modern China, these problems are further compounded by new considerations that derive from novel circumstances:

1. Unlike other minority groups, such as the Mongols, the Tibetans and the Chuang, the Muslims are not attached to any particular territory, although they admittedly constitute a majority in areas such as Ninghsia and Sinkiang and a very sizeable minority in Kansu and Yunnan. They can be found everywhere throughout the country, and every large city is likely to have its Hui section.
2. Unlike other minority groups in China whose home base may be included *in toto* within the confines of the People's Republic (e.g. Tibet), the Muslims, whose focus of identity remains with the universal umma of Islam, regard themselves as a Chinese branch of an alien culture, not a minority-guest culture in China. The daily validation of their membership

in the universal umma is at the basis of Muslim ritual, and one of the 'Pillars of Islam' is the tenet of hadj, the pilgrimage to Mecca—the Holy Place of all Muslims.

3. Despite Chinese attempts to differentiate within the Muslim community in China between the Hui of China proper, the Uighurs of Sinkiang and the other Turkic minorities of Central Asia—Uzbek, Kirghiz and Kazakh—a general sentiment of Islamic brotherhood unites, potentially if not practically, all those splinters into one living social and cultural group which, given certain circumstances, may seek political expression as well. However, as long as the *divide et impera* policy of the Chinese state prevails, the ethnic and linguistic differences between the Hui and the other Muslim groups in China are being cultivated in order to preclude the menace of an all-China Muslim front. Thus, when reference is made in state announcements to the population of Sinkiang, the purpose is to serve the policy of emphasising parochial peculiarities and to stem the rise of Muslim unity throughout the land.

4. Islam is not only a culture but also a totalistic way of life which inseparably encompasses politics and religion, and irrevocably strives to bring to bear the Islamic political theory; this carries with it the seeds of Muslim statehood. When a Muslim minority happens to live in a non-Muslim state, it remains in many ways outside that polity and nurtures separatistic ideals which can materialise when the opportunity presents itself.

5. More recently, because of the mounting power and wealth of some Islamic countries, Islam has become a success story. Moreover, the new institution of the Islamic Conferences, which have been convening yearly since 1969, has given a new impetus to popular, if not political, Pan-Islamic sentiments. One may conjecture that in the post-Gang of Four era, as China seems to be less rigid toward the outside world, Chinese Islam may be affected by these Pan-Islamic currents, and consequently by separatistic trends, as has been the case with other Muslim minorities in Asia (the Philippines, Thailand and Burma).

The above survey and analysis of the incongruencies between the guest Muslims and the host Chinese leave not much ground for optimism when one reflects upon the current plight of Muslims in China. Indeed, it appears that averting a Muslim minority uprising in China is possible only as long as a thin, and often precarious, balance can be maintained between a strong-handed policy that does not encroach too bluntly upon the cultural-religious viability of the Muslims, and a liberal and generous policy which remains short of total autonomy. Whether the Chinese newly adopted constitution was truly perceptive of these Islamic realities, and therefore provided for 'giving back to ethnic minorities the right to preserve or reform their own customs and ways', only time will tell. Previous pledges of national minority rights 'to autonomy, to arm themselves and to hold on to their religious beliefs', voiced by Chou En-lai, and Mao's re-confirmation of their right to self-determination, had proved empty rhetoric.

Now, with powerful Teng Hsiao-p'ing at the helm of China, and in light of the wide open-door policy that has been adopted in the post-Gang of Four era, it is very likely that the international intercourse will affect the life of many Chinese, not least of all the minorities. The Muslim community in China will become ever more conscious of its Islamic identity if a freer movement of Muslims manifests itself between China and Muslim lands. Chinese Muslims will, no doubt, become more and more aware of the Muslim success story in the contemporary world, where mosques are sprouting in Washington, London, Geneva and even Seoul, on an unprecedented scale and with untold splendour. They will become conscious of the legendary wealth wielded by some Islamic countries, not least of which are precisely those, like Libya, who have been backing Muslim separatist movements in other Asian lands (Thailand and the Philippines). They will take cognisance of the most powerful of all Islamic states, Saudi Arabia, where the Holy Places of Islam are located and where local sharifs claim descent from the Prophet himself. The holy pilgrimage to Mecca will regain a new impetus with a growing number of Muslim pilgrims making the journey, and some of them may even stay and settle there, if allowed, as had been the case with many of their compatriots who fled from China in the early 1950s.

In recent years, the enhanced stature of Islam has engendered a keener and deeper interest of the Muslim centre in the minorities of the periphery. This renewed interest manifests itself in the recurrent information printed in the Arabic press, and particularly in the resolutions adopted yearly by the Islamic Conferences, which have been meeting regularly since 1969, bringing under one roof delegates of forty-odd Muslim or self-styled Muslim countries, representing over eight hundred million people.

The recognition by the Marcos government of the Philippines of the Islamic Conferences as a partner for negotiating the autonomy of the 'Moros'; and the Filipino 'going to Canossa' (Libya) to discuss the terms of the autonomy, in 1977, only gave legitimacy to the earlier decision by the Conference calling upon the Filipino government to halt its military operations against the Muslims and adopt the necessary measures for the immediate withdrawal of its troops (from Filipino sovereign territory!) and honour its commitment to grant autonomy to Muslims in the southern Philippines. Other resolutions in that same Conference favoured the Muslim community in Cyprus over the Greek and condemned the French for their continued occupation of Mayotte.

In today's world, where there prevails a universal reluctance to antagonise Muslims, converging with China's new liberal policies towards the minorities, circumstances may well allow, and indeed demand, a renewed Muslim awakening in the PRC. We have already observed that too brutal pressures on Muslims or, paradoxically, too lax measures may well bring about the same result: more reticence on the part of the Muslims to adapt to the Communist Chinese rule. A difference exists none the less in the likely end results: while under extreme oppression the Muslims (like other minorities) may rebel and call for secession, they are also liable to be ruthlessly suppressed (e.g. the case of Tibet, Ch'inghai and Sinkiang in 1958–9), and Western public opinion might keep silent, or at least helpless about it, out of consideration for China's defence of her 'territorial integrity'. If, however, demands for secession arise under a liberalised and more open system, the Chinese would have so much stake in maintaining world public opinion on their side (see the case of dissidents in the USSR), that they might well have to respond to Muslim demands for a looser definition of autonomy.

If the cleavages among the Chinese leadership during the Cultural Revolution on matters of minority policy are instructive as a precedent, it is evident that the experienced administrators ('experts') usually favoured concessions to customs and traditions of minorities, while the ideological zealots ('reds') professed an immediate and total integration of these groups. The Gang of Four's 'red' policy towards minorities had already expressly come under fire, well before March 1978, and an 'expert' pledge of the new People's Congress was heard to restore minority rights. If it is true that Teng Hsiao-p'ing, the strong man of the PRC (or his hand-picked successors for that matter) is willing to 'strive for modernization at a greater cost to the core values of the Revolution', then he might conceivably also be prepared to pay the price of a relaxed policy towards Muslims (and minorities in general), as a correlative cost of modernisation and liberalisation. It would be again paradoxical that non-doctrinaire statesmen such as Teng (or his disciples and protégés) would be the men to restore Marxist doctrine on the minorities to its original thrust.

A Cautionary Summing Up

The picture of Chinese Islam depicted above can at best reflect the broad lines of the mainstream of Muslims in China, but is by no means applicable to every Muslim in every Muslim community throughout the empire. Ambiguities, uncertainties, paradoxes and puzzles remain which defy definition, generalisation and analysis. For example, Chinese Muslims were described as trying to avoid contact with the Chinese and to focus their activities, economic and social, within their communities. Yet, many Muslims not only took part in the Chinese system but became prominent in it, especially (though not exclusively) in the military domain. Examples abound: Cheng Ho, the famous maritime explorer of the Ming who preceded

Columbus by over a century, was Muslim; many high-ranking Muslim officials climbed through the examination system to some of the highest posts in Chinese government, as did Ma Hsin-i, Governor General of Fukien and Chekiang in the late Ch'ing.

This ambivalent attitude can be explained in terms of the pragmatic approach of Islam to the necessities of life, because Chinese Muslims did not, indeed could not, isolate themselves from a society on which they depended in many respects. But one might also think that Muslim inroads into the highest positions of power in the government, especially in the military, (which was the paradigm of power) may be attributed to a sublimation of their frustrations. They could thereby show to the Chinese who despised them that they, too, could make it to the top, despite their underprivileged position. Moreover, Muslims in top positions may have been thought able to intervene from within the system on behalf of their co-religionists, and that in itself justified their deed, since in the final analysis they helped protect and preserve Islam rather than turning their backs on it. The Holy Qur'an justifies such a measure: 'Good deeds exonerate evil doings.'

The record shows that in China many Muslim communities and Muslim individuals have drifted away from their heritage and acculturated more fully to the host culture than the mainstream of Chinese Islam, especially in isolated places where maintaining one's distinctiveness could become a matter of daily embarrassment and a constant nuisance rather than a source of pride and superiority. So we hear of Muslims who practised ancestor worship and local spirit worship, of Muslims who adopted Chinese mourning practices, and even of Chinese who respect some tenets of Islam but are unaware of their Islamic origin. There are missionary accounts of Muslims who would gather to listen to Christian preaching and find similarities between their faith and Christianity, a thing unheard of in the lands of Islam.

These phenomena are due to the organisational fragmentation of Chinese Islam and the absence of supra-communal authority that could look after the needs of small and isolated communities and save them from extinction. As Skinner has remarked, 'the greater number of individuals who carry a species or a culture, the greater its chances of survival'. Local compromises that Islam had made during its expansion, and the incorporation of *urf* (local custom) into the Shari'a, had brought about the spread of the faith. But that was achieved under a victorious conquering Islam, whose self-confidence allowed it to compromise.

This compromise, far from plastering over the incompatibilities between these two self-confident cultures, on the contrary exposed the built-in limitations of each of them to come half-way to meet the other. Therefore, Muslim dormant aspirations, which are inherent in the Islamic system of belief, erupted into a full-scale confrontation with the

Confucian state, when coexistence was no longer feasible under the Ch'ing Dynasty.

The fact that the rebellions of the nineteenth century were suppressed did not lead to the submission of the Muslims, nor did the latter ever reconcile thereafter with the idea of a sizeable Muslim population ruled by the Chinese host culture. The Chinese, under the Republic, made tremendous efforts to appease the Muslims by recognising them as one of the 'five peoples of China'. Sun Yat-sen himself became devoted to this aim, because he was aware of the numerical and political weight of the world Muslim community, of which Chinese Muslims considered themselves part and parcel. The problem, however, was not one of compromise, because both the Islamic and the Chinese political traditions are such as to leave no room for accommodation. The Chinese state has always been, and still remains, unitarian and shunning the idea of a multi-state federation, an idea which was accepted, at least in theory, by the Soviet Union. The Muslim ideology requires assumption of the political power, as the will of Allah has to be worked on earth by a political system; therefore, no Muslim would find his identity within a non-Muslim unitarian state. No wonder then that even under Communist rule, outbursts of Muslim particularism erupted when the lax period of the Hundred Flowers gave the Muslims the opportunity to express themselves. More unrest may be in the offing if the present-day liberal policies and opening up of China proceed.

Further Reading

Andrew, G.F. *The Crescent in Northwest China* (London, 1921)

Cordier, G. *Les Musulmans du Yunnan* (Hanoi, 1927)

D'Ollone *Mission d'Ollone: Recherches sur les Musulmans Chinois* (Paris, 1911)

Israeli, R. 'Established Islam and Marginal Islam in China: From Eclecticism to Syncretism', *Journal of the Economic and Social History of the Orient*, XXI (1978), pp. 99–109

—— 'Islamization and Sinicization in Chinese Islam' in N. Levtzion (ed.) *Conversion to Islam* (Holmes and Meier, New York, 1979), pp. 159–76

—— *Muslims in China: A Study of Cultural Confrontation* (Curzon and Humanities Press, London and Atlantic Heights, 1980), p. 260

—— 'Muslim Minorities Under Non-Islamic Rule', *Current History* (April 1980), pp. 159–64, 184–5

—— 'Muslims in the People's Republic of China', *Asian Survey*, vol. XXI, no. 8 (Aug. 1981), pp. 901–19

Yang, C.K. *Religion in Chinese Society* (University of California, Berkeley, 1967)

26 Islam in Indonesia

E.U. Kratz

Introduction

Indonesia, independent since 1945, is the fifth largest nation in the world. About 90 per cent of its population consider themselves Muslims, and the Republic of Indonesia, though not an Islamic state in the constitutional sense, has the world's largest number of Muslim citizens.

Roughly 62 per cent of Indonesia's total population which, in 1985, was estimated at over 160 million, reside on the island of Java which is one of the most densely populated parts of the world. A high percentage of the population lives in rural areas based on subsistence economy. The difference between city and country life, between the urban elite and the rural masses is distinct.

There is still some confusion in the literature about the ethnographic description of the peoples of Indonesia whom one may find referred to as the 'Malays', or, even less correct, as Proto- and Deutero-Malays. The use of the word *Malay* as a generic term is misleading since, strictly speaking, it only applies to one of the several hundred ethnic groups inhabiting the islands. These groups tend to differ widely with regard to their traditional social structure and political organisation. Only a few founded states in the past. Examples are the Javanese and Balinese, the Malays of Sumatra and the Malay Peninsula and the coastal parts of other major islands, the Buginese and Macassarese of southern Sulawesi (Celebes), the Acehnese and the Batak of northern Sumatra, some groups in the Moluccas, and the Minangkabau of western Sumatra. Whereas some of these states, foremost among them the Javanese empire of Majapahit (fourteenth century) had a firm territorial base, others such as the Malay empires of Srivijaya (tenth century) and of Melaka (Malacca, fifteenth century) gained their wealth and power almost exclusively through trade and commerce.

It was only with the arrival of nationalism at the beginning of this century that the numerous ethnic groups and nations moved towards the formation of one Indonesian nation.

Language and Script

The national language is Indonesian, a close relative of Malaysian, the national language of Malaysia. Indonesian is now widely used in all social situations and, generally speaking, has pushed the other languages of Indonesia (about 250 different languages and an equal number of dialects which are spoken as first languages) into the role of merely regional, provincial languages. Ethnic and linguistic borders generally coincide.

Both Indonesian and Malaysian are dialects of Malay which used to be the lingua franca of the archipelago and which was of considerable importance in the spreading of Islam throughout the area. Lexically, Malay began to grow in different directions only as a result of colonial influences when, following the Treaty of London (1824), the Malay Peninsula and the archipelago became divided into, respectively, a British and a Dutch region of dominance. Today, the governments of both Indonesia and Malaysia are concerned to bring the two languages closer together again.

Linguistically, Malay which is the mother tongue of only about 5 per cent of the population, belongs to the western branch of the Austronesian language family. This group of languages (once called Malayo-Polynesian) stretches across the Indian Ocean and the Pacific from Madagascar to the Easter Islands and includes the languages of the Philippines as well as some of the languages of Formosa and mainland South-east Asia, for example, that of the Cham, an isolated group of Muslims living in present-day Cambodia and Vietnam. The vast majority of languages and dialects spoken in Indonesia also belong to the same western or Indonesian branch of the Austronesian language family.

In the past, not many of these languages developed their own systems of writing. Generally only those ethnic groups which formed states in the course of their history acquired scripts and their own written, literary traditions. However, not all Indonesian ethnic groups with a script have left a written heritage as rich as that of the Javanese, Balinese, Malays, Buginese and Macassarese. Non-Islamic texts of a religious nature appear prominently among some, such as the Balinese and the Batak. A major part of the indigenous texts was written on perishable materials such as palm-leaf or locally produced paper, hence surviving copies are of a fairly recent date and not older than a few centuries. Nevertheless, some of the texts can be traced to a much earlier time, reaching as far back as the thirteenth and fourteenth centuries. Epigraphy tends to go back further and we have been left with inscriptions on stone dating back to the fourth century CE.

Indian scripts and other locally developed variants of those scripts were widely in use prior to the arrival of Islam and the introduction of *Jawi*, as the modified Arabic script which is close to its Persian variant is generally called. Nowadays, only the Islamic Javanese and their close cousins the Hinduistic Balinese still employ on occasion their own Indic scripts when using their regional languages, Javanese and Balinese. Of the two groups, at least the Javanese were familiar with the Arabic script, which they called *pegon* and which was used almost exclusively in the context of Islamic learning. Macassarese and Buginese, too, preserved their own Indic-derived script after the arrival of Islam. However, unlike the Javanese and Balinese, that script has not been much used in recent times.

Today the Latin script is officially and commonly in use although, until only a few decades ago and prior to the introduction of a (secular) public education, the writing of *Jawi* was a more common skill. This skill did not, however, receive the recognition of the Dutch colonial authorities and only those able to read and write the Latin script were officially considered to be literate.

Colonial Background

Mention has been made of the year 1945 when Indonesia declared its independence. However, Indonesia had to combat the Dutch for its sovereignty, and it was not until 1949 that the Netherlands gave up their claim to Indonesia, which they had maintained after their sudden and unexpected defeat by the Japanese and their swift withdrawal from the colony in 1942.

The centuries between the first arrival of the Dutch in 1596 and their defeat in 1942 have been considered by both colonialists and nationalists to be of special importance. Nationalists are prone to refer to that period as one of continuous colonial rule, whereas colonialists, particularly during the latter days of their rule and after they had lost control altogether, liked to insist on the existence of a special spiritual bond as a result of that centuries-long contact.

A closer look at the dates reveals the following picture. From the first Dutch voyage in 1596 until 1799 contact between the peoples of the archipelago and the Netherlands was maintained through the VOC, the United Dutch East India Company, a privately funded trading organisation. The company, whose main purpose was commercial gain, had a small number of territorial bases of limited size and, through a combination of political circumstances, treaties and alliances with local rulers and the selective use of military force, succeeded in edging out European and Asian competitors such as the Portuguese, British, French and Chinese. Eventually it monopolised the overseas trade of the archipelago and virtually controlled the interinsular trade. The VOC was considerably helped by interethnic conflicts which led it to become involved in the internal power struggle among Indonesian nations. This involvement became strongest on the island of Java, where at times the VOC could be found fighting in alliance with some of the staunchest Islamic states on the north coast. The VOC's political and military control over Java was almost total by the end of the eighteenth century. After the financial collapse of the VOC in 1799, which was caused by mismanagement and corruption, its dissolution and the assumption of power by the Dutch government on 1 January 1800, Dutch colonial rule began in earnest, notwithstanding a brief British interregnum in Java and other islands which lasted only from 1810 to 1817 and which had its cause in the Napoleonic wars.

With the exception of Java, large-scale territorial occupation did not take place before the nineteenth century. A survey published in 1938 at the height of colonial rule shows that until 1619 only Batavia with its surrounding countryside and the islands of Ambon in the Moluccas were under direct Dutch control. By 1684 a stretch of West Java, some parts of South Sulawesi, and Menado in North Sulawesi had been added. Most of Java followed in the eighteenth century and by 1830 the whole of Java was under Dutch rule. Between 1824 and 1898 South and West Sumatra, Deli in North-east Sumatra, West and South-east Kalimantan (Borneo), the northern part of Bali, Lombok and further parts of North Sulawesi and of the islands of Seram in the Moluccas were joined to the Dutch East Indies, partly as a result of changes in the economic policies of the colonial authorities which by then allowed the influx of private European capital into the archipelago and the increased settlement of land-hungry European planters. The rest of the archipelago, i.e. East and North Sumatra (which includes Aceh), most of Kalimantan and Sulawesi, Nusa Tenggara, the Moluccas and the whole of West Irian were put under direct Dutch control only between 1898 and the 1930s. The Portuguese colony of East Timor, never an Islamic area, was not incorporated into the Republic of Indonesia until 1977.

In 1942 the Japanese overran South-east Asia and with it the Dutch East Indies. They ruled the territory until 1945. This period, though brief in time, was of tremendous significance for the future development of Indonesia. The strict policy of the Japanese of severing all links with European civilisation boosted the self-confidence of Indonesians in a manner the Japanese had not anticipated, and despite the harshness of Japanese rule, it helped to accelerate the process of Indonesian self-identification.

In courting nationalist politicians the Japanese also paid great attention to Islam as a political force, thus planting the seeds of later frustration, when the newly independent republic seemed to revert to a religious policy more akin to that of the former Dutch rulers.

Unity in Diversity

The motto of the Republic of Indonesia is *Bhinneka Tunggal Ika*, i.e. 'Unity in Diversity'. This slogan goes back to the famous fourteenth-century Javanese poet Mpu Tantular of Majapahit. According to nationalist ideology Majapahit extended in size and authority as far as the now independent state of Indonesia. On the basis of our historical knowledge we can assume, however, that if Majapahit ever reached the size postulated, its various parts were rarely in a relationship of direct dependency to the rulers of Majapahit, whereas today all islands and peoples of the archipelago are an integrated part of a centralised administration which is more penetrating than that of any government ever preceding it.

A desire for political unity, regional rebellions of the recent past notwithstanding, has been widely shared ever since the rise of nationalism at the beginning of this century. Ironically Islam, the professed faith of the absolute majority of the country's population, which during the days of colonial rule and pre-Independence nationalism helped to link the peoples of Indonesia, has seemed more recently to be losing some of this unifying strength on account of (non-ethnic) theological rifts among Muslims themselves. The desire for political unity is probably more clearly demonstrated in the way in which the many ethnic groups have accepted Malay as their national language and made it into Indonesian than in a common religious expression.

Nevertheless, neither this political will nor the distinct ethnic and linguistic background which the peoples of the archipelago have in common should let us overlook the marked social, cultural and material differences traditionally existing between the various islands and groups. Thus, historically a certain dichotomy can be observed between the western and eastern parts of Indonesia, and between the coastal regions and the interior of most islands: the peoples living on the islands in the west were in the course of their history exposed to Hinduism, Buddhism and Islam to a much larger degree than most of those living further to the east. In fact, such contact seems to have decreased the further east one goes, with the exception of parts of the Moluccas such as the original Spice Islands, Ternate and Tidore, which saw the emergence of strongly Islamic kingdoms not much later than other more westerly situated islands. Those places apart, in the west one finds more often states with a highly institutionalised and hierarchical social structure; in the east tribal systems prevail. Whereas in the west most people have settled permanently, in the east more groups are still semi-nomadic.

This is not to say that the social structure and economic patterns described as common for eastern Indonesia cannot be found in the west as well. There they emerge in areas of retreat in the interior, away from the coastal regions which are inhabited by 'newcomers' such as the Malays. Given the nature of the environment it is also hardly surprising that some groups of semi-nomadic Malays have made the sea their permanent home.

The Influence of World Religions

Already prior to the arrival of the Europeans the archipelago had been of importance to the great nations to its east and west for many centuries as a major producer of spices, precious woods, resin and gold; goods that were traded as far as Rome in the west and China in the east. The trade to the west is presumed to have passed via India and it is interesting to note that Indian, far more than Chinese culture, exerted an obvious influence upon the islands. The international importance of the Malay empire of Srivijaya as a centre of Buddhist learning is recorded in Chinese sources of the seventh century; and the ninth-century Buddhist monument of Borobudur and its eleventh-century Hindu counterpart, the temple complex of Prambanan, both located in central Java, still bear witness to the heights which Indian religions and cultures had reached in Java and Sumatra prior to the arrival of Islam.

There is no agreement as to how Indian religions and culture came to the region. Merchants, sailors, adventurers and holy men from India and Indonesia itself are supposed to have jointly and individually helped to disseminate Indian culture in a peaceful manner. The fourteenth century Siva-Buddha cult of Java suggests that at times Buddhism and Hinduism, of which the latter proved to be more resilient as can be witnessed in present-day Bali, presented themselves jointly. However, Indian religions and values were not accepted totally or uncritically. The caste system, for example, never assumed the rigidity it had developed in India and the people of Java and Bali, to whom the *Ramayana* and *Mahabharata* are still living traditions, succeeded in combining their own mystical heritage with the new ideas. Only at court do Indic ideas and concepts seem to have been accepted to a greater degree, and, under the guidance of Indian and Indonesian priests, the royal elite made elements of Indian culture such as script, cosmology, time-reckoning, law, court rituals, and symbols of power and authority like the cult of the *devaraja* or god-king, their own. Still, neither then nor later again when Islam arrived, was there a wholesale destruction of earlier spiritual and social traditions. Inherited values and concepts were adapted and modified to become compatible with the main principles of the newly arrived religions which in turn, too, had to adapt to their new surroundings.

It has already been mentioned that groups in the islands' interior and in eastern Indonesia tended to be least affected by cultural change and it is in the interior that people seem to have resisted most the advances of Hinduism, Buddhism and Islam. Nevertheless, it is there that in more recent times Christianity first gained a foothold. Yet, large-scale missionary efforts did not begin until the second half of the nineteenth century and were mainly confined to non-Islamic areas.

The attitude of the Dutch Reformed colonial authorities to Christian missionary activity seems to have been one of ambivalence and was much determined by the political climate at home. In the days of the VOC attempts were made to stamp out Islam locally and prospective pilgrims were banned from using the company's ships for the voyage. From the nineteenth century onwards a more circumspect policy can be observed resulting from a government instruction of 1803 which decreed religious neutrality and which culminated in the policies adopted before the turn of the twentieth century and in the wake of the Aceh War on the advice of C. Snouck Hurgronje. It would not be wrong, however, to say that the colonial authorities generally regarded any form of Islamic activity with suspicion. As for Christian missionary activities, Bali was 'off limits', while Irian Jaya, which was not formally integrated into the territory of the Dutch East Indies until the mid-nineteenth century, and which was effectively put under Dutch administration only in the 1920s and 1930s, was divided into Protestant (northern) and Catholic (southern) halves. Still it is revealing to see that in Indonesian the term *Kristen* (from the Dutch for Christian) refers to Protestants only whereas their Catholic fellow Christians have to be content to be known merely as *Katolik*.

Affiliation to a particular religious community follows ethnic lines broadly (hence the high percentage of Muslims if we remember that the Javanese, who in their overwhelming majority are Muslims, account for about 62 per cent of the population) although there are always exceptions. Most Batak groups tend to be Protestant, as do the Toraja in Central Sulawesi and the Menadonese on the northern tip of that island who, together with the Ambonese, were in contact with the Dutch for longest. In contrast, the peoples of Jakarta and its surroundings, who for centuries had been closest to the centre of colonial power, always remained Muslims. Peoples in Nusa Tenggara, the south-eastern part of Indonesia where the Portuguese first arrived and stayed longest, tend to be Catholic. In Irian Jaya the majority of people accounted for are Christians.

After 1965 Christianity is said to have made some inroads in Java, whereas Islam on the other hand is reported to have increased its numbers in some traditionally non-Islamic areas. In all perhaps 6 to 7 per cent of the population follow the Christian faith, a few are Hindus (Bali) and Buddhists, and only a small percentage of Indonesians adhere to (tribal) creeds, little influenced by the larger world of the archipelago.

The Historical Process of Islamisation

There are few historical facts available about the early history of Islam in the archipelago. Epigraphical and other material evidence is rare and late and the very early history of Indonesian Islam remains obscure as far as Western scholarship is concerned. Yet, it is particularly with this early period that Indonesian Muslims, scholars and theologians have concerned themselves intensely and therefore it seems appropriate to quote their conclusions, last formulated at a seminar held in 1963 and reaffirmed in 1978 in Aceh. The 1963 seminar in Medan (North Sumatra) stated with regard to the early history of Islam in Indonesia:

1. That following the sources known to us, Islam entered Indonesia for the first time in the first century Hijra (seventh to eighth century Christian Era) and came directly from Arabia.
2. That the area first reached by Islam was the Sumatran coast; and that after the establishment of an Islamic community, the first Islamic Raja was to be found in Aceh.
3. That in the further process of Islamisation Indonesians played an active part.
4. That those early *muballigh*, apart from spreading Islam were also active as traders.
5. That Islam spread in Indonesia in a peaceful manner.
6. That the arrival of Islam in Indonesia brought high learning and culture to the shaping of the Indonesian national identity.

(A final point demanded the setting up of a research body in order to study further the history of Islam in Indonesia.)

Apart from the first point, academic research and opinion appear to agree broadly with the spirit of these resolutions. There is little that can be said in comment on the first resolution from a historical point of view as we lack non-circumstantial evidence in its support. While the presence of Muslims prior to the dates suggested by archaeological and epigraphical evidence is undisputed, there exists uncertainty about the direction, nature and extent of this initial contact with Islam. In opposition to this reservation on the part of Western scholars, however, we have to record the view of a distinguished Indonesian theologian, Kiai Haji Saifuddin Zuhri, who, as a Minister of Religious Affairs, took part in the 1963 discussions and who wrote recently that the fact which distinguished Western Orientalists from Indonesian believers was that those Western Orientalists did not share the Indonesians' faith and, hence, might approach the question of the arrival of Islam in a biased manner.

To date, the available recorded evidence presents itself as follows:

Earliest archaeological proof of the presence of Muslims is provided by a tombstone imported from southern India and dated 1082 or 1102 CE. It was found in Leran near Gresik in Central Java. The stone commemorates Fatima bint Maimun who appears to have been a foreigner but of whom nothing else is known. The fact that there should be the tombstone of a foreigner is not surprising given the great commercial attraction of the archipelago by itself as well as its role as a natural staging-post between the Middle East and India on the one side, and China on the other. There had been Islamic communities in southern China since the ninth century and settlements in Champa date from the eleventh century onwards. Tenth-century envoys from Srivijaya to the Sung court of China seem to have been recruited from among the non-Indonesian, foreign Muslim merchants.

The first known and confirmable eyewitness account of parts of the island of Sumatra is given by Marco Polo who visited North Sumatra in 1292. Of the eight kingdoms of Sumatra, to which he refers as Lesser Java, only one, Ferlec (Perlak), which appears to have been situated in present-day Aceh, was Islamic. Marco Polo, who provides us with the first description of any Islamic state in the Malay world, writes that 'the people of Ferlec used all to be idolators, but owing to contact with Saracen merchants, who continually resort here in their ships the people in the city have all become Muslims'. Those in the mountains, according to Marco Polo, do continue to 'live like beasts'. In addition to Marco Polo's account we have the evidence of the tombstone of the founder of the (Acehnese) kingdom of Samudra-Pasai, Malik as-Saleh, which is dated 1297 CE.

The first known Malay inscription using *Jawi*, the slightly modified Malay version of the Arabic script in use throughout the archipelago, unfortunately cannot be dated precisely as part of its date is no longer there. The inscription, which is of an Islamic and legal nature, was written in either 1303 CE or 1387 CE and hails from Trengganu, a place on the Malay Peninsula. Interesting is the use of Sanskrit words where one might expect Islamic terms to be chosen, as in the reference to Allah, here called *dewata mulia rava* (noble, exalted god(s)).

In 1345/6, according to Ibn Battuta, Malik az-Zahir ruled over the North Sumatran state Sumutra. An Islamic cemetery in Troloyo in East Java covers a period between 1371 and 1475 CE. To be noted here is the presence of Chinese Muslims in the region.

Early in the fifteenth century the rulers of Melaka (Malacca) adopted Islam and it is said that as a result of the conversion of Malacca many other places within its sphere of influence on the Malay Peninsula and on the eastern coasts of Sumatra also adopted the new religion. Unfortunately we know nothing about the connections between Trengganu, which had received Islam prior to Malacca, and Malacca itself at that crucial time at the beginning of the fifteenth century, nor do we know more about the even earlier relationship between Samudra-Pasai and the Kedah region of the Malay Peninsula. Thus it may well be that the role of Malacca as an instigator of Islam in its nearest neighbourhood will have to be reconsidered.

In 1518 the first Islamic state in Java, Demak, emerged on the island's northern coast. Further states were to develop soon among the port-cities of Java which seem to have been more enthusiastic in their acceptance of Islam than the people in the interior of Java.

In the course of the sixteenth century many of the coastal regions of Kalimantan (Borneo) which were in close contact with the port-cities of Java adopted the religion too. Early in the seventeenth century South Sulawesi (Celebes) was converted but not before its major rulers had had a very close look at what Christianity might have to offer in reconciliation with their traditional beliefs. Aceh, which during that century had assumed a leading role among the Malay states after the fall of Malacca to the Portuguese in 1511, developed into a centre of Islamic culture and learning. Towards the second half of the eighteenth century all of East Java turned to Islam.

The process of Islamisation of the archipelago is widely considered to have come to its conclusion by the beginning of this century.

Given what seems an accelerated process of Islamisation from the sixteenth century onwards, it has been argued that, following the fall of Malacca in 1511, Christianity and Islam were in competition for the favour of the peoples of the archipelago and that, in the struggle against the Europeans, Islamic rulers forced their faith on their dependent territories. Also, it is argued, the VOC neglectfully and out of mercantile interests threw away a real opportunity and failed in its statutory duty 'to foster the progress or propagation of the true Christian religion' and thus left the archipelago to Islam. This may well be so as far as the VOC is concerned; however, as this brief chronological survey aims to show, the other arguments need specific proof in every single case. It is conceivable that some rulers weighed up both Islam and Christianity as shown so well by Pelras (1985) in the case of seventeenth-century South Sulawesi but, when the Europeans first sailed into Malay waters, Islam had already been present in parts of the region for several centuries. In places Islamic knowledge and learning had reached such heights that the Portuguese, during the very brief period of influence they enjoyed in the sixteenth century, would have found it difficult to offer a serious spiritual alternative to Islam with their own brand of Christianity. The Dutch, who only emerged early in the seventeenth century, and then only as one group of foreign traders among others, were not at this point very interested in the question of converting the heathen.

It is correct that forced conversions to Islam did occur, but this is no reflection on the peaceful penetration of Islam from outside. Where there was coercion, it would seem that at times the concept of jihad offered a welcome means of carrying on traditional interethnic rivalries and settling commercial conflicts.

Theories of the Islamisation of the Archipelago

A number of equally attractive, yet unsatisfactory and incomplete theories and hypotheses have been put forward to explain the conversion of the archipelago in a logical and coherent fashion (Drewes, 1968). The formulation of a satisfactory general theory has not been helped by the diverse nature of the societies and cultures met in the archipelago nor by the chronologically and geographically uneven evidence which at close range does not fit into any one general pattern.

Al-Attas, for example, has formulated a general theory of the Islamisation of the Malay-Indonesian archipelago (al-Attas, 1976). In it he recognises three stages, each characterised by its own particular features and broadly supported by historical evidence. The first stage according to al-Attas is characterised by a marked stress on *fiqh* (jurisprudence). Legal scholars play an important role, particularly at court. This phase is set between the thirteenth and fifteenth centuries. In the second phase (fifteenth to eighteenth centuries) mysticism (*tasawwuf*) and Sufism play the key role in taking Islam to the people. The third phase (nineteenth century onwards) saw the integration and consumation of both. Phase One, still following al-Attas, saw the conversion of the body; Phase Two that of the soul; and Phase Three the consolidation of both.

It is obvious that the theory of al-Attas mainly reflects events as far as they are documented locally for separate parts of North Sumatra and the Malay Peninsula. Java seems to play a smaller role in his considerations. The theory assumes an initial Islamisation from above, from the court and ruler, and leaves the conversion of larger numbers of the common people to the second phase. This does not seem to have been the case everywhere, however, and the absolute chronological framework proposed by al-Attas does not fit in with developments elsewhere in the archipelago. The stoutly Islamic region of South Sulawesi was not converted until the seventeenth century, for example. Finally, if one were to disregard the absolute chronology proposed and were to look at the principle behind al-Attas' theory, while one would agree that Islamic law plays a vital role in the consolidation of any Islamic community, and that adherence to the law is part of the conversion of the 'body', yet it may not always have been the first step in the process of conversion, unless the meaning of law is reduced to that of obedience to some basic ritual obligations. In many cases this first phase may well have come second thus making the theory less applicable in a general way.

Johns has stressed recently that speculation on the origins of Indonesian Islam, on its precise where and when, sidesteps the far more important issue of how Islam established itself in the archipelago within the religious framework of Islamic learning and teaching; not following any grand design but developing slowly and at times rather laboriously, establishing itself in one community and another, its own fate tied in with the economic rise and decline of its environs. According to Johns there is no single scheme of Islamisation, and what holds true for one place at one moment quite often is inapplicable at another, since the particular ethnic, social, political, historical and economic aspects of a town, state, region and island have differed considerably in time and place. Moreover, many theories disregard the actual process of transmission of Islamic learning from master to pupil and fail to see the important spiritual link between the heartlands of Islam and the archipelago (Johns, 1980:181), overlooking the religious character of Islam in favour of theologically less relevant issues.

The problem of dealing with Islam in the region has been aggravated further by a modern inclination to look at the territory of the Republic of Indonesia as a self-contained unit and to see the development of Islam in the past within the boundaries of the modern state. However, political unity, it has been pointed out, is a development of the recent past and it is probably more helpful to look at the archipelago (together with the Malay Peninsula) as a larger unit irrespective of modern political boundaries. Hence the term 'Indonesian' is used here in a broad cultural and anthropological sense rather than in a political one without, however, forgetting that behind the single term Indonesian a wide range of diverse societies is hidden.

At close range conditions do not only differ from island to island but also from one (ethnic) region to another. The 'religion of Java' as described by Geertz, to take one example, does not extend to West Java. Java as an ethnic and cultural entity only covers the centre and the east of the island in geographical terms. West Java is inhabited by the Sundanese who in their cultural expressions and in their language differ markedly from their Javanese cousins. And even in present-day Java, the island most exposed to outside influence among the islands of the archipelago, we still find small communities in the mountainous interior which have been able to isolate themselves from the rest of the island for centuries. Until today the Badui of West Java and the Tenggerese of eastern Java seem to have avoided the major impact of Islam and Christianity alike.

Aceh, the inhabitants of which feature so prominently in most accounts for their uncompromising religious stand, and which frequently functions as a paradigm for Islamic Indonesia, only covers the northern tip of Sumatra.

The Minangkabau on Sumatra's west coast, whose commitment to Islam is equally beyond doubt, have struggled more than any other ethnic group over the relationship between *adat* and *syaria*, between traditional law and custom as reflected there most conspicuously in a matrilineal kinship system on the one hand and Islamic law on the other.

A study of the process and nature of Islamisation is made even more difficult by the fact that serious gaps in our empirical knowledge of almost all regions have to be admitted. Only for the twentieth century do we come across a larger body of well-documented studies (Boland and Farjon, 1983). However, one criticism (Boland, 1982:1–6; Johns, 1980) which has been levelled against these more recent studies is their narrow disciplinary viewpoint and concentration on particular aspects of social life which are only a result of developments within Islam at the expense of a study of the actual dynamics in Indonesia itself.

The Spiritual Process of Islamisation

As has been said, it seems generally agreed that Islam came in a peaceful manner and that it was carried into the archipelago by traders in a slow process which continued over many centuries. Conversion myths indicate that everywhere Islam met with established systems of government. However, the suggestion implied in some conversion myths that Islamisation was initiated from the top should not be generalised.

Islam spread along the main sea and trade routes and blossomed first, it appears, within the less Indianised communities of the archipelago. North Sumatra and especially Aceh Darussalam, the porch of Mecca (*serambi Mekah*), as it was known over centuries to all those Muslims who set out for the hadj via Acehnese ports, played an important role.

There is scarcely any hard evidence of a direct and sustained contact with the Islamic heartlands in that early period. Evidence tends to point more to a closer contact with India. Here Gujarat features prominently. Widely used terms such as *lebai* (mosque official) which comes from the Tamil for trader (*labbai*) also indicate southern India as a connecting point in the transmission of Islam. Other terms often referred to when stressing the Indian link are inconclusive evidence as their use may have grown out of the Indonesians' already established familiarity with Indic concepts. So, Sanskrit *puasa* has taken preference over the Islamic term for the fast, *saum*. *Santri*, the term now used to describe the devout Muslim, is equally rooted in Sanskrit and in pre-Islamic traditions of learning and isolation from this world.

Only in the eighteenth and nineteenth centuries do we find larger groups of immigrants from the Hadramaut who, although intermarrying locally, lived in a closely knit community. The influence of these immigrants on the activity, behaviour, customs and everyday life of Indonesian Muslims, barring some exceptions, appears to have been neither strong nor large scale.

It would seem that wandering mystics and Sufi orders were of particular importance in the spread of Islam to the geographical periphery of the Islamic world. And, looking at the process of Islamisation with this perspective, the question of the precise origins of Indonesian Islam becomes irrelevant since travelling mystics might have come from all directions of the compass. This too would explain why Islam first took a hold along the trading routes and sea passages and why urban settlements were so important in the spread of Islam, since it was in urban societies that one would find the many traders and craftsmen who, as members of their respective guilds, followed the one or the other mystical tradition.

Johns, who has been most persistent in his study of South-east Asian Islam as a religion, attributes the initial success of Islam to the fact that Sufis more than others were able to accommodate traditional, pre-Islamic mysticism, which is still strong in Java, in their own doctrines and teaching. He writes:

> It is possible to characterize the Sufis as they presented themselves to the Indonesians as follows: they were peripatetic preachers ranging over the whole known world, voluntarily espousing poverty; they were frequently associated with trade or craft guilds, according to the order (tarikah) to which they belonged; they taught a complex syncretic theosophy largely familiar to the Indonesians, but which was subordinate to, although an enlargement on the fundamental dogmas of Islam; they were proficient in magic and possessed powers of healing; and not least, consciously or unconsciously, they were prepared to preserve continuity with the past, and to use the terms and elements of pre-Islamic culture in an Islamic context (Johns, 1961:15).

The citizens of those newly developing and obviously thriving urban Islamic communities considered themselves not so much as members of any local state but as members of a community stretching from the Middle East to China with the Arabian Peninsula as its spiritual centre and with Arabic as the main medium of international communication. Indonesian scholars who had spent years of their life studying in Arabia stayed in constant contact with their teachers and there seems to have been a regular and frequent exchange between theologians on both sides of the Indian Ocean. Theological doctrines and religious orders seem to have risen and fallen in the archipelago echoing developments in Arabia. Doctrinal controversies in the Middle East were fought in the archipelago with equal zest. The heterodox mysticism of Hamzah Fansuri and that of his follower Syamsuddin al-Sumatrani or Syamsuddin of Pasai which followed the *Wujudiya* concept of Ibn al-Arabi was fiercely contested later in the seventeenth century by Nuruddin ar-Raniri who upheld a more orthodox teaching of the *Wujudiya*.

Again there exists only a fragmentary record of the intellectual network and the dominant *silsilah* or chains of transmission existing over the centuries between the archipelago and Arabia. Yet from what we know so far, we gain the impression of a regular and intensive interchange. The *Jawah*, as the pilgrims, students and teachers from the archipelago were referred to in Arabia, constituted a considerable body of semi-permanent settlers in Mecca and other places of Islamic learning, as was described so clearly by Snouck Hurgronje for the rather late period of nineteenth-century Mecca. And, as can be gleaned from the correspondence sent to the reformist journal *Al-Manar* in Cairo from various parts of the archipelago, which has been studied recently by J. Bluhm, the religious queries of the Muslims of the archipelago were given serious theological consideration by authoritative scholars, right down to the twentieth century.

Traditional Islamic Literature

Although the relationship between Middle Eastern masters and Indonesian pupils can rarely be traced with exactness, we are fortunate to have a fairly large corpus of texts which is able to show some of the issues of concern to Indonesian Muslims. Here too, however, the distribution of documentary evidence is uneven. Moreover, research on the many theological manuscripts preserved in the archipelago and in European libraries has never been intensive. Some of the texts have been studied by scholars, but our knowledge of religious literature as a whole is still incomplete. Most literary texts which have survived the passage of time do not go back further than the sixteenth century and in fact most manuscripts in our possession are copies dating from the nineteenth century when European interest in indigenous writings began to increase and scores of manuscripts were acquired to be preserved mainly in what was then Batavia and in European public collections. This is not to say that there are no local and private collections but in general we know even less about the contents of those private collections than we do about the actual holdings of the National Library in Jakarta and of the European libraries. A large private library of religious manuscripts kept at a *madrasah* at Tanah Abee in Aceh is one such example.

The literatures of the archipelago most studied until now are probably those of the Malays and Javanese. It is regrettable that there has been little research pertaining to Islamic literature in other Indonesian languages; however, we know that many of the Islamic texts in regional languages including Javanese appear to derive from Malay sources. The comparatively small volume of Islamic texts in regional languages also indicates that most Muslims were able to understand and read Malay, the lingua franca of the archipelago, and it illustrates clearly the importance of Malay in the spread of Islam among the peoples at large. Literature in Javanese of course is of particular relevance since the Javanese form the largest ethnic group in the archipelago. (It goes without saying that the true Islamic scholar would frown upon the use of Malay and Javanese for reading and writing, a disdain which has been preserved into this century, and which is also reflected in the attitude of many theologians towards modern fiction.)

Whereas in Java there is obvious proof of a pre-Islamic literary tradition, the evidence with regard to Malay literature is less conclusive. This has given rise to the claim that traditional Malay literature as we know it today is probably not older than Islam itself and that in fact Malay literature is an Islamic literature which developed almost exclusively within the framework of an Islamic concept of the arts as it is manifested in Persian and Arabic literature. The apparent lack of any manifestly pre-Islamic literary texts is taken as clear evidence to support this contention. This is not the place to argue the point; it should be said, however, that the lack of earlier materials does not necessarily imply their previous non-existence. Just as in Java the development of the figurative arts appears to have been brought to an end with the consolidation of Islam, one could imagine that earlier literary traditions had similarly disappeared in the Malay world. Even the works of the heterodox mystical writer Hamzah Fansuri have not come to us in their totality as some seem to have been destroyed already in the seventeenth century by the opponents of his theology. Thus, if today traditional Malay literature, which is written exclusively in *Jawi*, is seen as an Islamic literature, it does not follow that this Islamic literature has not superseded an earlier literature and that in this present literature there are no elements of an earlier literature which only for lack of comparative material is difficult for us to distinguish from its more recent manifestations.

A large part of the Islamic literature in Malay and Javanese is anonymous. It is frequently undated and the age of a manuscript is no indication of the age of a text. The exact place of origin of a text and manuscript too is often difficult to establish. A major part of this literature is theological and didactic in nature and pertains to the study of the traditional disciplines of Islamic learning. Another part is devoted to the study of Arabic as a language. *Adab* literature, i.e. non-religious prose fiction and poetry, is rare prior to the twentieth century.

Roolvink distinguishes the following types of Islamic literature (Roolvink, 1971):

1. Qur'anic tales, or stories about prophets and other persons whose names are mentioned in the Qur'an. These extremely popular tales are of an edifying nature and serve to complement and explain certain stories found in the Qur'an. Of the Qur'anic stories the *Hikayat anbia* was and still is among the most popular. The stories generally agree with Arabic traditions.
2. Tales about the Prophet Muhammad himself. The stories are centred around the life of the Prophet and concentrate on the miracles he performed. Most of these stories seem to have become known in the archipelago through Persian versions.
3. Tales about contemporaries of the Prophet, both his companions and his adversaries. Most famous of the stories in this category is probably the *Hikayat Muhammad Hanafiyyah* which has been traced back to its Persian original. Just as the reading of many of the stories related to the life of the Prophet Muhammad was deemed to award protection against various evils, reading of the *Hikayat Muhammad Hanafiyyah* was considered to increase the courage and fighting spirit of the Muslim warrior. In fact, at one time its powers were considered to be so strong, that on the eve of the Portuguese attack against Malacca in 1511 the Sultan of Malacca initially refused the request of his soldiers to have this *hikayat* read to them and offered the *Hikayat Amir Hamzah* instead. It has been argued that this particular text, the *Hikayat Muhammad Hanafiyyah*, is the prototype of the Malay *hikayat per se*.

4. Heroes of Islam. Beginning with the story of Alexander the Great (*Hikayat Iskandar Dzulkarnain*) which seems to have been modelled on some Arabic-Persian version, this group includes what seems to be the original Malay creation of the story of the eighth-century Sufi Ibrahim ibn Adham, the *Hikayat Sultan Ibrahim*.
5. A special group can be classified as *kitab* literature, i.e. theological literature in the stricter sense written by and for theologians and religious teachers and not for the faithful at large. In this group too fall the Javanese *primbon* which are sometimes no more than scrap-books kept by pupils of a *pesantren* (a school of Islamic learning). The *kitab* literature is very comprehensive and, as can be expected from a literature where faithfulness, accuracy and above all legitimacy are all important, here we find the names of authors, translators, editors and adaptors mentioned more frequently. A large number of texts in the *kitab* tradition stem from the eighteenth and nineteenth centuries.

Given the didactic purpose of this literature and considering the spiritual traditions in which the writers saw themselves, most of the works in this category do not strive for originality. However, there are exceptions and again we have to turn to seventeenth-century Aceh and the Islamic literature written there in Malay, leaving aside the considerable literature in Acehnese itself which has been discussed at length by Snouck Hurgronje.

Four outstanding theologians, writers and thinkers each in his own way made their presence felt in the Aceh of the sixteenth and seventeenth centuries. Reference has been made already to Hamzah Fansuri (d. *c.* 1600). However, Hamzah's reputation does not rest just on his heterodox views. He is considered the first original and creative poet with an individuality of his own known to us from Malay literature. Hamzah is credited with the 'invention' of a particular form of quatrain called *syair* and its introduction into Malay literature. Echoing traditional Malay as well as specifically Islamic, i.e. Perso-Arabic, forms of poetry, Hamzah created a poetic form of his own which was to leave a lasting stamp on Malay poetry by pushing other forms into the background. Only in this century and with the development of a more modern literature did the *syair* begin to lose its importance as it was no longer able to serve as a creative means of expression. Originally employed by Hamzah to express his own mystical emotions, experiences and thoughts, the *syair* developed into the most common form of poetry and came to be employed in a religious and non-religious context. With Hamzah, too, for the first time we see the attempt made to express mystical, religious thought in a language accessible to those who did not know Arabic and Persian sufficiently well.

Hamzah not only wrote poetry. In a number of prose works he set out his own concept of *Wujudiya* which was so vigorously opposed a few decades after his death by a native of Rander in India, Nuruddin ar-Raniri. Nuruddin stayed only a few years in Aceh (1637–44) during which time he wrote a number of books in both Arabic and Malay. Today perhaps best known is his *Bustan as-Salatin*, a compendium of knowledge with original chapters on the history of Aceh and the genealogy of its rulers. If Hamzah had a follower in Syamsuddin al-Sumatrani, or Syamsuddin of Pasai, who died in 1631, then Abdurrauf of Singkel (*c.* 1615–93) stood in the orthodox tradition of Nuruddin. Abdurrauf is credited with the first full commentary on the Qur'an in Malay, the *Tarjuman al-Mustafid* which, in its present form has recently been identified as a composite text enlarged by his pupil Daud Rumi, according to P. Riddell. Abdurrauf, who had spent about 20 years of study in Arabia before returning to his home country of Aceh in 1661, had among his teachers Burhan al-Din who authorised him to set up the Syattariah order in Aceh.

According to Roolvink, Nuruddin's *Bustan* falls already into the category of *adab* literature to which another seventeenth-century text can be added, the *Tajj us-Salatin* by Bukhari Djohori, a mirror of conduct written in 1603 and based on Persian models.

The nineteenth century saw the creation of what is probably the most remarkable indigenous Islamic work in the *adab* tradition, the *Tuhfat al-Nafis* by Raja Ali Haji. The work is outstanding for several reasons. Normally it does not seem to have been common for members of the aristocracy to be literate (let along devoutly religious), and, although there have been rulers and aristocrats of high learning throughout the history of the archipelago, it would seem that the majority of aristocrats would have acted as patrons only, leaving the actual writing to court scribes who were often of lowly rank. One of the exceptions to this pattern was the family of the deputy ruler of Riau which was of Bugis descent and, although there are few words of Buginese in the *Tuhfat* it is worth remembering that the Buginese had a well established literary tradition of their own. Apart from Raja Ali Haji, his father and a sister are also known to have been actively engaged in literary work. Raja Ali Haji and his father, incidentally, were said to have been the first nobles from the Riau court to have made the pilgrimage. Raja Ali Haji himself wrote theological and didactic prose and poetry. A 'linguistic' study of Malay also stands to his credit. However, his most famous work, the *Tuhfat al-Nafis*, is the first historical work in Malay which not only sets out its sources with previously unknown precision but also covers a world much larger than the one known from most Malay historical texts, as it encompasses most of the Malay world and not just the world of one state. This is understandable historically as the work aims to describe and justify the advance of five Buginese brothers, of whom Raja Ali Haji is a descendant, into the western Malay world, and their current military and political strength. But the book also has a strong moral and, according to B. Andaya and V. Matheson, ethical undertone and Raja Ali appears to have been influenced in particular by al-Ghazali and his *Nasihat al-Muluk*. In the *Tuhfat al-Nafis* he strives to show how the course of history and the well-being of a state and internal harmony are determined by the proper conduct of subjects and ruler who do not follow their desires, *hawa nafsu*, but logic and reason, *akal* and *ilm*.

Generally speaking, in the nineteenth century, apart from the increase in the *kitab* literature already mentioned, we also find a larger number of texts whose 'subject matter . . . derived from international Islamic literature, their surroundings set in the central lands of Islam' (Roolvink, 1971:1234). It should be noted, too, that the late nineteenth century saw, hand in hand with the development of the press, the development of a more secular non-Islamic literature.

Of religious literature in Javanese which differs from that in Malay, mention perhaps should be made of the so-called *suluk* literature, i.e. anonymous, mystical songs whose creation has been attributed in part to the nine *wali*, the cultural heroes who are said to have brought Islam to Java. Despite their lyrical form the *suluk* songs are of a didactic nature. Popular too is the so-called *Menak* cycle of prose stories centred around Hamzah which is most directly related to the Malay version of the *Hikayat Amir Hamzah*.

Tensions within the Islamic Community

As is to be expected those Indonesian Muslims who take their religious obligations very seriously and who would strive to lead an exemplary life, devoted entirely to Islam as taught and practised in the Islamic heartlands, and even more those who are engaged in scholarship, have always formed a minority among their neighbours. The majority of the others, however, although probably less orthodox in their religious life, and upholding inherited values and local traditions to a larger degree than was common among orthodox Muslims, are no less convinced personally of their own religious sincerity. Hints of friction between the two can be found in doctrinal conflicts of seventeenth-century Aceh, and clear signs of a rift are apparent, too, if one looks at the development of Islam in Java over the centuries.

In Java today, *santri* is the general term used to describe the practising, 'orthodox' Muslims, but the term still carries the connotation of men and women who remove themselves from this world in order to spend their lives in devotion in the *pesantren*, literally the place of the *santri*.

The importance of the Javanese *pesantren* and similar institutions elsewhere for the religious life of Indonesian Muslims in past centuries cannot be overestimated. Although partially reduced in significance by the progressive *madrasah* (see below) in this century, the rural *pesantren* has been regaining some of its popularity of late. Relying heavily on donations and the active and material assistance of its members, the *pesantren* is usually led and owned by a *kiai*, as he is known in Java, or *ulema* as he is known elsewhere in the archipelago. A *kiai* has to be a man of learning and a gifted spiritual leader. In fact the reputation and fortunes of a *pesantren* depend very much on the recognition enjoyed by its leader, the kiai. It is interesting to observe that whereas the institution of the *pesantren* has survived for centuries, individual *pesantren* rarely seem to have been able to keep up momentum and to maintain a high standard of excellence beyond the life of their outstanding founder.

In the past, the Javanese *kiai*, who are closely linked through an intricate network of marriages and teacher/pupil relationships, have, by their positive example and spiritual leadership, been a major rallying point for the surrounding community beyond the limited confines of the *pesantren* as such, and although reluctant to be involved in matters of this world, they could become leaders in times of social and economic distress.

The single-minded concentration of the *santri* on reaching paradise, however, has not always met with general understanding. A Sundanese folk-story (as retold by Ajip Rosidi), for example, tells of the hadji who spends all his life in devotion; even the rock on which he always performs his prayers is worn down. He expects paradise as if it were his by right, and so turns away from Allah and becomes an evil-doer and an apostate when he learns that instead of him a notorious criminal, who accepts that he has to redeem his sins in hell, has been chosen by Allah to go to paradise.

Then there are the *abangan*, people whose philosophy and religious beliefs owe very little indeed to Islam and a considerable amount to traditional Javanese mysticism and traditional Javanese religious conventions and practices, also described as *Javanism*, and now officially recognised as a creed called *kebatinan*.

The distinction between *santri* and *abangan* has been discussed in a contemporary setting by Geertz in his influential book, *The Religion of Java* (Geertz, 1960) which besides the *santri* and *abangan* types also identifies a third type which Geertz calls *priyayi*. This is how Geertz characterises the three types:

> *Abangan*, representing a stress on the animistic aspects of the over-all Javanese syncretism and broadly related to the peasant element in the population; *santri*, representing a stress on the Islamic aspects of the syncretism and generally related to the trading element (and to certain elements in the peasantry as well); and *prijaji*, stressing the Hinduistic aspects and related to the bureaucratic element (Geertz, 1960:6).

Geertz's division has not remained unchallenged, and it has been pointed out in particular that the third *priyayi* type is not cultural but one of sociological relevance only, and that the term is not indicative at all of the religious attitudes of the members of this particular social class, 'the traditional, legitimate elite' (Bachtiar, 1973:88). A *priyayi* just as any member of any other social class may be *santri* in his religious attitude or he may be *abangan* or, as would be even more typical:

> A *prijaji*, as *Pater familias*, may on certain occasions enact the prescribed ritual of the ancestor cult associated with the *pusaka*, the family heirlooms, to venerate the

> ancestors; as a prominent member of the community he may, when occasion demands, arrange to hold a *slametan*, a communal dinner, at his house; on Fridays, as a good Moslem, he may go to the mosque to pray together with the other members of the Islamic religious community, or, at least, does not fail to appear for the public prayer on Idul Fitri to celebrate the end of the Ramadhan, the fasting month; as a member of a theosophy group he regularly attends the monthly meetings of the local lodge to discuss theosophical problems; as a member of a political party he takes every opportunity to propagate his party's political ideology, and as a dutiful Indonesian citizen he is always present at mass meetings where the national ideology holds sway; then, also, as a Western educated man he may participate in discussions which are very much dominated by Christian values or European logic with, perhaps, a dash of Aristotelian philosophy or modern French existentialism; but when in the dark of the night he walks home from a meeting he may be a little frightened of the evil spirits that are believed to be on the lurk for their prey. (Bachtiar, 1973:95)

Ricklefs (1979) argues that the conflict between those Javanese who are fully committed to Islam in a stricter form (the *santri*) and those to whom Mecca and all it stands for are at times peripheral (and to whom, for example, several pilgrimages to the grave of one of the nine *wali* would make the hadj superfluous), is more significant in present-day Java than the frequently invoked opposition of *santri* and *abangan*, if we take *abangan* to mean those Indonesians to whom, ultimately, Islam is irrelevant to the conduct of their spiritual life.

According to Ricklefs, historically three periods can be distinguished in the Islamisation of Java as opposed to its conversion to Islam: 1. the fourteenth to the eighteenth century; 2. the nineteenth century; 3. the twentieth century.

The first period is one of marked religious tolerance characterised by two development processes, the gradual Islamisation of the people of Java and the accompanying Javanisation of the non-Javanese Muslims who had brought Islam to and settled in Java. In that period pre-Islamic, Indic and authentically Javanese cultural and religious concepts generally continued to live side by side with Islamic concepts in mutual tolerance.

For a number of reasons the nineteenth century saw a change in that relationship. Direct colonial rule and exploitation, which imposed a considerable burden on Javanese society and its economy, coincided with the emergence of a new type of Muslim among the many who, to the displeasure of the colonial authorities with their fear of Pan-Islamic activism, made use of the improvements in overseas transport in order to go on the pilgrimage. These newly returned hadjis naturally would have become influenced not only by the conduct of other Muslims in Mecca, but also by Wahhabi revivalism and by the reformist ideas emerging from Egypt, thus reversing the trend brought about by the interference of the VOC which, particularly in the eighteenth century and through its trading and shipping monopoly, had broken up the international network of Muslims which had been so characteristic of the earlier period of Islam in the archipelago. As a result of that new experience in Mecca a rift was bound to develop between the returning hadjis and the traditional religious teachers, the *kiai*, who might have accommodated non-Islamic spiritual traditions in their teaching and religious practices. And, in consequence, the *abangan*, too, were faced perhaps for the first time, with a decision about which of the two, Islam or Javanism, to choose. Naturally this affected *priyayi* and non-*priyayi* alike, and hand in hand with the consolidation of colonial rule, part of the traditional, indigenous elite (the *priyayi*) which was to gain most from an integration into the colonial system began to turn to Western ideas while upholding traditional Javanese values and consciously rejecting the Islamic option.

In the twentieth century those divisions began to harden and it appears that the distance between the three has now become so great as to split Javanese society to an unprecedented degree. Ricklefs even believes that while the commitment to orthodox Islamic faith and practice has been greatly strengthened within the *santri* community in the past century, the percentage of all Javanese who are Muslim (most of them *abangan*) has probably declined. This of course has been realised by Muslims who today consider the conversion of the Javanese as their primary task (Boland, 1982:191).

The changes in colonial policy and the increased impact of colonial rule, and equally important for Indonesian Islam, the changes occurring in the Middle East with the emergence of the Wahhabi movement and with the development of the reformist thought of Muhammad Abduh, obviously not only had an impact on Java but affected the other regions of the archipelago as well. Looking at the spiritual development of Islam in the archipelago in general, nineteenth- and twentieth-century Islamic revivalism and reformism were of singular importance throughout as everywhere they forced Muslims individually to rethink their own religious position. If Ricklefs observes that these issues, revivalism and reformism, more than any other issue split Javanese society, his observation also holds true for other regions and ethnic groups of the archipelago right to the present day. Once Muslims began to insist on the pervasiveness and all-embracing nature of their religion, this religion became a divisive issue which not only separated rulers and ruled, colonisers and colonised, but also continued (and continues) to disturb the traditional internal coherence of indigenous communities. Given the nature of state rule, first that of a colonial government doing everything in its power to maintain control over its territory, and then that of a newly-born nation strongly concerned to confirm its own authority over a heterogeneous array of traditional societies, any form of regional and internal conflict, religious or otherwise, was bound to develop into a confrontation with central authority.

This became apparent first during the Padri War (1803–38) in which the Dutch became involved from 1821 onwards. The *padri*, so named after the Acehnese port of Pedir from which many Sumatran Muslims set off for the pilgrimage, as argued by some or, as argued by others, because the Malays had adopted the Portuguese lingua franca term for cleric, were pilgrims who had returned to Minangkabau in West Sumatra from Mecca, deeply impressed by the conquest of the city by the Wahhabi in 1803 and by their puritanism. Their immediate aim was to raise Islam in Minangkabau to a similar level of purity as they had seen in Mecca by turning against local *adat* and against what they perceived to be a general laxity in morals and customs of a non-Islamic nature. By emphasising the role of *fiqh* it was also hoped to restore greater order and security in social and economic life. In their efforts the *padri* soon resorted to fanatical and dogmatic violence and turned not only the traditional secular elite against them but also those Muslims who were closely associated with the traditionally strong Sufi orders of the region. Most prominent amongst those orders was the Syattariah which was said to have been brought to Minangkabau by Burhanuddin, a pupil of the Acehnese mystic Abdurrauf who was mentioned earlier.

When the Dutch returned to West Sumatra in 1821 they sided with the *adat* party, i.e. all those opposed to the fanaticism of the *padri*, and in 1837 the power of the *padri* was broken after their most prominent leader, Tuanku Imam of Bonjol, had been forced to surrender. Apart from smaller local uprisings in the nineteenth (and the twentieth) century two other, and for the Indonesians equally unsuccessful, major wars of the nineteenth century, the Java War (1825–30) and even more so the Aceh War (1873–*c.* 1912) also had a religious aspect, at least as far as the indigenous combatants were concerned. Prince Diponegoro of Yogyakarta, the rebel leader of the Java War had a strong religious (mystical) background and to many of his followers he seemed to combine the qualities of the Mahdi of Islam and the promised just king (*ratu adil*) of Javanese mythology.

Aceh, always fiercely independent and politically orientated towards the Middle East, strongly resisted Dutch attempts to subjugate it and after a vain effort to gain the support of Turkey among others, it settled down to fight the jihad on its own. As the Aceh War dragged on at great expense to the Dutch, the religious element in the Acehnese resistance was analysed and astutely exploited by the colonial authorities on the advice of C. Snouck Hurgronje (1857–1936) who, before accepting a Chair in Leiden, resided from 1889 until 1906 in the Dutch East Indies, as an advisor to the colonial government first on Eastern languages and Islamic law and then from 1898 onwards on 'native matters', with a special brief for Aceh. Snouck Hurgronje more than anybody else formulated a view of and policy towards Indonesian Islam, the impact of which was to last far into the twentieth century. As Boland has pointed out, for example, the office to which Snouck Hurgronje had been attached, the Department for Native Affairs, known to Indonesians as the Bureau of Religious Affairs, was the direct predecessor of the independent Republic's Department of Religious Affairs (Boland and Farjon, 1983:17).

Basically, Snouck Hurgronje advocated a policy of discrimination by which a distinction was to be made between Islam as a religious, personal and private affair, and Islam as a political force. To that aim government should grant absolute freedom to and not interfere with the purely religious expressions of Islam. The hadj, contrary to previous policy, should not be discouraged (nor, for that matter, should it be encouraged). Government should interfere as little as possible with the application of Muhammadan law, as long as this law did not itself interfere with or contradict the regionally quite diverse *adat*, i.e. local traditions and customs with legal consequences, in the definition of Snouck Hurgronje. Ultimately, however, both *adat and syaria* had to be subject to (European) civil law.

Outside the purely religious sphere Islamic activities were to be curbed and severely restricted and, finally, efforts were to be made to help Islam and Indonesian Muslims to leave the era of narrow dogmatism in order to catch up with Western civilisation and modern liberal thought (Benda, 1983:20–31).

During the Aceh War, Snouck Hurgronje's approach succeeded in gradually splitting religious and *adat* leaders, as the *adat* leaders were more easily accommodated and the war ended with the defeat of the *ulema*, the religious leaders. However, about 40 years later, in 1946, the *ulema* were to have their revenge when in the course of the so-called Social Revolution many of the *adat* leaders were killed indiscriminately. Similar events occurred in Java in reverse order where Communists turned on the *santri* in 1948 only to be persecuted and massacred in return in the wake of another political upheaval, the *Gestapu* affair of September 1965 which led to the formation of the New Order regime.

A further event of considerable impact and with clear political dimensions also had a prominent Islamic aspect to it, namely the regional *Darul Islam* rebellions which beset West and East Java, South Sulawesi, South Kalimantan and Aceh between the late 1940s and 1965 through periods of intermittent guerrilla warfare directed against the central government. As van Dijk has pointed out, Islam was a major rallying point for the rebels but, 'less a criterion whereby to distinguish friend from foe' (van Dijk, 1981:394). The regional rebellions had a number of causes, many of which were unrelated to religion as such. Yet, support for the rebellions reflected the belief of many of the rebels that it would be possible to overcome the various shortcomings blamed on central government if Indonesia were to become an Islamic state.

Of the rebellious regions whose activities were rarely co-ordinated and who strove for the establishment of an Islamic state, Aceh probably gained most. Unlike the other areas it was granted the status of a Special Region in 1959. This privilege had so far been bestowed only upon the capital city of Jakarta and the one-time capital city of Yogyakarta. Within the limits of existing law Aceh was also to have considerable autonomy especially with regard to religious education and the application of *adat* and *syaria*.

Modernists versus Traditionalists

Among Indonesian Muslims there are as in most (religious) communities traditionalists and modernists with many shades and colours in between; a considerable problem which troubles many attempts at analysis of a wide range of Islamic movements and activities in the archipelago is that of defining particular expressions of Indonesian Islam other than by using popular labels such as orthodox, neo-orthodox, scripturalist, revivalist, traditional, fundamentalist, reformist, modern and progressive. The indiscriminate use of these labels is rather misleading and helps to distort the complex image of the faith of many Indonesians, as these terms are used in a variety of non-theological contexts. In the Indonesian case, for example, are not the so-called fundamentalists modern in their desire to purge the faith from things un-Islamic and, are not the so-called modernists fundamentalist in their insistence on the original word? Be that as it may, Indonesian Muslims like other religious groups disagree on a number of theological issues, and these differing theological views have found an echo in the formation of a range of competing social and political organisations. These organisations within Islam are habitually divided and have hardly ever been able to form a united front against the secular nationalists. Only under the strong Communist pressure before 1966, when many Islamic organisations were banned by the government, could a larger unity among Muslims be observed. In less troubled times, 'modernists' will accuse 'traditionalists' of rigid dogmatism, blind obedience to established teachers, the *kiai* and the *ulema*, of insufficient intellectual inspiration and of escapist unrealism in the face of worldly (and Western) challenges. To the 'traditionalists' on the other hand the 'neo-orthodoxy' of the reformers is anathema. Traditionalists do not understand why modernists are not content to go to Mecca to further their education there and why they feel it important to adopt organisational and educational principles coming from the West and to absorb Western learning in their studies as is obvious from the foundation of the originally urban *madrasah*, i.e. religious schools set up by the religious reform organisation Muhammadiyah, which besides the traditional Islamic subjects of learning also include secular subjects in their curricula. The modernists' aim of taking Islam out of the mosque and the *pesantren* and carrying it to the people is to them a highly suspicious ambition, although the traditionalists, too, have embraced the concept of *dawa*, which has come to stand for Islamic 'propaganda' and missionary efforts in general. Ultimately traditionalists can not understand why modernists mean to discard scholastic knowledge and why they favour individual reasoning (*ijtihad*) over the unquestioning acceptance of established *fatwa* and the accumulated wisdom of past centuries of learning. The distinction drawn between religious *musts*, where no reinterpretation is possible, and worldly matters which have to be solved in an Islamic spirit but in step with the times is alien to them. The traditionalists would never agree to the suggestion by some modernists of abandoning the *syafii* school of law which is generally adhered to and developing a separate Indonesian school of law more in accordance with local conditions.

Yet, despite these many controversies which have plagued Indonesian Islam in the last two centuries, no clear-cut distinction is possible between traditionalists and reformists as there are many points of overlap between the two. Both want a 'better' Islam. Both want to rid Islam of non-Islamic embellishments and both want Islam given its proper place in society. But when it comes to the question of how to achieve this aim, it has so far been impossible for the two to achieve a lasting consensus. Suspicion, distrust and outspoken hostility have quite frequently marred their relationship, thus weakening both sides and depriving them of the opportunity to achieve their common goal together.

The discussion of the divisive issues is far from over, yet it is quite obvious that during the process both sides, gradually and perhaps even quite unconsciously, have absorbed many of each other's thoughts. This has happened in the case of the *adat*, for example, which, very much alive and continuously evolving, has in many instances adopted elements of Islamic law, so that these are no longer recognised as belonging to *fiqh* but are now considered an integral part of the traditional law. The slow process of osmosis between traditional and modern thought can also be clearly observed in the attitudes of the two sides towards contemporary non-theological literature.

A new, original, creative and individual form of *belles-lettres* in Malay and Indonesian began to develop from the turn of this century onwards. Basically secular in orientation it has since attracted writers who use the stylistic conventions of contemporary fiction to express their religious feelings, emotions and convictions. Yet, those Muslims who consciously wanted to express their own, inner feelings were faced with the dilemma that *belles-lettres* used to be held in low esteem by traditional Muslims. A criticism made by the modernists against the traditionalists was that because of the latter's preoccupation with the hereafter they were totally ignorant of, let alone part of, cultural and literary developments in the Islamic world at large. When in the 1930s young modernist Muslims began to publish their own, modern Islamic and Indonesian literature in response to the developments in secular fiction, their activities were soon declared *haram* by traditionalists who based their opposition on Sura 26, *Al-Suara The Poets*, in verses 221–6, which read in Arberry's translation:

> Shall I tell you on whom the Satans come down?
> They come down on every guilty impostor.
> They give ear, but most of them are liars.
> And the poets—the perverse follow them;
> hast thou not seen how they wander in every valley
> and how they say that which they do not?

To which the modernists replied by quoting verse 227:

> Save those that believe, and do righteous deeds,
> and remember God oft,
> and help themselves after being wronged;
> and those who do wrong shall surely know by what
> overturning they will be overturned.

Since the 1930s the traditionalists especially have shifted their position, it has to be admitted, and from a position of total rejection they have moved slowly to one of reluctant tolerance. However, the discussion still continues as to how the Islamic nature of literature ought to manifest itself. Should literature serve solely as a medium of *dawa* and should this function have priority over artistic criteria as the traditionalists demand, or should literature be given the freedom to express its Islamic character in whichever way the artists individually think best? In other words, should the message of Islam be explicit or implicit in a work of art?

Islam in Contemporary Society

The question of how far the involvement of Muslims should go in matters of this world has of course not only affected their stand towards literature but concerns all spheres of social and political life. Here again it becomes difficult to draw clear lines. Traditionalists might have attempted to keep themselves away from this world and might have been persuaded more easily to accept any worldly rule whatever as long as they were allowed to live their religion in peace. But on the other hand, in the history of the archipelago traditionalists more than others have been involved in local uprisings and the struggle for an Islamic state. Ironically the modernists, who in many ways speak the language of the secularists, perhaps because of their involvement in the world, found themselves in sympathy with the ideals of the *Darul Islam* too. Masyumi, the political party of the modernists, was barred under Soekarno for its reluctance to dissociate itself convincingly from the rebellions, and for the same reason not even under the New Order was Masyumi allowed to reorganise itself.

The roots of the weakness of Indonesian Islam as a political force go back to colonial days and beyond. As was said earlier, already in pre-colonial times strict Muslims were usually more concerned with the life thereafter than with the world around them. Admittedly, if one takes for example the sixteenth- and seventeenth-century city-state of Aceh, there is evidence that this state maintained diplomatic relations with Turkey as the seat of the caliphate. (Turkish soldiers served as auxiliary forces with the Acehnese and Turkish cannons were much in use.) Court life in Aceh was moulded on the example provided by the Mogul court. Local rulers in Sumatra and Java (Banten) were concerned to have their authority sanctioned and their credentials certified in Mecca. When in the second half of the seventeenth century a succession of sultanas came to reign over Aceh, a timely *fatwa* from Mecca brought an end to this tradition. Despite these examples and despite the courtly literature of seventeenth-century Aceh, it is questionable how far the government of the traditional Indonesian states was truly Islamic in nature as advocated by Raja Ali Haji in the nineteenth century. It would seem that Islamic titles often had little more than token significance and served merely as an additional device to underpin ideologically a ruler's authority and legitimacy. Few rulers are known ever to have made the pilgrimage.

In the twentieth century it was therefore not totally surprising that whenever Islam strove to assume real control over the secular authorities, it was to meet resistance. Nevertheless, in the eyes of Muslims it is tragic that, although the origins of the nationalist movement are closely linked with the foundation of a modernist Islamic organisation, the *Sarekat (Dagang) Islam* (Islamic (trading) Union), in 1911, the relationship between state and mosque has worsened so much that, since the defeat of the Communists by the New Order, organised Islam is now considered, to an unexpected degree, a major political threat to the state.

The basically secular foundation of the state and the pluralism of Indonesian society had obvious implications for the legal and political life of its Islamic citizens. There exist courts of religious (i.e. Islamic) justice whose jurisdiction, however, hardly extends beyond the family sphere and relates only to marriage, revocation, divorce, custody and guardianship (Hooker, 1983). This of course is resented by many Muslims and it is an indication of the strength of their feelings that an attempt by the government in 1974 to bring the marriage law into line with civil law in general faltered in the face of Islamic opposition. Then, for the first time in the history of the Republic, a pressure group (Islamic students in this case) invaded Parliament and staged a demonstration inside the building which led the government to rethink the proposed bill.

Despite this particular success, Muslims have been least successful on the political front. The fact that adherence to the *syaria* was not made compulsory for all Indonesian Muslims in the Constitution of 1945 remains an unresolved issue. One draft of the preamble of that constitution which sets out the state philosophy in five tenets known as the *Pancasila* had as its first principle 'the belief in one God with the duty for all Muslims to follow the *syaria*'. This particular draft, which contains in seven Indonesian words

words this special proviso for Muslims and which is now known as the *Piagam Jakarta* or Jakarta Charter, was not acceptable to all those involved in drafting the Constitution, and in the final and constitutional version of the *Pacasila* the first tenet now reads (in an official translation):

1. Belief in the one supreme God.

The four remaining principles are (in the same translation):

2. Just and civilized humanity.
3. The unity of Indonesia.
4. Democracy led by the wisdom of deliberations among representatives.
5. Social justice for the whole of the people of Indonesia.

Generally, the political strength of Muslims bears no relation to their numerical strength and violent (re)actions by fundamentalist groups can be seen as an indication of sincerely felt frustration and as a response to unfulfilled aspirations rather than as proof of widespread grass-roots support for the aims of any particular theology. The *Darul Islam* rebellions of the 1950s and early 1960s which mostly affected the islands of Java, Sumatra and Sulawesi, and which were brought to an end only after a prolonged military campaign, were one such indicator and response. Recent violent outbreaks seem to be as much inspired by current developments in countries such as Iran as reflections of how Indonesian Muslims perceive their own present situation in a basically secular state which strongly supports religion as a principle, but which ultimately seems to regard religious life and activities as an entirely private matter.

Again, the constant internal divisions among the Muslims themselves have not improved their position in political life. Prior to the early 1970s there were almost as many Islamic political parties and other organisations in Indonesia as there were opinions and views. A decision by the government to 'streamline' the party political system in 1971 resulted in the abolition of all existing Islamic and other parties and the formation (by government decree) of three new parties and functional groups to express the political wishes of the electorate at large. The Partai Persatuan Pembangunan (PPP) or United Development Party was designed to express the political aspirations of all Muslims but, as was to be expected, so far it has not been able to overcome its internal problems and conflicts. Members of the two major Islamic parties of the past, the traditionalist *Nahdatul-Ulama* and the progressive *Masyumi*, form clearly definable factions pursuing their own goals and interests within the new party. Hence the PPP has rarely been able to offer a united front or a common policy. The chronic weakness of Islam as a political force has been demonstrated again in 1985 when the Partai Persatuan Pembangunan accepted the Constitutional version of the Pancasila as the party's guiding principle. Admittedly all political and social organisations in

Indonesia had been asked to demonstrate their loyalty to the state by pledging allegiance to the Pancasila unless they wanted to be considered hostile to state and country; however, in denouncing the famous 'seven words' of the Jakarta Charter, the only party meant to defend the interests of Muslims had clearly given ground once more. The PPP was even forced to abandon its recognised symbol, the *kabah*, which never seemed to have found the approval of the government, and it had to replace it with the star-shaped symbol from the national coat of arms which stands for the first *sila*. The case of the PPP has not been helped either by the recent withdrawal from the party of the *Nahdatural-Ulama* whose own efforts to rethink its position and role promise to be of significant interest in the future.

With Islamic law and Islamic courts operating only on the periphery of society, with Islamic higher education under government control through the National Islamic Institutes (IAIN *Institut Agama Islam Negeri*), with (*abangan*) mysticism now classed as a govenment recognised faith called *kebatinan*, with the imposed formation of only one Islamic party in which traditional factions are still clearly at work, and which has had a limited response from the electorate, with a secular army whose loyalty is to the state in its present form, there is, at the moment, little Muslim activists can do democratically to alter their political status. Faith has indeed become the outsider (McVey, 1983).

Bibliography

Al-Attas, S.M.Ng. 'A general theory of the Islamization of the Malay–Indonesian Archipelago in Sarbro Kartodirdjo (ed.), *Profiles of Malay Culture* (Ministry of Education and Culture, Jakarta, 1976), pp. 73–84

Bachtiar, Harsja W. *The Religion of Java: a Commentary* (Madjalah Ilmu-Ilmu Sastra Indonesia, 1973), pp. 85–118.

Benda, H. *The Crescent and the Rising Sun: Indonesian Islam under the Japanese Occupation, 1942–1945* (W. van Hoeve, The Hague, 1983)

Boland, B.J. *The Struggle of Islam in Modern Indonesia* (Nijhoff, The Hague, 1982), Verhandelingen KITLV 59

—— and Farjon, J. *Islam in Indonesia, a Bibliographical Survey* (KITLV Bibliographical Series 14, Dordrecht, 1983)

Dijk, C. van *Rebellion under the Banner of Islam* (Nijhoff, The Hague, 1981) Verhandelingen KITLV 94

Dobbin, C. *Islamic Revivalism in a Changing Peasant Economy* (Curzon, London, 1983)

Drewes, G.W.J. 'New light on the coming of Islam to Indonesia?' in *Bijdragen tot de Taal-, Land- en Volkenkunde*, 124 (1968), pp. 133–459

Geertz, C. *The Religion of Java* (The Free Press, Glencoe, 1960)

Hooker, M.B. (ed.) *Islam in South-East Asia* (Brill, Leiden, 1983)

Johns, A.H. 'The role of Sufism in the spread of Islam to Malaya and Indonesia' in *Journal of the Pakistan Historical Society*, 9 (1961), pp. 143–61

—— 'From Coastal Settlement to Islamic School and City: Islamization in Sumatra, the Malay Peninsula and Java' in J.J. Fox *et al.* (eds.) *Indonesia, Australian Perspectives* (ANU, Canberra, 1980), pp. 163–82

McVey, Ruth 'Faith as the Outsider: Islam in Indonesian Politics' in James P. Piscatori

(ed.) *Islam in the Political Process* (Cambridge University Press, Cambridge, 1983), pp. 199–225
Noer, Deliar *The Modernist Muslim Movement in Indonesia 1900–1942* (Oxford University Press, Singapore, 1973)
—— *Administration of Islam in Indonesia Inthaca* (Modern Indonesia Project Mon. 58, Cornell, New York, 1978)
Pelras, C. 'Religion, Tradition and the Dynamics of Islamization in South Sulawesi', *Archipel*, 29, pp. 107–35
Ricklefs, M.C. 'Six Centuries of Islamization in Java' in Nehemia Levtzion (ed.) *Conversion to Islam* (Holmes & Meier, New York, 1979) pp. 100–28

27 Islam in the Middle East

Denis MacEoin

The Middle East region, comprising the Arabian Peninsula, Mesopotamia and the Levant, contains within it the three earliest centres of Islamic civilisation: the Hejaz, dominated by Mecca and Medina, where the Prophet Muhammad preached and where the first Islamic community developed under his aegis and that of the first three caliphs; greater Syria, centred on Damascus, the capital of the Umayyad dynasty from 661 to 750, and containing Jerusalem, Islam's first *qibla* and its third holy city; and Iraq, where the new capital of Baghdad became the centre of a vast empire under the Abbasids, where the consensus that grew into Islamic orthodoxy was first hammered out, and where the chief elements of classical Islamic civilisation were developed.

In the course of time, of course, the centres of power in the Islamic heartlands were to shift elsewhere—to Fatimids, Ayyubids and Mamluks in Egypt, to the Ottoman Turks with their capital in European Byzantium and to the Safavids in Iran. Turks and Persians ruled where Arab dynasties had once held sway. And Islam itself spread and consolidated its power in fresh regions: India, Africa, the Far East. The Arabian Peninsula remained much what it had been before the advent of Islam, a backwater, of significance only for the holy cities of Mecca and Medina and the myth of the untainted nomad roaming its deserts. Iraq and the Levant became Ottoman provinces.

Religiously, the fortunes of the region followed its relegation to provincial status. The great focuses of Islamic scholarship lay elsewhere, in Fès, Cairo, Istanbul, or Isfahan, and even when individual scholars of merit originated in provincial centres, they generally gravitated to the great cities where their talents could be best put to use. Organised Sufism spread throughout the Ottoman Empire but left the Arabian Peninsula virtually untouched. Mecca and Medina retained their quality of holiness, of course, and continued to attract the pious and pilgrims, playing in this respect an important role in bringing together scholars and holy men from the length and breadth of the Islamic world. In some cases, their experiences in Mecca were to become turning-points in the lives of men who rose to positions of eminence elsewhere. In the early nineteenth century, for example, the Sufi reformer Ahmad ibn Idris al-Fasi (1760–1837) attracted large numbers of pupils to Mecca, where he had settled in 1818. Although the movement he founded had little direct impact in Arabia, pupils such as Muhammad Uthman al-Mirghani and Muhammad ibn Ali al-Sanusi established brotherhoods—the Mirghaniyya and Sanusiyya—that were to have an enormous impact in the Sudan and Libya respectively.

Removed as they were from the centres of power, these regions came for the most part more slowly than others into the orbit of the European powers and, in consequence, faced the problems of Westernisation and modernisation rather later than the rest of the central Islamic world. Areas like Oman, Yemen and what is now Saudi Arabia remained remote and deeply rooted in tradition until well into the twentieth century. Change, when it came, often came swiftly and with devastating results. Unlike Turks or Levantines or coastal North Africans, who had never been wholly isolated from the world around them, the inhabitants of the inland reaches of the Arabian Peninsula were denied the comforts of a gradual induction into the ways of the Technical Age that was invisibly but inexorably tightening its grip on their borders.

Islamic society and, in particular, Islamic religion possessed resources which rendered them, if not impervious to outside influences, at least capable of resisting wholesale capitulation to them. In many less developed societies, the impact of Western culture was generally productive of profound changes in the religious life of the people, generating indigenous movements of spiritual renewal from the cargo-cults of Melanesia to the nativist churches of sub-Saharan Africa. Islam, on the other hand, had a wide panoply of religious texts, functionaries, institutions and routines that made resistance to Western pressures in that sphere relatively easy and even inevitable. This is not to say that religion in the Islamic world has remained unaffected by changes mediated by agencies of the West. Whole areas of life have passed out of the sphere of religious control, from education, law and even commerce to neighbourhood associations and the family. But the chief developments in the religious sphere have either represented a closing of ranks against the forces of secularisation or a continuation of internally inspired currents of renewal or reaction, such as the Tijani and Sanusi brotherhoods of North Africa, the Sudanese Mahdist rebellion, the Iranian Babi sect, or even more modern movements in Iran, Egypt, and elsewhere.

Nevertheless, although religious developments have taken their own course and Islam has retained its internal autonomy against

Western systems of thought and behaviour, external factors have played an enormous role in ensuring the success or failure of specific trends or movements, whether indirectly by influencing the general economic and social climate or directly by the despatch of gunboats or the organisation of *coups d'état.* Throughout the nineteenth and twentieth centuries, then, the fortunes of Islam in the Middle East have been closely tied to internal political changes (themselves as often as not the result of Great Power intrigues or direct intervention) on the one hand and to external pressures on the other.

Central Arabia

Of all the Islamic movements to rise to prominence in the past few centuries, none has had a greater or more lasting impact than that of the Wahhabiyya, an uncompromising assertion of Islamic orthodoxy and orthopraxy directed against all innovations in doctrine and practice deemed to have entered the faith since the third century. In their desire to return to a pristine synthesis of faith and morals, purified of all accretions and dedicated to the implementation of the puritan ideal in every sphere of human activity, the Wahhabis prefigured or inspired numerous movements of Islamic revival down to the present day.

The founder of the movement, Muhammad ibn Abd al-Wahhab (1703–92) was a native of the central Arabian province of Nejd, a region nominally under the rule of the Ottoman Empire but in practice divided, like the rest of the peninsula, among competing clans and tribal groups. In 1744, Ibn Abd al-Wahhab, expelled from his home town of Uyayna, joined forces with the ruler of Dariyya, Muhammad ibn Saud (d. 1765), in a religio-political alliance that was to transform Wahhabism from one man's obsession into the ideology underpinning a small Arab empire.

Wahhabi doctrine was simple, uncluttered by speculation, and forcefully expressed. Terming themselves *muwahhidun* or *ahl al-tawhid* (exponents of the divine unity), the followers of Ibn Abd al-Wahhab eschewed anything and everything that seemed to them tainted with heresy. Wahhabism was not, in the strict sense, a new sect within Islam but a revival of orthodox Sunnism based on the teachings of the fourteenth-century scholar Ibn Taymiyya and the rulings of the Hanbali law-school, the strictest of the four recognised within the Sunni consensus. The particular targets of Wahhabi wrath were the Sufi brotherhoods (which had by that time reached unprecedented heights of influence throughout the world of Islam), Shi'ism, and the cult of saints common to both groups. Among the bedouin who rallied in increasing numbers to the growing military power of Ibn Saud and his descendants, a host of pre-Islamic customs, including the worship of sacred trees and stones, were rigorously attacked and eradicated. Attendance at public prayer was made compulsory, the smoking of tobacco forbidden, and all ostentation, luxury and recreation from music to chess vigorously suppressed.

Throughout the late eighteenth and early nineteenth centuries, Wahhabi armies spread terror across the peninsula and beyond, reaching into Syria and Iraq. Medina was taken in 1804 and Mecca in 1806: Wahhabi arms ruled the most sacred sites of Islam, and Wahhabi intransigence began the process of remodelling society along the lines laid down by strict and unremitting orthodoxy. Shrines, even visible tombstones, were demolished (at one point even the tomb of the Prophet in Medina came near destruction), strict observance of the law was imposed, and zeal unleashed for the waging of an ongoing jihad against the 'idolatrous' practices of the Shi'i and Sunni communities on their borders.

The inevitable riposte, when it came at last, was sudden and effective. Authorised by the Ottomans to intervene, the semi-independent ruler of Egypt, Muhammad Ali Pasha, embarked on a series of campaigns led by himself and two of his sons, in the course of which Wahhabi rule was broken for a while. But however hard pressed it became in subsequent decades, Wahhabism continued to exercise a profound influence throughout central Asia, above all in Ibn Abd al-Wahhab's native Nejd, where the Rashid dynasty of Hail was in control throughout the second half of the nineteenth century. Its fortunes so closely linked to the military success of the Saudi family, Wahhabi Islam became retrenched and isolated, but it was far from spent as a force in the world.

In the opening years of the twentieth century, a new Saudi leader of immense ability, Abd al-Aziz ibn Saud, recaptured the old dynastic capital of Riyadh and embarked on a campaign of conquest that was to lead in a matter of decades to the creation of the Kingdom of Saudi Arabia. Like his ancestor, Muhammad ibn Saud, Abd al-Aziz relied as much on the indomitable faith of his bedouin troops as he did on their swords. In 1912, a movement of renewal began among the Wahhabis of Nejd. Calling themselves Ikhwan or 'Brethren', a rapidly-growing band of bedouin established centres known as *hujar* (sg. *hijra*), from which they preached an intensified version of the Wahhabi creed. The use of the term *hijra* for their settlements was a deliberate invocation of the early Islamic theme of emigration, of movement away from idolatry and unbelief towards true faith and the perfect society. It is a theme that has been taken up again most recently by the Egyptian group responsible for the assassination of President Sadat, the *Jamaat al-Takfir wa 'l-Hijra*, the 'Association of Excommunication and Emigration'.

In 1916, Abd al-Aziz ordered those bedouin who owed allegiance to him to abandon herding and join forces with the burgeoning Ikhwan movement. Animated by a fundamentalist zeal that remained untempered by any external influence, the Ikhwan launched what was effectively a holy war throughout the peninsula, taking Mecca and Medina by force in 1924 and pushing the borders of the Saudi kingdom further and further afield. The curious parallel, not only with the original Wahhabi conquests but with the early days of Islam itself, was emphasised in the striking fashion whereby converts to the Ikwan would speak of themselves as having 'become Muslims', describing the period prior to their conversion as *jahiliyya* or 'ignorance'—a term normally reserved for the days of irreligion before the coming of Muhammad. It was as if Islam itself was being reborn in its original homeland.

But as the power of the Ikhwan increased, so too did their intransigence. Wholly preoccupied with religion to the exclusion of everything else, they imposed a stark puritanical regime on all the territories they conquered. Under their rule, a man could as easily be put to death for his knowledge of Islam coupled with their version of it as for his ignorance of its tenets. Prayer was rigidly enforced and every conceivable form of recreation, however seemingly innocent, banned through the efforts of *mutawwiun*, bands of 'enforcers' whose task it was to ensure the observance of a strict Wahhabi ethic. Before long, Abd al-Aziz himself began to recognise that, whatever the advantages of Ikhwani dedication, these were far outweighed by their fanaticism and the danger it posed to the new state he was attempting to create. The Ikhwan for their part began to criticise the ruler for introducing what they regarded as impious innovations and for mixing with non-Muslim foreigners.

In 1928, bands of Ikhwan began to attack other Saudi subjects in Nejd, and in the following year Abd al-Aziz launched a military campaign against them, as a result of which he was able to put an end to their influence throughout the country. The defeat of the Ikhwan did not, however, in any way spell the end of Wahhabism in Saudi Arabia, merely the curtailment of its most fanatical and least workable expression. The Saudi state remains firmly rooted in the Wahhabi creed down to the present day: 'Just as the critical fact in the Saudi economy is petroleum, so the quintessence of its very being is Islam' (Ralph Braibanti). Until the Iranian revolution of 1979, Saudi Arabia was the only state in the Islamic world to come close to the fundamentalist Islamic ideal. The country's constitution remains the Qur'an, supplemented by the provisions of Islamic tradition and the rulings of the Hanbali law-school. The country's legal system consists of two parts: the Shari'a or religious code and a body of state-issued 'Regulations'. The latter do not, however, operate as an independent system as does customary law in some Muslim states, but are regarded as no more than decrees which enable the Shari'a to be properly implemented. In the 'Fundamental Instructions for the Hejaz issued by Abd al-Aziz in 1926, it states that 'His Majesty is bound by the provisions of the noble Shari'a. The ordinances [of the state] shall always be in accordance with the Book of God and the Sunna of His Messenger and the ways of the Companions [of the Prophet] and the pious ancestors.'

Under the brief rule of Faisal (1964–75), Saudi Arabia took an increasingly influential role in the development of Islam at the international level, reviving earlier ideas of pan-Islamic unity that had been increasingly displaced by an ethos of national autonomy modelled on Western patterns. An extremely pious man, Faisal sought to combine political ambition with a variety of activities designed to enhance a sense of unity in the world of Islam at large. Even before he became king, Faisal sought to counteract the political radicalism promoted by Nasser throughout the Arab world by invoking Islam as an alternative, unifying ideology appropriate for all Muslims, both Arab and non-Arab. In 1962, the Saudi government sponsored an international Islamic conference in Mecca, at which delegates discussed ways in which Muslims could combat the twin threats of radicalism and secularism. The conference resulted in the formation of the World Muslim League, an international body with headquarters in Mecca, the purpose of which was to further the interests of Islam and Muslims throughout the world. In 1969 and 1970, Faisal was again instrumental in calling the first Islamic summit (held in Rabat) and the first Islamic conference of foreign ministers (in Jedda).

As against its growing role as leader of the international Islamic community (a role much enhanced by custodianship of Mecca and Medina, the preservation of a respected puritan order and the financial power brought by petro-dollars), Saudi Arabia has had to face tensions at home which serve in many ways to symbolise the clash between Islamic and secular values in a singularly vivid manner. Although other oil-rich countries have experienced similar tensions in the course of modernisation, Saudi Arabia has felt the strain of rapid change more acutely than most precisely because of its perceived status as a nation somehow entrusted with the preservation of authentic Islamic faith and practice in a world fast receding from them. Saudi *ulema* have generally been slow to admit the legality of innovation, even in such relatively innocuous areas as sport, television, or telephones, let alone more serious concerns such as the education and employment of women or the codification of Shari'a law. In thus attempting to find expression for Islamic identity while seeking to enter fully into international life at all levels, Saudis face an unenviable dilemma. It remains to be seen whether Islamic banking can function as a viable method within the international monetary system or whether Islamic universities can integrate traditional values concerning knowledge with the methods and ideals of Western science, particularly in the social and religious sciences.

In 1979, the seizure of the Grand Mosque in Mecca by a messianic sectarian group led by Juhayman ibn Sayf al-Utaybi showed that the vigour of Islamic fundamentalism has been weakened but far from extinguished in the kingdom. The Ikhwan are unlikely to become a serious threat again, but in a state where piety and puritan values are officially encouraged on the one hand and vast wealth creates unprecedented opportunities for dissipation and corruption on the other, it would not be surprising if Islamic extremism did not make headway among the younger generation. What happens in Saudi Arabia is bound to prove of immense significance for the entire Islamic world.

Oman

The state of Oman, on the south-eastern corner of the Arabian Peninsula, facing both the Persian Gulf and the Arabian Sea, represents an interesting and individual parallel to Saudi Arabia. Since the eighth century, the people of Oman have owed their allegiance to the Ibadi sect, the only surviving branch of the Khariji movement, the earliest schismatic grouping in Islam. Like the later Wahhabis, the Kharijis promulgated a simple, puritan faith at the point of the sword, but insistence on political autonomy and an extreme position on the question of who could legitimately be regarded as a member of the Islamic community excluded them from the mainstream of Sunni orthodoxy (and did, indeed, do much to encourage the formulation of the moderate majority consensus).

The modern history of Oman illustrates with unusual clarity the nature of the tensions facing conventional Islamic societies confronting the challenges of life in a changing world. The Omani case is particularly instructive in that it presents an unparalleled and paradoxical combination of a sequestered, backward-looking sector on the one hand and a moderate, liberalising sector in close contact with the world at large on the other—the two groups separated as much by geographical factors as by intellectual differences.

Until the seventeenth century, Oman had generally been dominated by the forces of Ibadi conservatism, but since then a number of related developments have allowed more liberal elements to come to the fore. In 1648, the ruling Ibadi imam threw the Portuguese out of Masqat (Muscat), a port they had occupied since 1508. This enabled the imam to unify the country for the first time in centuries and to lay the basis for the expansion of Omani economic and political influence throughout the Gulf and along much of the East African coastline. In so doing, however, a tension was created between the imam's traditional role (in so far as he was a religio-political leader) as a preserver of the status quo and a growing need to adapt to the changes wrought in Omani society by the access of new power and wealth. The increasing concern of the imams with secular matters and the creation of a hereditary dynasty in contradiction to the Ibadi principle of free election led to a growing rift between conservatives and moderates, the first rift of its kind in the Islamic world in the modern period.

Following a brief interval of Persian rule, a new imamate was established by the Al Bu Sa'id clan in 1749, but in 1783 the religious leadership deposed the second member of the dynasty on the grounds that he had introduced heretical innovations. As a result, the Al Bu Sa'id became secular rulers with their territorial control centred on the coastal region, while the interior of Oman remained in the hands of the conservatives, who sought a return to the rule of a properly constituted imamate. Ibadi conservatism was, if anything, strengthened by the emergence of militant Wahhabism on the inland borders of the country in the late eighteenth and early nineteenth centuries.

During the first half of the nineteenth century, maritime trade between coastal Oman and ports in Africa, Iran and India expanded considerably, increasing the power of the moderates and isolating the conservative hinterland even further. But from the 1860s a rapid decline in Oman's economic fortunes began, triggered in part by the entry of advanced European shipping into the Gulf. In 1868, a coalition of religious conservatives under Sa'id ibn Khalfan al-Khalili and tribal leaders from the interior launched a successful fundamentalist revolution that aimed to reverse the trend of secular rule and to re-establish an orthodox imamate along traditional lines—a forerunner, in many respects, of the more recent Iranian revolution.

Although it lasted only three years until 1871, the fundamentalist regime established by al-Khalili and his followers represented in stark terms the escalating tensions between traditional and modernising values. The head of state was an elected imam, but real power resided in the hands of al-Khalili, who held the official posts of Governor of Muscat and chief religious judge (qadi) of Oman. Like the Wahhabis, the Ibadi leaders employed *mutawwiun* to enforce their rule on the populace, particularly the somewhat mixed and secularised inhabitants of the coast. Divided between religious leaders and tribal soldiers, the *mutawwiun* imposed a puritanical regime throughout the country and caused serious damage to the commercial life of the seaboard region, for whose problems they had no sympathy.

A moderate regime was re-established by Turki ibn Sa'id in 1871 and with the help of the British (who were now the strongest power in the Gulf) he succeeded in putting down two further conservative rebellions. During the later nineteenth century, following the death of al-Khalili in 1871, new elements emerged within the conservative party dedicated to the restoration of the imamate in the interior. By the early twentieth century, some of the tribes in al-Sharqiyya and Uman provinces had begun to shut themselves off entirely from outsiders, and in 1913 a new conservative coalition was formed under the religious leadership of Shaykh Abd Allah ibn Humayd al-Salimi. British policy remained opposed to the idea of conservative rule on the coast, and between 1913 and 1920 Anglo-Indian forces aided the Sultan of Muscat to defend his territory against conservative arms, while the latter consolidated their power in the interior, establishing a new imamate with its capital at Nizwa. The result was the effective partition of Oman into two autonomous regions—the Sultan-controlled coastal strip and the imam-controlled hinterland. Unfortunately, Sa'id ibn Taymur (who became Sultan of Muscat in 1932) was himself as reactionary as his conservative rivals in the interior, and during his reign (which lasted until 1973), Oman followed an official policy of almost total isolation. Very few foreigners were ever permitted to visit the country, there were restrictions on travel abroad by Omanis, and there was a ban on virtually anything Western, from medicine and books to radios, spectacles, cigarettes, music and even trousers.

Following the death of the reigning Ibadi imam in 1954, Sa'id ibn Taymur was able (with the inevitable British help) to capture Nizwa and begin the reunification of the country. Dissatisfaction with his rule led, however, to growing unrest, culminating in a palace coup in 1973 and the accession of his son Qabus to the sultanate. Since then, Oman has witnessed frenzied and probably irreversible change, a process much accelerated by the discovery of major oil deposits in the country in the 1960s and the consequent influx of enormous wealth.

Although its Ibadi allegiance renders it in many ways atypical, Omani experience in the past two centuries illustrates with remarkable clarity several of the main dilemmas facing traditional Muslim states in the modern world. The clash between conservative and moderate wings of the faith, the polarisation of forward-looking secular rule and backward-looking religious traditionalism and, above all, the central role of a Western power in tilting the balance in favour of the former, are all problems that have affected Muslim countries to a greater or lesser degree.

Yemen

A somewhat similar anomaly is presented by Yemen (the Yemen Arab Republic, to be distinguished from the modern People's Democratic Republic of Yemen to the south). In the ninth century, the country came under the control of the Zaydi sect of Shi'ism, whose imams ruled the region from the northern highlands. The theocratic rule of the Zaydis was frequently tempered by foreign domination and more regularly by the presence in the country of a large proportion (60 per cent) of Sunni Muslims belonging to the Shafi'i law-school, who retained autonomy in religious matters but accepted the temporal rule of the Zaydi leaders. Yemen fell naturally into two main areas, with Zaydis predominating in the northern and central highlands and the eastern desert and Shafi'is in the Tihama coastal strip, the foothills and the south.

Although Yemen came under the technical suzerainty of the Ottomans in 1520, the Zaydi imams were left in effective control of the country between 1630 and the 1840s, when an expedition sent to expel Wahhabis from the region reimposed the authority of Istanbul, leaving the imams with a much restricted sway over their traditional centres in the north. In 1904, a new ruler, Yahya ibn Muhammad, succeeded to the imamate. It was his vision to restore the full vigour of theocratic rule, and in 1906 he demanded that the Ottomans reintroduce the Shari'a law-code in place of the secular systems of Turkish and customary law. The final collapse of Ottoman power in the First World War allowed Yahya to take control in 1919, whereupon he embarked upon a campaign to make the authority of the Shari'a absolute throughout the country. He attempted to replace traditional legal experts with religiously-trained jurisprudents, but failed to eradicate customary practice completely. By the 1930s, a compromise was effected whereby the administration of law was divided between judges from both the customary and religious traditions. Yahya also tried to preserve his vision of a medieval-style theocracy by introducing numerous measures designed to isolate Yemen from outside influences, such as a ban on radios, gramophones and similar Western innovations.

Increasing opposition from progressive elements led to Yahya's assassination in 1948, but his son Ahmad rapidly regained control and continued to impose reactionary policies on the country. As a gesture towards lessening the tensions between the Sunni majority and the ruling Zaydi minority, Ahmad appointed Shafi'is to positions in the administration; but neither this nor his willingness to enter into alliances with other Arab states sufficed to detract the political opposition from the widespread repression encouraged by his rule. Ahmad's death in 1962 and the succession of his son Muhammad al-Badr (who attempted to introduce reforms in the face of criticism from the religious leadership) failed to prevent the outbreak of a protracted civil war between royalist and republican forces that lasted until 1970. The establishment of a republic has left the way open for the introduction of modern techniques and commodities, but the long-term effects of this change have yet to be assessed.

The modern Yemeni experience is interesting for several reasons. Although the YAR continues to acknowledge the Shari'a as the source of all law and remains an Islamic state, the link between theocratic rule and political, social and economic repression (or just plain obscurantism) has left its mark. With the advent of modern communications, the conservative Zaydi interior of the country, like the strictly Ibadi hinterland of Oman, is being brought increasingly under central control, with little chance of reversion to traditional patterns. Zaydi fundamentalism is ultimately less of a threat to the republic than the Marxism of the PDRY to the south. Whereas Twelver Shi'ism became a revolutionary force in Iran because of its identification with the oppressed masses, Zaydism is still identified with reactionary rule and is only likely to be able to generate a revolutionary appeal by turning to earlier models of Zaydi political action within a context of extreme social dislocation brought about by modernisation.

The Fertile Crescent

Outside the Arabian Peninsula, isolation (whether natural or self-imposed) is no longer a major determinant of religious or political attitudes. That is not to say that the physical constraints of geography have not had a role to play in the patterning of religious affiliation (as in the mountains of Lebanon and Syria or the marshes of southern Iraq); but the great sweep of fertile lands that loop the peninsula in the north have never been as wholly remote from currents of change as the more secluded sectors of Arabia proper. As a consequence, Islam in these regions has never been quite so home-grown as Nejdi Wahhabism or Omani Ibadism. Along with Egypt, the Palestine/Syria region (including Lebanon) has been closely involved with all the major developments of the modern period, from the spread of the reformist ideas of Muhammad Abduh and Rashid Rida to the rise of the fundamentalism of the Muslim Brothers and related groups or the elaboration of the principles of Arab nationalism and its relationship to Islamic (or, in Lebanon, Christian) identity.

On the whole, religion has been a less significant force in the modern period than politics, although there are visible signs that the balance may be shifting again (or, at least, that religious factors are re-entering the political arena in a significant way). In Syria, for example, none of the constitutions promulgated since independence in 1941 has recognised Islam as the state religion. Inevitably, this has led to a state of confrontation between religious conservatives and the state, a confrontation which has at times exploded in violence, as in the anti-constitution riots of 1973 or the more recent massacres of the Muslim Brothers in Hama and elsewhere. In Lebanon, the enormous potential for internal divisions along religious lines made it imperative from the beginning that the new state be run on a secular rather than confessional basis, providing a formula for national unity that proved remarkably successful until a deterioration in the political consensus and the introduction of external agents of stress led in recent years to a recrudescence of interreligious feuding.

At the same time, the religious balance is an increasingly sensitive and potentially destabilising factor in at least three countries: Lebanon, Syria and Iraq. The rapid growth of the Lebanese Shi'i population in this century means that the Shi'a are now probably the largest religious minority, while their increasing militancy and the fragmentation of the Christian, Sunni and Druze elements in the country combine to make them potentially the most important force in Lebanese politics. Whereas Shi'i fundamentalism in Iran has gone largely unchallenged by the small Sunni minority there, the Lebanese situation offers the long-term prospect of a clash between Shi'i and Sunni extremists.

In Syria, the Alawi (Nusayri) faction exercises a disproportionate influence through its effective control of the ruling Ba'th party and the armed forces. Here again, it is likely that the Sunni–Shi'i division will overflow into armed violence. Although the Alawis have traditionally been regarded with suspicion by mainstream Shi'is and condemned by them as *ghulat* or 'extremists', they were recently accorded official recognition as legitimate Muslims by the Imam Musa al-Sadr, leader of the Lebanese Shi'i community until his disappearance in 1978. The brutal treatment meted out to fundamentalist Sunnis by the Alawi ruling elite in Syria (which includes President Hafiz Asad) is almost certain to lead to further conflict along sectarian lines.

By contrast, the Iraqi Ba'thists are predominantly Sunni (although the reverse was true at the time of the party's inception there), a situation that reflects the traditional imbalance of power in the country, where a Sunni minority rules over a largely rural and impoverished Shi'i majority. It is not only its proximity to Iran that threatens Iraq, but also the presence within its borders of a religious community which, however deprived it may be in economic terms, has developed an articulate political presence in the past two centuries. It was in the Iraqi shrine centres of Najaf and Karbala during the late eighteenth century that Shi'i scholars first developed the theories of clerical supremacy that gave them a growing voice in political affairs, particularly in neighbouring Iran. In the present century, the Shi'i clergy were active in leading opposition to British rule after the First World War. Although this role waned somewhat from the 1930s, after the coup in 1968 the Shi'a of Iraq again turned in large numbers to their religious leaders. A number of Shi'i groups, of which the Dawa party is the most prominent, are active in organising opposition to the present regime.

Conclusion

However much Islam expands into new regions, however much it diversifies through emigration, factionalism and conversion, however much it exchanges old identities for new, it is hard to doubt that the Arab Middle East will remain its symbolic core. Its three holiest cities are there: Mecca, Medina and Jerusalem (al-Quds). The Jewish state in Palestine and the continued occupation of Jerusalem are not so much grievances for the displaced Arab population of that region as profound symbols of an alien presence at the heart of Islam itself. Israel stands for much more than a small enclave carved out of Arab soil, just as European Turkey was once more than the Ottoman outpost. It stands for the West as a whole, for the alienating processes of modern life, for the conflicts brought about by the radicalising innovations of contemporary thought and behaviour. The metaphors used express this vividly: a cancer, a growth, a tumour. For Muslims everywhere, the well-being or sickness of the Middle East has become an index of the vitality or weakness of Islam. If the cancer is the West and all it stands for, it is not yet clear what the cure should be: radical surgery to excise the tumour, chemotherapy to modify it, or homoeopathy, using like to cure like.

For better or worse, modernity has left its stamp on the Middle East. In the process, some of the most isolated and inward-looking corners of Islamdom have been confronted in the course of decades with dilemmas that even societies long innured to the forces of technological and social change have found intractable. Destinies set long ago by sectarian visionaries and serious-minded theologians have been checked or deflected by forces unprescribed-for in religious law or the classical theories of Islamic government. Thus far, responses to change have been remarkably consistent, whether they be those of Wahhabis, Ibadis, Zaydis, or Twelver Shi'is: a rejection of modernity on the part of the conservatives followed by a reluctant bowing to the pressures of life in a world that will not tolerate seclusion. Until recently, the future seemed to lie with the modernists: Islam could and would adapt to Western ideals of freedom, democracy, female emancipation and unremitting progress (even if the Western powers set a poor enough example of such virtues themselves). But now the demands for a return to tradition are being heard with growing insistence on every university campus and in mosque after mosque throughout the Islamic East.

In the past two centuries, Islam has undergone very little rethinking of its doctrinal essentials. The authority of the Qur'an still goes unchallenged, the authenticity of the *hadith* collections is still largely unquestioned, the basic assumptions of the theologians concerning God, revelation, faith or morals remain intact. What challenges there have been have all been to the operation of Islam in society, to the functioning of an integral Islamic polity rather than to the practice of Islam as a faith. Thus, Shari'a law has been threatened by the introduction of secular law-codes, the sense of Islamic community (*jamaa* or *umma*) by the fragmentations of modern nationalism, the continuity of the *sunna* as an embodiment of orthodox practice by wave upon wave of innovation (the very term for which, *bida*, is the nearest Arabic translation of 'heresy') and the traditional emphasis on Islam as a source of proper knowledge by the spread of Western education at all levels. A separation of religion and state wholly alien to Islamic experience has been allowed to develop along lines inspired by the Christian ideal.

As modernisation brings its strains and stresses ever more deeply into the lives of ordinary people, the inevitable reaction is beginning to occur. For fundamentalist Muslims, it seems very easy to pinpoint where things went wrong and to propose an all-purpose solution to the multitude of problems facing modern societies. The Islamisation of all areas of life from government to dress is held out as the universal panacea for all the ills of a society gone astray from the course of its own destiny. In most places, this involves an idealisation of the past, while in others it calls for a radical shift from traditional practice. Nevertheless, there are places like central Arabia, Oman and Yemen where the theocratic ideal has been nearer to realisation than elsewhere. It remains to be seen what impact neo-fundamentalism will have on such societies and what implications any moves in that direction may have on Muslim communities elsewhere. Perhaps the real crisis Islam has yet to face will come if and when the fundamentalists recognise the potential of Western technology as a means of implementing their vision of the perfect society. If that should ever happen, one of the greatest achievements of classical Islam—the delicate balance preserved between the perfectionism of the urban clerics and the more casual practice of the rural hinterland—will have been rendered truly a thing of the past.

Further Reading

There are no really suitable studies of this subject, but the following may prove useful in a limited degree.

Arberry, A.J. (ed.) *Religion in the Middle East*, vol. 2, *Islam* (Cambridge University Press, Cambridge, 1969)

Cantwell Smith, Wilfred *Islam in Modern History* (Princeton University Press, New Jersey, 1957)

Curtis, Michael (ed.) *Religion and Politics in the Middle East* (Boulder, Colorado, 1981)

28 Islam in Tropical Africa to c. 1900

J.O. Hunwick

Introduction

In 1985 there were approximately 130 million Muslims (or roughly one-sixth of the total world Muslim population) living in Africa between the tropics of Cancer and Capricorn. They are mainly concentrated in the Sahelian and Sudanic (or savannah) belts lying to the immediate south of the true Sahara and between the Atlantic and the Red Sea and in the Horn of Africa and along the East African coast down to northern Mozambique. A little over half of this number live in West Africa, with one country alone—Nigeria—accounting for about one-third of the sub-Saharan African total (estimated 43 million). The Nilotic Sudan accounts for a further 14.5 million, or 73 per cent of the total population of the Republic of the Sudan, 13 million or 40 per cent of Ethiopia's population (including Eritrea) is Muslim, while some 18 million live in the Horn and East Africa.

Sub-Saharan Africa's contact with Islam goes back, on its fringes, for some twelve centuries when seafaring merchants from southern Arabia and the Gulf began to trade on the coasts of what are modern Somalia and northern Kenya, and North African merchants first crossed the Sahara to make contact with populations along the banks of the Rivers Senegal and Niger and in the area to the north of Lake Chad. Since then Islam's progress has, even if slow, been steady and though in the twentieth century it has had to face the challenge of Christianity allied with imperialism, it has continued to attract Africans looking for a 'universalist' faith in a world where local and ethnic loyalties have been giving way to outlooks that are increasingly national and international. This brief essay will attempt to chart the dissemination of the faith in tropical Africa and to note some of its more significant historical manifestations in the pre-colonial period. In particular, emphasis will be placed upon the agents of Islamisation, regional traditions of Islamic learning and orthopraxy and the interplay of faith and politics in African kingdoms.

The Nile Valley

Within ten years of the death of the Prophet Muhammad (d. 632 CE/10 AH), the former Byzantine province of Egypt had been incorporated within the expanding Islamic empire. Penetration into Upper Egypt brought the Arab Muslims for the first time into contact with a sub-Saharan African state, the Christian kingdom of Nubia. It was, however, to be another seven centuries before Islam made serious inroads beyond the Second Cataract of the Nile and in the intervening period relations between the Muslim dynasties of Egypt and the Nubian kingdoms were governed by a treaty of non-aggression which was guaranteed by an annual exchange of gifts: 360 (or later 400) slaves from the Nubian side and from the Egyptian side a quantity of cereals and cloth of equivalent value. There were obvious benefits to both sides beyond these gifts. The Nubians were left undisturbed politically and religiously and had, by the terms of the treaty, the right to travel and trade in Egypt. The Egyptians, whose political interests were rather in the area of the Fertile Crescent, could be assured of peace on their southern border and trading opportunities in a land which produced gold and precious stones and was the gateway to a vast hinterland.

The Arabisation and Islamisation of the northern Sudan only gained impetus after the advent of the Mamluk dynasty in Egypt in 1250. A combination of Arab intermarriage with Nubian royal women and military pressure led in 1323 to the fall of Dongola, the capital of the Nubian state of Maqurra and the installation of a Muslim ruling family. Although Christianity survived in Nubia well beyond this date, the way was now open for nomadic Arabs from Upper Egypt and some who crossed the Red Sea from Arabia to establish themselves in the Nile valley and adjacent plains. The western coastlands of the Red Sea were also exposed to Islam from a similar period. The port of Sawakin, close to present-day Port Sudan, came into prominence in the fourteenth century in succession to the more northerly Aydhab. The port and the area were controlled by a Beja group called the Hadariba to which various nomadic Arab groups became assimilated. Perhaps associated with the Hadariba rulers was the enigmatic Abd Allah al-Jamma who carved out for himself a state based on Qarri on the Nile about a hundred miles north of modern Khartoum. Extending his influence southward he conquered Soba near the confluence of the two Niles, capital of the declining Christianised state of Alwa (Alodia). Somewhat farther up the Blue Nile he came into conflict at Arbaji with the rising power of a group of southern Nilotic origin, known to history as the Funj. The defeat of the Abdallab, traditionally placed in 1504, marked the founding of the Funj state with its capital at Sinnar on the Blue Nile.

The first ruler of this state, Amara Dunqas, became a Muslim, perhaps to facilitate trading relations with his Muslim neighbours (especially Egypt), and although many non-Islamic institutions remained vigorous (the office of *Sid al-qom*, official regicide, is a noteworthy example), the Funj rulers did much to foster Islam, encouraging holymen (*fuqara*) to settle in the Gezira by granting them lands and various fiscal immunities and creating a state bureaucracy literate in Arabic. The seventeenth century witnessed an influx of Muslim teachers, jurists and Sufis from Egypt and Arabia as well as the growth of an indigenous class of holymen, trained originally outside the Funj state, but later increasingly at Sudanese centres such as Arbaji. At its height, around 1700, the Funj state extended from the Dongola region in the north to Fazoghli in the south, with a somewhat looser hegemony being exercised over Kordofan and the Nuba mountain kingdom of Taqali. The second half of the eighteenth century, however, saw the decline of the Funj state, symbolised in the establishment of the Hamaj regency in 1760 followed by a period of intrigues and revolts resulting in loss of authority over Kordofan and the disaffection of several of the northern provinces. When the forces of the Ottoman Viceroy of Egypt, Muhammad Ali, invaded the Sudan in 1821 the Funj state was in no condition to offer effective resistance.

The sixty years of Turco-Egyptian rule in the Sudan did little to promote the cause of Islam. Despite the fact that the ruling elite were Muslims and an Islamic judicial superstructure was established, the personal conduct of the Turco-Egyptian officials and the corrupt and exploitative nature of their regime led them to be categorised as 'infidels' by the more learned and devout of the Sudanese. Such was certainly the view of the self-proclaimed Mahdi Muhammad Ahmad who led a jihad (holy war) to dislodge the 'Turks' (1881–5) and who, together with his successor, the Khalifa Abdullahi Ta'ayishi (1885–98), strove to create a genuine Islamic state in the Sudan. Though their political efforts were brought to nought by the Anglo-Egyptian conquest of 1898, the Mahdi's teaching and preaching certainly contributed to a profounder Islamisation of many groups in the Sudan. On the other hand, the Sudanese understanding of Islam has been as much shaped by the activities of the Sufi orders—the Qadiriyya and Shadhiliyya at first and then, in the nineteenth century, the Khatmiyya, Rashidiyya, Dandarawiyya, Tayyibiyya, Tijaniyya and Sammaniyya—with their spiritual hierarchies, special litanies (*awrad*), cult of the thaumaturge (*wali*) and tomb visitation (*ziyara*).

Dar Fur and Wadai

Far to the west of the Nile valley lie the regions of Dar Fur (now in the west of the Republic of the Sudan) and Wadai (now in eastern Chad). Both began to come in contact with Islam around the year 1600. Nomadic Arabs probably reached northern Dar Fur in the late sixteenth century and in the following century holymen from the Nile valley ventured westwards, after the first ruler of the Keira dynasty, Sulayman (*fl.* 1650) accepted Islam. At about the same time the Muslim sultanate of Wadai was founded by a holyman of Nile valley origin, Abd al-Karim, who married into the Tunjur ruling family and then led a revolt against it, establishing a dynasty which endured until the French conquest of 1911. The Keira dynasty of Dar Fur was similarly long-lived, surviving, despite a period of evanescence during the Turkiyya and the Mahdiyya, until the incorporation of the area into the Anglo-Egyptian Sudan in 1916 and the killing of its last sultan Ali Dinar. Islamic influences came to these areas not only from the Nile valley but from West Africa also, since they lay along the pilgrimage route from the Lake Chad region to the Nile valley and Red Sea.

Not only did West Africans sometimes abandon their pilgrimages and settle at various points along the route (including points much farther east), but the route was also a conduit for migrant holymen and scholars. Like the sultans of Sinnar, the rulers of Dar Fur settled immigrant holymen on estates (*hakura*), granting them immunities (*jah*) both physical and fiscal; farther west still, the mais of Borno granted holymen similar privileges (known as *hurma* and enshrined in a *mahram* document) and there are traces of such a system in sixteenth-century Songhay. The object of rulers in settling holymen near their court was to be able to tap their blessedness or 'holiness' (*baraka*), to acquire protection from them through the amulets they could write and so that the prayers or Qur'an readings they could offer on the ruler's behalf would bring upon them God's favour in this world and the next. Encouragement of Muslim holymen should not, however, be taken as a sign of the commitment of these Sudanic rulers to an Islamic political or social order. The courts of Sinnar, Dar Fur, Wadai, Borno and Songhay, while adopting certain Islamic trappings (e.g. an Arabic chancellery, the title *wazir* (chief minister) in some cases, patronage of imams (prayer leaders) or qadis (judges), retained in large measure their older African character, reflected in a high degree of royal autocracy, a complex hierarchy of offices with indigenous titles, traditional taxation systems and, in Borno and Dar Fur at any rate, an influential role for the royal women.

West Africa

While the Nile valley was one obvious, though very late, conduit for the passage of Islam to tropical Africa, the central and western Sahara boasted numerous routes between the lands of the Mediterranean and the lands of the Sahel and some of these were exploited from the late second century of Islam. After conquering Egypt the Arab armies pushed westwards into Cyrenaica and in a second wave in the 660s reached the former Roman province of Africa (roughly the area of modern Tunisia) and founded Qayrawan in 670.

From there further expeditions were launched westwards leading to the pacification of all of North Africa up to the Atlantic Ocean. Then, instead of turning southwards across the inhospitable Saharan wastes, the Arab armies crossed the Straits of Gibraltar (711 CE) and began the conquest of the Iberian peninsula. An important consequence of this was that West Africa was never, in part or whole, involuntarily incorporated into the Islamic imperium or Arabised culturally or linguistically. Islam was introduced instead by the agency of North African traders, both Arab and Berber, who followed older trans-Saharan trails from oasis to oasis and from well to well until they made contact with settled peoples associated with established polities on the Sahelian fringes of the south.

The principal routes used in the period 800–1200 were, from west to east: a route from Sijilmasa via the Dra valley and the Mauritanian Adrar down to Awdaghast (site at modern Tegdaoust) and thence to Ancient Ghana in the south-east (in the area of modern south-east Mauritania) and the kingdom of Takrur (astride the lower Senegal River) in the south-west; a central route from Warghla (where routes from Qayrawan, Tahert and other central and eastern Maghribian centres met) down the Mzab valley, across the barren Tanezrouft, the Adrar-n-Ifoghas and down the Tilemsi valley to Gao on the banks of the Niger; and thirdly, a route from Tripoli through Jabal Nafusa, the Fezzan and the Kawar oasis towards Lake Chad. The effect of this trade on the progress of Islam is clear, if slow. Though the ruler of Ancient Ghana refused to abandon the faith of his fathers, he allowed Muslim merchants to settle close to his town of residence and even to build a mosque within his town. Soninke merchants who traded the gold obtained from beyond the River Senegal were among the earliest West Africans to become Islamised and their descendants, known variously as Wangara, Dyula or Jahanke, carried the faith far and wide in the course of their trading activities and were, within specialised clans of theirs, to nurture a lively tradition of Islamic learning. By the second half of the fifteenth century they were to be found in modern Ivory Coast and Ghana, in Gambia and Guinea, in the cities of the Middle Niger (notably Jenne and Timbuktu) and in Kano and other urban centres in northern Nigeria. A ruler of Takrur embraced Islam shortly before the middle of the eleventh century and the area he ruled (later known as Futa Toro) became a place of settlement for Muslims of surrounding areas. The ancestors of the great nineteenth-century reformer of northern Nigeria, Shaykh Uthman b. Fudi originated from there as did the Sufi scholar and empire-builder al-Hajj Umar b. Sa'id (d. 1864).

Gao's role in the implantation of Islam seems at first less obvious. A ruler of the Za dynasty there became a Muslim probably about the middle of the tenth century and his successors and those of the following Sunni dynasty (*c.* 1275–1493) were at least nominally Muslims. Evidence from tombstones also points to an apparently short-lived dynasty of 'kings' and 'queens' at Gao in the late eleventh and early twelfth centuries and perhaps of Sanhaja (Almoravid) origin, lauding themselves with Islamic epithets including the term *mujahid*—'warrior for the faith'. But, to whatever extent it was practised (and often practice must have been minimal), Islam was essentially a religion of the elite—rulers, courtiers and long-distance traders. Among the Songhay living downstream from Gao, indigenous cults were still flourishing in the mid-twentieth century, while Gao itself was never, even in its heyday under the Askia dynasty (1493–1591), a noted Islamic centre. That honour belonged to Timbuktu, some 250 miles to the west, which grew into a major commercial centre in the second half of the fourteenth century and in the fifteenth attracted to it a coterie of Muslim scholars—Arab, Sanhaja, Dyula and Fulani—who settled themselves around the Sankore mosque and established there a tradition of teaching by no means inferior to that of the great North African centres. Under the Askias the city enjoyed a fair measure of autonomy and its qadis were respected and honoured by most of them. The pattern of aloofness of the scholars from centres of political power is a common one in the Sudanic belt. It perhaps began when Muslims began to trade with non-Muslim rulers, at first at a distance of several days' journey—Awdaghast to Ghana, Tadmakka to Gao, Bilma to Kanem—and later in twin towns two or three hours distant, as in Ancient Ghana and at Sane-Gao. Even when rulers were self-proclaimed Muslims the most scrupulously pious among the scholars put little trust in such professions of faith. Holymen and scholars would thus often cluster in towns apart: Setico on the River Gambia, Diakhaba on the River Bafing and Goundiouro on the River Senegal in Ancient Mali, Timbuktu in Songhay, Kalumfardo in Borno, Jadid al-Sayl in Dar Fur and Arbaji in the Funj kingdom. Sometimes a whole town such as these was 'privileged' and custom forbade the ruler to enter without permission or to send his men there in pursuit of his enemies.

The scholars who, in best Islamic pietist tradition, held themselves aloof from the rulers, castigated those who lived at court or serviced the monarch's spiritual needs as 'venal scholars' (*ulama al-su*). Al-Maghili, a scholar from Tlemcen who, after counselling the rulers of Kano and Katsina, wrote replies to religious questions posed by Askia al-hajj Muhammad of Songhay (1493–1528), had harsh words for the venal scholars and even called for a jihad against them. The tradition of Islamic reform he inspired also proclaimed that soi-disant Muslim rulers who oppressed their subjects, were negligent of Islamic rituals or patronised indigenous cults, were to be branded 'unbelievers' (*kuffar*) and should be overthrown by the nearest true Muslim ruler to them. These doctrines of Islamic revolution were later invoked by Shaykh Uthman b. Fudi in his struggles against the rulers of Hausaland and Borno and by al-Hajj Umar in his justification for jihad against the Bambara rulers. Al-Maghili was also responsible for popularising (if not actually introducing) the concept of the 'regenerator' of religion (*mujaddid*) who would be sent by God at the beginning of every

Islamic century to purify men's faith and practice, a doctrine that was taken up and developed by later West African scholars such as Ahmad Baba of Timbuktu (d. 1627) and al-Mukhtar al-Kunti (d. 1811).

Kanem-Borno and Hausaland

The third great trans-Saharan route which ran from Tripoli through the Fezzan down to the Lake Chad region, was in use from the late eighth century and continued to be important right down to the colonial period. As early as the mid-eleventh century a ruler of the emerging state of Kanem became a Muslim and by the mid-thirteenth century one of its rulers was known to the Andalusian geographer Ibn Sa'id as 'celebrated for his pursuit of the jihad and for acts of religious charity'. He may have been the same ruler who sent an embassy to the Hafsid ruler of Tunis and established a college-hostel (*madrassah*) in Cairo for Kanemi students. By the late fifteenth century the ruler of Borno, an offshoot of Kanem situated to the west of Lake Chad, was using the title *amir al-muminin*, 'Commander of the Faithful', stressing the religious basis for his legitimacy, while the late-sixteenth-century ruler Mai Idris Aloma fought a series of jihad-like campaigns to Islamise or drive out remaining non-Muslim groups in Borno. Study of the Islamic sciences, already established in the thirteenth century, flourished in the sixteenth when we see the first local chronicles appearing, while in the following two centuries Borno scholars established a reputation well beyond the confines of the state. Nevertheless, as in most Sudanic states, political institutions remained indigenous and social customs were only slightly modified by Islamic norms. In the early nineteenth century Muhammad Bello, son of Shaykh Uthman b. Fudi, openly condemned the Bornoans as unbelievers, accusing them of pagan sacrifices, disregard for Islamic female dress norms and gross irregularities in their Islamic legal system. Al-Kanemi, ruler of Borno, despite an elegant rebuttal of the charge of paganism, did not in fact deny that there was some truth behind the accusations.

The above controversy took place within the framework of a jihadist movement which originated in the north-western corner of what is modern Nigeria, inspired by Shaykh Uthman and largely conducted by his brother Abd Allah and his son Muhammad Bello, leading to the establishment of a large Islamic state with its capital at Sokoto (founded 1809). The jihad was principally directed against the rulers of the Hausa states who were accused, in lengthy polemics, of being unbelievers. Islam had, in fact, probably begun to infiltrate Hausaland as early as the thirteenth century from Kanem-Borno, was strengthened in towns such as Kano and Katsina by immigrant Dyula in the fourteenth and fifteenth centuries and in the countryside by influxes of Islamised Fulani from the fifteenth century onwards. In the fifteenth and sixteenth centuries both Kano and Katsina were visited by Muslim scholars of repute from North Africa and Timbuktu and by the seventeenth century Katsina had developed its own teaching and writing traditions. The ruling family in Kano became Muslim from about the mid-fourteenth century, those of Katsina and Zaria in about the mid-fifteenth, Kebbi no later than the early sixteenth, Zamfara and perhaps also Gobir in the mid-seventeenth century.

The jihad raised by Shaykh Uthman against the Hausa rulers highlights the tension which grew over the centuries between traditional West African ruling elites whose ancestors had made a formal profession of Islam and scholarly elites of teachers and preachers whose perception of Islam was a social and political one grounded in the notion of a perfect system of law—the Shari'a—being universally applied in a society governed by the idealised principles of the 'Rightly-guided' caliphs and the institutional theory of the late Abbasid period. The commitment of the rulers to Islam was often no more than formal and ceremonial—appearance in public at Friday and festival prayers and fasting by day and feasting by night during the month of Ramadan. Holymen were often retained at court to recite the Qur'an, to lead prayers, make amulets for the ruler and courtiers and to accompany armies into battle. A few rulers even made the pilgrimage to Mecca. But the point of such pilgrimages, as well as other overt manifestations of piety by rulers, was to reinforce the ruler's authority while preserving the status quo rather than to create a state based on Islamic principles. They were not reformers but eclectic statesmen whose problems were to defend their territory, suppress rebellion, gather taxes and maintain the authority and prestige of their lineages. Little thought was given as to whether their practice accorded with Islamic theories in such matters. This blending of the traditional with the imported Islamic, each being blended in very varying proportions in different times and places, was typical of Sudanic Muslim societies down to the thirteenth Islamic century (1785–1882), not only at the level of the ruling elites, but more broadly throughout these societies. Among the Muslim scholarly elite, however, a tradition of reform, based on the Maliki school of law, had been establishing itself in West Africa from the late fifteenth century. At the political level the scholars had done no more than try to influence the rulers, from near or far, to uphold the Shari'a and observe its teachings. It was only in the thirteenth Islamic century that the scholars themselves initiated action to overthrow existing structures and to take the reins of government into their own hands. By way of illustration we shall look in more detail at the movement of Shaykh Uthman b. Fudi in northern Nigeria, comparing it and contrasting it with that of the Mahdi Muhammad Ahmad in the Nilotic Sudan.

Revival and Reform: W. Africa and the Sudan

In Muslim Africa the thirteenth century of the hijra (1785–1882 CE) might be categorised as a century of revival and reform. There were two underlying factors influencing this trend towards religious regeneration (*tajdid*). In the first place the twelfth century of the hijra (roughly the eighteenth Christian century) had witnessed the growth of wider reformist movements in both Sufi and juristic circles which bore fruit in the thirteenth: the battle against antinomianism and anthropolatry in Sufi circles had given rise to reform in certain orders such as the Naqshbandiyya and the Khalwatiyya, while in juristic circles the dead hand of the *madhhab* (school of jurisprudence) system was being lifted by scholars of the Hadith school of Medina who favoured *ijtihad* (scholastic initiative) in the search for a return to the Sunna of the Prophet. This led in turn, on the one hand, to the growth of new Sufi orders such as the Egyptian Sammaniyya with its Sudanese offshoot the Tayyibiyya and the highly Sunna-oriented orders deriving from Ahmad b. Idris al-Fasi (d. 1836), such as the Mirghaniyya/Khatmiyya and Rashidiyya in the Sudan and the Sanusiyya in Libya; on the other hand, it led to the greater juristic eclecticism of Muhammad b. Abd al-Wahhab in Arabia, Shaykh Uthman b. Fudi in Nigeria and al-Hajj Umar in Guinea and Mali.

The second factor influencing the trend towards religious regeneration in the nineteenth century was the widespread belief in tropical Africa that the thirteenth century of the hijra would witness the appearance of the Mahdi, that final reformer of Islam who would introduce an era of justice and righteousness and the triumph of true Islam leading immediately to the Day of Judgement. Shaykh Uthman was keenly aware that the time of the Mahdi was close at hand and though he denied that he was himself the Mahdi, he saw himself as the harbinger of the final reformer. There were also Mahdist overtones to the movement of al-Hajj Umar and several migrations eastwards to 'meet the Mahdi' originating from northern Nigeria later in the century. Finally, at the very close of the thirteenth century, in 1881, came the 'manifestation' (*zuhur*) of the Sudanese Mahdi Muhammad Ahmad.

There are several points of both comparison and contrast between the movements of Shaykh Uthman and Muhammad Ahmad. In the first place both were rural-based movements claiming a monopoly of religious orthodoxy and orthopraxy, directed primarily against urban-based ruling elites who considered themselves Muslim but were adjudged by the reformers to be so corrupt as to have passed beyond the pale of Islam. In the case of Shaykh Uthman these were the rulers of the Hausa states and in the case of Muhammad Ahmad they were the Turco-Egyptian officials who governed on behalf of the Khedive of Egypt. In both cases they were accused of fiscal oppression, arbitrary justice and loose living. Both reformers took the view that whoever opposed them was also to be classified as an infidel. Shaykh Uthman invoked the Qur'anic principle that the believers are friends one to another and that whoever prefers an unbeliever over a believer is himself an unbeliever; this he then applied to whoever supported or encouraged the Hausa rulers, including the ruler of Borno. Similar arguments were made by al-Hajj Umar against Ahmad b. Shaykh Ahmad Lobbo, ruler of the Islamic state (*diina*) of Hamdullahi, who supported the Bambara of Segu against the reformer. In the case of Muhammad Ahmad belief in his mission as Mahdi was taken to be an article of faith, backed by the consensus of Muslim thinking (*ijma*) about the obligation to support the 'Mahdi of Allah' at the End of Time. Both men used similar techniques to muster their following and to distinguish the 'true' Muslims: declaration of mission, withdrawal (hijra) from the land governed by the infidels and finally struggle (jihad) against them.

The basic difference between the two men lay in the nature of the authority each claimed. Shaykh Uthman's authority was temporal and limited, originally grounded in obedience to him as a shaykh of the Qadiriyya order and respect for him as a scholar of the law (*faqih*) and publicly proclaimed in his designation by his followers as Commander of the Faithful (*amir al-muminin*) and thus supreme ruler of an ever-growing Islamic state after his hijra. As a Sufi he founded no new order but remained a devout Qadiri, while as a jurist he remained a Maliki and a self-confessed traditionalist (*muqallid*), despite a tendency towards eclecticism which led to a degree of anti-madhhabism (opposition to the schools of jurisprudence) late in life. Muhammad Ahmad's authority, on the other hand, was seen as cosmic and permanent until the end of the world. He claimed the absolute allegiance of all Muslims by virtue of his having been sent by God to take charge of the community (umma) of Islam, to reform it and lead it to triumph over all other religions. Though a Sufi of the Tayyibiyya suborder, as Mahdi Muhammad Ahmad had a spiritual authority which abrogated that of the orders, and devotions centred on his prayer manual, the *Ratib*, were to replace usual Sufi litanies. Similarly, in matters of jurisprudence, his authority was unique and *sui generis*. He issued authoritative edicts both through letters and proclamations (*manshurat*) and pronouncements in public gatherings (*majalis*), many of which were subsequently recorded in writing. Though a full study of his *fiqh* (jurisprudence) has yet to be made, available evidence seems to indicate the predominate influence of the Maliki *madhhab*.

Both of these movements led to the creation of Islamic states, but their subsequent histories were very different. Shaykh Uthman's state eventually covered most of north-western and west-central Nigeria as well as Adamawa on the Nigeria–Cameroon borderland and parts of south-western Niger. Centred on Sokoto (and hence sometimes called the Sokoto Caliphate) the Islamic state was administered through provincial emirs descended from original jihadist flag-bearers who were responsible to the *wazir* of Sokoto. Leadership of the state was in the hands of descendants of Shaykh Uthman, beginning with his son Muhammad Bello, and they used the title *amir al-muminin* or the Hausa equivalent *Sarkin Musulmi*. The Sokoto state survived the British conquest of 1902–3 to become the basis for indirect rule. Since Nigerian independence in 1960 it has survived two civilian and several military administrations and the emirs still command authority, if not much direct political power.

In the Sudan the basis of an Islamic state administration had barely been laid when the Mahdi died (June 1885) without having brought about the triumph of Islam or filling the world with 'justice and righteousness'. Undismayed, his closest companion, Abdullahi, succeeded him with the title of *Khalifa* and consolidated his gains, ruling over a state that was a good deal less tightly knit than the Sokoto state until the Anglo–Egyptian conquest (often called the 'reconquest') of 1898. Unsuitable, both for political and administrative reasons, to be used as the basis for indirect rule, the Mahdist state ceased to exist after 1898, though sentiment for the Mahdist cause and devotion to Muhammad Ahmad's descendants survived through a quasi-*tariqa* (brotherhood) organisation known as the *Ansar* and eventually a political party, the Umma party. The Mahdi's great-grandson, the Oxford-educated al-Sadiq, continues to play a major role in Sudanese political life.

The Horn and East Africa

Turning now to the Horn of Africa and East Africa proper, it is clear that these areas had a very different historical experience of contact with Islam from West Africa or the Nile Valley. In the first place these areas received Islamic influences directly from the Arabian Peninsula—from Yemen, the Hadramaut or Oman—and this gave their Islam a strongly Arab stamp, particularly on the coasts of Kenya and Tanzania. In the second place, though Islam spread with a certain degree of evenness among nomadic or semi-nomadic peoples of the Horn (Somali, Afar and parts of the Galla), further south its progress was, until the nineteenth century, limited to the islands (Zanzibar, Comoros, Pemba, Kilwa, Mombasa, Pate, Lamu and so on) and some settlements immediately on the mainland coast. Though Arabs and Persians who came to the East African coast came for trade, they had no contact with the interior, nor, so far as we can tell, did they make any attempt to proseletyse among the coastal Bantu. Instead, they gradually assimilated some of them through slavery, concubinage and marriage, forming a new and distinct Muslim culture out of Arab and Bantu elements. The most obvious sign of the synthesis of the two cultures is the language, Swahili, which gave its name to the culture as a whole and is a highly Arabised Bantu koine spoken from Brava to Kilwa historically and in the twentieth century as a lingua franca over Kenya, Tanzania and parts of eastern Congo. Thirdly, Islam was not associated with large centralised states in East Africa in the way it was in West Africa and the Sudan, nor did the area witness Islamic militancy by and large, the notable exceptions to this rule being the jihad movement of Ahmad Gran (d. 1543) against the Christian kingdoms of

Ethiopia in the early sixteenth century and proto-nationalist jihad of Muhammad Abd Allah Hasan against British encroachment on Somali territory in the first two decades of the twentieth century.

The history of the spread of Islam in the Horn and in East Africa is very imperfectly known. There were trading contacts between south Arabia and the coastlands of the Horn from long before the rise of Islam and these continued on naturally into the Islamic era. The chief trading items were incense and aromatics from the northern coast of the Horn and ivory, slaves, leopard skins and other products from further south. In Islamic times, at any rate, gold was obtained from the Zimbabwe goldfields through the port of Sofala in Mozambique. There was population movement between Arabia and Africa also across the narrow straits of the Bab al-Mandab from very early times and this route and other short sea crossings, such as that from Aden to Zayla, continued as passages for trade and migration in Islamic times. A brisk trade in slaves from the Kenya–Tanzania coast is one indicator of a Muslim presence there from the mid-ninth century. These 'Zanj' were known to early Arab writers such as al-Jahiz (d. 868) and were the principal actors in a massive revolt against Abbasid rule, generally called the Zanj Revolt, in 868–83. By the mid-twelfth century al-Idrisi, the Moroccan geographer, reported that the majority of the inhabitants of Zanzibar were Muslims. Kilwa too, was probably also a Muslim enclave from a similar period and by the early thirteenth century Mogadishu was also. In 1329–30 the great traveller of Tangier, Ibn Battuta, visited the Horn and East Africa and his account leaves us in no doubt that Zayla, Mogadishu, Mombasa and Kilwa were well organised Muslim city-states at the time. While the people of Zayla were Shi'a, those of Mombasa and Kilwa (and, by inference, those of Mogadishu too) were Sunnis belonging to the Shafi'i *madhhab*. The people of Kilwa were said to be zealous in pursuit of the jihad, but this may have been no more than an excuse for slave-raiding; it certainly does not seem to have led to the creation of any sizeable Islamic territory.

The history of Muslim settlement and influence on the East African coast and neighbouring islands is rich and complex and no justice can be done to it in a summary such as this. We must content ourselves here with noting that there are three main cultural influences: the so-called Shirazi culture whose origin can be traced to a variety of groups from the Gulf who gained political ascendancy first on the northern coast between Mogadishu and Lamu in the thirteenth century and in the following century on more southerly Muslim settlements down to Zanzibar and Kilwa. Secondly, an Omani influence which became predominant after the period of Portuguese hegemony (*c.* 1500–1650) and was particularly marked in nineteenth-century Zanzibar under the rule of the Bu Sa'idi sultans. The Omanis were Kharijites of the Ibadi persuasion, but they seem to have had no doctrinal influence on local Muslims; rather, their particularism served to keep them aloof from their Sunni Shafi'i subjects. The third influence was that of the Arab families originating from the Hadramaut, many of whom claimed to be *ashrāf* (descendants of the Prophet Muhammad). The ancestors of some of these clans arrived on the Swahili coast as early as the mid-sixteenth century. Families such as the Ba Alawi, the Al Jamal al-Layl and the Ba Faqih combined in them the hereditary *baraka* (blessedness) inherent in *ashrāf* and the acquired respect due to men of learning. They maintained close links with their brethren in south Arabia and returned there in pursuit of the higher study of the Islamic sciences.

Islam made little progress in the East African interior until the nineteenth century. Prior to this time the Arab merchants of the coast had been content to let the trade of the interior come to them and, unlike the West African Sahel where the Islamisation of rulers of large states encouraged wider adoption of the religion, the immediate hinterland of the East African coast offered no centralised states which might become launching pads for proselytisation further inland. In the first half of the nineteenth century, however, under the energetic rule of the Omani-Zanzibari Sultan Sayyid Sa'id (1806–56), trade routes were opened up into the interior to satisfy the increasing world demand for ivory and the demand of the central Muslim world for slaves in a period of increasing European pressure to suppress the slave-trade. As Arab coastal traders established trading posts in the interior at such places as Tabora, Karagwe and Ujiji and took local wives or concubines, so these places became centres for the dissemination of Islamic influences. Such influences even reached as far west and north as the kingdom of Buganda where the Kabaka Mutesa (1856–84) seems to have made a rather opportunistic profession of the faith. In the middle decade of his reign he virtually established Islam as the state religion, but in 1876 he put to death some two hundred young zealots whose criticisms threatened his authority and thereafter tried to impress incoming European explorers and traders with his interest in Christianity. Islam survived, however, as a minority faith and today almost 10 per cent of the Ganda are Muslims.

Conclusion

What, finally, has been the legacy of Islam in tropical Africa? Firstly, in those societies which were already reaching out to wider horizons, whether through trade, war and conquest, nomadism or other factors, the transcendent monotheism of Islam provided a more appropriate spiritual support system than ethno-specific polyspiritual systems operating within a micro-cosmic environment. Though Islam could not tolerate indigenous ancestor and spirit cults, it could fill the void with parallel forms of its own: the scholarly genealogy (*isnad*), the Sufi ancestry (*silsila*), the cult of the Prophet or the *tariqa* founder, belief in a chief spirit of evil—Iblis—and lesser such spirits (*shaytan, ifrit* etc.) as well as a host of task-oriented spirits (*jinn*) which, as possession spirits, became almost indistinguishable from their African counterparts (e.g. in the *zar* in Ethiopia and the Sudan, the *bori* in Hausaland and the *holey* among the Songhay).

Secondly, Islam claimed, and was widely believed, to have superior methods for harnessing cosmic forces: through the Qur'an itself, the 'Word made Book' which could, in part or whole, be read, written, hung about the person or dwelling, drunk off a slate or wrapped in goatskins as a community talisman; and through the mediator of the Word, the imam, the teacher, the Sufi *shaykh* and, above all, the ubiquitous 'holyman' (variously called *Alfa* (Songhay and Yoruba), *Karamokho* (Manding), *Malam* (Hausa), *Feki* (Sudanese Arabic), *Wadaad* (Somali) etc.) who acted as chaplain, medicine-man, rain-maker, arbitrator, protector, preceptor of boys and supervisor of *rites de passage* in the communities he dwelt among.

Thirdly, Islam introduced many societies to a linear as opposed to a cyclical view of creation. For Islam reincarnation is anathema. Man is born, lives his life in accordance with or in opposition to divine law, dies, is judged and rewarded with paradise or punished with hell. He has no second chance; hence the stress placed upon scrupulous observance of rituals and taboos expressed with a self-discipline which outside observers have often castigated as fanaticism.

Fourthly, the advent of Islam opened up for communities in tropical Africa a macrocosm which took them not merely beyond the confines of village or tribal society, but incorporated them into a vaster pan-Islamic cultural system and into a world economy. In the Sahelian belt from the Atlantic to the Red Sea long-distance trade was in the hands of Muslim merchants and the goods they introduced from the Mediterranean, Europe and the Middle East were themselves vectors of social and economic change, fostering in urban centres forms of pre-industrial capitalism and the growth of elites. The principal goods they exported northwards were the products of exploitation and oppression: gold and slaves. The interchange between tropical Africa and the worlds of the Mediterranean and south-west Asia was not only a material one. The pilgrimage to Mecca took men and women on international travels and exposed them to new cultures, new ideas, new foods, forms of dress, architecture, crops and so on, while the return home established for them a new and higher social status. Men also travelled in search of learning, both within the Sahelian lands and up and down the East African coast and further afield to North Africa, Egypt, Jerusalem, Medina and other cities of Islam. Books travelled even further and it is no surprise to find books written in Baghdad, Cordoba, Bukhara or Nishapur being studied in Mombasa, Arbaji, Timbuktu or Katsina, just as works by Fulani or Sanhaja scholars might be read in Morocco, Egypt or India. The multifaceted exchanges which Islam facilitated in tropical Africa find their permanent reflection in Arabic loan words which have been absorbed by many African languages, the heaviest borrowings being in Swahili, Somali, Hausa, Fulfulde and Manding. The Arabic script was also borrowed (sometimes slightly modified) to write a number of languages spoken by African Muslims during the eighteenth and nineteenth centuries and even today, despite the Europeanisation of education, this art is not altogether lost.

Lastly, Islamisation has tended to foster certain social attitudes, practices and organisational patterns. In the first place, medieval interpretations of Islam (which are still current in many areas) have favoured a patriarchal form of social organisation and stark dichotomies between free and slave, Muslim and non-Muslim. In such a system free Muslim males monopolise political and economic power, women are excluded from the forces of production and generally kept in seclusion, while slaves form a prominent part of the labour force and sometimes of the military. The patriarchal system is reflected in the jurisprudence of medieval Islam which rarely allowed a woman to act in her own behalf, but required her to act through a guardian (*wali*), often classifying her, from the point of view of legal competence, along with slaves, minors and lunatics. Tropical African societies responded in varying ways to the explicit or implicit social norms of the wider Muslim world. In some societies (e.g. Dar Fur, Borno, Hausaland and among the nomadic Tuareg) women had considerable political influence and social freedom; in some societies (e.g. Songhay, the Hausa states, Borno) slaves could attain to administrative office and (as in Songhay) there might be elaborate emancipation systems which over the course of three or four generations integrated slaves into the societies they served in.

But the stronger the influence of self-styled apostles of orthopraxy became, the more likely those societies were to emphasise sharp differentiations of role and status between men and women, sharp social distinctions between free and slave and to stress the 'uncleanness', barbarousness and enslaveability of non-Muslims, this latter process being sanctified through the doctrine of jihad—struggling for the dominance of the faith of Islam. Hence, in the name of Islam (though contrary to its actual teachings) clitorodectomy has been practised almost universally in Muslim tropical Africa as a means of controlling women's sexuality, while in the Sudan and Somalia older and harsher forms of genital mutilation (including infibulation) are evidence of the extremes to which patriarchalism can be taken. Hence too, in the name of Islam (though contrary in most cases to the letter of its law) certain African societies (e.g. in Central Africa, the southern and south-western Sudan, the 'Middle Belt' of West Africa) have been decimated or at least severely disrupted and degraded by the activities of Muslim slave-raiders and traders. Over the centuries (*c.* 800–1900 CE) many millions of men and women in the prime of their lives were uprooted from their own societies and forcibly reimplanted in alien societies either within tropical Africa or in distant societies on the shores of the Mediterranean, in the Fertile Crescent, the Arabian Peninsula or in India. Slavery is, of course, now a thing of the past, but some of its effects still linger in the social stigma attached to slave ancestry in some African societies and the general social inferiority of persons of tropical African origin in Arab-Muslim societies. The status of women in African Muslim societies, however, remains an area of intense debate as the increase of fundamentalist interpretations of Islam tends to reinforce a harsh patriarchalism which women, from their educationally and economically disadvantaged position, are likely to find it increasingly hard to combat.

Further Reading

Clarke, Peter B. *West Africa and Islam* (Edward Arnold, London, 1982)

Hiskett, Mervyn *The Sword of Truth: the Life and Times of Shehu Usuman dan Fodio* (Oxford University Press, New York, 1973)

—— *The Development of Islam in West Africa* (Longman, London, 1984)

Holt, P.M. *The Mahdist State in the Sudan, 1881–1898*, 2nd edn (Clarendon Press, Oxford, 1970)

—— and Daly, M.W. *The History of the Sudan from the Coming of Islam to the Present Day*, 3rd edn (Westview Press, Boulder, Colorado)

Hunwick, John O. *Sharīʿa in Songhay: the Replies of al-Maghīlī to the Questions of Askia al-Ḥājj Muḥammad* (Oxford University Press for the British Academy, London, 1985)

Levtzion, Nehemia *Ancient Ghana and Mali* (Methuen, London, 1973)

Lewis, I.M. (ed.) *Islam in Tropical Africa* (Oxford University Press for the International African Institute, London, 1966)

Martin, B.G. *Muslim Brotherhoods in 19th-Century Africa* (Cambridge University Press, Cambridge, 1976)

O'Fahey, R.S. and Spaulding, J.L. *Kingdoms of the Sudan* (Methuen, London, 1974)

Pouwels, R. *Horn and Crescent: Cultural Change and Traditional Islam on the East African Coast, 800–1900* (Cambridge University Press, Cambridge, 1987)

Saad, Elias N. *Social History of Timbuktu: the Role of Muslim Scholars and Notables, 1400–1900* (Cambridge University Press, Cambridge, 1983)

Trimingham, J.S. *Islam in the Sudan* (Oxford University Press, London, 1949)

—— *Islam in Ethiopia* (Oxford University Press, London, 1952)

—— *Islam in West Africa* (Clarendon Press, Oxford, 1959)

—— *Islam in East Africa* (Clarendon Press, Oxford, 1964)

—— *The Influence of Islam upon Africa,* 2nd edn (Longman, London, 1980)

29 Islam in Tropical Africa in the 20th Century

Peter Clarke

The Colonial Era

By comparison with its previous history in tropical Africa, discussed elsewhere in this volume (see pp. 470–85), Islam has made rapid progress there during the twentieth century. In Eastern Africa, from modern-day northern Kenya to northern Mozambique, it was largely confined to the coastal areas and to Arab and Persian traders and settlers until the closing decades of the nineteenth century. But from then on Islam was to penetrate inland and secure an increasingly larger following among the indigenous peoples, especially in what is today Tanzania. In western Africa also, where for many centuries it had been for the most part the religion of court and commerce and of the inhabitants of the towns, leaving many of the rural areas virtually untouched, Islam was to make great strides during the colonial era (*c.* 1885–*c.* 1960). Areas classified as non-Muslim or 'pagan' at the onset of colonialism, such as the southern region of the Ivory Coast, had a strong and growing Muslim presence by the end of the Second World War. And in Nigeria, towns like Lagos and Ibadan, each of which has several million inhabitants, are now predominantly Muslim, whereas a little over one hundred years ago the Muslim population of both towns when taken together was no more than a few thousand.

Although the pace of its development has varied and the depth and the extent of its expansion has been uneven, there is no country in either eastern or western Africa where Islam has not made significant headway during the last one hundred years. This is also the case in the Nilotic Sudan where, while the north has been largely Muslim for some considerable time, vigorous attempts have been made much more recently, especially by Nimeiri's government before it collapsed in 1985, to promote Islam in the south of the country. There is also evidence of expansion in parts of Central

Africa, for example in Malawi and Zimbabwe, and in South Africa. There are an estimated 360,000 Muslims in South Africa today, the first group having been brought to the Cape from Batavia (Jakarta) in the former Dutch East Indies in the second half of the seventeenth century, some as slaves and others as political exiles who had fought against Dutch imperialism. Then in the late nineteenth and early twentieth centuries there was an influx of Indian Muslims, a majority of them traders, who settled in Durban, Johannesburg and Cape Town. In the past decade or so, an increasing number of Africans has been turning to Islam, though they still constitute only a very small proportion of the total Muslim population.

There is no one, single explanation for this expansion of Islam during the colonial era. In a number of instances where expansion occurred this was facilitated, at certain stages at least, by colonialism. While colonial policy towards Islam was hardly ever consistent there were cases where it directly assisted Muslims, former Italian Somaliland and Eritrea being examples. This did not mean, however, that Italy especially favoured Islam and as a matter of principle as well as policy sought to advance its cause. It was much more a matter of expediency, involving the use of Islam to achieve political objectives in 'Christian' Ethiopia. By way of contrast Italy showed much less inclination to bolster or support Muslims in Cyrenaica and her other North African possessions where Islam was seen as more of a threat to her colonial ambitions.

The policies of the Belgian, British, French, German and Portuguese colonial regimes towards Islam were also shot through in varying degrees with pragmatism. Belgium, however, was perhaps more consistent than the rest for after a rather short-lived, initial alliance with the Arabs in the Congo (Zaire) she went on to display unmitigated hostility towards Muslims. Britain and France, on the other hand, were much more given to twists and turns in their relations with Islam. The former, while supporting the claims of the Muslim establishment in Zanzibar to the East African coast, somewhat paradoxically opposed Islam in Kenya, Uganda and Central Africa.

Short of trained personnel and money in their East African Protectorate as elsewhere, the British, following their positivist as well as pragmatic inclinations, at first considered the possibility of producing a class of administrators from among the Arabs and 'higher Swahilis' who alone, it was believed, possessed any notion or sense of justice, politics or government. However, when Nairobi replaced Mombasa as the seat of the colonial administration in East Africa and with the arrival of Sir Harry Johnson as governor of Uganda in 1899, Islam came to be seen as a potential danger to British interests. It then became government policy to encourage the spread of Christianity, using Uganda as a line of defence against the further penetration of Islam. In former German East Africa government reaction to what were considered to be the potential dangers of Islam came later and only after representations and strong protest from Christian missionaries.

In West Africa Britain's policy varied from one territory to another and even within the same territory. In northern Nigeria, for example, while the British policy of indirect rule, which consisted of administering the Muslim areas through the Muslim chiefs or emirs and the existing Muslim institutions, may in some respects have weakened the authority of these local rulers, it nevertheless did much to protect the Muslim way of life and culture. Christian missionary activity, for instance, was, with one or two exceptions, confined to areas outside the walls of Muslim towns and in general to the so-called 'pagan' areas such as the Jos Plateau in present-day Plateau State. Elsewhere in Nigeria, for example in the west among the Yoruba, Muslims received no such 'protection'.

French official policy towards Islam in the final analysis was equally pragmatic, ranging from outright hostility to accommodation, to support, influenced from the outset by the resistance to French imperialism encountered in, among other places, Algeria and of course in West Africa itself. Numbered among those Muslims who have gained esteem and fame for their resistance to French imperialism are the Senegalese al-Hajj Umar al-Futi (*c.* 1794–1864) and Samori Turé (1830–1901) from Guinea (Conakry). These were two West African counterparts of the Sudan's Muhammad Ahmad, the Mahdi (d. 1885), and Somalia's Muhammad b. Abd Allah (1864–1920/1). Resistance took many forms and it was not only those who resorted to armed struggle that were regarded as hostile by the French. Muslims expressed their opposition in a number of different ways, some of them religious, and most often simply by tacit forms of non-co-operation. There were, of course, those who collaborated and accepted in return certain privileges and benefits.

Moreover, like their British counterparts in northern Nigeria and the Germans in East Africa, French colonial administrators not only believed that Islam as a culture and civilisation was superior in every respect to traditional religion but also, since some Muslims were literate, sought to make use of them at the outset as interpreters, clerks, educators, judges and chiefs, even in non-Muslim areas, and this had the effect of extending Islam's influence in parts of Senegal just as in British-occupied northern Nigeria and former German East Africa. However, over against this, the administration was also to restrict the activities of the marabouts, Muslim clerics, and not only those who may have been charlatans, but even respected members of the Muslim intelligentsia. This happened in Guinea (Conakry) where, because of a supposed threat from Muslim fanaticism, the administration staged a thoroughgoing assault on Islam between 1911 and 1912 in which some leading marabouts were executed while others were imprisoned or exiled. Muslim schools were also closed down. What the French wanted, and this applies to the other colonial powers, was a malleable, pliable Islam that would serve their purposes.

The reason, then, for the progress made by Islam in sub-Saharan Africa during the colonial era is not to be attributed solely or directly to what some Christian missionaries saw as the pro-Islamic policies of colonial regimes. Indirectly, as we have seen, this expansion initially, and in some instances throughout the period of colonialism, did have something to do with the colonial occupation by, among other things, bringing Muslims in former British and German East Africa and in parts of former British and French West Africa into the interior in greater numbers than ever before and placing them in positions of authority and influence. Moreover the development of the road and rail networks, and of the modern sector of the economy, facilitated the expansion of Islam as they did that of Christianity in this period (see pp. 243–56).

Other Explanations of Islam's Expansion

Others, and most notably Robin Horton, have attempted to explain Islam's, and Christianity's expansion in Africa during the period under discussion not in terms of colonial policy but because these religions answered needs that had arisen within Africa's traditional religious system as a result of the increasing modernisation and consequent opening-up of political and economic frontiers that began to occur in the late nineteenth century.

It is difficult to do justice to Horton's complex argument by attempting to summarise it in the small amount of space permitted here; nevertheless, what he seems to be suggesting, albeit somewhat paradoxically, is that to understand Islam's development—we will confine the discussion for the most part to Islam, though much of what is said applies to Christianity also—the principal object of study should be the rituals, ethics and belief system of the local, 'indigenous' religions and/or traditional religions as they are sometimes called and not those of Islam.

These religions, he suggests, have a dual character or two-tier structure, the first or lower tier being that of the lesser spirits and the higher or top tier that of the Supreme Being. In a particular socio-economic and political context (that is in those local, small-scale African societies that are relatively isolated from and have little contact or exchange, political, economic and cutural, with other societies), the people tend to acknowledge and have recourse consistently to the lesser spirits to explain, interpret, control and predict what happens and will happen in their world. By way of contrast, the inhabitants of those societies where the economic, political and cultural frontiers have been greatly widened through extensive trade and in other ways, tend to give far more significance to the role and importance of the Supreme Being in their life. In other words, the more small-scale a society in terms of being highly integrated, largely homogeneous, self-sufficient and self-sustaining and for the most part untouched and untrammelled by outside influences, with a precise, clear and well-defined socio-cultural framework, the greater the dependence of such a society on the lesser spirits. And the converse also holds: as societies open up they look increasingly to the Supreme Being, the higher of the two tiers in their cosmology, to explain, interpret and control their world.

This opening-up and consequent shift from dependence on the lesser gods to the Supreme Being is characteristic, Horton seems to be arguing, of much of Africa from the second half of the nineteenth century, and was stimulated by the development of nation-states, the creation of new road and rail networks and the extension of the modern sector of the economy. These developments in particular prised open the boundaries, cultural, political and economic, of small-scale societies, greatly enlarging in the process their scale of economic, cultural and political interaction with the wider world. The response of people to these changes in the socio-economic organisation of their communities was to turn their attention in a more systematic way to the top tier of their cosmology, the Supreme Being, to explain, predict and control the wider world which they now inhabited. For, according to Horton's theory, while the principal sphere of activity of the lesser spirits is the microcosm or small-scale, enclosed society, that of the Supreme Being is the macrocosm of open, pluralist and structurally more differentiated and complex society.

This understanding of religious change and development suggests that there exists an intricate interdependence between patterns of belief and patterns of social organisation and that shifts of emphasis or changes of belief are more than anything else a response to changes in social organisation. Horton is adopting here what is termed in philosophy and social science circles an intellectualist approach to African belief systems, that sees them primarily as theoretical systems for the purpose of explaining, predicting and controlling space–time events. From this perspective, therefore, he would maintain that as and when significant social changes occur, such as those mentioned above, these belief systems will be adapted to explain the new situation and to enable people to cope with it intellectually, and also psychologically and emotionally. What has all this to do with the development of Islam in Africa during the past one hundred years or so? Well, from Horton's perspective what we have been witnessing during this period is not so much the development of a monotheistic faith in the form of Islam, or as we have already pointed out Christianity, but more the remoulding and reshaping of the traditional belief systems of Africa, which he suggests have considerable adaptive potential, in response to the unprecedented levels of social change consequent upon the 'dramatic improvements in communications and accompanying economic and political developments that overrode the boundaries between the various microcosms'.

Previously insulated from the wider world people were forced by these changes to confront and adjust to it as the stable boundaries of their local societies began to crumble under the impact. But they did not have to turn to Islam or Christianity to provide themselves with a sense of meaning and community in this wider world or for an explanation of the new order or the means to deal with it for they were already in possession of the substance of an explanatory system in that the traditional cosmology was grounded in the notion, albeit largely unelaborated, of a Supreme Being as moral guardian and underpinner of this wider world. And it was to the development and application of this notion that they turned in the new situation. From being at the periphery of their lives in the local, insulated community situation, the Supreme Being is now brought to the centre of the stage, as it were, being moved from a position of moral neutrality to one of moral concern, while rituals previously few and far between are devised for the purpose both of approaching and securing his guidance and assistance. Meanwhile the lesser spirits recede into the background, being largely irrelevant in the new order.

For its part Islam, and in a somewhat different way from Christianity, while it cannot claim to have initiated this shift in emphasis in the traditional cosmology, turning people away from their concern with the lesser spirits to a more active belief in and worship of the Supreme Being, and thereby advancing its cause in Africa, did, nevertheless, contribute something to the process. For, as we have seen, this shift, as Horton explains it, was due to a great extent to the economic and political developments which broke down the boundaries that had kept local communities isolated from each other and dependent on the lesser spirits. Therefore what Islam and Christianity did in their different ways was to act not as innovators, bringing to Africa a new concept of God, but as 'catalysts' or 'triggers' for changes that were 'in the air anyway'.

According to this version of events, then, what has taken place is not so much an advance of Islam as something distinctive and new but a development in traditional African belief systems and/or cosmologies. If Islam has spread rapidly in Africa in recent times, and it has, the explanation for this (and the same applies to Christianity) is not to be found in its own message and missionary endeavours, but in the revolution in communications linked with the above-mentioned economic, educational, social and political innovations. These created the conditions in which it became far more meaningful for people to become in practice more thoroughgoing monotheists in the sense of explaining and acting out their lives in what was a different and expanding world by reference and recourse to the Supreme Being rather than to the lesser spirits. In pushing the belief in and worship of the Supreme Being to the fore in the traditional African cosmology in the sense of giving it greater intellectual, emotional, psychological and practical relevance, these changes facilitated the acceptance of some of the beliefs and practices of the two world religions and in particular those which coincided with the responses of that cosmology to the new or modern situation.

In modern times, then, Islam's progress in Africa can be accounted for by the fact that as a monotheistic religion, centred on a belief in the oneness and uniqueness of God, yet tolerant of mixing and syncretism and concerned with the explanation, prediction and control of space–time events, it has responded to the rapid changes that have opened up local African communities in a way that is largely compatible with the developments within the traditional African cosmology. In other words, becoming a Muslim has not involved a radical shift in perspective, or, to put it another way, the rejection of essential elements within or the underlying purpose of the traditional cosmology as it began to develop in response to profound socio-economic and political change.

This is not to suggest the existence of complete harmony and compatibility between the two belief systems in theory or even in practice but rather of a number of important and significant equivalences which made it possible for Islam to expand by accommodating itself or by being accommodated to an African society experiencing great change which affected the way people related to and interpreted the role of the Supreme Being.

This is an interesting and thought-provoking explanation of religious change in late nineteenth- and twentieth-century Africa and should, therefore, be taken for what it is intended to be, that is a very general theory based as much on 'an imaginary situation', to use Horton's own words, as on hard fact. The situation is an imaginary one in the sense that one cannot assess the actual developments in the African traditional cosmology resulting from its encounter with the modern, as Horton attempts to do, while at the same time leaving Islam and Christianity to one side, for in their different ways they were also an integral part of the genesis of that modernity, contributing not only religious ideas and practices but also as the pioneers of some of its basic economic, social, educational, political and more generally cultural ingredients.

However, Horton's theory has not only challenged but has also been challenged by a number of historical, philosophical, theological and other interpretations of religious development in general and of Islam and Christianity in particular in the African setting. Some critics have argued that, among other things, it is all very circular setting out to prove what has already been decided is the case, or that it presents a monocausal and highly reductionist explanation of religious development. It is also, in this writer's opinion, a very passive, mechanistic view of conversion, presenting the convert as someone who merely adapts her/his religious beliefs in response to social change without ever actively pursuing, in a positive, creative sense a different or alternative understanding and explanation of reality.

Moreover, is it the case that the Supreme Being assumed the active, interventionist role in people's lives as a result of the opening-up of African society in the way Horton suggests and almost exclusively in that context? The evidence for this, as Fisher in particular has shown in his detailed set of replies to Horton, indicates otherwise. Fisher points out, among other things, that following Horton, there are examples of African societies where one would expect to find the Supreme Being at the centre of a people's worship yet one does not and where one does not expect to find this, it happens to be the case. So Fisher would maintain that Islam, and Christianity, were far more dynamic and innovative than Horton's theory suggests, and that their progress has to be explained with this in mind.

Furthermore, in linking religious change so closely to change in social structure Horton seems to pay too much attention on the one hand to the idea of a causal relationship between the social order and the conceptual order and too little to the actual findings of scholars such as Evans-Pritchard who, in for example his study of the Nuer, convincingly argues that the evidence is against this kind of positivist interpretation of religious development.

Other explanations of Islam's progress in Africa include what we might call the 'market value' theory of Islamic expansion along the lines of Weber's Protestant ethic thesis. The ethic of Islam, it is claimed, is a commerce-oriented one (see Qur'an Sura 198), and the alliance of market and mosque has facilitated this religion's phenomenal advance in Africa especially in more recent times. This, however, does not explain why some communities unassociated with trade converted to Islam and why others that were did not.

Then there are those who, starting from a different perspective and premiss from Horton, maintain that Islam's development is attributable in the main to the fact that it is, more so than Christianity, an 'African religion'. Certainly it must have appeared to many but by no means all to have been less bound up with colonialism than Christianity and to have fitted in better with, among other things, African family patterns. But these were not the only criteria or measuring-rods used by Africans to determine the relative merits and demerits of these two world religions. Moreover, Islam is proving no less attractive today in areas where polygyny has become a rarity and Christianity has been thoroughly indigenised. It seems worthwhile considering here in a little more detail, in the light of this view of Islam as an African religion, the interaction between these two religions.

Islam and African Traditional Religion

Although, as we have seen, Horton's theory of the development of Islam, and Christianity, in Africa is at a level of generalisation that admits of many pieces of contrary evidence, it has the advantage of directing attention at traditional, local religious systems, pointing to their capacity to adapt and to their inherent dynamism. Challenged by the forces of industrialisation, urbanisation, Western education and by both Islam and Christianity, traditional religion can be said not only to have held its own in certain respects but also to have influenced the shape and form that these two world religions have taken in the African setting.

Islam has often confronted the traditional religions of Africa both at the level of belief and practice, yet the relevance and immediacy of such things as masked cults and the figurative art of shrines did not always diminish under the impact of Muslim practice. Furthermore some Muslim communities have shown great tolerance towards indigenous representational art, and in some instances have even contributed to its maintenance and development. In Bonduku in the Ivory Coast, for example, Muslims have not only participated in the Gbain cult, an anti-witchcraft masking tradition, but have also assumed positions of responsibility and control over this cult. There are other masking traditions in this area which are believed to be Muslim in origin, such as the Do masquerade, where the masks have been carved by Muslims themselves, the injunctions of the Qur'an and 'sound' *hadiths* (traditions) against imagery and representational art forms in general notwithstanding.

Just as some Muslims have been prepared to maintain and develop aspects of African religious art and rituals, traditional religionists, for their part, have provided a ready home to Islamic imagery and custom, one of the most interesting examples being the place given in masquerades and spectacles to the image of al-Buraq, the winged steed which is said to have carried Muhammad on his night journey (*Isra*) from Mecca to Jerusalem and then on his nocturnal ascent (*Miraj*) to the dome of the seven heavens.

While Islam and African traditional religion have, then, made something of each other in the sphere of art and in other areas such as divination, the former has also sought to eradicate many traditional beliefs and rituals, to make a clean break with the past, and on occasion this has been one motive, though by no means the only one, for the jihads (holy wars) of the nineteenth century referred to elsewhere in this volume (see pp. 470–85).

But what perhaps is most noticeable in many parts of Africa where Islam has established itself is the blend or synthesis that has taken place over time, born out of its interaction with African society and culture. This can be seen not only among the Muslim Yoruba of south-western Nigeria but possibly even more clearly in the Swahili world of eastern Africa. There the language is an intermixture of Arab and Bantu elements, and the literature, which dates back at least to the seventeenth century, is written in a modified Arabic script and includes at the same time much that is Islamic by way of theology, history and hagiography and Bantu by way of proverbs expressing the world-view and wisdom of the African. The end result is not, as one might imagine, a Swahili culture that is but a pale reflection of Islamic civilisation but a distinctive culture with its own identity.

The Sufi Brotherhoods and the Muslim 'Cleric'

Returning to the theme of Islam's progress in sub-Saharan Africa during the colonial era, it seems to this writer that improved communications, the expansion of the economy and the creation of new towns facilitated that progress. So also did the reliance on and protection afforded Islam in certain instances by colonial governments, arising from the fact that there existed in some areas an established Muslim state with a ready pool of literate Muslims, many of whom were trained in the Muslim way as clerks, administrators and teachers and were, therefore, useful to the colonial regime. But this last point is in need of qualification for, as we have seen, colonial governments also placed obstacles in the way of Islam's development.

Equally, if not more important in the spread of Islam in this period and since, were the Sufi brotherhoods, notably the Qadariyya and Tijaniyya in West Africa as a whole from the first half of the nineteenth century, while others, emerging in the twentieth century, were to gain large numbers of followers in particular countries, the Mouride brotherhood in Senegal being a case in point.

The role of the Muslim 'cleric', often a trader as well, was also crucial as was that of the charismatic leader such as the Senegalese Shaykh Ibrahim Niass, who perhaps did more than anyone else in the twentieth century to popularise the teachings of the above-mentioned Tijaniyya brotherhood throughout West Africa, and through his international links to connect his followers with Muslims in the rest of the world. The Muslim cleric was the principal carrier of Islam. Known by different names in different societies, for example malam in Hausa-speaking areas and marabout in parts of French-speaking Africa, he wandered from village to village and town to town, living with the people wherever he went and often came to play the role of teacher, philosopher and guide of the local community. His Christian counterpart would be the catechist whose role in spreading Christianity has been discussed elsewhere in this volume.

By the time the colonial era began to draw to a close in much of sub-Saharan Africa in the late 1950s, Islam had penetrated and established itself in areas which it had previously hardly even touched, the Tabora district of Tanzania and the southern region of the Ivory Coast being but two of many examples. By the 1950s an estimated 34 per cent of the total population of West Africa was Muslim, and all of this was accomplished without the aid of a Western school system, which Muslims for a variety of reasons opposed, chiefly because they saw it as an instrument of Christian evangelisation, and Western hospitals. Muslims, of course, did have their own schools, their trading networks and their physicians which many people found relevant and appropriate to their needs.

Islam in Tropical Africa since Independence

Already by independence Muslims in parts of Africa had become better organised and more integrated as a community and had begun once again to strengthen their links with the rest of the Muslim world, and these trends continue to be among the most striking aspects of Islam's development in tropical Africa in the post-colonial period. However, though numerous national, regional and interregional organisations have been set up, as far as integration and organisation are concerned the pace has been uneven and the results patchy, from one region of the continent to another.

Links with the wider Muslim world have been strengthened by the increase in the number of African Muslims performing the hadj (pilgrimage)—over 100,000 Nigerians left for Mecca in 1977, making them after the Indonesians the largest group of pilgrims in that year—and through such organisations as the Islamic Conference Organization, the Arab League and the Organization of African Unity.

It is, however, difficult to see in what way these contacts have influenced the foreign policies of African states, nor is it clear to what extent if any Islamic resurgence in recent years in Iran and elsewhere in the Muslim world has affected the life and attitudes of the majority of ordinary Muslims in tropical Africa. On the other hand, educated Muslims, and less convincingly some heads of government, Nimeiri in the Sudan before he was forced to resign being an example, have tried to extend the scope of Islamic law, Shari'a, and turn their societies into thoroughgoing Islamic states. Somewhat less marked, gradual changes are also occurring in other spheres, including the political sphere. For example, in South Africa there are signs that the Muslim community is becoming more politically conscious and prepared to join in the struggle against apartheid. Elsewhere Islam presents itself as embodying a form of socialism which is not only in keeping with the allegedly classless character of pre-colonial African society but also provides a genuine, relevant and up-to-date alternative to the Western, capitalist world and what is referred to as 'other godless socialisms' found in the Sovier Union and elsewhere.

The move towards greater unity amongst themselves and with the wider Muslim world and the drive to present Islam as the most relevant political, social, economic and cultural option available to Africans—which, of course, could end by making it simply one more option among many to be rejected like others if it fails—these are some of the main trends in contemporary Islam in tropical Africa. Muslims, however, are far from constituting a community characterised by rigid uniformity. As in the past there are also today a variety of strands to Islam south of the Sahara and a variety of responses to the wider world.

While, therefore, significant changes are taking place in African Islam, which is on the whole more confident of itself and of its rights and relevance, as was seen in the Shari'a debate in Nigeria in 1977–8, there is also much that remains more or less unchanged since the colonial period. And this last point is as true of the ways in which this religion advances as it is of the reasons why it continues to appeal and attract converts in ever-increasing numbers.

Further Reading

See also J.O. Hunwick's Further Reading list in his contribution to this volume, 'Islam in Tropical Africa to c. 1900', pp. 470–85.

Bravmann, R.A. *Islam and Tribal Art in Africa* (Cambridge University Press, Cambridge, 1980), paperback edn

Clarke, P.B. *West Africa and Islam* (Edward Arnold, London, 1982)

—— and Linden, I. *Islam in Modern Nigeria. A Study of a Muslim Community in a Post-Independence State* (Grünewald, Mainz, and Kaiser, Munich, 1984)

Cruise-O'Brien, D.B. 'Islam and Power in Black Africa' in A.S. Cudsi and A.E. Hillal Dessouki (eds.), *Islam and Power* (Croom Helm, London, 1981), pp. 158–69

Fisher, H.J., 'Conversion Reconsidered . . .', in *Africa*, vol. XLIII, no. 1 (Jan. 1973). Fisher has also replied to Horton's thesis in other later editions of this journal

Horton, R. 'African Conversion', in *Africa*, vol. XLI, no. 2 (April 1971) and vols. 4 and 5, nos. 3 and 4 (1975)

30 Islam in Contemporary Europe

Peter Clarke

Introduction

The arrival of several million Muslims in Western Europe during the past twenty-five years has introduced into the region, in so far as the history of religion at least is concerned, something radically new. Not so long ago in many Western European countries Islam was little more than an exotic appendage to the everyday religious, cultural, political and social way of life of the wider society in Western Europe. For many, learning about Islam was above all else a matter of erudition, something that could be carried on quite adequately from a distance, for it was a religion that existed and was practised by people 'out there', beyond the boundaries of Western Europe, so to speak. Now, however, it is becoming increasingly evident that it has to be understood from within, for it is central to an understanding of the religious, cultural and social life of over 2 per cent of the population of Western Europe, and as such has important implications of a legal, educational, political, ideological and religious kind for the rest of Western European society. Already, as we shall see, Islam is performing a similar role in determining the future of the various Muslim ethnic minorities in Western Europe to that played by religion among the various Christian and Jewish immigrants to the United States in the last century. In what follows we consider the numerical growth of Islam in Western Europe, the profound changes in the social composition of the Muslim community there, and in addition provide a brief survey of the fortunes of Islam in Eastern Europe and the Soviet Union during the past twenty-five years, focusing on this religion's persistence in these parts, despite the combined onslaught of Slav nationalism, and Marxism–Leninism which has sought to eradicate all traces of it. There will be only passing reference to Islam in Turkey since that is considered elsewhere in this volume (see pp. 390–407).

Attention is also given to the various ways in which religion functions as a framework for personal and social identity in different political and cultural contexts. And we consider how believers, in this case Muslims, when confronted with a different culture and way of life attempt either to preserve their beliefs and practices in what they see as their original and/or orthodox form or to adapt them to this new socio-cultural milieu. The changing response to Islam is also considered, as is that of the appeal of Islam in the West, for there is a small but increasing number of Western European-born converts to the Muslim faith.

Western Europe

As we have already indicated, the growth of Islam in Western Europe in the past twenty-five years has been striking. Although there are no reliable statistics available it is generally agreed among researchers in this field that France, West Germany and Great Britain, in that order, have the largest Muslim populations in contemporary Western Europe. In each case, and the same applies in other Western European countries such as Belgium and Holland, this unprecedented growth of the Muslim community in what are traditionally non-Muslim areas can be attributed in large measure to the influx of migrant Muslim workers during the 1960s, for the most part single men who were later to be joined by their families.

France

While in France estimates of the size of the Muslim population vary from two to five million, the figure most often quoted is about two and a half million. The majority of these Muslims originate from France's former North African colonies with over three-quarters of a million from Algeria, almost half a million from Morocco, and some two hundred thousand from Tunisia.

North African immigration began with the arrival of Algerians in France in the 1870s following the French suppression of the rebellion in the Kabylie Mountains in 1873. Between then and 1905 most of the immigrants settled in Marseilles, working mainly as domestics or petty traders. The first two decades of the present century and in particular the years 1916–19 saw the emergence of what is termed 'industrial immigration' as increasing numbers of Algerians, mainly Kabyles, were recruited to work in the factories in Marseilles and Paris and in the mines in Lens and elsewhere in the north of the country. This was followed during the interwar years and the Second World War by a marked decline in the number of immigrants from Algeria, and from Morocco and Tunisia, while at the same time some of the earlier immigrants were now returning home. Reconstruction after the Second World War saw the arrival in France of a new wave of North Africans, a majority of them once again Algerians and, although there was a fall off during the Algerian war of independence (1957–62), this trend continued until the mid-1970s when the number of second generation Algerians born in France began to outstrip new arrivals. The period 1960–75 also saw a very significant increase in Moroccan and Tunisian immigration.

There are also in France over 120,000 Muslims from Turkey, some 70,000 from tropical or Black Africa (the majority coming from former French West Africa, in particular Senegal), an estimated 16,000 from Yugoslavia and a few thousand from Pakistan.

From a demographic point of view the Muslim population in France, and the same can be said of West Germany, Great Britain, Belgium and Holland, has undergone considerable change in recent times. This has been due in the main to the increase in the proportion of Muslim women relative to the total Muslim population as a whole since the late 1960s, and in those of both sexes under the ages of twenty-five and fifteen respectively. As to the rise in the number of Muslim women in France in the past twenty years or so, this has been of the order of 150 per cent in the case of Moroccans, almost 70 per cent among Tunisians and around 55 per cent in the case of the Algerians. One of the more important consequences of this is the greater stability that it has given to the Muslim community in France and those other countries in Western Europe just mentioned.

Moreover, alongside this increase, there has been, as we have already said, a significant rise in the number of Muslims under the ages of twenty-five and fifteen respectively. Close on 50 per cent of the Algerian, Moroccan and Tunisian Muslims in France are under twenty-five and two-thirds of the under twenty-fives are fifteen years of age or under. Both of these developments have led to a change in the direction and orientation of the Muslim community in France and, as we shall see, in a number of other countries in Western Europe. For example, a growing number of Muslims in France while retaining their religious and cultural links with North Africa are, nevertheless, very involved in the task of creating and developing a French Muslim community, an exercise which demands not only that they reconsider what constitutes the essentials of Islam but also the most effective ways of achieving this goal.

In France Muslims have been pressing for changes in certain existing educational, legal and political arrangements and practices to enable them to live and practise their religion in a largely secular, non-Muslim context. On the political front, as an example, for many see progress here as the key to progress in other areas such as law and education, Muslims in France have joined other immigrants in the campaign in recent times for local voting rights. This is something that has been permitted for some time in the United Kingdom to citizens of member states of the Commonwealth and the Irish Republic. Moreover, Sweden, followed by Denmark, granted immigrants both the right to vote in local elections and to be elected, in the early 1970s.

However, at the time of writing, this right still does not exist either in France or West Germany, although it should be noted that in the case of the former there are some Muslims of North African origin who have French citizenship and, therefore, enjoy all voting rights. A majority of these French Muslims, as they are called, are from the middle or lower middle classes, college educated, and number about eight thousand in Paris. By way of contrast, the vast majority of the rest of the Muslim population is employed in construction work, or in Renault car or Michelin tyre factories, or as lorry drivers, while others have been 'successful' in that they have moved on from such employment to become owners of small grocery shops and the like.

From the point of view of many of the older generation of Muslims in France one of the most serious problems lies in the education of the young, many of whom are illiterate in Arabic. However, some of the latter, despite their parents' insistence that they learn at least sufficient Arabic to understand the Qur'an, do not accept this, maintaining that there is no need of a specialised language to read and recite the Qur'an and even point out that they understand it better in French. Nevertheless, more parents are demanding a complete Muslim education for their children, a majority of whom according to recent surveys and reports are having little success in the state education system.

One of the strongest arguments used by the parents in support of a much more rounded and thoroughgoing Muslim education which would include the culture, customs, language and traditions of their own country of origin—Algeria or Morocco or Tunisia, for example—is that the evidence shows that where the young are trained and educated in the 'traditional' or Muslim way and have a grounding in their mother tongue they are far less likely to become delinquents.

The younger Muslims of school age, however, remain by and large unimpressed by the case advanced by their parents for a thoroughgoing Muslim education. Moreover, unlike many of the older generation of Muslims in France, very few of these younger Muslims have a desire to return 'home', that is to go back not only to what is still considered to be their country of origin but the one to which ultimately they are supposed to owe their allegiance. The main problem, however, for those of this mind is that they believe that they are far from being fully accepted by the wider French society and therefore fall, as it were, between two cultures. As a consequence some, a minority, have turned to a more fundamentalist version of Islam as a framework for establishing and protecting their identity.

Estimates of the number of converts to Islam among the French themselves, and among other non-Muslim immigrant groups in France in recent times, vary from several thousand to as many as one hundred thousand, women converts being the most numerous. The reasons given for conversion range from disenchantment with Western materialism to the desire for firm guidance and direction in terms of one's function and role in the family and in life generally. Islam's teaching on the place of women in the family and society is said to attract many women converts, especially among the non-Muslim immigrant population.

Although the pace is slow, what is perhaps most interesting in the case of Islam in France, and this is also noticeable in Britain and elsewhere in Western Europe, is the process of increasing secularisation of the younger generation of Muslims on the one hand, which however is partly offset by the 'reconversions' made by an active, missionary Muslim movement that sees its religion less and less in terms of North African Islam or an Islam incarnated in any particular culture or tradition. This is an attempt to create a Muslim community with which second and third generation Muslims can identify.

West Germany

Although there has been a small Muslim presence in the Federal Republic of Germany or West Germany for close on three hundred years, the modern history of Islam in that country only began to take shape in the 1960s with the influx of large numbers of Turkish 'guest workers'. Today the Muslim community in West Germany is estimated to be just under two million, making it after the Lutheran and Catholic churches the third largest religious body in the country and, as we have already seen, the second largest Muslim grouping in Western Europe. It is composed in the main of the Turkish guest workers just mentioned, many of whom have been joined by their families and who to all intents and purposes are immigrants with little prospect or intention of returning home. The next largest group after the Turkish Muslims are those from Yugoslavia, who number around 100,000, followed by an estimated 45,000 North African Muslims, mainly from Morocco and Tunisia. Others include Shi'ites from Iran, about 20,000, perhaps 10,000 Sunnis or orthodox Muslims from Jordan, some 5,000 Muslim refugees from the Soviet Union, and between 1,000 and 2,000 German-born converts to Islam.

Numerically, therefore, Islam in West Germany is predominantly of the Turkish Sunni (orthodox) kind. But it is worth noting that although Shi'ite groups, for the most part Iranian, are much smaller, the relatively high proportion of their members who are either academics or in business enables them to exert a much greater influence than their numbers would otherwise allow.

The Muslim population is concentrated mainly in the North Rhine-Westphalia and Baden-Württemberg regions, and in Berlin, which with a Turkish community of around 100,000, has the largest Turkish population of any city outside Turkey. Cologne is another city with a large Turkish population of around 60,000 and one in which many Muslim organisations, associations and fraternities have their headquarters.

It would be misleading, however, to give the impression that the Muslims in West Germany form a highly organised and tightly integrated community. There can exist considerable difference of opinion between the various Muslim organisations over, for example, matters of policy regarding such issues as the means to be used to achieve official recognition from the State which has not as yet recognised Islam as a statutory organisation with specific civil rights. Moreover, it would seem that a majority of Muslims are no more than nominal members of one or other Muslim association or fraternity. These loosely knit bodies are usually attached to one or other of the seven hundred mosques, many of which are no more than makeshift arrangements in the form of a room set aside in the home.

Nevertheless, they help to provide Muslims in West Germany with an element of community and cohesion at the local or city level, and through their links, albeit at times very tenuous, with federal and international Muslim organisations, at the national level and in the wider world of Islam respectively.

Several international Muslim organisations and brotherhoods have representatives in West German cities, and included among these are the Muslim World League, the Muslim Brotherhood and the Naqshbandiya Brotherhood which is also found in Britain and France. Further, several Muslim institutions have close links with the Turkish government's Department of Religious Affairs and have been concerned as much, if not even more so, with Turkish affairs than with the interests of Muslims in Germany. And this no doubt helps to perpetuate in the minds of the German people the image of Islam as a 'religion of foreigners'. Moreover, nothing has been done to dispel this image of Islam by Turkish governments which through such organisations as the Directorate for Religious Affairs Abroad, established in 1972, took responsibility for, as it was stated, 'our countrymen abroad', and especially for maintaining solidarity and unity among them, their links with the ideals of the Turkish nation and for the provision of religious instruction. On the other hand, there are Turkish movements in West Germany, for example those groups that together form the Organization of National Vision, that oppose not only their government's claim to have responsibility for the education and religious instruction of Muslims but also the existence of a secular state in Turkey. As far as many West Germans are concerned, therefore, the country has become something of a battleground between the Kemalists, that is those Turkish Muslims who support the principle of the secular state established by Kemal Atatürk (see 'The Turks and Islam', pp. 390–407) and the integralists, those who seek to revive the Islamic state in Turkey. All of this, then, only seems to confirm the suspicion people have that the Islam in their midst has more to do with Turkish politics than religion.

This, however, is not an accurate description of the actual situation, for there are a number of Muslim organisations that stress that Islam in the Federal Republic is not a passing, foreign phenomenon and concentrate much of their time and energies on missionary work with the aim of turning their fellow believers into active, conscious Muslims for the purpose of creating an authentic Muslim community in the West German setting. These groups are preoccupied above all else with obtaining statutory recognition for Islam in West Germany and with the question of Muslim education, both of which have given rise to considerable public debate and even argument, especially in recent times and not least among Muslims themselves.

An estimated one in ten pupils in West Germany's schools today are Muslim and mainly Turkish, and by law they are entitled to Islamic religious education. But, as we have already pointed out, there is no agreement among Muslims themselves as to how this should be provided. The state authorities, for their part, have resorted to a number of different solutions, some opting to take responsibility for the development of a Muslim curriculum together with the related teacher training for those interested, Muslim or otherwise, while other authorities have decided to provide Islamic religious instruction, taught by Turkish teachers following a Turkish curriculum, for classes of bilingual Turks. Although not to every Muslim's satisfaction, the first of these developments, along with such changes as the virtual ending of 'homeland' burials, is slowly providing Turkish Islam in the Federal Republic with a more recognisably local character.

The problem of integration, however, remains acute and is generally attributed to the refusal of Muslims to accept the fact that they are part of a modern, pluralistic society. Muslim parents—they are not alone in this—are seen to oppose on religious grounds many practices such as coeducation, the use of contraceptives before marriage and marriages with non-Muslims, all of which the majority allegedly regards as a matter of personal choice.

Moreover, as in France, the second generation of bilingual Muslims, many of whom were born in West Germany, experience a most acute emotional and psychological problem posed by partial integration. In what since the 1970s has become a special branch of German literature, the thoughts and feelings of these Muslims on this question, expressed in German and in their own words, have been published. What is quite clear from these accounts is that many of these second generation Muslims have, in varying degrees of seriousness, an identity crisis. Some speak of having their feet on two planets, others of planning their return 'home' when they wake up in the morning only to have become more accustomed to Germany by noon, while others write of travelling every day for thousands of kilometres 'there and back' in their imaginary train, of 'living between wardrobe and suitcase'. One writes:

I carry two worlds in me,
but neither is a whole,
they both are bleeding unceasingly
Their front line goes through my tongue
I keep picking at it like a prisoner
playing on a wound.

Born and educated in Germany, these young Muslims are often not accepted by the wider society where in recent times there has been something of a backlash against foreign workers and where financial inducements have been offered to those who are prepared to leave. On the other hand they are told by their parents that they were 'not meant for that country (Germany)', that it 'was not made for them', that their real world is at 'home'—Turkey or some other Muslim land. It is little wonder, therefore, that second generation Muslims frequently ask the question, 'Who am I and where do I belong?'. Again, as in France, some resolve the issue by turning to Islamic fundamentalism for a framework and a reference point for their identity.

It would be misleading, however, to convey the impression that all second generation Muslims in West Germany are suffering from a deep-seated identity crisis or that all they meet with from the host population is either cold indifference or outright hostility. For example, the Federal Protestant Church in Germany (EKD) at its meeting in June 1983, requested, among other things, that in mapping the way forward in education the state take very seriously the religious and cultural heritage of Muslim children and stressed that it was incumbent on the Church to take up the cause of Muslims living in Germany in accordance with the 'biblical principles of charity and hospitality'.

There are, however, German Evangelicals who take what traditionally might be termed a very conservative view of Islam and whose attitude not only conflicts with but causes concern to the main-line German Protestant churches mentioned above. The former reportedly identify Islam as an 'anti-Christian' religion, even an obstacle to salvation that should be fought on all fronts, and request their members to use every means including the school to convert Muslims.

Currently, however, there would appear to be more German-born converts to Islam than there are Muslim converts to Christianity. Some of the former have been won over to Islam by the fervently 'evangelical' and missionary-oriented Muslim sect of Indian origin, the Ahmadiya movement founded in Qadian by Ghulam Ahmad in the 1880s. Beginning in the 1950s, this movement established mosques in Hamburg, Frankfurt and elsewhere in West Germany, while much earlier this century it had already started its missionary work in Britain. Today the number of converts of German origin in recent times is somewhere between one and two thousand and, along with many of the several thousand naturalised

Muslims in Germany, they seek to create an Islamic culture appropriate to the German setting.

Great Britain

The modern history of Islam in Britain began around the middle years of the nineteenth century with the arrival of Muslim seamen who came in the main from Aden, the Yemen, the Horn of Africa, in particular Somalia, Iran, Bengal, Gujarat and Sind. From the 1850s to the outbreak of the First World War the Muslim community in Britain was composed of these seamen, a majority of whom settled in the ports of Bristol, Cardiff, Liverpool, London and Tyneside, a small number of students and professional groups, mainly from India, and a few British converts. Some of these converts were professional people—academics, mainly in the sciences, barristers, solicitors, civil servants, diplomats and contract engineers—from the middle and upper classes, while others were local women who converted to Islam on marrying Muslim seamen.

Among the better known of these early converts were the solicitor William Quillian, who founded an Islamic institute and a mosque in Liverpool, and Lord Headley, who announced his conversion to Islam at a public meeting in Caxton Hall in December 1913. The former came to be known as the 'Shaikh of Islam in Britain' and on several occasions was appointed to represent the Sultan of Turkey, Abd al-Hamid II. Lord Headley for his part, in close co-operation with the Indian Kwaja Kamaluddin, a lawyer by profession and a member of the Ahmadiya movement which had established a mosque at Woking in Surrey, founded the British Muslim Association for the purpose of spreading Islam in Britain.

However, it was to be a succession of political events, most notably the partitioning of India and the foundation of the state of Pakistan in 1947, and government legislation on immigration, that was to lead to the expansion of the Muslim community in Britain. Anxious about the fate of their relatives following on the 1947 partition, Muslims already living in Britain encouraged their kinsfolk to join them. This led to a relatively small but at the time significant increase in the numbers of Muslims in Britain, a majority of whom came from the rural areas of Pakistan. This was followed for most of the 1950s by a steady flow of immigrants from Pakistan to Britain, a flow which was to increase markedly when it became widely known that Britain proposed to introduce restrictions on entry through the Commonwealth Immigrants Act of 1962. A similar situation occurred in the late 1960s when, as a result of the indigenisation policies of East African governments, many East African Asians came to feel insecure. This sense of insecurity was heightened by the knowledge that the British government was to withdraw automatic right of entry to Britain from certain classes of British passport holders, in particular those who were descendants of people of British origin. This restriction on immigration came in an Act of Parliament in 1968, but before it was introduced, a further influx of immigrants, many of them Muslims, arrived in Britain.

Since these restrictions on immigration were introduced the growth of Islam has been the result in the main of the arrival of the dependants, mostly women and children, of those Muslims already resident in Britain. Prior to the 1960s the Muslim community in Britain was composed in the main of Muslim men, a majority of them either semi-skilled or unskilled, in search of work, and many of whom intended to return home one day to their families. That situation changed with the above-mentioned arrival of dependants which was to result not only in a significant increase in the number of Muslims born in Britain but also in the growth of a more stable Muslim community there.

In contemporary Britain a majority of the Muslim community, between 360,000 and 400,000, originate from the rural areas of Pakistan and Bangladesh, with the next largest grouping coming initially from India. Other sizeable groups of Muslims include the Turkish Cypriots, Arabs from the Middle East and North Africa, East African Asians and Shi'ite Muslims mainly from Iran. There are also smaller groups of Somalis and Yemenis, most of them descendants of those nineteenth-century Muslim communities already mentioned, and others from West Africa.

Not only is the Muslim community in Britain culturally heterogeneous, it is also somewhat fragmented by sectarianism—for example there are a number of Shi'ite groups, and others such as the Ahmadiya which are not considered to be orthodox—and also as a result of the quest for work which has taken Muslims to different parts of the country. There are relatively large concentrations of Muslims in the south-east, the east and west Midlands, the north-west and Yorkshire and Humberside. However, though the Muslim community in Britain displays considerable diversity and is far from being a homogeneous, integrated body, organisations and institutions have been established for the purpose of co-ordinating activities and generating greater co-operation and unity. Recently the British Council of Mosques was set up for these purposes among others. There is also the United Kingdom Islamic Mission which operates through an association of mosques—there are around two hundred and fifty registered mosques today in Britain compared with nine in 1960—for the purpose of providing religious instruction for Muslim children in state schools.

As in France and West Germany, education is a major concern of the Muslim community in Britain. While there is no unanimity as to how exactly this should be achieved, most if not all Muslims want their children to receive a thorough grounding in the Qur'an and Islamic studies. Some would prefer this to be done by Muslim teachers within the state system, providing that provisions can be made for, among other things, single-sex education, attendance at mosque and the observance of prayer times and dietary laws. Then there are those who wish to see the establishment of Muslim schools along the lines of Catholic or Jewish schools, and one such school, the Islamia Primary School in the London Borough of Brent. This solution is not favoured by among others the National Union of Teachers (NUT). This union, in its discussion paper on Muslim schools published in October 1984, while agreeing that there was a case for single-sex schools, believed that the setting up of separate Muslim schools could be divisive.

It would appear that the first of the two proposals mentioned above would find considerable support among many of the less well-to-do Muslims, while the better educated, middle-class Muslim appears to be in favour of the second. It is worth noting here that this Muslim middle class, although small when compared with the percentage of the total population in Britain that is categorised as middle class, is by comparison with Muslims elsewhere in Western Europe quite large and influential, and its stance, therefore, on such matters as education and marriage is often taken to be representative of Muslim opinion generally. Evidence suggests, however, that many working-class muslims are less conservative in their views on these and other matters than their middle class co-religionists.

Differences of opinion also exist on the question of the Shari'a, Islamic law. Some Muslims in Britain and elsewhere in Western Europe maintain that since the Shari'a is a totally integrated legal system based on a divinely revealed source, the Qur'an, it is not possible for them on grounds of faith to accept anything less than a separate system of family law, with its own autonomous judiciary. Muslims of this persuasion in Britain, therefore, request Parliament to make provision for this in the country's legal system and establish the necessary courts. Parliament, however, would not have control over the content of Muslim law, nor could there be any appeal to a higher, non-Muslim court. Other Muslims are of the opinion that Islamic family law could be built into the existing legal system in one of several different ways, for example by the establishment of family tribunals before which Muslims could choose to appear and whose decisions would be subject to appeal in the traditional way in a court equipped to take into consideration Islamic practice. This last mentioned approach would have the virtue of maintaining the essential unity of the legal system.

While very few are indifferent or hostile to Islam as a religion the views of the younger generation of Muslims born in Britain on questions such as education and arranged marriages show that there is a good deal of heart searching and even criticism. This cannot be separated from the realisation that for the vast majority at least there is no alternative to being a Muslim in Britain, in the sense of professing and living an Islam that is pruned of what are regarded as inessentials, including some of its 'foreign' cultural trappings.

Something of this heart searching and criticism can be illustrated by reference to the question of arranged marriages, where research shows that while some Muslim girls have confidence in this system and respect it, others reject it for the reason that it deprives them of the right to choose. Moreover, some of the latter argue that their parents' reasons for insisting on such marriages have little or nothing to do with Islam and all to do with social pressure combined with a desire to preserve a particular way of life, culture and tradition. Nevertheless, the alternative, love marriages as they are known, are widely believed to be more likely to fail than arranged marriages.

Intimately bound up with the question of arranged marriages is the equally thorny question of Western education already discussed. Girls, who under the system of arranged marriages are normally married by the age of sixteen, may wish to continue their education and enter upon a professional careeer before getting married and this can lead to tension in the home. Some Muslim men, moreover, are of the opinion that Western education radically alters the attitude of Muslim girls, rendering them incapable of performing with any conviction and enthusiasm the role of wife and mother in the traditional way, and therefore are reluctant to marry such girls. Moreover, the latter, for their part, are not always prepared to accept the traditional role assigned to them and realise the difficulties this might give rise to if marriage arrangements are not sufficiently flexible to allow full consideration to be given to their feelings and aspirations.

There are, however, many Muslim girls who accept that, despite whatever they themselves may want to do with their lives, they will not be going beyond secondary school to train for a career and, as a consequence, pose little or no threat to the traditions and customs of their parents. All of this means that there are very few 'out marriages' among Muslim girls and even where Muslim men are concerned, almost all of the very few that have 'married out' have only done so after their prospective partners had agreed to convert to Islam.

As is the case in France, West Germany and in other Western European countries, Muslim parents tend on the whole to depict the wider society as permissive, regarding its standards on matters of sexuality in particular as being extremely low. They are, therefore, concerned and anxious to shield and protect their children from the 'evil' influences of that wider society and this has led in some instances to a strengthening of the institution of purdah and to an increase in the number of those Muslims who favour single-sex schools.

However, while many Muslim parents are clear in their own minds as to what they want for their children, an increasing number of the latter live in conflicting worlds—the home and the wider society—and are not, as we have seen, fully accepted in either. As a result they tend to develop dual images of themselves in their anxiety to satisfy the demands of two cultures. Then Islam often becomes the *via media* or escape route between the two, although this is not necessarily the same Islam, in all its details and cultural trappings, that their parents commend. The former insist more on an Islam that rises above any particular culture and that can be meaningfully practised in any society. They tend, therefore, to be scripturalists, to emphasise that the life of a Muslim must be grounded exclusively in the Qur'an and *hadith* (tradition) and that practices and obligations that cannot be found there are not to be regarded as authentic. There are also those who simply accept things as they are; for some of them the home provides an escape from the tensions of the wider society, while for others it is the other way round.

These young Muslims are not alone in the pursuit of an Islam stripped of some of what they see as unnecessary cultural baggage acquired in other lands. British-born converts to Islam—there have been several thousand of these in the past twenty years—are also anxious to encourage the development of an Islam that is more recognisably Qur'anic and in accord with authentic tradition than that which they sometimes see advocated and practised by some of their fellow believers. Like their counterparts in West Germany and elsewhere in Western Europe, the British converts insist that, while Islam does not necessarily always conflict with them, it nevertheless can and indeed must be seen to transcend the particularities and peculiarities of any one culture, otherwise it will not succeed in its universal mission.

If this move towards a more scripturally based form of Islam gathers support the most likely outcome will be, somewhat paradoxically, a more marked adaptation of this religion to the attitudes, perspectives and way of life of Britain, something that is also occurring in the case of other religions transplanted to Britain, among them Buddhism and Hinduism.

Islam Elsewhere in Western Europe

After France, West Germany and Britain, Holland with an estimated 320,000 Muslims, the majority of whom are originally from Turkey, followed closely by those from North Africa, and with a substantial minority from Indonesia, has the largest Muslim population in Western Europe. Belgium has close on 200,000 Muslims, over 50 per cent of whom are from North Africa, while Turkish Muslims account for most of the remainder. Cyprus, with 18 per cent of its over 600,000 inhabitants Muslim, and Greece with around 140,000, most of whom once again are of Turkish origin, come next. In the case of Greece this figure marks something of a decline in the number of its Muslim inhabitants in this century. In both Austria and Italy the number of Muslims is somewhere between 40,000 and 50,000. The Muslims in Austria are in the main Turkish labourers, most of the others coming from Yugoslavia, while a majority of those in Italy are from Eastern European countries, in particular Albania, Yugoslavia, Bulgaria and Hungary, with a small number from the Horn of Africa. In 1984 the foundation stone of the Rome mosque was laid and over twenty Muslim countries have promised to help pay for its actual construction, the estimated cost of which is twenty-eight million pounds sterling.

Turkish migrant workers once again make up the majority of the 17,000 Muslims in Switzerland, and also of those in Sweden where the Muslim population is estimated at 25,000. It is perhaps worth pointing out here that not all Turkish immigrants are Muslims. For example, in Sweden some are Christian and a majority of these are Syrian Orthodox. Denmark's Muslim population is around 15,000 and in this case, as in so many others, most are Turkish migrant workers with the remainder coming from North Africa and Pakistan. Norway has a somewhat smaller Muslim community estimated at around 12,000 and centred mainly on Oslo. Over 50 per cent of these Muslims originate from Pakistan, the remainder being evenly divided into Moroccans and Turks. Finland's closely knit Muslim community of under 1,000 is of Tartar origin. Its existence in Finland dates back to the last century and beyond, and it is strictly endogamous and at present in decline. The total Muslim population in the Iberian peninsula probably numbers no more than 6,000 over 5,000 of whom live in Spain, a mere handful in a land where Islam and Arabism had once established deep and firm roots. The 1,000 or so Muslims in Portugal originate from the African states of Guineau-Bissau and Mozambique, and from Pakistan.

Western Europe's Changing Image of Islam

The Western view of and response to Islam has undergone considerable change during this century and during the past twenty-five years in particular. And this is most notable in the case of the Christian churches who once perceived Islam as the principal threat to the survival and expansion of Christian civilisation and summarily dismissed it as a post-Christian heresy. Of course, history is not all on the side of Islam which considered what were once Christian lands as *dar al harb* or the abode of war *par excellence*.

Today, and for some time now, these same churches, leaving aside some of the fundamentalist movements, for example the German Evangelicals as mentioned above, are increasingly inclined to adopt a more open, tolerant attitude towards Islam. This change in attitude is clearly marked in the case of the Roman Catholic Church among others.

This church, which had once resorted to scripture to justify the crusades and in a variety of different ways, for example through the introduction of a number of solemn feasts such as the Transfiguration and through other liturgical means, had made Christians aware of the 'peril of Islam', only officially altered its attitude toward and response to this religion as recently as the 1960s. In its document, *Nostra Aetate*, on non-Christian religions the Second Vatican Council (1963–5) presented what has been interpreted as a 'positive if cautious and minimalistic' view of Islam stating, among other things, that the Catholic Church, 'looked with esteem on Muslims who adore one God, living and enduring, merciful and all powerful, Maker of heaven and earth and Speaker to men'. The document also acknowledged that over the centuries quarrels and hostilities had arisen between Muslims and Christians and encouraged both to forget the past and to 'strive sincerely for mutual understanding'. This pronouncement, though it did not go as far as Muslims would have wished—for example it said nothing very precise on the essence of the Muslim faith or on belief in the prophetic mission of Muhammad—did mark a breakthrough and vindicated in part the work of such Catholic scholars as Massignon who described Islam as the 'religion of faith', encouraged Christians to embark upon a 'spiritual Copernican revolution', and to return to the origin of Islamic teaching, 'to that point of virgin truth that is found at its centre and makes it live'.

Another Catholic document, *Guidelines for a Dialogue between Muslims and Christians*, followed *Nostra Aetate* in 1968. Moreover, the European Conference of Churches (ECC) meeting in the Austrian town of St Polten in February 1984 while recognising the important theological differences that existed between the two faiths nevertheless emphasised the need for Christians and Muslims in Europe to co-operate more closely on practical issues such as peace and justice. It insisted, further, that the political rivalry and competition that once characterised relations between the two faiths should be laid to rest and encouraged Christians and Muslims to shoulder responsibility together and 'before God for the world and its future'.

Despite this constructive approach on the part of the churches, negative images of Islam, reinforced from time to time by events in Iran, Libya and elsewhere, persist and are likely to do so for some time to come. Perhaps the most widespread of these images is that of Islam as a backward, primitive, and given the understanding of some of its teachings, for example those on slavery, and of its laws regarding theft and adultery, an inhumane religion.

The Muslim image of Christianity is also very often a distorted one based, as it sometimes evidently is, on mere hearsay, myth and even unauthentic documents such as the Gospel of Barnabas. According to recent research in West Germany on Muslims' images of Christians, typical responses included the following: 'Christians have several gods, one of whom is Jesus', and 'Christianity is belief in three persons: Mary, Jesus and God the Father.' Changing these false images is an extremely difficult and contentious task, and one that demands a great deal of trust and confidence in each other on the part of both Muslims and Christians. Both are world religions and seek to convert others to their faith and this can affect the extent to which either one is prepared to adopt the necessary means to disabuse its followers of any wrong notions they may have of the other. Certainly, as has been mentioned, some Christian evangelical churches in Germany show no signs of rethinking their views of and attitudes toward Islam and, although there has been some softening in tone and attitude in recent times, Muslim sects such as the Ahmadiya tend to present a highly subjective view of Christianity.

However, there is evidence in the Western European context that an increasing number of Muslims are concerned both to know more about Christian beliefs and practices and to forge closer ties with Christians. In a poll of nine hundred practising Muslims between the ages of sixteen and sixty-five, conducted in 1984 in West Germany by a Muslim organisation (Islam Archiv Deutschland), attached to the Muslim World Congress, between 70 and 80 per cent favoured 'more friendship' and 'closer personal relations with Christians both for themselves and their children', and an even higher percentage 'welcomed suggestions of social and educational co-operation'. And rather surprisingly over 50 per cent of the parents stated that they would not object to their sons marrying Christians while, not so surprisingly, only 30 per cent would allow their daughters to do so and only then on condition that their future sons-in-law became Muslims.

It would appear that, theological differences apart, the potential for Christian–Muslim co-operation and understanding in the Western European setting is considerable, and that although the 'spiritual Copernican revolution' in the Christian approach to and understanding of Islam called for by Massignon has not yet fully materialised there has been, none the less, something of a profound change in both these areas.

Islam in Eastern Europe and the Soviet Union

Eastern Europe

The development of Islam in Eastern Europe, where it has a relatively long history, once again owes much to the influence of the Turks and this time mostly as conquerers rather than migrant workers. The process of Islamisation began in Eastern Euruope with the rise of the Ottoman Empire in the fourteenth century. By the late fourteenth century this empire had occupied parts of modern-day Bulgaria and by the fifteenth century a substantial part of the Balkan peninsula, including Bosnia and Hercegovina in present-day Yugoslavia, had fallen under its control. It is interesting to note that even today Muslims in Bosnia are still referred to by others in the region and by themselves as Turks. The words Turk and Muslim are virtually interchangeable in this part of the world, although numerous Slav and Christian elements have survived in the marriage and other customs of the Turkish/Muslim population, particularly among Muslim craftsmen and peasantry, the Muslim elite having preferred to adhere much more strictly to Islamic/Turkish practice. Nevertheless, in the case of craftsmen and peasantry also Islam has been a key factor in the creation of a separate identity. Today in Yugoslavia, close on three million, or just over 10 per cent of the total population, are Muslims and while their situation is by no means as difficult as that of their co-religionists in many Eastern European countries, for example Albania and Bulgaria, it is not always an easy one. The government, no doubt concerned about any development that might upset the balance of nationalities in Yugoslavia, a concern shown in its sentencing in Sarajevo in 1983 of Muslims who were said to have been linked to the proclamation of an Islamic Declaration, appears on occasion to have restricted the rights of Muslims by placing obstacles mainly of a bureaucratic nature in the way of, among other things, mosque construction.

However, in comparison with Yugoslavia the difficulties encountered by Muslims in other Eastern European countries have been much greater. In Albania there has been a systematic attempt by the state to eradicate all traces of Islam. Under Ottoman control for almost five centuries (1431–1913), some two-thirds of this isolated country's population were converted to Islam. And once again, as in Yugoslavia and also Bulgaria, being a Muslim came to be synonymous in people's minds with being a Turk. This is an important point to remember when considering the energy devoted to the eradication of religion by the government in Albania since 1948. The attack on religion is both an attack on what is considered to be 'unscientific, primitive superstition', and at the same time it is part of a policy of nation-building in that it is an attempt to forge a new Albanian identity with Marxism–Leninism as its centre-piece.

After struggling to regain its independence from Turkey, Albania was forced into a union with Italy in 1939 and then at the end of the Second World War came under the political domination of Yugoslavia until 1948 when, with the rupture in Yugoslav–Soviet relations, it seized the opportunity to re-establish its independence. This is briefly the historical and political background to Albania's isolationism and xenophobia since 1948 and goes some way to explaining its vigorous and even at times ruthless campaign against what it considers to be foreign or deviant ideologies, including religion, which is dismissed as one of the trappings of the 'bourgeois-revisionist' world. In order to ensure ideological purity in the form of Marxism-Leninism, through the Communist Party's progress and domination over all spheres of life, traditional religious institutions, Catholic, Muslim and Orthodox, have been systematically displaced. However, despite the imprisonments, the campaign against it in the media and attempts to 'cleanse' the education system of all traces of religion—it is true that in the past Christian and Muslim schools were established with conversion as one of their principal goals—religious beliefs and practices are still widespread in modern-day Albania. And the main reason for this, it would appear, lies in the fact that in Albanian society the family, and through the family local custom and tradition (of which religion forms an integral part), continue to exercise the greatest formative and long-lasting influence over behaviour and attitudes.

It is this subtle influence that has counteracted government campaigns in schools, universities, the media and the workplace to eradicate religion, particularly, although not exclusively, in the rural areas, where Islamic dress continues to be worn, purdah practised, prayers said in public and facing east, and marriages performed in the traditional Islamic way. Moreover, there is very little evidence where marriages are concerned of people marrying others of a different faith.

While the campaign against Catholicism in particular as an anti-Albanian religion, an instrument of 'foreign' imperialism, continues unabated, both the current domestic and foreign policy objectives of the regime make a relentless, all-out offensive against either of these religions, and particularly Islam, unlikely. In fact, in recent years the Party has made relatively few, direct attacks on Islam, perhaps in order not to pre-empt the possibility of an improvement in relations with Arab states and out of recognition that certain Muslim practices and prohibitions, like certain Catholic ones, further some of its own objectives.

The Party, for example, would like to see a significant increase in the population which now stands at just over two and a half million, and for this reason gives strong support to the idea of the large family and resolutely opposes abortion, as do both Islam and Catholicism. However, what ultimately protects Islam from an all-out attack by the regime, is the fact that Albanian society remains so strongly influenced at the grassroots level by the Muslim way of life.

Bulgaria, like Albania, has attempted to eradicate the influence of religion among its people. Once a Christian kingdom, Bulgaria also came under Ottoman control from the second half of the fourteenth century until the Treaty of Berlin in July 1878 when it became an autonomous principality.

Even though thousands died or fled during the 1877–8 war of independence, a majority of the population of the new principality were Muslims and were to experience serious economic set-backs under the new dispensation as a result of the upheavals and the land reforms introduced after 1878. No longer the majority, they were hit once again by the nationalisation of the land by the Communist regime between 1949 and 1955. Their Muslim way of life was further undermined by the regime's policy of assimilation, or more accurately of enforced Bulgarisation, which coerced Muslims who previously had only very limited contacts with Bulgarians to leave their enclosed communities and integrate with the rest of society.

The Bulgarisation policy also insisted on intermarriage between Muslims and non-Muslims, and in the 1950s on the nationalisation of all Turkish/Muslim schools, incorporating them into the state system to create what are called 'unified schools'. Subsequently no more than two hours a week was to be given to the teaching of Turkish while all religious education was ended. The closure of mosques by the government has also had a serious, adverse effect on the Muslim way of life. Each village or community is allowed only one mosque but even then services in the mosque are controlled in that Qur'anic teaching therein is prohibited. In addition, burial in Muslim cemeteries and the public celebration of Muslim festivals are not allowed. Further, the policy of Bulgarisation even extends to forcing Muslims to adopt Bulgarian names, and according to reports, some of those who refused to comply have either been imprisoned or put to death. In Bulgaria then, as in Albania, Islam is officially regarded as an enemy both of national integration and of the state ideology of Marxism–Leninism. And perhaps more so in Bulgaria than in any other Balkan state colonised by the Ottoman Turks the attack on Islam is bound up with nationalist sentiment, for it was the Bulgarians who bore the brunt of the battle against the Turks during the Balkan Wars (1912–14) for complete independence.

Romania, also for centuries under Ottoman control until gaining a measure of autonomy in 1878 and complete independence during the Balkan Wars just mentioned, has an estimated quarter of a million Muslims, the vast majority of whom are also of Turkish origin and subject to certain restrictions.

Elsewhere in Eastern Europe Muslim communities tend to be much smaller. For example, in present-day Poland there are only 3,000 or so Muslims, almost all of whom are of Tartar origin and whose presence in the country dates back to the fourteenth century. These Muslims are to be found in the main in the district of Bialystok, north-east of Warsaw, where they have two mosques, while the foundation stone for another in Gdansk has already been laid. Hungary, likewise, has a small Muslim population of around 2,000 and there are probably even fewer in Czechoslovakia and East Germany.

In most of Eastern Europe there is little if any evidence of a growth in Islam. In fact, in most instances the contrary is the case and this is due in part to the restrictive and in some instances repressive measures of the state, to the upsurge of Slav nationalism in the nineteenth and the first half of the twentieth century which involved a determination to eradicate all trace of Ottoman rule, and to the fact that during the past hundred years or so significant numbers of Turks have emigrated from Bulgaria and other Balkan states. The situation of Muslims in the Soviet Union both resembles and differs from that of their co-religionists in Eastern Europe, and it is to a brief discussion of this that we now turn.

Islam in the Soviet Union

The percentage of professing Muslims in the Soviet Union has increased steadily throughout this century and now stands at over 11 per cent of the total population, which makes for a Muslim community today of between thirty and thirty-five million members. And if the birth-rate indicators showing a decline in births among Russians and a rapid rise among the Muslims of Central Asia are reliable, then the inevitable outcome will be a shift in the relative weight and influence of nationalities in the USSR.

Most Muslims are Sunnis or orthodox and are concentrated in the Caucasian and the Central Asian republics, some of which were wrested from Ottoman control by Russia in the nineteenth century. In one of these, the Soviet Socialist Republic of Azerbaijan, which at one time belonged to Iran, there is an important minority of Shi'ites of the Twelver or Ithnashariya sect, the majority Muslim group in Iran (see pp. 354–67). There is also an Ismaili or Sevener Shi'ite community of around 100,000 members in Pamir.

Since the Bolshevik Revolution of 1917 the Soviet attitude to Islam has varied greatly, periods of severe repression and the wholesale closure of mosques and educational establishments alternating with a degree of toleration. Before 1917 there were, according to observers, over 27,000 mosques in the whole of Russia and this number had been reduced to less than 1,000 by 1970. Moreover, during the same period all institutions for the training of Muslim clerics were closed except for one, the Mir-i-Arab Madresah in the ancient Uzbek town of Bukhara, first founded in 1535, closed after the Revolution and reopened in 1948. Further, by the early 1970s there was only a very limited number of editions of the Qur'an in Arabic in circulation.

Media treatment of Islam has frequently presented it as an anti-scientific ideology which gives people a false approach to life and destroys initiative and creativity, and has very often attacked such practices as the payment of dowry and the Muslim attitude to women. In Baku, capital of Azerbaijan, there is an important symbolic statue of a Muslim woman casting off the chadour.

Moreover, observances such as the fast during Ramadan and the pilgrimage to Mecca, while they are performed are restricted, as is Muslim education and the activities of the Sufi brotherhoods. Even the role of the Muslim family in perpetuating what is referred to as a backward 'ideology' has come in for strong criticism. However, for some time now the Soviet Communist Party has sought to counter Islam's considerable and growing influence without, at the same time, alienating the Muslim nations of the Third World whom it seeks to influence and from whom it seeks support, and some of whom have been inspired by the ideas, zeal and commitment of the well-known Muslim socialist Sultan Galiev. Generally, however, the response of Muslim leaders in the Soviet Union to Communist ideology and practice has also been ambiguous, appearing anxious on the one hand to demonstrate the compatibility between Islam and

Communism, while on the other preaching the supremacy and eventual triumph of Islam over all other systems and ideologies.

But, whatever the public stance of Muslim leaders and Party officials on the compatibility or otherwise of the two systems, there is very little intermingling between Muslim and non-Muslim in the Soviet Union. Intermarriage, for example, is rare and where it does take place it is almost always between Muslim men and Slav women with the children being brought up Muslims. The vast majority of Muslims in the Soviet Union continue to find in Islam the basic framework of their identity. Meanwhile, the Soviet government, while faced in its dealings with Muslims with many of the same problems as those confronting governments in Western Europe, has the added difficulty of being perceived to be and in fact of being in the position of a colonial power.

One is left, finally, with a picture of Soviet Islam as a restricted but none the less vigorous and active community set against the background of a modernising state which grants limited toleration to national traditions, customs and languages, providing always that Soviet ideology is not openly questioned.

Conclusions

The main concern here has been to outline the development of Islam in Western Europe during the last quarter of a century. Some of the implications of this development both for the wider society as a whole and for second generation Muslims in particular who form a majority of the estimated six million Muslims in Western Europe, have also been considered. And while there is much that is uncertain about the future shape and orientation of this community what is clear from the very fact alone that so many of its members are European by birth, education and in other ways, is that Islam has moved during the past twenty-five years from the position of an exotic appendage to an established component of Western European society, thereby adding to its already considerable ethnic, cultural and religious resources and complexity.

Further Reading

Three of the most valuable sources of information on contemporary Islam in Europe are:

Abedin, S.Z. (ed.) *Journal* (Institute of Muslim Minority Affairs, Umram Publications, London)

Nielsen, J.S. (ed.) *News of Muslims in Europe* (Centre for the Study of Islam and Christian–Muslim Relations, Selly Oak Colleges, Birmingham)

—— (ed.) *Muslims in Europe*, Research Papers (Centre for the Study of Islam and Christian–Muslim Relations, Selly Oak Colleges, Birmingham)

Other useful references include:

Antes, P. and Kreiser, K. 'Muslims in Germany—German Muslims?' in J.S. Nielsen (ed.) *Muslims in Europe*, Research Papers, no. 28 (Dec. 1985)
Anwar, M. *The Myth of Return. Pakistanis in Britain* (Heinemann, London, 1979)
—— and Garaudy, R. 'Social and Cultural Perspectives on Islam in Western Europe' in J.S. Nielsen (ed.) *Muslims in Europe*, Research Papers, no. 24 (1984)
Bennigsen, A. and Lemercier-Quelquejay, C. *L'Islam en Union Soviétique* (Payot, Paris, 1968)
—— *Les Musulmans oubliés. L'Islam en Union Soviétique* (PCM/petite collection maspero, Paris, 1986)
—— and Galiev, Sultan *Le Père de la révolution tiers-mondiste* (Fayard, Paris, 1986)
—— and Windbush, S. *Muslim National Communism in the Soviet Union. A Revolutionary Strategy for the Colonial World* (University of Chicago Press, Chicago, 1979)
Dassetto, F. and Bastinier, A. *L'Islam transplanté* (Editions EPO, Bruxelles, 1984)
Krieger-Krynicki, A. *Les Musulmans en France* (Maisonneuve & Larose, Paris, 1985)
Lamand, F. *L'Islam en France* (Albin Michel, Paris, 1986)
Malewska-Peyre, H. *Crise d'identité et deviance chez les jeunes immigrés* (Documentation Française, Paris, 1981)
Mince, J. *La Generation suivante* (Flammarion, Paris, 1986)
Morsy, M. (ed.) *Les Nords Africains en France* (CHEAM, Paris, 1984)
Nielsen, J.S. 'Muslim Immigration and Settlement in Britain' in J.S. Nielsen (ed.) *Muslims in Europe*, Research Papers, no. 21 (March 1984)
Rocher L. and Cherqaoui, Fatima *D'une foi à l'autre. Les conversions à l'Islam en Occident* (Editions du Seuil, Paris, 1986)
Wallraff, G. *Tête de Turc* (La Découverte, Paris, 1986)

The author would like to thank the Leverhulme Trust for the award of a fellowship which enabled him to carry out much of the research contained in this chapter.

31 Islam in North America

S.S. Nyang

Introduction: The Slave Trade and the Arrival of Islam

Islam in North America is now a fact and the three million Muslims living in this part of the world provide definite proof of its establishment in the pluralistic democratic societies of Canada and the United States. The history of this religion can be traced back several centuries. There are scholars who believe that the earliest encounters of Islam with the New World predate the age of Columbus. Working on certain literary fragments of Arab writers of pre-Columbian times, in western Sudan, these scholars maintained that an expedition was outfitted and sent out by Abu Bakr and Mansa Kankan Musa who ruled the ancient empire of Mali. This hypothesis about pre-Columbian Muslim arrival in the New World was also supported by Harvard University Professor Leo Wiener, who argued in the 1920s that Arabo-Islamic and Mande influences began during this period. Instead of relying on Arabic literary fragments to develop his case for a pre-Columbian Muslim arrival in the New World, Leo Wiener based his conclusions on linguistic evidence derived from an analysis of the languages in Mexico and areas of Mande peoples in West Sudan. Though Wiener wrote a longer study arguing his point, he failed to convince the mainstream American historians. To most of these scholars, the arrival of Islam dates back to the slave trade when many African Muslims began to arrive on the American shores. Allan D. Austin has done an excellent job of bringing together all the available literary fragments which deal with the life and experiences of Muslim slaves in North America. This work shows that many of the Muslims who came to America were literate and had some knowledge of the Qur'an and Islamic teachings. Apart from the much celebrated Kunta Kinteh whose saga has been fictionalised and immortalised by his descendant, Alex Haley, there were men like Ayub Ibn Sulayman Diallo, Yarrow Mamout (which should read Yorro

Mahmud), Muhammad Bah and others whose stories were recorded by contemporary writers.

The case of Yorro Mahmud is a good example and illustration of the life and condition of some of the Muslim slaves who came to America. Although Allan D. Austin has given us a useful account of his life and times, as described in the diary of Charles Willson Peale, my research has led me to the State of Maryland archival data which confirmed the existence of one Yarro (most probably our Yorro Mahmud) who was freed on 22 August 1796 by Upton Beall (not Bell as stated in Allan Austin's volume). This state document also reveals that assessments for Georgetown, 1809–19, listed negro Yorrow as a tax payer. An examination of the records at the National Archives should tell us which land in Georgetown was owned by Yorro Mahmud.

Another interesting piece of information about Yorro is the order of manumission which he asked his owner to write. In the State of Maryland archival record entitled Montgomery County LRG no. 385 (1796), Yorro's master, Upton Beall, wrote the following:

> At the request of Yorro the following manumission is recorded this 22nd day of August 1796 to wit know all men by these presents [*sic*] that I Upton Beall of Montgomery County and State of Maryland do manumit and set free negro Yorro from this day forward to act for himself as a free man in all things given under my hand and seal this 22nd day of August, anno domini seventeen hundred and ninety six
>
> Upton Beall
> Clerk

What is striking about this order of manumission is the fact that the executor was not the Clerk of Court at the time. Yet, in looking into the will of this former slave master, we find that he freed two blacks listed simply as Mary and Hope.

From the limited data given in Charles Willson Peale's diary, we now know that Yorro was a pious and devout Muslim who abstained from the consumption of pork and alcohol. He was said always to be an industrious hard-working man. He saved up his money and bought property in Georgetown, although he lost his first savings of one hundred dollars when the young merchant to whom he had entrusted it went bankrupt. This event did not make him despair. Rather he opened an account with the Columbia Bank and managed to save up to 200 dollars. It was with this money that he purchased land in Georgetown.

In looking at the Islamic experience during the slave trade, one finds that Yorro Mahmud's biography provides much food for thought and comparative analysis. His experience in Maryland shows how a young African Muslim got sold into slavery in the Americas in the 1720s and then worked his way to freedom almost seventy-six years later. Assuming that Yorro was a boy of fourteen when he landed in the US, he would have been ninety years old when Upton Beall signed his order of manumission. However, if Yorro was really aged thirty-four years instead of fourteen as his owners and their friends believed, then he was 133 years old when he sat for the portrait for Peale.

Equally fortunate but much more lucky in terms of ultimate relationship with slavery in America was Ayub Ibn Sulayman Diallo, the Bundu prince who was captured and brought to America as a slave in 1730. Prince Ayub's saga is quite a story. Being fluent in Arabic and well grounded in Qur'anic studies, he impressed many people around him. He tried to escape several times but without success. However, once his master knew of his religious background he decided to let Ayub practise his religion with greater ease. Taking advantage of his less oppressive situation he wrote a letter in Arabic to his father asking that he be ransomed. This was not to happen until 1733, when all arrangements were finalised and he set sail for England. There he was well received and he had the opportunity to associate with British royalty. From England Prince Ayub found his way back to Bundu.

Another Muslim whose experience is useful to the student of the Islamic movement in America is Abdur Rahman. Son of Ibrahima Sori Mawdo, second Almamy of the Futa Jallon, this African Muslim member of a Fulbe ruling class became a slave in nineteenth-century America. His story is told in Terry Alford's *Prince Among Slaves* (1977). Dr Austin's study, *African Muslims in Antebellum America: A Sourcebook* (Garland Publishing Company, New York, 1984), provides the sources from which Alford started his study. What is interesting about Abdur Rahman (erroneously Anglicised as Abdul Rahahman) is that he managed to escape the humiliations of American slavery through the assistance of Americans who had had contact with him and his family in Africa. Like Diallo, he was captured as a young man in his mid-twenties. Like Diallo also, he kept his faith in Islam throughout his stay in America. What is, however, striking about Abdur Rahman was the drama surrounding his release from American captivity. Having been recognised and identified by Dr Cox in Natchez, Mississippi, Abdur Rahman was the subject of many efforts by his friends to set him free. Before Dr Cox passed away in 1816 he had not only befriended the young Fula prince, but had also made a number of people aware of his plight. In October 1826, Abdur Rahman, outraged by a heartless decision to sell his daughter, sent a letter in Arabic to the Sultan of Morocco asking for his assistance. This Muslim ruler intervened on behalf of Abdur Rahman and the American President obliged. This led to the ransom and freedom of Abdur Rahman. He secured his manumission from Mr Thomas Forster, who accepted no official remuneration but insisted on the condition that Abdur Rahman return to Africa. This man, who had arrived in America in his mid-twenties, served for almost forty years as a slave before his departure at the age of sixty-five. The tragedy of this Muslim prince's life was that at the moment of liberation, he found himself free but members of his family were still in slavery. He succeeded in securing the freedom of his wife but failed to carry with him other members of his family. This certainly was a blow and the poor man died on his way to an historical reunion with his long-lost kin in Futa Jallon.

Besides these three remarkable Muslim slaves, there were others who were neither as lucky as Ayub and Abdur Rahman who returned to Africa, nor fortunate enough to gain freedom for the rest of their days in America. But regardless of this fundamental difference between the 'fortunate slaves' and the 'condemned slaves', the fact remains that these early Muslims in North America heralded the rise of Islam in American society. Though none of them left descendants who practise Islam, the legacy and history of their battle to remain Muslim on American soil now serve as a source of inspiration to Afro-Americans who flock to the Islamic caravan.

Islam and the North American Dream

Having discussed the Islamic experience of the Muslim slaves from Africa, let us now treat the next phase in the North America encounter with the religion of Islam. This should shed some light on the institutionalisation of Islam in North America.

The first Muslim immigrants who came in search of the 'North American Dream' were from the Mediterranean region of the world. Following the construction of the Suez Canal, and in response to the political unrest developing within the Ottoman Empire, a small but growing number of Syrian and Lebanese Arabs began to seek their fortunes elsewhere. Some of these moved to West Africa, others to South America and yet others to the United States. At the beginning of this mass emigration, the great majority from the Ottoman Empire were Christian Arabs. But with the increase in the number of tales of Arab successes in the United States, many of the Muslims reluctantly sailed out of the Middle East for the New World. There is the story of the Lebanese Muslim who, after learning from the captain of the ship he was supposed to board for the United States that there were no mosques in America, quickly jumped off the boat. This hesitant Muslim was gradually replaced by the adventuresome Muslim who wanted to go to the United States in the hope of striking it rich quick and then returning home. Many of these men never went back home. Their fates resemble very much those of the latter-day Muslim immigrants who went to England in the 1950s and 1960s and decided to stay for good. For those who went to America, the decision to stay was occasioned by a new sense of freedom and the realisation of the American dream of acquiring wealth and property beyond their wildest expectations back home.

The Arab Muslim immigrants settled along the

Eastern Seaboard and in the Midwestern parts of the United States. Indeed, the first mosques and Islamic centres in continental United States were built among the Arab settlers living in the Midwest. Also, the first breakthrough of Islam among the native-born Americans, particularly the black Americans, took place in the Midwest, although I would hasten to add that some of the earliest Muslim organisations, such as the International Muslim Union (1895), the African Moslem Welfare Society of America (founded by the Sudanese Imam Muhammad Majid in 1927) and the Muslim Society of the celebrated Muhammad Webb, the American diplomat to the Philippines who later converted to Islam in the 1890s, were based in New York, Pittsburgh and New York respectively. These early organisations, with the exception of Webb's, were primarily formed by immigrant or visiting Muslims.

Between the 1900s and the 1930s, the number of Muslim immigrants began to increase significantly. The Muslims of eastern and southern Europe, following the examples of their non-Muslim neighbours, began to emigrate to the United States in search of the American dream. These were the Albanian and Yugoslavian Muslims who were fleeing from the political situations in their countries. Many of these men and women settled in the Eastern Seaboard and the Midwest. Besides these two European Muslim communities, there were also those from the Soviet-dominated areas further to the north. Some of those from Poland have been traced by some writers to the descendants of Genghis Khan. They too settled in the New York/New Jersey area and carved a place for themselves in the biscuit industry. The immigrants from Ruthenia settled in New York (Brooklyn area) before branching out into the neighbouring areas. These Muslims organised themselves into the Mohammedan Society of America with headquarters in Brooklyn. An unpublished study done by a Slavic scholar in the United States traced their point of entry to the country to the turn of the nineteenth and the beginning of the twentieth century.

Another early group of Muslim immigrants who came in search of the North American Dream and later settled in the United States were the Muslims of Punjab in British India. Following in the footsteps of their Sikh neighbours, these Muslims responded to the food shortages of their country at the turn of the century by going to the United States. They settled on the West Coast as farm workers, and Willows, California, was one of their earliest settlements. Today the descendants of these early Muslims are scattered in the western United States and Canada. Of course, some of these Pakistani and Indian Muslim immigrants also settled on the Eastern Seaboard. Like their other Muslim and non-Muslim brethren from the non-European world, they were students, seamen, traders and stowaways who decided to make America their home. Many of them married into American families. In fact, the most widely reported case of an American-Pakistani marriage is that of Fazal Khan, who came to the United States in 1912 and married a black American lady in the Eastern Seaboard. His case became national American news because his American daughter, Lurey Khan, following the example of Alex Haley, author of *Roots*, journeyed to Pakistan in search of her Pakistani roots. There were many cases like these, and today in Pennsylvania, Delaware, Maryland and in the New York/New Jersey area, we find many descendants of early Muslims among white and black American families.

One other case which deserves wider attention is the claim of the late Shaykh Daoud Faisal and his wife Sister Khadija. This couple, who founded the Islamic Mission of America, played an important role in the early propagation of Sunni Islam. In a recent interview, Sister Khadija revealed her Pakistani roots by showing me photographic evidence of her early life. The offspring of a Pakistani Muslim and a black Caribbean mother, she settled in the United States, where she met and married her husband, who was himself the child of a Moroccan father and a Grenadian lady from the West Indies. All these meetings of Muslim immigrants were brought about by their common search for a new and better life in America. Their common quest for the American Dream made them fertilisers for the Islamic seed in their new homeland.

In looking into the relationship between Islam and the North American Dream, one can therefore argue that the search for fortune and the realisation of their dreams motivated many of these early immigrants to plant the seed of their faith in North America. In order for these men and women to survive they embarked upon new careers and new ventures. Following the footsteps of many of the earlier immigrants to the United States, these Muslims, among other things, engaged in peddling wares in and out of the main cities of the Eastern Seaboard. Here the early career of the Prophet of Islam in trade and commerce provided an example to Muslims trying to earn their keep while simultaneously maintaining their faith in a foreign land. Many of these immigrants spoke little or no English at all, and their lives were centred around the small communities within which they lived. They travelled short and long distances selling the goods and merchandise they obtained from their fellow-countrymen or from big wholesalers bent on making fast profits from the services of these recently arrived foreigners. The pattern developed in the north-east and along the Eastern Seaboard (ranging in distance from Quincy, Massachusetts, to Baltimore, Maryland, where the word Arab, with an emphasis on the A, is still used to describe a street vendor and a pedlar). American business historians tell us that foreign-born Americans dominate the field of small business. This is largely the case because it is the only arena where they can operate without dealing very intimately with the rest of society and suffering discrimination and prejudice at the hands of those who see their poor English and lack of familiarity with Americanisms as weaknesses and liabilities. Given these realities and owing to the fact that the Muslim immigrant who was serious about his faith had to pray five times daily at the appointed times for *salat* (prayer), one could see how peddling became attractive not only because it was something familiar to the Muslims from the East and the Old World, but also because it granted some leeway to these men and women trying to carve a social and economic niche for themselves in their adopted homeland.

The pattern of peddling which developed along the Eastern Seaboard was reproduced in the Midwest, an area which attracted the interest and attention of many of the early Muslim immigrants. There are several studies of Arab and other Muslim immigrants who migrated to that part of the United States. Some of these immigrants settled in rural areas where they could obtain land and practise farming; other moved into the urban areas where they took up peddling as an occupation; and some others started to hire themselves out to the emerging motor industry. As a result, there developed an Arab and Muslim neighbourhood along the streets near the auto plants in Highland Park and Hamtramch in Detroit, Michigan. At the beginning the Muslim segment of this predominantly Arab neighbourhood was very small, but as time went on the number rose gradually. Letters describing the successful encounters of Arab Muslims with the American Dream and the comparative comfort of life in America started a chain migration. According to a *Detroit Monthly* study two years ago (see Further Reading), 'Over time, almost entire villages were transplanted to the Detroit area. Most of the southern Lebanese here, for example, trace their roots back to two border villages, and there are organizations of Arabs who all come from particular towns, such as Beit Hanina and Ramallah in former Palestine.'

The Nation of Islam

It was in the Midwestern part of the United States that the mysterious pedlar-cum-teacher Farad Muhammad revealed himself to the late Elijah Muhammad, founder of the Nation of Islam. This powerful organisation, whose earlier efforts in the name of Islam were denied and rejected by Old World Muslims, later went through a radical transformation under the current leader Imam Warith Deen Muhammad. Fundamentally changed to reflect more accurately the true teachings of Sunni Islam, this largest body of Sunni Muslims in the United States can be said to be one of the contemporary efforts of Muslims to be assimilated into the mainstream of American society and to realise as all other American citizens the fruits and benefits of the American Dream. Though this may sound anathema to those who knew the old Nation of Islam (NOI), the fact remains that the American Muslim Mission is currently trying to achieve for its predominantly black Muslim membership what all the three dominant American religious establishments have done for the Protestant, the Catholic and the Jewish Americans. An interesting point about the American Muslim Mission is that its original founder taught his followers an ethic which has been characterised by some of the American researchers of the movement as 'very similar to the work ethic of the Puritans'. This emphasis on self-pride and on the dignity of self-help and self-development within the framework of their community has ironically resulted not in the distancing of the black Muslim from the mainstream of American society but in propelling him towards greater engagement with the American Dream. By moving into the field of small businesses, these American Muslim converts became more and more self-confident in their belief and hope of realising their dreams within the American society. With this change in perception and attitude came the new feeling that America can be made habitable for Muslims and all others. This native American attempt at reconciling Islam and the American Dream is still in an embryonic stage and a counter-movement from the more militant and more rebellious groups of the old Nation of Islam is beginning to unfold.

Self-preservation

Besides the native American response to the Islamic message, there is also the response of the long established and Americanised Muslim immigrants to the American Dream. This group of Muslims from different parts of the Old World has also emerged in recent years to assert its Muslim identity within the framework of Americanism. One of the earliest efforts at reconciling the Islamic faith and the American Dream was that of the members of the Federation of Islamic Associations. Founded by Arabs from the Levant and the Fertile Crescent, but later joined by other Muslims from elsewhere, this group of Muslims was drawn mainly from immigrants and naturalised Americans who had succeeded or were trying to succeed in America. Like the other immigrants and children of immigrants, they too pursued the American Dream and 'reinforced the Puritan strain in the American tradition (and) . . . enhanced the conservative streak which runs all through American culture'. In the special case of the Muslim immigrants, one can argue that their determination not to see the community lose its identity in the American environment led them to throw up barriers. Activities like dancing, gambling, drinking and dating American-style, which serve as vehicles for American encroachment, were banned and discouraged. Yet there were cases when even these efforts at self-preservation proved unsuccessful. This was particularly true among the Arab Muslim immigrants in the Midwest. This effort of the Federation of Islamic Associations to reconcile its members with the American Dream was made possible by the various local Islamic centres and organisations ministering to the needs of the Muslims at the local level. By organising these centres at the national level, some semblance of unity was developed, although I would hasten to add that greater mobilisation of the Muslim community was to take place much later.

Recent Muslim Migrants

With the 1965 liberalisation of American immigration laws, Asians began to migrate in greater numbers than previously. As a result, we witness for the first time the greater migration of Muslim professionals from Turkey, Iran, India, Pakistan, Indonesia and the Arab world. Mehdi's recent study of Arabs in the United States shows that 'of the more than 100,000 who have arrived since 1945, 70 per cent are Moslem in contrast to earlier decades'. This increase in the Muslim population in American society was not confined to the category of professionals; it was also evident in the growth of Muslim students coming into the United States. Whereas in the early thirties, Muslim students constituted a very negligible percentage of America's foreign students, by the mid-sixties and seventies, the figure had climbed to 120,000 students. This was facilitated by decolonisation in the Muslim world and the greater American involvement in the education of these societies. One important result of this phenomenon was the birth of the Muslim Student Association whose success story has led to its transformation into the Islamic Society of America, a new and much broader-based organisation catering to both its old student constituents and the professional class of Muslims who in many cases were former student members of the old MSA. These new Americans and new immigrants have all been generally identified with values emphasising success in American society. Although the Iranian Revolution created some problems for the safety and effective operation of many Muslims, particularly those from the Middle East, the fact remains that since the release of the American hostages, Iranian-American Muslims are once again doing business as usual and many are still hoping to have a successful rendezvous with the American Dream.

Conclusions

In conclusion, one can say that the arrival of Muslims in greater numbers in American society was made possible by the changes in the American immigration laws and the birth and development of home-grown Islamic movements. The appeal to Muslim immigrants of the American Dream is by no means unique and peculiar, for most of these men and women were either refugees from tormenting political situations in their own countries or were lured by the greater opportunities of American society. Their case is similar to that of many others from the Old World. Another point that can be made is that the planting of Islam in the United States is another contribution to the cultural diversity of this society. Writing before the changes of the 1960s, Will Herberg could say in his *Protestant, Catholic, Jew*, that, 'By and large, to be an American today means to be either a Protestant, a Catholic, or a Jew ... Unless one is either ... one is "nothing"; to be a "something", to have a name, one must identify oneself and be identified by others, as belonging to one or another of the three great religious communities in which the American people are divided.' Under present conditions and given the gradual growth of Islam among indigenous Americans, one can say that Herbert's statement needs some revision. The growth in the Arab/Asian immigrant population has swelled the numbers of Buddhists, Sikhs, Baha'is, Hindus and of course Muslims.

Another conclusion to be drawn is that, with the successful planting of Islam in American society, it is quite conceivable that some day American Muslims could be one of the major pillars of support of world Islam, and American Muslim centres, like those of other branches of the Abrahamic tradition, will play an important role in the cultural development of their brethren elsewhere in the Muslim world. All these developments, however, will depend on the successes of the native-born as well as the immigrant Muslims who have opted for American citizenship and strive to see their Muslim dreams wrapped in the greater American Dream. Last but not least, one can also conclude that Muslims and other American believers in the religious heritage of mankind will maintain and pass on their respective traditions only if they succeed in holding their own against the very powerful forces of secularism and materialism in American society.

Further Reading

Austin, Allan D. *African Muslims in Antebellum America: A Sourcebook* (Garland Publishing Company, New York, 1984)

Bosquet, G.H. 'Moslem Religious Influence in the United States', *Moslem World* (Jan. 1935), pp. 40–4

Braden, Charles 'Islam in America', *The International Review of Missions*, vol. XLVIII, no. 191 (July 1959), pp. 309–17

Cheyfitz, Kirk, and Warblow, Kathy 'Arabs and Islam, Detroit is the American Mecca', *Monthly Detroit*, vol. 3 (Feb. 1980)

Ghayur, Arif 'Muslims in the United States: Settlers and Visitors', *Annals of the American Academy of Political and Social Sciences*, no. 454 (Mar. 1981)

Lincoln, C. Eric *The Black Muslims in America* (Saunders of Toronto, Toronto, Canada, 1961)

Muhammad, Akbar 'Muslims in the United States. An Overview of Organizations, Doctrines, and Problems', in Yvonne Haddad, Byron Haines and Ellison Findly (eds.) *The Islamic Impact* (Syracuse University Press, New York, 1984), pp. 195–218

Nyang, Sulayman S. 'Islam in the United States of America: A Review of the Sources', *Islamic Culture*, vol. LV, no. 2 (April 1981), pp. 93–109

Tunison, Emory H. 'Mohammad Webb, First American Muslim', *The Arab World*, vol. 1, no. 3 (1945), pp. 13–18

Winters, Clyde-Ahmad 'A Survey of Islam in the Africa Diaspora', *Pan African Journal*, vol. 8, no. 4, pp. 425–34

Part 4 The Religions of Asia

Editor:
Friedhelm Hardy

32 Introduction

Friedhelm Hardy

In one sense, there are innumerable religions in Asia. Some of these are tribal religions, belonging to relatively small social groups which so far have resisted an integration into wider cultural and social structures. Others are folk religions, relatively amorphous practices and beliefs which underlie the more structured 'high religions'. But in a different sense, only three or four religions are of primary importance, both in terms of the complexity of their beliefs and of their geographical spread. Thus Christianity found a home in south-western India from the earlier part of the first millennium CE. From the late fifteenth century, a succession of colonial powers and missionary activities gave rise to sizeable Christian communities in other parts of India and in Asian countries like the Philippines, Vietnam, Sri Lanka and China. But far greater has been the impact of Islam. From the seventh century CE onwards, it created a whole string of Islamic countries (Iran, Afghanistan, Pakistan, Bangladesh, Indonesia, Malaysia) and also acquired numerous followers in countries like India, central Russia and China. Nevertheless, both Christianity and Islam belong historically to the Near East, and in spite of their presence further east, they changed relatively little of their basic, 'semitic', character. Thus it is primarily Buddhism followed by Hinduism which appear as the older and truly 'Asian' religions.

From its original home in India, Buddhism spread into all the neighbouring countries, and from there further afield to Central Asia, Mongolia, China, Korea, Japan, Indonesia and Indo-China. Its history in India itself was complex, and often three 'phases' are distinguished to which three different types of Buddhism correspond. Depending among other things on the period during which a particular Asian country came to know of Indian Buddhism, one of these types was adopted.

Buddhism itself (along with a much lesser known parallel movement, Jainism, which remained restricted to India) evolved out of an older religious cosmos. The latter developed in the course of the centuries a whole spectrum of concrete expressions and, commonly summarised as 'Hinduism', has influenced the majority of Indians over more than three millennia. In medieval times, Hinduism influenced the whole of Indo-China and Indonesia extensively. It was Islam that eliminated these influences (except for the small enclave of the island of Bali), just as it put an end to Buddhism in India, Iran, Central Asia and Indonesia.

Although Buddhism and Hinduism have played an essential role in the 'national' histories of most Asian countries, only occasionally did they develop into 'national' religions. Tibet is perhaps the best-known example of such a fusion of the religious with the political; Sri Lanka and, to some extent, Japan can be added to the list. But in most cases, Hindus and Buddhists (Jains etc.) lived together in the same political system. It is possible to get glimpses of such a multi-religious situation from modern Nepal for instance. Moreover, the expansion of Buddhism (and to some extent, of medieval Hinduism) was primarily due to missionary and mercantile activities without military and 'colonial' aspects.

For a variety of reasons, other Asian religions deserve to be mentioned. Thus of considerable historical interest is Mazdaism (often styled Zoroastrianism). On the basis of linguistic similarities between a whole range of languages (including Greek, Latin, Old Slavonic, Old Germanic and Sanskrit), scholars reconstructed an original Indo-European language. It appears that, in the prehistoric past, the people speaking that language broke up into various groups and gradually moved into a variety of regions. One such group (called the Indo-Iranians) moved eastward, there, in its turn, to split up further: some entered Iran, and others continued their journey towards the east, to settle in north-west India. Whilst the group that entered India is associated with the oldest form of Hinduism, the immigrants into Iran developed Mazdaism which remained prominent in that country till the arrival of Islam. The Parsees of modern India are the descendants of refugees from Islamised Iran.

With Shamanism and Taoism, we can still catch some glimpses of religious practices and beliefs which belong to a world unaffected by the religions ultimately deriving from Indo-Iranian sources. On the other hand, a religion like Sikhism represents a relatively modern offshoot of Hinduism with Islamic features in its background. Even more recent is a whole range of religious developments which in part are due to modern, Western stimuli. The 'new religious movements' of Japan have particularly attracted scholarly attention. But it would be a serious mistake simply to contrast these modern developments with fixed systems (like Buddhism). The history of all these ancient religions is extremely dynamic; they constantly change, partly by interacting with the many folk religions upon which they have imposed themselves as a more complex superstructure. To enter into the spirit of the Asian religions means to realise this dynamism.

Introduction

During the last two hundred years or so, much information about, and many impressions of, the East have accumulated in our own culture. Inevitably, a fair number of stereotypes and unquestioned assumptions have crystallised in our perception of those other cultures. 'The mysterious East' is a commonly used expression in which these various preconceptions are gathered together. The word 'mysterious' is sometimes used to suggest 'incomprehensible', alien to such an extent that our own way of thinking cannot cope with it. If this were true of the East, the implications for what human nature is would be catastrophic, for it would suggest that different groups of people cannot actually relate to each other in a meaningful, namely human, manner. But if we consider the case of language as a parallel here, such a drastic position becomes unnecessary. An unknown language sounds extremely strange and incomprehensible, but so far no language has been discovered which cannot be learnt by an outsider. Some languages may be more difficult to learn than others, but in principle human speech is culturally transferable. In other words, no group of people which has a language in common is essentially isolated from other such groups with different languages. The onus would be on the person putting forward the theory of the Eastern incomprehensibility to prove that religion constitutes a case totally different from that of language.

But even if the Eastern religions were in principle 'comprehensible', they still could be 'mysterious' in the sense of being 'irrational'. In fact, this is probably the more frequent implication when we hear about the mysterious East. Again this is an assertion loaded with implied assumptions about human nature. It implies that only some people (in this case naturally us) are logical, systematic in their thinking and coherent. Other people do not possess such mental qualities, and not reason, but emotion (or something else) remains as the only means of comprehending the mystery. This particular understanding of the East is found not only in its critics, but also in its admirers. Rationality is to some the culmination of human existence, and to others the fundamental evil of Western society. Since the East is seen not to be rational, it cannot be regarded as fully developed in human terms (as the critics would see it), or it must be applauded as far more perfect (as the admirers would postulate). This is a remarkable consensus of opinion, at least as to the fundamental assumption, in whatever way it may then be evaluated. But is it true? Superficially, it is very easy to construe real-life situations (let us say, for a situation-comedy) where the Eastern reaction indeed appears incomprehensible and irrational. Take the following example. A tourist enters an Indian restaurant and asks the waiter: 'Isn't there any food here?' Imagine the answer to be 'Yes, sir.' Naturally we would find it very logical that the tourist should sit down at a table and wait for his meal to arrive. Nothing happens. The waiter has disappeared, and no food appears. The tourist begins to fidget, and finally shouts for service, the waiter reappears and answers once again 'Yes, sir!' to the question whether there isn't any food in the place. Repeat this a few times, and you have a comedy. But you have not proved that the East is irrational. All that we can say is that either the waiter does not use the English word 'yes' accurately, or that the tourist does not know how to interpret an Indian 'yes'. The Indian languages do not actually possess a word that corresponds to our 'yes'. They possess words of negation and affirmation. So all the waiter does when he replies 'yes' is to agree with our tourist. 'You are quite right: there is no food here.' Once this is realised, the whole scenario spontaneously turns into a perfectly rational affair. The confusion is merely due to the premisses by which the word 'yes' is used and understood.

On a more serious note it is still possible to make a similar point. It can be shown without difficulty that Eastern logic is identical to ours; the differences lie in the premisses of Eastern thought. Any system of thought is based on a set of axioms—fundamental facts that are regarded as so totally self-evident that they are not reflected upon and usually carried along as unconsciously made assumptions. It is here where the differences lie. The fact that a culture does not normally spell out such premisses, and that most of its members would not even be able to do so when asked, lies at the centre of the 'Eastern mystery'. Yet the logic which is then brought into operation is precisely the same as ours, but does not appear as such because of the dislocation of the premisses. Let us look at some examples to illustrate this in greater detail.

We take it utterly for granted that a thing is identical with itself. A chair is a chair, and nothing else. Moreover, such a self-identical object is a constant which we can insert into propositions. For example, 'this chair is brown and made out of oak wood.' We would be very loath to question any of this. To scrutinise it further would seem to be an extreme form of hair-splitting. And yet, empirically speaking, such a premiss is questionable, at least to the extent that it ought to force us to acknowledge that our premiss actually implies a decision about how we want to look at reality. Empirically, the chair is a most transient object. It comes about through the gluing together of various pieces of wood, taken from trees that have grown out of tiny seeds, and even if no fire or woodworm or any other destructive agent came near it, its life-span as a 'chair' is infinitesimally smaller than the life-span of the universe. The decision that we have made is to abstract from the transience (as defined above) and pretend—for totally legitimate, pragmatic reasons—that a chair is a chair. But a different decision could be made, which includes the element of transience in the basic understanding of what an object is. In that case, we are less likely to encounter propositions about 'objects', and more likely descriptions in terms of processes (the growth of trees, the joining together of different bits of wood and the gradual disintegration of this union). It is still possible to make perfectly logical statements about chairs, statements that need not make explicit the process characteristics of objects. But it is not difficult to imagine a situation comparable to the one envisaged above in the restaurant, in which talk about chairs can easily give rise to amazing misunderstandings. The 'uncomfortable chair' of one person may well be the 'pain-inflicting process stimulated by a temporarily solidified mass of transient phenomena' of another person (including some Western philosophers). Now why anybody would want to come up with such a perception of reality (and this kind of talk about it) depends on many other factors. It is needless to add that such factors fall squarely into what we call the Eastern religions.

Let us pursue this for a case where 'identity' is a crucial issue in the human destiny: the self-identity of the person. It is only through looking at the unusual or abnormal that we become aware of the implicit assumptions in our own culture. The schizophrenic appears to consist of more than one 'person'; alcohol can 'bring out a different person'; drugs can cause altered states of consciousness. But in all these cases our culture has decided to regard them as unimportant in relation to the definition of a person. In all three examples something is happening that ought not to. The 'real' person is disturbed or interfered with. Now let us turn to Asia. Here we find it culturally accepted that a person may leave his body. Thus the shaman roams about freely and enters the bodies of animals and other human beings. Or the body of one person is used by another being, in the cults of possession. Or the meditator experiences embodiment as an animal or a different human being. Or the same meditator experiences a widening of his self-awareness: the conventional boundaries surrounding the 'I' are removed and the 'I' plunges into a far more comprehensive reality. Some of this is directly observable to others, like a possessed person, through whom a different being speaks and acts. In other cases, the rest of society has to rely on the testimony of the person experiencing it. As in the example from the Western context, a decision as to the validity of such experiences for the definition of personhood has to be made. The fundamental difference between East and West here is simply that Asia has accepted such phenomena as issues worth discussing and reflecting upon and does not discard them as 'abnormal'. It is clear that regardless of how precisely a religion may sort matters out, the very fact of deciding to accept any of these experiences as a valid source of insight must have far-reachng consequences for the formulation of human destiny.

Let us look at another example. It is probably fair to say that our traditional view of the world regards it as an object lying outside ourselves. In religious terms it is a creation out of nothing and thus, ultimately, of no real concern in the relation between God and man. To the extent that Christianity has formulated this as a dogma it has explicitly identified it as an axiom. The East knows of no such thing as creation out of nothing. The world tends to be accepted as a factually given entity, like man. From this follows logically the assumption of a very intimate connection between man and the world. Within the world can be found a rhythm, a structure or pattern (e.g. the *Tao* or the *Dharma*) which is decisive for man's own destiny and fulfilment. Religion spells out how to harmonise one's individual being with this universal rhythm. Aspects of this have been labelled 'fatalism' by certain Western observers. Yet when this term is required to denote more than merely a somewhat placid personality type, content with accepting things as they are, it does not do justice to this view of the world. Wherever we find the belief in such a cosmic rhythm, it goes along with the assumption that 'ordinary' man has not yet achieved his harmonising with it. Thus he must do something: he is called for action. He is faced with a definite choice, and it is his choice alone. Even when the past is brought into this conception, as in certain ways predetermining the current life, it is never seen as preventing the essential actions asked for. Man remains in control of his destiny, at least where it is supposed to matter most. Moreover, the cosmic rhythm is often envisaged as containing undreamt-of powers which can be used by the man who knows how to get at them. Whether Taoist or Tantric, the pursuit of such powers guided by religion can certainly not be regarded as 'fatalistic' (or, for that matter, as 'world-negating' or 'spiritual').

Such a premiss of a cosmic rhythm implies another important difference from traditional Western thought. We are used to looking at the world as containing good and evil as objective entities, as universal, cosmic forces. Historically, this derives from the Judeo-Christian tradition, which in turn, some claim, may have been influenced by Mazdaism (Zoroastrianism). The powers of goodness are with God, and evil is associated with the devil. This type of binary, objectifying thought is alien to the religions further East. Objectively, there is only the world with its inbuilt rhythm and structure. As long as, subjectively, man harmonises himself with this rhythm, he does what is 'good'. The evil experienced in life is the price paid for there existing many beings who do not join into this rhythm. Such an ethical neutrality of the world in relation to man can become particularly disconcerting for a Western observer when it presents itself in a theistic form. We are so strongly accustomed to link the concept of God with that of ultimate 'goodness' that a 'neutral' God is inconceivable. Yet it is equally rational to argue that, given the nature of God as Absolute, by definition he must transcend whatever categories and attributes our contingent human mind can come up with.

We may conveniently continue this exploration of premisses by staying with the theme of theism. It goes without saying that for us religion has to do with God, or at least with gods. If we stick by this definition, a considerable amount of material found in Asia must be excluded, because there is no God here, and often not even gods. That sometimes, in a rather uncritical manner, the concept 'god' was applied to entities like the Japanese *kami* or the Indian *deva*, is another story. By themselves, the *kami* or the *deva* do not necessarily offer us the concept of 'god'

On the other hand, if we say that religion has to do with the ultimate, that it provides a transcendental reference point and guides man towards his fulfilment, then we have no problem here. Theism then reveals itself as a particular mode of envisaging or concretising this transcendental. Whether it is Buddhism, or Jainism, or Taoism (the traditional trouble-makers in the philosophical discussion about the nature of religion), they all provide us with such transcendental pointers: human destiny comprises more than the monolinear process of birth, life and death. That the charge of nihilism could have been made against these religions has actually nothing to do with the mysterious premisses of Eastern religious thought, but is merely due to our insufficient factual knowledge about these religions.

For the same reason, the existence of true monotheism has not been brought properly into focus. Certainly for India (and a case could perhaps be made also for Amida Buddhism in China and Japan) we must acknowledge monotheistic religion. Details on these will be found in the section on the Indian religions, and at this point we may simply note that behind our conventional term 'Hinduism' a great variety of truly monotheistic systems are hidden. From this emerges the rather important general conclusion that the contrast West: East is not one of monotheistic: polytheistic (or whatever). The phenomenon of monotheism allows us also to learn something further about the hidden premisses that make our understanding of the East so troublesome. Wherever the concept of an absolute God is found, his definition as a 'person' implies assumptions about certain characteristics that inhere in this 'person'. Inevitably, the way such characteristics are envisaged derives from human experience. Thus God is a 'he'; he is the 'father'. Moreover, a relational element may be introduced: God is the Father relating to the Son through the love personified in the Holy Spirit. In essence, Indian theism does the same, but makes decisions about how to concretise such characteristics which differ considerably from what we are used to in the Judeo-Christian tradition. Given the fact that about half the human population is female, it is perhaps not all that surprising to find that from the fertile religious ground of India a 'she' has also emerged as God. And instead of choosing the father–son relational model, India tends to use the husband–wife model. Such choices may appear strange to us (and may even shock us initially because of the love-life explicitly acknowledged through the husband–wife relationship), but they are not 'mysterious'.

Thus what has been suggested here so far is the possibility of detecting a level of (usually unconsciously made) premisses or axioms which provide the foundation for sometimes extremely complex edifices of viewing the world and man's destiny in it. Moreover, it has been suggested that it is not necessary to postulate a different kind of logic or rationality at work in such edifices, when they appear in different civilisations. The initial choice as to which premiss to adopt (for example, is God a 'he' or a 'she'?) concerns logical alternatives, whatever the motivation behind a particular choice may be. Again, the manner in which from a set of such chosen premisses a whole religious system is developed appears to follow the same logic and reasoning, for example when 'grace' is associated with the female side of the deity. Thus at least in principle the religions of the East do not present unassailable obstacles to our comprehension.

In practice, things are obviously more difficult and it might perhaps be of some use to look at a few examples of this kind of difficulty. We are not now talking about fundamental things like 'premisses' of thought, and have moved to a far more superficial level, the level of practicalities. Initially, the world of the East was indeed 'mysterious' for the simple reason that little factual information was available. Naturally, when during the last two hundred years or so an increasing amount of information became available, attempts were made to bring some order into this material. Phenomena that appeared related were grouped together under a common heading, the 'isms', and the whole began to make much more sense. Terms like Taoism, Buddhism, Hinduism, evolved as useful tools for surveying the rich Asian religious scene. But, however useful they may be, certainly the specialist remains aware also of how imperfect, tentative and inefficient they still are. They are no more than temporarily put-up pointers, in need of constant revision and improvement. The need for this has nothing to do with the mysteries of the East and is entirely due to our own imperfect factual knowledge. But unfortunately, our 'isms' have taken on an independent existence as well. They have moved outside the confines of academic discourse and have entered into the parlance of society at large. This has meant that here for instance 'Hinduism' is now understood to be 'the same sort of thing as Islam etc.' But in reality, a term like 'Hinduism' denotes a very large cluster of 'religions' each of which by itself would be 'the same sort of thing as Islam'. It is here where perhaps the most common justification for the belief in the mysterious and irrational East lies. Let us stay with 'Hinduism' to demonstrate this. With great effort a fair amount of factual knowledge has been acquired by the student. Thus from the rather over-full pigeon-hole labelled 'Hinduism' he knows that there is a belief in Viṣṇu (a male personal god). He also knows that there is a belief in *brahman* (an impersonal world-soul). He finally knows that there is belief in meditation as achieving final fulfilment. Since all this comes out of the same box marked 'Hinduism', he quite appropriately attempts to correlate these pieces of information. But however hard he may try, the puzzle simply does not fit. His more polite reaction will be to speak of the mysteries of the East. Similarly, in addition to his knowledge of Viṣṇu he may pick up information about the belief in Śiva (like Viṣṇu, a male personal god). The logical conclusion would be to say that 'Hinduism' is polytheistic, because a number of gods are believed in. But what has actually been done here is comparable to some Martian's attempt to formulate a logically coherent explanation of religion in Britain, by drawing information indiscriminately from the different churches, chapels, mosques, synagogues, etc. In other words, the bits and pieces of the puzzle can be put together, but in a coherent way only if we accept that they do not all belong to a single 'mysterious' religion, which we call 'Hinduism'. The seeming chaos can be turned into order, but only in the form of many ordered wholes. Naturally, what has been said here about Hinduism applies also to many of the other Asian religions.

There is one final observation that might be felt to be useful in our struggle with the incomprehensible East. Anybody acquiring a knowledge of Eastern religious material constantly repeats the question: 'what does this mean?' In itself this is a perfectly legitimate question. The problem lies in the way that a possible answer is perceived. In the Semitic traditions, religion has defined itself consciously and rigorously. Every component of its complex edifice is carefully explained, in terms of its meaning, through the system as a whole. Institutionalised 'authority' acts as the final arbiter in cases of doubt or ambivalence. But this kind of centralised meaning-definition is simply absent in the East. An enormous number of religious symbols are handed down from generation to generation, but their meaning and significance may vary greatly, depending on the individual context in which they occur. The implication of this is that the search for what religious symbols actually mean to the religious individual becomes troublesome and laborious. But there is nothing irrational or confused in this.

'Mysterious East' has one further connotation: it is perceived to be attractive, challenging, inviting exploration and pleasurable. Nothing could be further from the intentions of this present exploration than the desire to prove that such a perception is inaccurate or inappropriate. All that has been suggested here is a bit of commonsense and a lot of patience—patience when trying to fit the pieces of the puzzle together, and patience in waiting for the specialists to keep on adding further information. We are far from having acquired all the pieces of all the puzzles. Once upon a time, the East appeared as a devastating, deadly threat (and the connection of the Mongols with supposedly peaceful Buddhism is worth exploring in this context). There is no need to perceive the 'challenges' that have been spoken of here in this vein. For some it might be an exciting discovery to find a God who is a 'she'; to others it might enhance their understanding of a God who is a 'he'. Some might derive great comfort from the discovery of monotheism as far away as India or Japan; others might deepen their belief in devotion in view of beliefs about meditationally gained altered states of consciousness. But there is no threat here, only the possibility of interesting insights.

33 Philosophical and Religious Taoism

Bulcsu Siklós

In a sense it is inappropriate to treat the two totally separate phenomena of the title under the single rubric of Taoism. Philosophical and religious Taoism share the use of the word *tao* and not very much else—most of Lao-tzu's recommendations were and still are blatantly ignored by followers of religious Taoism. The latter term itself has come to be used as a blanket title denoting everything recognisably 'religious' in China which was not obviously Confucian or Buddhist, when it is perhaps best defined in antithesis to China's age-old indigenous 'popular' religion. To counter the insidious influence of the latter was the prime concern of the early followers of the Way of the Heavenly Masters.

The Philosophical Taoism of Lao-tzu and Chuang-tzu

Lao-tzu and his eponymous classic, also known as the *Tao Te Ching*, are both equally obscure and shadowy. Ssu-ma Ch'ien, who was author of the *Shih chi* (Historian's Records) and wrote in the first century BCE, some three centuries after Lao-tzu, is as much in the dark about him as we are today. Ssu-ma Ch'ien tells us that Lao-tzu was a native of the state of Ch'u, that his family name was Li, that he was a court archivist, that he met Confucius (551–479 BCE) and that, dissatisfied with the state of the Chou dynasty, he wandered westwards through the pass at Han Ku where he was persuaded to write a summary of his philosophy by the Keeper of the Pass, Yin Hsi. All of this is apocryphal; indeed there is no real reason to assume that there ever was a Lao-tzu or that the *Tao Te Ching* is the work of one man; nevertheless there is no harm in continuing to call the author or authors 'Lao-tzu'. The division of his work into two books, the *Tao Ching* and the *Te Ching*, gave it its alternative name. There is no reason to believe that this division goes back further than the first century.

Early Chinese is not grammatically difficult—if anything it is too simple and ambiguous—but the interpretation of a text like the *Tao Te Ching* is often a matter of *ad hoc* hermeneutics, with an end result far removed from the author's original intentions. It would be hard enough to glean the meaning of many sections of the *Tao Te Ching* even if the text were not rife with abbreviated characters, and if it were punctuated. One would think that the very obscurity of Lao-tzu's *magnum opus* would have deterred translators, but that has not been the case. It is often said that only the Bible has been translated into English more often.

Here are two versions of the opening lines of the *Tao Te Ching*:

The way that can be spoken of
Is not the constant way:
The name that can be named
Is not the constant name.
The nameless was the beginning of heaven and earth;
The named was the mother of the myriad creatures.

(TTC I:1, tr. D.C. Lau, 1963)

Lodehead lodehead-brooking: no forewonted lodehead
Namecall namecall-brooking: no forewonted namecall.
Having-naught namecalling: Heaven-Earth's fetation
Having-aught namecalling: Myriad mottling's mother.

(TTC I:1, tr. P.A. Boodberg, 1979)

The character *tao* (道) is composed of two elements (a head/person 首 and to walk/go 辵), and has the basic meaning of 'way' or 'road'. By extension it has the meaning of a 'ruled district/province', the more abstract sense of 'the (virtuous) way' or 'doctrine' and the verbal meanings of 'to enact a law', 'to state', 'to tell' and 'to instruct'. The word *tao* is thus by no means the exclusive property of Taoism—most early Chinese philosophers, Confucius included, made ample use of it, usually in the sense of an ethical code of some sort. In early popular religion tao signified the power or ability to perform magical feats, as well as the power of kings whose authority often rested on such magical skills. It was by following the order or principle of the world, apparent in the daily, monthly, seasonal and yearly alternations of *yin* and *yang*, the 'feminine' and 'masculine' principles, that the ruler came to possess tao. Perhaps it was the inclusion of that strangest of books, the *I Ching* (Book of Changes), among the canonical books of the Confucians that prompted early philosophical inquiry into the tao underlying the 64 hexagrams representing pure yang, pure yin and all the various intermediate states.

Lao-tzu used the word 'tao' provisionally, as can be noticed in the above passage. He seems to have considered his tao to have been twofold, nameable and unnameable, the unnameable being the 'constant' tao, the fundamental principle behind the named tao which produces the universe ('heaven and earth') and all beings ('the myriad creatures'). This interpretation is somewhat at variance with what Lao-tzu seems to be saying, where the nameless tao is actually responsible for the creation of the universe. We should not worry ourselves overmuch—it should be stressed that commentators, both Chinese and Western, ancient and modern, have differed in their interpretations of these and the following terms. Lao-tzu sometimes calls the nameable tao 'Being' and states (XL) that Being was produced by Non-being, which in turn is symbolised by the Mysterious Female (the nameless tao in its fecund aspect) and the Valley Spirit (the nameless tao in its void aspect). The terms *yu* and *wu*, 'being' and 'non-being' could also mean 'having' and 'having-not', referring to the presence or absence of perceptible features in each.

Lao-tzu unifies both taos under the rubric *hsüan*, 'the Obscure', which really seems to hit the nail on the head. All this is perhaps best summed up in Lao-tzu's own phrase:

> The way begets one; one begets two; two begets three; three begets the myriad creatures.
>
> (TTC XLII:93)

This sentence itself, expressing a slightly different point of view from those of the opening section already quoted, has given many commentators considerable trouble, contradicting as it does the general yet perhaps naïve concept of the tao as the One. (This misinterpretation led Catholic translators of the Bible into Chinese to translate 'God' by 'tao'.) Chuang-tzu in particular refutes this interpretation—in any case the word tao is uncountable—and there is surely no way of reconciling the concept of tao and its various manifestations to the Western ideas of universals and particulars. This is very reminiscent of the way in which the Neoplatonist Damascius held to the doctrine of the unnameable principle behind all nameables (in contrast to, say, Plotinus, for whom the One was the highest principle).

So how does the tao—the unnameable tao—appear to the mystic?

> As a thing the way is
> Shadowy, indistinct.
> Indistinct and shadowy,
> Yet within it is an image;
> Shadowy and indistinct,
> Yet within it is a substance.
> Dim and dark,
> Yet within it is an essence.
>
> (TTC XXI:49)

Although the sage has access to the tao via meditation and trance, Lao-tzu never indicates that the experience is ecstatic (or rather, enstatic) or involves any feeling of union or any experience of light or totality or any of the other typical signs of mystical achievement.

Meditational and breathing exercises, and perhaps sexual techniques, are of use to the sage wishing to attain the tao:

> When carrying in your head your perplexed bodily soul can you embrace in your arms the One
> And not let go?
> In concentrating your breath can you become as supple
> As a babe?
> Can you polish your mysterious mirror
> And leave no blemish?
>
> When the gates of heaven open and shut
> Are you capable of keeping to the role of the female?

(TCC X:24)

In this poem, the term *p'o* or 'bodily soul' (the *yin* 'soul' which descends into the earth at death, as opposed to the *yang* 'soul', the *hun*, which ascends to heaven) comes to have the meaning of 'semen' according to the commentators. Likewise the 'gates of heaven' are glossed as the mouth and nostrils. It is only because everything produced by the tao—the nameable tao, heaven and earth, the myriad beings—returns to the tao that it is possible for the sage to attain the tao prematurely.

If we can ignore, perhaps unfairly, Lieh Yu-k'ou's *Lieh Tzu* (the extant text of which is based on a version some 600 years later than the author's presumed dates (fourth to fifth centuries BCE), and which is of dubious authenticity), the other early Taoist work to have survived is the *Chuang Tzu* of Chuang Chou (fourth century BCE). Once again the author is often called by the name of his work. Biographical details of Chuang-tzu's life are few and far between, and are perhaps even thinner on the ground than in Lao-tzu's case. The difference between the two authors is considerable, not necessarily philosophically but stylistically. Where Lao-tzu is lofty and mysterious, obscure and even humourless, Chuang-tzu is worldly, lively, playful and, above all, human:

> A man was terrified of his shadow, and disliked his footprints. Intending to get rid of them, he started running, but the more often he raised his feet as he ran, the more the number of footprints became, and however fast he ran, his shadow still followed him. Telling himself that he was not going fast enough, he ran faster and faster without stopping, until finally he was exhausted and dropped dead. Foolish man, if he had stayed in the shade, he would have had no shadow; if he had been still, there would have been no footprints.

How different is this to Lao-tzu's

> I do my utmost to attain emptiness;
> I hold firmly to stillness.

(TTC XVI:37)

A lot of the energy expended on the dozens of translations of Lao-tzu's work would have been better spent on the *Chuang Tzu*.

There are two aspects of Chuang-tzu's thought which are worth emphasising, though one is hardly doing justice to him by ignoring other aspects such as his emphasis on spontaneity. Firstly, Chuang-tzu advocates a type of relativism based on what might be termed a 'meta-view' encasing various linguistic and conceptual terms. As we have seen, Lao-tzu was also aware of the limitations of language in describing the tao—indeed the recognition of this limitation could be regarded as a hallmark of true mysticism—but this finds far fuller expression in the *Chuang Tzu*. Secondly, Chuang-tzu wrestles with the problem of what it is exactly that controls mental activities such as perception, and thereby parallels the tao in its controlling aspect. For the controller of mental activities Chuang-tzu uses the term *hsin*, originally meaning 'heart' (the organ), but also translatable as 'mind'. Locating the essential core of man at the heart is not, of course, exclusively Chinese. The *hsin* was also a valve for the tao, a double mirror which reflected both the tao and the external world indiscriminatingly, much as the mirror-like wisdom of the *dhyānibuddha* Akṣobhya reflects the Buddhist *tathatā* or 'suchness'.

The works of Lao-tzu and Chuang-tzu exerted considerable influence in literary, court and academic circles, and indeed continue to do so in the Far East of today. In the West, Lao-tzu's conception of tao in particular has been grist to the mills of numerous thinkers, self-styled mystics, academics and, more recently, of those wishing to compare 'Eastern mysticism' with the ideas of modern physics.

Despite all this, the Taoism of Lao-tzu and Chuang-tzu never became a religion as the term is commonly understood. There was no room for faith, prayer, ecstasy, a priesthood, no way of involving the ordinary man, and no way of truly accommodating government, authority or conventional morality. It was the way purely of the solitary sage, the anchorite possessed of superior wisdom (*ming* or 'light') who achieves everything through the superficially paradoxical technique of 'not-doing' (*wu wei*), through not interfering with the natural order. *Wu wei* does not mean total abandonment of activity. Rather, it is a way of rolling with the punches, as it were; or, even better, not even being there when the punch is thrown. Strictly speaking, the Taoism of Lao-tzu and Chuang-tzu should have no place in this book.

Religious Taoism

There exists another type of Taoism which involves a variety of religious features; 'Taoism' will henceforth be used here to denote this religious material. This Taoism is an oddly assorted mixture of beliefs and practices with very little in common at first sight. A firm definition is however possible—all modern Taoist schools, however disparate their practices, recognise the primacy of the first *T'ien shih* or Heavenly Master, Chang Tao-ling (*fl.* 126–45 CE) and the revelations received by him, even if they do not venerate the present Heavenly Master. By this definition (proposed by M. Strickmann, in Welch and Seidel (1979), pp. 123–92) alchemy, breathing techniques, meditation, yoga and so forth are seen not necessarily as Taoist arts but as methods, often pre-existing ones, adapted for use by Taoists and hence only admissible into the body of Taoism when practised by Taoists conforming to the above criterion. This definition is useful mainly because, as pointed out in the introduction, Taoism becomes Taoism through contrast with the indigenous religious practices of ancient China from which certain methods were borrowed and certain practices (for example, sacrifice) very strongly rejected.

From a very early period, the primary concern of the Taoist has been the attainment of a state usually called immortality. Unification with the tao is concomitant with the achievement of a state transcending putrefaction and death, but many Taoists seem to have interpreted this not in the purely spiritual sense of Chuang-tzu but in a totally literal sense. The term *hsien*, meaning an 'immortal', originally might well have referred to Philosophical Taoists who had taken Lao-tzu's anchoretic injunctions to heart.

Numerous different types of immortality could be attained. One could become an immortal on our plane and simply inhabit a perfected body here on earth, or, perfected, one could depart bodily to higher realms; if death was somewhat premature, one could descend to the palaces within the earth to continue one's studies or actually to become the contents of an other-worldly athanor wherein one's body would be forged into one conforming to transcendent standards. This last process is very reminiscent of the trancic dismemberment and 'reassembly' undergone by shamans throughout North Asia, especially as there are indications that the prospective Taoist immortal merely died a 'temporary death' (*chan ssu*) during which his alchemical transformation took place. It is perhaps from experimentation with fungal, herbal and mineral means to achieve this state of temporary death that the later obsessions with the alchemical process developed, as well as the search for miraculous herbs and mushrooms, and the fabulous mountains and islands on which they were said to grow.

The human body is a microcosmic model of the universe, and, as such, can be affected by drawing on the powers of the external world. The body contains three Cinnabar Fields (*tan t'ien*), respectively located in the head, heart and just below the navel. These Cinnabar Fields imprison the Three Maggots or Worms, which can only be set free by their host's death. It is thus in their interest to hasten the ageing and death processes, which can in fact be halted if the practitioner abandons consuming the grain, meat and wine on which the Worms feed, and consumes only such herbal and mineral preparations as can hasten the Worms' demise. The meditative absorption of deities symbolising the tao (the deified Lao-tzu among them) into the Cinnabar Fields from their abodes in the Big Dipper also lengthens the practitioner's life and keeps the Worms at bay.

Alchemy has already been mentioned in its role as the means by which elixirs of immortality could be obtained, but, just as in Europe, the true alchemist, the practitioner of Internal Alchemy, looked down on the humble 'puffer' trying, often unsuccessfully, to concoct his potions. Using meditative procedures the internal alchemist imitated the external alchemical process by creating cinnabar in his lowest Cinnabar Field through uniting the sexual energy with the subtle aspect of breath, and then ascending from the resultant chaotic stage (comparable to the stage of blackness and putrefaction in European alchemy) to a stage where the Yellow Flower finally blossomed and rendered the adept perfected. The components of cinnabar (mercuric sulphide, HgS) are exactly those which form the basis of the stages of the Lesser ('mercury') and Greater ('sulphur') Works of European alchemy. The end result was also conceived of in a more external sense as the Mysterious Embryo, rebirth into which would enable the adept to escape his inexorably ageing body and join the ranks of immortals in any one of many heavens.

The *fang shi* or court 'magicians' of the Ch'in and Early Han periods (230 BCE–24 CE) seem to have been the forerunners of the Taoists proper. The Han dynasty itself was founded with the assistance of a magician who claimed to have received instructions from a manifestation of Lao-tzu, and later on official cults were established to honour the deified Lao-tzu as well as certain other deities who were to become part and parcel of everyday Taoist worship. Of prime importance were the *wu ti* or Five Emperors, symbolising any group of five (the Five Elements: wood, fire, earth, metal and water, or the Five Organs: liver, heart, spleen, lungs and kidneys, for example). Many of the aphorisms of the *fang shih*, as well as cosmological theories and methods for commanding the spirits are to be found in the *T'ai-p'ing Ch'ing-ling shu*, the Great Peace General Command Book, a text revealed by the spirits to a semi-legendary figure, Yü Chi, which became the basic handbook for many later groups and which also influenced Chang Tao-ling (*fl*. 126–45), the founder proper of Taoism.

Chang Tao-ling was by all accounts extremely well read in the Classics, and expressed an interest in alchemy, perhaps dating from the time he arrived in Szechuan—alchemy in general seems to have been a primarily southern and western Chinese affair. His disciples were required to pay a tax of five bushels of grain to his administration (hence the Confucian derogatory term for the sect, Wu-tou Mi-tao or Five Bushels of Grain school), an administration which Chang Tao-ling and his grandson and successor Chang Lu established very much on classical lines, following Lao-tzu's recommendations, among others.

Yü Chi's writings also inspired a certain Chang Chiao to establish another movement, this time one which was militant in the extreme and made the fatal error of actively trying to overthrow the by now sickly but not yet impotent Han dynasty. The Way of Great Peace, as it was known, was soundly suppressed for its pains, while its followers were renamed the Yellow Turbans after the headgear they wore to their deaths.

With the increasing influence of Buddhism during the North–South Period (265–581), the best minds of China had to come to grips with some of the best that India could offer in the way of philosophy, cosmology and personal salvation. The Religion of Numbers, as the Chinese termed the—to them—arcane lore of Śākyamuni, inspired several major changes in Chinese (and, more specifically, Taoist) religious practice. That linchpin of Chinese thought and morality, filial piety, was extended to cover all sentient beings through the Mahāyānist idea that all living beings throughout the universe had at some time been the parents of every other being. As a practical manifestation of this, increasing influence came to be laid on burial practices, ensuring a smooth transition for the deceased from this life through the intermediate state to a favourable rebirth. All the Taoist orders came to consider the newly created, Buddhist-inspired liturgies of the *San Tung* (Three Arcana), the first Taoist Canon, as basic to their practice.

The sect which seems to have been most influenced by Buddhism, and the founding of which dates from this period of strong Indian influence is the Mao Shan or Shang Ch'ing (Highest Purity) sect, based on a series of revelations received by Yang Hsi in *c.* 364 from several immortals, and notably from a manifestation of a perhaps legendary woman, Wei Hua-ts'un (251–334?). The Mao Shan sect was essentially monastic and much more concerned with contemplation than with collective worship. Mao Shan treatises in general show considerable Buddhist influence, yet the prime Taoist concerns with immortality and internal alchemy are still predominant. Eschatologically, some see a reflection of Maitreya, the coming Buddha, in the idea or the *Hou sheng* or Coming Sage who will at some future date, after the extermination of all evil, establish *t'ai p'ing* (Great Peace) on earth.

During the Sui and T'ang Dynasties (581–905), Indian Buddhist Tantrism reared its mysterious and colourful head(s) in China. Taoism responded by incorporating a vast selection of *mudrās* (hand gestures) and pseudo-Sanskrit *mantras* (spells, or potent formulas) into its liturgical corpus. Public ritual started increasing in popularity at the expense of meditation, one result of which was the increasing fragmentation of Taoism. T'u Kuang-t'ing (842–926) is worthy of note as being the last truly ecumenical master of ancient Taoism. The rise of sectarianism continued unabated during the Sung and Yüan periods (960–1341), a phenomenon that may be seen as akin to that of the Reformation—though, not atypically, the rivalry was less intense than in Europe, perhaps because the differences were ritual or methodological rather than doctrinal, and frequently stemmed merely from a Taoist response to new developments in Buddhist practice. It should not be thought, however, that the relationship between Taoism and Buddhism was as rosy as may be gathered from this short survey. Debate was often acrimonious in the extreme. The founding of the North Chinese Ch'üan Chen sect in particular was an obvious effort to match the rigorous, simple yet effective techniques, both meditational and monastic, of Ch'an (Zen) Buddhism. It is commonly stated that Ch'an itself was influenced by Taoism to no small degree, especially in its attachment to spontaneity and in its—theoretical—rejection of scriptural authority and outward form. However, these practices belong to the repertoire of the 'Philosophical Taoist', and are as far divorced from religious Taoism as they are from more ritualised Buddhist schools such as T'ien T'ai.

The old sects still continued to function, often in revitalised form, or under different names. The Cheng I sect was not much more than the officially sanctioned continuation of the Heavenly Master sect. Also during this period the imagination of Taoists was captured by Buddhist Tantrism, not in its Indian form this time, but in its seemingly more demoniacal Tibeto–Mongol form as practised by the Yüan court. Various sects arose, all specialising in different versions of what is known as *lei fa* or Thunder Magic, a technique whereby the energy of a thunderstorm is absorbed by the practitioner through breathing techniques, *mudrās* and *mantras*, and is then employed to light the inner fire of the alchemical furnace or to exorcise evil. Members of certain sects, notably the Shen Hsiao, were often accused of abusing the powers thus gained and not following strict canonical rules. Indeed, the Shen Hsiao is still regarded as somewhat unorthodox.

Official patronage of Taoism continued through the Ming period (1368–1644). The present Taoist Canon, the *Tao-tsang*, was first printed in the reign of Cheng-t'ung in 1447 in some 1,100 volumes, unbelievably enough a considerable reduction in size compared to earlier versions. The tripartite division of the Taoist Canon is reminiscent of the *tripiṭaka* of the Buddhist Canon, but, strictly speaking, the division corresponds more to the Three Vehicles of Buddhism, i.e. Hīna-, Mahā- and Vajra-yāna.

Sectarianism was gradually brought under control in the Ming and Ch'ing periods (1644–1911) by issuing licences to all practising Taoists once they had learnt the canonical registers and one particular brand of Thunder Magic. This of course just led to an increasing dichotomy between the 'official' orders and proliferating local orders which were in effect practising illegally. Taoism lost considerable influence under the generally pro-Buddhist Ch'ing, though it is doubtful whether its stock was as low as is commonly thought, especially as true Taoist practice found today in Taiwan and Hong Kong seems to be refined, sophisticated and based very much on old canonical standards.

Bibliography

Lao-tzu *Tao Te Ching*, translated with an introduction by D.C. Lau (Penguin, Harmondsworth, 1963)
Boodberg, P.A. *Selected Works of Peter A. Boodberg* (Berkeley, 1979)
Saso, M. *The Teachings of Taoist Master Chuang* (Yale University Press, New Haven, 1978)
Welch, H. *The Parting of the Way—Lao Tzu and the Taoist Movement* (London, 1958)
—— and Seidel, A. (eds.) *Facets of Taoism* (Yale University Press, New Haven, 1979)

34 Mazdaism ('Zoroastrianism')

Julian Baldick

Mazdaism, the principal religion of pre-Islamic Iran, counted approximately 30,000 adherents there in the 1970s, and had about 87,500 followers, known as the Parsees, in India, Pakistan and Sri Lanka in 1976. The faith is characterised by an emphasis upon a struggle between Good and Evil. It is of interest not only in its own right, as manifesting a complex mixture of archaic and variegated ingredients, but also for the study of the gods and legends of many peoples, from Ireland to India. Another source of interest is the spectacular methodological progress made in this field, particularly on the continent of Europe, during the last fifty years, which has given new life to the history of religions.

One must pay attention to the methods used by the specialists, since Mazdaism is one of the more difficult religions of the world to investigate. The original sources are few, extremely corrupt and largely incomprehensible. As a result scholars have come to widely divergent conclusions, so that the student risks bewilderment. Because Mazdean texts lend themselves to the most diverse interpretations, we are forced to concentrate upon the logic displayed by modern writers in their reconstructions, in order to determine which are the more convincing. We need not take seriously anyone who claims to know 'what actually happened' among the ancient Iranians.

The terms 'Mazdaism' and 'Mazdean' will be used here, in line with modern international practice, and as corresponding to the terminology of the worshippers of Ahura Mazdā, the 'Wise Lord', who appears as the chief (and to some as the sole) god of the religion. Since non-British writers use this terminology in works available in English it seems inappropriate to keep the old-fashioned words 'Zoroastrianism' and 'Zoroastrian', formed after a European version ('Zoroaster') of the name of the alleged founder, Zarathushtra, a figure whom scholars now tend to date to around 1000 BCE. Such usage would be comparable to speaking of

'Mahometanism' instead of the correct and now universally accepted 'Islam'.

In approaching Mazdaism it is important to bear in mind that because of its archaic, 'fossilising' character it presents features which go back to the Indo-Europeans, the linguistic ancestors of a variety of peoples in Asia and the West. Owing to the scantiness of Iranian and Mazdean materials we are obliged to resort to comparisons with the religions of other nations. Much disagreement has surrounded the question of where the Indo-Europeans originally lived, but now it is considered to have been somewhere in south Russia or Siberia.

Even fiercer controversy has raged around the theories concerning Indo-European religion propounded by the French scholar Georges Dumézil. In Mazdean studies the quarrels have been bitter, but here Dumézil has found the support of many specialists. This is not surprising, since it was largely from the Mazdean scriptures, the Avesta, that he reconstructed the alleged 'threefold ideology of the Indo-Europeans'.

The Indo-Europeans, he claims, maintained that society should be organised into classes according to three 'functions': 1. sovereignty, linked with religion in its magical and juridical aspects; 2. war; 3. fertility, in its economic and erotic aspects. These 'functions' inspired the mythology expressed in the Indo-European languages. Now we may observe that this does not get one very far in studying Greek or Indian religion, given the enormous inventiveness of the Greeks and Indians, who quickly submerged their Indo-European heritage in a rich flowering of legends. But the ancient Iranians do not appear to have produced much more than an ideoloy of this kind. They expressed it in their religious texts and national epic, and put it into practice, maintaining a rigid class system until it was broken by Islam.

We must now turn to a sub-group of the Indo-Europeans, the Indo-Iranians, when they were in their original homeland, before dividing and migrating as Indians to India and as Iranians to Iran, possibly between 2000 and 1500 BCE. Here reconstructions are completely theoretical, and belong almost entirely to the field of historical and comparative linguistics. The Indian and Iranian materials certainly present many religious features in common, but these have given rise to much academic dispute, notably concerning the various deities and the 'structures' to which they might be assigned.

The view which has prevailed for most of the twentieth century, but has been impressively challenged, is that the Indo-Iranians worshipped two kinds of gods, seen as opposing one another: on the one hand, gods called *daēva-* by the Iranians and *deva-* by the Indians, and on the other hand gods called *ahura-* by the Iranians and *asura-* by the Indians. As a result, the first class were to be demoted to the status of demons (*daēvas*) by the Iranians; the second class, in this theory, were similarly demoted to the status of demons (*asuras*) by the Indians. The work of demotion on the Iranian side is credited to the alleged founder of Mazdaism, Zarathushtra, who is supposed to have made Ahura Mazdā the sole or chief god, and 'reformed' the old Iranian religion.

This conventional theory is weak and would now appear to be obsolete. In any case, since it presents a hostility between two classes of gods in Indo-Iranian times, the idea of a later 'reform' is unnecessary, as was pointed out by the late Marijan Molé: the *daēvas* could have been demoted to the status of demons by a natural development, as opponents of the venerated *ahuras*, without the intervention of a 'Reformer'.

That this theory 'is false from beginning to end' has been argued by a distinguished British linguist on the Indian side, Thomas Burrow. He points out that it is absurd to say that a class of gods called the *asuras* were demoted into demons. For the individual Indian beings titled *asura-* were never so demoted, and so it is ridiculous to claim that the *asuras* as a class were demonised. Besides, it is wrong to speak of an original class of gods called *asura-* in opposition to gods called *deva-*. The term *asura-*, meaning 'lord', was probably used by the Indo-Iranians as a name to denote the original Indo-European sovereign sky-god, who appears as Jupiter among the Romans, and as Dyaus in the earliest Indian hymns, where the name is combined with the title *asura-*. In these hymns *asura-* is a designation for some higher gods. The term, as the Indian evidence shows, came to mean 'demon' by a gradual process of development, but the gods remained gods. On the Iranian side the sovereign sky-god presumably continued to be called 'Ahura', a name which was to form part of the combined designation 'Ahura Mazdā' ('the Wise Lord'). As for the Iranian use of the term *daēva-* as 'demon', it probably results from contact with the Indians as the latter stopped on their long migratory process towards India. The Iranians would have seen some of the Indian gods, unfamiliar to themselves, as demons. Thus some individual deities on the Indian side are named as demons in Mazdaism.

Burrow's argument has been accepted by the leading Italian specialist in Mazdean studies, Gherardo Gnoli, while the principal German specialist, Helmut Humbach, has reached similar conclusions. So instead of explaining things with reference to an original Indo-Iranian state of affairs, the scholars are now moving to a context of later contacts between Indians and Iranians. We may observe that in this perspective also no 'Reformer' is needed.

At this point we must consider some hard evidence: an inscription. It seems that some Indians, instead of making their way towards India, went to the Near East, where the names of some of their gods are preserved in an inscription of around 1380 BCE. Since the same names appear together in the earliest Indian hymns, we have the first attested 'structure': 1. Mitra and Varuṇa; 2. Indra; 3. a couple called the Nāsatyas. Dumézil claims these as representing his triad: religious sovereignty, war and fertility.

These gods have been connected with the most archaic, and in the usual view the oldest part of the Avesta (the Mazdean scripture) namely the Gāthās, hymns attributed to Zarathushtra himself. Differing dates have been proposed for Zarathushtra, but nowadays academic opinion seems to be crystallising in favour of *c.* 1000 BCE, in the prehistoric period. The language and style of the Gāthās closely resemble those of early Indian hymns. In these Gāthās Ahura Mazdā is extolled, and is surrounded by six Entities, elsewhere called the 'Holy Immortals' and viewed as archangels. Dumézil has argued that these six Entities are old Indo-Iranian gods reappearing in disguise: the five gods of the inscription plus a goddess, called on the Indian side Sarasvatī, who corresponds to all three 'functions', but especially to fertility. He establishes the correspondences as follows in Table 34.1, notably in accordance with the material elements associated with the Entities by Mazdean literature:

Table 34.1

Indian Deity	**Entity**	**Material Element**
Mitra	Good Thought	Cattle
Varuṇa	Order (or Truth)	Fire
Indra	Power	Metals
Sarasvatī	Devotion	Earth
Nāsatya I }	{ Health	Water
Nāsatya II }	{ Non-Death	Plants

This correspondence is demonstrated by various arguments external to the Gāthās, and also by counting the frequencies with which the Entities are mentioned or associated with one another within the Gāthās. This method has the advantage of avoiding the difficulties posed by the incomprehensibility of the Gāthic verses themselves.

Dumézil's analysis has been accepted by many specialists and rejected by others, who took offence at the suggestion that their cherished 'monotheistic Reformer' had dishonestly slipped the old gods in under new names. We need not take so simple a view of things. Dumézil has observed that there are unresolved questions. Does the name 'Zarathushtra' cover the ideas of a man or a group? Was there one reform, two or a long series? We may feel that such a series could be better termed a 'development'. For Dumézil's work is really still enclosed in the traditional academic reconstruction, in which Zarathushtra rejected an old polytheism, established monotheism, and then had his work undone by unfaithful successors, who brought back the old gods (under their own old names). In this tale of a founder betrayed by succeeding priests we may perhaps see another illusion of Protestant scholarship. The evidence seems rather to suggest not so much a replacement of polytheism by monotheism, with the subsequent restoration of polytheism, but more a development into a continuing henotheism, that is a belief in one god without abandoning belief in others, but giving them less attention. The old Iranian gods continued to be worshipped under their old names, but subordinated to Ahura Mazdā and his 'Entities'.

It would appear, then, that if we no longer need the idea of a Reform, or a denunciation by Zarathushtra or others of old gods common to the Indians and the Iranians, Dumézil's theory of a correspondence between the Entities and the Indian gods needs some adaptation if it is to be preserved. Presumably the answer would be that the *functional properties* of old Indo-Iranian deities, deities corresponding to but by no means always identical with those found on the Indian side, have been transformed into the Entities. At any rate we may agree that it is correct to concentrate not so much upon the names of gods and Entities, but rather upon how a god or Entity works.

We must now consider the Gāthās themselves and the question of Zarathushtra's existence. As regards the Gāthic hymns, recent research on the continent of Europe has brought scholars to conclude that their character is above all a liturgical one. It is undoubtedly correct to concentrate upon comparison with the early Indian hymns, and this is the conclusion to which such comparison leads.

British work in this field, however, has been of a biographical and moralistic kind. It has been well summarised by the American scholar R.N. Frye: 'For W.B. Henning and his school it seems that one should understand Zoroaster as a meticulous thinker who carefully chose his words, and acted in an eminently rational manner. His language too was grammatically correct, though later corrupted, and he behaved as proper prophets should.'

It must be borne in mind that Henning accepted the traditional date for Zarathushtra: 258 years before Alexander the Great (336–323 BCE). His argument was that nobody would invent '258'. He failed to notice that it had been produced by subtracting 42 years of Zarathushtra's life from 300.

Ideas put forward by Mary Boyce have remained highly controversial. Her dating of Zarathushtra successively to *c.* 1000, 1500, 1700–1500, 1400–1200 and 1400 BCE has not prevented her from recounting how he lived, received revelations and visions, organised his community, and established its rituals. She is the first Western specialist to take Mazdean legend as a serious source for Zarathushtra's life. Her method has been to project back into the past all later doctrine and practice, and then claim that she has shown the continuity of Mazdaism, which she has taken for granted as her starting-point. The academics have reacted with heavy irony, notably with regard to her presentation, as historical fact, of veneration of purely imaginary Indian and Iranian deities.

The moralistic tradition of the British school has been continued by specialists in America, who have produced 'metaphorical' interpretations of the Gāthās. Thus 'a fertile cow and a steer' is seen as a metaphor for 'the good vision' and Zarathushtra. Plants represent the believers, and the pasturage 'peace and freedom'. This has been greeted with derision from French and Belgian scholars, and a rebuke from Humbach.

The best arguments concerning Zarathushtra were presented by Molé. He observed that the diversity of academic opinions about Zarathushtra (a witch-doctor, a politician, a prophet and so on) showed the impossibility of reconstructing his personality. Since the Gāthās are liturgical texts, it is dangerous to try to extract historical information from them. When they refer to alleged incidents and people these may be real or legendary. Nothing proves that Zarathushtra composed the Gāthās. It is impossible to determine whether he existed or not. Translations of the Gāthās are highly speculative and influenced by a traditional academic picture of Zarathushtra as resembling an old-fashioned image of a prophet of Israel. This is based on later legend, imbued with Judeo-Christian and Islamic influences. Zarathushtra in the Gāthās appears as an archetypal priest.

Against Molé, it has been claimed that ancient Greek authors speak of Zarathushtra as a real person. But this is of no historical value: they are writing centuries after the Gāthās. Molé seems right in pointing to the most obvious parallel to Zarathushtra: Orpheus, the mystical founder of the Greek religion of Orphism, with whose name hymns were also associated. Also against Molé, it has been said that the Gāthās have a 'unity of tone and subject' which proves the historicity of Zarathushtra. But scholars who differ on everything else come close to agreeing that out of the 238 stanzas of the Gāthās almost 190 are incomprehensible. So what weight can be given to such a subjective opinion?

We must now consider what can be found in the Gāthās. In spite of assertions by the Anglo-American moralistic school that they provide an 'ethic' it is difficult to see what this is. To pray for good fortune for one's family and bad fortune for one's enemies hardly seems ethical.

The Gāthās are permeated by the praise of Ahura Mazdā, the 'Wise Lord'. There are bad gods, *daēvas.* Beneath Ahura Mazdā there is a Holy Spirit, Spenta Mainyu, and an Evil Spirit, Angra Mainyu. The text is clear enough, the specialists have pointed out, to show that Ahura Mazdā is *not* identical with the Holy Spirit, as Mazdaism later believes. So in the Gāthās we do not have an absolute dualism, but rather an opposition of two spirits beneath a sovereign god. The evidence suggests henotheism, belief in one god while not denying the existence of others. It seems unwise to assume that we have monotheism here. The Gāthās do not mention another leading god of Mazdaism, Mithra (the Indian Mitra), but it would appear unfounded to imagine that he is one of the bad gods, the *daēvas.* Since the

Gāthās are hymns to Ahura Mazdā, there is no reason to expect Mithra to be mentioned, let alone to take absence of mention to imply condemnation. Such an unwise assumption has accompanied the idea that Zarathushtra's unscrupulous successors brought back Mithra and the other old gods in betrayal of the 'Founder'.

This idea has dominated discussion of other hymns in Mazdean scripture, which show the worship, not just of Ahura Mazdā and the Entities, but of other gods as well. These are all called part of the 'Younger Avesta', although some of them could be of the same period as that of the Gāthās. The so-called 'Younger Avestan' dialect may be as old as the Gāthic one. Some of these non-Gāthic hymns are certainly extremely old. Burrow dates some to before 900 BCE. If they are not so old as the Gāthās, they can be taken to contain earlier materials. The usual interpretation is that they represent the return of the old gods, readmitted but only in a subordinate position. Such a view is just as hypothetical as that which posits an inner core of believers faithful to the Gāthās and Ahura Mazdā alone. It is important to avoid calling the non-Gāthic gods 'pagan' gods. This term is no longer acceptable in the history of religions. With regard to Mazdaism it seems all the more misleading and absurd as the traditional academic reconstruction appears to be collapsing.

Let us briefly mention some of these gods. Mithra (the meaning of whose name has been much disputed, 'contract' still seeming the best translation) is to be venerated alongside Ahura Mazdā (like Mitra alongside Varuṇa among the Indians). Verethraghna, 'Victory', we shall also encounter again. Aredvī Sūrā Anāhitā, 'Moist, Mighty, Immaculate', is seen by Dumézil's followers as representing the three functions—fertility, war and religious sovereignty—in her name, but also, like the Entity 'Devotion', corresponding in particular to that of fertility.

Other deities are Apąm Napāt, 'Offspring of the Waters', who has an Indian counterpart of similar name, and has been convincingly linked with the Roman water-god Neptune and the Celtic Nechtan; Haoma, a plant corresponding to the Indian Soma, and now considered to have been a hallucinogen, the preparation and consumption of which are central to the Mazdean liturgy; and Ātar, 'Fire', the veneration of which is the most famous aspect of Mazdaism, with the distinctive fire-temples of the Mazdeans leading the Muslims to call them 'fire-worshippers'.

Another feature is constituted by supernatural beings called the Fravashis. They are both the guardian angels and the higher souls of the faithful. They survive after death to be venerated by the living. They participate in battles against demons on a cosmic level, on the side of Ahura Mazdā, and in the terrestrial fighting of the believers. In general, they correspond most closely to the Valkyries, the martial maidens of Norse mythology.

We must now pass on to the historical period, and the great Persian Empire of the Achaemenid kings, which lasted from *c.* 550 to 330 BCE. Here our sources are scanty and unreliable. The most used is the Greek writer Herodotus (*c.* 485–425 BCE), famous not only as the so-called 'Father of History' but also as the 'Father of Lies'. It is difficult to see what credence can be given to this author, who in matters of Persian religion is demonstrably ignorant and misleading in the extreme. Priority must be given to the oriental materials. The inscriptions of the Persian kings themselves give a one-sided, official propagandist picture. Archaeology gives us altars, sculpture and also inscribed tablets relating to expenditure, which are by far the best source.

The empire of the Persians was preceded by that of another Iranian people, the Medes. Of these six tribes are mentioned by Herodotus, notably the Magi, a name which is also that of the priests under the Persians. This obviously leads to speculation that the Magi might originally have been a specialised priestly tribe among the Medes. That the Medes had a fire-cult and altars in temples, and a holy mountain with rooms for priests or pilgrims, is known from archaeological evidence. One surviving fire-altar clearly could not have been used for the everlasting fire characteristic of Mazdaism. Further reconstruction of Median religion is entirely speculative.

After the Medes we come to the Persian Achaemenid kings themselves, and the vexed question of whether they were followers of the religion attributed to Zarathushtra or not. A vast amount of ink has been spilt for and against. The best answer is one given by Frye, that this is a false problem, and anachronistic, since it wrongly assumes the existence at that time of a modern concept of a Mazdean religion. It would seem better to speak of 'Mazda-worship' rather than 'Mazdaism' in this period, since there is no sign of a fully-fledged system of beliefs or an organisation of believers.

The founder of the empire, Cyrus (560/559–530 BCE), is not someone of whose religious activities much can be said. In Babylonia he did homage to the Babylonian god Marduk and expressed the wish that a variety of lesser gods should intercede on his behalf. The sculptural evidence shows that he had his palaces in Iran decorated with reliefs of Assyrian magical figures. We know that his policy was to allow the various peoples of his empire to follow their own religions.

Darius I (522–486 BCE) has left inscriptional evidence of his feeling of indebtedness to Ahura Mazdā (much repeated and emphasised) and his hostility to the Lie. But by the Lie he appears to mean his enemies, and by the Truth his own power. He says that he was helped by Ahura Mazdā and 'the other gods that are'. Much has been made of his failure to mention other gods by name, but tablets show that in his reign and that of Xerxes (486–465 BCE) the state paid for the worship by Iranian priests of Mithra and non-Iranian deities, as well as employing them in the cult of mountains and rivers. Again, everything points to henotheism.

Xerxes is known to have destroyed the temples of some gods. He did this in Babylon to the cult of Marduk, and in an inscription he says that he did it to *daivas* (false gods). Again, scholars are divided as to who and where these were. He mentions his personal worship of Ahura Mazdā. As in the case of Darius, this is hardly surprising: since Ahura Mazdā is a sovereign god, it is only natural that a sovereign should concentrate his worship upon him. It has been claimed that a 'Zoroastrian' calendar was adopted by the Achaemenid court in this reign or not long after, but this too has been much disputed.

Artaxerxes II (405/4–359/8) mentions Mithra and the goddess Anāhitā along with Ahura Mazdā in his inscriptions. Much has been made of this, and also of the fact that he erected statues of Anāhitā, identified with the Greek Aphrodite. But it would be unwise to draw any conclusions by way of contrast with the previous absence of Mithra and Anāhitā from royal inscriptions, as we have seen.

Exaggerated claims have been made for alleged Iranian influences on Greek philosophy during the Achaemenid period. Classical scholars accept very little of what has been attributed to ancient Greek thinkers to support this. To project later Mazdean time-speculation ('Zurvanism') back into the Achaemenid period and then claim that it inspired Greek interest in Time is anachronistic: probably the inspiration went in the reverse direction. Similar excessive claims, sometimes now disproved, have been made for Iranian influences on Judaism, Christianity and the Roman religion of Mithraism.

The conquest of the Achaemenid Empire by Alexander the Great (336–323 BCE) was to bring centuries of domination by Greek culture, and a rupture of continuity in Iranian civilisation. This has proved a considerable embarrassment to modern writers subsidised by the Iranian monarchy in order to emphasise such continuity. For Iran itself we have no evidence about indigenous religion in the period of Alexander's successors, the Seleucids. A colourful attempt has been made to find a spirit of Mazdean resistance to the Greek yoke, by redating apocalyptic texts to this period. In works of this kind, in which prophecies of impending liberation are repeatedly revised after they have failed to be fulfilled, it is indeed normal to find literary strata of earlier generations. But in the absence of external corroboration one must be doubtful here.

In the third century BCE an Iranian people, the Parthians, came to the fore. They were gradually to displace the Seleucids in Iran, and ruled until the third century CE. Of religion under the Parthians again very little is known. It may have been in their period that the final portions of Mazdean scripture were composed, since these mention Greco-Roman measures in contrast to Iranian ones in the earlier parts of the Avesta. In these later portions we find plenty of details relating to ritual purity and the utmost severity towards sexual licence. It is not clear when the Avesta was first written down, but it was certainly after a very long period of oral transmission.

The veneration of Greek deities, identified with Iranian ones, was popular. Of particular interest is an inscription in what is now Turkey, which appears to give striking support to Dumézil's theories. As in the Indian inscription of *c.* 1380 BCE, we find listed first the two sovereign gods, Ahura Mazdā, identified with the Greek Zeus, and Mithra, identified with Apollo, Helios and Hermes; then the war-god Verethraghna, identified with Heracles and Ares; finally, 'my all-nourishing fatherland Commagene', where the function of fertility is evident enough.

Other aspects of Iranian religion in the Parthian period are the everlasting fire, known from a classical source to be associated with the monarchy, as later in Iran; and temples dedicated to Anāhitā, in whose honour prostitution was practised. But there is no evidence of any official religion in the shape of Mazdaism as we later know it or any formally constituted sect thereof.

In the third century CE a new dynasty, that of the Sassanians, took power and ruled until the Arab conquest in the seventh. This dynasty controlled a large and powerful empire, and under it Mazdaism came to fruition as an official, established state religion. But this process of establishment took a long time, and it was only in the sixth century that it was actually completed.

Study of Mazdaism as it emerges in this period is complicated by a phenomenon called 'Zurvanism', which, following Frye, we can see as time-speculation in Iranian form. Some scholars have seen this as a separate sect or indeed as a religion in its own right, but in recent years it has become more normal to see it as a tendency or even just as a popular myth.

In the Avesta there is already a minor god called Zurvān, 'Time'. According to Damascius (sixth century CE) it was reported by Eudemus of Rhodes in the late fourth century BCE that the Iranians believed the first principle to be either Time or Space. This first principle would either have given rise to Ahura Mazdā and the Evil Spirit directly or to light and darkness before them. In the third century CE the new religion of Manichaeism calls its supreme god Zurvān, which shows the exalted position now occupied by the deity, as does his occurrence in proper names. Obviously, under the Parthians veneration of Time had become important in Iran, as it had in the West. During the Sassanian period Christian writers speak of a myth in which Zurvān is the original father of Ahura Mazdā and the Evil Spirit, and attack it as the essential dogma of Iranian religion. But afterwards, in the Islamic era, it is condemned by the Mazdeans and virtually disappears except for traces discovered by modern scholars.

Various theories have been put forward to explain this. There has been an unfortunate use of the words 'orthodoxy' and 'heresy'. It must be remembered that the emerging Mazdaism was, like ancient Roman religion, essentially a set of rites. As in Rome, it was a matter of 'doing the done thing' and honouring the gods, while plenty of Greek philosophical ideas were absorbed. In such a perspective what a man believes about the original source of the gods will not get him labelled a 'heretic', whereas in Christianity such speculation about God will. Now to the Christian writers of the Sassanian period the myth of Zurvān, a god who offers sacrifice in order to have offspring, is absurd and disgusting, and consequently splendid material to use to discredit their opponents. Accordingly they present it as the central doctrine of the Mazdeans. For later, Muslim writers, who were apt to invent a 'heresy' at the slightest pretext, people who believe in the myth of Zurvān have to constitute a separate sect. From this it is only a short step to the reconstruction of a modern Christian scholar, with a Mazdean 'orthodoxy' confronting a 'Zurvanite heresy'. In this perspective an original (but imaginary) Mazdean 'orthodoxy' is replaced by 'Zurvanism' in the Sassanian period only to reimpose itself under Islam.

Shapur I (240–72 CE) is of interest as the patron of Mani (d. *c.* 274), the founder of Manichaeism, a religion which grew out of the Gnostic movement, characterised by its emphasis on a hidden knowledge reserved for an elite. Manichaeism, like Christianity, was an international religion; Mazdaism, like Judaism, was a national one. Shapur I calls himself 'Mazda-worshipping', but attributes his successes to the aid of 'the gods' in general and lays stress upon the cult of them. Since the most important Mazdean priest of the ensuing period speaks of 'Ahura Mazdā and the gods' in inscriptions, the materials point to henotheism.

After Shapur I's death Mani was executed and the Mazdean priesthood increased its power. Its leader, Kerdir, has left fascinating inscriptional evidence of a journey which he made into the next world. This is undoubtedly characteristic of shamanism, the magical religion of Central and North Asia, and perhaps shows a practice surviving from the Iranians' original homeland.

The reign of Shapur II (309–79) has sometimes been seen as establishing a kind of Mazdean 'orthodoxy', but it would appear that on the contrary Mazdaism itself was not firmly established as the state religion until the sixth century CE. On the other hand, the conversion of the Roman Empire to Christianity led to severe persecution of Christians in Iran, who were seen as belonging to the enemy. In the fifth century they proclaimed their independence from Western Christianity, but this did not prevent an unsuccessful attempt by the Persian Empire to impose Mazdaism upon its Christian subjects in Armenia.

At the end of the fifth century we must note the remarkable movement led by the reformer Mazdak, celebrated for socialistic or communistic tendencies. Mazdakism (with a 'k', not to be confused with the main-line Mazdaism) has usually been seen as a gnostic religion, founded some time before and growing out of Manichaeism. Against this Molé has argued that it was a sect of Mazdaism. But when we have an account by a Muslim who met Mazdakites and had read their writings, the doctrines are not Mazdean but undoubtedly Manichaean, maintaining that the first principle was Light, which had been partially transmuted into darkness. Moreover, it seems that their faith was called 'the joyous religion' in direct opposition to the Mazdean self-appellation 'the good religion'. Mazdak himself gained the favour of the king Kavad (488–531), who seems to have used the movement to break the power of the greater nobles. But at the end of Kavad's reign Mazdak was executed and his followers persecuted. Apparently it was in a reaction to his movement that the monarchy, now closely allied with the lesser nobility, collaborated with the priesthood to make the Mazdean religion the firmly established faith of the empire. This was done by Khusro I (531–79). He allowed Mazdean priests to persecute Christians, while he himself acted as a patron to Greek philosophers. He declared that Mazdaism, while not the only path to truth, was self-sufficient, and vigorously repressed religious teachings that he did not like.

There was a rise in conversion to Christianity (notably from the more privileged classes) in the last century of Sassanian rule. Khusro II (590–628) had a Christian wife and was devoted to St Sergius, but persecuted Christians when his territories were invaded by the Roman emperor. The intolerant character which Mazdaism now possessed, along with its insistence on class distinctions, undoubtedly weakened the Sassanian realm, as did the antiquated and national character of the religion, which was unable to compete with faiths campaigning for recruits and offering universal truths in contrast to its preoccupation with rituals and taboos. In 642 what remained of the Persian Empire's army was destroyed by the conquering Arabs, and in 651 the last Sassanian king was killed. Iran was now to be taken over by the rising religion of Islam.

We must briefly turn to the general characteristics of Mazdaism in the Sassanian period. Here Dumézil's principal disciple in this field, Jacques Duchesne-Guillemin, has argued that four divinities dominate the scene, Ahura Mazdā, Mithra, Verethraghna and Anāhitā. Since the goddess Anāhitā represents fertility, he points to a correspondence with the inscriptions of the Indians and Commagene noted above. Moreover, the Sassanians insisted on the division of society into classes: priests, warriors and a class representing the economic aspect of fertility (cultivators, craftsmen and merchants), along with a new class of bureaucrats.

The Arab conquest of the seventh century CE and the subsequent Islamicisation of Iran produced a complete reversal of fortunes for Mazdaism, as Michael Morony has well shown. From being the proud masters of society, the Mazdean priests were to become desperately defensive inferiors. Under the Sassanians they had been the guardians of privilege, with religious observance being the hallmark of social distinction, and a lowly estate in this world seen as foreshadowing a poor place in the next. Since riches were seen as good, the asceticism of Manichaeism was viewed as evil. Now the rise of Islam brought converts to the new religion, as well as more conversions to Christianity. There were economic incentives to turn Muslim: discriminatory taxation, and the prospect of employment in the army and bureaucracy. From being persecutors, the Mazdeans now became victims of persecution. Muslim rule also brought new movements of a libertine and insurrectionist character, aimed largely against the Mazdean clergy as linked with the old nobles. Various aspects of Mazdaism would be attacked in these religious uprisings, in which Islamic and Manichaean elements were put together in a common hostility to the traditional ideology of the nobility. Moreover, now that the Mazdean priesthood could no longer itself exercise repressive powers, it had to resort to moralising instead. The priests now had to come to terms with poverty and exalt its virtues. They had to face the economic realities of living with non-Mazdeans and soften their insistence on ritual purity.

It was against this background that the main Mazdean texts in Middle Persian were composed in the ninth and tenth centuries CE. The language of the Avesta (Mazdean scripture) had long since died, and the Mazdeans now had very little idea of what was meant by it. The Middle Persian translations of the Avestan texts are so bad that on their own they are enough to destroy the myth of the so-called 'continuity' of Mazdean teachings. In argument with the Muslims the Mazdeans now proclaimed an absolute dualism, with Ahura Mazdā identified with the Holy Spirit, and consequently balanced by the Evil Spirit. This was in contradiction with the original Gāthic position, in which Ahura Mazdā was above both Spirits.

This absolute dualism has been seen as a 'restored orthodoxy', after a 'heretical' period in which Zurvān, Time, was venerated as supreme. It would seem, however, as Morony well observes, that there never had been or was to be a doctrinal 'orthodoxy'. The Mazdeans found it convenient, in discussion with Jews, Christians and Muslims, to minimise their worship of divinities other than Ahura Mazdā, explaining that they were merely objects of veneration rather than gods. So in dialogue with Jews and Christians they tended to present themselves as monotheists. Often, in other contexts, they seemed to formulate their opinions in henotheist, polytheistic or dualist ways. Why a dualist one in answer to Islam?

The answer is perhaps to be sought in the atmosphere of controversy within Islam, from the eighth to the tenth centuries, about how a good God allowed evil in the world, and in the circumstance that the Muslims generally presented God as the Creator of all actions, even evil ones. To this the Mazdeans had an excellent answer in absolute dualism: there are two first principles, one good, one evil. To be sure, this view seems to have existed before Islam, but now it was to be remorselessly emphasised as the simplest and clearest answer to Muslim propaganda.

In this perspective the condemnation of 'Zurvanism', the tendency to venerate Time as the first principle, is entirely understandable. In the context of argument with Muslims this exaltation of Zurvān would have been an embarrassment in debate, weakening, obscuring and complicating the Mazdeans' clear-cut dualist case. Moreover, the old myth of Zurvān, a god sacrificing in order to have a child and then getting two, would have appeared an obscene absurdity in the Middle Eastern interfaith polemic of the ninth and tenth centuries CE.

Although these Mazdean writings of the early Islamic period undoubtedly contain plenty of much older materials, one has to allow for both priestly 'filtering' and Muslim influences. The latter would appear to be evident in the Middle Persian legend of Zarathushtra himself. At any rate plenty of Judeo-Christian traditions had been at work in the 'biography' of Zarathushtra, presented as a prophet. Here the late Jean de Menasce did well to speak of the difficulty of determining the figure's historicity.

Of the greatest interest in this literature is the story of a Mazdean called Artā Virāf, who takes a hallucinogen, goes into a period of apparent death, and visits heaven and hell. This state of apparent death is a further indication of the influence of shamanism, previously observed in the extraterrestrial journey of the priest Kerdir.

Also of interest is the continuing emphasis on incestuous marriage, a phenomenon attested beyond a shadow of doubt in Mazdean and non-Mazdean sources, contrary to nineteenth-century attempts to deny its previous existence. It is indeed noteworthy that this practice continued for so long under Muslim rule, before being replaced, sometime after the eleventh century, by cousin-marriage, and was considered in detail in the Mazdean literature of the early Islamic period, as meritorious and to be encouraged, whether children were to be expected or not. We are given evidence that women were forced against their will to marry their brothers and fathers, although the agreement of the bridegrooms was necessary.

Finally, we may note the emphasis in this literature on the division of society into four classes and the activities thereof, explicitly set out: in the priesthood, religion, education and justice; in the warrior class, horse-riding and foot-soldiering; in the peasant class, breeding and commerce; in the artisan class, preparation of bread and other food.

There were still plenty of Mazdeans in Iran in the tenth century, but at this time an important emigrant community established itself in India. The Mazdeans of India were to be known as the Parsees. Meanwhile, in Iran, Islamic influences continued to make themselves felt in practice and belief. Mazdean influences on Islam, on the other hand, have been much exaggerated. Elements such as 'the wine of the Magi [the Mazdean priests]', when found in Muslim mystical poetry, are literary motifs of a libertine or symbolic character, and do not indicate transmission of Mazdean ideas. The 'Oriental' philosophy of Suhrawardī (d. 1192), often cited to show continuity with the Iranian past, shows only a minimal acquaintance with Mazdaism.

Various sources, in succeeding centuries, show the difficulties faced by the Mazdean communities in Iran and India: persecution and enforced conversion to Islam, and ignorance among Parsees of their own religion, owing to the difficulty of communication with their Iranian counterparts, seen as the fount of authority. There was to be increased emigration from Iran to India, where attempts to combine Mazdaism with other religions and Greek philosophy, under the guise of a mystical unity, met with considerable success in the seventeenth century.

In the eighteenth century the great and intrepid French pioneer Anquetil Duperron discovered the Mazdean scriptures and introduced them to Europe. Unfortunately an absurd fit of pique among British orientalists led them to reject his materials as forgeries. But from then on it was possible for the Parsees, via European scholarship, to rediscover their own religious heritage, as the linguistic study of the Avesta partially rescued it from the confusion produced by the Middle Persian interpretations.

This rediscovery was assisted by a remarkable change of fortune among the Parsees. British rule, by freeing them from the Muslim yoke, gave them an opportunity to enrich themselves by finding favour with, and adapting themselves to, the new masters. They did this with immense dedication and success. The grateful British responded by adopting a markedly uncritical attitude towards the Parsees. This was in stark contrast to the lack of esteem usually displayed by the British rulers towards their other subjects.

The leaders of the newly-enriched Parsees, complaining of the ignorance and backwardness of their priests, set about encouraging the study of their religion. When a European scholar informed them that Zarathushtra was a monotheist they gladly accommodated themselves to what appeared a convenient position. Meanwhile modernist reformers were instrumental in what Christine Dobbin has called 'the largely successful struggle of the Parsi community to emancipate itself from the despotic authority of the community's heads'.

The economic success of the Parsee merchants in the nineteenth century has been attributed to a religious inspiration inherent in Mazdaism, and comparable to the 'Protestant work ethic'. Against this it may be said that religious and ethnic minorities generally tend to enrich themselves when not impeded by artificial restrictions. The Parsees' success was to be reversed when the Hindus acquired the necessary skills.

On the other hand, the subsequent decline of the Parsees can be partly attributed to a new phenomenon. At the end of the nineteenth century some Parsees were much influenced by the Theosophical movement of Helena Blavatsky (1831–91), and decided that everything in the Avesta had a secret, inner meeting, reserved for themselves as an elite. It would seem that, like their European counterparts, they were trying to defend their privileged social position against rising competition, and sought to camouflage insufficiency of information and reasoning powers by a claim to wisdom naturally possessed or directly vouchsafed. These Theosophical Parsees found a natural ally in their priests, who have usually found employment by ingratiating themselves with wealthy patrons, and consequently tended to be lacking in knowledge and intellect. In an ideology which conferred enormous mystical powers on the syllables of their texts the priests found a welcome weapon against the menace of rationalism.

The twentieth century has seen a sharp fall in the fortunes of the Parsees. Obviously, the end of the British Empire was a major reason for the decline of its collaborators. The Parsee population has sunk in numbers, leading to considerable academic investigation, largely inconclusive, into the causes of low birth- and marriage-rates. The discovery of the widespread extent of poverty among fellow-Parsees has greatly surprised and shocked their wealthier co-religionists.

Meanwhile, the fortunes of the Iranian Mazdeans followed a different pattern from the eighteenth century to the present day. The chaos of eighteenth-century Iran, with its horrific massacres, was particularly severe in its consequences for them, and brought yet more enforced conversion to Islam and emigration to India. In the nineteenth century discriminatory measures were particularly oppressive, and hampered economic activity. However, in the second half of the century Parsee and British intervention created new opportunities for Iranian Mazdeans to leave village life for urban, professional careers. Thus in the twentieth century they continued to rise in the social scale, with a consequent decline in Iranian Mazdaism itself. For just as in the Muslim world in general Westernisation and economic progress have brought a decline of Islam within the ranks of the middle classes, so too Iranian Mazdaism has wilted before an impatient, progressive younger generation.

A highly romanticised picture of Mazdaism in modern Iran has been painted by Boyce, in an uncritical attempt to show that little had ever changed, and to suggest that there had been few differences of opinion within the community. Fortunately Michael Fischer has demonstrated that the reverse is the case: plenty of rites and legends have been taken over from the Muslims, and the feuding between Iranian Mazdeans has been particularly bitter. A large number of them were so appalled by the reactionary mindlessness of their elders that they left the faith for the new religion of Baha'ism.

The Islamic revolution of 1978–9 in Iran has naturally produced plenty of worries for the Mazdeans, who had been prospering under the monarchy now overthrown. Since the monarchy had glorified Iran's Mazdean past in contrast to Islam, there were now, not surprisingly, to be some unfortunate excesses directed against them.

Returning to the history of Mazdean studies in the West, we may note that at the moment the most exciting and impressive work is being done by Philippe Gignoux, who has pointed the way to future improvements by concentrating on the anthropology of northern Eurasia. This gives us three significant parallels with Mazdaism, attributable to influences upon the Iranians in their original homeland: 1. the important and original significance of the *bones* as constituting the source of life itself (perhaps it is to this reason that one may attribute the source of Mazdaism's method of disposing of the dead: exposing the corpse on the 'Towers of Silence' for the bones to be picked clean by dogs or vultures—a practice usually explained by the need to avoid polluting earth or fire with dead matter); 2. the presence of a multiplicity of souls within a single human being; 3. extraterrestrial journeys, accompanied by the use of psychotropic drugs and a state of apparent death.

In general, it may be said that Mazdaism strongly resembles other national religious traditions in its ritualism, in its forgetting of its original significations and in its conservatism. This conservatism, however, should not be seen as absolute, nor should it be confused with 'continuity': the original elements were to be combined in different patterns, and were modified by enormous accretions. The latter had to come from the outside: from Greek philosophy and other religions. But to learn from others is hardly discreditable.

Mazdaism's insistence on the primordiality of Evil is a salutary antidote to the modern myth of man's natural innocence. But its attribution of all that is bad to a demonic Other has discouraged self-criticism and provided an excuse for repression in the manner of twentieth-century states. Its emphasis on class distinctions, accompanying the loss of its empire, is of particular interest with regard to Britain today.

Further Reading

The Cambridge History of Iran, vols. 2–4 (Cambridge University Press, Cambridge, 1975–85)

Dumézil, Georges *The Destiny of a King* (University of Chicago Press, Chicago, 1973)

Duchesne-Guillemin, Jacques *Symbols and Values in Zoroastrianism* (New York, 1966)

—— *Religion of Ancient Iran* (Bombay, 1973)

Morony, Michael '*madjūs*' in *The Encyclopaedia of Islam*, 2nd edn

Zaehner, Robert Charles *The Dawn and Twilight of Zoroastrianism* (Weidenfeld & Nicolson, London, 1975)

—— *The Teachings of the Magi* (Sheldon Press, Oxford, 1976)

35 The Classical Religions of India

Friedhelm Hardy

Preface to Chapters 35–44

The religious situation in India has been infinitely more complicated than conventional labels like 'Hinduism' or 'Buddhism' suggest. On the one hand, a typological analysis will have to distinguish a wide spectrum of essentially different religious attitudes and expressions; on the other hand, such types appear frequently in 'Hindu', 'Buddhist', etc. garbs. The present chapter on **The Classical Religions of India** attempts to present this typological differentiation, along with its considerable overlap between different traditions. Instead of dividing the material artificially into 'Hinduism', 'Buddhism', etc. or simply presenting conventional norms put forward by some representatives of these traditions, it describes what is actually found there.

Vedic Religion (pp. 575–81) looks at the oldest documented type of religion. Brought into India by the Āryas, it has interacted in many ways with other indigenous traditions, offering points of reference not only in later Hindu religions, but also in those cases where it it consciously rejected.

The Renouncer Traditions (pp. 582–603) share certain typical assumptions which distinguish them from Vedic ritualism. While the Upaniṣads attempt a new synthesis, both Jainism and Buddhism reject such a possibility and replace rituals by asceticism and meditation.

A further component emerges as *Epic and Purāṇic Religion* (pp. 604–26), which introduces monotheism and devotion to the Hindu traditions. In Buddhism too, at least comparable features emerge as part of the Mahāyāna (pp. 627–36).

As well as the great range of religious practice described, India developed sophisticated modes of reflection by utilising philosophical and theological tools that allow a tradition to rationalise and justify its premisses. Whilst such modes have a more overtly Buddhist,

Hindu and Jain orientation, they remain nevertheless embedded in an overall Indian intellectual pursuit. (*Mahāyāna Buddhism and Buddhist Philosophy* (pp. 627–36); *Hindu Philosophies and Theologies* (pp. 637–45); *Later Jainism* (pp. 646–8)).

Finally, any account of the classical Indian religions must take note of religious developments that either place themselves above the mainstream or that reject the latter outright: *The Esoteric Traditions and Antinomian Movements* (pp. 649–58) attempts some assessment of these.

The remaining chapters of Part Four of *The World's Religions* describe further aspects already touched on in this chapter, and in particular the developments of the classical Indian religious tradition inside and outside the sub-continent. Not all areas on the typological spectrum described earlier have been studied to the same extent. Some, like the esoteric traditions (popularly known as 'Tantrism') have only very recently become the object of serious scholarship and a special study of **Śaivism and the Tantric Traditions** (Chapter 36, pp. 660–704) has been included to explore this subject in greater detail.

The classical heritage of the Indian religions has, over time, been broken up into more self-contained entities. This process has been the result of a variety of factors.

The influx of Western ideas gave rise to conscious reflections, for instance in India, on the Hindu traditions—a **Modern Hinduism** (Chapter 37, pp. 705–13) has to be placed now alongside the continuing older traditions.

From within the antinomian movements the Sikhs developed a very specific and distinct self-awareness which makes it possible to treat **Sikhism** (Chapter 38, pp. 714–25) as a separate religion.

Forms of Buddhism were taken to many other Asian countries, and once established there, developed along relatively self-contained lines. **Theravāda Buddhism in South-East Asia** (Chapter 39, pp. 726–38) explores this process for an early transplant from India. In the cases of **China** and **Japan**, and then **Tibet** and **Mongolia** (Chapters 41–4, pp. 756–817), we are dealing with two later stages of Indian Buddhism. On the other hand, **Nepal** (Chapter 40, pp. 739–55) has preserved a situation that in some respects corresponds to that of classical India before 1200 CE when Hindus and Buddhists were still living side by side within one society and culture.

General Remarks on the Religious History of India

India, the land to the east of the river Indus, must have held great promise for anybody living in the arid regions of Central Asia or the mountains of what is today Afghanistan. Fertile and rich in natural resources, green and full of wonders, it exerted an irresistible attraction to the nomads roaming through the semi-desert to its north-west. But if it meant an earthly paradise, it was well guarded: in the north, the Himalayas, and in the north-west the Hindu Kush mountains provided an almost impenetrable barrier. Yet during the more than three thousand years of Indian history, time and again peoples managed to enter it. Although it is certain that neither the Arabian Sea, nor the jungles of the north-east acted as complete barriers, from the point of view of the religious history of India up to the colonial period, the influx of peoples from the north-west was decisive. Thus Indian religious history begins with the arrival of nomads who called themselves the Āryas, the 'noble ones', sometimes around the middle of the penultimate millennium BCE.

But it was not an empty country the Āryas entered. Other peoples were already living there, who had to be conquered or pushed into less desirable regions. Filled with an aggressive spirit and superior in terms of arms and military tactics, the Āryas appear not to have found this difficult. Yet they may not have been directly responsible for the disappearance of a much older civilisation, which had flourished along the river Indus (and is known accordingly as 'Indus Civilisation'). Perhaps an inner decay of this culture made it possible for the Āryas to move south. Very little of what the archaeologist has unearthed throws light on the religion of this unknown people, and nothing can be inferred from it, as far as the later Indian religions are concerned.

The spread of these Āryas and their culture and religion over the region took hundreds of years. Soon after 1000 BCE the Aryan heartland had shifted to the region around what is today Delhi, and less than five hundred years later the country along the more eastern part of the Ganges river had become the Āryāvarta, Aryan homeland. The third century BCE witnessed Aryan culture establishing itself further south in the

Deccan, but it took almost a millennium for it to settle properly in the extreme south (from the sixth century CE).

What will be discussed in the following pages as the Indian religions are all the result of the interaction, in a vast number of different ways, of the Aryan heritage with local and regional traditions. In most cases, the latter are extremely difficult to identify, particularly for the earlier period—historical documentation on the whole has been produced by the Aryas alone. But what scholars have discovered during the last few decades about non-Aryan cultures and religions in India adds up to enough evidence to reject the claims that we are dealing here with a homogenous and continuous, monolinear history of religious phenomena. Sometimes very fundamental transformations occurred as a result of regional influences.

Where does our evidence for this hypothesis derive from? First, there is the presence of linguistic groups which do not belong to the Indo-European Sanskrit and its subsequent developments (or to the languages in the north-west which derive from, or are related to, Old Iranian). Of primary importance here are the Dravidian languages. The term was coined by Bishop Caldwell (who even suspected that the Hebrew words for some of the exotic articles brought to Solomon were of Dravidian origin—an assumption that today looks rather far fetched). The major languages in this group are spoken in South India: Tamil, Telugu, Kannada (or Kanarese) and Malayalam (which is the mother tongue also of the 'Syrian' Christians in Kerala). But outside the south many other peoples also speak Dravidian languages, for example in the more inaccessible regions of central and eastern India. The presence of a Dravidian language, Brahui, in modern Pakistan, is perhaps the most convincing evidence for an earlier pan-Indian Dravidian presence. Furthermore, we have other peoples speaking languages which either link them with those spoken in Burma, Thailand, Kampuchea (the Mon-Khmer languages, with their most important Indian representative Santali), or with Tibet and China. Finally, as a curiosity may be mentioned Burushaski high up in the Himalayas (in Hunza) for which scholars have found no link to any other known language. The continuation of linguistic autonomy of a great variety of peoples in the country can be taken as a symptom of their relative autonomy also in terms of culture and religion.

Closely related to this is a second aspect. At least in one case we still possess a corpus of literature (in Tamil) which goes back to the very beginning of the Common Era. It documents for the extreme south a culture which is as yet hardly influenced by the north. The Tamils drew for centuries on this so-called *caṅkam* literature to express their perception of Hinduism. For instance, the Āḻvārs and Nāyaṉārs, and the *Bhāgavata-Purāṇa*, bear witness to the extent of this southern transformative power.

A third aspect is important here; this could be called 'incomplete' or 'multiple' history. Whilst we are used to thinking in terms of historical processes, say the French Revolution or the Industrial Revolution, which affected Western society to such an extent that (in degrees) nobody was left out of them, the case in India has been different. Whatever major historical events took place (the invasion of the Āryas, or of the Hūṇas in the fifth century CE, the conquest of most of the country by Muslims, or Portuguese and British colonialism), they only had a very limited effect on the Indian peoples at large, and it tended to take centuries before even this effect reached its peak. The result of this is that even today in India we can find (a few) people who belong to the Stone Age in terms of their lifestyle, and, at the other extreme of the spectrum, nuclear reactors. What lies in between is enormously variegated. In reality we ought to speak therefore of many histories of India.

All this meant, in terms of Indian society, that many groups of people, who spoke different languages, belonged to different histories and practised different religions, over a period of hundreds of years learnt to live together and interact socially. At the same time, the mere scale of such social differentiation must have been perceived as a threat to the sense of identity of the individual group within such an amorphous whole. Whilst modes of social interaction and of sharing cultural and religious elements thus evolved, modes of maintaining a separate identity were also established. Conventionally, these two sides of the same coin are treated together under the heading of the 'caste system'. But the social reality of India has been far more fluid and flexible, with enormous regional and historical variations. Of particular interest in the present context is the role of religion. Though almost always blamed for the negative sides of the so-called caste system, religion has in fact frequently played a very positive role by setting up new social structures designed to overcome certain repressive or discriminatory aspects of the social conventions.

In one sense, the history of the Indian religions could be described as the process of infusing the Aryan heritage into the whole of India. Except for the tribes (of which there exist even today quite a number, involving millions of people), most Indians were affected by this—though they may then have strongly reacted against it. This Aryan heritage itself, symbolised by 'the Veda' and the brahmin, did not however remain constant in the course of history. This latter aspect is almost totally ignored by the representatives of such a—very traditional—approach to Indian religious history. In different regions and social milieux, these symbols underwent considerable transformations and modifications. One could be tempted to describe the function of the brahmin as that of a 'clearing-house': he receives religious material and returns it in a form that bears the stamp of his style and values. The Purāṇas are perhaps the most typical expression of this process.

In another sense, the history of the Indian religions dissolves into a large number of separate histories, according to individual traditions, cultural-linguistic regions, and social groups and milieux. The conventional labels of 'Buddhism', 'Jainism' or 'Sikhism' neither exhaust the (very large) range of the traditions we can identify outside the most unhelpful title of 'Hinduism', nor do they, for the most part, even define proper 'religious systems'. The section on Sikhism, which has evolved as perhaps the most self-contained of these 'isms', will illustrate this particular approach. Two further sections will demonstrate to what extent even in relatively small regions (Kashmir and Nepal) the religious scene is differentiated and yet witnesses the constant interaction of these variegated traditions.

In a third sense, writing the history of the Indian religions could mean first, to establish some kind of typology of the religious content, of fundamentally distinct expressions of the religious, and then, secondly, to trace the documentation of each of these types. Now precisely because of the 'multiple history' mentioned above, each subsequently documented type adds to, but does not replace, the previous ones. The sections on traditional Indian religions follow this approach, and thus it is not necessary here to elaborate on it. The four basic types which became documented at subsequent stages are: ritualism, mysticism, devotionalism and antinomianism. Systematic reflections on them appear from the last millennium BCE onwards. Both our four types and also the structures of thought found in the reflective traditions cut right across the conventional four labels of 'Hinduism', 'Buddhism', etc. Further initial confusion is created by the fact that, in real life, the four different types are almost always mixed up with each other, in endless forms. For example, devotion to God combines with a set of ritual practices and daily meditational exercises.

From among the four basic types of the religious, 'antinomianism' (usually under the title of 'Tantrism') has in particular attracted popular interest. Reliable and critical scholarship on this material is, on the other hand, the least readily available. In view of this situation, more space has been given to the 'esoteric traditions', 'Śaivism in Kashmir' and 'the Religions of Tibet', than could perhaps be justified otherwise.

During the nineteenth and early twentieth centuries Indians on the one hand reacted to the influx of Western ideas and criticisms (see the separate section on this). Already this reaction involved a new type of reflection on the religious heritage (e.g. what were the 'scriptural authorities' for the 'orthodoxy' of temple worship). On the other hand, Westerners also showed curiosity and interest in the Indian religions, thereby further stimulating this new type of self-reflection. Now traditionally the Indian religions had evolved their own modes of self-reflection and conceptualisation (see on this in particular the sections on Buddhist and Hindu philosophies, and on Śaivism in Kashmir). Whatever was still known of this older conceptualisation (it tended to be Śaṅkara's Advaita-Vedānta more than any of the others), was offered to the enquiring West(erner), along with *ad hoc* 'explanations', which represent more the questioner's own prejudices than the informant's factual and critical understanding. 'The Hindu Trinity', 'idol worship' and indeed 'Hinduism' are samples of this process.

Vedic Religion

Whatever the religions may have been which were practised by the other peoples of ancient India, the documented religious history of the sub-continent begins with the arrival of the Āryas in the north-western regions. Hindus and Western scholars agree that a corpus of scriptures, known as the Veda ('[sacred] knowledge') and associated with those ancient Āryas, forms the basis of all subsequent developments of Hinduism. But it is important to realise that what either group means by this differs fundamentally.

In the Hindu understanding, the Veda consists of eternally existing (however that may be defined by individual schools) sacred scriptures. These are 'revealed' at the beginning of each cosmic age to seers (*ṛṣis*) who 'see' the Veda and teach it orally to their disciples (who thus 'hear' it). From this mode of transmission, the Veda is also known as *śruti* (lit. 'hearing'), a term denoting primary, ultimate revelation. Moreover, Vyāsa, one of the primordial sages, is regarded as the compiler of these scriptures, putting them together as a definitive corpus. This consists of four main traditions (Ṛg-, Sāma-, Yajur- and Atharva-Veda) which in turn are divided into four genres (Saṃhitā, Brāhmaṇa, Āraṇyaka and Upaniṣad). This corpus constitutes the highest religious authority and pervades all forms of Hinduism, however variegated they may appear on the surface.

But for the scholar, this monolithic block of 'the Veda' falls apart into chronologically different stages and socially separate layers of a literary development that may have lasted for perhaps as long as a thousand years. The latter half of the second millennium BCE has emerged as the most likely period for the beginnings of Vedic literature. For such a date there are few other documents of comparable bulk in the history of religion anywhere else in the world. Yet here we are dealing with religious documents in an unusual sense, for these are not written sources (like, for example, Sumerian cuneiform tablets). The Veda is primarily an oral literature, but transmitted across the centuries in such a meticulous manner that very little change or distortion has occurred.

Frequently, the term 'Veda' (or 'Vedas', for the four traditions Ṛg-, Sāma-, etc.) is used in a more restricted sense. Instead of denoting the entire corpus, it excludes the latest of the genres, that is the Upaniṣads. To speak of 'Vedas and Upaniṣads' has indeed certain advantages, for it highlights the major differences between the earlier hymns and the later Upaniṣads. The latter group of texts reflects a type of religion which is very different from early Vedic ritualism.

The centre of the religious practice of the Āryas was the sacrifice: rituals performed around and through the fire. The symbolism and the motivation behind such sacrifices can without difficulty be derived from the theme of 'hospitality', an important element in nomadic life all over the world. Thus the sacrifice is a meal, but it is shared not only between members of a group of Āryas, but also with beings of a different order called *devas*. The sacrificial meal aims to establish bonds of loyalty and mutual responsibility between men and *devas*. But who are those *devas*? To determine what 'deva' here means is almost identical with defining Vedic religion—a task which scholarship is far from having completed. Certainly these *devas* are 'beings' of some kind; they are normally invisible to the human eye, possess individual names and many personal characteristics. They are more powerful than man, and in many ways interfere in his life, both in a positive and negative manner. They can be addressed by man, be propitiated and requested to grant specific favours. Yet at the same time, they also manifest a puzzling association with natural phenomena, such as fire, rain, thunderstorm, etc. In these contexts, they are more like 'things' or 'events'. But if we acknowledge that we are dealing here with an archaic form of thought which does not yet make a clear conceptual distinction between a 'person' and other forms of agents observable in nature, at least this ambiguity need not cause undue problems. How the different *devas* are perceived, in their individuality and their interaction among themselves and with man, constitutes the perception which Vedic man had of himself within the world. Moreover, such a perception would provide the theory (however unconscious it may have been) underlying the sacrificial practices. Thus the *devas* are non-human forces at work everywhere in the world which can to some extent be manipulated through ritual means.

But there is one further problem here: the Sanskrit word *deva* is etymologically related to the Latin *deus* and the Greek *theos*, a fact that produced the conventional translation of *deva* as 'god'. The description of the *devas* offered above makes it clear to what an extent the *devas* are 'natural' beings and not 'supernatural'. To derive an understanding of Vedic religion from the nature of the *devas* alone would thus be very misleading. In fact, early scholars went even further and thought they had discovered suggestions here as to the 'origin of religion' itself. The strong association of the *devas* with natural phenomena was seen as evidence that nature, when 'personified' and 'deified', gives rise to religion. Yet logically the concept of 'god' itself cannot be derived from, only projected upon, natural phenomena. Moreover, the link between *deva* and *deus/theos* was also developed in a different direction, but again without yielding fruitful results (at least as far as an understanding of Vedic religion in its own right is concerned). In this case, the common linguistic heritage from the Indo-European past was seen as the paradigm also of a common religious past. This may well have been the case, and the reconstruction of it is certainly an exciting enterprise in its own right. But as a religious system, Vedic religion developed its identity precisely because it moved away from that common heritage. Sanskrit *agni* (fire) may be related to the Latin *ignis*, and the Greek god Ouranos may reveal some similarities with the *deva* Varuṇa. But the insights into Vedic religion from such correlations are extremely small.

The *devas* themselves makes up a motley crowd. Attempts at counting them by listing different proper names have almost reached the figure 1,000. Most of these are male, with only a few and insignificant female *devas*, that is, *devīs*. However, only a few *devas* are really central to Vedic religion. Not surprisingly, the sacrificial fire itself, under the name of Agni, is one such *deva*. Through him man communicates with the other *devas*, for offerings addressed to them are handed over to him. Similarly, since the dead are cremated, Agni conveys people into the dark and rather nebulous realm of Yama, the *deva* of death. And it is Agni who carries the nourishment to the ancestors (*pitṛs*, literally 'fathers') living in that realm. To provide this nourishment regularly (through the monthly *śrāddha* ritual) is the primary duty of any son. But the sacrifice is not just a conveyance of food. It also involves the production and offering of a liquid called *soma*, which is the material manifestation of the *deva* Soma. No definite conclusions about the identity of the plant from which the juice was derived have been reached by scholars. But it is clear that the liquid extracted from it possessed hallucinogenic properties. In this strictly controlled ritual context, a portion of the *soma* was also drunk by the human participants. The degree to which this has any bearing on the kind of poetry which was produced for these rituals has not yet been ascertained.

A very different kind of *deva* is Indra. He is the most frequently invited guest to the sacrifice, and in the way he is described we can see many features of the aggressive, conquering Āryas themselves. Then there is Varuṇa, a much less transparent figure. Both he and Indra are associated with the natural order, Indra using his valour to remove obstructions to it and Varuṇa supervising the actions of man and punishing any transgressions. It has become customary to list even in the shortest catalogues of Vedic *devas* two further figures, Viṣṇu and Rudra/Śiva. The reason for this is that *devas* of those names acquire central importance at a later stage in the history of Hinduism. But in the Vedas, they play a very marginal role.

There cannot be any doubt that Vedic religion had its mythology—traditional stories about *devas* and their past deeds—but our understanding of it is very imperfect. This has to do with the nature of our sources. Besides the offerings of food and of *soma*, the sacrifice involved recitation of poems addressed to the *devas*. An invitation to come and join the meal is expressed in such a poem, usually dedicated to one particular *deva* or a smaller group of them. These poems also flatter the *deva(s)* because of heroic deeds done or grand qualities like liberality. Suggestions are made as to the rewards desired by the sacrificer for his efforts. Given this literary form, we cannot expect a coherent narrative of whole myths; we find only sporadic fragments and allusions. Judging from later literature, it would appear that such fragments did not actually derive from one single, coherent mythology and that many different versions were current at the time. The freedom of poetic imagination and mythological inventiveness must have been considerable.

From an unknown date onwards, such poems composed for the sacrifice began to be collected, initially within priestly families as treasured heirlooms. Eventually such collections were put together as one bulky corpus, which now constitutes the main part of the Ṛg-Veda (*ṛc*, *ṛg*: hymn). In addition to the 'recitation' (performed by the *hotṛ*-priest), a much more musical mode evolved which became associated with another class of priests, i.e. the *udgātṛ*. No new poetry was created for this, and thus the Sāma-Veda contains mostly material already found in the Ṛg-Veda. Very different material was collected in a third corpus, the Yajur-Veda. Here we find the sacrificial formulas, and, depending on the recension, also the details of ritual acts, which made up the ritual function of the *adhvaryu*-priests.

These three Vedas thus arose from the functional differentiation within the priesthood responsible for the Vedic fire-sacrifice. But there is a fourth collection, the Atharva-Veda. In the first half at least we find material of a very different kind, which may well be contemporary with the early hymns of the Ṛg-Veda. 'Popular religion' is perhaps the best label to describe it. Rituals are presented to us here which do not involve the *devas* at all and which are perceived to be effective merely through their accurate performance, joining the correct verbal formulas to the appropriate ritual action. No professional priest is necessary, and the results aimed for are even more down-to-earth than that which the fire-sacrifice is supposed to yield (for example, winning the love of a woman).

This presence of two rather different religious-ritual traditions in the same society is interesting; it might also have had implications for the subsequent developments. For we notice that in the course of time the *devas*—after all very unpredictable and free agents—become less and less important and the sacrifice itself moves into the centre of the religious view of the world. In terms of underlying rationale, such a view is comparable with what we find in the Atharva-Veda. Thus at least hypothetically one might be able to speak of a transfer of popular ideas on to the hieratic sacrifice. But what is clear is that in the course of time the structure of the sacrifice became enormously complicated. Consequently a whole specialist literature evolved which dealt with these ritual details (adding accounts of the origin of rituals etc.). These sometimes very lengthy texts were called the Brāhmaṇas. At a certain stage, a third genre was formulated, the Āraṇyakas. It seems that, for reasons of their particularly powerful and thus potentially dangerous nature, certain rituals could only be performed in the forest (*āraṇyaka*: belonging to the forest), away from house and home. Material on these was collected outside the Brāhmaṇas.

The amount of textual material that has been discussed by now is quite staggering. For in the course of time, the three types of priests differentiated further into more than a dozen separate 'branches' (*śākhās*), each one with its own independent Brāhmaṇa (and Āraṇyaka). In this form it has been handed down from generation to generation. That texts which in print fill many hundreds of pages should be learnt by heart *in toto* is by itself an amazing achievement of human memory. That it should be done with almost perfect accuracy is sheer genius. We can infer this accuracy among other things from the fact that the type of language found here corresponds to what linguists would expect historically, that the grammar is consistent over the whole corpus and that different versions agree essentially. To achieve such precision, various devices were invented. Thus the texts were learnt not just once (that is, as actually recited), but many times over: having them split up into separate, individual words, arranging the words in various patterns of *ba*, *dc*, etc. That such dedication, over many years of study, should be shown to this material, clearly suggests that the Vedas themselves had acquired extreme religious status.

What does all this add up to in terms of religion? In the past, Vedic religion has often been described as 'polytheism', to which a second evolutionary stage, called 'henotheism' was added. This concept derives from a stylistic peculiarity found in many Vedic hymns, where one *deva* is addressed with the attributes (and names) of many other *devas*. Whilst this second presumed stage is of limited significance, 'monotheism', which scholars postulated as the third and final evolutionary stage of religion, did not grow out of the Vedas at all. Instead, the development took a different direction. Thus instead of pursuing the discussion of the *devas* further, it seems preferable to listen in to the discussions which the ancient Indians themselves had about these matters. For indeed the Vedic Indians did ask questions about the nature of man and the world and about what principles ordered and governed them. Already at an early stage, a concept *ṛta* evolved which denoted some cosmic order or harmony. Varuṇa in particular was its guardian, acting as the agent of retribution for any infringement of *ṛta*. This suggests that behind the multiplicity of *devas*, some unifying principle, abstract and impersonal, was envisaged. Similarly we find the concept *brahman*, denoting at this early stage a particular 'sacred', cosmic power. In fact it was this power which accounted for the efficacy of the sacrifice, since it was located within the brahmin priest, and that in turn because he had absorbed it by learning the Vedas. Such conceptions were then developed along much more conscious, searching lines. A great interest in the world, in the laws governing it and in its origin and structure, came to the fore. The sacrifice was used as a major conceptual model for exploring these issues. A search began for the one principle underlying and controlling all other forces in the world. For, and this appears to be the motivation, if this one could be controlled or manipulated ritually, total control over the world and man's destiny could be gained. In a large number of 'creation myths', a whole spectrum of suggestions of such a one principle is made. What better way to demonstrate the power of the one over the many than to show how out of the one the many evolved? Well-known examples are Vāc (Speech, that is the Vedas), Skambha (the cosmic axis), Puruṣa ('Man', the sacrificial victim, out of whose dismembered body the world with its beings and social classes evolved). It is clear from the multiplicity of such conceptions that we are not dealing here with any kind of normative ('Hindu') account of creation comparable with what we find in the book of Genesis. But eventually all these extremely variegated speculations settled on *brahman*, a term that now also denotes the one at the beginning and at the centre of all the many things and beings that make up the universe. It goes without saying that this must have added enormously to the prestige of the priests and of their sacrifices where *brahman* was located in a very special way. All these speculations found their textual home within the Vedic literature discussed above: as Book X and part of Book I of the Ṛg-Veda, as the second half of the Atharva-Veda and in scattered form in the different Brāhmaṇas. In the light of these observations, the role of the *devas* cannot exclusively be regarded as central to Vedic religion. Neither in the perception of the sacrifice as 'automatic' nor in the way a single ultimate principle is envisaged do personal features or *deva*-figures play any decisive role.

It is often said that the Veda is to the Hindus what the Bible is to Christianity. But for all practical purposes, such a comparison is at most misleading, if not totally inappropriate. Whilst it is certainly true that any reasonable description of Hinduism would have to refer constantly to 'the Veda', it would only be slightly exaggerated to say that its actual content is irrelevant (at least as far as the hymns and the sacrificial material are concerned). The reality of the Veda is primarily conceptual. Certainly the fact that they are not a written scripture is important here. But to explain why this was not done requires a look at the social context. They were the carefully guarded 'religious knowledge' of a certain group of people, and thus not a proclamation of beliefs addressed to the whole of Indian society. Moreover, parallel to a decrease in the linguistic comprehensibility went an increase of the purely functional role of this literature. Both in grammar and vocabulary, the earlier Vedic hymns are in a pre-classical form of the Sanskrit language. In the course of time, these hymns thus became increasingly more incomprehensible, even to those people who knew classical Sanskrit or whose mother tongue was derived from it. Their style and poetic conventions and their allusive mythology also became increasingly remote and archaic. But this created no obvious problems, for as was observed above, the actual content was of no importance, once a more reflex conception of *brahman* as central cosmic power had evolved. What remained important was the learning of the hymns, for *brahman* would thereby be absorbed, and the recitation of them, for *brahman* would thereby be applied to a ritual act. The Brāhmaṇas are far more easily accessible, but their relevance for the professional priest as his handbook is a primarily practical one. Moreover, whatever new forms of religion evolved during the following millennia, none could claim to be 'orthodox', or acquire social respectability, unless some connection with the Veda could be shown, however tenuous, putative or artificial this link might be. Much of what to the uncritical observer appears as the 'continuity of the Vedic tradition' in Hinduism reveals itself at closer inspection as a secondary recourse back to the ancient past, and not as historically grown extensions.

In many other ways did the Vedas stimulate further intellectual and religious developments. A whole range of academic disciplines evolved, all of which derived from concerns connected with the Veda, and are thus known as the *Vedāṅgas*, the 'limbs' of the Veda: for example, astronomy (to determine the precise time and date for a sacrifice), grammar (to maintain the comprehensibility at least of the ritual treatises) and geometry (for the precise construction of altars). But more important, because it was of far greater general relevance, was the formulation of the ideal of a 'Vedic life'. In particular two such disciplines concerned themselves with the study of domestic rituals and with life in society. The earliest textual expressions of these subjects are the various *gṛhya*- and *dharma-sūtras* which we still find included in the repertoire of the various *śākhās*. Of particular interest here is the concept of 'dharma' (a development of that of *ṛta*). But the 'classical' view of *dharma* and thus of the orthodox, Vedic life is not merely a development of Vedic religion, but a relatively late synthesis of two very different traditions. Traceable as far back as *c.* 800 BCE, that is when Vedic literature had reached the stage indicated above, we find a very different kind of religious reality. This is the 'renouncer tradition', and we must turn to it, before pursuing the topic of the ideal religious, Vedic life.

The Renouncer Traditions

The rewards requested from the *devas* in the Vedic hymns have a decidedly this-worldly character: sons, long life, victory in battle, etc. And the motivation behind the later sacrificial system is the maintenance of the cosmic order, implying the same idea of prosperity on earth. The early section of the Atharva-Veda deals even more with the minutiae of ordinary, daily life. Behind the speculations about the One lies a quest for the one power that controls all others in this world. This emphasis on 'worldly' matters may well be due to the very shadowy and rather unattractive conception of an afterlife in a gloomy underworld.

Then suddenly a new set of concepts becomes documented, from around 800 BCE onwards. These ideas are so much at variance with what we have encountered so far that some kind of discontinuity must be assumed. Here now we find expressed a conception of transcendence, a reality beyond all limitations of space, time and matter. Moreover, this reality contrasts sharply with ordinary life which appears limited, painful and undesirable by comparison with it. In addition, the span of this 'ordinary life' is extended greatly, for a potentially unlimited chain of such existences is envisaged for each living being. This is the idea of transmigration or rebirth. Each life is the result of previous lives, and in turn conditions further lives. Nevertheless, a qualitative leap into the realm of transcendence, of liberation from transmigration, is possible. It is simply a question of knowing what causes further rebirth and what the means are of escaping from it. Here also, in the perception of such means, the discontinuity with Vedic religion is apparent. No ritual, no *deva* could ever achieve it, only 'knowledge'. From the way that this 'knowledge' is described to us, and the more explicit statements about the method we are given, it can be inferred that we are dealing with ascetically, meditationally gained 'altered' or 'higher' states of consciousness. Desire and ignorance inevitably appear as the crucial cause of rebirth, and ascetic practices coupled with meditation are advocated as eradicating them. We find shared presuppositions about the need for sexual abstinence, poverty, homelessness and a radical avoidance of harming any form of life. These constitute the 'renunciation'.

The source of such ideas is obscure, but it is extremely unlikely that the *soma*-induced state of altered consciousness has had any causal link with them. It appears to be more likely that somewhere 'outside' the Vedic tradition these religious ideas were picked up and/or cultivated by some Āryas. What precisely this 'outside' could mean is impossible to answer; local tribal religion has been suggested. But it is clear that in some sense the follower of this type of religion places himself outside Aryan society and Vedic religion. He becomes a 'renouncer'.

This brief introductory sketch has gathered together material which textually has been preserved in three very different religious traditions and therefore is normally treated under three separate headings. These are the Upaniṣads, Jainism and Buddhism. But either by assuming a straightforward continuity between the Vedas and Upaniṣads, or by treating for instance Buddhism in isolation from its context within the renouncer tradition, many important features would be distorted. On various (mainly linguistic and geographical) grounds, the earliest texts known as Upaniṣads have been dated around 800 BCE. Then there are hints that Jainism is not the original creation of the alleged founder, the Mahāvīra (of the sixth or fifth century BCE), but the remodelling of a somewhat earlier religion associated with the name of Pārśva. Thus when the Buddha taught around the sixth century BCE, he had to address himself to a centuries-old tradition. The sophistication of his teaching would support his relatively late position within the renouncer tradition.

Whilst Jainism and Buddhism rejected *in toto* the Vedic religious tradition (and thus turned 'heterodox'), the Upaniṣads appear to attempt a synthesis or compromise. But whatever the theoretical position was in relation to the Veda, in terms of social behaviour the three varieties represent one movement: the renouncer tradition which defined itself as superior to ritualism. But what was felt to be even more important by each type within this tradition was a definition in relation to the other types. There are enough traces left in the literature to catch glimpses of an extremely variegated and dynamic internal discussion, and the three contestants mentioned here are no more than the eventual 'winners'.

The Upaniṣads

The word 'upaniṣad' denotes a particular genre of texts; its literal meaning has however remained obscure. 'Intimate teaching' might be a possible explanation. These Upaniṣads have come down to us as part of a neat and tidily structured package: the Veda (as Indians would use the word). In the previous chapter it was mentioned that over the centuries each Vedic *śākhā* acquired three genres of text: a Saṃhitā, Brāhmaṇa and Āraṇyaka. To these three we must add now the Upaniṣad. Indeed many of the genuinely old six or so texts belonging to this genre are simply known by the name of the *śākhā* to which they belong (like the *Aitareya-* or *Kauṣītaki-Upaniṣad*). This applies only to the Ṛg-, Sāma- and Yajur-Veda; but the Atharva-Veda also attracted later Upaniṣads. So we end up with a clear four-by-four structure. Moreover, another fourfold pattern is applied to this, that of the four stages in a man's life (for which see below). The fourth stage, that of the 'renouncer' (*saṃnyāsī*), is correlated to the fourth genre, that of the Upaniṣad.

This is the way traditional Hinduism interprets the situation. But the very neatness of the structure raises doubts about its historical validity. In view of the general remarks made above it appears more likely that we are dealing here with material which attempts to correlate extraneous and recently accepted religious ideas with the conceptions expressed in the earlier portions of the Vedic corpus. This may be an extreme way of envisaging the situation, but whatever its shortcomings may be, it has the advantage of focusing more sharply on the central religious issues than the traditional assumption of a direct continuity.

The *Chāndogya-* and the *Bṛhadāraṇyaka-Upaniṣads* have been identified as some of the oldest, and indeed historically most important, Upaniṣads. The title of the latter, bṛhad-*āraṇyaka*, highlights that the boundaries of the genres are by no means clear-cut. Thus the Upaniṣads also contain a large number of speculations on the One, along the cosmological lines of the earlier literature. And the aim is still to 'come to know it'. But the purpose of such knowledge has changed. To 'know it' now means to achieve that qualitative leap into the realm of liberation. This is how a direct link with earlier Vedic thought could be established. In trying to define what such a transcendental reality could be, the Upaniṣads draw on the images, concepts, terms and symbols of earlier Vedic literature. Some more independent speculations around symbols like fire, water and air are also expressed, but without doubt the concept of *brahman* emerges from all this as the sole survivor. This nevertheless expanded the denotation of the term far beyond what the earlier literature meant by it. Now *brahman* was not just the 'sacred' power pervading the sacrifice and the Veda itself, and not just the One out of which the many arose, but also the One into which man merges back by achieving his liberation from the cycle of rebirths (*saṃsāra*). Moreover, *brahman* is an experiential reality, available through meditation.

In more technical terms, this appears as follows. Ordinary man finds himself in *saṃsāra*, coursing from one life to the next. What remains constant is his innermost self, his *ātman*. But this *ātman* is surrounded and in fact imprisoned, not just by the different physical bodies which are cremated after death, but also by a subtle, invisible body. This *sūkṣma-śarīra* absorbs the 'qualities' of all the actions done in a given life, called *karma*, which after the disintegration of one body germinates, as it were, a new body appropriate in view of the past actions. This is by no means restricted to human bodies; rebirth as an animal, as one of those many categories of non-human beings known to ancient Indian folklore, or as a *deva* is equally well possible. Thus whatever status the *deva* may have possessed in earliest Vedic religion, it is now brought down to that of belonging to the transient order. By eradicating *karma* and 'coming to know' *brahman*, the *ātman* can liberate itself, to become reunited with *brahman*, like the spark with the fire from which it arose. That is *mokṣa* or *mukti*, the state of liberation. The 'coming to know' itself is mentioned under different names, but eventually the common and well-known term 'yoga' becomes universally used to refer to such forms of meditation.

The older Upaniṣads still lack a systematically defined terminology and neither, for that matter, do they draw on one coherent system of thought. The imagination coupled with critical, conceptual analysis is still at work to come to terms with the transcendental experience of *brahman*. Metaphor is one commonly used means of expression. When we thus find the relationship between *brahman* and the world (including man) envisaged as that of a fire and its sparks, or of a spider and its web, it is clear that an 'ontological' dependence is suggested between two real things: *brahman* and the multiple, variegated world of phenomena. Both are real, but the many derive from and depend on the One. There cannot be any question here of the world being an 'illusion', as some forms of later Hindu thought would present it. Other metaphors tell us about the achievement of liberation. It is like the merging of different rivers into the one ocean (in which they lose their identity and name), or the pollen of many flowers that make up the honey. This clearly suggests an ultimate identity of *ātman* with *brahman*, an identity in which the former is absorbed into the latter. An expansion of the self is experienced in which the whole universe is encompassed. In this context the names of at least the two most important teachers appearing in the early Upaniṣads must be mentioned: Uddālaka and Yajñavalkya. In their teaching we encounter attempts at a more systematic exposition, which could be described as 'progressive abstraction'. Thus Uddālaka has his disciple bisect a tree's fruit, then its seed, until only an invisibly small particle remains. Yet it is here, beyond the range of the human eye, in the 'essence' of the tree, that *brahman* is present, and 'that you are' is the famous conclusion drawn from it. With Yajñavalkya we find similar instances of such abstraction. From seeing to hearing to thinking to 'true knowledge' we are led along the scale of most immediate and object-bound information about reality to its most abstract, direct and non-objective form. In a famous passage (*Bṛhadāraṇyaka* II, 4) he removes his wife's doubts about this. Once the *ātman* has reunited with that which lies at the heart of all things and all events in the world (including perception itself), it makes no more sense to speak of a subject–object relationship, and the form of awareness that is connected with such a relationship is transcended in pure, that is non-objective, consciousness. Dream appears in such explorations as a useful metaphor, and more so, as an intermediary stage between the experience of *brahman* and ordinary consciousness. For in it we can already witness a degree of demolition, as far as the ordinary relationship between phenomena in the space–time–matter continuum are concerned. Following the logic of this first transition, *brahman*, as much as the experience associated with it, then appears as altogether outside that continuum. A famous formula summarises all this by describing *brahman* through the attributes of pure being (*sat*), consciousness (*cit*) and bliss (*ānanda*). But we also detect a note of despair in all this mystical exuberance, despair about the limitations of human thought and language when it comes to grasping *brahman*. Thus *neti neti* is suggested as the most appropriate way of referring to *brahman*: all that can be said about it is 'not, not'.

What has been sketched so far is typical of the older, genuinely *śākhā*-associated Upaniṣads. But in terms of the literary history of the genre, this was merely the beginning of many further developments. Thus, still well within the BCE period, Upaniṣads were produced in which the thinking took on a more systematic form, on the basis of what would seem to be somewhat different premisses. We are in fact dealing here with early expressions of a system, the Sāṃkhya, which will be discussed further in its appropriate context, that of the Hindu philosophical traditions. Still somehow linked to *śākhās*, yet another type of Upaniṣad evolved. By now we are probably in the last few centuries BCE. In works like the *Śvetāśvatara-Upaniṣad* we encounter for the first time a type of religion that can be styled monotheistic. More on this will be found in the section on the gods and God. By now the genre had established itself as most prestigious, and a large number of further Upaniṣads was produced over the next centuries. Few religious movements resisted the attempt to point at an Upaniṣad as the final authority for their particular beliefs. Even the famous *Bhagavadgītā* of the Mahābhārata epic presented itself as 'the Upaniṣad sung by Bhagavān', although this particular claim was never accepted by the Hindu traditions. In most cases, such late Upaniṣads were nominally connected with the Atharva-Veda—another sign that this Veda played a role separate from that of the other three Vedas.

It is not known from what period onwards attempts began to be made to survey the older, originally *śākhā*-specific Upaniṣads and treat them as constituting one coherent corpus of teaching. The *Brahma*- or *Vedānta-sūtras* ascribed to Bādarāyaṇa became the most prestigious work offering such a survey. It provided the basis for the most important of the so-called six schools of Hindu philosophy, the Vedānta. But later forms of Hinduism have taken recourse to the thought of the Upaniṣads in many other ways. On the one hand linked to the Veda, and on the other hand enormously variegated in content, the Upaniṣads offered the most obvious basis for any claim of 'Vedic orthodoxy'.

In the chapter on Vedic religion, mention was made of the ideal of the orthodox, Vedic life. Taken in its most radical form, the teaching of the Upaniṣads would have to appear in direct contrast to the this-worldly ritual religion of earlier Vedic literature. Indeed, we still find traces of a conscious mockery of sacrifices to the *devas* expressed in some

Upaniṣads. The ideal of renunciation challenged all conceptions of a life, however 'pious', which included wealth, sexuality, a home and possessions. But the Upaniṣads did not just externally draw on Vedic speculation about the One and attach themselves to the Vedic *śākhās*. An internal decision was implied in this: that both religious attitudes could be combined. Eventually this was conceptualised as the four stages in a man's life (the *āśramas*), and somehow overlapping with this, as the four human goals (*puruṣārthas*). Together with the assumption of a fourfold division of society (the four *varṇas*), all this crystallised in the concept of *dharma*, a cosmic order which set the norms for human behaviour and action. Provided that a man belongs to one of the higher three *varṇas* (which means that he is a true 'Ārya'), his life should proceed in four stages. First there is a period of celibate studentship, dedicated to the study of the Vedas. Then follows marriage, enjoyment of sexuality, procreation of children and pursuit of wealth. After this, a gradual withdrawal from the world should begin, culminating in rejecting all ties with family and home and becoming a *saṃnyāsī*, a 'renouncer'. Whilst during the earlier stages Vedic ritual religion is appropriate, the quest for *brahman* along the lines of the Upaniṣads characterises the final stage. *Mokṣa* is now the only legitimate *puruṣārtha*; *dharma* (in the sense of Vedic religious activities), *artha* (pursuit of wealth) and *kāma* (sexuality) cease to be relevant. This general pattern is further differentiated according to the specific requirements made of the different *varṇas*. Thus a *brahmin*'s primary link is with *dharma* and religion, a *kṣatriya*'s with warfare, and a *vaiśya*'s with trade and agriculture. The *śūdra* is left out of all this; Vedic religion is not available to him, and only through serving the other three groups can he hope to be reborn into a *varṇa* where Vedic religion and *brahman* are cultivated. This is in a nutshell the conventional understanding of the (*varṇāśrama-*) *dharma*. A vast amount of critical, literary activity evolved around it in India. The very brief summaries of early discussions contained in the *Dharma-sūtras* were replaced by lengthy treatises, the *Dharma-śāstras*. The one attributed to Manu (from around the beginning of the Common Era?) is the most famous one. But other such treatises show that no final, positive definition of *dharma* in terms of universally accepted specific norms evolved. This remained an area of discussion and divergent views. But there are further restrictions on the application of this material to the real life. On the whole, this is normative thought, suggesting an ideal, not a social reality. As we shall see, Jainism and Buddhism reject all this outright, recommending renunciation exclusively. On the other hand, it is by no means the case that the tradition advocating *dharma* unanimously accepts the ideal of *mokṣa* or renunciation. Holding on to views from a period prior to the emergence of the renouncer traditions, many strands of the *dharma* literature advocate man's 'fulfilment' directly through the adherence to the three goals *dharma*, *artha* and *kāma* alone. Much more generally, the actual relevance even of beliefs in *saṃsāra* and *karma* was quite restricted. There is ample evidence in Hindu scriptures of later periods to suggest that such ideas were not necessarily always at the forefront of the religious consciousness.

Early Jainism

The figure of Prince Vardhamāna, who became the Mahāvīra ('great hero') and from whom Jainism takes its historical origin, leads us back into the sixth century BCE. There is evidence to suggest that at that time a religious community associated with the name of Pārśva was in existence and that Vardhamāna had some connection with it. Thus it is possible that Jainism has roots beyond the Mahāvīra in a strand of the renouncer tradition of the eighth century BCE or so. The extreme archaism of much of the teaching associated with his name would speak in favour of such an assumption. However, the history of Jainism begins with the Mahāvīra, and even in his case it is very difficult to distinguish between legend and history, and between his own teaching and that of later generations. For although the Jains possess an enormous amount of canonical and post-canonical scriptures, by their own testimony anything resembling a canon was only finalised in the fifth century CE, a thousand years after Vardhamāna's preaching.

What appears fairly certain is that in the sixth century BCE, in a region of eastern India which corresponds roughly to the modern state of Bihār, a prince called Vardhamāna renounced his life as a *kṣatriya* and householder, spent many years as a renouncer in search of liberation by exposing himself to almost impossible physical hardships, obtained the state of a Jina ('conqueror') and died after many years of preaching, at an age of at least seventy years. From this title *jina* are derived 'Jainism', for the religion initiated by the Jina, and 'Jaina' (or 'Jain' in its modern Hindi form), for his followers. The religious movement founded by the Mahāvīra has evinced a surprising continuity and coherence till the present day. Although it is today by no means as numerous and influential as it was during certain phases of its history and in certain regions of India (though never outside it), unlike Buddhism it survived the onslaught of Islam, and moreover, did not split into the great variety of different school traditions as did Buddhism. Only a single bifurcation occurred in the history of Jainism (around the first century CE), and even this effected only a relatively small area of disagreement. One branch maintained that monks must not wear any clothes—thus the title *digambara*, 'dressed in space', evolved. The other branch regarded this as excessive and allowed for the wearing of one 'white dress'—*śvetāmbara*. The latter tradition maintains that a sizeable amount of the Mahāvīra's teaching has been preserved and lists about 45, partly very extensive, scriptures as its canon. According to the Digambaras, all of the Jina's teaching has been lost in its original form and it is only available through the later writings of teachers like Umāsvāti and Kundakunda. But both believe that the tenets of Jainism derive from an omniscient being (the Mahāvīra) and thus doctrinally do not allow for any fundamental transformations and developments.

Although both Jainism and Buddhism originated in the same region of India at roughly the same time and reveal amazing similarities of detail, in essence we are dealing with very different religions. It has been suggested that this may be due to the very different personalities of the Buddha and the Mahāvīra, the latter appearing as austere, authoritarian and interested in philosophical discussion. But it is not the thought of the Upaniṣads that provides the background for that discussion; it is nature-philosophical speculation.

The Jains assume the existence of only one world system, and the archaism of their teaching reveals itself in the fact that even liberation is still located within it—at the very top of the universe. Below that are found a whole range of heavenly realms, then—as the central disc—the world of human beings, and finally subterranean realms and many layers of increasingly painful hells. This whole structure is filled with an infinite number of *jīvas*, 'souls', which except for the liberated ones at the very top are all embodied in some form or other (as *deva*, human being, animal, denizen of hells. This invisibly fine material *karma* enters the *jīva*, whenever an ordinary knowledge, power and happiness. But since eternity, the souls are caught up in *saṃsāra*, the cycle of rebirth. Here again the archaism of Jaina thought reveals itself, because the reason for the *jīva*'s entanglement in *saṃsāra*—also here styled *karma*—is actually conceived of as being loaded by heavy matter (*karma*) which pushes it downwards into the heavens, human world or even hells. This invisibly fine material *karma* enters the *jīva*, whenever an ordinary act—in thought, word and deed—is performed by an embodied being. Once inside a *jīva*, this *karma* in various degrees reduces or eliminates the innate characteristics of unlimited vision, knowledge, etc., stimulates further action by giving rise to desires and passions, and thus causes further rebirth. Later Jain scholasticism went to amazing lengths of spelling out a great variety of types of *karma* and their respective effects on the new embodiment. Some amount of *karma* inside a *jīva* is used up during a life-span of an individual, through his moments of happiness (positive *karma*) and sufferings (negative *karma*). But at the same time, more *karma* is thereby let into the *jīva*.

The outlines of Jain teaching on liberation are clear from this sketch: man (the other classes of embodied beings cannot do so) must attempt to ward off the influx of further *karma* by controlling all his actions, and to eliminate the *karma* already present inside the *jīva*, by burning it up, as it were. A strictly regulated ethical life followed by a check on all one's senses will weaken one's passions and desires and thus reduce the amount of *karma* flowing into the *jīva*. Ascetic practices (which in certain circumstances may go as far as starving oneself to death) serve as the fire to consume *karma* already present. Quite literally, one form of such *tapas* involves exposing oneself not just to the sun of the Indian summer, but adding to it by keeping fires burning all around oneself. When eventually the *jīva* has been cleansed by these means of all the *karma* filling it, no weight holds it down in this world of transmigration, and with its innate qualities fully realised, it moves into the realm of liberation, at the top of the universe, never to return into the world of matter.

Such an ideal is obviously designed for the full renouncer only. But in practice, allowances are made for the fact that *karma* may well prevent a full commitment to the Jain path. Thus Jainism has extended its programme to laymen and nuns, offering spiritual practices in preparation for a rebirth in which liberation becomes possible. But no allowances were made for brahmin ritualism and for the social structure and restrictions associated with it. Vedic rituals were rejected as useless, and the Jaina path was open to all, whatever their social background. With enormous zeal the Jains have from earliest times onwards developed the practical details of their spiritual path, from the moment a being becomes convinced of the truth of the Jain teaching to the achievement of final liberation. Thus for the laymen we find the five *aṇuvratas* (minor vows): not to kill, tell lies or steal, and to preserve marital faithfulness and put a restraint on possessions. *Guṇavratas* may be observed voluntarily: to avoid acts that could be harmful to living beings, impose restraints on one's travelling and eating, etc. The layman is brought even closer to the monastic life through the *śikṣāvratas* which involve often severe forms of fasting and sexual abstinence, all kinds of religious ceremonies and a commitment to supporting the monks.

With the monks, the *aṇuvratas* turn into the *mahāvratas*, the 'great vows', where marital fidelity is replaced by complete chastity. Many further lists of virtues to be cultivated and of spiritual practices are given. Among these, three may be mentioned in particular. The cultivation of *samiti*, 'carefulness', aims at eliminating all forms of unconscious or instinctive activity and producing a conscious awareness of everything one does. The twelve *anuprekṣās* are meditational exercises on set topics, such as the transience of beings, the impurity of the human body, the difficulty of gaining liberation and the supreme value of the Jain teaching. The practice of *parīsaha*, 'endurance', encourages the monk to become indifferent not only to relatively mild forms of tribulation like hunger, thirst, cold, insect bites and insults, but also to physical persecution and martyrdom. But everything listed so far primarily achieves merely the prevention of further *karma*. *Tapas* is the true means for the monk to burn up existing *karma*. Besides long periods of fasting, adopting painful physical postures and other means already mentioned above, *tapas* also includes meditation. However, unlike the Buddhists and also the Upaniṣads, the Jains emphasise the need for physical austerities, and it is regarded almost as a by-product that thereby mental effects (ultimately, the infinite knowledge of the *jīva*) are achieved.

This teaching is contained in the very bulky canon of the Śvetāmbaras. But even they agree that this canon no longer contains the oldest scriptures (*pūrvas*, which by both branches are associated with Pārśva).

The extant 45 or so works are gathered together in six groups (Aṅgas, Upāṅgas, Prakīrṇas, Chedasūtras, Mūlasūtras and two individual treatises). Cosmology and cosmography, with lists of the various beings populating this vast universe, are mixed with doctrinal and disciplinary matters. But many of these works illustrate a feature in which Jainism excels in later times: the telling of stories. Time and again abstract matters are given concrete application by showing how for specific individuals (legendary figures, the Mahāvīra himself, or imaginary persons) *karma* operates in real life. Most of the texts are in a form of Prakrit called by scholars Ardhamāgadhī. Though developed here as a literary language, it probably comes close to the actual language spoken by the Mahāvīra. For centuries, the Jains cultivated the Prakrits for literary purposes. Thus a slightly different Prakrit was employed by them for writing increasingly complex and voluminous commentaries on the canonical scriptures. Only towards the end of this enterprise was Sanskrit used. In turn, this commentarial literature is followed by the more systematic writings of the Jain philosophers. Umāsvāti (of the early centuries CE) is still accepted by both branches as authoritative. From his exposition of Jain teaching, two well-known schemas may be mentioned. The first is that of the five *astikāyas*, 'chunks of reality'. This consists of space, of movement (called *dharma*), of rest or obstruction (*adharma*), of the infinite number of souls (*jīvas*) and of *pudgalas* (material entities, in their smallest form *aṇus*, 'atoms'). From this list it is immediately obvious how 'realistic' or 'proto-scientific' the whole is conceived of. No world-soul (like the Upaniṣadic *brahman*) or transcendental reality outside space, time and matter is envisaged. The second schema summarises the essentials of Jain teaching on the path to liberation, in the form of the seven *tattvas* or fundamental truths. Here reality is simply divided into *jīva* and *ajīva*, the remaining four *astikāyas* which are insentient. The third *tattva* is that of *āsrava*, the 'influx' of material *karma* into the *jīva*, and the fourth (*bandha*) denotes the 'bondage' to *saṃsāra* effected thereby. With the fifth, *saṃvara* or 'warding off' of new *karma*, we enter the Jain path, to proceed with *nirjarā*, 'the removing' of existing *karma*. *Mokṣa*, 'liberation', signifies the final goal.

Jainism is manifestly a very austere religion with its emphasis on physical austerities and self-inflicted pains. At the same time, it is very rigid in its fundamental doctrinal framework. Nevertheless, in spite of these basic characteristics, Jainism has developed fully fledged cultural features, taking from and feeding back into the non-Jaina Indian cultural and religious scene. However, most of these developments belong to a later age, and thus will be taken up in a separate section below.

Early Buddhism

Another religion which grew out of the fertile ground of the renouncer tradition is perhaps the most important one in the context of Asian religious history: Buddhism, the teaching of Siddhārtha, the Buddha. There cannot be any doubt about his historicity, although the precise details of his life are lost in the jungle of later hagiographies. Still, it seems likely that he lived his long life during the sixth and fifth centuries BCE in north-eastern India, that he was of *kṣatriya* descent, that he abandoned his home and family to search for a means to liberation, that he believed he had succeeded in this at the moment of his 'enlightenment' and that he spent the rest of his life teaching others about it.

Later generations felt this to be a far too lifeless account, and a variety of 'lives' of the Buddha appeared which in ever-increasing detail filled in concrete 'biographical' incidents. Moreover, these versions widened the scope and surrounded the specific life-story with all kinds of cosmological and religious features. Thus works like Aśvaghoṣa's *Buddhacarita* and the anonymous *Lalitavistara* and *Mahāvastu* do not merely narrate a story, but spell out in popularly accessible narrative terms their individual perception of Buddhism. Naturally, when the Buddha is presented as spending his early years till well after his marriage in the utmost luxury and pleasure, this highlights the alluring charm of ordinary life. When he then, out of curiosity, explores the world outside the palace walls and encounters an old man, a sick man and a corpse, in a most striking and immediate manner it is shown that ordinary life is characterised by old age, illness and death. Or when we hear that Siddhārtha tried yoga with two brahmin teachers and then practised severe asceticism which brought him to the verge of death, yet found both methods unsatisfactory, this can be interpreted as a self-definition of Buddhism in relation to other movements in the renouncer tradition. It calls itself the 'middle way' which avoids the excesses of self-indulgence and fanatical asceticism. It is not difficult to see in the latter a reference to Jain *tapas*, and in the former an allusion to the easygoing, almost corrupt pretences of self-satisfied brahmin religion. As we have seen above, there may even be some historical truth in this, for both the brahmin and the Jain concern for meditation and asceticism appear to have preceded the life of the Buddha by two or so centuries. This must have affected the interpretation of Buddhism: as a relatively late phenomenon in the renouncer tradition, it could survey the spectrum of teachings already available. And in a sense it wanted to transcend and synthesise the various alternatives that were on offer. Certainly early Buddhist teaching is more abstract and 'modern' by comparison with that of Jainism and the early Upaniṣads. The same feature makes it that much more difficult to understand.

Two key periods in the life of the Buddha attracted the attention of his followers initially. One was Siddhārtha's enlightenment (*bodhi*) which transformed him into a *buddha*, an 'enlightened one'. This event is the most central aspect of the whole of Buddhism. For not only was this the point at which Siddhārtha personally achieved liberation, not only was this the source of his insight into the nature of reality, it was also the event that propelled him into teaching and thereby offering to others the same enlightenment. The second key period is that of the last few months before his death. Its importance derives from the need of the young community to define its institutional structures. Apparently the Buddha refused to appoint a successor, claiming that just as the goal of *bodhi* was the same for all, all followers of his were the same and all decisions had to be made by them in unison. This resulted in a religious history remarkably different from that of Jainism. Whilst the latter adhered to far more rigid structures, Buddhism developed a wide spectrum of interpretations of the Buddha's teaching and also of different social groups of Buddhists advocating them. Again, this great flexibility and variety adds to the difficulties in understanding 'Buddhism'.

The reconstruction of earliest Buddhist teaching is fraught with difficulties. A large number of Indian sources relevant to this task have been lost over the centuries, and this fact would naturally strengthen claims by the sole direct survivor of ancient Indian Buddhism, the Theravāda of Ceylon (Sri Lanka) to be the only legitimate, 'orthodox' form of Buddhism. A relatively recent scholarly interest in the fragments of the Indian material which have survived, and a more critical, unbiased look at other traditions outside India, suggest that such a simplistic picture of orthodox versus distorted Buddhism will have to be altered considerably. What follows here is a tentative sketch of what in the light of this might be regarded as the earliest Buddhist teaching.

Hagiography tells us that the key theme of the Buddha's first sermon was that of the Four Noble Truths. It is not difficult to regard this schema as central to Buddhist teaching generally. Modelled on ancient Indian medical procedure, it provides a critical analysis of the human situation, investigates the causes of the 'disease', states that a cure is possible and prescribes the medicine for it. It does not, however, present any theoretical framework for its pragmatic procedure, no definition of 'what it means to be healthy' (in terms of the medical model). And whilst it emphasises very strongly that there is an illness, that is, 'suffering' (thereby giving rise to an initial appearance of depressing negativism), it regards true happiness (the liberation from this 'suffering') as a self-evident phenomenon. We shall return to this attitude at a later stage.

The First Noble Truth states that there is 'suffering' (*duḥkha*, Pali: *dukkha*). Most evidently it reveals itself in the painful events of birth, illness, old age and death. Implied in this is also the assumption of rebirth, the endlessly repeated occurrence of these events. It is further implied that all beings are involved in it, man as much as animals and *devas*. Yet outside these events life is also characterised by 'suffering': to be with what we do not want, not to be with what we want, in short, every wish unfulfilled, is *duḥkha*. To this is added one further component which makes it clear that we are not just dealing with 'aspects' of life, but with its essential nature. To be a person is identical with 'suffering'. Such a person is now analysed in terms of five major layers or interacting components, 'the elements of grasping' (*upādāna-skandhas*). On the most superficial level one could say that 'suffering' is experienced in all five, or 'in thought, word and deed'. But more is alluded to through this schema. These five components want to describe the empirical person, and that in terms spelled out more clearly in the Second Noble Truth. With that focus in mind, the picture of the 'person' would look like this. There is the physical side, the body (*rūpa*, lit. 'form'). This body is endowed with the sense-organs, and through these information about the outside world is received. But man is not a computer which mechanically absorbs data. Thus this information 'affects' him, namely acquires an affective, emotional colouring. This is *vedanā*, 'emotions'. Since the senses inform us through five different channels, offering us (affectively coloured) visual, aural, etc. data, all this is put together into one composite whole, a single mental image associated with the corresponding sights, sounds and so forth (*saṃjñā*). Moreover, all kinds of additional assumptions are made with regard to such a perceived object, partly due to the influences of past *karma*. Then the will reacts, by setting in motion an act of reaching out to acquire or enjoy the object, or to reject and destroy, depending on the decision we have made as to the positive or negative qualities of the object. All this is summed up in the term *saṃskāra*. Finally, these are not mechanical processes, for we are aware of all this and constantly impose thoughts on to them, associating them with an (autonomous) 'I'. This is *vijñāna*.

The Second Noble truth mentions the cause of suffering: we suffer because we relate to objects in precisely the manner indicated above. We 'thirst' (the keyword used in this context, *tṛṣṇā*, Pali: *taṇhā*) for the enjoyment of objects that appeal to us, and by implication hate those that do not. But there is one further implication here, which alone makes sense of this analysis: no object in human experience can actually provide the happiness we hope for when desiring its enjoyment. Thus even if every wish of ours were kept being fulfilled, we would still continue to desire more. This now implies a form of ignorance, and it is indeed through such a concept (*avidyā*) that the Second Noble Truth is expanded. Again, this 'ignorance' can be specified as concerning the understanding a person has of what he is and what he could gain from any object. This means that the acquisition of any desired object would only make sense if it could add something lasting to someone lasting. But, empirically, no such 'lasting' entities are found. All five *upādāna-skandhas* are transient (thought, *vijñāna*, appears and disappears most rapidly among them). So the whole way we react to the world and perceive ourselves is mistaken. These three interrelated ideas (desire, ignorance, incorrect conception of 'I' and 'mine') are summarised as the three *āsravas*. Because of the three *āsravas* operating in the person, life is suffering.

Now in the context of renouncer thought, this is not yet a sufficient explanation. For 'life' here implies transmigration. Can the analysis of the Second Noble Truth be applied to this idea as well? This appears to be the purpose of another schema, variously known as 'conditioned origination', 'dependent co-production', etc. (*pratītya-samutpāda*). The title is symptomatic of its abstruseness. We are given a list of twelve concepts, starting with *avidyā*, 'ignorance'. The following two, *saṃskāra* and *vijñāna*, are already known to us. The fourth, *nāma-rūpa*, denotes the person (and in that sense is synonymous with the five *skandhas*). The fifth, 'the six spheres', concentrates on the sense-organs of such a person, which are in 'contact' (*sparśa*) with the outside world. Due to this, *vedanā*, and in turn *tṛṣṇā*, arise. As the ninth element, *upādāna* is mentioned. This 'grasping' conditions *bhava* ('conception of a foetus'), birth, and—as the twelfth—old age, death, grief, lament, suffering, depression and despair. The rationale of the whole list is: if such and such a phenomenon occurs (say, 'ignorance'), then it follows inevitably that the subsequent phenomenon will also occur (thus, *saṃskāras*). Now we have encountered above a dual interpretation of the cause of suffering: as 'desire' and 'ignorance'; and both terms reappear in the list. Moreover, the list seems to refer twice to the whole person (with *nāma-rūpa* and, indirectly, 'birth'). In view of this, the following interpretation may be the most original one among the traditional analyses of the list of twelve conditions. It is first shown how rebirth occurs with the concept of 'ignorance' as starting-point; then the same processes are once again described, but with 'desire' as the focal point and with different subsequent terms. But later Buddhist traditions evolved a whole range of different interpretations. The complexity of such a description of *saṃsāra* is partly due to the fact that here once again no reference to anything lasting in the 'person' (as defined by the five *skandhas*) is made. Transmigration is described merely as a chain of interconnected, transient processes which continuously yield suffering.

The Third Noble Truth simply states that it is possible to get out of this vicious circle of constantly desiring true happiness and yet constantly being thrown back into suffering. Thus, at this point, Buddhism turns cheerful and optimistic. The Fourth Noble Truth spells out the method by which liberation can be achieved. In view of what has been said above, the principles can be predicted: the eradication of desire and ignorance. This is presented as the Noble Eightfold Path. Various interpretations of it have evolved in Buddhist reflection, but the following might be the most original. The whole is a map of the spiritual path which Buddhism is advocating. We start with that initial moment when someone hears the Buddhist teaching and is struck by how sensible it all appears. Thus he feels inclined to commit himself to it and enter the path laid out in front of him. (This would be the first two stages: correct insight and resolve.) Then follow steps on the path which are basically ethical and ascetic, clearly intended to eradicate desire. A beginning is made with 'correct speech', which is followed by 'correct conduct' (*śīla*). Buddhism has formulated four or five primary ethical rules: not to harm any living being, not to steal, not to commit sexual misdemeanour (which in the case of the monk turns into total sexual abstinence) and not to tell lies and insults. To this was added a prohibition of intoxicants. These five make up the *pañca-śīla*, 'fivefold conduct'. At a certain point, the rejection of various professions is enjoined ('correct livelihood'). For example, to make a living out of hunting or being a soldier would be irreconcilable with the ideal of not harming any creature.

After 'correct effort' the path moves out of the life of a layman into that of the fully committed Buddhist, the monk. Ethic is here complemented by meditational exercises, alluded to by 'correct mindfulness (*smṛti*, Pali: *sati*)' and 'correct meditation (*dhyāna*, Pali: *jhāṇa*)', designed to overcome ignorance. Detailed information on the structure and rationale of Buddhist meditation techniques can be found in the old scriptures. Rather surprisingly perhaps, no major differences appear in a comparison with what Hindu yoga traditions have to offer. After appropriate moral preparation, the first exercises involve the cultivation of positive mental attitudes. Then a radical awareness (*smṛti*) of all one's thoughts, words and deeds is aimed at which intends to eradicate unconscious attitudes, instincts and prejudices. In this connection may be mentioned an exercise called 'application of mindfulness' (*smṛtyupasthāna*). First the body, then the emotions and the mind (*citta*), and finally all empirical phenomena are meditated upon as transient and lacking any kind of lasting inner core. This leads over to an increase of the concentrative faculties and mental clarity, and the mind now reaches out into higher states of consciousness (*dhyāna*). Ultimately this allows for the direct perception of the Buddhist teaching as true, of the nature of reality, and of the chain of causes and effects that have resulted, after innumerable rebirths, in the current existence. Alongside these insights, the experience of true happiness occurs, for suffering has been overcome and there will be no further return into its realm. Liberation has been achieved. Whether presented to us in the hagiography about the Buddha's own enlightenment or in the texts talking about Buddhist meditation, this is the content of the culmination of the Buddhist path.

This is, in a nutshell, the teaching implied in the Four Noble Truths and, in a sense, of early Buddhism. But we have to remind ourselves that it appears within the renouncer tradition, and in fact at a relatively late stage. Thus we may assume that this teaching comments in a variety of ways on the thought available at the time and defines itself in relation to it. It clearly shares with many of the other renouncers a total rejection of the Vedic religious system. The possibility of achieving enlightenment and liberation is latent in every man, and thus Buddhism addresses itself to all. To restrict true religious knowledge to a small minority, to have an elite guard the access to it and to claim that it is available only through a revealed corpus of sacred, equally well-guarded scriptures—all this appears to Buddhism as a parody of true religion. Now given the fact that a metaphysical framework of liberation which involved concepts like '*ātman*' and '*brahman*' inevitably had ideological connotations (as shown above), this is one reason why early Buddhism would find it difficult to adopt a similar framework. Furthermore, it did not want to accept the idea of an individual, permanent 'soul' or *jīva*, as found for instance with Jainism. The observable transience of all phenomena suggested to them the absence of a lasting, inner core in man. Whatever other reasons there may have been, the Buddhists decided to take a strictly empirical and pragmatic line and reject all speculation about the nature of a soul, a self, an *ātman* or a *jīva*, as unproductive. If it makes sense to assume the all-pervasive presence of suffering, the only logical conclusion to draw from this is the need for a practical course of action. To eradicate suffering by removing desire and ignorance is the only legitimate task; to sit back and speculate would be a fatal waste of time.

The absence of any explicit teaching about metaphysical issues like the existence of a 'soul' or some such inner core in man and the nature of the state of liberation has created considerable consternation not just among Western scholars, but also among Indian thinkers outside, and indeed inside, the Buddhist tradition. In fact, it could be argued that the subsequent history of Buddhist thought is no more than a struggle to interpret this Buddhist teaching and the nature of the Buddha himself (which implies, the nature of anyone 'enlightened') more in terms of a philosophical system. But such a turn to metaphysical speculation had very practical implications for the religious life. Given the absence of any centralised authority or initial metaphysical doctrines, there was obviously enormous scope for a great variety of positions to emerge. It is here where Jainism and Buddhism differ radically.

Perhaps not surprisingly, the charge of 'nihilism' was levelled against the Buddha's teaching. But if the Buddhist goal had been to overcome suffering by plunging into a total 'nothing', it would have been easy enough for the Buddha to say so. Instead we find frequent statements in which early Buddhism explicitly distances itself from 'nihilism' (which was indeed preached by some of the renouncers). An episode is told in which the Buddha was asked directly whether he accepted the existence of a soul or not. He kept silent. Afterwards he explained himself. Had he said yes, his teaching would have been interpreted as similar to those schools of thought that postulated an eternal soul (e.g. the Jains). Had he said no, it would have made no sense to the person who had asked the question. In short, neither answer would have served any spiritual purpose. Or here is another illustration of this practical orientation. If a man were hit by a poisoned arrow, he would not waste his time asking who shot the arrow, whether he was fat or slim, what his family background was, what kind of bow was used and so on.

Instead he would try to find a doctor as soon as possible. *Vis-à-vis* the fundamental fact of suffering, not metaphysical speculation but spiritual practice is urgently required. Then we have an episode where the metaphor of a burning fire is compared to earthly existence. It can be defined in terms of its place and of the time it burns, and also of its material causes (the fuel). But once it has gone out, such qualifications cannot apply any more. By 'gone out' the contemporary audience may well have understood that it has merged back into the amorphous, latent state of the cosmological element, fire. This seems to suggest that once the Buddha (and by implication, any enlightened being) has died, all qualifications in terms of space, time, matter, name, etc. do not apply any more. Like the ocean, he has become unfathomable and unchartable. If all this meant simply 'nothing', this would be dreadfully roundabout and verbose. After all, enlightenment is a totally fulfilling experience; it implies the happiness of knowing that suffering has been destroyed, or 'blown out'. The word *nirvāṇa*, which does mean 'blowing out', need not be pressed to refer to annihilation in an ontological or metaphysical sense. It is perfectly sufficient to read it as referring to the annihilation of the three *āsravas*, that is, ignorance, etc. The very fact that such an experience is possible implies that it takes place somewhere. It can certainly not be in *vijñāna* (as defined above), the most fleeting of the *skandhas*. Where else it could be is not stated; only when we come to Mahāyāna Buddhism will attempts at answering this question be found.

By making these ideas available to others and evolving concrete structures within society, the Buddha's teaching became a religion. He is presented to us as extremely sociable, and adaptable to a great variety of audiences. Here, in his attitude towards ordinary people, the principle of the 'golden middle' is applied. He is said to have succeeded in recruiting a large following from a great variety of backgrounds. The predominant lifestyle they adopted seems to have been, at least initially, that of the homeless, itinerant mendicant. What better way of backing up one's meditations about the transience of all things than by leading such an unsettled life, which brings one in contact with all kinds of people? However, like the Jains, the early Buddhists did not insist on an either/or decision. They accepted that in many cases people would benefit from closer contact with the mendicants without actually joining them. Thus we have the category of lay followers. The most obvious difference between the two groups lies in total sexual abstinence for the mendicant and a strictly regulated sexual life within his marriage for the layman. There seems to have been a certain reluctance to allow women to 'renounce', but eventually this became possible, although such 'nuns' were always kept in an inferior position. Thus, like the Jain community, the Buddhist one consists of four components: *bhikṣu* and *bhikṣuṇī*, *upāsaka* and *upāsikā*. Whilst the laymen provide the mendicants with their, theoretically meagre, requirements (simple food, an occasional ochre robe, etc.), the mendicants in return preach the Buddha's *Dharma*—his teaching—to them, to prepare them for a full commitment to the spiritual path in a later rebirth.

From early times onwards, settled monastic life provided an institutional alternative to homeless mendicancy. This monasticism seems to have started as a result of the Indian weather. Heavy downpours during the three months of the rainy season make travelling on foot almost impossible. Thus for these three months even the mendicants remained in one place. As a result of the laymen's zeal in showing their appreciation through lavish donations towards the construction of proper edifices for these 'rain retreats', and presumably also due to the temptations of a life more comfortable than the homeless wandering, the period expanded, until in the end mendicants remained the whole year in these new homes.

Sedentary monasticism stimulated the development of monastic ethics and of rules governing the communal life. At the very basis of these rules lie the ethical presuppositions of the renouncer tradition generally. But in the emphasis on intention, as opposed to a mechanistic conception of moral behaviour (more typical of the Jains), we may well sense the influence of the Buddha. Such rules were initially formulated as the *prātimokṣa*, a catalogue or litany of monastic injunctions. It has been suggested that the *prātimokṣa* was originally linked with the fortnightly communal meetings in the monasteries, acting as the 'confessional mirror' each monk had to confront. Any infringement of the rules had to be confessed, and the appropriate penance be done. Eventually, then, a full system of monastic ethics evolved, in which each rule was elaborately defined in terms of its range of application. This then is the *Vinaya*. The more than 200 rules are divided into seven groups of graded severity. Four injunctions are essential; a violation of any of them will result in the permanent expulsion from the monastic community. They are: sexual intercourse, theft, killing and the proclamation of superhuman faculties. All remaining injunctions allow for atonement. With group seven the rules are so peripheral to Buddhist spiritual discipline that they are no more than guide-lines for good manners (like not licking the fingers while eating).

Thus the *Vinaya* inculcates ethical attitudes, while at the same time it lays down precise rules for the monk's behaviour both inside and outside the monastery. In theory the whole *Vinaya* is subordinate to two other major responsibilities: to pursue one's liberation and to preach the Buddha's *Dharma*. But given the *Vinaya*'s complexity, in practice it might well have usurped central importance in the minds of many a monk. To observe the rules would in that case have become the primary spiritual goal. It will be seen below (in the section on the Mahāyāna) that certain critics at least assumed the existence of such an attitude.

Parallel to the evolution of monasticism and a complex monastic rule went another development, namely the formulation of the Buddha's teaching. What the Buddha taught was not written down, nor was it turned into a literary corpus like the Vedas. It emerged in the context of formal and informal public addresses, to a great variety of audiences and over a long period (traditionally, forty years). It seems reasonable to assume that the Buddha did not 'compose' a totally new sermon for each of the thousands of occasions when he preached. Instead, a fair number of 'repertoire pieces' of teaching must have evolved over the years. Now many of his disciples would have listened to hundreds and thousands of such sermons (*sūtras*, Pali: *suttas*). Key ideas, recurring patterns, typical structures and such repertoire pieces must have engrained themselves deeply in their memories. Thus there is no need to doubt that even some generations after the Buddha's death the essence of his teaching, in that form, was still available, though obviously very little of it verbatim. Again, it seems likely that efforts were made at certain stages to co-ordinate and regulate the available store of such memories and weed out the inevitable apocryphal material. Yet it is highly unlikely that the whole of the Buddhist movement could remain involved in such efforts, as the generations since the Buddha passed by; the geographical spread of Buddhism was far too wide for that. What is important here is the fact that we cannot assume the existence of some 'original Buddhist canon'. Instead, there is sufficient evidence to suggest that a variety of such Buddhist canons evolved only gradually, in a variety of Buddhist communities belonging to different geographical areas. It seems that the Buddha himself laid the basis for this proliferation, by preventing the creation of a 'canon' (in Sanskrit) of his teaching. Just as the teaching was delivered in the vernacular, his disciples conceptualised it and preached it by means of their respective vernaculars. But the fact that Buddhism (and its literatures) disappeared from India around 1200 CE gave rise to a rather different impression of this situation. The only 'complete' canon that has come down to us belongs to the Buddhist tradition of Ceylon (Sri Lanka). It appears that during the third or second century BCE settlers from central north India brought their Buddhism to this island. Pali was the vernacular in which the Buddhist teaching had been retained by them, and it remained the language of Buddhist learning long after texts began to be written down. But Pali was not the Buddha's mother tongue. Fragments of other 'canons' in other Indian vernaculars testify to the existence of traditions outside the Pali one. None, however, are written in what must be assumed to have been the Buddha's native language, some form of Māgadhī.

Besides the *Vinaya* and the sermons on *Dharma*, early Buddhist literature knows of a third component, the *Abhidharma*. It grew out of reflections on the sermons and did not attempt to present itself as the direct teaching of the Buddha. Thus we are dealing here with a relatively late literary product. Earliest Buddhism refrained from presenting its teaching in any systematic or metaphysical framework. The *Abhidharma* in a sense attempts to fill this gap. It is difficult to say what its original intentions were. It could have been the need to provide structured guidance for meditation, or to justify Buddhist ideas philosophically, or simply the temptation to draw on fashionable intellectual discussions and provide a Buddhist position in them. Whatever the precise circumstances may have been, the *Abhidharma* develops a systematic view of the world, man and his destiny. The key concept is that of the *dharmas* (not to be confused with the *Dharma*, the Buddhist teaching, or the Hindu concept). The whole of reality is cut up into *dharmas*, that is the smallest possible units. As far as matter is concerned, we obtain 'form-*dharmas*', of different kinds corresponding to the different elements earth, water, fire, etc. These would be the atoms of other schools of Indian thought. But similarly emotions, volition, thinking, etc. are also dissected into 'feeling-*dharmas*' etc. Here typically Buddhist ideas are now employed. All *dharmas*, of whatever kind, are characterised by three interrelated features: they are transient, lack an inner permanent core or essence and are suffering. These are the *tri-lakṣaṇas* (triple characteristics) *anitya*, *anātman* and *duḥkha*. That anything which is transient cannot be regarded as possessing some permanent substance, and in turn cannot therefore be approached as providing true happiness—these are old Buddhist ideas. But to have it applied to all *dharmas* is new. Not only that: 'transience' itself is radically redefined. Every *dharma* lasts but a moment, to be replaced by a similar one the next moment. The three *āsravas* (naturally also made up of *dharmas*) account for this replacement and thus for continuity in time. Only one *dharma* is not conditioned in this manner, and that is *nirvāṇa*. Such ideas were developed in the various treatises which together make up the *Abhidharma* and in the commentaries on them.

These now are the three basic categories (or 'baskets', *piṭaka*) of Buddhist 'canonical' literature: *Vinaya*, *Sūtra* (also called *Dharma*) and *Abhidharma*. However, as a culture Buddhism produced a variety of further literary works which found their way into the 'canon' (in the Pali, as the 'miscellaneous section' of the *Sutta-piṭaka*). Here we find among others a collection of ethical maximes (*Dharma-pada*, Pali: *Dhamma-pada*), poems by early monks and nuns (*Thera-* and *Therī-gāthās*), stories about the Buddha's previous existences (*Jātakas*) and poems, partly very ancient, on the spiritual path (*Suttanipāta*).

So far the emphasis has been on 'learned' and monastic Buddhism. We do, however, possess evidence also for developments outside the monasteries, among the laymen of the Buddhist community. Thus with striking immediacy one of the last Maurya emperors, Aśoka, speaks to us through his inscriptions (third century BCE). The Buddhist *Dharma* to him is clearly a humanitarian ethic, a concern for the well-being of people and also of animals. No philosophy, no meditation and no monastic institutions are referred to. Besides these inscriptions, we have from roughly the same period architectural remnants, the *stūpas* (or *caityas*) of Sāñchī, Bhārhūt, Amarāvatī, and so on. In origin, a *stūpa* is a burial mound for nobles of pre-Buddhist north-eastern India. Its role in Buddhism is not well defined. Legend says that portions of the Buddha's ashes were kept on top of the hemispherical structure. In terms of normative Buddhism, a visit to these sites could be no more than a reminder of the Buddhist spiritual ideal. But there must have been at work a strong popular cult as well, which approached the *stūpa* in a different way. It is clear that acts of worship were performed here, very much like what went on in popular village religion, with offerings of flowers and incense, and with music and dance. The *Vinaya* would prohibit monks participating in these rituals. Since no literary documents about these religious practices are known (though some connection with aspects of Mahāyāna Buddhist literature has been suggested), it is impossible to say what precisely the religious content could have been. For some people participating, the Buddha may well have been like a *deva*, but the more sophisticated participants must have envisaged the nature of the Buddha and his relationship with the *stūpa* cult in some other, more typically Buddhist, manner. What is important is to realise that, from an early period onwards, Buddhism expresses itself not merely as a monastic system, but as a religion with decidedly popular aspects.

Buddhism spread over India very rapidly, and by the second or first century BCE we can assume its presence in most Indian regions (including Ceylon/Sri Lanka and what today is Pakistan). Inevitably, regional variations developed. Moreover, we have the variations in terms of monastic versus laymen's and popular Buddhism. Thirdly, there is the initial absence of a rigid authority. If one takes these three features into account, it is not difficult to envisage earlier Indian Buddhism as an extremely dynamic and multifarious religion. However, there is another side to this. Such a fluid and dynamic scene has the potential for all kinds of tensions and disagreements. Some of these must have been about doctrinal issues, others about details of the monastic discipline; some could involve an ideological struggle between monastic institutions and laymen, and yet others may well be neutral, merely regional variations observable only to the traveller. The evidence available, however fragmented and ambivalent it may be, is sufficient to show that all these dynamic developments cannot be explained merely in terms of a series of 'councils' and consequent 'schisms'.

Inevitably such variety is interpreted for us through the eyes of Sri Lankan Buddhism which naturally presents itself as the single 'orthodox' tradition. Besides, its relative isolation from Indian developments allowed it to preserve a fairly 'archaic' appearance. But it must not be forgotten that the Pali canon began to be written down only around 100 BCE, and that only around 400 CE was a final corpus and its definitive interpretation established. Of the other 'sects', we know in most cases little more than their names. Moreover, it is far from clear what the rationale of such nomenclature may have been. In many cases we may be dealing merely with titles used by a regional group of Buddhists (of whatever doctrinal and disciplinary persuasion). Sometimes such a name itself created the idea of a 'heterodox' position.

One group in central India called itself the *Lokottara-vādins*. This title has been interpreted to mean 'transcendentalists' and became associated with the idea that these Buddhists believed in a supernatural (or quasi-divine) Buddha-figure. However, one of their canonical scriptures, the *Mahāvastu*, has been preserved, and an unbiased study of the text yields a different picture. This 'life-story' of the Buddha presents him indeed as capable of deeds far beyond the potential of ordinary human beings. But then he was indeed special. As the many *jātaka* stories included in the *Mahāvastu*, and the text as a whole, make clear, he was a being who over many past existences accumulated an enormous store of *puṇya* (positive *karma*). Inevitably a person who can draw on such a store will be able to do things well 'beyond what is possible to ordinary people' (this is an alternative translation of *lokottara*).

Traditionally, the first schism occurred between the *sthaviras*, the advocates of 'orthodoxy', and monks, and the *mahāsāṅghikas*. The latter term has variously been interpreted, for instance as 'the majority' or 'those believing in a wider community' (that is including laymen). The Pali for *sthavira* is *thera*, and thus Sri Lankan Buddhism presents itself as the direct continuation of that *sthavira-* or *thera-vāda*, the 'teaching of the elders'. It does, however, acknowledge a variety of 'sectarian' offshoots from its own 'mainstream' lineage. From some of these, like the *Sarvāsti-vāda* (the 'teaching that everything exists'), some literature has been preserved. Details on most of the further varieties of the *Mahāsāṅghika* are not available. But in terms of historical importance, this whole discussion of Indian sectarian developments is relatively insignificant, when compared with a very different kind of internal argument, which eventually crystallised as the Mahāyāna and the Hīnayāna. This will be discussed in a later section.

Obviously, the spread of Buddhism was partly due to direct missionary activity: mendicants travelling far and wide and preaching the *Dharma*. But in addition we must also envisage movements of whole groups of people, on a large scale. In some instances, this may have been due to banishment on account of disputes. But in most cases this was just part of the general spread of 'Aryan' people over the sub-continent. As new Aryan kingdoms were created in 'frontier regions' (like Āndhra and Ceylon/Sri Lanka during the third century BCE or the Tamil country somewhat later), they attracted groups of immigrants, and these included Buddhists. But it was relatively rare in India for a king to profess openly to be following Buddhism; Aśoka seems to have been very much the exception. This was different in Sri Lanka, where up to the present day Buddhism has been able to enjoy the patronage of the ruling power, in an uninterrupted line.

Epic and Purāṇic Religion

With the spread of Aryan culture over the whole of India, Vedic religion could establish itself as the most prestigious superstructure for most of the social groups affected by it. But at the same time, during this expansion an enormous range of other forms of religion was encountered, which in turn stimulated new syntheses of a staggering variety. It is not easy to survey or order this mass of material. That the global title of 'Hinduism' has been given to it must be regarded as an act of pure despair. In the context of the present survey of the Indian religions, three major aspects may be distinguished very tentatively: popular theism, sophisticated systematisations and esoteric and antinomian movements. The present section attempts to explore the first aspect, whilst the remaining two will be dealt with further below. Because this popular theism has found its primary textual expression in the genre of the Purāṇas, and on a more limited scale in the Epics, it may be referred to as epic-purāṇic religion. Since the literary situation is particularly complex, it appears justified to deal with it separately at the beginning. This is followed by a discussion of the typically epic-purāṇic gods and also of the emergence of a God-concept. A third section will look at typical modes of expressing devotion to these divine beings, and at the 'Hindu' religious life generally.

The Epic-Purāṇic Literature

To say that the brahmin's role in Indian society (which naturally excluded to some extent social enclaves like the Jains and the Buddhists) was defined by taking care of the religious needs of people does not actually restrict religion itself to what the brahmin had to offer. In other words, the brahmin's religion—however prestigious and normative it may be in itself—is only one expression of ancient Indian religion. Precisely because other types of religion were current even in early Aryan society, brahmin religion remained flexible, fluid and integrative. The brahmin received and moulded all kinds of religion which thereby acquired respectability and social standing.

Where now were such other types found, who were their guardians and what was their content? Given the state of our knowledge about ancient India, such questions are not easy to answer. We may begin by shifting our focus away from the brahmin to the members of the second class (*varṇa*), the *kṣatriyas* or warriors. This may take us by surprise, for we would not immediately suspect the existence of additional types of religion in this social group. But already the Upaniṣads showed a number of cases where a brahmin approached a *kṣatriya* for information on *brahman*. And although both the Mahāvīra and the Buddha opted out of their conventional lives, they did so as members of *kṣatriya* clans. These initial considerations can be complemented by the following points.

We must imagine the political situation in northern India during the first half of the last millennium BCE to have been extremely loose and undefined. Scattered all over the region were pockets and enclaves of Aryan settlements, which were particularly dense in the area known as the Āryāvarta. This is the region between the rivers Jumna and Ganges in central north India, and somewhat further east along the Ganges. To say that Aryan society was split up into various 'tribes' would give rise to confusion, in so far as we have used the word 'tribe' to denote indigenous peoples outside the Aryan influence. To speak of 'nations' or 'states' would introduce an anachronism, since it suggests a centralisation of political control and a solidity of the political unit that began to emerge only from the fifth century BCE onwards. Perhaps the word 'clan' may be used here. Whatever the precise status of the rulers of these clans may have been, these 'kings' (*rājas*) maintained courts and a court culture. In a world that was surrounded and pervaded by non-Aryan peoples, an awareness of a common Aryan bond was cultivated by the clans, not least through marriage ties binding together different 'royal courts'. But central to our discussion is the role of the *sūta*, the royal bard.

This bard was the professional expert in epic literature, or better, epic culture. Naturally, this included an element of public entertainment; but he also conveyed learning of all kinds in subjects useful to a ruler and his court. Above all, it was an important means of maintaining the awareness of the common Aryan bond between the clans, and of spelling out the position of the dynasties in the history of the world. And it is this last mentioned characteristic which accounts for the fact that the literature which eventually evolved from these bardic performances must be considered to be one of the most important textual documents of the Indian religions, particularly Hinduism. Conventionally this literature is referred to as the Epics and the Purāṇas, but how it came about is quite a long and complicated story. The following is a tentative summary of it.

Like the Vedic literature, the performances of the royal bards were not written down, at least not for many centuries. But unlike the Vedic counterpart, we are not dealing here with fixed material that was transmitted in a meticulously accurate and verbatim form. But it was certainly not the case that every bard, at every performance, made up the whole. Instead we must assume a number of thematic cycles, each one at least in outline fixed. In addition there were 'skeleton stanzas' which the bard knew by heart and around which he could improvise his narrative. Of particular importance in the history of Indian religion were four such thematic cycles, two involving all the clans, and the other two being originally purely local. Thus we have cycle A which deals with the memories, surely partly historical, of a particularly devastating war which two rival groups of Aryan clans fought. The cause of this war was a controversy over dynastic succession, and its extremely destructive outcome left deep wounds in the people's memories. We hear about two groups of cousins, the five Pāṇḍavas (including Yudhiṣṭhira and Arjuna) and the hundred Kauravas (led by Duryodhana). The former are the rightful heirs to the kingship, but lose in a game of dice their title (and common wife) for a number of years. It is when their period of exile has come to an end that the Kauravas' obstinacy in holding on to royal power necessitates the devastating war. The Pāṇḍavas do win, but it is a painful victory in view of the large-scale bloodshed.

Cycle B was primarily concerned with the genealogies of the various Aryan dynasties and the heroic deeds of outstanding members of them. The intention here was clearly to offer the kind of reference which, in theory, should make bloodshed over dynastic disputes unnecessary. Moreover, a wider frame is provided here for the histories of the Aryan kings. Not only did the clans intermarry, but their common origins were traced back to the very beginning of the world, to the first man, Manu. This offered in turn the opportunity to deal with such religious matters as the 'creation' of the world itself, its evolution and its final destiny.

Cycle C takes us to the town of Ayodhyā (near the modern Oudh); again the central theme is that of dynastic dispute over succession. But elements comparable to those of the fairy-tale are also mixed into it. Due to a promise made by the king to one of his minor queens, his son Rāma, although the legitimate heir to the throne, has to go with his wife Sītā into exile. During this stay in the forest, Sītā is abducted by an ogre Rāvaṇa. Accompanied by an army of monkeys, Rāma marches to Laṅkā, the island stronghold of the ogre, and rescues her. Moreover, all ends well when he finally recovers his kingship.

Cycle D finally takes us to the town of Mathurā, where a vicious usurper Kaṃsa is threatening the life of the legitimate crown prince, Kṛṣṇa, who is his nephew. The latter grows up secretly in the forests among cowherds. There he reveals supernatural strength by warding off dangers from the herdsmen, and equally supernatural handsomeness which infatuates all the girls and women. Eventually he defeats the usurper in Mathurā, and various other kings in the Āryāvarta who are Kaṃsa's allies.

This simple list of four thematic cycles is merely an abstract attempt at reconstructing something like a starting-point for the extremely complex history of bardic-epic literature in India. What makes it so complicated is the fact that all four cycles have had their independent developments, while at the same time an enormous amount of intermingling and fusion between them took place. Moreover, when written versions did become available, in most cases they were random accounts, not consciously 'literary' works in which the variety of current oral versions was unified and systematised. Added complexity arises from the fact that many such 'random' versions were recorded.

Cycle A was developed along truly encyclopedic lines (a development that even around 1000 CE had not yet reached its end). As a story about human self-destructive tendencies, it implied profound questions about ethics, the role and responsibility of the king, the meaning of human life on earth, caught as it was between fate and man's own will, and about a possible significance of the bloody events in the context of cosmic history. Such questions were considered on a grand scale, and a vast array of what different religious and intellectual traditions (including, quite prominently, Buddhism) had to contribute to them was laid out. Since the war involved more or less all Aryan clans, our Cycle B could be used to provide the historical background, and inevitably an interaction between the religious material (origin of the world, etc.) took place. Material typical of Cycle C could be incorporated, since it offered a thematic parallel (exile in the forest of the legitimate crown prince and eventual victory of righteousness). Cycle D contributed even more directly, since one of the main protagonists of the Pāṇḍavas is Kṛṣṇa, the prince of Mathurā. As described so far, this grand encyclopedic synthesis became crystallised as a definite text in the form of the *Mahābhārata*, arguably the world's largest epic. A complete translation would run to over three or four thousand pages. But it is the work of many people, over a period of at least 1,500 years, and belonging to different regions. Almost drowned in this enormous mass of text is a small, originally perhaps independent, work, the *Bhagavadgītā*. Of all the Hindu scriptures, this is probably the single most important one. In it we find one of the earliest formulations of a fully fledged theology, centring around the God-figure Kṛṣṇa.

The *Mahābhārata* also acquired, perhaps around the third century CE, an 'Appendix'. The primary reason for this addition was the need felt for further information on Kṛṣṇa. Material typical of our Cycle D could be used for this purpose on a large scale. But it was not presented in isolation: Cycle B laid itself around Kṛṣṇa's life as its frame and context. Here again even 1000 CE does not appear to mark the end of the literary developments of the *Harivaṃśa* (as this 'appendix' was called). The Kṛṣṇa-figures offered by the *Mahābhārata* and the *Harivaṃśa* may be part of a coherent narrative, but in character they are very different from each other. And when Kṛṣṇa appears as one of the major God-figures of medieval Hinduism, it is the Kṛṣṇa of the *Harivaṃśa* who provided the primary inspiration for it (with the *Bhagavadgītā* providing its theology).

Our Cycle C acquired literary shape in a relatively simpler manner. Moreover, unlike the other texts spoken about so far, the *Rāmāyaṇa*, 'the story of Prince Rāma', was given sophisticated poetic expression, which in turn means by one author (at least for the bulk of the work). The Indian tradition names him as Vālmiki. His date may not be too far removed from the change into the Common Era. But this sophisticated epic does not signal the end of Rāma's own history: subsequent individual works demonstrate a process of increasing deification of Rāma (more on this aspect in the following section).

This leaves us with one last thematic cycle (our B). The Indian tradition neatly summarises the complex literary developments of this cycle in the concept of the 'eighteen great Purāṇas'. If historically the process had been so simple, we would—in the light of the observations made so far—have to speak of eighteen separate recordings of Cycle B material. Yet reality is much more complicated. An ancient core can indeed be identified: views on the origin of the world, its structure and past history, the royal dynasties and the deeds of past heroes and instructions on how to perform rites in honour of ancestors generally. Such a core is still present in many of the extant texts (though by no means in identical verbal form). But then a vast amount of more or less related material was added to such a core, in different regions, by different individuals, at different times. Even after such 'recordings' were fixed and could be identified by individual names (for example, 'Viṣṇu-Purāṇa'), they set in motion a further history of additions (not infrequently by drawing on other such textually 'fixed' Purāṇas). Although there are unlimited possibilities of what could be added to a Purāṇa, and for whatever reason, certainly from our point of view it is the enormous amount of religious material which is of interest. Kṛṣṇa and Rāma figured as heroes already in the dynastic histories typical of our Cycle B. When the 'eighteen grand Purāṇas' crystallised finally as the texts that we have now, every major and minor Hindu god or God-figure had been dealt with in this literature, sometimes on a gigantic scale.

The final products (i.e. the actual text or versions of it that we now possess) belong to different periods. Thus, for example, the *Mārkaṇḍeya-Purāṇa* and the *Viṣṇu-Purāṇa*, even with their respective interpolations, may well belong to around the middle of the first millennium CE. Others, like the *Śiva-Purāṇa* or *Brahmavaivarta-Purāṇa*, appear to be compiled as late as the middle of the second millennium. But not all this material is 'anonymous' and the product of compilers over many centuries. Perhaps the most famous of all these Purāṇas, the *Bhāgavata-Purāṇa* (ninth or early tenth century CE), must in essence be the conscious literary creation of one person (in south India). In turn, the *Devī-Bhāgavata-Purāṇa*, which in some lists replaces the *Bhāgavata-Purāṇa*, is a conscious imitation, some centuries later, of the former and comes from north-east India.

By now we have almost lost track of the bards who were originally involved in the cultivation of epic literature. Indeed, at some stage interest in purely local, dynastic and genealogical matters ceased, and topics of pan-Indian relevance (such as the origin of the world and the stories associated with the gods) began to dominate epic literature. It seems likely that this transformation went hand in hand with a shift towards brahmin involvement in the epic and purāṇic enterprise. Indications of this are, for instance, the formulation of the concept of *smṛti*, literally 'memory' but denoting in this context 'tradition' as opposed to *śruti*, 'Vedic revelation'. *Smṛti* was put forward as secondary in importance to the Vedas, and as the literature spelling out the implications of the Vedic heritage. The idea of the 'fifth Veda' for the Epics brought this literature even closer to brahmin culture. As brahmin-cultivated carriers of the story material about the heroes and the gods, and of popularly expressed philosophical and theological ideas, the Epics and Purāṇas had an enormous influence on Indian religion.

But it was not just in their Sanskrit form that the Purāṇas and Epics provided inspiration to much of Indian religion. Innumerable translations, adaptations and very free renderings into the many vernaculars enhanced the accessibility of this material. Yet that is still not the end of the story. In many ways, the classification of the Purāṇas into 'eighteen grand ones' is totally artificial. To a large extent the selection of these (and the lists even of the grand eighteen vary in part) from among a very much larger number of available Purāṇas has been arbitrary. The remainder, called Upa- or 'secondary' Purāṇas, are not necessarily more recent, more 'sectarian' or more regional than many of the 'classical' eighteen.

By now we have been discussing a literature that in print would fill many thousands of pages. Yet the Purāṇas were such a popular genre of religious literature, that the list of them ought to be enlarged by thousands of further works. These are now known as the Sthala- or 'local' Purāṇas. Each one is associated with a more or less famous temple or place of pilgrimage and narrates, amongst other things, the deeds of the relevant god in that particular locality. When discussing the temple, more will have to be said about this literature.

The Hindus are not the only participants in this enormous literary enterprise. There are some indications that the Indian Buddhists also showed interest in the genre of the Purāṇas (the *Mahāvastu* could be classified like this); but the Jains developed their versions of the Epics and Purāṇas into a whole literature of grandiose proportions. More will be said about this in a later section under the heading of the Jain *Mahāpurāṇa*.

In summary then it must be stated that an exploration of the Epics and Purāṇas does not allow for easy short cuts. These are not just twenty or so texts of minor religious significance, but actually imply a whole literary history of enormous textual proportions. These works were of such popular and widespread influence that even today in many a South Asian country the stories of Rāma, Kṛṣṇa and the Pāṇḍavas constitute some of the most famous themes of various art forms. Although the old Hinduism in many of these countries has been superseded by Islam or Theravāda Buddhism, epic and purāṇic heroes still figure not just in the various literatures, but also in dances and in the puppet theatre.

The Hindu Gods and God

Conventionally, Buddhism and Jainism are characterised as 'atheistic'. We have seen how misleading such an attribute can be, since our concept 'atheism' denotes not merely the absence of a God-figure, but also a conscious rejection of anything transcendental. For Hinduism the case has been slightly more complicated. In some perceptions, it has been similarly called 'atheistic'. In other perceptions, and this is perhaps the more common one, it is labelled 'polytheistic'. The term 'polytheism' acknowledges the presence of a God-figure in a religious system, but in the plural. Thus it is said that Hindus worship many such beings we call God. But obviously this implies a very profound difference in the understanding of what such a 'God' could be. Thus how could he be omnipotent, if he has to share his power with many other peers? As we shall see, this model of understanding theistic Hinduism is actually extremely unhelpful. This may be illustrated initially by looking at another commonly made assumption. It is often said that Hindus worship three gods, and these are in fact called the 'Hindu Trinity'. The gods involved are: Brahmā, Viṣṇu and Śiva. The first is supposed to create the world (at the beginning of each cosmic cycle), the second to maintain it in being, and Śiva, at the end of a cosmic cycle, to destroy it again. There is a certain attraction to this simple and neat conception; unfortunately, it cannot be substantiated from the religious literature. Not that texts do not talk about such a Trinity—they do, frequently. But then they add a further idea which is ignored by the proponents of the theory of a Hindu Trinity. What is added invariably implies that over and above these three figures lies a single reality. This 'one above the three' controls the activities of creation etc. Brahmā and the others, who carry out these functions, are merely manifestations of that highest being, or they relate to it in some other, equally secondary, form. That the Indian traditions evolved a very large number of interpretations of what or who this ultimate, single reality is may not come as a surprise in view of what has been said already about the dynamism and proliferation of religious conceptions in these traditions. It is an issue that deserves a more detailed exploration.

We have seen that the religious status of the Vedic *devas* is relatively undefined. The late Vedic period more consciously and systematically pursued the quest towards some overall, single principle behind the rich array of *deva*-figures. But for reasons unknown to us a dual discontinuity occurred. First, as already discussed, the renouncer traditions brought their devastating critique to bear on the whole range of *devas*. Now they are unequivocally defined as members of the natural order, beings that like ourselves move in the realm of space, time and matter. A second discontinuity occurred which has not yet attracted the same attention. What has previously been discussed as the epic-purāṇic traditions certainly knows of *devas*. But strangely enough, figures appear here about which the Vedas have either nothing, or extremely little to say (Nārāyaṇa, Kṛṣṇa, Rāma, Viṣṇu, Śiva). The central *devas* of the Vedas, that is Agni, Soma, Indra, do not appear at all, or in an insignificant role (Indra). Glimpses of local folk religion, which the Buddhist and Jain canonical literature offers us, point at a god figure Brahmā. As to the religious status of these epic-purāṇic *devas*, the contexts in which we hear about them is in most cases so unspecific that we cannot comment on this. Yet in certain instances the evidence suggests beyond any doubt that something novel has happened: the concept of a single, all-powerful, eternal, personal and loving God has emerged. This is the concept of 'Bhagavān'. And to the extent that secondary implications of the Christian concept of 'God' can be ignored (e.g. creation out of nothing), it is indeed appropriate to translate Bhagavān with 'God', without giving rise to too many confusions.

But who is this Hindu Bhagavān? At least to us as the outside observers he is not one, but many. Śiva, Viṣṇu, Kṛṣṇa, Rāma, Kārttikeya and Gaṇeśa may be mentioned as the most important Bhagavān-figures. But to speak of many Bhagavāns has nothing to do with 'polytheism', for in terms of Indian society, different groups of people have their one and only Bhagavān. That means, the concept itself is an empty slot, to be filled by concrete characteristics which then make up a specific Bhagavān-figure who serves as (the one and only) God to a given group of people. To describe this with any precision would require the methods of sociology, and not of theology. Theologically speaking, there cannot be anything over and above Bhagavān. Sociologically speaking, a society—particularly as variegated as India—can know of many such figures.

It would be extremely interesting to know the answers to two interrelated historical questions: how did the concept of Bhagavān arise, and what are the sources from which the concrete characterisations were derived? Unfortunately, our known textual documents do not offer us much information on this. The two crucial texts that so far have come to our attention suggest somewhat different answers, and that really only about our second question. The *Śvetāśvatara-Upaniṣad* and the *Bhagavadgītā* are the seminal expressions of true monotheism in India. The latter introduces us to a Bhagavān-figure, Kṛṣṇa, totally unknown in earlier, Vedic literature. Thus both the concept and its visualisation in specific form make a sudden, inexplicable appearance. The *Śvetāśvatara-Upaniṣad*, on the other hand, draws very heavily on those Vedic hymns in which a *deva* Rudra is addressed. This Rudra is called '*śiva*', which means 'benevolent', and this attribute was subsequently used increasingly as this Bhagavān's proper name. But even if we allowed for a direct continuity between the Vedic *deva* Rudra and Bhagavān Śiva, no such conceptual continuity for the concept of 'Bhagavān' itself can be derived from this. Thus perhaps one of the most exciting questions in the study of Indian religions has to be left unanswered, at least until further evidence comes to light: how, during the last few centuries BCE, monotheism arose in India.

A considerable amount of scholarship has concerned itself with the problem of the historical continuity between the Vedas and subsequent religion. This has obscured another process, of equal importance: the artificial recourse to Vedic material at a much later date. A well-known textual example is the famous *Bhāgavata-Purāṇa* (ninth or early tenth century CE). Its language is not the Sanskrit of the other Epics and Purāṇas, but an artificial recreation of the Vedic (namely pre-classical Sanskrit) language. Here is a work that by sounding Vedic claims to be Vedic in its teaching. This recourse to the Vedas for the purpose of legitimisation is already apparent in the case of the *Bhagavadgītā*. The text itself throws out many references back to Vedic ideas and figures, including a very minor one to the Vedic *deva* Viṣṇu. Since the rest of the *Mahābhārata*, an ocean in which the *Bhagavadgītā* is no more than a tiny drop, focuses on Viṣṇu, amongst other things as a Bhagavān-figure, subsequent ages sought to identify this Viṣṇu with Kṛṣṇa. It is at least possible to ask whether in the case of the *Śvetāśvatara-Upaniṣad* such a process also underlies (some of) the seeming Vedic continuity.

This is clearly an extremely important aspect of the Hindu traditions, and throws considerable light on the role the Vedas have played in their history. But it must not obscure another important process: the constant recourse to folk-religious (and even tribal) material. In a sense it is precisely because the Hindu traditions were constantly involved in drawing on non-Vedic sources, that the need for Vedic legitimisation arose. We have already encountered one illustration of this process, the *Harivaṃśa*. Kṛṣṇa plays an extremely important role in the whole of the *Mahābhārata* as a prince and primary initiator of action, and naturally as Bhagavān in the *Bhagavadgītā*. Yet his youth is left a blank here. By drawing on local, folk-religious mythology, the *Harivaṃśa* filled this blank. Scholars tend to agree that the Kṛṣṇa of the *Mahābhārata* and Kṛṣṇa the cowherd, fighting ogres and infatuating all the women and girls, historically and sociologically belong to different traditions.

Another well-known illustration is the figure of Skanda. When we consult the earlier standard Sanskrit texts, we are told that Skanda is the son of Śiva and his wife Pārvatī. Śiva was known to be such a dedicated ascetic that a demon ventured to ask that his death be at the hands of Śiva's son. Somehow the *devas*, with the primary help of Pārvatī, managed to have Śiva break his ascetic vows and procreate a son, Skanda or Kārttikeya. As initially totally separate from all this we find in the ancient Tamil-speaking south a god Murukaṉ: handsome, vigorous, fighting demons and wooing girls. This Murukaṉ now became identified with Skanda, and the two mythologies fused to a new, composite whole.

A third illustration is less well known and modern, so that we can still observe the actual process at work. In Mahārāṣṭra we find a regional god, Khaṇḍobā. Evidence suggests that we are dealing here with an originally autonomous god-figure belonging to a regional and independent religious system. But when the evidence we possess about the iconography, mythology and devotion associated with Khaṇḍobā is projected on to the time-scale, we notice that this god is increasingly brought into the proximity of Śiva and turned into a secondary manifestation of him. Yet this process is by no means complete even today.

A final example takes us back to Rāma, the hero of the *Rāmāyaṇa*. Already in south India during the first millennium CE, this prince of a 'secular' epic began to enjoy a directly religious attention (particularly through his association with Viṣṇu, for which see below). But it was in north India, during the later sixteenth century, that a cult of Rāma as Bhagavān found its textual expression in the *Rāmcaritmānas* of Tulsīdās.

These four examples are no more than illustrations of a process that has been taking place on a very large scale. Naturally it was broken up into innumerable smaller events, in different regions and different social milieux. Moreover, this process of 'integration' also involved modes in which man related to these Bhagavān-figures.

Earlier epic-purāṇic and even Vedic *devas* are still relatively few in number. The number of *deva*-figures known in tribal, folk and regional religions, all over the vast expanse of the Indian sub-continent, is practically unlimited. Such a range is staggering not just for us as the outside observers, but has always been so for the more observant Indian. It has been rather underestimated as to what extent Indian reflection itself has been at work to bring some order into, and to conceptualise, this complex situation. Some examples may illustrate this.

The approximation of Kṛṣṇa and Viṣṇu in the *Mahābhārata* has been mentioned above. One particular way of envisaging this relationship proved extremely useful and prolific. This is the concept of the '*avatāra*'. It denotes a 'descent' of Viṣṇu into the realm of space, time and matter, entirely due to his own free will (and not, for example, due to the laws of *karma*), and involves on the whole a full life cycle, from (normal) conception and birth to (natural) death. Historically (and that means around the beginning of the first millennium CE) the first *avatāra* thus to be envisaged was Kṛṣṇa. But soon it was felt that a number of other figures of religious importance could be accommodated successfully too. The history of this incorporation is complex and certainly not monolinear, nor did it ever achieve a final completion. Thus when conventionally ten such *avatāras* of Viṣṇu are mentioned, it can be regarded as no more than one, particularly successful, schema. As such it deserves a few more comments. The obvious point to note here is the plurality of such *avatāras*. We are not dealing with a single, unique event in the history of the cosmos when God incarnates himself on earth; he does so time and again. Secondly, many of these *avatāras* are not recognisably human (like the Fish, Turtle, Boar, Man-Lion). Then we notice an attempt to structure the pattern of the ten in a kind of 'evolutionary' manner: from the ocean (Fish) we gradually move to the dry land (even the Boar still jumps into the ocean). Then the movement is from not-yet-human (Man-Lion, Dwarf) to fully human (Kṛṣṇa, Rāma, Paraśu- or Bala-Rāma). Finally, with Kalki, we reach the end of time, or better, of a cosmic cycle. That this pattern is intended as a means of integrating existing religious cults is made clear not just from the fact that many of the myths told about the Boar or the Turtle are actually fully fledged creation myths, but also that in some versions the Buddha appears as an *avatāra*.

The so-called Hindu Trinity is a further illustration. Certainly, through reference to Viṣṇu and Śiva, a religious system could not just differentiate itself from the systems in which Viṣṇu or Śiva was Bhagavān, but also impose itself on to them, at least claiming, if not always succeeding in this claim, that it is their fulfilment. Better known cases are religions in which Rāma or Kṛṣṇa or the Goddess (on whom see below), or even Rudra, appear as the single, ultimate Bhagavān over and above the three *devas* of the 'Trinity'. To apply to such cases what has been learnt about the relationship between Śiva and Rudra, or Viṣṇu and Kṛṣṇa, for other contexts makes no sense, since those relationships have never been defined with universal relevance.

Perhaps because it had, historically, a 'Viṣṇuite' flavour, the concept of *avatāra* was used rather hesitantly by non-Viṣṇuite religious traditions. Yet we find many illustrations of a wider appeal, particularly in vernacular contexts which are less concerned with such subtleties. Here, for example, Khaṇḍobā may be seen as an *avatāra* of Śiva, or various goddess-figures as *avatāras* of the Goddess.

Another mode of bringing some order into the vast array of available gods reminds us of the way the ancient Greek organised their pantheon, namely through family relationships. This approach is thoroughly purāṇic, which means that it merely served as a method and not a pattern which could claim pan-Indian relevance. A particularly charming example is that of the south Indian popular god-figure Aiyappaṉ. Here in the south the worshippers of Viṣṇu and Śiva socially constitute a particularly strongly demarcated binary opposition. To link Aiyappaṉ with either Śiva or Viṣṇu would have meant a definite decision in favour of one side or the other. So the following ingenious solution was proposed: he is the son of both Śiva and Viṣṇu! The story takes us back to the time when the *devas* and the *asuras* (demons) had churned the milk-ocean and recovered the drink of immortality. The *devas* felt loath to let the *asuras* have their legitimate share, and Viṣṇu changed himself into an extremely attractive woman, to entice the *asuras* and take the nectar from them. Somehow Śiva was unaware of this, and when he saw the transformed Viṣṇu, he lusted after her.

How is all this perceived through the eyes of an individual member of Indian society? The conceptual distinction between *deva* and Bhagavān is less useful than it appears at first sight. For in most cases a particular Bhagavān-figure may look the same as a *deva*. By 'looking the same' is meant here: possessing the same external characteristics (including name) and having the same or very similar stories told about his mythical deeds. From this follows that the individual (or, in practice, far more often, the group to which he belongs, and this more frequently by birth than choice) makes a decision as to how to regard such a figure. To take Viṣṇu as an example: Viṣṇu could thus be the Bhagavān for some people, a minor manifestation of Śiva for others, a godling for a third group, possibly an evil demonic being for a fourth and Īśvara (the personal, but ultimately illusory, creator) for a fifth. But this does not mean that every single religious individual in India ends up with a Bhagavān. As we have seen already it is quite possible to be religious and not be theistic.

There is another complication here. An individual may belong to a given religious system which in terms of its own normative premisses cannot acknowledge a given figure to be Bhagavān. Yet when looking into the religious life of that individual, it might well be possible that it differs from what the norm says. Sometimes this is conceptualised in the idea that every Hindu has his own '*iṣṭa-devatā*', his personally chosen deity. There may be a kernel of truth in this, to the extent that we do find a fair amount of flexibility in some milieux. But on the whole there are considerable constraints at work as to the range of such choices. One such constraint is implicitly ideological. It has been mentioned that traditional Hinduism evolved its own ways of ordering the vast mass of god-figures available in society. Both here and when it comes to making a decision as to whether or not a given figure is Bhagavān, by no means everything available is perceived to be on an equal level. One can isolate a whole scale of values, according to which *devas* are judged. Any kind of Vedic association would be most prestigious, and below that, a role in the Epics and earlier Purāṇas. Figures outside this range acquire respectability only by subterfuge, that means, as illustrated above, by becoming 'identified' with Vedic or purāṇic gods, or acquiring a, naturally relatively late, Sanskrit Purāṇa that deals with them. Otherwise, such deities will be regarded as socially 'low' by the Hindu 'mainstream'. 'Tell me who your *deva* is and I will tell you who you are' could well paraphrase the situation.

How all this comes to life in the devotion and actual 'religion' of real people will be shown in the following section. Yet surprising though it may seem, a major chunk of material relevant under the present heading has not yet been discussed. This concerns the divine in feminine form.

The more observant reader will have noticed that on the whole the *devas* and Bhagavān figures discussed are male. Whilst from the viewpoint of the Semitic traditions this may not appear remarkable, from the point of view of the Indian religions this would be only half the story. The *devīs* and Bhagavatī, the corresponding feminine forms of *devas* and Bhagavān, still require discussion. For two reasons, this material is mentioned only at this stage. First, there is the state of scholarship which till very recently has ignored this type of religion. But, secondly, that itself is actually due to the way the divine feminine was perceived in India. For on the whole, religion involving *devīs* or Bhagavatī is not quite the same as the types knowing *devas* or Bhagavān. The difference is basically social and ideological. That means *devī*-religion must be envisaged as belonging to a 'lower' stratum of society, although, as we shall see, occasional inroads were indeed made into the 'mainstream'.

The middle of the first millennium CE marks the culmination and end of what could be called 'classical' Hinduism. Yet important new phenomena now begin to make their appearance in Sanskrit literary works. For a variety of reasons it looks plausible that we are not dealing here with 'new' phenomena as such, but with facets of the religious heritage which due to social and political upheaval succeeded in attracting the attention of literati. One such facet (on another, see the section on the esoteric traditions) is the emergence of a novel, and in various ways revolutionary, concept of a personal absolute deity: God as woman.

The crucial text is the *Devīmāhātmya*, 'the glorification of the Goddess'. This short work, of *c.* 550 couplets, found its way into one of the oldest Purāṇas, the *Mārkaṇḍeya-Purāṇa*, and this position secured its preservation and popularity. The nature of this Goddess is demonstrated here through three stories, which were taken up by later writers in endless variations and transformations and which also found visual expression in a large number of sculptures. In the first of these, an older creation myth about Viṣṇu has been transformed to show that the Goddess allows for Viṣṇu to create the world, for Brahmā to reveal the Vedas, and for all demonic obstacles to be removed. The remaining two myths refer to two instances when demons have ousted the *devas*. They are unable to fight their enemies, and it is the Goddess (variously called Ambikā, Caṇḍikā, Durgā, Gaurī) and various gruesome secondary manifestations of her (such as Kālī and Cāmuṇḍā) who by their supreme power demonstrate what puny godlings they are. The second story involves a demon in the shape of a water-buffalo (Mahiṣa), whose slaughter by the Goddess has been a particularly favourite theme in Indian art. The third myth tells us about two demon brothers, Śumbha and Niśumbha, the former of whom was passionately in love with the Goddess, but suffered cruel death through her because of his arrogant advances. On all three occasions, the text makes it clear that we are dealing with earthly manifestations of an eternal, immanent and transcendent deity, to be venerated and lauded by all beings on earth. And indeed various hymns are sung by the (male) gods, to ask her for help or to sing her praise after her victories.

A surprising number of prominent post-Gupta Sanskrit court poets produced poetic masterpieces in honour of the Goddess. Mention may be made here of two of them, Bāṇa (who composed the *Caṇḍīśataka*, in the seventh century) and Ānandavardhana (who wrote the *Devīśataka* in Kashmir, in the ninth century). Bāṇa fuses in his poem the mythical incident of the Goddess thrusting her foot down on Mahiṣa's head with an amorous situation found in conventional Sanskrit court poetry: the lover attempting to placate his beloved who is furious at some unfaithfulness of his. Through this ingenious device the whole becomes transparent for the human situation generally, in which earthly happiness and liberation from *saṃsāra* are found through submission to the Goddess, ritually expressed through placing one's head on her feet. By this logic, the demon Mahiṣa also found his salvation! Similarly Ānandavardhana envisages the Goddess, ultimately, as the apex of wisdom, mental clarity and Vedic revelation—nothing here about the theory that the feminine equals unreflecting nature! Every facet of Hindu religion is in one way or other connected here with the Goddess as its ultimate rationale and motivation.

Documents from later periods reveal to us that the triumph of the Goddess, as celebrated in the above mentioned myths and texts, had its parallel in the religious history of India, or at least, certain regions. In north-eastern India in particular, during the earlier part of the second millennium, a whole range of new Purāṇas was produced which promulgated a religion of the Goddess as infinitely superior to the traditional male gods. On the whole, no new myths evolved; instead, the vast classical repertoire was reinterpreted, in order to make transparent the final agent in them. Wherever we find greed, delusion, ignorance, violence and wherever we encounter goodness, search for truth and salvation, these are instances where the presence of the Goddess can be felt. We are dealing here with a grandiose and daring attempt to encompass everything that is an object of human experience, with all its contradictions and dynamics, within the ultimate ground of being, the Goddess. The instincts as much as the desire for more controlled and conscious actions, cruelty and kindness, which anybody can easily identify within himself, along with the variegated nature of the external reality—famine and rich harvest, poverty and affluence, war and peace, illness and health—all this derives from, and converges in, the Goddess. The final culmination of this vision was reached in Rāmprasād Sen (1718–75), a poet who composed in the vernacular Bengali moving songs of altercation and submission, accusation and devotion addressed to the Goddess (variously called Kālī, Durgā, etc.). In turn, Rāmprasād inspired a whole crowd of later poets to continue the genre he had created.

Two important questions deserve closer attention: how can we explain the rise of this religion of the Goddess, and what reactions did it provoke in other circles?

In a general way it seems possible to reflect on the historicity of religious symbols and their social concatenation. Given the major upheaval caused by the collapse of the Gupta empire, it could be argued that this external disintegration of a dominant culture allowed religious symbols—already perceived as far more significant and comprehensive in relation to the concrete human situation—to emerge from subcultures which could now replace symbols which had become outdated, elitist and too limited in their range of application. This general reflection can be linked with a more specific one. The study of rural, village, or folk religion (however one may want to style it), reveals that in these milieux cults of *devīs*, 'goddesses', are widespread, if not to say, dominant. Moreover, it is possible to reconstruct regional cults which at one time may well have centred around autonomous Goddesses. The figures of Manasā (in north-east India) and Yellammā (in the Deccan) are candidates for this. To the extent that it is possible to extrapolate from this relatively recent evidence, we may infer that already in works like the *Devīmāhātmya* popular religion has found literary expression, within the genre and the conventions of hallowed tradition. In a typically Indian fashion, such regional figures are integrated by subsuming them, as her 'manifestations', in the great Goddess.

Less speculative is the question of the reaction provoked. Here a well-known contrast between 'grassroot' and elite religion and religious value-systems can be perceived to apply. Thus much more typical of the purāṇic attitude is the dominant role of the male *devas* or of Bhagavān, who acquire *devīs* as their wives. In that subordinate role, such a *devī* may be associated with some activity secondary to his divine nature. She may then be called his *śakti*, 'power'. 'Śāktism' is the term used in the Indian conceptualisation of Goddess-religion (and it has been adopted uncritically by Western scholars). It should be clear from what has been said above that such a concept does not accurately describe the nature of Bhagavatī.

Worship and Devotion

Given that the early Āryas were a semi-nomadic people, it is not surprising to find a lack of interest in particular places or localities. The sacrifice would be performed by erecting brick altars for the occasion, and the fire could be carried from one place to the next. Similarly the different offshoots of the renouncer movement re-emphasised this mobility. Meditation and asceticism did not require specific places. However, when the Āryas established more permanent settlements in north-eastern India, along the banks of the Yamunā (Jumna) and Gaṅgā (Ganges), we witness the emergence of spatial symbols. The realm itself was conceptualised as the Āryāvarta, the country of

Aryan culture *par excellence*. Even centuries later, when the *Dharma-śāstras* attempted to systematise the details of the Hindu *Dharma*, they suggest, as the final resort in cases of disagreement between different traditions, going to the Āryāvarta and observing the behaviour of true Āryas there. Besides, individual towns were drawn into a process of mythologisation. Above all it is Benares (Vāraṇāsī) that became associated with all kinds of religious and cultural ideas. Among other places may be mentioned Prayāga (Allahabād) where the Yamunā and the Gaṅgā meet. Even where at a later stage theistic notions were superimposed on these archaic ideas (as Benares is associated with Śiva), these remain secondary. It is being in Benares and dying there and having one's ashes scattered into the river that is important (as if it were the return into the womb of a primordial 'mother', Gaṅgā). Naturally it will vary enormously how individual Hindus will conceptualise and perceive the custom of going to Benares, a custom that has attracted millions every year up to the present day. Related to this, although not connected with dying and death, are similar customs, such as celebrating the *kumbhamela* in Prayāga. In the further history of the Aryan expansion many new places emerged that attempted to emulate Benares in its appeal. Different catalogues were produced of such 'holy towns', but nothing comparable to a universally agreed-upon list has evolved. Moreover, in many cases the rationale for a town's 'holiness' is primarily theistic (e.g. in the case of Kāñcīpuram, Rāmeśvaram and Śrīraṅgam in Tamilnadu and Puri in Orissa).

Typologically in sharp contrast with early Aryan 'mobile' religion and with amorphous religious associations of towns in the Āryāvarta, are the folk religions. As the Āryas spread out over the whole of India, they encountered innumerable hunter and agricultural societies with their different religions. Given the lack of information on most of the latter, any characterisation has necessarily to be hypothetical. But from information found in early Buddhist and Jain scriptures, and on Buddhist buildings (from the third century BCE), from stray references in secular Sanskrit and vernacular literature, and also because of the 'multiple history' explained above, it becomes possible to make certain general statements. These different religions appear to be localised, which means that the objects of worship are perceived to be permanently resident in specific places. This in turn allowed for increasing complexity of the structures and modes of worship over the centuries in one and the same locality. Our earliest, indirect documentation comes from the Buddhist *stūpa*, an edifice associated with such localised cults, though presumably with a transformed, Buddhist, motivation. In these local cults generally, offerings are made in a specific place with food, water, flowers, clothes, incense, perfumes, camphor and lamps. In many cases this will also involve the slaughter of animals, and alcohol. The rites are accompanied by song, music and dancing. All this goes by the name of '*pūjā*'. The choice of the place itself may not have been arbitrary: crossroads, special trees, ponds, ant-hills, caves and springs appear to have been particularly favoured spots. Quite clearly all this presupposes the presence of one or more non-human beings in honour of whom these rites are performed. Our texts conceptualise these beings as *yakṣas*, *gaṇas*, *nāgas*, etc. But it is likely that within the relevant religious community these beings were originally conceived of as 'gods'. Presumably for ideological reasons (i.e. to emphasise their non-Vedic nature) it was difficult to regard them as '*devas*'. However, once the cults of the epic and purāṇic gods, and indeed, Gods, had gained prominence, a complex interaction with these folk-religious cults began. Existing centres of worship could be reinterpreted as abodes of such a *deva/Deva* (or even *devī/Devī*), new ones could be created by using the existing forms, and *devī*-figures could be 'married' to the newcomer, the (epic-purāṇic) Aryan *deva*.

Parallel to all this runs a trend to give concrete form to the being believed to be permanently present in a given place. Even in modern India, one can still find the whole spectrum of the various possibilities represented. At one end of this spectrum, there may be no formal sign at all, other than the conventional markings of a 'sacred place of worship' (a flag, clean earth, some line of boundary, etc.). Then we may find a stone, usually marked by a red spot on it or actually painted red. Next, the stone may be given a degree of sculpturing: chiselled-out eyes, a rough nose or mouth. When we come to Śiva religion, the stone will have the shape of a *liṅga* (often set inside a *yoni*). Particularly with the Vaiṣṇavas, but also with the worshippers of the Goddess, we reach the other end of the spectrum: full-figure sculptures with all the details of, say, folds of dress, physiognomy and jewellery. This spectrum runs parallel to a shift in the understanding: whilst the uniconic stone may serve merely to mark the presence of a formless divine being, the iconic, sculptured images tend to be interpreted as the actual 'body' of the god. Yet all this has nothing to do with 'idolatry' (a charge often levelled against this type of religion), as we shall see below.

Given that a particular cult centre enjoyed popularity in a wider region and over a longer period of time, its formal structures could develop enormous complexity. In the extreme, we may end up literally with 'temple towns' (see for example Śrīraṅgam). In fact, any traveller to India will immediately encounter Indian religion through its temples, many thousands of which—small or very large—are scattered all over the country. The temple is indeed the most prominent mode for all types of the Indian religions to manifest themselves externally.

Just as we find a logical spectrum for the representation of the divine being, the complexity of even the largest temple can be explained in terms of many such spectra. Thus one such spectrum would be: from improvised roof (say a stone placed horizontally on top of two vertical stones, protecting the central figure from the rains) to 'hut' to 'house' to 'palace'. The sacred space may be demarcated by a line drawn on to the ground, or a simple fence, or even by tall and thick walls. The entrance could be built up as an arch or even as a *gopuram*, massive towers above the heavy entrance gates. The images can multiply: as a king has his courtiers and queens, the god has his wives, attendants and the saints of the past who sang in his honour. Each one of these may acquire a separate shrine. The greater the complexity of the architectural structures, the greater is the need for maintaining contact between the god and his subjects. Thus festivals evolved during which the god is carried out from his palace and in procession blesses the town or the village. Obviously no large stone image could be used for this purpose, and thus there is a duplication of the statue in bronze or a variety of precious metals. The utensils of *pūjā* require proper, professional care in their production. Thus a flower garden provides the myriad of flowers used by the garland weavers; the food offered (used to feed sometimes hundreds of temple employees and pilgrims) has to be cooked in large kitchens and the grain stored in sizeable storerooms. Music, song and dance are institutionalised and new professional groups emerge: temple musicians and '*devadāsīs*', dancing girls, who sing and dance in front of the temple image. The god or goddess may acquire large supplies of jewellery and dresses in the course of centuries, and special strong-rooms have to be built for these. To carry heavy water vessels is one of the tasks of the temple elephants (who naturally have their own stables). For the procession, large wooden carts may be constructed. The carts of the temple in Puri were so enormous that they provided the English language with the word 'juggernaut' (from the Sanskrit name of the god taken in procession, Jagannātha, 'Lord of the Universe'). Clockwise circumambulation turns into a major walk, through halls of thousands of pillars. In terms of architectural styles, there is a marked difference between the north and the south; Kerala has preserved an altogether different style.

Alongside these trends towards sometimes staggering size and complexity went the development of ritualism. There was obviously the need to codify the innumerable daily, seasonal and special ritual ceremonies: how to bathe the images, how to dress them, how to express the devotional submission of the community to the god, etc., and also how to construct the buildings themselves. Only professionals could learn all this, and thus a number of mostly hereditary traditions arose which specialised in these matters. As in the case of the philosophical systems, such traditions developed their own metaphysics and theologies, thus providing a wider frame for this ritualism. Thus with the Vaiṣṇavas, we find for example the Pāñcarātrins (with their sizeable Saṃhitās) and the Vaikhānasas (who claim to represent one Vedic *śākhā*). With the Śaivites, a whole literature called the Āgamas evolved. As to the overall symbolic model for the temple ritual, the treatment of a respected guest provides the inspiration in more limited contexts; the whole paraphernalia of a king's court and courtly ritual, that for the larger temples.

Whatever the individual theology may be that was

developed in such traditions, it is clear that the image of the deity tended to be regarded as his or her 'embodiment'. That means, the deity itself is not the stone or the metal: by its own nature, the manifested divine is beyond such material constraints. Moreover, food offerings are not literally perceived to be eaten by the deity: the physical contact with the deity's 'body' purifies it and renders it fit for human consumption. Thus it is not justified to treat all this as 'idolatry'. Among Vaiṣṇavas, a particular theological concept evolved, that of the *arcāvatāra*. Similar to the historical 'incarnations' of Viṣṇu, we now have permanent 'incarnations' in the *arcās*, the temple images. Generally speaking, an enormous literature arose for thousands of these temples all over India which tells stories about how the god came to abide permanently in a given temple, what kind of miraculous features are associated with it and what benefits certain individuals gained from visiting the temple. These are the Sthala-purāṇas, repertoires of localised mythology.

A considerable amount of the Indian religious reality is at least to some extent connected with temple worship. This is a form of devotion very few religious movements could altogether ignore. Thus even the Jains constructed temples on a large scale, installed images of their Tīrthaṅkaras (i.e. the Mahāvīra and his predecessors) in them, and instituted *pūjā* (often by hiring Hindu *pūjārīs* for the purpose). There is no reason to doubt the presence also of Buddhist temples in India; very likely the Hindu idea of the Buddha being one of Viṣṇu's *avatāras* was developed in such a temple environment. Even radical antinomian movements that began by totally rejecting temple worship tended to end up worshipping images of their founders and saints in temples (as, for example, in the case of the Nāthas). But the religious significance of the temple varies with different groups. Thus in the strictest terms of Jain doctrine, no Tīrthaṅkara can actually embody himself in a temple statue.

But it does mean that from the viewpoint of an individual member of Indian society, he is surrounded by a (random) collection of different temples. In most cases this person will not bother to study the theologies that would be integral to each individually. He may visit many temples, for different reasons probably unique to him, and worship there. Visits of Hindus to Muslim shrines and even Christian churches are commonplace. But temples want to have an appeal beyond the immediate neighbourhood. Great efforts are made to celebrate the seasonal festivals on as lavish a scale as possible, and thereby attract large numbers of pilgrims. It is difficult to say what factors account for the popularity of certain temples; it need not be size (whch often is the direct result of visits by large groups of pilgrims). In terms of 'sanctity', there is little to choose between them, for each Sthala-purāṇa tries to make the most grandiose claims. Theologically, there is often no need at all for it, since the same Viṣṇu is encountered in all the different Viṣṇu temples. Thus we must assume a whole cluster of motives (including unconscious and random ones) to be at work here.

Visiting the local temples and going on pilgrimage are two important modes of expressing religion in concrete terms. But others may be mentioned. First there are the festivals which are annually celebrated in the homes of people (thus comparable to Christmas, etc.). Naturally they follow the traditional Indian calendar, and thus often the name itself includes the particular day. For instance, Nāg-pañcamī, a festival held in honour of the Nāgas (i.e. 'mythologised' serpents), falls on the 'fifth day' (*pañcamī*) of the month Śrāvaṇa (July/August); Gaṇeś-caturthī, in honour of the elephant-headed 'god of learning' Gaṇeśa, is celebrated on the 'fourth' day (*caturthī*) of Bhādra (August/September). Once again, given the size and variety of India and its religions, we need not be surprised to find enormous regional and social differences in what festival is celebrated and how it is interpreted. Sometimes a festival is purely regional, like the Durgā-pūjā in Bengal during the month of Aśvin (about October). But often one can recognise a common core, as in the spring festival of Holi or the autumn festival of Dīvāli/Dīpāvali. But how even such 'pan-Indian' festivals are given a religious significance depends on the area, caste and religious allegiances of people. It is therefore basically wrong to claim that 'Hindus celebrate x' and offer one such religious interpretation, as if that exhausted the subject. All that can be said is that certain festivals gave gained wide recognition all over India and may have entered into the *Dharma-śāstras*; any Kṛṣṇaite, Rāmaite, Vaiṣṇava, Śaivite, etc. symbolism of it is in most cases secondary.

A further important form of religious expression in the home (apart from domestic *pūjā* and the festivals mentioned above) is the *vrata*. These are rituals usually involving some form of voluntary deprivation (fasting, sexual abstinence, etc.), often in fulfilment of a vow (*vrata* means, amongst other things, vow). Among the higher castes, a brahmin may be employed to recite the 'story' (*kathā*) which narrates the benefits of such a *vrata* and its divine origins. Such ritualised readings of other, major religious works (like the *Bhagavadgītā*, *Devīmāhātmya*, *Bhāgavata-Purāṇa*) may also take place as part of public festivals.

Naturally, there is yoga, which does not necessarily require any external structure. However, it may well be practised as part of daily visits to a temple. A more committed approach would involve leaving the fetters of society behind and turning itinerant mendicant. Alternatively, there is the institution of the *maṭha* or *āśrama* (ashram), comparable to monasteries in the case of permanent residents, and to retreat houses in the case of temporary visitors. Yoga is not a necessary part of *maṭha* or *āśrama* life, since the more emphatic theistic traditions may not cultivate it and concentrate on *pūjā*, *bhakti* and so on instead.

More important than the external forms through which religion expresses itself is the inner content. However, this is an area which does not lend itself easily to direct scrutiny. Nevertheless, there are certain obvious misconceptions which ought to be avoided here. Thus the

Indian material makes it abundantly clear that what we would call 'theology' does not necessarily describe religious content in an integral or adequate manner. Obviously a theological system is easily recognised; moreover, it presents a religious content in a rational, accessible manner. But it would be a grave mistake to describe the whole of the Indian devotional traditions merely in terms of a set of theological systems. Often the concern of Hindu theologians has been marginal to the actual devotion with which it aligned itself. More often, religious movements did not, or not fully, conceptualise their own religious premisses. That means that what will be said in a separate section about the various philosophical and theological strands in Hinduism can, and in fact must, be regarded as an enterprise at least relatively independent of the actual devotion. The case of the Goddess mentioned above is a good illustration.

The early texts that offer us a monotheistic conception also provide the key term for the devotion associated with it: *bhakti*. For instance in the *Bhagavadgītā*, this *bhakti* denotes a fundamental loyalty to Kṛṣṇa which expresses itself through the cultivation of yoga and adherence to the established (Hindu) *Dharma*. In its highest form, it becomes 'love', and that as a mutual relationship between Kṛṣṇa and the devotee. Historically, this rather abstract *bhakti* becomes predominantly associated with temple worship: in the temple image the devotee finds most frequently the concrete divine presence to which he reacts with *bhakti*. For the first time, this is documented for south India where in the context of Śiva and Viṣṇu temples a highly ecstatic type of *bhakti* emerged. Here *bhakti* also acquires a concrete form of expression which then gains universal popularity in India: the song (to be sung by a professional, or by a group of devotees). Most frequently, it is called *kīrtan* or *bhajan*. In fact, an enormous literature evolved over the centuries in all the vernaculars and also in Sanskrit. Famous poets contributed to this store, and sometimes the genre reaches the sophistication of classical Indian poetry (as in Ānandavardhana's poem in honour of the Goddess, or Vedāntadeśika's hymns addressed to Viṣṇu). Often such religious songs were collected and turned into the sacred scripture of a particular religious community; their poets become 'saints' and receive ritual treatment. Thus in the Tamil country we have the Āḻvārs and Nāyaṉārs (500–1000 CE). Their often extremely sophisticated poems were collected in the *Divya-Prabandham* and the *Tiru-Muṟai* respectively, and these corpora were integrated into Śrī-Vaiṣṇavism and the (south Indian) Śaiva-Siddhānta. Moreover, the poetry (and devotion) of the Āḻvārs provided the basis for many passages in the famous *Bhāgavata-Purāṇa* (ninth or early tenth century). From the thirteenth century, Mahārāṣṭra had its '*sants*' (most famous among these are Jñāneśvar, Nāmdev and Tukārām), who in connection with the cult of Viṭhobā of Paṇḍharpur composed thousands of poems of a Kṛṣṇaite/Vaiṣṇavite nature. From the fifteenth century onward, the region around Mathurā attracted many pilgrims and devotees. The scenes of Kṛṣṇa's youth were 'rediscovered' by them. Many founders of Kṛṣṇaite movements settled here permanently or at least established close links with their representatives there. Some of these movements managed to formulate theologies within the Vedānta (like that of Caitanya's disciples, or of Vallabha). Many others contented themselves with the composition of vernacular poetry and provided a less rigid structure for the religious practice of their followers. Different aspects of Kṛṣṇa's life tended to be emphasised. It was his early mischievous childhood on which the Vallabhites focused, or his love for the cowgirl Rādhā, which was marked by separation, on which the Caitanyaites concentrated.

Again in the south, from the early beginning of the second millennium onwards, the cult of Rāma began to flourish. Kampaṉ's Tamil *Rāmāyaṇa* illustrates the process of deification which the epic figure of Rāma was undergoing. Closer to Rāma's home country in north India, Tulsīdās, in his *Rāmcaritmānas* (*The Lake of Rāma's Deeds*) expressed the culmination of this development by envisaging Rāma as God (i.e. Bhagavān) and not as *avatāra*.

The devotional poetry in honour of other gods and God-figures is far less well studied. Śaivite material seems to be particularly amorphous. But in eighteenth-century Bengal, Rāmprasād Sen composed *bhakti*-songs in honour of the Goddess which immediately gave rise to a popular tradition of composing, and singing, such *kīrtans*. Of an even more recent date are the popular cults of Gaṇeśa in Mahārāṣṭra and of Aiyappaṉ in Tamilnadu (to mention only two examples).

With the regional gods we often find religious 'professionals' who specialise in the ritualised recitation of poetry, stories and even plays in honour of and about, say, Yellammā (Mahārāṣṭra and south), or Khaṇḍobā/Mallāri (Mahārāṣṭra and Karṇāṭak). Of distinctive, often striking, external appearance, these professional religious performers (who belong to lower castes in most cases) can be found all over India. Their individual institution may either be hereditary, or they may have been offered at birth to a particular temple. Their devotional rituals tend to be performed in people's homes or on the street, and this is another feature which adds to the 'random' availability of many different religious cults and institutions in any one locality.

Thus, for most individuals in Indian society, the religious life expresses itself through domestic *pūjā* and *vratas*, visits to temples and *maṭhas*, singing *bhajans* or *kīrtans*, celebrating the popular festivals, patronising wandering performers and consulting *svāmīs* or gurus. Only a small part of this variety has been codified in the *Dharma-śāstras*, like the 'sacraments', *saṃskāras*, of higher castes—the sacred thread ceremony, marriage, etc. Some aspects may have acquired a strong textual, theological and institutional basis. But most of it has been handed down loosely from generation to generation and has been developed by individual groups.

By now it should be clear how many 'random' factors actually determine an individual's religion. In addition, there are strong family and caste traditions of allegiance to a particular form of religion. Yet there remains ample scope for the individual in his choice of what he relates to among the many things on offer in his society. Moreover, we must not ignore the important role of charismatic figures. These may be itinerant mendicants, people associated with a temple or a *maṭha*, or religious 'amateurs'. More often than not, they are performers of some kind, gifted poets or singers or story-tellers. Their role may simply be to combine entertainment with edification, to perform rituals, or to advise on spiritual matters. But sometimes their charisma is powerful enough to create new social structures, by bringing together whole groups of families (and individuals) in a new form of religious allegiance. Since the scale of personal, religious commitment varies enormously in India, it is very difficult to decide when such a new structure ought to be called a 'sect' or a 'religious system'. Criteria developed in the West simply do not help here. Where such a new movement is consciously antinomian, it is relatively easier to identify it. The majority, nevertheless, tend to regard themselves as 'orthodox', which given the purely functional role of the Vedas can mean a wide range of things. But one point is clear: we are dealing here with one aspect of social dynamism which contradicts any rigid conception of the Indian 'caste system'. Social structures, orthodox or antinomian, created by such charismatic figures, very frequently override existing caste barriers, and in turn may give rise to new castes themselves.

To acknowledge these flexible aspects of traditional 'Hinduism' is not the same as uncritically accepting fashionable ideas about 'tolerance'. Any religious leader, however much he may emphasise his 'orthodoxy' and display 'orthopraxy', inevitably challenges others. In fact the heavy emphasis on proving one's orthodoxy (in the most elaborate case, by writing a Sanskrit commentary on the *Bhagavadgītā*, the *Vedānta-Sūtras* or the *Bhāgavata-Purāṇa*) evinces the existence of pressures in Indian society to conform. And the history of Hinduism does know of violent interreligious struggles. Thus the much advertised 'tolerance' is a matter of degree and form; it may express itself in areas where the Western traditions have not shown it.

The enormous variety of religious expressions we have observed in this exploration of epic and purāṇic religion is due to the fact that the 'Hindu' can express his religion spontaneously, whilst drawing on a wide spectrum of given symbols and models. The absence of any centralised practical and doctrinal authority has been mentioned above. But all this does not mean that India did not reflect on its own religious realities. It has been pointed out above how such reflections are expressed in mythical symbols (the 'Trinity', the *avatāras*, etc.) But over and above this level of reflection, India produced a most imposing tradition of philosophical and theological enquiry, on the basis of the religious realities mentioned so far. Historically, Buddhists, Jains and Hindus shared, in their own specific ways, in this enterprise. It is time for us to turn to these developments.

Mahāyāna Buddhism and Buddhist Philosophy

When Buddhism disappeared from India around 1200 CE, inevitably its Indian literary sources also vanished. What was not directly destroyed during the Muslim pillaging of the monasteries disintegrated in the course of time, since nobody was left who could, or wanted to, copy out the manuscripts. Thus the Buddhist community in Sri Lanka became practically the sole custodian of ancient Indian Buddhist material. Indeed the Chinese and the Tibetans made an enormous effort to translate Indian Buddhist literature, and thus, at least in this form, a very sizeable amount of Indian material was saved. However, these translating activities took place during later periods of Indian Buddhist history and concerned themselves on the whole with the materials prevalent at that time. All this had the following result for the traditional Western perception of Buddhism. From China and Tibet forms of Buddhism were known that appear to differ quite radically from that found in Sri Lanka. Since the latter had preserved archaic Indian material, and also quite naturally presented itself as 'orthodox' Buddhism, the types found in China and Tibet tended to be regarded as 'late', as transformations and distortions, almost beyond recognition, of an original Buddhism. The 'Mahāyāna' or 'Northern Buddhism' and the 'Vajrayāna' were seen as successively later developments, to contrast with the 'Theravāda' or 'Hīnayāna' as the original stage. Theism, ritualism, nihilism, magic, obscenity—such have been the labels applied to Northern Buddhism; in themselves, they reveal an interesting diversity of interpretation. Basically for two reasons, such a view of Buddhist history in India now requires drastic reinterpretation.

First, not everything had been lost or destroyed; manuscripts (though often in a fragmentary state) of Buddhist Sanskrit texts were discovered in areas (such as Nepal, Kashmir and Central Asia) where the climate (both literally and socially) was more favourable to the preservation of this fragile material. Secondly, a critical exploration of this literature (usually with the help of Chinese and Tibetan translations) has begun to yield interesting insights. Thus in many cases very complex works (which in that form may belong to, for example, the fourth or fifth century) reveal themselves as crystallisations of a long literary development, metastructures incorporating sometimes very old material (perhaps as old as the second century BCE). This now means that we are dealing here with chronological parallels to much of Pali Canon material preserved in Sri Lanka, and not with necessarily much later stages. Indications have been given above how this would affect our understanding of earlier Indian 'sectarianism'. But here we have to look at a far more fundamental division, that of the Theravāda (or Hīnayāna) versus the Mahāyāna. In fact, it might well be possible to go so far as to regard these two major strands as parallel developments out of the common core of 'original Buddhism'.

Considerable effort has been spent on trying to identify a particular region of India, or a particular Buddhist community, as the original birthplace of the Mahāyāna. The two main contenders have been north-western India and the Āndhra country in the south. However, such a quest has not proved particularly useful. Early Mahāyāna in itself is not easily defined, and the model of a one-point origin appears not to be appropriate. By looking at the earliest identifiable material in extant Mahāyāna literature, a variety of themes emerges, and it seems best to regard these as documenting a dynamic discussion within Indian Buddhist communities, which eventually crystallised as a 'revivalist' movement all over the country. Institutions surrounding the (non-monastic) *stūpa* cult, and the role of the *dharma-bhāṇaka* (lay preacher?) have been suggested as possible points of departure for Mahāyāna teaching.

Let us first look at this literature. Sanskrit appears to have been used by Indian Buddhists at a relatively late period. After all, there were strong ideological and practical reasons speaking against this. Initially scholars thought that the popular Mahāyāna works were written in a 'corrupt' form of Sanskrit. By now however it is clear that under the cover of 'corrupt' Sanskrit one or more vernacular languages are hidden, often superficially Sanskritised. Thus this is material comparable to Pali, another representative of such vernaculars. A fair amount of the oldest literary strata that can be reconstructed consists of small, self-contained poems on the spiritual life; fragments of dramatic plays may be recognised, and inevitably there are many *jātaka* tales. At least in terms of logic, if not strictly in terms of history, the next stage was that such early material was gathered together and set within an overall narrative frame, initially still in the vernacular. The 'sermon' (the *sutta*, Skt. *sūtra*) served as the literary model for such a frame. The intention of this device is clear: to present these ideas as the actual teaching of the Buddha, delivered by him on a specific occasion and in a specific place. Further developments then included a linguistic transformation; the old vernacular material is preserved, but now provided with a Sanskrit 'translation'. Other expansions involved the elaboration of the frame-story (sometimes to a very great extent), the addition of further material of similar kind and reflections of a particular work on its own religious significance, and indeed ritual treatment, as 'sacred text'. The outcome of all this was that hundreds of such (Mahāyāna) *sūtras* evolved, a few of which obtained a bulk of hundreds of pages of text individually. Much of it has actually been preserved in Chinese and Tibetan translations. On the whole it is *sūtras*, of which Indian originals have been preserved, which are the better known ones. Here may be mentioned the *Lotus-Sūtra* (*Saddharma-puṇḍarīka*), *Pure-Land-Sūtras* (*Sukhāvatī-vyūha*, shorter and longer), *Diamond-Sūtra* (*Vajracchedika*), *Laṅkāvatāra-Sūtra* ('delivered in Laṅkā'), *Sūtra of Golden Light* (*Suvarṇabhāsottama*), *Jewel-Heap-Sūtra* (*Ratnakūṭa*) and *Flower-Garland-Sūtra* (*Avataṃsaka* or *Gaṇḍavyūha*). The *Perfection-of-Wisdom-Sūtras* (*Prajñā-pāramitā-sūtras*) make up a miniature literature of their own. The oldest version is the one in 8,000 *granthas* (a counting unit of 32 syllables); the verses (called *Ratnaguṇasaṃcayagāthā*) which accompany that prose text may be even earlier. Later versions reach up to 100,000 *granthas* (the size of the *Mahābhārata*), and yet later ones reduce the bulk once again, as in the *Heart-Sūtra* (*Hṛdaya*) of only a few units. Among those with lost Indian originals may be mentioned the *Sandhinirmocana-sūtra* ('explication of the mysteries' might be the meaning of the title), the *Vimalakīrti-nirdeśa-sūtra* (which deals with the instructions given by the rather antinomian Buddhist layman Vimalakīrti), the *Śūraṅgama-samādhi-sūtra* and the *Āryā- Śrīmālā-sūtra* (in which Queen Śrīmālā figures as teacher). From this brief literary survey it must be evident that the greatest obstacle to an accurate understanding of the Mahāyāna is simply the enormous bulk of its literature, with its as yet barely charted history of a thousand years.

The rise of the Mahāyāna could perhaps be described by reference to a tension well known also in other religious movements: that between institution and charisma. Earliest Buddhism maintained a spontaneous link between spiritual perfection and social interaction by being an itinerant movement. But consequent upon the development of settled monasticism, the emphasis had to shift. The distance between monks and laymen had to increase, the elaborate rules must have absorbed a considerable amount of spiritual energy, and the ultimate goal itself moved further and further away into some distant future existence for the individual. In the formulation of the goal itself, that is *nirvāṇa*, the (philosophically realistic) *Abhidharma* appears to have developed, in certain instances, a relatively negative and sometimes perhaps even nihlistic conception. Certainly its 'monolinear' approach to spiritual progress (which allowed for no more than individual and separate streams of continuity) reduced the possibility of spiritual achievement through personal interaction. Furthermore, the grander the image became that was presented of the Buddha, and the more enormous the store of his personal *puṇya* and its consequent 'superhuman' potentials became in the stories of his life, the less immediate and ordinarily repeatable became his enlightenment.

This appears to characterise the perception of institutionalised Buddhism by at least certain segments of the Buddhist community. A reaction set in which in a variety of ways criticised individual aspects, or in fact the whole, of the Buddhist establishment. Attempts were made to restore the Buddhist teaching to its charismatic origins, and in that sense it may be possible to speak here of a 'revivalist' movement.

The following may convey some impressions of the ideas put forward by the 'revivalists'. The Buddha brought back into the world the medicine that cures the suffering of humanity: his *Dharma*. Transmitted from generation to generation, it must be spread to as many people as possible, to put an end to their *duḥkha.* Thus for someone to receive it and not to pass it on and administer it is a fundamental breach of the Buddha's intentions. Moreover, the spreading of the *Dharma* cannot simply be a mechanical act. Every human skill must be involved, searching for and applying the most appropriate means to communicate it in different contexts to different kinds of people. The concept of 'skilfulness in means' (*upāya-kauśalya*) evolved which denotes the mode in which the *Dharma* is dynamically transmitted through history and infused into society. Even the different types of Buddhism that existed in India were interpreted as expressions of the Buddhas' skilfulness in means. 'Rationalist' interpreters of Buddhism have found it difficult to accept the belief in many past Buddhas and in Buddhas found in many other world-systems. But we are dealing here in principle with a universal Buddhist idea and not a specifically Mahāyāna conception. Thus time and again in cosmic history Buddhas arose to reinstitute the *Dharma*. And, in fact, our present aeon will witness the appearance of one future Buddha, Maitreya. All that the Mahāyāna did, apart from developing such ideas further, was to derive from it its emphasis on the social responsibility (*karuṇā*, 'compassion') of the individual recipient of the *Dharma*.

But this could also be developed into another direction. Given the belief in the existence of many past Buddhas, in the accumulation of vast amounts of *puṇya* over endless periods, and in the existence of many cosmic realms other than our own world, a cult like that of the Buddha Amitābha (or Amitāyus) could 'logically' develop. The names of this Buddha mean 'possessing unlimited light' and alternatively, 'unlimited life'. Whether or not this Buddha-figure is derived from some Iranian god, does not affect his role and function in one branch of the Mahāyāna. On the other hand, it is important not to read back into the Indian understanding of Amitābha developments that took place in China and Japan, where the 'Amida' form of Buddhism became extremely popular. The Indian conception could be summed up as follows. Here is a past Buddha who through his enormous amount of merit could actually create a world-system ideally suited for the achievement of enlightenment. Ordinary human beings could become reborn in that world due to the merit acquired from worshipping Amitābha.

The Sanskrit name of that ideal world is *Sukhāvatī*, 'the blissful one'; other names are: 'The Pure Land' and 'The Western Paradise'.

Yet another very different line is pursued by a further segment of the early Mahāyāna. It concentrates its attack of institutionalism on certain implicit assumptions made in the monastic life. Ingeniously it uses ancient concepts, but redefines them. The key term here is that of 'emptiness' (*śūnyatā*). The pursuit of spiritual perfection in the monasteries implies certain 'realist' (in a philosophical sense) assumptions. There it is taken for granted that there is virtue, the Buddha, *nirvāṇa* and the process of personal continuity. Now the question is asked in what sense such items can be said to 'exist'. As to the nature of the person (including that of the Buddha), earliest Buddhism had already been teaching that it is *anātman* (or *śūnya*), lacking an eternal core or individual essence. In the *Abhidharma*, this had been generalised: all *dharmas* are *anātman*. But, these critics point out, to strive through many lives towards *nirvāṇa* actually means to ignore such fundamental facts. Thus instead of conceiving of a 'monolinear' progress through time, from *saṃsāra* to *nirvāṇa*, what ought to be envisaged is a 'qualitative leap' of insight—corresponding to the Buddha's own enlightenment. This qualitative leap beyond *nirvāṇa*, or outside both *saṃsāra* and *nirvāṇa*, is styled the 'supreme enlightenment' (*samyak-sambodhi*), or the 'perfection of wisdom' (*prajñā-pāramitā*). What has created particular difficulties for early interpreters of such ideas is the fact that '*nirvāṇa*' here has actually undergone a conceptual transformation. In early Buddhism, it may well have denoted a state of realisation which transcended the realm of *duḥkha*. Now it is used to denote merely the end of *duḥkha*. Another term created similar difficulties: 'emptiness'. Originally it denoted little else than the lack of an *ātman*. However, the *Abhidharma*, and the subsequent Theravāda philosophies which derived from it, used *anātman* as one of the three characteristics of all *dharmas*. Implicitly or explicitly, these *anātman dharmas* were regarded as momentarily real (and, in that sense also, any sequence of *dharmas*, their continuity in time, had to be seen as 'real'). At this point we have come back to the critique levelled by the proponents of the emptiness teaching against the 'realist' trends of the monastic life. Developing ideas originally formulated in the schema of the 'conditioned origination', they state that nothing which is 'conditioned' can be regarded as 'real' (in the sense of possessing autonomous existence or essence). To take an example of ordinary life: we can perceive of 'cows' only by virtue of there being non-cows (such as horses, pigs, etc.). 'Cows' are thus 'conditioned'. When this approach is pursued to the highest level of abstraction, even *nirvāṇa* (as perceived in institutionalised spirituality) is 'conditioned' by *saṃsāra*, and vice versa. Neither can therefore be regarded as possessing autonomous reality. Both are 'empty'. This does not now imply that what is 'empty' is 'nothing'. Myriads of phenomena are there, for us to perceive, including our own 'persons'. But none of these *dharmas* possesses an ontological status which could be denoted by terms like 'real', 'unreal', etc.

All we can say is that they are empty, because they are conditioned. At this point, what earlier on has been called a 'qualitative leap' can be defined in more precise terms. If all *dharmas*, including *saṃsāra* and *nirvāṇa*, are empty (*śūnya*), it becomes possible to speak of *śūnyatā*, 'emptiness' as the common ground of all *dharmas* (and the term *dharmadhātu*, 'root of *dharmas*', is indeed found). *Śūnyatā* is ultimate truth, all *dharmas* make up the realm of relative truth. This realisation of *śūnyatā* is the qualitative leap beyond *saṃsāra* and *nirvāṇa*. It is however important to keep in mind that such ideas are not primarily intended as 'philosophy'. They are an attempt to back up logically the spiritual programme put forward, and the critique levelled against the striving for personal perfection and *nirvāṇa*. The true spiritual path aims at the realisation of emptiness in all phenomena, including the Buddha, his teaching, *nirvāṇa* and virtue. This is the supreme enlightenment and the perfection of wisdom. But clearly *śūnyatā* is not something outside, or separate from, the *dharmas*. Thus, whilst the traditional, institutional approach aimed at leaving *saṃsāra* behind in the realisation of *nirvāṇa*, a dialectical attitude is suggested here. The 'perfection of wisdom' can only occur within the realm of the *dharmas*. This dialectic is now given a particular application. The realm of relative truth is, as earliest Buddhism has taught, the realm of suffering, *duḥkha*. Any insight into its fundamental nature cannot now ignore the (relative) reality of *duḥkha* and of suffering beings. The very insight into this is experienced as stimulating an active drive towards making the medicine of the Buddha's teachings available. This is conceptualised as the 'perfection of compassion', *karuṇā-pāramitā*.

Mahāyāna literature refers to the type of Buddhist it criticises by means of the term *śrāvaka*. This is the person who receives the *Dharma* externally and makes use of it purely for personal spiritual advancement towards *nirvāṇa*. Contrasted with him is the *bodhisattva* who aims at the 'qualitative leap' of 'supreme enlightenment' and combines the pursuit of wisdom and compassion. Again, the terms '*bodhisattva*' and 'perfection (*pārami*[*tā*])' are ancient Buddhist. Popular *jātaka* literature is filled with stories depicting the Bodhisattva (that is, the Buddha-to-be in past existences) cultivating the perfection in various virtues. It is not difficult to see how the Mahāyāna could derive its generalised *bodhisattva* concept from this. Besides *śrāvaka* and *bodhisattva*, we find contrasting terms denoting the different spiritual programmes. What has been characterised here as the 'revivalist' movement presented itself as the 'Mahāyāna' and labelled the *śrāvaka* tradition the 'Hīnayāna'. Our understanding of these terms is not as clear as one would wish for. Possibly the most original meaning of *yāna* is that of a '[spiritual] road'. A contrast could be construed between a 'broad' or 'high' (for *mahā*) road and a 'narrow' or 'low' (*hīna*) one. But *mahā* could also denote 'large', in the sense of incorporating more. This 'more' in turn may refer to an enhanced role of laymen, or to the claim frequently made of being the all-embracing, culminating form of Buddhism (thereby actually including the *Hīnayāna* as a lower stage). Alternatively, *yāna* has been interpreted as denoting a 'vehicle'. Whilst it is clear that '*śrāvaka*' and 'Hīnayāna' are used as derogatory terms, it is not clear whether 'Hīnayāna' referred to any specific institution or Buddhist community. More likely the term was originally intended as a critique of generally prevalent attitudes.

What has been sketched so far can relatively safely be regarded as fairly early Mahāyāna teaching. There are however further aspects which have as yet evaded a more precise chronological location within Mahāyāna history. Thus a considerable amount of material is concerned with the glorification of particular meditational exercises (called *samādhis*) and the specific insights and 'miraculous' powers gained through them (e.g. the *Samādhirāja-* and *Śūraṅgamasamādhi-sūtras*). Then we find reflections on the actual 'locus' of supreme enlightenment. Given that man lacked an inner, autonomous core, it seemed preferable to locate the ultimate spiritual experience in some real beyond the individual. In this connection the concept of the *tathāgatagarbha*, 'the seed of all Buddhas', is developed. Enlightenment is perceived as a potential (the 'seed') latent in all men and, moreover, as ultimate reality which in some sense gave rise to the world of phenomena. Or again, a closer relationship between the realm of *dharmas* and the perceiving mind was established. An ultimate insight into the nature of reality could only be regarded as 'achieving' anything (i.e. liberation) by virtue of reality itself being 'mental'. We can move away from the realm of suffering not by changing our perception of *saṃsāra* and so on, but by realising that—quite literally—they are no more than figments of our imagination. Another very different aspect of the Mahāyāna is the development of ritualism in connection with specific Bodhisattva and Buddha-figures. Once again legend and myth are busy elevating particular figures to objects of worship and veneration. Conceptually, the '*trikāya*' evolved as an attempt to provide a systematic exposition of this. Reality is envisaged here as 'three levels' (or 'realms', lit. 'chunks, bodies'). There is the realm of the phenomena (*nirmāṇa-kāya*), with its Buddhas in 'flesh and blood'. Then there is the realm of the highest truth (*dharma-kāya*), ultimate Buddhahood, emptiness, and at the same time the seat of the eternal *Dharma*. In between these two is a third (*sambhoga-kāya*), a heavenly realm filled with Buddhas such as Amitābha and Bodhisattvas like Avalokiteśvara.

From all these different trends it becomes clear that both in its beginnings and during its later history the Mahāyāna was a multifarious movement, mirroring the dynamism of the 'sects' of both the Indian Theravāda and Mahāsāṅghika. But the Mahāyāna expressed itself not merely through its enormous *sūtra* literature. On the basis of the latter, far more systematic philosophical and scholastic traditions arose. Some of this speculation found expression in further *sūtras* (see, for instance, the minute scholasticism about the spiritual career of a *bodhisattva*, divided into ten stages or *bhūmis*, found in the *Daśabhūmika-sūtra*, or the lengthy catalogue of *samādhis* in the *Gaṇḍavyūha-sūtra*, or the *tathāgatagarbha* theory formulated in the *Āryā-Śrīmālā-sūtra*). But on the whole it was in identifiable philosophical schools and by individual thinkers that these more systematic trends occurred.

One of the earliest figures to emerge is Nāgārjuna (second century CE?) He became the founder of the school of the Mādhyamika. His main concern was to place on a philosophical foundation the teaching of 'emptiness' as lying 'in between' (*madhyama*) the 'real' and the 'unreal'. Perhaps to the following century belonged Sāramati who created a system very different from that of Nāgārjuna. One truly 'real' is assumed here, a cosmic self-luminous Mind which due to extraneous impurities projects, as it were, the world of phenomena. Such ideas influenced Maitreyanātha (*c.* 300 CE?), who developed the idea of a cosmic mind further, while he tried, at the same time, to eradicate the blatantly substantialist views of Sāramati. It has been suggested that Maitreyanātha was the actual founder of the second grand school of Mahāyāna philosophy, the Vijñāna/Vijñaptimātra ('Consciousness-Only'), also called Yogācāra. Better known representatives of this school are Asaṅga and the (senior) Vasubandhu (both fourth century CE).

In a sense, Mahāyāna philosophy reached its culmination during the fourth and fifth centuries CE. Indeed it continued for centuries after this period (e.g. in the famous Nālānda in eastern India and in Kaṭhiavār in the west). But fundamentally new ideas were not produced any more. The religious focus shifted to other areas (which will be discussed in the section on the esoteric traditions.) The various philosophical schools that continued elaborated on the details of existing thought and attempted various syntheses of different trends. Thus out of the combination of ideas found in the Yogācāra and Sautrāntika (a Hīnayāna school) evolved the epistemological school associated with the south Indian Dinnāga (fifth/sixth century CE). Whilst certain followers of the Mādhyamika school (like Buddhapālita, fifth century, or Candrakīrti, seventh century) restricted themselves to elaborating on Nāgārjuna's arguments and substituting a more satisfactory logic for them, others went further and attempted a synthesis with Yogācāra thought. Among these may be mentioned Bhāvaviveka of the sixth century. These different attitudes to the thought of Nāgārjuna gave rise to considerable controversy within the Mādhyamika, and two branches are distinguished: the *Prāsaṅgikas* (restricting their efforts to demonstrating the impossibility of all positive propositions) and the *Svātantrikas* (who were prepared to accept the more positive line of the Yogācāra teaching). With all these thinkers, Mahāyāna thought had entered into a philosophical discourse of enormous complexity and technical acumen. It would be impossible to discuss the details of this material here.

But whilst the philosophers were busy refining their systems, and whilst in other areas the esoteric traditions were influencing

Buddhist religious life, a much more popular strand continued. This was an increasing trend towards a devotionalism centred around specific grand Bodhisattva-figures. Avalokiteśvara appears to have been particularly popular, as some late *sūtras* (like the *Kāraṇḍavyūha*) and late additions to older ones (particularly to the *Lotus-Sūtra*) demonstrate. We also find figures like the 'goddess' Tārā being worshipped.

All the various forms of Mahāyāna Buddhism, with its different literary works, were taken up by the Chinese, and through their mediation transmitted to other Asian countries, like Korea and Japan.

How did the 'Hīnayāna' deal with all these developments? In one sense it attempted to keep abreast in the philosophical discussion that was going on under the banner of the Mahāyāna. Thus it created its own systematic expositions. But in another sense, it simply closed itself off against the attack of the Mahāyānists. We must not forget that from an early date onwards the 'Hīnayāna' became fragmented into many different 'sects', 'schools' and communities, scattered over a very large area. Thus it is impossible to expect a concerted and generally co-ordinated response to Mahāyāna philosophical critique. Instead we find in various individual schools separate attempts at developing traditional beliefs and practices into coherent philosophical systems that could rival, as far as the sophistication of its analysis was concerned, with its Mahāyāna competitors. Best known among these is the school of the Sarvāstivāda, which appears to have spread from Mathurā all over northern India and to have found in Kashmir one of its most important strongholds. In the (junior) Vasubandhu (fifth century) this school's thought reaches its culmination. Historically, however (as the title of Vasubandhu's main work itself bears out: *Abhidharma-koṣa*, 'Treasure of the *Abhidharma*'), the thinking is primarily an elaboration on the older *Abhidharma* and thus cannot positively relate to Mahāyāna metaphysics with its open or implied critique. More nebulous is our information on another school, that of the Sautrāntika (associated with the names of Harivarman, third century CE, and the same Vasubandhu of the fifth century, through his own commentary on his *Abhidharmakoṣa*). The contrast between the Sarvāstivāda and the Sautrāntika has been described as that of philosophical realism versus nominalism. 'Sarvāsti-vāda' itself means the 'teaching that claims "everything exists"', and refers to the belief in the reality of all *dharmas* (including the past and future ones). The Sautrāntikas, on the other hand, rejected such ideas and proposed a merely nominal reality for many *dharmas*. Since '*nirvāṇa*' was included among the latter category, the school may well be described as nihilist. *Nirvāṇa* here is, ontologically speaking, 'nothing'. Both because treatises of the Sarvāstivāda and the Sautrāntika became known relatively early in the West, and also because its teaching draws on seemingly archaic ideas, such Hīnayāna ideas tended to influence Western interpretation of Buddhism as such.

When we turn to Sri Lankan Theravāda, we also find here for the same period (the fifth century or so) attempts at systematising the religious thinking on the basis of the *Abhidharma*. Buddhaghoṣa, particularly through his treatise *Visuddhimagga* (Pali, 'Path of Purification') produced the culminating works here. But in many ways the radical extremes of the Sarvāstivādins and Sautrāntikas are avoided by him.

Buddhist philosophy, particularly Mahāyāna thought, may be regarded as leading intellectually in India for a number of centuries. There is nothing really comparable, in terms of sophistication, on the 'Hindu' side till the seventh century or so. When such systems emerge (and that means not merely dealing with religious issues in a general sense, but presenting themselves as consciously 'Vedic'), they reveal many traces of Mahāyāna ideas and of the Buddhist philosophical method generally.

Hindu Philosophies and Theologies

For a variety of motives, the Indians have shown, from an early period onwards, a considerable interest in a more systematic analysis and understanding of the world, man and religion. 'Systematic' denotes here an analytical, logically coherent and wide-ranging approach, carried out through increasingly sophisticated and carefully defined methods. Whilst it is possible to maintain a distinction between philosophy and theology in principle, the overlap and interaction between these two disciplines has been far greater in India than in the West. This is partly due to the fact that 'religion' here need not involve the concept of a personal absolute, and partly there was the need perceived by many thinkers to present their teaching within an 'orthodoxy' and 'orthopraxy' which at least nominally had Vedic authority. Thus purely philosophical systems tended to be expanded through references to religious matters. And even in cases where their premisses were directly based on religion, no concept of 'God' was necessarily involved. To describe them as 'theologies' would emphasise this religious concern, though it would be misleading, if it were associated in all cases with a *theos*, 'God'.

Traditionally, the whole arena of Hindu speculation has been conceptualised as the 'six (orthodox or Hindu) *darśanas*'. The word '*darśana*' itself denotes a 'vision' or a 'conception' of the world and man's destiny in it; it therefore fuses observation with religious practice. But for a number of reasons, the schema is extremely unsatisfactory. It was formulated at a late stage of the Indian history of thought when most of the thinking listed in it had already lost its relevance to live discussion. It obscures basic distinctions between very different types of systematic thought and their different motivations. It restricts the range of what India produced in the form of critical thought, and ignores all aspects of a historical development and interaction. Moreover, Hindu thought has not been an isolated and self-contained tradition, for over hundreds of years Buddhist philosophy, particularly that of the Mahāyāna, played a leading role in India and necessitated 'Hindu' reactions to it.

When we turn to the individual members in the group of the six *darśanas*, some further general comments are necessary. Already the later portions of the *Ṛg-Veda* demonstrate a great interest in a systematic analysis of the world. More than intellectual curiosity is involved here, for this knowledge is perceived as power, ultimately the power to control one's own destiny and, in the Upaniṣads, to reach out for liberation. Two trends may be distinguished even at this early stage: a proto-scientific (sometimes even mechanistic) approach, and attempts to create a metaphysic for 'mystical' experiences. In addition, ancillary disciplines were developed that served as tools for both approaches. But as always in India, such neat logical distinctions get considerably blurred in real life. In this context it is important to note that these forms of intellectual activity developed their own institutional structures. Professional school traditions evolved, where specific teaching was handed down and elaborated over the centuries. The primary core of such traditions would vary enormously. But given that at least to the professional within any of these traditions it made up 'his whole life', we need not be surprised to find that these cores were expanded and surrounded by a metaphysical framework. Sooner or later, every philosophical school tradition attempted to offer a 'deeper meaning' of its subject matter. Presumably this was primarily intended as a religious conceptualisation internal to the tradition, for the professional representatives. But it may well have been directed also towards society at large, justifying itself in this manner. However, what society made of it is yet another affair. It might adopt the whole package, core discipline and metaphysical framework (as was certainly the case of the Vedānta), or ignore the metaphysics and restrict itself to what the tradition had to offer in practical terms (as seems to have been the case frequently with the *Yoga-* and *Nyāya-darśanas*). Moreover, what precisely constituted a 'metaphysical frame' for a core discipline varied with time. At the beginning, this might be no more than reflections on *saṃsāra* and *mokṣa*. Theistic and 'mystical' matters evolved only later as topics to be considered. The schema of the six *darśanas* abstracts from all this and pretends that all six traditions can be lined up parallel to each other.

Let us begin by exploring the developments in the 'proto-scientific' strand of Indian speculation. Probably the most impressive results were reached, at an early period, in the area of language. They were motivated by the need to preserve the older form of the Sanskrit language that itself was rapidly changing and in fact developing various vernacular 'mother tongues'. At first sight, language consists of an unlimited number of words, put together as sentences. At closer analysis, the number of words reveals itself as finite (say, a hundred thousand). Modifications to a word (the morphemes) show themselves to be far more limited, and also suggest the existence of different types of words (verbs, nouns, adjectives, etc.). In turn, a 'root' can be abstracted from this, to which the various morphemes are added. Thus what results from such an analysis is a system consisting of

1. a catalogue of all roots, 2. sets of morphemes and 3. an account of how to combine the two. Such a system was indeed produced; its final form is associated with the name of Pāṇini and belongs to the fifth century BCE. It is presented in the form of about 4,000 formulas (called *sūtras*), systematically arranged and incomprehensible without the explanation of the commentaries.

In its own right, grammar could hardly claim a place in an account of the Indian religions. But Indian thought perceived a close affinity between language and the world, and in addition applied the methods and the principles of analysing it to other areas. As to the affinity with the world, whole metaphysics evolved. Language in the abstract (this may be called the Vedas or *śabda-brahman*, the *brahman* of words) possesses eternal, autonomous being. It then generates its concrete structures, actualises itself through the spoken word and gets concretised in the objects corresponding to the words. Thus to study the world means to study its words, and, beyond that, language in its prototypal form; language is the avenue towards the transcendental. Such ideas were expressed in various forms and traditions, including the Mīmāṃsā and the school associated with the name of Bhartṛhari. Rather different usage is made of this conception in the esoteric traditions.

As far as the method is concerned, both in approach and in the presentation of its results parallels to other areas of enquiry were perceived. Here was an ideal example of ordering an amorphous and seemingly infinite set of phenomena, by reducing this 'chaos' to a limited set of primary factors and the rules governing their combination and interaction. Obviously this could be applied to the whole world of human experience. From an early period, Indian thought envisaged four or five primary elements that made up all material forms (earth, water, fire, air and possibly ether). Correlations of these five to the five human sense-organs (eye for sight, etc.) were attempted (earth being an object for all five, ether—as carrier of sound—only for the ear). At an early date, forms of atomism emerged which postulated that matter (i.e. the elements) consisted of four or five types of innumerable atoms. To account for 'life', that means for example organic growth, movement, the healing faculty of the human body, perception and consciousness, the existence of a 'soul' or 'life-principle' (often called *jīva*) was postulated. Elements, *jīvas*, and space and time which made up the continuum within which matter and life occurred, tended to be regarded as eternal. On the basis of this raw material, whole cosmological systems could be built which described not just the outside world but also the nature of man. It is quite possible that sometimes such systems carried a conscious mechanistic intention, directed against more 'mystical' or transcendentalist forms of thought. But one of the earliest expressions of this approach is Jain philosophy, and as we have seen, this system is clearly intended to explain how in Jain terms liberation from *saṃsāra* comes about. The Buddhists made much more tentative use of this material, in their *Abhidharma* (from the third century BCE onwards). On the Hindu side, the most typical representative is the *darśana* Vaiśeṣika. As a full metaphysical programme with its (in this case very negative, almost nihilistic) teaching on liberation, it has had relatively little influence. However, one of its achievements was the development of the concept of the 'categories', which along with its cosmology had far wider impact. Reality is now perceived not simply as made up of various 'things', but different types of entities. Thus a substance is distinguished from its attributes which can only occur in conjunction with it. Transformations of substances inhered by attributes are seen as movement, a third category of being. Objects and beings are not discrete entities, but share common characteristics. Thus 'cow' refers to a whole set of animals that all have the same attributes. On the other hand, a category 'difference' (*viśeṣa*, from which perhaps the system derived its name) distinguishes 'cows' from 'horses'. Finally, the sixth category is even more abstract, since it refers to the relation between the other five. It is inherence, as for example an attribute inheres in a substance. Buddhist thought reacted very strongly against this kind of view of reality; it basically rejected the concept of autonomous substance.

Out of a concern for debating techniques arose an interest in the structures of human thought and reasoning, and in their relationship with language. Eventually this crystallised as the *Nyāya-darśana*, which at a still later stage added a kind of theistic frame to its teaching. Often the Nyāya and Vaiśeṣika were regarded as complementary and thus fused into one.

The scholastic study of the ancient Vedic ritual treatises revealed all kinds of contradictions and variations between different branches of the tradition. Thus complex and sophisticated methods of exegesis evolved. This was linked with speculation on the Vedas themselves as the authority for these rituals, and on *Dharma* (according to which these rituals had to be performed) and its role in society. This gave rise to another *darśana*, that of the Mīmāṃsā.

Originally at least, these systems of thought tended to bypass the issues that were raised in the Upaniṣads: *saṃsāra* and *mokṣa*, the *ātman* and *brahman*, and 'altered states of consciousness'. Jainism drew directly on 'proto-scientific' thought to present its own views within the renouncer tradition, and the Buddhists initially refused to put up any kind of systematic, metaphysical account, and even in the *Abhidharma* presented a very idiosyncratic view of the same proto-science. The earliest attempts within the 'Hindu' tradition to deal with such matters centrally still bear the mark of 'proto-scientific' thought, and it may be argued that differences from the actual teaching found in the Upaniṣads are due to this impact. Anyway, the *darśana* Sāṃkhya addressed itself directly to the questions of *saṃsāra* and liberation. A very idiosyncratic cosmology was suggested, in which all phenomena other than the eternal and individual souls (called *puruṣas*) are derived from one ultimate substance, *prakṛti*. The latter consists of three aspects (*guṇas*, qualities or components) *sattva*, *rajas* and *tamas*. Since the latter unequivocally means 'darkness', the other two are most easily explained as 'dust' or 'haze' (*rajas*) and 'brilliance, light' (*sattva*). Because of these three different ingredients, *prakṛti* time and again evolves increasingly 'gross', material forms. The result is a view of the person consisting of a body (made up of five subtle elements—which carry the *karma* after a person's death—and the corresponding gross elements); five senses and five primary faculties of movement; a 'mind' (*manas*). All these are regarded as evolved out of *ahaṅkāra*, the sense of 'I', and the latter in turn grows out of *buddhi* (intellect) which itself is the first stage in the differentiation of *prakṛti*. A *puruṣa* is fettered by this whole structure, but internally unaffected by it. By locating most aspects of the empirical person in the realm of *prakṛti*, it becomes almost impossible to say anything at all about the nature of the *puruṣa*, for even thought and consciousness are still part of *prakṛti*. The intention seems here to be to prevent any kind of action (even a mental one) being associated with the *puruṣa*—an extreme form of the belief in *karma*. In ordinary circumstances (namely in *saṃsāra*), the *manas* feeds into the 'self-awareness' (*ahaṅkāra*) all kinds of false ideas, which are derived from the contact of the senses with their corresponding objects in the material world. By systematically removing the *guṇas rajas* and *tamas* from the whole structure, the *ahaṅkāra* can be purified. Moreover, it is possible then to influence the *buddhi*, which at the moment of deepest insight realises that its own nature is evolved from *prakṛti* and that there exists a fundamental difference of the *puruṣa* from anything connected with *prakṛti*. At this moment the link between *puruṣa* and *prakṛti* is severed, and unimpeded by *saṃsāra* the *puruṣa* achieves liberation.

The Sāṃkhya is a difficult system to interpret. The oneness of all being of the Upaniṣads is maintained here only to the extent that all phenomenal being is unified in *prakṛti*. But the *puruṣas* are very many and remain so even in the state of liberation; there is no *brahman* into which they merge. To what extent the purification of the *buddhi* is regarded as a purely 'intellectual' affair has also been a problem, and to what extent we are actually dealing here with meditational exercises in the form of yoga. Certainly historically, the Sāṃkhya aligned itself very closely with the *Yoga-darśana*. This link itself is problematic, for it has been suggested that the earliest text of the *Yoga-darśana* indicates a metaphysics very much at variance with that found in the later commentaries which all appear to project Sāṃkhya ideas on the *sūtras*. What is important here is the fact that Indian traditions have looked on the *Yoga-sūtras* as the classical account of yoga meditational exercises.

The rationale of these are clear. After preparations of a general ethical and moral kind (*yama*, that is avoiding negative actions like lying and stealing, and *niyama*, that is cultivating positive virtues like contentedness and endurance), the technical side of yoga can begin. This involves the choice of a place conducive to inner quiet and a bodily posture that allows for comfort, relaxation and concentration (*āsana*). A new rhythm is imposed on one's breathing intended to slow down and calm our mental processes (*prāṇāyāma*). Our faculty to filter out sense data that are accidental in a given situation is consciously developed further (in *pratyāhāra*, withdrawal of the senses from their objects). Now follow the inner yogic exercises. *Dhāraṇā* (concentration) seeks to increase the length of time a thought can focus on a particular mental object, and thereby to increase its penetrating powers. 'Meditation' (*dhyāna*) develops this further towards a merger between the meditating mind and its object, and this culminates in *samādhi*, where full mental clarity and an ultimate insight into the nature of reality are achieved. Naturally this achievement is seen as constituting liberation (*mokṣa*).

The *sūtra* (or a similar device) constitutes the formal expression of all these types of teaching. But unlike the Buddhist *sūtra*, the word refers here to extremely concise formulas which are incomprehensible without a commentary. Such explanations tended to be given orally and are therefore not available to us. Even in those cases where literary commentaries were produced, frequently they have not come down to us. This then made it possible for later commentators to read all kinds of interpretations back into the enigmatic *sūtras*. In the case of the sixth of the *darśanas*, the Vedānta, this is particularly apparent.

When discussing theistic and 'mystical' matters, the Epics and earlier Purāṇas used concepts derived from, or related to, the Sāṃkhya system. Even a group of relatively early Upaniṣads resorted to the Sāṃkhya for their speculative material. Although what can be recognised as 'Sāṃkhya material' does not quite correspond to the classical formulation of the system (as found in Īśvarakṛṣṇa's *Sāṃkhyakārikās* and its commentary *Yuktidīpa*, both fifth or sixth century CE), it can by no means be said that we are dealing here with an integral systematisation of the thought of the earliest Upaniṣads. In fact, a systematic metaphysic which could conceptualise *saṃsāra* and *mokṣa* in terms of *brahman* and *ātman* was developed only at a relatively late date. A concept of the 'transcendental experience' of *brahman* was not easily formulated against the background of other philosophical schools. The *Brahma-* or *Vedānta-sūtras* ascribed to Bādarāyaṇa (possibly fourth/fifth century CE) are the earliest known attempt to systematise the teaching of the early Upaniṣads. In turn they served as the scriptural authority for the whole of the *Vedānta-darśana*. 'Vedānta' itself means 'end of the Vedas' and denotes the Upaniṣads, as the Veda's final portion. Thus by its very title this system claims the highest Vedic authority. But from the critical outsider's point of view, the systematisation offered by Bādarāyaṇa is no more than one way of analysing the wide spectrum of Upaniṣadic thought. Moreover, it contains a major unresolved tension. While the cosmos is envisaged as a real transformation (*pariṇāma*) of *brahman*, the liberation of the *ātman* is seen as a monistic merger into *brahman*. Later commentators had to decide which of these two positions to adopt for a fully coherent framework.

Thus Gauḍapāda (in his comments on the *Māṇḍūkya-Upaniṣad*, *c.* seventh century CE) interpreted the world of phenomena as a purely illusory imposition (*vivarta*) upon the universal Mind (equivalent to *brahman*). But it was the south Indian Śaṅkara (between 650 and 750) who through his commentary on the *Brahma-sūtras* established the classical exposition of this approach. He proposed two levels of reality (or 'truth'), an empirical and an ultimate one. The world of the phenomena is explained as the effect of universal ignorance (*avidyā*) upon pure consciousness (*brahman*); individuality as the effect of (individual) ignorance on the *ātman* which in essence is identical with *brahman*. From the ultimate point of view, *brahman* is the sole real. *Avidyā* cannot possess separate, autonomous existence. This dependent relationship between *brahman* and *avidyā* is styled *a-dvaita*, 'non-dual'. Since *brahman* alone possesses true being (*sat*), Śaṅkara cannot accept the existence of a Bhagavān. Thus the God-figures of Hindu religion are conceived of as ultimately illusory aspects of *avidyā*. Overtly in Gauḍapāda, and still implicit in the structure of Śaṅkara's thought, are many Buddhist influences, particularly from the Mahāyāna. But by identifying, for instance, Mind-Only with *brahman*, not only does the Vedānta turn substantialist; it also becomes consciously Vedic, that is Hindu, and anti-Buddhist. Of somewhat doubtful historical value are the accounts that have Śaṅkara imitate the Buddhists by also founding a variety of monastic orders. But monasticism certainly did develop in the tradition of the *advaita-Vedānta*. The increasingly subtle discussion of the precise relationship of *brahman* with *avidyā* (or *māyā*, 'illusion') gave rise to a number of further schools.

The non-classical Sāṃkhya of the Epics, Purāṇas and some Upaniṣads knows of Bhagavān over and above *prakṛti* and the *puruṣas*. In Śaṅkara's system, there was no place for such a figure. But by drawing on the popular devotion to Viṣṇu current in South India at the time (i.e. the tradition of the Āḻvārs), and on theological ideas found in the Pāñcarātra, Rāmānuja (twelfth century CE) created a blatantly monotheistic system. He also applied the cosmological realism of Bādarāyaṇa to the relationship between *brahman* (who is Viṣṇu here) and the *ātman*. The universe, with its beings and its material objects, is as it were Viṣṇu's body. For their existence they depend totally on him (thus again this is *advaita*), and they are his real external expression—he is 'differentiated' into, or 'qualified' by, them (*viśiṣṭa*). Thus the system known as the *viśiṣṭādvaita*. Later theologians (like Vedāntadeśika, thirteenth/fourteenth century CE, and his contemporary Piḷḷai Lokācārya) focused on the problematic relationship between the operation of Viṣṇu's grace and human merit. Eventually, Śrīvaiṣṇavism, that is the religious movement of the *viśiṣṭādvaita*, split into two branches. One side maintained that in no way could human merit (acquired through virtue and religious works) be a condition for Viṣṇu's saving grace. As the cat simply grabs its kitten at the moment of danger and carries it off to safety, Viṣṇu simply comes and saves. The other branch insisted that by this logic either everybody should be in the state of salvation, or Viṣṇu would be a cruel lord. At least in some small measure man must make himself ready to receive the divine grace, as the baby monkey must at least hold on to its mother's neck in order to be carried into safety.

The period between the thirteenth and the sixteenth centuries witnessed the formulation of many further theistic varieties of the Vedānta. Madhva (thirteenth century) formulated a strictly dualistic system, with Viṣṇu as *brahman*. Even in the state of liberation, the soul does not lose its individual identity. Nīmbārka (before the sixteenth century), Vallabha and Caitanya's disciples, particularly Rūpa and Jīva Gosvāmī (all sixteenth century) focused on Kṛṣṇa as *brahman*. It is impossible here to provide further details on all these theological developments within the Vaiṣṇava or Kṛṣṇaite Vedānta.

A commentary on the *Brahma-sūtras* was one of the most prestigious ways of formulating a theology and thereby establishing the orthodoxy of a religious system. But theologies were created in India in many other ways; the example of the *Devīśataka* by Ānandavardhana has already been mentioned in a previous chapter. Thus alongside the Pāñcarātra, the Śaiva Āgamas had also been transmitted from north India to the south. Against the background of the earlier Śaiva mystics (the Nāyaṉārs), a theology was developed on the basis of the Āgamas which is called the Śaiva-siddhānta. Meykaṇṭaṉ, Aruḷnanti and Umāpati (1200–1300 CE) are some of the more important theologians involved in this; they all wrote in the vernacular Tamil. The devotionalism derived from the Nāyaṉārs added features in the south which made the system look rather different from its earlier namesake in Kashmir. In a similar manner, Pāñcarātra ritualism acquired a devotional dimension through the Āḻvārs and Śrīvaiṣṇavism.

Theism and mysticism (in the sense of meditationally gained 'knowledge') are, however, not the only areas to which this type of critical and systematic thought was applied. The materials typical of the esoteric traditions (about which more will be said in following sections) also became the object of philosophical investigation. Kashmir was particularly fertile in the production of such systems.

From these various observations it should have become clear that, in spite of the enormous spectrum of different views contained in the labels of the Vedānta, and of the 'six systems' generally, Hindu religious speculation does not restrict itself to these traditions. As far as the religious content of this speculation is concerned, a similar variety and flexibility presents itself. Man may be envisaged as capable of achieving his own liberation (through meditation, or through rituals which in turn may be exoteric or esoteric); or he may be regarded as totally dependent on divine grace, or a subtly balanced combination of both views may be proposed. Attempts may be made to gather together the totality of all that exists in one ultimate unity, or irreconcilable and unfusable differences of categories of reality may be perceived to persist even on a fundamental level, or again, combinations of both positions may be proposed. The possible varieties are unlimited, and over more than a millennium Hinduism has formulated a large number of them. That such intellectual dynamism was possible is due to a number of factors: a particular interest of Indian society at large in such matters and its readiness to support its institutionalised forms, but perhaps most of all, the absence of any central and all-embracing doctrinal authority. Naturally, the emergence of ever new religious teachers and movements made the formulation of ever new systems necessary.

Later Jainism

The apparent austerity of Jainism was complemented by a considerable culture-forming power, at least in certain regions of India and during certain periods. Moving from Gujārāt and Rājasthān southwards in the western half of India, via Mahārāṣṭra and Kārṇāṭaka. and ending in Tamilnadu, we travel through regions which at some time or other during the last two millennia have been strongly influenced by the Jains. Thus many of the various languages spoken in these regions were actually moulded by Jains as vehicles of literary expression. The Jain literature in Tamil, Kannada and Gujarati in particular is of staggering size. Besides, the Jains continued cultivating Prakrit (in its Māhārāṣṭrī form), frequently resorted to Sanskrit and made ample use of Apabhraṃśa (a literary language derived from an early medieval vernacular of the Gujārāt/Rājasthān area). Northern Mahārāṣṭra can be regarded as a very rough dividing line between the Śvetāmbara and Digambara branches, the latter belonging to the southern part.

In the south, Jainism flourished during almost the whole of the first millennium CE, though much later works were still produced in Tamil. In Gujārāt the Jains began to dominate the political and cultural scene towards the close of the first millennium CE, and, though suffering heavily from Islamic persecution, have maintained their prominence till the present day.

In the history of Tamil literature, the Jains are not only known for their ancient moralistic classics (like the *Tirukkuṟaḷ* and *Nalāṭiyār*). They also cultivated a large amount of local, originally secular, folklore and epic material. The best-known work in this category is the epic *Cilappatikāram* (perhaps of the fifth or sixth century CE). The year 892 CE saw the completion of another major literary enterprise. Began by Jinasena, continued by his disciple Guṇabhadra and finished by the latter's disciple Lokasena, under the title of the *Mahā-Purāṇa* (*Ādi-* and *Uttara-Purāṇa*) a grandiose vista of world history and the role of the Jaina saviour-figures in it was expressed in the prestigious Sanskrit. To the many later works dealing with these themes and written in various vernacular languages must be added, on the Śvetāmbara side, Hemacandra's *History of the 63 Great Men* (written in Sanskrit in the twelfth century in Gujārāt). On a gigantic scale Jainism has produced here its own version of the epic and purāṇic literature. Starting therefore with the origins of our present cosmic age, the figure of Ṛṣabha is presented as the Jain culture-hero, who not only made the Jain teaching available to our aeon, but also instituted social structures and so on. Twenty-three further such *tīrthaṅkaras*, religious founders, followed after him, the penultimate being Pārśva and the last one, the Mahāvīra. Alongside these figures, twelve universal emperors (*cakravartins*) are mentioned (three of whom also count as *tīrthaṅkaras*). In addition, from the Kṛṣṇa and Rāma stories were developed three series of nine Vāsudevas (equivalent to Kṛṣṇas), anti-Kṛṣṇas and Baladevas (equivalent to the Kṛṣṇas' half-brothers). These are the 63 heroes. By telling the life-stories of all these, the Jains could not only incorporate the material which also found expression in the *Mahābhārata*, *Rāmāyaṇa* and earlier Purāṇas; they could also draw on and develop a vast store of other stories, myths and legends.

Generally, the Jains were the great tellers of religious stories in India. This literature, obviously intended for the edification of lay people, is vast. In endlessly variegated form the key tenets of Jainism are shown to apply to a person's life: the pernicious effects greed and lust, hatred and violence have on subsequent existences. From among this almost unsurveyably large range of material, the story of Yaśodhara may be singled out because of its particularly frequent and sophisticated treatment; perhaps best known is the *Yaśastilaka-campū* of Somadeva, 959 CE. Because king Yaśodhara had permitted the 'sacrifice' of a cock made of dough, for many further existences he had to pay for this minimal act of violence by suffering the utmost cruelties.

Without apparently suffering a loss of their essential teaching and religious identity, the Jains adopted a variety of other features from their environment. Although in terms of their teaching the veneration of images cannot make any sense, the Jains took to temple building on a large scale. Images of the *tīrthaṅkaras* have been installed, *pūjā* is being performed and hymns full of the spirit of *bhakti* are sung. The *tīrthaṅkaras* in the state of *mokṣa* may not be addressable through these forms of devotion. But as well-intended pious acts these religious expressions are generally acknowledged to produce merit. But in fifteenth-century Gujārāt—possibly under the influence of Muslim ideas—a Jain layman, Loṅkā Śāha, founded a movement (the Sthānakavāsins) in opposition to the widespread Śvetāmbara acceptance of temple worship.

Given the extent to which Jain doctrine had been formulated from early times, it was far more difficult for the Jain philosophers to participate in the discussions and trends that dominated the Indian scene. What was developed over the centuries as the *syādvāda*, the 'teaching that [things] may be [this, or may be that]', must be regarded as a primarily defensive device. This means that there are always a whole range of possible viewpoints (a list of seven evolved) from which any item can be approached. No single statement can thus encompass the whole truth. However, a thinker like Kundakunda (a Digambara from the Deccan, perhaps fourth century CE) showed that adjustments to the current trends in Buddhist and Hindu thought were possible. The archaic emphasis on the materially conceived *karma* as the cause of *saṃsāra*, and the corresponding cultivation of physical modes of eradicating it, stood in stark contrast to most of Hindu and Buddhist thought. Where these did not focus on 'ignorance' as the cause of *saṃsāra*, and on meditation as the primary spiritual practice, they emphasised devotion, *bhakti*, and the role of divine grace. Kundakunda made 'ignorance' (*ajñāna*) the primary cause of *saṃsāra*. By distinguishing now a level of relative from that of ultimate truth, he argued that only on the former does the soul (*jīva*) appear to be active, and thus appear to be generating further *karma*. On the level of ultimate truth, the *jīva* merely perceives its own nature, and that as totally distinct from everything material. To realise this is, according to him, liberation. Such a new focus, away from *tapas* towards meditation (which naturally is the means for the *jīva* to realise the ultimate truth), was also made use of in a different context. Although the Jains on the whole did not participate in the 'tantric' developments to be mentioned in the next chapter, or merely externally adopted the usage of certain *mantras* and *yantras*, we do find traces of an antinomian attitude similar to that of the nominally Hindu *sants*. Apabhraṃśa works like the *Paramappapayāsu* (end of first millennium?) attack external religious practices (including the adherence to labels like 'śvetāmbara' and the inferior role of women in religion) and advocate the cultivation of inner spiritual values and of 'knowledge'.

It is very difficult to compare the role of Jainism with that of Buddhism in the context of the Indian religions. Given the almost total disappearance of Buddhist literature from India, it is impossible to assess the cultural face of Buddhism during the period studied here. Yet this itself may suggest a hint of an explanation. Possibly Buddhism suffered so much worse under the hands of the Muslims because it had far less contact with its lay populace—because it lacked the 'cultural face' Jainism consistently developed.

The Esoteric Traditions and Antinomian Movements

It was roughly the middle of the first millennium CE that witnessed the emergence of a whole new branch of religious literature. This consists of texts which tend to call themselves 'tantras'. It is not just the original meaning of the word 'tantra' which is disputed and far from clear. The nature of the material itself found here is still extremely obscure and its critical study has only just begun. The chapter on 'Śaivism and the tantric traditions' will summarise the results of current scholarship as far as material from Kashmir is concerned. Here some general comments will be made. Precisely because little critical study of the esoteric material has been available till very recently, all kinds of claims and global assessments by popularist writers could be made. Thus a concept 'Tantrism' (with the related adjective 'tantric') has gained great popularity, with its implied assumption that we are dealing here with a well-defined and coherent system of religious ideas and practices. But in reality, no such systematic coherence exists throughout the vast literature of the Tantras.

Historically speaking, it seems possible to explain the literary emergence of esoteric material by reference to the changed social and cultural circumstances in northern India after the collapse of the Gupta empire. A 'normative' and intellectual superstructure collapsed which made it possible for religious undercurrents to rise to the surface and find literary expression. It seems extremely unlikely that a new type of religion itself originated during this period. Indeed, externally not much is actually 'new' here. For most of the material found, earlier parallels could be cited. If anything, it is the combination of such material that is novel. Furthermore, it is the attitude and the purpose behind its application which are expressed now in a literary manner.

The term 'magic' is frequently used to describe or define the material found in the Tantras. But this is not a useful approach. It is in no way possible either to set up objective criteria for what features distinguish 'religion' from 'magic', or to reduce the enormous spectrum of religious activities in India to such a simplistic polarity. For example, the *mantra* is a particular combination of syllables (which may or may not have a direct linguistic meaning). Knowing it and reciting it is universally regarded as an act of actualising the particular power latent in the *mantra*. But Vedic hymns consist of '*mantras*', the worship of God in the temple is accompanied by *mantras* and yogic meditation may well be accompanied by the muttering of them. Yet in all three cases it is hardly possible to regard this as 'magic' or 'esoteric', or to ignore the distinctions between these three types of religion. However, if a person actually believes in the existence of an all-powerful God and then expects to gain personal access to that power directly through the recitation of the appropriate *mantra*, then this must be regarded as a fourth type. To call it 'magic' will still obscure those cases in which the practice has a consciously expressed transcendental objective ('to achieve liberation'). 'The tantric approach' will be used here as the term to refer to the type of religion which pursues the objective of gaining 'power', for whatever reason.

The following could be put forward as a very tentative general framework within which this type of religion could be assessed. Man lives in a universe which is pervaded by all kinds of forces. Many of them are destructive and threatening, others relate in a more positive manner to his life. What conventional society has on offer as the means of controlling these forces is believed to be limited and restrictive as to the realisation of man's full potential. There is, however, a knowledge available which the more adventurous and mature person can draw on and thereby improve that realisation radically. But it is esoteric, well guarded by a secret tradition. With the help of this esoteric knowledge it becomes possible to expose oneself to even the most dangerous and powerful of such universal forces and not just survive, but actually control them and absorb them for one's own fulfilment.

Such a global description implies various important features. The world-view is that of ordinary people, not that of the philosopher or theologian. The value-system of ordinary society is maintained. For example, a potentially fatal force is still perceived as such here. But by means of the esoteric knowledge it is now possible to come in contact with precisely the taboo areas shunned by ordinary society because of these dangerous forces. Finally, just as this knowledge itself, so its application remains a secret affair. Clearly we are dealing here with a form of antinomianism, but because of its secret nature it must be distinguished from other types (which are discussed below) which publicly reject certain conventional assumptions about what is 'dangerous' or forbidden. Naturally, in real life there will be a fair amount of overlap and fusion, but at least conceptually the differences of these types of antinomianism ought to be maintained.

When such ideas were given literary expression (however secret the texts themselves may then be kept), it became possible to draw upon the mainstream of the Indian intellectual scene. That means that the whole store of the philosophical and theological discussion could be utilised for the conceptualisation of this religion. Particularly prominent were the advaita-Vedānta, Śaiva theology, and the Mahāyāna, and that also means that typically 'Hindu' and typically 'Buddhist' formulations evolved. Yet the presence of mainstream terminology and concepts must not be mistaken for an intrinsic relationship between the tantric approach and other forms of Buddhist and Hindu religion.

Thus there are at least three layers that have to be distinguished. They are not just historical, but also social. At the basis, we have the 'raw material' upon which then the 'tantric approach' is imposed. This in turn was given metaphysical interpretation and thus linked with Buddhist and Hindu thought.

Attempts to define 'Tantrism' through catalogues of its 'raw material' necessarily fail, because all items of such a list are more or less Indian universals. *Mantras* and *yantras* (or *maṇḍalas*), powerful strings of syllables and combinations of visual patterns, are all-pervasive in Indian religion. So are *mudrās,* particular gestures of the hands and fingers, and *pūjā*, the rituals employed to propitiate, venerate or worship powerful non-human beings. The concept of *śakti* ('power'), abstract or personalised (particularly as a 'goddess'), occurs frequently in monotheistic and other systems of thought. Certain elements are socially restricted, which means they are 'natural' and legitimate for some classes of society, but not for others. Among these may be mentioned the consumption of meat and alcohol and the celebration of orgiastic fertility festivals (like Holi), Inevitably the concern for 'purity' of some classes of society necessitates the (legitimate) existence of other classes that remove (and thus handle) 'impurity'. Finally, certain phenomena would probably universally be regarded as taboo, like acts of wilful killing or the consumption of bodily excretions (faeces, urine, spittle, vomit, etc.), particularly of another person. All this is perceived not as objectively 'bad' (or even 'impure'), but as subjectively harmful and destructive.

To understand how the 'tantric approach' deals with this situation, it would be of primary importance to define the social position of the *tāntrika*. Unfortunately, little direct information on this is available, and we have to rely on the whole on inference. But given the fact that we are dealing with actual texts in Sanskrit (however incorrect it may be in some cases) and that certain rituals can be analysed as conscious and systematised acts of breaking social taboos, it appears appropriate to locate this position somewhere above the tribals, peasants, artisans and villagers generally, with whom some of the features (like alcohol, meat, 'impurity') occur naturally. For only from the vista of 'middle class' (or better, of higher castes) certain practices could appear as 'taboo'. Though it is useful for a social identification of the 'tantric approach' to concentrate on the breaking of taboos, this is obviously a far too limited overall definition. Certain types of ascetics have been suggested as more original practitioners of tantric rites.

At the heart of this religion lies the pursuit of power. Thus by drawing the right diagram (*yantra* or *maṇḍala*) and reciting the appropriate *mantras*, powerful beings can be brought down into the centre of the *maṇḍala* (or into the person himself). *Pūjā* may then be offered, and that could mean to oneself as the seat of that power which has been made to enter the body. Furthermore, many forces normally perceived to be dangerous can be invoked and/or treated ritually through items equally perceived to be dangerous: blood, alcohol, etc. The setting itself could be a realm ordinary people would never enter, in particular the cremation ground, and that during night-time. Although of no such overall importance in the Tantras themselves, one particular ritual has dominated the imagination of many Western writers on the subject. These are the five M's—a ritual involving five features which all begin with the letter *ma* in Sanskrit. At the beginning, there is *mada*, alcohol, consumed by the participants. Then there are dishes of *matsya* (fish) and *māṃsa* (meat). This is followed by *mudrā*, which in this context probably does not refer to gestures of the hand, but to a particular dish perceived as an aphrodisiac. Finally, there is *maithuna*, sexual intercourse. A host of interpretations have been proposed for this; moreover, there is enormous variation as to the precise context and the concrete details. Particularly when envisaged as practised in a cremation ground at night by male and female members of a secret cult who are not married to each other, it is not difficult to see in it a ritualised breaking of taboos. Powers are utilised which according to ordinary perception are so dangerous that they are kept 'taboo', that is, outside one's own person and realm. Moreover, the organisation of the ritual itself could suggest a progressive stimulation of sexual energies towards the final climax. But given the ritual context, such a climax is not perceived as merely physical. A force is released or realised which can be used for spiritual purposes.

How all this may work (whether specifically the five M's or any other such rituals) depends on many factors, which include theories of a quasi-physiological nature. Accordingly, we may find that ejaculation is prevented. Whilst emission of semen is regarded as 'waste' of energy, the ritualised intercourse rechannelises this energy, pushing it upwards a (nominal, i.e. non-physiological) duct. This is part of a more comprehensive model, which itself may be found in a wide range of contexts (including 'mainstream', post-classical yoga). Two primary, complementary powers are located inside the human body, one in the head and the other at the base of the spine. By activating the lower one, pushing it upwards and letting it unite with the top one, an initially 'diffuse' person can become integrated and in total control of all his faculties. Alternatively, the union of man and woman can be explained as achieving a fusion of powers that normally occur only separately.

Any application of the tantric approach to the practical raw material implies some specific conception of its rationale and mode of operation. Whilst in principle it may not be impossible to establish a chronological scale of such conceptions, in practice only the more advanced levels of this conceptualisation are available to us. In other words, with the present state of scholarship these religious practices only make sense to us when they are spelled out within a known metaphysical framework. As indicated above, such a framework is not fixed or unique; a variety of very different traditions may be employed in different contexts. In Hindu environments, a whole array of associations around the concept of '*śakti*' can be made use of. Philosophically, an in itself immutable and passive absolute can be envisaged as active (for example, as creating, maintaining and destroying the world) by envisaging *śaktis* inhering in it. Theologically, this may be concretised as Śiva and his goddesses, his *śaktis*, or as Kālī and her 'powers'. The tantric approach may now present itself as the concrete, ritual means of personally realising the unity of Śiva and his *śaktis*, of establishing individually the union of the absolute with the world of phenomena. In different words, liberation within the world can thus be achieved. Generally, the links with Śaivism are quite pronounced in tantric literature, and Śaivite symbolism and terminology is ubiquitous. But often it is not Śiva, but Kālī, who appears at the centre of such systems. Moreover, there are examples of a Vaiṣṇava and Kṛṣṇaite character. The Bengal Sāhajīyas draw heavily on the Kṛṣṇaism to which Caitanya gave shape in the sixteenth century, and from the twelfth century south Indian Śrīvaiṣṇavism knows a *Lakṣmī-Tantra*, a work quite popular in the official temple worship of the Pāñcarātra.

More complex is the Buddhist application of this material. But even here it is possible to correlate the intentions with standard Buddhist ideals. Late popular Mahāyāna Buddhism may have venerated Bodhisattvas and Buddhas on a large scale, but, in terms of Mahāyāna metaphysics, these could never be regarded as 'objective' realities or beings. Instead, they shared with all other phenomena the basic characteristic of being 'empty'. Particularly with the help of a model like that of the *trikāya* it was possible to emphasise the emptiness of all Buddha- and Bodhisattva-figures, while stating their 'reality' on the level of phenomenal existence. On this level, worship in temples and prayers addressed to them made sense. To proceed further and manipulate such figures ritually was in fact far less 'sacrilegious' than in a monotheistic Hindu system. For on the plane of absolute truth, no omnipotent absolute being can be envisaged. Moreover, the evolution of specific Bodhisattva- and Buddha-figures, with their mythologies, was a special development out of the original ideal that every good Buddhist should be a *bodhisattva*. The tantric approach allowed for precisely such an identification between the individual person and the—artificially projected—image of a (mythologised) Bodhisattva. As to the breaking of taboos, it could be argued that any view of the world that maintains as absolute a division of the respectable versus the forbidden is still limited and, in fact, characterised as fundamental ignorance. All phenomena are relative, because they condition each other. Ritually breaking taboos is a concrete way of transcending the level of the conditioned. Finally, the grand ideal of the Mahāyāna is the union of the perfections of wisdom and compassion. Now just as in Hindu contexts the conception of two complementary forces could be presented in Tantric contexts as the union of Śiva and *śakti*, Buddhism could envisage it as the ritual concretisation of the union of *prajñā* and *karuṇā*.

But in some ways, the Buddhist conceptualisation of the tantric approach differs fundamentally from the Hindu varieties. Thus it does not break any metaphysical taboos; there is no clash here between the conception of an omnipotent highest reality (say Bhagavān Śiva) and its tantric manipulation. That means, in its intentions tantric Buddhism is not esoteric, is not the alternative to an insufficient and mistaken mainstream religion. It simply presents itself as an easier, more efficient means of achieving standard Buddhist ideals, through methods that are appropriate for a feeble and decadent age. Thus when we sometimes find this form of Buddhism described as a third '*yāna*' (most often, 'Vajrayāna'), this is not really parallel to the critical self-definition of a Mahāyāna *vis-à-vis* the Hīnayāna. Tantric Buddhism applies the abstract insights of Mahāyāna thought to concrete, ritualised practice.

The tantric approach is not uniform in other respects as well. By no means all applications can be called religious in any sense of the word. Often quite practical aims are being pursued: increase of wealth, power (in a political or economic sense), victory in military matters, health, etc. As far as the latter aim is concerned, there is an overlap with an enormously complex and variegated range of material which all deals with 'healthy living' and curing diseases. This includes the use of drugs, elixirs, medicines, yoga and sexual practices. In such contexts we may well encounter the ideal of 'liberation' expressed as 'bodily immortality'. Secondly, where the tantric rituals are envisaged as operating on some internal aspect of the person, say mental or meditational, it was logical to internalise the ritual itself with its concrete, physical utensils, or present the latter through innocuous substitutes. A traditional classification of left- and right-hand Tantra refers to this possibility. Only the left-hand variety would physically and literally execute the rituals; the other variety obviously ceases to be truly antinomian.

Tantric Buddhism dominated the Indian scene during the last few hundred years of Buddhist presence in the sub-continent (until *c.* 1200 CE). China took in pre-Tantra Buddhism, and acted as a kind of filter when tantric material began to appear for a brief period. Only a minute amount of tantric materials was taken over, to become the Chen-yen (Japanese: Shingon) school. Tibet on the other hand encountered Buddhism during the flourishing phase of its tantric expression, and it is fundamentally this type of material which was translated and preserved in the Tibetan Canon (where hundreds of Tantras can be found). The Tibetans adopted tantric Buddhism not as an already fixed system, but as a still dynamic affair, and they actively continued the conceptualisation of the tantric approach in terms of Mahāyāna thought. But it would be unrealistic to assume that the north Indian Buddhist 'universities', where tantric Buddhism was cultivated, received from many Asian countries students and endowments merely because of the lofty ideal of achieving supreme enlightenment. As a system of gaining 'power', in a variety of senses, it had an attraction far beyond the strictly religious realm. The same applies to tantric Hinduism. Here the history has continued up to the modern time, although the practice of left-handed rituals must be assumed to have become extremely rare, if ever it played a significant role among non-ascetics. The boundaries between more abstruse forms of yoga, medicine, alchemy, *pūjā* and right-hand *tantra* have become almost totally blurred during the second millennium CE.

In some senses related to, and in other senses radically different from, the tantric approach is another component of the Indian religious scene. This may be called the 'antinomian movements'. What links them with the material discussed so far is a conscious rejection of certain socially accepted taboos, and of a belief in the efficacy of official religion. What is different is the rejection of any external expression of religion, including the forms of tantric ritual. Moreover, this antinomianism expresses itself publicly, without resorting to clandestine alternative or additional practices. Again, it is easy enough to draw conceptual distinctions; in reality the differences are blurred, particularly in the case of the 'right-handed' *tantra*, which has become 'domesticated'.

Such antinomian movements have occurred in most regions of India over most of its history. The following observations can do no more than provide a very general characterisation of these movements. While it is inevitable that every religion creates its own external forms of expression, the antinomian critics point out that a mere adherence to such outside manifestations cannot be regarded as 'true religion'. Institutionalisation allows for ossification: the inner life has died away, while the shells of outer form remain. Rituals, sacrifices, temple worship, yogic postures, social structures, sacred language, nocturnal tantric rites in cremation grounds—these and many similar phenomena may all be practised in a purely external, mechanical manner, without a commitment to an inner purification. Moreover, they may act as obstacles to the live religious realisation.

No study of the Indian religions would be accurate which did not pay attention to the permanent dynamism of evolving such forms (as signs of religious expression) and criticising them when they are perceived to have lost the life they are meant to contain. A classic example is obviously early Buddhism. Already here we see many factors at work which time and again during the following centuries generate similar antinomian attitudes. The Buddha quite consciously rejected 'Brahmanism', with its restrictive claim that only a minority of the population could have access to 'true religion', that the latter was contained in the Vedas, and that only the brahmins could be the legitimate guardians and ritual functionaries of this religious reality. The Mahāyāna in turn reacted against institutionalised forms of a slightly later Buddhism. In the course of the centuries, other areas of attack can be identified in 'Hinduism': its temple worship, folk rituals, forms of esoteric yoga and indeed tantric practices. What is set up as the live alternative is an inner religion that produces a real change in the person, non-ritualistic expressions, a fluidity that avoids solid and permanent structures (both literally and metaphorically), usage of the vernacular directly accessible to all members of a society and democratic and non-elitist social structures. The last mentioned point has often been called 'attack on the caste system', but this label is not very useful, for on the whole the attack was restricted to aspects of the social system which were discriminatory in religious matters alone. Generally it did not affect features like marriage or economic status. In terms of metaphysics, we can find time and again Buddhist undercurrents at work (for instance, in some of the Tamil Cittars). With the Mānbhāvs of Mahārāṣṭra some Jain influence might be detected. Advaita-Vedānta with its conception of oneness of all beings could be applied, and radical forms of monotheism (around Śiva or Viṣṇu) also produced antinomian movements. Frequently, commonsense and arguments derived from what resembles our 'proto-science' are used to demonstrate the meaninglessness of rituals etc. In northern India, after the gradual permeation of society by Islamic ideas, Sufism in particular (itself a potentially antinomian phenomenon) began to interact with the traditional Indian attack on ossified religion. The arrival of Western ideas about religion and democracy added a further theoretical basis for antinomian attitudes. In many cases at least, what has conventionally been described as 'reform Hinduism', with the West priding itself in having provided the inspiration, ought to be regarded as modern representatives of the age-old antinomian dynamism.

The information on antinomianism during the first millennium CE is relatively sparse; a separate section deals with various Śaivite movements that can still be identified. Towards the last few centuries of this millennium, the Apabhraṃśa language established itself as a lingua franca over wide areas of northern India. Derived from various local vernaculars, it produced a literature which included antinomian strands. Thus we have from this period Saraha's *Dohākośa*, a work that officially would belong to Tantric Buddhism, but in terms of its ideas is perhaps more typical of the antinomianism discussed here. The religious realisation is *sahaja*, 'innate' in man, and will occur 'spontaneously', once all external and ossified religious forms have been removed. The Jains also expressed similar ideas in works like the *Pāhuḍadohās* and *Paramappapayāsu*.

From around the thirteenth century, a more pronounced regionalism emerges, with the return to the actual contemporary vernaculars. Various antinomian movements were directly involved in this linguistic and literary change. Thus during the twelfth century, in what is today the state of Kārṇāṭaka, originated the Vīra-Śaivite or Liṅgayite movement, with Basavaṇṇa as its primary instigator. Monotheism (with Śiva at the centre) provided the metaphysical framework, but by attacking temple worship, brahmin rituals and the restrictions of the caste system (which in this particular case seems to have included the 'secular' side as well, i.e. marriage), the Liṅgayites are clearly antinomian. A large store of religious poetry in the vernacular Kannada (Kanarese) was produced by Basavaṇṇa and other poets like Allama-prabhu and the poetess Mahādevīyakka. The thirteenth century witnessed in neighbouring Mahārāṣṭra the rise of the Mānbhāvs (Mahānubhāvas) to whom Cakradhar gave its structure. This movement is characterised by a pronounced anti-Vedism and emphasis on asceticism. At a later stage, it developed the concept of the five Kṛṣṇas (which includes Cakradhar, the Hindu figure of Kṛṣṇa and the central deity, Parameśvara). It produced a sizeable literature in Marāṭhī. Both movements have continued up to the present day; the Liṅgayites in particular, with five million followers in 1959, constitute an important influence in Kārṇātaka. In Tamilnadu, Śrīvaiṣṇavism under Maṇavāḷa mā muṉi (fifteenth century CE) derived from the total submission to Viṣṇu's saving grace an alternative social structure which discarded all the paraphernalia of 'orthopraxy'.

In many other instances, less well-defined movements occurred. Thus in the Tamil-speaking region, we find a whole string of individual poets (from well back in the first millennium CE onwards), who are called Cittar (from Sanskrit Siddha) and who all share certain typically antinomian ideas. Northern Buddhism also knows of a series of Siddhas (which includes Saraha mentioned above). The theoretical centre of Siddha religion is at least the cultivation of *siddhis*, 'miraculous' powers gained through esoteric yogic practices. Closely related are the Nāthas who all over northern India have produced a more clearly defined movement. From Bengal must be mentioned the Bāuls, whose poetry has had a considerable impact on Bengali thought and religion. Here the interaction between Sufi and antinomian Hindu ideas is particularly strong, and indeed members of both religions join the (loosely defined) movement which still exists today.

Finally, in the Hindi-speaking regions of northern India we find another string of individual antinomian poets, the Sants. In most cases, these 'saints' did not create religious institutions as permanent frames for their ideas. Often from humble origins and also from Muslim backgrounds, they sang their religious songs on the market-places and by the roadside. Their deity is ultimately ineffable and beyond all human comprehension and conception. Thus they refer to it indiscriminately as Allah, Rām, etc. Divine saving grace is available everywhere; by purifying the heart and removing the obstacles of external religious forms, man can open himself up for it. Perhaps the most famous individual among the *sants* is Kabīr (fourteenth century). But it was Gurū Nānak (fifteenth century) and his nine successors who created a well-defined religious organisation within the overall framework of the sant tradition. This is the religion of the Sikhs (on which see the separate section pp. 714–25).

As an example of the continuity of the antinomian movements well into the nineteenth and twentieth centuries may be mentioned Nārāyaṇa-guru. He belonged to a relatively low caste of Kerala, but managed to acquire the Sanskrit learning which on the whole had been restricted to the highest castes. Not only did he make the teaching of Advaita-Vedānta available to his own caste-fellows by transposing it into the vernacular Malayalam language. From its teaching on the oneness of all beings he also derived a social programme that challenged established modes of religious practice.

No discussion of antinomian movements in India would be complete without a reference to the further histories of such movements within the context of Indian society. They all may set out to challenge society at large, in a variety of ways. But most end up once again contained within the overall social fabric, for example as yet another caste or caste-cluster. Internal hierarchies and status symbols evolve which produce a new form of stratification. The spontaneous religious poetry in the vernacular of the past poets gets collected and turns into a 'sacred scripture' (often no longer comprehensible due to linguistic changes in the community). Hagiographies of the grand saints of the past are produced, and often Sanskrit is resorted to in order to define the belief-system within the framework of the Vedānta. Temples are erected and modes of *pūjā* are developed, not just in honour of the central deity, but also of the images of the past saints (often regarded as incarnations of the deity). Even such *sants* who refused to create institutional structures for their religious message may be drawn into this development. Thus around the figures of Kabīr and Ravidās religious movements arose long after their deaths. Yet it would be a mistake to regard this return to external forms of expression simply as the reassertion of some ultimately static reality. The continuous emergence of new antinomian movements maintains a dynamism, and however formalised individual movements may become in due course, something genuinely new may well be added to the whole. For example, the way Mānbhāvs venerate Kṛṣṇa in their temples, Sikhs deal ritually with their Sacred Book and even the Jains worship at temple images of their Tīrthaṅkaras, is something new which cannot be subsumed under some general and fixed heading 'Hindu temple worship'.

Further Reading

Bechert, H. *Buddhismus, Staat und Gesellschaft in den Ländern des Theravāda-Buddhismus*, 3 vols. (Frankfurt/Wiesbaden, 1966–73)

—— and R. Gombrich (eds.) *The World of Buddhism* (Thames & Hudson, London, 1984)

Bhattacharyya, B. *Introduction to Buddhist Esoterism*, 2nd edn (Varanasi, 1964)
Brockington, J. *The Sacred Thread* (Edinburgh University Press, Edinburgh, 1981)
Carrithers, M. *The Forest Monks of Sri Lanka* (Oxford University Pres, Delhi, 1983)
Collins, S. *Selfless Persons—Imagery and Thought in Theravāda Buddhism* (Cambridge University Press, Cambridge, 1982)
Conze, E. *Buddhist Thought in India* (Allen & Unwin, London, 1962)
—— *A Short History of Buddhism* (Allen & Unwin, London, 1980)
Dasgupta, S. *A History of Indian Philosophy*, 5 vols. (Cambridge University Press, 1922–49)
Dasgupta, S.B. *An Introduction to Tantric Buddhism* (Berkeley, 1974)
Dayal, H. *The Bodhisattva Doctrine in Buddhist Sanskrit Literature* (Kegan Paul, London, 1932)
Dhavamony, M. *The Love of God According to Śaiva-Siddhānta* (Oxford University Press, Oxford, 1971)
Edgerton, F. *The Beginnings of Indian Philosophy* (Allen & Unwin, London, 1965)
Frauwallner, E. *Geschichte der indischen Philosophie*, 2 vols. (Otto Müller, Salzburg, 1953 & 1956)
——*Die Philosophie des Buddhismus*, 3rd edn (Akademie-Verlag, Berlin (GDR), 1969)
Foucher, A. *The Life of the Buddha* (Middletown (Con.), 1963)
Gombrich, R. *Precept and practice—Traditional Buddhism in the Rural Highlands of Ceylon* Clarendon Press, Oxford, 1971.
Gonda, J.*Vedic Literature* (Harrassowitz, Wiesbaden, 1975)
Gupta, S., D. Hoens and T. Goudriaan *Hindu Tantrism* (Brill, Leiden, 1979)
Hacker, P. *Prahlada—Werden und Wandlungen einer Idealgestalt*, 2 vols. (Steiner, Wiesbaden, 1959)
Hardy, F. *Viraha-bhakti—The Early History of Kṛṣṇa Devotion in South India* (Oxford University Press, Delhi, 1983)
Hawley, J.S. and D.M. Wulff (eds.) *The Divine Consort—Radha and the Goddesses of India* (Berkeley Religious Studies Series, Berkeley, 1982)
Hiriyanna, M. *Outlines of Indian Philosophy* (Allen & Unwin, London, 1967)
Jaina, P.S. *The Jaina Path of Purification* (Motilal Banarsidass, Delhi, 1979)
Keith, A.B. *The Religion and Philosophy of the Veda and Upanishads* (Harvard University Press, Cambridge, Mass., 1925)
O'Flaherty, W.D. *Asceticism and Eroticism in the Mythology of Śiva* (Oxford University Press, London, 1973)
—— *Hindu Myths* (Penguin Books, Harmondsworth, 1975)
Rahula, W. *What the Buddha Taught*, 2nd edn (Gordon Fraser, Bedford, 1972)
Ramanujan, A.K. *Speaking of Śiva* (Penguin Books, Harmondsworth, 1973)
Sangharakshita, B. *A Survey of Buddhism* (Shambala, Boulder (Colorado) and Windhorse, London, 1980)
Schubring, W. *The Doctrine of the Jainas* (Motilal Banarsidass, Delhi, 1962)
Schumann, H.W. *Buddhism—An Outline of its Teachings and Schools* (Rider & Co., London, 1973)
Sontheimer, G. *Biroba, Mhaskoba und Khaṇḍobā* (Steiner, Wiesbaden, 1976)
Spiro, M.E. *Buddhism and Society—A Great Tradition and its Burmese Vicissitudes* (New York, 1970)
Vaudeville, C. *Kabīr*, vol. 1 (Clarendon Press, Oxford, 1974)
Williams, R. *Jaina Yoga* (Oxford University Press, London, 1963)
Zaehner, R.C. *Hinduism* (Oxford University Press, London, 1966)
Zvelebil, K. *The Poets of the Power* (Rider & Co., London, 1974)

36 Śaivism and the Tantric Traditions

Alexis Sanderson

The term Śaivism here refers to a number of distinct but historically related systems comprising theology, ritual, observance and yoga, which have been propagated in India as the teachings of the Hindu deity Śiva. A Śaiva is one who practices such a system. To understand the term to mean 'a worshipper of Śiva' or 'one whose deity is Śiva' is less precise; for a Śaiva may well be a worshipper not of Śiva but of the Goddess (Devī). Though she is commonly represented as the consort of Śiva and, theologically, as that god's inherent power (*śakti*), it is none the less the defining mark of certain forms of Śaivism that she is seen as transcending this marital and logical subordination.

The scriptural revelations of the Śaiva mainstream are called Tantras, and those that act in accordance with their prescriptions are consequently termed Tantrics (*tāntrika*). The term *tantra* means simply a system of ritual or essential instruction; but when it is applied in this special context it serves to differentiate itself from the traditions that derive their authority from the Vedas (direct revelation: *śruti*) and a body of later texts that claim to be Veda-based (indirect revelation: *smṛti*). This corpus of *śruti* and *smṛti* prescribes the rites, duties and beliefs that constitute the basic or orthodox order and soteriology of Hindu society. The Tantrics however saw their own texts as an additional and more specialised revelation (*viśeṣaśāstra*) which offers a more powerful soteriology to those who are born into this exoteric order. The Tantric rituals of initiation (*dīkṣa*) were held to destroy the rebirth-generating power of the individual's past actions (*karma*) in the sphere of Veda-determined values, and to consubstantiate him with the deity in a transforming infusion of divine power.

The Śaivas were not the only Tantrics. There were also the Vaiṣṇava Tantrics of the Pāñcarātra system, whose Tantras, considered by them to be the word of the deity Viṣṇu, prescribed the rituals, duties and beliefs of the devotees of Vāsudeva in his various aspects (*vyūha*) and emanations (*vibhava*, *avatāra*). In addition to these two major groups of Tantrics there were Sauras, followers of Tantras revealed by the Sun (Sūrya); but while we have access to a number of Vaiṣṇava Tantras and to a vast corpus of Śaiva materials, the Saura tradition is silent. An early Śaiva Tantra (*Śrīkaṇṭhīyasaṃhitā*) lists a canon of 85 Tantras of the Sun, but not one of these these nor any other Saura Tantra has survived.

The production of Tantric revelations was not limited to those who accepted the supernatural authority of the Vedas. It went on, though on a much smaller scale, among the Jains, while the Buddhists added an enormous Tantric corpus to their canonical literature during the period *c.* 400–750 CE. By the end of this period the system of the Tantras, called 'the Way of the Diamond' (Vajrayāna) or 'of Mantras' (Mantrayāna), was generally recognised among the followers of the Greater Way (Mahāyāna) as the highest and most direct means to liberation (*nirvāṇa*), and its esoteric deities were enshrined in the monasteries as the high patrons of the faith. The Tibetans, who received Buddhism at this stage of its development, preserve, in the Tantric section of their canon, translations from the Sanskrit of almost 500 revealed texts and over 2000 commentaries and explanatory works. Of these more than three quarters concern Tantras of the most radical kind, those of the Higher and Supreme Yogas (*Yogottara-tantras* and *Yogānuttara-tantras*).

All these Tantrics were similarly related to the traditional forms of religion, the Buddhists to the monastic discipline and the Vaiṣṇavas and Śaivas to Vedic orthopraxy. They were excluded by the traditionalists because they went beyond the boundaries of these systems of practice. But the Tantrics themselves, while excluding these exclusivists, included their systems as the outer level of a concentric hierarchy of ritual and discipline.

In those communities in which it was possible or desirable to add to the exoteric tradition this second, more esoteric level, there might be forms of the Tantric cult in which this transcendence entailed the infringement of the rules of conduct (*ācāra*) which bound the performer of ritual at the lower, more public, level of his practice. Thus some rites involved the consumption of meat, alcohol and other impurities, even sexual intercourse with women of untouchable castes (*antyaja*). These practices originated as part of the magical technology of certain extremist orders of Śaiva ascetics. They passed over into the married majority; but when they did so, they survived unrevised only in limited circles. The general trend—and this was also so in the case of Tantric Buddhism—was to purify the rites by taking in everything except the elements of impurity. This left the essential structure intact: one worshipped the same deity, with the same complex of emanations or subordinate deities, *mantras*, deity-enthroning diagrams (*maṇḍalas*), and ritual gestures and postures (*mudrās*). The spread of the Tantric cults in Indian religion is largely the history of this process of domestication and exotericisation.

The followers of these cults, even in their undomesticated form, should not be seen as rebels who rejected a ritualised social identity for a liberated cult of ecstasy. This popular view of Tantrism overlooks the highly-structured ritual contexts (Tantric and non-Tantric) of these un-Vedic practices. A person who underwent a Tantric initiation (*dīkṣā*) was less an anti-ritualist than a super-ritualist. He was prepared to *add* more exacting and limiting ritual duties to those which already bound him. Indeed he has much in common with the most orthodox of Hindus, the *śrauta* sacrificer, who transcended the simple and universal domestic rites prescribed in the secondary scripture (*smṛti*) to undertake the great rituals of the primary and more ancient revelation (*śruti*). Though the *śrauta* and the Tantric occupied the opposite ends of the spectrum of Hinduism they shared the character of being specialists of intensified ritual above the more relaxed middle ground of the *smārtas* (the followers of *smṛti*). This similarity is carried through into their doctrines of liberation from rebirth (*mokṣa*). Both the *śrauta* tradition articulated by the Bhāṭṭa Mīmāṃsakas and the Tantric represented by the Śaivas stood apart from the mainstream by holding that the mere performance of the rituals prescribed by their respective scriptures is a sufficient cause of final liberation (see pp. 691ff.). It is this ritualism which largely accounts for the rapid decline of the Tantric traditions in recent decades. The complex obligations and time-consuming rituals which the Tantric takes on for life can hardly be accommodated within the schedule of the modern employee.

Un-Vedic though it was, the Tantric tradition was destined to have a far greater influence than the *śrauta* on the middle ground. While the *śrauta* tradition all but died out, the Tantric came to pervade almost all areas of Indian religion. The distinction between the Vedic and the Tantric in religion continued to be crucial, and it was drawn in such a way that the Tantric continued to be the tradition of a minority; but what was called Vedic here was essentially Tantric in its range of deities and liturgical forms. It differed from the properly Tantric principally in its *mantras*. This became the chief formal criterion: in Vedic worship (*pūjā*) the actions that compose the liturgy were empowered by the recitation of Vedic *mantras* drawn from the *Ṛgveda* and *Yajurveda* rather than by that of the heterodox *mantras* of the Tantras. At the same time these de-Tantricised reflexes of Tantric worship were non-sectarian. While properly Tantric worship was more or less exclusive, being emphatically centred in a particular deity, Vedic domestic worship was inclusive. Its most typical form is the *pañcāyatanapūjā*, the worship of the five shrines, in which offerings are made to the five principal deities, Śiva, Viṣṇu, Sūrya, Gaṇapati and the Goddess (Devī). The scriptural authority for these neo-Vedic rituals was provided by the indirect revelation (*smṛti*) and in particular by the ever-expanding Purāṇas, though the exact text of worship is generally a matter of unascribed tradition. Such worship is therefore called *smārta* ('*smṛti*-based') or *paurāṇika* ('Purāṇa-based'), or, where the properly Vedic or *śrauta* tradition is completely absent, simply *vaidika* ('Veda-based'). Its form in a particular community is largely the product of the history of the various Tantric traditions within that community. An example of this will be given below, when we consider the religion of medieval Kashmir (see pp. 701–4).

What follows falls into two parts. In the first I present Śaivism on the evidence of what survives, mostly unpublished, of its earliest scriptural sources. In most of this material the domestication of which I have spoken above has yet to begin. We shall therefore be looking in the main at traditions of Śaiva asceticism. Here the married man (*gṛhastha*) is altogether absent or at best subordinate. In the second part (pp. 690–704) we shall consider what happened to these traditions when they were domesticated. Our evidence here is the literature of the Śaiva community of Kashmir from the ninth century onwards.

This second body of texts is our earliest datable and locatable evidence for the Śaiva traditions. How much earlier than these Kashmiri works the scriptures to which they refer were composed cannot be decided yet with any precision. At best we can say that the main body of these early Tantras must have been composed between about 400 and 800 CE. To this we can add some relative chronology. We know even less about where these Tantras were composed or about the areas within which they were followed. However I incline to the view that when these traditions became the object of sophisticated Kashmiri exegesis between the ninth and thirteenth centuries they were widely represented throughout India. It is certain that the Kashmiri and the Newars of the Kathmandu valley looked out on much the same distribution and interrelation of Śaiva Tantric cults at this time, and it is highly probable that each community inherited these traditions independently by participating in a more widespread system, which may have included even the Tamil-speaking regions of the far south of the subcontinent.

The Kashmiri exegesis considered in the second part is a local tradition of much more than local impact. In a very short time it was acknowledged as the standard both in its theological metaphysics and in its liturgical prescription among the Śaivas of the Tamil south. This was the case in the Śaiva Siddhānta (see pp. 691–2), the Trika (see pp. 692–6), the Krama (see pp. 696–9), and the cults of Tripurasundarī (see pp. 688–9) and Kubjikā (see pp. 686–8). Consequently, while the Hindu culture of Kashmir declined in influence and vitality after the thirteenth century with large-scale conversion to Islam and periodic persecutions, the Tantrics of the far south continued the classical tradition, and through their many and outstanding contributions to Tantric literature guaranteed it a pan-Indian influence down to modern times. These southern and subsequent developments are unfortunately beyond the scope of this essay.

The Atimārga and the Mantramārga

The teaching of Śiva (*śivaśāsana*) which defines the Śaivas is divided between two great branches or 'streams' (*srotas*). These are termed the Outer Path (Atimārga) and the Path of Mantras (Mantramārga). The first is accessible only to ascetics, while the second is open both to ascetics and to married home-dwellers (*gṛhastha*). There is also a difference of goals. The Atimārga is entered for salvation alone, while the Mantramārga promises both this and, for those that so wish, the attainment of supernatural powers (*siddhis*) and the experience of supernal pleasures in the worlds of their choice (*bhoga*). The Atimārga's Śaivism is sometimes called Raudra rather than Śaiva. This is because it is attributed to and concerned with Śiva in his archaic, Vedic form as Rudra (the 'Terrible'), the god of wild and protean powers outside the *śrauta* sacrifice. It has two principal divisions, the Pāśupata and the Lākula.

The Pāśupata Division of the Atimārga

The ascetic observance (*vrata*) which is this system's path to salvation is the Pāśupata. It bears this name because its promulgation is attributed to Rudra as Paśupati (the 'Master [*-pati*] of the Bound [*paśu-*]'). Paśupati is believed by the followers of this tradition (the Pāśupatas) to have appeared on earth as Lakulīśa by entering and re-animating a brahmin's corpse in a cremation ground. Thus yogically embodied he gave out the cult's fundamental text, the *Pāśupata Aphorisms* (*Pāśupatasūtras*). Our principal source for the detail of the tradition is Kauṇḍinya's commentary on this text. It has been suggested on slender evidence that this commentator belongs to the fourth century. The Pāśupata cult itself, at least that form of it which derives itself from Lakulīśa, is at least two centuries older.

The Pāśupata observance (*pāśupata-vrata*) was restricted to brahmin males who had passed through the orthodox rite of investiture (*upanayana*), which gives an individual access to his Veda and full membership of his community. The stage of life (*āśrama*) from which such a brahmin became a Pāśupata was irrelevant. He might be a celibate student (*brahmacārin*), a married home-dweller (*gṛhastha*), a hermit dwelling in the wild (*vānaprastha*), or a peripatetic mendicant (*bhikṣu*). Transcending this orthodox classification he entered a 'fifth' life-stage, that of the Perfected (*siddha-āśrama*).

The final goal of the Pāśupatas was the end of suffering (*duḥkhānta*). It means just this, but was also conceived positively as the assimilation of Rudra's qualities of omniscience, omnipotence and so forth at the time of one's death. This was the state of final liberation and it was to be achieved through four stages of discipline. In the first the ascetic lived by a temple of Śiva. His body was to be smeared with ashes and he was to worship the deity in the temple by dancing and chanting, boisterous laughter (*aṭṭahāsa*), drumming on his mouth (*huḍḍukkāra*), and silent meditation on five *mantras* of the *Yajurveda*, the five *brahma-mantras* which in course of time would be personified as the five faces of Śiva.

In the second stage he left the temple. Throwing off all the outward signs of his observance he moved about in public pretending to be crippled, deranged, mentally deficient or indecent. Passers-by being unaware that these defects were feigned spoke ill of him. By this means the Pāśupata provoked an exchange in which his demerits passed to his detractors and their merits to him. By acting in this way he was simply making unorthodox use of a thoroughly orthodox principle. He was exploiting his ritual status as one who had undergone a rite of consecration (*dīkṣā*) to initiate an observance (*vrata*); for in the *śrauta* system one bound by the observance (*vrata*) consequent on consecration (*dīkṣā*) for the Soma sacrifice was similarly dangerous to anyone who might speak ill of him.

Purified by this period of *karma*-exchange, the Pāśupata withdrew in the third stage to a remote cave or deserted building to practise meditation through the constant repetition of the five *mantras*. When he had achieved an uninterrupted awareness of Rudra by this means, so that he no longer required the support of the *mantras*, he left his place of seclusion and moved into a cremation ground to wait for death. While previously the Pāśupata had begged for his sustenance he now lived on whatever he could find there. This fourth stage ended with his life. Entering the stage of completion (*niṣṭhā*) with the falling away of his body and the last traces of suffering, he was believed to experience the infusion of the qualities of Rudra. The cause of this final liberation was not thought to be any action of his, but simply the grace or favour of Rudra himself.

The Lākula Division of the Atimārga

The second division of the Atimārga, that of the Lākula ascetics, developed from within the original Pāśupata tradition. It accepted the authority of the *Pāśupata Aphorisms* and maintained both the *mantras* and the basic practices of its prototype. However, its special discipline required a more radical transcendence of Vedic values. After his consecration (*dīkṣā*) the ascetic

> should wander, carrying a skull-topped staff (*khaṭvāṅga*) and an alms-bowl fashioned from a human cranium. His hair should be bounded up in a matted mass (*jaṭā*) or completely shaved. He should wear a sacred thread (*upavīta*) [the emblem of orthodox investiture (*upanayana*)] made from snake-skins and he should adorn himself with a necklace of human bone. He may wear nothing but a strip of cloth to cover his private parts. He must smear himself with ashes and decorate himself with the ornaments of his God. Knowing that all things are Rudra in essence he should

hold firmly to his observance as Rudra's devotee. He may eat and drink anything. No action is forbidden to him. For he is immersed in contemplation of Rudra, knowing that no other deity will save him.

Niśvāsatattvasaṃhitā (MS), ch. 4.

Here the ascetic took on a more radical aspect of Rudra's nature as the outsider within the Vedic religion. He became Rudra the brahmin-slayer. For it is ruled in orthodox sources that one who is guilty of this terrible crime may exonerate himself only if he removes himself from society for twelve years, lives in a cremation ground and carries the skull-bowl (*kapāla*) and the skull-staff (*khaṭvāṅga*) when he goes forth to beg for food. Thus the Lākula's observance, generally called that of the skull (*kapālavrata*), is also known as that of exile, 'of those that are outside the world' (*lokātītavrata*). It is also referred to as the Greater Pāśupata Observance (*mahāpāśupatavrata*). While the Pāśupata ascetic's outsideness was limited to the system of life-stages (*atyāśramavrata*), the Lākula skull-bearer was to abandon the more basic notion of the pure and the impure.

The Kālāmukha ascetics who are known from many south Indian inscriptions from the ninth to thirteenth centuries were part of this Lākula division of the Atimārga. Doxographic material from this region records among their practices bathing in the ashes of the cremated (their milder predecessors had been content with the ashes of cow dung), eating these ashes and worshipping Rudra in a vessel filled with alcoholic liquor. This mode of worship was common in the rituals of the Kaula Śaivas (see pp. 679–89), but there is no reason to think that it was connected here as there with rituals involving sexual intercourse. It appears that these followers of Rudra the solitary penitent were bound by strict vows of celibacy.

The Lākulas had their own canon of scriptures concerned with both theology (*jñāna*) and ritual (*kriyā*), the eight *Authorities* (*Pramāṇas*). Of these nothing survives but their names and a single quotation from one of them, the *Pañcārtha-Pramāṇa*, in the works of the Kashmiri Kṣemarāja. For their doctrines we have an account of Lākula soteriology and cosmography in the *Niśvāsatattvasaṃhitā* quoted above, and a few scattered discussions in later Śaiva sources from Kashmir. From this we can see that the Lākulas had already developed most of the detailed hierarchy of worlds (*bhuvanādhvan*) which characterises the later Mantramārga. The Lākula ascends to his salvation through a succession of worlds, each governed by its own manifestation of Rudra. The highest of these is the world of the Rudra Dhruveśa. Reaching this he attains liberation, a state of omniscience void of activity.

In the closely clustered systems which form the Mantramārga the soul of the initiate is raised through such a world-hierarchy at the time of his consecration. The difference is that the hierarchy has been further extended. It contains that of the Lākulas, but adds a number of new worlds above Dhruveśa's. The Lākula cosmos was itself the outcome of such a process of extension. For immediately below Dhruveśa is the world of the Rudra Tejīśa. This was the final goal of the Vaimalas, a superseded group about whom our surviving sources tell us little but this. Further down the scale are the worlds of the Rudras Kṣemeśa and Brahmaṇaḥsvāmin. These were the cosmic termini of two other obscure Pāśupata groups, the Mausulas and the Kārukas.

The Mantramārga

It is clear that the cosmos of the Mantramārga grew out of that of the Atimārga by the same process of competitive extension which set the Lākulas above the Vaimalas, and the Vaimalas above the Mausulas and the Kārukas. And there are other continuities between the two Paths in the fields of ritual, iconography, *mantras* and observances (*vrata*). However, in spite of these continuities, there is a fundamental difference of character between the two main branches of the Śaiva tradition. While the Atimārga is exclusively liberationist, the Mantramārga, though it accommodates the quest for liberation, is essentially concerned with the quest for supernatural experience (*bhoga*).

This difference might be thought to correspond to that between the aspirations of the original ascetics and the newly admitted married householders. On the contrary, it corresponds to that between two varieties of ascetic. For in the Mantramārga it is the ascetics who are principally concerned with the attainment of powers, the path of liberation being largely the domain of the men in the world; and it is the methods by which power may be attained that are the main subject matter of the Mantramārga's scriptures. The gnostic home-dwellers, who would come in time to dominate the Mantramārga, are here the unmarked category of aspirant. They are defined by the fact that they do *not* involve themselves with the concerns which generated not only the greater part of their texts but also the system's internal diversity. For it was for the sake of the power-seeker that there developed the extraordinary variety of rites, deities and *mantras* which sets the Mantramārga apart from the purely gnostic Atimārga.

The history of the expanding hierarchy of the Rudra-worlds shows that the Mantramārga is later than the Atimārga. None the less, the dichotomy between the liberation-seeking and the power-seeking forms of Śaiva asceticism is more ancient than the present corpus of Mantramārgic texts. The latter contain more archaic strata at which the superior deities of the developed Mantramārga give way to the earlier Rudra. If we compare these text-elements with the Rudra cult of the Atimārga, we see that the dichotomy which underlies the later form of the division is between a solitary and celibate Rudra in the Atimārga and a Rudra associated with bands of protean and predominantly female spirits in the background of the Mantramārga. In the fully developed and diversified Mantramārga this association is but one aspect of that with feminine power (*śakti*) conceived more universally. It is this association which most obviously marks off the Mantramārga from the *śakti*-less Atimārga. We shall see that within the Mantramārga the major divisions correspond to different representations of this association.

The Tantras of the Śaiva Siddhānta

While our evidence for the Atimārga is very sparse, the Mantramārga can be studied in an enormous body of Sanskrit texts. The scriptures of the Mantramārga fall into two groups. On the one hand is the well-defined and relatively homogeneous canon of texts (the ten *Śiva-Āgamas*, the eighteen *Rudra-Āgamas* and attached scriptures) that constitute the authority of the tradition known to itself and others both in the scriptures and later as the *Śaiva Siddhānta*. On the other hand is a much more diverse, numerous and variously listed body of revelations known as the scriptures of Bhairava (*Bhairava-Āgamas*) or collectively as the Teaching of Bhairava (*Bhairavaśāstra*).

The Śiva forms of both are visualised as skull-bearing denizens of the cremation grounds. In the Śaiva Siddhānta, however, the god lacks the aura of terrifying and ecstatic power which is emphasised in his manifestations in the tradition of Bhairava ('the Fearsome'). Similarly, while the concept of feminine power (*śakti*) is found throughout the Mantramārga, it tends in the Śaiva Siddhānta to move away from personification as the Goddess or goddesses towards metaphysical abstraction. It is seen here principally as the creative power of the male Deity, manifest in the cosmic and soteriological process and embodied in his *mantra*-forms. In the daily ritual of the initiate the deity is worshipped, like the Rudra of the Atimārga, without a female consort. Linked to this is the purity of the mode of his worship. There is none of the offering of alcoholic drinks, blood and meat that typifies the rituals of the rest of the Mantramārga, with its greater emphasis on feminine and transgressive power.

The Tantras of Bhairava: Kāpālika Śaivism

The Tantras of Bhairava, so called because they take the form of his answers to the questions of the Goddess (Devī, Bhairavī), have been variously listed and classified in different parts of the corpus. The classification given here corresponds, I believe, to the main structure of the Śaiva tradition outside the Śaiva Siddhānta at the time when the Kashmiri began their work of post-scriptural systematisation in the ninth and tenth centuries.

Within these Tantras there is a primary division between those of the Seat of Mantras (Mantrapīṭha) and those of the Seat of Vidyās (Vidyāpīṭha). The latter are either Union Tantras (*Yāmala-tantras*) or

Power Tantras (*Śakti-tantras*). Within the latter one may distinguish between the Tantras of the Trika (or rather of what was later called the Trika) and material dealing with cults of the goddess Kālī. Tantras which teach the cult of Tumburu-bhairava and his four sisters (Jayā, Vijayā, Jayantī and Aparājitā) are fitted into this scheme as a third division of the Vidyāpīṭha. But this is artificial. It accommodates a tradition whose importance had been superseded by that of the Mantrapīṭha (the cult of Svacchanda-bhairava) to the extent that it was no longer part of the main structure. No more will be said of this minor tradition here.

Figure 36.1: The Structure of the Mantramārga

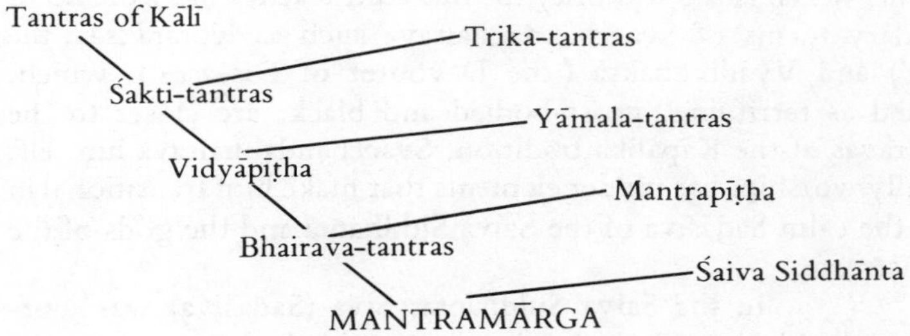

This arrangement is hierarchical. Whatever is above and to the left sees whatever is below it and to the right as lower revelation. It sees itself as offering a more powerful, more esoteric system of ritual (*tantra*) through further initiation (*dīkṣā*). As we ascend through these levels, from the Mantrapīṭha to the Yāmala-tantras and thence to the Trika and the Kālī cult, we find that the feminine rises stage by stage from subordination to complete autonomy.

The Mantrapīṭha and the Cult of Svacchandabhairava

At the beginning of this ascent is the Seat of Mantras (Mantrapīṭha). This term expresses the fact that this group of Tantras emphasises the masculine, while in the Seat of Vidyās (Vidyāpīṭha) it is the feminine that predominates (the nouns *mantra* and *vidyā*, which both signify the sacred sound-formulas, being masculine and feminine respectively).

The basic cult of the Mantrapīṭha is that of Svacchandabhairava ('Autonomous Bhairava') also known euphemistically as Aghora ('the Un-terrible'). White, five-faced (the embodiment of the five *brahma-mantras*) and eighteen-armed, he is worshipped with his identical consort Aghoreśvarī, surrounded by eight lesser Bhairavas within a circular enclosure of cremation grounds. He stands upon the prostrate corpse of Sadāśiva, the now transcended Śiva-form worshipped in the Śaiva Siddhānta.

The traditions of the Bhairava Tantras are Kāpālika, the basic form of their ascetic observance being that of the skull (*kapālavrata/mahāvrata*). The difference between this and the Lākula form of this observance is largely a matter of the basic difference of the Mantramārga stated above. The term Kāpālika is reserved here for this Mantramārgic segment of the Śaiva culture of the cremation grounds.

This Kāpālika background is evident from the iconography of the divine couple. Worshipped within an enclosure of cremation grounds they themselves wear the bone ornaments and brandish the skull-staff (*khaṭvāṅga*) of the Kāpālika tradition. None the less these features are not emphasised here to the extent that they are in the Vidyāpīṭha. Though the *Svacchandatantra*, which is the authority for this cult, teaches the worship of certain secondary forms of Svacchandabhairava such as Koṭarākṣa ('the Hollow-Eyed') and Vyādhibhakṣa ('the Devourer of Diseases'), which, being visualised as terrifying, gross-bodied and black, are closer to the standard Bhairavas of the Kāpālika tradition, Svacchandabhairava himself, the deity of daily worship, has milder elements that make him transitional in type between the calm Sadāśiva of the Śaiva Siddhānta and the gods of the Kāpālika mainstream.

In the Śaiva Siddhānta, Śiva (Sadāśiva) was worshipped alone. In the Mantrapīṭha he is joined in worship by his consort as the personification of *śakti*. Iconically she is his equal. But the larger ritual context shows that she is still subordinate. Her feminine presence is not reinforced by secondary goddesses in the circuit (*āvaraṇa*) that surrounds the couple. Furthermore Svacchandabhairava is worshipped alone after he has been worshipped with his consort. His appearance with Aghoreśvarī is his lower form.

The Vidyāpīṭha

With the ascent to the Vidyāpīṭha the Śaiva entered a world of ritual in which these last restraints on *śakti* dissolved. He was consecrated in the cults of deities who presided in their *maṇḍalas* over predominantly female pantheons, and who passed as he ascended to the left from Bhairavas with consorts, to Goddesses above Bhairavas, to the terrible Solitary Heroines (*ekavīrā*) of the cults of Kālī.

If in the cult of Svacchandabhairava the Kāpālika culture of the cremation grounds was somewhat in the background, here it is pervasive. The initiate gained access to the powers of these deities by adopting the observance of the Kāpālikas. With his hair matted and bound up with a pin of human bone, wearing earrings, armlets, anklets and a girdle, all of the same substance, with a sacred thread (*upavīta*) made of twisted corpse-hair, smeared with ashes from the cremation-pyres, carrying the skull-bowl, the skull-staff and the rattle-drum (*ḍamaru*), intoxicated with alcohol, he alternated periods of night-wandering (*niśāṭana*) with worship (*pūjā*) in which he invoked and gratified the deities of the *maṇḍala* into which he had been initiated. This gratification required the participation of a *dūtī*, a consecrated consort, with whom he was to copulate in order to produce the mingled sexual fluids which, with blood and other impurities of the body, provided the offering irresistible to this class of deities.

The Cult of Yoginīs. Accessible from the main cults of the Vidyāpīṭha, and underlying them in a more or less constant form, is the more ancient cult of Rudra/Bhairava in association with female spirits (Yoginīs). In the Atimārga and thence in the Mantramārga the series of cosmic levels (*bhuvanādhvan*) is governed by Rudras. When the initiate passed into this subjacent tradition he found that this masculine hierarchy was replaced by ranks of wild, blood-drinking, skull-decked Yoginīs. Radiating out from the heart of the Deity as an all-pervasive network of power (*yoginījāla*), they re-populated this vertical order of the Śaiva cosmos, appropriated the cycle of time (ruling as incarnations in each of the four world-ages (*yuga*)), and irradiated sacred space by sending forth emanations enshrined and worshipped in power-seats (*pīṭha*) connected with cremation grounds throughout the sub-continent.

The goal of the initiate was to force or entice these Yoginīs to gather before him and receive him into their band (*yoginīgaṇa*), sharing with him their miraculous powers and esoteric knowledge. The time favoured for such invocations was the fourteenth night of the dark fortnight, the night of the day of spirits (*bhūtadina*); and the most efficacious site was the cremation ground, the foremost of their meeting-places. The Śiva worshipped in these rites is Manthāna-Rudra (or Manthāna-Bhairava), a four-faced and therefore secondary or archaic form. Not 'married' to the Goddess as in the cults of entry, he is rather the wild ascetic who leads the Yoginī hordes (*yoginīgaṇanāyaka*).

The cult of Yoginīs is not concerned with these protean powers only as the inhabitants of a theoretical and liturgical universe, and as goddesses enshrined in the cremation ground power-seats. For they were believed also to possess women and thereby to enter into the most intimate contact with their devotees. Of these incarnate Yoginīs some, having been conceived in the intercourse of the consecrated, are considered divine from birth. Others appear in girls of eight, twelve or sixteen who live in the vicinity of the power-seats, these being of three degrees of potency. Others are identified in untouchable women from the age of twenty-seven as Ḍākinīs and other forms of assaulting spirit.

All Yoginīs belong to the family (*kula*) or lineage (*gotra*) of one or other of a number of higher 'maternal' powers, and in any instance this parentage is ascribed on the evidence of certain physical and behavioural characteristics. An adept in the cult of Yoginīs can identify members of as many as sixty-three of these occult sisterhoods, but is most vitally concerned with the eight major families of the Mothers (*mātṛ*) Brāhmī, Māheśvarī, Kaumārī, Vaiṣṇavī, Indrāṇī, Vārāhī, Cāmuṇḍā and Mahālakṣmī. For at the time of consecration he entered a trance in which the possessing power of the deity caused his hand to cast a flower into a *maṇḍala* enthroning these Mothers. The segment into which the flower fell revealed that Mother with whom he had an innate affinity. This established a link between him and the incarnate Yoginīs, for these families of the eight Mothers were also theirs. On days of the lunar fortnight sacred to his Mother the initiate was to seek out a Yoginī of his family. By worshipping her he aspired to attain supernatural powers and occult knowledge.

The Union Tantras (Yāmala-tantras): the Cult of Kapāl'īśabhairava and Caṇḍā Kāpālinī. Above this Yoginī cult, in the front line of the Vidyāpīṭha. the first level of the ascent of Śakti towards autonomy is seen in the Union Tantras. The principal cult here is that of Bhairava Lord of the Skull (Kapāl'īśa-, Kapāleśa-, Kapāla-bhairava) and his consort 'the Furious' (Caṇḍā) Goddess of the Skull (Kāpālinī). This is taught in the twelve thousand stanzas of the strongly Kāpālika *Picumata-Brahmayāmalatantra* (MSS). In the cult of Svacchandabhairava, in the Mantrapīṭha, the secondary deities surrounding the couple in the *maṇḍala* were male and solitary. Here they are female, with subordinate male consorts in the densely populated *maṇḍala* installed for exceptional worship, and alone in the much simpler pantheon of the private daily cult (*nityakarma*). Bhairava rules these secondary deities as the unifying holder of power (*śaktimat*, *śakticakreśvara*), in accordance with the general Śaiva conception of the divine nature. But this supremacy on the iconic plane is transcended by *śakti* on that of the deity-embodying *mantras*. For the essential components of the *mantras* of the nine deities who form the core of the greater *maṇḍala* and are the pantheon of daily worship are the syllables of the *mantra* of Caṇḍā Kāpālinī: (OṂ) HŪṂ CAṆḌE KĀPĀLINI SVĀHĀ ('... O Caṇḍā Kāpālinī ...!'). Thus Kapālīśabhairava (HŪṂ), his four goddesses (Raktā (CAṂ), Karālā (ḌE), Caṇḍākṣī (KĀ) and Mahocchuṣmā (PĀ)) and their four attendant powers or Dūtīs (Karālī (LI), Danturā (NI), Bhīmavaktrā (SVĀ) and Mahābalā (HĀ)), are aspects of a feminine power which transcends the male–female dichotomy which patterns the lower revelations.

The Power Tantras (Śakti-tantras): the Cult of the Triad (Trika). Above the Yāmala-tantras are the Śakti-tantras. These contain the scriptural authority for the system that in its later Tantras is called the Trika, and also that of the esoteric Kālī cults.

In the Tantras of the Trika (*Siddhayogeśvarīmata* (MSS), *Tantrasadbhāva* (MSS), *Mālinīvijayottaratantra*) the cult of Yoginīs permeates all levels; for the cult of entry is itself a development of that tradition. The focus of the Trika is directly on the network of Yoginīs (*yoginījāla*) as the hierarchy of cosmic manifestation, from the innermost resonance of the deity's power to its gross transformations as the sense-data that populate individualised consciousness.

The Trika's system of ritual and yoga leads to liberation and power by treading the steps of this emanation in reverse. The worshipper ascends to the core within the circuits of lesser Yoginīs. This core is the triad of goddesses, Parā (see Figure 36.2), Parāparā and Aparā, worshipped alone or with subordinate Bhairavas and visualised as enthroned on three white lotuses that rest on the tips of a trident (*triśūla*) (see Figure 36.3). This trident is superimposed in imagination along the central vertical axis of the worshipper's body so that the trifurcation rises through a space of twelve finger breadths above his head, the whole from its base at the level of his navel to this summit being identified with the series of cosmic levels from gross matter to the Absolute. The central goddess, Parā, is white, beautiful and benevolent. Single-faced and two-armed she holds a sacred text and exhibits the gesture of self-realisation (*cinmudrā*). Parāparā and Aparā, to her right and

Figure 36.2: Parā

left, are red and black respectively. Raging Kāpālika deities, they brandish the skull-staff (*khaṭvāṅga*). Externally the three are worshipped with offerings that must begin with alcoholic liquor and red meat, and on such 'thrones' as a *maṇḍala*, a square of ground prepared for this purpose (*sthaṇḍila*) or an image painted on cloth (*paṭa*) or incised on a human cranium (*tūra*).

***Figure 36.3: The outline of the* Maṇḍala *of the* Trident *and* Lotuses *(triśūlābjamaṇḍala) as prescribed in the Trika's* Devyāyāmalatantra**

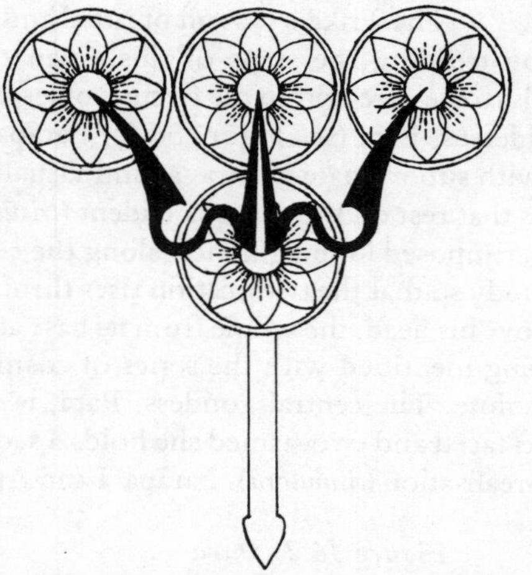

Parā has two aspects, for she is worshipped both as one of the three and as their sum and source. In this higher aspect she is called Mātṛsadbhāva (Essence of the Mothers), the summit of the hierarchy of the female powers which populate the cult of Yoginīs. Later all this would be interpreted along more metaphysical and mystical lines. Mātṛsadbhāva was read as Essence of (All) Conscious Beings ([*pra-*]*mātṛ-*) and the three goddesses were contemplated as the three fundamental constituent powers of a universe which was consciousness only. Parā was the power of the subject-element (*pramātṛ*), Aparā that of the object-element (*prameya*) and Parāparā that of the cognitive field or medium (*pramāṇa*) by virtue of which they are related, while their convergence in Mātṛsadbhāva came to express the ultimate unity of these three within an Absolute of pure consciousness contemplated as the liberated essence of the worshipper.

The Jayadrathayāmala and the Cult of Kālī. Beyond the cult of the three goddesses, at the extreme left of the Mantramārga, is the *Jayadrathayāmalatantra* (MSS). Also known as the King of Tantras (*Tantrarājabhaṭṭāraka*) it expounds in 24,000 stanzas the Kāpālika cults of over a hundred manifestations of the terrible goddess Kālī as the Destroyer of Time (Kālasaṃkarṣiṇī).

There are two main levels in the Tantra. The first, which is taught in the first quarter of the work (probably composed earlier than the rest), is that of the cult of a golden-limbed, twenty-armed Kālasaṃkarṣiṇī with five faces of different colours, that which faces the worshipper being black. Conventionally beautiful but holding such Kāpālika emblems as the skull-staff (*khaṭvāṅga*) and the severed head (*muṇḍa*), wearing a tiger skin dripping with blood, trampling the body of Kāla (Time) beneath her feet, she holds a trance-possessed Bhairava in a two-armed embrace in the centre of a vast, many-circuited *maṇḍala* of goddesses enclosed by cordons of male servant-guards and an outer ring of cremation grounds. In the elaborate form of worship both the goddesses and the guards embrace consorts. Here then is a Yāmala (Union) cult very similar to that of Kapālīśabhairava and Caṇḍā Kāpālinī taught in the *Picumata-Brahmayāmala* but centred in Kālī rather than Bhairava.

In the remaining three quarters of the text Bhairava is excluded from worship altogether. He is now just the highest of the male deities whose power Kālī transcends, the seventh at the summit of the hierarchy of the dethroned, coming above Indra, Brahmā, Viṣṇu, Rudra, Īśvara and Sadāśiva. Lying beneath her feet or dismembered to adorn her body, Bhairava suffers in his turn the humiliation which he inflicted on Sadāśiva in the Mantrapīṭha. With his fall the pantheons of worship are entirely feminised. But the femininity which remains is not that of the Yāmala systems. There *śakti* is worshipped in the form of beautiful and passionate consorts. Here the triumphant Goddess reveals herself to her devotees as a hideous, emaciated destroyer who embodies the Absolute (*anuttaram*) as the ultimate Self which the 'I' cannot enter and survive, an insatiable void in the heart of consciousness.

Typical of the conception of the Goddess in this second and more esoteric part of the Tantra is Vīrya-Kālī (Kālī of the [Fivefold] Power) (see Figure 36.4). Visualised in the centre of an aura of blinding light and contemplated as the innermost vibrancy (*spanda*) of consciousness she is black and emaciated. She has six faces and her hair is wreathed with flames. She is adorned with the severed heads and dismembered limbs of the lower deities. She rides on the shoulders of Kālāgnirudra (the Rudra of the Final Conflagration). In her twelve hands she carries a noose, a goad, a severed head, a sword, a shield, a trident-*khaṭvāṅga*, a thunderbolt (*vajra*), a ringing bell, a *ḍamaru*-drum, a skull-cup, a knife, a bleeding heart and an elephant-hide. The Rudra who is her vehicle (*vāhana*) is black on one side of his body and red on the other, symbolising the two breaths, the ingoing (*apāna*) and the outgoing (*prāṇa*), whose fusion and dissolution into the central axis of power reveals the state of thoughtless (*nirvikalpa*) awareness that holds the Goddess in its heart. The fivefold power (*vīrya*) that she embodies as 'the essence of the entire Vidyāpīṭha' is that by virtue of which the 'waveless' (*nistaraṅga*), self-luminous ground of reality projects itself as content in consciousness, and then re-absorbs this content, returning to its initial tranquility: this cyclical movement being the pulsation of consciousness from moment to moment as well as the pulsation of consciousness in cosmic creation and destruction. She passes from pure Light (*bhāsā* (1)) within the Śiva-void (*śivavyoma*), through incarnation (*avatāra* (2))

Figure 36.4: Vīrya-Kālī

as the impulse towards extroversion, to actual emission (*sṛṣṭi* (3)) of content, which appears as though outside consciousness, to her Kālī phase (*kālīkrama* (4)), in which she re-absorbs this content, and finally to the Great Withdrawal (*mahāsaṃhāra* (5)), in which she shines once again in her initial state as the pure Light. By contemplating this sequence (*krama*) in worship the devotee of Kālī is believed to realise the macrocosmic process within his own consciousness and thereby to attain omniscience and omnipotence.

In the fourth quarter of the *Jayadrathayāmalatantra* we are introduced to what the text claims to be the ultimate form of the Kālī cult. Here Mahākālī (Great Kālī) is worshipped in a black circle with a vermilion border surrounded by a ring of twelve such circles containing Kālīs who differ from her in their names but are identical in appearance. The relation of dependence between the Goddess and Śiva-Bhairava has already been transcended in the pure *śakti* cult of the higher level of this Tantra. Now even the hierarchy of source and emanations which remained within *śakti* herself is ritually dissolved, in a *maṇḍala* which expresses the perfect identity in essence (*sāmarasya*) of the Absolute and its manifestations, of the state of liberated transcendental (*sarvottīrṇa*) consciousness (*nirvāṇa*) and its finite projections, as the state of transmigratory existence (*bhava*, *saṃsāra*). Worshipped externally in orgiastic rites, the thirteen Kālīs (12+1) are to be realised internally in mystical self-experience, flashing forth as the ego-less (*nirahaṅkāra*) void through the voids of the senses during sexual union with the *dūtī*. This system known here as the Kālīkrama or Kālīkula, links this Tantra with the Krama to be described below (see pp. 683–4 and 696–9).

***Figure 36.5: The Trika's* Maṇḍala *of the Three Tridents and (Seven) Lotuses* (tritriśūlābjamaṇḍala) *with the twelve Kālīs in its centre, as prescribed by the* Trikasadbhāvatantra**

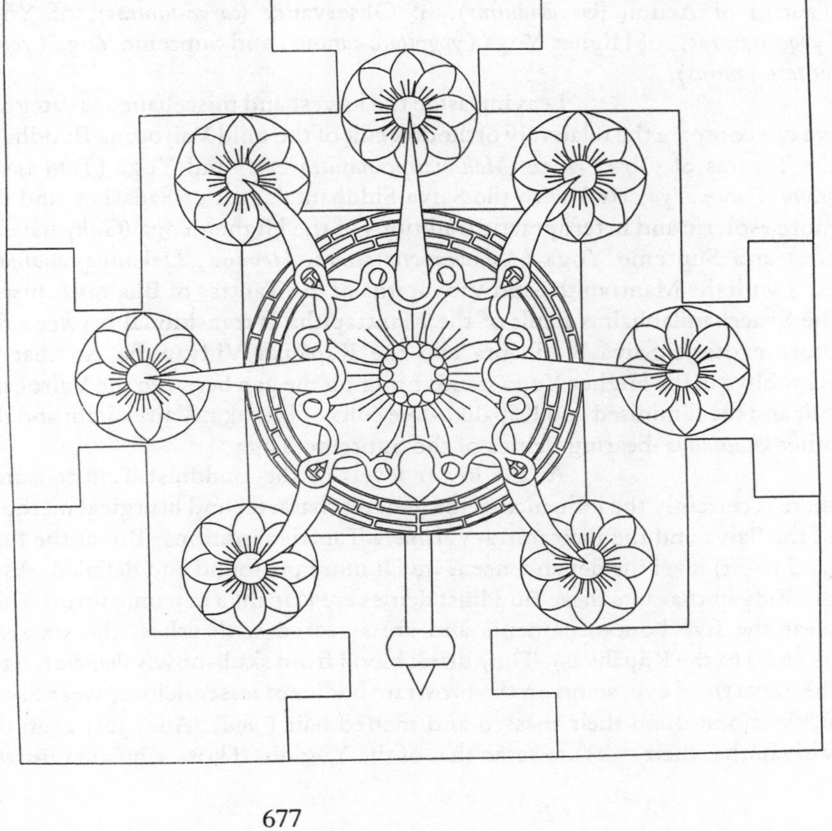

The Kālī-based Trika. The cult of the three goddesses and that of Kālī were not sealed off from each other in the manner of rival sects. The *Jayadrathyāmala* shows that the devotees of Kālī had developed their own versions of the cult of the three goddesses. The Trika in its turn assimilated these and other new and more esoteric treatments from the left. Consequently we find a later Trika stratum in which Kālasaṃkarṣiṇī has been introduced to be worshipped above the three goddesses of the trident (*Devyāyāmalatantra*). Finally there is a radical reorientation in which a system of sets of deities, worshipped in certain forms of the Kālī cult as the embodiment of the phases of cognition, is superimposed on to an elaborated version of the ancient triad as the inner structure of the point in which the three goddesses converge into the mystical fourth power, which is their interpenetration (3×3) in unity. In the centre of this convergence are the twelve Kālīs of the Kālīkrama (or Kālīkula) in their twelve circles (see Figure 36.5).

The Vidyāpīṭha and Esoteric Buddhism. By the eighth century CE the Buddhists had accumulated a hierarchy of Tantric revelations roughly parallel in its organisation and character to that of the Mantramārga. Their literature was divided in order of ascending esotericism into the Tantras of Action (*kriyā-tantras*), of Observance (*caryā-tantras*), of Yoga (*yoga-trantras*), of Higher Yoga (*yogottara-tantras*) and Supreme Yoga (*yogānuttara-tantras*).

Leaving aside the lowest and miscellaneous category we can compare the relatively orthodox cult of the mild Vairocana Buddha in the Tantras of Observance (*Mahāvairocanasūtra* etc.) and Yoga (*Tattvasaṃgraha*, *Paramādya*, etc.) with the Śaiva Siddhānta's cult of Sadāśiva, and the more esoteric and heteropractic traditions of the Higher Yoga (*Guhyasamāja* etc.) and Supreme Yoga (*Abhidhānottarottara*, *Hevajra*, *Ḍākinīvajrapañjara* etc.) with the Mantrapīṭha and Vidyāpīṭha of the Tantras of Bhairava. Just as the Svacchandabhairava cult of the Mantrapīṭha is transitional between the more exoteric Śaiva Siddhānta and the Kāpālika Vidyāpīṭha, so that of Akṣobhya in the Higher Yoga stands bridging the gap between the Vairocana cult and the feminised and Kāpālika-like cults of Heruka, Vajravārāhī and the other *khaṭvāṅga*-bearing deities of the Supreme Yoga.

At the lower levels of the Buddhist Tantric canon there is certainly the influence of the general character and liturgical methods of the Śaiva and the Pāñcarātra-Vaiṣṇava Tantric traditions. But at the final (and latest) level the dependence is much more profound and detailed. As in the Vidyāpīṭha cults these Buddhist deities are Kāpālika in iconic form. They wear the five bone-ornaments and are smeared with ashes (the six seals (*mudrās*) of the Kāpālikas). They drink blood from skull-bowls (*kapāla*), have the Śaiva third eye, stand on the prostrate bodies of lesser deities, wear Śiva's sickle moon upon their massed and matted hair (*jaṭā*). And, just as in the Vidyāpīṭha, their cults are set in that of the Yoginīs. Those who are initiated by introduction to the *maṇḍalas* of these Yoginī-encircled Buddhist deities are adorned with bone-ornaments and given the Kāpālika's *khaṭvāṅga* and skull-bowl to hold. Those who wish to do so may take on the long-term practice of the Kāpālika observance itself (Vajra-Kāpālikavrata), living in the cremation grounds, consuming meat and alcohol and offering erotic worship.

The Buddhist-Kāpālika Yoginī cult which gives these Tantras of Supreme Yoga their distinctive character and the greater part of their subject matter—indeed, they refer to themselves as Yoginī-tantras on the whole—borrows much of its detail and textual material directly from parallel Śaiva sources. Thus most of the material in the *Abhiahānottarottaratantra* and *Saṃpuṭodbhavatantra* listing the characteristics by which Yoginīs of different sorts may be recognised, and the sign language and syllabic codes with which they must be addressed (*chommā*), has been lifted with some Buddhist overwriting from such Vidyāpīṭha texts as the *Yoginīsaṃcāra* of the *Jayadrathayāmalatantra*, the *Picumata-Brahmayāmalatantra* and the *Tantrasadbhāva*.

The Kaula Reformation of the Yoginī Cult

The Yoginī cult, like the main cults of entry into the Vidyāpīṭha, was the speciality of skull-bearing ascetics removed from conventional society. It might reasonably have been expected to remain so but for Kaulism. This movement within esoteric Śaivism decontaminated the mysticism of the Kāpālikas so that it flowed into the wider community of married householders. In that of Kashmir it found learned exponents who used it to formulate a respectable metaphysics and soteriology with which to stand against the Śaiva Siddhānta.

The rites of the Yoginī cults and the fruits they bestowed were called *kaulika* or *kaula* in the texts which prescribed them, these terms being adjectives derived from the noun *kula* in its reference to the families or lineages of the Yoginīs and Mothers. Thus a Kaulika rite was one connected with the worship of these *kulas*, and a *kaulika* power (*kaulikī siddhiḥ*) was one that was attained through that worship, above all assimilation into these families (*kulasāmānyata*).

Kaulism developed from within these Yoginī cults. It preserved the original meaning of the term *kula* and its derivatives but it introduced a new level of esotericism based on a homonym. For *kula* was also taken to mean the body and, by further extension, the totality (of phenomena), the 'body' of power (*śakti*). This last meaning neatly encompassed the original, for this cosmic 'body' was said to consist of the powers of the eight families of the Mothers. One was believed to enter the totality (*kula*) through that segment of its power with which one had a special affinity, determined as before by the casting of a flower during possession (*āveśa*).

Furthermore, these eight Mothers of the families were made internally accessible by being identified with the eight constituents of the individual worshipper's 'subtle body' (*puryaṣṭaka*), these being sound, sensation, visual form, taste, smell, volition, judgement and ego. The worshipper was therefore the temple of his deities; the central deity, out of whom these Mother-powers are projected, in whom they are grounded and into whom they are re-absorbed, was to be evoked within this temple as the Lord and/or Lady of the Kula (Kuleśvara, Kuleśvarī), as the blissful inner consciousness which is the worshipper's ultimate and trans-individual identity.

In the cults of the Vidyāpīṭha the propitiation of the deities involved sexual intercourse with a *dūtī*. This practice is continued in Kaulism. Indeed it moves to the very centre of the cult. However while its principal purpose in the Vidyāpīṭha was to produce the power-substances needed to gratify the deities, here the ritual of copulation is aestheticised. The magical properties of the mingled sexual fluids are not forgotten: those seeking powers (*siddhis*) consumed it and even those who worshipped for salvation alone offered the products of orgasm to the deities. However the emphasis has now moved to orgasm itself. It is no longer principally a means of production. It is a privileged means of access to a blissful expansion of consciousness in which the deities of the Kula permeate and obliterate the ego of the worshipper. The consumption of meat and alcohol is interpreted along the same lines. Their purpose, like that of everything in the liturgy, is to intensify experience, to gratify the goddesses of the senses.

The Kāpālika of the Vidyāpīṭha sought the convergence of the Yoginīs and his fusion with them (*yoginīmelaka*, *-melāpa*) through a process of visionary invocation in which he would attract them out of the sky, gratify them with an offering of blood drawn from his own body, and ascend with them into the sky as the leader of their band. The Kaulas translated this visionary fantasy into the aesthetic terms of mystical experience. The Yoginīs became the deities of his senses (*karaṇeśvarīs*), revelling in his sensations. In intense pleasure this revelling completely clouds his internal awareness: he becomes their plaything or victim (*paśu*). However, when in the same pleasure the desiring ego is suspended, then the outer sources of sensation lose their gross otherness. They shine *within* cognition as its aesthetic form. The Yoginīs of the senses relish this offering of 'nectar' and gratified thereby they converge and fuse with the *kaula*'s inner transcendental identity as the Kuleśvara, the Bhairava in the radiant 'sky' of enlightened consciousness (*cidvyomabhairava*).

Kaulism developed into four main systems. These were known as the Four Transmissions (*āmnāya*) or as the Transmissions of the Four Lodges (*gharāmnāya*) (eastern, western, northern and southern). Each has its own distinctive set of deities, *mantras*, *maṇḍalas*, mythical saints, myths of origin and the like.

The Kaula Trika: the Eastern Transmission (Pūrvāmnāya). The first context in which we find this Kaula esotericism is the Trika. The Kaula form of the cult of the three goddesses of the trident was well established among the Kashmiri by the beginning of the ninth century; and our first detailed exegesis of the Kashmiri Trika, at the end of the tenth century, shows that there had long existed a hierarchical distinction between the lower, Tantric form of the cult (*tantra-prakriyā*) and the new Kaula tradition. Kaula sources outside the Trika, such as the *Ciñciṇīmatasārasamuccaya* (MSS), indicate that the Kaulism of this branch of the Vidyāpīṭha is the closest to the origin of the tradition.

The basic Kaula pantheon consists of the Lord and/or Goddess of the Kula (Kuleśvara, Kuleśvarī) surrounded by the eight Mothers (Brāhmī etc.) with or without Bhairava consorts. Outside this core one worships the four mythical *gurus* or Perfected Ones (*Siddhas*) of the tradition (the four Lords of the Ages of the World (Yuganātha)), their consorts (*dūtīs*), the offspring of these couples and their *dūtīs.* The couple of the present, degenerate age (*kaliyuga*) are Macchanda (the Fisherman), venerated as the revealer (*avatāraka*) of Kaulism, and his consort Koṅkaṇā. Of their sons, the twelve 'princes' (*rājaputra*), six are non-celibate (*adhoretas*) and therefore specially revered as qualified (*sādhikāra*) to transmit the Kaula cult. They are worshipped as the founders of the six initiatory lineages (*ovalli*). At the time of consecration one entered one of these lineages and received a name whose second part indicated this affiliation. Hand-signs (*chommā*, *chomā*, *chummā*) enabled members of the *ovallis* to reveal themselves to each other (a remnant of the more elaborate code-languages [also called *chommā*] of the Kāpālika Yoginī cults and their Buddhist imitators); and each *ovalli* had lodges (*maṭha*) for its members in various parts of India. In this last respect they maintained the earlier tradition of Śaiva asceticism.

The Trika's Kaula cult added little to this matrix. It simply worshipped its three goddesses Parā, Parāparā and Aparā at the corners of a triangle drawn or visualised enclosing the Kuleśvara and Kuleśvarī of the centre. The worship could be carried out externally, on a red cloth upon the ground, in a circle filled with vermilion powder and enclosed with a black border, on a coconut substituted for a human skull, a vessel filled with wine or other alcohol, or on a *maṇḍala.* It may also be offered on the exposed genitals of the *dūtī*, on one's own body, or in the act of sexual intercourse with the *dūtī.* Later tradition emphasises the possibility of worshipping the deities within the vital energy (*prāṇa*)—one visualises their gratification by the 'nectar' of one's ingoing breath. We are also told that the seeker of liberation may carry out his worship in thought alone (*sāṃvidī pūjā*). However even one who does this must offer erotic worship with his *dūtī* on certain special days of the year (*parvas*).

The Kaula tradition of the Trika saw itself as essentialising Tantric practice. In this spirit it offered a much condensed form of the liturgy followed in the Tantra-system, emphasising spontaneity and intensity of immersion (*tanmayībhāva*, *samāveśa*) over elaborate ritual. Thus the usual preliminary purifications (*snāna*), the internal worship (*antaryāga*) which always precedes the external in Tantric rites and the offerings in the sacrificial fire (*homa*), which follow and repeat the worship of the deities, may all be discarded as superfluous. Moreover, the worshipper may advance from an initial stage in which he worships the full Kaula pantheon until eventually he worships only the central Kuleśvara.

The same condensation and intensification determines the form of consecration (*kaula-dīkṣā*). The guru opens the initiate's path to salvation and power by ritually annulling in advance whatever future experiences other than his present goal might await him at the various levels of the cosmos. He unites him with the deity at the summit of the subtle levels of the universe and then equips him with a 'pure' or divine body so that after this elevation to the immaterial plane of the deity he can re-enter the world as an initiate. In the Tantra-system of the Trika, as in all Tantra-systems, this destruction of karmic bonds involves an elaborate sequence of offerings in the sacred fire (*hautrī dīkṣā*). The initiate may be entirely passive during this process. In the Kaula system all this is achieved with minimal ritual, while the initiate is required to manifest signs of possession (*āveśa*) and is said to have direct experience during his trance of his ascent from level to level of the cosmos.

The Tantra-system with which this Kaulism is contrasted is not exactly the Trika-Tantrism of the ascetics. It is rather that tradition's domesticated form as it was practiced by the married householders from whom the Kaula Trika received its initiates. One might conclude, then, that this Kaulism, with its emphasis on possession and mystical experience, offered the married Tantric enthusiast an acceptable substitute for the intensity of the Kāpālika Tantric tradition to which he was directly linked through his deities and *mantras*, but from which he was necessarily excluded by his status as a married home-dweller.

The Kaula Kālī Cult: the Mata, the Krama and the Northern Transmission (Uttarāmnāya). After its appearance in the Trika, Kaulism next emerges in the Kālī cult. We must distinguish here three major traditions, (i) the Doctrine (Mata), (ii) the Sequence(-system) (Krama), also called the Great Truth (Mahārtha), the Great Way (Mahānaya), or the Way of the Goddess (Devīnaya), and (iii) the cult of Guhyakālī.

(i) The Mata. The Kaula Mata is rooted in the tradition of the *Jayadratha-yāmalatantra*. Its essence or culmination is the worship of the twelve Kālīs, the *kālīkrama* which, as we have seen above, was believed to irradiate or possess the consciousness of the adept and his *dūtī* during sexual intercourse, obliterating the binding structures of differentiated awareness (*vikalpa*).

This Kaulism, like that of the Trika, rests upon a broader base of Tantric practice, but unlike that of the Trika this base is unrestrainedly Kāpālika. The most striking feature of this Tantric Mata is the prevalence of deities who have the faces of animals, or who have numerous such faces in addition to a principal anthropomorphic face. In the centre of its pantheon are three terrific goddesses of this second type, Trailokyaḍāmarā (Terroriser of the Universe), Matacakreśvarī (Goddess of the Circle of the Mata), and Ghoraghoratarā (She who is More Terrible than the Terrible).

Our only detailed account of the Kaula form of the Mata is the *Ciñciṇīmatasārasamuccaya* (MSS). Given there as the Kaulism of the Northern Transmission (Uttarāmnāya) it is expounded through two mystical texts of twelve and fifty verses respectively associated with the probably mythical gurus Vidyānandanātha and Niṣkriyānandanātha. In style and content these are closely related to the Kālīkrama section in the *Jayadrathayāmalatantra*.

(ii) The Krama. A much more elaborate or rather better documented Kaula system of Kālī worship is found in the literature of the Krama. The outstanding characteristic of this tradition is that it worships a sequential rather than a simply concentric pantheon. A series of sets of deities (*cakras*) is worshipped in a fixed sequence as the phases (*krama*) of the cyclical pulse of cognition (*saṃvit*). These phases are Emission (*sṛṣṭikrama*), Maintenance of the emitted (*sthitikrama*) (also called Incarnation (*avatārakrama*)), Retraction of the emitted (*saṃhārakrama*) and the Nameless fourth (*anākhyakrama*) (also called the Phase of the Kālīs (*kālīkrama*)), in which all trace of the preceding process is dissolved into liberated and all-pervading consciousness. This sequence differs somewhat from that seen below in the cult of Vīryakālī, and considerably as far as the actual deities who are worshipped in these phases are concerned. The final phase, that of the Nameless, is identical to that of the thirteen (12+1) Kālīs seen in the Mata. Indeed this set of deities is the feature which is most constant through the different forms of the Kālī cult.

The main scriptural authority for this form of the Krama is the *Devīpañcaśataka* (MSS). However there was a variant Krama tradition based on the *Kramasadbhāva* (MS). This adds a fifth sequence, that of pure Light (*bhāsākrama* (see p. 676)), to the four above. It also worships a system of sixty-four Yoginīs (also called Śākinīs) in five phases as the prelude to the cult of the Kālīs of the Nameless. In the period of the Kashmiri exegetes elements from each of these two traditions were brought together (see pp. 697–8 for the interpretation of this cycle of sixty-four Yoginīs). None the less there remained a permanent division in the tradition between tetradic and pentadic *krama*-worship, deriving from the *Devīpañcaśataka* and the *Kramasadbhāva* respectively.

The scriptures of this tradition considered themselves to be above the Vidyāpīṭha, and it is true that, though there are continuities with the *Jayadrathayāmalatantra*, they are more sophisticated in a number of respects. Thus the cult has *mantras* but lacks the grosser level at which the deities take on iconic form. External worship is greatly simplified and looked upon as inferior to worship in the mind, it being understood that the order of worship (*pūjākrama*) is no more than a reflection of the ever-present order of cognition itself (*saṃvitkrama*).

This claim to superiority is also expressed by the fact that the two scriptures mentioned reject the universal convention of the Bhairava Tantras which has Bhairava teach the Goddess. Here the roles are reversed. The Goddess teaches Bhairava. For she embodies what he cannot know, the cycle of cognitive power which constitutes his own self-awareness.

While on the whole it is not possible to say at present where the majority of the Tantras originated, the scriptural tradition and the later commentators are unanimous in attributing the Krama revelations to Oḍḍiyāna, the Northern Seat of Power (*uttara-pīṭha*). This was in the Swat valley in what is now Pakistan, some 300 kilometres north-west of the valley of Kashmir. The same place figures prominently in the hagiographical histories of Buddhism as the major centre from which the traditions of the Yoginī-tantras (=*Yogānuttaratantras*) were propagated. With the advent of Islam and the subsequent collapse of urban and monastic culture in that region, all traces of its Tantric traditions have disappeared.

(iii) The Cult of Guhyakālī. It is a common phenomenon in the history of the Tantric traditions that such refinements as those of the Krama are quickly written into the lower, more concretely elaborated rituals which they sought to transcend. So there has flourished, from at least the tenth century to the present, a cult in which the mystical deity-schemata of the Krama are fleshed out with iconic form as the retinue of the Goddess Guhyakālī. The source of this concretisation is the Tantric tradition of the Mata. In her three-faced and eight-armed form, Guhyakālī's faces are worshipped as the three Mata goddesses Trailokyaḍāmarā, Matacakreśvarī and Matalakṣmī (=Ghoraghoratarā). Thus she is seen as the transcendent unity of that tradition. Further, in her principal form she is virtually identical with the third of these goddesses. Eight- and finally fifty-four-armed, black and ten-faced, she dances on the body of Bhairava in the centre of a cremation ground (see Figure 36.6).

The earliest datable evidence of this cult is also our earliest datable example of a Tantric ritual handbook providing detailed instructions on worship with all the *mantras* to be recited. This is the *Kālīkulakramārcana* of Vimalaprabodha, an author first mentioned in a Nepalese manuscript dated 1002 CE. This and many other practical texts of her cult have circulated and circulate still in the Nepal Valley, where she is the esoteric identity of Guhyeśvarī, the major local Goddess from our earliest records (*c.* 800 CE) to the present. The Newars, who maintain the

Figure 36.6: Guhyakālī

early traditions of the region, preserve her link with the Northern Transmission. For them Guhyakālī is the embodiment of that branch of Kaulism. Linked with her in this role is the white Goddess Siddhalakṣmī (always written Siddhilakṣmī in Nepal), one of the apotropaic deities (Pratyaṅgirā) of the *Jayadrathayāmalatantra* and the patron goddess of the Malla Kings (1200–1768 CE) and their descendants.

A version of the cult of Guhyakālī seems also to have flourished in Mithilā (in northern Bihar) on the authority of the *Mahākālasaṃhitā*. The connection with the Krama sequence-worship is very attenuated here. Though her icon is as elsewhere, she is unusual in being worshipped with a consort and one who is not a form of Śiva, as one might have expected, but the Man-Lion (Narasiṃha) incarnation of the rival God Viṣṇu. But that too has its precedent in the *Jayadrathayāmalatantra*. For in its fourth quarter that Tantra teaches the cult of a Kālī Mādhaveśvarī to be worshipped as the consort of this same Viṣṇu-form. Indeed this seems to have been a major tradition in Kashmir, for Abhinavagupta, the great Kashmiri Tantric scholar, gives this cult in his *Tantrāloka* as one of two forms of Kaulism connected with the Trika.

The Kaula Cult of Kubjikā: the Western Transmission (Paścimāmnāya). Intimately connected with the Trika is the third form of Kaulism, the cult of the Goddess Kubjikā. It is distinct from the Trika in that it adds the cult of a new set of deities, so that the Trika recedes from the front line of devotion into the ritual, yogic and theoretical body of the system. Its dependence on the Trika is revealed by the fact that much of its principal and earliest scripture, the *Kubjikāmata*, consists of chapters and other passages taken with minor overwriting from the scriptural corpus of that tradition.

***Figure 36.7: Kubjikā with Navātma on Agni, according to the visualisation text of the* Nityāhnikatilaka**

The high deity of the new pantheon is the goddess Kubjikā ('the Humpbacked' or 'Stooped'). Black, fat-bellied, six-faced and twelve-armed, adorned with snakes, jewels, human bones and a garland of severed heads, she embraces her consort Navātma ('the Nine-fold' [embodying the nine-part *mantra* H-S-KṢ-M-L-V-Y-R-ŪṂ]). He is five-faced and ten-armed. Also black, but youthful and handsome, he dances with her on a lotus which grows from the navel of Agni, the god of Fire, who lies in the centre of a lotus visualised by the worshipper in his cranial aperture (*brahmarandhra*) at the summit of an axis of brilliant light rising from the power-centre (*cakra*) in his genital region (*svādhiṣṭhāna*) (see Figure 36.7).

The tradition of the *Kubjikāmata* is *śākta*, which is to say that it is a Śaiva cult which emphasises the Goddess (*śakti*) rather than Śiva/Bhairava. In this sense all the Transmissions are *śākta*. However in the Western Tradition (Paścimāmnāya) there is a parallel system known as the Śāmbhava. It is Śāmbhava as opposed to *śākta* because it stresses Śambhu (equivalent to Śiva, i.e. Navātma) rather than *śakti* (=Kubjikā). Similarly masculinised variants existed in the Trika and the Krama. In the first there is the Kaula cult, in which Parā, Parāparā and Aparā are worshipped as the powers of Triśirobhairava (Bhairava the Three-headed); and in the second Manthāna-bhairava may take the place of the thirteenth Kālī in the Kālīkrama. This Śāmbhava system, however, was much more widely propagated. It is found in the *Śambhunirṇayatantra* (MS) and in much south Indian postscriptural literature (e.g. Śivānandamuni's *Śambhunirṇayadīpikā* (MS), Tejānandanātha's *Ānandakalpalatā* (MSS), and Umākānta's *Ṣaḍanvayaśāmbhavakrama*). It was even taken into the mainstream of the purified Kaulism propagated by the south Indian Śaṅkarācāryas of Śṛṅgerī and Kāñcīpuram, being the esoteric content of the ever popular *Ānandalaharī* attributed to Śaṅkara.

In this system Navātma also called Naveśvara or Navaka is worshipped as Solitary Hero (*ekavīra*). Alternatively the divine couple (Navātma and Kubjikā) assumes six variant forms to preside over the Six Orders (*ṣaḍanvaya-*) located in the six centres (*cakras*) along the central power-axis of the body and equated with the five elements (earth, water, fire, wind and ether) and mind (*manas*). These six levels are further populated by six series of divine couples (*yāmala*), 180 in all (the 360 'rays'), drawn from the pantheon of Kubjikā in the earlier cult of the Western Transmission.

The system of the six power-centres (*cakras*) (*ādhāra*, also called *mūlādhāra*, in the anus, *svādhiṣṭhāna* in the genital region, *maṇipūra* in the navel, *anāhata* in the heart, *viśuddhi* in the throat and *ājñā* between the eyebrows) is also characteristic of the yogic rituals of the *Kubjikāmata*. Later it became so universal, being disseminated as part of the system of *kuṇḍalinī-yoga* beyond the boundaries of the Tantric cults, that it has been forgotten in India (and not noticed outside it) that it is quite absent in all the Tantric traditions except this and the cult of the goddess Tripurasundarī. The yoga of these two traditions sets them apart from the earlier Kaula traditions of the Trika and the Kālī cult. It is noteworthy in this respect that these two newer forms of Kaulism also mark themselves off from the earlier by worshipping as their founding Siddhas Mitranātha, Oḍḍanātha, Ṣaṣṭhanātha and Caryānātha, while the Trika and the Kālī cults share the series Khagendranātha, Kūrmanātha, Meṣanātha and Macchandanātha also called Matsyendranātha.

The Southern Transmission (Dakṣiṇāmnāya) and the Cult of Tripurasundarī. Under the heading of the Southern Transmission the *Ciñciṇīmatasārasamuccaya* describes the cult of Kāmeśvarī (the Goddess of Erotic Pleasure), a slim, two-armed and single-faced maiden (*kumārī*) surrounded by a retinue of twelve. Eleven of these are goddesses with such appropriate names as Kṣobhinī (the Exciter) and Drāviṇī (the Melter). The twelfth is male, Kāmadeva, the Indian Eros.

This cult of erotic magic is the prototype or part of the prototype of the Kaula cult of Tripurasundarī (the Beautiful Goddess of the Three Worlds), also called Kāmeśvarī, the Goddess who is worshipped in and as the nine-triangled *śrīcakra*, red, red-garmented, garlanded with red flowers, single-faced and four-armed, carrying a noose (*pāśa*), an elephant-goad (*aṅkuśa*), a bow and five arrows (the five arrows of the Love God), and

Figure 36.8: Tripurasundarī on Sadāśiva

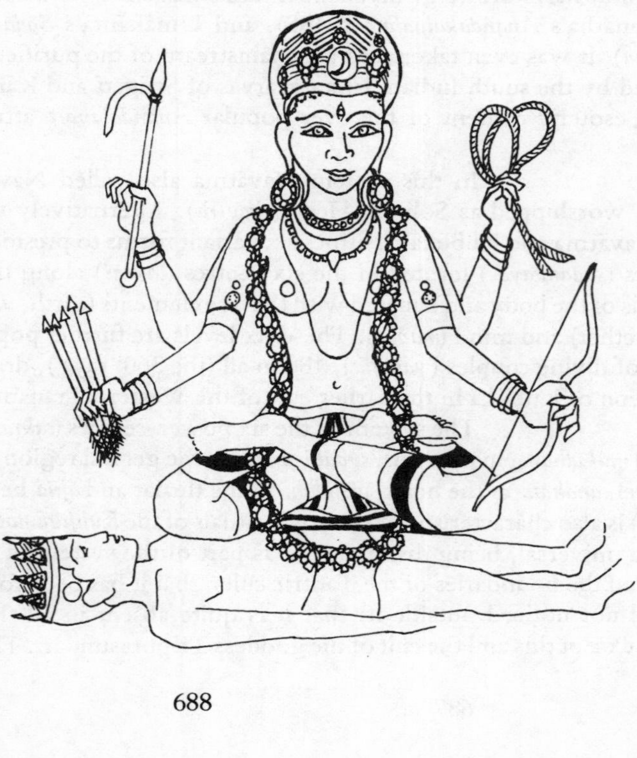

seated above the lower gods Brahmā, Viṣṇu, Rudra and Īśvara, on the prostrate body of a white Sadāśiva (see Figure 36.8).

The classical form of this cult remembered that it had a special link with the older Southern Transmission; but it had come to see itself as transcending this quadripartition of the Kaula traditions. It called itself the Upper or Supreme Transmission and considered the four divisions to be subsumed within it. In a later elaboration of the cult known as the Kālī-Doctrine (Kālīmata) worship of Tripurasundarī incorporated more or less artificial and inaccurate versions of the pantheons of these other systems. To these new liturgies corresponded the almost universal ascendancy of this form of Kaulism throughout the middle ages down to the present.

The cult of Tripurasundarī is certainly the latest of the traditions of the Mantramārga covered here. Its basic scripture, the *Nityāṣoḍaśikārṇava*, clings to the edge of the Śaiva canon, being known in this canon only to itself. The southerners, who took this cult very seriously—it became so powerful that it was adopted, in a purified form, by the orthodox authority of the Śaṅkarācāryas of Śṛṅgerī and Kāñcīpuram—considered it to be Kashmiri in origin. However, this is quite possibly because they failed to distinguish the scriptural tradition itself from the Kashmiri theological and exegetical system within which they received it from the north and within which they continued to work. From Kashmir itself the evidence is inadequate. The Kashmiri Jayaratha (*fl. c.* 1225–75 CE), who wrote a learned commentary on the *Nityāṣoḍaśikārṇava* (his *Vāmakeśvarīmatavivaraṇa*), refers to a long tradition of local exegesis, but we cannot conclude from his evidence more than that the cult was introduced into Kashmir at some time between 900 and 1100 CE.

Figure 36.9: Śrīcakra

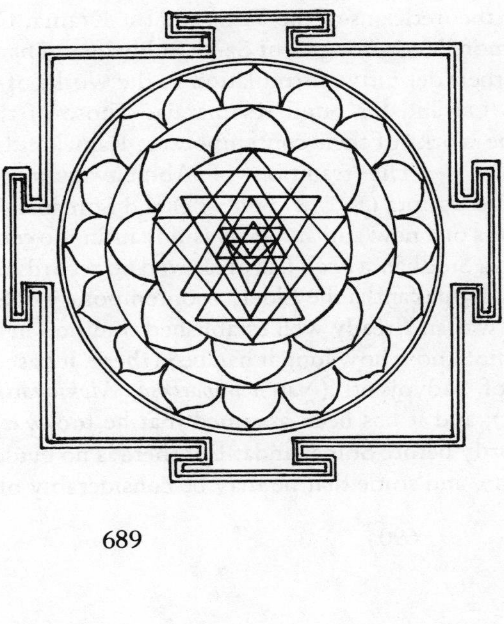

The *Nityāṣoḍaśikārṇava* is an unsophisticated text which concentrates on external ritual and on the various supernatural effects which such ritual can bestow on the worshipper, particularly in the quest for control over women. For a deeper meaning the tradition had to turn to the *Yoginīhṛdaya*. Here one could find the internal correspondences of the external elements, the metaphysical meaning of the sequence of creation and re-absorption which the deity-sets of the densely populated *śrīcakra* were believed to embody (see Figure 36.9). Thus the text of the ritual, though apparently concerned with erotic magic—the names of many of the constituent goddesses make this clear enough—could become the vehicle of ritualised, gnostic contemplation. However, although the *Yoginīhṛdaya* is scriptural in form (a dialogue in which Bhairava teaches the Goddess), there is no evidence of its existence before the thirteenth century in south India, shortly before Amṛtānandanātha (*fl. c.* 1325–75) wrote the first known commentary. Certainly it was composed when the non-dualistic Śaiva system of the Kashmiri exegesis of the Trika and the Krama had become the norm in the reading of the Kaula cults in south India, that is after *c.* 1050 CE. This is clear from the fact that it frequently echoes such popular texts of the Kashmiri tradition as the *Pratyabhijñāhṛdaya* of Kṣemarāja (*fl. c.* 1000–50).

The Post-scriptural Śaiva Traditions of Kashmir from the Ninth Century

The Common Base

From the middle of the ninth century these Tantric Śaiva traditions of the Mantramārga emerged from their scriptural anonymity into an extensive body of Kashmiri exegesis. In this literature we encounter two schools. On the left were the theoreticians of the Trika and the Krama. On the right was the staider and more Veda-congruent Śaiva Siddhānta. The doctrines of the former reached their definitive formulation in the works of Abhinavagupta (*fl. c.* 975–1025 CE) and his pupil Kṣemarāja. Those of the latter school culminated in the works of their contemporary, Rāmakaṇṭha.

The tradition of Abhinavagupta was recent. It looked back to Vasugupta (*fl. c.* 875–925 CE) and Somānanda (*fl. c.* 900–50 CE) as the founders of a new and anti-Śaivasiddhāntin movement among the learned. The Śaiva Siddhānta itself has preserved no records of its presence in Kashmir beyond Rāmakaṇṭha the Elder, a contemporary of Somānanda. We know that there was an already well established tradition in Kashmir at that time, but we do not know how long it had been there. It based itself above all on the works of Sadyojyoti (*Nareśvaraparīkṣā*, *Mokṣakārikā*, *Paramokṣanirāsakārikā*, etc.); and it has been assumed that he too was Kashmiri, and that he lived shortly before Somānanda. But there is no evidence that Kashmir was his home, and some that he may be considerably older.

Both schools addressed themselves principally not to the specialist seekers of powers so prominent in the scriptures themselves but to the seekers of liberation (*mumukṣu*), to those with no specific goal, who seek self-perfection through conforming to the physical and mental rituals of the Śaiva tradition. This, the unmarked category, was the sect's broad base in society, the community of married Śaiva householders. It is in accordance with this breadth that Śaivism appears in both schools not merely as a system of doctrines but first and foremost as a set of social facts independent of or presupposed by doctrine. Thus beneath the fundamental differences in theology which separate the schools there is complete solidarity in a basic faith that it is enough to be a Śaiva in a purely ritual sense, that the least gnostic (privy to special knowledge) of their common audience will attain liberation simply by being processed by the rituals of the community.

The Kashmiri Śaiva Siddhānta

The Kashmiri Śaiva Siddhānta enclosed and reinforced this exoteric base. It propagated an anti-gnostic ritualism which immunised the consciousness of the Tantric performer of ritual against the mystical and non-dualistic tendencies of the Kāpālika and Kaula left, and encouraged him to internalise without inhibition the outlook and values of non-Tantric orthodoxy.

According to Rāmakaṇṭha the scriptures of the Śaiva Siddhānta teach that salvation can only be attained by ritual. To be bound to the cycle of death and rebirth (*saṃsāra*) is to be ignorant of one's true nature, but knowledge of that nature cannot bring that bondage to an end. This is because the absence of liberated self-awareness is caused by impurity (*mala*). This cannot be removed by knowledge, because it is a substance (*dravya*). Being a substance it can be destroyed only by action and the only action capable of destroying it is the system of ritual prescribed in the Śaiva scriptures.

The rite of consecration (*dīkṣā*), through which one enters upon one's ritual obligations, destroys all the impurity (*mala*) which would otherwise be the cause of further incarnations. The daily (*nitya*) and occasional (*naimittika*) rituals which one is bound to perform after consecration cause, said Rāmakaṇṭha, the daily decrease of the impurity which the rite of consecration has left intact, the impurity which is the support of one's current physical and mental existence. But since the passage of time itself accomplishes this end, bringing one daily closer to the liberation at death which is the promised effect of consecration, it is hard to believe that this theory that ritual after consecration has a positive effect can have been in the forefront of the awareness of the Tantrics of the Śaiva Siddhānta. More compelling must have been the negative argument offered by Rāmakaṇṭha, as by the Bhāṭṭa Mīmāṃsakas, that one performs one's ritual duties in order to avoid the evil consequences of not performing them. For if one omits them, or breaks any other of the rules (*samaya*) which bind the initiate, one must perform a penance (*prāyaścitta*); and one is told that if this penance is neglected one's liberation guaranteed by the rite of consecration may be postponed by another incarnation, even by a period in hell.

The Kashmiri Trika

The Kashmiri authorities of the Trika attacked this ritualism of their Śaiva Siddhāntin contemporaries. They claimed that they had exaggerated certain tendencies in the scriptures of the Śaiva Siddhānta by means of sophistic exegesis. Thus, said the Trika, these scriptures place a greater emphasis on ritual than those of the left, but they do not go to the extent of claiming that salvation can be gained by no other means.

According to the left, the Śaiva Siddhānta contains the truth as modified by Śiva for the benefit of those not mature enough to enter the less conditioned and more demanding paths of his esoteric revelations. The extreme positions of the current Śaiva-Siddhāntin exegesis were believed to have arisen from failure to see this essential continuity of the Śaiva revelation. Thus the left attacked certain interpretations of these scriptures—and it must be said that in the main its criticisms are justified—but it never denied the efficacy of the religious practices of those who followed the prescriptions of these scriptures, even if they accepted the right's biased exegesis. The left was content to believe that the most hardened Śaiva-Siddhāntin ritualist would attain perfect liberation at death by the power of Śiva manifest in the mechanism of ritual. It drew its strength not from exclusion but from the propagation of a universally applicable *theory* of ritual. This theory promised liberation to all Śaivas while motivating ascent into the esoteric left through further consecrations in which the meaning of ritual proposed by the theory could be realised with ever greater immediacy and intensity. The culmination of this intensification is liberation, not at death but in life itself.

The left maintained that there are those who have attained this mystical transformation spontaneously or by means of gradual, ritual-less insight. Thus while the Śaiva Siddhāntins held that liberation could not be attained except through ritual, the authorities of the Trika maintained that liberation, while attainable by ritual alone (Śaiva-Siddhāntin or esoteric), could also, though more rarely, be attained by mystical experience and gnosis. Further, their theory divided the performance of ritual itself into two levels. Ritual without internal awareness would lead to liberation at death, as we have seen; but ritual could also be a means of liberation in life. Gnostic meaning encoded into the manipulations and formulas of the ritual could be so internalised through daily repetition that it would no longer require this external medium of expression in action. It could become purely mental, a ritual of self-definition in thought. The Tantric was exhorted by the left to see the sequence of ritual (*pūjākrama*) as a mirror in which he could perceive and contemplate his ultimate nature. Thereby he could attain liberation, for to be fully aware *of* this ultimate nature is to be liberated *as* this nature. By means of daily repetition he was to achieve a state of mind in which he believed that he was and always had been that which his ritual defines.

The ritualist of the Śaiva Siddhānta maintained that the scriptures taught no self beyond that of a purified and blissless individuality. For him salvation was not a merging into a transcendental godhead. It was simply that state of the eternally individual self in which its *equality* with Śiva previously concealed by the substance of impurity had become fully manifest. He did not become Śiva; he became *a* Śiva, omniscient and omnipotent but numerically distinct. Thus the Kashmiri Śaiva Siddhāntins stressed the difference between the Śiva who had never been bound, the 'original Śiva' (*anādiśiva*), and those who were Śivas through liberation from bondage, 'released Śivas' (*muktaśivas*). The latter were held to be capable of performing the five cosmic functions (*pañcakṛtya-*: creation, maintenance of the created, retraction of the created, and the binding and liberating of other selves), but to refrain from so doing because of the non-competitive spirit inherent in liberation.

Equally absolute in the Kashmiri Śaiva Siddhānta was the doctrine that matter and consciousness are entirely separate. According to Rāmakaṇṭha, following Sadyojyoti's interpretation of the scriptures, selves know and act upon a world whose existence is entirely independent of them, though it is arranged to fulfil their karmic needs. Śiva causes the entities of our universe to emerge by stimulating an independently eternal, all-pervasive, and unconscious 'world-stuff' (*māyā*). Thus are created the various spheres, bodies and faculties by means of which eternal selves can experience the effects of their past actions (*karma*) and eventually attain release from their beginningless state of bondage through Śaiva consecration (*dīkṣā*).

In the Kashmiri Trika the seeker of liberation (*mumukṣu*) is to realise through his ritual a self which breaks through these exoteric barriers of pluralism, realism and reified impurity. For the self of his worship and meditation is an absolute and omnipotent consciousness which, by manifesting contraction of its infinite powers, *appears* as separate individuals, their streams of experience, and the 'outer' objects or 'causes' of those experiences. He thinks of the three goddesses convergent in the fourth as this infinite and all-containing self, seeing their structure as that of his own consciousness. As this awareness deepens through immersion in the ritual, his individual consciousness, which is these powers contracted without change of structure, dissolves into its uncontracted prototype (cf. p. 673).

The Doctrines of Vibration (Spanda) and Recognition (Pratyabhijñā)

According to the Kashmiri Trika these doctrines of the ultimate non-plurality of centres of consciousness, of the non-existence of any reality except as projection within this all-containing consciousness, and consequently of the immateriality of impurity (*mala*), have been revealed by Śiva in all the Tantras of Bhairava. This is to say that they were read into this corpus or presupposed in any reading, for the surviving texts themselves hardly support this sweeping claim.

None the less, these doctrines are not entirely post-scriptural. For the view that the Deity is non-dual, dynamic consciousness (*saṃvidadvayavāda*, *śāktādvayavāda*) was already present at the far left of this corpus, in the literature of the Kāpālika and Kaula cults of Kālī (in the Mata and the Krama). From the middle of the ninth century the Trika, which was then permeated by the Kālī cult (see p. 678), produced theological metaphysicians who elevated these doctrines towards respectability within the Śaiva mainstream by abstracting them from their heterodox ritual context, by formulating them in a less sectarian terminology and by defending them philosophically against the doctrines of the Buddhists. This new direction began precisely during the period at which royal patronage in Kashmir started to shift from Pāñcarātra Vaiṣṇavism to Śaivism.

The first stage of this development is seen in two works of the ninth century: the *Aphorisms of Śiva* (*Śivasūtra*) and the *Concise Verses on Vibration* (*Spandakārikā*). The first was 'discovered' by Vasugupta. The second was composed by Vasagupta according to some, or by his pupil Kallaṭa according to others.

The *Śivasūtra* is too brief and allusive a work for us to be able to form a precise picture of its doctrine apart from its inevitably biased interpretation in the commentaries of Bhāskara (*fl. c.* 925–75) and Kṣemarāja (*fl. c.* 1000–50). We can see only that it sought to outline the non-ritual soteriology of an esoteric Śaiva tradition closely related to what we find in the *Jayadrathayāmalatantra* and the Kālī-based Trika.

The *Spandakārikā*, being more discursive, can be much more clearly understood independently of the commentaries. The work's fifty-two verses, offered as the key to the theology of the *Śivasūtra*, proposed that Śiva is all-inclusive reality, a single, unified consciousness, which manifests itself as all subjects, acts and objects of experience by virtue of an inherent and infinite dynamism. This dynamism, the essential nature of the Deity, was termed the Vibration-Reality (*spanda-tattva*). Liberation was to be attained by realising this vibration (*spanda*) in the source, course and end of all states and movements of consciousness.

Kṣemarāja, the author of an important commentary on this work, was probably right when he claimed that the scriptural background of this text is the Krama and the Mata with some elements of the

Trika. For the concept of 'vibration', or rather the use of this term to denote the inherent dynamism of a non-dual consciousness, which is the signature of this doctrine, is well-established in the *Jayadrathayāmala* and other texts of the Kālī cults.

The second stage of this scholarly underpinning began in the early tenth century with the *Perception of Śiva* (*Śivadṛṣṭi*) by Somānanda (*fl. c.* 900–50). While the *Spandakārikā* preserved some of the heterodox flavour of the goddess-orientated traditions of the far left, Somānanda, though he was certainly an initiate in those traditions, formulated a Śaiva non-dualism along more orthodox and rigorously philosophical lines. His pupil Utpaladeva, also a *guru* of the Trika and the Krama, gave this non-dualism its classical form in his *Concise Verses on the Recognition of the Deity* (*Īśvarapratyabhijñākārikā*). Claiming to follow his master he offered a 'new and easy path to salvation' through the recognition (*pratyabhijñā*) that it is one's own identity (*ātman*) which is Śiva, the Great Deity (Maheśvara). This transpersonal Self (*ātmeśvara*) is to be seen as that which contains all subjective and objective phenomena, holding this totality in a blissful synthesis of non-dual awareness. Through this recognition, which is forcefully defended against the Buddhist doctrine of impersonal flux, one is released from the cycle of death and rebirth (*saṃsāra*). For one's true identity is an already-liberated and never-bound 'I'-consciousness outside *time*, *form* and *location* (the three bases of (the appearance of) bondage in the continuum of transmigratory existence). This state of limitation is to be contemplated as the spontaneous play of this 'I'-consciousness. The pure autonomy (*svātantrya*) of the self expresses itself by manifesting its own 'contraction' in the form of limited centres of consciousness perceiving and acting within time, form and location, in accordance with the causal power of their acts (*karma*). Thus there arises the 'binding' appearance of essential differences between a world 'out there', a self 'in here' and other selves. Liberation is the realisation that all this is internal to the awareness which represents it as external. Consciousness thereby throws off its state of 'extrinsicist contraction', and knows itself only as the pre-relational, pre-discursive unity of manifestation (*prakāśa*) and self-cognition (*vimarśa*).

The philosophical position of Utpaladeva's Doctrine of Recognition was analysed and supported in great detail by Abhinavagupta (*fl. c.* 975–1025), a pupil of his pupil Lakṣmaṇagupta, in a commentary of the *Concise Verses* (*Īśvarapratyabhijñāvimarśinī*) and in a much longer commentary on Utpaladeva's own exegesis of his verses (*Īśvarapratyabhijñāvivṛtivimarśinī*).

The Doctrine of Recognition and the Trika

The Kashmiri Trika is known to us principally through the works of this same Abhinavagupta, particularly through his *Tantrāloka*, *Tantrasāra*, *Mālinīvijayavārtika* and *Parātriṃśikāvivaraṇa*. In the first three of these he expounds the doctrine and ritual of the Trika on the basis of the *Mālinīvijayottaratantra*. In the fourth he develops a more concentrated form of Trika worship, which focuses only on Parā, the highest of the three goddesses. Because the goddess is worshipped here as Solitary Heroine (*ekavīrā*), that is without the customary offerings to aspects and emanations, this tradition is sometimes distinguished from the Trika proper as the Ekavīra. For the same reason it is known as the Anuttara, 'that above which there is nothing'.

His exegesis of both of these forms of the Trika is based on the Doctrine of Recognition. Utpaladeva's concepts and terminology provide his metaphysical groundwork and are fed into Trika ritual. Thus, to give but one example, the phases of the worshipper's divinisation of his person with *mantras* (*nyāsa*) is required to be understood within the framework of Utpaladeva's four levels of contraction in which the self manifests itself in progressively grosser forms as the sensation-less void (*śūnya*), internal sensation (*prāṇa*), the mind (*buddhi*) and the body (*deha*).

Thus we may speak of at least three major phases in the evolution of the Trika. At the beginning are the *Siddhayogeśvarīmata* and related texts (see pp. 672–4) which teach the cult of the three goddesses alone. Then this triad is transcended and subsumed within Kālī (see p. 678). Finally we have the Pratyabhijñā-based Trika of the Abhinavagupta with its two aspects, the first being the Kālī-based cult of the *Tantrāloka*, and the second the condensed cult of Parā as Solitary Heroine.

The Kashmiri Krama

The Krama passed from its scriptural phase into chartable history with Jñānanetra *alias* Śivānanda in the first half of the ninth century. Said to have been instructed supernaturally by the Goddess herself in Oḍḍiyāna, he was the source of well-attested *guru* lineages in Kashmir and beyond. His tradition is remarkable for the theoretical structure of its ritual. It synthesised and adjusted the scriptural prototypes (principally those of the *Devīpañcaśataka* and the *Kramasadbhāva* (see pp. 683–4)) to produce a liturgy which could be thought of as the unfolding of the imperceptible sequence of cognition (*saṃvit-krama*) in the perceptible sequence of worship (*pūjā-krama*).

After contemplating various pentads as the structure of his bodily and mental existence and seeing them as emanations of a set of five goddesses representing the cycle of cognition—thus he consecrates his person as the true site of worship and seat of power (*pīṭha*)—the worshipper proceeds to a five-phased worship which enacts the progress of cognition from initial to terminal voidness. Each phase is equated with one of these same five goddesses.

In the first, that of the goddess Vyomavāmeśvarī (She who Emits the [Five] Voids), he worships the whole pentadic cycle (the

Five Voids) as condensed within the initial and eternal vibration of thoughtless consciousness.

In the second, the phase of the goddess Khecarī (She who Pervades the Void [of Cognition]), he worships the twelve Lords of the Wheel of Light (*prakāśa-cakra*). These are identified with the twelve faculties of cognition (the introvertive mental organ [*buddhi*] and the five senses) and action (the extrovertive mental organ [*manas*], speech, manipulation, locomotion, excretion and sexual pleasure). He mediates on these as illuminated by cognitive power as it moves from its initial vibration (*spanda*) in the five voids towards the extroverted representation of objects facing a subject.

In the third stage, that of the goddess Bhūcarī (She who Pervades the [Outer] Field), the constituents of the preceding phase have moved outwards and incorporated into consciousness the representation of the five external sense-data (sound, tactile sensation, visible form, taste and odour). This extroversion entails the suppression of the introvertive mental organ. Thus there are now sixteen constituents: the preceding twelve reduced to eleven and increased by five. These he worships as the sixteen Yoginīs of the Wheel of Sensual Bliss (*ānanda-cakra*).

The fourth stage is pervaded by the goddess Saṃhārabhakṣiṇī (She who Devours in Retraction). It represents the first stage in the reversion of cognitive power to its prediscursive source, the internalisation of the object of sensation that occurs in the awareness that one has perceived it. The extrovertive mental organ (*manas*) which was distinct in the preceding phase is now submerged and the introvertive mental organ (*buddhi*) re-emerges. These sixteen are increased to seventeen by the addition of ego-awareness (*ahaṅkāra*). They are worshipped as the Lords of the Wheel of Fusion (*mūrti-cakra*).

The fifth and final stage is that of the goddess Raudreśvarī (The Terrible). Here he worships the sixty-four Yoginīs of the Wheel of the Multitude (*vṛnda-cakra*). The ego-awareness which emerged in the preceding phase is represented as suddenly expanding to obliterate all that conceals the radiant voidness of the transpersonal Absolute within consciousness. This obliteration is worshipped in five stages as sixteen, twenty-four, twelve, eight and four Yoginīs.

The first sixteen of these Yoginī emanations dissolve the latent traces (*vāsanā*, *saṃskāra*) of the field of objective sensation worshipped as the Wheel of Sensual Bliss (*ānanda-cakra*). In the second stage the traces of the twelve constituents of the cognitive Wheel of Light (*prakāśa-cakra*) are obliterated. Twenty-four Yoginīs are worshipped here, because each of the twelve has two aspects, a latent and an active. In the third phase twelve Yoginīs penetrate this cognitive field with pure, non-discursive awareness. Now there remain the latent traces of the subtle body (*puryaṣṭaka*) consisting of the five sense-data (sound, etc.) and the three internal faculties (the extrovertive and introvertive mental organs together with ego-awareness). By worshipping eight Yoginīs here he enacts the elimination of these elements. The four Yoginīs worshipped in the fifth and last phase of the Wheel of the Multitude (*vṛnda-cakra*) represent the obliteration of a subtle residue which the preceding eight left untouched: the deep latent impression of the threefold inner mind and of objectivity reduced to a single, undifferentiated sensation of contact (*sparśa*).

He now worships Raudreśvarī herself as the sixty-fifth power, the non-relational ground of these sixty-four Yoginīs, consciousness in its pristine purity. He identifies her with Maṅgalā *alias* Vīrasiṃhā, the goddess incarnate of Oḍḍiyāna. He thereby equates the Krama's Absolute with the lineage of teachers, male and female, who have embodied this Absolute and transmitted it to him. For after Maṅgalā he worships Jñānanetra and then the *gurus* who descend from Jñānanetra to himself.

Finally he worships the four Sequences (*krama*), those of Emission (*sṛṣṭi*-), Maintenance (*sthiti*-), Retraction (*saṃhāra*-), and the Nameless (*anākhya*-) which pervades the three as their ground. The twelve Kālīs of this fourth sequence are to be worshipped during sexual intercourse with the *dūtī*. They are understood as the gradual withdrawal of cognitive power into Kālasaṃkarṣiṇī (Kālī the Destroyer of Time), the waveless void of the absolute Self. Here the worshipper realises the absolute autonomy (*svātantrya*) of the Goddess (Consciousness) through which she assumes the form of the universe without contamination or diminution of her nature.

Three major works of this Kashmiri Krama survive, all entitled *Mahānayaprakāśa* (Illumination of the Great Way), that of Śitikaṇṭha (in Old Kashmiri with a Sanskrit auto-commentary), that of Arṇasiṃha (MS) and the third anonymous. The last is the source of our exposition of the phases of pentadic worship leading up to that of the four Sequences.

The function of the ritual sequence of this tradition is said to be that it prepares the initiate for the non-sequential (*akrama*) intuition that will enable him to transcend it. It is designed to condition awareness with the image of its true nature, so that eventually it will provoke a spontaneous and instantaneous 'swallowing of dichotomising cognition' (*vikalpagrāsa*), the annihilation (*alaṃgrāsa*) of the mechanisms of individuation and projection through which the innate (*sahaja*) purity of awareness appears *as though* it were sullied in the natural processes of ideation and perception. The worshipper is to pass through the ritual to reach the liberating conviction that absolute reality is this pure awareness, and that the phases and levels of cognition are co-extensive with it as its innate vitality. Liberation (*mokṣa*) here is the resolution of the distinction in self-perception between a transcendental or internal state of *nirvāṇa* and an imminent or external state of finite, transmigratory existence (*bhava*, *saṃsāra*).

This system of contemplative worship was not the Krama's only means of enlightenment. It believed that there were those who were capable of reaching the goal without it. For these two higher paths are described. In the first, that of Oral Instruction (*kathana*), the *guru* was to provoke the disciple's intuition through certain mystical aphorisms (*kathā*, *chummā*). The emphasis here is on sudden enlightenment (*sāhasa*). In the second path the goal was believed to be attained without any instruction, either spontaneously or through some non-verbal stimulus such as the *guru*'s glance.

Both this intuitionism and this view of ritual as a mode of liberating insight are thoroughly in harmony with the position which Abhinavagupta expounds for the Trika. Indeed in this respect the Trika was greatly indebted to the Krama. It had already accommodated important elements of this system in the second phase of its development (see p. 678). In the third phase, during which this enriched Trika was grounded in the Doctrine of Recognition, we find Abhinavagupta drawing directly on the postscriptural Krama of the lineage of Jñānanetra, adapting it as the basis of the Trika's claim to be the ultimate in Śaiva revelation. Kṣemarāja, his pupil, who offered no detailed exegesis in the Trika itself, unambiguously asserts that it is the Krama that embodies this final truth. Clearly the prestige of the Krama-based Kālī cult was widely felt in esoteric Śaiva circles. The *Manthānabhairavatantra* places it above the Trika at the summit of the hierarchy of the Śaiva traditions, allowing it to be transcended only by the Western Transmission (Paścimāmnāya), the tradition of the text itself. Another work of that Transmission, the *Ciñciṇīmatasārasamuccaya*, goes further. It gives the realisation of the Krama's Kālīs in the Sequence of the Nameless as the highest, internal worship within the cult of Kubjikā itself.

The Kashmiri Cult of Svacchandabhairava

We have seen that Śaivism in Kashmir was split between two centres of authority. On the right was the ritualistic Śaiva Siddhānta with its anti-mystical pluralism and extrinsicism. On the left was the gnostic non-dualism of the Trika and the Krama. The right saw the left as heretical while the left saw the right as the exoteric base of the Śaiva hierarchy, leading to liberation but only at death.

It might be imagined therefore that it was the tradition of the Śaiva Siddhānta which was the source of the practice of the greater part of the Śaiva community, and that the Trika and the Krama were the preserves of enthusiasts dependent on this exoteric or common Śaivism both for the candidates for these 'higher' initiations and as the form of their own more public identity in the wider society. This then would be the sense of the frequently quoted maxim of the left which requires one to be privately Kaula, publicly Śaiva and Vedic in one's social intercourse.

However, the interrelation of the traditions was more complex in Kashmir. For the Śaiva cult of the majority was not that of Sadāśiva taught by the Siddhānta, but that of Svacchandabhairava. Since the latter derived its authority from the *Svacchandatantra* of the Mantrapīṭha section of the Tantras of Bhairava (see p. 670), it was, strictly speaking, a tradition of the Kāpālika-based left. None the less, the Kashmiri practised a thoroughly domesticated form of the cult, and in the tenth century the Śaiva Siddhānta, though not its source, had taken advantage of this to bring it under the sway of its doctrines. The Śaiva Siddhānta was, therefore, the principal doctrinal authority among the Śaivas of Kashmir, at least during the tenth century.

It is hardly surprising, then, that the non-dualistic tradition of the left should have tried to oust the Śaiva Siddhānta from this position of power once it had itself attained a degree of respectability during the course of the tenth century. This vital task of establishing the authority of the new exegesis beyond the confined territory of the Trika and the Krama was accomplished by the works of Kṣemarāja. While his teacher Abhinavagupta limited himself to the exposition of the esoteric traditions in harmony with the Doctrine of Recognition, Kṣemarāja (*fl. c.* 1000–50) popularised the essential doctrine and applied it through commentaries to the cult of Svacchandabhairava and its annexes. In the first case we have such works as his *Essence of Recognition* (*Pratyabhijñāhṛdaya*) and his commentaries on two popular collections of hymns, the *Stavacintāmaṇi* of Bhaṭṭa-Nārāyaṇa and the *Stotrāvalī* of Utpaladeva. In the second case we have his elaborate analytical commentaries on the *Svacchandatantra* and the *Netratantra*.

In both of these commentaries Kṣemarāja states that his motive is to free the understanding of these texts from the dualistic exegesis that was traditional in his day. The importance of the *Svacchandatantra* has already been stated. The *Netratantra* was the authority for the cult of Amṛteśvarabhairava and his consort Amṛtalakṣmī. The worship of this pair was closely linked with that of Svacchandabhairava and Aghoreśvarī in the Kashmiri tradition, as can be seen from the surviving ritual handbooks (*paddhatis*) in use until recently among the Tantric family priests.

In purely doctrinal terms Kṣemarāja's commentaries do violence to both of these texts, at least as much as that of which the dualistic commentaries must have been guilty. Neither Tantra fits either exegetical straitjacket. In the area of ritual, however, Kṣemarāja had a clear advantage. When, for example, he attacked the then current practice of substituting water for alcoholic liquor in Svacchandabhairava's guest-offering, he was simply reinstating the text within the tradition of the Bhairava Tantras to which it properly belonged. This recontextualisation would have seemed all the more plausible in the light of the fact that when the deity-system of the Svacchanda cult of common Śaiva worship in Kashmir extends beyond its immediate boundaries, it does so not to the right and the

Śaiva Siddhānta but to the left and the goddess cults. Thus we find the *Picumata-Brahmayāmala*'s Caṇḍā Kāpālinī with her eight *śaktis* (see p. 672), Kuleśvarī and the eight Mothers with the Bhairavas (see p. 681), the Kaula alcohol deity Ānandeśvarabhairava, the Trika's Parā and Mālinī (as Goddess of the Eastern Transmission), Kubjikā (as Godess of the Western Transmission), several aspects of Tripurasundarī and a number of goddesses from the *Jayadrathayāmala*.

The literature of this common Śaiva worship current in Kashmir shows that this attempt to throw off the influence of the Śaiva Siddhānta was entirely successful. How quickly this was achieved cannot be seen from the evidence so far uncovered. We can say only that the corpus of the anonymous texts of Śaiva ritual in Kashmir is completely non-dualistic in the manner defined by Abhinavagupta and Kṣemarāja, that this corpus records a tradition which must go back at least five hundred years, and that there is no trace of any Kashmiri literature in the doctrinal or liturgical aspects of the Śaiva Siddhānta after the eleventh century. But the most striking indication of its ascendency is its influence outside the sphere of the properly Tantric.

Śaiva Non-Dualism and the Non-Tantric Tradition in Kashmir

When the Pratyabhijñā-based Trika was emerging in Kashmir both the Vedic and the Tantric traditions were fully deployed. The first was active in both its *śrauta* and its *smārta* forms (see pp. 660–2), while the second could be seen not only in the various forms of Śaivism outlined above but also in the Vaiṣṇavism of the Pāñcarātra.

At some point, probably during the Muslim period from the fourteenth century, the Kashmiri *śrauta* tradition of the Kāṭhaka-Yajurvedins disappeared entirely. All that remained of the Vedic tradition were the domestic rites (following the ordinances of Laugākṣi) together with a repertoire of non-Tantric deity-worship (*devapūjā*). In Kashmir, as elsewhere, this *smārta* tradition of worship mirrors the Tantric at a safe distance. This is to say that it has borrowed Tantric deities and liturgical forms, but uses Vedic rather than Tantric *mantras* within this framework.

The Tantric Vaiṣṇavism of the Pāñcarātra also disappeared, but not without leaving behind clear evidence that it was once a powerful influence in Kashmiri religion. For the Tantric tradition mirrored in the *smārta* worship of the region is not the Śaiva as one might have expected but precisely the principal cult of the earliest scriptural Pāñcarātra, that of Vāsudeva in his form as Vaikuṇṭha (see Figure 36.10), in which a mild human face is flanked by those of his incarnations as the Man-Lion (Narasiṃha) and the Boar (Varāha), with that of the wrathful sage Kapila behind.

Thus there remained only the simple dichotomy between a *smārta* tradition influenced by the Pāñcarātra and the Tantric Śaiva

Figure 36.10: Vaikuṇṭha

tradition which, as we have seen, was itself simplified by the decline of the Śaiva Siddhānta.

It should not be imagined, however, that the non-Tantric excluded and condemned the Tantric in Kashmir. While this may have been the more usual position in the rest of India, as earlier in Kashmir itself, the evidence of recent centuries shows a more or less unified community. The Vedic tradition came to be outside the Śaiva only in the sense that the former comprised the rituals of those who had undergone the common investiture (*upanayana*) of the Brahmanical tradition but had not yet undergone or never underwent special consecration in the form of the Tantric Śaiva *dīkṣā*. Thus they were not bound by the additional and more exacting duties of Tantric worship. However, outside the special domain of ritual these brahmins were as Śaiva as the rest. Texts dealing with their duties teach side by side with non-Tantric ritual a thoroughly Tantric form of *yoga*. This is designed to cause *śakti* as macrocosmic power within the microcosm of the body (*kuṇḍalinī*) to rise from her state of latency in the region of the anus (*mūlādhāra-cakra*), to ascend through the central channel (*suṣumṇā*) imagined along the internal vertical axis of the body, to transcend the body through the cranial 'aperture of Brahmā' (*brahmarandhra*), and finally to come to rest in union with Śiva at a point twelve finger-breadths above the head (*dvādaśānta*). This form of *kuṇḍalinī-yoga* is derived, as we have seen (see pp. 687–8), from the later Kaula tradition of the cults of Kubjikā and Tripurasundarī. As for duty in the form of the cultivation of liberating knowledge (*jñāna*), this is the study of the mystical soteriology of the Trika expounded by Abhinavagupta, which is to say the practice of all but the ritual of that system.

Thus the whole society of Kashmiri brahmins had become Śaiva. It was no longer necessary, as the earlier tradition had insisted, to take Tantric consecration, thereby binding oneself to perform Tantric worship, if one wished to have access to Tantric yoga and mystical doctrine.

This separation, which enabled Tantric Śaivism to pervade the community so completely, is not a recent phenomenon. Its roots can be seen at the turn of the millennium in the works of Abhinavagupta and Kṣemarāja themselves. For it is in the essence of their opposition to the Śaiva Siddhānta that they saw ritual as a lower and transcendable mode of self-knowledge (see pp. 700–1). The rule that only those who had been consecrated and bound to Tantric ritual could attain liberation was preserved only in the letter. For the definition of consecration was stretched into the metaphorical so that it could bypass ritual in the special case of 'consecration by the deities of one's own consciousness'. This sort of thinking was justified by appealing to the authority of the most heterodox area of the Śaiva Mantramārga; but it served in the end to make a private Tantric identity accessible to all Kashmiri, while the Śaiva Siddhāntins, for all their ostentatious orthopraxy, declined and disappeared from the scene. For though the Siddhānta argued that it was pure in the sense accepted by the non-Tantric, it did not do so out of any desire to extend its domain across boundaries of ritual qualification (*adhikāra*) into the wider community. Its concern was rather to claim high social status for its adherents as a distinct and exclusive group within that community. The Śaiva Siddhānta has survived to this day in south India among an endogamous community of Śaiva temple-priests, the Ādiśaivas, as the basis of their profession and the guarantee of their exclusive hereditary right to practise that profession. It seems very probable that the Kashmiri Śaiva Siddhāntins were protecting similar rights. If they died out it may have been because centuries of Islamicisation had deprived them of their institutional base. Certainly nothing survives in Kashmir that is remotely comparable to the richly endowed Śaiva temples which continue to provide the livelihood of the Ādiśaivas in the Tamil south.

Finally, just as the esoteric Śaiva traditions in Kashmir flowed into the non-specialised brahmin majority, so when these same traditions went south they took root among the Śaiva brahmin community that surrounds the Ādiśaiva enclaves in that region. The cult of Tripurasundarī (see pp. 688–9) became particularly well established. In purely Tantric circles it was propagated within the theological system of the Pratyabhijñā-based Trika; but, much as in Kashmir, it came to pervade the wider community of Śaiva brahmins known as the Smārtas. Purged of its Kaula heteropraxy, it became there the special cult of the renunciate (*saṃnyāsin*) Śaṅkarācāryas, who are the ultimate spiritual authorities of this community. Its emblem, the *śrīcakra* (see pp. 689–90), was installed in the major Śaiva temples to assert their claim to pre-eminence even within the domain of the Ādiśaivas.

Further Reading

On Pāśupata doctrines:

Hara, Minoru 'Nakulīśa-Pāśupata-Darśanam', in *Indo-Iranian Journal*, vol. II (1958), pp. 8–32

On the Pāśupatas, Kālāmukhas and Kāpālikas:

Lorenzen, David N. *The Kāpālikas and Kālāmukhas: Two Lost Śaivite Sects* (Thomson Press (India), New Delhi, 1972)

On the doctrines of the Śaiva Siddhānta:

Brunner, Hélène, 'Un chapitre du *Sarvadarśanasamgraha*: Le *Śaivadarśana*', in *Mèlanges Chinois et Bouddhiques*, vol. XX (*Tantric and Taoist Studies in Honour of R.A. Stein*) (Institut Belge des Hautes Études Chinoises, Brussels, 1981), pp. 96–140

On the mysticism and ritual of the Śaiva Siddhānta:

Brunner, Hélène, 'Le mysticisme dans les āgama śivaites', in *Studia Missionalia*, vol. 26 (1977) (Gregorian University, Rome), pp. 287–314

—— *Somaśambhupaddhati*, vols. 1–3 (1963–77) (Institut Français d'Indologie, Pondicherry). See the introductions to these volumes for an excellent account of Śaiva ritual. The other traditions of Tantric worship (the Pāñcarātra, the Trika, the cult of Svacchandabhairava, etc.) differ from this only in their deities, *mantras*, *maṇḍalas*, *mudrās* and such constituents. The ritual framework is largely constant.

On the Trika and related systems:

Gnoli, Raniero (trans.), *Luce delle Sacre Scritture (Tantrāloka) di Abhinavagupta*, (Unione Tipografico-Editrice Torinese, Turin, 1972)

Padoux, André *Recherches sur la Symbolique et l'Énergie de la Parole dans certains Textes Tantriques* (Institut de Civilisation Indienne, Paris, 1963)

Sanderson, Alexis 'Purity and Power among the Brahmans of Kashmir' in Michael Carrithers, Steven Collins and Steven Lukes (eds.), *The Category of the Person* (Cambridge University Press, Cambridge, 1985), pp. 191–216

37 Modern Hinduism

Glyn Richards

Any attempt to give an account of Hinduism in the nineteenth and twentieth centuries within the compass of a short article must of necessity be selective. What I propose to do in the following essay is to select those leaders of thought who may be regarded as both inheritors of the Hindu religious and social traditions and contributors to the renewal of Hinduism and the development of modern India.

It is not without justification that Rāmmohan Roy (1772–1833) has been described as the father of modern India. His enthusiasm for reform may be attributed in part to the influence of Islamic thought and Western ideas, but, as his *Vedānta grantha* shows, he is also indebted to Vedāntic teaching concerning the unity and supremacy of *Brahman* as Eternal Being and One without a second. His defence of Hinduism against the attacks of Christian missionaries is an indication of the influence of his Brahminic upbringing and the part it played in moulding his desire to restore the religious purity of Hinduism. He endeavoured to do this through his journalistic and literary activities and through the formation of the *Brāhmo Samāj*, a society he founded in 1828 to promote the worship of the one eternal, immutable God and the rejection of image worship so characteristic of popular devotion. If the intellectual bent of the *Brāhmo Samāj* deprived it of popular appeal, it nevertheless succeeded in creating an atmosphere of liberalism and rationality in which a reinterpretation of the Hindu tradition could take place.

Roy's emphasis on logic and reason is reputed to have characterised one of his earliest Persian works entitled *Tuhfatul-ul-Muwahhiddin* (Gift to Deists), in which belief in a Creator, the existence of the soul and life after death, are claimed to be the basic tenets of all religions (though such tenets could hardly be attributed either logically or reasonably, e.g. to Buddhism). The same work dismisses as irrational beliefs in miracles, anthropomorphic deities and the efficacy of rituals in man's salvation. It was his earnest endeavour to convince his fellow-countrymen and prove to his European friends that what he called superstitious and idolatrous practices had nothing to do with the pure spirit of the Hindu religion. He was not convinced of the symbolic nature of the images worshipped and maintained that Hindus of his day firmly believed in the existence of innumerable gods and goddesses.

His opposition to idolatry is matched by his rejection of some of the social customs of Hinduism, especially suttee, the practice of burning widows on the funeral pyres of their husbands. His advocacy of the provision of education for his fellow-countrymen, particularly in mathematics, natural philosophy, chemistry and other useful sciences, was aimed at the elimination of such customs, the cultural improvement of the native population and the harmonisation of Western science and Eastern spirituality for the benefit of mankind. His pursuit of this goal justly earned him a place of eminence as one of the most creative personalities of nineteenth-century India.

A fellow member of the *Brāhmo Samāj*, whose opposition to idolatry matched that of Roy, was Devendranāth Tagore (1817–1905). It was his firm belief that the ultimate good of India would derive from the rejection of tantric and puranic myths and legends and the acceptance of *Brahman* as revealed in the Upaniṣads. He showed great enthusiasm for the purification of the Hindu religion and joined the campaign to provide free education for Hindu children. A man of sensitive spirit, Tagore in his later years inclined to mysticism and his piety earned him the title Maharishi, 'great sage'. He attracted many able young men to the *Samāj*, including Keshab Chunder Sen (1838–84), who became equally committed to religious and social reform.

Sen's enthusiasm to propagate the message of the society led him to found the *Indian Mirror* and the *Dharmatattva*, journals of religion and philosophy, and to establish branches of the *Samāj* in many parts of India. Like Roy he rejected idolatry as erroneous and superstitious, but unlike his predecessor he recognised the popular need for visible and tangible expressions of the divine and the intense love, reverence and faith manifested in the worship of images. Hence his claim that Hindus ought to be grateful for the gods and goddesses of India and the legends of Hindu mythology. His unbounded enthusiasm and vitality proved a mixed blessing to the society and schisms ensued which resulted in the founding of the *Brāhmo Samāj of India* in 1865, and subsequently the setting up of the *Sādhāran Brāhmo Samāj* in 1878 by his disenchanted followers.

Sen's close acquaintance with Christian teaching provided him with the terminology he needed to express the principles of his New Dispensation. This he refers to as equivalent to the Jewish and Christian Dispensations; as the fulfilment of Christ's prophecy; as the harmonisation of all scriptures and all religions; and as proclaiming the message of love which prohibits all distinctions between Brahmins and Śūdras, Asiatics and Europeans. Its uniqueness for him lay in its insistence on the direct, unmediated worship of God. His acceptance of the divinity of Christ and the title of Jesudās, the servant of Jesus, suggests that he completely embraced the Christian faith. In fact he considered Christ to be an Asiatic and his concept of the Incarnation is not 'once and for all' but the manifestation of God in history through great men and prophets. Christ, he claims, held the doctrine of divine humanity, which is essentially a Hindu doctrine and at one with the Vedāntic notion of man's unity with the Absolute.

Sen's belief in the providential nature of British rule would not have been shared by Dayānanda Sarasvatī (1824–83), whose promotion of Hindi as a national language was not unrelated to the development of national self-consciousness. He was fully aware of the intimate relation that pertained between language, religion and nationalism, and was convinced that political independence was the natural corollary of the restoration of Vedic ideals. It was his firm belief that the Vedas contained true revelation and were the authoritative source of the Hindu religion. Through the generosity of his followers he founded schools to teach the Vedas but this proved an unsuccessful experiment. More successful was his insistence on the place of morality in true religion and his denunciation of idol worship as contrary to the teaching of the scriptures. In his view God, being formless and omnipresent, cannot be conceived of existing in any particular object, and the evil practice of idol worship was responsible for widespread ignorance and mendacity in the country.

The *Ārya Samāj*, founded by Dayānanda in 1875, provided him with the organisation necessary to propagate his religious and social ideals. Among the rules adopted by the society, belief in God, the authority of the Vedas and the rejection of idol worship and incarnational doctrines were paramount. The duty of all members of the *Samāj* was to promote spiritual monotheism, Vedic authority and social reform. The reforms he advocated related to child marriage, widow remarriage and *niyoga*. He was aware of the problems of early widowhood and child marriage and the relation between the dowry system and female infanticide. The eradication of the practice of child marriage, he believed, would reduce the number of widows and he advocated *niyoga*, the temporary legal union of widows and widowers, as an interim solution to the problem of early widowhood. He approved of the education of both sexes, insisting that it was the basis of mutual respect between husband and wife. The best form of marriage, in his view, was marriage by choice (*svayaṃvara*) after the education of the contracting parties had been completed. Education itself should involve Hindi and Sanskrit and a case should be made for making them the medium of instruction in schools.

Dayānanda's aggressive nationalism and deep desire to lead his fellow-countrymen back to the Vedas earned him the title of the

'Luther of India', a description which is not entirely inappropriate.

Of the mystics of modern India pride of place must go to Rāmakrishna (1836–86), who from an early age is reputed to have experienced mystical trances. Though lacking formal education he possessed an abundance of native intelligence and for the greater part of his life served God at the Kālī temple at Dakshineswar. Through his association with followers of the Tantric and Vedānta schools he acquired an understanding of yogic techniques and the ways of *bhakti* (devotion) and *jñāna* (knowledge) as means of union with the divine. His personal experiences of other religious traditions, especially Islam and Christianity, enabled him to make the claim that different religions are simply different paths to the same goal. As Kālī, the Divine Mother, and *Brahman* are two aspects of the same reality so the mystical experience of Christ is at one with the mystical experience of Allah. God may be called by different names but he is one and the same. There is no necessity to choose between the formless Absolute and the personal God, for God with form is as real as God without form and the difference between them is no more than that between ice and water. The impediment to spiritual development is worldliness which is *māyā*. It is man's ignorance of his true self that causes him to become enmeshed in *māyā* in the first place, and release is attained through discrimination which recognises God alone as real and eternal. Social reform, including the elimination of caste distinctions, should derive naturally from the love and worship of God.

Rāmakrishna's disciples, of whom Vivekānanda was the most prominent, proclaimed his teaching throughout India but were more explicitly committed to social reform than their master, establishing schools, orphanages and hospitals in order to give practical expression to their religious ideals.

Another of India's mystics was Rabindranāth Tagore (1861–1941) whose views concerning the interrelation of God, man and nature would classify him as a nature mystic. The Absolute is manifested in creation and both man and nature are revelations of God. The same power that creates the universe enlightens man's consciousness and the main goal of life is to realise the Absolute through the immediate apprehension of the divine in one's own soul. Spiritual progress is achieved through a life lived in close proximity to nature, hence the rural location of Viśva Bhārati University founded by Tagore in 1921 to promote his religious and cultural ideals.

Man's kinship with nature is coupled with his identity with his fellow man. God's immanence in creation implies man's involvement with social justice and the needs of all God's creatures. In a world suffused with the spirit of God nothing can be deemed untouchable so the rigidity and exclusivism of the caste system must be rejected as contrary to the cultivation of spirituality. Similarly, the selfish pursuit of materialistic goals, which intensifies the inequality between those who have and those who have not, undermines the social system and degrades man himself. The same applies on a national level when selfishness takes the form of patriotism devoid of concern for humanity as a whole which resorts to force to achieve its ends. Concern for the nurture of the soul determines Tagore's attitude to every aspect of life and gives a marked distinctiveness to his social, cultural and religious ideals.

One of the foremost mystical philosophers of India is generally accepted to be Aurobindo Ghose (1872–1950), who, after a period of political activity in close association with Bāl Gangādhar Tilak (1856–1920), which resulted in his being jailed on a charge of advocating terrorism and violence, withdrew to the French settlement of Pondicherry where he spent forty years in study and contemplation. The fruit of those years is his philosophical system of integral yoga which he describes as Vedāntic. The essence of his system is that the Absolute by a process of involution and evolution manifests itself in, and expresses itself through, grades of reality, or levels of being, from matter to spirit. The Absolute is the starting-point of the evolutionary ascent from lower forms of matter through mind to supermind and spirit, and the involutionary descent of the spirit through supermind to mind and matter. For Aurobindo every aspect of reality is permeated by the Absolute and the veil between mind and supermind is where the higher and lower levels of reality meet. The development of divine consciousness depends on rending the veil through involution and evolution and the divine life produced manifests that fullness of spirituality which can be described as gnostic being. Because of their divine cosmic consciousness gnostic beings are able to effect the transformation of lower levels of being and the whole of nature.

What Aurobindo seeks to do in his philosophy of synthesis is to reconcile matter and mind, mind and spirit, finite and infinite, God and man. Though complex and highly esoteric in terminology his system is marked with spiritual insights which succeeded in inspiring enthusiasm among intellectuals in particular for the cultural heritage of India.

Two of the more systematic philosophers of India are Vivekānanda (1863–1902), and Rādhakrishnan (1888–1975), an acknowledged academic who was elected President of his country. Both were interpreters of Advaita Vedānta. The Vedāntic doctrine of the divinity of man is a significant tenet in Vivekānanda's teaching and one aspect of the message he proclaimed at the World Parliament of Religions in Chicago. Another aspect of his message is the essential unity of all religions and the basic oneness of existence. For Vivekānanda there is but one life, one world and one existence. God permeates all that exists from stones and plants to human beings, so the difference between one life and another is one of degree and not of kind. It would be contrary to Vedāntic teaching to claim that animals were created in order to provide man with food. Similarly, he upholds the ideal of a universal religion not in the sense of a single ritual, mythology or philosophy, but in the sense that every religion proclaims an aspect of the universal truth according to its insights. Each religion is a pearl on a string and no one form of religion will do for everyone. Religion is in essence one but diverse in application, and toleration teaches us not to look for defects in religions other than our own. The Advaitist or qualified Advaitist does not say that dualism is wrong; it is a right view, yet a lower one which is on the way to truth. So the finest pearl on the string after all, for Vivekānanda, is Advaita Vedānta!

Rādhakrishnan claims that in his philosophical writings he seeks above all to convey his insight into the meaning and purpose of life; to provide a coherent interpretation of the world; and to promote the religion of the spirit. He sees no discontinuity between human life and spiritual life or between animal life and human life since all forms of life are expressions of the divine spirit. Spiritual existence is the fulfilment of human life and the ultimate goal of the cosmic process. This means that the world is not illusory but a manifestation of the divine spirit. It depends on the immanent creative activity of God without which it would cease to be. So the reality of the world is a dependent not an ultimate reality, which is precisely what the doctrine of *māyā* seeks to convey. Knowledge of the primordial divine spirit is possible through rational analysis of empirical data, but certainty comes through the immediate, intuitive apprehension of the nature of ultimate reality which is the result of *jñāna*, gnosis, or integral insight. It is a state of ecstasy; it is what is meant by being at one with God. This is an experience common to all religions, hence the importance of learning about the basic principles of all the great religions of the world and recognising the folly of missionary activity. No one religion can claim to be exclusive; religious traditions are imperfect expressions of the essence of religion which is truth. And since all men are bound together in one spirit, a life of service and sacrifice is inevitable for those who would promote the religion of the spirit and defend the ideals of freedom and justice.

One of the most remarkable men of twentieth-century India was Mohandās Karamchand Gandhi (1869–1948). Though he resented being called a saint, since he thought it too sacred a term to apply to a simple seeker after truth, there can be no doubt that he was a 'great soul' and most worthy of the title Mahātma. Fundamental to his thought is the concept of Truth (*Satya*), the existential quest for which forms the basis of all aspects of his teaching. He is faithful to the traditions of Hinduism when he affirms the oneness of Truth and Being, Consciousness, Bliss (*Saccidānanda*), and when he describes Truth as the most significant term that can be used for God. Yet his preference for the idea of God as formless Truth does not prevent him from recognising that God is personal to those who need to feel his presence, thereby accepting the *anekāntavādin* position that reality has many forms. He acknowledges that perfect Truth is beyond man's empirical grasp and that he must hold on to such relative truth as he is able to apprehend through his understanding of the essential teaching of his own religious tradition. All religions, he claims, possess truth but no single religion can embody the whole truth since it is a human construct and therefore imperfect. This has implications for missionary activity but it does not prevent those who wish to change their religious affiliation from doing so, or others from making a plea for toleration.

The reverse side of the coin to Truth is *ahiṃsā*, non-violence, and as far as Gandhi is concerned the attainment of one involves the realisation of the other. Ends and means are convertible terms in his philosophy, but it does not mean that he is unable to conceive of situations when violent action might be justified. Like perfect Truth, perfect non-violence is beyond man's grasp and in situations of moral dilemma one must do what it is morally possible for one to do while remaining informed by the spirit of *ahiṃsā*. The same applies to *Satyāgraha*, or holding firm to Truth, which is the technique of *ahiṃsā*. Its method is conversion rather than coercion, and although it involves civil disobedience and non-co-operation it seeks to establish social justice by the power of love and gentle persuasion.

In Gandhi's thought no distinction is drawn between Truth, Reality and the Self or *Ātman* which all men share. Belief in the indivisibility of Truth and the oneness of God involves belief in the oneness of humanity. We may have many bodies but we have but one soul. These metaphysical presuppositions point clearly to the interrelation of morality and religion and imply that we have an inescapable moral obligation towards our fellow men. This is illustrated in Gandhi's emphasis on *sarvodaya*, the welfare of all, which is revealed in his concern for the status of Harijans (Untouchables) and women in Indian society. He proclaims the need for the abolition of the caste system, child marriages, enforced widowhood and purdah which were harmful to the moral and spiritual growth of the nation. Radical social changes were required to improve the lot of the outcastes and the status of women and only the restoration of the purity of the Hindu way of life would suffice to effect the changes needed.

The social, economic and political implications of Gandhi's emphasis on *sarvodaya* are far reaching. His economic policy is people-oriented and rejects developments that dehumanise and degrade people's lives, including unbridled industrialisation; his alternative educational system fosters rather than undermines the cultural heritage of the nation; and his political goal of *Svarāj*, self-rule, promotes Indian self-respect and the determination of his people to accept responsibility for managing their own affairs.

It is not without significance that Gandhi subtitles his autobiography 'the story of my experiments with Truth'. He sought to live his life in the spirit of Truth and in accordance with the religious and ethical ideals of the Hindu way of life.

One of Gandhi's most ardent admirers and enthusiastic followers was Vinobā Bhāve (1895–1983). He was impressed by Gandhi's views on the importance of indigenous languages, the plight of the poor and the need for purity in personal and public life. In the ashram at Wardha he laboured diligently to prove himself a true disciple and became one of the first *satyāgrahīs* when the civil disobedience movement began. After Gandhi's death he inaugurated the *bhūdān* movement designed to encourage wealthy landowners to donate land voluntarily to those who had none and succeeded over a period of six years in acquiring four million acres for distribution. The method he adopted was persuasion rather than coercion in accordance with the principle of *ahiṃsā*.

Another of Vinobā Bhāve's activities involved the decentralisation of government and the development of self-sufficient, self-governing village units. *Grāmrāj*, village government, was an extension of *svarāj* with each village having the power to manage its own affairs. This meant the progressive abolition of government control, (*rāj-nīti*), and the establishment of government by the people (*lok-nīti*). For Vinobā the best form of government is freedom from government and this is what he means by *sarvodaya*.

With the decentralisation of government and the development of *grāmrāj* goes the responsibility for educating people to manage their own affairs. Vinobā's concept of *nai talim* (new education) meant the introduction of a programme directed towards establishing a *vidyāpīṭh*, a seat of knowledge or university, in each village. It involved also the establishment of village industries and the recognition of the principle of social equality. In short, his new education programme was education for the whole of life.

Many parallels exist between Vinobā and Gandhi but the former developed his theories in his own way and the *bhūdān* movement was his distinctive contribution to resolving the problem of the poverty of India.

Further Reading

de Bary, Wm. Theodore (ed.) *Sources of the Indian Tradition*, vol. II (Columbia University Press, New York/London, 1958)

Embree, Ainslie T. (ed.) *The Hindu Tradition: Readings in Oriental Thought* (Vintage Books, New York, 1972)

Naravane, V.S. *Modern Indian Thought: A Philosophical Survey* (Asia Publishing House, Delhi, 1964)

Richards, Glyn (ed.) *A Source-Book of Modern Hinduism* (Curzon Press, London/ Dublin, 1985)

—— *The Philosophy of Gandhi* (Curzon Press, London/Dublin; Barnes & Noble Books, New Jersey, 1982)

38 Sikhism

C. Shackle

Sikhism is the most recent in origin of the recognised Indian religions. There are now more than ten million Sikhs in India (largely concentrated in the north-western state of Punjab and the surrounding areas), where they significantly outnumber the combined totals of all Indian Buddhists and Jains. As a consequence of successive waves of emigration over the past hundred years, there are also perhaps a further one million Sikhs settled in other parts of the world, the most important communities of this diaspora being found in North America and in the United Kingdom, where the numbers of Sikhs are now comparable to those of British Jewry.

Throughout its development from the time of its origins in the early sixteenth century, Sikhism has nevertheless remained closely linked to its homeland in the Punjab, where most of its holy places are located and where the great majority of its adherents still live. Most Sikhs are consequently Punjabi by culture and by language. Indeed, the word 'Sikh' itself (correctly pronounced to rhyme with 'wick' rather than with 'week') is the Punjabi for 'disciple'. Without some understanding of the general background of historical events in the Punjab, it is therefore impossible to form a proper appreciation of the somewhat complex stages of development through which the Sikh religious tradition has evolved, whether these concern its attitudes to other religions in the area, or its own remarkable transformation over time from an initial core of pacific inner-directed adoration so as to accommodate a subsequent strong emphasis upon disciplined militancy.

Guru Nanak

Guru Nanak, the founder of Sikhism, was born to Hindu parents in a village west of Lahore in 1469. For knowledge of his life we are almost entirely dependent upon the much later prose hagiographies (*janamsakhi*) which were composed in the Sikh community during the seventeenth century. Like all such pious accounts, to whose compilers minute historical accuracy is of far less concern than their principal aim of mythological glorification of their subject, they must be used with some caution as biographical records.

In very broad outline, however, the picture given by the hagiographies may be accepted, not least their frequent references to the great diversity of religious life in sixteenth-century Punjab. As one of the first areas of India to be conquered by Muslim invaders, the Punjab had for some four centuries been subject to strong Islamic influences. Ultimately subordinate to the authority of the sultans in neighbouring Delhi, Muslims had long been politically dominant, and the state authority supported the institutions of orthodox Islam and the clerics who serviced them.

By this period Islam had long since ceased to be exclusively an alien import or just the religion of a foreign ruling class. Intense missionary activity, largely the initiative of Sufi preachers with their more tolerant interpretation of Islam and often charismatic personalities, had brought about mass conversions of substantial groups of the local population. The shrines of such great Sufi saints as Shaykh Farid (1173–1265) of Pakpatan, administered by their spiritual successors, were firmly established as major centres of popular devotion.

Amongst the Hindus, too, a variety of religious traditions was to be found. While perhaps less rigidly enforced in this border region than in its heartland in the Gangetic plains, the dominant orthodoxy was that of Brahminical Hinduism, upholding the necessity for the strict observance of caste distinctions. But the claims of the Brahmins to exclusive spiritual authority had never gone completely unchallenged. The Punjab had long been, for instance, an important centre of the Nath yogis, claiming descent from the semi-legendary Gorakhnath, who inspired considerable awe by the powers they allegedly derived from the intensive practice of *haṭha-yoga* techniques.

More recently, as all over northern India, various devotional movements had come to exercise an increasing appeal. The most prominent of these movements of devotion had as their object a personalised God (*saguna bhakti*), and the most popular cults focused upon incarnations of Vishnu, especially Krishna. In these cults, which may in one sense be seen as the response of a revitalised Hinduism to the spiritual challenge presented by the political dominance of Islam, the emotional togetherness of the congregations of the faithful listening to hymns of adoration composed in easily understood contemporary language stood in sharp contrast to the hierarchical separation of castes encouraged in the traditional Sanskritic rituals performed by the Brahmins.

Finally, there were also devotional movements directed towards the worship of an impersonal God (*nirguna bhakti*), which derived from the teachings of a loosely associated group of reformers known as the Sants. Almost all of very humble caste, these Sants included the cotton-printer Namdev (1270–1350) from Maharashtra, the weaver Kabir (1440–1518) from Benares and his younger contemporary, the leather-worker Ravides. Though naturally varying in their expression, the teachings of the Sants tended to be more radical than those propounded by the personalised cults. Not only were traditional learning, rituals and caste-observances pronounced useless, but devotion to images too was regarded as an obstacle to the salvation which could only be attained by heeding the voice of God in the human heart. In their expression of this central doctrine in their vernacular verses and hymns, the Sants relied not just on vivid local imagery, but on terminology drawn both from the personal cults and from the system of yogic terms earlier developed by the Nath yogis to describe the workings of the inner spiritual process. In a very real sense, therefore, the teachings of the Sants, which were diffused by informal transmission of their compositions rather than by the sort of formalised religious institutions which they so frequently attacked in others, represent a summation of the reformist currents of medieval Hinduism, though never achieving a fully integrated expression of the constituent elements involved.

The fact that Guru Nanak was able to achieve such an integration in his teachings may be attributed in some measure to his background. Whereas the Sants had come from low castes, Guru Nanak was a member of the Khattri caste, traditionally involved in business and administration. His father was a village accountant (*patvari*), the lowest rank in the revenue administration, and when Guru Nanak himself left home, it was to be employed as the steward of a local Muslim magnate. Both the imagery and organisation of his compositions and the coherence of his teachings reflect this early professional background.

The traditional accounts provide no certain clues as to the nature of Guru Nanak's early spiritual development. As a boy and youth, he is said to have been a dreamer, little interested in worldly affairs, and even after his marriage, which resulted in the birth of two sons, and his employment as an administrator, he continued to be absorbed in matters of the spirit. His great moment of transformation is said to have occurred when he was about thirty years old and went, as was his practice each morning, to bathe in the river. On this occasion he was taken before God, and did not emerge for three days, when he came out uttering the famous words, 'There is neither Hindu nor Muslim', which are taken as the charter of Sikhism's character as a separate, third religious tradition. (They should also serve to give the lie to the common misconception that Sikhism is some sort of syncretic synthesis of Hinduism and Islam.)

This profound experience caused Guru Nanak to abandon his job and his family for an extended series of travels, traditionally depicted as a series of triumphs over all rival religious leaders, during which he was accompanied by his devoted follower, the Muslim minstrel Mardana, who would accompany the Guru's hymns.

This long period of wandering, during which the first Sikhs would have been drawn to give their allegiance to him, came to an end in about 1520, when Guru Nanak settled down on land given him by a wealthy follower at Kartarpur, where he was to be based for the rest of his life. It was during this final phase, when he resumed domestic life as the head of a religious settlement, that his teachings were ultimately refined and future guide-lines for the Sikh community's subsequent development were established. After selecting one of his disciples as his successor, Guru Nanak died at Kartarpur in 1539.

Guru Nanak's Teachings

Guru Nanak's hymns, composed in a mixture of Old Punjabi and Old Hindi, are preserved in the Sikh scriptures. His teachings, expressed in poetry of great power and beauty, are therefore far better recorded than are the circumstances of his life. As has been indicated, these place him as a religious thinker firmly within the Sant tradition of devotion to a non-anthropomorphic God on the one hand, but on the other, by the quality and coherence of the insights which they collectively reveal, as the founder of a new religion.

At the centre of Guru Nanak's theology lies the issue of how salvation is to be attained, given the inherent dichotomy between God the creator and the observer and controller of his creation, whose oneness and unknowability is continually underlined, and unregenerate man, whose psyche (*man*) is totally clouded by his false sense of a self-determined identity that can operate without reference to the will of God (called *haumai*, literally 'I–me'). The fate of such a psyche-dominated man (*manmukh*) can only be to suffer the torments of death, hell and transmigration. The solutions offered by other religious specialists, whether Brahmins, yogis, Krishna-cultists or Muslim *qazis*, are totally belied by the personal corruption of their parasitic existence, to whose criticism many of Guru Nanak's most vivid verses are dedicated.

This apparently hopeless divide can, however, be bridged. One of the most striking tributes to Guru Nanak's quality both as religious thinker and as poet lies in his adaptation of Muslim political terminology to express theological insights. So God, conceived as the ultimate ruler whose designs are in the last resort unfathomable, does in his graciousness provide the means by which his true servants may approach him. For these to be apprehended, their fidelity must first be demonstrated both by the rejection of idle asceticism in favour of the practical discipline of earning one's own living honestly and sharing its fruits with others, and by the inner discipline of opening one's heart to the inward meditation on his 'name' or divine qualities (*nam japan*, *nam simran*), both by private devotion and by participation in congregational worship, where fellow-aspirants to salvation join in listening to hymns with inner attention.

With these preconditions fulfilled, the devotee may be fortunate enough to be the recipient of the divine sovereign's look of favour (*nadar*), also expressed as being able to hear the call (*sabad*) in one's heart. In this active aspect of himself as communicator, God is usually described as the Teacher (*guru*) or True Teacher (*satiguru*). Those privileged in this way to receive the divine message, through Guru-direction (*gurmukh*), may apprehend the full significance of the divine order (*hukam*) and attain the ultimate bliss of freedom from the cycle of birth and death so as to participate in the heavenly joys of the company of saints (*satsang*), who sing in eternity at the gates of God's ineffable court the praises of his glory.

Guru Nanak's Successors

However distinguished from them by superior internal cohesion, it will be seen that Guru Nanak's teachings share with those of the earlier Sants a profound emphasis upon inward spirituality rather than the outward organisation of religious life. A vastly greater number of verses are devoted to the praise of the heavenly company of saints and to the mysterious workings of the Divine Guru in the human heart than are allotted to rules for honest everyday existence.

It was, however, important that the original nucleus of the Sikh community established under Guru Nanak's direction in his later years at Kartarpur (literally, 'City of the Creator') should be maintained and developed, if it were to achieve its purpose of creating the conditions by which the faithful on earth might aspire to the ultimate achievement of the heavenly model so powerfully set before them in Guru Nanak's hymns. The subsequent successful evolution of Sikhism along its separate way stands in sharp contrast to the amorphous character of the groups stemming from the other reformers of the time, and is to be attributed not only to the coherence of Guru Nanak's message, but also to his provision for continuing effective leadership after his death.

While Sikhism has from the beginning laid much stress on the irrelevance of caste distinctions, it appears from early lists that most of the early converts were from a Khattri background similar to that of its founder. Certainly, all the Gurus were from various sub-groups of Khattris. But the succession was not at first hereditary. Guru Nanak passed over the claims of his son Sri Chand, disqualified by his asceticism, in favour of his disciple Angad (1504–52), who in his turn chose in preference to his own sons his elderly disciple Amar Das (1479–1574), originally a Khattri convert from Vaishnavism. Thereafter the hereditary pattern asserted itself with Guru Amar Das's selection of his son-in-law Ram Das (1534–81), succeeded in his turn by his youngest son Arjan (1563–1606), the direct ancestor of all the later living Gurus (see Figure 38.1).

Figure 38.1: The Sikh Gurus

1. Nanak (1469–1539)
2. Angad (1504–52)
3. Amar Das (1479–1574)
4. Ram Das (1534–81) / married daughter
5. Arjan (1563–1606)
6. Hargobind (1595–1644)

(son)
7. Har Rai (1630–61)
8. Har Krishan (1656–64)

9. Tegh Bahadur (1621–75)
10. Gobind Singh (1666–1708)

Although each succession was disputed at the time, the splinter groups founded by disappointed claimants dwindled more or less quickly into insignificance, while the institutions of the main community were developed and strengthened by the Gurus to ensure its cohesion as it grew in numbers, especially in the Punjab. The Guruship itself, conceived as an office passing from one to another successor as one lamp is lit from another (*joti jot samauna*), provided the central focus for the Sikhs. The collection of Guru Nanak's hymns was supplemented by the subsequent compositions of the later Gurus, whose spiritual identity was symbolised by their common use of the poetic signature 'Nanak'.

A network of local communities was established, each having as its centre of congregational worship a temple, corresponding to the modern Sikh *gurdwara* ('house of the Guru'), to which there might be attached a free kitchen (*langar*), symbolically open to all, regardless of caste. These local communities were organised into regions, each under the authority of the Guru's appointed representatives, responsible for transmitting his teachings and instructions and for collecting his tithe for remission to his centre.

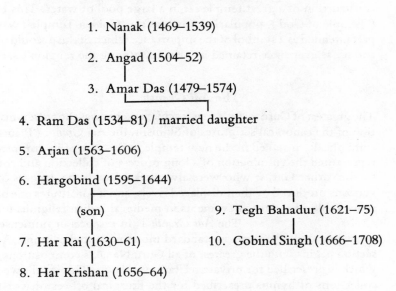

In the early years, this centre, at which all Sikhs were expected to gather before their Guru on the day of the New Year (*Baisakhi*), shifted with each accession to the Guruship. Guru Ram Das, however, established his centre on a new site granted him at Amritsar ('Lake of Nectar'), and it was here that his son Guru Arjan completed in 1604 the construction of a great temple set in a large pool of water. This Harmandir ('Temple of God'), popularly known as the 'Golden Temple', was surely in part intended as a symbol of the importance which Sikhism could now claim, and it has ever since retained its primacy among the religion's sacred sites.

The *Ādi Granth*

The greatest of Guru Arjan's many achievements was, however, his compilation of the canonical scriptures of Skihism, the *Ādi Granth* ('Primal Book'), symbolically installed in the new temple in the year of its completion. This represented the culmination of a long process of collection and composition by the earlier Gurus, who were always faced with the dangers of heretical versions produced by their displaced rivals, and it constitutes one of the most remarkable editorial achievements in medieval Indian religious literature.

The *Ādi Granth* is in essence an immense hymnal, consisting of 1,430 pages in standard modern printed editions. A prefatory section begins with the greatest of all Guru Nanak's compositions, the *Japji*, which is prescribed for private recitation at dawn. This is followed by short collections of hymns prescribed for the liturgical offices of worship in the evening (*sodar rahiras*) and then before retiring (*kirtan sohila*). The bulk of the scripture is then arranged, in accordance with its hymnal character, by the mode (*rag*) in which the various compositions are to be performed. Within each of these thirty-one modal headings, hymns are arranged first in order of metrical length, then by author. A concluding section includes a number of miscellaneous compositions for which no place could appropriately be found under the main headings.

The language of the *Ādi Granth* naturally varies somewhat from author to author, sometimes from genre to genre, but seldom diverges greatly from the poetic idiom so memorably established by Guru Nanak. Its archaic character, whose difficulties are compounded by the conciseness of expression favoured in medieval Indian religious poetry, means that it is no longer fully approachable by Sikhs today without some special study, and much effort has gone into the compilation of commentaries and translations. The use of the sacred Gurmukhi script (a distinctive relative of the Devanagari script used to write Sanskrit and Hindi) both in the *Ādi Granth* and for modern Punjabi has, however, served to blur the distinction between the two.

The great bulk of the contents of the *Ādi Granth* naturally consists of hymns by the early Sikh Gurus. It is possible to give some idea of their relative contribution by enumerating the compositions attributed to them, although the varied length of these makes this only a rough guide. At their core, and as their major inspiration, lie the hymns of Guru Nanak (974), briefly supplemented by the scattered couplets of Guru Angad (62), and extensively restated in the hymns of his last contemporary Guru Amar Das (907). The new note first struck by Guru Ram Das (679) was developed on a collosal scale by the largest single contributor to the volume, its compiler Guru Arjan (2,218), whose enormous *œuvre* explores almost every possibility suggested by his predecessors, and includes the *Sukhmani* ('Peace of Heart') as both its most famous item and as the longest of all the hymns in the collection.

Also included in the *Ādi Granth* are a few eulogies of the Gurus by the bards attached to their courts. Much more remarkable is the incorporation of hymns by other teachers, whose works first entered the Sikh tradition in a collection compiled during the time of Guru Amar Das. Designed to demonstrate the universal truth of the Gurus' message by analogy, these included extensive contributions from Namdev (60), Kabir (541) and Ravidas (41), besides the Sufi Shaykh Farid (116). While it is subordinate in status to the *gurbani* ('Utterance of the Gurus') proper, the inclusion of this *bhagat-bani* ('Utterance of the Saints') is striking testimony to the breadth of the religious vision of the early leaders of Sikhism.

The Seventeenth Century

The seventeenth century was a time of transition, during which the Sikh community, while continuing to grow in size and importance, was substantially altered in character by the influx of converts from the farming Jat caste with more warlike traditions than the Khattris who had formed the majority of the first disciples. These changes had the dual consequence of making the Gurus more prominent politically and of increasing the suspicion with which they, as leaders of a growingly warlike sect in a region close to Delhi, came to be regarded by the Mogul emperors.

Guru Arjan himself was the first to fall martyr to this inherent tension between the Sikhs and the Mogul authorities when, following his support for an unsuccessful claimant to the imperial throne, he was executed at Lahore in 1606. His son Guru Hargobind (1595–1604) was also imprisoned by the Moguls for a time, and is credited with being the first Guru to claim both spiritual and temporal authority (*piri miri*). As a symbol of the latter he constructed opposite his father's Harmandir the Akal Takht ('Throne of the Immortal Lord'), which has ever since remained the symbolic organisational centre of Sikhism. His successor Guru Har Rai (1630–61) was driven by imperial hostility to take refuge in the hills north of the Punjab, and his son, the child Guru Har Krishan (1656–64), died in custody in Delhi.

By the time of Guru Tegh Bahadur (1621–75), the organisation of the Sikh community was thus falling into increasing disarray, since the Gurus were increasingly constrained from exercising authority over their local representatives. Guru Tegh Bahadur's own efforts at reform were ended by his execution in Delhi on the orders of the Emperor Aurangzeb. His son Guru Gobind Singh (1666–1708) was brought up by his followers in the safety of his refuge in the hills at Anandpur, though even there he was brought into increasing conflict with the neighbouring chieftains.

The Khalsa

Guru Gobind Singh, revered by Sikhs as the greatest of Guru Nanak's successors, effected a radical and lasting transformation of both the organisation and the outlook of the Sikh community by his institution of the quasi-military order of the Khalsa (a technical term used to designate land under direct imperial control, also suggesting the sense of 'Company of the Pure'), which abolished the authority of intermediate spiritual representatives and invested the community itself with ultimate power and responsibility.

The symbolic foundation of the Khalsa took place when the Sikhs gathered before their Guru on the Baisakhi festival at Anandpur in 1699. The Guru asked for five volunteers, from different castes, who were taken into a tent and apparently executed. But as they were led out, it was revealed that goats had been slain in their place, and that these heroic 'five beloved ones' (*panj piare*) were to form the nucleus of the new order of the Khalsa. Their initiation was symbolised by the administration of baptism, involving the drinking of sweetened water (*amrit*) sanctified by the utterance of prayers during its preparation and mixing with a dagger. The five disciples then in their turn administered baptism to the Guru, symbolising the transfer of authority to the community.

The code of conduct (*rahit*) expected of all initiates of the Khalsa, as laid down by Guru Gobind Singh and subsequently elaborated, emphasises both the equality of its members and the martial spirit expected of them by awarding the Rajput titles of Singh ('lion') to men and Kaur ('princess') to women, irrespective of caste origin. Also incumbent on all male members is the observance of the five outward tokens known from their Punjabi names as the 'five Ks' (*panj kakke*), including unshorn hair (*kes*), a comb (*kangha*) to hold it, a dagger (*kirpan*), a steel bangle (*kara*) and a pair of breeches (*kachh*). To these should be added the turban, which has long been the best-known symbol of the Sikh identity. The baptismal vows also include distinctive dietary restrictions, including total abstinence from the consumption of tobacco and from all meat which has not come from animals butchered by beheading (*jhatka*).

The new militant spirit of the Khalsa was given verbal expression in the hymns composed by Guru Gobind Singh. Some of these were added to those by the earlier Gurus prescribed for the three daily offices, thus a baptised Sikh is expected to add to Guru Nanak's *Japji* in his morning prayers the recitation of Guru Gobind Singh's *Jap Sahib* and ten short poems (*das savaie*). Guru Gobind Singh's compositions are collected in the *Dasam Granth* ('Book of the Tenth Guru'). While of comparable size to the *Ādi Granth*, it is much more heterogeneous in character, containing a great amount of material obviously not by the Guru himself, and has never enjoyed the same canonical status.

The status of the original scriptures was further heightened as a consequence of Guru Gobind Singh's remodelling of the Sikh community. During a brief respite from the almost perpetual fighting against the Moguls and their local allies in which much of his life was spent, and during which all his four sons were killed, he re-edited the *Ādi Granth* so as to include his father's compositions, although not his own. In this final form, the scriptures received the authority of the Guru, and consequently received the honorific title of *Guru Granth Sahib* by which Sikhs usually refer to their holy book. With Guru Gobind Singh's death in 1708, the line of living Gurus came to an end, and Sikhs have since revered the scripture which they composed as their spiritual guide. The *Guru Granth Sahib* occupies the central place in all *gurdwaras*, and elaborate reverence is paid to it in the rituals of the larger temples.

Subsequent Developments

The decentralisation of authority involved in the creation of the Khalsa inevitably brought to an end the long period of the primary theological formulation of Sikhism by Guru Nanak and his successors. But the new order proved most successful in ensuring the community's survival during the long succession of wars which followed the collapse of the Mogul Empire early in the eighteenth century, as invaders from Afghanistan battled with the local Muslim governors for control of the Punjab. Inspired by the war-cry *raj karega khalsa* ('the Khalsa shall rule'), the Sikh guerrilla bands eventually emerged victorious, and the heroic age of Sikh history culminated in the kingdom established in the name of the Khalsa at Lahore by Maharaja Ranjit Singh (1799–1839).

But while the Khalsa thus proved well able to deal with the threat to the community's existence by hostile Muslim political forces, the rapid reversion to Hinduism by many fair-weather converts following the final British conquest of the Punjab from the Sikhs in 1849 showed it had been less effective in maintaining the distinctive character of the reformist teachings of the Gurus. As was so often the case in colonial history, the loss of political power led to a period of intense self-questioning and the rearticulation of reformist ideals.

Some of the most trenchant of these mid-nineteenth-century reformers fell foul (through their excessively stated claims to spiritual authority) of the doctrine of the abolition of the living Guruship in Sikhism, and they and their followers were hence regarded as more or less heretical by the main body of Sikhs. As from Guru Gobind Singh's time, this included not only the baptised Khalsa Sikhs but also large numbers of *sahajdhari* ('slow-adopting') Sikhs who followed the Gurus' teachings and the temple rituals, but without adopting the Khalsa baptism and the discipline thereby entailed. In this fluid situation, with many families having both Hindu and Sikh members, and many temples having in the course of time fallen into the hands of hereditary quasi-Hindu administrators, it was all too evident to the founders of the main late nineteenth-century reformist movement, the Singh Sabha, that Sikhism risked being reabsorbed totally into the capacious Hindu tradition from which it had been born. An intensive programme of propaganda was accordingly instituted, directed both towards inculcating stricter adherence to the Khalsa discipline within the community, and outwardly to combating the aggressive assertion by such reformist Hindu sects as the Arya Samaj that the Sikhs were no more than heretics to be reclaimed for Hinduism.

Largely successful in their primary objectives, the reformers' campaign assumed an increasingly political emphasis with the struggle in the 1920s to assert the community's physical control over its major shrines. The British authorities at first supported the legal claims of the traditional administrators, but were eventually forced by the massive demonstrations organised by the newly formed Akali Dal ('army of the Immortal Lord') to hand control of the great temples and their massive endowments to the Sikh activists in 1925.

Contemporary Sikhism

At the centre of contemporary Sikh organisations lies the Gurdwara Management Committee, or SGPC, set up to administer the major temples in Punjab. This is an elected body, which has always been under the control of one or another group of the Akali Dal, the main Sikh political party. In keeping with the long-standing traditions of Sikhism, the SGPC is run by lay members, and the officials of the temples, whether readers (*granthi*) or musicians (*ragi*), are its paid servants, without the sacerdotal status of 'priests' in the accepted sense of the term.

In lesser temples, too, whether in the Punjab or in the diaspora, a similar pattern of management obtains, with lay members having chief responsibility for running the temple and the *langar* attached to it, for ensuring compliance to the Khalsa discipline, and if necessary undertaking the excommunication of members for grave infractions, such as the cutting of hair, or fixing penalties for lesser offences. A summary code of guidance, laying down the fundamental rules of Sikh belief, religious and personal life, was issued by the SGPC in 1946.

The evolution of Sikhism has, however, been such that its purely religious aspect is only somewhat artificially to be regarded in complete isolation from its contemporary political expression. The political activism to which the reformists' energies had become increasingly directed received further impetus through the circumstances in which the British Empire in India was dissolved in 1947. This involved the partition of the Punjab between the successor states of India and Pakistan and a massive transfer of population between the two halves of the province, with the whole Sikh population of the western districts being forced to migrate to India.

A long campaign by the Akali Dal eventually secured the establishment of the Sikh-majority state of Punjab in India in 1966. But the dream of a fully independent Khalistan ('land of the Khalsa') has continued to appeal to some Sikhs. It received further impetus from the campaign of violence instigated by Sant Jarnail Singh Bhindranwale (1947–84), a village preacher with a message of charismatic fundamentalism, and from the Indian Army's storming of Sikhism's holiest shrine, the Golden Temple complex at Amritsar, in June 1984, when Bhindranwale and his followers were killed and from the continuing subsequent repercussions of this military assault.

As has, however, been indicated by subsequent events in India and the polarisation of feeling among many sections of the Sikh diaspora, it would be unwise to disregard the appeal of the new fundamentalism in attempting any assessment of the contemporary profile of Sikhism, which continues to contain within itself the effects of the several stages of development which have gone into its making.

Further Reading

Cole, W.O. and Sambhi, Piara Singh *The Sikhs, Their Religious Beliefs and Practices* (Routledge & Kegan Paul, London, 1978)

Grewal, J.S. and Bal, S.S. *Guru Gobind Singh* (Chandigarh, 1967)

Harbans Singh *The Heritage of the Sikhs*, 2nd edn (New Delhi, 1983)

Khushwant Singh *A History of the Sikhs*, 2 vols., 2nd edn (Delhi, 1977)

Macauliffe, M.A. *The Sikh Religion*, 6 vols. (Oxford, 1909), reprinted as 3 vols. (Delhi, 1963)

McLeod, W.H. *Guru Nanak and the Sikh Religion* (Oxford University Press, Oxford, 1968)

—— *The Evolution of the Sikh Community* (Oxford University Press, Oxford, 1976)

—— (ed.) *Textual Sources for the Study of Sikhism* (Manchester University Press, Manchester, 1984)

Shackle, C. *An Introduction to the Sacred Language of the Sikhs* (University of London, SOAS, 1981)

—— *The Sikhs* (revised edn) (Minority Rights Group Report no. 65, London, 1986)

39 Theravāda Buddhism in South-East Asia

W.J. Johnson

The use of the Pali term 'Theravāda' ('Doctrine of the Elders') to define their particular school reflects the fact that the Theravādins present themselves as belonging to that branch of Buddhism which has continued to preserve the 'orthodox' or 'original' teaching of the Buddha. Less chauvinistically, the term refers to the doctrines and practices of the one monastic school to have survived from among the unknown number of Indian schools that had branched out from an original Sthaviravādin (Pali, *Theravādin*) trunk, itself the result of a schism early in Buddhist history. This survival of Theravāda is synonymous with the survival of its Pali scriptures, the only complete recension of the Canon extant in an ancient Indian language. In a wider sense, 'Theravāda Buddhism' is that form of Buddhist culture which has dominated religious, political and social life in Sri Lanka, Burma and Thailand, and, until very recently, Laos and Cambodia as well. It has been the interaction of these two aspects of Theravāda—of the 'school' with the wider culture—which has given rise to the characteristic features of the religion's history.

The history of Theravāda in India remains obscure, and perhaps impossible to extricate from the history of Buddhism in general, although it is known that it was the dominant tradition in a number of important centres in the South-east of the subcontinent, in Andhra Pradesh and Tamil Nadu. Thus at one time there were Tamils who were Theravāda Buddhists. In Sri Lanka, however, where Theravāda established itself firmly as the national religion, the historical situation is clearer. The major source for this history is the Pali verse chronicle, the *Mahāvaṃsa*, or 'Great Chronicle', written by a Sinhalese monk late in the fifth century CE. This was based on another chronicle, the *Dīpavaṃsa*, compiled a century earlier, possibly by nuns. These are, of course, essentially Buddhist histories, whose aim is to establish the inextricability of Theravāda Buddhism from Sinhalese (or Sinhala) national identity. However, their account of Theravāda after its arrival in Sri Lanka is probably broadly accurate.

According to the *Dīpavaṃsa*, the Pali Canon was taken to Sri Lanka and South-east Asia by missionaries sent out by Aśoka in the middle of the third century BCE. Although scholars are extremely sceptical about the claim for South-east Asia, there seems no reason to doubt that Theravāda made its first appearance in Sri Lanka at about this time. Whether the Canon itself arrived all at once in the heads of the first missionaries or more gradually, it is likely that the Pali commentaries (which Buddhaghosa, writing in the fifth century CE, claims Mahinda, the missionary son of Aśoka, brought with him and then translated into Sinhala) arrived over a longer period of time. It is even possible they originated in Sri Lanka itself. Certainly, additions continued to be made to the commentarial literature until about the middle of the first century CE, at which time the corpus was probably closed. It is this body of material that Buddhaghosa himself superseded in the process of translating it from Sinhala into Pali and editing it into what became its definitively orthodox form.

About half a century before the body of commentarial work had been closed, there had occurred what was probably the most significant and far-reaching event in early Theravāda history. During a period of turmoil, late in the first century BCE, when Sri Lanka was threatened by foreign invasions and famine, the decision was taken to commit the Theravāda Canon to writing. This happened between 29 and 17 BCE. Until then the Canon had been transmitted orally from generation to generation of monks. The monastic community, the Saṅgha, was the sole repository of the Buddha's Doctrine (*Dhamma*; Sanskrit, *Dharma*), and it was through the Saṅgha alone that the laity had access to that Doctrine. Perhaps it was only when it was presented with the threat of its own imminent destruction that the Saṅgha made the conscious decision that its first duty—indeed, its primary function—was to preserve the Doctrine for future generations. This decision and its consequence, the writing down of the Pali Canon, had far-reaching consequences for the nature and subsequent history of the Saṅgha itself.

As important as the Canon for the Theravāda tradition is the Pali *Visuddhimagga*, or 'Path of Purity', an original work composed in Sri Lanka in the early fifth century CE by the same Indian monk, Buddhaghosa, who edited the commentaries. This compendium of Buddhist doctrine has been the touchstone of Theravādin orthodoxy ever since. Its intended 'readership' was the monastic community, an audience reflected in the work's dual function as a summary of doctrine and a handbook for meditators. The dominant theme is the cultivation of that moral and mental purity which, allied to the necessary prerequisite of learning, together make up the practical path to enlightenment. After Buddhaghosa other monks soon wrote definitive Pali commentaries on those parts of the Canon he had left untouched, including a Pali version of the commentary on the *Jātaka* stories about the 550 previous births of the Buddha. And presently Pali subcommentaries on these works also appeared. By reverting to a classical language (Pali), Buddhaghosa and his followers effectively internationalised the Theravādin tradition. That is to say, they prepared the way for Sinhala orthodoxy to become the standard form of Theravāda Buddhism throughout South-east Asia. Such 'internationalisation', combined with the universalistic ethic expounded in Buddhist teaching, meant that Theravāda had some invaluable instruments with which both to consolidate its expansion and to renew itself in times of decline.

In the terms of its self-definition the history of Theravāda Buddhism is synonymous with the history of its monastic community, the Saṅgha, in that it is only through the Saṅgha that the teaching is preserved and handed on. Two monastic rites are crucial to the establishment and survival of the Saṅgha: higher ordination (Pali, *upasampadā*) and the fortnightly communal recitation of the Disciplinary Code (Pali, *pātimokkha*) after the confession of faults. To convey the authentic tradition of the Buddha's Doctrine, the higher ordination ceremony must be valid, and the validity of any particular ordination depends on its being at the end of an unbroken line of valid ordinations going back to the Buddha (the continuity being preserved by the presence of a quorum of monks who are themselves validly ordained). This can only be guaranteed if the monks who belong to a particular Saṅgha lead morally pure lives according to the Discipline (*Vinaya*). Such purity is ensured and expressed by the fortnightly *pātimokkha* recitation, for a monk who has committed a transgression against the Disciplinary Code may not attend and thus endorse his commitment to the Code without first having purified himself by confessing his fault. When the 'unity of the Saṅgha' is referred to, it is precisely this unanimous adherence to a single Disciplinary Code that is meant. Anything less than unanimity constitutes a split in the Saṅgha, i.e. the formation of a new sect. This is not a matter of choice: it is considered essential that every monk within an area defined by a formally established monastic boundary, or *sīmā*, should personally attend a *pātimokkha* ceremony once a fortnight. Without the prior establishment of an area of bounded monastic territory, no formal act of the Saṅgha, whether ordination ceremony or *pātimokkha*, can take place. Thus whenever the Saṅgha (i.e. 'Theravāda Buddhism') wishes to establish itself in a new region or country, it requires immediate material support from the laity in the form of a gift of land. Beyond that, it needs daily support in the form of alms, and ultimately it needs to recruit new members from the local population to sustain itself. In return for all this material support, the monks provide the infinitely more valuable gift of the Buddha's teaching, and spiritual good in general, especially merit.

From its origins in India the Saṅgha had been supported by the rich and influential. This was a pattern that developed in Sri

Lanka and South-east Asia into what is sometimes called a 'symbiotic' relationship, i.e. a mutually beneficial relationship between the Saṅgha and the ruling power or king (in essence, the chief layman). It is important to note that, once Buddhism becomes established as the religion of a nation-state such as Sri Lanka, the significance of the Discipline undergoes a substantial change. Thus if one takes the slogans 'No Buddhism without the Saṅgha' and 'No Saṅgha without the Discipline', and adds to those the further slogan, 'No Sri Lanka/Burma/Thailand without Buddhism', it becomes clear that the preservation of the Discipline, i.e. of the moral purity of the Saṅgha, is the essential component in the preservation and proper functioning of the nation. In this context, the monk, who is the embodiment or exemplar of moral purity, of Discipline, becomes a figure with public responsibility. It is no longer, if it ever was, simply a matter of cultivating his own enlightenment (although, of course, the two roles are not necessarily incompatible). Moreover, the king, as the embodiment of the state, feels that ultimately it is his duty to preserve the institutions of society, especially the Saṅgha. Much of later Theravāda history is therefore patterned by the recurrent efforts of kings to preserve or re-establish the purity of the Saṅgha, since the prosperity of the nation is ultimately seen to depend upon its moral example. The precedent for such royal interference in the affairs of what, ideally, was the self-governing Saṅgha had been set by Aśoka, who had undertaken a purification of the Saṅgha—albeit in accordance with *Vinaya* rules—in India in the third century BCE. And it was Aśoka who remained the inspiration and model for later monarchs in their dealings with the monastic community. That is to say, they saw it as their duty to defend the Saṅgha by expelling its corrupt members and, in some cases, by introducing ordination traditions from countries which were believed to have a superior variety.

Corruption of the Saṅgha has two principal aspects: luxurious living, i.e. a laxness in Discipline and thus a diminution of moral purity, and a consequent disharmony that threatens to split the unity of the community. In other words, practice by some members of the Saṅgha which diverges from the norm laid down in the *Vinaya* leads to a situation where all members do not acknowledge the same *pātimokkha* rules, and a split occurs. Given this analysis of corruption, there can be little doubt that royal patronage was itself a factor in bringing about that very decay of the Saṅgha which the kings' periodic 'purifications' were intended to reverse. For state patronage cast monks in new roles which were frequently quite at odds with the Discipline. Perhaps the most immediately obvious of these was that the monasteries became great landlords. From late in the first century BCE land grants to monks and monasteries became a frequent occurrence in Sri Lanka, so much so that monastic land-holding became a major feature of the economy, until between the ninth and twelfth centuries CE monasteries were probably the greatest landlords in Sri Lanka. And while legal fictions could be devised to justify the Saṅgha's communal involvement with property, it was more difficult to accommodate the economic business of individual monks to the Discipline, particularly the practice of inheriting personal monastic property. Inevitably the way of life of wealthy monks and monasteries came to differ substantially from the canonical ideal. Similarly, the central role of the Saṅgha in the welfare of the state led some monks into politics. Perhaps the most typical role for the monk in the Theravāda countries, however, has been that of the 'village-dwelling' scholar and preacher who, from the laity's point of view, acts as a ceremonial specialist and is often involved in astrology and medicine as well. In essence the 'village-dweller's' function is to make merit for the laity. Classically, the complementary opposite to the 'village-dwelling' monk is the 'forest-dwelling' ascetic (Pali, *āraññika*), who retires alone to pursue insight and enlightenment through meditation. But such groups of monks have always been in a small minority, following a special vocation within the Saṅgha, and have persistently been drawn back into the 'village' mode of life, which in practice constitutes the monastic norm. Their status, however, is very high since they are popularly regarded as holy or 'ideal' monks.

Sri Lanka was the first and, for the first millennium CE, the only Buddhist state. Whatever Theravāda Buddhism there was elsewhere in this period has left little trace of itself, although there is some evidence for its presence in both Burma and Thailand by the seventh century CE. However, the Sinhala-derived orthodoxy that came to dominate much of South-east Asia established itself only gradually from the late eleventh century onwards, after the rise of the monarchical states and the corresponding possibility of royal patronage. The Burmese king Aniruddha is credited with the establishment of Theravāda in upper Burma (*c.* 1057 CE) by having the ordination tradition and the Canon brought from Sri Lanka. At the end of the twelfth century a Burmese monk returned from Sri Lanka to Burma to set up a separate *nikāya* or 'fraternity', the 'Sinhalese Saṅgha', which became the main indigenous monastic tradition. And again in the fifteenth century, the reforming king, Dhammaceti, imported the ordination tradition afresh from Sri Lanka, at the same time unifying the Saṅgha and establishing a monastic hierarchy.

Theravāda probably reached Thailand via the Burmese 'Sinhalese Saṅgha' in the thirteenth century, and with the help of further injections of purity from the Sinhalese tradition gradually overcame the Mahāyāna and Hindu forms of religion which had preceded it. By the mid-fourteenth century the Sinhala Theravādin orthodoxy was also established in Laos and Cambodia—probably, in the latter case, coming from Thailand and initiating the subsequent close connection between the Buddhism of the two countries.

In Sri Lanka itself the Saṅgha was in decay during the two centuries of Tamil invasions and civil wars at the beginning of the second millennium, and it was probably during this period that the order of nuns died out. This decline was only halted with the 'purification' and unification of the Saṅgha undertaken by Parakkama Bāhu I in 1164/5. He set up a single authority structure for a national Saṅgha, headed by a monk known as the 'king of the Saṅgha' (*Saṅgharāja*), who was aided by two deputies. This kind of political organisation was imitated in Theravāda countries in South-east Asia, and in Thailand in particular it was elaborated into the institutionalised hierarchy of offices which is so evident today. The effect of this reform movement was felt in Sri Lanka until the fifteenth century, but thereafter the Saṅgha suffered an even more serious erosion of standards, so much so that the indigenous ordination tradition was lost, and between the end of the sixteenth century and 1753 it is likely that there were no true monks in Sri Lanka but only those who had taken lower ordination. Again the original export of the Sinhalese ordination tradition came to the rescue, and in 1753 it was returned from Thailand, where centuries before it had found its way, via Burma, from Sri Lanka itself. Contemporary *nikāyas* in Sri Lanka, however, belong to ordination traditions introduced from Burma in the nineteenth century.

From the nineteenth century onwards Buddhism in the Theravāda countries has had to face the pressures of colonial rule and the competition of Western ideologies. In Burma, for instance, royal patronage of the Saṅgha ceased abruptly when the country was incorporated into the British Empire in 1885. And while this did not mean the collapse of Buddhism as such, it did mean that the Saṅgha lost its organisational structure. In general during the colonial and post-colonial periods individual monks as well as the Saṅgha became deeply involved in independence and nationalist movements. In this era there has also been the periodic appearance of millenarian sects, especially in Burma, often using the expected imminent arrival of the future Buddha, Maitreya, as their point of focus. Also Western 'rationalist' interpretations have been fed back into Theravāda cultures, leading to 'modernist' movements which reject many traditional Buddhist beliefs and practices. Furthermore, the introduction of Western education and the spread of literacy have caused the Saṅgha to lose its monopoly of religious authority, and the idea has developed that each person is responsible for his own salvation, and thus for the welfare of the religion in general. Yet thanks to Buddhism's strong scriptural foundation, there have continued to be 'fundamentalist' and reform movements, even among meditators, basing themselves on the revival of scriptural knowledge. On a tragic note, two great Theravāda traditions, those in Laos and Cambodia, were brought to an abrupt halt in 1975 when the communists and the Khmer Rouge took over. In Laos the Saṅgha can now be said at the very least to have lost its traditional influence, while in Cambodia Buddhism was completely destroyed, with most of the monks being murdered. It is obviously too early to say whether these traditions will again be able to revive themselves, or to speculate as to what form such a revival might take.

What was Buddhism's relation to the pre-Buddhist or 'folk' religions it encountered as it spread throughout what are now the Theravāda nations of Sri Lanka and South-east Asia? In this respect, it should be remembered that Buddhism originated in the context of another culturally dominant religion, Brahminical Hinduism, and, more generally, in an Indian culture which, like others, held beliefs about demons and spirits as well as about 'higher' gods. Thus Hindu gods (*devas*) and demons have been part of the Buddhist world-view from its inception, and play their part in the Pali Canon. Typically, the merit acquired at Buddhist ceremonies is always subsequently offered to the gods so that they can respond with this-worldly protection. The Buddha never denied the existence of supernatural beings, he simply viewed them as irrelevant to his soteriological system for bringing about the end of suffering. Similarly, the Buddhist view of gods and spirits has continued to be that, while they may be harmful or beneficial with regard to worldly ends, they are ultimately insignificant precisely because they belong to *saṃsāra*, the world of cause and effect. Thus they are as much subject to the law of *karman* as human beings. Buddhism, however, is not concerned with worldly ends, its purpose rather being to bring that cycle of *saṃsāra* to an end. So in all Theravāda countries followers of the Buddha have retained non-Buddhist beliefs in spirits and gods. In Burma, for instance, the cults of the Nats (animistic spirits) co-exist naturally with Buddhism, since the concerns of the former are to attain material well-being and to avert danger, while the latter's interest is in moral purity, future lives and, ultimately, final release from worldly existence. Such gods and spirits are easily accommodated within the Buddhist cosmic hierarchy, governed by the law of *karman*, with the Buddha at its apex. Thus while all deities are seen to embody Buddhist values, and remain connected to all other beings, including man, by the law of *karman*, they, and the practices associated with them (such as possession), are at the same time appropriated to Buddhism with very little change in meaning. In this way Buddhism was able to spread and become a popular religion throughout Sri Lanka and South-east Asia without coming into conflict with indigenous religions. This is not to say that Buddhism, because of its ethical purity, is not itself often used magically as a protection against dangers of the present existence—but that, paradoxically, is precisely because it is not itself concerned with such particular dangers. The real religious conflict, of course, arises between different soteriologies.

So far, I have looked at some of the main themes and events in the history of Theravāda Buddhism, and little has been said about Buddhism as it is practised today. The rest of this chapter will therefore provide a sketch of some 'modern' practices. This has sometimes been called 'popular' Buddhism, but one should beware of what is often implied by such categorisations, namely, that there has been some gradual corruption or decay from a 'pure' Buddhism, or that Buddhism has become syncretistic. Modern studies have shown that from a very early period Theravāda has been nothing if not 'popular'. The religion practised in the villages of Sri Lanka and South-east Asia until very recently differs very little from what was happening 1,500 years ago, and probably very little from the practice of Buddhism soon after, or perhaps even during, the Buddha's lifetime. For the overwhelming majority of both laity *and* monks this accommodation of normative, Theravāda doctrine—of the Canonical ideal of renunciation leading to *nibbāna* (Sanskrit, *nirvāṇa*)—to the needs of life in the world is what constitutes, and always has constituted, orthodox Theravāda Buddhism.

For lay people to define themselves as 'Buddhist', it is sufficient for them to declare that they 'go for refuge' to the Buddha, the *Dhamma* and the Saṅgha (the 'Three Refuges'), and that they will abide by the Five Precepts (not to kill, steal, be unchaste, lie, or take intoxicants). However, in the Buddhist liturgical calendar there are days in the lunar month of intensified observance (*uposatha* days) when, ideally, a lay person takes the Eight Precepts. These are the basic five, with the modifications that all sexual activity is excluded, that one should not watch entertainments or use adornments, and that one should not use luxurious beds. This is close to lower ordination or novitiate (*pabbajjā*), which entails taking the Ten Precepts. The latter are the same as the Eight, but abstention from entertainments and adornments are treated as separate precepts, and an injunction against using money is added. To take the Ten Precepts it is not necessary to be ordained; indeed, since the Theravāda order of nuns is extinct, following these precepts is formally the closest that women can come to ordination. Nevertheless, there are some women who behave very much as nuns might, leading ascetic lives, either in religious communities or alone, but without the same recognition that monks enjoy. A novice (*sāmaṇera*) can enter the order at about the age of seven, and can go on to take higher ordination and thus become a monk (*bhikkhu*) at twenty. Although monks are always free to leave the Order, ordination in Sri Lanka is assumed to be for life. In other Theravāda countries, however, there is a far more flexible system of temporary ordination. And perhaps the majority of the male population in these countries has spent at least some time, however short, as a novice.

In theory, the single aim of Buddhist practice is to attain *nibbāna*, the extinction of desire and so the end to re-birth and suffering. Classically, this goal is attained by progressing via moral purity, self-restraint and the practice of meditation, to the achievement of wisdom, a path which only the monk or nun can hope to tread successfully. In practice, however, *nibbāna* has proved to be too remote, too difficult either to understand or to achieve, and thereby simply too unattractive as an immediate religious goal for the vast majority. Beyond that, the Buddhist teaching that existence is 'unsatisfactory' or 'suffering' (*dukkha*) is evidently only partially or intellectually accepted by most people: they can see or imagine states of wealth and power where suffering is outweighed by happiness and pleasure, and those states, however impermanent, still seem desirable. So the ideal goal becomes not *nibbāna* but a better re-birth, if possible as a god in heaven, or at worst in an improved station on earth. Lip-service is still paid to *nibbāna* as the ultimate goal, but it has been indefinitely postponed. Some day one may be in a position both to merit and to understand it; until then it is better to proceed by stages. Interacting with this attitude, there is the widespread popular belief that Buddhism has declined so far that it is no longer possible for men to attain *nibbāna*.

How then is one to achieve the modified goal of a better re-birth? The answer is through the acquisition of merit (Pali, *puñña*), and virtually all Buddhist religious practice, whether by laity or monks, has merit as its aim. Moreover, such merit-making is perceived as being quite compatible with doctrine, since it all contributes towards *nibbāna* in the end. It also develops psychological states, such as feelings of peace, happiness and generosity, which are in themselves mentally purifying and thus steps along the road to *nibbāna*. What is merit and how does one go about attaining it? Simply, merit is the 'karmic' recompense for good deeds which produces a better re-birth: the more merit acquired the better the re-birth. Bad action, particularly action which violates the Buddhist moral precepts, produces demerit and thus karmic retribution in the form of a worse re-birth. As understood by the unsophisticated, merit is therefore a kind of intangible spiritual 'currency' which can be reckoned and 'transferred', and which increases in proportion to the amount 'invested'. There is a well-known but uncanonical Pali verse list of 'Ten Good Deeds' which includes all the possible ways of earning merit: generosity, observing the precepts, meditation, transferring merit, empathising with merit, serving (one's elders), showing respect, preaching, listening to preaching, and holding right beliefs. The inclusion of the moral precepts in this list is, of course, a nod towards the Canon, but following them is seen principally as a way of avoiding demerit; the only way to feel certain that one is actually acquiring and increasing merit itself is to take action. The most rewarding merit-making activity is generosity (*dāna*). Principally, this means giving food and other goods to monks in exchange for religious services, chiefly preaching, presiding at funerals and the chanting of *paritta* texts (see below). Because the Saṅgha follows and disseminates the Buddha's doctrine (*Dhamma*), it is considered to be 'the supreme field in which to sow merit', the most worthy recipient of respect and donations. This, of course, runs counter to the usual reading of Buddhist ethics—that karmically it is the intention of the actor which counts in any particular deed. Here the amount of merit acquired is in direct proportion to the *perceived* spiritual worthiness of the *recipient*. There is a Burmese saying that feeding a hundred dogs is the equivalent in merit of feeding one human being, feeding a hundred laymen the equivalent of feeding one novice, feeding a hundred novices the equivalent of feeding an ordinary monk, and so on. In other words, merit-making requires the co-operation of both laity and monks, and from the layman's point of view the most important function of the Saṅgha is to provide him with the opportunity to make merit by giving, not only through daily alms but also through the monastic feeding ceremonies that accompany every important public event. Thus the everyday relationship between the Saṅgha and the lay population is typified by the invitation to monks to take part in various rituals where they can, as it were, become both the 'targets' for extensive generosity and the generators of further merit. This is clearly a long way from the ideal of the monk as world-renouncer. Ideally, the monks' major religious activities are limited to obeying the Discipline and studying the scriptures; in practice, however, most monks spend most of their time performing merit-making rituals for laymen. Yet since few monks consider *nibbāna* to be a realistic goal, such activity is in fact beneficial for them as well, for preaching and propagating the *Dhamma* is one of the ways in which they acquire merit and thus the chance of a better re-birth. This is a spiritual economy in which both parties benefit and the store of merit goes on increasing.

Nearly all public Buddhist acts are seen as occasions for mutual merit-making: the laity feed the monks, and the monks reciprocate by 'preaching'. This may take the form of sermons, or readings from texts. Traditionally, the main content of sermons is derived from the *Jātaka* collection and in particular from its preface, the *Nidānakathā*, which is the principal Theravādin source for the Buddha's biography. Another popular source is the commentary on the *Dhammapada*. The most distinctive form of preaching, however, is the formalised and often lengthy recitation of Pali scriptures known as *paritta*, literally 'protection' texts. These are essentially a magical means of bringing good luck, of improving one's health and wealth. Similarly, after every public Buddhist ceremony the merit acquired is offered to the gods so that they can reciprocate by helping in the worldly realm which is their proper sphere of influence. How merit can be 'transferred' or 'shared' in this way requires some explanation. The original context for transferring merit is probably the funerary ritual. This, quite remarkably when one considers other religions, is the only 'life-crisis ritual' at which Buddhist monks officiate (albeit simply as preachers), and thus it is the only such ritual officially sanctified by Buddhism. A week after the death the monks are formally fed, again three months later, and thereafter at annual commemorative rites. And it is on these occasions that the merit, which goes in the first place to the donor, is ritually 'transferred' to the dead person. According to the normative theory of *karman* this should be impossible: the responsibility for an individual's fate lies in his own hands—strictly speaking, in his intention or volition, which alone decides the karmic quality of his thoughts and actions, and thus settles his future. However, it is clear that people have a pressing emotional need to do something for their dead relatives, and if that contradicts the law of *karman* they are quite happy to ignore or leave unformulated that contradition. In fact the more sophisticated, especially the monks, have developed a subtle and complex justification for the 'transfer of merit' based on the doctrine that the moral weight of an action lies in its intention. The donor can *intend* to transfer his merit to somebody else (a god or a dead relative) and so, without actually losing any, acquire more. Similarly, the intended 'recipient' is given the chance to applaud or empathise with the intention of the 'donor' to share his merit, and thus the 'recipient' too can perform an action (i.e. have an intention) which makes merit. Such a rationale is clearly strained, but the whole question of merit and its transfer draws attention to another area in which there has been a shift in the perception of a classical Buddhist teaching, namely, the doctrine of 'no-self' (*anattā*). Clearly, if a man is concerned that he should have a good re-birth, and believes that his dead relatives can have merit transferred to them, then he can hardly feel in any deep sense that an individual has no lasting personality and that the only continuity between this existence and the next one is karmic. The abiding wish for the survival of some personal essence after death cancels out the counter-intuitive doctrine of 'no-self', even when lip-service is paid to it. (The question of whether many people really understand this difficult doctrine is a related but somewhat different one.) This, no doubt, is also one of the reasons why *nibbāna*, the state which requires that the 'selflessness' of the person should be fully realised, remains a deferred ideal.

In addition to those mentioned above, a number of other Buddhist practices, all connected with devotion, can be seen as opportunities to produce material welfare through the transfer of merit. However, the best motive for acts of devotion is said to be that they are part of that complex of mental training which constitutes the Buddhist path: in so far as they calm the mind they produce spiritual welfare. From very early in Theravāda history the related practices of building *stūpas*, going on pilgrimages, and worshipping relics have been commonplace. Indeed, these three activities as well as the transfer of merit have canonical authorisation (in the *Mahāparinibbāna Sutta*). *Stūpas* originated as burial mounds for the Buddha's relics. They proliferated under the belief that all enlightened beings were entitled to such tombs, eventually even all Theravādin monks. However, only *stūpas* said to contain the relics of a Buddha are worshipped. The relic may be something like a piece of bone, or it may be a part of the Buddha's 'Dharma-body', i.e. a part of scripture. *Stūpas* are thus, in one sense, 'reminders' of the Buddha; and by a relatively late classification relics were divided into body relics (such as bone, teeth or hair), objects used by the Buddha (such as begging bowls, but also the Bo tree under which he attained enlightenment) and places associated with his life, and 'reminder relics', which included statues. In one way, all sacred objects are reminders to devotees of the (dead) Buddha, bringing them psychologically that much closer to him. Pilgrimage, which is by no means an obligation for Buddhists, is mainly to *stūpas* and sites associated either with the historical Buddha or with one of the many Buddhas who are supposed to have preceded him. Such sites, supported by various myths concerning miraculous visits from Gotama Buddha, exist in all Theravāda countries. Thus it is chiefly by the doctrine of relics that Buddhist worship and the practices associated with it are justified. Yet worship remains an individual and simple affair, one in which flowers or incense are offered before a Buddha image, and some Pali verses recited, very much in accordance with its stated function as a way of purifying the mind. To put this in more general terms, while the Buddha himself is the principal object of religious emotion and the focus of devotion, it is the monks who, as 'sons of the Buddha' and living exemplars of Buddhist ideals, receive the greatest veneration. Thus the very reason for the existence of a village temple, for instance, is that it is the residence of at least one monk.

Throughout the history of Theravāda the great majority of laity and monks have practised their religion in the ways outlined above—pursuing various devotional practices and making merit for themselves and others. There have, however, certainly intermittently and perhaps always, been some monks who have concentrated entirely on the ideal practices of meditation and asceticism, and so followed the path to *nibbāna*. The tradition is probably not an unbroken one. However remote the hermitage, its monks are still dependent on the laity for food, and such is the veneration in which meditating monks are held, and so great is the potential merit to be gained from giving to them, that they are constantly in danger of being drawn back into 'village' activities, i.e. into the monastic norm of preaching and teaching. In one case in modern Sri Lanka it is necessary to 'book' a year in advance to give a group of forest-dwelling meditators a meal, so great is the demand. It is likely that a pattern was established from a relatively early date in Theravāda history whereby monks setting themselves up as meditators had to revive the tradition from written sources rather than from any living master. The classical source is Buddhaghosa's *Visuddhimagga*. There, meditation (*bhāvanā*) is described in terms of moral and mental self-discipline, the total cultivation of the individual which results in wisdom (*paññā*). That purification which leads to and is synonymous with *nibbāna* is the objective, and it is renunciation which is seen as the height of moral purity. When it actually comes to 'sitting in meditation', two techniques are prescribed: meditations for 'tranquillity' (*samatha*), and 'insight meditation' (*vipassanā*), the distinctively Theravādin form. One proceeds from the first to the second, the aim of the latter being to realise in one's own experience the psychological reality of the Buddhist doctrine that all things are impermanent, unsatisfactory, and that there is no self. Realising this truth, desire is discarded and *nibbāna* achieved. Hermitage revival movements in the twentieth century have also depended on Buddhagosa; however, there have been a number of new developments, some of them heterodox, notably the teaching of 'insight' meditation to laymen and the setting up of meditation centres.

The meditating monks who live in the forests attempt to act by the Buddha's moral code and embody the ideals expressed in his doctrine in their own ways of life. In a sense, by purifying themselves they purify the entire Saṅgha, turning it back towards its ideal past. And throughout the history of Theravāda Buddhism, it is the Saṅgha that has in turn provided the rest of the population with an ideal of civilised behaviour, an ideal which is encapsulated in the *Visuddhimagga*'s prescription to meditators: that a man should first of all wish himself well, but then he should go on and do the same for others.

Further Reading

Bechert, H. and Gombrich, R.F. (eds.) *The World of Buddhism* (Thames & Hudson, London, 1984)

Carrithers, M. *The Forest Monks of Sri Lanka* (Oxford University Press, Delhi, 1983)

Gombrich, R.F. *Precept and Practice: Traditional Buddhism in the Rural Highlands of Ceylon* (Oxford University Press, Oxford, 1971)

—— *Theravada Buddhism: A Social History from Ancient Benares to Modern Colombo* (Routledge & Kegan Paul, London, 1988)

Spiro, M.E. *Buddhism and Society, A Great Tradition and its Burmese Vicissitudes* (University of California Press, Berkeley, 1982)

40 Buddhism and Hinduism in the Nepal Valley

David Gellner

Introduction

The Kathmandu Valley is a roughly circular bowl about twenty-five kilometres in diameter set high in the Himalayan foothills. The rich black soil of the valley, and its strategic position on ancient trade routes between Tibet and India, meant that it became an outpost of South Asian civilisation from the fourth century CE onwards. The Chinese Buddhist pilgrim Hsüan Tsang (Xuan Zang), passing through the plains of India in the early seventh century, heard that the Valley possessed both Hindu temples and Buddhist monasteries close together, and that there were 'about 2,000 [Buddhist] monks who study both the Great and the Little Vehicle'. Numerous inscriptions in elegant Sanskrit and many beautiful sculptures, still today sited in temple compounds or in wayside shrines, attest to the high level of culture attained in the Licchavi period (fifth to ninth centuries CE).

Subsequently the Kathmandu Valley experienced a period of weak and decentralised government, lasting about 500 years. We know very little about the first 300 years or so, but after that there is much more evidence. Then in 1382 King Jaya Sthiti Malla ascended the throne and united the Valley under one ruler for the first time in many centuries. Although he reigned for only thirteen years his influence seems to have been profound: many of the religious and cultural practices still alive today can be traced back to his reign or to the time of his immediate successors. His descendants ruled over the Valley, which was subsequently divided into three separate kingdoms, until 1768–9, when it was conquered by Prithvi Narayan Shah, the ancestor of the present king. This was the crucial step in the establishment of the modern kingdom of Nepal, which stretches far beyond the narrow confines of the Kathmandu Valley.

From an ethno-political point of view the backbone of Prithvi Narayan Shah's dynasty was provided by the Brahmin and

Kṣatriya castes (pronounced locally as 'Bāhun' and 'Chetri' respectively). The Brahmins were priests of course, but they were also administrators, judges and landowners. The Kṣatriyas were soldiers, policemen, politicians and farmers. Still today the King of Nepal must by law come from the Kṣatriya caste. These groups, and associated untouchable service castes, are known as 'Parbatiya'. They migrated throughout the hills of Nepal, taking their language, now called 'Nepali', with them. Nepali had become the lingua franca of the hills even before the time of Prithvi Narayan Shah; now it is the national language and is fast gaining ground among the various tribes-cum-castes (e.g. Magar, Gurung, Rai, Limbu) who inhabit the Nepalese hills.

The Parbatiyas migrated also to the Kathmandu Valley, but they are not its traditional inhabitants. These are the Newars, an ethnic group defined primarily by its language, Newari. This is a Tibeto-Burman tongue but through almost two millennia of influences from the south it has absorbed a very large number of Indo-European words, especially in those contexts (e.g. religion) in which the *written* word is important. The Newars have their own caste system which, thanks to the fact that they are traditionally city dwellers, is more complex and elaborated than that of the Parbatiyas. Figure 40.1 gives a very simplified representation of it.

Figure 40.1: Newar Caste System

<table>
<tr><td>Newar Brahmins

High Caste Hindus (administrators, businessmen, astrologers)</td><td>Buddhist priests and monks (goldsmiths, artisans)

High Caste Buddhists (businessmen, artisans)</td></tr>
<tr><td colspan="2">Farmers</td></tr>
<tr><td colspan="2">Various Artisan and Service Castes</td></tr>
<tr><td colspan="2">Untouchables</td></tr>
</table>

Since the establishment of modern Nepal by Prithvi Narayan Shah many Newars have emigrated from the Kathmandu Valley, their 'homeland', and become traders and shopkeepers throughout the hills of Nepal. The Newars also provide most of Nepal's artisans—carpenters, masons, sculptors, potters, coppersmiths and goldsmiths. Within the Kathmandu Valley, as is shown on the chart, they constitute a complete social system. Unlike the Parbatiyas, who are all strong Hindus very similar to those of north India, the Newars have the unique characteristic of possessing both Buddhist and Hindu religious traditions side by side, and both in a very archaic form. In general terms, much of what I shall say applies to the Parbatiyas also, especially to those living in the Kathmandu Valley. But my description is primarily of the Newars, since they are the inheritors of the Valley's ancient civilisation, a fact of which they themselves are extremely proud.

In spite of the political changes which have occurred, the Shah dynasty has maintained most of the traditions associated with that ancient civilisation. From 1846 to 1951 the Rana family of hereditary prime ministers held absolute power. They pursued a deliberate policy of isolation from British India so that Nepal knew little of the complex changes set in motion by the colonial power with its laws, factories and new ways of thinking. Modernisation has only come to Nepal in the years since 1951. So far change has been more eye-catching than thoroughgoing and the old ways still vastly outnumber the new.

Thus it is that one can see in the Kathmandu Valley a unique and ancient urban culture still functioning today. Three- and four-storey houses of brick and wood, with intricately carved windows; three- and five-storeyed 'pagoda' temples, their roofs covered with beaten copper and held up by beautifully carved wooden struts; numerous sunken water fountains in which a continuous stream of water—often brought long distances underground—flows from several carved stone ducts; public meeting-houses, wayside shelters, temples, monasteries and shrines of all sorts at every corner; the meticulous farming which gets three crops a year from irrigated fields and skilful artisan work of all kinds—all this is visible to any casual observer. Moreover, he or she cannot fail to notice a devotion to religion which overflows into festivals, fasts and rituals on almost every day of the year. Many visitors to the Valley have remarked that there seem to be almost as many temples as houses, as many gods as men.

The rituals and festivals of the Newars are, like most of their culture, extremely ancient. Some new cults may have risen to prominence, some new observances have been initiated, some new castes have emerged, but the basic structure of their religion and society seems to have remained much the same since the fourteenth century. Thanks to a combination of geographical isolation and political circumstance, the Valley avoided both Muslim rule and also (with the exception of some ill-fated visits by Jesuits in the seventeenth century and Capuchins in the eighteenth) the attentions of missionaries. Many traditions even go back beyond Jaya Sthiti Malla. The rites of the Buddhists can be traced back to the great monasteries of Bihar and Bengal in the late first millennium CE. Only here, in this little corner of South Asia, has this type of Indian Buddhism survived. Here too are forms of Tantric Hinduism which are equally ancient. The cultural conservatism of the Valley, and its temperate climate, have also meant that many ancient Buddhist and Hindu Sanskrit manuscripts, lost in the rest of South Asia, have survived here.

A Religion Based on Worship

Religion in the Kathmandu Valley is primarily a set of practices and these are all based on the idea of worship, doing *pūjā*, to a superior. Usually the superior in question is a deity, but it can also be a priest, elder or monk, someone considered to incarnate a deity, or anyone worthy of respect; and there are two popular family festivals, held on consecutive days, in which respectively one worships one's own body, for good health, and elder sisters worship their younger brothers, for long life.

The simplest worship consists simply of bowing one's head with folded hands; also indicative of respect, though not constituting worship as such, is the practice of keeping the deity or other superior on one's right hand. If offerings are made, the simplest is a few grains of rice or, these days, a coin. A more elaborate worship is made by offering a set of five things together: flowers, incense, light, vermilion powder and food (e.g. rice, sweets or fruit). To these may be added an offering of water, representing the bathing of feet, and thread tied in a circle, representing cloth. All of these offerings may be made by an individual on his own; but in rituals which require the specialist services of a priest the number of offerings increases rapidly. Some of these offerings are kept at home by each family, others may be bought at shops specialising in the sale of ritual perquisites, and some are so unusual—such as the rhinoceros meat required when performing ancestor worship—that the priest will bring along a minute quantity himself. Certain deities accept animal sacrifice: the various forms of the Hindu Goddess (e.g. the Eight Mothers and the Nine Durgās), Bhairava, Gaṇeśa and Bhīmasena. But to sacrifice an animal to high and pure deities—Mahādeva (Śiva), Nārāyaṇa (Viṣṇu), the Buddha or the Buddhist *bodhisattvas*—would be a heinous sin. However there is another class of deities, the secret or Tantric deities, who may be seen and worshipped directly only by those with special empowering initiations; while not normally receiving actual blood sacrifice they must be offered cooked meat and alcohol.

The offerings made in worship must be new and fresh—offering a half-eaten banana would be a terrible insult, and contradict the basic emotional attitude of worship, namely respectful acknowledgement of one's inferiority and, often only implicitly, a request for protection. Likewise the offering must be kept pure, that is, it must be kept away from contact with impurity, a category which, as in the rest of South Asia, includes saliva, excrement, menstruating women, dogs, leather, Untouchables, the soles of the feet and so on. When worship has been performed it is usual to receive back some of the offerings as a blessing: vermilion powder as a spot on the forehead, flowers put behind the ear (right for men, left for women), water or food—including the meat of a sacrificed animal—to consume.

A Westerner from a secular society can only be amazed at the time, energy and resources that Newars devote to their religion. Every day offerings must be made and every year hundreds of festivals are observed, some confined to a particular village or quarter of the city, others common to all Newars alike. In addition every lineage has its own deity which must be worshipped once or twice a year, as do many castes or professional groups. High-caste families have their Tantric deities requiring regular worship. There are gods for toothache, earache, smallpox and infertility, gods who will help you find things you have lost, gods whose worship can help to remove the sin of adultery. Birth, entry into adulthood, marriage, the attaining of the ages 77, 80 and 99, and death are all marked by religious observances which involve the whole family and many relatives.

Newars also have a unique and characteristic religious organisation called *guthi*: these group together a number of men usually, but not invariably, of the same caste, for some socio-religious purpose or other. Every Newar belongs to at least one *guthi*, a funeral association which takes charge of the cremation of its members. But there are hundreds of others, e.g. those responsible for the maintenance of wayside shelters, *guthis* set up to ensure the annual performance of a particular fast, or charged with the building of the cart of a popular deity, to mention only a few. *Guthis* are funded by lands and other donations, gifted either by the founder or subsequently as an act of religious merit, or by annual contributions from its members. Each year or month, depending on the rhythm of the *guthi*'s activities, a different member takes charge of its organisation. At the conclusion of his turn he must give a feast for all the members. The dishes to be served are laid down by tradition and participating in it is also a religious act, since the food is consecrated by the presiding divinity. Similar feasts are eaten by the family, and its guests, at the conclusion of every life-cycle rite, and at every important annual festival.

Underlying this efflorescence of religious activity is a complex but stable society, built on respect and hierarchy. Different castes are related to each other, just as men are related to gods, in certain fixed and traditional ways, which are re-enacted every year as inevitably as the seasons. The historian or anthropologist can detect that certain rituals have gone out of, or come into, fashion (e.g. the fast of Svasthānī, mentioned below), that the caste system is mutating and that new types of religious activity have emerged. But the Newars themselves remain extremely attached to their traditions and to the idea that they are unchanging and ought not to change.

Newar religious practices can be divided into the compulsory and the optional. The sheer quantity of compulsory observance is very slowly decreasing, but there seems to be at least as much optional religious activity as there ever has been.

Obligatory Religious Practices

Every family has its own god-room situated high and near the back of the house, i.e. as privately as possible. For the women of the house, keeping the god-room, the kitchen and the storeroom (considered the abode of Lakṣmī, the goddess of wealth) clean and briefly worshipping all the deities present, is part of their daily religious duty. That done, one person from the house, again usually female, visits the shrines of the locality, making offerings at each.

Men who have taken some kind of initiation must also perform a daily ritual: this is a lifelong personal obligation they have undertaken. Mostly this ritual consists in the recitation of sacred formulas and prayers; depending on the type of initiation and the individual's piety, it may last for anything from ten minutes to two or three hours. Until this daily worship has been performed no food may pass his mouth. The difficulty this obligation imposes means that those who take initiation are usually old or at least middle-aged. In any case neither young men, unless of the priestly castes, nor children are expected to take any great interest in taxing religious observances.

Just as cleaning the house each morning is a religious act for women, so cleaning the shrine and bathing the deity is an obligatory daily task for men who are temple-priests, either permanently or in rotation, and for those families that have established their own private shrines. In every temple of any size the first thing that occurs early in the morning is this 'regular worship' before outside worshippers may present their offerings. At the temples of popular deities huge crowds gather during which the priests recite prayers and bathe the deity. The water is then sprayed onto the assembled worshippers as a blessing. Out of simple faith and devotion this regular worship occurs, scaled down, at thousands of other small shrines and temples every day, though no one may be there to observe or bring offerings. The high and pure gods, and for the most part the Tantric deities, are the preserve of the priestly castes of the two religions—Brahmins and Karmācāryas (Hindu Tantric priests) for Hindu gods, and Vajrācāryas (literally 'master of the diamond [Vehicle]') and Śākyabhikṣus ('Buddhist monks') for the Buddhist deities. But many other deities, worshipped in common by the followers of both religions, are served by priests of other castes: Gaṇeśa shrines for instance are usually served by farmers and even the Untouchables have temples where they have the right to keep all offerings, namely those of the Mother Goddesses that ring the city and protect it from external evil influences.

Every month, calculated according to the moon's cycles, certain holy days recur: the no-moon day, the eighth (sacred to the Bodhisattva Lokeśvara), the eleventh (on which no meat may be sold, sacred to Nārāyaṇa), and the full-moon day; in the waning half of the month, there is the fourteenth (sacred to various deities); also holy are the days that the sun passes into a new zodiacal sign and initiates a new solar month (likewise sacred to the Bodhisattva Lokeśvara). On all these days religious observance brings greater merit: both men and women take greater pains with their daily worship, visit more shrines and say more prayers than usual. At large temples special rituals mark these holy days. Similarly each day of the week is holy to a particular deity, for instance Tuesday to Gaṇeśa, Saturday to Mahākāla and to many of the Mother Goddesses. On these days their shrines will be many times more crowded than on normal days.

Every year numerous annual festivals are celebrated in the home. On these days it is forbidden to eat cooked rice, the consumption of which involves mild impurity (that is why one's daily ritual must be completed before eating). Instead parboiled flattened rice, buffalo meat cooked in various ways and numerous tasty vegetable and bean dishes are eaten. But this feast occurs only after the head of the household and his wife have performed the ritual necessary to that day. The following day daughters of the household who have been given away in marriage to other families must be invited along with their children; on a few important festivals their husbands will also be included in the invitation. In this way women maintain frequent contact with their natal home, and their children come to regard their maternal uncles with special affection. Men say that they have a religious duty to feed their married sisters and daughters whenever they celebrate anything because, by marrying into another family, they have lost the right to inherit from their own parents.

In addition to the annual festivals which everyone observes there are many particular to individual areas, castes or *guthis*. People also observe their own birthdays by making offerings at various temples. Membership of most *guthis* is optional, but it is not something lightly abandoned. If one's ancestor has founded a Buddhist *caitya* (Buddhist cult object), or donated a tympanum, for example, to a temple, every year the anniversary of the donation must be marked by a reconsecration: the family priest must be called, a fire sacrifice lasting several hours (during which all participants fast) must be performed, and finally a feast served.

The various stages of life are also marked by religious ritual. Only by ritual can a house be purified after a birth or a death. These occasions implicate relatives too, so that Newars often describe how closely they are related by mentioning the degree of mourning they are obliged to observe for each other's death. During these periods of impurity it is forbidden to worship deities, except indirectly or from outside a given area. Auspicious stages of life are also defined religiously: a child's first rice-feeding is a time of great joy and the help of the gods is required to ensure its healthy growth. In later life Newar girls pass through a ceremony in which they are 'married to a *bel* fruit'; according to Buddhist priests the girls are marrying the god Kumāra, and according to Brahmins, Nārāyaṇa. The *bel* fruit is, on learned interpretations, just a witness, but for ordinary Newars these are academic matters. Ritually speaking the girl is then married, and married for life, so that even if her human husband dies she is not supposed to suffer the indignity of being a widow (in practice however high-caste women do suffer some stigma). Girls must also undergo a twelve-day rite in which they stay in a room without seeing the sun; its purpose is, it seems, to defuse the danger of their imminent menstruation. Boys pass through a single though complex rite called 'tying the loin-cloth'; for Brahmins and high-caste Hindus this also involves the donning of the sacred thread; boys of the Buddhist priestly-monk caste spend four days as a Buddhist monk. All these rites mark the transition to adulthood, so that the boy or girl is now considered a full member of his or her caste and family.

Marriage, too, is a long and complex ceremony, sanctified at every stage with worship of the gods. If an old person reaches 77, 80 or 99 years they are also entitled to a further rite which consecrates them as becoming ever more divine themselves. All members of their lineage come to show their respect and do obeisance to them. Finally death is marked by ceremonies extending over many years. Every year, at least for the first two years, and usually for many years afterwards, a deceased father receives worship and 'feeding' from his eldest son, a mother from her youngest son. The complex ceremonies performed on behalf of the dead are felt to be a great help in times of bereavement, since they give those left behind concrete measures to take on behalf of their loved one.

The higher castes, both Hindu and Buddhist, are more punctilious in observing these various life-cycle rituals than the low castes. In fact more ritual involvement in general is part of the way in which 'high' caste is defined. The life-cycle rites are seen, especially in the Hindu view, as purifying; some Buddhists tend to play down the importance of particular rites, but they, like all Newars, see the undertaking of the rules and restrictions involved in ritual in general as a sign of commitment to the religious life.

Public Festivals

The most spectacular side of Newar religion is its public festivals. These form an intermediate category between the obligatory and the optional: they must take place, and for those directly involved in organising them there is no choice; but everyone else takes part for the fun and religious merit of it.

One type of public festival involves visiting every shrine of a particular deity within the city. In Lalitpur the most popular festival of this sort is called 'The procession of [offering] light': thousands of worshippers circulate without stopping and without eating on a route laid out beforehand, visiting and making offerings to every *caitya* in the city, which takes from 5 am to about 8 pm to complete. Ten different sections of the city take it in turn to organise the festival. In the same way there are processions to every Bhīmasena shrine, to every Gaṇeśa, to every Kṛṣṇa and so on at different times of the year, events in which hundreds of people participate.

In chariot and palanquin festivals it is the god who circulates for the benefit of worshippers on a prescribed route around the town. The most famous of these is the chariot festival of the god called Matsyendranāth by Hindus, Karuṇāmaya by Buddhists and Buṃgadyaḥ by most ordinary Newars. It is also the festival with the tallest chariot and lasts longer than any other. All sections of the population observe the festival with great enthusiasm but it is perhaps the farmers who show the greatest devotion since Matsyendranātha is believed to bring the rain on which their crops depend. Chariots with huge wooden wheels are expensive and time-consuming to make so most deities circulate on a palanquin carried on the shoulders of four or more men. In these festivals different tasks are laid down by tradition for different castes. These duties are usually jealously guarded privileges, a source of pride to the groups and individuals concerned.

In most public festivals the king plays a significant role. Before 1768 each of the three major cities of the Valley, Kathmandu, Bhaktapur and Lalitpur, had its own king and he would be present as principal sponsor of the festival and guarantor of the material and spiritual well-being of the kingdom. In smaller settlements the local headman, as representative of the royal power, played and often still plays the role of 'king'. When the present dynasty established its capital in Kathmandu the kings continued to be present at some rituals and kept up the rituals associated with royalty in the other two cities, Bhaktapur and Lalitpur. Nowadays, though he is rarely present himself, the sword of the king must always be brought along. Some of the festivals centre around the royal palace of each city, in particular the autumn festival known as Dasaiṃ in Nepali, Mohanī in Newari, Durgā Pūjā or Navarātrī in Sanskrit. This is at the same time an archetypal family ritual, observed in every house in the country: all offices close and absent relatives return home. Theologically the festival celebrates the victory of Durgā over the buffalo demon; this myth is given vivid expression by the sacrifice of hundreds of buffaloes to the king's tutelary deity, Taleju, a form of Durgā, who is at the same time a Tantric deity and whose *mantra* is believed to guarantee the king's power. Thus while this is a nation-wide, indeed *the* nation-wide and state festival, it is also above all the festival of the ruling and warfaring (Kṣatriya) class. Other festivals in which the king has an important role are Ghoḍe (horse) Jātrā and Indra Jātrā in Kathmandu (the presence of the Vedic god Indra is another sign of the antiquity of the Newars' religion), Bisket Jātrā in Bhaktapur and the Matsyendra Jātrā in Lalitpur.

In many festivals dancers impersonate gods; when they put on their masks they begin to tremble as a sign that the god has entered them. The most famous of these are the Nine Durgās from Bhaktapur who dance for nine months of every year, visiting twenty-one quarters of the city and the nineteen towns and villages which used to comprise the kingdom of Bhaktapur. There are many other such dance groups: the Eight Mothers of Lalitpur (danced unusually by Buddhists); a similar group from the village of Theco nearby; the dancers attached to the Naradevī temple in Kathmandu; and many more. Lākhe (demon) dancers circulate in association with many festivals. There is a special set of dances in Lalitpur over many nights during the month of Kārtik. These include farces and devotional dances, culminating on the final night in the dance of the half-man half-lion Narasiṃha (an incarnation of Viṣṇu with royal connections) who is acted nowadays by a Brahmin, destroying the demon Hiraṇyakaśipu, acted by a man of the painter caste. In the old days, people say, the painter was really killed; now he merely becomes unconscious and is revived with holy water.

Optional Religious Practices

For the pious individual there is a vast panoply of ways to invest his or her energy. One of the most popular with women is the one- or two-day fast. For Buddhists and those with Buddhist priests, this means above all the *aṣṭamī vrata*, a fast in the name of Bodhisattva Amoghapāśa Lokeśvara, which occurs each month on the eighth day of the waxing moon. Often a group will form, sponsored by one or more rich men who wish to earn merit, and undertake to perform the fast at each of the twelve holy bathing places in the Valley. Another Buddhist fast involves performing the same rite at eight Hindu temples of Viṣṇu and Śiva, who are classed as *bodhisattvas* in the Buddhist scheme of things. Once a year a popular fast is performed to the Buddhist goddess Vasundharā and there are many *guthis* to ensure that it takes place without fail.

Hindus fast for the god Nārāyaṇa (Viṣṇu) on the eleventh day of the waxing moon, and also often perform a fast over several days called the *Satya Nārāyaṇa pūjā* when they have some special reason to celebrate or a particular wish to be fulfilled. At the end of the holy month of Kārtik a few women undertake a five-day fast to Karuṇāmaya or Nārāyaṇa and at the end of it are fetched by their husband and led home in triumph with a band playing. In the old days this fast was often undertaken for a whole month with the women consuming nothing except the holy water in which the deity had been bathed. Every year in the month of Māgh (January–February) Hindu women, both Newar and non-Newar, observe the fast of Svasthānī, a uniquely Nepali goddess identified with Śiva's wife Pārvatī.

Even if they cannot fast they read the stories associated with the fast and the goddess every evening. This practice, like of that of Gai (cow) Jātrā, has spread from the Newars to other groups in Nepali society and is almost universal throughout the middle hills of modern Nepal.

A less taxing but longer-term practice is simply the service of a deity, visiting his or her temple every day for a month, or even a year. This is undertaken by both men and women, though men predominate. Some treat this as little more than a regular morning walk; but in the month of Kārtik, when it is both dark and very cold at 5 am, rather more commitment is required. At certain important shrines regular devotees join in the recitation of Sanskrit prayers every morning, a form of devotion which is open to all and highly valued. On holy days, in the morning, and sometimes also in the evening just for the fun of it, groups of men gather to sing hymns: the ancient style is highly percussive and the words are usually in old forms of Maithili and Bengali, imported from the plains of India centuries ago; the newer style, introduced in the last sixty years or so, makes use of the accordion and in this style new hymns, composed in the local vernaculars (Newari and Nepali) are sung. These hymn groups are usually organised as a *guthi* with certain fixed duties and an annual feast, but membership is optional.

Those with money have numerous possibilities for approved forms of merit-making: donating a fitting or decoration to a temple, founding a Buddhist *caitya* or Hindu Śivaliṅga, building a wayside shelter, establishing a *guthi* for the annual performance of a ritual to one's favoured deity. In recent times more modern forms of religious activity have received sponsorship: publishing religious pamphlets (usually in the name of a dead parent or relative), writing for religious magazines, establishing health clinics, religious schools and other types of social service. Buddhist meditation camps and Buddhist, Hindu or interdenominational conferences have become regular events.

Another way of dividing up religious practices is to consider the individual's motivations. Where compulsory religious practices are concerned the motives are obviously diffuse: there is no need for an individual to ask him or herself why it is being done and the practice goes on out of a general desire to satisfy the gods, perpetuate tradition and avoid any ill consequences (divine retribution, social obloquy) which might follow the evasion of one's religious duty. Optional religious practices on the other hand are undertaken with more precise aims in mind. Sometimes this is merely to win religious merit and peace of mind: it is very widely felt that religious practices protect one from domestic disasters while omissions and mistakes, particularly in the ritual due to a powerful deity, incur misfortunes sooner or later. But other rituals and practices are undertaken with a very specific aim in mind: the birth of a son, success in an exam, new job or business, to cure an illness, or to ensure a safe return from a long journey. Such rites vary in the extent to which such personal and specific desires are explicitly acknowledged: Buddhist fasts or the reading of the text, *The Perfection of Wisdom in Eight Thousand Lines* (Aṣṭasahasrika-Prajñāpāramitā-Sūtra), are officially carried out 'for the good of all beings', and it is only within that framework that one may ask for a particular favour. Other rituals, which some priests perform, or which women (and a few men) possessed by goddesses such as Hariti, the Buddhist goddess of smallpox, recommend to their petitioners, pretend even less to an altruistic motivation: everyone knows what they are for and there are few who have never patronised this type of ritual, though many outwardly condemn them.

One final type of optional religious practice which is equally important in Buddhism and Hinduism is initiation into the cult of a given Tantric deity. In one way this is the most onerous practice of all, for henceforth come what may one must perform the required ritual and say one's prayers every day before eating. Tantric initiations are restricted to high castes and to certain closely defined groups within other castes (e.g. men of the painter caste, who must be allowed into Tantric shrines in order to paint images and wall-hangings). The deities associated with Tantric practice are strictly secret; their shrines are enclosed rooms on the first floor of a monastery or of special god-houses, or on the second floor if in a private home. It is widely believed that looking at a Tantric deity whom one is not entitled to see causes blindness or madness. But for those who are entitled, and who fulfil faithfully their obligations to their deity, a good controlled death, and the attainment of liberation in this life, can be hoped for.

Tantric deities are usually represented in coitus with a female partner and sexual symbolism is central to Tantric ritual. It cannot be too heavily emphasised however that, though everyone knows of their existence, these deities and rituals really are secret: only thus is it possible for them to coexist with the highly moral and ascetic tendencies of exoteric (non-Tantric) Buddhism and indeed Hinduism. Through the use of meat, alcohol and sexual symbolism, which in other contexts are forbidden or disapproved of, the secret truth is taught that everything is emptiness (for Buddhists) or Śiva (for Hindus). Tantric deities are taken to be the highest, innermost and ultimate nature of the divine, of which other divinities and indeed the whole world are just outer forms. Thus it is that, though for most of the population their significance is opaque, the whole of Newar religion is permeated by Tantric symbols. And priests invoke the presence and protection of Tantric deities on behalf of their clients as part of almost every ritual, whether or not the client himself has initiation.

The Relation of Hinduism and Buddhism and the Problem of Belief

Many questions will occur to the Westerner confronted by this religion: what role does religious belief have for Newars? Is not this mass of ritual and worship just a confused jumble, a syncretistic pottage? What kind of Buddhism is it that encourages ritual, hierarchy and secrecy? Do we have anything to learn from such a completely different attitude to the sacred and the 'meaning of life'?

I have indicated the role which respect for tradition plays in the religious life of the Newars, and I have tried to show that this relates primarily to rites and practices. Newar children are taught no catechism nor to read their own scriptures (unless they come from the priestly castes). Rather, from an early age, they participate in festivals and undergo life-cycle rites under the instruction of their family priest and helped by their mothers. Young girls learn to help their mothers and the other young women of the household in making offerings, and themselves teach their younger siblings how to make obeisance to deities. As they grow older both men and women, particularly (though not only) of the upper castes, learn to recite prayers in Sanskrit and often make use of them in their daily ritual. But they are far from understanding them word for word; the point is not to analyse them but to recite them in an attitude of devotion. Reciting prayers, whether or not a manuscript or printed book is used to jog the memory, is also an activity, not a confession of faith. When fasts and some other rites are performed at a certain point the priest reads out the 'story' which goes with the practice; but it is written in an archaic style, he reads it out fast and the participants know the broad outline already; consequently, attention is lax and this too is simply another ritual.

While ritual is carefully codified and maintained by specialists, belief is not: there are no institutions for collective expressions of given articles of faith. Belief is an individual concern. Providing one conforms outwardly to the rites traditional to one's family, one can, if one wishes, believe things apparently in opposition to it. Some Buddhists privately prefer Hindu deities, and I know one prominent Buddhist intellectual whose family background is strongly Hindu. Women on the whole restrict their interest to rites and to the moral stories recited on various occasions by the learned priests of the two religions. Men on the other hand, particularly as they get older and begin to retire from worldly affairs, often take a lively interest in theological matters. It is not uncommon for them to discuss them amongst themselves. But the opinions they express represent their own reflections on past experience, with scraps they have heard from priests or their own older relatives. Doctrine is not codified and the only way to solve a dispute is to ask a priest. And since the organisation of priests is weak and consensual, and in any case concerned with ritual matters rather than doctrine, there is no authority empowered to decide such questions as there is in Western churches. Consequently it is ritual, and not belief, which determines whether one is a Buddhist or a Hindu.

According to one definition, the definition which tends to be given by priests themselves, all those with a Buddhist (Vajrācārya) family priest are Buddhists ('followers of the way of the Buddha'), and all those with a Brahmin family priest are Hindu ('followers of the way of Śiva'). For all compulsory rituals one must call one's traditional family priest and he, on his side, is obliged to come or send a substitute if he cannot. At optional rites however one may invite whomsoever one wishes; and one consequence of this is that certain families, and some castes, which are traditionally Buddhist, that is, have a Vajrācārya family priest, nevertheless invite Brahmins to perform rituals for them whenever they have the chance. The main reason for this is that the rulers of Nepal have been Hindu for a very long time and therefore Hinduism has higher social prestige; further, it is widely felt that Hindus have a better chance than Buddhists of obtaining government jobs, even though there is no systematic prejudice against them and the official view is that Buddhism is just a 'branch' of Hinduism.

Newar Buddhism is unusual in lacking a celibate monastic order. (As a result of recent influence from Tibet and South-east Asia there are now both Tibetan Mahāyāna and Theravāda monks in the Newar community; but these exist as an adjunct to traditional Newar religion and need not be considered here.) Instead of a celibate monkhood Newar Buddhism is led by a caste of *married* monks, made up of two subsections, one being the Buddhist priests, the Vajrācāryas, and the other, somewhat larger, called Śākyabhikṣu ('Buddhist monk') or Śākyavaṃśa ('of the Buddha's lineage'). The idea of married monks may seem strange but it is in fact one of the marks of Mahāyāna, as opposed to Theravāda, Buddhism to put less stress on celibacy and formal monasticism. This is equally true of Japanese Buddhism and of the un-reformed Tibetan schools.

The menfolk of this Buddhist caste, the Vajrācāryas and Śākyabhikṣus/Śākyavaṃśas, all pass through a rite as boys in which they spend four days as monks. In this way they become members of a particular monastery in which they have certain rights and duties for the rest of their life. The immediate neighbourhood of the monastery is inhabited by its members, though many also move, e.g. to set up as gold- or silversmiths elsewhere. In that case they return for important festivals and to fulfil their obligations in the monastery. (Only in the last thirty years have members who have lived for generations many days' travel away from their monastery started to break away and found new monasteries.) Other Newars respect them as a holy order and at certain festivals come to give them gifts as monks. It could be argued that such gift giving, *dāna*, is characteristically Buddhist; though conceptually not very far from worship, *pūjā*, it does seem to play a greater role in Buddhism than Hinduism.

The Buddhist monk caste has control of monastery deities, a category which includes some of the most popular gods in Nepal. As Buddhist priests they also have much the same position for Buddhist lay people as Brahmins do for Hindus. As monks, however, they tend to think of themselves as the only true Buddhists. And herein lies an important difference of values between them and Hindus: Hindus would never say that Brahmins are the only true Hindus; Hindus are inclusive and will tend to accept Buddhists as Hindus, although they assign them a rank lower than Buddhists would ascribe themselves. Buddhists on the other hand tend to define anything which is not on a strict definition Buddhist as non-Buddhist, and therefore as Hindu.

This explains how Buddhists can acquiesce in certain castes who have Buddhist priests being defined as Hindus. In fact, however, most Newars are neither clearly Buddhist nor clearly Hindu. They worship all deities with equal fervour; they carry out all the rites that tradition prescribes; if they have definite opinions this is a personal matter and not one which implicates anyone else. It is only the priestly castes at the top of the hierarchy, and one or two others immediately below them, who are careful not to allow themselves to be defined as members of the other religion. For all other Newars, perhaps 70 per cent of the total, the question of which religion they belong to is rather academic. This does not mean that they cannot tell the difference: they know very well what it is, but they say: 'We honour all deities equally, we respect both Brahmins and Vajrācāryas, we have our traditional practices as every caste and every nation does. There is no need to denigrate one religion and praise another, but one should keep up one's own traditions and respect what is good in all of them.'

There are two reasons why this is a tenable attitude for them. Firstly there is the fact that neither religion denies the existence or forbids the worship of the gods of the other. The Buddha is recognised as an incarnation of Viṣṇu; and Buddhists worship Viṣṇu and Śiva as *bodhisattvas*. One of the most popular gods of Nepal is known to outsiders by his Hindu name Matsyendranāth; but Buddhists, as I have already pointed out, call him Karuṇāmaya, an epithet of the Bodhisattva Avalokiteśvara; and most ordinary Newars, who are all enthusiastic worshippers, call him simply 'the god of [the village] Buṃga', thereby avoiding the question of whether he is a Hindu or a Buddhist deity. For them he is simply a powerful protector, who sends the monsoon rains, and the question of which religion he belongs to is irrelevant. They see the fact that he is worshipped equally by all tendencies of both religions as proof that such distinctions are academic. At the highest level of the pantheon then, the two religions offer competing explanations of the same divinities. But as with the social hierarchy, which has a clear distinction between Buddhist and Hindu at the top, but not at the bottom, the divine hierarchy is also clearly distinct only at the higher levels. Lower down where 'blood-drinking' gods such as the Eight Mothers or Gaṇeśa are concerned, it is not necessary to have alternative names. Both religions accept them as lower deities, though—again, as in the social hierarchy—Hinduism's inclusive tendency makes it more enthusiastic than Buddhism in doing so.

The second reason for the ordinary Newar's attitude to questions of religious attachment I have already described: it is that the primary religious activities are worship and ritual (which is just elaborate worship). This means that doctrine, polemic and even myth are 'second-order' activities; that is, they start from the fact of worship and on the whole reflect rather than determine it. This broad truth applies to both religions, so that a single act of worship to a deity of itself aligns one with neither religion. It is only by systematically worshipping Viṣṇu and Śiva, and avoiding Buddhist shrines and purely Buddhist festivals, that one defines oneself as a Hindu, and vice versa.

The primacy of praxis has a further consequence. Unlike the catechismal beliefs of religions like Christianity and Islam, which leave a relatively small scope to different interpretations, the simple action of worship is open to a wide variety of meanings. I have indicated how most Newars prefer simply to worship while remaining neutral about the question of whether their worship is Hindu or Buddhist. But even within a given religion the action of worship, which is common to every Newar of whatever background or education, can be seen naïvely as the propitiation of powerful beings; it can be seen as one's religious duty which leads to a better rebirth; or it can be seen as a discipline which calms the mind and produces good results for all concerned. In the Tantric systems, involving initiations and the complex worship of secret deities, it can be seen as a technique for identifying oneself with those deities and thereby with the essence of the universe, thus overcoming the limitations and duality of the ordinary world. Newars do not usually stop to consider which of these views they hold, though most of them will be aware, even if only vaguely, of them all. The peaceful coexistence of these various theories permits all Newars, of whatever background, to participate in the same tradition and religious culture.

It would be wrong to conclude therefore that the Newars' religion is an unsystematic syncretism of different elements and traditions which ought to have been kept separate. It is however held together by principles which are different from those we are familiar with from Western religions; and the way in which Hinduism and Buddhism define their relation to each other is quite foreign to Western religions. Moreover Buddhism and Hinduism, in coexisting as they do, are perfectly consistent and true to their own history.

By putting praxis at the centre of their religion, and making the degree and extent of it so much a matter of personal choice, the Newars' religion exhibits great tolerance—tolerance of different practices, of different viewpoints, of individuals' choices. Struggles with faith and a permanent sense of guilt are entirely unknown to them. At the same time their religion provides a framework, which everyone shares, of festivals, life-cycle rites and consecrated social relationships. One can but admire the simple faith, the far-reaching piety and the sheer enthusiastic enjoyment which such a religion inspires. Unfortunately however for those who might wish to emulate it, the Newars' religion is based on a stable social hierarchy, on respect for hereditary differences and rights and on a powerful belief in tradition, all of which, even in Nepal, are now rapidly being undermined by the inexorable process of Western-inspired change.

Further Reading

Allen, M.R. *The Cult of Kumari, Virgin Worship in Nepal* (INAS, Tribhuvan University, Kathmandu, 1975)

Bennett, Lynn *Dangerous Wives and Sacred Sisters—Social and Symbolic Roles of High-caste Women in Nepal* (Columbia University Press, New York, 1983)

Gutschow, Niels *Stadtraum und Ritual der newarischen Städte im Kathmandu Tal, Eine architekturanthropologische Untersuchung* (Kohlhammer, Stuttgart, 1982)

Lévi, Sylvain *Le Népal, étude historique d'un royaume hindou*, 3 vols. (Leroux, Paris, 1905)

Locke, John K. *Karunamaya, The Cult of Avalokitesvara-Matsyendranath in the Valley of Nepal* (Sahayogi, Kathmandu, 1980)

Slusser, Mary S. *Nepal Mandala, A Cultural Study of the Kathmandu Valley*, 2 vols. (Princeton University Press, Princeton, New Jersey, 1982)

Toffin, G. *Religion et société chez les Néwars du Népal* (CNRS, Paris, 1984)

41 Buddhism in China

Bulcsu Siklós

To many, the idea that Buddhism could, within a few hundred years, become an established, state-supported religion in, say, Europe would be far-fetched to say the least. Yet, almost to its own surprise, the age-old, highly conservative and excessively xenophobic civilisation of China managed to make Buddhism its own within a short period of time. This was perhaps the greatest coup ever pulled off by Buddhism, and one without which the Indian religion would have been restricted to playing a purely peripheral role in world history once its influence in its homeland had waned.

Ignoring certain groundless claims for the earlier introduction of Buddhism, many of Buddhist invention, it seems probable or at least possible that Buddhist monks started filtering in to western and northern parts of Han China during the first few years of our era from Central Asia. Obviously the process must have started before the Emperor Ming (58–75) had his dream of a flying golden deity interpreted by his ministers in a Buddhist light, resulting in the dispatch of several envoys to Central Asia. The implication, of course, is that Buddhism was already known, or rather, known about in China prior to this event, evidence for which can be culled from several sources, notably from the biography of Prince Ying of Ch'u. This states that by the year 65 there was a Buddhist community of some size in at least one peripheral part of western China, one which had possibly existed since *c.* 2 BCE. By the end of the first century CE, a community had likewise been established at Lo-yang, the capital, which even penetrated court circles to a degree where imperial shrines were set up for the worship of the Buddha alongside the deified Lao-tzu. Translation activities were also engaged in under the direction of a Parthian monk, An Shih-kao (arrived in China in 148) who laid emphasis on texts revealing meditational and breathing techniques, while his Scythian co-worker Chih-ch'an concentrated on translations of the *Prajñāpāramitā* (Perfection of Wisdom) literature. The monks of this period were without exception non-Chinese, though undoubtedly Chinese laymen played a considerable role in supporting the new community in various ways.

Buddhism during the Han period (until *c.* 220 CE) was doctrinally somewhat primitive, and not much effort was made to translate texts dealing with basic Buddhist philosophical issues. The central tenets seem to have been an acceptance of the idea of reincarnation and of the concept of *karma* understood in a very literal and moral sense, coupled with a totally un-Buddhist belief in the permanence and indestructibility of the 'soul' (how could rebirth take place otherwise?). Emphasis was laid upon simple meditational and yogic techniques paralleled by similar Taoist practices, although certain traditional objects of meditation, such as corpses in various stages of putrefaction, were considered unsuitable.

In this early period Buddhism's path was smoothed considerably by the Taoist theory of *hua-hu*, the Conversion of the Barbarians, according to which Lao-tzu had, after his disappearance westwards, travelled to India, converted its 'barbarian' inhabitants and become known as the Buddha. This was no more than a Taoist defence mechanism—why become a Buddhist when one could equally well approach the doctrine in its original Chinese form—but it basically backfired by obscuring the distinctions between the two systems. Why not be a Buddhist if Buddhism was just as Chinese as Taoism? It was in fact not until the end of the Han dynasty (220) that Buddhism began to gain, in Chinese eyes, a semblance of independence from Taoism.

Certain doubts concerning the innate superiority of Chinese culture assailed the populace after the fall of the Han which was the beginning of a period of chaos that only really ended with the accession of the short-lived Sui dynasty in 589.

In the south, the Eastern Chin dynasty (265–420) maintained the Chinese heritage they had inherited from the Han, but with a lot less self-confidence, given the loss of the northern heartlands and its traditional culture. There had been no sectarian developments as such during the Han period, but by Eastern Chin times there was a considerable polarisation between those Buddhists stressing the aforementioned Hīnayāna meditational and ritual practices, and those putting emphasis on by now better understood theories and practices based on the *Prajñāpāramitā-sūtras* dealing with the concept of *śūnyatā* (emptiness) and its identity with *rūpa* (form). The latter slowly came to dominate Chinese Buddhist thought in the fourth century, and also became an object of interest to Philosophical Taoists who admired the similarity to Lao-tzu's idea of the material world originating in Non-being. Such concerns naturally led to the frequent use of Taoist terminology to express Buddhist concepts in translation, a method known as *ke yi* or 'matching the meaning'; this disappeared after the authoritative translations of Kumārajīva came into vogue in the fifth century. The Chin court was also affected by Buddhism to no small degree. Courtiers and emperors alike became devoted lay followers, while monks vied with each other for imperial favours. A further development was the establishment by Tao-an (312–85) of a cult for the worship of Maitreya, the future Buddha currently residing in the Tushita Heaven in which devotees could be reborn. In turn Tao-an's chief disciple Hui-yüan (344–416) is credited with the establishment in 402 of the Pure Land (Ching-t'u) school dedicated to the worship of Amitābha, the Buddha symbolising the process of transformation (indicated by the element fire) and discriminative wisdom who is said to be the presiding Buddha of the Western Pure Land, a paradise where the *dharmakāya* (Truth Body) of supreme enlightenment can manifest itself in perfected, non-human form. This early version of the Pure Land school was not noted for the missionary zeal that characterised its later variants, and was in fact highly intellectual in its approach. Hui-yüan's best-known and most controversial disciple, Tao-sheng (*c.* 360–434), categorically stated that such Pure Lands did not exist as such, given that the Buddha-nature existed and could be realised within each individual's consciousness. Tao-sheng was also committed to the idea, later characteristic of Ch'an (Zen), that enlightenment was a sudden experience attained without any gradual progression. Either one is enlightened or one is not.

The course of Buddhism ran very differently in northern areas of China under a succession of non-Chinese dynasties. Acceptance was far easier simply because such dynasties naturally gravitated towards a religious system they considered civilised and yet, like them, 'barbarian'—the very reason why the acceptance of Buddhism by the Chinese themselves was often such a slow process.

In the north, various Altaic and Tibetan groups held power, initially amidst ceaseless fighting, for varying lengths of time over areas of varying size. Their leaders came to value the advice, both social and military, and the magical prowess of the Buddhist monks in their domains, and provided a degree of institutionalised support previously unknown. The most notable Central Asian monk to make the later Ch'in capital Ch'ang-an his home was Kumārajīva (344–413), known mainly as the translator of most of the fundamental texts which became so important in later periods. His pioneering translations of the Madhyamaka (Middle Way) classics of Nāgārjuna (second century) led to the establishment of the San-lun or Three Treatise School which provided a forum for much discussion on 'relativity' (the emptiness of phenomena in view of their dependent origination). Further afield in the kingdom of Pei-liang the fourth century saw the rise of Tun-huang, originally a cave-temple complex at the junction of the main caravan routes from Central Asia which attracted numerous monks especially at times of political and social upheaval. Tun-huang retained its importance for about a thousand years up to the end of the Sung period (1126), and is of particular value because of the remarkably well-preserved Buddhist murals on the cave walls. This era also saw the first of many Chinese pilgrims starting on the long journey to India in search of the original textual sources for their religion.

The Turkic rulers of the Northern Wei (386–535) initially encouraged Buddhism in their extensive northern domains, but soon afterwards the machinations of two of the Emperor Wu's (424–51) ministers, a Taoist, K'ou Ch'ien-chih, and a Confucian, Ts'ui Hao, led to a series of restrictions on the religion which culminated in an anti-Buddhist persecution initiated in 446. The motive for this persecution was quite simply the desire on the part of the nation's rulers to Sinicise their 'barbarian' subjects by eradicating their 'barbarian' religion. The fact that the religion happened to be Buddhism was irrelevant.

The normalisation of attitudes which followed Wu's death and the renewed patronage of the nation's leaders led to the development of two primarily economic institutions unique to Northern Wei Buddhism—the Sangha and Buddha Households. The former consisted of groups of agricultural families who were required to pay a certain amount of grain per year to the local monastic office which stored it ready for immediate distribution in times of famine. The latter were groups of criminals who would be usefully employed performing various household duties for their monasteries as well as cultivating monastic lands. Buddhism under the Northern Wei went from strength to strength, especially after the transfer of the capital to Lo-yang which could soon rejoice in a plethora of the most magnificent temples and pagodas yet seen in China. For the first time too there is evidence that Buddhism managed to exert a strong influence on the lives of ordinary people rather than just on court circles. Academic work on Buddhist topics and newly translated texts also proceeded apace during this era, much of it laying the foundation for the later sectarian developments in the T'ang era (618–907).

In the south a series of short-lived native dynasties followed the fall of the Eastern Chin in 420 during what is known as the Nan-Pei Ch'ao (Northern and Southern Dynasties) period (420–589). Imperial encouragement of Buddhism continued, occasionally reaching new heights as during the reign of the Liang Dynasty's founder, the Emperor Wu (502–49), who seems to have considered himself a Chinese version of the famed Indian Buddhist ruler Aśoka. During this period, one of the most studied treatises was the *Satyasiddhiśāstra* (Treatise on the Completion of Truth) of Harivarman (third century), essentially a Hīnayāna treatise putting forward a reductionist view of emptiness (i.e. the view that objects partake of the nature of emptiness since emptiness is the end result after the object has been reduced to ever smaller component parts), an idea that was successfully criticised by the San-lun school on the grounds that emptiness is inherent in objects of all scales by virtue of their interdependence. This era also saw the introduction of the 'idealist' works of the brothers Asaṅga and Vasubandhu (fourth century), founders of the Indian Yogācāra school expounding the idea that it is the mind (not, however, regarded as a single entity) which is responsible for the nature or character (*tathatā*, literally, the 'thusness') of all phenomena which are as a result objectively unreal. The translator of most of these works into Chinese was the Indian monk Paramārtha (arrived in China in 546), also known by his Chinese name Chen-ti.

Opposition to Buddhism in the south, both Taoist and Confucian inspired, remained at a crudely nationalistic but verbal level. Buddhist–Taoist debate revolving around the question of which religion enjoyed historical primacy was prevalent throughout the sixth century, resulting in large numbers of forged texts emanating from both camps. In the north, after initial successes, the fortunes of Buddhism waned yet again under the Emperor Wu (561–77) of the non-Chinese Northern Chou (557–81) who, like his Northern Wei namesake, seems to have been anxious to ensure the Sinicisation of his state by suppressing Buddhism. The full-scale suppression decided upon by the emperor, involving the forcible secularisation of all monks and the destruction of temples, statues and scriptures, came in the years 574–7. Surprisingly enough the decree was extended to cover Taoism, primarily because of the emperor's acceptance of the various arguments against the native religion put forward by the Buddhists in earlier acrimonious debates between the two religions. Wu's successor repealed the decree, and a few years later both the Northern Chou and the (Southern) Ch'en Dynasties disappeared as Yang Chien reunified the country in 581, establishing the Sui Dynasty (581–618).

Considerable encouragement was given to Buddhism during the few years of Sui rule. Buddhism was looked upon as a national ideology, capable of unifying the populations of the north and south in a more effective way than Taoism could, doctrinally fragmented and uncentralised as it was. The Japanese in particular took the Sui attitude of imperial patronage and bureaucratised support very much to heart during their concurrent importation of Buddhism.

Initially the T'ang Dynasty (618–907), though officially Taoist, espoused a policy of tolerance towards all religions found in the land, primarily as T'ang control extended over large areas of Central Asia inhabited by adherents of Islam, Manichaeism and Nestorian Christianity who in time came to form sizeable minorities in major towns. Buddhism had by this time been an established religion in China for long enough for it to adopt specifically Chinese forms at both ends of the social spectrum. Laymen of all classes intoned the name of Amitābha and happily took part in the mass Buddhist festivals which were such a characteristic of the T'ang. Monks provided instruction in basic Buddhist practices for the populace often through the mediums of drama, story-telling and painting, and also set up charitable organisations to assist the poor, ill and dying. One practice much in vogue was that of *fang-sheng* or the release of living creatures about to be killed for food.

Although most of the Buddhist schools which flourished during the T'ang originated far earlier, hardly any can in any real sense be traced back to pre-existent Indian schools. Sectarian distinctions in China were based primarily on the degree of reliance placed upon specific *sūtras* and Indian commentaries, though, typically, stress laid upon one particular *sūtra* by one school did not preclude the study and appreciation of other texts, even of those uniquely favoured by philosophical opponents. The use of the term 'school' rather than 'sect' reflects more clearly the type of relationship that existed between philosophically opposed groups.

The T'ien-t'ai school, the doctrines of which were first promulgated by Hui-wen (*fl.* 550), Hui-ssu (515–77) and Chih-i (538–97), rose to prominence primarily because it attempted to provide a clear and logically consistent systematisation of the vast corpus of Buddhist doctrine, thereby explaining the philosophical discrepancies which had so troubled earlier Chinese Buddhists. The T'ien-t'ai classification was primarily chronological, relating particular *sūtras* to specific periods in the Buddha's life and providing an underlying justification by referring to the pan-Mahāyānist idea of *fang-pien* or 'skilful means' which stated that the Buddha had provided mankind with a vast range of texts and ideas, sometimes contradictory, to enable each person to find the system meeting his or her own requirements and agreeing with each person's pre-existent philosophical stance. The Buddha, finding that the *Avataṃsakasūtra* (Flower Garland Sūtra), given shortly after his enlightenment, was too profound for most, decided upon a graded system of teachings which culminated in the *Saddharmapuṇḍarīkasūtra* (True Dharma Lotus Sūtra, usually just known as the *Lotus Sūtra*). Though a lot of T'ien-t'ai commentarial literature deals exclusively with the *Lotus Sūtra*, the school managed to provide a place for every text, whether Hīnayāna or Mahāyāna, within its all-encompassing system. Indeed, philosophically, a great deal of T'ien-t'ai thought, notably the stress on totality, the mutual interpenetration of all phenomena and the identification of the whole with its parts, is based on the *Flower Garland Sūtra*. As an independent school the T'ien-t'ai in China did not outlive the Hui-ch'ang persecution of 845.

The Hua-yen (*Avataṃsaka* or Flower Garland) school was, as the name implies, based more exclusively on the *Flower Garland Sūtra*, and stressed the relationship between the underlying universal principle or *li* ('noumenon') and phenomena or *shih*, unlike T'ien-t'ai which tended to concentrate on the interrelationship of the phenomena of the universe with each other. Tu-shun (557–640) is regarded as the founder of this uniquely Sino-Japanese school which eventually disappeared from China after the disastrous persecution of 845. The cosmological ideas of the Hua-yen school have attracted increasing interest in recent times in view of their similarity to certain modern concepts in the field of physics. The holistic view outlined above, coupled with concepts such as the emergence of the phenomena of the physical universe from emptiness ('self-creation') may at one time have been considered both naïve and unrealistic, but the whole system has managed to stand the test of time more successfully than many other ancient philosophical systems, both Oriental and Western.

A school of less prominence was the Fa-hsiang (Characteristics of the *Dharma*) school, based on the works of Asaṅga and Vasubandhu introduced during the Liang dynasty (sixth century CE). The school's concern with the analysis of phenomena was matched by its concern with the mechanisms of consciousness and the multiple mind. The five sense consciousnesses are complemented by a mental consciousness which sorts the sense data and provides conceptions for the volitional mind to select from, deal with and analyse. The volitional mind also looks inwards into the (subconscious) store-consciousness wherein all thoughts and karmic effects are automatically stored without discrimination, thereby providing a mechanism for the operation of *karma*.

The main ideas of *Tantra* have been mentioned elsewhere; suffice it to say that an independent Tantric (Chen-yen or *mantra*) school existed in China for a short period, imported by three Indian worthies, Śubhakarasiṃha (Shan-wu-wei, arrived in China in 716), Vajrabodhi (Chin-kang-chih, arrived in China in 720) and Amoghavajra (Pu-k'ung chin-kang, ?–774). Confucian orthodoxy was bound to object to the sexual practices encouraged by certain kinds of Tantrism, and the school as a result disappeared totally after 845.

Several less important schools are also of interest. The San-chieh (Three Periods) school, founded by Hsin-hsing (540–94) during the Sui era had as its main tenet the idea, found in many other schools, that the Buddha's doctrine passes through three historical stages, each stage lasting 500 or 1,000 years (opinions differed). During the first stage, the true doctrine exists in unaltered form. The second stage sees the appearance of a 'counterfeit' doctrine merely approximating to the original. During the third stage, the doctrine begins to decay and disappear. As an aside, it is surely praiseworthy that Buddhism in most of its forms remained faithful to its fundamental theory of impermanence by including itself amongst all phenomena subject to this law, thereby avoiding the historically wrong-headed insistence found so consistently in other religious systems that no process of decay or dissolution could possibly affect the expression of their own eternal truths. The San-chieh school firmly held that the third stage was already at hand, and its resultant pessimism led to a dissatisfaction with all traditional methods of reaching enlightenment. However, regarding the age as corrupt and the populace and authorities of the time as inferior to those of earlier eras hardly endeared the school to the imperial authorities, and resulted in the school's proscription in 713, with what little remained of it disappearing in 845.

The Lü (*Vinaya* or Disciplinary) school, also known as the Nan-shan (Southern Mountain) school was founded by Tao-hsüan (596–667) and was, as its name indicates, concerned almost exclusively with the clarification and exegesis of monastic rules, primarily of those of Hīnayāna origin. Never enjoying a wide following, it ceased to exist as an independent school in 845.

The Chu-she (*Kośa* or treasury) school was in effect founded by Paramārtha with his translation of Vasubandhu's *Abhidharmakośa* (Treasury of the *Abhidharma*), an essentially Hīnayāna treatise. The school essentially maintained that the basic phenomena or *dharmas* of the universe, both physical and mental, actually existed, with only the objects constructed from these *dharmas* being subject to the law of impermanence. By the eighth century the school had for obvious reasons merged into the related Fa-hsiang school, only to perish along with it in 845.

Though many of the T'ang emperors actively encouraged Buddhism, at certain times attempts were made to ensure the prominence of Taoism and to subject Buddhism to various controls. These measures were often advantageous to Buddhism itself—the defrocking of careerist monks and the limits put on monastic wealth enabled the religion to maintain the adherence of its Chinese followers. The atmosphere of relative tolerance came to a sudden end in the 840s and culminated in the well-known persecution initiated by the Emperor Wu-tsung in 845. The persecution was Taoist-inspired, although undoubtedly other factors, primarily economic, played a part in influencing the emperor. Strict controls were introduced in 843 to limit the authority not merely of Buddhism but of Manichaeism as well. In 844 all minor temples were closed or destroyed and all unregistered monks along with all monks under the age of 50 were ordered to return to lay life. In 845, all temples and monasteries, with one exception per prefecture, were destroyed and all temple and monastic wealth confiscated by the state. Happily, no effort was made to exterminate systematically the practitioners of Buddhism, though localised abuses undoubtedly occurred. Wu-tsung died in 846 (probably as a consequence, it should be said, of excessive consumption of Taoist elixirs of immortality) and his successor, Hsuan-tsung, re-established the principle of tolerance characteristic of the early T'ang.

The monastic community had, however, been fundamentally damaged by the events of 845 and did not manage to recover. More ritualistic and scholastic schools were unable to survive without their monasteries and scriptures, especially as their organisational continuity and financial base had disappeared. The only two schools to survive the destruction of the Buddhist infrastructure were Pure Land and Ch'an (Zen)—Pure Land because it was, and still remains, essentially a popular devotional form of Buddhism, and Ch'an because of its anti-intellectual and contemplative emphasis, as well as its clear conscience in face of the charges of economic parasitism levelled against other schools.

The beliefs of Pure Land Buddhism—and the word 'beliefs' is used deliberately—are in the main quite simple and are mostly derived from the *Sukhāvatīvyūha-sūtras* (Pure Land *Sūtras*) originally researched in the early fifth century by Hui-yüan. As mentioned earlier, the Pure Land is presided over by the Buddha Amitābha; invoking his name results in the believer's rebirth from a lotus bud in the paradise from where progression to a state of enlightenment is far easier. Emphasis is thus uniquely placed on reliance on an external deity—a feature almost without parallel in Buddhism, but one which enabled the religion to spread to the proverbially illiterate peasant, as well as to those from all social classes who quite simply had neither the time nor the inclination to meditate for the many years required for attaining enlightenment in more self-reliant systems.

The word *ch'an* is the Chinese equivalent of the Sanskrit term *dhyāna* ('contemplation'), and is sufficient indication of where the Ch'an school places its emphasis. The origins of this school are traditionally traced back to the Indian master Bodhidharma who, after arriving in the Northern Wei kingdom in 520, reportedly sat in contemplation for nine years facing a wall, impervious to the imprecations of his eager disciple-to-be, Shen-kuang, who at last resorted to cutting off his own arm in order to prove his earnest desire for the doctrine, but was rewarded by becoming the second patriarch of Ch'an after his master's death. When in the seventh century Ch'an started to enjoy some degree of popular support, a question arose concerning the legitimacy of the claim of Shen-hsiu (600–706) to be the sixth patriarch of Ch'an. The resultant acrimonious debate led to the division of Ch'an into Northern and Southern Schools, and the disappearance of the former when the primacy of the Southern School's candidate, Hui-neng (638–713), was established. The entire disgraceful episode, of much greater complexity than may be apparent from the above sketch, clearly shows that Ch'an, despite its claims to the contrary, was just as prone to worldly involvement as any of the other more ritualistic schools.

The anti-intellectualism of Ch'an, smacking of Philosophical Taoism, stemmed from the belief that since enlightenment was a state obviously beyond common experience it was also beyond rationalisation. Any rational planned activity (including devotion, *sūtra* recitation, and indeed structured meditation) is therefore useless—in fact, worse than useless since it hinders the ability of the mind to function in a purely natural, unconstrained and spontaneous manner. When it does so function, it is possible for the individual to achieve an awareness of underlying reality, an experience known as *wu* (*satori*, the Japanese term, is perhaps better known), usually translated as 'enlightenment'. It is at least possible to wonder whether the Ch'an experience of sudden enlightenment is quite the same thing as the experience of *nirvāṇa* achieved using more conventional graded methods.

The main techniques employed by the Lin-chi (in Japanese, Rinzai) branch of Ch'an are well known. The master will try various methods—beating and shouting seem to be popular—to jolt the disciple out of the rut of his conventional modes of thinking; alternatively, the master will provide the disciple with a *kung-an* (in Japanese, *kōan*), a paradox of sorts, the answer to which once again necessitates recourse to something other than normal intellectual ways of tackling a problem. Ch'an activities and dialogues can seem peculiar:

> When Shih-lin Ho-shang saw the Layman P'ang coming, he raised up his whisk and said: 'without falling into Tan-hsia's activities, try saying something.'
> The Layman snatched away the whisk and held up his own fist.
> 'That is precisely Tan hsia's activity,' said Shih-lin.
> 'Try not falling into it for me,' returned the Layman.
> 'Tan-hsia caught dumbness; Mr P'ang caught deafness,' rejoined Shih-lin.
> 'Exactly,' said the Layman.
> (The Recorded Sayings of Layman P'ang, pp. 68–9.)

The Ts'ao-tung (in Japanese, Sōtō) branch of Ch'an is far more conventional, relying on graded instruction, reasoned logical argument and seated meditation for attaining the 'truth beyond words'.

After the fall of the T'ang, the country was once again unified under the Sung in 960. Pure Land and Ch'an struggled on much as before, though the country was in dire financial straits. Military and domestic expenditure was inordinately high, and one government fund-raising scheme, that of selling monk certificates (a system introduced under the T'ang in 747), contributed to the decline of the remaining monastic community. A monk was exempt from the taxation and corvée which was such a burden on the average citizen, and hence a monk certificate, apart from being an absolute necessity for every monk, was a desirable commodity for many others. The Sung bureaucracy obviously felt that the advantage of such a ready source of income outweighed the disadvantages of a monastic community full of unqualified monks only nominally Buddhist. Furthermore the Buddhism of the Sung, dominated as it was by Ch'an and Pure Land anti-intellectualism, was in no fit state to counter the arguments of neo-Confucianism, the major intellectual movement of the era which spent much of its time objecting to Buddhism's other-worldly and unfilial concerns. Concurrently, Buddhism was disappearing in India, thereby bringing to an end centuries of fruitful contact between the two countries.

The Mongol Liao Dynasty (907–1125) which controlled much of north China, Mongolia and Manchuria encouraged Chinese forms of Buddhism in its domains, as did the later Manchu Chin (Jurchen) Dynasty (1115–1234). The Mongol Yüan Dynasty (1206–1368), while itself espousing Lamaism, did not discourage specifically Chinese forms of Buddhism in its empire, although during the initial stages of the Mongol conquest of

China, the material damage to the remaining temples and monasteries was considerable. A special relationship developed between the Mongol administration and the Lin-chi subschool of Ch'an after the monk Hai-yün (1201–56) was appointed religious advisor to the khanate. At the imperially arranged debates between Taoists and Buddhists during the mid-Yüan period, Ch'an masters were also asked to put forward the Buddhist view alongside Tibetan lamas. In China itself, politically motivated Buddhist societies flourished, whilst Buddhist intellectual life continued to deteriorate.

The Chinese Ming Dynasty (1368–1662), the founder of which played on the soteriological hopes of the populace awaiting the arrival of the Buddha Maitreya by linking the new dynasty to the concept, initially promoted the activities of the two surviving schools. A Taoist–Buddhist system of granting merit/demerit points for specific charitable and uncharitable acts was much in vogue; at this time, also, attempts were made to show that Buddhism and Confucianism were philosophically compatible. Efforts were likewise made to syncretise Ch'an and Pure Land and to spread the end result amongst the laity. The success of the lay movements of this period led for the first time to a situation in which the leadership of Buddhism in China started passing from monastic to lay hands.

Chinese Buddhism under the pro-Lamaist Ch'ing (1662–1911) was just as inactive as it had been under the Ming, suffering yet another major blow during the pro-Christian and disastrously iconoclastic T'ai-p'ing (Great Peace) rebellion. The rebels as a matter of policy destroyed all Buddhist temples, libraries and works of art in areas under their temporary control; so thorough was the destruction that a large percentage of Buddhist canonical and commentarial literature had to be reintroduced from Japan and privately reprinted and distributed. The names of Yang Jen-shan and Wang Hung-yüan should be mentioned in connection with this re-introduction; it has been reported of the former that he was responsible, almost single-handedly, for the redistribution of approximately one million Buddhist treatises throughout China.

The Republic of China, established in 1911, barely tolerated Buddhism in its efforts to 'modernise' the country, whilst the spread of Marxism caused even more concern to the beleaguered Buddhist community. Although the monk T'ai-hsü (1889–1947) tried to counter such ominous developments with a comprehensive programme of reforms designed to make Buddhism more palatable to the country's new rulers, the age-old religion, barely recovered from the battering it received at the hands of the T'ai-p'ing rebels, charged with social and economic parasitism as well as philosophical wrong-headedness, finally succumbed to Maoism. It remains to be seen if it can survive this latest assault.

Buddhism in China

Further Reading

Bary, W.T. *et al.* (eds.) *Sources of Chinese Tradition* (Columbia University Press, New York, 1960)

Chang, G.C.C. *The Buddhist Teaching of Totality—The Philosophy of Hwa-Yen Buddhism* (Allen and Unwin, London, 1972)

Ch'en, K.S. *Buddhism in China—a Historical Survey* (Princeton University Press, New Jersey, 1964)

Welch, H. *The Practice of Chinese Buddhism 1900–1950* (Harvard University Press, Cambridge, Mass., 1967)

—— *The Buddhist Revival in China* (Harvard University Press, Cambridge, Mass., 1968)

Wright, A.F. *Buddhism in Chinese History* (Stanford University Press, California, 1959)

Yang, C.K. *Religion in Chinese Society* (University of California Press, Berkeley, 1961) a study of contemporary social functions of religion and some of their historical factors

Zürcher, E. *The Buddhist Conquest of China* (Leiden, 1959)

42 Buddhism in Japan

Bulcsu Siklós

The images of traditional Japan that spring to mind are almost all Buddhist inspired. Shintō, it is true, has its part to play, but the quiescence of the Tea Ceremony, the artistry of the swordsman or flower arranger, the skill of the Nō actor or the haiku poet all have their basis in Buddhist or more precisely Zen practice. These images, so unlike the ones connected with Buddhism elsewhere in Asia, would also lead one to believe that Japanese Buddhism is somehow more Japanese than it is Buddhist, that it has been altered more than any other type. There is perhaps some validity in this view but, even though the Japanese initially adopted Buddhism as an aspect of Chinese culture rather than as an independent religion, in its fullest expression it remains as canonical and hence as Indian as any other type.

Probably in the year 552, the king of the Korean kingdom of Paekche, hard pressed by the expansionist desires of the two neighbouring kingdoms of Koguryō and Silla, decided to send a bronze image of the Buddha, accompanied by several volumes of scriptures in Chinese as well as a letter highlighting the beneficial effects of Buddhism, to the Japanese court. This hardly had much of an effect; in short it was presumably the loss of the Japanese outpost of Mimana on the Korean coast that led to a certain degree of realisation concerning the political, economic and indeed cultural backwardness of Japan when compared to the continent, and which rapidly led to a desire for all that their great neighbour China could offer. Resistance to Buddhism during this initial period was considerable, the traditionalists objecting to the worship of the Buddha on the grounds that it would offend the native deities who would (and, let it be said, did) respond by causing various epidemics and droughts throughout the land.

The responsibility for promoting the new religion fell to Prince Umayado, better known as Shōtoku Taishi (Crown Prince

Shōtoku, 572–622), son of the Empress Suiko (593–628), whom Japanese Buddhists generally regard as the founder of their religion. Doubtless Buddhism would have made little headway without imperial support from the earliest times; support which was generously provided since it enabled the court to present a unified front replete with continental sophistication to the traditionalists of the Mononobe and Nakatomi clans desperately trying to maintain the status quo. The doctrine was no longer proffered by Paekche but was imported by the Japanese court itself directly from the north Korean kingdom of Korai which maintained close contacts with the Chinese Sui dynasty.

The Buddhism of this period was of course non-sectarian and hardly considered inimical to the Japanese spirit as its native practitioners took due care in keeping to the required Shintō observances. Indeed Buddhism was thought of merely as a superior form of magic, its superiority obvious in view of its architectural, artistic and ritual complexity—certainly a provincial noble on his first visit to the imperial capital would have been left in no doubt as to the deficiencies of the autochthonous faith. This said, the commentaries attributed to Prince Shōtoku suggest that at least some Japanese in this early period felt attracted to Buddhism because of its philosophical subtlety and vast range of meditative techniques, although such appreciation was limited to those with a good knowledge of Chinese since no Buddhist text had yet been translated into Japanese.

The first permanent capital at Nara, established in 710, rapidly became the nucleus from which Buddhism spread to the rest of the country. The forty-fifth emperor, Shōmu (701–56, reigned 724–49), ordered the construction of two Provincial Temples (*kokubunji*) in each province, one for monks (*kokubunsōji*) and the other for nuns (*kokubunniji*) who were required to perform observances to ensure the continuity of the state and successful harvests. The *kokubunji* were regarded as branches of the Tōdaiji in Nara, founded in 745, the central hall of which is even today the largest wooden building in the world, housing an immense bronze statue of the Buddha Vairocana (in Japanese, Dainichi nyorai or Biroshana), extremely popular because of the belief that the Shinto solar deity Amaterasu was no more than a local manifestation of this Buddhist divinity.

During this period, six separate schools of Buddhism managed to establish themselves at Nara, all of them equivalents of contemporary Chinese schools. Prior to the Nara period, the year 625 had seen the official establishment of two schools, the Jōjitsu (Chinese, Ch'eng-shih) school based on Harivarman's Hīnayāna treatise, the *Satyasiddhiśāstra* (Treatise on the Completion of Truth) much studied in China during the Liang Dynasty, and the Sanron (Chinese, San-lun or Madhyamaka) school. The Hossō (Fa-hsiang or Characteristics of the *Dharma*) school was introduced in 654, followed by the Kusha (Chinese, Chu-she or Treasury) school in 658. The eighth century saw the introduction of the Kegon (Chinese, Hua-yen or Flower Garland) school and the Ritsu (Chinese, Lü or Disciplinary) school.

As one might expect, corruption was rife in the Nara monasteries; unlike in China there was no Confucian bureaucracy imbued with anti-Buddhist sentiment ready to expose the most glaring abuses of monastic privilege. It was partly to escape the crowds of sycophantic monks that the Emperor Kanmu (782–805) decided to transfer his capital from Nara to Heian (present-day Kyōto) in 794 after a ten-year unsuccessful relocation to Nagaoka.

The Heian period (794–1185) saw the introduction of the Tendai (Chinese, T'ien-t'ai) and Shingon (Chinese, Chen-yen or Tantric) sects, with the word 'sect' being rather more appropriate here than 'school', as we shall see. The eclectic and universal approach of the former enabled it to gain rapid support soon after its official introduction by the Nara monk Saichō (Dengyō Daishi, 767–822), who had been sent to China by the Emperor Kanmu expressly for the purpose of finding the most suitable branch of Buddhism to propagate in the new capital. Saichō's initially close relationship with the importer of Shingon, Kūkai (Kōbō Daishi, 744–835) led to Tendai assuming certain distinctly tantric characteristics, further emphasised by Ennin (Jikaku Daishi, 794–864), absent in the parent form, while the eclecticism of Tendai in time spawned the Lotus Sūtra-based (and uniquely Japanese) Nichiren sect.

A dispute in 993 over the succession to the abbotship of the main Tendai monastery, the Enryakuji on Mount Hiei, led to the establishment of an alternative branch of Tendai at the Miidera in Ōtsu. This was no mere scholarly dispute; in time both monasteries came to maintain large numbers of 'warrior monks' (*sōhei*, also appropriately known as *akusō* or 'bad monks'), little more than mercenaries in priestly garb. The practice grew quickly, with most major monasteries realising the advantage of having a force of no mean military capability under their control which could—and frequently did—attack, loot and reduce to ashes the monasteries of opposing sects. In times of governmental instability successful attacks could also be launched on the imperial capital itself, if a particular claim, usually material, needed pressing.

The main Shingon monastery on Mount Kōya, tranquilly located further from the capital near Ōsaka, was less prone to indulgence in such activities. The sect's political influence was accordingly smaller, but its religious influence was considerable, and not merely on philosophically similar sects such as Tendai. In fact, no post-Nara sect is entirely free of Shingon influence, given that Kūkai's short two-year stay in China resulted in an inevitable simplification of tantric ritual (for example, Shingon recognises only two main *maṇḍalas*, both presided over by Vairocana—one can compare this to the Lamaist situation with literally hundreds of *maṇḍalas* and a far larger range of presiding deities). For other sects there was thus no great difficulty in adapting esoteric ideas to their own needs.

A short-lived and little-known twelfth-century sub-sect of Shingon, the Tachikawa, is of interest as numbered amongst its practices were activities such as ritualised sexual intercourse. One might think that this indicates that the Indo-Tibetan Highest Yoga Tantras (the *Anuttarayogatantras*), replete with sexual symbolism and methods for sublimating sexual energies, had secretly found their way to Japan, but it seems that Tachikawa sexual ritual was based on Taoist practices involving the unification of the male *yang* (in Japanese, *yō*) and female *yin* (in Japanese, *in*) principles.

The confusion, corruption and strife reigning at the end of the Heian period (eleventh to twelfth centuries) led to an outbreak of religious pessimism and an explanation in terms of the Buddhist concept of *mappō* (the End of the Doctrine) or *mappōji* (the Period of the End of the Doctrine), the last and most degenerate of the three eras into which Buddhists often divide the history of their religion after Śākyamuni (see for example the San-chieh school of sixth-century China). Certain Tendai monks felt that the time had come to begin the active proselytisation of the cowed and illiterate populace and for the emergence of a broad-based, popular form of Buddhism worlds apart from the scholasticism, elaborate ritual and political intrigues of the established sects. Drawing on the experiences of Chinese Pure Land proselytisers, the main method popularised was the *nenbutsu* (recitation of the Buddha Amitābha's name) with the aim being rebirth in the Pure Land (*jōdo*). It took a while for these beliefs and practices to form the basis for a new sect *sensu stricto*, though even prior to the Kamakura period (1185–1333) when the capital was relocated to Kamakura by the first shogunal family, the Minamoto, certain individuals had widely and exclusively recommended the *nenbutsu*. The itinerant preacher Kūya (903–72) taught the invocation through the medium of popular songs, while the less unorthodox Chingai (1091–1152) saw it as an adjunct to standard Shingon practice (in other words, he still felt that meditation was of prime importance), though he encouraged simple recitation if there was no viable alternative given the circumstances of the practitioner.

The unwitting founder proper of Japanese Pure Land Buddhism was Hōnen (Genkū, 1133–1212). His dissatisfaction with Buddhism as it then was, along with a wide reading of the works of his visionary precursor Genshin (Eshin sōzu, 942–1017) enabled him to come to the conclusion that the only worthwhile practice was the *nenbutsu* itself (meditation, always the corner-stone of Buddhist practice was, to him, pointless). His emphasis on *tariki* ('other power'), the power of Amitābha (in Japanese, Amida) to save, and his abandonment of another key concept, that of *jiriki* ('self-power' or 'self-reliance') brought him perilously close to monotheism and left him open to the various charges that were levelled against him by the other sects. For example, a petition presented in 1205 to the Retired Emperor Go-Toba asked for the movement to be halted on the grounds that it 1. was not an imperially recognised sect, 2. used uncanonical images which showed monks of other sects failing to reach illumination whilst even criminals were represented as illumined if they recited the *nenbutsu* correctly, 3. ignored Śākyamuni, 4. condemned practices other than the *nenbutsu* wholesale, 5. rejected the Shintō gods, 6. condemned practices other than the *nenbutsu* which did actually lead to the Pure Land, 7. used the *nenbutsu* without the accompanying meditation, 8. rejected the codes of monastic discipline and 9. was a threat to stable government due to its popular base. The Pure Land sect in time showed itself to be, quite clearly, guilty on all counts.

Hōnen was no intellectual match for individuals like Kūkai or Saichō, yet he comes across as a far more reasonable—and indeed Buddhist—personage than his chief disciple Shinran (1173–1262), for whom one sincere invocation was enough to ensure rebirth in the Pure Land. The Pure Land sub-sect he founded, the Jōdo Shinshū (True Pure Land Sect, often known simply as the Shinshū or 'True Sect') abolished monasticism totally, permitted the marriage of its priests (thereby establishing a blood succession to the patriarchy) and became, perhaps predictably, increasingly militant. The eighth True Pure Land patriarch Rennyo (1415–99) did much to encourage intolerance and fanaticism amongst his followers, often disaffected peasants who, in the utterly chaotic political situation of the sixteenth century, frequently rebelled against local feudal lords or took to attacking the monasteries of other sects. When one of the most powerful of these *daimyō*, Oda Nobunaga (1534–82) attempted the military reunification of the country the armies and temples of the True Pure Land were obvious targets for annihilation.

A marginally more sophisticated and contemplative form of Pure Land Buddhism, the Ji ('Time') sect, founded by Ippen (1239–89), was also influential from the mid-fourteenth to the early sixteenth centuries, before losing much of its support to the True Pure Land. The tenets of the Ji sect betray Shingon influence; for example, the *nenbutsu* is regarded as complementary to visualisation with the end result being the identification of the practitioner with the physical form (and thus the mental state, so to speak) of Amitābha himself.

Zen (Chinese, Ch'an) ideas and methods were introduced into Japan in the seventh century by the Hossō monk Dōshō (638–700) as part of Hossō practice, and certain Chinese masters, notably Tao-hsüan (in Japanese, Dōsen, 596–667) visited the country to discuss Ch'an ideas with representatives of the Nara sects. The Tendai founder Saichō was instructed in Zen by a disciple of Tao-hsüan and was apparently impressed enough to include the techniques of this particular Chinese form of Buddhism among the wide-ranging practices of his new sect. Just as in the case of Pure Land, however, it was not until the Kamakura period (1185–1333) that Zen managed to establish itself as an independent sect.

The Rinzai (Chinese, Lin-ch'i) sub-sect of Zen was formally introduced into the country by the (originally) Tendai monk Eisai (Zenkō kokushi, 1141–1215) after his return from China in 1191. Initial opposition from the Tendai sect disappeared once the Shōgun Minamoto Yoriie (1182–1204) gave his approval and protection to Rinzai Zen. He also requested that Eisai found a new monastery (the Jūfukuji) in the shōgunal capital Kamakura, thereby initiating a fruitful and long-lasting relationship between Zen and the increasingly important military class (the *samurai*).

The Sōtō (Ts'ao-tung) sub-sect of Zen was introduced by the (once again) Tendai monk Dōgen (Buppō zenji/Shōyō daishi, 1200–53) after his study trip to the continent lasting from 1223–7. Eisai, under whom Dogen reportedly studied for a short period, had always been willing to compromise with the other sects (it is even reported that he regularly performed Shingon rites), but Dōgen on the other hand was so convinced of the superiority of his *zazen* ('seated Zen') techniques that he felt no need to encourage any other practice and further expressed particular hostility to the *kōan* (Chinese, *k'ung-an*) method of Rinzai Zen. The Sōtō *kōan* is something entirely different. Dōgen simply defined the term *genjō kōan* ('manifestation and achievement of *kōan*') as if it were a synonym for the ultimate present reality, the *dharmakāya* (principle or 'body' of truth). Just as the bird flies in the air without being concerned with or understanding the air, so the practitioner should act naturally and limit himself to existing in the present without worrying about the ultimate. The present moment or in other words the practitioner's present state is itself the ultimate and is therefore the basis of enlightenment. Dōgen also avoided such Rinzai concepts as the *busshō* or 'Buddha Nature' to make his disciples realise that there was of course no actual abiding permanent essence to be sought out within one's mind. The Buddha Nature is simply impermanence.

The wholesale adoption of Zen by the warrior class, a process initiated and promoted by Musō Soseki (Musō kokushi, 1275–1351), spiritual mentor of several shōguns and emperors, led to a widespread secularisation of Rinzai methods. The harmony of nature in miniature was expressed in landscape and rock gardening, the plastic equivalents of monochrome ink painting (*sumie*) and calligraphy, all of which were objects of contemplation for the practitioner. The *samurai* applied Zen to the martial arts and were responsible for the popularisation of the Tea Ceremony (tea itself had been reintroduced to Japan from China by Eisai). Literature also adopted specifically Zen forms. Haiku poetry attempted to capture the simplicity and harmony of the rock garden or ink painting in a mere seventeen syllables, with the best of these poems often being used as objects of contemplation much on the lines of the Rinzai *kōan*. Probably the most original Zen-inspired cultural innovation of the Muromachi period

(1336–1598) was the Nō drama. Nō developed from the *sarugaku* ('monkey music') of early feudal times into a highly stylised and unremittingly gloomy form of drama in which the actors wore elaborate costumes and masks and chanted their lines to the accompaniment of music on a bare stage.

Zen was to the *samurai* all that Pure Land was to the peasant. Each inspired new forms of art and literature, each provided a behavioural code moulded to the needs of its practitioners and each became thereby more purely Japanese.

The last major Japanese Buddhist sect to develop, the Nichiren sect, is also the only one with no continental equivalent whatsoever and further is probably the only Buddhist school or sect anywhere to take its name from its founder. Nichiren (1222–82), a man of humble origins (as he himself always stressed), initially studied Pure Land doctrines at a small provincial Tendai temple until some unknown traumatic event (legend states it was the sight of his Pure Land master dying in agony) turned him against Pure Land and brought on his almost insane hatred for Hōnen. This, along with his increasing admiration for the Lotus Sūtra, led to his pilgrimage in 1242 to Mount Hiei where he hoped to find 'true' Buddhism, true according to the criteria he devised. Any sect based not upon a canonical text but on an independent Indian treatise was ruled out as a repository of 'true' Buddhism—primarily the Sanron, Hossō, Kusha and Jōjitsu. Further, Zen was ruled out on account of its claim to have a separate transmission outside the scriptures. Pure Land was dismissed on personal grounds, while Kegon and Shingon he considered inferior to Tendai which he eventually chose as the nearest approximation to his ideal. According to Nichiren, it was the abandonment of the Lotus Sūtra (the final expression of the Buddha's teaching in the Tendai view) by the Japanese nation which had led to the state of political chaos, to the increasing Mongol threat and to the ruination of the imperial family following the exile of the Emperor Go-Toba (1180–1239) after his unsuccessful attempt to reassert imperial supremacy.

Nichiren's feelings about the other sects are neatly summed up in his *Essentials of the Honmon Sect* (*Honmon-shūyōsho*):

> The followers of *nenbutsu* will fall into the lowest hell,
> Followers of Zen are devils,
> Shingon destroys the nation,
> The Ritsu are national enemies
> And Tendai is an outdated calendar.

According to Nichiren, only by relying on the Lotus Sūtra can equal emphasis be laid upon each of the *sanshin* or Three Bodies (Sanskrit, *trikāya*) of the Buddha. The *hosshin* (Sanskrit, *dharmakāya*), the 'body' or state of ultimate reality manifests itself as, or rather is symbolised by Vairocana, the central object of worship in Shingon; the *hōjin* (Sanskrit, *sambhogakāya*), the 'Enjoyment Body', the 'body' or state enjoyed by an enlightened being in higher realms (e.g. the Pure Land) manifests as (among others) the Buddha Amitābha, stressed as we have seen to the exclusion of everything else by the Pure Land sects, and finally the *ōshin* (Sanskrit, *nirmāṇakāya*), the 'Emanation Body', the intrusion of the *dharmakāya* into our realm has as its prime example the historical Buddha, much revered in Zen.

The method advocated by Nichiren to reach the state of Buddhahood was the *daimoku* ('Great Title'—the title of the Lotus Sūtra) recitation in the form *namu myōhō renge kyō* ('homage to the wondrous Lotus Sūtra'). This is less banal than it may at first sound, since title exegesis, on the premiss that the title of a canonical text should in itself be a summary of the text itself, had long been a concern of most of the Chinese schools of Buddhism, given that the range of meaning of the individual characters making up the title could be so large. Hence according to Nichiren the absolute manifests itself as the five-character title (*myōhō* meaning 'wondrous', descriptive of the absolute; *renge* meaning 'lotus', signifying the universal law of cause and effect; and *kyō* or '*sūtra*' signifying the text's origin from the *nirmāṇakāya*, Śākyamuni), while the subject (i.e. the practitioner) is present in the initial homage (*namu*).

Nichiren's initial preaching activities hardly endeared him to the government or indeed to any of the other sects. His total intolerance led to the promulgation of views so extreme that they are almost without parallel in the Buddhist world. Just as an example, Nichiren seriously proposed on several occasions the physical eradication of his Buddhist opponents. Quite simply he did not consider the killing of Pure Land followers a sin.

With the breakdown in law and order particularly in the fifteenth century, Nichiren followers, perhaps predictably, also took up arms with as much enthusiasm as the followers of Pure Land. These *hokke ikki* (Lotus Rebellions) were especially frequent during the period 1532–6, when Nichiren armies dominated Kyōto until their annihilation by a huge force from Mount Hiei.

To the outside observer, the Nichiren sect seemed a well-disciplined, unified organisation but it was in fact far more prone to internal dissension than the Pure Land sects. Disagreements mainly centred around the question of exactly how tolerant the sect should be—less tolerant groups led by purists such as Nichijū (1314–92), Nichijin (1339–1419) and Nisshin (1407–88) adopted the principle of *fuju-fuse* ('no giving and no receiving', in other words, no compromise whatsoever with anyone not a member of the sect) which gradually came to provide the name for a new sub-sect led by Nichiō (1565–1630). The Fuju-fuse sect became an object of persecution during the Tokugawa period (1600–1867), remaining officially prohibited until 1876.

The popular view often portrays the six Nara schools along with Tendai and Shingon as having nothing more than reactionary and corrupt roles during the Kamakura and Muromachi periods; yet all of them responded, sometimes successfully, sometimes not, to the new developments of Pure Land, Zen and Nichiren by introducing old practices to the population at large. To counter the worship of Amitābha, the worship of Shaka (Sanskrit, Śākyamuni) was encouraged; likewise the worship of Miroku (Sanskrit, Maitreya, the coming Buddha), of Monjushiri (Sanskrit, Mañjuśrī, the Bodhisattva of wisdom), of Kannon (Sanskrit, Avalokiteśvara, Bodhisattva of compassion) and of Jizō (Sanskrit, Kṣitigarbha, the Bodhisattva of the earth, regarded as the protector of children). In the intellectual and doctrinal field, efforts were made to combine Sanron (Madhyamaka) concepts with those of Shingon, notably by Myōhen (1142–1224), resulting in the disappearance of the Sanron as an independent school. A lot of work was also done on the monastic code (the *Vinaya*) to counter its wholesale rejection by the popular sects, while the esoteric sects, Shingon and Tendai, continued to flourish, the latter especially maintaining its political and military influence.

In 1600 the Tokugawa family managed to establish unified effective military rule over all Japan, and followed this by moving the capital to Edo (present-day Tōkyō). The first Tokugawa shōgun, Ieyasu (1603–10), was totally determined to ensure that Tokugawa rule could endure unopposed into the foreseeable future, and as a result decided to limit contact with the outside world, and especially with Christianity which was regarded as a social menace. Christianity was stamped out with military thoroughness by Ieyasu's successors Hidetada (1616–23) and Iemitsu (1623–51), much use being made of the ingenious *fumie* ('treading picture'), usually a brass plaque with a representation of Christ engraved on it which the suspected Christian was required to defile by stepping on it. Refusal usually meant a slow death.

The Tokugawa government was of course fully aware of the divisive and rebellious nature of certain Buddhist sects, but since the military effectiveness of these sects had been severely curtailed by the weapon confiscation programme of Ieyasu's predecessor Toyotomi Hideyoshi (1536–98), it decided that a system of temple registration along with the encouragement of learning was sufficient to maintain discipline and governmental control. The Tokugawa themselves were members of the Pure Land sect, so this sect flourished; the other sects kept themselves busy by rebuilding and refurbishing temples and monasteries damaged in the preceding era. Certain shōguns were in fact noted for their religious enthusiasm, the best-known of whom is the fifth shogun Tsunayoshi (1680–1709) who, amongst other things, issued various Buddhist-inspired edicts protecting animals in general and dogs in particular. His conception of Buddhist morality was perhaps unusual; on one occasion he had a man executed for injuring a dog.

The new-found peace and prosperity of the Tokugawa period was welcome, but in the long run the price Buddhism paid for the advantage of political stability was stagnation.

Zen was the exception, mainly as a result of the activities of Hakuin (1685–1768), a man perhaps more mindful of canonical literature than the Rinzai ideal demanded. Hakuin was particularly concerned with revitalising the *kōan* but his fame also extends into the fields of calligraphy and poetry. The Huang-po (in Japanese, Ōbaku) branch of Chinese Zen also entered the country with the arrival of the Chinese priests Yin-yüan (in Japanese, Ingen, 1592–1673) and Mu-an (in Japanese, Mokuan, d. 1684) and was much respected by the Tokugawa authorities.

Confucianism and Shintō were both much studied during the later Tokugawa period with most men of letters expressing a strong nationalistic interest in the latter. Buddhism's close association with the shogunate as well as its general deterioration left it in a vulnerable position when imperial power was restored and the country opened up to the West at the beginning of the Meiji period (1868–1912). Shintō was established as the state religion in 1870 under the name of *daikyō* ('Great Religion'), and the Shintō-inspired and fortunately short-lived *haibutsu kishaku* ('destroy the Buddhas and discard the scriptures') movement was initiated, resulting in considerable material destruction to Buddhist temples and monasteries and in the secularisation of many priests. An interest amongst the Japanese in all things modern and Western further resulted in an interest in Christianity, another threat to the Buddhist establishment.

Various sects sent representatives to Europe and America to study the methods and organisation of Christianity and also to study new developments in Western thought. Soon after, however, once the constitution of 1889 had assured Buddhism's equality with all other religions found in the land, there was a certain degree of Buddhist-inspired realignment between Buddhism, Shintō and Confucianism against Christianity.

In modern times, at a popular level dissatisfaction with Buddhism became widespread and resulted in the proliferation of 'new religions' drawing their often carelessly formulated ideas from Buddhism, Christianity and Shintō. Three of the better known new religions are recognisable as vaguely Buddhist: the Reiyūkai ('Society of Friendship with Souls'), based on simple morality and the Confucian concept of filial piety; the Risshō kōseikai ('Society for the Establishment of Correct and Friendly Relations') founded in 1938 and concerned with repentance; and last but by no means least the somewhat cultish and intolerant Sōka gakkai ('Value-Creating Study Group') which claims that happiness is dependent on 'profit', goodness and beauty, the three of which can only be understood through detailed study, recitation of the *daimoku* (the title of the *Lotus Sūtra*) and the donation of large sums of money to the organisation.

Further Reading

Eliot, C. *Japanese Buddhism* (Routledge & Kegan Paul, London, 1935)

Matsunaga, D. and A. *Foundation of Japanese Buddhism*, I–II (Los Angeles–Tokyo, 1974–76)

Sansom, G.B. *Japan—a Short Cultural History* (New York, 1943)

Saunders, E.D. *Buddhism in Japan with an Outline of its Origins in India* (University of Pennsylvania Press, Philadelphia, 1964)

Suzuki, D.T. *Essays in Zen Buddhism*, First Series (1927), Second Series (1933), Third Series (1934), London

Takakusu, J. *The Essentials of Buddhist Philosophy* (University of Hawaii Press, Honolulu, 1947)

Tsunoda, R. *et al.* (eds.) *Sources of Japanese Tradition* (University of Columbia Press, New York, 1958)

43 The Religions of Tibet

Tadeusz Skorupski

Tibetan Buddhism or Lamaism

Historical Perspectives

It was in the seventh century CE that Tibet emerged as a formidable military and political entity on to the world scene. The same century also witnessed the formal introduction of Buddhism and the beginning of historical records. Our knowledge about religious beliefs and historical events in Tibet prior to the seventh century remains very limited and it is derived mainly from legendary and quasi-historical accounts. The earliest literary sources suggest that the Tibetan Plateau was first occupied by semi-nomadic groups of people who in the course of time formed into rival factions. These factions were led by chieftains who established their headquarters in fortified strongholds in the major valleys of the central and eastern tributaries of the Tsangpo River (i.e. Brahmaputra). To the north of those valleys a nomadic pattern of life seems to have persisted up to modern times. The darkness of legends began to yield to apparently more historical accounts when some of those local chiefs joined together to recognise the chief who controlled the Yarlung Valley as their leader. This valley is situated to the south of Lhasa which later became the main city in Tibet.

It was the confederacy led by the chief of Yarlung that became the nucleus of Tibet as a country. He was known by the title of Pugyal Tsangpo (sPu-rgyal btsan-po) and his kingdom became known as Pugyal-Bod. The exact meaning of the word 'bod' (? 'native land') is not easily discernible but it has become the name applied by Tibetans to their own country ever since. We possess several versions of a legendary account, first recorded in the fourteenth century, which describes how the first king descended on the sacred mountain of Yarla Shampo (Yar-lha sham-po) in Yarlung. He was greeted by people who according to different accounts are said to have been sages, chieftains or simply shepherds. Since he descended from the sky, they resolved to make him their king. The first king, Nyatri Tsanpo (gNya'-khri btsan-po or, in Tun-huang documents, Nyag-khri) and his successors were considered to have been endowed with a distinct sacral quality, and they were referred to by such titles as 'Divine Mighty One' (Lha-btsan-po) or 'Divine Son' (Lha-sras). They were supposed to have descended from the highest point of heaven by way of a 'sky-cord' (dmu-thag) which passed through the various intermediate levels between the sky and the earth. As they were of divine origin they did not die but at the end of their earthly sojourn they returned to the sky by means of the same 'sky-cord' without leaving behind any mortal remains.

In the sixth generation of the first king's family, during the reign of the king called Drigum (Dri-gum, 'Slain by Pollution' or Gri-gum, 'Slain by Sword'), there took place the change to the normal mortality of the kings. Endowed with immortality and magical powers, Drigum became arrogant and proud, and constantly challenged his entourage to fight with him. Finally, one man called Lo-ngam consented to confront the self-confident king on the condition that the king would not make use of his magical weapons. On the agreed day, the king's opponent attached spear-points to the horns of one hundred oxen and loaded their backs with sacks of ashes. As the oxen became annoyed and struggled together the bags with ashes burst open and the ash-dust clouded the air. Amid the general confusion and poor visibility the king was killed; or in another version he cut his 'sky-cord' and was compelled to remain on earth. From that time onwards the kings left their mortal remains on earth and were duly entombed in the royal burial grounds at Chonggye ('Phyong-rgyas) in the Yarlung Valley.

According to the Buddhist tradition, it was during the reign of the twenty-eighth king, Lhatho Thori (Lha-tho-tho-ri) that a sacred object in the form of a *stūpa* and a Buddhist text were lowered from the sky and deposited on the top of the king's palace; but at that time no one was able to discern the symbolism of the sacred object or to read the text.

The thirty-second king, Namri Lontshan (gNam-ri slon-mtshan), who ruled at the time of the Sui Dynasty (581–618), is the first Tibetan ruler to be referred to by name in Chinese records. When Namri was assassinated (*c.* 627) his young son Srongtsan Gampo (Srong-btsan sgam-po, 627–50) succeeded to the throne. It is with this famous king that Tibet sets foot on the firm ground of history. Srongtsan Gampo initiated a period of military aggression and expansion that continued till the ninth century. A rapid and successful conquest of immediate neighbouring lands such as Zhang-zhung to the north-west and other parts of the vast territories to the north, east and south, brought the Tibetan military troops into contact with various principalities of Central Asia, China and India. Srongtsan Gampo married several noble ladies, of whom one was a Chinese princess (Wen

Ch'eng) and one a Nepalese princess (Bhṛkutī). These two princesses are given much credit by the Buddhist tradition for bringing Buddhist images with them and for supporting the propagation of the new religion. It was for their benefit that the king erected Buddhist temples in Lhasa: the Jokhang and the Ramoche.

There exists a popular legend among the Tibetan people which informs us that the Tibetan race originated from the copulation of a monkey and an ogress. The later Buddhist tradition made use of this legend to demonstrate that it was a predestined plan that the Tibetans were converted to Buddhism. The Bodhisattva Avalokiteśvara, who is regarded as the patron of Tibet, decided in the remote past to convert the 'Land of Snows' (i.e. Tibet) to the Buddha's doctrine. Assuming the form of a monkey he went to meditate in solitude on a mountain summit. He was duly induced to copulate with a rock-demoness and from their union were born the ancestors of the Tibetan people; during the course of their evolution their monkeyish tails shrivelled and the hair of their bodies disappeared.

It was during the reign of Srongtsan Gampo that the time finally came to convert Tibet. The king himself is regarded as an emanation of Avalokiteśvara, and his Chinese and Nepalese consorts as emanations of Tārā in her white and red manifestations. Buddhist temples were erected at different places geomantically determined so as to peg down the demoness prostrate on her back beneath the whole expanse of the Tibetan land. The symbolic implication of this operation indicates the beneficial impact and civilising force of the newly introduced religion. The pinned-down demoness was seen in some respects as Tibet itself, whose ancestral inhabitants were described as red-faced demons, flesh-eaters and blood-drinkers. It is alleged that at death the king and his two wives were absorbed into the statue of Avalokiteśvara installed in Jokhang, the main cathedral at Lhasa which became one of the holiest places of worship and pilgrimage. Srongtsan Gampo is credited with the promulgation of a code of civil laws, some religious instructions and a prophecy about the permanent establishment of Buddhism in Tibet in later generations.

Although the pious Buddhist tradition in Tibet looks upon Srongtsan Gampo as the greatest king and champion of Buddhism, more critical scholarship does not attribute many religious activities to him. It is, however, agreed that Buddhism was introduced or recognised formally at this time, although on a rather limited and moderate scale. A few temples were certainly built and Buddhism was allowed to put down its initial roots as a recognised religion amidst the strong indigenous religious beliefs and practices. There is no evidence in contemporary sources to suggest that the king became a convert. On the contrary, there are strong and convincing indications that he remained faithful to his ancestral religion which cherished the cult of the kings as divine beings. He was buried in the traditional manner in the Yarlung Valley in an elaborate ceremony which included the ancient rituals of animal and probably human sacrifice. The true motives for introducing or rather recognising Buddhism seem to have been, in the first instance, the acquisition of cultural and educational elements from the neighbouring and more sophisticated civilisations in order to develop and govern the country with efficiency. It was during the reign of Srongtsan Gampo that the Tibetan script is said to have been invented by Thonmi Sambhota on the pattern of the contemporary Indian Gupta script.

It was during the reign of the fifth monarch after Srongtsan Gampo that Buddhism appeared in official records. The king, Trisong Detsen (Khri-srong lde-brtsan, 740–*c.* 798), considered as the second 'Religious King' and an emanation of Mañjuśrī, was inclined favourably towards Buddhism which he sponsored and defended against the indigenous priests and the ministers at the royal court who supported them. After a period of internal intrigues and bitter struggles within the royal court, the king and the supporters of Buddhism emerged victorious over opponents who represented the interests of the ancient beliefs and practices.

Trisong Detsen invited to Tibet the Indian *paṇḍita* Śāntarakṣita, who inspired the construction of the first Buddhist monastery in which Tibetans were trained and ordained as monks. The monastery which was built at Samye (bSam-yas) is said to have been modelled on the renowned Buddhist monastic university of Odantapuri in northern India. The Buddhist tradition suggests that opposition from the indigenous religious factions and the local deities still persisted, causing obstructions and evil omens. Padmasambhava, a great tantric master and magician from Oḍḍiyāna, was therefore invited to confront and convert the powerful local deities. These two masters, Śāntarakṣita and Padmasambhava, represented two different forms of Buddhist practices. While Śāntarakṣita taught the conventional monastic and scholastic theories and practices based on the *Vinaya* and the Sūtras, Padmasambhava was a tantric master and a *siddha*, who specialised in mystical and ritual exercises, and the magical coercion of demoniac powers. These two forms of Buddhism permeated each other and have constituted ever since a characteristic feature of Tibetan Buddhism. Padmasambhava encountered innumerable difficulties but overcame them by means of his magical abilities and brought to submission various demoniac powers, forcing them to swear an oath to become the protectors of the new religion. Over the years Buddhism in Tibet has succeeded in the elimination of various indigenous practices, such as animal and human sacrifice. It did not eradicate the local deities but rather absorbed and accommodated them within the already well-populated pantheon brought from India by placing them among the lesser or mundane deities (*laukika*) as sworn-in protectors (*dam-can*).

Trisong Detsen and his court took an oath to protect and to support the Buddhist religion. Members of the ever-increasing monkhood, mostly those from noble families, received important state positions.

The monastery of Samye was exempted from tax and given material support. The monks were outside civil legislation and were granted immunity from bodily punishment.

It seems quite certain that the initial Buddhist inspiration did not come exclusively from India, as the later Buddhist tradition in Tibet suggests, but also came in considerable force from Central Asia and from China. The somewhat contrasting teachings brought from India and China led to a formal debate held at Samye under the patronage of the king. The debate was to produce a conclusive decision as to whether Indian or Chinese practices and teachings should be followed. The Indian group was led by Kamalaśīla, a disciple of Śāntarakṣita, who was invited on the recommendation of his master. The Indian party argued in favour of the conventional Mahāyāna which propounded the theory of the gradual progress of a *bodhisattva* towards the final attainment of Buddhahood. According to this teaching, it is necessary to accumulate vast quantities of both knowledge and merit during the course of innumerable world-ages in order to succeed in one's progress towards Buddhahood. Such a method was seen as being beneficial not only to oneself but also to all living beings. In general terms it was a doctrine that favoured the conventional pattern of philosophical pursuits and moral training that required the stability of monastic life and the practice of morality. The Chinese party led by Hwa-shang, an adept of Ch'an (Zen in Japanese) Buddhism, assumed the position that the absolute nature of Buddhahood can be realised by anyone who was able to acquire, and to abide in, a state of complete equanimity. Conventional morality and philosophical speculations were seen as unnecessary or even harmful because they could impede one's pure contemplation of emptiness (*śūnyatā*). After a period of two years the final verdict was passed in favour of the Indian party. Hwa-shang and his companions were expelled from Tibet and their scriptures were eliminated. However, according to the sources found at Tun-huang, it was the Chinese party that won the argument. The acceptance of the Indian form of Buddhism may well have been motivated by political reasons, for we know that Tibet and China were in constant military struggle.

In the reign of the seventh king, Ralpachen (Ral-pa-can, 815–38), who is also remembered as the third 'Religious King', intense efforts were made to produce a systematic translation of Buddhist scriptures into Tibetan. A number of trained Tibetans who worked side by side with Indian scholars translated many canonical works and philosophical treatises from Sanskrit and from other languages in which the scriptures were recorded. The system of translation was standardised and a Sanskrit–Tibetan dictionary of technical terms, called *Mahāvyutpatti*, was compiled to aid the translators in using the same Tibetan equivalents for the Sanskrit terms. Unfortunately for Buddhism, Ralpachen, who had sponsored the work of translating Buddhist scriptures generously, and had subsidised the building of religious establishments, was assassinated by his older brother Langdarma (gLang-dar-ma, 838–42) who was opposed to Buddhism and supported the indigenous beliefs and practices. The Buddhist tradition looks upon this king as the epitome of an anti-Buddhist ruler. During his short rule the monastic establishments are said to have been damaged and the monks were unfrocked, killed or exiled. Langdarma himself was finally assassinated by a Buddhist monk. It was with him that a glorious period of Tibetan history ended. The claimants to the throne fought each other, political unity collapsed and the great Tibetan empire disintegrated within a short period of time. The whole period of Buddhist history in Tibet from the time of Srongtsan Gampo to Langdarma is generally known as the 'First Diffusion of the Doctrine'.

The next period of Buddhist history in Tibet is known as the 'Second Diffusion of the Doctrine'. After a period of over one hundred years of being eclipsed and limited to isolated communities, Buddhism received a new and decisive impetus for revival in the territories to the west of central Tibet. The defeated and exiled descendants of the royal dynasty established the three kingdoms of Maryul (sMar-yul), Guge (Gu-ge) and Purang (sPu-hrang) in the vast lands of west Tibet. One of the rulers of west Tibet is particularly renowned for his zealous and ardent propagation of Buddhism. He was Yesheö (Ye-shes-'od), the king of Purang who sent a group of young men to Kashmir and India to study and to bring back Buddhist scriptures and teachers. One of the young men sent abroad was the famous Rinchen Zangpo (Rin-chen bzang-po, 958–1055). Having spent seventeen years in Kashmir and India, he made himself competent in the monastic discipline (*Vinaya*) and the Mahāyāna doctrines. After returning he translated many Buddhist works and re-established monastic discipline and the monastic life. He is also credited with the foundation of many monasteries and temples throughout the whole of west Tibet, two of which, Tabo in Spiti and Toling in Purang, still survive. Through the activities of Rinchen Zangpo and his collaborators Buddhism grew quickly and expanded through the whole of west Tibet.

Another inspiring stimulus resulted from the invitation to Tibet of Atiśa from India. Atiśa (982–1054) was one of the most prominent teachers of his time. He was well-versed in the conventional Mahāyāna and in the Tantras. During his sojourn in Tibet he conferred tantric initiations on Rinchen Zangpo and on his own followers, including his chief Tibetan disciple Dromten ('Brom-ston, 1008–64). Although Atiśa taught the Tantras, he also stressed the need for a life according to the monastic discipline. Thus he introduced, along the lines of the great monastic centres of learning in India, a well-balanced situation in which tantric studies and practices were pursued within monasteries whose members were obliged also to observe the monastic discipline according to the *Vinaya*. Atiśa propagated the cult of Avalokiteśvara and Tārā, stressed the importance of the conventional Buddhist morality and the pursual of the gradual path as represented by a *bodhisattva*'s career. It is under Atiśa's inspiration that there developed the general pattern of Tibetan Buddhism that was practised within the monastic context.

The revival of Buddhism in the eastern parts of Tibet is epitomised by the activities of three men who left the central parts of the country and escaped to the east during the persecution that started with Langdarma. It is said that they carried with them the *Vinaya* books. In due course a number of men from central Tibet came to them and were ordained as monks. The newly ordained monks returned to their native localities or dispersed throughout the country and established monastic centres.

During the period between the tenth and the thirteenth centuries many Tibetans travelled to India in search of Buddhist scriptures and spiritual masters. After returning to Tibet many of them lived as solitary or wandering *yogins*; some of them dedicated their time to translating Buddhist texts and only a few established monastic orders. By the beginning of the fifteenth century all the major religious orders of Tibetan Buddhism were established, four of which survived and played a dominant role in the religious life of Tibet till its loss of independence in 1959. As the monastic establishments grew in number and became populated by large groups of monks, the different heads of the religious orders acquired more and more political power and eventually control over the country. By the seventeenth century the descendants of the royal family and different princes who attempted to gain control over Tibet were defeated or eliminated.

The major religious orders developed simultaneously, each order following a particular tradition while accepting in principle the totality of the Buddhist heritage brought from India. The followers of Atiśa became known as Kadampas (bKa'-gdams-pa, 'Bound by Command'). Dromten, Atiśa's chief disciple, founded the monastery of Reting (Rva-sgreng) in 1056, which became the main centre of this order. It followed a strict monastic discipline, observing in particular the rules of celibacy, abstention from intoxicants and from the possession of worldly wealth. Great stress was placed on receiving a direct instruction from one's teacher. It is said that when Dromten once asked Atiśa which was more important, the scriptural text or the teacher, Atiśa replied that personal instructions received from the teacher were more important. Such an attitude was to guard against false teachers and to preserve the continuity of the lineage of teachers and their oral instructions; it also became a feature of other religious orders and traditions. The Kadampas led a rather secluded pattern of life, passing their time in study and meditation. Their main teachings and practices aimed in the first instance to achieve the purification of the mind (blo-sbyong), and then to produce the realisation of moral and esoteric aspirations. The adepts were trained to understand the nature of their own minds and to achieve spiritual maturation as represented by the highest levels of emptiness (*śūnyatā*) and compassion (*karuṇā*). The concept of enlightenment as viewed from the point of absolute truth was equated with emptiness, and considered from the viewpoint of conventional or relative truth, was seen as compassion; emptiness represented the 'Body of Essence' and compassion the 'Body of Form'. The Kadampa order played a crucial role in Tibetan Buddhism because of its insistence on and practice of the *Vinaya*. By the fifteenth century this order had declined to some extent and was later transformed, or rather absorbed, into a new religious order founded by Tsongkapa.

Drogmi ('Brog-mi, 992–1072) was the founder of the Sakyapa (Sa-skya-pa) order. He travelled to India and spent some eight years at the monastic university of Vikramaśīla where he studied the *Vinaya* and the *Prajñāpāramitā* texts. He pursued the study of the Tantras under the guidance of Śāntipa and Virūpa who were renowned as *siddhas*. He received initiation into a number of Tantras, among them into the *Hevajra Tantra*, which he translated into Tibetan and which became the chief tantric text for the Sakyapas. On his return to Tibet, he founded the monastery of Myugulung (Myu-gu-lung) in 1043. His disciple Konchog Gyalpo (dKon-mchog rgyal-po) founded the monastery at Sakya (Sa-skya) in 1073. It was this monastery that gave its name to the whole monastic order. Konchog Gyalpo was a member of the powerful 'Khon clan and it was this family that produced the successive abbots or chief lamas (bla-ma) of Sakya who have continued as the heads of this order until the present time. The succession of abbots within the family was established on the uncle-to-nephew pattern. While the abbot remained celibate, his brothers or close relatives continued the family line and controlled the monastery's worldly affairs. When the abbot died, he was succeeded by one of his nephews. The Sakya monastery, strategically positioned and lying on a trade route to Nepal, flourished and became powerful within a very short period of time.

The apex of Sakya political power was reached in the thirteenth century. The Mongol ruler, Godan, attempting to gain some control in Tibet, summoned the Sakya abbot to his court in 1244. The abbot expressed a formal submission of Tibet to the Mongol khan and in return he was appointed as the regent of Tibet. The next Sakya abbot, Phagpa ('Phags-pa, 1235–80), won the confidence and favour of Kublai Khan, the Emperor of China. Phagpa was appointed as viceregent of Tibet and personal chaplain to the Emperor. The monasteries in Tibet received exemption from taxation and various other privileges. It was at that stage that Tibet became subject to a single political head for the first time since the collapse of the monarchy in the ninth century. Phagpa developed a 'priest-and-patron' relationship with the Emperor. The abbot provided spiritual instruction and the Emperor gave his powerful support to the Buddhist religion. In the fourteenth century the Sakya power in Tibet dwindled away with the decline of the Mongol dynasty in China.

During the thirteenth century a new school branched off from the Sakya order. It became known as the Jonangpa school after the monastery of Jomonang founded by Thugje Tsongdru (Thugs-rje brtson-'grus). The philosophical teachings of this school were considered by many Buddhist masters as unorthodox and extremist. It was opposed with great vigour by the Fifth Dalai Lama. The Jonangpa possessions and monasteries were taken over by the Gelugpas and their writings became prohibited.

Marpa (Mar-pa, 1012–96) is considered retrospectively as the founder of the Kagyupa (bKa'-brgyud-pa) order. At the outset of his religious career Marpa became a disciple of Drogmi from whom he learned Sanskrit. He made three journeys to India, where he studied for sixteen years. While in northern India, he became a disciple of Nāropa from whom he received the teachings known as the Six Doctrines of Nāropa (Nāro chos drug). He also studied with Maitripa from whom he received the transmission of the meditational practices known as *Mahāmudrā*. On returning to Tibet he settled in his native land, Lhobrag, and led what appeared to ordinary people to be the life of a married householder, taking care of his fields and possessions. To those who became his intimate followers, Marpa was known as an accomplished master of tantric practices, qualified to bestow initiation into the most advanced esoteric practices. He traced back his spiritual lineage to the Indian *siddhas* and through them to Vajradhara, the personified principle of Buddhahood. He attracted a handsome group of disciples of whom Milarepa (Mi-la-ras-pa, 1052–1135) became the most famous for his saintly life and his esoteric songs. Milarepa lived an ascetic life, passing many years in solitary meditation in caves on the slopes of the Himalayas. It was to him that Marpa bequeathed the so-called 'lineage of practices' (sgrub-brgyud) that comprised the various yogic exercises brought by Marpa from India. Neither Marpa nor Milarepa were ever ordained as monks. They represented a type of yogic and tantric practice which was different from Atiśa's teachings and practices taught within the monastic context. They represented the esoteric practices that were pursued along the pattern of the Indian *siddha* tradition. They introduced a new genre of religious literature to Tibet and a type of religious poetry that combined the Indian *dohā* tradition and their own spontaneous contributions that reflected their spiritual feelings.

Milarepa had many disciples to whom he imparted his spiritual heritage. One disciple played a crucial role in the formation of this tradition into an organised religious order. He was Gampopa (sGam-po-pa, 1079–1153) of Dvagspo. During his youth, prior to joining Milarepa, Gampopa studied medicine (hence his nickname the 'Doctor of Dvagspo') but at the age of twenty when his wife died suddenly, he turned his thoughts towards religion. He entered the Kadampa order and received monastic ordination. Later on he became Milarepa's disciple. It was through his efforts and writings that he was able to formulate a unified tradition which combined the teachings and practices inherited from Milarepa with the monastic discipline acquired from the Kadampas. He reinterpreted the *Mahāmudrā* teachings in order to adjust them to the monastic life. Thus the whole yogic tradition brought by Marpa became organised into a religious order. It was Gampopa who became the real founder of the Marpa Kagyupa school. All the Kagyupa schools collectively became known as the Dvagspo Kagyupa because of the reforms introduced by Gampopa. Gampopa passed on the monastery that he founded to his nephew, Dvagspo Gomtshul (sGom-tshul or Tshul-khrims snying-po, 1116–69). The Dvagspo Kagyupa proper was identified with Gampopa's monastery and lineage. The founders of the four major branches (che-bzhi) of the Dvagspo Kagyupa were disciples of Gampopa or of his nephew Gomtshul.

The Tshalpa Kagyupa branch was established by Gomtshul's disciple Zhang Yudrak (Zhang-g.yu-brag-pa brtson-'grus 'grags-pa, 1123–93) who founded the monastery of Tshal Gungthang ('Tshal-gung-thang). This branch reached its peak during the early Yuan period in China when the Tshal Gungthang monastery became the centre of an influential myriarchy. Its strong political position was lost when one of its myriarchs opposed Tai-situ Changchub Gyaltsan (Byang-chub rgyal-mtshan). The discovery by Dungtsho Repa (Dung-mtsho ras-pa shes-rab rgyal-mtshan) in 1315 of a *terma* (gter-ma, 'treasure'; see below, p. 791) text—the Sems-khrid—that apparently had been concealed by Gampopa, brought the Tshalpa branch closer to the Nyimapas.

The Kamtshang (Kam-tshang) or Karma Kagyupa branch, the leading sect of the Kagyupa order at the present time, was established by Dusum Khyenpa (Dus-gsum mkhyen-pa, 1110–93) who built the monastery of Tshurpu (mTshur-phu) in 1189 which became the head monastery. It was in this sect that the tradition of reincarnating lamas was introduced for the first time. This system of reincarnation of particular lineages of teachers or lamas was soon adopted by other religious traditions in Tibet and became one of the permanent features of Tibet's religious and political life. The Karmapa sect played a dominant role in the affairs of Tibet from the late fifteenth to the early seventeenth centuries. The sect lost its power to the Gelugpas. There are several important reincarnations that come from the Karmapa branch. They are the Gyalwa Karmapa (considered as the head of this sect), the Zhamar (Zhwa-dmar, 'Red Hat'), the Zhanag (Zhwa-nag, 'Black Hat'), the Gyaltshab, the Situ, the Pabo (dPa'-bo) and the Trebo *tulkus* (*sprul-sku*). The Karmapa sect has produced two sub-sects: Zurmang and Nedo Kagyupas, both of which developed close relations with the Nyimapas.

The third branch of the Kagyupa order became known as the Baram ('Ba'-ram) Kagyupa and was founded by Darma Wangchuk (dBang-phyug). This sect enjoyed some popularity in Khams, the eastern province of Tibet. During the later decades of the nineteenth century this branch became almost completely absorbed by the Nyimapas through the *terma* practices discovered by Chogyur Lingpa.

Gampopa's fourth disciple Phagmo Trupa Dorje Gyalpo (Phag-mo-gru rDo-rje rgyal-po, 1110–70) founded the monastery of Densathil (gDan-sa-mthil) and established a new branch which almost immediately split into eight sub-sects. The main Phagmo Trupa Kagyupa tradition became closely associated with the Densathil and Tsethang (rTse-thang) monasteries which acquired power and wealth through the patronage of the noble family of Lang (rLangs). This family soon began to provide the Densathil monastery with abbots and lay administrators on the uncle-to-nephew basis. As secular affairs gained a predominant importance over religious concerns, the Phagmo Trupa teachers became patrons rather than religious practitioners. The actual teachings transmitted to Dorje Gyalpo were put into practice by his disciples who, as already mentioned, established eight distinct sub-branches (chung-brgyad or zung-bzhi ya-brgyad), issuing from the main Phagmo Tru tradition. Some of the eight branches of this tradition are as follows. The Drigung ('Bri-gung) Kagyupa was initiated by Drigung Kyobpa Jigten Gompo ('Bri-gung skyob-pa 'jig-rten mgon-po, 1143–1217). It is one of the more interesting sub-sects because of its particular body of teachings and its political involvement in Tibetan affairs during the Chinese Yuan and Ming dynasties. It has survived till now and within its own sub-sect it has produced several further sub-sects, of which Lhapa Kagyupa became the most prominent. This sect became the main contender with the Drugpa Kagyupa for dominance in Bhutan.

Tsangpa Gyare (gTsang-pa rgya-ras ye-shes rdo-rje, 1161–1211) who founded the monasteries of Namdrug (gNam-'brug), Longdol (kLong-rdol) and Ralung (Rwa-lung) is considered to be the founder of the Drugpa Kagyupa tradition which became the predominant sect in Bhutan. Many spiritual teachings preserved by this sub-sect were passed to Tsangpa Gyare through Lingrepa (gLing-ras-pa Padma rdo-rje, 1128–88). The teachings that are considered to be the most important for the Drugpa sub-sect focus on the Ronyom Kordrug (ro-snyom skor-drug, 'One Flavour Six Cycles') which employed different practices to achieve the same goal, which is a *terma* instruction concealed by Milarepa's disciple, Rechung (Ras-chung) and rediscovered by Tsangpa Gyare. Another interesting system of spiritual precepts introduced by Tsangpa Gyare was the Tendrel (rten-'brel), an esoteric presentation and interpretation of the *pratītyasamutpāda* (Conditioned Origination). All the major monastic centres established by Tsangpa Gyare were passed on to his nephew Sangye Bonre (Sangs-rgyas dbon-ras dar-ma seng-ge, 1177–1238). The members of the Gya (rGya) family continued as the heads at Ralung until 1616, when Nawang Namgyal (Ngag-dbang mam-rgyal, 1594–1651), a reincarnation of Padma Karpo (Padma dkar-po, 1527–93), was forced by his enemies (the house of gTsang) to flee to Bhutan, thus becoming the founder of the country. The Ralung monastery, along with its affiliated establishments, was taken over by the Tsang authorities and given to Pagsam Wangpo (dPag-bsam dbang-po), Nawang Namgyal's rival for recognition as Tsangpa Gyare's and Padma Karpo's reincarnation. Prior to the dispute Ralung remained at the centre of the Bar ('Middle') Brug School. The unresolved dispute as to who was the true reincarnation of Padma Karpo led to the division of this school into the northern (Byang-'Brug) and southern (Lho-'Brug) branches of the Drugpa. The Drugpa produced several minor traditions which did not develop to the extent of gaining much recognition. The two major traditions that produced important religious works are the Todrug (sTod-'Brug) founded by Gotshangpa (rGod-tshang-pa mgon-po rdo-rje, 1189–1258), and the Medrug (sMad-'Brug) established by Lorepa (Lo-ras-pa dbang-phyug brtson-'grus, 1187–1250). Of the remaining six sub-sects established by Tsangpa Gyare's disciples it will suffice to mention here the Talung (sTag-lung) tradition initiated by Talung Thangpa (sTag-lung thang-pa bkra-shis-dpal, 1142–1210). This tradition, like the Drigung Kagyupa, became strongly influenced by the Nyimapa teachings.

The Kagyupa tradition as a whole, like all the other traditions, has produced a vast body of religious literature. The doctrinal differences between the various Kagyupa branches are not of any great significance, nor are they sources for dispute. Their differences are limited mainly to emphasising certain spiritual practices, following particular texts, and especially to preserving their own lineages. The Kagyupa order played a powerful role on the political scene. The Phagmo Trupa family subdued the political strength of the Sakya abbots and assumed the rule of Tibet. It efficiently controlled the political affairs of the country during the fourteenth and fifteenth centuries, and it retained, at least nominally, the title of the rulers until the seventeenth century. The Phagmo Trupa leaders lost their power to the Karmapa sect which in turn was superseded after a short period by the Gelugpa order.

A similar but quite distinct tradition known as the Shangpa (Shangs-pa) Kagyupa originated with Khyungpo Nalchor (Khyung-po rnal-'byor, eleventh century CE). This sect took its name from the valley in which Khyungpo founded the monastery of Zhong-zhong. Before travelling to India, Khyungpo studied the Dzogchen traditions and the *Mahāmudrā* precepts of Nirūpa. The principle teachings of this sect centre around the Six Doctrines of Nāropa (see below, p. 801). However, those teachings were received by Khyungpo not from Nāropa, as was the case with Marpa, but from the Ḍākinī Niguma, the sister of Nāropa, who received direct inspiration from the Buddha Vajradhara himself. This tradition assumed a definitive form in the fourteenth century through the activities of Barawa Gyaltshan Pelzang ('Ba-ra-ba rgyal-mtshan dpal-bzang). In later centuries it almost disappeared as a separate school but its teachings can still be found persisting among other religious traditions.

The next religious tradition in Tibet to be described

here is the Nyimapa (rNying-ma-pa) order which presents a completely different case. This order developed without any centralised leadership or systematically organised hierarchy. It avoided becoming involved in the political quarrels pursued by the other orders, and its religious centres remained small and scattered for a long time. The Nyimapa order was established as a kind of reaction to the other religious traditions that came into existence with the Second Diffusion of Buddhism in Tibet. The Nyimapas (the name means 'The Ancient Ones') claimed that their religious traditions went back to the royal period when Buddhism was first introduced to Tibet. They were in possession of the scriptures translated during the early period, especially a set of Tantras which had been translated by them before the Second Diffusion. They took the person of Padmasambhava for their archetype and founder. They soon elevated him to the status of a divine figure, a second Buddha who assumed various manifestations of which eight are recognised as principal. In theory he was considered as equal to Śākyamuni Buddha, who was seen as one of Padmasambhava's manifestations, but in practical terms he eclipsed him completely. The Nyimapas attributed to Padmasambhava and his immediate disciples all their teachings in one form or another; their doctrines stand apart from those of the other orders. The Nyimapas recognise two kinds of transmission of their doctrines and scriptures. The Kama (bka'-ma) or Oral Tradition (which is also recorded) is considered to be an uninterrupted continuation of teachings passed on from master to pupil from the time of Padmasambhava. The second form of transmission is represented by a sort of visionary or revelation-like transmission that can occur at intervals in time. This transmission can take the form of a mind-transmission (dgongs-gter) from a departed master to the visionary or a pure-vision (dag-snang). The form of transmitting teachings which is especially developed and highly valued among the Nyimapas is the tradition of the so called *termas* (gter-ma, 'treasure') or rediscovered treasures, usually in the form of texts or objects. The Nyimapas suggest that during his visit to Tibet, Padmasambhava, foreseeing the persecution of Buddhism, had hidden a number of texts in various places with the intention that they should be discovered at an auspicious and appropriate time in the future. The period of treasure-discoverers (gter-ston) began in the tenth century with Sangye Lama (Sangs-rgyas bla-ma). The most important and valuable period of the rediscovered texts evolved between the eleventh and fourteenth centuries. The tradition of rediscovering texts continued in subsequent centuries until the twentieth century and it has always remained open to new discoveries.

The systematisation of the philosophical and religious doctrines of the Nyimapas was initiated on a large scale in the fourteenth century by Longchen Rabjampa (kLong-chen rab-'byams-pa, 1308–64), who produced seven works known as 'Seven Treasures'. It was he who produced the doctrinal bases for the Dzogchen (rdzogs-chen) or 'Great

Perfection', an esoteric system of teachings and practices, whose origins are difficult to trace, and which are valued as the most important among the Nyimapas. The Dzogchen teachings were somehow traced back to Vairocana who lived in Tibet in the eighth century and who is said by the Nyimapas to have been Padmasambhava's disciple. The Nyimapas were severely attacked and criticised by other religious orders for the Dzogchen teachings, especially for possessing scriptures whose origins could not be traced back to India. This criticism applied in particular to the *terma* texts and to certain Tantras. Some more radical critics rejected those texts completely as nothing more than mere fabrications. However, objective research has shown convincingly that considerable portions of those texts contain very ancient materials. By the seventeenth century the Nyimapas succeeded in gaining respect for their tradition as a valid form of Buddhist teachings and practices. For a long period a great majority of the Nyimapas were married men, many of whom acted as 'village priests' (sngags-pa). They pursued yogic and tantric practices on which they embarked without any theoretical preparation. For them the mystical experience always remained the chief goal. In the eighteenth century a reform movement began in eastern Tibet which stressed the necessity of studying the doctrines in a systematic and scholastic manner, and also the practice of the *Vinaya*. Among the Nyimapas there are thus men who take tantric vows and receive various esoteric initiations and consecrations, and live as married men or *yogins*, and those who live in monasteries following the *Vinaya*.

In the nineteenth century a new movement arose known as Rime (ris-med) or 'ecumenical approach' which attempted to formulate a non-sectarian approach to the presentation of the Buddhist doctrines. Generally speaking, the Tibetans were always eclectic and non-aligned in many respects, especially in the sense of following renowned religious teachers rather than particular schools. But this time an attempt was made to unify all religious systems and to eliminate sectarian differences and quarrels. The broad orientation of this movement was a return to the original sources and teachings that were recognised by all schools. The participants of the Rime movement came from several orders but it was from among the Nyimapas that there came the most important personalities such as Kontrul Lodro Thaye and Khyentse Wangpo.

Whenever it refers to religious orders in general, the Tibetan religious tradition speaks of four orders: Sakyapa, Kagyupa, Nyimapa and Gelugpa. The Gelugpa (dGe-lugs-pa) order was founded as the last of the four major sects, but within a short space of time it became the most powerful in political terms. It was founded by Tsonkapa (Tsong-kha-pa, 1357–1419). In his youth Tsongkapa travelled from monastery to monastery, mainly in central Tibet, and pursued his studies with competent teachers of various schools. Being exceptionally gifted he acquired a profound knowledge of the *Vinaya*, the Mahāyāna philosophical doctrines and the teachings of the Tantras. By the age of forty he had become influential as a religious master. At the same age he entered the Kadampa monastery of Reting. His main ambition was to revive the strict monastic life which is said to have become relaxed by this time: many monks abandoned the celibate life and indulged in worldly affairs. Tsongkapa emphasised the religious ideals of strict monastic discipline, the life of celibacy and abstention from intoxicants. In his philosophical and doctrinal instructions he based himself on Atiśa, and in particular on the great Indian thinkers such as Nāgārjuna, Asaṅga and Diṅnāga. He produced a masterly exposition of Mahāyāna Buddhism in a work entitled *Lam-rim-chen-mo* or 'The Great Exposition of the Gradual Path' which was composed as a commentary on Atiśa's *Bodhipathapradīpa.* The tantric doctrines were explained in another work entitled *Ngags-rim-chen-mo* or 'The Great Exposition of the Tantra Stages'.

In 1409 Tsongkapa founded the monastery of Ganden (dGa'-ldan). Two other very important monastic centres, Drepung ('Bras-spungs, in 1416) and Sera (in 1419) were established by his disciples. Within a short time, he gained a considerable following and his school constantly expanded to receive overt support from many monks of other orders, and particularly from lay people who were tired of religious people who involved themselves in politics and worldly affairs. In 1408 he established the annual New Year religious function, called the Great Prayer, in the Jokhang at Lhasa, which was to serve as a yearly rededication of Tibetan people to Buddhism. His learning and saintly personality inspired such a distinct religious movement that the Kadampa monasteries in which his followers lived became completely absorbed and ceased to exist as a separate order. In the initial stages Tsongkapa's followers were called the New Kadampas but soon they became named as the Gelugpas or 'Those of the Virtuous Order'. The Gelugpas attempted to maintain strict monastic discipline and follow scholastic pursuits without themselves engaging, like the other orders, in political disputes. The support of political factions was often represented by aristocratic and princely descendants of the royal families. Very soon, however, they too became involved in political games. The third successor of Tsongkapa, Sonam Gyamtsho (bSod-nams rgya-mtsho, 1543–88), visited Mongolia in 1578 and conducted a series of teachings. He gained the sympathy of Altan Khan from whom he received the title of Dalai Lama. This title was applied retrospectively to his two predecessors and a reincarnation lineage was established. The political supremacy over Tibet by the Gelugpa order was assumed during the life of the Fifth Dalai Lama (1617–82) who received military assistance from Gushri Khan of the Qosot Mongols. The civil and military administration of the country became the responsibility of a regent (sde-srid) appointed by the Dalai Lama, and the khan assumed the role of a 'Religious Protector'. Later on a somewhat similar system was maintained with the Manchu emperors of China. From the Fifth Dalai Lama until 1959 when the Fourteenth Dalai Lama fled to India, the rule of Tibet remained with the Gelugpa order. The Fifth Dalai Lama bestowed the title of Panchen Lama on his teacher, the abbot of Tashilhunpo monastery (bKra-shis lhun-po). The reincarnating lamas of this lineage gained a powerful position and wealth, and they often played an active role in the political and religious life of Tibet.

Main Characteristics of Tibetan Buddhism

The numerous texts that were brought from India during the two diffusions of Buddhism were eventually translated into Tibetan and divided into two major groups: *Kanjur* (bka'-'gyur) and *Tanjur* (bsTan-'gyur). The *Kanjur* included the works which contained the 'Buddha's Word' and the *Tanjur* comprised numerous commentaries and treatises composed by Indian masters. The *Kanjur* resembles the classical *Tripiṭaka* only in a very general manner. Apart from the *Vinaya* and a number of the early *sūtras*, it contains many Mahāyāna *sūtras*, the *Prajñāpāramitā* literature, the *Ratnakūṭa* collection, the *Buddhāvataṃsaka* and the texts belonging to the four classes of the Tantras. It consists conventionally of 108 volumes. The *Tanjur* has no evident Indian prototype. It consists of 225 volumes and, apart from philosophical and exegetical texts concerned with doctrines, it contains works on medicine, crafts, iconography and the like. The *Kanjur* and *Tanjur* jointly contained more than 4,500 works of various lengths. The systematisation and classification of the canonical texts were largely done by Buston (Bu-ston Rin-chen-grub, 1290–1364). In deciding which texts should be included in the Canon, Buston took a firm position that only those works which could be related to their Indian originals should be included. Such an assumption led him to exclude from the Canon a large number of texts, particularly the tantric works translated during the earlier period. The Nyimapas who cherished those Tantras claimed that they were transmitted through a *ḍākinī* (mkha'-'gro-ma, a class of female deities) or that they were found as *termas*. The old Tantras, being rejected by the 'New Buddhist tradition' (gsar-ma-ba) were made by the Nyimapas into a collection known as the 'Old Tantras' (rNying-ma'i rgyud-'bum). Similarly they assembled their *terma* texts into several collections. While the Nyimapas recognise the authority of the *Kanjur* and *Tanjur*, their teachings and practices are based mainly on the collections of their own. Apart from these, the religious masters of all traditions in Tibet produced a bewildering number of works, individual or collective (gsung-'bum), that were concerned with various aspects of Buddhist doctrines and practices.

Tibetan Buddhism has produced a large number of original thinkers but still the Tibetans generally assume that their contribution to the doctrines is limited to classification and clarification of obscure or difficult points. Practically all the doctrines, not always with convincing proof, are referred back to Indian texts or masters. The broad and fundamental doctrines of all Tibetan schools have the same Indian foundation. They all derive their philosophical orientation from the philosophical schools of India, in particular the Mādhyamika, the Vijñānavāda, the Vaibhāṣika and the Sautrāntika. The differences between the schools are not rooted in contradicting or opposing doctrines, although disputes happened, but rather in their allegiance to particular exegetical or philosophical traditions, or again, as is the case particularly among the Nyimapas, in their attachment to textual transmissions or a body of practices. The division into sects should not have pejorative implications but should rather be seen as the result of separate religious traditions, similar to the Christian orders of the Middle Ages.

Indian Buddhism produced many teachings and practices, especially in its later stages, which could not easily be preserved as a living tradition by one religious order. All the Buddhist schools in Tibet recognise the authority of the canonical texts except for the excluded texts mentioned above. The Mūla-Sarvāstivāda *Vinaya* is the only *Vinaya* that has been translated into Tibetan and that constitutes the foundation of the monastic life of all the religious orders. The ultimate goal is the same for all adherents to Buddhism. It is deliverance (thar-pa) from *saṃsāra*'s bonds and passing into *nirvāṇa*. The notion of *nirvāṇa* and its relationship to *saṃsāra* was not firmly defined during the early period of Indian Buddhism. As the philosophical theories evolved, especially among the Mahāyāna schools, the concept of *nirvāṇa*, which had previously been conceived of as 'an escape' from *saṃsāra*, was gradually replaced by a 'positive' interpretation of an 'Absolute'. This was variously perceived as pure light or luminosity, as pure consciousness in which discursive thinking which differentiates subjects from objects does not exist, or as 'emptiness' (*śūnyatā*). However, one does not arrive at these highly advanced concepts of pure mind or consciousness, or of absolute emptiness, during the early stages of one's spiritual career. Nor does one attempt to understand them or put them into practice at this stage. The whole training begins with some more general and yet fundamental assumptions. The Buddha's *Dharma* is not something just to be accepted without reservations but above all it is to be understood, reasoned out in one's own mind, and mystically experienced. The path of liberation begins with a correct vision of the nature of things, and with appropriate conduct. This conduct will be suitable to reach the final goal which is the awakening of one's spiritual entity to the highest truth that transcends the phenomenal world of illusive appearances and dichotomic concepts. One becomes aware that all things are impermanent in the sense that all things perceived in this world and all concepts cannot be thought of as real but as being without any true nature and value. Having understood the deceptive character of all phenomenal appearances, one gains a further awareness of a state that reaches beyond transitory phenomena. In order to free oneself from the bonds of this world and to reach beyond its limits, one embarks on the path of appropriate practices.

Tibetan Buddhism follows the path of the Mahāyāna ideals. One takes a vow to attain the supreme state of Buddhahood. It is the *bodhisattva* career that one attempts to pursue. The goal is not just one's own personal deliverance but also the deliverance of all living beings. The doctrinal position of this career is defined and advocated in the *Prajñāpāramitā* scriptures. The long path towards enlightenment begins with accumulation of merit and knowledge. One must acquire moral purification and intellectual alertness in order to separate oneself from worldly impurities and to become a receptacle for the supreme enlightenment. The *bodhisattva* path is graded into ascending levels, usually conveniently divided into ten stages of spiritual progress centred around the Ten Perfections (*pāramitā*). The process of cultivating the thought of enlightenment (*bodhicitta*) is thus presented by the Mahāyāna as a long and arduous path that is pursued for two or three incalculable world-ages (*asaṃkhyeya*).

The Mahāyāna introduced some other important concepts of which the notion of the three Buddha-Bodies is one of the most important. While phenomenal existence on the level of conventional truth appears to be real, in reality it is false. Through the acquisition of an intuitive knowledge that enables one to abolish all concepts of duality and erroneous perceptions of phenomena, one approaches the level of absolute truth which, as already mentioned, can be expressed by several technical concepts. This highest truth or the quintessence of all things constitutes the nature of the supreme Buddhahood which can be conceived of as the self-abiding Buddha-Body (*svabhāvikakāya*). Such an inconceivable state may assume a threefold manifestation: Absolute Body (*dharmakāya*) which is beyond all forms and concepts; Glorified Body (*sambhogakāya*) which becomes manifested in numerous Buddhist paradises, the abodes of Buddhas and Bodhisattvas; Manifested Body (*nirmāṇakāya*) which corresponds to a Buddha manifestation in a human body. This concept of a threefold and cosmic manifestation of the supreme Buddhahood gave rise to a great variety of Buddhas described in scriptures and depicted iconographically. The same concept became a doctrinal foundation in Tibetan Buddhism for numerous lineages of reincarnating lamas. It is asserted that different Buddhas or Bodhisattvas can become manifest in different people. A particular Buddha or Bodhisattva may 'reveal' himself in one person or in several. Furthermore, several people can become emanations of different aspects of the same Buddha; emanations of his Body, Speech, Mind or Activities. The principle of reincarnating lamas is interpreted in two ways. While a particular lama represents a Buddha emanation, at the same time he is also considered to be a reincarnation of his predecessor who also represented the same Buddha emanation. The reincarnating lamas are called *tulkus* (*sprul-sku*, emanated-body). When a *tulku* dies, a search is made to find a child that possesses certain established indications of being a reincarnation of the departed predecessor. There are numerous lineages of reincarnating lamas among the Nyimapas and the Kagyupas. The Gelugpas have two prominent emanations: one is the line of the Dalai Lamas who are emanations of the Bodhisattva Avalokiteśvara, and the other is the line of the Panchen Lamas as emanations of Buddha Amitābha. The reincarnations can appear at any time, discontinue or become suspended.

To avoid certain discord and to justify various practices, Tibetan Buddhism adopted the Indian classification of doctrines and practices into three vehicles (*yāna*). This classification asserts that the Hīnayāna was taught for people who are endowed with average intelligence. The Mahāyāna was destined for those of superior capacities, and the Mantrayāna or Vajrayāna was devised for people with the highest intellectual and spiritual abilities. Such a gradation of teachings and practices enables people of different mental categories and walks of life to embark on a suitable path. The lower vehicles are recommended for the lay people and in particular for the religious as a preparatory stage for the most advanced practices. Thus stress is placed here on the necessity and utility of the gradual path. One must accumulate merit and knowledge, and acquire a gradual purification through many reincarnations. Within monastic training it is this general orientation that constitutes the core of intellectual studies and daily practices of meditation.

The tantric practices and meditation which are styled as the rapid path towards the highest goal that may be achieved in one life-span are justified and accessible only to those who are sufficiently prepared to understand them and to execute them. So far as the philosophical doctrines are concerned, the Tantras accept as their foundation the doctrines of the Mahāyāna, in particular those of the Mādhyamika and the Vijñānavāda schools. The Tantras are not preoccupied with speculation. Their chief goal is to induce and acquire a mystical experience. In a general way, one could say that the Tantras represent a ritualised and yogic application of the Mahāyāna philosophical concepts. Two of those concepts, *saṃsāra* and *nirvāṇa,* stand at the centre of tantric considerations. The Tantras assert that a mystical experience of their non-duality leads to the realisation of the supreme Buddhahood. The duality of concepts and appearances is seen as remaining at the root of all imperfections and through its elimination one achieves the highest spiritual perfection.

To the two concepts of *saṃsāra* and *nirvāṇa,* we may add some other pairs of concepts which also portray the same state of reality from somewhat different angles. These are 'means' (*upāya*) and 'wisdom' (*prajñā*), 'compassion' (*karuṇā*) and 'emptiness' (*śūnyatā*). The concepts of 'wisdom' and 'emptiness' refer to absolute truth, and the concepts of 'means' and 'compassion' may be conveniently seen as parallels of relative or conventional truth. Various activities and practices within *saṃsāra* that lead to the supreme wisdom are seen as the means towards it. The same means pursued out of compassion for all living beings are referred to as the compassion that induces the dawn of emptiness. It can be asserted, in a general way, that *saṃsāra* as a whole is the means for achieving *nirvāṇa* for it is within it that the various practices of purification, meditation and intellectual training are pursued. The ascent towards the supreme goal is not merely a one-way effort but rather it should be viewed as a mutual merging of the two extremes, as it were, represented by the pairs of concepts just mentioned. As one's inner disposition becomes more purified one becomes a receptacle for the highest perfection that begins to unfold itself.

Thus the Tantras propound that it is a merging of these dualistic or dichotomic assumptions that should be experienced and retained within oneself through meditation and yogic practices. For the purpose of tantric exercises, the Tantras made use of a large variety of symbols to represent those abstract concepts: the *vajra* (means) and the bell (wisdom), the moon and the sun, the vowels and the consonants, the male and the female. Similarly the same concepts can be personified as deities. Different deities can be seen either as embodying the totality of Buddhist perfection or a part of it. Thus for instance Vajrasattva or Samantabhadra represents the supreme state of Buddhahood, while the Five Tathāgatas of the Yoga Tantra represent a fivefold manifestation of Buddhahood. Once united in a tantric embrace the deities represented as male (means) and female (wisdom) symbolise the non-duality of all concepts and manifestations.

A *maṇḍala* which represents a cosmic diagram is perhaps the best example of tantric ideals and aspirations. If we take for instance the *maṇḍala* of Vairocana, the deities are distributed as follows. At the centre of the cosmos is Vairocana with his female partner. To the four cardinal points of the compass are distributed the other four Buddhas (Akṣobhya etc.) with their goddesses (Locanā etc.). The subsequent circles of the diagram are occupied by a group of Bodhisattvas and lesser deities. As the deities become more distant from the centre, they assume a lesser importance. Each deity is attributed a particular aspect of Buddhist perfection and is conceived of as counteracting certain aspects of human imperfection. A *maṇḍala* can be depicted iconographically and used as an aid in meditation or, in the case of more advanced practitioners, it can be visualised directly. The meditational exercises of visualisation are called evocations (*sādhana*). During an evocation one first imagines or creates mentally the foundation of the *maṇḍala* diagram or the cosmic palace which symbolises the physical world. Next one envisages the deities which are distributed to their assigned places. So far this performance has recreated the illusory world of phenomena. The next stage consists of emanating rays of light from one's heart by means of which the divine manifestations that pervade the envisaged deities are summoned from the absolute sphere and are known as the knowledge-deities. The meditational state has now succeeded in uniting as it were the phenomenal and transcendental spheres. The next moment leads to identifying oneself with the deities of the *maṇḍala*. One attempts to assume and to retain the transcendental perfection of the deities. At the end of such an exercise the *maṇḍala* is dissolved. The practice of evocation can be performed by visualising a group of deities or just concentrating on one particular deity. It can be performed as a meditational practice or it can be expressed externally in a ritual with recitations, chanting, music and presentation of offerings.

Another practice based on the same principle is to think of one's own body as a *maṇḍala* or as being endowed with different mystic levels (*cakra*) or channels which can enable one to achieve meditational trances. This kind of practice is derived from the common lore of Indian yogic tradition. Yet another method makes use of a female partner. In such trances the *yogin* (means) identifies himself with a particular Buddha while his female partner assumes the role of the Buddha-Goddess (wisdom). While the *vajra* and the lotus are united (which here means during sexual intercourse), the jasmine drop (semen) representing the thought of enlightenment (*bodhicitta*) must not be lost but should ascend through the *yogin*'s body to the summit of the head where the culminating moment of esoteric trance is achieved. This kind of practice can only be performed by well trained *yogins* and their chosen partners, both of whom are required to possess absolute control over their bodies. Such practices are never performed within monasteries, and the monks who take monastic vows perform only tantric meditations which do not impede the vow of celibacy.

The various tantric methods, and especially the mystic experience to which they lead, cannot be easily communicated or conveyed to others mainly because such practices are liable to misconceptions and misuse. In all tantric practices stress is placed on the continuation of living transmission of teachings and practices. The mere knowledge of tantric texts is said to have no value. A suitable master is required to guide his disciples in their meditational and ritual exercises, to instruct them and to bestow initiations upon them. So that the tradition may become efficient, the disciple must first receive a direct textual transmission (*lung* or *upadeśa*) from his master; this is often done by reading the text aloud. An oral transmission of texts is regarded as important for two reasons: it is a formal permission to study the texts and it produces a certain spiritual capacity for understanding them. After a period of studying and listening to instructions, the disciple receives tantric initiations (*dbang*, *abhiṣeka*). The tantric consecrations vary in number and nature. Some of them are preliminary and general, others are highly advanced; the higher Tantras have four major consecrations.

The recognition of the superiority of mystical experience over intellectual speculation led to the admission of the possibility of many forms of individual experience. Such an assumption allowed the tantric practitioners to make use of various yogic practices available in India, and of magical performances that they considered appropriate and suitable to their personal taste. However, all those yogic practices and magical skills had to be interpreted within the context of Buddhist ideals. The tantric tradition, like other Buddhist schools, has produced a vast body of texts known as *Tantras*: hence the name Tantric Buddhism. The Tantras are often divided into four classes: Action (*kriyā*, *bya-brgyud*), Performance (*caryā*, *spyod*), Yoga (*rnal-'byor*) and Highest (*anuttara*, *bla-na-med*). The Action Tantra is characterised by external practices such as ritual offerings to deities, recitation of *mantras*, magic rites and rituals whose chief aim is to acquire certain spiritual but also mundane benefits. The Performance Tantra makes use of the elements contained in the previous category but it adds the practice of mental concentration and meditation. The Yoga Tantra, which stands at the centre of all the tantric practices, makes use of psycho-physical yogic exercises and meditation. The external rituals are not essential but they are used as additional aids. It is in this class of Tantras that the methods of evocation and identification with deities have been fully developed. The Highest Tantra is considered to advocate the most advanced esoteric practices in which the experience of non-duality of phenomenal and transcendental spheres and the illusory character of their duality are mystically achieved through the aid of a female partner. This category of Tantras very often speaks of the highest spiritual experiences as the Great Bliss (*mahāsukha*, *bde-chen*) which represents a transposition into mystical level of the joy experienced in the tantric union. Many people are puzzled by the tantric practices that involve sexual yoga. In the case of Tibet one general observation can be made here. During the initial period of Buddhism in Tibet there existed it seems a considerable number of yogic adepts who made use of sexual yoga. We have written evidence, a letter of the king of Purang, which condemns such practices. In due course, when the monastic orders and discipline became established, such practices were limited to individuals who pursued their practices outside monasteries. There are still today married lamas among the Tibetan orders, especially among the Nyimapas; those people do not follow the *Prātimokṣa* rules (the *Vinaya*) but take tantric vows. It should be said that the Tibetans have a great respect for the Tantras as a means of mystical experiences and especially as a source of powerful magic rituals which can be employed to achieve various results. In the monasteries life flows according to the *Vinaya* rules, the doctrinal outlook is that of the Mahāyāna, and the rituals are often of the Tantras; very often tantric deities are depicted on the walls of monasteries.

So far we have considered the features of Tibetan Buddhism which are largely applicable to all the religious orders. There exist certain differences between the orders. The major differences amount to following particular traditions of texts and practices. The Sakyapa order, as far as the tantric tradition is concerned, gives a predominance to the *Hevajra Tantra* and related texts. The doctrinal and exegetical assumptions are centred around the teaching which places in apposition the practical path towards the supreme goal and its fruit (*lam-'bras*). While one advances along the path of religious practices, one at the same time acquires the fruits of one's efforts in proportion to those efforts. Like the Gelugpas, the Saskyapas study the Mādhyamika philosophy. The Gelugpas are the greatest champions of the Mādhyamika doctrines. They attach importance to dialectical studies and intellectual training. The writings of Tsongkapa and his two chief disciples, Khedrub and Gyaltshab (mKhas-'grub-rje and rGyal-tshab), provide a general framework for intellectual training. Among the Tantras, the Gelugpas specialise in the *Kālacakra Tantra*. The Kagyupas present a more complex tradition. Apart from the traditions brought by Marpa and the eclectic systematisation of Gampopa, they have also adopted certain Nyimapa practices. The practices systematised by Gampopa centre around the *Mahāmudrā*—'Great Seal'—teachings. The Great Seal stands for the ultimate non-duality. The teachings were brought from India but Gampopa reinterpreted them within the general and wide context of Buddhist philosophy and practice. The Six Doctrines of Nāropa are of course a particular feature of this order, but they also spread to other traditions. The first of Nāropa's doctrines making use of the haṭha-yoga techniques explains the practice of meditation used to acquire the ability to sustain or retain bodily heat in adverse and cold circumstances. The second doctrine explains visualisations that lead to becoming aware of the illusory character of one's body. The third doctrine centres on the illusory nature of dreams and related states. The pure light nature of absolute reality is taught in the fourth doctrine. The transference of consciousness is the subject of the fifth doctrine. Here one learns how to transfer one's consciousness at the moment of death into one's chosen deity or to dissolve it into the universal luminosity. The sixth doctrine is similar. It teaches how to animate dead bodies. The transmission of the sixth doctrine discontinued with the sudden death of Marpa's son.

The Nyimapas have produced their own most interesting body of literature. They do not preserve the classical tradition of scholastic training nor group their teachings on the Indian pattern. They emphasise spiritual practices in preference to intellectual pursuits; one learns as one experiences is the general orientation. Their doctrines are not systematised into three vehicles but into nine. The *Śrāvaka*, *Pratyekabuddha* and *Bodhisattva* Vehicles (*yāna*) are classed as the three lowest vehicles. The first three Tantra classes (*kriyā*, *caryā*, *yoga*) constitute the three lower vehicles of the Vajrayāna. The three highest vehicles *Mahāyoga*, *Anuyoga* and *Atiyoga*, consist of the tantric texts belonging to the Highest Tantra, the old Nyimapa Tantras rejected by Buston, and other similar texts. As the highest and most valuable body of teachings the *Atiyoga* explains the doctrines and practices known as *Dzogchen* (*rdzogs-chen*, literally 'Great Perfection'). The *Dzogchen* teachings, introduced by Vairocana, centre around the Tantras that do not have *maṇḍalas* containing numerous deities to be contemplated. The practice focuses on luminosity-emptiness, that is uncreated, without beginning or end, a primordial self-existence named as Samantabhadra (Kun-tu-bzang-po). Samantabhadra represents a state even beyond the Buddhas, the most refined and pure intelligence of which all beings are possessed. Deliverance from the phenomenal world is gained through the elimination of all impurities caused by the projections of the mind. One must therefore eliminate all mental activities. The actual practice often involves regular periods of meditation on Light which is frequently performed by gazing at the sun. A successful effort should culminate in becoming completely absorbed and dissolved bodily into the Light, assuming the form of a rainbow ('ja'-lus). The *Dzogchen* practices were criticised and condemned by many masters of other schools as being a disguised form of Chinese Ch'an (Zen).

Certain practices introduced in Tibet survived as living traditions through different masters but without belonging to any particular order. Of those the Chö (gCod, 'cut off') practices are perhaps the most original. They were brought to Tibet by Phadampa Sangye from India, it is alleged, along with related practices called *Zhi-byed.* The Chö school in Tibet was established by a woman-*ḍākinī* called Macig Labdron (Ma-gcig lab-sgron-ma). Its philosophical and doctrinal foundation is grounded in the *Prajñāpāramitā* literature. Thus its final goal is the same as that of other orthodox traditions. The practices, however, are very different. They centre around the terrifying aspects of human nature and phenomena in general. Its practitioner wanders off to places such as dreadful cemeteries, awesome mountains, haunted crossroads and so on. While meditating one evokes and then provokes the spirits and wrathful demoniac powers around one and then one tries to control them. The culminating moments of such meditational sessions involve the act of cutting up one's own body into pieces and offering it to the host of terrifying beings around. At the end of meditation one reabsorbs within oneself all the hallucinatory apparitions born from one's own mind. The ultimate goal is to become aware of the illusory nature of phenomena, the non-existence of one's self, and to gain the supreme Wisdom.

Interaction with Popular Religion

Apart from the orthodox and monastic Buddhism as represented by the different religious orders and traditions described in the previous pages, there exists in Tibet a popular religion, totally garbed in Buddhist attires, but in truth constituting a mixture of Buddhist and non-Buddhist elements. The general and overall attitude of ordinary people is Buddhist. They place their trust and take refuge in the Three Jewels (*Triratna*): Buddha, his *Dharma* and his *Saṅgha*. They practise Buddhist morality and accumulate merit through various actions such as charitable deeds, prayers, prostrations before images and sacred constructions, circumambulations of temples and *stūpas*, donations to monasteries and going on pilgrimages. Some more educated people read sacred texts and many Tibetans dedicate their lives completely to religion at advanced stages in life when they pass all their worldly responsibilities on to their children.

For the Tibetans at large, the world of everyday life is crowded with various categories of spirits and demoniac powers. Some of the more important deities are referred to by their proper names but a large majority of them are reduced to generic appellations. Each place, village or town, valley or plot of fields has its own local deity (*sa-bdag*, 'master of the earth') who controls it. This class of deities, like others, must not be provoked or made angry for it can cause diseases, death or loss of property. Another category of spirits called *lu* (*klu*) controls underground waters, lakes and rivers. They too must not be disturbed by polluting water. Some deities considered to be very powerful inhabit mountain passes or the summits of numerous mountains. Some of the mountains are dedicated to different Buddhas or Bodhisattvas but the majority of them are in the control of deities whom the Buddhist tradition classes as *laukika* or belonging to this world. Many of the most powerful local and mountain gods were converted to Buddhism and made into 'Religion-Protectors' (*chos-skyong*, *dharmapāla*). On occasions of crossing mountain passes, or near the places where the local deities are said to dwell, people make food offerings and recite prayers which are Buddhist in nature. There exists a great variety of rituals for propitiating the different categories of lesser deities, for offering ransoms or even fierce rites to eliminate them altogether. The entire life of Tibetan people is orientated towards self-defence and constant efforts are made to appease and to placate the powers that surround them. Each individual is accompanied by some deities. On one's right shoulder is the enemy-god (*dgra-lha*) who protects against enemies and who is a remote echo of the primitive period of nomadic hunters. The right armpit carries the paternal-deity (*pho-lha*), the left armpit the maternal-deity (*mo-lha*) while the uncle-deity (*zhang-lha*) rests in the heart. These three deities represent the continuity of the family. They seem to represent the paternal and maternal ancestors who watch over the safe continuity of the family lineage. The hearth is inhabited by the hearth-god (*thab-lha*), the storeroom by the abundance-god (*bang-mdzod-lha*), and the house-god (*phug-lha* or *khyim-lha*) dwells in the central pillar of the house. The house itself can be interpreted in cosmological terms. Thus, for instance, the central pillar represents the world's axis and the ladder connecting the ground floor with the upper storey, having thirteen rungs, symbolises the thirteen levels of heaven. The personal deities are also attributed different parts of the house as their habitations.

The Buddhist doctrine of the non-existence of a soul is generally accepted but popular belief firmly asserts that each individual has a soul which is called *la* (*bla*) which has a definite form. The *la* resides in the body and it can become separated from it on certain occasions, such as moments of fainting, mental disorder or death. It can also be abducted by evil spirits. There are special rituals to recall the *la* that wandered astray or to regain it from a malevolent spirit. Another element resting within the body is called the life-force (*srog*) which is identical with the duration of one's life. It penetrates the whole body, flows through with the breathing and its main seat is the heart. It represents the life-principle as opposed to the state of death. Certain astrological forces are represented by the so-called wind-horse (*rlung-rta*) on which depend one's health and prosperity.

The oldest Buddhist doctrines in India maintained that one was reborn soon after death. The sum of one's good and bad actions (*karma*) conditioned the next rebirth. The later Buddhist tradition introduced the concept of an intermediate period between death and rebirth. It was asserted that during that period the departed ones could be aided to gain, if not a complete deliverance, then at least a better rebirth than the one imposed by the rule of *karma*. In Tibet this period, reckoned as lasting for forty-nine days, has become associated with some very ancient concepts, especially that of a soul as comprising the whole person. This type of soul-concept is not easily discernible because, once again, it is garbed in Buddhist terms. The ancient term itself is not employed but it is subsumed in the Buddhist technical term of consciousness (*vijñāna*, *rnam-shes*). At the moment of death, or soon after it, one receives instructions called *phowa* (*'pho-ba*) which describe to one the process of death and the immediate events that follow it. Through those instructions one should understand that there is nothing to be feared and that the only successful conduct to assume is to confront with calmness the manifestations that appear before one. It is assumed that immediately after death one has a vision of a beam of light. If one follows this luminous vision one should be able to cut off all the successive rebirths and to reach the supreme state of deliverance. If one hesitates, even for a moment, one begins to fall back into one's next rebirth. The luminous beam is paralleled with a similar beam of darkness which becomes predominant as the intermediate period evolves. The moment of death is considered as extremely important. One must not be disturbed for one's consciousness might be perturbed and become an evil ghost or take possession of another man. There are special exercises that teach how to perform by oneself the act of dying when the death cannot be avoided. Those who acquire this knowledge very frequently die while fully aware. Usually they assume the bodily posture of their chosen deity and then transfer their consciousness directly into the heart of the deity or to the sphere of pure consciousness or luminosity. In the case of ordinary people, once physical death is ascertained the consciousness receives instructions through the reading of a text known as *Liberation through Listening in the Intermediate State* (*Bar-do-thos-grol*), better known in the West as *The Tibetan Book of the Dead*. This text explains what happens at each successive day of the intermediate period. Once the consciousness begins to relapse into the world, it passes through a series of visions consisting of seeing various deities both peaceful and terrifying, traversing dangerous abysses, enduring attacks of all kinds and meeting ordinary people and members of the family. As the fall becomes deeper and deeper, the beam of light gradually dwindles away and with it the last chances of following it. Finally the consciousness becomes aware that it needs a body to act like all other people around it. It perceives copulating people and desires to unite itself with the seed of life, gaining thus its next rebirth.

The Tibetans, like many other civilisations, make use, but on a very much larger scale, of divination and astrological calculations. They employ many techniques to discern various omens and events. Most of the divination methods are contained in special books and their astrology includes Indian, Chinese and Tibetan materials. There exist people who specialise in divination and astrology. The more simple methods are used by people at large. While engaged in trading, travel or a particular enterprise, the Tibetans often consult specialists to find out whether there are any obstacles arising from demons or evil people. The difficulties are overcome by the use of amulets, ransom offerings presented to demons or by appropriate rituals. The Tibetans also make use of oracles, who act as media and become possessed by different deities. A particular deity will take possession of its medium, who goes into a trance during a seance. Oracles are found not only in villages but also in monasteries. The Dalai Lamas have always consulted the state oracle at Nechung near Lhasa.

The aspiration towards the Buddhist *nirvāṇa* is certainly present among ordinary people, but in general they aspire to gain a better rebirth. The high religious aspirations of people are often expressed in their desire to reach the legendary country of Shambhala, the land of abundance, peace and freedom from all suffering. Shambhala is believed to lie to the north of Tibet beyond impenetrable mountain ranges. Its rulers continue the line of pious kings who, of course, profess Buddhism and know the most advanced esoteric teachings. When the time will come, the king of Shambhala, like the epic hero Gesar, will lead his armies to destroy evil and establish a universal kingdom of just and virtuous happiness on the earth. The land of Shambhala can only be reached by those endowed with spiritual purity, for only good people have a chance to traverse the dangerous mountains and snares that separate Tibet from Shambhala. Some more sophisticated accounts speak of Shambhala as being in the hearts of people who live a moral life.

Indigenous or Pre-Buddhist Beliefs

There are two distinct, somewhat opposed, and yet similar religious traditions in Tibet. One is represented by Buddhism, brought from India, and the other is Bon, which claims different origins but in fact represents a heterodox form of Buddhism from the eleventh century onwards. Both these religions claim—and are followed in this by some Western scholars—that Bon and its followers, called Bonpos, represent the ancient religious beliefs of Tibet. Critical scholarship has proved decisively that such an assumption does not portray the true situation. Ever since Buddhism was introduced in Tibet, it gradually eliminated the ancient beliefs, especially those that were in a direct contrast to its doctrines. Some of the more acceptable practices, and especially myths as we have seen, were subsumed into both Buddhism and carried forward by Bon, in both religions under an appropriate terminology. Thus all the materials in Tibetan religious sources that contain or refer to the ancient beliefs are given a suitably transformed interpretation. The description of the ancient beliefs, therefore, can only be limited to generalities and certain accounts that appear almost certainly to have existed in Tibet before the introduction of Buddhism in the seventh century; some of the ancient elements have already been mentioned above.

The oldest indigenous Tibetan beliefs seem to have centred around the sacral and divine character of the very early kings. The transition to the earthly mortality of the kings did not eliminate their sacral nature but it necessarily introduced new elements which were largely connected with funeral rites. The interment of the kings, from Drigum onwards, involved elaborate ceremonies to assure their peaceful stay in the realm of the dead. The kings were buried with a whole set of worldly possessions, including animals and probably their companions. The funeral rites included special ransom ceremonies which aimed to prevent evil powers from disturbing the dead, and also, it seems, to seal off, as it were, the world of the dead from the living. On such occasions animal sacrifices were performed and suitable verses were recited. The belief in the realm of the dead led to the cult of ancestors which was expressed through periodical offerings made by families to their departed forefathers. It seems quite certain that bloody sacrifices were still practised on special occasions, such as the swearing of solemn oaths or the instalment of the kings, even during the initial stages of Buddhism in Tibet. A great number of the ancient practices seem to have been concerned with divination and astrological calculations to determine the causes of people's misfortunes and ailments, and to procure suitable cures to eliminate them. The sources of people's troubles were often attributed to local gods and demons of all kinds. The usual manner of counteracting and preventing harmful influences of various evil powers was achieved through the use of ransom offerings.

The specialists who performed the funerary rites, divination or made offerings to different categories of spirits were known as *bon* or *shen* (*gshen*). Those priests engaged by the royal court were credited with various magical powers, skills in ritual sacrifices and abilities to perform spectacular feats such as flying in the air. The religion, as such, seems to have had no name but at times it is referred to in texts as 'divine conventions' (lha-chos) in contrast to 'human conventions' (mi-chos), or again as 'the custom of heaven and earth' (gnam-sa'i-lugs). Some scholars assert that it was called *tsug* (gtsug) or *tsuglag* (gtsug-lag). The origin of the world is attributed to a category of celestial beings called *cha* (phyva). The heavenly dwelling consisted of thirteen levels and the earth had nine. The *cha* gods, presided over by a leader (sku-lha), controlled the cosmic events according to the Law (tsug). The harmonious rule of the universe was retained by the Law with some gods remaining in heaven and other gods taking residence on the earth. The universal order was disrupted by a demon released from the ninth subterranean level. Moral decay evolved and only some people sustained the Law. The general immoral chaos will end and good people will regain the control epitomised by the Law but, in the meantime, they remain in a peaceful state in the abode of the dead.

Another discernible feature of the ancient beliefs is the cult of mountain deities. Certain mountain peaks were treated as sacred and it seems that the early Tibetan tribes had their separate mountains. The deities living on those mountains belonged mostly to the group of the most powerful category known as *tsan* (btsan, 'mighty'). Even today there are many mountain peaks which are considered sacred.

Bon Religion

The Tibetan word for religion is *chö* (chos). It had its particular meaning in the ancient times but with the introduction of Buddhism it was employed to translate the Sanskrit technical term *Dharma*—the Buddha's doctrine. The ancient interpretation of this term dwindled away and only certain aspects of it continue among popular beliefs. The term 'Bon', which in the ancient times referred to a category of priests, was employed from the eleventh century onwards to denote a whole body of religious teachings in the same way as the Buddhist *Chö* (*Dharma*). Both Buddhist *Dharma* and Bon traditions are fundamentally the same so far as the philosophical doctrines are concerned. The Buddhist tradition traces itself to India while Bon asserts its origins in the country to the west of Tibet which it calls Tazig (sTag-gzig, asserted to be Iran). The Bon religion, it must be pointed out, incorporates a large portion of ancient beliefs but in a completely transformed manner; so, too, does the Buddhist tradition, as already mentioned.

The Bon teachings were first propagated on earth by Shenrab Mibo (gShen-rab mi-bo), whose historicity is not attested; the name itself is an epithet. His life story is patterned on that of Śākyamuni but it incorporates many original accounts. Shenrab was born in Olmo Lungring ('Ol-mo lung-ring) situated in Zhang-zhung (the western part of Tibet near Mount Kailasa) or in Tazig, depending on different accounts. Olmo Lungring, designed as an eight-petalled lotus with the sky above it in the form of an eight-spoked wheel, had a mountain at its centre which consisted of nine successive levels symbolising the 'Nine Ways of Bon'. From the four sides of Mount Yungdrung (g.Yung-drung) there flowed four rivers towards the cardinal points. To the south of the mountain there was a palace in which Shenrab was born. The palaces to the west and north were inhabited by Shenrab's wives and children. Olmo Lungring was separated from the rest of the world by an impenetrable mountain range and access to it was gained by an arrow-path (mda'-lam); once Shenrab shot an arrow thus creating a passage. In the past ages, Shenrab and his two brothers studied with a Bon sage. When they had completed their training, they went to the supreme lord of compassion, Shenlha Ökar (gShen-lha 'od-dkar), who advised them how to help beings living in misery. The oldest brother guided living beings during the previous world-age. The second brother, Shenrab, became the teacher of the present world-age and his younger brother will teach in the future.

At the age of thirty-one, Shenrab renounced the world and lived in austerity teaching his doctrines. His propagation of Bon was constantly obstructed by a powerful demon Khyabpa. On one occasion, while pursuing Khyabpa who stole his horses, Shenrab arrived in Tibet; it was his only visit. Before leaving Tibet, Shenrab pronounced a prophecy foretelling Tibet's conversion and gave some instructions to local people on how to placate various deities and exorcise demons. Having returned to Olmo Lungring he died after a period of illness and passed into *nirvāṇa*. Shenrab's son Mucho (Mucho ldem-drug) continued to teach the doctrines, put them on record and then translated them with a group of translators so that they could be propagated in many countries. The tradition that spread to India became the origin of the Śākya clan from which issued Śākyamuni Buddha as an emanation of Shenrab; other sources assert that Shenrab and Śākyamuni were brothers.

Bon was propagated in Tibet (the name of Tibet or Bod is seen as being derived from the term 'Bon') well before the arrival of the first king. The Bon scriptures were brought to Zhang-zhung by Mucho's six disciples and translated first into Zhang-zhung languages and then into Tibetan. The first diffusion of Bon in Tibet ended with the death of Drigum who died in retribution for suppressing Bon. The Bon doctrines were revived during the reign of Drigum's son Pude Kung-gyel (sPu-lde gung-rgyal) and continued to flourish until the reign of Trisong Detsen as the religion of Tibetan people. With the conversion of Trisong Detsen to Buddhism and his support of it, Bon began to be persecuted. The Bonpo adherents were forced to become Buddhists, many were exiled and some killed. Dranpa Namkha (Dran-pa nam-mkha'), one of the chief Bonpo figures of the eighth century, deliberately became Buddhist in order to preserve Bon. With the help of his companions he recorded many Bon scriptures and hid them in different places for future rediscovery by his successors. As evil omens occurred and Trisong Detsen became ill, the Bonpos were allowed to resume some of their practices in certain parts of Tibet.

The period from the eighth to the eleventh century is submerged in darkness and silence. The Bonpos speak of a third diffusion of Bon in the eleventh century which coincided with the second propagation of Buddhism. The Bonpos assert that as far as the continuation of monastic ordinations was concerned, both Buddhists and Bonpos went to eastern Tibet to receive monastic vows from the same group of people. From the eleventh century onwards the Bon tradition often refers to itself as the New Bon (Bon-gsar). The first Bonpo texts were rediscovered by three laymen at Samye. A large number of texts were rediscovered by Shechen Luga (gShen-chen klu-dga', 996–1035), a married man who practised asceticism. Shechen found so many *terma* texts that some of his Buddhist contemporaries accused him of plagiarism. He acquired a good number of followers who spread Bon. Three of Shechen's disciples were entrusted with the continuation of three different traditions. To Druchen Namkha ('Bru-chen nam-mkha'), whose family came from Gilgit ('Bru-zha), he entrusted the study of metaphysics and cosmology. The Druchen family patronised the Bon religion until the nineteenth century. Then it ended its male line, when for the second time the Panchen Lama's reincarnation was found in this family. The second disciple, Zhuye Legpo (Zhu-yas legs-po), continued the Dzogchen teachings, while the third one, Paton (sPa-ston dpal-mchog), upheld the tantric tradition. In the course of the following centuries, the Bonpos built a number of monasteries all over Tibet.

The Bonpo scriptures were systematised in the fifteenth century by Sherab Gyaltshan (Shes-rab rgyal-mtshan), who classified them into two major groups, the *Kanjur* (bka'-'gyur) and the *Katen* (bka'-rten). The *Kanjur* texts attributed to Shenrab consist of 116 volumes and include doctrinal expositions. The *Kanjur* also includes texts that narrate ancient cosmogonic myths and three biographies of Shenrab. The *Katen* group of 131 volumes, like the Buddhist *Tanjur*, contains commentaries, rituals, works on arts and crafts and so on. One text that is particularly cherished by the Bonpos is called *Zhang-zhung Nyengyu* (Zhang-zhung snyan-brgyud) and represents an uninterrupted tradition of *Dzogchen* teachings.

The fundamental teachings, like those of the Buddhist, propound the nature of impermanence, the law of karma, and the path towards enlightenment. The Bonpos recognise the *bodhisattva* ideal and the three Buddha-Bodies. The technical terminology differs from the Buddhist one but it expresses the same concepts. On the whole the Bonpo doctrines as recorded in their scriptures represent an amalgamation not only of texts that parallel those of the Buddhists but also of a vast quantity of magical rituals, various legendary accounts and cosmogonic myths, some of which echo old Iranian and Central Asian cosmogonies.

The Bon doctrines are classified in two different ways. One classification divides them into five categories under the name of 'The Four Portals and the Treasury as Fifth' (sGo-bzhi mdzod-lnga). The second classification includes all the elements of the first one and is called 'The Bon of the Nine Successive Stages' (Theg-pa rim-dgu'i bon) or simply the Nine Vehicles of Bon.

The first vehicle, 'The Vehicle of the Shen of Magic', deals with different methods of prediction such as astrology, divination, examination of omens, medical diagnosis and with ransom rituals. 'The Vehicle of the Shen of Worldly Appearances' explains the origins of gods and demons, exorcism and different ransom rituals to gratify or to subjugate gods. The third vehicle, 'The Shen of Magical Illusion', deals with fierce rituals that aim to destroy completely the adverse powers. Some of those rituals include a *linga* (effigy) which represents the enemy to be eliminated. The person or demon concerned is summoned to reside in the *linga* and then ritually destroyed. The fourth vehicle, 'The Shen of Existence', is concerned with funeral ceremonies. The next vehicle, 'The Vehicle of Lay Followers', refers to the religious practices to be performed by lay people. Stress is placed on pursuing life according to the ten virtues and the six perfections. The monastic life is dealt with in the sixth vehicle. It describes in detail the monastic discipline and ordinations. The last three vehicles deal with tantric teachings and practices. The 'Vehicle of Pure Sound' propounds higher tantric practices, theories of spiritual realisations and rituals. 'The Way of Primeval Shen' explains different states of meditation, circumstances of tantric practices, the manner of choosing masters and tantric partners, and various tantric requirements. 'The Supreme Vehicle' is represented by the *Dzogchen* teachings that have very much in common with those of the Nyimapas.

The Bonpos survived until the present time. In Tibet they were greatly outnumbered by the Buddhist population. The Tibetan Buddhists have always frowned upon the Bonpos and considered them to be dangerous magicians. However, on the whole they were left in peace, apart from a few open attacks on them, and a number of them studied in Buddhist monasteries. Some Tibetans speak of white and black Bonpo magic. White magic refers to harmless magical activities and black magic to fierce and demoniac performances. The Bonpos themselves know these terms but do not retain a living tradition of such practices. It all seems to be a mere echo of the remote past.

Further Reading

Hoffmann, H. *The Religions of Tibet* (Greenwood Press, London, 1961)

Karmay, S.G. *The Treasury of Good Sayings: A Tibetan History of Bon* (Oxford University Press, Oxford, 1972)

Nebesky-Wojkowitz, René de *Oracles and Demons of Tibet* (Graz, 1975)

Snellgrove, D.L. and Richardson, H.E. *A Cultural History of Tibet* (Weidenfeld & Nicolson, London, 1968)

Snellgrove, D.L. *The Nine Ways of Bon* (Oxford, 1967; reprinted Boulder, Colorado 1980)

—— *Indo-Tibetan Buddhism, Indian Buddhists and their Tibetan Successors* (London, 1987)

Stein, R.A. *Tibetan Civilization* (Faber & Faber, London, 1972)

Tucci, G. *Tibetan Painted Scrolls*, 3 vols. (Rome, 1949)

—— *The Religions of Tibet* (Routledge & Kegan Paul, London, 1980)

Waddell, L.A. *Buddhism and Lamaism of Tibet* (London, 1895; reprinted New Delhi, 1974)

44 Buddhism in Mongolia

Bulcsu Siklós

It may come as a surprise to some to discover that the religion most prevalent in areas inhabited by Mongolians was, and to an extent still is, Buddhism. Other types of Mahāyāna Buddhism, the types practised in Tibet, China and Japan, are easily distinguishable both from each other and from the parent Indian form, while Mongolian Buddhism, even when its existence is acknowledged, is usually treated as identical to its Tibetan antecedent, and hence subsumable under it.

The Mongols were relative latecomers both to Buddhism and to the historical scene. It is true that Mongolian tribes, often in alliance with other Altaic peoples, had made numerous inroads into China itself from early in Chinese recorded history, but even so, the sense of historical continuity relating the Mongols to world events and enabling them to be treated independently of other (in Chinese terms) 'barbarian' groups in matters of religion dates only from the thirteenth century, after Činggis (Jengiz, Gengis, etc.) Khan's unification of the Mongol tribes into a cohesive whole. The religion of the Mongols of this time and earlier could be classed as Shamanism, although it is hardly possible to treat all the Mongolian tribes together, the distinction between the majority nomadic groups and the more northerly sedentary tribes being particularly important to bear in mind. It has been suggested that Central Asian nomadic nations in general came quite late to Shamanism, perhaps borrowing most of their shamanic concepts from the forested areas further north.

The Mongols also came into contact with various Iranian religious concepts during this early period, primarily through their association with the Uighurs, a Turkic-speaking people who had converted to Manichaeism in the eighth century. The number of religious terms and divine appellations taken over from Iranian languages and still in use is quite considerable—for example the chief of the traditional shamanist grouping of the 33 *tngri* or 'gods' is known as Khormusta in Mongol, and is equivalent to the problematic Zurvanite deity Ohrmazd, principle of light, and to the Mazdean Ahura Mazdā. In fact, looking at the various *tngri*, whether in the above grouping of 33 or in the commoner grouping of 99 (44 'eastern' and 55 'western') or indeed looking at Mongolian shamanic practice in general, it is almost impossible to sort out all the various Iranian, Taoist, Manchu-Tunguz shamanist and, later, Buddhist ideas which might have come into play in forming what might be called the Mongolian shamanic synthesis.

During the thirteenth century, whilst Mongolian armies were busy laying most of Asia waste, the Mongol emperors were encouraging a great number of foreign administrators and religious practitioners to come to the Mongol court, with the delegation of various tasks to these non-Mongols being done fully on the grounds of suitability, and not on the grounds of supposed cultural superiority. It is probably on similar grounds that the Mongols decided to adopt the Uighur alphabetic script (derived ultimately from Syriac through Sogdian), rather than the more prestigious and unsuitable Chinese script, the adoption of which would have drawn the Mongols into the Chinese cultural sphere and led them down a totally different religious path from the one they eventually followed.

The numerous Tibetans at the Mongol court were in the main representatives of the most influential political and religious force in Tibet at that time—the Sakya (Sa-skya) sect of Tibetan Buddhism. Although in time the Sakya lamas came to be regarded as religious specialists at the court, much as Uighurs were regarded as administrative specialists, the initial contacts of the Mongols with Tibetan Buddhism were exclusively political, and stemmed from the extremely wise Tibetan decision to submit unconditionally to the Mongols. Any other decision would surely have led to the near-total destruction of Tibetan civilisation and of that particular form of Buddhism which is now associated so strongly with Tibet. The loss would have been compounded by the fact that the North Indian antecedent of Tibetan Buddhism was at this time systematically being extinguished by the Muslims.

The Sakya monks at the Mongol court managed to arouse a considerable amount of interest in Buddhism, especially during the reign of Khubilai (Kublai) Khan (1260–94), who seems to have taken a personal interest in the new religion. This was in the main due to the practical instruction he received in Buddhist practice from the most important figure in the history of this, the 'First Conversion' of the Mongols, a certain 'Phags pa blo gros rgyal mtshan or, for short, 'Phags pa (1235–80). His adroitness in arousing Khubilai's interest in Buddhism led to the initiation of Kubilai himself and his consort, Camui, into the tantric cycle of Hevajra, and to the conversion of the whole imperial court. Numerous honours were heaped upon 'Phags pa, who was also asked to create a new script in which, hopefully, all the main languages of the Mongol Empire could be written. Known as the 'phags pa or dörbelǰin ('square') script, it was rather cumbersome and did not outlive the Yüan (Mongol) dynasty.

Just as during the Second Conversion of the Mongols to Buddhism, which dates from the time of the later Ming dynasty, the worship of Tantric deities in their wrathful aspects was much more prominent than any other aspect of Lamaism in Mongolian religious life. Apart from Hevajra, mentioned above, and other major meditational deities assigned Buddha rank, several of the protector deities (of Bodhisattva rank, considered responsible for safeguarding the Doctrine) were extremely popular. Such wrathful deities, bedecked with ornaments of human bone, spattered with human blood and fat, and often portrayed in a state of sexual union with female partners, seemed to have appealed to the Mongol court and high-ranking military—certainly these deities were considerably more terrifying and licentious than the old shamanic gods. It should also be mentioned that the practice of Tantra in many ways stands very close to that of Shamanism. There is not too much difference between the tantric assimilation of one's 'body, speech and mind' to those of the deity, achieved through visualisation, and the shamanic assimilation of the deity into oneself, in other words, the attainment of possession. Naturally, tantric practice precluded the social function of the shaman, and added certain soteriological, eschatological and indeed philosophical ideas to the world-view of the Mongol practitioner. This last aspect should be stressed, since it is commonly stated that the Mongol court limited itself to misunderstanding, and consequently indulging in, the violent and sexual side of Tantra. This side of Tantra certainly was part of the appeal of Buddhism, but the closeness of a large part of its basic practice to Shamanism and its more elaborate imagery helped ensure the victory of this very special form of Buddhism over the various other religions competing for support at the imperial court—Taosim, Nestorian Christianity, Manichaeism, Islam and even Catholicism.

The First Conversion of the Mongols to Buddhism did not go very deep, and was confined almost exclusively to the Mongol aristocracy and military. The average Mongol still worshipped the old gods, the gods of natural phenomena, the god Eternal Blue Heaven and many others, and had probably never seen a lama or even heard of Buddhism. So, although by the time of the last Mongol emperor, Toγan Temür (1333–68), part of the *Kanjur* (the first section of the Tibetan Canon) had been translated into Mongolian and several monasteries founded, Shamanism remained the characteristic religion of Mongolia at large.

The eclectic and analytical studies of that most learned of Tibetan mystics, Tsonkapa (Tsong-kha-pa, 1357–1419), provided the inspiration for the development and growth of the first indigenous

Tibetan school of Buddhism, the Gelugpa (dGe-lugs-pa). Throughout north China in the early Ming period considerable interest was shown in this highly esoteric and 'magical' form of Buddhism, and the resultant presence of large numbers of Gelugpa lamas caused considerable resentment in orthodox Chinese and imperial circles. This resentment culminated in the anti-Buddhist persecutions of the late Ming, in the face of which lamas fled in large numbers to the more congenial environment of south and west Mongolia, initiating the Second Conversion of the Mongols to Lamaism, this time in its Gelugpa form. The fragmented political nature of Mongolia at this time ensured that certain Mongol groups, initially seeking political support from a mostly unified Tibet, managed to make Buddhism their own within a few decades, whilst other, more isolated groups remained shamanist and had to wait until the nineteenth century for their first proper contact with Lamaism.

During the early stages of the Second Conversion in the mid-sixteenth century, south-east Mongolia had a true *cakravartin* (universal—and pious—monarch) in the person of Altan Khan. His meeting with bSod nams rgya mtsho resulted in the rapid conversion of all south-east Mongolian tribes to Lamaism, the outlawing of certain shamanistic practices (notably sacrifice) in the area, the consolidation of Gelugpa authority in Tibet itself and the conferral of the title Dalai Lama on bSod nams himself. The title 'Dalai Lama' is an abbreviation of the Mongolian *bilig-ün dalai lama*, 'Ocean-of-Wisdom-Teacher'. Since bSod nams conferred the title of 'Dalai Lama' posthumously on two of his predecessors, he counts as the third in the lineage of *rgyal-bas* (lit. 'victors' i.e. Dalai Lamas). After the death of the Third Dalai Lama, the Gelugpa returned these favours by accepting a newly-born relative of Altan Khan as the reincarnation of the Dalai Lama—a privilege indeed.

The process of conversion continued in similar ways until all Mongol territories were affected. One of the most common methods employed was straightforward bribery:

> In order to begin the spread of the Buddha's doctrine . . . the Tüsiyetü Khan of the Khorchin lets it be publicly known that he will give a horse to whoever learns by heart the summary of the Doctrine, and a cow to whoever can recite the *Yamāntaka-dhāraṇi* by heart.
> (From a biography of Neyiči Toyin (1557–1653); quoted from Heissig, pp. 36f.)

Gelugpa authorities frequently objected to this sort of activity, especially as it encouraged tantric practice without prior training or initiation, but in the long run it was probably to their own advantage that their warnings were scarcely heeded.

Merely teaching *mantras* and various invocations at a popular level would hardly have ensured Lamaism's lasting success in Mongolia. Institutions for the study of the doctrine, monastic training, translation, printing and so forth were soon established in most Mongol territories. Most characteristic were the numerous unattended temples known as *süme*, prevalent in nomadic regions, at which nomadic lamas would assemble only on festival days to perform specific rites before once again rejoining their herds.

Before we go on to discuss Ch'ing times, one individual of considerable interest should be mentioned, Öndür gegen (1635–1723), the first in the reincarnation lineage of the *rJe btsun dam pa khutuγtu*, who was primarily responsible for the ground gained by the Gelugpa in Khalkha ('Outer') Mongolia at the expense of other Tibetan schools. It may indeed have been a gesture of reconciliation on the part of the Gelugpa that Öndür gegen himself was recognised as an incarnation of the historian Tāranātha who had belonged to the heterodox Jo nang school of Tibetan Buddhism. The Jo nang pas were considered aberrant by all other schools for holding the concept of a type of 'emptiness' which was non-relative. Their monasteries were taken over by the Gelugpa in the seventeenth century.

The Manchu emperors of the Ch'ing dynasty saw in Lamaism a useful means by which to pacify the Mongols, arch-troublemakers that they were, and took on the role of chief patrons of Lamaism in all Mongol areas under their control (collectively known as Inner Mongolia). Lamaism flourished as never before, especially from the time of the K'ang Hsi Emperor (1654–1722) onwards. K'ang Hsi himself seems to have taken a personal interest in the alien religion, and was instrumental in summoning Ngag dbang blo bzang chos ldan (1642–1714, the first in the reincarnation series of the *lCang skya khutuγ tus*) to Peking to take up permanent residence there as the chief incarnate lama of Inner Mongolia. This encouraged the growth of his capital as a Lamaist centre and prevented Mongols being drawn to the natural headquarters of the Doctrine, Lhasa. The Manchus were concerned about the possibility, real in their eyes, of the development of a lamaist 'state' directed from Lhasa with the Mongols supplying the military wing. They even went so far as to construct a smaller version of the Potala, the Dalai Lama's Lhasa palace, at Jehol, the emperor's summer residence.

The Yung Cheng Emperor (1723–36) was by all accounts an ardent Buddhist with an interest in Zen as well as Lamaism. He turned his childhood palace into the famous Yung-Ho-Kung, which soon became the major Lamaist temple in Peking where the *lCang skya khutuγtus* would, with Imperial co-operation, pick the names of prospective reincarnations of high-ranking lamas from a huge golden urn.

More and more high-ranking incarnates were being drawn to Peking throughout the seventeenth and eighteenth centuries, out of the many who had been newly confirmed by the Manchu Court. This honour was freely given to any lama who had rendered some service to the court or to Lamaism in general, and so the number of incarnates grew to almost unmanageable proportions. By 1900 there were 14 incarnate lamas in Peking itself, about 160 in Inner Mongolia, some 120 in Outer Mongolia and 35 in the Kokonor region, a total of some 326—more than the total number of Gelugpa incarnates recognised by the Manchu court for Tibet itself.

Perhaps the most remarkable figure of eighteenth-century Lamaism in Mongolia was the *mergen lama-yin gegen*, bLo bzang bstan pa'i rgyal mtshan, who was single-handedly responsible for the compilation of what could be termed a Mongolian national liturgy incorporating elements both of Buddhism and of Shamanism. A scholar of considerable ability, he tried to amass as many authentic texts relating to Shamanism as he could, and produced vast numbers of liturgical texts treating the worship of shamanistic deities in Buddhist guise.

The end of the eighteenth century marked the beginning of the decline of Mongolian Lamaism. Literary and religious activity still continued, though in Inner Mongolia it was becoming increasingly difficult to finance large-scale projects because of the impoverishment and instability of the Ch'ing (brought about in part by increasing European intervention). The situation was better in Outer Mongolia; it was from here that Lamaism started spreading northwards to Buryat Mongolia which was still fully shamanist in the early nineteenth century—indeed, many parts of Buryat Mongolia remained exclusively shamanist until the establishment of Soviet rule.

With the formation of the Mongolian People's Republic after the death of the eighth and last *rJe btsun dam pa khutuγtu* in 1924, both Shamanism and Lamaism were constitutionally prohibited in what had been Outer Mongolia. In Inner Mongolia after the fall of the Ch'ing in 1911, Lamaism managed to hang on, even though it was officially unsupported and frowned upon. The political and economic situation in Inner Mongolia was utterly chaotic during the first half of this century—monasteries owed vast amounts of money and were liable to be sacked or destroyed by any number of roving bands of marauders. Worries were compounded by reports of persecutions of Buddhists in both the Mongolian People's Republic and in Buryat Mongolia, especially after the so-called 'Lama Risings' of the 1930s, and Inner Mongolia, just like Tibet, was unable to escape the inevitable destruction of all its cultural institutions during the Chinese Cultural Revolution of the 1960s.

Further Reading

Heissig, W. *The Religions of Mongolia* (Routledge & Kegan Paul, London, 1980)

Lessing, F.D. *Yung-Ho-Kung—An Iconography of the Lamaist Cathedral in Peking*, vol. 1 (Stockholm, 1942)

Miller, R.J. *Monasteries and Cultural Change in Inner Mongolia*, Asiatische Forschungen, vol. 2 (Wiesbaden, 1959)
Pozoneyev, A.M. *Religion and Ritual in Society—Lamaist Buddhism in Late Nineteenth-Century Mongolia*, ed. J.R. Krueger (Bloomington, Indiana, 1978)

Part 5 Traditional Religions

Editor:
Peter Clarke

45 Introduction

Peter Clarke

The term 'traditional' as used here to refer to the Australian Aboriginal, African, Melanesian, Maori and North, Mesoamerican and South American Indian religions covered in this section of the volume is not meant to suggest that these religions are static and unchanging, but is simply one way of distinguishing them from the major world religions which have spread themselves more widely across many different cultures and which tend to be, therefore, less confined to and by any one specific socio-cultural matrix. Indeed, it is very likely, given that they are, with some exceptions, in a sense non-literate and for that reason among others highly eclectic, that traditional religions have been more flexible and tolerant of change than those excluding, literate religions or religions of the book, the world religions as they are called, whose literary mode of supernatural direction and guidance leaves them in theory at least less room for manoeuvre. Moreover, while the use of the label *traditional* can be somewhat misleading, it is perhaps less so than *primitive* which has been applied to these religions, not only in the sense of early or primeval, but also in the sense of 'lower' and less 'rational' than the religions of what have often been described as the more 'civilised', 'advanced' societies. This view of traditional religions was based not on empirical data but on a theory of social and intellectual development or evolution current in the nineteenth century. According to this evolutionist approach, the term *primitive* referred on the one hand to a stage low down on the scale of social and intellectual development reached by prehistoric man and on the other to those contemporary, non-literate peoples whom, it was assumed, had remained at this same low social and intellectual level. It is clear that evolutionists of this mind tended to make too close a connection between social structure and thought, making development in the latter totally dependent on development in the former. In this century beginning after the First World War, and increasingly from the 1930s, researchers began to produce convincing evidence that not only undermined the two last mentioned propositions but also the premiss concerning the alleged inferiority of the 'primitive' mind, showing that non-literate peoples, though technologically very far from advanced, had developed, none the less, highly complex systems of thought and belief.[1] One ethnologist, the Austrian, Father Wilhelm Schmidt, went so far as to maintain that the hunting-gathering, forest Pygmies of central Africa, far from being animists or fetishists, later 'degenerations' of religion, were in fact monotheists, and that since they represented the oldest surviving culture on earth this was the earliest form of religion. It hardly needs to be said, however, that any attempt by the ethnologist or any other scholar to trace the earliest form of religion has encountered and will continue to encounter unsurmountable obstacles, the main one being the lack of historical data.

This has also been a problem for the student of traditional religion and perhaps explains why these religions have come to be regarded not only as static but also the product of and confined to a particular society. The contributions on African and Native American religions in particular show how misleading this view of traditional religion can be. In both instances, as in many other cases, the traditional religions in question spread across numerous political, economic, geographical and cultural boundaries and underwent considerable development and change.

For the most part, it has been the social scientist and, in particular the social anthropologist, who has provided most of the information we have about these religions, some focusing their attention almost exclusively on the functions of these religions within the social system, others on their symbolic and philosophic content and others (Chapter 46 on Shamanism being an example) on both function and meaning.

But what about the possible application of other disciplines, such as history, to this subject? Can this discipline, for example, contribute to a deeper understanding of traditional religions? The fact that many of these religions are in a sense non-literate religions not only makes the task of documenting their history extremely difficult but also opens it up to a great deal of speculation and conjecture. But, as several of the contributions to this section show, this should not deter the student from attempting such a study. The kind of written historical document rightly valued so much by the Western-trained historian although of great importance is not everything. The historian can usefully attempt a study of traditional religion by the judicious use of oral tradition and other materials such as those provided by the archaeologist, art historian and linguist among others, as a number of the contributions to this section, and in particular those on African and Native American religion, show. Moreover, in some instances traditional societies have their own 'written' records of their history, as the chapter on Native American religion illustrates. The 'outside world' has also documented, but not always very accurately or objectively as we have seen, something of the beliefs and practices of these religions, and here again we can look to all the contributions to this section for examples. It is both possible and fruitful, then, to attempt the historical study of 'traditional' religions.[2] Moreover, a study such as this might usefully examine these religions in a wider cultural, geographical and religious context. Although their contact with literate cultures and the wider world in general has been uneven it is, however, the case, that for a relatively long time many of the traditional religions, far from existing in a self-contained traditional universe have been part of a complex sphere of relationships that extended to contact with the world religions, and which in varying degrees involved contact with the world of books, most often at first the religious books or scriptures of Christianity and Islam, or the ideas contained in those books. And the result has very often been, not the complete demise of the former but, as the contribution on Melanesian religion illustrates, the development and modification of the beliefs and practices of both the traditional religion and the world religion in question.

But how long can traditional religion survive the impact of these world religions, regarded increasingly by many in traditional societies as religions of progress, and the process of 'modernisation' itself? This question is addressed directly in the contribution on Australian Aboriginal religion. There are examples, as the author of the account on North American Indian religion shows, where in the past forces from outside have brought about the virtual collapse of traditional religion. Moreover, elsewhere in this volume contributors have pointed to the rapid growth of Christianity and Islam over the past one hundred and fifty years in, for example, Africa, and to the fundamental changes brought about by these two world religions in the social and religious life of African societies. Under their impact and that of the forces of modernity all things traditional, including religion, appear to have literally fallen apart.

But changes and developments have not all been in one direction only. As is the case in Melanesian religion, and the same holds for African religion, traditional religion has not only shown in the recent past a remarkable capacity to develop and adapt its own beliefs and practices when confronted by both the world religions and 'modernity' but has also greatly influenced much of the belief and practice of these same world religions and to an extent the direction in which the forces of modernity have sought to steer traditional society. Moreover, there are examples, the Maori religion being one and Afro-Brazilian religion another, where what is in essence a traditional religious life has developed a way of interacting with and settling down alongside a world religion in a modern setting.

Furthermore, although fewer people now refer to themselves as traditional religionists, these religions continue to appeal for a variety of different reasons to many from all walks of life, whether Western-educated or not. In parts of Africa, as one contributor shows, not only have traditional religions 'intermixed with the main movements of twentieth-century change' and 'turned out to be alive and important at the heart of revolutionary movements' but they have also countered new ideas and approaches in a number of fields, including modern medicine and technology, which have not been able to undermine confidence in that important insight at the heart of traditional religion: that solutions to health and environmental problems have an important relational dimension. And we see from the contribution on Australian Aboriginal religion how important Aboriginal myth and ceremony have been in determining Aborigines' legal rights to land. Traditional religions, then, though under threat, continue to be of importance to many both at the level of meaning and function and it would, therefore, be premature to predict their demise.

Notes

1. For an example see E.E. Evans-Pritchard, *The Nuer* (Oxford university Press, Oxford, 1956).

2. In addition to the contributions to this section of the volume see also T.O. Ranger and I.N. Kimambo (eds.), *The Historical Study of African Religion* (University of California Press, Berkeley, 1972).

46 Shamanism

I.M. Lewis

Shamanism is not, as Weston La Barre comprehensively claims, the origin of *religion*, but rather of *religions* in whose decline and fall it certainly plays a highly significant role. By 'shamanism' we mean the religious activities of inspired priests or shamans who control cosmic spiritual forces and regularly incarnate them. The term *shaman*, more familiar in American and continental than in British ethnography, is generally traced to the language of the Tungus reindeer herders of the Lake Baikal region of the Soviet Union and, according to the great Russian medical ethnographer Shirokogoroff, like its Manchu cognate *saman* means literally 'one who is excited, moved, or raised'. Its first appearance in a major European language seems to have been in seventeenth-century Russian. More particularly among the Tungus, a shaman is a man or woman who has acquired the power of mastering spirits and who knows how to introduce them into his body. Frequently the shaman permanently incarnates his spirits, controlling their manifestations, and going into states of trance on appropriate occasions. As Shirokogoroff expresses it, the shaman's body is thus a 'placing' or receptacle for his spirits, and it is through his power over these incarnate forces that the shaman has the authority to treat and control afflictions caused by malign, pathogenic spirits in other victims. The Tungus shaman is consequently literally a 'master' of spirits, although, as we shall see, the spirits can, at times, overpower their tamer and controller. In this classical arctic setting, shamanism is firmly embedded in the Tungus clan structure. So the shamanistic master of spirits guarantees the well-being of his clansmen, controlling the clan's ancestral spirits which would otherwise wreak havoc amongst his kin. These domesticated spirits can, moreover, be employed to counteract hostile alien spirits and to divine and treat local illnesses and other problems and misfortunes. Here the main diagnostic and therapeutic ritual is the public shamanistic seance in the course of which the shaman seeks to establish contact with the spirits of the upper or lower worlds. Shirokogoroff vividly describes the typical setting:

> The rhythmic music and singing, and later the dancing of the shaman, gradually involve every participant more and more in a collective action. When the audience begins to repeat the refrains together with the assistants, only those who are defective fail to join the chorus. The tempo of the action increases, the shaman with a spirit is no ordinary man or relative, but is a 'placing' (i.e. incarnation of the spirit); the spirit acts together with the audience and this is felt by everyone. The state of many participants is now near to that of the shaman himself, and only a strong belief that when the shaman is there the spirit may only enter him, restrains the participants from being possessed in mass by the spirit. This is a very important condition of shamanizing which does not however reduce mass susceptibility to the suggestion, hallucinations, and unconscious acts produced in a state of mass ecstasy. When the shaman feels that the audience is with him and follows him he becomes still more active and this effect is transmitted to his audience. After shamanizing, the audience recollects various moments of the performance, their great psycho-physiological emotion and the hallucinations of sight and hearing which they have experienced. They then have a deep satisfaction—much greater than that from emotions produced by theatrical and musical performances, literature and general artistic phenomena of the European complex, because in shamanizing the audience at the same time acts and participates.

Shamanism, Spirit-Possession and Ecstasy

Mircea Eliade argues that: 'The specific element of shamanism is not the incorporation of spirits by the shaman, but the ecstasy provoked by the ascension to the sky or by the descent to Hell: the incorporation of spirits and possession by them are universally distributed phenomena, but they do not necessarily belong to shamanism in the strict sense.' While we must welcome Eliade's recognition of the link between shamanism and ecstasy, which we shall develop here, it will be clear that his attempt to distinguish between shamanism and possession does not accord with the Tungus primary evidence. This, however, has not deterred the ingenious Belgian structural anthropologist, Luc de Heusch, from taking this supposed distinction between shamanism and possession and making it the corner-stone of his ambitious, formalist theory of religion. Shamanism, de Heusch maintains, is the ascent of man to the gods, possession the reverse. As an 'ascensual metaphysic' the first is, naturally, the opposite of the second which is an 'incarnation'. Where, in the former, man ascends, in the latter the spirits descend. Possession, moreover, according to de Heusch, can itself be divided into two types. The first, characterised as 'inauthentic' assumes the form of an undesired illness, a malign demonic assault which must be treated by the expulsion or *exorcism* of the intrusive demons. The second, a sublime religious experience, is in contrast a 'joyous Dionysian epiphany'. This highly prized state of exaltation is cultivated in what becomes a 'sacred theatre'.

These misleading contrasts, based on the tone of the emotional experience involved, are further confounded by later writers notably by Douglas in her *Natural Symbols*, although Bourguignon, who writes of 'negative' and 'positive' possession, clearly appreciates that the distinction may not have such far-reaching implications. The truth is that, just as there is generally little point in distinguishing between shamanism and possession since both occur together in the arctic *locus classicus* and widely elsewhere, so the distinction between benign and malign possession *experiences* can be highly misleading. In the first place, it is simply not true that what is perceived as a negative or even traumatic event is necessarily interpreted in the same vein as irrefutable evidence of demonic intervention. On the contrary, amongst the Tungus and all over the world, traumatic *episodes*, personal calamities and even physically crippling afflictions regularly serve as the harbingers of the divine call. This is not to say, of course, that where experiences of this kind are actually interpreted as signs of satanic possession they are not treated by exorcism. But, frequently, the situation is far from being as clear-cut as this neat intellectual dichotomy might seem to imply. There is not invariably any direct parallelism between the emotional quality of an experience and its interpretation: what begins as an illness requiring treatment to appease the spirit responsible may gradually develop into a mutual accommodation where, as we would say, 'the patient learns to live with his problem'. In this extended process, which is likely to include intermittent recurrence of the original symptoms, a new and binding relationship develops between the human subject and the spirit with the increasing domestication of the latter. The final step in this long-drawn out initiatory process occurs when, having fully demonstrated his power to control spirits, the ex-patient begins to diagnose and treat similar spiritual affliction in others.

Thus, as St Paul's traumatic experience on the road to Damascus reminds us, what ends in ecstasy may begin in agony. Indeed, those who vainly seek divine inspiration from other shamans may only succeed in achieving it after much self-inflicted mortification. So, in a characteristic account, an Eskimo shaman explained to one observer, Rasmussen, how, after unsuccessfully attempting to learn the shamanistic mysteries from others, he wandered off on his own into the wilderness of the arctic Tundra. There, he explained to Rasmussen,

> I soon became melancholy. I would sometimes fall to weeping and feel unhappy without knowing why. Then for no reason all would suddenly be changed, and I felt a great inexplicable joy, a joy so powerful that I could not restrain it, but had to break in to song, a mighty song, with room for only one word: joy, joy! And I had to use the full strength of my voice. And then in the midst of such a fit of mysterious and overwhelming delight I became a shaman, not knowing myself how it came about. But I was a shaman. I could see and hear in a totally different way. I had gained my enlightenment, the shaman's light of brain and body, and this in such a manner that it was not only I who could see through the darkness of life, but the

same bright light also shone out from me, imperceptible to human beings but visible to all spirits of earth and sky and sea, and these now came to me to become my helping spirits.

The importance of recognising the ambivalent character of the announcement of the shamanistic vocation cannot be overestimated. It is precisely for this reason that no absolute value can be attached to displays of reluctance in responding to the call. The universal mystical convention, here, is to protest one's unworthiness, so that the more one does so (e.g. through suffering affliction) the more one asserts the imperative importance of the divine command. Thus, manifest reluctance becomes the conventional mode of signalling the urgency and significance of the divine call. It consequently becomes impossible to attempt to assess the 'authenticity' of inspiration in these terms.

We may conveniently note here, also, that possession and trance do not necessarily always coincide. Trance is a physiological state; but possession is a cultural construct and may be used to interpret the condition of people who are clearly not in any sense in states of trance. Thus, a possessed person may only experience trance from time to time, and especially in shamanistic rituals. Indeed, as Oesterreich acutely observes of the traditional Christian exorcist rituals, as practised, for example, at Loudon, it is frequently only at the climax of the rites designed to expel the spirits that the afflicted victims actually fell into trance!

Shamanism and spirit possession are, then, cultural theories of trance, of states of altered consciousness, and more widely of illness and affliction. The ambivalence which we have been stressing is fully consistent with the fact, well known to mystics of all religions and periods, that religious ecstasy can be readily produced by two apparently diametrically opposed methods: by sensory deprivation (e.g. fasting, wandering alone in the wilderness and so on), and by sensory over-stimulation with hallucinogenic drugs, music, dancing and so on. (Illnesses and other traumas may sometimes include elements of both these extremes.) Since we are now liable to overemphasise the role of drugs, we should note here that even LSD is regarded generally by pharmacologists and psychiatrists as possessing no 'drug-specific' features, being rather as Groff suggests an 'all-powerful, unspecific amplifier and catalyst of mental processes'. We must applaud the painstaking labours of R.G. Wasson and others in attempting to chart the global distribution of hallucinogenic mushrooms, and we must recognise the importance of these powerful stimulants even in some of the classic shamanistic cultures. Thus as Jochelson, who travelled among the shamanistic peoples of Siberia at the turn of the century, reports of the Koryak:

> Fly-agaric produces intoxication, hallucinations, and delirium. Light forms of intoxication are accompanied by a certain degree of animation and some spontaneity of movements. Many shamans, previous to their seances, eat fly-agaric to

> get into ecstatic states ... Under strong intoxication the senses become deranged; surrounding objects appear either very large or very small, hallucinations set in, spontaneous movements and convulsions! ... attacks of great animation alternate with moments of deep depression.

Yet while acknowledging the significance of drugs here and elsewhere, we must not get things out of proportion as, for instance, John Allegro so manifestly does in his curious book *The Sacred Mushroom and the Cross.* We must not fall into the trap of assuming that shamanism and ecstasy can only be produced with the aid of such powerful pharmacological aids. As we have seen many other well-tried techniques exist in which drugs play no part at all. And from the widest perspective, it is probably in illness and affliction that we find the commonest route to the assumption of the ecstatic vocation.

Cults of Affliction

The shamanistic career, as Siikala has shown, has, characteristically, a tripartite structure, comprising three main phases or episodes. In the first phase, the subject suffers illness or misfortune which is diagnosed as possession by a spiritual power. In the course of treatment by a shaman, the patient is typically induced to behave in a trance-like fashion such that the possessing agency speaks 'in tongues', announcing its reasons for plaguing its victim. In the ensuing dialogue between the shaman and spirit, a bargain is struck, according to which, in return for stated gifts and regular acts of devotion, the spirit consents to allow the patient to recover. This initiation rite removes the immediate affliction at the price of the patient's entry into the ecstatic cult group led by the shaman. The 'cure' is in effect to become a chronic patient. So what began as an involuntary, uncontrolled and unsolicited affliction achieves its apotheosis in regular religious devotion as a cult member where possession is voluntarily solicited (although it may also come at times unbidden). This is the second, longer phase. Here, it is important to note, that once the devotee has learnt the technique of ecstasy, the simplest and lightest of stimuli will regularly succeed in producing trance. So, for example, whenever a cult member hears her spirit-tune being sung or played she is likely to go into trance with the greatest of ease. As M.J. Field points out, in shamanistic cultures, people are conditioned to go into trance at the appropriate time and place much as those in Western Europe are conditioned to fall asleep in a comfortable bed in a dark, quiet room.

With increasing mastery of the spirits, the ex-patient enters the final phase, that of becoming a shaman with the power to cure and control spirit-caused afflictions. This pattern recalls T.S. Eliot's image of the 'Wounded Surgeon' and is remarkably similar to the initiatory 'training analysis' ritual (i.e. simulated illness and cure) by means of which psychoanalysts are recruited and trained. We must not conclude, however, that shamanism is merely an inferior, rustic form of psychoanalysis or psychotherapy. There are significant parallels in both directions. But we must remember, as Shirokogoroff long ago noted, that if the shaman's therapy only works in the treatment of the psychological aspects of his patients' complaints, his practice is not limited only to psychogenic or psychological illnesses. The range of disorders which he is asked to treat is far wider than that normally encountered in psychiatric practice in Europe or America.

If, consequently, the shaman's role transcends that of the primitive psychiatrist, what of his own mental state? Here the received tradition that shamans are generally mentally unstable, even acute schizophrenics, or at best 'half-healed madmen', requires drastic revision. As Shirokogoroff himself observed amongst the Tungus, 'The shaman may begin his life career with a psychosis, but he cannot carry on his functions if he cannot master himself.' The truth thus is, as we should expect from the range of disorders present in those diagnosed as possessed, that like priests and psychiatrists, the personalities of shamans reveal an equal diversity of types. Indeed, as the uniquely qualified anthropologist and psychiatrist, M.J. Field, has observed of African spirit mediums, effective shamans require strong, stable personalities. Hence the shaman's calling is *not* 'the resort of inadequate maladjusted neurotics and hysterics'. To see these facts in their proper perspective, we should again recall that in shamanistic cultures the initial onset of divine election is highly stereotyped.

We can conveniently begin displaying the utility of our tripartite model of affliction, cure and control by reference to Tarantism as it exists today in the remote and poorer parts of southern Italy. Here, as de Martino shows, entry into the cult is achieved by experiencing an illness or affliction for which the tarantula spider is held responsible. The 'tarantula' has in fact become a composite figure intimately associated with the Apostle Paul. The standard treatment in Salento involves the performance of rituals, with a musical accompaniment (in which the Tarentella is played) at the local chapel, dedicated to the Saint. In these, the Saint is greeted with the extraordinary invocation: 'My St Paul of the Tarantists who pricks the girls in their vaginas; My St Paul of the Serpents who pricks the boys in their testicles.' A typical case-history of a tarantist involves a lovelorn eighteen-year-old orphan girl. This poor creature was prevented from marrying her lover by her poverty, and was 'bitten' at the height of her despair by the deadly tarantula and so forced to join the ranks of the *tarantati*. Later, when she was forcibly abducted by another man, St Paul suddenly appeared before her, commanding her to leave her betrayer and follow him. In the end, a compromise was achieved. The poor girl reluctantly accepted her mortal union as long as she could continue her spiritual adventures with regular participation in the tarantist rites.

Elsewhere, typically, those so recruited into such shamanistic cults are offered the opportunity of eventually becoming shamans themselves. So, in Haitian Voodoo, in the West African *bori* cult, in the north-east African *zar* cult (which has spread from Ethiopia throughout Islamic Africa and along the Persian Gulf coast to Iran), and in countless other similar movements, chronic patients graduate to becoming doctors. Where they exist as underground heretical sects, or Dionysian mystery religions, only tolerated by the male establishment because they masquerade as therapy, such ecstatic cults appeal particularly to women, and the most committed enthusiasts and those most likely to become shamanistic cult leaders tend to have persistent difficulties with men and problems in sustaining the ideal female role. They consequently appeal especially to infertile women, those with gynaeocological disorders, and those who find the burden of male chauvinistic ascendency particularly galling and hard to bear. This gives these marginal shamanistic cults an aura of female militancy and a claim to be regarded as the authentic founders of Women's Liberation. Married women, with generally successful family lives who are less committed adherents, may, nevertheless, occasionally succumb to possession afflictions, requiring costly treatment in the cult. This is particularly likely to happen at times of domestic crisis. So, for example, a husband's opening moves to contract a second marriage in a polygynous society constitute a typical provocation. The treatment in such circumstances can be so costly that the husband is no longer in a position to proceed with his marital negotiations. Wives, consequently, are always potentially vulnerable, and the treatment demanded by their familiars—costly clothes, jewellery, perfumes and other luxuries—can represent a considerable drain on the family budget. Other women, following the manner of Marie of the Incarnation, dedicate themselves to ecstasy when they are widowed, or have completed their child-bearing role and seek relief from menopausal depression and a new career outside the family. The fact that such incomplete women are regarded by the opposite sex as half-men serves to underline the aggressive, masculine tone of these cults and their Liberationist flavour. These sex-war aspects are further highlighted by the frequent hatred which the spirits involved are said to display towards men, and by the flauntingly aggressive sexuality which some leading women shamans display. Moreover, while possessed, many of the women concerned behave like men, and seize weapons and other accoutrements which symbolise masculinity in their rituals. Their rituals and songs may indeed be a complete parody of those of the world of male-dominated establishment religion. Of course, there is conflict between women in relation to men as Wilson maintains; but this occurs in a wider setting of more generalised sexual conflict in which women manifestly chafe at their subordinate position.

Shamanistic Religions

Ecstasy is not, however, a female monopoly and cannot therefore be explained in the biological terms which the etymology of the word hysteria (i.e. 'womb') suggests. In stratified societies men of low socio-economic status join the ranks of the enthusiasts, either in a single, mixed cult, such as that of Dionysus, or, as in the Sudan and Egypt and widely elsewhere, with two parallel cults—one for upper-class women, and the other for the lowest orders irrespective of their sex. As might be anticipated, in the Indian caste system, while priests belong to the highest caste (Brahmin), shamans, who may rival them in power, are drawn from the lowest castes. In this setting shamanism thus offers an important route to power for the lowliest of men. And, of course, when possessed by a divinity shamans of low status become gods who can openly denounce their superiors and treat them with contempt. So, for instance, M.J. Field reports how in Ghana, 'An obscure little rural priest was moved by his spirit to travel a hundred miles to Kumasi where, endowed with the authority of possession, he forced his way into the presence of the Ashantihene and told him some unpalatable truths'. The mighty Ashanti king was forced to listen to him with respect and reverence.

More generally, and as we should expect, those whose social circumstances render them peculiarly receptive to the ecstatic call change as society changes. So, for example, the ex-slave Cuban cult known as *Santeria* has undergone a remarkable sea change in the years since Fidel Castro's rise to power. Despite its lowly origins translated to the Cuban refugee community in Miami, this has become a flourishing middle-class movement appealing to all those who oppose Fidel Castro and desperately seek an alternative Cuban identity. Similar connections appear to exist between the immensely popular *Umbanda* of contemporary urban Brazil and its more rustic, African precursor, *Candomblé*. With its ambiguous relationship to Catholicism, closely paralleling that of Haitian Voodoo, *Umbanda* is increasingly the effective religion of the urban masses. The most intriguing member of its mixed Afro-Indian-American spirit pantheon is that which, with its childlike innocence and uncertain parentage, seems to merge all these elements in a new, uniquely Brazilian identity as Pressel points out. The potential for dynamic developments of this kind seems to be a marked feature even of the ostensibly most conservative of ecstatic cults. Enthusiasm is a volatile force and spirits readily become literally the 'winds of change', being often, indeed, described as 'winds'.

When, under conditions of external pressure (whether of physical or socio-political origin), ecstatic cults develop into fully-fledged main-line shamanistic religions, they repudiate their lower-class connections. Enthusiasm which celebrates the position of the dominant classes in society can scarcely afford to allow itself to be controlled by the lower orders. Under such conditions, ecstasy becomes one of the principle expressions of orthodox, establishment power. This is generally true of classical arctic shamanism among the Eskimos, Tungus and other Siberian peoples and equally the case in the numerous tiny South American Indian communities where hallucinogenic drugs play such an important role. Although it is debatable whether all small hunting and gathering communities live under as acute environmental pressures as the Eskimos, or as precariously, prima facie there does seem to be some connection between this type of economy and central shamanistic religions. The view that the effervescent, shamanistic style of religiosity is a response to acute pressures of one kind or another tends also to find confirmation in the circumstances surrounding the rise and decline of new religions. Strident, new messianic 'religions of the oppressed' are invariably founded by inspired shamanistic prophets and religious dynamism characteristically finds expression in divine possession. The dialectical interplay between this incarnatory prophetism and an established priesthood can indeed be seen in the original and more recent Tungus material collected by Shirokogoroff and Hoppal respectively. The Tungus distinguish between those shamans who hold stable, priestly offices within the clan and their more volatile colleagues who have no fixed position. It is naturally those who are least secure and most ambitious who affect the most florid forms of ecstasy. In much the same way, the wild prophetic founders of the American Indian Ghost Dance subsequently assumed the more sober roles of priestly shamans. In the syncretic Shinto-Buddhistic tradition in Japan, the figure of the ascetic shaman (*shamon*) plays a complementary role to the spirit-inspired medium (*miko*). In feudal Japan, apparently, it was not unusual, as Blacker shows, to find an ascetic husband married to a female medium. Today, however, perhaps as in the Soviet Union with the marginalisation of these beliefs, women shamans seem to be increasingly prevalent in a society which the Japanese scholar K. Sasaki describes as 'a hotbed of spirit possession and shamanism'.

Yet if shamanism seems to thrive in circumstances of constraint and privation which it seeks to evade or transcend, there is also evidence to suggest that exactly the opposite conditions may generate the same response. Thus, as Douglas and others have claimed, formless anarchy or comparable conditions when society relaxes its grip on its members, appear also to promote the emergence of ecstatic shamanistic movements. At this point the Marxist and Durkheimian arguments intersect and, as so often with social phenomena, the extremes meet. This conjunction is, of course, fully consistent with our earlier observation that individuals can achieve states of ecstasy either through over- or under-stimulation. Nor, in this context, should we lose sight of the actual techniques employed to achieve ecstasy. Although the availability of powerful psychedelic drugs is not a necessary and sufficient condition for shamanism, it must influence the ease with which trance states can be achieved.

The Love of the Gods

The ecstatic encounters which shamanism, whether combined with spirit possession or not, always involves are described all over the world and in every period of history in remarkably similar terms. The gods and their devotees may address each other in different countries in different languages, but they all employ the same terms of endearment. The language of spiritual intimacy is truly international, and 'possession' here has strong sexual undertones. In this tradition, St Teresa of Avila speaks of the 'Wound of Love', of 'Rapture', and of 'Union', and Marie of the Incarnation records her experiences with her 'Beloved', 'Dearest Spouse'. Less well-known shamanistic devotees in other cultural settings regularly use the same vocabulary, being 'married' to their celestial 'spouses', even in Haiti to the extent of holding marriage certificates! Amongst the Saora Indian tribesmen of Orissa a shaman is often chosen by the direct intervention of a Hindu spirit who proposes marriage. Here, as elsewhere, such spiritual unions compete with their mortal counterparts, frequently leading to most complex matrimonial arrangements. In the case of the arctic Chukchee, for instance, those shamans who happen to be homosexuals (as some are) may be wedded simultaneously to mortal and immortal husbands. More generally, as in the ancient world, these cosmic love-matches may be blessed with children—as in the case of the Virgin Mary. (The famous nineteenth-century English ecstatic, Joanna Southcott, who died of what has been described as a 'hysterical pregnancy', was less successful.) It is thus not surprising that those ecstatics who love the gods should also regularly describe themselves as their 'children'. This filial idiom compounds the marital metaphor in Christianity where Christ's mother's union with God makes him God's Son. The Tukano Indians of Colombia are even more explicitly oedipal. With the aid of hallucinogenic drugs, Tukano shamans achieve beatific visions which they directly compare to incestuous intercourse. The supreme aim of their visionary quest is actually to be 'suffocated', as they describe it, in a mystic uterine union. The theme of a return to the womb (and of birth and re-birth) is, of course, frequently encountered in psychoanalytic treatment and in experiences with psychedelic drugs in medical and non-medical settings.

Closely connected with this uxorial and filial imagery is the more earthy language of the stables which plays an equally prominent role in the vocabulary of shamans and mystics. In this idiom, the gods regularly 'ride' their human 'mounts' as Apollo straddled the oracle at Delphi, and cult members are consequently widely described as the 'horses', or, as with women in the Hausa *bori*-cult, 'mares' of their familial spirits. The Manchu and Tungus, who also follow this imagery, go so far as placing real (as well as human) horses at the disposal of the spirits. These spirit-mounts are brought into the house and, with silk ribbons attached to their manes, made to stand in front of the ancestor spirit shrines. They may not be ridden by women or clansmen wearing mourning dress.

These equestrian and sexual descriptions of shamanistic relations with the gods raise interesting problems. Can the most sublime religious experience be reduced to erotic fantasy and dreaming? Is it all simply a matter of sublimation: or is it rather that the human sexual act offers the most readily available template for transcendent experience and hence the natural language with which to strive to capture the ineffable?

Further Reading

Basilov, V.N. 'The Study of Shamanism in Soviet ethnography' in M. Hoppal (ed.) *Shamanism in Eurasia* (edition Herodot, Gottingen, 1984), pp. 46–66

Blacker, C. *The Catalpa Bow, a Study of Shamanistic Practices in Japan* (Allen & Unwin, London, 1975)

Bourguignon, E. 'World Distribution and Patterns of Possession States', in R. Prince (ed.), *Trance and Possession States* (Montreal, 1967)

—— (ed.) *Religion, Altered States of Consciousness and Social Change* (Ohio, 1973)

Douglas, M. *Natural Symbols* (Barrie & Jenkins, London, 1970)

Eliade, Mircea *Shamanism: Archaic Techniques of Ecstasy* (Routledge & Kegan Paul, London, 1964)

Field, M.J. 'Spirit Possession in Ghana', in J. Beattie and J. Middleton (eds.) *Spirit Mediumship and Society in Africa* (Routledge & Kegan Paul, London, 1969)

Hoppal, M. *Shamanism in Eurasia* (edition Herodot, Gottingen, 1984)

Hori, I. *Folk Religion in Japan* (Chicago University Press, Chicago, 1968)

Jochelson, W.I. *The Koryak. Report of the Jessup Expedition, 1900–1901* (New York, 1905–8)

La Barre, W. *The Ghost Dance: The Origins of Religion* (New York, 1970)

Lewis, I.M. *Ecstatic Religion* (Penguin, London, 1971)

Metraux, A. *Voodoo in Haiti* (London, 1959)

Pressel, E. 'Umbanda Trance and Possession in Sao Paulo, Brazil', in Goodman, F.D., Henney, J.H. and Pressel, E., *Trance, Healing and Hallucination* (New York, 1974)

Rasmussen, K. *The Intellectual Culture of the Iglulik Eskimos* (Copenhagen, 1929)

Shirokogoroff, S.M. *Psychomental Complex of the Tungus* (London, 1935)

Siikala, A.L. *The Rite Technique of the Siberian Shaman* (FF Communications 220, Helsinki, 1978)

Voigt, V. 'Shaman—Person or Word?' in M. Hoppal (ed.), *Shamanism in Eurasia*, (edition Herodot, Gottingen, 1984), pp. 13–21

Wasson, R.G. *SOMA. Divine Mushroom of Immortality* (New York, 1968)

Wilson, P.J. 'Status Ambiguity and Spirit Possession', *Man*, 2 (1967)

47 Australian Aboriginal Religion

K. Maddock

The vast island continent of Australia was thinly peopled by a few hundred-thousand dark-skinned hunters and gatherers when British settlement began in 1788. James Cook, who had sailed up the east coast eighteen years earlier, wrote that they might 'appear to some to be the most wretched people upon Earth, but in reality they are far happier than we Europeans'. The ancestors of the Aborigines, as they are now known, probably entered Australia more than 40,000 years ago, but no one knows from where they came or to whom they are biologically or linguistically related.

Today's Aborigines, who comprise one or two per cent of the Australian population, are diverse in character and situation. Many follow an essentially European mode of life, speak only English and biologically are less than half Aboriginal. Others are purely Aboriginal, speak several Aboriginal tongues and pursue a way of life based partly on hunting and gathering. Such diversity results from the forces and pressures exerted through colonisation and from their uneven impact in different areas.

Knowledge of what can loosely be called Aboriginal religion relies on observations since 1788. The Aborigines knew no writing and any earlier sojourners among them left no records, so greater time depth can be obtained only by inference from what has been learned during the past two hundred years. But attempts at reconstruction run into the difficulty that Aboriginal religious practice has greatly changed over that period—vanishing altogether in some areas, showing signs of nativism or Christian influence in others and generally adapting itself to new political and socio-economic circumstances.

For example, our best accounts include those of A.W. Howitt, who worked in south-east Australia late last century, and of his contemporaries Baldwin Spencer and F.J. Gillen, who worked together mainly in the Northern Territory. Howitt wrote detailed descriptions of the Bora (a protracted initiatory ceremony focused on tooth avulsion), but the two performances he attended were inspired by him and carried out by Aborigines who, by that time, were depleted in numbers and much changed in mode of life. Spencer and Gillen wrote comprehensively about the *intichiuma* ceremonies of the central Australian Aranda (these rites were thought to ensure the abundance of plants and animals), but the series they first witnessed was staged in gratitude to Gillen, whose intervention a few years before had put a stop to police terror directed against Aborigines—it seems that the location and some other details of the performance differed from past practice.

No unity of faith or practice existed among Aborigines in a sense comparable to what is found in any of the great divisions of Christianity or Islam. Aboriginal horizons were highly circumscribed—a person's social universe might comprise five hundred or a thousand souls, beyond whom lived people of whom little was known but much might be suspected. Except in more arid parts, an Aboriginal's life would have been largely spent in a tract of a few thousand, or perhaps only a few hundred, square miles. Should we not speak, then, of there being many religions, just as there were hundreds of languages? Perspectives were also very limited in a time sense. Genealogical memory and memories of past events usually ran back no more than two or three generations. Earlier than that, or separated from it by an indefinite lapse of time, lay the creative period when nature and culture were fashioned by a multitude of beings who, commonly half-human and half-animal but with supranormal powers, made a mysterious appearance from beneath the earth or from the sky or from distant horizons before vanishing. This was not creation out of nothing, for something already existed, but it lacked form and active life, being pictured perhaps as a watery expanse or a waste of level ground. It is these beings and their world-formative deeds who are commemorated in the myths and rites of Aboriginal religion. More than that, many are conceived still to exist, in some sense, and, whether existent or not, they have a continuing tangible relevance, for they laid down the rules of the social order and the natural setting is filled with their bodily memorials—here a circular water-hole is the eye of a half-human cockatoo, there the trees lining a watercourse are the tails of half-human snakes and somewhere else a rocky ridge is the backbone of a half-human marsupial.

A paradox can readily be seen in Aboriginal religion (or religions). On the one hand, spatial and temporal perspectives were very restricted, but on the other hand, Aborigines throughout Australia's three million square miles were joined by their shared ancestry and by their long isolation from the rest of the world. We must therefore recognise that chains of connection ran in every direction and back to time immemorial, even if the Aborigines themselves did not know it. So, even granting that it is more accurate to speak of *religions* than of *religion*, we can reasonably expect common religious features. Also we can expect that divergent features will, in many cases, prove to be historical variations on indigenous themes.

E.A. Worms, a Roman Catholic priest, has made the most determined modern effort to distil the essence of Aboriginal religious belief and practice. He sees the religions of the continent as forming an organic whole, characterised by eight common features:

1. Absence of esoteric doctrine;
2. Belief in a personal sky-being;
3. Belief in auxiliary spirits, often the sons of the sky-being, who taught sacred rites and gave sacred instruments;
4. Belief in holy objects left behind by the sky-being, in which his power is contained;
5. The use of liturgical drama to renew and symbolise the sky-being's creative acts;
6. The practice of initiation, including tests of hardship;
7. Traces of sacrifice and prayer, in the wildest senses of those words;
8. The existence (presumably within each community) of a leading liturgist or medicine-man.

Considered in the light of all the fieldwork carried out in Australia, Worms's list is too specific to be accepted as valid, though Worms himself might have defended it as an enumeration of the shared features of the religious complex out of which the present-day Aboriginal religions have developed. A personal sky-being, for example, is known in many areas, most notably in the south-east, where he is depicted as an All-Father, human in form, mighty in power and continuing to take an interest in life on earth, even though he has withdrawn to the sky. In particular, he was associated with the Bora ceremonies, at which he might make a personal appearance. But in other areas no such outstanding being is known or else the most obvious counterpart is female (the All-Mother of some northern areas) and is associated more with the earth or the water than with the sky (she may, for example, be identified as a rainbow serpent who admittedly appears in the sky—as a rainbow—but more usually dwells in fresh water).

To take another example, Worms is right to recognise the importance of spirits who gave sacred instruments or taught sacred rituals (the intimate connection between the two is shown in the fact that the name of a ceremony is often the name of the instrument used in it, such as gong or bullroarer). But they cannot always be seen as relatives of the sky-being (or his counterpart). Thus myths of the Gunabibi, a major northern ceremony, credit it in some areas to a human-like father and son and to a pair of snakes, while in other areas the leading mythical figures are a pair of human-like sisters and a snake. None of these beings has any special association with the sky.

Worms allowed for the obvious differences among Aboriginal religions by distinguishing what he called 'incidental accretions'. They include such features as the prevalence of secondary spirits and of snake and other animal symbolism and the exclusion of women from much of the men's ritual. When one considers the reports now available on various northern and central ceremonies it is hard to escape the conclusion that some 'incidents' are as essential as any of the suggested common features. Of the eight, one can be confident of the universality (or near universality) only of the third, fourth, fifth and sixth—and even they must be modified so that a sky-being is no longer insisted upon.

Worms's approach has been little emulated, though the time is now ripe for fresh attempts making use of the mountain of information collected by fieldworkers over the last two decades. So far the more usual approach has been in accord with W.E.H. Stanner's view that the best avenue for the understanding of Aboriginal religion is through the study of the surviving regional cults (or ceremonies). In them we see religion in action.

The rich perspectives opened by this approach are well shown in W. Lloyd Warner's classic monograph on the Murngin of north-east Arnhem Land. In the late 1920s, the time of his study, they were performing these major ceremonies (as well as a number of others of lesser scope):

1. Djungguan;
2. Gunabibi;
3. Ulmark;
4. Marndiella;
5. Dua moiety's Narra;
6. Yiritja moiety's Narra.

Each ceremony is a complex whole, including a series of ritual acts and dances, a series of songs and a set of ritual parapher-nalia. It is performed at grounds constructed for the purpose and is associated with a body of myth—and hence with the world-formative deeds of the creative period. Religious performance cannot be isolated from the social system, for the roles which actors play are allocated according to important social divisions—of sex, for example, or of moiety.

To speak of Murngin religion as comprising a number of ceremonies may leave the impression that it lacks overall system. In fact, Warner sees unity as coming especially from myths, which provide a symbolic underpinning for the ceremonies. Thus the first four of the six ceremonies listed above belong to the myth cycle of the Wawilak sisters and the last two to that of the Djunkgao sisters. Each myth is in effect an organising focus for two or more cults, providing not only their charter, in Malinowski's sense, but an interpretative rationale through which many ceremonial episodes can be understood as present-day re-enactments of events occurring in the creative period.

The Wawilak myth, for example, tells of two sisters who set off from the interior on a northwards journey to the sea after committing incest. As they travelled they named the plants they gathered and the animals they killed; they also named places and countries and, from time to time, changed language to that now associated with the area through which they were passing. When the younger sister felt a child within her (the fruit of incest) she told the elder, and they hurried on to a water-hole associated with the rock python. There they made a fire and began to cook the plants and animals collected on their journey, but each sprang from the fire and ran like a man to the water, into which it dived. Next the elder sister gathered bark for a bed for the younger, but in doing so she menstruated into the water. The pollution aroused the python. He rose to the surface, the water level also rose to flood the surrounding country and soon rain began to pour down. Hastily the sisters built a house. They fell asleep within it, but were soon awoken by the rain, which was becoming heavier and heavier.

In a vain effort to stop the rain the sisters sang the songs of the Gunabibi, Djungguan, Marndiella and Ulmark. Then in desperation they sang of rock python and menstrual blood. At this the python made them fall asleep by magic, after which he swallowed them. He regurgitated them, swallowed them again and finally regurgitated them a second time. Later the spirits of the sisters appeared in a dream to two men, to whom they taught the four ceremonies.

The Wawilak myth is more than an original tale. It enables symbolic sense to be made of what is done in the ceremonies associated with it. In the Gunabibi, for example, the bullroarer (one of the 'holy objects' of Worms) is identified with the python, the various animals referred to in songs or mimed in dances are among those the sisters saw and named on their journey and a structure of forked sticks, erected at a late stage and serving as a focus of action for both men and women, is the house in which the sisters took shelter. We can also see the myth as rationalising the religious division of labour and responsibility between the sexes—a theme elaborated in a different way by the myth of the Djunkgao sisters.

It would be a mistake to explain the ceremonies as having been derived from the myths. Rather the ceremonies, as large-scale collective actions of stereotyped form, could more plausibly be invoked to explain the myths, for the latter are not learned in word-perfect fashion and can vary a good deal in the telling. But, when Murngin religion is looked upon as a more or less functioning whole, myth and ceremony are best seen as complementary variables.

Many of the cults described in the literature are not confined to one locality. Those of the Murngin, for example, are performed by other Arnhem Land peoples. The Gunabibi, in particular, enjoys a wide distribution, being known over many tens of thousands of square miles of northern Australia. But, as is to be expected from the lack of an overarching 'church', considerable variations can occur in details of performance from one locality to another, and the associated myths can be quite different. Thus, to the south-west of the Murngin, the Gunabibi is explained by a myth about a father and son, both properly married, who set off on a journey inland from the sea after a water-dwelling monster swallowed ceremonial performers and regurgitated them as bone.

In addition, there can be important differences in the purposes fulfilled by ceremonial performances. Emphasis may be laid especially on the passage of youths into manhood and on the separation of masculine from feminine elements in society—certainly that is how Warner depicted Murngin religion. But ceremonies may also be understood as a means to transform spirits of the dead from a wandering state to a state in which they may enter ancestral waters—and from which, in the belief of some areas, they may undergo reincarnation. Ceremonies may be centred on the disposal of the bodily remains of the dead, or they may aim to ensure the perpetuation of plant and animal species. Invariably they incorporate a division of labour and responsibility, for which reason it is by no means fanciful to see them as occasions on which Aborigines colourfully and dramatically map out their social structure. And, because the associated myths and songs are located at known places, or lines of places, in the landscape, the ceremonies are also a kind of geographical mapping. Some of these functions—the social and geographical mapping, for example—probably pertain to all ceremonies, but others are contingent and can change from one area to the next even as regards the 'same' ceremony. Thus assisting in the transformation of spirits of the dead provides some of the purposive core of the Gunabibi south-west of the Murngin, but it is no part of the Gunabibi among the Murngin themselves. They secure that end through other ritual observances.

These considerations suggest that the future development of the study of Aboriginal religions will do well to follow two complementary paths. On the one hand, we need to elucidate the system of ceremonies (understood as complex wholes) of particular peoples. On the other hand, we must aim to trace the chains of connection between the systems of different peoples. In ascertaining the relations of transformation between different ceremonies in the same locality or between the 'same' ceremony in different localities, we may hope to reach more or less plausible conclusions about processes of religious growth, change and decay on the continent. Given the shared ancestry of the Aborigines and their long isolation from the rest of the world, it might well turn out that these processes could best be understood on the analogy of the incessant dealing and re-dealing of a pack of cards.

But have Aboriginal religions (as distinct from the study of them) a future? They have vanished from parts of Australia, and where they survive the context of performance—and therefore the significance of performance—is by no means what it would have been in pre-colonial times. Formerly, for example, most Aborigines spent much of the year on the move in small groups in a quest for food. Performances of major ceremonies were occasions of heightened social life, when perhaps a few hundred people would come together for a few weeks. Disputes might be settled and marriages arranged, as well as ceremonies performed. The switch to a largely sedentary existence and to assured food supplies has changed all that. The social order in which Aborigines live can no longer be wholly explained by the deeds of the spirit beings of the creative period. Greatly improved communications have exposed Aborigines not only to profound differences in attitude and belief among Europeans but to considerable variations in Aboriginal practice according to location or region. Not all influences are corrosive. Thus the definition of Aboriginal land rights in South Australia and the Northern Territory has incorporated the mythic and ceremonial aspects of traditional relations to land. Accordingly it would be premature to foretell the demise of Aboriginal religions. The likelier outcome, at least in the near future, is the emergence of very widespread religious movements based on a selection of themes and elements from the more detailed but spatially more restricted cults of the immediate past.

Further Reading

Charlesworth, M., Morphy, H., Bell, D. and Maddock, K. (eds.) *Religion in Aboriginal Australia: An Anthology* (University of Queensland Press, St Lucia, 1984)

Howitt, A.W. *The Native Tribes of South-East Australia* (Macmillan, London, 1904)

Spencer, B. and Gillen, F.J. *The Native Tribes of Central Australia* (Macmillan, London, 1899)

Stanner, W.E.H. *On Aboriginal Religion* (Oceania Monographs, Sydney, 1964)

—— 'Religion, Totemism and Symbolism', in R.M. and C.H. Berndt (eds.) *Aboriginal Man in Australia* (Angus and Robertson, Sydney, 1965)

Warner, W.L. *A Black Civilization* (Harper, New York, 1937)

Worms, E.A. 'Religion', in H. Shiels (ed.) *Australian Aboriginal Studies* (Oxford University Press, Melbourne, 1963)

48 Melanesian Religions

V. Lanternari

The inhabitants of Melanesia traditionally gain their livelihood mainly by horticulture, with gardens of yams and taro, and in the coastal areas by fishing. Pig-raising is also practised in a number of isles and in the interior region of New Guinea. As in practically all sedentary societies who take their livelihood from cultivated plants, a fundamental feature of the native Melanesian religion is the cult of ancestors. Belief in the deceased persons' spirits gives rise to a number of ceremonies, which are carried out by the members of each clan in honour of their ancestors. The ancestors' cult is a means to control individual behaviour and to preserve the moral code. It also helps to strengthen social cohesion and to maintain the cosmic order. Finally, it re-establishes symbolically, on each occasion, continuity between past generations and the living, that is to say between tradition and the present life.

Knowledge of the necessary rituals is often passed on from father to son or, in matrilineal societies, from maternal uncle to nephew. In the Fiji group there was a class of hereditary priests who officiated at ancestor cult ceremonies and became possessed. In this state they spoke with the voice of the spirit and were consulted as oracles. Sometimes, as in the Solomon Islands, ancestral spirits are believed to inhabit fish or other animals. Among some tribes, they are believed to inhabit their skulls which are recovered some time after death. They are moulded with coloured resins and clays, then they are collected in men's houses or placed on a figure modelled in clay and fibre (*malekula*), or in a special model-hut (New Georgia). The skulls actually represent the deceased persons. Their power is considered to be favourable or harmful according to the proper or improper fulfilling of ethical and ritual duties by their clan heirs.

On the northern coastal region of Irian the *korwar* figures are a notable form of religious art production. *Korwar* is the wooden or stone statue of a deceased forefather. Some time after death a statuette is made by the relatives of the deceased, into which his soul is then lured. The very skull of the departed person may be placed on a headless *korwar* statue. Among the Fly River and Purari River tribes and in New Britain the frontal portion of the skull was modelled in the form of a mask. Generally speaking, masks are worn by initiates during sacred ceremonies, particularly in the initiation rites. Actually, the uninitiated believe that the masked performers are spirits and regard them with awe and terror. The initiates, though conscious of the deception, nevertheless feel a sort of identification with the spirits they represent.

Sometimes the cult of the dead, together with the males' initiation rites and the New Year fertility feast, merges into one single multivalent ceremony, in which an atmosphere of symbolic death-regeneration is produced. This ceremony is more generally concerned with the adolescent life crisis of puberty, with the growing of crops and with propitiation for the whole tribe's destiny in its relationship with the cosmic order. The *Nanga* ceremony of Fiji is an example of this kind of complex ritual. On this occasion, the young novices are led to the sacred stone platform in the centre of the village. Here they meet an awesome group of actors whose arrival is announced by the sound of sacred flutes representing the ghosts' voices. The actors-initiates are masked and disguised in frightening apparel; they threaten the novices in terrifying mimes. Frightened by the scene, the novices ritually die; but after some time they are reborn and collectively recognised as adult members of the society. Thus the return of the dead is dramatically represented as a symbolic rite of human and cosmic regeneration. Offerings of crops and meat are produced for the spirits from the heaps of yams and the swine which have been prepared for the celebration. Prayers are said to obtain the spirits' co-operation in fostering prosperity and general well-being.

Another and somewhat different example of the merging of initiation rites with mortuary ceremonies and with a general regeneration feast is the *Malanggan* ritual in New Ireland. The name itself, *Malanggan*, is also shared by special kinds of ceremonial objects of great artistic interest. The *Malanggans* are either intricate, wide horizontal carvings, or meticulously executed multifigured, vertical carved poles. Both types are embellished by printed patterns of a stylistically impressive effect. The *Malanggan* carvings are solemnly presented by adult initiates to the novices during the initiation rites, which are performed on the occasion of the great *Malanggan* celebrations in memory of the departed.

In Melanesia, the spirits of recently deceased persons are believed to exercise individually a direct influence on the living, while the spirits of those who died in the more remote past are collectively evoked on the occasion of periodical rituals. On these occasions they are honoured with food offerings and particularly the first-fruits. Then they are formally and vigorously expelled and invited to go back to their abode. The inhabitants of many of the Melanesian islands believe that the ghosts have their dwelling on a smaller isle in the west.

This belief becomes relevant with reference to the newer development of syncretistic movements generally called Cargo-cults. They have emerged among the inhabitants of a great number of islands, in response to the arrival of the white peoples' boats with their surprising products (cargo), so different from anything the natives had ever seen. The initial identification of the white people with the spirits of the dead was favoured by the traditional mythical belief concerning the western abode of the ghosts and their maritime journeys. People were easily induced to mythologise about the cargo and to ascribe its creation to a spiritual world with which the white man was in contact. Thus, since the white man brought the goods, the cargo was a gift from the dead. The occurrence of Cargo-cults in myriads of societies or groups, independently of one another, in response to similar events such as the encounter with an unknown kind of human being and new material objects, demonstrates the creative potentiality inherent in the traditional system of beliefs and myths. It also proves that the cult of the dead is a fundamental component of the structure of Melanesian religion. This cult is centred on the widespread belief that the spirits or ghosts are the original givers of wealth, of prestige and of mastery to the natives.

As for the traditional ceremonies, in which the spirits of the deceased are honoured with every kind of offering, we conclude that through the ritual activity a profitable psychic equilibrium is fostered by the people for themselves. Through the rite, in fact, a mutual giving-receiving relationship is established between the living and the supernatural powers. Further, by paying homage to the spirits people hope to obtain the practical reward of good fortune for themselves.

On the whole, ritual activity in Melanesia generally revolves around three main critical moments of the individual's or community's life: death, initiation and the New Year. Initiation rites are of two main types: initiation of all boys into adult status, which is typical of New Guinea, Bismarck Archipelago, the Solomon Islands and New Caledonia; and initiation into age-grades or secret societies (the 'degree-taking' rites), which are common in New Britain (*Duk-duk*), New Ireland (*Igiet*), Florida (*Matambala*), Banks Islands (*Tamate*) and northern New Hebrides (*Qatu*). The initiated are ritually and collectively instructed by the elders on their moral duties, myths, ancestors' deeds, the general prescriptions and taboos and sometimes also magical rites. They are supposed to communicate, during the rituals, with the spirits through the voice of the sacred flutes or of the bull-roarer. In the north-eastern region of New Guinea a monster, called Balum, symbolically swallows the new initiate, as a symbol of death and rebirth and also as a test of courage. The novice, in general, is subjected to a period of segregation, and to physical proofs of pain-tolerance, in many cases through such sexual mutilations as penis-incision or circumcision. While the initiation to adulthood is shared by all young men, the initiation into secret societies is reserved for men who can afford the expense. They get, from the initiation, special privileges of a political and judicial kind. The women's initiation to adulthood is also widespread, but it has an individual character as opposed to the collective character of the men's initiation. Furthermore, the female initiation is reduced to a feast in which the girl receives some gifts, changes her clothes and is instructed about her impending duties as wife and mother. In fact, this type of initiation corresponds to the celebration of her first menstruation. Both men and women are supposed to marry only after initiation.

For initiated men the revelation of cult secrets to women or to the uninitiated is regarded as a serious breach of tradition. Since the observance of the general moral code is imposed on the initiated men, an outstanding function of the initiation rites is to ensure a correct and harmonious proceeding of the social life. Contraventions meet not only with human blame and censure, but also with automatic spiritual punishment such as sickness and misfortune, attributed to the intervention of the spirits.

In recent times European contact has brought about a decline of the traditional ways of life, mostly in the religious, socio-ethical and economic spheres. Christian missionaries have intervened against initiation rituals and other feasts, which they regarded as unacceptable manifestations of paganism. The forced abandonment of customary ritual activities, the attraction of modern cultural models, the diffusion of alcoholic beverages and the changes in the old value orientations caused by the new forms of economic enterprise introduced by the Europeans, have produced the collapse of old spiritual sanctions, and the deterioration of moral standards. The uneasiness and the feeling of frustration caused by these factors underlie the spreading of the Cargo-cults which clearly express a deep yearning for the renewal of the traditional way of life. Significantly, the Cargo-cults are promoted by native prophets under charismatic inspiration. Following dreams and visions, they become the spokesmen of widely shared aspirations and sentiments.

So far we have considered Melanesian religion mostly in the phenomenological contexts of death and initiation. Both are tightly interwoven with a third mythico-ritual context: the religion of the New Year. A very well-known example of the New Year feast in traditional Melanesian societies is the *Milamala* feast of the Trobriand Islanders, as it is described by Malinowski in his classical work, *Coral Gardens.* The Trobrianders celebrate the *Milamala* after the principal harvest of the yam crop has been completed, in August. The celebration lasts one lunar month; its name is shared by the month itself, and contains the notion of abundance (*malia*). On this occasion heaps of yams are ostentatiously distributed in the village, while the store-huts are full of the new tubers. *Milamala* is primarily a joyful celebration of the products of cultivation. Nevertheless, the newly produced yam crop is taboo. It cannot be eaten before the end of the ceremony. A fundamental aspect of the ceremony, in fact, is the return of the spirits of the dead (*baloma*) to the village, *en masse*. The hungry spirits are welcomed and an offering of the first-fruits is given to them. Heaps of yams are prepared on special platforms along the paths of the village, which the spirits are supposed to visit every night. They eat the essence of the yams. And only then, when the offerings have been accepted, is the consumption of the new food permitted.

This ritual symbolically underlines the acknowledgement of the spirits' ownership of the cultivated plants and of food in general. The offering of the first-fruits to them, together with the imposing of the food taboo on the living, clearly signifies the restitution of property to its spiritual owners and the symbolic annulment of the yearly work of cultivation and of the product itself, as if a sacrilege had been perpetrated against the supernatural powers, particularly the spirits of the dead. In the final part of the feast—which is at the same time a feast of the crops and of the dead—the *baloma* spirits are ritually expelled by a solemn declaration, and people then indulge in eating, dancing and sexual licence.

This ritual behaviour—the celebration of crops, the food taboo, the ceremonial return of the dead, the first-fruits offering to them and the final expulsion of the spirits and the orgy—is observable, in more or less the same forms, among the majority of the Melanesian peoples, whose belief systems and culture have been examined by scholars. Moreover, from a more general point of view, it is worth pointing out here that among practically all societies of primitive or archaic cultivators, a structural interplay can be observed between the ideological sphere pertinent to cultivation and production, and the one pertinent to the world of the dead. Among these societies the cult of the dead is of great significance and in one particular form this cult is represented by the eschatological complex of the return of the dead viewed as the forerunners of a general regeneration.

Further, it is reasonable to assume that the New Year feast of the Melanesians can be interpreted as the ritualised expression of the feeling of a link between the tilling of the earth—mother of plants—and the violation of the ancestors' seat—the earth itself where the dead are buried—so that the rites of the temporary food taboo, of welcoming the *baloma* spirits once a year, of the first-fruits offering to them, reveal the significance of a symbolic and articulate action viewed as expiating the inevitable guilt committed. In this way the fear that in the future food production may fail is overcome. The final feasting, the joyful and frantic indulging in eating and dancing and in the sexual orgy after the expiatory role of the previous rites and after the expulsion of the spirits, play the complementary role of clearing the way for the community to proceed trustfully and joyfully towards the new cycle of life and of agricultural activity. The Melanesian New Year feast, therefore, can be regarded as paradigmatic of how an eschatological world-view is expressed by a ritual drama in which the resurrection of the dead is represented in its living and sensible reality.

By way of contrast, among those tribes who practise pig-raising, ritual life centres on a solemn pig festival, which is carried out at intervals of several years. The pig festival is substantially a rite of social promotion, within the context of the dynamic competition between individuals who aim to acquire social prestige and to emerge as leaders ('big men'), or who wish to maintain the role and power they have previously acquired. Ambitious men gain or maintain personal power by arranging and managing a great pig festival. The procedure is based, firstly, on the ability of wives to procure and rear as many pigs as possible, within a period of several years. It is also based on the ability to mobilise kin, friends and clients of the candidate for leadership, in order to obtain their co-operation in the rearing of a great number of pigs. When the candidate or 'big man' believes that the right moment has arrived to display his riches, in the form of all the pigs amassed by himself and by his clients, the pig festival begins. It takes the form of a tremendous fight to kill the animals, and of a huge sacrifice of hundreds of swine. This sacrifice has a number of mythical references. For example, according to a Kiwai myth in New Guinea, man and pig are identified and the killing of a pig is at the basis of death for humankind. That is the reason why the pigs are not killed by their personal owners, but by others. The religious character of the feast is also marked by the ritual dedication of the animals to the spirits or to mythical beings as the culture-heroes, or (among the Marind-anim of New Guinea) to the swine-Dema. The Dema are mythical beings of the Marind-anim; all natural objects, plants, animals and humankind itself derive from the Dema.

The social function of the pig festival is to create or to re-establish the special rank of 'big men' who exercise religious, social and political power within the federation of the affiliated kin, friends and clients who have co-operated with them. The principle of reciprocity is central to the relationship between leader and co-operators. The former is supposed and is even obliged to return the favours he received from the latter. Where he is unable to fulfil his obligations, he loses his power and rank. On the other hand, each 'big man' has also to face competition from every other ambitious individual who may at any time try to rise in rank and status by arranging his own pig festival. We see from the Melanesian pig festival that myth and ritual are interwoven with the dynamics of the social structure. The pig festival includes in its structure also some of the same rites as the New Year festival, such as the offerings to the spirits, the initiation of young men and such beliefs as the return of the dead.

A final observation is worth adding: the sacrificial massacre of hundreds of pigs is followed by what amounts to a frenetic bout of eating. The excessive consumption of meat on this occasion can only be understood and rationalised if seen within the framework of a dialectical relationship between ordinary and extraordinary behaviour, and particularly between profane time and sacred time, that is to say between daily life and feast. Actually, the waste of goods and food in the feast is one of its structural rules, since the purpose of the feast is to express the reversal of ordinary everyday conditions, relationships and situations. Thus daily poverty and hardship are denied—in strongly symbolic language—by the exaggerated consumption of food in the feast.

A concept widely diffused in Melanesia is *mana*. According to classical authorities such as Rivers, Hocart and Codrington, it is at the very heart of most religious beliefs and practices, and also of the world of magic. *Mana* is a supernatural and impersonal power or influence, which operates in and influences all the events or phenomena which remain outside the ordinary competence or domain of men. Though impersonal, *mana* is always activated and directed by certain kinds of people. Originally it belonged to all kinds of spirits and ghosts, and to certain individuals. Even some inanimate objects possess *mana* because they are inhabited by a spirit. These objects are characterised by unusual and strange forms. In New Britain the sorcerers have power from *mana* to cause illness and even death. In Guadalcanal (Solomon Islands) a sorcerer may obtain *mana* from a ghost (*tindalo*) inhabiting a special bird, *naroha*. The sorcerer goes to a place where that bird can be found and asks him for *mana*. Among the Fijians the *mana* is associated with ghosts, spirits, chiefs and medicines. In many tribes all around Melanesia the spirits of the dead are held to be the principal sources of *mana*. Bones of deceased persons, for instance, are employed to build arrows in Lepers Island. The effect should be to bestow *mana* on the arrow and to get success in striking the prey. Bones or teeth are also employed to make charms. In New Guinea the belief in *mana* exists only among the south-western and Papua-Gulf tribes.

Since a rigid distinction between magic and religion is fundamentally doubtful, we can consider here some of the so-called magical practices that are common almost everywhere in Melanesia. As is well known, magic is aimed at preventing individual or collective calamities of every kind. Malinowski's idea was that magic intervenes in those circumstances and situations regarded as being beyond human control. He underlined a series of magical operations of the Trobrianders in the preparation of canoes for their *kula* expeditions, in order to ensure the success of the expedition itself. Magical practices are also carried out, he wrote, on yam farms, in order to ensure that the plants grow well, and to protect the plantations from the intrusions of wild pigs.

A number of traditional practices, of magico-religious significance, especially head-hunting, cannibalism and human sacrifice, were suppressed after the arrival of Europeans. Head-hunting was originally practised for the purpose of acquiring and displaying skulls, a mark of warriors' virtue. Among the Marind-anim of New Guinea, once a year a head-hunting expedition was organised against the enemy. All the able-bodied members of the tribe participated in it. A special hut was prepared where the skulls were placed as glorious trophies and as bringers of new force to the tribe. The heads were also used in the fertility rites, as a magical source of vitality.

Cannibalism was practised by some of the tribes inhabiting the smaller Melanesian islands and New Guinea, mainly in the initiation ceremonies. Among the Kiwai people a ritual prescription for novices in the initiation rituals was to kill an enemy as a test of courage. Cannibalism followed on this occasion, the principal purpose of it being to seize the force and vitality of the victim. Human sacrifice occurred sporadically, mainly in the Solomon group, on such occasions as the launching of a canoe.

The suppression of certain traditional customs after contact with Europeans, the introduction of new cultural models from the Whites and the appearance of the European ships off the coasts from the end of the last century, profoundly affected the world-view of the indigenous inhabitants and the same disturbing effect was produced by the arrival of the first planes in the open glades of the forest in New Guinea. A messianic and millenarian atmosphere soon began to pervade all parts of the region. Ancient mythological topics, particularly those of the periodical return of the dead, were revived, reshaped and adjusted to new configurations. What was traditionally, in the yearly feast of the dead, simply the periodic expectation of the return of the dead and of a temporary renewal of life, now, in the new cults, became the enthusiastic expectation of a definitive and eschatological regeneration of the world.

This happened on a great number of islands and among many peoples, and it gave rise to a completely new process in the local history: the rise of millenarian Cargo-cults. In other instances the myth of a culture-hero of the past was revived, for instance in the case of Manseren Manggundi in the Schouten Islands of New Guinea. In every case, both the spirits of the dead and the culture-hero were held up as messianic heralds of a new era of good fortune and blessing. According to the myth, Manggundi was a beneficent, popular hero reputed to have access to the source of all riches and foods. He also had power to lead men to the threshold of the Golden Era by bestowing on them the riches he controlled. But the myth also narrated that men did not acknowledge him when he first came among them, so that, hurt and discouraged, the hero departed, promising none the less to return. The myth is a clear 'rationalised' representation of the poor conditions of life of the aborigines, and also an expression of a longing for a better future.

The myth of Manggundi was revived more recently, when in 1938 a number of prophets established millenarian movements. They announced the regeneration of the world, combining in their teachings the traditional ideas of abundance and immortality with the new idea of emancipation from colonialism. Inspired by dreams, they preached the advent of a Utopia (*koreri*) marked by liberty and riches.

In Dutch New Guinea another prophetic cult was created among the Muju people in 1913 by Karoem. This prophet was visited by a spirit, who showed him how to lead the Maju out of their backward condition to one of wealth, well-being and fulfilment. All taxes and tributes imposed by the administration, and all contributions to mission churches, would be abolished. A great city would rise up, including a factory, a mint and shops. A huge ship laden with goods for the inhabitants would arrive at the port. The dead would come to life. Karoem was arrested by order of the Dutch government, but his prophecies spread far and wide among the Muju people who tried, in public assemblies, to contact the spirits in order to prepare for the advent of the New Day. In many cases, as one can see from the examples we give, these movements pave the way for the more or less organised expressions of socio-political ferment and discontent. Always, they are a response to the critical experience of culture shock, derived from the encounter with 'modern' and attractive but frustrating forms of civilisation.

One of the best-known examples of Cargo-cults is the so-called 'Vailala Madness' of the Orokolo tribes on the Gulf of Papua. It arose soon after the First World War in response to European influence and missionary preaching. The founder, Evara, was visited by the spirits. In a state of trance, characterised by frantic excitement which very quickly affected the assembled crowd, and which the whites viewed as manifestations of collective hysteria, Evara prophesied the arrival of a ship guided by spirits of the ancestors. They would bring the cargo of rice, meal, tobacco and guns for the people. The cargo, the prophet said, did not belong to the whites but to the Melanesians. The former, in fact, would be miraculously expelled from the island and their cargo would then pass into local hands. The psychic and physical excitement which spread among the prophet's followers is one very typical feature of this cult, and another is its millenarian notion of the return of the dead. This concept, while based on traditional belief, was developed and revived in new ways after Evara had heard a white missionary deliver a sermon on the resurrection of the dead. Thus we can see the direct influence of Christianity on the rise of the Melanesian messianic cults in modern times. It is important to note, however, that European Christianity as it was and still is preached by missionaries was modified in the light of local needs and hopes. For example, in this case the biblical concept of the Resurrection was reinterpreted, adapted and made relevant to expectations and material requirements of the indigenous population.

Furthermore, the founder, Evara, introduced special rituals and insisted on the observance of certain ethical and moral norms. He commanded his followers to attend the feasts in honour of the departed; he ordered them not to steal, not to commit adultery and to observe Sunday rest. Special 'temples' were erected for worship, the main purpose of which was to facilitate the speedy arrival of the cargo, and the regeneration of the world. Some followers called themselves 'men of Jesus Christ', and were at least nominal Christians. Meanwhile so great was their faith in the immediate arrival of the miraculous cargo and in the dispensation of goods in the Golden Age that they abandoned all those agricultural and commercial pursuits which traditionally gave them a livelihood. Although desirous of the material benefits that Europeans had to offer, Evara and his followers were totally opposed to white domination. After a number of incidents, the colonial administration intervened and arrested several chiefs of the movement. As Peter Worsley points out, Vailala Madness expressed both the eagerness of these people to possess European goods and at the same time their desire to expel the whites. The followers of the Cargo-cults not only abandoned work, but sometimes even destroyed their gardens and killed their pigs, indulging in dancing and feasting. They placed offerings on the graves of the dead, and in some cases they constructed roads for the spirits of the dead who were supposed to come from the sea.

Some recent experiences from the Second World War were also incorporated into some cults. For instance the members of the Marching Rule, a Cargo-cult which spread in the Solomon Islands, came to expect the arrival of the Americans whom they viewed as the heralds of a this-worldly 'paradise'. Other prophets took rational initiatives of a social and reformative character. Among these were Yali in the Madang District of New Guinea (1946–50), and Paliau in Manus Island, Great Admiralty Islands (1946–54).

Generally speaking, then, in the Cargo-cults we can see the adaptation and development of traditional myths and rituals found in the great yam feasts and elsewhere: the idea of the return of the dead, of the boat of the dead, the ritual suspension of work and the offerings to the spirits. The socio-culture crisis brought about by the disturbing presence of the Europeans, the expectations of the periodic return of the dead and of renewal of life, typical of the yearly traditional feasts, becomes in the new cults the expectation and the symbolic foundation of a definitive and eschatological renewal of the world. Nevertheless, in spite of their mythico-ritual basis, which is taken as their starting-point, the cargo-movements are often vehicles of modernisation and social improvement.

Further Reading

Burridge, K.O. *Mambu, a Melanesian Millenium* (Methuen, London, 1960)

—— *New Heaven, New Earth* (Basil Blackwell, Oxford, 1971)

Brunton, R. 'Misconstrued Order in Melanesian Religion', *Man*, 1 (1980), pp. 112–28

Lanternari, V. 'Origini storiche dei culti profetici melanesiani', *Studi e Materiali di Storia delle Religioni* (1956), pp. 31–86

—— *The Religions of the Oppressed. A Study of Modern Messianic Cults* (Alfred Knopf, New York, 1963)

—— *La Grande Festa. Vita rituale e sistemi di produzione nelle società traditional* (Liguori Editore, Bari, 1976)

Lawrence, P. *Road Belong Cargo* (Manchester University Press, Manchester, 1964)

Sahlins, M. 'Poor man, rich man, big-man, chief. Political Types in Melanesia and Polynesia', *Comparative Studies in Society and History*, no. 5 (1953)

Worsley, P. *The Trumpet Shall Sound. A Study on Cargo-cults in Melanesia* (MacGibbon and Kee, London, 1957)

Wagner, R. 'Ritual as Communication: Order, Meaning and Secrecy in Melanesian Initiation Rites', *Annual Review of Anthropology*, XIII (1984)

49 Maori Religion

T.P. Tawhai

If you ask a Maori in, for example, a settlement such as Ruatoria where Maoris constitute a majority of the population, what he understands by religion, expect him to scratch his head in thought, before at length replying 'Whose religion?' Religion and Christianity may be synonymous words for him, but what they mean will vary between 'a human recognition of a superhuman controlling power', on the one hand, and 'the preaching of one thing and too often the doing of something else', on the other. It was religion in the latter sense that the Christians who 'brought Jesus to civilise the natives' in earlier days seemed to follow, showing up their God in an adverse light in the eyes of the ancestors, whose traditional gods acted swiftly and usually harshly. For all that, the ancestors were well able, soon after their contact with Christianity, to distinguish the Message from the messengers. The Maori of Ruatoria will accept that Christianity is an integral part of his fellow Maori's life, but that each will also have his own brand of religion, for historic and other reasons; for instance Maoris have the same religion as their forebears. While the Christian God provides Maoridom with its first Redeemer, he appears mostly to ignore needs at the temporal and profane level, leaving this domain to the ancestral gods who continue to cater for those needs. The *tohunga*, formally trained experts in various academic disciplines, say that in the 'long ago' the gods took an active interest in the affairs of humans, and interaction among them and the ancestors was the norm rather than the exception. Thus, in the long ago, marvellous events occurred, which would account, at least in part, for a past which today sounds more like fable than anything else.

Such issues as whether there was at some stage an entity that can be said to be the origin or architect of creation, and whether such an origin or architect had a single material form, if any, were and continue to be subjects of much speculation. Our typical Maori's tribal upbringing makes him familiar with the capacity of superhuman controlling powers to exist as they choose—in a single form, or transformed at will into numerous manifestations.

What immediately concerns him are such issues as the effectiveness of the relationship between a person and a superhuman controlling power in magnifying that person's capacity to work his will; or the constraints and obligations upon that person in order to sustain the relationship. The ability to accommodate these issues rests a great deal upon knowledge based in turn upon *korero tahito* (ancient explanations). These may be called 'myths', if that word refers to material the main purpose of which is to express the beliefs and values of people.

That the *korero tahito* persist in influencing the Maori's mind is evident during *hui* (large social gatherings). Whether it is the occasion of a *huritau* (birthday), or *tangi* (a gathering to deal with a bereavement), each elder present uses the forum. Gazing around in assessment of those present, he rises in his turn to his feet and with measured dignity expounds in solemn rhetoric. To make his points he invokes the imagery of the tribal myths, with apt gesture, and with references to the symbolism, for example of the art and carving of the meeting-house.

The following passage is transcribed and translated from a speech by a *tohunga* Arnold Reedy, recorded in 1966. It conveys something of the way in which biblical ideas and *korero tahito* continue to interact, in the Maori way of thinking.

> Should I happen to meet with [the Apostle] Paul I would probably say to him, 'By Gosh, Paul, those thoughts conflict greatly in my mind.'
>
> The reason is that Adam is the ancestor of the Hebrews and of the Israelites. Whereas ours is this other: Io the Parent. That's ours. From Him/Her are Papa and Rangi and then the Tamariki. Such is the Maori *whakapapa*, right from Tikitiki-o-rangi.
>
> There, then is the difference between our God and the God of the Hebrews. The God of the Hebrews and Israelites they say has His residence in Heaven. Ours, and the God of our ancestors, resides there too. But they know that Tikitiki-o-rangi is the name of the residence of Io; it's there. Io has a house there, Matangireia by name. It has its own forecourt. All those sorts of things are there.
>
> What er . . . Paul is saying looks, to use an English term, very much confused, in my view.
>
> Because, take Adam: Then said the God of the Hebrews, 'Let us create man after our image.' And so the God of the Hebrews created Adam. But when that Adam was born into this world, others resided there too, and he considered them: 'What an ineffectual state of affairs.' For sexual organs simply dangled there with nowhere to go, nowhere.
>
> Let us observe the formalities in our discussion! [an elder's (female) voice] . . .
>
> People were born. What Paul is telling us here is that nobody was born. How did he manage it? He took hold of one of his ribs and yanked it out, and then said, 'This is Eve.' They had union and Cain and his younger brothers were born, the generations of whom Paul speaks; these are the Hebrews and the Israelites.
>
> Look here, ours, not so; ours goes this other way. The *tamariki* of Papa and Rangi

resided, but that God continued to reside above, the beginning and the ending. The visaged one, the faceless one. Io, Io the Parent, he is the beginning, he is the ending.

But the *tamariki* of this couple [Papa and Rangi] resided between them. Gradually, eventually, a stifled sense overwhelmed them; they of course being all male, there were no female ones. Some began to say, 'Let us kick our parents into separating, so that we may emerge into the ordinary world of light.' Others spoke. Tu Matauenga began to say, 'Let us slay our *matua*, slay them.' And others were saying, 'No, that is too shameful.' From that time hence, Tu Matauenga is god of war, of bloodshed.

Some began to say, 'How shall we proceed?' Tane lay down and raised his feet. Hmm! He began to kick, causing gradual separation, and hence was called by that name of his, Tane-toko-Rangi [Tane sunderer of the sky]—and so, there is separation, there is separation.

But at the separation of Papa, I of course do not agree with what Paul says; there is strong conflict in my mind, the matter is this other way. They were separated and the *tamariki* emerged.

Rongomaraeroa was guardian of fern; that's the Minister of Agriculture. Is it not so? Tu Matauenga, Minister of War—War Department. Er . . ., Tane-nui-a-rangi: that was god of the forests.

Minister of Forests . . .

Tangaroa, Tangaroa of the Marine Department. They now have these posts, they have. (Money had not been invented at that time.)

But here is the problem. These people were all male; there was no female. These people considered their situation: 'By golly, comrades, this is a distressing state! Just us, wherever you look it's the same.' Each one with his (male) sexual appendages. Gradually they became highly distressed by their own company. They began to ponder, 'What shall we do, what shall we do?'

'It is well!', Tane-nui-a-rangi informs them, 'it is well. I have the prescription for our disorder.' He, Tane-nui-a-rangi, proceeded to the beach at Kurawaka and arrived. He began to heap up sand, more sand. He pondered his appearance, and began to mould (the heap) into shape similar to his own. But he added length to the hair . . . etc.

'O Ropi [the female elder, Mrs Ngaropi White], these are the words of Wi-o-te-rangi, O Ropi.'

The Maori on the street of Ruatoria, nowadays at least, is content with the knowledge that he has access to the expertise of *tohunga* like Arnold Reedy. To outsiders he is inclined to present a front of learning, as a defence against anything that might question the worth of his tribal culture; the treasures transmitted to him by his ancestors.

Before turning to the main task I will note something about myself. The aim is to indicate some of the traditional constraints under which I write, and also to provide some data concerning the reliability of individual sources. I am of Ngati Uepohatu, a tribe whose unextinguished fires, lit by our explorer ancestor Maui, burn in the Waiapu valley near East Cape. The continuously burning fires refer to the state of being unconquered, and in turn refer to the tribe's unsullied prestige; that is the purity, *inter alia*, of its *korero tahito*. Maui is the legendary Maui Tikitiki a Taranga (Maui of the topknot of Taranga, his mother) who as our *korero tahito* explains discovered and settled Aotearoa (New Zealand). The name Aotearoa means 'long twilight', unlike the brief equatorial ones Maui and his crew were used to. Maui had voyaged out and Mount Hikurangi of Aotearoa had seemed to thrust up out of the sea as he sailed toward shore. Noah on the other hand had waited patiently and it was the waters which subsided thereby exposing Mount Ararat. (I think this reflects something of the philosophies of the two peoples. The Maori view is that things come to those with the courage to get them. The Judaic view is that things come to those who can wait.)

My understanding is that each tribe has its own system of ancient explanations. The apparently permanent migration of some Maori into the tribal territories of other Maori has complicated the picture in some ways. And in relation to that and other matters, I recall an often quoted precept of the ancestors which goes: if you must speak, speak of your own. I speak of *korero tahito* and accordingly speak of Ngati Uepohatu ones. Our *korero tahito* have in the telling more or less depended in the past upon such factors as the appropriateness of the emotional climate in which it is told, the messages stated by the surroundings on the occasion, the body language of the narrator and the attributes that the human voice lends to words. Written presentation takes these things away. More than that, it tends to rigidify what has and should remain pliant. Flexibility in our *korero tahito* enables them to accommodate the capacity of the narrator to render them more relevant to the issues of the day. It is therefore with misgivings and a sense of danger that I must explain that this telling is only for this time, and that tomorrow I would tell it another way.

Te Po

Te Kore evolved through aeons into *Te Po. Te Po* also evolved through generations countless to man to the stage of *Te Ata* (the Dawn). From *Te Ata* evolved *Te Aoturoa* (familiar daytime) out of which in turn evolved *Te Aomarama* (comprehended creation). The state of *Whaitua* emerges (the present tense is used to animate the narrative) with the recognition of space. There are several entities present. Among these are Rangi potiki and Papa who proceed to have offspring namely: Tane, Tu Matauenga (Tu for short), Rongomatane (Rongo for short) and Haumie tiketike (Haumie for short). The *korero tahito* ends.

In the Maori conception the creation is a great kin unit, and thus is thought of as having a genealogical structure. The genealogy begins with Te Kore. In the dialect of the Maori on the street of Ruatoria, the article *te* has both negative and positive meaning, rendering Te Kore as an ambiguous name or title. Te Kore can mean either 'The Nothing' or 'Not The Nothing', and in the Maori's thinking ambiguity is a trait of the superbeing and superior things. For reasons I have been unable to ascertain, Te Kore is hardly mentioned, and the common reference is instead to Te Po. The *tohunga* Arnold Reedy when asked what Te Po was, replied: 'The never-ending beginning.'

Te Po is not thought of as object, or as context. It is said that Te Po is oneness, meaning among other things that Te Po is both object and context.

The employment of the genealogical framework means that to reach Te Po would take a journey in mind, and a return in spirit to former times. During such former times the awareness of our pre-human ancestors operated at the intuitive level only. The situation is sometimes likened to that of a person who is in the grip of sleep, and in that unconsciousness nevertheless senses that although it is night now, dawn is at hand.

Reproduction occurs at the intuitive level. Te Po logically would be the forebear of the Maori on the street in Ruatoria. However the Maori has a strong impression that Te Po is not subject to logic, that Te Po is remote not only on account of the lapse of time but probably more importantly on account of magnitude. It is such as to appear to him to render it fanciful and perhaps even dangerous for him to contemplate Te Po as one of his pre-human ancestors. (The danger is not from Te Po whose magnitude and remoteness put in doubt an interest by Te Po in earthly activities and their performers. An assertion as to genealogical connection has the effect of boosting one spiritually, the boost being dependent on the spiritual level of the one being connected to genealogically. The danger is that at higher spiritual levels, different laws of nature operate and may not necessarily contribute to human survival.)

While Te Po is recognised as a superhuman controlling power, Te Po is not invoked as are some younger superhuman controlling powers. As far as the Maori is concerned the controlling power of Te Po is indirect, controlling those superpowers to whom we can relate directly.

The Tamariki of Rangi and of Papa

The *tamariki* [*Tamariki* translates as 'children'. The word in fact refers to persons of the group who belong in the generational category to which one's natural children do or would have belonged. The group can be as large a one as the tribe] named are Tane, Tu, Rongo, Haumie and Tawhiri matea (Tawhiri for short). Tawhiri, son of Rangi, is half-brother to the others and is eldest. The *tamariki* perceive it is dark, their world consisting as it does of the valleys and hollows between the bodies of Rangi and Papa who are in close embrace. The feeling of cramp and a longing for light is general. There does not seem to be any prospect of change. Except for Tawhiri, the *tamariki* agree to a proposal to separate Rangi and Papa, the former to be removed afar off and the latter to be retained as nurturing parent. [Rangi potiki and Papa, supported by Tawhiri, resist separation. This is the first time in the *korero tahito* that there is opposition to differentiation or expansion, and the intervening factor is *aroha* (love, sympathy). The separation is physical only. Rangi sends his *aroha* down in the rains, which are his tears, to Papa, who responds by sending up her greetings at dawn in the rising mists. Although physically apart they are united in spirit, their *aroha* binding them as one. The saying that '*aroha* is the one great thing' may have originated here, and it is tempting to suppose that some ancestors appreciated the process of condensation without which life on this planet as we know it would not exist.] The retention of one parent is the idea of Tane, as is also the advice that force only adequate to accomplish separation and no more should be applied. All four brothers in turn attempt to bring about separation but it is Tane's effort alone that brings success and in that role he gains the title of Tane-toko-Rangi (Tane who sets Rangi asunder). [Tane, Tane mahuta, Tane-toko-Rangi and so on is similar to Dad, Mr Chairman at the Rugby Club meeting, Major in the army and so on: the same individual wearing different hats.] With the change in role the name of Rangi becomes Rangi nui (the sky) and that of Papa becomes Papa tuanuku (the earth).

Tawhiri brooding over the maltreatment of Rangi and of Papa projects thoughts that assume material form as the clouds, rains, sleet, storms. In the spirit of revenge Tawhiri unleashes these upon his brothers. They wreak havoc with all except Tu who withstands their assault. Tu, who had urged the others to present a united front against the assault, and who had been ignored, now turns upon his brothers and uses them for food and for his other needs. The *korero tahito* ends.

The addition to intuitive perception of sensory perception proves expansive and the plot of complex interrelationships is seen to thicken. Expression of experiences now requires physical terms such as cramp, but also emotional terms such as *aroha* (sympathy, love) and the feelings that make for the spirit of revenge. Possession by the *tamariki* of human attributes provides a basis for assuming that, exalted as they are, they are sufficiently human as to be approachable by the Maori. Sometimes as themselves, but more often in their forms as manifestations, the *tamariki* are recognised superhuman controlling powers. Thus Tane manifest as Tane mahuta (trees and birds) is invoked by those who have business in the forest. Rongo manifest as Rongomaraeroa (sweet potato) is invoked during the cropping season.

The purpose of religious activity here is to seek to enter the domain of the superbeing and do violence with impunity: to enter the forest and do some milling for building purposes, to husband the plant and then to dig up the tubers to feed one's guests. Thus that activity neither reaches for redemption and salvation, nor conveys messages of praise and thanksgiving, but seeks permission and offers placation.

From this *korero tahito* together with the Te Po one we see that humans consist of a tangible and an intangible part. Implicitly both originate in Te Po. The intangible part is *wairua* (soul). There is also the *mauri* (essence or potential) but how it relates to *wairua* is unclear. The word 'essence' is appropriate in that it conveys the idea of that which cannot be analysed further. The word 'potential' is appropriate in so far as it refers to the unrealised. *Mauri* construed very briefly in terms of power is *mana*. The privileges and constraints that accompany the possession of *mana* is the *tapu*. And the dread or awe that surrounds the possession of *mana* is the *wehi*. A chief is often welcomed with the words: *haere mai te mana te tapu me te wehi*.

'Welcome to the powerful, the privileged and the awesome.' The Maori on the street of Ruatoria speaks of the *mauri* of carving, the *mauri* of oratory and so on. And by that he means the spiritual climate that surrounds the carver and his carving, especially during the creative process, the spiritual climate that surrounds the orator and his words, especially during the moments of delivery.

Tane and Hine-ahu-one (Earth Maiden)

Tane observed that the *tamariki* without exception were male and so set about redressing the imbalance. Using the female substance, the earth, Tane formed the first anthropomorphic female and mediated the spirit into her through his breath. He called this manageable female Hine-ahu-one and begat from her a daughter called Hine-titama. Tane took her to wife. One day she asked him who her father was, and his reply was that she might ask the walls of the house. [The walls of the house were of timber and Tane was referring to his many roles: the father, husband, giver of shelter and so on.] When she learned the answer she fled in shame and eventually arrived at Rarohenga, the underworld. [The shame did not, as is sometimes supposed, spring from the incest but from a violation by Tane of a fundamental principle of social relations, namely sharing. So long as there was only one woman Tane was entitled to her exclusively. As soon as there were more than one under his jurisdiction he was bound to share. This he failed to do.] Tane followed and implored her to return with him to the world of light. She declined, saying that she would remain to welcome their descendants into her bosom after the completion of their lives in the world of light and that he should return there and welcome them into it. Tane tearfully agreed. In her new role Hine-titama is called Hine-nui-i-te-po (Great lady of te po). The *korero tahito* ends.

The *tamariki* lack the generative power and on this account there is some sense of failure. The Maori on the street of Ruatoria has only vague notions about the whole thing. The power that the *tamariki* lack is possessed by Hine-ahu-one who transmits it to her daughter Hine-titama. Hine-titama bears children for whom it is clear for the first time that this life has an end. Henceforth it may be said that people are born only to die and because of this the womb has sometimes been referred to as *te whare o te mate* (the house of death). The Maori on the street of Ruatoria is disinclined to subscribe to this piece of inverted logic. As descendant of Maui he knows the myth that tells how his ancestor met his end: strangled while attempting to enter the womb of the slumbering Hine-titama in her role as Hine-nui-i-te-po. In his view it is an ignominious end. Some say Maui wished to return to the pre-born state and others that he wanted to obtain immortality. But the *korero tahito* about Ruaumoko tells us of man's innate wish to be born, and as for immortality, the *wairua* (soul) lives forever.

At the end of this life the physical part of the dead return, rather than proceed, to the bosom of the ancestress Hine-nui-i-te-po. The *po* in her name has made for an interpretation such as the 'grand lady of the night'. I wonder whether the reference is not Te Po—the 'grand lady of Te Po'? If this is so then the boundaries of Te Po lie on the other side of conception and through the doorway that is death. This interpretation of that part of her name seems to be borne out in the addresses made to the dead in the form of farewells and travelling directions: *haere atu ki ou tipuna te hanga tamoko kei Te Po* ('precede us to your ancestors, the tattooed ones at Te Po').

Tane and Tu

These two had contrasting personalities. Tane was peaceable and philosophic while his younger brother was aggressive and a man of action. The brothers clashed. For his part in that affair Tane was given the lordship of Tikitiki-nui-a-rangi—the fourth heaven—and with the role the title Tane-nui-a-rangi. [The creation includes many heavens and also basement levels. The numbers are in question; mention is made of twelve heavens and at least four basement levels. The higher the level the more spiritual the environment.] Tu for his part lost the power to travel to the different heavens. The *korero tahito* ends.

In retrospect we can trace the growth of expansion and can say that it is a propensity in the creation. It was present at the level of awareness or consciousness and then extended into the physical level; more specifically into the realm of bodily experience and of geographic realms.

In the Tane and Tu *korero tahito* the field of expansion is *mana*. The *mana* of Tu is in the temporal field; that of Tane-nui-a-rangi is in the divine field, with one foot nevertheless in the temporal field. This situation has not, however, been taken to mean that the flow of *mana* from the realm of Tane into that of Tu is more fluid than vice versa. This expansion is not expressed as a feeling or reaching toward a God or origin at this stage or for a long time to come. Emphasis is sometimes placed upon the element of confrontation, the situation that appears to have developed when the two *mana* came into contact. However this *korero tahito* is not mentioned among explanations of the rites invoked when different *mana* are brought together; as for example, the rites invoked when visitor and host come together on the occasion of a *hui*.

Tane-nui-a-rangi

An information release from Naherangi—the eleventh heaven—reached Tane-nui-a-rangi; that three baskets of knowledge had been made available at Naherangi for the taking. Competition would be intense. The chances that Tane-nui-a-rangi would win the baskets appeared slight indeed, but of those closely associated with man's genealogical tree he was the one with the greatest chances of success in that venture. It transpired that Tane-nui-a-rangi was successful notwithstanding fierce harassment by Whiro, lord of one of the infernal regions. Tane-nui-a-rangi has the three baskets with him at the moment in his fourth heaven. The ancient explanation ends.

The source of much knowledge, the difficulties that were faced in order to obtain it, the willingness of no less than Tane-nui-a-rangi to face those difficulties, the high motivations required of students before they are considered fit persons to come in contact with knowledge of a superior kind, all these are indications that knowledge should be prized.

(I had thought that the significance of the number three—the number of baskets—would have struck people not in a numerical sense but as representing a balance of knowledge to enable one to live a balanced life. Like the three-fingered hands on many carvings, the three represents a useful, because balanced, piece of anatomy.)

Maui Tikitiki a Taranga

Taranga has a miscarriage and miscarriages are normally born dead. There was a social role for the dead foetus, and that was to provide the focal point for the rites to appease the soul thought to have been angered by this denial of the opportunity to live life. But this miscarriage has been born alive, and of course society has no role and therefore no place for the person whose time of arrival is not yet.

Taranga cut off her tikitiki—topknot—wrapped the foetus in it and flung the bundle into the sea. This is washed ashore in due course and morning finds the bundle entangled in kelp upon the beach. Sunshine causes the placenta encasing the foetus to shrink and strangulation is averted when a seagull pecks away the placenta. More dead than alive the foetus is espied by Tane-nui-a-rangi who removes it to Tikitiki-nui-a-rangi. The foetus survives as the child Maui-tikitiki-a-Taranga—Maui of the topknot of Taranga. Among other activities Maui delves into the three baskets of knowledge. When Maui is capable of deciding whether to remain in Tikitiki-nui-a-rangi or to return to the world of men he opts for the latter. The ancient explanation ends.

The abnormal circumstances in which Maui first sees light singles him out as unusual. The apparent withholding of his mother's personality to prop up his own during the first hours of life precludes him from being a social being. He is then denied a place on the breast of Papa tuanuku—a right of every human. Thus the gates opened to humans into this life have been shut in his face.

Physically too, the chances of enjoying life are waning. Nature itself seems to have reversed its function. The protecting placenta is threatening to strangle him, and the energy-giving rays of Tama-nui-te-ra (the sun) is threatening to deprive him of what scarce energy remains to him. Starved as well, it appears he is being discouraged from this life and forced to turn his face to the next. The reference to him as *my mokopuna*, by Tane-nui-a-rangi, confirms that Maui is indeed more of the next world than of this. One with such a disposition is ready to delve into the baskets of knowledge.

Conclusion

Sir Apirana Ngata, considering in 1930 doing a doctorate in Maori social organisation, left as the introductory part of rough notes the following:

> The thesis is that after 140 years contact with the kind of civilisation the English brought to these islands there are indications that the Maori is settling down to a regime under which he finds he can exist side by side with the Pakeha [European] or at some distance from the Pakeha, not merely physically but rather socially, economically, morally and religiously so as to make the Maori communal life possible in the same country.

This chapter bears out Ngata's thesis, in respect at least of the Ngati Uepohatus during the 1980s.

Further Reading

Alpers, A. *Maori Myths and Tribal Legends* (John Murray, London, 1964)

Best, E. *Maori Religion and Mythology* (2 parts) (Government Printer, Wellington, 1976 and 1982) (first published in 1924)

Binney, J., Chaplin, G. and Wallace, C. *Mihaia—the Prophet Rua Kenana and His Community at Maungapohatu* (Oxford University Press, Wellington, 1979)

Metge, J. *The Maoris of New Zealand* (rev. edn) (Routledge & Kegan Paul, London, 1976)

Reed, A.W. *Maori Myth and Legend* (Reed, Wellington, 1972)

Salmond, A. *Hui—A Study of Maori Ceremonial Gatherings* (Reed, Wellington, 1975)

Schimmer, E. *The World of the Maori* (Reed, Wellington, 1966)

Simmons, D. *The Great New Zealand Myth: a Study of the Discovery and Origin Traditions of the Maori* (Reed, Wellington, 1976)

50 African Traditional Religion

T.O. Ranger

African religion has been much misunderstood, and misunderstood in ways which have made it very difficult to treat historically. Those who have been hostile to African religion have called it primitive; those who have been favourable to it have called it primal. Both words imply an unchanging continuity with the earliest times. African religion has been contrasted, both unfavourably and favourably, with the dynamic 'religions of the book', with their belief in a divinely ordained historical process and their assertion of the primacy of man over nature. Critics of African religion have said that its collective character has constituted a tyranny over individuals and that its conservative character has acted as a brake on progress. Admirers of African religion have praised its contributions to solidarity, stability and community. Critics have depicted African religion as the product of human fear in the face of an all-powerful and arbitrary nature. Admirers have praised its humility and ecological sensitivity. Yet these opposing evaluations arise from essentially the same analysis of African religion which both critics and admirers have seen as having escaped the blessing, or the curse, of historical development.

The Protestant missionaries of the nineteenth century were men committed to modernising change—to the trinity of Christianity, Commerce and Civilisation. They saw African religion as a powerful force holding Africans locked into an impoverished past. To many of them it hardly deserved to be called a religion at all, and if it were to be considered as a religion then it was only a very primitive and immature one. These missionaries ran together every sort of African belief and practice, confusing religion and witchcraft belief under the general heading of 'superstition', and describing every African ritual practitioner as a 'witch-doctor'. Missionaries were confident that revealed Christianity could lead Africans into a dynamic and progressive future. Ironically, though, their picture of African religion was made use of by evolutionary anthropologists who often sought to discredit all religion by revealing its irrational beginnings. Such anthropologists used data on African religion as evidence for the beliefs of the earliest human societies, out of which the historical religions had evolved.

In the twentieth century both missionary and anthropological assumptions changed but not in the direction of treating African religion more historically. Indeed, in reaction against the bogus history of the evolutionists most anthropologists ceased to ask historical questions at all. They produced instead subtle and illuminating studies of how African religion functioned to maintain the organic stability and coherence of traditional African societies. Functionalist anthropologists were often sharply critical of missionaries, whom they saw as ignorantly interfering with, and sometimes destroying, age-old and delicate mechanisms of social balance.

Many missionaries, however, also came to be much more sympathetic towards African religiosity and many of them sought to learn from functionalist anthropological studies. These missionaries came to admire precisely those qualities in African religion on which the anthropologists laid most emphasis. They liked, and hoped to reproduce within an 'adapted' Christianity, the communal values and social stabilities which they thought were guaranteed by African religion. It was no coincidence that these attitudes were most widespread and influential when colonial economies ran out of steam in the 1930s and when stable African rural communities were the ideal of both missionaries and administrators. Since Western historical 'progress' seemed to have led to disaster, African a-historicity began to look much more attractive. Many people's models of African religion were built up at this time by bringing together a collection of opposites to contemporary European beliefs rather than by any objective study of African religion itself.

Such models were taken over by a number of other groups who became particularly interested in African religion. One of these was the Pan-Africanist school, which argued for a single, common African consciousness arising from a fundamental religion of 'soul-force'. Pan-African consciousness, which it was believed had been preserved by Afro-Americans also, was contrasted with the technological aridity and competitive individualism of Europe. Another group which took over an a-historic model of African religion was the comparative religionists. Anxious to treat with respect all religious traditions of the world, they coined such terms as 'the primals' to describe the oral religions of the Third World. In books about religions in Africa such scholars set out to pay as much attention to African religion as they did to Christianity and Islam. The ways in which they treated these different religions, however, varied greatly. Christianity and Islam in Africa were treated very historically, with relatively little said about the imaginative experience of African Muslims or Christians. African religion, on the other hand, was not treated historically at all, but described entirely in experiential terms. This mode of treatment did as much injustice to African religion as it did to African Christianity and Islam.

Finally, African theologians writing in the last twenty years have offered the same a-historical picture of African religion. One of these, John Mbiti, has published the most widely influential studies of African religion. In these he has emphasised that African religion knew no future tense and possessed no founders, converts or prophets. African religion was coexistent with African societies; every member of a society was born into its religion. Mbiti regards this total integration of religion and society as wholly admirable and laments that it could not survive the rate of change and scale of interaction which have characterised modern Africa. He looks to national and indigenised African Christian churches to play the same role in the future.

It may well be asked whether so many different scholars, writing from so many different perspectives, can have been mistaken in their shared view about the a-historicity of African religion. The view clearly has a foundation in real contrasts between African religion and the historic religions of the book. But to say that African religions have not been historical in the same way as Islam and Christianity is not to say that they have no history at all. Intellectual developments of the last twenty years have led to at least an initial understanding of what that history has been.

One of these intellectual developments, of course, has been the general rise of historical studies of Africa. Thirty years ago most people doubted whether it was possible to write the history of any aspect of pre-colonial African societies, let alone of their religion. Today there is a vast body of historical literature about Africa, though it remains true that African religious history is the least fully developed. Nevertheless, it is now the case that we know that most African societies have undergone such profound economic, social and political changes that if African religion were coexistent with society it must also have changed profoundly. Moreover, the whole notion of an African 'society' has come under question. Many historians argue, for instance, that the tribal units into which twentieth-century Africa seems to be divided are of relatively recent origin. If this is the case, then it makes no historical sense to talk of 'Kamba religion' or 'Zulu religion' prior to the nineteenth century. Such constructs have their own and very recent history.

It seems clear, then, that African religion has a history—or perhaps more accurately that African religions have a history. The problem is to discover how to document and describe that history. Here African religious historians are able to draw on the whole battery of skills and methods which have been developed by African historiography as a whole. One of these is the collection and assessment of oral traditions. It turns out that some types of African religious institution—cults which possess shrines and priesthoods—have their own mechanisms for transmitting oral traditions. It also turns out that many bodies of oral tradition refer back to key religious figures, and especially to prophets and to bodies of prophecy.

In assessing this material, historians are greatly helped by intellectual developments within anthropology. Anthropologists have become interested in process and in transformation, and especially in cultural and ideological processes and transformations. Many of them draw a distinction between the 'imageless discourse' in which Europeans talk about change and an African 'argument of images' in which change is expressed and facilitated. In short, in Africa the metaphorical and ritual language of religion, so far from reiterating changelessness, is the very form which change takes.

Finally, there has been an increased interest in African religious history because it has become obvious that African religion is still playing a dynamic role in many parts of contemporary Africa. One example of this was the crucial influence exerted by spirit mediums in the Zimbabwean guerrilla war of the 1970s. These men and women, believed to be the mediums for spirits of founding heroes, 'made history' in two ways. They mediated between peasants and guerrillas so as to produce a single ideology of resistance. And they creatively restated oral tradition and redefined traditional history so as to integrate the guerrillas into the past as well as the present. In this case, then, African religious figures commanded history as process. Any historian of the Zimbabwean war has to take African religion into account whether he is a historian of religion or not.

What, then, can we begin to say about African religious history? We have to start off with a different model of African religion. For much of pre-colonial Africa we have to replace the idea of bounded tribal entities, each with its own 'religion', by a much more open and complex pattern. We have to think of broad regions of interaction between village-based agricultural peoples. Across these regions there flowed movements of hunters, and traders, and people in search of salt, and pilgrims to shrines. There were, therefore, many different levels of relationship between people. There were relationships with kin and neighbours but also relationships with other hunters and traders and pilgrims. There were relationships with the cultivated land, but also with the hunting bush and forests. African religious ideas were very much ideas about relationships, whether with other living people, or with the spirits of the dead, or with animals, or with cleared land, or with the bush. In many parts of Africa, though not invariably, all such relationships were thought of as relationships with spirits—spirits of ancestors, spirits of the land or the water or the bush, spirits of dead foreigners. The idiom of spirit was an idiom of personification, dramatising the personal rather than the merely metaphorical content of relationships. What Europeans have come to think of as absolutely impersonal phenomena—such as epidemic diseases—were also personified in African religious thought, and were represented by named spirits. All these spirits could manifest themselves by taking possession of living men or women.

These ideas—of relationship, spirit and possession—helped to make possible ordered interactions between people and helped to establish codes of conduct. Thus cults of the land enforced ecological rules—determining where and when fire could be used, when planting could begin, what crops should be grown. Cults of ancestors legitimated ideas of inheritance and laid down who could marry whom. Cults of alien or a-social spirits helped to establish rules of communication between traders and the communities through whom they passed. At the same time, the idea of relationships expressed through the idiom of spirits allowed for explanations of misfortune. Misfortunes were understood in terms of breach of relationships, either deliberate or inadvertent. Normality could be restored by determining to which spirit reparation was to be made.

So far this model has no doubt seemed a very functionalist one and, with its emphasis on rules, a very conservative one. But a number of points can at once be added. First, religious ideas were by no means restricted to personifying and policing relationships. There was speculation about the moral character of power; about the nature of personal identity; about what constituted 'good' and what 'evil'; about whether one could reasonably expect good fortune to be the norm or whether life was intrinsically ambivalent or even tragic. There was plenty of room for divinities as well as personifying spirits, and often the most important relationships were themselves thought of as involving divinities, so that some cults of the land addressed themselves to the spirit of a Creator God, as controller of rain and fertility. Second, the regions so far described, and the flows of people and ideas across them, were themselves the product of long historical processes and were constantly subject to change. The introduction of new crops, the rise of a trade in ivory, the emergence of strong polities which could exact tribute, and the development of new religious ideas and cults, could all significantly change the pattern. Thirdly, these systems of regional flows could not and did not produce a single, common, coherent religion, coexistent with 'society'. Each set of relationships involved different people at different levels and scales of interaction. So, recent historians of African religion have often talked about 'cults'—a territorial cult, concerned with relationships with the land; hunting guilds, concerned with relationships to other hunters and to wild animals; ancestral cults; so-called 'cults of affliction', bringing together strangers believed to be affected by the same spirit of disease and hence often emerging in zones of extensive trading. The geographical areas in which each of these cults operates vary greatly; so too does their personnel. Cults overlap each other and quite often compete with each other. Some esoteric cults initiate selected elders in a special, tragic or fatalistic understanding of the world, while the majority of people are engaged in less demanding and more optimistic rituals.

Hence there is great scope for innovation in this model. Contrary to Mbiti's propositions, there can be founders and prophets and converts. The presiding spirits of some territorial cults are remembered as having been in life historical prophetic figures, martyred by jealous rivals or arbitrary chiefs. A stranger could enter a region with a message about a hitherto unknown spirit of affliction or about a hitherto unknown means of eliminating the evil of witchcraft. New religious movements spread across whole regions with surprising regularity and rapidity. Often the founders or emissaries of such movements claimed a special authority given to them by God; they had died and returned to life with a special commission from God. Often this special commission was to restore old rules which had been broken, but even such conservative prophets could in effect produce change. Other prophets articulated new messages which called for change or legitimated it. In such a religious situation there was great dynamism rather than stasis; pluralism rather than a single, collective religion.

Of course, this open set of regional flows was often radically modified by the emergence of strong political units, whch sought to define their boundaries and to give a distinct identity to their subjects. This sometimes happened because of an unusual environment which gave special opportunity for co-ordinated exploitation, so that a ruler could advance claims to 'own' and control the land in a very particular way. In such a case, the rulers could take over a territorial cult completely, replacing the original presiding spirits, and turning it into a cult of dead kings. This happened, for instance, in the kingdom of Barotseland, on the flood plain of the Zambezi. Or the rulers could claim a special, privileged relationship with the territorial spirits, so that only they could be possessed by them or come to embody them, as happened in the kingdom of the Kuba in north-eastern Zaire, where a state-induced 'agricultural revolution' took place. Sometimes, on the other hand, a powerful kingdom emerged because its rulers could control the flow of trade, in which case territorial cults were much less significant to the state. Other polities depended on control of great cattle herds. Yet others depended on the development of a new military strength, either because of new techniques and weapons or new forms of social organisation. In such cases, cults of authoritarian militarism grew up.

In some cases, the ruling classes of African states became so powerful that they exerted control over most levels of religious association. Thus, the ancestral cult could become centralised so that at its apex were the spirits of dead kings; cults of initiation could be centralised so that young men and women were only inducted at the command and under the supervision of the king; trade flows could be so commanded by the state that cults of possession by alien spirits were set aside; new ideologies of military power could develop, bringing with them a prestige which made people strive to become identified solely as members of the state. All this could happen, though such a degree of control over all religious layers was rarely achieved even by the most powerful state. But even where it did happen the result was not simply one all-dominant consensus religion. Recently, for example, students of the Asante state have been revising views of the nature and function of Asante religion.

Hitherto the myths and rituals of Asante religion had been seen as ensuring an absolute consensus and submission to the divinely ordained authority of the king of Asante. But recent studies have shown that precisely because state power made rebellion or political opposition almost impossible, dissent within the Asante state took the form of counter-myth and counter-ritual. The Asante state was one of the most powerful in Africa. Elsewhere, even strong states had to coexist with long-established regional cults whose zones of influence overlapped with that of the state. And throughout Bantu-speaking Central Africa, abuses of chiefly power were regularly countered by the rise of prophets, whose role was to expose the corruption of rulers and to restore a right political order.

This picture of the variety, scale and dynamism of African religion not only contrasts sharply with older models of static, small-scale 'tribal' religions, but also means that historians have had to change their ideas about what happened when African religion encountered mission Christianity and colonial capitalism. Hitherto it had been thought that small-scale and stable religions could not handle the challenge of large-scale rapid change. In some remote places African religion 'survived'; elsewhere, bits and pieces of it continued to operate. But essentially, it was thought, African religion had become archaic, incapable of change or growth and fated to decay. The historic religions, with their sense of the future, their gift of literacy, and—in the case of mission Christianity—their commitment to the values of capitalist enterprise, were manifestly bound to triumph in the modern period. Now that we know more about the pre-colonial vitality of African religion, however, we have to question this sort of interpretation.

In its place a very different picture has begun to emerge. To begin with, we are coming to understand that African religion responded to the crises of the nineteenth century with a variety of thoughtful innovations. Economic crises—the rise of the slave trade in East Africa and its collapse in West Africa; political crises—the collapse of many long-established states and the emergence of new polities led by military adventurers; ecological crises—the spread of human and animal epidemics; the increasing awareness that powerful outsiders were pressing in upon Africa: all these meant that 'intellectuals' within African religious systems endeavoured to develop new ideas and forms that made more sense and gave more control of the world. In some cases they developed the idea and role of the High God, whose 'macrocosmic' authority seemed appropriate to the greatly increasing scale of societal interaction. In other cases, though, cults of possession by minor spirits became more widespread and influential, as a means of linking people together over wide regions.

In many places there was a sense of an almost millenial moment so that there were attempts to cleanse society by means of movements of witchcraft eradication, with public confession and destruction of charms, whether protective or malevolent. Throughout East, Central and Southern Africa great prophets emerged whose names and pronouncements are still vividly remembered today. These prophets were bearers of truth from God and only incidentally predictors; their lives and sayings allowed African peoples to feel that colonial conquest and capitalist transformation were not inexplicably imposed from outside but were events taking place in an indigenous drama.

It seems clear that many nineteenth-century missionaries were received by African societies as part of this complex movement of reinterpretation. Some missionaries were received as witchcraft eradicators, to whom people flocked to throw their charms on bonfires; others are remembered to this day as prophets. Others were accepted as knowing important things about the High God, even if they were ignorant about other spirits and about witches. From this moment on it becomes almost impossible to write about any of the religions of Africa—African religion itself, Islam, mission Christianity, independent African Christianity—in isolation from each other. There has been great religious pluralism in twentieth-century Africa, but, as we have seen, there was much religious pluralism in pre-colonial Africa too.

It also seems clear that African religion has not turned out to be incompatible with 'modern' societies. Certainly, African religious leaders were often prominent in armed resistances against European invasion and conquest. But their relation to the colonial world was not merely one of conservative repudiation, with the result that African religion remained influential only in the most remote communities. Instead the twentieth century has seen the same ferment of religious speculation and innovation as the nineteenth. Some scholars have shown how African religion could adapt to people becoming peasants; others have shown how it could adapt to people becoming migrant labourers. Cults of affliction and witchcraft eradication movements have been as vital under colonialism as they were before it. African cults of chiefship have often been supported by colonial powers who supported chiefs in what was called Indirect Rule. And colonially-backed chiefs have often been denounced by prophets at the head of popular movements. So-called 'secret societies' have formed the basis for self-help associations of urban migrants.

The variety of forms of African religion have thus proved relevant to colonial Africa. So also has the underlying and fundamental realisation of African religion—that morality is a matter of relationships, and relationships not only with living persons. The rise of Western medicine has certainly not undercut this insight; nor has the rise of scientific agricultural expertise. Crises of health and crises of environment demand relational rather than merely technological solutions. Moreover, the modes of communication of African religion—its argument of images—retain their power, enabling African rural communities to generate powerful metaphors for comprehending and operating within their world.

In conclusion, therefore, not only historians of religion but historians of social, cultural and economic change in Africa have come to realise that they must understand the idioms and history of African rural religion. So far from being set aside from, it has been intermixed with the main movements of twentieth-century change. African religion has turned out to be alive and important at the heart of revolutionary liberation movements. More than ever it needs to be understood historically and dynamically as well as experientially.

Further Reading

Binsbergen, W.M.J. van *Religious Change in Zambia. Exploratory Studies* (Routledge & Kegan Paul, London, 1981) (for an examination of twentieth-century African religious change by a historically conscious anthropologist)

Fernandez, J. *Bwiti: An Ethnography of the Religious Imagination in Africa* (Princeton University Press, New Jersey, 1982) (for an analysis of the argument of images in an innovatory African cult)

Lan, D. *Guns and Rain* (Heinemann Educational, London, 1985) (for an account of how spirit mediums made history during the Zimbabwean guerrilla war of the 1970s)

Mbiti, J.S. *African Religions and Philosophy* (Heinemann Educational, London, 1970) (for a non-historical account by an African theologian)

Parrinder, G. *Religion in Africa* (Penguin, Harmondsworth, 1969) (for a non-historical account by a distinguished comparative religionist)

Ranger, T.O. and Kimambo, I.N. (eds.), *The Historical Study of African Religion* (Heinemann Educational, London, 1972) (for a statement of the possibility and importance of a historical approach)

Ray, B.C. *African Religions. Symbol, Ritual and Community* (Prentice-Hall, New Jersey, 1976) (the most useful general introduction, which summarises the major anthropological works on African religion and is aware of the historical questions)

51 North American Traditional Religion

G. Cooper

The majority of the original inhabitants of the North American continent migrated there from north-east Asia across the Bering Straits, over a time-span of perhaps 12,000 to 60,000 years ago. Arriving as hunters, the movement of peoples across North America (and further south into Central and South America) led to the development of numerous tribes, displaying a wide variety of languages and lifestyles. Most tribes continued to rely primarily on hunting and gathering, but in certain areas, notably the east and south-west, tribes became more sedentary as they learned to grow crops, mainly maize, squash and beans. The most densely populated areas in aboriginal America lay along the eastern and western seaboards, where food supplies were most plentiful.

Particular tribal religions thus result from a development of some thousands of years in varying ecological, economic and cultural conditions. Furthermore, systematic investigation into native American religions did not begin on any major scale until the end of the nineteenth century, when all tribes had been affected in some degree by white culture. Consequently it becomes almost impossible to make generalisations about North American native religions, for we are dealing with many different and distinct religions and not one homogenous system.

There are none the less certain common elements underlying North American indigenous religions. No tribe has a word for 'religion' as a separate sphere of existence. Religion permeates the whole of life, including economic activities, arts, crafts and ways of living. This is particularly true of nature, with which native Americans have traditionally a close and sacred relationship. Animals, birds, natural phenomena, even the land itself, have religious significance to native Americans: all are involved in a web of reciprocal relationships, which are sustained through behaviour and ritual in a state of harmony. Distinctions between natural and supernatural are often difficult to make when assessing native American concepts.

Conceptions of time among native Americans are cyclical and concerned with reciprocal relationships, such that ritual becomes not mere re-enactment of mythic events, but rather the mythic event re-occurs in the present. Linked to this is the power of names and words: songs, prayers and myth-telling are viewed as spiritual forces which directly affect the world, giving it form and meaning and effecting changes.

Conceptions of the world derive from mythology. Hultkrantz has noted four major types of myth in North America. Firstly the cosmological myths, describing the cosmos, its origins and the interrelationships of its phenomena. This of course includes the Creation myths, of which there are a number of types. The most widespread is the Earth Diver, in which animals dive for mud in the primeval sea. Other major types are creation by world parents (the Father-Sky and Mother-Earth symbol being pervasive in North America), by Spider, from conflict between two beings, and the Emergence myth, which, strictly speaking, is more an account of human origins from worlds below the present one than a pure creation myth. Secondly there are institutional myths, which account for the existence of cultural and religious institutions. Thirdly there are ritual myths, which serve as 'texts' for ritual and ceremony and, finally, myths of entertainment or mythic tales, which are subject to elaboration and invention by the raconteur and are thus not of the same sacred character as other myths, but which, none the less, have important religious significance.

A distinction should be made between myth, which deals with the activities of deities and mythic beings in primordial times, and legend, where activities occur in historic times between humans and supernaturals. In North America, such a distinction is often difficult to make, since the two often merge. The Oglala Sioux account of the acquisition of the sacred pipe, for example, is, strictly speaking, a legend, but has the same sanctioning power as myth. A major function of mythology is to highlight the correct relationships between the phenomena of the world, thus providing not only sanction and explanation, but also moral and educational guidance. A greater elaboration and precision in myth and a closer correlation of myth with ritual is to be found among the horticulturalists, notably in the south-western USA. This closer relationship of myth and ritual allows not only greater precision of myth, but also of cosmology. In the horticultural societies, there is a more clearly defined three-layered world of heaven-earth-underworld than generally occurs among the hunting peoples, whose concepts of the underworld are vaguer. In the south-west, many more worlds are described, since here the myth of Emergence from previous worlds predominates. The concept of the world tree or pole is widespread, as are symbols of the cross, representing the four directions, and the circle.

Some variation is to be found in the notion of a Supreme Being. Despite a conviction by many early Western scholars that such a conception did not exist in North America, it has been clear for some time that this was erroneous. One reason for the confusion may well be that the Supreme Being is often only vaguely outlined and plays little role in immediate religious concerns. As such, the Supreme Being exists as a *deus otiosus*, remote from everyday affairs. This is not to suggest that conceptions of the Supreme Being necessarily lack sophistication. The Supreme Being of the Oglala Sioux, for example, involves aspects of transcendence and immanence of great subtlety. None the less, the Supreme Being usually remains remote, being prayed to at times of particular criticality, and other sacred beings play more prominent roles in everyday religious activity; in cultic activity the Supreme Being generally has an inconspicuous role. Even in mythology the Supreme Being does not, with the exception of certain cosmogonic myths, play a major role. The most prominent role in native American mythology generally is filled by the Trickster-transformer-culture-hero.

This latter figure reflects a widespread native American interest in the process whereby the world has been fashioned into its present nature, rather than in the original creation. The Trickster-transformer-culture-hero is a mythological character combining three different roles in one and is to be found throughout North America in different guises, being Coyote in the Plains, Basin, south-west and California areas, Raven or Mink on the north-west coast, Hare in the south-east and Bluejay in the Plateau area. Among hunting peoples, he tends to display the full range of roles—Trickster, a prankster or fool, whose activities provide the source for numerous and widespread 'Trickster tales'; Transformer, whose activities transformed the basic 'stuff' of the world into the present condition; and Culture-Hero, who, through daring adventures, provided numerous benefits (fire, water, daylight etc.) and cultural skills and customs to human beings, rendering the earth safe for human habitation. Among tribes where agriculture is prominent, it is often the Trickster elements alone that are found, cultural benefits being due to other beings. The 'Trickster tales', found throughout North America, provide one of the most entertaining series of myths and are extremely popular. Even though such myths can be considered as entertainment tales, being subject to elaboration and invention and therefore not having the same sanctioning power as other myths, which are sacred and hence unalterable, these tales none the less have important instructive and explanatory purposes and have significant religious value.

There are other mythological beings of importance, although many are regionally specific. Among the more widespread are the Thunderbird, which produces thunder and lightning, and the Hero Twins, culture-heroes who, in some areas, are associated with warfare.

Without doing injustice to native American concepts, it is possible to make a distinction between the sacred beings of myth and those of everyday life. There are exceptions such as the Thunderbird, which attracts significant cultic attention on the Plains, but generally mythological beings, whilst providing sanction for the cosmos and affecting the nature of the world, are often not so prominent in everyday religious concerns. Here we find, especially among the hunting peoples, where the close correlation between myth and ritual found among agriculturalists is lacking, that other sacred beings figure more prominently. Chief among these is the Master or Mistress of Animals, the divine leader and protector of game. He or she exercises stewardship over wild animals, especially those hunted by humans, and ensures that correct ritual is carried out by humans when hunting and burying the bones of animals. The Master or Mistress of Animals varies in character. Among the Eskimo, there is a female deity, Sedna, who controls sea animals from a home beneath the sea and, at times of game shortage, must be placated by a shaman, who makes a trance journey to her home. Elsewhere there may be a guardian animal for each of a number of species, often in hierarchical order, or there may be one for all species, as, for example, buffalo on the Plains. Among the Kwakiutl of the north-west coast, there are two guardians, one for land and one for sea, representing a wider cosmic dualism. In some hunting societies, the Master/Mistress of Animals can virtually be identified with the Supreme Being, reflecting the importance of game in hunting societies.

The seeking of a personal relationship with the sacred through vision is one of the most distinguishing features of many tribes. Deliberate 'vision quests' occurred throughout much of North America, typically involving a period of purification and prayer, followed by seclusion in a remote place for a period of days, during which time the supplicant fasts and prays until a vision is attained. Among the Eastern Woodlands and Prairie tribes, boys were expected to undertake the quest at puberty and acquire a guardian spirit, usually in animal form, which would lend supernatural power, usually throughout the individual's life. Among the Plains tribes such activity was observed by men, who regarded the vision quest as a means of gaining and renewing spiritual power. Visions were also associated with mourning, supplication, success in hunting and warfare and in curing. On the north-west coast, the vision became more a form of spirit possession, occurring during the winter ceremonial initiation rites. Unsought or spontaneous visions were generally regarded as more powerful than sought visions, but occurred more rarely and were the prerogative of the few, generally those who became shamans.

The acquisition of a guardian spirit was a practice found in all areas of North America, except the south-west. The most common way of acquiring one was through vision, but in some areas it was possible to inherit or purchase a guardian spirit, although the spirit involved had to agree to the transfer. Taken as a whole, the nature of guardian spirits seems limitless, varying from mythic beings to demons, the weather, even kettles, although by far the most common were animals and birds, occasionally appearing in anthropomorphic guise. Usually different spirits had different degrees of power or possessed different kinds of specialised power. Through the acquisition of a guardian spirit, an individual gained access to power, the nature of such power varying with the spirit, such as to lend either general power, giving aid in hunting or warfare, or a more specific, perhaps greater, power, such as the ability to cure illness or to prophesy. The relationship to the spirit was sustained through following instructions given by the spirit, including the use of certain songs and prayers, the observation of various taboos and the preparation of a 'medicine bundle', containing objects relating to the particular spirit. Spirits could be demanding and argumentative and the strong relationship between an individual and the guardian spirit in some cases amounted almost to a personal religion. On the Plains, individuals having the same guardian spirit formed societies, occasionally engaging in competitive demonstrations of power.

Individuals acquiring a guardian spirit which gave the power of curing generally formed a distinct group. Those who acquired this power through an unsought vision were regarded as particularly powerful and usually became shamans—those who entered trance to perform a variety of tasks, of which curing was the most important. True shamans and shamanism proper were to be found in the Arctic and north-west coast areas, although shamanism demonstrates its influence throughout the continent and many individuals displayed power derived from visionary experience who cannot be termed shamans in the strict sense. Unfortunately, the wide variety of individuals and activities centred around curing and the lack of an adequate morphology of such specialists means that they can only be referred to by the imprecise term 'medicine-men'. They can, nevertheless, be clearly distinguished from the more priestly figures, found in the south-west among the Navajo and Pueblo tribes, whose power is derived from the learning of traditional rites, rather than personal contacts with spirits.

Disease concepts traditionally rested on notions of soul-loss, taboo-violation or witchcraft, the latter two often resulting in the idea of object-intrusion—the lodging of an object in the patient's body. Curing rituals thus involved soul-retrieval, characteristic of shamanism, or object-extraction, all requiring the assistance of spirits to lend power. In the Eastern Woodlands and Plains there developed a curing ritual referred to as the 'Spirit Lodge' or 'Shaking Tent', in which a bound medicine-man attracted spirits to a darkened lodge or tepee to effect his release and cure the sick. Underlying all curing rituals is the basic notion of restoration of harmony.

One other sacred specialist deserves mention—the sacred clown. Found predominantly in the Plains, south-west, California and north-west coast areas, the clown displayed varying regional characteristics. In the Plains, he observed backward or contrary behaviour; among the Sioux this resulted from a vision of the Thunderbird. In the south-west, among the Pueblos, clown groups engaged in sexual, social and ceremonial satire. Although such behaviour occasionally appeared to have more entertainment than religious value, the clown was regarded as being a particularly powerful and sacred figure, displaying links with fertility as well as having psycho-social functions.

Women's participation in religious affairs was generally more limited. In some tribes women attained visions, although this was not common, and whilst medicine-women could be found, especially in Oregon and California, as a whole they were not as numerous as men. Child-bearing and rearing was considered their primary role. The ability to bear children gave women a singular power of their own, which, particularly among the hunters, was considered antithetical to power wielded by men. Female power was manifested most obviously in menstruation and women were normally isolated during this time for fear of 'polluting' sacred objects and ritual activity. Among the Athapascans especially, the girl's first menses was marked by an important puberty ceremony.

Ritual and ceremonial life demonstrates great richness and diversity. A brief summary of selected tribes in different areas must necessarily suffice to give some indication of this richness.

The Ojibwa of the north-east lived by hunting, fishing and gathering in a relatively harsh environment. In common with other hunting tribes in many parts of North America, individual rites predominated, centring round visions, attention to dreams and the acquisition of guardian spirits, termed *manitos*, which inhabited trees, rocks, birds, animals and other natural phenomena. Most rites involved the use of tobacco, regarded as a sacred plant. The largest ceremony was the *Midewiwin* (literally 'mystic doings'), a society of medicine-men which held an annual ceremony for the purposes of initiating new members and curing illness. Initiates, on payment of the requisite fees, could progress through a number of initiatory levels. The ceremony culminated in a public performance in a specially constructed medicine-lodge, in which the initiates were shot with *migis* (small white clam shells), which drove out sickness and renewed life.

On the Plains, the Oglala Sioux, whose traditional culture as we know it developed with the introduction of the horse in the early eighteenth century, likewise derived their living from hunting, predominantly buffalo, and here again individual rites predominated. Seven rituals associated with the use of the sacred pipe, originally given to the Sioux by the sacred White Buffalo Calf Woman, constituted the bulk of Sioux rituals. Whilst they included individual rituals, such as the purificatory Sweat Lodge and the Vision Quest, one in particular—the Sun Dance—was a major communal ceremony. This ceremony was held annually during the summer and involved the construction of a special lodge, at the centre of which was raised a cottonwood tree, representing the world pillar. The ceremony took place over four days and provided an opportunity for individual sacrifice as well as renewal of the relationship of the whole tribe to the sacred, being in essence a world-renewal ceremony.

Some of the richest, most dramatic ceremonialism occurred on the north-west coast, where stable and plentiful food supplies and sedentary living patterns in villages on the beaches allowed the development of rich material and ceremonial cultures. Among the Kwakiutl tribe, clans traced their ancestry to mythical animals who, in primordial times, became humans and founded the different lineages. There was a strong emphasis on status and rank and, through inherited rights, individuals were initiated into religious societies during a long winter ceremonial period. Pre-eminent among these societies was the *hamatsa* cult, relating to the great deity *Baxbakualanuxsiwae* (Great Man-eater). Initiation involved seclusion in the woods, spirit possession and public ritual with the appearance of dancers wearing elaborate masks and costumes and representing supernatural beings. The potlatch ceremony was a ceremonial distribution of wealth, related to rank and, like all Kwakiutl ceremonialism, reflected underlying motifs of transformation, death and rebirth.

Agricultural ceremonialism was found in some form wherever crops were grown. The most prominent forms occurred among the Pueblos of the south-west, particularly the Hopi of Arizona. Relying on scanty rainfall for the growing of maize and other crops, Hopi ceremonialism is linked to both myth and the agricultural cycle. Social, political and ceremonial organisation was traditionally interlinked and a number of different religious societies perform ceremonies at particular times of the year from November (the start of the New Year) onwards. Involving secret rituals in ceremonial chambers, called *kivas*, and with public dances on the concluding days, ceremonies incorporate rituals of recreation, initiation and the attraction of *kachinas*—spirits who bring rain and other blessings to the tribe. Masked dancers appear as *kachinas* in both private and public rituals. Other Pueblo groups to the east, whilst stressing fertility, show stronger emphasis on curing ceremonies, carried out by organisations of medicine-men. Although these practices show clear shamanic influences, Pueblo religious specialists rely solely on learned traditions as the basis of their power and not on visionary experience.

The Navajo, pastoralist neighbours of the Pueblos, likewise rely on the learning of word-perfect ritual as the basis of their ceremonialism. Arriving in the south-west around 1500 CE as small hunting bands, this tribe provides a good example of a people who have adopted more elaborate religious conceptions and practices (in this case from the Pueblos) and, in so doing, have developed basic shamanic curing rituals into complex and lengthy ceremonials for the curing of illness, which constitute virtually the whole of Navajo ceremonial practice. During these ceremonials, some of which last nine days and nights, the patient is identified with holy people through prayer, song and the use of dry-paintings or sand-paintings, which depict mythic events associated with the particular ceremonial; in fact each ceremonial is a reoccurrence of a myth, the patient being identified with the hero and original patient, who, through exorcising of evil and identification with holy people, is restored to a state of harmony.

These brief examples can only suggest the richness and diversity of native American ceremonial life, which tends to be almost exclusively concerned with this life. Native American religious life generally displays little concern with eschatology. The afterlife was commonly seen as a happier continuation of this life, behaviour in this life having little effect on one's fate after death. In all of North America, bar the south-west, the belief occurs in one form or another that human beings are equipped with two kinds of soul: a bodily soul, granting life and movement and consciousness to the body, and a dream or free soul, identical to the person, which can leave the body and visit far-away places, including the land of the dead. This free soul can be directed at will by shamans and indeed the general belief can be traced to the pervasive influence of shamanism. The dead, with few exceptions, were feared in varying degrees and it was considered important to maintain a clear separation between living and dead.

The traditional religious life of the native Americans is the result of development over many thousands of years. Even before the arrival of the Europeans, ecological, economic and cultural factors meant that native American religions have never been static systems of belief and practice. However, the incoming Europeans had a radically different and more overwhelming influence on traditional cultures. Policies towards the native Americans varied, but the net result was the introduction of diseases and military conquest, which killed millions and led to the extinction of numerous tribes, the taking of land and the suppression of traditional culture and religion. The loss of land and traditional lifestyles has affected different tribes in different ways. Little remains of traditional religious culture in some areas, whereas other areas (for example in the south-west, where the desert land was of little interest to whites) retain strong traditional religions.

The south-west was the initial area of penetration by Europeans into North America when the Spaniards arrived in the sixteenth century and proceeded to impose political and religious domination on the Pueblos. Despite nominal conversion to Catholicism, traditional ceremonialism survived virtually intact and today the two systems of belief coexist with relatively little friction. Elsewhere, missionary activity, coupled with the banning of traditional ritual in the 1880s, has led to the nominal conversion of most native Americans to Christianity. I say nominal because it is in fact often impossible to make clear distinctions between Christians and traditionalists. Whilst there are strict adherents to both of these belief systems, they are not necessarily mutually exclusive, many native Americans fluctuating between the two, depending on circumstances. Of overriding importance is their sense of identity as, firstly, members of a particular tribe and, secondly, as native Americans.

In this regard, two religious responses by native Americans to encroaching white culture and religion are of importance. The first is the Ghost Dance movement of the late nineteenth century, which originated with the Piaute prophet, Wovoka, who beheld God in a vision. He was told that the old life would return and the dead come back to life, provided that the Indians regularly performed dances. This millenarian movement, combining Christian and indigenous elements, swept across the Great Basin and Plains areas in 1889–90, assuming a distinctly anti-white tendency among the more warlike tribes, particularly the Sioux, who introduced 'Ghost Dance shirts', said to offer protection against bullets. The movement culminated in military action against the Sioux, ending with the murder of Chief Sitting Bull and the massacre of a large band of Sioux at Wounded Knee in 1890. With this defeat and the failure of the millenium to materialise, the movement died away. It was, none the less, a significant attempt to posit a positive future for peoples whose ways of life were being destroyed.

A more successful syncretic response is the Peyote Cult. The ritual taking of peyote, an hallucinogenic cactus, developed in Mexico and spread northwards into the Plains during the latter part of the nineteenth century. It is now firmly established in a number of tribes and, although its spread was vigorously opposed by both Christians and traditionalists, it clearly provides a means of gaining power for the dispirited and, by combining Christian (the use of the Bible, Christian prayers and ethics) and traditional (singing, drumming, visions and the incorporation of indigenous spirits) elements, it provides a new ritual form which is distinctly Indian, but which allows accommodation to a changing world.

It has often been assumed that, with the overwhelming influence of white culture and the corresponding destruction of traditional native American ways of life, that the traditional religions have become virtually extinct. This is an inadequate and erroneous conception. Whilst traditions often display outward signs of collapse, native American religions have always been dynamic, incorporating historical changes and disruptive elements within them. The effects of white culture have been especially dramatic and severe, but the persistence and survival of the basic identity of so many Indian tribes is a testament to their ability to withstand change and adapt new situations to the essential characteristics of their own traditions.

Currently, therefore, native American societies display a variety of religious beliefs and practices, ranging from the purely traditional, through syncretic forms such as peyotism, to Christianity. One important recent factor has been the rise of what has been termed 'red power', reflecting a widespread determination by native Americans to pursue more forcibly such issues as land rights and sovereignty, guided by an increased concern with arresting the erosion of their traditional cultures and religions. This is resulting in much resurgence and revitalisation of traditional religions. These religions are thus by no means extinct, indeed they continue to give strength and meaning to native Americans and offer scholars of religion a rich source of revealing and significant insights into the religious life of human beings.

Further Reading

Beck, P. and Walters, A. (eds.) *The Sacred* (Navajo Community College, Tsaile, 1977)

Brown, J.E. *The Sacred Pipe* (University of Oklahoma Press, Norman, 1953)

Cooper, G.H. *Development and Stress in Navajo Religion* (Almqvist and Wiksell, Stockholm, 1984)

Feraca, S.E. *Wakinyan: Contemporary Teton Dakota Religion* (Museum of the Plains Indian, Browning, 1963)

Gill, S.D. *Songs of Life: an Introduction to Navajo Religious Culture* (E.J. Brill, Leiden, 1979)

—— *Native American Religions: an Introduction* (Wadsworth, Belmont, 1982)

Goldman, I. *The Mouth of Heaven: an Introduction to Kwakiutl Religious Thought* (Wiley, New York, 1975)

Hultkrantz, A. 'Spirit Lodge, a North American Shamanistic Seance' in C-M. Edsman (ed.), *Studies in Shamanism* (Almqvist and Wiksell, Stockholm, 1967), pp. 32–68

—— *The Religions of the American Indians* (University of California Press, Berkeley, 1979)

—— 'Myths in Native American Religions' in E.H. Waugh and K.D. Prithipaul (eds.), *Native Religious Traditions* (Wilfred Laurier University Press, Waterloo, 1979), pp. 77–97

LaBarre, W. 'The Peyote Cult', *Yale University Publications in Anthropology* (Yale University Press, New Haven, 1938), vol. 19

Landes, R. *Ojibwa Religion and the Midewiwin* (University of Wisconsin Press, Madison, 1968)

MacNeish, R.F. *Early Man in America* (W.H. Freeman, Oxford, 1973)

Mooney, J. *The Ghost Dance and the Sioux Outbreak of 1890* (University of Chicago, Chicago, 1965; originally pub. 1896)

Slotkin, J.S. *The Peyote Religion: a Study in Indian–White Relations* (Free Press, Glencoe, 1956)

Waters, F. *Book of the Hopi* (Viking, New York, 1963)

52 Latin American Traditional Religion: Three Orders of Service

Gordon Brotherston

In the native New World, as anywhere else, religion responds to geography, economics and language, phenomena which over that continent prove to be extremely varied. Yet underlying a diversity of local cults and practices, certain doctrines or 'orders of service', proper in the first instance to religion, may be discerned as nothing less than paradigmatic. A clear case is the trance journey, typified by a visit to the nether world: prevalent in cosmogony throughout North America, including Mexico and parts of Central America, this other-worldly quest has been widely instituted as a principle of religious initiation in such traditional priesthoods as that of the Midewiwin, on the uppermost Mississippi. Noting the tests, rhythms and astronomical correlatives of the trance journey takes us into what may be considered a true shamanist substratum of the whole northern sub-continent, comparable with that analysed by Mircea Eliade, and by Ake Hultkranz in his study of the North American Orpheus motif.

Other such paradigms appear rather to confine themselves to cultural areas already established in scholarship, and indeed stand as a privileged diagnostic of those areas. Examples come from greater Mexico or Mesoamerica, and from South America. In the teeming pantheons of the former, an area which owes its very definition to the existence of pre-Columbian scripts, iconographic and hieroglyphic, as well as screenfold books of paper and parchment that deal pre-eminently with religion, we find a remarkable triple pattern which holds good over great distances and time-depths and which corresponds intimately with the particular agricultural and urban development of the area. Further south, we find rather a monotheistic emphasis, in the cult of Viracocha, the chief deity of the vast empire of the Inca known as Tahuantinsuyu or 'Four Districts' in Quechua: stretching down the Andes from present-day Colombia to Chile, this area forms a highly distinct world within South America. This is due not least to the pastoral economy unique to it in America and hallowed by Viracocha, which in its own way transformed the myriad cults, beliefs and myths of the surrounding lowlands that have provided the main focus for the four monumental volumes of Lévi-Strauss's *Mythologiques*.

In considering these three cases, we may appeal to a wide range of evidence not least from the disciplines of archaeology, anthropology and history. Here the guiding principle has been above all literary: throughout the emphasis is on native texts, that is, on statements made by native Americans themselves and where possible recorded in their language and by their means and media. In sheer technical terms, such an approach has been facilitated by the growing scholarly attention to the whole issue of script and visual language in the New World, from the scrolls of the Midewiwin, through the great bibliographical heartland of Mesoamerica, to the *quipu* or knotted-string records of the Inca. Acknowledging these original sources helps to validate the deeper coherences of native American religion, as these are evinced for example in a comparison between the pages of a pre-Columbian screenfold book and sand-paintings used in Navajo ceremonial today. It also helps to make up for some of the grosser distortions of the past, which arose in the main from Christianity's perceived need to justify, in religious terms, the invasion and expropriation of native America that began with Columbus.

The Shaman's Trance Journey

A striking introduction to all that concerns the trance journey is provided by the Ottawa-Algonkin shaman Chusco (Muskrat). Born a few years after Pontiac's rising in the early 1760s, Chusco bargained with General Wayne at Greenville (1793); he was prominent in the Midewiwin but his wife's involvement with the Christian mission at Mackinac led to his apostasy in the last ten years of his life (1828–38), during which time he divulged Mide secrets to Henry Rowe Schoolcraft. In this way he came to contribute to the one-verse epic of Indian America in English, Longfellow's *Hiawatha* (i.e. Manabozho), a work which draws heavily on Schoolcraft.

In Schoolcraft's *Algic Researches* (1839), Chusco's narrative bears the title 'Iosco or a visit to the sun and moon: a tale of Indian cosmogony, from the Ottawa'. The opening incorporates tales told by Indians who by one means or another had visited the Old World: travelling east, Iosco and five companions first cross the sea and end up in a gilded European capital. Still determined to encounter the sun and the true source of life, the six press on with their journey, and only from this point does the cosmogony proper begin. Changing entirely, the landscape becomes subterranean, and after three days which 'were really three years' the six meet the rattle-wielding Manabozho. In conversation he offers them guidance and notes that on arriving they had passed over three-fourths of their way and that they are to spend the remaining time with him, a day which also is really a year, making four in all. Before setting off again, in twos, each of the three pairs makes a wish about how long they should live, with the result that only the humblest pair, Iosco and his companion, succeed in crossing a chasm that then opens before them.

On the other side these two meet the moon, a woman in white 'approaching as from behind a hill'. She tells them that they are now half-way to her brother's (the sun) and that from the earth to her abode was half the distance; and she promises in due time to lead them to her brother then absent on his 'daily course'. In this half-way position they stay with her until the 'proper time' arrives to meet the sun. The story goes on:

> When the proper time arrived, she said to them, 'My brother is now rising from below, and we shall see his light as he comes over the distant edge: 'come,' said she, 'I will lead you up.' They went forward, but in some mysterious way, they hardly knew how, they rose almost directly up, as if they had ascended steps.

At a point 'half-way' between the edge of the earth and 'midday', Iosco then converses directly with the sun, being in effect blessed by him. Then, having reached the point of plenitude, the 'Heart of Heaven' or midday, they set off down again, making the last half of the descent 'as if they had been let down by ropes'.

With its references to Europe and the Old World, Iosco's solar quest was no doubt Chusco's own, and reflects the struggle he felt in himself between Mide and Christian teaching. In any case, the tale lives up to its cosmogonical epithet; it leads us up from the lower to the upper paths of the solar walk. For in time and space Iosco follows the apparent course of the sun and moon; and the 4+4 day-years he spends between west and east evoke the four-year leap day span of the sun, each year acquiring the quarter-day later defined between east and west; and they evoke as well the utas and the eight-year octaeteris over which the yearly sun and the moon again get back in step with one another (8 years equal 99 moons). As for Manabozho, the third figure in the story encountered prior to the moon in the underworld, he has been equated with the Nanabush of the Lenape *Walam Olum* and the great Hare or Rabbit Michabo. Just this identity is widely attributed to the Morning Star Venus in North America, among the Sioux, where as a hunter he steps over the eastern horizon before the sun (by rising heliacally), and in Mexico, where the sign for Venus is equivalent ritually to the sign Rabbit. Along the solar walk of the northern Blackfeet Algonkin, the Morning Star, together with his parents sun and moon, makes up the 'big three', the trio of the brightest bodies in the sky; and it is the case astronomically that the octaeteris experienced by Iosco includes Venus (over 5 synodic periods) just as much as the moon and sun, a point developed below.

The moral concerns implicit in Iosco's quest were anticipated in a famous story recounted by Pontiac, likewise an Ottawa and a Mide shaman, as well of course as the great military opponent of the English. Faced with the task of closely uniting his diverse forces he described a pilgrimage similar to Iosco's, undertaken by a member of the 'grandfather' tribe of the Algonkin nations and the Huron alike, a Lenape (Delaware) of the Wolf clan. The only record that survives of Pontiac's words stems from the inimical pen of Robert Navarre who, witnessing the narrative, deplores it as 'the principal of the blackest of crimes against the English nation, (i.e. Pontiac's rising) and perhaps against the French, had not God in his grace ordered it otherwise'. Despite Navarre's hostility as interpreter, the outline of the narrative comes through clearly and suggests the same paradigm of native religion and cosmogony. It is also perhaps significant that the day chosen by Pontiac to relate it, 27 April 1763, was reported as the fifteenth of the moon, i.e. full moon.

Anxious to know the 'Master of life', the Lenape sets out on his journey, making much the same preparations as Iosco does. Overall this again lasts eight 'days', and it leads to a choice between three paths that grow strangely luminous in the twilight of the eighth day. This motif conjoins the two lots of three paths evoked in Iosco: those of the bright trio on the solar walk (sun, moon, Venus), and those chosen respectively by the three pairs of travellers, only one of which led to midday in the sky (that of the sun). This reading is strengthened by the fact that again only one path, the third, takes the Lenape hero the whole way through the day; the other two go only 'half-way' and issue into a large fire 'coming from underground', which is where Iosco encounters Venus and the moon and where the unsuccessful pairs of his companions go no further. Having travelled the right path, the Lenape is shown the way to his goal by the moon, who likewise appears on a mountain as a white woman.

Several details in Pontiac's narrative, notably the instructions given to the Lenape by the Master of life, are quite possibly Christian in origin and were perhaps inserted to win over the evangelised Huron and even the French to his cause. Yet there can be little doubt about its adherence to the solar-walk paradigm of Chusco's story, and hence about its indigenous spirituality.

In literary-historical terms Chusco's and Pontiac's narratives are best understood as products of the Midewiwin, the predominantly Algonkin priesthood that had and has its heartland in Ojibway territory at the sources of the Mississippi, the Great Lakes and Hudson Bay. For they both invoke doctrines basic to that body, notably those relating to the hunt and to the initiation of novices by degrees, which feature Manabozho as guide, intermediary and instructor of the Mide, the moon and its phases, and the quest for life's sources in the noon sun. Mide charts on birchbark graphically record the novice's path through a series of degrees which like the 'days' of the solar walk conform to an ideal total of 4 (+4), while certain chronological symbols specify fast and feast periods each of four actual days. More graphically still, symbols recording antiphonal verses intoned during initiation, which also normally fall into stanzas of four, depict both the physical course of the solar walk which the candidate aspires to make and the celestial travellers along it, sun, moon and Venus.

Hence pictographic texts copied and interpreted by Sikassige, Little Frenchman, Kweweshiash and other Mide shamans begin with the entry into the Mide lodge, the collecting of fees, and preparatory activities like taking a sweat bath and digging down into the earth for 'medicine' with which to enhance perception for the journey itself. This may start 'below' and follow the course, for example, of the otter sacred to Manabozho, or the beaver renowned for his capacity to travel great distances before resurfacing. Or it can be celestial: the candidate rises up on and into the arch of the sky by steps or like a bird and there encounters the Great Spirit (Gitche Manito) depicted as the sun. To a figure mounting the celestial arch from the east like 'the sun pursuing his diurnal course till noon', and like Iosco and the Lenape traveller, correspond the words: 'I walk upon half the sky'; similarly the moment of plenitude at noon or midday is registered by a figure atop the arch, to which Sikassige puts the words: 'The spirit has given me power to see'. (See Figure 52.1a, b.)

Figure 52.1: Mide Symbols for the Solar Walk

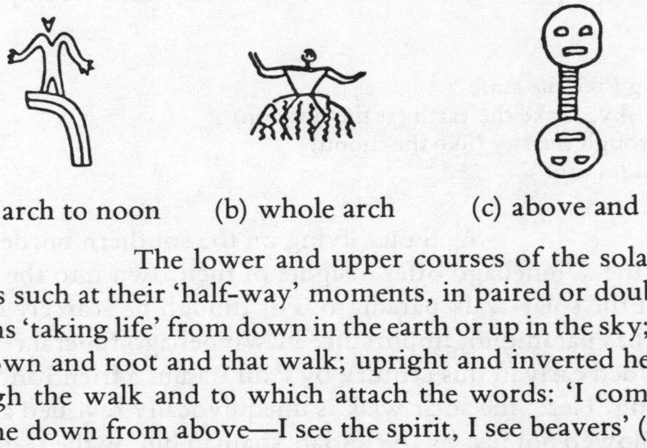

(a) half arch to noon (b) whole arch (c) above and below

The lower and upper courses of the solar walk are epitomised as such at their 'half-way' moments, in paired or double-headed symbols: arms 'taking life' from down in the earth or up in the sky; trees with foliage at crown and root and that walk; upright and inverted heads which rotate through the walk and to which attach the words: 'I come up from below, I come down from above—I see the spirit, I see beavers' (Figure 52.1c). In a single-stanza song 'for beaver hunting and the Metai Mide' collected by Tanner, the down-up opposition occurs in the first and last symbols, a subterranean lodge and a flying eagle. This text is also notable for the chronology encoded in its second symbol, which depicts the four 'day-years' familiar from Chusco and Pontiac. Referring to marks drawn on a fasting figure, on chest (2) and legs (4), come the words: 'Two days must you sit fast, my friend; four days must you sit fast'. 'Binding' the legs the four lines mean actually sitting fast for four days but as far as the candidate's inner devotion goes Tanner's informant assured him that they are understood simultaneously to mean four years.

A definite link between these Mide texts and the extended alphabetic narratives of Chusco and Pontiac is provided by Catherine Wabose, an apostate like Chusco, who described her first solar walk both verbally and in a pictographic Mide chart. Prepared by a ritual fast of four days, she sets off on a mysterious path stretching down between the setting sun and the new moon at the western horizon; having passed figures equivalent to the full moon and Venus (see Figure 52.2b, d), she rises to the heart of the sky, the climax of the vision, before again descending, on a snake. The importance of the moon's phases is clear from Wabose's and one of Little Frenchman's symbols (see Figure 52.2c) while moon and Venus, in the posture of the guide Manabozho, are similarly conjoined in single stanza of

Figure 52.2: Mide Symbols for the Three Travellers

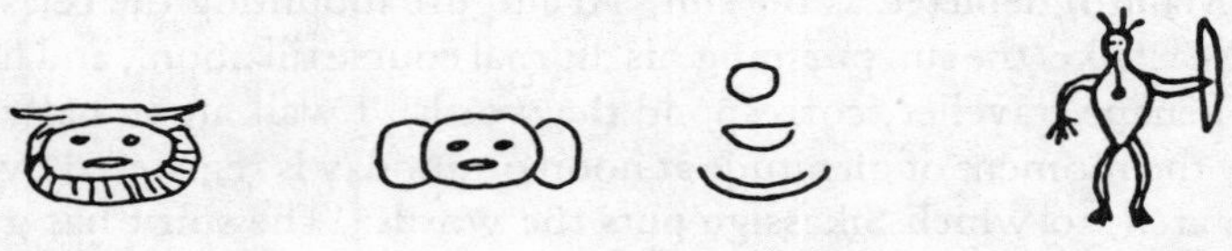

(a) sun (b–c) moon (d) Manabozho

hunter's pictographs also recorded by Schoolcraft. The accompanying words read:

I am rising (like the sun)
I take the sky, I take the earth (at the horizon)
I walk through the sky (like the moon)
Venus guides me.

As Sioux living on the southern border of the Mide heartland, the Winnebago offer insights of their own into the meaning and function of the solar-walk paradigm. For though he scarcely comments on the fact, it has paramount importance in Winnebago funeral rituals meticulously recorded early in this century by Paul Radin, a friend and collaborator of C.G. Jung. Here, the solar walk is unequivocally revealed as the route to true life followed not just by the initiate shaman but by the soul after death.

Instructed by a great-grandmother figure, the Winnebago soul sets off on a path that takes him past the underworld fire of the Lucifer-like Herucgunina, leads him step by step over the eastern horizon, and brings him up to the circle of his relatives in the heart of the sky. He (or she) is told:

My grandchild, Earthmaker is waiting for you in great expectation. There is the door to the setting sun. On your way stands the lodge of Herecgunina, and his fire.

> Those who have come [the souls of brave men] from the land of the souls to take you back will touch you. There the road will branch off towards your right and you will see the footprints of the day on the blue sky before you. These footprints represent the footprints of those who have passed into life again. Step into the places where they have stepped and plant your feet into their footprints, but be careful you do not miss any. Before you have gone very far, you will come into a forest broken by open prairies here and there. Here, in this beautiful country, these souls whose duty it is to gather other souls will come to meet you. Walking on each side of you they will take you safely home. As you enter the lodge of the Earthmaker you must hand to him the sacrificial offerings. Here the inquiry that took place in the first lodge will be repeated and answered in the same manner. Then he will say to you, 'All that your grandmother had told you is true. Your relatives are waiting for you in great expectation. Your home is waiting for you. Its door will be facing the mid-day sun. Here you will find your relatives gathered.

Texts such as this bring together the Mide tradition (compare the 'footsteps' with Iosco's) with the Plains Ghost Dance of the 1890s, in which Sioux and Algonkin alike re-enacted the circular dance of their relatives in the heart of the sky.

Besides this, the Winnebago ritual observed by Radin touches on the matter of the 4+4 day-years experienced by Iosco and other travellers along the solar walk. For the Winnebago wake lasts four days, during which period the mourners concentrate on helping the soul on his way beyond death, until he has passed the critical half-way encounter with Herucgunina. Indeed, what the mourners say and do, whether or not they exaggerate or lie about their own capacity to help, directly affects the soul's passage. For his or her part, the traveller enters another type of time, the 'ancient' time of the spirits, in which the true period of mourning is said to be not four days but four years. Similarly, sacrificial victims among the Aztecs contemplated a journey to the underworld with the words: 'over four years we shall be carried on the wind'. In other words, as in Tanner's fasting symbol, it is a question of two dimensions of time, earthly and spirit, days and years, which run concurrently, correlated by means of an astonomically significant cipher. (For the shamans not far north of the northern Algonkin a day *is* a year.)

Geographically, the solar-walk paradigm may be understood as part of a larger tradition of native American ritual and chronology whose coherence is especially marked in the northern half of the continent, extending from the Atlantic coast and the south-east, across the Plains to the south-west and Mexico. For in Mexico and Mesoamerica, the walk is clearly mapped out in native script, hieroglyphic and iconographic, in the screenfold books of ritual. On the *mappa mundi* pages of the Fejervary and Laud screenfolds, for example, it may be traced through the cardinal stations of native astronomy in the tropics, the east and west horizons, with zenith and nadir each half-way between; such is the case too with the Venus tables in the hieroglyphic Dresden screenfold. For this is the route followed by the culture-heroes of Mesoamerican cosmogonies implicit on those pages and written out alphabetically in such works as the Nahua 'Cuauhtitlan Annals' and 'Legend of the Suns', the Quiche-Maya *Popul vuh*, and the lowland Maya Books of Chilam Balam. True to the astronomical analogue, these travellers pass through the underworld (Mictlan, Xibalba), rise again at the eastern horizon, and reach the moment of plenitude in the heart of the sky.

In the 'Legend of the Suns' the 'feathered serpent' Quetzalcoatl descends to Mictlan to acquire the bones from which to make woman and man; on his way back up east, this Venus-figure faces a strange hazard, one astoundingly reminiscent of that faced at the same astronomical position by the Morning Star of the Blackfeet Algonkin: he is set upon and pecked at by birds. In the *Popul vuh*, whose underworld 'test-theme' has been fruitfully compared with that in the cosmogonies of the south-west, the hero Twins descend to Xibalba to avenge their father who had been murdered there and got no further than this half-way station; they themselves pass through and like their Mide counterparts step up into the eastern sky, where they actually become sun and moon:

> And thus they took their leave,
>   Having completely conquered all of Hell (Xibalba)
> And then they walked back up
>   Here amid the light,
> And at once
>   They walked into the sky.
> And one is the sun,
>   And the other of them is the moon.
> Then it grew light in the sky,
>   And on the earth.
> They are still in the sky.
>
> (tr. M. Edmonson)

This same stepping up past the eastern horizon recurs in the far more esoteric lowland Maya version of what is basically the same cosmogony in the Chumayel Book of Chilam Balam. In a long and complex chapter of that book (pages 42–63), levels of reality are successively claimed through the establishment of the basic sets of Mesoamerican ritual themselves, the midwife's 9, the augur's 13, and finally the 'alphabet' of Twenty Signs, against each of which a tenet of Christian dogma is critically examined. Embodied as the *uinal*, this last set begins his cosmic journey under a great-grandmother's tutelage, exactly as in Winnebago ritual which indeed is echoed with surprising closeness when it comes to 'getting into step' at the eastern horizon (here also a pun and an Eleatic paradox):

> He started up from his inherent motion alone.
> His mother's mother and her mother, his mother's sister and his sister-in-law, they all said:
> How shall we say, how shall we see, that man is on the road?
> These are the words they spoke as they moved along, where there was no man.

When they arrived in the east they began to say:
Who has been here? These are footprints. Get the rhythm of his step.
So said the Lady of the world,
And our Father, Dios, measured his step.
This is why the count by footstep of the whole world, xoc lah cab oc was called
lahca oc 12 Oc.
This was the order born through 13 Oc,
When the one foot joined its counter print to make the moment of the eastern
horizon,
Then he spoke its name when the day had no name.
as he moved along with his mother's mother and her mother, his mother's sister
and his sister-in-law
The uinal born, the day so named, the sky and earth,
the stairway of water, earth, stone and wood, the things of sea and earth realized.

1 Chuen, the day he rose to be a day-ity and made the sky and earth.
2 Eb he made the first stairway. It ebbs from heaven's heart
the heart of water, before there was earth, stone and wood

It is on reaching the 'heaven's heart' that the *uinal* completed his journey and himself: the twenty constituent Signs join hands to form a circle of relatives reminiscent alike of the centre of the Aztec Sunstone and the Ghost Dance songs.

In all, the Mesoamerican texts lend a truly epic dimension to the solar-walk paradigm and relate it specifically to the emergence of man in the grand evolutionary scheme of multiple creation or suns. And in so doing they enrich our astronomical reading of the 4+4 cipher, further developing the day-year time-shift noted in texts from further north; compare, too, the lots of 4 day-years in the lives of the Navajo Sun's children in the same world-age context. Duly observed in the Aztec Atamale ceremony the 4+4 years of the octaeteris are formally embedded in the very mechanism of the Mesoamerican calendar, which groups years into leap-day spans of four recurrent Signs and in which the second burial ceremony occurred after four years. For their part the Dresden Venus tables take the octaeteris (of 2920 days) as their base; and they clearly establish the much cited eight days of the solar walk as the official length of that planet's inferior conjunction or underworld passage from west to east. This fact strongly corroborates our previous detections of Venus figures in Mide and related texts. The principle of the Dresden tables is Venus's subsequent ascension in the east, its heliacal rising as Morning Star. Detailed in the iconographic screenfolds, this dramatic moment is ritually acknowledged in the Nine-night chants of the south-west and on the Plains, and appears for example in the Sioux story of the rabbit hunter who manages to outpace the sun. It also dominates the 'Cuauhtitlan Annals' version of One-Reed Quetzalcoatl's self-incineration in 895 CE and his apotheosis as Venus, for prior to his heliacal rising, the passage through the underworld falls into two lots of 4 days, the official length of inferior conjunction either side of Mictlan. In a passage of great beauty, adapted by D.H. Lawrence in his novel *The Plumed Serpent*, we learn how Quetzalcoatl's heart makes the same journey, having burned to incandescence:

> So that where Quetzalcoatl burnt himself is called the place of Incineration.
>
> And it is said that when he burned, his ashes rose up and every kind of precious bird appeared and could be seen rising up to the sky: roseate spoonbill, cotinga, trogon, blue heron, yellow-headed parrot, macaw, white-fronted parrot, and all other precious birds. And after he had become ash the quetzal bird's heart rose up; it could be seen and was known to enter the sky. The old men would say he had become Venus; and it is told that when the star appeared Quetzalcoatl died. From now on he was called the Lord of the Dawn.
>
> Only for four days he did not appear, so it is told, and dwelt in Mictlan. And for another four days he sharpened himself. After eight days the great star appeared called Quetzalcoatl on his ruler's throne. And they knew, on his rising, which people, according to Sign, he penetrates, shoots into and loathes.

In conclusion here it may be fairly claimed that the solar walk was and is a paradigm in native North American religion. Integral to it are a pattern of days and years of astronomical significance and the principle of the time-shift itself. With Chusco this leads further into the inner dimensions of the day, forenoon and afternoon; in Mesoamerica it leads outwards towards a vast evolutionary story recorded at length in the *Popul vuh* and counted by aeons, hundreds of millions of years, in the hieroglyphic inscriptions.

Mesoamerica's Priests, Farmers and Warriors

When rejecting Franciscan efforts to Christianise them in 1524, in the Aztec capital Tenochtitlan (today Mexico City), the priesthood of that place pointed out that they already had a religion of their own, one with roots deep through the vast extent of the Aztec tribute empire, and Mesoamerica itself. Rather than insist on this point, the Aztecs preferred, as they put it, to open the treasure casket just a little, to allow a glimpse of their indigenous tradition. And they did so in a finely structured piece of rhetoric, which touches in turn on the three gifts of their gods, each being allotted a stanza that begins with the words '*They* gave' or 'give' (*yehuan-maca-*) and ends with the question 'where?' (*in canin*). This part of their speech is worth quoting in full, because of its precise detail, and because it has not been widely published in direct English translation:

> They gave us
> their law
> and they believed,
> they served, and they taught the honour among gods;
> they taught the whole service.
> That's why we eat earth before them;

that's why we draw our blood and do penance;
and that's why we burn copal and kill the living.
They were the Lifelord
and they became our only subject.
When and where?—In the eldest Darkness.

They give us
our supper and our breakfast,
all things to drink and eat,
maize and beans, purslane and sage.
And we beg them
for thunder-Rain and Water
on which the earth thrives.
They are the rich ones
and they have more than simply what it takes;
they are the ones with the stuff,
all ways and all means, forever,
the greenness of growth.
Where and how?—In Tlalocan
hunger is not their experience
nor sickness, and not poverty.

They give also
the inner manliness, kingly valour
and the acquisitions of the hunt:
the insignia of the lip, the knotting of the mantle,
the loin-cloth, the mantle itself;
Flower and aromatic leaf, jade,
quetzal plumes, and the godshit you call gold.
When and where?—It is a long tradition.
Do you know
when the emplacement of Tula was, of Uapalcalco,
of Xuchatlappan, of Tamoanchan,
of Yoalli ichan, of Teotihuacan?
They were the world-makers who founded
the mat of power, the seat of rule.
They gave
authority and entity
fame and honour.
And should we now destroy the old law,
the Toltec law,
the Chichimec law,
the Colhua law,
the Tepanec law,
on which the heart of being flows,
from which we animate ourselves
through which we pass to adulthood,
from which flows our cosmology
and the manner of our prayer?

In each of the three stanzas, the divine gift in question achieves meaning in human and sociological practice, which in turn is distinguished as that of the priest, the farmer and the warrior. The first of these groups or classes, the priests, draw their power from self-denial and penitence, a shamanist way which goes back to the palaeolithic and the eldest darkness (*inoc yoayan*). In the Mesoamerican cosmogony and system of world-ages recorded in the *Popul vuh*, this is the time when humans were first distinguished from animals by their capacity in principle to worship 'Heart of the Sky', with the copal incense that the Maya riddle in the Book of Chumayel and the Fire-god on the Fejervary title-page together identify as the 'brains of the sky'. At the start of this world-age or 5,200-year Era, the high priest of its first city, the lowland Tula named below, is characteristically shown holding a copal incense-burner, as he is in the Rios Codex of Tenochtitlan (page 9). Evocative of the native American theory of evolution, with its lowly reptiles and iridescent birds, his name Quetzalcoatl (feather-snake or plumed-serpent) is the one by which the Aztec priests referred to themselves. This is the figure whose underworld trance journey, discussed above, made possible the creation of the human beings of this world-age.

After the priests come the farmers, the American agriculturalists who, after their economic success with gourds, manioc, chillis and other millennial crops, surpassed themselves with the invention of maize, probably not long after 3000 BCE, the staple highly adaptable to altitude and soil type whose protein value is much increased when paired with beans. The space-time of this invention is the rain-god's lush abode at midday or zenith, Tlalocan: with his goggle-eyes and toothy mouth (like the rain-god of the Hopi further to the north), Tlaloc enjoys the power to bring down the waters above, as in the Flood which ended the first world-age. In his role as the ninth of the midwife's night or lunar figures, which served as year-guardians, the rain-god Tlaloc was also the most propitious protector of the annual maize crop, as the Fejervary screenfold confirms (see Figure 52.3). Maize and beans with their respective flours, purslane and sage, are the primary agricultural produce shown to be due annually in the Mendoza

Figure 52.3: The Rain-god and the Maize Plant

Codex and the tribute accounts of the Aztecs, while the staple maize becomes the very substance of mankind in the *Popul vuh* cosmogony. In the religion of the Toltecs, and even more in that of the Aztecs, Tlaloc's rain was not freely given. It was bargained for, in exchange for the blood of sacrificed victims whose flowing tears would simulate and so stimulate the flow of rain: before dying, the victim would imagine his journey up to Tlalocan, the 'house of quetzal plumes', Tlaloc's abode at the heart of the sky, passing on the way through the 'place of the unfleshed', the abode of 'the frightening prince' or Lord of the Underworld—once again the trance journey.

Third come the hunter-warriors, the founders of empire, whose first impulse is to acquire and enhance the urban centre with luxury goods of clothing, incense and jewellery, likewise listed in the tribute books, in the same sequence. Indeed, with this third group political history begins, in a series of emplacements whose whereabouts the Franciscans could not have been expected to know any more than they are likely to have cared to. The roll-call of six particular cities begins with Tula or Tollan, the great lowland metropolis which stands as the first named city in a wide range of Mesoamerican texts, including the *Popul vuh* from highland Guatemala, and the Rios Codex of Tenochtitlan where its appearance (page 9) is synonymous with the start of the present 5,200-year Era. And the list ends with Teotihuacan, which our archaeology is now confirming flourished up to no later than the end of the classic era, that is, about 800 CE. The hunter-warrior profession is shown also to have been at the origins of four laws or calendrical usages diagnostic of four of the principal imperial traditions of western Mesoamerica: the Toltec which goes back ultimately to the first city Tula, probably on the Gulf Coast; the Chichimec, which includes the Aztec themselves and other Valley of Mexico tribes; the Colhua which possibly linked Texcoco, to the east of the Valley, with Tilantongo and the Mixteca; and the Tepanec, Otomi-speaking and to the west, the demise of whose capital Azcapotzalco led to the rise of Tenochtitlan. Whatever may one day prove to be a full and correct reading of this concise historical scheme, there can be no doubt about the warrior's role in it, or about his opposition in principle to the sedentary farmer, under the initial and primary aegis of the priesthood, representatives of which were after all delivering the speech in question.

Of considerable interest in itself, and distinguished by initial verb tense in the speech, this last typal opposition between planter and hunter-warrior recurs elsewhere in Tenochtitlan literature. Written in Aztec or Nahuatl like the Priests' Speech and the depository of an extensive collection of poetry from the tribute empire of that city, the *Cantares Mexicanos* manuscript distinguishes the *xopancuicatl* or 'burgeoning song' of the planter from the *yaocuicatl* or war-song of the warrior; written in native or iconographic script, the Boturini screenfold when depicting the Aztec migration into the Valley of Mexico appeals to the same division, in order to characterise the separation of the eastern agriculturalists of Huexotzinco with their *milpas* and the western hunters of Malinalco with their arrows and nets. In architecture, it was emblemised in the twin temples atop Tenochtitlan's main pyramid, the one dedicated to the rain-god Tlaloc, the other to the war-god Huitzilopochtli.

Modelled on Tezcatlipoca ('smoking mirror'), who with the priestly Quetzalcoatl and the agricultural Tlaloc completes the 'trinity' of major Mesoamerican gods, this Huitzilopochtli of the Aztecs deserves a brief commentary in his own right. For in the Aztecs' account of their migrations from Aztlan (somewhere in northern Mexico or the southern United States), when they were poor and despised, this figure is an unprepossessing character, carried with them along the road. This is how he appears in the Boturini screenfold, bundled up like a mascot and with a modest Humming-bird (huitzilin) disguise. When they attained power in Tenochtitlan, however, the Aztecs provided the world with a much grander image of the patron who had urged them on to glory. He was made into a solar god, his sanctuary next to Tlaloc's then being given to him. He was also said to have been miraculously conceived by Coatlicue (Snake Skirt), the earth-mother, who was impregnated by a ball of fluff or down when she was sweeping. Her family felt dishonoured by her unexplained fat belly and swore to kill her. As they closed in, Huitzilopochtli leaped out of Coatlicue's womb, fully armed like Tezcatlipoca, and slew them to a man. This feat has the solar analogy of sunrise 'killing' the stars and epitomises the power to strike instantly and definitely. In his annals of Tenochtitlan and the Valley of Mexico, the Nahua author Chimalpahin, writing about 1600, discussed this transformation of Huitzilopochtli from tribal mascot to sun-king. He showed how the Aztecs (like the imperialists of our own century) deliberately created and reshaped myths for political ends. In this respect, Huitzilopochtli is especially notable as one who was claimed to have been conceived miraculously. The moral and kinship problems caused by this special origin are resolved in his tremendous martial energy alone, this being provoked by doubts about legitimacy which are never explicitly denied.

Once acknowledged for what it is in the Priests' Speech, the Tenochtitlan triple paradigm of Aztec religion proves on inspection to be endemic to Mesoamerica as a whole, over a wide geographical area, at horizons long prior to that of the Aztecs, and in media that include sculpture and architecture as well as literature. A striking example comes from the city of Palenque which flourished in the Maya lowlands five hundred or so miles to the east, nearly a millennium before the Aztecs delivered their speech (see Figure 52.4). The text in question consists of three panels set in three temples atop pyramids that rise to the north, east and west of a plaza in the city (temples said to be of the 'Cross', the 'Foliated Cross' and the 'Sun' respectively); while the latter two match each other in height, the northern one rises far higher. Each of the panels has the same format: a central design flanked by columns of Maya hieroglyphic writing, the greater stand-

Figure 52.4: The Palenque Trilogy

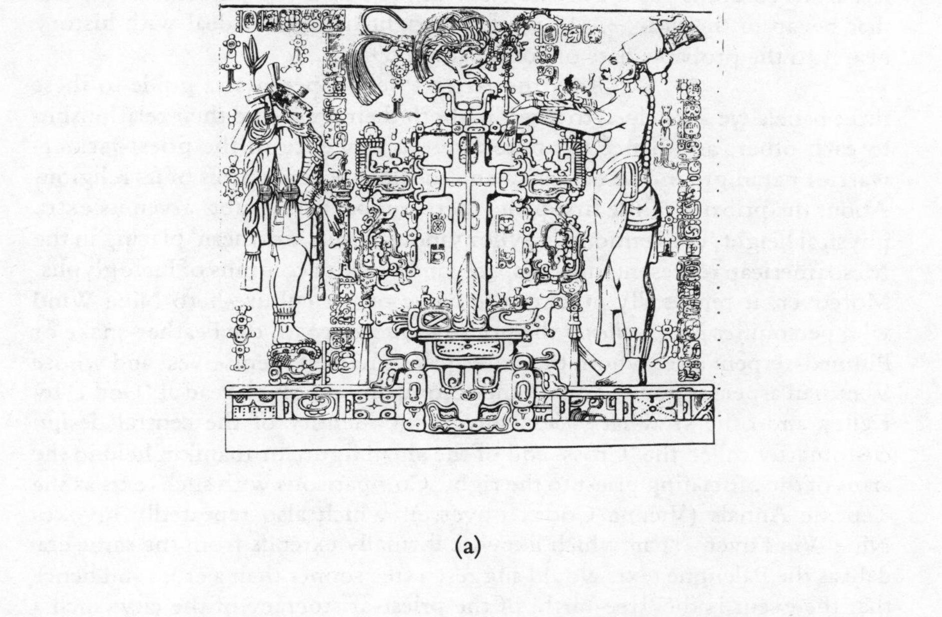

(a)

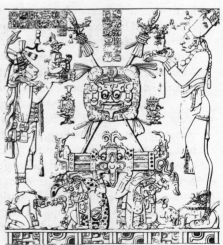

(b) (c)

ing of the northern panel here being reflected in the fact that it has an extra column to left and right. Calendrically, all three follow a pattern whereby the left-hand columns record events early in the Maya and Mesoamerican Era that began in the year −3113 while the right-hand ones deal with history nearer to the probable date of composition 692 CE.

Using the Aztec Priests' speech as a guide to these three panels we are helped to interpret both their detail and their relationship to each other, and hence to appreciate the resilience of the priest-farmer-warrior paradigm in Mesoamerica and the holistic tendencies of its religion. About the priority of the first panel there can be little doubt, given its extra physical height, conventionally synonymous with a 'northern' placing in the Mesoamerican representation of space, and its extra columns of hieroglyphs. Moreover, it repeatedly invokes the name of the culture-hero Nine Wind who personifies *par excellence* the priestly Quetzalcoatl, the Feather-snake or Plumed-serpent after whom the Aztec priests named themselves, and whose Venusian aspect is pointed out in the accompanying glyph read as 'God 1' by Kelley and others. What is less sure is the identity of the central design customarily called the 'Cross' and of the small figure or manikin held in the arms of the officiating priest to the right. Comparisons with such texts as the Tepexic Annals (Vienna Codex obverse), which also repeatedly invokes Nine Wind over a span which likewise formally extends from the same era date as the Palenque text, would suggest a tree sooner than a cross and hence that the event is the 'tree-birth' of the priest-aristocracy of the city; such a birth theme is certainly present in other cradled figures at Palenque first reproduced by Stephens, could possibly be read from the 'Euripos' arrangement of signs for the inferior and superior planets to the left and right of the central tree stem, and appropriately echoes the fact that of all the male Mesoamerican gods Quetzalcoatl Nine Wind was the one most thoroughly identified with heritage and genealogy.

As for the other two panels facing each other east and west, they demand to be read as the stories of Palenque's farmers and warriors, complementary to each other as are their respective horizons beneath the 'northern' zenith. The farmers' 'Foliated Cross' is in fact not a cross at all but their consummate genetic achievement, the maize plant which began to transform Mesoamerica's economy not long after the −3113 Era date and whose sustenance is identified in the *Popul vuh* creation story with the flesh of this Era's people. The jade-skirt worn by the left-hand officiating figure, which has been cited as evidence of the local monarch Pacal's desire to own all qualities, male and female, finds a deeper echo within Mesoamerican culture in the skirted Tlaloc that guards the maize in the Fejervary screenfold. Diametrically opposite, to the west, stands the Sun panel which is architecturally designed so as to relate to a solstice sun motif also elaborated in the Temple of the Inscriptions and the shaft of Pacal's tomb below. At its most obvious, however, the actual centre-piece of the panel includes the shield and crossed spears of the warrior, below which crouch two captives, in the knightly uniforms of the jaguar and the eagle. The diagonal cross of the spears, moreover, schematically recalls the format of Mesoamerican tribute maps, like that of Tenochtitlan on the title-page of the Mendoza Codex. As for the recently detected Jupiter relevance of dates on this panel, it would also support rather than contradict this military reading.

Overall, the structural parallels between these two representations of religion, Aztec and Classic Maya, are the more striking given what otherwise amounts to major differences between those two cultures. The long-nosed Chac of the Maya farmer resembles Tlaloc only in part, while the chief weapon of his warrior gods, the blowpipe, is absent from the arsenals of Tezcatlipoca and Huitzilopochtli. Indeed, the roots of the triple paradigm must lie as deep in Mesoamerican cultures as the notion of Tula itself, the first named city, and take us back to the first Olmec settlements on the Gulf Coast, midway between Aztec and Maya, where the oldest surviving representations of Quetzalcoatl have been found.

The Good Shepherd of the Inca

To the south, in the course of their invasion of the New World, Europeans encountered in the Andean highlands a civilisation which for all its common native American traits, in curing, weaving and metallurgy for example, exhibited others quite distinctive to it. Indeed, the Inca empire Tahuantinsuyu penetrated by Pizarro remains to this day a source of theoretical enquiry, as a result of its highly organised religion and state system, which served to hold together many thousands of kilometres of territory, radiating out from the capital Cuzco, its means of communication being the *quipu*. Nowhere else in the Americas was such thorough control of population and economy achieved over such a vast geography; nor was there a religion even nearly so institutionalised and monotheistic.

At the same time, this region was the exclusive home of the four American camelids: the llama and the alpaca, the huanuco and the vicuña. Having in common with the Old World camels a remote and long vanished ancestor in the North American Ohio Valley, these animals differ somewhat in size and in quality and colour of wool, the first two having been domesticated and the other two not. While the larger llama, probably derived from the huanuco, has served largely as a pack-animal, the alpaca has been best known for its wool; the finest wool, however, belongs to the wild and rare vicuña. (The exact dates and places of domestication are still the subject of research, though bone evidence from Ayacucho points to as early as 4000 BCE.)

Given these two characteristically Andean phenomena, sociological and zoological, the question naturally arises whether they were connected, and if so, how. A prime aid towards any answer is the corpus of texts native to the region, which in many cases have only recently been published and edited. Written in Quechua and Spanish, and transcribed in part from *quipu* originals, these texts include the encyclopedic *Nueva coronica y buen gobierno* sent by Guaman Poma as a letter to Philip III of Spain and which structurally reflects, in its first part, Inca state organisation; the *Huarochiri Narrative* composed entirely in Quechua, which focuses chiefly on cosmogony and Christian attempts to incorporate native religion; other narratives like the *Relacion de antiguedades* of Santacruz Pachacuti, which includes a plan of the Inca temple Coricancha, as well as the Quechua originals of the Situa liturgy, in which the great god Viracocha is worshipped.

In the first instance, these native texts confirm the categorical change signified by domestication as such, that is, loss of wildness. Nowhere is this more fundamentally stated than in the general American cosmogony of world-ages, where the eclipse that ends the second age prompts a domestic revolt against masters who have lost their capacity to worship and respect the life-spirit. In Mesoamerica, this upheaval is led by mortars and kitchen utensils tired of unfeeling use, and not least by the Dog and Turkey, the two creatures whose long-standing alliance with American man is elsewhere celebrated in rituals that survive even today, for example in the south-west of the United States. That in Tahuantinsuyu this same contract was perceived to have extended to llamas is clear from the *Huarochiri Narrative*, where during the eclipse the revolt of the utensils is accompanied by one on the part of these creatures, who turn on their masters in herds. Later in the same *Narrative*, this motif recurs in the binary opposition established between the few wild vicuña who help the poor Huatyacuri and the teams of llamas enlisted by his rich antagonist (Chapters 4 and 5). For their part, Quechua poetry and drama nostalgically invoke the aesthetic attraction of the 'wild' llama, be it that of the beloved as a silky-haired, farouche vicuña, or that of the rebellious Ollantay who defies the Inca as a 'straying lamb'. Consistent with the terms of this domestic contract is the inclusion of the tamed creature as a ritual ally and even social companion. The actual process of inclusion is well-illustrated in Guaman Poma's report of the religious ceremonies proper to the month Uma Raima (October; see Figure 52.5), in which supplicants for rain included not just human children and dogs, whose tears and howls were elicited as sympathetic magic, as in Mexico for example, but a black llama as well. In Inca cosmogony it was the plaintive quality of the llama's faint cry or song that warned humans of the Flood that ended the first world-age (*Huarochiri Narrative*, Chapter 3), while socially this beast, this time coloured red, became the singing companion of the emperor himself in court performances of the Quechua *yaravi*. Indeed, for these capacities the llama, like our Ram, was elevated to the stars as a principal constellation and guide.

Besides these functions, however, for which parallels can be sought elsewhere in native America, the tame camelids of the Inca

Figure 52.5

VTVBRE
VMARAIMI
quilla
carnero nigro
ayunaa lloras y pidir agua
a dios - con la ham
procicion que piden agua a dios runacamag -
uma

had others, exclusive to them. For from all that has been recorded about the Inca state, it is clear that these creatures alternatively served just as units of value, mere items of exchange devoid of particular status or rights, and that as such they were transacted on the grand decimal scale of the *quipu*, whose first and most enduring use appears to have been to tally herds. In Umu Raimi, while one black llama sang for rain one hundred of his white brethren were simply slaughtered; and at the festival of Pariaca 'several thousand' were offered to his priests, such amounts being calculated and checked by means of the *quipu*, according to the *Huarochiri Narrative* (Chapter 9).

As a standardised arithmetical unit of value, especially for the purposes of Inca state religion, the llama in this respect can be well compared with other such units used both within Tahuantinsuyu and in urban economies beyond, like Mesoamerica. Hence, on the one hand it resembles Mesoamerican tribute units of precious feather, stone and metal in its durability; and on the other, in its immediate usefulness, it resembles rations of woven cotton and food, like the mantles and the bushels of maize and beans separately rendered as tribute to the Aztec emperor, for its wool could be variously spun according to quality, its flesh eaten fresh or as *charqui*, its dung spread as manure and so on. Besides uniquely combining these qualities the llama had two others. In the complete absence of any analogue except humans themselves, the llama served as transport, carrying about 45 kilos for up to 20 kilometres a day, chiefly crops from the estates of Empire and Religion back to the capital Cuzco, and thus provided labour as well as commodity value. Secondly, it increased and multiplied itself as sheer capital (whence 'cattle'). Inca attention to breeding, to the selection of prime males literally in 'races' and to penis size, is reported by the *Huarochiri Narrative* (Chapters 9 and 10).

Combined, these qualities of the domesticated Andean camelid, llama and alpaca, endowed it with a value that could not easily have been restricted to the type of domestic contract honoured throughout native American culture. How and where its particular qualities were exploited over time need still to be researched, but the process must have begun with domestication itself. For his part, Guaman Poma (pages 57–78) speaks of a sharp increase of llama and people in the age of the warlike Auca who succeeded the Purun, the first to measure out owned land distinguishing pasture from fields (*chacra*). Without doubt the process led to a new definition of land use and ownership, the edge between tutelary and wild territory being a powerful feature of Andean ideology still today. This meant another social definition of the agriculturalist, whose particular rivalry with the shepherd, rather than with the hunter-warrior, as elsewhere, is likewise evident in the modern ritual of the Collas in Bolivia. And it led to another formulation of religious control, of a flock obedient to its emperor-god, innocent of 'sin', and hence sheltered from the ravenous dangers beyond the frontier fence.

In the latter part of the story, a critical moment was certainly reached in the mid-fifteenth century, with the Inca Pachacuti's conquest of the Lake Titicaca region, the 'Collasuyu' renowned for its huge pastoral wealth and its own imperial past. For it was under this emperor and his son and heir Tupac Yupanqui that the Inca state was given its definitive shape, in dispositions which all point to the importance of pastoralism as an ideological as well as an economic force. Whereas the guarding of llamas could be relegated to boys and girls of twelve acting out of 'love' for the Inca, which is how Guaman Poma depicts it (pages 204 and 225), in incorporating the Collas the Inca emperors, in conjunction with the local chiefs, assigned the large herds they had appropriated to the care of professional shepherds. Though they worked full-time, these new appointees were privileged to retain their right to agricultural land, which was worked for them by their kin. Entrusted with the *quipu* accounts of Empire and Religion, these favoured few became pastoral retainers who among other rights could leave their post, patriarchally, to a son. At the same time the central administration set up by Pachacuti and Tupac Yupanqui made quite explicit the more general and significant equation between the llama flock and the human folk as complementary arithmetical components of the state, the latter being likewise counted on the *quipu* to the last unit and according to the ten categories and ages listed by Guaman Poma. This much is evident in the very term used for the police, *michic* or shepherd, responsible for surveillance of the population and for reporting absences from work and religious festivals once again by means of the *quipu* (*Huarochiri Narrative*, Chapter 31).

The same equation between flock and folk is made above all in the monotheistic worship of Viracocha exemplified in the following hymn from the Situa liturgy:

Oh dew of the world
Viracocha
inner dew
Viracocha
you who dispose by saying
'Let there be greater and lesser gods'
great Lord
dispose that here
men do multiply
fortunately.

Father Viracocha
you who say
'Let there be
the upper world
and the lower world'
you who fortify
the world below
hear me

attend to me:
Let me live in peace and in safety,
Father Viracocha,
with food and sustenance,
with maize and llamas,
with all manner
of skills.
Abandon me not.
Remove me
from my enemies,
from danger,
from all threat
of being cursed, ungrateful,
or repudiated.

In the Quechua cadences of this liturgy, the supreme god and paternalistic principle Viracocha is repeatedly asked to keep both men and llamas in peace and safety under the care of his representative on earth, the Inca emperor, and to favour their 'increase'; he is also asked to keep his flock from straying into disobedience and sin, again concepts otherwise foreign to native American liturgy. Actual confession was helped by the payment of llamas, and there are even reports of a black llama serving literally as a scapegoat during the Situa ritual, collective sin being heaped upon it. Disobedience towards Pachacuti the 'good shepherd', and its retribution, certainly provides the whole message of the play *Ollantay*.

The catalogue of pastoralist traits peculiar to Andean religion could easily be lengthened. Yet those noted already are enough to justify the connection in principle between fauna and society in that area and in so doing to raise larger theoretical issues like the standardisation of value, land appropriation, the concentration of power within what thereby becomes the 'state', the deep complicity between the -isms of capital and social, and the pastoral roots of monotheism itself. Indeed, set in as it were the laboratory conditions of the New World the Inca Tahuantinsuyu offers useful pointers to features of our own religion long saturated with pastoralist ideology, from the fable of Cain the agriculturalist and Abel the keeper of flocks, to the doctrine of Christ both shepherd and sacrificial lamb.

Further Reading

Brotherston, Gordon *Image of the New World. The American Continent Portrayed in Native Texts* (Thames & Hudson, London and New York, 1979)
Dewdney, Selwyn *Sacred Scrolls of the Southern Ojibway* (University of Toronto Press, Toronto, 1975)
Eliade, Mircea *Shamanism: Archaic Techniques of Ecstasy (Routledge & Kegan Paul, London, 1964)*
Krickeberg, Walter *Pre-Columbian Mexican Religions* (Weidenfeld & Nicolson, London, 1968)

Part 6 New Religious Movements

Editor:
Peter Clarke

53 Introduction

Peter Clarke

> There are no gospels which are immortal, but neither is there any reason for believing that humanity is incapable of inventing new ones.[1]

While some would undoubtedly question the first part of the above quotation from Durkheim's *The Elementary Forms of the Religious Life*, recent history has put the second part beyond all doubt. Over four hundred 'new' religions have emerged in Britain alone since 1945 and many of these and others are to be found in the rest of Western Europe. The figure is very much higher for North America,[2] and post-war Japan[3] has also witnessed, as have parts of sub-Saharan Africa[4] from the 1890s, what amounts to a thriving industry in new religions. Although we have no reliable statistics, the clientele of post-Second World War new religions must be estimated in millions rather than thousands. Although it can be argued that the religions covered in this section, or at least some of them, are not *new* in a 'cultural' and 'theological' sense,[5] as used in this introduction the term *new* is employed chronologically to refer to all those religions that have established themselves in Western Europe, North America and Japan since 1945, and in Africa over a somewhat longer time-span. It is worth pointing out here that the new religions that are known about and documented may constitute only the tip of the iceberg; below the surface there would appear to be a large mass of new religions which has neither been located nor measured with any precision. We can mention in this context the phenomenon of neo-pagan, esoteric and related movements. It is also worth mentioning that a number of new religions have burst upon the scene, flourished for a time and died, but in some cases not before having profoundly influenced the behaviour, thinking and general lifestyle of many thousands of people, and also the legal system in a number of societies, a notable and recent example being the Rajneesh movement discussed in one of the contributions to this section of the volume.[6]

New religions in the West and Japan derive from many different cultures and can vary enormously in terms of content, ritual, attitudes towards the older, albeit themselves once new religions, and towards one another and the wider society. They have also posed a great many questions for that wider society and the mainstream religions, in particular Christianity, obliging the former, for instance, to re-examine, and in certain instances to refine and develop among other things its legal concepts and definition of religion, and the latter to focus more of its attention on the mystical dimension of its tradition. Further, students of religion, including sociologists, psychologists, philosophers, theologians and historians, have also been pressed by the phenomenal growth in recent times of new religions to examine and improve their techniques of research, and reappraise some of their long held conceptual creations and notions about, for example, the meaning, nature and purpose of religion, the nature and method of interpretation of religious discourse, the mechanics of religious conversion, the question of religious freedom and tolerance, the process of secularisation and the character of modern society (both themes are treated in Bryan Wilson's contribution to this section on secularisation), the principle of and meaning of the term membership and the social location, nature and limits of charismatic authority. Numerous attempts have also been made to explain the rise and impact of new religions and the response of the wider society to this phenomenon and these are issues addressed by some of the contributors in this section of the volume and elsewhere.[7]

There is also the equally interesting question as to why some movements succeed while others fail, a question to which several of the contributions in this section attempt to provide an answer, pointing to, among other things, the process of rationalisation that is proceeding apace in modern society, leaving little room for that charismatic authority, precarious in itself, on which a number of the new religions are based. Of course, in this context success and failure are relative terms. However, if we limit the criterion here to no more than staying power or length of survival they would appear to have much to do not only with charismatic authority and the forces of rationalisation but also with the overall composition, size, structure and organisation of a particular movement, its methods of recruitment and evangelisation, the relevance of its message, its financial circumstances, the image it conveys of itself to the outside world, the response it meets with from the wider society, including the kind of media coverage it receives, the character and structure of that wider society, where and how the movement decides to insert itself and the extent to which it can in travelling to new areas assimilate to the local culture in which it finds itself without loss of purpose or identity.[8]

Rather than examining the foregoing questions in any detail here we can consider briefly some of the conceptions and stepping-stones to 'salvation' mapped out by some of the new religions and common in one form or another to many. There is first of all strong opposition to the rational, intellectual approach to religious truth. The mind, it is claimed, obstructs the quest for such truth and must, therefore, be controlled, some movements going so far as to encourage the complete abandonment of intellectual activity. In advocating this approach and at the same time criticising what they refer to as 'arid intellectualism' new religions would appear to be mistaken about the position of the student of religion and in particular the philosopher of religion who, far from maintaining that belief in God, however defined and understood, arises by irresistible logic either from a scientific investigation of the 'sources' or the world, holds almost as an axiom that such a belief can be achieved only by means of a much more complex process which takes note of experience and intuition as well as reason. For the new religionist, on the other hand, the only path to and authority for 'faith', which, as we shall see below, can dissolve into 'knowledge' even in this life, is experience; an approach which can sometimes lead to the suspension of all doubt and criticism in order to allow time for the old habits of mind and ways of thinking to be cast off.

A number of new religions are the creation of a charismatic leader and tend to be dominated by her/his personality and, despite at times disclaimers to the contrary, these leaders place great emphasis on the 'virtue' of surrender, a logical step considering their views on the limitations of the mind and/or intellect. Moreover, the relationship between master and disciple is considered to be of fundamental importance in the process of realising and perfecting the self, the primary goal of some of the more popular new religions, as the contribution to this section of the volume on the 'Self-Religions' makes clear. This relationship entails the absolute surrender of the disciple, for whom all other relationships, and especially those with family or friends, must become of secondary importance.

Realising and perfecting the self consists of being the *cause* of all one does, of determining events rather than being determined by them, of exchanging one's status of slave to events and circumstances for that of master of all that happens. It consists of becoming a creator. Unlike Christianity, many of the new religions are persuaded of the perfectibility of human nature in the here and now and much of the theorising which predicates this is grounded in the 'belief' that the individual is divine, is God. Once an individual realises that he/she is divine then all things are possible. What we see here, echoing Feuerbach, is a concern not with God as other but with a God who lives in and for the individual and whose real meaning lies in a conception of man.[9]

Given these related 'beliefs' in the perfectibility of human nature and the divinity of man, and their Buddhist and Hindu derived ideas and practices, it is not surprising to find that in many new religions the idea of faith as found in Christianity, whereby in the here and now we see only in part or 'through a glass darkly', is replaced by that of 'knowledge'.

New religions accept that there is a distinction between faith and knowledge but insist that this need not persist throughout this life for one can come to 'know' fully *now* the 'divine' or 'God', and thus faith becomes redundant.

An emphasis on the millennium is to be found in Soka Gakkai (Value Creation Society), almost all Japanese new religions, as another of the contributions to this section shows, and in many other new movements such as the Unification Church, more popularly known as the Moonies,[10] the Worldwide Church of God and the Rastafarian movement.[11] This is not unexpected in the light of what has just been said about human nature, the source of the divine, faith and knowledge. Moreover, millennialism can serve many purposes, operating in situations of rapid social change and upheaval as an appropriate and effective ideology.[12] Although there are differences in interpretation, for most new religions the millennium is close at hand and offers an escape from contemporary society and entry to a new, golden age, at times depicted as a highly spiritual realm but more often than not as a Utopia.

While others see them as attempts to grapple with the problems generated by the twin processes of rationalisation and secularisation, the new religions regard themselves, much in the same way as Christian and Islamic fundamentalists, as the instruments for the creation of a perfect order of society and as being in the forefront of the movement to regain the territory lost by religion over the past two hundred years and more since the Enlightenment. They may, however, prove to be something of a Trojan horse, quickening a process of internal secularisation rather than extending the frontiers of religion. Their more immediate aims can vary, but what is most striking is the attempt by many new movements, particularly those of Japanese origin, to enable people to cope with ordinary living, to provide solutions to ordinary everyday problems, to what Durkheim considered to be 'profane' matters.

Notes

1. E. Durkheim, *The Elementary Forms of the Religious Life: A Study in Religious Sociology*, trans. Joseph Ward Swain (Allen & Unwin, London; Macmillan, New York, 1915), p. 428.

2. J. Gordon Melton, *Encyclopedia of American Religions* (Gale Research Co., Detroit, 1986); D. Choquette, *New Religious Movements in the United States and Canada: A Critical Assessment and Annotated Bibliography* (Greenwood Press, Westport, Connecticut/London, 1985).

3. H. Byron Earhart, *The New Religions of Japan. A Bibliography of Western Language Materials* (University of Michigan Centre for Japanese Studies, Ann Arbor, 1983).

4. H.W. Turner, *Religious Innovation in Africa* (Boston, Mass., 1979); R.J. Hackett, 'Spiritual Sciences in Africa', *Religion Today. A Journal of Contemporary Religions*, vol. 13, no. 2 (May–Sept. 1986), pp. 8ff.

5. F. Hardy, 'How "Indian" are the new Indian Religions', *Religion Today. A Journal of Contemporary Religions*, vol. 1, nos. 2/3 (Oct.–Dec. 1984), pp. 15ff.

6. J. Thompson and P. Heelas, *The Way of the Heart: The Rajneesh Movement* (The Aquarian Press, Wellingborough, 1986).

7. R. Wallis, *The Elementary Forms of the New Religious Life* (Routledge & Kegan Paul, London, 1984); I.I. Zaretsky and M.P. Leone (eds.), *Religious Movements in Contemporary America* (Princeton University Press, Princeton, 1974); E. Barker (ed.), *New Religious Movements: A Perspective for Understanding Society. Studies in Religion and Society* (Edwin Mellen Press, New York, 1982), vol. 3; B.R. Wilson (ed.), *The Social Impact of the New Religious Movements*, Conference Series, no. 9 (The Unification Theological Seminary, Barrytown, New York, 1981).

8. J.A. Beckford, *Cult Controversies: The Social Response to the New Religious Movements* (Tavistock Publications, London, 1985); P.B. Clarke (ed.), *The New Evangelists* (Ethnographica Publishers Ltd, London, 1988).

9. L. Feuerbach, *The Essence of Christianity*, trans. by George Elliot (Harper & Row Publishers, London and New York, 1957), p. 281 and *passim*.

10. E. Barker, *Becoming a Moonie: Choice or Brainwashing?* (Basil Blackwell, Oxford, 1985).

11. E. Cashmore, *Rastaman: The Rastafarian Movement in England* (George Allen & Unwin, London, 1979); also P.B. Clarke, *Black Paradise: The Rastafarian Movement* (Aquarian Press, Wellingborough, 1986).

12. N. Cohn, *The Pursuit of the Millennium* (Paladin, London, 1970); J.A. Beckford (ed.), *New Religious Movements and Rapid Social Change* (Sage/Unesco, London/Paris, 1986).

The author would like to thank the British Academy for a research grant which made possible his research on new religions in Western Europe.

54 North America

R. Wallis

Introduction

America possesses a free market economy *par excellence*. The mechanisms of the market extend not only to goods and services, but far into the sphere of culture, affecting even the realm of religion itself. Just as goods and services emerge and change in response to market forces, growing affluence, recession, the appearance of new consumer groups and new consumption desires, so too does the religious commodity. Existing suppliers seek to develop a new brand image, or continue to survive on the retained brand loyalty of old customers and sometimes their families, while forceful, even aggressive, marketing by new suppliers of salvation may lead to the capture of some section of the existing market, or the formation of new consumers from groups and strata hitherto ignored.

But the market is no longer a merely local phenomenon, even if the locality extends to the 50 states. The Western world and beyond have become enmeshed in the American market. Its products are promoted internationally through the multinational corporations. The Coca-Cola drinker keeps almost the whole world company. American cultural products too are enthusiastically exported, from films and television soap opera in Europe, to Pentecostalism in Latin America.

Not that the traffic is all one way, of course. Americans are willing to consume indigenous products of other economies and cultures, often, indeed, willing to believe that imported brands bear a certain superior cachet; although in time the product may become tailored and adapted the better to suit American palates and sensitivities.

The internationalisation of the market—at least in the non-Communist and affluent societies—both mirrors and extends an internationalisation of experience. Idiosyncracies of local production and culture are eroded by emulation and by the rationalisation of life in the pursuit of profit, efficiency, improved living standards and universal access to basic rights and privileges.

But although in one respect greater uniformity is the result—an airport hotel is much the same in London as in Los Angeles—in another, mass production encourages product diversification, to locate a niche in the consumer ecology unsatisfied by existing suppliers, servicing a particular clientele with distinctive consumer demands. Construing religion as a commodity thus leads to asking questions about factors operating to generate the consumer demands met by the new religions which have emerged or flourished on the American scene in the post-Second World War era.

Of course, the wave of new religions which emerged into prominence, even notoriety, in America after 1945 was by no means a unique phenomenon. There had been earlier waves. Immigration to a land of greater religious toleration had been a frequent recourse for embattled sects in earlier centuries. The Doukhobors, the Shakers, the Amish and a multitude of other religious groups found America to be an environment in which they might be left alone, if not accepted, and in which large tracts of available and cultivatable land permitted the formation of a comfortable agrarian style of life. The absence of an established church, jealous of its privileges and its flock, permitted the uninhibited development of indigenous religious innovations, and the American ethos of individualism and pragmatism ensured that there would always be an abundance of religious innovators, and of potential adherents for new beliefs and practices locally produced or imported.

Early in the nineteenth century Mormonism was to develop, recruiting in large numbers not only in America, but also in the British Isles. Alongside it, Millerism, a millennialist doctrine of the Second Coming developed in the eastern states, giving rise in turn to the Jehovah's Witness movement at the end of the nineteenth century. In the mid-nineteenth century, the Holiness movement was to spring from the Methodist tradition, giving birth in turn to Pentecostalism. Spiritualism too was a mid-century innovation, an American adaptation of European-originated Swedenborgianism. Christian Science and New Thought flourished in the late nineteenth century, and the World Parliament of Religions held in Chicago in 1893 gave a platform in America to Hindu thought in the form of Swami Vivekenanda and the Vedanta movement. Theosophy too, although in its early years centred in Britain and India, was founded in New York in 1875 and provided a further route for Eastern religious ideas to infiltrate American culture, spawning in turn a multitude of local heresies and adaptations. (An excellent source on all of these movements is B. Wilson's *Religious Sects*.)

The Variety of Modern New Religions

There is therefore, a considerable continuity between the new religions that emerged or flourished in post-Second World War America, and those that appeared in earlier generations. Indian thought found new vehicles in the Divine Light Mission of the Guru Maharaj-ji, Maharishi Mahesh Yogi and Transcendental Meditation, A.C. Bhaktivedanta Swami (also known as Srila Prabhupada) and the International Society for Krishna Consciousness (ISKCON), and later Bhagwan Shree Rajneesh and the Neo-Sannyas Movement (the 'Orange People' or Rajneeshism). Christian-originated movements were to arise from the radical conversionist tradition of American fundamentalism in the Jesus People and the more notorious Children of God (Family of Love). And Christian millennialist thought was to be reimported in the unusual form of a syncretic sect which combined Judeo-Christian adventism and Far Eastern Shamanic, Taoist and Buddhist thought in the form of the Unification Church of the Revd Sun Myung Moon (the 'Moonies').

From the 1950s, Zen Buddhism had found a small following among intellectuals and bohemians ('the beatniks' or 'beat generation'), and continued to thrive, if only among a rather small group of such people willing to suffer the rigours and austerity of Zen Buddhist discipline and practice and the rather arid intellectualism of its philosophy. The post-war occupation of Japan was to result in the return of GIs, often with Japanese wives, who had converted to the new religion of Nichiren Shoshu (Soka Gakkai), a Mahayana Buddhist heresy.

These movements were not, of course, all of a piece. Even among the Indian imports there were major differences. Transcendental Meditation provided only a meditational technique for the vast majority of its clientele. Customers would attend one or two preliminary orientation sessions, then a brief initiation at which they were given a *mantra*. Thereafter they were encouraged to meditate for twenty minutes twice a day. There was little expectation of any continuing involvement with the organisation or other adherents of the practice. The Divine Light Mission too offered a meditational technique, but also sought to encourage its followers, the *premies* or 'lovers' of Guru Maharaj-ji, to live communally, sharing a life of devotion to their guru, although often taking jobs outside the commune. Even more demanding as a way of life was that of devotees in the International Society for Krishna Consciousness, who adopted Indian dress, vegetarian food and a rigorous and ascetic mode of life in which sex, alcohol and tobacco were eschewed. Males were required to shave their heads but for a topknot by means of which Krishna would pull them up to heaven. Devotees rose before dawn in communal temples, for a demanding round of rituals before the temple deities, and *sankirtan*—chanting and witnessing in public—or street solicitation of funds in return for magazines, incense or records. While the Transcendental Meditation follower committed only the equivalent of one week's pay and forty minutes a day to the movement, the Krishna devotee committed himself twenty-four hours a day, subordinating his identity totally to its expectations.

The Jesus People and the Children of God involved a synthesis of lifestyle elements of the youth counter-culture—such as long hair, hippie dress and speech, rock music, and an emphasis on love and spontaneity—with American fundamentalism, a belief in the literal truth of the Bible, an expectation of imminent apocalypse and the Second Advent of Christ, a Jesucentric faith, and a commitment to the notion of the Holy Ghost still working in human lives as displayed through such signs as glossolalia, or 'speaking in tongues'. While the Jesus People (a disparate range of groups and movements which flourished in the late 1960s and early 1970s and was largely confined to North America) rose rapidly, peaked quickly and then virtually disappeared by the late 1970s, the Children of God were to survive, albeit in a rather different form. The Children of God emerged in the late 1960s in America as a more radical and zealous wing of the Jesus People. Its leader, Moses David Berg, a former itinerant preacher, was considerably older than most of his followers. Finding his message of cursing the apostate, materialistic worldly system and its compromising churches, and of the imminence of the Apocalypse and Christ's return eagerly accepted by many of the young people who came to hear him, Berg came to view himself as God's prophet for the End-time. He took a new young wife and began to introduce many new elements into the movement's system of belief and practice, including a belief in spirit guides, in Gadaffi as the probable Antichrist, in the likely return of Christ by 1993, and in the freedom of 'spiritual Israel', i.e. himself and his followers, to do 'all things' without sin, including engaging in increasingly indiscriminate sexual relationships.

Prominent among the new religions, however, was a range of groups and movements which—although hinted at in the structure and philosophy of Christian Science and the New Thought Movement—represented a relatively new departure. They diverged from traditional religions in being largely indifferent to the existence or will of any creator God. Rather, they construed the individual as a god in embryo or a spiritual being constrained by material or psychological bonds, and it was from ideas of psychological and psychosomatic therapy that such movements developed.

The Psychoanalytic Movement was the main progenitor of many of the psychological new religions. The more independently minded associates of Freud often departed from psychoanalytic orthodoxy by travelling in a more spiritual direction. Jung displayed a range of occult interests; Reich investigated forms of energy not located by conventional science, and the UFO phenomenon, as well as developing a form of therapy predicated on the assumption that psychological difficulties and traumas were absorbed into body musculature and would be released by physical as well as psychological techniques. Otto Rank shifted the locus of the major psychological trauma affecting adult behaviour back from the Oedipal conflict and other aspects of infant–parent interaction, to the trauma of birth itself. This development was crucial, because once the journey back had begun there was no intrinsically logical place to stop. Dianetics—the forerunner to Scientology—was to shift a stage further back from the birth trauma to traumatic experiences of intra-uterine life (the main one revealed by early Dianetics enthusiasts apparently being attempted abortion by the mother).

Dianetics was founded by L. Ron Hubbard, a pulp-fiction writer who had dabbled in hypnotherapy and the American occult underground. Employing regression and abreaction techniques adapted from medical hypnosis, Hubbard regressed his clients to earlier and earlier points in the life cycle, back to conception itself. Thereafter, although not initially encouraged by Hubbard, clients (known as 'pre-clears') began to produce 'memories' which they believed could not have come from this life at all. Thus a conception of reincarnation was combined with psychologically-oriented methods, and paved the way for a new religion, Scientology.

Scientology possessed a number of features in common with the other psychological religions and with related movements which offered a means of salvation from life's vicissitudes, even if they lacked overt spiritual reference. They shared a conception of man as perfectible. Human beings are believed to possess far greater potential ability, awareness, creativity, insight and capacity for emotional expression and experience than they currently display. Dianetics, for example, argued that the average human being used less than 10 per cent of his mental powers.

Through social conditioning and painful social interaction people lose their ability to manifest all their potential. They repress their emotional aspect, learn to act through the medium of constricting social roles and lose their spontaneity. However, they contain within themselves all that is necessary to be whole, to achieve their potential. Instead of *adding* anything, the individual may rather need to shed the constraints or impediments that have been acquired during the course of one or many lifetimes. By the practice of some technique, or series of techniques, often organised in a particular ritual format or training, the individual can break down conditioning and release the hidden powers beneath.

Just as had earlier been the case with Christian Science and the New Thought Movement, Scientology was to give rise to a myriad of smaller heretical movements and groups founded by individuals unwilling to subordinate themselves entirely to Ron Hubbard's authoritarian direction, and who believed that by synthesis or through their own insights or experiments, they too could develop such ideas and practices further. One of the most successful of such offspring was Erhard Seminars Training (or est) which synthesised ideas drawn from Scientology with practices from Gestalt therapy and a presentational technique drawn from Mind Dynamics, influenced in turn by Silva Mind Control, which reached back to New Thought and Couéism for inspiration. (Coué's most influential contribution to psychological development was probably the phrase—to be repeated several times every morning—'Every day, in every way, I get better and better'.) Est in turn gave rise to various other practices offering a slightly different package such as Lifespring, Actualizations and Insight.

These new psychological religions and related salvational systems adopted not only contemporary psychological ideas and practices, but also contemporary organisational structures and modern marketing methods. They promised not calendrically based collective worship, but rather individually-tailored, or consumer-convenient therapy, training, counselling or courses, available through weekend or evening sessions at a fixed fee and with cash discounts. The salvational commodity was purveyed through permanent outlets in major metropolitan locations, or by travelling teams which set up in large city centre hotels, offering their services to 150 or 200 clients at a time.

The major suppliers organised themselves as multinational corporations, often developing considerable expertise in international financial transfer and in corporate and public law. They marketed a particular range of brand-identified salvational services, striving to retain customer loyalty often by differentiating their product into a series of stages constituting a career which would take a considerable investment of time and money to complete. Some clients would be encouraged to make their hobby into a vocation by volunteering time to recruit or service clients, or by taking full-time employment with the corporation; or clients might be encouraged to pursue their course through the hierarchy of training with the expectation that they would be able to recoup their investment on completion, through professional practice.

Such large corporate suppliers inevitably attempted to maximise control over staff and committed clients, giving them a sometimes somewhat authoritarian character. Others required less exclusive commitment, and marketed their salvational commodity through facilities which provided a location for many different ideas and practices.

A major role in this respect was played by the Human Potential Movement which was a diffuse and eclectic congeries of ideas and practices drawn from the Psychoanalytic heretics; massage and other physical practices; humanistic psychology (Gestalt, Encounter, Transactional Analysis etc.); the corporate major suppliers such as Scientology, Primal Therapy, Arica etc.; and a variety of other sources. These ideas and practices were made available through centres which offered a rotating programme of therapy and training to a shifting clientele which might sample from among the advertised range of one centre and then another, without any necessary commitment to any one system, practitioner or purveyor. The most famous centre in the Human Potential Movement was undoubtedly the Esalen Institute at Big Sur in California, but more modest endeavours could be found during the late 1960s, and early 1970s throughout America, and in the major European metropolises.

One way, then, of considering the new religions of post-Second World War America is in terms of their origins, i.e. whether they are derived predominantly from indigenous religious traditions, from imported religious traditions, or from essential psychological sources.

Figure 54.1: Origins of New Religions in Post-War America

Derivation	Indigenous Traditions	Imported Traditions	Psychological
Examples	Jesus People Children of God	TM ISKCON DLM	Scientology est Silva Mind Control Inner Peace Movement Human Potential Movement

Unification Church

Rajneeshism

However, a classification in terms of origins can only take us a short way along the path to understanding such movements, their structure, functioning, development and sources of support. We can get somewhat further along if we conceive new religious movements as having three possible ways of orientating themselves to the world around them: they may reject that world, expecting or promoting its general transformation; they may embrace the world, accepting its goals and values, and promoting the means to cope with it more effectively; or they may merely accommodate to a world they view as potentially corrupting and dangerous, striving to cultivate their religious experience and heighten their religious sensibilities in an effort to provide a more effective example; in the world but not of it.

Figure 54.2: Orientations of New Religious Movements

World-rejecting	World-affirming	World-accommodating
ISKCON	est	Charismatic Renewal
Unification Church	Inner Peace Movement	House Churches
Children of God	Human Potential Movement	Subud
People's Temple	TM	

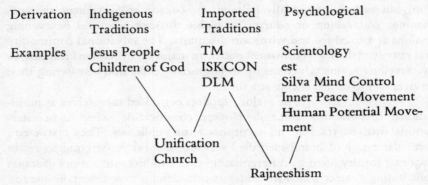

These three orientations produce different structures and patterns of behaviour and collective functioning. While there are clear examples of each in the new religions, many new religious movements may combine elements of two or more orientations, or shift between one and another over the course of time.

The world-rejecting movement typically adopts a communal way of life, recruiting the young or other radically disaffected groups on the social margins. Its hostility to the surrounding society may breed a lack of respect for social norms, a willingness to lie or break the law in what is seen as a good cause. Because of the sharp break involved in the transition from the conventional world to that of the movement, recruitment often involves intense, concentrated pressure to convert, with a high level of emotional display, and often an attempt to isolate the new recruit for a period from family or former friends until he is firm in the new faith. Rejecting the wider society will normally entail an unwillingness to engage in conventional occupations, and economic support will therefore be generated by street solicitation, street sales, unemployment and welfare payments, and other means which minimise the involvement of members in conventional social activities. The sharp break with the former life of members will often be marked by a new name and by handing over all possessions to the communal fund.

The world-affirming movement typically organises itself as a commercial operation, recruiting those who have a substantial investment in or commitment to the prevailing order, but who feel they are failing to attain some of the valued goals and attributes which their society makes available. Their full powers and potential can be unlocked by some practice or set of techniques which can be purchased in the same way as other luxury non-durables and services, from a convenient city centre outlet. The adherent becomes only gradually more deeply involved in the group as he invests progressively more time and money, acquires the language and conceptual scheme of the salvational group and begins to view the world in terms of it, and then finds that the only people who speak the same language and share the same interests as him are other members. Most followers must therefore inevitably remain deeply involved in the wider society. They not only see the movement as a recourse to improve their success in, and enjoyment of the world outside, but also have to earn sufficient funds in that world to pay for the therapy, counselling or training that the movement provides. There is no sharp break therefore on joining the group, and assimilation into its world-view and thought pattern, into complete commitment, may be a quite gradual process.

The world-accommodating movement likewise provides a recourse for people who generally continue to live and work in the world. However, they turn to such a movement not in order to become more successful or less guilt-ridden, but in order to heighten their experience of the supernatural, the transcendental, the divine. They are spiritually oriented people, often already committed Christians in the case of Charismatic Renewal and the House Church Movement, who have found the conventional religious institutions lacking in warmth and zeal, and unable to provide a clear *experience* of the spiritual world. Through 'speaking in tongues' and similar activities, neo-Pentecostals can feel themselves to have experienced the power of the Holy Spirit in their lives, reinvigorating their faith, recharging them to return to the materialistic world outside, and revivifying their commitment to moral and religious standards regularly challenged and affronted in that world. A number of small, non-Christian groups would also seem to follow this pattern: the Aetherius Society, Subud and various forms of Gurdjieffian and Ouspenskian study, for example. In addition, many groups tend to develop more in this direction over the course of time, from an originally world-rejecting stance. Some parts of the Jesus People shifted in this direction, and it is arguable that parts of the Unification Church and ISKCON are doing likewise.

Moreover, since these 'orientations to the world' and the syndrome of characteristics associated with each of them (see Wallis, *The Elementary Forms of the New Religious Life*) constitute 'ideal types', analytical constructs for the purposes of clarifying major features and central tendencies, we should expect to find that many actual new religions will contain—at least for a while—elements of two or more orientations. This may, indeed, have decided advantages at least during a movement's early years. The predominantly world-rejecting new religion risks completely alienating its social environment through the hostility it displays towards the wider society, and through its indifference to, or rejection of, normal social conventions. Such behaviour is likely to generate intolerable or at least very high levels of social control. This appears to have been what transpired in relation to the People's Temple, Synanon, and to a lesser extent the Children of God in various locations. Intense rejection of the world also jeopardises recruitment as potential converts come to find the distance between their world, and the world of the movement, too great to cross. Economic support is also jeopardised as a decline in new recruits may entail a drop in goods and income brought in with them, and sympathisers are likely to be alienated by the blanket condemnation and hostility toward a world which they still inhabit, thus rendering them less willing to donate, or to do business with such a group.

The predominantly world-affirming movement, with its very open boundaries, attracting in the public and requiring little initial commitment, risks the diffusion of its ideas and practices out through those boundaries, into the wider culture and other organisations beyond. Thus it risks the loss of any distinctive character for its salvational commodity as its ideas and practices are adopted by others and synthesised into quite different packages. Its clientele may therefore drop away as they find more or less the same commodity or service available elsewhere at lower cost.

The world-accommodating movement risks the classic problem of denominationalisation: the gradual attenuation of its distinctively enthusiastic character, and a loss of support as it becomes less clearly distinguishable from the established purveyors of salvation from which many of its followers originally came in dissatisfaction.

A new religion that can sustain elements of all three types may hope to attract three corresponding types of member. The now officially defunct Neo-Sannyas Movement of Bhagwan Shree Rajneesh, or Rajneeshism as it was called, may offer an example. Rajneeshism was founded in India in the late 1960s, but it was to attract a substantial American following, and in 1981 Rajneesh was to move to America, settling with a large number of his followers in central Oregon where he planned to found a large 'sannyasin' city.

Rajneesh preached a tantric-inspired philosophy which claimed that enlightenment came from acceptance and surrender to union with the cosmos. Achieving such a state involves 'dropping' the ego with its inheritance of social conditioning and patterns of learned belief, expectation and false needs. By total awareness of the present moment, by non-judgemental acceptance of oneself, one's feelings and circumstances, the individual will awaken from sleep, from mechanically responding to stimuli, and begin acting in harmony with the universe, spontaneously and in love.

Rajneesh initially attracted spiritual seekers and hippies on the guru circuit in the Indian sub-continent, but by the early 1970s, he was also attracting large numbers of Human Potential Movement therapists and group leaders, and through them in turn, many of their clients.

The faithful were gathered together around Rajneesh at an ashram in Poona in India, and later at Rajneeshpuran in Oregon. There they developed a programme of Human Potential activities which made those centres among the largest of all remaining providers of this salvational service. Smaller centres were also established throughout Europe, America and Australasia. The most intensely committed lived in the ashram or centre, and this inner elite constituted the most world-rejecting element of the movement. Not only did they carry out necessary administrative and fund-raising activities, but they also provided services and a role-model for less committed followers who continued to live in the world. Such people would remain in more or less conventional homes and jobs, but would visit the ashram or centre for a weekend or longer, to participate in activities there, revive their commitment, and return to the world with a strengthened vision of how life ought to be lived. Services were also provided through therapy, massage, group work and the like, for people with no great commitment to the Rajneeshee way of life, but who found in its facilities resources which equipped them better to cope with the conventional world.

Such a structure was particularly effective in that it provided a mechanism for supporting a world-rejecting elite from the gifts and fees of world-accommodating and world-affirming members and clients. It offered a graded, rather than entirely discontinuous pattern of entry from less committed client to totally committed and deployable member. It also provided a protective periphery of more conventional personnel to represent the movement and speak in its defence in the wider society (Wallis and Bruce, *Sociological Theory*, ch. 8).

Sources of Support

Where do the members of these new religions come from, and why are they attracted? The division of the field into the three analytical types facilitates the answering of this question. In the case of world-accommodating movements, we have almost answered it already. Such movements draw their support from the spiritually inclined who find that the established religious institutions offer little experiential confirmation of spiritual power in contemporary life. They are usually already committed to a religious faith or a spiritual quest, and find in the movement the concrete reassurance of the transcendent which they seek.

The world-rejecting movement draws its support from the social margins. The classic cases of such movements historically have found their support among the underprivileged and dispossessed, but in the modern world groups may feel themselves to be marginalised by their society, even though they may not objectively be poor or subjected to oppression. The world-rejecting new religions of the 1960s and 1970s largely found their following from among young people who had become part of the counter-culture, seeking to transform their society or their own situation through political radicalism, communal living, or drug use. The optimistic vision of change which informed the New Left, the student movement and anti-Vietnam war protests, the hippie and commune movements, had, by the late 1960s, become considerably tarnished. Student protests had led to violent deaths, communes had disintegrated, and the hippie playgrounds had become a focus of exploitation by drug dealers and freeloaders. Many young people active in, or sympathetic towards, these movements came to believe that human endeavour having failed, effective transformation could only come about through divine intervention. Post-war affluence had fostered optimism and a belief in the feasibility of progress and social justice. When secular means failed to produce it, some young people—often more spiritually inclined than before as a result of drug experiences—were prepared to believe that supernatural means might succeed where political endeavour and social innovation had failed. The world-rejecting new religions particularly appealed to the thwarted idealism of the young, their hostility to the corrupt, materialistic values of modern Western societies, and their commitment to a more intimate, caring community which would seek to promote a more mutually supportive, caring and principled world.

The world-affirming movement finds its clientele from among those who have been affected by the rationalisation of the Western world. The development of the economy and the advance of technology have created a situation in which the public sphere of life in the capitalist West has become dominated by the values of efficiency, predictability, rational planning and profitability. Success in the public sphere thus tends in most occupations to be incompatible with the fulfilment of a rich emotional life. Successful performance of public roles is often achieved at the cost of an impoverishment of private inner life. Emotion becomes harder to express, feelings are repressed. Spontaneity disappears as we become more deeply embedded in our public roles. The joy of discovery and experiment attenuate as our activities become more routinised, a habit rather than an adventure. Intimacy dissipates in the anonymity, impersonality, segmentalisation and privatisation of urban industrial society.

The world-affirming new religions provided, for those who were relatively successful in the modern world, resources for attaining the expressive release and intimacy denied them in their everyday lives. Through cathartic exercises, encounter, massage and the like, the adherent could escape the guilt and trauma of the past, the inhibition of the present, and attain some temporary community and the opportunity to indulge emotions and secrets normally repressed.

For those who were less successful, the world-affirming movements offered resources for releasing hidden abilities and powers, holding out the promise of achieving the valued goals of the conventional world, greater success in their jobs, increased intelligence, improved interpersonal relations and the like. Those who entered Scientology and est were often likely to be aspirants to corporate success. Those who went to Esalen or the Rajneesh ashram in Poona or Oregon were more likely to be drawn from social and educational backgrounds which gave a certain amount of choice as to the future, and sought to direct their lives into creative and imaginative occupations or those providing a service to other people, particularly in respect of human development. They were often teachers, social workers, therapists, performing artists and the like. But of course the attractions of liberation from social conditioning and constricting social roles was far more widely attractive at a time of affluence and economic expansion. Many people were willing to expend surplus income in a possible salvational programme in economically buoyant times. Come the recession, however, they were more likely to save on such expenditure, or to direct it to means of holding onto their jobs in more competitive times.

As for the world-rejecting movements, they too were affected by the changing economic climate, albeit indirectly. Recession meant that fewer young people took time out to follow some personal quest for fulfilment in the expectation that worthwhile opportunities would still be available should they decide to return to the conventional world later.

Recession meant that leaving the normal career path almost inevitably entailed unemployment. The counter-culture receded as a significant social phenomenon and fewer young people were on the streets or otherwise unattached, available to be recruited by a new religious movement which offered a vehicle for their idealism.

Conclusion

The evaporation of the counter-culture has meant that the recruitment base for the world-rejecting new religions has largely disappeared, and in consequence many of them have declined, while others have had to change their style, accommodating more to the wider society to secure new bases of support. The Unification Church has begun a parochial mission; ISKCON has begun to locate a new source of support among East Indians living in the West who wish to avail themselves of the devotional facilities of the movement, without becoming themselves totally committed to it.

A deepening of the religious life, a magical recipe for securing more of what this world has to offer, or a millenarian programme for the transformation of a world conceived to be altogether unsatisfactory, these are three responses to life's vicissitudes which recur constantly, in many societies and historical epochs. The new religions which emerged or flourished in America in the post-Second World War era reiterated these recurrent themes, but they did so in ways which sharply reflected and refracted the particular circumstances of the world in which they appeared or flourished.

Bibliography

Wallis, Roy *The Elementary Forms of the New Religious Life* (Routledge & Kegan Paul, London, 1984)

—— and Bruce, Steve *Sociological Theory, Religion and Collective Action* (The Queen's University, Belfast, 1985)

Wilson, Bryan *Religious Sects* (Weidenfeld & Nicolson, London, 1970)

55 Western Europe: Self-Religions

P. Heelas

Self-religions offer participants the experience of god. What they experience is themselves, the god within. The self itself is divine. Many will be perplexed by such claims. However, there is little that is new about this form of monism. The self-religions point to parallels, in both Western and Eastern traditions. Thus one of the first self-religions (Psychosynthesis, the Italian psychoanalyst-cum-mystic Assagioli founding the Instituto di Psicosintesi in 1926) cites the Renaissance Neoplatonist Paracelsus: 'In every human being there is a special heaven, whole and unbroken.' And the founder of est (the highly influential seminar training established by Erhard in 1971) observes that, 'Of all the disciplines that I studied, and learned, Zen was the *essential* one.' In fact Eastern traditions, whether the teachings of Patanjali, Sufism, or various forms of Buddhism (in particular Vajrayana), lie at the very heart of the self-religions. They are basically Eastern in nature.

But this is not to say that there is nothing new about them. They are Eastern manifestations in a particular Western context. They are new in that they fuse two domains which we have become accustomed to see as antagonistic—the religious and the psychological. The fusion has occurred by virtue of two innovations. On the one hand the self-religions have moved beyond the parameters of religion as established in the West. Participants do not worship and surrender to an externally envisaged theistic being. Instead, they live 'as' gods. On the other hand the self-religions have moved beyond the parameters of mainstream psychoanalysis and psychotherapy. Participants do not simply engage in psychological activities for reasons of therapy, growth, self-improvement or even to fulfil their human potential. Instead, they use psychological techniques to reveal the god within. That these movements are self-orientated qualifies what is normally understood by 'religion'; that they are religiously-orientated qualifies what is normally understood as 'self'.

These movements can easily be distinguished from new religions of a theistic nature. Hare Krishna, Transcendental Meditation and Meher Baba's movement, for example, are not self-religions in that god is attributed an external locus of agency. As new religious movements the self-religions can also be distinguished from those Eastern imports which might be monistic but which have not fused with Western psychological traditions and institutions. Yogananda's Self-Realization Fellowship, the paths of Sai Baba and Sri Chinmoy, and countless yoga and Buddhist schools are not new in the fashion of the movements under discussion.

The great majority of the self-religions active in Europe owe their immediate ancestry to developments in the United States. Going back a step, however, these developments in turn largely derive from events in Europe. One event, above all others, stands out: Gurdjieff's establishment, in 1922, of the Institute for the Harmonious Development of Man. Housed in a château on the outskirts of Fontainebleau, Gurdjieff's Institute paved the way for what was to follow. Gurdjieff taught that we are all capable of obtaining what he called 'objective consciousness', namely, the 'enlightened state'. But we do not know it. We are 'prisoners'. Gurdjieff introduced a model of human nature, a model which both explains why this is so and what can be done about it. Part of the model (reminiscent of behavioural psychology) is, as he puts it, that, 'Man is a machine. All his deeds, actions, words, thoughts, feelings, convictions, opinions and habits are the result of external influences, external impressions. Man does not love, hate, desire—all this happens.' We are trapped by the mechanics of our socialised selves. We are driven by how we have learnt we should present ourselves to win approval, and so on.

The remainder of the model has to do with the techniques which must be used to gain liberation, to awaken spirituality, to reach the 'real and unchanging "I"', to come to act, not to react. To use a Sufi term, Gurdjieff was perhaps the first to function as a 'context-setter' in the West. He provided the (often) group contexts, complete with rules and techniques, to effect transformation. All the basic ingredients of the self-religions are thus in evidence. And as well as provoking what was to come, Gurdjieff's 'The Work' is still alive and well. Although it is impossible to estimate how many are currently engaged in 'The Work' in Europe, if England is anything to go by the numbers are not inconsiderable. Between five and ten thousand attend centres (including the Gurdjieff Ouspensky School), and then there are those attached to such neo-Gurdjieffian movements as Arica, the Emin Foundation (700) and the School of Economic Science (5,000).

Other European figures have also contributed to the development of the self-religions. All belong to the psychoanalytical tradition. All have made contributions to that spiritualising of psychology which is such an important aspect of that fusion discussed earlier. Mention of the self-religion which I know best, namely London-based Exegesis, serves to introduce one such contributor. D'Aubigny, the leader, has had an office devoid of books, except the collected works of Jung. If for no other reason this is because Jung wrote of 'individuation', 'the psychological process that makes of a human being an "individual"—a unique, indivisible unit or "whole man"'. Bearing in mind that individuation involves integrating the 'ego-consciousness' and the 'unconscious', and that the 'unconscious' takes a decidedly mystical form, it is not surprising that Jung, like his contemporary Groddeck, should be on the reading list of contemporary context-setters.

It is also worthy of note that the fusion of psychological techniques and Eastern spirituality, the hallmark of all self-religions, was long ago formulated by Gurdjieff in a way which incorporates psychoanalysis:

> Man has become an uprooted creature unable to adapt himself to life and alien to all the circumstances of his present existence. This is what the psychological system of M. Gurdjieff asserts by means of psycho-analysis, showing by experiment that the world-picture of a modern man and its own effect on life are not the personal and voluntary expression of his entire being, but that on the contrary are only the accidental and automatic manifestations of several parts of him.

Developments within the psychological tradition have provided many of the ingredients of the self-religions (see Wallis in this volume for further details). The tendency to spiritualise psychology (as well as to psychologise spirituality) has made specific impact in that the psychotherapeutic tradition itself has generated a considerable number of self-religions. Clare and Thompson, for example, have gone so far as to write of 'the inexorable thrust which propels every new therapy into a creed of salvation'. As they continue, 'Reichian massage, Moreno's psychodrama, Rogerian psychotherapy—they each began as a relatively circumscribed approach to helping the mentally distressed and ill and ended up as a programme for living, a philosophical statement and a religious message.' Along similar lines Vitz has written a book with the revealing title *Psychology as Religion. The Cult of Self Worship*.

Heavily psychologised forms of self-religions are today well in evidence in Western Europe. As well as those already mentioned, one can think of forms of Transactional Analysis, Primal Therapy and Co-Counselling; of Rebirthing (a movement which is becoming increasingly popular); of various Esalen-like growth movements which have sprung up during the last twenty or so years, such as London's the Open Centre, the Human Integration Centre and the Constructive Teaching Centre of the Alexandra Technique (there is also, for example, the Skyros Centre in Greece); one can even think of certain drug addiction units, employing the

Minnesota model and engendering monistic sentiments. Then there is the International Society of Analytical Triology, with roots in the Freudian tradition but which, in common with all the self-religions, works with a much more optimistic, Pelagian, model of man. And there are the various centres of Transpersonal Psychology, Mind Dynamics and so on.

Together with Eastern traditions, Western therapeutic thought has also influenced one of the best known self-religions, Scientology. The movement appears to be enormous, 300,000 in Great Britain, 80,000 in West Germany, 30,000 in Sweden, 10,000 in Switzerland and 8,000 in Holland. These figures can be put in perspective by the admission, reported in *The Sunday Times* of 28 October 1984, that membership in Britain is actually 1,000. But it is clear that it is one of the larger self-religions. And it is also clear that it is one of the most radical.

A Scientological Operating Thetan, living as a *Homo Novus*, believes that he has moved beyond the illusory albeit real restrictions imposed by the everyday world. He has become a 'spiritual agent of infinite creative potential that acts in, but is not part of, the physical universe'. This allows Operating Thetans to communicate telepathically, perform psychokinesis and mentally materialise things. For reasons which will become apparent, such radical claims are not characteristic of the great majority of self-religions, including those which owe much to Scientology.

These are the est-like movements. Erhard of est and D'Aubigny of Exegesis both acknowledge their debt. So too, I imagine, would the leaders of those other est-like movements which are operative in Europe—the Church for the Movement of Inner Spiritual Awareness/Insight, Self Transformation, the Life Training/the Kairos Foundation, Relationships and the like. Movements of this variety are seminar based. With reference to est, what is offered is 'a sixty-hour educational experience which creates an opportunity for people to realize their potential to transform their lives'. Drawing on a whole range of techniques or 'processes', including many drawn from the 'therapies' mentioned earlier, seminars also include lengthy talks and interchange sessions. The aim is to allow each participant to see who he really is; the overall process is one of de-identification. As Erhard puts it, 'The person de-identifies with his mind, de-identifies with his body; he de-identifies with his emotions, he de-identifies with his problems, he de-identifies with his maya, he begins to see that he is not the Play.' Since Enlightenment is knowing what one really is, and since this is a 'machine', est trainers say, 'An asshole is a machine that thinks he's not a machine; an enlightened man is an asshole that knows he is a machine.'

Unlike Scientology, where there is a clear dualism between the mechanical self and the indwelling spiritual agency, monistic identification of the mechanical and the spiritual means that there is no *sui generis* god within to exercise 'magical' powers. As a trainer says, 'You're the source and creator of all you experience, you're a God, but what you, the individual entity bouncing around inside the big universe you've created, what you do is totally out of your control.' A far cry perhaps from the powers of the Operating Thetan. However, this is not to say that knowledge of mechanicalness is held to be without efficacy. The purpose of the seminar is to 'transform your ability to experience living so that the situations you have been trying to change or have been putting up with clear up just in the process of life itself'. The machine can come to be experienced as perfect (cf. Relationships and their cry, 'You are perfect just the way you are').

Those graduating from est and other est-like seminars typically report improvements ranging from physical well-being to such factors as a new sense of responsibility, greater self-esteem and confidence, greater communicative skills, being in control and 'the experience of personal power'. These results go some way in explaining the popularity of the movements. They are almost certainly the fastest growing form of self-religion in Europe. Some 70,000 have been involved with est in West Germany (5,000 are are full time), est is popular in Israel (est-Kibbutzim), and 8,000 have taken the seminar in Britain. These figures are higher if one includes graduates who have become involved in courses since the 'closure' of est in December 1984. Another, more direct indication of the growth rate of these movements is provided by the fact that Self Transformation Seminars has only been active in Britain since 1982, yet already realistically claims in excess of 7,000 graduates.

Like other self-religions, only perhaps more so, the est-like movements are not simply in the business of transformation. They are equally concerned with the transformation of business. In the United States this is well developed. The *Network Review*, reporting Erhard's organisation, for example, writes of the fact that 'Two independent enterprises, "Action Technologies" and "Transformational Technologies", join "Hermenet" in offering a wide range of new programs that make the technology of transformation widely available within the business and corporate communities.' In Europe it does not appear that things are yet so well organised. However, a number of companies employ est graduates (including Saatchi and Saatchi and Gold Greenlees Trott, reported in *Marketing*, 14 July 1983), a number of Exegesis graduates have decided to work together and so have formed or joined various businesses, and a number of movements put on courses or training for secular companies (Findhorn, whose philosophy is not so very different from that of est, has close ties with the Business Network and The New Initiative Ltd). Many concrete illustrations of how the self-religions as a whole attempt to transform mainstream institutions and life could be given. And these are not limited to business: est/the Network has the World Hunger Project; self-religions are moving into the fields of schooling, social work and so on.

Although the self-religions, especially those of an est-like variety, are expanding, they are not expanding as fast as they are in the United States. No European city comes anywhere near the 'one out of 34 adults have taken est' figure provided by this organisation for Boston. It is likely that Europeans are put off by what they perceive as a brash form of American positive thinking and idealism. On the other hand, and this helps explain why these movements are growing, the self-religions are by no means alien to the European sensibility. Gurdjieff, Jung and Frankl, to name but three, worked in this part of the world. To the extent that Erhard, for example, is a latter-day Gurdjieffian (it is surely not a coincidence that he devotes himself to what he calls 'The Work'), he can appeal to a similar clientele as those attracted to the Institute for the Harmonious Development of Man. Add to this the ever-increasing 'therapeutic awareness' of Europeans and the progress of self-religions hardly stands in need of further explanation. Therapy offers salvation through 'knowing oneself'; monistic spiritual paths offer a far from dissimilar route to salvation. The paths enhance one another. The desire to fulfil human potential is taken further by the addition of the god within. We have a transformed humanism. Feuerbach's and Durkheim's prediction, of religion and god becoming internalised, has in measure been validated. God, one might say, has been put to work by the psychological-therapeutic culture; has been put to use in perfecting a conception of man.

To close here is a list of some of those self-religions which have not already been mentioned: Silva Mind Control, Science of Mind, DMA, CAER (a human potential centre), Self-Formation, Play-world, the I am Institute of Applied Metaphysics, the Taking Risks workshop, the Emissaries of the Divine Light, the Centre for Psychological Astrology and much of the work of the Wrekin Trust. Many other movements have much in common with the self-religions but contain additional ingredients. Rajneeshism, especially active in Germany, and with offshoots such as Focus of Life, is one such instance. It is a self-religion in that there is talk of 'the psychology of the Buddhas', of the fact that we are all 'Gods and Goddesses in exile'. But there is also worship, and Rajneesh is more than a context-setter. Much the same goes for the Laughing Man Institute(s). Lifewave ('Man is the only God'), Eckankar, the 'I am' movement (Christian monism) and Inner Light Consciousness also have much in common with the self-religions but, so to speak, go well beyond the human self. Yet more movements are discussed by C.W. Henderson in his excellent survey, *Awakening. Ways to Psycho-Spiritual Growth.* Mysticism is certainly showing signs of being active in the modern world.

Further Reading

Clare, A. with Thompson, S. *Let's Talk About Me. A Critical Examination of the New Psychotherapies* (British Broadcasting Corporation, London, 1981), p. 142

Groddeck, G. *The Book of the It* (Vision Press, London, 1979), original 1923

Henderson, C.W. *Awakening. Ways to Psycho-Spiritual Growth* (Prentice-Hall, New Jersey, 1975)

Rhinehart, L. *The Book of est* (Holt, Rinehart and Winston, New York, 1976)
Vitz, P. *Psychology as Religion. The Cult of Self Worship* (Lion, Hertfordshire, 1977)
Wallis, R. *The Road to Total Freedom: A Sociological Analysis of Scientology* (Heinemann, London, 1976)
Webb, J. *The Harmonious Circle. The Lives and Work of G.I. Gurdjieff, P.D. Ouspensky, and their Followers* (Thames & Hudson, London, 1980)

56 *Japan*

A. Lande and Peter Clarke

Introduction: Common Features

An estimated two hundred 'new' religious movements, known as *Shinko-shukyo*, 'newly arisen religions' or the preferred title of the groups themselves, *Shinshukyo*, 'new religions', are to be found in present-day Japan. Very many of these are indigenous in that their beliefs and practices are for the most part derived from traditional Japanese religions, among which we include Buddhism and Confucianism although they both originated outside Japan. They have, however, a long history in that country and have been influenced, shaped and moulded by Japanese society over a relatively long period of time.

The non-indigenous new movements tend to have a more pronounced Christian or Hindu doctrinal dimension and include the Unification Church, more commonly known as the Moonies, which has an estimated two hundred thousand followers in Japan, and the International Society for Krishna Consciousness (ISKCON), also called Hare Krishna, with a very much smaller following.

From the perspective of the Japanese the indigenous new religions are neither unfamiliar nor exotic and if considered in a Western context they would seem to parallel more closely Christian revivalist movements rather than for example the new religions of India or the self-religions (see pp. 912–24 and pp. 925–31). In almost every instance these new religions are built around the personality of a charismatic founder, usually seen as an *ikigami*, that is as one possessed by a deity. Among the founders of new religions possessed by a Shinto deity are Miki Nakayama of *Tenrikyo*, the Teaching of Heavenly Truth, and Kawate Bunjiro of *Konkokyo*, the Teaching of the Golden Light.

The differences that are to be found in these new religions can often be attributed to the differences in the personality of the founders or leaders in question. Moreover, while each of these religions has its own spiritual and socio-cultural centre point or 'Mecca' they all tend to be highly syncretistic, holding to a mixture of beliefs and practices. Some of these derive from traditional Japanese religion, for example the belief in the continuing presence and power of the spirits of the dead, in the efficacy of various forms of magic, and in practices such as exorcism as a means of healing, and in purification through ancestor worship. There is also in many new religions a close link between Shamanism (see pp. 825–35 *re* Shamanism) and ancestor worship. Shamans are believed to enter into contact with the *kami*, spirits of the ancestors, receive and transmit messages from them and acquire from them powers of healing and prediction. Not only the new religions but Buddhism and Confucianism have given a central place to ancestor worship in order to appeal to the Japanese.

New religions such as *Risshokoseikai*, Establishment of Righteousness and Friendly Intercourse, began with the teaching that the family was the centre of human life and this was based in large measure on the belief in the continuing presence and influence of the ancestors. There are those, moreover, who believe that the worship of the ancestors is of great benefit to the nation. Further, the new religions lay great emphasis on the psychological, emotional and in general medical and social benefits to be derived from membership; virtually all of them are millenarian, stressing that the Kingdom of God on earth is near at hand and that great rewards both of a material and spiritual kind will be bestowed on the faithful. These religions are also characterised by a spirit of optimism and, with some exceptions, most notably Soka Gakkai, they teach the relativity of all religions.

We can now move on to consider in more detail examples of some of the better known of these new movements, beginning with those that have been strongly but not exclusively influenced by Shintoism, before turning to those that display a pronounced Japanese Buddhist character.

Nineteenth-Century Japanese New Religions

From the mid-nineteenth century until the end of the Second World War many of the Japanese new religions derived much of their mythology and many of their deities and rituals from Shinto sources while at the same time drawing heavily on other local religious traditions. Prior to 1945 these new religions had a somewhat ambiguous relationship with State Shintoism. On the one hand, since they worshipped Shinto deities and professed belief in Shinto myths they could be regarded, officially, as legitimate religions—in 1868 the Japanese recognised thirteen Shinto religions and Buddhism and Christianity—while on the other hand they could be and indeed were seen as alternatives to State Shintoism and as a consequence were at times persecuted and suppressed.

Three new religions which emerged during the period of religious revival in the mid-nineteenth century deserve particular attention. These are *Tenrikyo*, Heavenly Wisdom (the suffix kyo means religion or teaching), *Konkokyo*, Golden Light, and *Omotokyo*, the Great Origin. The first of these three, Tenrikyo, was founded by Miki Nakayama (1798–1887), the daughter of a farmer who received her first revelation in 1837. She taught that the Heavenly Kingdom was drawing near bringing a world of sickness and poverty to an end, and appealed in the main to farming communities who had lost their property and status during the Meiji land reforms. Tenrikyo has an estimated 153,000 teachers and 2,500,000 members for whom the object of worship is God the Parent, the creator and sustainer of all life, who is assisted by a number of lesser gods. Miki Nakayama, it is believed, is both the shrine of God the Parent and the mediatrix between this god and humanity. The movement also has a holy shrine or centre at Jiba in Tenri City.

Despite the fact that the Tenrikyo creation account placed Japan at the centre of the universe and presented the Japanese as the original and supreme race, ideas compatible with those held by the new centralising administration, the movement was, none the less, persecuted by Meiji officials. This, however, did little to curtail its growth and in 1909 it received official recognition.

Konkokyo was founded in 1859 by Bunjiro Kawate (1814–83) whose father was also a farmer and who likewise was the recipient of numerous revelations. It was in one of these many revelations that he was told that the prosperity of mankind was the ultimate purpose of the 'Parent-God of the Universe' and that without the realisation of that purpose God himself would be morally imperfect. While this movement retains many Shinto rituals and services it is, nevertheless, 'new' in that it has discarded other Shinto beliefs and practices such as exorcism and divination. But what distinguishes it most clearly from Shintoism, and the same can be said of Tenrikyo, is its belief in a mediator between God and man. This movement's 'holy centre' is at Asaguchi City and the principal object of its worship is the Parent God of the Universe who is believed to be the Spirit of the Founder. It has an estimated membership of just under half a million.

Omotokyo was founded in 1899 by Nao Deguchi (1836–1918), at one time a member of Konkokyo. Not surprisingly, therefore, she preached a message of world reformation which was similar in many respects to that preached by Miki Nakayama. Deguchi proclaimed that 'The Greater World shall be changed into the Kingdom of Heaven where peace will reign through all ages to come.' However, it was her adopted son Onisaburo Deguchi (1871–1948) who was largely responsible for the development and spread of Omotokyo. Onisaburo also propounded the 'Three Great Rules of Learning' which provided many Omoto offshoots with much of their doctrinal content.

The first of the three rules lays down the principle that the body of God is Nature, the second that the energy of God is the source of the Universe's movement and the third that every living creature possesses the soul of the true God. Therefore, everything is divine. Onisaburo also preached the imminent arrival of the Kingdom of God and became seriously involved in political issues criticising among other things Japan's annexation of Korea, Manchuria and Taiwan. Further, he presented himself as the only leader capable of ruling Japan, and by way of giving symbolic expression to this belief in his own unique ability to rule, he began to imitate the lifestyle of the Emperor.

The government responded in 1921 by arresting and imprisoning Onisaburo and by destroying the movement's temples. After his release Onisaburo became a firm supporter of the Emperor and membership of the movement grew rapidly, reaching a total of almost three million by the mid-1930s. But once again in 1935 Onisaburo was arrested and charged with lese-majesty and the movement was dissolved and its temples and other property destroyed. Omotokyo began to experience something of a revival after Onisaburo Deguchi's release in 1942, but it soon began to stagnate with the latter's death in 1948. Today Omotokyo has an estimated 7,000 teachers, some 150,000 members and two sacred temples or centres, Kameoka and Ayabe, in Kyoto Prefecture. It has also developed strong links with other religious traditions, including Christianity, both in Japan and in Western Europe and the United States. Moreover, although numerically quite small when compared with a number of the other Japanese new movements, Omotokyo continues to exercise a considerable influence on Japanese society. One of its main concerns has been world peace. It maintains that religion is the basis of society and that the pursuit of peace should begin with religion. Omotokyo also emphasises the close link between religion and art. According to Onisaburo, 'Art is the mother of religion', and the movement has organised a number of art exhibitions in the West for the purpose of demonstrating this relationship and for the promotion of world peace. These and other ideas, many of which are contained in the eighty-one-volume encyclopedia produced by Onisaburo Deguchi, have served as a source of inspiration for other Japanese new religions, among them *Sekaikyuseikyo*, Church of World Messianity, *Seicho no Ie*, House of Growth, and Perfect Liberty Kyodan. Indeed it makes sense to speak of these three movements as Omoto-derived new religions.

Twentieth-Century Examples

Sekaikyuseikyo, founded in 1934 by Mokichi Okada, at one time a member of Omotokyo, has for its main object of worship the True God of the Marvellous Light, and concentrates on healing. The principal healing rite is *jorei*, spirit purification, which consists essentially in raising the palm of a hand of a member wearing an amulet called *ohihari* towards a recipient, who may or may not believe in the movement's teachings. Critical of the Western medical approach to the treatment of illness as found in Japanese hospitals and in private medical practice, Okada developed a theory of healing which related sickness to spiritual clouds and also prescribed, among other things, the use of herbal medicines for the removal of such clouds. Further, believing like Omotokyo that religion is the source of peace, both inner and collective, this movement has constructed models of paradise at Atami and Hakone, situated between Tokyo and Kyoto, and these are not only meant to serve as prototypes of a world where peace reigns supreme but also to promote a consciousness of a new age of peace and harmony. Sekaikyuseikyo has over 800,000 members in Japan and has also established itself in the West, Latin America and Thailand.

Sekai Mahikari Bumei Kyodan, World True Light Civilisation, established in 1959 by Okada Kotama (1901–74), also lays great stress on the importance of healing through radiation transmitted via the hand. However, whereas Sekaikyuseikyo attributes evil and sickness to spiritual clouds, this religion believes that the cause of evil is to be found in unpacified spirits. It is chiefly known for its *o-kiyome*, purification, which is used to eradicate the misfortune and disease caused by the angry spirits of the ancestors and of the rest of the dead. Once these spirits have been placated then wholeness, harmony and peace can return to the troubled individual or society.

Mahikari like Omotokyo and Sekaikyuseikyo has its cosmic vision and grand theory of history. As for the present, this is a time of crisis described using both Buddhist and Christian imagery and myth—the Old Testament story of the Flood being one of the illustrations used to depict the contemporary situation—and people are warned that now is the time to enter the ark of salvation provided by Mahikari. So far an estimated 50,000 people have joined this movement which now has centres in a number of Western countries and which specialises not only in healing but also in clairvoyance, ecstasy and prophesy. There is also a splinter group *Sukyo Mahikari*, Religion of True Light, which broke away from the main body in 1978 and is at present building a temple or sacred centre for the 'Civilisation of Light' in the mountains north of Tokyo. In some Japanese traditions mountains are regarded as holy places and have been treated by shamanistic diviners and exorcists, among others, as *shintai*, that is *kami* objects charged with the power of the spirits. Traces of this mountain worship are to be found in some of the new religions and the climbing of a sacred mountain such as Mount Fuji, an act of worship in itself, is seen by members as a means of purification, of acquiring spiritual strength and of contributing to the well-being of the nation.

Seicho no Ie, House of Growth, also derives many of its beliefs from Omotokyo. Its founder Masaharu Taniguchi (b. 1893) was formerly a member of Omotokyo and in fact a scribe in the employment of Onizaburo Daguchi. In 1930 Taniguchi started a publishing house and since then this movement has stressed the 'word' in its spoken or written form as the principle of the cosmos. This is a clear example of Omotokyo influence. The words of the founder are believed to be the divine media *par excellence* and to have the power to heal, and it is for this reason that his books are read aloud. Taniguchi has paid great attention to the concept of the *word* or *logos* as found in St John's Gospel and has even written a commentary on this theme.

Seicho no Ie, then, is primarily about healing. It regards sickness as in essence an illusion or 'deceit of the mind' to be conquered by spiritual means and in particular through the healing power of the word. Like a number of other Japanese new religions this movement has altered its political views and its views of Japan on more than one occasion. Prior to 1945 it was an ultra-nationalist movement which proclaimed that Japan was the centre of the universe and its Emperor its overlord. Since 1945 these beliefs have been modified and although today members are among the strongest supporters of emperor-worship they now see the Emperor as the centre of the Japanese nation only.

Seicho no Ie has a large following in Japan, estimated at over three million members, and many branches in North and South America and several others in Europe and Africa. Its main temples or sacred centres are in the Nagasaki Prefecture and at Uji in Kyoto, while the principal object of worship is the Great God of the House of Growth.

Perfect Liberty Kyodan was first established in 1924 as *Hitonomichi*, the Way of Man, but was dissolved by the government in 1937 on the grounds that, like Omotokyo, it was a threat to the position of the Emperor. Reorganised in 1946 by Miki Tokuchika (b. 1900) under the name Perfect Liberty, it emphasised the importance of art as a religious pursuit. Its use of computers and other forms of modern technology for providing members and other interested parties with information, of English in contrast to Omoto's use of Esperanto, and of fashionably-dressed female attendants known as 'angels', all give to this movement the appearance of a modern, international organisation. This religion is also well known for its golf courses and other sporting activities and for its highly colourful display of fireworks put on to celebrate the founder's birthday, a display which is regarded as remarkable even by Japanese standards.

The members believe that God has revealed a number of precepts, one of which is that the individual is a manifestation of the divine and another that individuals suffer if they do not 'show forth' or express their 'divine' nature. Furthermore, they see artistic and religious pursuits as means to happiness which is the ultimate goal of Perfect Liberty Kyodan. Believers regularly assess by questionnaires the progress they have made towards this goal. The movement promotes itself at home and abroad under the slogan 'a joyful religion' and compares and contrasts itself with the 'gloomy' religion of Christianity which, it believes, places too much emphasis on sin and suffering. Perfect Liberty Kyodan which, according to some estimates, has over one million followers, has its main centre of worship at Osaka.

Nicheren Buddhism and the New Religions

It was suggested above that some of the Japanese new religions have been greatly influenced by Buddhism and particularly by the Nicheren tradition. Nicheren (1222–82), a Japanese monk of the Tendai sect, founded a distinctly Japanese tradition of Buddhism based on the Sutra of the Lotus of the Good Law, in Japanese *Hokkekyo*. This scripture was regarded by Nicheren as the final and supreme embodiment of Buddhist truth. Moreover, he not only initiated the worship of the Lotus Sutra, having himself devoted a strong faith in its supernatural powers, but also believed himself to be the Bodhisattva prophesied for the last days. The formula of worship, known as the 'sacred name' or *Daimoku* invocation, consists in the chanting of 'Nam-myoho-renge-kyo' (I take refuge in the glorious Lotus Sutra). This invocation, believed to have been inscribed by Nicheren on the sacred mandala or scroll known as the *Gohonzon* and housed in the main temple of the Soka Gakkai movement at Taiseki-ji, near Mount Fuji, is held to be the law of life and for all living beings the principal means of attaining enlightenment. Nicheren Buddhism, defined as the Buddhism of *True Cause*, is seen as transcending the Buddhism of Gautama Buddha, the Buddhism of *True Effect*, and the Lotus Sutra. Among the important elements of the Lotus Sutra stressed by Nicheren were a this-worldly concept of salvation, the religious equality of all social classes, the possibility for all to achieve the state of Buddhahood and the duty to evangelise and convert others to the Buddhist Way.

Nicheren was also concerned with the welfare of society as a whole and believed that true religion and proper worship were necessary conditions for its peace and happiness. He held that since the state did not honour true Buddhism, national disasters would befall Japan by way of divine judgement, and his prophecy was believed to have been fulfilled with the Mongol invasion of Japan in 1274 and again in 1281. Nicheren's prophetic powers and the veneration and respect he showed for the ancestors greatly enhanced his authority and led many to believe that he alone could save Japan from religious *malaise* and political domination. His teachings, which he spread with determination and even aggression for over thirty years, were characterised by a tendency to identify religion with national life, an intolerance of other people's beliefs and an apocalyptic mysticism based on Mahayana Buddhism. After the death of Nicheren a split occurred among his disciples and this resulted in the emergence of different Nicheren traditions roughly divided into *Nicheren-Shoshu* (Shoshu means true religion) and *Nicheren-Shu* (Shu means religion).

The Nicheren Shoshu Tradition and Soka Gakkai (Value Creation Society)

One of Nicheren's disciples, Nikko, acquired a considerable following and what he taught was later given shape and coherence by Nikkan (1665–1726). According to these teachings Nicheren is the eternal Buddha and Gautama Buddha is assigned the significance and role of a precursor. While the latter's teachings are said to be incomplete, the substance of what he taught is contained, it is maintained, in the Lotus Sutra, and in the invocation or *Daimoku*.

Soka Gakkai is the largest of the new religions belonging to the Nicheren Shoshu tradition and of the new movements in Japan as a whole. The movement was started in the 1930s by Tsuneburo Makiguchi (1871–1934), a teacher from Hokkaido in north Japan, who developed a theory of education based on Nicheren's teachings that emphasised that what was of value and profitable was paramount. Makiguchi, who was imprisoned during the war along with his assistant Josei Toda (1900–58), died in gaol. The latter after his release began the rebuilding of the movement, previously called *Soka Kyoiku Gakkai* and now known simply as *Soka Gakkai*.

The methods used by Toda to recruit more members, in particular the 'break and subdue', or *shakubuku* approach to 'false believers' proposed by Nicheren, brought strong criticism of the movement. Toda and his assistants literally pressed their beliefs upon people and the movement grew from several hundred at most in 1945 to around three-quarters of a million families in 1958. The majority of these recruits came from the working and lower middle classes and under Toda's successor Daiseku Ikeda (b. 1928) the movement increased its influence in Japanese politics under the umbrella of the *Komeito*, Clean Government Party, the third largest political party in Japan today. At the same time the *shakubuku* approach to evangelisation was moderated and this gave the movement a better image.

Soka Gakkai is a lay organisation. However, it has links with the priests of Nicheren Shoshu who since they are the guardians of the original *Gohonzon* are in a position to provide the movement with its spiritual legitimacy. Members of the movement are committed to chanting twice daily before a shrine which contains a replica of the *Gohonzon*, the invocation, *Daimoku*, and two chapters of the Lotus Sutra. Chanting, or *Gongyo*, it is believed, can alter karma, the law of cause and effect, and also, as many members testify, bring great benefits of an emotional, psychological and material kind for individuals in the present. There are also discussion groups, *zadakandai*, which usually take place in members' homes and it is on these occasions that followers recount the benefits they have received from chanting and the difficulties of an emotional, spiritual, psychological or material kind that they may be experiencing. Soka Gakkai seeks to bring religion down on to the factory floor or kitchen table, so to speak, and is very much a world-affirming religion. Members also undertake missionary work. This is the message they preach: religion and daily life are inseparable in the sense that the former, if true and practised regularly and correctly, unfailingly improves and enhances the latter. Moreover, those who can afford it make the 'pilgrimage' to Taiseki-ji, the *Kaidan* or place of dedication and instruction and the sacred place of Nicheren Buddhism.

All the positions of responsibility and leadership are filled by lay people. Lay leaders not only play a very important administrative role but also provide direction and counselling on personal matters. In terms of its organisation the movement is divided vertically into local, district, regional, national and international sections, and horizontally into a number of different groupings; for example, there is a section for young men, another for young women and another for children. But this horizontal grouping is not always maintained, especially in those areas where the membership is small.

Soka Gakkai, like other Japanese new religions, places great emphasis on art, music, dance, gymnastics, festivals, parades and education. It has its own university, a number of other educational institutions and an art museum. Furthermore, one of its major preoccupations, especially in recent times, has been with world peace, stressing that the safety and survival of the planet depends on the dissemination and application to daily life of true beliefs and practices.

The present estimated size of membership of this movement is ten million families and although the vast majority of these are in Japan it has been making steady progress in North and South America and Europe.

The Nicheren-Shu Tradition

Among the new religions that may be said to belong broadly to the Nicheren-Shu tradition are *Reiyukai*, the Association of Friends of the Spirit, founded in 1925 by Kubota Kakutaro (1892–1944) and Kimi Kotani (1901–71), and *Risshokoseikai*, the Establishment of Righteousness and Friendly Intercourse, begun in 1938 by two former members of Reiyukai, Naganuma Myoko (1889–1957) and Niwano Nikiyo (b. 1906).

Many of the Reiyukai teachings, being based as they are on the Lotus Sutra, are almost identical to those of Nicheren Buddhism discussed above. Initially, however, it placed even greater emphasis on ancestor worship which, as we have seen, it regarded as central to its belief in the family as the centre of human life. Moreover, like Mahikari it believes that suffering and evil are the result of neglect of the ancestors to whom, along with all other Buddhas and spirits of the universe, we are indissolubly connected.

Further, it believes that spiritual power is contained in the *mandalas*, those scrolls produced by its own founder and by Nicheren and which provide graphic illustrations of teachings. Through reading these scrolls believers can obtain direct access to the Buddhas and Bodhisattvas, that is those enlightened ones who delay entry to Nirvana in order to help suffering humanity. Moreover, it is believed that by reading the Lotus Sutra members can acquire merit for the ancestors. It was this movement that introduced the *Hoza* system, a method of group counselling which provided adherents with the opportunity to discuss in open forum, so to speak, their personal difficulties and problems. This system was adopted, as we shall see, by Risshokoseikai. It is also deeply committed to social and welfare programmes, including work for the physically handicapped and the Red Cross. The membership of Reiyukai is estimated at over two and a half million, some three thousand of whom are teachers. The Shaka temple in Tokyo is its holy centre and, as we have seen, its special object of worship and source of inspiration is the Lotus Sutra.

Risshokoseikai, it has already been pointed out, split off from Reiyukai in 1938 and made its own the *Hoza* group system which the latter had initiated. While in Reiyukai the believer acquires merit principally by chanting the *Daimoku* formula given above, in Risshokoseikai the stress is placed on personal development which must begin with the self. It is through self-transformation that the world will be transformed, also a central tenet of the self-religions discussed elsewhere in this volume (see pp. 925–31).

The concept of the Bodhisattva, defined above, is also central to Risshokoseikai teaching and practice, as is ancestor worship. The principal aim of group counselling and other practices is the fostering of the bodhisattva spirit which enables individuals to triumph over the law of karma and break through the cycle of *samsara* or rebirth. However, following Nicheren, and similar to the other Japanese new movements influenced by his teaching on the intimate relationship between religion and society, Risshokoseikai believes in an indissoluble link between the religious and social and political spheres. Religious development is not seen as a purely private and personal affair with no bearing on the wider society, for, as we have already indicated, religion is believed to have important social and political consequences and to be the foundation of individual and collective peace, stability and prosperity. This explains the movement's involvement in world peace, among other things, through its agency the World Conference of Religion and Peace. Also central to its belief and practice is the Nicheren mandala and the Lotus Sutra.

This movement's sacred centre or headquarters is the Great Hall in Tokyo and since its reorganisation after the Second World War it has made steady progress. According to a recent estimate there are as many as five million members, making it one of the largest of the new religions in Japan.

Conclusions: Some Problems of Classification

In the foregoing the focus has been on indigenous Japanese new movements and it has been implicit throughout that any attempt to classify these religions will encounter immense problems. It is extremely difficult, for example, to construct a typology of Japanese new religions on the basis of their content since many of them have drawn on a variety of religious beliefs and practices, and this in turn creates problems for those who might attempt a classification by relating them directly to either of the two major Japanese religious traditions, Shintoism and Buddhism. For example, *Tenshokotaijingukyo*, the Teaching of the Almighty God of the Universe, founded by Kitamura Sayo (1900–67), not only has a Shinto name and uses many Shinto terms and expressions but has also adopted a number of Buddhist and Christian beliefs and practices.

Moreover, the historian will want to ask whether it makes any sense at all to apply the term 'new' to many of the religions that have been discussed here. These religions have been referred to as 'Children of the Emperor system' and classified according to the Meiji (1868–1912), Taisho (1912–26) and Showa (from 1926) periods, with an additional historical period, the post-Second World War era, incorporated into this chronological framework. The post-Second World War period has witnessed what amounts to a veritable growth industry in new religions, many of which have a distinctively different character and orientation from the older, pre-Second World War and nineteenth-century movements, and fulfil somewhat different functions.

It is important, none the less, not to lose sight of the fact that although much has changed in the 'new religions' field during the past century and more many of the new movements form part of an ongoing historical process. In other words, we should not expect to find outbreaks of entirely 'new' new religions that are peculiar to and only intelligible in the context of one or other of these historical periods. If this is borne in mind then the emergence of Japanese new religions can be linked with political and economic developments during the Meiji, Taisho and Showa eras, that is from 1868 onwards. They were also, in part, a reaction to the rigid formalism and increasing irrelevance particularly during the nineteenth century and the first quarter of this century of the two mainstream Japanese religions, Shintoism and Buddhism, and a response to rapid post-Second World War industrial development, urbanisation and modernisation. And working within this historical framework the social historian of religion may well discover that what is 'new' is not to be found in the content of these movements but in the fact of their emergence as socio-religious organisations whose primary function has been the reworking and revitalisation of traditional religious beliefs and rituals in order to make them directly relevant to daily life in a society in transition.

Given the difficulties of classification on the basis of content, derivation, structure and historical context, perhaps the most satisfactory approach to the problem is that devised by the sociologist Bryan Wilson, who has constructed a typology of new religions based on their response to the world. According to Wilson, Japanese new religions, while they manifest a pronounced thaumaturgical dimension, especially in their early years, as they develop come to approximate more to the 'manipulationist' type of sect than to the 'thaumaturgical' type. By this Wilson means that their main concern becomes the provision of a modern, relevant faith for a society whose traditional belief systems are not easily accommodated to the new conditions created by the rapid process of industrialisation and urbanisation.

However, the fact that there is nothing necessarily fixed or determined about the doctrines, rituals, symbols and orientation of some of these new religions must in itself mean that even the most useful of typologies is in need of frequent refinement if it is to be of wide and general application. Sekaikyuseikyo, the Church of World Messianity, founded by Mokichi Okada (1882–1955) is but one of a number of examples of a Japanese new religion whose teachings, ritual and public official image has changed significantly since its emergence in 1935. This movement which began as a healing cult, and healing is still one of its central concerns, has called itself by several different names, indicating a shift at this public level from a Buddhist to Christian orientation, while at the same time making far greater use than was previously the case of Shinto ritual and of art as the medium for transmitting its message. Evidently such twists and turns and changes of emphases and orientation can greatly reduce the life-span and impose strict limits on the usefulness of any typology.

However, when considered within the chronological framework outlined above it would seem to be the case that most if not all of the modern Japanese new religions display the principal characteristic of revitalisation or renewal movements: they rework and reshape traditional beliefs, rituals and symbols in such a way as to make them relevant to the cultural, social and spiritual needs and aspirations of the present.

Further Reading

Blacker, C. *The Catalpa Bow. A Study of Shamanistic Practices in Japan* (George Allen & Unwin, London, 1975)

Byron Earhart, H. *The New Religions of Japan. A Bibliography of Western Language Materials,* 2nd edn (University of Michigan Center for Japanese Studies, Ann Arbor, 1983)

Kitagawa, J.M. *Religion in Japanese History* (Columbia University Press, New York, 1966)

Thomsen, H. *The New Religions of Japan* (Charles E. Tuttle Company, Vermont, 1963). (For a critique of this book and Western approaches to new religions in general see R.J. Zwi Werblowsky's review article in the *Journal for the Scientific Study of Religion* (JSSR), V, no. 2 (Spring 1966))

Wilson, B.R. *Religious Sects. A Sociological Study* (Weidenfeld & Nicolson, London, 1970)

57 Africa

H.W. Turner

In earlier centuries first Christianity and later Islam came as new religions in Africa, took root and expanded until today they are the dominant faiths of the continent. Their predominance was long confined to Africa north of the Sahara and east of the Nile but in recent centuries their expansion into sub-Saharan or 'black' Africa has led to a fresh and increasing interaction with the indigenous African religions. One massive result, more extensive in the Christian context than in the Islamic, has been the emergence of a wide range of new religious movements which draw on the local traditions and one or other of the introduced faiths to produce new syntheses. These are usually referred to as new religious movements and they should be distinguished from the missions, churches or communities associated with these two faiths, from other religious bodies that have more recently taken root in parts of Africa, such as Baha'i, the Mormons and Jehovah's Witnesses, as well as from the original primal religions of the African peoples. They represent a creative attempt to meet African needs in African ways by a reworking of all available religious and cultural resources.

Different Kinds of Movement

The thousands of movements across hundreds of African peoples naturally exhibit many varieties. Among these, five different groups may be distinguished according to their religious content and intention, and the various degrees of syncretism between the African and the Christian or Islamic contributions.

Neo-Primal Movements

These stand closest to the indigenous tradition but have adopted some important new features from one of the other faiths, such as a single universal divinity, God or Allah, the rejection of magic or the adoption of new elements such as preaching or parts of the Mosaic decalogue. Islamic-related examples have taken the form of new voluntary possession cults adding Muslim powers to local spirits, and in east Nigeria a sophisticated religion known as Godianism rejects Christianity and much of local tradition in favour of a new single God of Africa who is derived from ancient Egyptian sources.

Synthetist Movements

These consciously attempt a combination of elements from each tradition to form a new religion for Africans. Although there are few clear examples from the Islamic milieu there are many with a Christian component, such as the extensive Déïma religion in the Ivory Coast or those sections of the Bwiti cults in Gabon which are increasingly adopting Christian forms and ideas.

Deviationist Movements

These endeavour to depart from indigenous traditions by the adoption of an Islamic or a Christian content, but in fact so deviate from some of the basic elements of these faiths as to be unacceptable to them. In the Islamic context this may mean neglecting the Qur'an, as with the movement of Yakouba Sylla from the 1930s in the Ivory Coast. He claimed a new revelation from Fatima, the daughter of Muhammad, depreciated prayer and made fasting optional. In Nigeria since 1934 the God's Kingdom Society has claimed to be a Christian movement but has replaced Christmas with a Feast of Tabernacles and would be closer to the classic religion of Israel.

Africanised Movements

These intend to be either Islamic or Christian but are more concerned with practical relevance in Africa than with Christian or Islamic orthodoxies. In West Africa the reforming and missionary Islamic brotherhood founded by Hamallah in 1925 regarded its own holy city, Nioro, as more important than Mecca, developed a more exuberant form of worship and dealt with social problems by supporting greater freedom for slaves, the lower classes and women. Christian examples of this form are commonly called 'aladura' churches in Nigeria, 'spiritual' churches in West Africa, Botswana and other areas, and 'Zionists' in southern and central Africa. A general term for these would be 'prophet-healing' churches.

Orthodox Movements

Such movements aim to be fully Islamic or Christian and even to reform or renew their African communities, but do so by adapting to African situations and needs under African leadership and independently of outside influences. In Islam this concern usually leads to mahdist movements which are rather different from those dealt with here; by the nature of Islam strictly independent orthodox movements are rare. Christian examples, however, are numerous since about the 1880s. The largest and best known is the Kimbanguist Church in Zaire and central Africa, dating from 1921; in 1970 it became the first such body to be admitted to the World Council of Churches, after the question of its doctrinal orthodoxy had been dealt with.

It must, however, be remembered that these movements usually lack established traditions and strong institutions and so are free to respond to the rapidly changing African situation. They are also often still in the process of working out their new religious syntheses or forms. There is therefore considerable mobility in beliefs and practice so that a movement seemingly belonging to one of the above groups may within a few years be better understood in terms of a different group.

What are the Causes of these Movements?

If there is any general common factor it lies in the great social and cultural upheaval consequent upon increasing interaction with the world outside Africa. While this includes the Arab world, the main influence has come from the West and from its Christian religion, first in the exploration and colonial periods, and now in the era of independence, modernisation and development. These movements have sometimes been seen as essentially political protests against colonialism. This is only part of the truth for there has been a substantial increase in religious independency in the post-colonial period and many movements are not protesting against anything but are seeking positive spiritual goals.

Among the many factors that can be identified there are the stress and rootlessness arising from the great cultural, social and political disturbances, bringing new values and lifestyles, and from particular issues such as employment, marriage, alcohol and, above all, sickness. There is more ill health today in Africa than ever before in its history and the majority of the new religious movements offer some form of spiritual healing. Western medicine is too limited in extent and seems unable to reach the real cause of much African sickness; the Christian churches which first brought Western methods have relied on these and seldom offered spiritual healing. This is now prominent in the independent movements and makes a real contribution to some dimensions of African ill health.

This should be seen as part of the overall search for a spiritual power greater than that of the traditional faiths, and more freely available in relevant forms than through the older Christian churches. There is a further search for independent revelation from God direct to African founders and prophets, and often through visions and dreams. This means that African relations with the divine are no longer tied to Arab or Western channels and forms but have their own identity and status in the sight of God and man.

Some of their Common Features

Despite the diversity of the different groups surveyed above there tend to be certain features characteristic of these movements, which may be summarised as follows:

1. They begin with a founder who has a mystical experience of a new revelation from the spirit world, often described as dying, visiting heaven, being given a new way and then being sent back to earth to start the new religion. The latter is therefore no man-made invention but has divine authority.

2. The divinity is now seen as a single personal supreme being who has ultimate power and will help people if they obey him.

3. The founder is accepted as an authentic African prophet called by God, occasionally as a new Messiah; contrary to traditional locations of authority the founder is often young and is sometimes a woman.

4. There is a selective rejection and retention of different elements of local culture. Magic, divination and dealings with the occult are usually discouraged, but revelatory dreams and visions, polygamous marriage, drumming and dancing, food taboos and colour and other symbolisms are retained and perhaps reshaped.

5. Considerable creativity is shown in the development of new forms of worship. There are new hymns, vestments, styles of architecture, and new major festivals, often at a new holy mountain or community centre with a biblical name such as 'New Jerusalem'.

6. The new blessings or salvation offered include healing, guidance from God, protection from evil powers and membership in a new and disciplined community as a 'place to belong'.

7. Receipt of these blessings depends on following the new rites and the new ethic, which commonly stresses love, discipline and industry, bans luxury and alcohol and tobacco, and sometimes transcends tribe and nation.

8. Expansion by deliberate missionary activity is a major innovation as compared with primal religions. It is based on the new universal deity, on the revelation from this source, and on being a new open and voluntary society in distinction from traditional age-grade, vocational or secret societies. Thus

the Kimbanguist Church is established in a number of central African nations and some Nigerian independent churches have spread around West Africa and into Europe.

9. The contribution to modernisation and development may be quite substantial but is seldom recognised. A change of world-view has begun when magical control of power is replaced by rational and scientific methods; when their own past story and future hopes introduce the dimension of history into an outlook dominated by myth; when the traditional closed, sacral, tightly integrated society is replaced by the new open, desacralised, pluralist forms implied by these movements; and when evil begins to be internalised so that one takes responsibility for one's own misfortunes rather than always blaming them on external evil powers. Psychologically and culturally there is a break with the past and an openness to an innovative future. This is sometimes expressed in new low-technology economic activities and better farming, coupled with a new work ethic. The Mourides Islamic movement in Senegal, with its groundnut farming and other activities, is a notable example of new forms of organisation and discipline playing a major role in the national economy.

The Size and Distribution of the Movements

Not all areas of Black Africa have produced these new religious movements to the same extent. Islamic movements seem concentrated in West Africa and especially in Senegal. Christian-related movements are a second-stage response rather than a preliminary substitute and so have first appeared and have proliferated where this faith has been longest established, in Ghana and Nigeria, in South Africa and in Zaire. Certain tribes, such as the Lovedu in South Africa, and some areas, such as Cameroon and Tanzania, have produced few movements of this kind; the explanation is to be sought in terms of the particular cultural features and mission history of each area.

It was once widely believed that such movements arose only in Protestant mission areas and that Catholic areas were immune, partly because they did not provide the model of many denominations and did not freely translate and distribute the Scriptures. Earlier there was some truth in this but since the 1940s there have been notable movements arising within a Catholic milieu as well as many Catholic individuals who have joined these movements. The Eastern Orthodox tradition has been interacting with Black African peoples from about 1924, first indirectly through Marcus Garvey's African Orthodox Church in North America, and, when its authenticity was questioned, through the Alexandrian Patriarchate of the Greek Orthodox Church. The complex of Orthodox-related independency has developed mainly in East Africa and since the 1970s has been extended through the presence of a missionary bishop of the Coptic Orthodox Church in Nairobi.

Estimates of the total number of distinct movements reach as high as 20,000; in Ghana alone some five hundred were known in the 1970s. Some, however, are very small, with perhaps no more than twenty members. Others are large, with several million members—for example the Kimbanguist Church, and the Zion Christian Church in Southern Africa which was reported to have over three million assemble at its annual Easter festival at Zion City Moriah in the northern Transvaal in 1985. A fairly firm figure for South Africa, based on the 1980 census, indicates that about thirty per cent of all Blacks, about 5.9 million members, belong to these movements in that one country. While specific statistics in this field should be treated with caution it is clear that taken together these movements represent a massive new religious development in Africa.

Islam's Relations with Africa's New Religions

Compared with the colonial setting of much of the relation of Christianity to the peoples of Black Africa Islam has enjoyed considerable freedom in its dealing with African peoples. At certain points it has stood over against African traditions, especially where divinities were represented by images, where ancestor cults challenged the prerogatives of Allah, or secret societies stood for independent authorities in face of Islam's emphasis on the unitary community. At other points Islam has been able to accommodate readily to a wide range of African practices. Polygamy has been accepted and regulated, and the traditional male dominance in most African societies has been confirmed. Much divinatory practice has been retained, together with reliance on dreams as revelatory and the use of various forms of magic.

Traditional spirit-possession cults where the spirit power was present in human embodiment rather than in cultic image or object could develop in new ways by adding Islamic spirits, as found in the Qur'an. Many of the Islamic-related movements have been of this form and have exhibited the further novelty of being voluntary societies of adherents and initiates rather than public cults of the whole community, and of appealing especially to women. Among these cults we may mention the Zar cults of Ethiopia and the Nilotic Sudan, the various Bori cults among the Hausa of Nigeria in the nineteenth and twentieth centuries, and the spirit-possession movement among the Lebu women of Senegal, which operates alongside the more orthodox mosque religion of the men.

The Lebu people have also provided a more distinctive new religion founded by an illiterate fisherman, Seydina Limamu. In 1883 he experienced a call from God to fulfil the mission of Muhammad by reviving and expanding orthodox Islam through new fraternities of God-fearers (hence their name *layens*, from the Lebu word for God). As a charismatic saint, miracle worker and preacher, he imposed a strict ethic upon his followers and he himself was accepted by the orthodox and learned Muslims.

Opposition, however, arose from his more Africanising teaching, which rejected the obligation of pilgrimage to Mecca, the limitation of wives to four and the rigours of the Ramadan fast. The dominance of Arabic gave way to the religious use of the Lebu vernacular, Wolof, with a repertoire of songs and poems still widely used. He suffered much persecution from the French authorities. Since his death in 1909 the leadership has been held by two sons and then a grandson. The Laye movement survives as a small but religiously intense community being reintegrated into Islam. Limamu remains perhaps the most notable example of an African prophet inspired by Islam but equally concerned with the Africanisation of the faith.

The Positions of Islam and Christianity

While new Islamic-related movements still appear, as in the heretical movement of the prophet Maitatsine that has clashed violently with the government of Nigeria since the late 1970s, their paucity as compared with those related to Christianity requires some explanation. Since Islam lacks the distinction between Church and state, or religion and politics, there was more control of religious developments in Muslim areas. At the same time individuals had more freedom to achieve religious status or leadership than within the tighter organisation of Christian missions and churches with demanding requirements for ordination, and strong moral discipline. It is also possible to become a Muslim through easier stages than with Christian conversion and baptism.

On the other hand, independent forms of African Christianity have been encouraged by the extensive translation of the Christian Scriptures into hundreds of vernaculars and by the deliberate mission policy of developing non-Western indigenous forms. There has been no equivalent in Islam, with scriptures untranslatable in principle and a certain in-built disdain for 'primitive' African tribal cultures.

Nevertheless, there are many similarities between the movements these two faiths have engendered. Both have notable examples of new holy cities, often with the tomb of the founder, and serving as places of major festivals and of pilgrimage. Both have contributed to tribal revival and renewal: the Mourides for the Wolof, Limamu for the Lebu and Shembe's Nazarite Church among the Zulu. There is a tendency in both towards regarding the founder as a Messiah or Mahdi, but this usually fades with time, as it did with Limamu and with Shembe and Kimbangu. The passing of leadership by lineage descent is common in both, likewise disputes over the leadership and over property and money. In ritual and ethical matters there is much in common: the removal of footwear for worship, the emphasis upon prayer, the use of water for purification, the importance of dreams and visions, discipline through fasting and food and other taboos and the acceptance of polygamy. The presence of most of these features in classic

Islam also helps to explain why there has been less need of independent developments in that milieu.

Characteristic differences can also be identified. Movements in a Christian context have been more fissiparous, more hostile to Western forms and concerned to develop a religion adapted to Africa. They have also produced a number of young women founders, as seen in Alice Lenshina in Zambia, Victoria Akinsowon of the Cherubim and Seraphim in Nigeria, Gaudencia Aoko of the Maria Legio in Kenya and Marie Lalou of the Déïma religion in the Ivory Coast. Equally remarkable is the centrality of healing in the Christian context and the lack of a similar emphasis in the other group. In the latter the Qur'an tends to be a mystic sacred object, recited but not avidly studied; the Bible serves as a creative stimulus, within which African peoples find their own story and a normative reference point. It also serves as a means of contact for the increasing relationships between the church sector of the movements and Western mission agencies which offer help in Bible study and leadership training, and also with Christian councils, both national and international, which have admitted some bodies from this sector into their membership.

These new religious movements are still increasing and have come to represent a distinctive part of the religious scene in Black Africa, a major new phenomenon that neither African nor other nations can readily ignore.

Further Reading

Baëta, C.G. *Prophetism in Ghana: A Study of Some 'Spiritual' Churches* (SCM, London, 1962)

Barrett, D.B. *Schism and Renewal: An Analysis of Six Thousand Contemporary Religious Movements* (Oxford University Press, London, 1968)

Peel, J.D.Y. *Aladura: a Religious Movement among the Yoruba* (Oxford University Press for The International African Institute, London, 1968)

Sundkler, B.G.M. *Bantu Prophets in South Africa*, 2nd edn (Oxford University Press, London, 1961)

Turner, H.W. *African Independent Church: Church of the Lord (Aladura)*, 2 vols. (Clarendon Press, Oxford, 1967)

58 'Secularisation: Religion in the Modern World'

Bryan Wilson

From the perspective of religion, the single most important feature of the modern world is its secularity. Sociologists of contemporary affairs regularly refer to 'this secular age'; 'secular society' and 'the process of secularisation', and the Christian clergy and Jewish rabbinate (as the religious professionals of the dominant religious traditions of advanced Western countries) frequently acknowledge the prevailing secularity which has depleted their congregations and diminished their social influence. The term 'secularisation' is, however, unspecific, and the very width of its application has given rise to controversy and uncertainty. It may allude to religious practice (which, in such matters as congregational attendance, is perhaps the most easily available and apparently objective indicator). It may refer to religious institutions and the changes that have occurred in the internal character of their ideology, ritual and organisation. It may allude to the place of religion within the social system taken as a whole. There are other possible applications. The evidence with respect to the relative vigour of religion is various and not necessarily all one way, and whilst most commentators allude to secularisation as a readily assumed matter of fact of contemporary Western society, some apparently contrary indicators can be invoked and need to be taken into account.

One source of confusion arises from the confusion of secularisation with secularism. Secularisation is a sociological concept which refers to an aspect of processes of structural change in society. By way of illustration, we may take the structural change that occurs as work techniques develop. More extensive division of labour and increase in productivity follow. In turn, these developments historically facilitated urban growth. One consequence was the decline of the influence of the local community and the growth of a more impersonal society (the replacement of the *Gemeinschaft* by the *Gesellschaft*). In such a society, the role player (rather than the total ame the effective operational unit of the social system. This process brought consequential changes in other social institutions and in their value-orientations. Thus, to pursue the example further, education in Western countries once accepted religious dogmas as its basis, and was extensively employed to sustain the moral order and to assist the transmission of moral values. Today education has changed its character. The context of education has become—and increasingly becomes—scientific. Detached observation, empirical investigation, rational deduction and pragmatic application have come to characterise all academic disciplines, even including the humanities. These orientations have displaced erstwhile premisses of a supernaturalist, revelatory, or transmundane character, and have even modified where they have not entirely superseded more general humanistic and aesthetic dispositions.

Once secularisation is understood as a process occurring within the social system, as an objective fact denoted by an ethically-neutral term, it can be distinguished from a concept with which, especially in the minds of theologians, it is readily confused: namely secularism. Secularism is an ideology: that is to say, it denotes a negative evaluative attitude towards religion, and might even be appropriately seen as a particular 'religious' position, in the sense that secularism adopts certain premisses *a priori* and canvasses a normative (albeit negative) position about supernaturalism. Secularism may, in certain limited respects, have promoted secularisation, but it is more convincing to regard the secularity of modern society as a consequence of structural change (as posited by the secularisation thesis) rather than as a result of the advocacy of secularism. Even in the self-proclaimed secularist Soviet Union, sociologists attribute secularity much more emphatically to processes of structural change than to the state-sponsored advocacy of secularism.

Whilst the concept of secularisation originally referred to the sequestration of church properties by the political authorities, the concept has expanded to take into account the many diverse ways in which religious power and control has passed into non-religious hands. Secularisation may be defined as that process by which religious thinking, practice and institutions lose social significance, and become marginal to the operation of the social system. In advanced societies, religion has now lost that presidency over social activities which once it exercised, as various institutional orders of social life (the economy, the polity, juridical institutions, education, health, recreation) have ceased to be under religious control, or even to be matters of religious concern. Even in the most intimate areas of social relationship—in marriage, and in family matters—religion has no longer the influence that once it had. The process in which specialised institutions develop—functional differentiation, as it is termed by sociologists—has been a process in which religious ideas and practice have lost their social significance. The evidences are of many kinds, ranging from the dominant values expressed in society to the most personal concerns of everyday life. Thus, whereas the dominant ideal values of society were once formulated as the fulfilment of the will of God, today the transcendent and overarching social values are more likely to canvass the welfare of the people. Whereas once, to turn to personal intimacies, children were welcomed as God's gifts, and fertility was a primary focus of religious concern, today families are carefully planned, conception prevented, or foetuses aborted in the interests of rational family organisation.

As the social order has itself come to conform to rational precepts of action, so religious intimations respecting values and behaviour have given place to conscious calculation in economic terms of the utilisation of resources and the demand for material evidence of cost-efficiency, profit and expediency in their use. The growth of instrumental values, and the diminished potency of supernaturalist or transcendent ideals, affects religious institutions and religious professionals. A simple comparison of the stipends paid to professional groups indicates the relative weakness of the clergy and the diminished evaluation (even in money terms) of their social worth. A comparison of stipends over, say, the past two hundred years, would reveal the steady erosion of the value of clerical incomes in contrast to the experience of other professionals. The proportion of a society's gross national produce devoted to supernaturalist concerns (support of churches or other religious properties) would reveal the same emphatic trend.

It is clearly much less easy to document changes in the thought-processes of the general public, yet, if a liberal interpretation is made of what constitutes a religious mode of thought (and, in this sense, one may say patterns of thought which invoke superempirical concepts or processes) one may well conclude that modern man has become progressively less disposed to believe that supernatural influences operate in his day-to-day life. Whether the instances are those of pure superstition (which must count as part of the religious dimension when contrasted with rational pragmatic attitudes) or recourse to prayer, supplication, belief in revelation or mystical experience, there has been a dramatic change in the course of the last century. We may note, to consider a more fully institutionalised aspect of official (Christian) religion, that less regard is paid to rites of passage. Baptisms have shown considerable decline in recent decades; confirmations become less usual; marriages have become increasingly secularised: burial alone remains an activity firmly within the control of the churches, but this may be at least in part sustained by superstition and also by the fact that the churches operate a very considerable continuing control over the public facilities for burial in cemeteries and crematoria.

These elements of religious practice tell a broadly similar story to patterns of church attendance, although these patterns vary considerably as between Western societies. The steady decline in attendances in Europe during this century is not matched by the evidence from the United States, where church-going continues to be a popular activity, with something approaching half the population attending church on any given Sunday. However, this particular indicator of religiosity must itself be interpreted in the light of other evidence: church-going does not carry the same cultural meaning in all societies. Clearly, there are many motives for this very conspicuous form of religious activity, and sociologists have suggested that some of these are operative in a vigorous way in the United States which, by other evidences, some have regarded (with Japan) as perhaps the most totally secularised nation. Some of those additional motives are held to be the search for community in a society which has received successive waves of immigration and in which there is a very high incidence of geographic and social mobility. Others have maintained that, in a society without very long traditions and without a mystical and mythic sense of its own origins, church-going is a way of establishing national identity, so much so that it little matters to which church people go—all are equally potent as expressions of Americanness. Clearly, this hypothesis is one which is difficult to test, although here is abundant evidence that Europeans, from the time of de Tocqueville, have found religion in America to lack spiritual content of the kind with which they were familiar in Europe.

This last consideration relates to the internal secularisation of religious institutions. It has been contended that processes of secularisation are not merely patterns of diminishing religious influence over other areas of the social system, but are also evident in the changing quality of religious performances and beliefs. It is clear that in the case of Christianity there has been a steady erosion of many elements that were once considered central to the thought and practice of the Church. Some of this process of change has been gradual, such as is exemplified in the diminution of votive offerings to the effigies of saints, which has been recorded in, say, Catholicism in France, or in the gradual abandonment of anthropomorphic conceptions of deity which appears to have occurred very generally in Protestantism. Other changes have come as forthright and vigorous challenges to previous ideas and practices. Such have been the rejection by some modern bishops of central Christian truths including the virgin birth, the resurrection and even the Trinity, and by the dramatic liturgical changes introduced in the Catholic Church after the Second Vatican Council. Verbal formulas sometimes continue after their content has ceased to express the convictions of those who use them: thus, one may doubt how actively Christians, who weekly affirm belief in the Second Coming of Christ, actually believe this proposition.

All of these diverse evidences may be seen as facets of a secularisation process in advanced societies: they are, however, to be regarded as attendant phenomena rather than as the core manifestations of the process. The loss of religious influence over the major social institutions is the fundamental issue. Thus, the Christian Church once closely regulated economic matters in Western society, specifying dates for agricultural pursuits; regulating the practice of trade, by forbidding such devices as forestalling and ingrating; controlling the operation of craftsmen and stipulating the rules by which they worked. Today, the church has no influence in matters of this kind, nor in the more important and centralised functions of industrial and financial operations. Once, politics was an arena in which major churchmen played a vigorous role and even local clergy were often active: the affairs of the Church continued to occupy the minds of Prime Ministers in Britain up until the time of the First World War. Today, in contrast, church affairs are generally a very quiet bywater of the political mainstream. Less than a century ago, the presence of the Church in education was predominant, and Church Schools were still a majority of all schools, whilst university dons were mainly clergymen. That has all been swept away, as the structural differentiation of the social system has produced specialised agencies for different social functions. These phenomena, and the less formalised but equally apparent diminution of religious and/or church influence in health, recreation and family and moral affairs, represent the core of the secularisation process in advanced nations.

The structural differentiation of the social system is accompanied by the increasing dependence of society on the articulation of distinct roles, particularly in the economic sphere. Role relationships characterise advanced society in which interaction is governed by impersonal criteria: individuals who 'man' these social roles set aside their personal attributes and dispositions and confine their role performances to the relevant skills. It is this impersonality of role-articulated social systems which makes them uncongenial to religion. Religion has its natural locale in the small community, and functions best, as Max Weber long ago noticed, in circumstances where people interact as total persons in face-to-face contexts. In such situations, the moral precepts of Christianity have their fullest purchase: these moral injunctions are much less easily applied to the impersonal context and role-performances of the *Gesellschaft.* As modern society has been reorganised, with increasing tendencies for vital functions to be centralised (and 'societalised'), so religious influence, always greatest at the level of the local community, wanes, and so occurs the attendant phenomenon of diminished recourse to religious thought and practice. Modern man learns, of necessity, to function in a rational environment, in social situations which are increasingly 'man-made'. As men, in their role-performances, contribute rationally to the upbuilding of the social context, so the paradox occurs that the man-made environment is itself more rational (more the product of well-co-ordinated role performances) than are the individuals (as sensate human beings) who have created it. Thus, we have the spectacle of irrational man in rational society. The society is the product of role players, but each role player has another dimension to his life—the vibrant, sentient, emotional dispositions of his total humanity. Thus, although the major thrust of contemporary social organisation is to elicit from individuals rational responses to their situation (in the role, as profit-seekers, as negotiators of traffic system, electronic devices, the bureaucracy and the whole apparatus of the modern social system) of necessity, there remains still, in each individual, a fund of personal dispositions which are not satisfied by rational solutions. It is to these that modern expressions of religiosity, to which some have pointed as counter-evidence to the process of secularisation, frequently appeal.

Before turning to these creative religious responses to the current situation it may be instructive to examine one response by which some sought to resist and contain the process of secularisation in some European countries. The religious divisions which have been activated in the last century (between Protestants and Catholics in Holland, for example, and between Catholics and Free-thinkers in Belgium) led to the attempt by the churches to insulate themselves from secularising influences. The churches sought to create for their own following alternative agencies and institutions which fulfilled a variety of institutional functions. This process, known as 'pillarisation', saw the development of distinctively Catholic (or less significantly, Protestant) organisations, such as schools, universities, hospitals, insurance companies, trade unions, recreational organisations and even travel agencies. The attempt was to provide something like a state within a state, or at least to provide religious believers with a safe enclave within which the major requirements of modern life could be satisfied. The Catholic child, in Belgium, for example, would be born in a Catholic hospital, go to a Catholic school, on to a Catholic university, join a Catholic union or professional association, take out Catholic insurance and so on. These 'pillars', replicated for those of other persuasions, jointly made up the state. The Catholic pillar was a manifest attempt to prevent the influence of secularisation which elsewhere appeared as an autonomatic consequence of structural differentiation in society. But the pillarisation experiment may be said to have largely failed in the face of the impress of rational techniques and organisation. It may, first of all, be less cost-efficient than state systems because of duplication and loss of economies of scale. Beyond this, and more important, is the fact that the skills and competences of each profession (university teachers, doctors, bureaucrats) are increasingly dictated by essentially secular criteria. Studies of 'Catholic' hospitals and universities have found that they differ very little from their secular counterparts—professional ethics and advanced techniques dictate the style of these institutions and the personnel who operate within them, and these have been shown to be of greater saliency in determining institutional character than the confessional basis of their foundation and their work-force.

The concept of secularisation does not in any sense imply that the process by which religion loses influence is a regular, uninterrupted decline. Religious phenomena are themselves so diverse, and religion's influence over society has, in times past, been so pervasive at many levels, that any idea of a unilinear development must be at once rejected. Counter-currents occur, and there are clear reactions to contemporary secularity which, if they fall short of full-scale religious revival, indicate the persistence of a will to sustain religion on the part of some sections of the public even in the most secular societies. A review of the diverse contemporary manifestations of religiosity in the world might, indeed, at least superficially, lead to the conclusion that the present day was an age of unprecedented religious vigour. In the face of the overwhelming evidence of the diminution of influence discussed above such a view is untenable, but contemporary expressions of religion cannot be dismissed as merely incidental. Religion responds to certain deep-laid, perhaps atavistic, human needs, and, as such, something which passes for religion, no matter how different it may be from established, traditional and well-institutionalised forms, may well be a permanent phenomenon of human society, even if it prevails only at the margins and in the interstices of an increasingly rational structure.

The most conspicuous evidences of the vibrancy of religion come from societies in which social conflict is expressed in religious terms, in which men are, apparently, prepared to lay down their lives for the sake of religious convictions. The conspicuous cases are the civil strife in Lebanon and Ireland; the religious revolution in Iran; and the passive resistance to the Communist state in Poland. In each case, special factors are at work. In both Lebanon and Ireland it might not be too much to say that religion here functions as a legitimation of what are tantamount to tribal allegiances of populations which live on the periphery of the religious confessions to which they claim adherence. In such cases, marginal groups frequently over-identify with the values of the tradition to which they belong: Irish Catholics are notoriously 'backward' compared to Catholics in Europe, in the sense that they have retained the ultramontane and triumphalist stance of nineteenth-century Catholicism long after its abandonment in most other Catholic countries. Similarly, the Ulster Protestants represent an extreme fringe at the margin of Britain, more Protestant than the British, and capable of using this Protestant heritage to assert that they are, indeed, more British than the British. Over-identification is a well-known ethnic, nationalist and/or religious phenomenon, particularly among culturally deprived or retarded constituencies. All this being said, it must be recognised that the violent terrorism on both sides, but more pronouncedly on the supposedly Catholic side, owes nothing to the religious traditions in the name of which it acts. The marginality of Lebanon's mixed population of seventeen divisions of Muslim and Christian conviction might yield to similar analysis: religion becomes the symbol in terms of which embattled groups take cognisance of themselves.

The Iranian case is manifestly a case of resurgent religiosity, but religion proclaimed in an underdeveloped country in which religion is a rallying-ground against modernisation, or, perhaps more accurately, against the inequalities, corruption and social divisiveness which modernisation produced. Iran, as a less developed country, scarcely exemplifies a reversal of secularisation, although there is no doubt that secularisation—diffused from more advanced countries—might be retarded in contexts where external influences can be resisted, as for instance in pre-war Tibet. How long such self-imposed isolation can persist is a matter for speculation. The Polish case turns on different considerations. The Catholic Church has long been the repository of national identity for a much-conquered and long-occupied people, regularly deprived of their national leaders. Religion is here a surrogate for political expression in a context where such expression is prohibited. Religion regularly takes this role in contexts in which there is, apart from religion, no possibility of freedom of speech or action. The symbolic significance of the Catholic Church for Polish nationalism, and the recurrent recourse of Poles to the Church in search of national leadership (as has occurred also in Ireland and in Greece in times past) is a large part of the explanation of the revitalisation of religion in this instance.

In nations more advanced than any of these, there are also instances of religious revivalism. In these, quite different, circumstances, we may suppose that personal discontents with the increasingly impersonal, large-scale, societally-organised social system, induce a response in which religion—with its emphasis on personal relationships and transcendent values—is a ready-made focus for the expression of contemporary alienation. (This point might, of course, be made in strictly religious terms, expressed as man in search of spiritual values, mystical experience, or ultimate reality.) These examples of renewed religious vigour take many diverse forms, both within and without the existing church structures. Many of them are grass-roots movements which emerge to express some generalised consensus of protest against existing social or political arrangements, or to experiment with new forms of religious expression.

The so-called 'new American Right' appears as a loosely formed and diffuse agglomeration of people who appear to be principally concerned with the erosion of American moral values which they see as being embodied in fundamentalist religious positions. The influence of television religion ('the electronic church') and the impact of television revivalists has been significant in the emergence of this movement, the supporters of which accept the label of 'the moral majority'. This inchoate movement is, however, one of the least well-defined and most unorganised of modern religious constituencies claiming a large following among people who are not formally drawn into separately organised congregations. The influence which this form of religion exercises is difficult to assess, and claims of direct political weight are disputable. Its attempts to resist, for instance, the teaching of evolution in schools, or to demand equal time for creationist theories, have not produced convincing evidence of the movement's strength.

A more specifically religious reaction to modern society, and perhaps also to the rigidity of church structures, has been the movement known as Charismatic Renewal, which began in California in 1958. Charismatics believe, as has been believed since the beginning of this century by those sects which took the designation 'Pentecostal', that the gifts of the Spirit, as described in 1 Corinthians, are still in operation today. Most attention is paid to the gift of speaking to the congregation in 'unknown tongues'. All the major Christian denominations, including the Roman Catholic Church, have been affected by this movement, and many interdenominational prayer meetings have encouraged individuals to seek the experience of 'Spirit baptism' and the (usually subsequent) experience of exercising the gifts of the Spirit. The major churches have generally not resisted this spontaneous manifestation of religious enthusiasm, and some prominent church leaders (including Roman Catholic archbishops) have endorsed charismatic practice: on the other hand, the churches have not come forward to endorse as thoroughly orthodox this style of religious worship. Most of those who have accepted charismatic worship have remained in their church fellowships, and some congregations of main-line denominations have become well known for their manifestations of this enthusiastic phenomenon. The diffuse nature of the movement makes it impossible to say how many people have been drawn into charismatic practice, or how long they remain committed to this form of religion.

Charismatic renewal is perhaps significant for its incidental comment on both contemporary religion and church structures. The spontaneity, immediacy, emotionalism and, at times, anti-intellectualism, of this form of worship stand in sharp contrast to the formalised, hierarchically organised, solemn and ritualised order of the churches as they had developed into the present century. This movement represented an assertion of democracy, but it also implied a distrust of the mediated relationship to deity. If, as in the exercise of charismatic power, the individual believer can directly receive inspiration from a member of the Godhead, then the need for the church establishment and the ministration of priests may seem to be put in question. In this sense, charismatic renewal represented, whether its votaries were conscious of this or not, a latent and implied assault on the received structures of the churches. In practice, it may be recognised that despite this tacit criticism of religious leadership and the implicit democracy of this enthusiastic form of religion, many charismatic fellowships actually evolved new patterns of (sometimes very authoritarian) leadership: thus, a measure of control was exercised over what might otherwise have been highly volatile and disruptive religious activities.

Although the majority of Charismatics appear to have remained within their original church fellowships, this movement has also spawned new forms of religious organisation of a minimalist kind. Rejecting the formalism of church services, groups have come into being which emphasise the informality of worship by holding their meetings in houses, hence the collective name of 'house churches'. Some of these groups have tended to become at least loosely affiliated and there is evidence of an incipient process of denominationalism, even with the development of the purchase of new properties for religious meetings, so leading away from the idea of the house church. Some of those who have sought this style of religion have left their former churches altogether. In some cases, strong leadership has emerged, and different groups are identified by reference to the particular preacher whose teachings they accept. This movement owes something to earlier Nonconformist organisation and style, particularly that of Baptists and (Plymouth) Brethren.

The general decline in church practice in Europe, and the erosion of denominational differences (particularly in the United States) has seen the development of increased interest in amalgamations. Ecumenicalism has been part of the advocacy of many churchmen for several decades, but the process of amalgamation has not been especially swift. Some conspicuous examples have occurred, particularly the Church of South India. Generally amalgamations have been more easily effected in mission countries, since in those contexts denominational differences which were (at one time) of real social significance in the homeland more easily lost their particular *raison d'être*. Time and distance diminish these distinctions, and several amalgamations have taken place (in Scotland, the United States, Canada and Australia). In America, denominational labels had, by the mid-twentieth century, come often to represent little more than different organisations, the distinctive tenets of which had fallen into desuetude. In Britain, there have been some successful amalgamations among smaller bodies, and the United Reformed Church, composed of Congregationalists and Presbyterians, is the best known among these. Contrary to the expectations of some of those urging such mergers, however, these amalgamated bodies have not grown as a consequence of their new structure, but rather have experienced continuing decline.

Innovation within church communities, or at their fringes, is merely one form of contemporary religious activity, however. The sectarian tradition, in Protestantism, has persisted, albeit leading to the growth of a few sects rather than to a further proliferation of smaller groups. Some nineteenth-century sects and smaller denominations—Christadelphians, Unitarians and Quakers, have shown no capacity for growth in England; Irvingites have virtually died out; and the Exclusive Brethren have suffered a process of serious attrition. On the other hand, Jehovah's Witnesses, thanks in large part to the vigour of their doorstep evangelism, have continued to grow in England, and in most countries (particularly so in predominantly Catholic countries such as Italy, Portugal and Chile). Although it is well established that this movement has a considerable turnover of membership, perhaps associated with its particular preoccupation with the Second Coming of Christ and the periodic disappointments which the failure of prophecy occasions, none the less, the overall rate of recruitment is such that losses are, in most countries, more than compensated by continued gains.

Pentecostal sects, of which there are a great many, have also experienced considerable growth in recent decades, and particularly so in Third World countries. The Assemblies of God in particular has been successful, and this movement is now a vigorous presence in many parts of the world. It appears that the strength of traditional Pentecostalism has not been in any way vitiated by the development of Charismatic Renewal within the main-line churches, but it also appears that the Pentecostal sects do appeal to a different constituency, mainly of less well-to-do and less well-educated people and to people in less developed countries.

Two other major sects have shown great growth in recent decades, albeit in somewhat different countries. The Seventh-day Adventist Church, with several million members world-wide, succeeds in recruiting principally in Third World countries, the membership in which now considerably exceeds the membership in North America, Australia and Europe, where the movement has not experienced such dramatic patterns of growth. The Church, which maintains a vigorous programme of education and a health system of its own, finds its resources stretched by its recruitment of increasing numbers of people in poor countries. The Church in Britain has not escaped problems of racial tension because of its mixed composition of indigenous white and immigrant West Indian members.

The Mormons have also enjoyed a period of phenomenal growth with a membership of nearly six million, with continuing success in North America and in Europe, as well as in parts of the Third World. The Church, which organises its membership for social, welfare and recreational purposes as well as for religious practice, has been particularly successful in recruiting young families in European countries. Mormon temples, in which special rites are performed (including baptism for the dead by living proxies), have been built in many parts of the world for a membership which is no longer dependent on Salt Lake City for its facilities, although the church remains powerfully centralised and effectively organised from its American heartland.

A large number of new religious movements have sprung up in Western countries, particularly since the 1960s, but many of these remain relatively small even if well publicised, and it is a common characteristic that they encourage their members to accept work overseas and to engage in proselytising activity there. A number of these movements have drawn on oriental traditions which they have introduced to the West (Krishna Consciousness movement; Bhagwan Rajneesh; the Divine Light Mission; Transcendental Meditation, for example). Some, conspicuously the Children of God (later called Family of Love), grew up in the Christian tradition, although departing considerably from Christian morality in some respects. The Unification Church is conspicuously Christian but incorporates ideas which accommodate the assumptions of its Korean votaries. A different stream of contemporary religiosity flows from ideas that had some early expression in Christian Science and the New Thought movements which, in themselves, have shown little capacity for sustaining their numbers in the modern world: the modern variants of this tradition are represented by Scientology and some other 'human potential' movements, which emphasise the opportunity for individuals to increase their health, intellect and success in the world. Unlike the earlier representatives of this so-called gnostic tradition, which mainly recruited middle-aged votaries, most of whom were women, these movements tend to appeal to people in their twenties and early thirties.

Religious innovation is by no means confined to modern Western countries. New movements emerge regularly in other traditions, even if forms of worship and beliefs show less radical departures from the received tradition. The Sai Baba movement and the Swami Narayan movement are indications of the vibrancy of contemporary Hinduism and, unlike earlier variants of that tradition, these movements now seek to proselytise beyond the confines of India, initially among migrants but, in the case of Sai Baba, also among Westerners. Sometimes, too, the secular currents from other countries affect these new movements, as appears to be the case with the Brahma Kumaris in which women have acquired the conspicuous leadership positions in contrast to normal Hindu practice. Since feminism has not yet been significantly represented as a specifically religious intimation, we may suppose that this development owes more to secular ideas than to specifically religious ideas.

Japan is often regarded as one of the world's most secularised countries, yet it is in that country that some of the most successful and vigorous new religions have developed in the decades since the Second World War. These movements, Buddhist and Shintoist in inspiration, sometimes retain elements of traditional Japanese shamanism, particularly in the experiences claimed by their founders (several of whom were women). Many of these movements have a specific concern with healing practices. Some, such as Reiyukai and Rissho Kosei Kai, strongly counsel members to give all due attention to ancestral spirits and ancestor worship: others, chief among which is Soka Gakkai, entirely reject this aspect of traditional religious practice. Sociologically, the arresting fact about the new Buddhist movements is that, although they have attached themselves to one or another of the monastic sects of Japanese Buddhism, they are themselves entirely lay movements, with lay leadership and control. This process of lay revitalisation of otherwise increasingly ineffective and, at times, almost moribund ecclesiastical systems, is itself an eloquent commentary on one aspect of processes of secularisation.

New religious movements, whether in the Christian, Buddhist, or any other tradition, are not in the strict sense revivals of a tradition: they are more accurately regarded as adaptations of religion to new social circumstances. None of them is capable, given the radical nature of social change, of recreating the dying religions of the past. In their style and in their specific appeal they represent an accommodation to new conditions, and they incorporate many of the assumptions and facilities encouraged in the increasingly rationalised secular sphere. Thus it is that many new movements are themselves testimonies to secularisation: they often utilise highly secular methods in evangelism, financing, publicity and mobilisation of adherents. Very commonly, the traditional symbolism, liturgy and aesthetic concern of traditional religion are abandoned for much more pragmatic attitudes and for systems of control, accountancy, propaganda and even doctrinal content which are closer to the styles of secular enterprise than to traditional religious concerns. The new religions do evidently indicate a continuing interest in, perhaps a need for, spiritual solace and reassurance on the part of many individuals, but, in the West at least, they are also very much the creations of a secularised society.

An examination of the contemporary religious situation reveals that, at least in advanced countries, religion has necessarily abandoned many of its former functions. It no longer provides the overarching symbolic structure—the sacred canopy—in terms of which total societies take cognisance of themselves and affirm their supernatural origin. In considerable measure, religion has become a very private affair. In most societies there is a wide variety of religions and no religion is able to claim societal monopoly, nor even to represent the social system. Religion becomes—in a way which was not possible within the orthodoxies of the past—a matter of choice or preference. In consequence of this measure of privatisation, religion in the West ceases to claim a very significant societal position or to fulfil social functions. Religious movements might, of course, mobilise opinion. As voluntary bodies they are still perhaps the largest agencies for the expression of unconstrained opinion (in a way which is not true of trade unions—in which commitment is lower and which, in many countries, can scarcely be considered as truly voluntary organisations). Religious movements may serve primarily as mediating institutions between the individual and the increasingly powerful state, enclaves in which some vestige of communal association may be sustained. This is particularly evident in Japan, where, in this respect, their functions are of great importance. Religion may still have this significant function in societies which are increasingly impersonalised by formal, rational, bureaucratic structures and technological work operations.

In the face of persisting secularisation of the social order, we might expect religious movements, and particularly new forms of religion, to arise, perhaps as recurrent phenomena. Alienation is one source of religious demand, which, more in its associational features than in its doctrinal teachings, religion may serve to counteract. Alternatively, as long as society emphasises competitive success and the struggle for achievement, religions offering short cuts to social mobility, or enhanced personal power (whether intellectual, sexual, social or physical) may be expected to recruit a clientele. We may expect, with the speed of social change, religious expression to become diversified for different constituencies, as specified by age, education, social class and perhaps gender or sexual preferences. Religious diversity is quite consistent with secularised society, testifying in its own way to the limitations of what religion can actually do.

Further Reading

Bellah, R.N. *Beyond Belief: Essays on Religion in a Post-Traditional World* (Harper & Row, New York, 1970)

Hammond, P.E. (ed.) *The Sacred in a Secular Age* (University of California Press, Berkeley and Los Angeles, 1985)

Wilson, B.R. *Religion in Sociological Perspective* (Oxford University Press, Oxford, 1982)

Index

All India Muslim League 373
Allal el-Fassi 346–7
Almohad dynasty 336, 338, 342
Almoravid dynasty 335–6, 342, 348, 475
Ālvārs 572, 624, 643–4
Amar Das, Sikh Guru 718–19, 721
Ambrose of Milan 156, 159–60, 161
American Muslim Mission 527–8
Amitābha Buddha 630, 633, 758, 760, 764, 771, 772, 775–6, 797
Amoraim 113–14
Amritsar, Sikh centre 720, 725
Anabaptists 220, 223, 258
Anāhitā, Mazdean deity 558, 560, 561, 563
Ānandavardhana, Hindu poet 617, 624, 644
anātman (Sanskrit)=*anatta* (Pali), in Buddhism 631, 736
  see also ātman
ancestor cults
  in African religion 251, 867–9
  China 281, 411–12, 423
  in Maori religion 854–5, 858
  Melanesia 843–5, 847, 849
  in new religions 838
  in shamanism 825
  Tibet 811
Andaya, B. 442–3
Angad, Sikh Guru 718, 721
Anglicanism 66, 190, 223–4, 235, 260, 262; *see also* England, Church of
Anglo-Catholicism 240, 251
animism 8, 17–18, 275
  and Buddhism 732
  and Islam 337, 339, 444
Anselm of Canterbury 208
anti-clericalism 211, 234, 238, 239, 269
anti-popes 198, 202
anti-Semitism 65, 69, 136
  in Middle Ages 125–6
antinomianism 231, 478, 574, 626, 648, 654, 655–8
  and Tantrism 650
Antioch
  Patriarchate of 181
  theology of 162–5, 168, 170, 183, 187, 189, 194
Antony, hermit 151, 157–8
apocalyptic writings, Judaism 96, 99, 106, 109
Apocrypha 70, 73
Apollinaris, Bishop of Laodicea 162–3
Apologists 145–6, 148
apostles, *see* tradition, apostolic
Aquinas, Thomas 4, 30, 59, 209–10, 222, 227, 235
Arab League 496
Arabic
  in Africa 347, 349, 484
  in Far East 427, 433, 440
  and Judaism 117–18, 120
  maintenance of 501
  as official language 185, 188
  in Ottoman Empire 398
Arabs
  North Africa 329–31, 335
  and origins of Islam 314, 316, 356–7, 390
  and spread of Islam 369, 471, 473–4, 480–2
Āraṇyakas 575, 579
architecture
  Christian 147, 212, 226, 236, 266
  Islamic 387–8, 398, 414
Arian controversy 154–5, 156–7, 159, 162, 195
Arias, Mortimer 302
Aristotelianism
  and Christianity 201, 209
  and Judaism 119
Arjan, Sikh Guru 719, 720, 721
Arles, Council of 154
Armenian Church 188–9, 294
Arminianism 223, 260–1
art
  Buddhist 773–4
  Islamic 387–8, 398, 402, 494
arts, visual, Christian 147, 218–19, 229, 276
Āryas, in India 571–3, 575–7, 583, 603, 605–7, 618–19
Asanga, Buddhist scholar 634, 760, 762, 794
Asante state, religion 870
asceticism
  in Christianity 157–8, 159, 161, 170, 204
  in Indian religions 582, 589–90, 592, 618, 657
  in Islam 323, 333, 337–9
  in Judaism 108
  in Mazdaism 564
  in Theravāda Buddhism 730, 737
  see also Śaivism
Asharites 323, 376
Ashkenazi Jews 115, 117, 120–1, 122, 125
Askari, Hassan 304
Aśoka, Maurya emperor 601, 603, 727, 729, 759
'Assassins' 359
assimilation, of Muslims 308, 375, 413–19, 515–16, 526
Assyrian Church 184, 294
astrology, in Tibet 810, 811
asura (Mazdean deities) 553–4, 614
Ataturk, Kemal 401–3, 404–7, 503
Athanasius 156–7, 186, 243
Atharva-Veda 575, 578, 580, 582, 584, 586
atheism 52–60, 230, 233, 236, 237–8
  and Buddhism 6, 53, 610
  and Hinduism 610

Index

and Judaism 118, 122
Nepal
Buddhism and Hinduism in 533, 739, 741–2, 744–8, 750–5
history 739–40
modernisation 741
monarchy 739–40, 747
religion as worship 742–50, 754
Tantrism 742, 743, 747, 750, 754; *see also* Tantrism
Neri, Philip 225
Nero, persecutions 101, 143
Nestorianism 163–4, 167–8, 183–4, 187–8, 190, 272–4, 294
in China 760
and Islam 319, 323–4, 390
New Order, Indonesia 448
New Sect, China 410, 415–17
New Testament
attitudes to 68–9
canon of 103, 104, 146
as historical source 143, 236–7
New Thought movement 913, 915, 916, 964
New Year, in Melanesian religions 844, 846–7, 848
New Zealand, traditional religions, *see* Maori religion
Newars 663, 740–8, 751–5
and Tantrism 684–5, 750
Newman, J.H. 235
Ngata, Sir Apirana 863
Ngugi Wa Thiongo 287–8
Nicea
First Ecumenical Council (325) 153, 155, 156–7, 162, 168, 172
Seventh Ecumenical Council (787) 170–1
Nichiren, Buddhist sect 770, 774–6, 914, 938–41
Nichiren Shoshu tradition 938, 939–40, 914; *see also* Soka Gakkai
Nichiren-Shu tradition 940–1
Nicholas II, Pope 197
Niebuhr, H. Richard 263
Niebuhr, Reinhold 263
Niemöller, Martin 238
Nietzsche, Friedrich 237
Nigeria
Christianity in 488
Islam in 470, 474, 476, 478–9, 486, 488, 494, 497
nihilism, and Buddhism 538, 597, 629, 635
Nikodim, Patriarch 298–9
Nikon, Patriarch 179, 229
Nimeiri, of Sudan 486, 496
nirvāṇa
concept of 598, 601, 629, 631–2, 635, 661, 677, 698, 764, 795, 797, 805
and Islam 308–9
in Theravāda Buddhism (*nibbāna*) 733–4, 735–7
Nityāṣoḍaśikārṇava 689–90
Nizami, K.A. 381
Nizamuddin Auliya, Shaykh 375–6, 385
Nizaris 383
Nobili, Robert 273
Nō drama 768, 773
Nonconformity, England 235–6; *see also* Protestantism
North Africa
Christianity in 330, 334
early Church in 148, 150–1, 152–4, 156–8, 160–2, 243
Islam in 185, 186–7, 243–4, 329–52, 473–4
holy men 337–42
modern states 342–51
and tribal societies 329–31, 334–7, 340, 342, 345
North America
Christianity in 880–1, 956
Islam in 520–9
Judaism in 132–5
new religions 907, 912–24, 929–30
Orthodox Churches 66, 181–2, 262
traditional religions 823, 873–82
North India, Church of 278, 296
Nuruddin ar-Raniri 438, 442
Nyāya-darśana 638, 640
Nyimapa, Buddhist order 788, 790–2, 794–5, 796, 800–1, 810

oil, Middle East, impact of 349, 366, 461, 464
Old Believers 179, 229
Old Catholics 234
Old Testament
as history 71–5, 86–7, 89
difficulties 75–80
languages 70, 72, 88
as literature 75, 86–8
order 70–1
and religion of Israel 80–6, 89
see also Christianity; Judaism; Islam
Oman, Islam in 362–4, 457, 469, 480, 481
Omotokyo (Great Origin) 934–7
Öndür gegen 815
Oneida community 260
Oratorian Order 225, 226, 227
ordination, Theravāda Buddhism 728, 729–31, 733, 808
Organisation of African Unity 496
Origen of Alexandria 149–50, 154, 168, 243
Orthodox Churches 66, 167–73, 229, 233, 239, 274, 293
expansion 173–8, 181–3
modern 180–3